D1237061

An Economic History of the United States

FRANK W. TUTTLE
Professor Emeritus of Economics
University of Florida

JOSEPH M. PERRY
Assistant Professor of Economics
University of Florida

Published By

H27   **SOUTH-WESTERN PUBLISHING COMPANY**
Cincinnati • Chicago • Dallas • New Rochelle, N.Y. • Burlingame, Calif.

Copyright © 1970

by

SOUTH-WESTERN PUBLISHING CO.

Cincinnati, Ohio

Library of Congress Catalog Card Number: 69-11580

1 2 3 4 5 6 7 8 H 7 6 5 4 3 2 1 0

Printed in the United States of America

PREFACE

This book was planned and written to provide a different and, in some ways, unique approach to American history. The approach is primarily economic, providing analysis in economic terms of many problems not usually treated in this manner by traditional economic historians. It combines two popular viewpoints on economic growth: the chronological-institutional approach and the approach based on national income analysis. The chronological-institutional approach gives a view over time of the many institutional interrelationships that have developed in our economic system, but it does not present a way of evaluating their impacts on economic growth and welfare. The approach based on national income analysis provides such a measure, but it does not analyze the substructure that creates income and determines welfare. We believe our combination of the two approaches gives a better and more balanced view of American economic history than could be achieved by the sole use of either approach.

A number of features are found in our text that appear seldom or not at all in other American economic history texts:

(1) The use of time periods with new or different limits. For example, the first period of growth, which we call "Colonization and the Genesis of the American Economy—1607-1763," terminates in 1763, rather than in 1776 or 1783. Our reasoning is that 1763 marked a distinct turning point in the growth trend of the American colonies and coincided with several important political and economic changes in the colonial system. The 1607-1763 period is thus substantially different from the period beginning in 1763, which extends with few changes well beyond the time of the Revolution. We consider the War of 1812 the next turning point, since only at that time did the characteristics of a new national economy develop. Similar reasoning underlies the choice of other time period limits.

Another difference involving time periods is our inclusion of wars and preparations for wars at the end of periods, rather than at the beginning. We believe that wars and preparations for them are closely related to the events which precede them. However, they set in motion vast changes in the economic system which ultimately give rise to a period of growth with quite different characteristics. The one exception to this practice is the Revolutionary War, which is placed in the middle of a period.

(2) A strong emphasis on economic maturity and the path followed toward its achievement. Ways of measuring maturity are discussed at length. One often neglected measure, the complex of international debtor-creditor relationships, is analyzed to show how its neglect by policy-makers has affected economic policy and economic growth.

iii

(3) Adequate quantitative illustrations for points made in the text. Numerous tables of data are used throughout the book to illustrate and support discussions in the text. Our integration of text materials and data provide a more extensive and balanced discussion of historical events than could be achieved by the sole use of either.

(4) Discussion of topics not usually found in economic history texts. For example, the economic importance of leisure time is indicated at several points in the book. The nature and role of economic history are also given substantial discussion; much emphasis is placed on the unsolved problems of the discipline, thus avoiding a heavily dogmatic approach. The student will also find a number of short but rather unique historical anecdotes throughout the book, illustrating various points.

The imbalance in the number of chapters in the five parts is intentional. It reflects our opinion that economic developments in the recent past have exerted more influence on the world we know today than have events of the distant past. Accordingly, the parts devoted to colonial and antebellum times discuss only those events we consider to have a lasting impact on the economy.

We express our appreciation to Mr. John M. Hollingsworth, Indiana University, who prepared the illustrations for the text. Thanks go also to the staff of the Graduate Research Library at the University of Florida for their patience and perseverance in documenting obscure events and facts. Finally, we thank the College of Business Administration steno pool for the long hours spent preparing the manuscript. Responsibility for errors and omissions remains, of course, with us.

Gainesville, Florida

FRANK W. TUTTLE

JOSEPH M. PERRY

TABLE OF CONTENTS

Chapter 1. Nature and Content of Economic History   **1**

PART I

COLONIZATION AND THE GENESIS OF THE AMERICAN ECONOMY—1607-1763

Chapter 2. The Colonization of America   **23**

         3. Colonial Development   **47**

PART II

THE EMERGENCE OF A NEW NATION—1763-1815

Chapter 4. Discontent, Defiance, and Readjustments—1763-1783   **83**

         5. Establishing a New Nation   **109**

PART III

THE RISE OF A NEW NATION: INTERNAL AND EXTERNAL DEVELOPMENT—1816-1865

Chapter 6. Westward Expansion; Public Lands; Population
             Growth; Agriculture   **135**

         7. Money, Banking, and Finance   **160**

         8. Transportation and Communication   **179**

         9. Manufacturing; Business Organization; Labor;
             The Tariff   **203**

        10. The Rise of Domestic Commerce; The Decline of
             Foreign Commerce   **227**

        11. Intersectional Differences; War. Performance
             of the American Economy—1816-1865   **247**

PART IV

THE NATION MATURES: THE DEVELOPMENT OF ECONOMIC NATIONALISM—1866-1920

Chapter 12.   Population Growth and Distribution. Public Lands   275

13.   The Development of Agriculture—1865-1920   300

14.   Development of Independent Unit Banking. Triumph
of the Gold Standard   327

15.   New Techniques of Transportation and Communication 351

16.   Industrial Climate; Growth of Manufacturing   385

17.   Industrial Development, Concentration, and Control   417

18.   Labor: Organization and Legislation   443

19.   Markets and Trade: Domestic and Foreign   478

20.   Maturation: Performance of the American Economy   509

PART V

THE UNITED STATES IN A WORLD ECONOMY—1921-PRESENT

Chapter 21.   The Aftermath of War   547

22.   More on Prosperity   579

23.   Crisis, Panic, and Relief   611

24.   The New Deal: Reform and Recovery   641

25.   The War Years   670

26.   Reconversion without Depression   698

27.   Postwar Progress—Part I   725

28.   Postwar Progress—Part II   752

29.   The Performance of the American Economy   775

INDEX   801

Chapter 1

NATURE AND CONTENT OF
ECONOMIC HISTORY

A separate treatment of the economic history of the United States needs no defense. It is a segment of the history of the United States which has become such a voluminous serial that it must be broken down into areas of special interest. Not only are the special interest areas served by this procedure, but interpretations of movements and developments may be made which are not possible in a general account of American development.

Economic history does not deny the influences of noneconomic forces in the development of the American economy, nor does it ignore the leadership of outstanding personalities. However, it introduces these factors only as they exerted a significant economic influence.

ECONOMICS AND ECONOMIC HISTORY

The disciplines of history and economics contribute to the approach and methods used in economic history. The basic problems considered by economic history are economic in nature, however, and are common to other subdisciplines such as economic theory, labor economics, and international trade theory. A brief survey of economics will serve to introduce these problems in an integrated fashion. The specific nature of American economic history can then be explained in terms of the economic functions it analyzes.

The Nature of Economics

Economics is a study of the social activities engaged in by man in his efforts to obtain goods and services that are capable of satisfying his wants. This activity is made necessary by the fact that these goods and services are not free; they are scarce, they must be produced, and they cost money. The quantity of them that is available at a given time and in a given place is not sufficient to enable every person who desires to consume them to do so to the point of satiety. Since there is an insufficient quantity of these goods

1

to meet every person's needs, they command a price from those who are able and willing to pay for them. Man attempts to overcome this condition and degree of scarcity by engaging in economic activities.

To be *social,* these activities lead to the establishment of relationships with other persons, directly or indirectly. *Direct relationships* are those that are entered into in the presence of one or more persons. They may be in the nature of an exchange of goods for goods, an exchange of services for services, or an exchange of goods for services.

Indirect relationships follow direct ones, as, for example, a man may cultivate a garden by himself, but in so doing he uses tools that he has acquired from someone in the past. These tools, which may be a hoe, a rake, and a spade, are capital goods, which, in turn, are the products of labor. First, they were formed by labor that was applied to raw materials. After the raw materials had been fashioned into tools, they were sold to one or more dealers, who, in turn, made them available to the gardener upon payment of a price. All of the persons involved cooperated in making tools available, although they may not have known one another.

American Economic History

The economic history of the United States is the story of the ways and means by which the people of this country have obtained their living throughout the last three hundred years. It is the story of the struggles of man against nature in overcoming the unproductiveness of primeval forests and virgin lands, and in wresting mineral wealth from the bowels of the earth. It is also the story of man's struggle against man, often in a selfish and violent manner, to solve the basic problems of scarcity and human satisfaction. The results of these struggles, however, have enabled a large population to enjoy a higher scale of living in the mid-20th century than few persons dared dream of a hundred years ago.

The approach of the American people toward overcoming the scarcity of economic goods and services has been institutional. Various forms of business units have been used, including the individual proprietorship, the partnership, and the corporation. Basic economic activities in which people have been engaged include the rendering of labor services, including professional services such as those of physicians and lawyers; the carrying on of trade and commerce; the manufacturing of both capital goods and consumer goods; and the financing of these economic activities.

The degree to which scarcity was overcome determined the scale of living of a person or of a group. The fact that relatively few people were satisfied with any given scale of living gave rise to greater effort to improve upon it and to approach their desired standard of living. The *standard of living* is that level of the scale of living that people have set as their goal of attainment within the limits of any given stage of technology. Insofar as the national income was increased by the development of new consumers' goods that were made possible by the application of new technologies to productive processes, the standard of living was raised to include their utilization. *Economic history,* then, is the study of those social activities engaged in by man in his efforts to make a living and to improve his scale of living. Just as economic studies are concerned with production, distribution, exchange, and consumption, so is economic history concerned with the study of the development of these institutions, and in recording the results of their development on the economy.

Production. *Production* involves the manufacture and distribution of goods and the rendering of services. Economic history is concerned with the study of (1) the system of production—craft, household, and factory; (2) the ownership of the facilities of production—private or governmental (private ownership may be shared by partnerships and corporations, as well as by individuals); (3) the kinds and sources of power for manufacture and distribution—man, animal, and nonanimal, such as wind, water, steam, and electricity; and (4) the fuels used—wood, anthracite and bituminous coal, gas, and oil. Production of any kind is impossible without labor and guidance for this labor.

Organized production in the United States is and always has been motivated by the desire to make profits. Without going into an elaborate discussion of profits—their nature, how they arise, and their social justification—suffice it to say here that increments of business income over and above all costs of production, including wages of management, are profits. Historically, the receipt of positive profits by owner-entrepreneurs has contributed to an unequal per capita distribution of the national income. Time was when profits resulted from simple, direct two-way exchange in which little organization of the factors of production was necessary or existent. These transactions were effected with a minimum of administrative machinery and routine. Specialization was present in the single enterprise form of business unit.

As the volume of business increased and more specialization and division of labor were required of management and ownership, the partnership, and later the corporation, became prevalent forms of business organization. As relationships between the owners of business units and their operations, and between the business units and the public have become more complex, the corporate form of organization has become dominant. This is not to say that the single enterprise and the partnership have become passé. The latter are exemplified by the neighborhood store—as distinct from the neighborhood shopping center—the shoe repair shop, the barber shop, the beauty shop, possibly the bakery, and many other types of small business units.

Production in an economic system that is characterized by specialization and division of labor is useless in the absence of exchange, and economic history describes the money and monetary systems that have been used to facilitate the exchange of goods from the possession of the original producer to the ultimate consumer. Banks and banking systems have made their contributions to exchange, both domestic and foreign. Transportation systems have evolved from the horse and wagon era into the canal period, which in

turn gave way to the use of steam and electric railways, later to the motor
and air facilities of the present day. Turnpikes have given way to superhighways; canals and internal waterways, to railroads; sailboats, to modern
ocean liners; railroads and automobiles, to airplanes.

Distribution. *Distribution* contributes to a given scale of living through
the apportionment of the national income to and among those persons who
have contributed to its existence and to its size. Those who own land receive
economic rent, whether they use it or lease it to others. Those who perform
labor services receive wages; and interest is the return received for the use
of capital, regardless of its ownership. Entrepreneurs receive profits, which
may be either positive or negative. Economic history does attempt to explain
the apportionment but not to justify it; and it reveals some of the effects
of this apportionment upon the economic, social, and political segments of
our economy. Vested interests tend to be conservative in their economic and
political thinking. Insofar as they have resisted institutional changes that
might have altered the pattern according to which the national income would
be distributed, economic growth has been retarded. Urbanization and the
concentration of populations in commercial and in industrial areas are
aspects of the development of marketing and of industry. They also have
impacts on the distribution of income through the exercise of the power
that is given to landowners to exact higher rentals from their tenants. Changes
in the values of urban lands and in their uses in different locations constitute
another phase of the study of economic history.

Exchange. *Exchange values* are expressed in terms of money values. The
money values of commodities and services are their respective prices. In order
for prices to provide effective comparisons of commodity values at a given
time or to give expression to value changes over a period of time, the
common denominator of values should be one which is relatively stable in
value. It has been through the medium of and in terms of price that the
social dividend has been distributed among and between the productive
factors that gave rise to it. It has been in terms of prices that consumers have
been able to exchange the products of their respective specialities.

At times when the actual amount of money has not been adequate to use
in the exchange of goods and services, credit has been devised as a substitute. When businessmen needed money before final commodity values
had been actually determined on the market, they borrowed from banks.
Proceeds of loans from banks have been taken in the form of circulating
bank notes and in terms of *bank deposits*. Prior to about 1870, bank notes
were vastly more important than were *demand deposits*. During that period
of our development, the impacts of regulatory and control measures were
focused upon the conditions under which *circulating notes* not only were
put into circulation but maintained there at parity and ultimately redeemed.
When demand deposits became widely used, regulatory measures and control
devices were focused upon maintaining their continued use.

When the United States had reached a stage of maturity in its economic development, the weaknesses of independent unit banking led to the adoption of a regional central banking system. Federal Reserve banking became a reality just in time to facilitate the financing of the First World War. It has played an important role in our economic system since the day in August, 1914, when it was put into operation.

Consumption. The pattern of *consumption,* which is the end result of all economic activity, to a certain extent is the result of the distributive process. In an age of specialization and division of labor, few persons consume the products of their own efforts. Their abilities to consume the products of others depend upon their receipt of money incomes.

Consumer goods may be either nondurable or durable. The former, such as food and coal, are destroyed physically at once when they are consumed. Durable consumer goods, such as shoes, vacuum cleaners, and razors, are utilized over a period of time.

Not only is consumption necessary to keep body and soul together, it also contributes to the enjoyment of life and of living. One of the outstanding results of economic progress in any country has been the increasing amount of leisure time. The economic impact of this leisure time has affected the production of goods and services, especially in the field of commercial entertainment. There is scarcely a state in the entire United States that does not contain one or more natural phenomena that are exploited by entrepreneurs who attract tourists and other seekers of pleasure and entertainment. Most, if not all, of these places require an investment of capital and the application of labor in order to make them practical places in which others may spend their leisure. This use of leisure constitutes more than a passing of time. It involves spending of money that is used to pay (1) wages of attendants, (2) costs of items purchased, (3) rent for the use of equipment, and (4) interest on invested capital.

General Trends in Economic Progress. The continental United States has expanded from a narrow strip along the Atlantic Coast to embrace all of the territory between the Atlantic and Pacific Oceans from east to west and from the Canadian border to Mexico. In recent years Hawaii and Alaska have been admitted to statehood. If the only impact of absorbing this vast expanse of land into the United States had been to enable a correspondingly larger number of people to eke out an existence, the results would have been disappointing, to say the least. Without attempting to measure per capita income at this point, the mere fact that the scale of living of over 200 million people is much higher now than it was for less than four million people 180 years ago is prima facie evidence of economic progress. Instead of working from sunup to sundown every day for mere subsistence, labor in the United States works a 40-hour week or less at a legal minimum wage of $1.60 an hour in 1969. Before productive careers are entered upon, millions of young people, both men and women, devote from ten to twelve years of their lives to obtaining an education. During this time they are consuming much more than they are producing. This condition has existed for many, many years and all the evidence points to economic progress. For those who entered college or trained for a professional career, an additional four to eight years or more have been devoted to more specialized education and training. Education has tended to make people more productive on the one hand, while on the other it has taught them how to utilize their leisure time to advantage.

Basic Stimulatory Changes. A challenge to the reader is to detect economic changes that have led to increased national income. Expression of these increments cannot always be made in terms of cost and price. When a new technology has resulted in an increase in the output of a scarce product with the same or less labor effort, progress is indicated. When a given area of land has been cultivated every year without fallow and without a decrease in output per acre, progress is implied. When the labor segment of the population has acquired better housing facilities when working 40 hours a week than it had when it worked 72 hours a week, progress has occurred. When a larger proportion of the people own mechanical refrigerators than formerly owned ice refrigerators, progress has been made. If an increase in the total national income has not resulted in a higher *per capita* income, economic growth has not taken place. Mention has already been made of the scarcity of capital. In general, it has only been when the capital equipment of the United States has been increased in volume and/or in efficiency that real economic progress has been made.

Agriculture is no longer a full-time or part-time activity of almost every person or family unit even as a small-scale subsistence occupation. It has passed through one or more phases of development to which the term *agricultural revolution* has been applied, so prodigious have been the changes in its organization. Since the turn of the last century, farm employment has been in excess of farm population and both farm employment and farm population comprise less than 10 percent respectively of total employment and total population. The mining frontier did not conform to the traditional pattern of the agricultural frontier as it spread its way across the country. The development of this frontier caused an interruption in the steady progress of settlement in the westward movement of people, of agriculture, and of industry. It was a search for new furbearing animals that gave importance to the hunter-trapper in the march of progress across the nation. Fishing was one of the earliest of colonial industries; and, in spite of the many developments and improvements in the supplying of food, it has continued down through the years to command respect and attention. Since the middle of the 19th century, lumbering and fishing industries have employed 2 percent, more or less, as many workers as are engaged in farming.

No modern nation has had a problem of disposing of public lands comparable to that of the United States. The story of how this was done exemplifies the complexities of our economic life. The impact of this program has been felt in agriculture, railroad transportation, mining, forestry or lumbering, and banking; and its results appear in the background of some of our major economic upheavals or panics. Not only did public land policy provide stimulus to the development of railroad transportation west of the Mississippi River, it gave the development of agriculture a shot in the arm.

Outside the fact that the United States comprised one large trading area, the development of the railroad net, together with relatively stable money and banking systems, contributed much to an economy that ultimately raised the scale of living of its people to where it is today. Some of the changes that have occurred in the organization of marketing have been connected with the rise and fall of the wholesale establishment, the development of the department store, the chain store, the variety store, and the supermarket. The neighborhood shopping center is beginning to displace the downtown store, or at least to add to the convenience of the retail buyer and to provide parking space which is not metered.

Specialization. The economy of the American colonies developed patterns of geographic specialization, and industrial and occupational division of labor. These patterns were expanded as the westward movement carried pioneers into the frontier regions of the West. There no longer is an agricultural region and another of industry. Specialization of agricultural activities by regions or by locations has resulted in wheat belts, corn belts, dairy and poultry regions, cattle grazing areas, others for raising hogs, not to overlook the more recent movement of cotton and rice away from the Southeastern States into the Southwest and West. In other regions, tillable agriculture has given way to the cultivation of orchards—peach, apple, cherry, and pear—in widely scattered regions. Still other regions have become known for their growing of grapes, strawberries, or tomatoes. Truck farming has become a somewhat localized activity near urban centers, and the development of rapid transportation facilities and electric refrigeration has extended these areas in which the products of truck farms are distributed.

Industry first centralized in local regions, but more recently it has decentralized. Decentralization has not done away with specialization; it has created additional and more widely scattered areas of specialized industrial activity. The areas of specialization of those industries whose raw materials are natural resources have been expanded. Exploration and research have made available new deposits of mineral and petroleum resources. Mere mention of the discoveries of new deposits of iron and of new oil pools serves to illustrate this aspect of our development.

Industrial and professional division of labor has parallelled territorial specialization. First, a man becomes a doctor, which itself is a manifestation of specialized study and training. Within that area are many narrower fields of specialization—internal medicine, surgery, dermatology, pediatrics, and obstetrics, to mention a few. In automobile repair, which is a specialized activity, there are the classifications of body mechanic and motor mechanic. Almost every occupational field, apart from that of common labor, now exhibits a number of specialties, each requiring extensive training, and each employing workers of much higher productivity than that of common labor.

Uses of Economic Theory in Economic History

Economic history makes a special appeal to those persons who are interested in a study of economic theory and economic growth. It establishes an institutional framework within which economic principles or laws may be expressed and then tested. Theories concerning wages, the relationship between money and prices, the role of government in economic growth, and other problem areas can be effectively tested nowhere but in the laboratory of history; for nowhere else can the effect of the relevant variables be observed and analyzed.

Economic theory itself serves as a guidepost in the study of economic history. When considering the relationship between money and prices, for example, economic theory identifies the forces which are most important in establishing the relationship, and provides a point of view for the assessment of the relationship. Economic history and economic theory are thus of mutual importance and benefit.

Illustration of Economic Principles. While economic history is not a course in the principles of economics, or economic theory, its study provides many illustrations in support of economic principles. There is little doubt that Adam Smith and Thomas Malthus were familiar with the facts of economic history when the one formulated his principles of free trade, the other his theory of population. Economic history may have provided a model for formulating the iron law of wages. According to this "law," wages could never rise much above the subsistence level. The upsurge of population that followed wage increases increased the supply of labor in a few years and brought wages back down to the subsistence level. And how better to illustrate the widening of the extensive margin of cultivation and the accompanying changes that took place in supramarginal areas than by studying the effects of the westward movement of agriculture? To be more specific, the opening of the Erie Canal was followed by a migratory movement of people from New York and New England that resulted in the appropriation of what formerly had been submarginal land west of the Appalachian Mountains at the expense of creating new margins and in altering land utilization in older settled areas. Land rent appeared in the one area for the first time; it either disappeared or was preserved in other areas by forcing land to be put to more productive uses.

Economic history does not present a theory of wages, but it does recognize the fact that wages were higher in Colonial America than in England. It also recognizes the fact that the westward movement had the effect of tending to maintain a relatively high level of wages in states east of the Appalachian Mountains. Wages for factory workers tended to attract agricultural labor into the cities, not only during our early periods of development, but in an accelerated fashion after World War I. This movement was accompanied by a reorganization of agriculture and by a realignment of urban rents, especially in residential areas.

The economic history of the United States is rich in its illustrations of the functions of profits in a capitalistic economic organization. From the earliest days of trapping and fishing, down through the development of manufacturing in its many areas, the fields of trading and commerce, both domestic and foreign, were developed by those in search of profits.

Practical Knowledge of Economic Laws. While there is no evidence that the American colonists were well versed in the formal presentation of the principle of absolute cost advantage or comparative cost advantage or of the law of variable proportions of the factors of production, they became acquainted with them the hard way, the direct way, and they patterned their economic behavior accordingly. *Absolute cost advantage* of regions, or of products, exists when goods can be produced, or services rendered, at lower unit costs than are incurred in other regions or by other persons. *Comparative cost advantage* exists when the absolute advantages of producing certain goods, or of rendering certain services, are greater than in the production of others. Southern colonists discovered that they could make a better living by growing tobacco, rice, and some indigo and trading them for wheat, corn, and sugar than they could by attempting to grow all of the latter commodities they needed. Even subsidies failed to make it comparatively profitable to continue raising tobacco and indigo after the invention of the cotton gin. The culture of indigo practically disappeared. Tobacco became the main crop of North Carolina, Virginia, and Kentucky, regions in which growing cotton was unprofitable.

The *law of variable proportions* of the productive factors established the environment in which the decisions concerning the combinations of land, labor, and capital were made. It was in accordance with this law that extensive agriculture was more profitable than intensive agriculture. Land was abundant and cheap; labor and capital were scarce and costly. The colonists found it profitable to use that productive factor most whose cost was the least. Conversely, they used units of labor and capital sparingly because they were relatively high priced. It was under the guidance of this principle that farmers found it cheaper to move their barnyards, when they became so full of manure they could not be used, than it was to clean them. Labor and capital required to remove the manure and to fertilize the land cost more than to move their barnyards to another area that had to be cleared of trees and underbrush. The effects of the increase in population upon the economic rent of land, and of the increase of labor and capital upon wages and interest respectively, illustrate the law of variable proportions of the factors of production in a realistic fashion. Other examples could be cited at this point almost without end to show how economic theory may be made more realistic and fruitful by drawing upon the developments of economic history.

The Lessons of Economic History

Many lessons may be learned from a study of economic history. Many problems have been encountered by the farmer, by the businessman, and by labor in years gone by that were similar to those that are troublesome today. The way these problems have been handled in the past, and with what success, should enable us to avoid certain pitfalls in the latter part of the 20th century. Solutions to economic problems must be found within the limits of the framework of the economy and the level of technology. Even though they are different now than they were in years gone by, economic analysis makes it possible to project economic problems and their solutions into the framework of modern economic organization.

Examples of such reasoning are numerous. The failure of the British and colonial governments in their attempt to regulate the tobacco market showed the futility of attempting to control, at the producer level, the price of a product that was produced under fairly competitive conditions. The failure of the colonists in Maryland to adhere to their agreement to reduce their acreages planted in tobacco and the willingness of others to take advantage of that agreement foreshadowed many of the farm problems faced in the United States three centuries later. The successive changes that occurred in the character of New England agriculture may be accounted for only in terms of comparative advantage; farmers discovered that they could make more money furnishing milk to the people who lived in urban centers than they could in raising wheat for the market. The reasoning behind this change has remained important for many sections of the country, most recently the South, where diversification of agriculture occurred only tardily. The effect upon prices of rapid increases in the supplies of goods offered for sale is graphically illustrated by the experience of Americans after the close of the War of 1812, when renewed international trade brought floods of goods from abroad. These few instances serve to establish the point: most modern problems can be better understood with a knowledge of economic history. The present is a result of the past, and knowledge of the past is required to understand it.

THE ECONOMIC SIGNIFICANCE OF GEOGRAPHIC AND DEMOGRAPHIC FACTORS

In the absence of industrial and mechanical techniques, the economy of any region, no matter how large or how small, will be conditioned largely by its geographical factors—climate, topography, rivers and harbors, and the presence of known mineral wealth. In the vast expanse of the continental and conterminal United States, in the north temperate zone, roughly between the 25th and 50th parallels, are found rich and varied natural resources, many of which have been harnessed to meet man's needs. Their influence on the American economy will be revealed in somewhat spectacular fashion.

RELIEF MAP OF THE CONTIGUOUS UNITED STATES

Major Geographic Determinants

The flow of the rivers gave direction to early settlements and to commerce. The character of the soil, combined with rainfall and temperatures, determined what crops could be grown, given favorable climatic conditions and an adequate growing season. The presence or absence of timber and forests not only conditioned the extent to which lumbering was carried on, it likewise determined the extent to which lumber was used in construction. An alternative was stone or brick, later concrete and steel.

The presence of mountain ranges, such as the Appalachian chain in the eastern United States and the Rocky Mountains in the western part, both of which have a general north to south direction, conditions rainfall, winds, and temperatures. The development of coal, lead, gold, zinc, petroleum, copper, silver, iron, bauxite, and other mineral resources has given rise to the mining community and to the oil town, both of which have contributed much to our economic development.

Natural harbors have contributed to the development of commercial seaports, such as Portland, Boston, New York City, Charleston, New Orleans, Los Angeles, San Francisco, and Seattle. Other factors that make for good seaports are the character of their hinterlands and the presence of abundant natural resources. Also, products must be imported as well as exported, and unless there is some way of utilizing the imported products, or of distributing them where they can be used, economic development will be nil or slow.

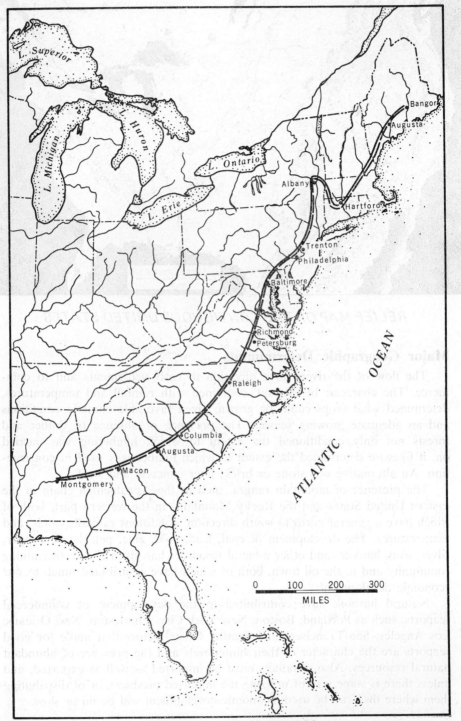

THE FALL LINE OF RIVERS

Before the age of the railroad and steam-propelled transportation facilities, waterways provided the avenues for commerce and wind was the propelling force. In New England and eastern New York and Pennsylvania, the general flow of the rivers is from north to south; while from Maryland to the south the general direction of their flow is from northwest to southeast. The smooth flow of these rivers from the Piedmont region to the coastal plain is interrupted by a sudden drop in elevation that provides a natural barrier to the movement of shipping, either upstream or down. This sudden drop, or fall line, is a geographical formation that extends southwest from about 15 miles inward from the coast in Maine to approximately 150 miles from the coast in Georgia. The line is continuous and fairly regular except for a break in New York State. The Hudson River is navigable to Albany which is 150 miles upstream.

Regional Differences

New England climate and soil were forbidding to the carrying on of a general type of agriculture. The climate was somewhat severe in winter, and the growing season was short. The soil was thin and rocky; and its fertility, in general, was limited by a lack of humus. Spring freshets enriched the Connecticut River Valley and others to a comparatively high level of fertility. Forests abounded in white pine, spruce, hemlock, fir trees, and some harder woods, including maple, oak, beech, and birch.

To the west and south of New England, while the winters were on the severe side, the growing season was longer and a somewhat general type of agriculture could be carried on successfully. Ample rainfall together with a rich humus contributed to bountiful crops which were unknown to New England. Here, again, spring freshets deposited rich silt in the river valleys to enrich the soils. Forests teemed with hard and soft woods and were the habitat of squirrel, bear, beaver, deer, muskrat, and other wild animal life.

Temperatures from Maryland and Virginia to the south were milder than in other regions of the Atlantic Coastal States to the north and the growing season was longer. Frosts occasionally nipped vegetation in the Carolinas and Georgia. The soil was deep and fertile, and swamp areas lent themselves to the cultivation of rice.

In the broad expanse of territory from the Appalachian highland on the east to the Rocky Mountain plateau on the west lie the rich alluvial valleys of the Mississippi River and its tributaries, the Ohio River to the east, the Missouri River to the west. The latter are fed by numerous smaller rivers, each one of which has its own smaller alluvial valley. Here are located some of the richest farmlands in the entire United States. Extending west from the Appalachian Mountains, trees are in abundance until the treeless plains of Illinois establish a new pattern for lands to the west of the Mississippi River. The forests of the Appalachian region extend into the South and add cypress, long leaf pine, short leaf pine, slash pine, and the loblolly pine, among others, to the list of trees.

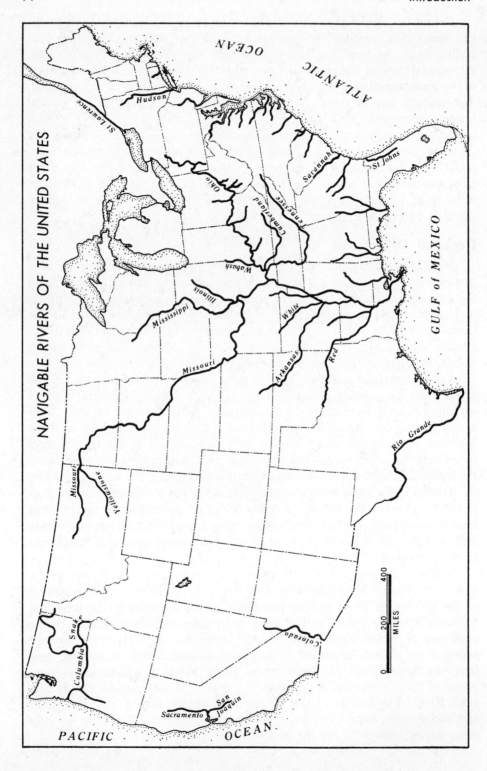

NAVIGABLE RIVERS OF THE UNITED STATES

The Appalachian Mountain chain extends from northeast to southwest, from New York to Alabama, and is rich not only in trees but in mineral wealth, principal among which are coal—anthracite and bituminous—iron ore, and petroleum. While these mountains were discouraging to east-west traffic across them, there are gaps that enabled the early settler to wend his way with difficulty through them.

Average rainfall is ample to support both agriculture and industry, becoming somewhat lower near the one hundredth meridian. To the west of this north-south line, drawn through the eastern boundary of the Oklahoma panhandle, the land is extremely fertile; but the less than an annual average twenty inches of rain is inadequate to support a tillable agriculture or to meet the needs of industry. Iron ore, bauxite, lead, zinc, copper, and coal are among the minerals found in this region.

The topography of the Rocky Mountain region has given rise to an economy of its own. Among its mineral wealth are found deposits of coal, gold, silver, lead, iron ore, and copper. Because of the lack of adequate rainfall in low elevations, most of the timber resources of this region are found in high altitudes. The cooler temperatures of the Northern States give rise to a more bountiful forestation of conifers than is found in New Mexico and Arizona. While tillable agriculture is carried on in this region, it is not one of the important agricultural areas of the United States. The Pacific Coastal States of California, Oregon, and Washington present a very different picture from a climatological point of view. Some of the richest agricultural lands in the United States are watered by abundant rains, and some of the most productive farms in the country are found in these states. Timber resources, likewise, are unique in the form of the giant redwood and sequoia trees. Douglas fir and other conifers grow in dense, luxurious forests.

The Role of People

To say that there are no more natural resources in America today than there were when the Indians roamed the country is a platitude, but it does call attention to the fact that natural resources without people who are willing to use them and without technology do not make for economic progress. Land, labor, and capital do not fall spontaneously into any form of business organization. Human direction and decision must be focused on combining them into efficient production units. The United States has been blessed with a people of ambition, of intelligence, of energy, of courage, of faith in humanity, and of mechanical ability. This has followed the mingling of races by natural increase as well as by immigration. To a certain extent it was those people who were dissatisfied with conditions in Europe and later in other parts of the world, who came to America voluntarily or who were sent here involuntarily because they were not in sympathy with the status quo, who were responsible for the economic development of the United States.

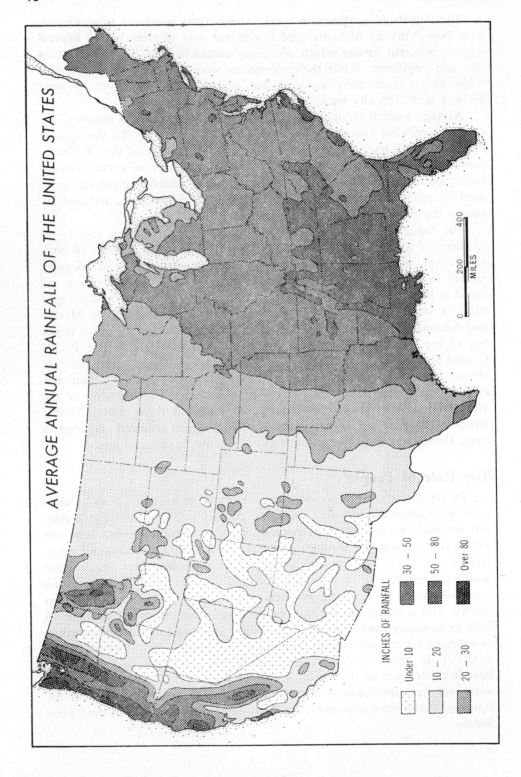

AVERAGE ANNUAL RAINFALL OF THE UNITED STATES

INCHES OF RAINFALL

Under 10

10 – 20

20 – 30

30 – 50

50 – 80

Over 80

MILES

0   200   400

Technology as a Modifying Factor

The development of technology has offset to some extent the dependence of an economy upon natural resources of a given kind at a given place. The mention of one or two developments of this sort will serve to illustrate the point and to provide the basis for further analysis by the reader. In many areas forests have been denuded, and during the years of this century many persons have become concerned with programs of conservation of natural resources. Others attacked the problem of an increasing scarcity of lumber and an increase in its price by attempting to find substitutes for wood. Brick, concrete block, asbestos shingles, terrazzo flooring, and aluminum window frames are substitutes for lumber in the construction of houses and other types of buildings. This list is not intended to be complete. The development of high tension wires and of electrical transformers has reduced the dependence of industry upon the direct application of power generated by falling water.

One of the aspects of modern western economies is the extent to which science and technology have modified the earth's surface. Canal waterways have been dug where nature did not provide rivers. Harbors have been enlarged and deepened where natural facilities were inadequate for the purposes at hand. Swamps have been filled in; others have been drained. Mountains have been tunnelled. Chasms and gorges have been bridged. Artificial lakes have been constructed to prevent a too rapid runoff of surface water. Man has provided what nature did not.

Economic Dislocations

The study of economic history reveals that innovations have resulted in dislocations of productive factors, sometimes of entire plants and industries. These dislocations have given rise to many of the economic crises that have marred an otherwise steady advance in our economic development. Opening the Erie Canal to traffic resulted in the dislocation of many farms and farmers in the New England States. The adaptation of internal combustion engines to farm tractors resulted not only in the dislocation of thousands of horses (farm capital) but of millions of acres of farmland upon which oats had been grown, the market for which was rather restricted to horse feed. The development of the railroad caused the dislocation of other forms of transportation. The encroachment of urban lands upon suburban areas has dislocated many farmers and owners of suburban residential properties. Many of the problems of economic history have arisen from the dislocation of the productive factors at given levels of technology.

ORGANIZATION OF THIS BOOK

The economic development of the United States may be divided conveniently into five major periods:

1607-1763—Colonization and the Genesis of the American Economy
1763-1815—The Emergence of a New Nation
1816-1865—The Rise of a New Nation. Internal and External Development
1866-1920—The Nation Matures. Development of Economic Nationalism
1921-present—The United States in a World Economy

One section of this book will be devoted to each of these periods, in which the significant events and economic trends will be presented and analyzed. In accordance with the stated policy of deemphasizing developments in the early years of our existence and of placing more emphasis on more recent occurrences, Parts IV and V each contain as many chapters as are found in the first three parts combined.

The choice of dates to frame a period must always be arbitrary. History is a continuum, and man's attempts to break it into periods or stages always does some damage to the reality of historical change. The concept of an historical period is not only a matter of its initial and terminal dates, it is shaped by the continuity of a type of economic development and by endogenous and exogenous factors.

There can be no doubt as to when the Colonial Period began. From a political point of view, it may have extended to the signing of the Declaration of Independence in 1776 or to the signing of the second Treaty of Paris in 1783 which formally brought to a close the Revolutionary War with England. We have chosen 1789, the year the Constitution of the United States was ratified, as the terminal year of the Colonial Period. When reference is made within the text to the Colonial Period, the years involved will be 1607-1789.

From an economic point of view, one phase of the Colonial Period may be considered to have terminated in 1763 in which year the signing of the first Treaty of Paris brought to a close the Seven Years War between England and France. Drastic changes occurred after this year in our relationships with England, as well as in the development of our own economic institutions. Thus in our division within the text, we will recognize 1763 as the year which marked the beginning of the last phase of the Colonial Period and the Emergence of a New Nation.

Many or most of the economic institutions and relationships that existed prior to 1763 continued long after the signing of the second Treaty of Paris in 1783 or the writing of the Constitution of the United States in 1789. The Colonists were struggling to assert themselves against the opposition of foreign aggressors. By the close of the War of 1812, the United States was relatively free of foreign interference, and it was strong enough to embark on positive economic programs.

Since the composite of economic developments after 1816 resulted in an armed clash between those who believed that the individual States should be permitted to exercise the right of economic determinism and those who believed that this right should rest upon a strong central government, the major economic developments that took place and the economic institutions that were adopted during the years of war are discussed along with the conditions that gave rise to the Civil War. While foreign economic relationships continued to loom large in our program of economic development, it was during this period that internal trade and commerce commanded the attention of entrepreneurs to the extent that they challenged the leadership of foreign trade as employers of labor and in the origin and use of capital. Problems of a market economy beset those engaged in agriculture. The factory system was extended and enlarged, and labor sought organizational relief to the problems of wages, hours, and working conditions.

The American economy reached a state of maturity in the 50 years following the close of the Civil War, and the development of economic nationalism gave expression to this fact. Again, our entry into a world conflict made manifest the position the United States had attained not only in its internal development, but in its external economic relationships. Even though the Armistice was signed in November, 1918, this period is extended to 1920, as the immediate impacts of war shaped our economy until then.

The year, 1921, marks the entry of the United States into a world economy on a peacetime basis; at least it marked the beginning of a period that did not experience an armed conflict of major proportions for another 20 years. A rather complete reorganization of our internal economic institutions and relationships was initiated this same year. The Great Depression of the 1930's was international in its causation as well as in its impacts. Government attempted to shape and control our economic institutions in a positive manner rather than negatively. World War II initiated an inflationary price trend that has been difficult to control effectively.

QUESTIONS FOR REVIEW

1. Define the discipline of economic history. How does it differ from economics? How are economics and economic history related?

2. What are the factors of production? What problems have grown out of the fact that the proportion between these factors has not remained constant?

3. How has consumption contributed to economic growth?

4. Is the expansion of economic activity the same as economic growth? Explain your answer.

5. What is economic theory? How is it used in economic history?

6. Why does economic history include a study of the geographic characteristics of an area?

7. What is meant by "economic impact"? by "economic dislocation"? Give examples of each.

SUGGESTED READINGS

Clapham, Sir John. "Economic History as a Discipline," *Enterprise and Secular Change,* edited by Frederic C. Lane and Jelle C. Riemersma. Homewood, Ill.: Richard D. Irwin, Inc., 1953.

Heckscher, Eli F. "A Plea for Theory in Economic History," *Enterprise and Secular Change,* edited by Frederic C. Lane and Jelle C. Riemersma. Homewood, Ill.: Richard D. Irwin, Inc., 1953.

Johnson, E. A. J., and Herman E. Kroos, *The American Economy.* Englewood Cliffs, N.J.: Prentice-Hall, Inc., 1960. Chapter 6.

Robertson, Ross M. *History of the American Economy.* 2d ed. New York City: Harcourt, Brace & World, Inc., 1964. Chapter 1.

Schumpeter, Joseph A. "The Creative Response in Economic History," *Economic Change in America,* edited by Joseph T. Lambie and Richard V. Clemence. Harrisburg, Pa.: Stackpole Books, 1954.

——————. "Theoretical Problems of Economic Growth," *Economic Change in America,* edited by Joseph T. Lambie and Richard V. Clemence. Harrisburg, Pa.: Stackpole Books, 1954.

Wright, Chester W. *Economic History of the United States.* 2d ed. New York City: McGraw-Hill Book Company, 1949. Chapter 1.

PART I

Colonization and the Genesis
of the American Economy—1607-1763

The early years of the Colonial Period were characterized by struggles for existence in all of the colonies. Early colonial populations were more homogeneous in their attitudes towards the mother country than were later ones, and they accepted English domination more graciously. The longer the colonists had been here and the more heterogeneous the populace, the greater became the desire for more freedoms, both political and economic. Since the settlement of and migration to the American colonies were, in part, in the nature of protest movements, it is not surprising that their overall development was characterized by resistances to regulations that were imposed upon them and partially enforced against them. Even though some of the provisions of the Navigation Acts of the mid-17th century, which will be presented in Chapter 2, accrued to their benefit, the very idea of England attempting to regulate their external trade relations was repugnant to them.

In the early years, it was the development of economic institutions that established the background for the expressions and manifestations of greater independence of thought and action. By the critical year of 1763, the colonists had not developed any particular sense of political or economic unity, but they did have their own system of land tenure and their systems for the conduct of external and internal trade. Semblances of monetary and banking institutions had appeared in each of the colonies.

The political situation was made worse by the overseas struggle between England and France for colonial supremacy. The French supported the Indians in their resistance to the colonists' encroachments upon their lands and hunting grounds. This support spurred the Indians to raid colonial frontier settlements. General histories of the Colonial Period present the details of these depredations in their accounts of the French and Indian War. The termination of this war in 1763 initiated a new era of colonial unrest, which constitutes the subject matter of Part II of this text.

Chapter 2

THE COLONIZATION OF AMERICA

The successful establishment of English colonies in North America was the last step in a long process of European economic expansion. Beginning with the resurgence of Mediterranean trade in the 11th century, and aided by the broadening effects of the Crusades, trade and commerce grew rapidly to meet the desires of people for goods that only faraway lands could provide. The exploration of unknown areas and the opening of new trade routes to the Orient were stimulated by the efforts to satisfy those desires. A century of voyaging by Spanish and Portuguese ships opened new trade routes with the East around the southern tip of Africa and enlarged the 15th-century world through the discovery of a hitherto unsuspected New World. As nations grew in power and as the desire for greater power spread, rulers looked to the newly opened lands for both markets and essential raw materials. The widespread goal of national self-sufficiency seemed attainable if only the new lands could be exploited. Colonization proved to be one effective means of exploitation which preserved strong governmental control. Spain, Portugal, France, and Holland instituted programs of colonization and settlement for trade purposes during the 16th century. England entered the colonization movement relatively late, but her settlements in the New World were based on the same economic and political motives that had stimulated non-English colonization in earlier years. This late start ultimately proved to be no hindrance, as the English colonies on the mainland were to flourish, rebel, and gain their independence as the United States of America.

THE GROWTH OF TRADE AND COLONIZATION

After a period of decline and relative economic inactivity during the Dark Ages, trade in Europe revived during the early 11th century, as Italian city-states, such as Venice and Florence, expanded trade with Asia Minor and the Far East. Commercial activity stimulated by expansion gradually spread to other European states, so that by the 12th century, both southern and northern Europe were enjoying higher levels of trade and primitive manufacture. Feudal institutions, which had tightly controlled

European economic life during the late Middle Ages, began to disintegrate. The resulting freedom of activity permitted widespread participation in commerce by groups from many levels of society. A monetary basis for the exchange of goods and services was provided by the network of banks of deposit, merchant bankers, and moneylenders, and by the growth of a widely accepted gold and silver coinage.

The Nature of Trade

Foreign goods were widely demanded by Europeans only after the Crusades had brought the Christian West into contact with the Muslim Near East, introducing new ideas and new tastes into western society. Luxury goods of all sorts, including fine fabrics, jewelry, perfumes, cutlery, and glassware were in great demand by the affluent mercantile and ruling classes. Spices and pepper proved to be necessities when it was found that they could be used to preserve meats and produce during a time when refrigeration was either unknown or impractical. Apothecaries found eastern drugs useful additions to their stocks in trade. Many kinds of new foods and beverages became common as Europeans expanded their previously limited diets. National demands for gold and other precious metals added to the importance of trade. With metallic money being widely used to finance armies and navies, its accumulation became a requisite for the development of national economic and political power. Governmental control or taxation of trade provided an opportunity for amassing needed funds or influencing the flow of money over national boundaries.

In return for the exotic goods of the East, Europeans exchanged staples such as salt, wine, hides, woolen cloth, and basic metals. Gold and silver also financed a part of the eastern imports, being readily acceptable by Oriental merchants in either bullion or coined form. It was only natural that interregional trade would foster intraregional trade. Northern and southern European merchants began to develop channels of trade with one another. The channels so created quickly eased the difficulty of trade within the continental countries. An efficient system of trade routes and commercial institutions reduced both the cost of transport and exchange of commodities, and the time required in transit. Land and coastal trade routes were supplemented by the fairs of France and the Hanseatic cities which evolved into major financial and commercial markets. The goods of European producers ultimately found buyers not only in the East, but also in neighboring towns and countries.

Trade and Change

Social and economic change was thus a major characteristic of the period between A.D. 1000 and 1500. More important, however, was the willingness of peoples to incorporate those changes into their manner of living. New attitudes and new beliefs were accepted, principal among them being the thought that man could find out about the world in which he lived and could use his knowledge to his advantage. This belief helped to support the trade and exploration that rising incomes and increasing demands for goods had initiated.

Trade and Trade Routes

The early trade routes between Europe and the Near East involved a combination of land and sea transport. Most of them followed a general east-west direction. After crossing France, they traversed the Mediterranean Sea, the Black Sea, or the Caspian Sea en route to the Near East and the riches of the even more distant Orient. The strategic location of the Italian city-states, foremost among which were Venice, Genoa, and Florence, permitted them to control or even monopolize a great part of this east-west traffic. In addition to providing shipping services for other countries, these city-states levied taxes on goods going in either direction, generally raising their delivered prices and aggravating the balance of trade problem felt by the participating countries. Mercantilistic reasoning could not condone the continuation of the Italian trade monopoly.

The Reaction to Italian Dominance. Most of the western and northern European nations began to seek an alternative to trade that was channeled through Italian ports. In particular, a search was begun for trade routes that would eliminate the Italian middlemen, yet give free access to Far Eastern ports. Prince Henry of Portugal devoted the last part of his life to encouraging exploration along the West African coast and into the Atlantic, in the hope of finding new and more direct sea routes to the Orient. His efforts bore fruit when Bartholomew Diaz rounded the Cape of Good Hope in 1488. A sea route to India around the tip of Africa was the result.

Just as important as the exploration of African waters was the westward movement into the Atlantic. By 1470, the Portuguese had recolonized the Azores, and adventuresome sailors were talking of a sea route to the Orient lying in a due western direction. Educated people of the time no longer believed the earth to be flat. This fact, combined with vastly improved ships and navigational instruments, led to the belief that ships could sail due west to the fabled Indies. No one dreamed that a continent lay in the way.

In 1492, the Genoese adventurer, Christopher Columbus, found this continent. He and subsequent explorers labored under the illusion that the lands they had found were in extreme eastern Asia. Within a decade or so, Europeans recognized that they had opened up a New World, and rushed to exploit its treasures. A major shift in trade routes occurred.

The Westward Movement of Trade Routes. The focus of trade during the early 16th century quickly moved from the Mediterranean to the Atlantic. Although trade with the Far East was still important, it was carried out largely by sea around Africa, using routes into the Atlantic from either the Mediterranean Sea or the North and Baltic Seas.

Apart from the trans-Africa trade, the new interest in the Americas also helped to shift the trade routes westward. Major east-west sea lanes were opened for trade with the Caribbean area during the early 16th century. Then came exploration of Central America, large parts of South America, and accessible southern areas of North America, that gave rise to expansion of sea trade between western Europe and the New World.

As might be expected, old trading centers which flourished on the Mediterranean trade declined in importance, and new centers emerged or grew in importance with the Atlantic trade. Most of these cities served as *entrepots,* or else were manufacturing or processing centers that depended on New World materials for their growth. Typical among these new centers were Cadiz, San Lucal, and Palos in Spain; Lisbon in Portugal; Bordeaux and Calais in France; London and Plymouth in England; Antwerp and Amsterdam in the Low Countries; and several German ports, such as Hamburg and Bremen.

Colonization

The establishment of colonies was easily justified as a means to self-sufficiency and the protection of national interests abroad. All of the major trading nations engaged in colonization, although their timing and methods varied. Spain, Portugal, France, Holland, and England were the principal colonizing powers.

Early Colonial Policies. All the major colonial powers except England began colonization during the early 16th century. Almost without exception, their colonies were only trading posts or fringe settlements, involving a small number of personnel from the mother country and depending on the cooperation or enslavement of native peoples for their success. The Dutch were able to set up trading posts in the East Indies, for example, but could not develop them further because of limitations of manpower and resources in the mother country.

Spain's efforts were also typical. She sought short-run, "get-rich-quick" returns on a minimum of short-term capital investment, rather than less spectacular profits arising from permanent and extensive settlement. She was exploitative, not developmental, and did not strive for a permanent foothold in her possessions. French settlements took the form of trading posts, fishing ports, and religious missions during the first great wave of colonization, and, therefore, lacked permanency. A balanced and growing population, interdependent in their economic activities, is necessary for long-term life of a colony.

English Colonial Policies. The major difference between English colonization and that of her competitors lay in the role of the government. While Spanish, French, and Dutch settlements were sanctioned, supported, and regulated by government, English settlements from the beginning were largely private enterprise undertakings. The English Crown supported colonization, and issued charters and grants to the groups and individuals who wished to plant colonies on the North American mainland. In 1696, the Board of Trade and Plantations was set up to supervise colonial activities and see that they were conducted in consonance with mercantilistic [1] ideals.

The English colonies were thus private organizations, established for the purpose of making profits for their owners, and oriented from the beginning toward extensive settlement and relocation of colonists in a productive environment. These goals were strengthened by the desire of many English citizens to make their home in the New World where abundant land and religious freedom could be found. It is true that almost all the English colonies on the mainland ultimately reverted to the Crown. By this time they were established economically and were permanent.

Early American Settlements

The earliest settlements in New England and in Virginia were made by individuals or groups of persons who were seeking profits in their new ventures. The people who settled America in the early 17th century found it inhabited by Indians who had no organization worthy of the name *economy*; hence, it was incumbent upon them to establish the skeleton framework of an economy within the limits of which they could produce, first, food, clothing, and shelter, and later other desirable articles of wealth that would make life and living more pleasurable and less rigorous. The search for profits had become the driving force that furthered economic endeavor in Europe, and the quest for profits lay behind the early settlements in America. When it became evident that the forces of free enterprise were not strong enough to overcome the barriers to financial success, government stepped in and adopted a program of development that strengthened the feeling of economic nationalism and its realization. The colonies in America were given royal charters and in this manner were recognized as integral parts of the British empire. Local governments were provided, but they were presided over by representatives of the Crown. Customs officials and court judges were also appointed by the Crown. Control over money and currency and limitations on manufacturing and trade, domestic and foreign, were exercised at the level of British government.

While the profit motive was strong in the hearts of those who dispatched settlers to North America, it was a combination of religious and economic discontent that caused the latter to spread out and to establish additional colonies. Roger Williams sought refuge from religious persecution in Plymouth and founded the colony of Rhode Island in 1636. In a few years that colony contained several fishing ports. Shipbuilding, shipping, and whaling were important industries; and the first textile mill in America was erected by Samuel Slater in 1790 at Pawtucket.

---

[1] See page 34, "British Colonial Policy" and "Mercantilistic Attitudes and Laws," for a definition and discussion of British mercantilistic policy and laws.

About the same time, one of the initial phases of the westward movement in America occurred on the occasion of the migration of settlers from Massachusetts. These people not only were disgruntled at the religious dogmatism of the Puritans, but were equally dissatisfied with the soil and topography of the farmlands nearby. The valley of the Connecticut River provided more fertile soil, and the distance removed them from the wrath of the Puritans. Hartford and Windsor were settled in 1638 and New Haven a few months later. New Hampshire was founded in 1637 by refugees from religious persecution in Massachusetts.

When Charles II granted a charter in 1664 to establish a colony in New York, he dealt a direct blow to the Dutch who had been trading up and down the Hudson River. To the west of the lower Hudson River, John Carteret and Lord Berk were granted what is now New Jersey. It was in that colony that one George Fox established Quakerism, but it was in Pennsylvania on the western side of the Delaware River that it experienced its greatest development. In 1681 William Penn was granted the largest amount of land ever granted by the Crown to an individual.

Because George Calvert was unhappy over the long winters in Newfoundland, winters that lasted from October to May, he migrated south in 1632 and obtained a Royal Charter that gave him a slice of Virginia to the north, which he called Maryland. Virginia lost another slice of land, this time to the south, when the Carolina colony was chartered in 1663. Charleston was founded in 1680 and was destined to become not only the nucleus of the colony of South Carolina, but one of the most important coastal towns in all of Colonial America.

Causes of Immigration

The peopling of the colonies could not have proceeded as rapidly as it did without substantial inflows of immigrants from abroad. And immigrants would not have been impelled to leave their homelands for a strange new country without a strong stimulus for movement. The causes underlying immigration deserve some discussion. For purposes of clarity, they may be divided into forces of "pull" and forces of "push."

Forces of "Pull." The forces of "pull" were those that attracted people from their place of living and led them to take up their homes in a new environment. Foremost among the forces that attracted people to this country was the opportunity to own land—an opportunity not open to many Englishmen or continental Europeans because of status or income. Not only was American land to be had very cheaply, but there were few social and legal barriers to its ownership by all who had the desire. The land hunger of the immigrant could often be satisfied by no more expense than the cost of passage to the colonies. It is true, however, that those colonies in which a landed aristocracy was built up passed laws of *entail* and *primogeniture* to protect and perpetuate those aristocracies. *Entail* prevented land from being sold to persons outside the families of the respective owners, and *primogeniture* passed title or a major share to the oldest son upon the decease of the owner. But there was land enough for all, especially as the frontier moved westward to and beyond the Appalachians.

In order to hasten the peopling of the Virginia colony, the *headright system* was used to give encouragement to immigrants leaving their homeland in order to settle in Virginia. Under that system, fifty acres of land were given to a person who transported, or was responsible for the coming of, a new settler to America who remained there three years. Later, the system gave the head of a family fifty acres for every member of his family who immigrated and fifty acres for every servant he brought into the colony. Similar plans were used in Maryland and other Southern Colonies. In addition to settling more colonists in America, these plans contributed to the progress of the westward movement as most of the land granted under the headright system was located on or beyond the frontier.

Another pull factor was a desire to engage in some kind of economic activity which many persons could not enter at home because of some legal or customary barrier. To many readers, this factor more properly may appear to be one of push, but since some initiative was required on the part of those who emigrated, it more properly belongs to the forces of pull. Another pull factor, and again one that could have been a push factor just as well, was the opportunity for freedom of worship in America. The student who is familiar with the dogmatism of the Puritans may well question the honesty and integrity of their belief in this principle as it applied to persons other than themselves. Since western economy was becoming decidely more capitalistic, another force on the pull side was the opportunity or prospective possibility of making profits. People could be found in all walks of life in the several colonies whose objective was the making of profits. They were landowners, some were merchants, others were artisans. Those who were engaged in shipping and in shipbuilding are known to have made profits that were large in terms of the environment in which they originated.

Forces of "Push." Forces of "push" were those conditions in the settler's homeland that made it undesirable for him to remain, given the alternative of moving to the New World.

The low level of wages in England was one of the factors of push rather than of pull, because many of those who sought an escape from low wages at home became landowners or merchants in America, whose incomes did not consist of wages. Another push factor was the increasing number of paupers and beggars who were sent to America in large numbers. While these people were not welcomed by the colonists, and Benjamin Franklin raised his voice in objection to their being sent over, it must be said to their credit that many of them led productive and respectable lives and contributed to the progress of the colonies. Unfortunately, among the push forces was a certain amount of kidnapping of children and pauper adults from the streets of English cities. These persons became *indentured servants* [2] involuntarily and were forced to serve terms of indenture that ranged from five to seven years. Undoubtedly, those whose terms were for seven years were sold by their captors at a profit above the actual cost of transportation from England to America, and it may have been these persons who escaped from their indenture to take up free land on the frontier. Many prisoners were given the choice of the death penalty or imprisonment, or of being sent to America, and they chose the latter. Among these prisoners who came to America to get a new start on life were political dissenters and some who were guilty of civil offenses. When the Edict of Nantes was repealed in 1685, many French Huguenots migrated to America where they settled largely in the Middle or Southern Colonies; and there are many surnames in the Carolinas that serve as constant reminders of the coming of those hardy people. Many Germans came over in the 18th century to escape persecution. Most of those people were from the upper Rhine valley, the German Palatinate; and they settled in Maryland and Pennsylvania, in both of which states much German culture is still found.

CHARACTERISTICS OF THE COLONIAL ECONOMY

Much insight into later American growth can be gained from an understanding of the economic characteristics of the colonies. Land was in such abundance it was almost free. Labor could not be measured in terms of population, because many of the settlers came to America to work for themselves rather than for others. Almost every head of a family was an entrepreneur either in agriculture, in fishing, or in trade and commerce. What capital existed was of the crudest kind. The settlers brought little with them; and they did not produce enough to save, which is necessary to create capital. The economic institutions with which colonists were familiar, the resources they were able to use, the technology they implemented, and the governmental policies they faced—all combined to shape the future of the American settlements.

Colonial Economic Institutions

Although it is difficult to rank the basic economic institutions of the colonies in order of their importance, an analysis of the more important ones is necessary in order to understand colonial economic development. In addition, coverage of these institutions will shed some light on the attitude the colonists took toward England during the latter part of the Colonial Period, especially after 1763.

The institution of *private property* in land and in consumers' goods was basic to the successful cooperation of the colonists in providing the bare necessities of life, let alone some of the comforts and luxuries of the times.

---

[2] For a further discussion of indentured servants, see page 43.

Until the men of John Smith were permitted to own the land upon which they worked and were given ownership rights to the product of their toil, they put forth little effort and the entire colony was faced with extinction. Probably the most concerted effort to transplant the English manor to America was along the banks of the Hudson River in New York, but it was not until the settlers were given ownership rights to the land that the colony became well populated.

The *profit motive* was uppermost in the minds of the colonists. Even though many of them were devout church members, and they maintained a high level of ethical and moral standards in their social patterns, they were not abashed over the possibility of making a profit from their commercial transactions. In fact it was the search for profits that motivated the colonists to ignore or to evade many of the trade restrictions laid down by the mother country. It was the profit motive that was responsible for the failure of the colonists to cooperate to their utmost in complying with the terms or the program of British colonial policy.

Not only did many colonists come to America because of the opportunity to own land, many of them came because they wanted the right to choose their manner of earning a livelihood. Western European countries had begun to cast off the cloak of custom and tradition. The enclosure movement resulted in the breakdown of the manorial system in England. Landed estates were transforming their arable lands into pastures. Cattle grazing replaced tillable agriculture. Fewer farmhands were needed to tend cattle than were required to cultivate manorial lands. Serfs had been driven from the land, and tradesmen in urban centers attempted to restrict the activities of newcomers. Enforced unemployment prevented many persons from giving expression to their personal talents in earning their living. They saw what other persons were accomplishing when they were given freedom to pursue their own economic interests. They thought there would be more latitude in the exercise of *freedom of enterprise* in America. In exercising this right, freedom in the exchange of goods and the *use of money* was a *sine qua non*. Not only were the colonists irked at the efforts of England to create a shortage of money and currency in the colonies, they deliberately violated a prohibition against the issuance and use of bills of credit after 1741. In order to keep the colonies and colonists dependent upon the mother country intercolonial or domestic trade was discouraged, if not forbidden, as was the manufacture of furs, and iron beyond the secondary stage. These efforts by England made little difference to the colonists who were over here to help themselves rather than being here for the glory of Old England.

That the advantages of *economic specialization*[3] and *division of labor* were well known to the people who settled America and who contributed

---

[3] Economic specialization, regional or product, is based upon the principle of *comparative cost advantage*. This principle was discussed in Chapter 1, page 9, under "Practical Knowledge of Economic Laws."

to its growth there is no doubt; this accounted for the appearance of tradesmen and specialty occupational groups. Many of the settlers in other colonies made no effort to sustain themselves in supplying all of their wants for goods, clothing, shelter, and some of the comforts of life. Fishermen knew that while they were out catching fish in greater quantities than they and their immediate families could consume, others would be cultivating and harvesting wheat, corn, pumpkin, and other products in greater amounts than they would need; and trade between the groups would solve the mutually respective problems of oversupply and scarcity of goods. They wanted the privilege of determining the prices of goods without the interference of governmental regulation or of a monopoly control group. *Free pricing* was another one of the institutions with which they were familiar, and they resented any action by any organized group that would tend to introduce price control or price rigidity.

Sectional Differences

For purposes of closer economic analysis, it is convenient to divide the American colonies into Northern or New England, Middle, and Southern Colonies, because of the many basic differences in the economic character-istics that were found in these respective groups of colonies. This technique will be utilized in a general way in the following sections that deal with population, growth of cities, and labor supply. These differences were not the result of personal preferences or whims of outstanding leaders in the colonies; they were adjusted to the natural environment—climate, coastline, topography, character of the soil, natural resources—of the several colonies. To a certain extent the economic institutions of Colonial America were transplantations of the economic institutions of Europe, with local adaptations as made necessary by the environmental conditions. There was no *one* system of landholding in all of the colonies, for example. Each group of colonies tended to solve the labor shortage in its own way. The same prod-ucts could not be grown throughout the entire length of the Atlantic coastal area. The one factor that was important to all of the colonies, wherever they were located, was the importance of their external trade relations; but even in this area of economic activity, the pattern of development was not the same for all of them, nor was the relative importance of their commodity exports and of their commodity imports of the same significance. They did not place equal emphasis upon trade, shipbuilding, and the carrying trade. Their degree of dependence upon England, as well as upon the rest of the known world differed, as did the nature and kinds of domestic industries.

New England Colonies. Massachusetts, New Hampshire, Rhode Island, and Connecticut comprised the New England group of colonies. The area which was later to become Maine was a part of Massachusetts, and Vermont was still an integral part of New York. This group of colonies was more homogeneous in its characteristics and economic development than were other groups. Except for the differences in name, the New England Colonies were quite similar in their agricultural development, their industries, and their dependence upon the sea for a livelihood.

Agriculture at more than a subsistence level was difficult to achieve in New England, due to the rocky soil, hilly terrain, severe winters, and short growing season. Some coastal areas, and a few low-lying regions such as the Connecticut River Valley, did provide extensive arable lands. But these were never enough to make commercial farming possible on a significant scale. The real strength of New England's economy lay in its proximity to the productive fishing banks off the Atlantic Coast, its ample forests with wood supplies suitable for shipbuilding, and its many rushing rivers which served as the source of power for the waterwheels of mills and yards. From the beginning of settlement, conditions in New England caused its inhabitants to be outward-looking toward the sea and its riches.

Middle Colonies. The Middle Colonies included New York, New Jersey, Pennsylvania, Delaware, and Maryland. This group was less homogeneous than the New England group in terms of economic development. New York, for example, had many characteristics in common with the New England Colonies; while Maryland enjoyed the extensive agriculture which was a trait of the Southern group. All of the Middle Colonies, nevertheless, enjoyed a common climate and a common mix of agriculture and industry.

Agriculture was very much favored by a longer growing season, adequate rainfall, and broad lands which proved to be extremely fertile when cleared. Pennsylvania and New York were the leaders in this category. Water transportation into the inland areas was facilitated by the many navigable rivers of the region. Trade which combined the movement of goods from hinterland to seacoast with the movement of goods over the Atlantic was thus made possible. Adequate natural resources, including iron ore, wood, and waterpower, supported some domestic industry. The Middle Colonies enjoyed a balanced type of growth that was to prove of great advantage in later years.

Southern Colonies. The Southern Colonies consisted of Virginia, North and South Carolina, and Georgia. Towards the close of the Colonial Period, the areas which now make up Tennessee and Kentucky were being explored, but they were parts of North Carolina and Virginia respectively at the time. The Southern group was almost as homogeneous as the New England group in regard to its pattern of development, but the emphasis was different.

Climate and location conspired to make the Southern Colonies ideally suited for agriculture, to the detriment of trade and industry. Southern lands were broad, adequately fertile, and readily accessible by water. They received plentiful rainfall during a growing season that permitted two successive crops in the lower South. Under existing conditions, tobacco and rice could be grown profitably from the time of earliest settlement. Southern pine forests provided important naval stores for the sea-oriented English possessions, while furbearing animals of many sorts supported another extractive industry. The Southern Colonies, unlike the New England Colonies, looked inland for their future.

British Colonial Policy

British colonial policy was mercantilistic. *Mercantilism* was a program of economic policies and controls that had for its purpose the building of a strong, economically independent, national state. In the application of mercantilistic principles to the relationships between England and her colonies, the latter were to be subservient to the former. It was this attitude of the English people, given expression in acts of Parliament, that created a strong undercurrent of unrest throughout all of the colonies, and that kept rising to the surface in the form of one protest movement or another. The early manifestations of unrest were spasmodic, unorganized, disorganized, and of short duration.

Mercantilistic Attitudes and Laws.[4] British mercantilism as applied to the American colonies was directed towards creating a shortage of money in the colonies. Without money, it would be difficult to trade among and between themselves, or so thought the English, and trade as it was related to the colonies would become overseas trade. How correct they were in their thinking is made manifest by the statement, which is true, that the outstanding feature of the American colonial economy was its external trade relations.[5] It was not difficult at first for England to enforce the mercantile ideal of interregional trade relations which resulted in commodity exports exceeding in value commodity imports, with the difference paid in money, and gold and silver money, too. While this condition was known as a favorable balance of trade to the English, it was decidedly unfavorable for the colonies, all the more so because there were no natural deposits of gold and/or silver known to exist in the original thirteen colonies. The only money metals that were available for shipment to England were those (1) that the colonists received in settlement of favorable balances between themselves and countries other than England, or (2) that were acquired by acts of depredation, called piracy or *privateering,* upon the vessels of other nations that plied the waters of the Atlantic Ocean. *Privateering* was a form of legalized piracy that was conducted under the terms of a license obtained from government. Spanish vessels that were laden with gold and silver ob-

---

[4] Because of the large number of mercantilistic writers in England, it is difficult to determine where the mainstream of mercantilistic thought lay. However, the most important ideas of the time may be found in the works of Gerald de Malynes (1586-1641), Thomas Mun (1571-1641), Sir William Petty (1623-87), and Sir James Steuart (1712-80).

[5] See, for example, Guy S. Callender (ed.), *Selections from the Economic History of the United States: 1765-1860* (Boston: Ginn and Co., 1909), pp. 6-83; and Douglass C. North and Robert P. Thomas (eds.), *The Growth of the American Economy to 1860* (New York City: Harper and Row, Publishers, 1968), pp. 56-110.

tained from Mexico and from South America fell prey to the depredations of privateers who were based in Colonial America and in the British West Indies. The English were not unmindful of the fact that trade was going on among the colonies and areas that were external to the English sphere of influence. Some of this trade was contrary to the spirit of the Navigation Acts,[6] but it was tolerated because its end results brought new gold and/or silver into the dominion of England. Another possible or potential source of metallic money was the amounts brought over by immigrants, but this source turned out to be unfruitful in the long run. Immigrants to the American colonies were not wealthy in terms of money holdings at the time of their arrival. Many of them had little or no savings to bring, and again it was contrary to mercantile policy and practice for foreign countries to permit immigrants to take specie with them.

As the colonial economy advanced, due to the exercise of the talents of the colonists, many of whom were artisans of one kind or another, England found it necessary or desirable to enact laws that had for their purpose discouraging the development of manufacturing industries in the colonies. For instance, an English manufacturer of hats who noticed that the colonial market for hats was declining, and who knew that one or more of his former employees had migrated to America, petitioned Parliament to forbid the manufacture of hats in Connecticut by any person who had not served an apprenticeship. This prohibition was effective in all of the American colonies. In order to preserve the market for processed iron, processing iron beyond the "pig" stage in America was forbidden. In view of what already has been said about these kinds of restrictions, nothing more need be added other than to remind the reader that both hats and iron continued to be manufactured in the American colonies.

The Navigation Acts.[7] While the Navigation Acts that were passed in the middle of the 17th century were aimed primarily at the lucrative trade that was carried on by the Dutch, their impact was felt in the American colonies. They tended to stimulate the shipping and shipbuilding activities of the colonies, first, by restricting the carrying trade between England and her colonies to ships of British registry, and, secondly, by requiring that three fourths of the ships' crews be British subjects. By admitting ships that were built in the colonies to British registry, and by including American colonists as British citizens for purposes of enforcing these Acts, shipbuilding and shipping were made still more attractive and profitable. This interpretation opened the door to the germination of an industry in which, after a few years of development, the colonists had a comparative cost advantage. Before that advantage was acquired, the Crown offered bounties for the build-

---

[6] The Navigation Acts were English laws aimed at regulating colonial trade for the benefit of the mother country.

[7] Although Navigation Acts were passed by the English Parliament over a period of several centuries, the acts most important to conditions in the American colonies were those of 1651, 1660, and 1663.

ing of ships and for the production of naval stores in general—pitch, turpentine, tar, rosin, masts, and spars. Although ships were built all along the Atlantic Coast, New England, New York, and Charleston were areas in which this activity was concentrated. In order to encourage their production, the colonial legislatures of Connecticut and Virginia required the planting of both flax and hemp, and later bounties as high as £6 per ton were offered to overcome a cost disadvantage experienced by producers of hemp in Maryland, North Carolina, and South Carolina.

The *principle of enumeration* was adopted to assure the shipment of raw materials from the colonies to England where they served as raw materials for manufacturing industries, and to prevent them from being shipped to countries that were economic competitors of England. Among these products were sugar, tobacco, raw cotton, indigo, rustic and other dyewoods, ginger, naval stores, rice from South Carolina, copper ore, beaver skins, whale fins, hides, potash and pearlash, iron and lumber. The final step in that direction was taken in 1766, when the shipment of nonenumerated articles, the most important of which were fish, rum, and grain, was restricted to England, Ireland, and to the countries south of Cape Finisterre.

Ships that were destined to dock at a colonial port had to have papers showing that they had come directly from a British port. Trade could be carried on directly between the British West Indies and the American colonies, but those coming from European countries were required to stop first in England. This policy was consistent with mercantilism, the principles of which dominated the thinking of the British people. Ships also were required to take their cargoes directly from the country of their origin to England; but this specification, along with many others, was honored in the breach. Coastwise shipping among and between the American colonies was restricted to colonial or to British ships.

Regional Differences in Policy. Due to differences in natural environment, the respective groups of colonies did not fit alike into the program of British mercantilism, which is another way of saying that the colonies did not all serve alike the purposes for which they were established and promoted. England had no intention of developing a colonial empire that would be competitive with the economy of England itself. According to accepted mercantile doctrine of that day, the economy of a colony should not be competitive with that of the mother country; it should be supplementary. While it is true that the trade relations of all of the colonies with England were their most important economic characteristic, the trade between England and the Southern Colonies was more supplementary to that of England than was the trade between England and either or both of the other groups. As will be brought out in the following paragraphs, the agricultural activity of the southern colonists produced crops that could not be produced in England and were much in demand there, while the products of New England were somewhat highly competitive with those of England. The economy of the Middle Colonies was partly competitive with, partly supplementary to, that of the mother country. The degree of competition between the economies of the colonies and that of the mother country conditioned the degree of economic independence of the colonies. The Southern Colonies were much more dependent upon England than were the Northern or Middle Colonies as a source for goods and supplies and also for the export market for tobacco, rice, and indigo. The New England Colonies were more independent of England than the other two groups because of their more diverse economic interests and the capabilities of the colonists themselves. Their settlements were more in the nature of communities, somewhat balanced and more varied in activity than were those in the South. The Middle Colonies occupied a position less pronounced in either direction. In certain areas a strong dependency appeared; in others they expressed a high degree of independence. The Middle Colonies did have a somewhat peculiar function in carrying out England's mercantile program, and that was in connection with precious metals. The final step in maintaining a favorable balance of trade was the shipment of specie (metallic money), or at least gold and silver metal, to England. It was the trade between the Middle Colonies and the Mediterranean countries, the Azores, and the Madeira Islands that provided either the bills of exchange or the metals themselves needed to complete that payment.

Colonial Production and Consumption

When the white man first settled in America he did not find an economic system worthy of the name. The Indians still were in the agricultural stage of development, and their techniques were somewhat crude though effective. Hunting and fishing also were engaged in by the Indians, and again their techniques were primitive. It was in protest against the loss of their hunting grounds that the Indian fought the white man in the latter's progress across the continent. The Indian had no use for money, as much of his life was communal. What trading or exchanging there was took place on a *barter* basis. The white man soon learned that wampum and sea shells would serve as media of exchange between him and the Indian. He also learned that a black shell was valued more highly by the Indian than a white one; so in order to get more for his money, the white man dyed seashells black. That deceit, which was practiced for profit, affords one of the earliest, if not the first, attempts at counterfeiting money in America.

Household Activities. A brief review of the products of household industry reveals clearly why so little has been written on domestic trade within the colonies. Household industries were those that could utilize the raw natural resources of America, and those for which the processes could be completed almost entirely by hand, with little capital entering into these processes at any stage of their development. Since foodstuffs were the principal items of consumption in every household throughout Colonial America, it was natural that household industries were focused upon meeting the needs for food. Each household supplied itself with foods that are now supplied by bakeries, creameries, cheese factories, packing houses, canning factories, sugar refineries, and last, but by no means least, breweries and wineries. When some form of drink was not an article of consumption it formed the basis of trading with the Indians, or with the people who inhabited areas external to the colonies.

The farmer was also a lumberman and did his own millwork with ax and saw. Using twisted limbs and branches, he fashioned crude scythe, pitchfork, shovel handles, sled runners, ox yokes, and harness hames. Wheels for his carts were solid ends of logs cut crosswise several inches thick. Floors and sides to his wagons, or carts, were rough sawed boards. Seats, when used, were nothing but boards laid from side to side. Since distances for hauling anything were short and riding was extremely rough and uncomfortable, drivers of oxen and/or horses usually walked alongside.

North of Maryland the rural household manufactured its own linens and woolens, and the women and children made clothing for the entire household. The colonies in which tobacco was not only the principal crop but a product for export did not develop the variety of household industries found elsewhere. It was easier to trade tobacco for the clothing and other products needed in the homes or on the plantations than it was to make them. It was only in times of low prices for tobacco, or of crop failures, that cloth and clothing were the products of household industry; and, consequently, skills in weaving, cutting, and sewing were not developed. Intercolonial trade, of which the Southern Colonies were a part, was more important than the domestic trade that went on within these same colonies.

Except for the food the colonists brought with them, and some corn and other cereal grains that they may have obtained from some friendly Indians, their food consisted of a combination of wild game and fish. The growing season varied from six to eight weeks for some plantings in New England to four to nine or ten months for the staples of Pennsylvania, Virginia, and the colonies to the south. Because of the pattern of settlement in all of the colonies, lands in the river valleys were brought under cultivation before farms in the hinterlands appeared, where the first settlements were made by those in search of furs, skins, pelts, and hides. In these settlements, attempts to grow food were scarcely worthy of the name agriculture—the ground was broken with a stick, the seed dropped in and nature did the rest. Harvesting amounted to nothing more than picking by hand, or cutting with a crude knife blade. There was little or no communication between the pioneer frontier houses, many of which were in isolation, and farms or settlements that were nearer the coast. Trade was unknown, and what industry existed was confined to the household.

Commercial Activities. The American colonists had hoped to discover deposits of gold and silver ores. They also had hoped to produce spices, sugar, silk, and indigo—products the English had been importing from Far Eastern countries. They were disappointed in the limited variety of natural resources that were available to them. They may be classified as products of the forest, products of the ocean, and products of the land. There was an abundance of forests all the way from Maine to Georgia, and the products of these forests—naval stores and lumber—formed the basis of much of the export trade of early New England, New York, and South Carolina. Furs also were obtained in abundance and were much sought after by the English. Albany, in New York, and Charleston, in South Carolina, were among the most important fur-trading centers of the period.

Products of the ocean were fish, including whales, cod, haddock, and mackerel. Whale oil was an important product in maintaining the English economy, and it provided a valuable export for the New England Colonies. New Bedford, in the Massachusetts colony, was the center of the whaling industry; and Gloucester, Salem, and Marblehead, all in Massachusetts, were among the prominent fishing ports. Fish were important locally as food for domestic consumption and for export purposes. Fish entered into the colonial trade with England, with Continental Europe, and also with the West Indies. The poorer grades of fish were an important part of the diet of slaves in the Southern Colonies as well as in the West Indies.

Products of the land were grown for food and for purposes of the export trade. Wheat and flour were exported from Philadelphia and Baltimore in the Middle Colonies and from Richmond in the South, tobacco and indigo from Maryland and the Southern Colonies. In exchange for these products the colonists received housewares, clothing, sugar, spices, farm tools, domestic animals, shoes, and a few luxury wares. Other items of import which not only served to break the monotony of a limited diet but afforded opportunities for production and trade were rye, barley, onions, cabbage, apples, carrots, beets, turnips, pears, parsnips, lettuce, peaches, apricots, plums, and cherries. Red clover, bluegrass, grapes, and alfalfa were also imported into the American colonies; and while raspberries and blackberries were native to both sides of the Atlantic Ocean, different varieties of each provided the basis for an extensive interchange of goods between the American colonists and Europeans. The home diet consisted of wild game, fowl, fish, pumpkin, squash, gourds, watermelons, peppers, tomatoes, and potatoes, in addition to a large variety of nuts and berries. In South Carolina and other regions in which floodwaters could be controlled, rice was an important product; and it was for the cultivation of rice, more than of tobacco, that slaves were imported into the Southern Colonies.

Population: Growth and Development

Data on the size of the population and the rate of population growth and its distribution among the colonies cannot be confirmed by checking the census data, as far as an actual count is concerned, but the Bureau of the Census has come up with some interesting figures that are usually con-

sidered as not far from being correct. The increase in population from a
mere 210 white people in 1610 to something short of four million in 1790,
when the first census was taken, was phenomenal, and occurred in the
face of a low net gain in population by natural increase.

Table 2-1

Population of the American Colonies

Year	Population	Average Annual Increase %	Year	Population	Average Annual Increase %
1610	210	. . . . . .	1740	889,000	3.5
1650	51,700	2,450.0	1750	1,207,000	3.5
1700	275,000	43.2	1760	1,610,000	3.3
1710	357,500	3.6	1770	2,205,000	3.5
1720	474,388	3.2	1780	2,781,000	2.6
1730	654,950	3.8	1790	3,929,000	3.5

Source: *A Century of Population Growth, 1790-1900* (Washington: U. S. Department
of Commerce, Bureau of the Census, 1909), p. 9.

Table 2-2

The Distribution of Colonial Population
(1610 Actual Count; Remainder in 000)

	1610		1650		1700		1750		1790	
	Pop.	%	Pop.	%	Pop.	%	Pop.	%	Pop.	%
New England	. . .	. . .	27.2	52.6	106	38.5	346	28.7	1,009	25.7
Middle	. . .	. . .	3.0	5.8	53	19.3	296	24.5	1,017	25.9
Southern	210	100	21.3	41.6	116	42.2	565	46.8	1,903	48.4
Total	210	100	51.5	100.0	275	100.0	1,207	100.0	3,929	100.0

Source: *A Century of Population Growth, 1790-1900* (Washington: U. S. Department
of Commerce, Bureau of the Census, 1909), p. 9.

In 1610, the Southern Colonies (Virginia) contained 100 percent of
the white population in America; but, by 1650, the proportion of the population living in the Southern Colonies had declined to 41 percent in round
numbers. During these years the New England Colonies had grown to contain a little under 53 percent of the population, while the Middle Colonies
had just begun to make an impression with about 6 percent. Undoubtedly,
the large proportionate increase in the population of the Middle Colonies
in 1700, 1750, and 1790 occurred at the expense of New England. This
must not be interpreted as meaning that colonists migrated from New
England to the Middle Colonies in large numbers. It was more a matter of
newly arrived immigrants settling in the Middle Colonies instead of in
New England. Factors of pull to the Middle Colonies were more attractive
than were similar forces to New England. By 1790, the Middle Colonies

had experienced the most rapid increase in population due to the influx of Germans and others into Pennsylvania and Maryland. Almost 26 percent of the colonial population was found in the Middle Colonies in 1790; the Southern Colonies contained about 48 percent; while New England was confronted with a situation that has continued down through the years, a decline in the proportion of total population living there to approximately 26 percent.

The Nature of Immigration. The British colonies were British in name and control only, because they were peopled by nationals from almost all of the European countries. The French Huguenots made their contributions to colonial economic life not only in South Carolina, but in Massachusetts, New York, Virginia, and other colonies. The Scotch-Irish migrated to America in large numbers in the early part of the 18th century, and along with the Germans they settled along the frontier from New York to Georgia. They were of sturdy stock, self-reliant and courageous, some of them of fiery temperament; and they cherished political as well as economic freedom. Their contributions to the American economy are without number; and without their rugged determination, the outcome of the rebellion of 1776 might have been different.

Dutch, Swedes, Germans, Scotch-Irish, French, Italians, Portuguese, Danes, Swiss, Poles, Australians, and probably others—Jew and Gentile, Catholic and Protestant—and their offspring populated young America; exploited its natural resources; extended its frontier to the West; engaged in commerce and industry; and became political, civil, church, and social leaders of their respective communities. Someone has described an American as ". . . a mixture of English, Scotch, Irish, French, Dutch, German, and Swedes. From this promiscuous breed, that race now called American has risen. I could point out to you a family whose grandfather was an Englishman, whose wife was Dutch, whose son married a French woman, and whose present four sons now have four wives of different nations." It is not surprising that these people did not feel that they were an integral part of England and that, when the yoke was tightened after 1763, many of the colonists became restless.

It has been estimated that there may have been as many as 200,000 Germans and other aliens in Colonial America at the outbreak of the American Revolution. While that figure constituted less than 10 percent of the entire population, there were many others of mixed parentage who were not enthusiastically loyal to England, or to any other country, for that matter. While there is no evidence that these people were aggressively opposed to England, undoubtedly their passive resistance gave encouragement to local Tory leaders.

The Contribution of Immigrants. Benjamin Franklin and Thomas Jefferson were somewhat concerned over the migration of so many foreigners into this country. They knew that the so-called best people in Europe were not migrating. They also knew that many persons, undesirable from one point of view or another, were being sent over against their will. None of these people brought any money with them and few of them were skilled artisans, but records indicate that the stimulus of a new environment instilled a new spirit into them, and they made valuable contributions to American life. There was something ahead of them for which to work. Life was not dulled by the monotony of custom and tradition; it was sharpened by new contacts, new environment, new relationships. Yes, there were loafers and dregs upon society and those who would not conform to accepted ways of living. Some of these became the pioneers who opened up new territory to the West. Some of them sought freedom from society's chains by taking to the sea; and, unfortunately, others continued along their slovenly way of life. Taking everything into consideration, the American colonies benefited more than they lost from immigration.

Labor Supply

The American colonies were in short supply of two factors of production—labor and capital. It is with how the scarcity of labor was overcome, and to what extent, that this section deals. An increase in the population did not measure the extent to which additions were made to the supply of labor. *Labor,* as used in economic studies, refers to that segment of the population that is available and willing to work for other people for wages. One of the pull factors that attracted immigrants to Colonial America was not only the relatively high wage rates that were paid, but also the opportunity to leave the wage earning class and become landowners and/or entrepreneurs. Records reveal the fact that some artisans were induced to come to America by the lure of high wages, higher than they were in England, but a great deal lower than those to which the readers of this book are accustomed. One of the perennial complaints by employers in all categories of economic activity was over the high levels of wages that were demanded by labor and even then many jobs were not filled. Since the time-honored method of a free economy—wage payments—failed to allocate the population resource factor to labor, other methods or systems were utilized in an effort to solve the problem. Many farmers who found they could not make a good living in New England either moved to an urban area or started their trek toward the West. Those who remained on the farms were unable to meet the level of urban wages, yet at times they needed assistance beyond that which was rendered by members of the family. The solution was a happy one, in that the farmers of a given community tended to make a gala occasion out of their mutually cooperative efforts to overcome the labor shortage. Several farmers would pool their efforts in helping one farmer, whose only obligation was fulfilled by the wife serving a bountiful dinner topped off with plenty of rum or cider in season. The shortage of labor along with the scarcity of capital contributed to limiting business and manufacturing firms to relatively small-sized units. Farm units in the

Middle Colonies were somewhat larger than those of New England, and cooperation was not a satisfactory answer to the labor problem. The system of indenture, both voluntary and involuntary, was depended upon, especially in Maryland and Pennsylvania, to furnish an ample, though at times unsatisfactory, supply of farm workers.

Indentured Servants. Indentured servants came over voluntarily or involuntarily. The former were those who were dissatisfied with economic, social, or political conditions and who did not have enough money to cover their transportation costs to America. Without attempting to account for all of the variations to the pattern of indenture, the basic conditions will be outlined. An immigrant bargained with a ship captain whereby his transportation to America would be paid by a colonist who was unable to obtain free labor by the proffer of wages. The colonist would be reimbursed by the "servant" working for him for a term of years, usually from four to seven. Involuntarily indentured servants were those who were sent to America against their will. They may have been kept on the ship until the captain was able to find someone who was willing to pay their transportation costs. Inmates of poorhouses in England were increasing, and the increasing costs of maintaining them imposed greater tax burdens on English landowners. It was to escape the paying of higher taxes that paupers were sent to America. Vagabondage in England was on the increase. Their enforced migration to America did not remedy the causes of their increase, but it did ease the financial burdens that accompanied it.

Slavery. Plantation farming in the Southern Colonies required almost year-round, low cost labor; and the growers turned to the system of slavery to supply the labor necessary to the cultivation of tobacco, indigo, and rice. Cotton did not become a major crop until after the close of the Colonial Period. The white man found it unpleasant and unhealthful to work in rice fields all day in the hot sun. Standing in water some of the time was not to his liking, and he became easy prey to malaria and hookworm.

Visitors to Colonial America were prone to compare the lot of the indentured servants with that of the slave, which was about as difficult as trying to evaluate the lot of the slave. Slaves represented a permanent investment of capital, and their natural increase accrued to their owners. Indentured servants represented a temporary "investment" of capital at best, and their natural increase did not accrue to their "owners." After having made these general statements, critics proceeded to deduce that in order to protect a long-run investment, slaves were treated with more consideration than were indentured servants. Records reveal that some masters of slaves and some masters of indentured servants treated their labor with kindness and consideration; others were quite cruel. The personal factor may have been as important as that of investment in determining the lot of forced labor. Looking at the question from another angle, the indentured servants who came to America for religious or political reasons may have had as much culture, education, and training as the masters who paid for their transportation; and, undoubtedly, they were treated more kindly than were some of the paupers and prisoners and those who were hijacked from the streets of London or Liverpool.

The indentured servants had something to look forward to, a future in which they would be free. Custom or law required that the master provide clothing and tools or equipment at the termination of the period of indenture; and it was with these few personal belongings that these people started life anew, and frequently on a new frontier. They wanted to get away from the scene of their bondage so that the stigma of that experience would not follow them in later life. They also wanted their children to mature in an environment that would not always look upon them as offspring of bond servants.

Growth of Cities

While Colonial America was predominantly rural and agriculture was the most important economic activity from the point of view of those engaging in it and with regard to the value of product, urban life was developing progressively all through the 17th and 18th centuries. Cities and towns began to develop at major trading or transshipment points up and down the Atlantic Coast.

Important Cities. Most of the important urban communities in the New England Colonies were along the seacoast, adjacent to natural harbors. Throughout most of the 17th century, Marblehead and Lynn were larger and more important than Boston. New Bedford derived its primacy from whaling. Whales were the source of tallow for candles, and whale oil lubricated much of the machinery in the colonies and in Europe throughout the 18th century.

As may be expected from what has already been said, there were more urban areas in New England and the Middle Colonies than there were in the South; and, by 1730, of the three cities having at least 8,000 inhabitants, the Middle Colonies had two—Philadelphia and New York—and New England had one—Boston. Charleston did not attain that size until 1760 and Baltimore until 1780. In addition to good harbor facilities, Philadelphia and New York had larger and more productive hinterlands than did either Boston or Charleston, which contributed to or stimulated trade and commerce.

Available data indicate that Boston was the largest city in the colonies until sometime during the decade of 1750 to 1760 when it was surpassed by Philadelphia. Census estimates reveal that Boston declined in population from 1740 until after the termination of the Colonial Period. The first United States census of 1790 showed Boston to have had a larger population than at any time during the Colonial Period, and the same thing may be said for all of the other cities whose populations are cited by the Bureau of the Census.

Table 2-3

Population of Cities Having at Least 8,000 Inhabitants—1710-1790

Year	Philadelphia	New York	Boston	Charleston	Baltimore	Salem	Newport
1710	. . . . .	. . . . .	9,000	. . . . .	. . . . .	. . . . .	. . . . .
1720	. . . . .	. . . . .	11,000	. . . . .	. . . . .	. . . . .	. . . . .
1730	8,500	8,500	13,000	. . . . .	. . . . .	. . . . .	. . . . .
1740	10,500	11,000	17,000	. . . . .	. . . . .	. . . . .	. . . . .
1750	13,400	13,300	15,731	. . . . .	. . . . .	. . . . .	. . . . .
1760	18,756	14,000	15,631	8,000	. . . . .	. . . . .	. . . . .
1770	28,000	21,000	15,520	10,863	. . . . .	. . . . .	9,000
1780	30,000	18,000	10,000	10,000	8,000	. . . . .	. . . . .
1790	42,444	33,131	18,038	16,359	13,503	7,921	. . . . .

Source: *A Century of Population Growth, 1790-1900* (Washington: U. S. Department of Commerce, Bureau of the Census, 1909) p. 11.

While Boston was experiencing a decline in population after 1740, Philadelphia and New York were growing steadily, the latter until 1780 when a decline was noted, the former continuously to the date of the first United States census in 1790. While foreign trade was still important to all of the colonies, the growth of Philadelphia at the expense of Boston and New York is an early indication of the influence of the westward movement and of the fact that the development of the West was becoming relatively more significant even at that early date than was trade overseas.

Urban Occupations. That these cities were real urban areas that had many of the characteristics of modern cities is manifest from the list of occupations in Philadelphia enumerated in the census of 1790. While 1790 is after the termination of the Colonial Period, there is no reason to believe other than that these occupations had been existent for a number of years. Without making a theoretical analysis, they throw some light on the degree to which specialization and division of labor had been developed and that formed the basis for trade and exchange.

Among those who rendered professional services were found artists, attorneys-at-law, clergymen, doctors of physic, surgeons and dentists, government officials, and schoolteachers. Domestic and personal services were rendered by barbers and hairdressers, boarding and lodging housekeepers, keepers of inns and taverns, and nurses and midwives. The largest single classification consisted of the 41.6 percent of the heads of families who reported. They were engaged in manufacturing and mechanical pursuits, such as bakers; blacksmiths; brewers; brickmakers and potters; butchers; cabinetmakers; carpenters and joiners; clock and watchmakers; copper, gold, and silversmiths; harness and saddlemakers; leather curriers and tanners; mantuamakers and seamstresses; metalworkers; painters and glaziers; plasterers; bookbinders; rope makers; shoemakers; stonecutters; tailors; textile workers;

tinners; weavers; and wheelwrights. The most numerous of these groups were tailors, house carpenters, and shoemakers respectively.

Trade and transportation were represented by bankers, brokers, clerks, and accountants, draymen and carters, hucksters and peddlers, merchants, and sea captains. That retailing was along small-scale lines is manifest from the fact that almost 25 percent of those enumerated were listed as merchants or dealers.

QUESTIONS FOR REVIEW

1. What were the economic causes of the westward movement of European trade routes in the 15th century?
2. Define the forces of "pull" and those of "push" in explaining why European people emigrated to the United States.
3. (a) With what institutions of capitalism were many of the colonists familiar? (b) How did their familiarity with these economic institutions affect early economic development?
4. (a) What is meant by saying that the English colonial policy was mercantilistic? (b) In what ways did the provisions of the Navigation Acts fit into colonial development?
5. (a) Explain the proportion of the productive factors as found in Colonial America. (b) What were some of the effects of this proportion on the organization for production?
6. In a discussion of indentured servants, develop the following points: (a) Who were they and how may they be classified? (b) Why were they used, and where? (c) What economic impacts did their utilization have upon the economic development of the colonies?

SUGGESTED READINGS

Callender, Guy S. *Selections from the Economic History of the United States, 1765-1860*. New York City: Augustus M. Kelley, Publishers, 1965. Chapter 3.

Craven, W. Frank. "The Early Settlements: A European Investment of Capital and Labor," *The Growth of the American Economy*, 2d ed., edited by Harold F. Williamson. New York City: Prentice-Hall, Inc., 1951.

Harper, Lawrence A. "The Effect of the Navigation Acts on the Thirteen Colonies," *United States Economic History: Selected Readings*, edited by Harry N. Scheiber. New York City: Alfred A. Knopf, Inc., 1964.

Johnson, E. A. J., and Herman E. Kroos. *The American Economy: Its Origins, Development, and Transformation*. Englewood Cliffs, N.J.: Prentice-Hall, Inc., 1960. Chapters 1-6.

Nettels, Curtis P. "British Mercantilism and the Economic Development of the Thirteen Colonies," *American Economic History: Essays in Interpretation*, edited by Stanley Coben and Forest G. Hill. Philadelphia: J. B. Lippincott Co., 1966.

Chapter 3

COLONIAL DEVELOPMENT

The economic development of the colonies, although halting and uncoordinated during the early 17th century, gradually accelerated as population grew and markets emerged. Whether actively encouraged by the Crown or left to their own devices, colonists in most areas were able, by the end of the Colonial Period, to rival Europeans in terms of their mastery of agriculture and craft skills. Colonial products were traded over most of the known world, as well as among the colonies themselves, and were usually carried in ships built in New England. Because of varying geographic and resource characteristics, however, development followed different patterns in the three major groups of colonies. The basic differences lay in the relative importance of agriculture and trade, with financial problems accentuating the differences.

THE NEW ENGLAND COLONIES

Nature endowed the New England area with a climate and topography that were a challenge to the farmer and something less than a blessing to the adventurer who had come to make his fortune. Yet this inhospitable land, precisely because of these characteristics, nurtured the trade and industry that were to bring wealth and power to many a merchant family. Since the New England Colonies were among the first settled by the English, their development was well begun by the middle of the 17th century, providing much of the experience needed by later settlers and establishing a beachhead from which civilization could move into the hinterlands. But timing was mainly a subsidiary factor in determining the nature of development. Climate and topography, more than anything else, dictated that agriculture would attain commercial scale in few areas and that trade would be the main source of New England revenues.

Agriculture

Agriculture in the four New England Colonies was the first concern of the settlers, partly because of the difficulty of bringing food across the Atlantic from England, and partly because of the relative inefficiency of

47

agricultural methods at the time. Even in England, much labor and much effort were required to wrest a livelihood from the soil. In the New World, a large part of the settler's working day was usually devoted to his crops, which not only supported him during the growing season, but also carried him through the lean months of winter. Beginning with the planting of crops around Plymouth in the 1620's, farming slowly spread up and down the Atlantic Coast and into the accessible river valleys, as settlements spread and the Indians were pushed back.

Basic Agricultural Conditions. The pioneers of New England were confronted with a formidable situation that was discouraging to those who attempted to employ European methods of tilling the soil. Not only was the general climate a handicap, with its frigid winters and its short growing season, but the thin, rocky soil made it very difficult to plant and cultivate crops. Only the rainfall was adequate, ranging from 40 to 60 inches per year along the coast. Additional difficulties were caused by the hilly terrain, which required considerable animal and human labor to transform it into properly drained and productive fields.

Areas through which rivers flowed, such as the Connecticut River Valley, were relatively fertile, in part because of the periodic overflowing of the streams that deposited fresh soil on the fields along the banks. The general conditions in New England were, nevertheless, unfavorable for the growth of large-scale farming and marketable surpluses of farm produce.

The size of the New England farm was, therefore, relatively small; and it contained just about as much acreage as the family unit could cultivate. Allowing for variations in local conditions and environments, five acres could usually be cultivated effectively by one man. Farm equipment consisted of hand-powered tools—hoe, sickle, rake, plow, spade, shovel, and pitch fork. Each farm unit had its complement of farm animals—horses, oxen, cows, hogs, chickens, and possibly turkeys—the actual number of each being determined by the needs of the respective farm families. There was little or no specialization in any agricultural activity, and surpluses that appeared were sold to those who lived in towns. The market for these products was small because many families who lived in towns had their own cows, hogs, and chickens. Farm labor, as a distinct wage-earning class, was practically unknown or nonexistent. Women and children were used as needed for outdoor work. African slaves were tried but were found to be unprofitable. A few domestic slaves were kept in towns that were located along the southern shores.

Cultivation of the soil was almost unknown, but the pioneer farmers learned from the Indians that maize which was planted in hills rather than in rows grew better when dead fish were buried in each hill. Trees were girdled in order to kill them, thus clearing the ground for planting and letting sunlight through to the soil. The dead trees were often burned and their ashes mingled with the soil to provide additional plant nutrients. Pumpkins and beans were planted along with the maize, which provided stalks up and around which the bean vines could climb. In this manner the New England farmers obtained the largest crops from limited acreage.

Capital equipment consisted of nothing more than crude, hand-powered tools, some of which the settlers had brought over with them. During inclement weather and the long cold winters, farmers devoted some of their time to fashioning tools and other equipment that were used on the farm and around the house. Rakes, hoes, shovels, yokes for oxen, plow handles, wagon shafts and bodies, and pieces of harness were among the products of home industry that were used on the farm. Seldom were these products the objects of trade. Skills of the local blacksmith were called upon when necessary to supply iron parts when needed. Harness was made of rope when leather strips were not available. Harness makers, or leatherworkers, took their place along with blacksmiths in supplying products of their specialities to a community.

Land Tenure. The earliest New England settlements imitated the organization of the English manor. The colonists lived in a compact village of small houses and shops, usually surrounding or lying next to a commons. The commons afforded pasturage for the sheep and cattle of the village. Crops were grown on fields located outside the village, often organized in the medieval three-field system, with strips of land planted in different crops. Villagers normally cultivated a part of the fields to which they had exclusive right, but the ownership of the fields lay in the village as a whole. The town council or town meeting served as the center for decisions concerning cultivation of these fields. Cooperation and common ownership of the productive land were the bases of this system.

The passage of time brought more settlers to New England, however, and many of them decided to become members of the established communities. Population pressure ultimately forced settlement on lands beyond the common fields. Individual family farms sprang up; and soon even parts of the common fields were being consolidated and converted to self-contained farming units, each with its own farmhouse and outbuildings. Ultimately, the land was parcelled into farm sites of a few acres each, owned outright and farmed by large numbers of colonists and their families. Only a few large farms existed as exceptions. The small family farm was in line with the democratic ideas of the New Englander, and it also permitted the pursuit of relatively intensive methods of cultivation by members of the family.

Major Crops and Livestock. History reveals that wheat has always been a frontier crop, and New England was no exception. But wheat was grown there strictly for domestic consumption. Other products of New England farms were buckwheat, corn, barley, rye, oats, and potatoes, in addition to all sorts of garden vegetables and fruits. Squash, pumpkins, and hay were produced in abundance; and apples loomed large in the New England diet in the form of cider, pies, dumplings, and apple butter. Most or all of these crops were produced for local or domestic consumption, and not many found their way into the other colonies or into export channels.

Sheep, cattle, and hogs were grazed in the pastures; but little or no care was taken of them. Hogs served the double purpose of disposing of garbage and becoming a source of food. Horses and oxen were the draft animals, and they were left to roam the forests. Wire fencing was unknown and rail fences were difficult to split, although trees were in great abundance, so the New England farmers built stone walls around their cultivated fields. In so doing they accomplished two objectives. They disposed of the rocks on their lands, and they kept the livestock from roaming in their cultivated fields, and both of these at the lowest cost in labor, time, and money.

Many animals perished during the long, severe winters as no shelter or food was provided for them. Visitors from England and the Continent were strong in their condemnation of the colonists, not only in New England but in the other colonies as well, for their lack of care of their farm animals. This criticism was extended to include indifference towards livestock breeding, which had become somewhat selective in Europe in the 17th century.

Trade

Since both soil and climate frowned upon agriculture, and since there were large supplies of naval stores, numerous good harbors, and abundant fisheries along the New England coast, it is not surprising that settlers soon turned to trade as an occupation. Fishing, shipbuilding, the carrying trade, and trade with other colonies gradually became the lifeblood of New England, providing employment and income that agriculture could not yield. The forbidding climate pushed the New Englander off the land and onto the sea lanes, where his fortune lay.

External Trade. A large part of colonial trade was carried on with England, with other English colonies in the Caribbean and elsewhere, and with foreign nations. Primary industries in the colonies, shipbuilding, and fishing provided the raw materials for such trade; and New England ships provided the carrying capacity.

Industries Associated with Trade. The Atlantic Ocean was in essence a huge marine farm that was exploited by New England workers. If such workers lived in the vicinity of New Bedford, Massachusetts, they may have engaged in whaling. Whale oil was the basis of a colonial domestic industry— the making of candles and providing oil for wick lamps and for street lamps. Cod, mackerel, halibut, and haddock were caught in the waters off the coasts of Maine, Massachusetts, and Newfoundland. Marblehead, Salem, and Gloucester were among the towns from which fishermen sailed. These fishermen were among the best sailors in the world. They manned the vessels that plied the coastwise trade as well as those that sailed to the West Indies, to Africa, to the Mediterranean Sea, to Continental Europe, and to England. In addition, the Madeira Islands and the Azores gave port to colonial vessels.

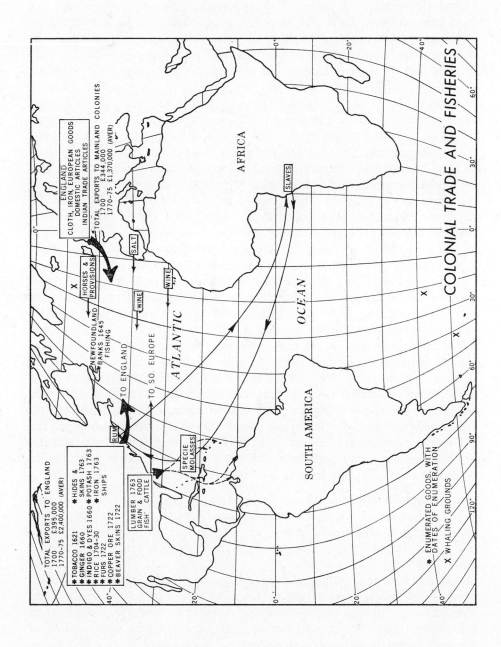

COLONIAL TRADE AND FISHERIES

ENGLAND
CLOTH, IRON, EUROPEAN GOODS
DOMESTIC ARTICLES
INDIAN TRADE ARTICLES

TOTAL EXPORTS TO MAINLAND COLONIES
1700 £344,000
1770–75 £1,370,000 (AVER)

TOTAL EXPORTS TO ENGLAND
1700 £395,000
1770–75 £2,400,000 (AVER)

✱ TOBACCO 1621   ✱ HIDES &
✱ GINGER 1660   SKINS 1763
✱ INDIGO & DYES 1660 ✱ POTASH 1763
✱ RICE 1704–30   ✱ IRON 1763
✱ FURS 1722   SHIPS
✱ COPPER ORE 1722
✱ BEAVER SKINS 1722

LUMBER 1763
GRAIN & FOOD
FISH · CATTLE

✱ ENUMERATED GOODS, WITH
   DATES OF ENUMERATION
X WHALING GROUNDS

HORSES &
PROVISIONS

NEWFOUNDLAND
BANKS 1645
FISHING

SALT

WINE

WINE

TO ENGLAND

TO SO. EUROPE

RUM

SPECIE
MOLASSES

SLAVES

AFRICA

ATLANTIC

OCEAN

SOUTH AMERICA

Shipbuilding, the naval stores industries, and the carrying trade were stimulated by the interpretation of the Navigation Acts; and the New England Colonies experienced a degree of prosperity that they otherwise would not have attained. Since there was a cost advantage involved, English capital in shipbuilding was exported to America, and artisans who were skilled in building ships emigrated there. New England pines, spruces, and firs were in great abundance; and lumber and naval stores were among the principal exports of New England, either in raw form or in the finished stage of production. More of the naval stores exported from New England ports came originally from the hinterland of Charleston, South Carolina, than were produced in New England itself. These products loomed large in the coast-wise trade between New England ports and those of the Southern Colonies.

The Navigation Acts gave colonial sailors the status of Englishmen, and the enumerating of articles for export from the colonies to England gave the ships cargoes to carry. This is not to imply that enumerated articles did not find their way to other parts of the globe. There was a lucrative trade between the New England Colonies and the West Indies—English, French, and Spanish. Much of the trade with the latter areas was illicit; but, since it was extremely profitable to the New England colonists and probably to those in the French and Spanish West Indies to trade with each other, some goods were carried openly between them, while others were smuggled or secreted in one way or another. Fish, timber, and cooperage products such as barrel staves and hoops, casks, and tuns were exported to the French West Indies; and rum, sugar, and molasses were the cargoes on the return trip. Sometimes the exports from the colonies were sold for cash for all or part of their value, and this proved to be one of the sources of silver money that circulated in early America. The Spanish piece of eight was one of the silver coins that was obtained in trade with the Spanish West Indies and that circulated in the colonies. Even though the trade between the colonies and the French and Spanish West Indies was not encouraged, and in some instances even forbidden, violations of English mercantile practice were tolerated since they brought new money into the realm.

Triangular Trade. All of the external trade of the New England Colonies was not direct, two-way trade. Several patterns of triangular trade were developed with individual seaports in New England serving as a vertex of the triangles. One pattern was to send rum to Africa, where a ready market was found among African and Arab traders who sold slaves. The slaves acquired in exchange for the rum were carried to a port in the West Indies. Many West Indian ports served as the third vertex from which sugar and molasses were brought to the mainland. Another pattern was the export of furs, timber, naval stores, and fish to England where they were exchanged for such manufactured goods as hardware, clothing, and household articles. These were taken to the British West Indies; and the triangle was completed by carrying sugar, molasses, and rum to New England.

English mercantilism decreed that no goods from the colonies could be carried directly to continental countries, but had to be landed first at an English port. Since fish from the colonies competed in England with fish caught by English fishermen, this commodity was permitted to be taken directly to the Catholic countries. However, products from these countries could not be taken to America without first touching English shores. Consequently, fish were sold for Spanish or French money, which was used in the purchase of goods from England, which, in turn, were taken to America to be sold. An alternative to this pattern was to use the money received for fish in the purchase of wines and trinkets which were exchanged with African traders for slaves, which were then brought to the West Indies or to the Southern Colonies to make up for the labor shortage in either or both places. Sometimes *drafts,* or *bills of exchange,*[1] drawn on English banks were accepted by the traders in payment for the fish they sold along the Mediterranean shores. At this point it is in order to remind the reader that the colonists were familiar with the practice and advantages of three-cornered trade and with the use of the bill of exchange as a means of payment and also as a device for transmitting money.

Figures 1 through 5 on Chart 3-1 on page 54 show schematically the most common patterns of triangular trade. For the sake of simplicity, the colonial vertex of the triangles is located in the New England Colonies. In reality, New York, Philadelphia, Baltimore, Charleston, Savannah, and other cities were additional ports through which passed goods that were destined to reach foreign ports. Similarly, many ships from foreign ports tied up at docks or wharves in these same cities. Still another pattern of trade was for rice or naval stores to be shipped coastwise from Savannah and Charleston respectively to some more northern port, whence they were shipped overseas. Many goods that first touched American shores at Baltimore and ports north were shipped coastwise to Charleston and Savannah. After putting in at the Madeira Islands or the Azores, many ships went to Mediterranean ports before sailing to England. There were literally dozens of patterns of multicornered trade, all of them advantageous to the colonists. They were almost the only means by which the colonists could acquire precious metals, thus helping to finance their unfavorable trade balances with England; and they were an easy way of acquiring some commodities that could not be obtained readily in a direct, two-way trade. From the English point of view, one of the unexpected and unanticipated advantages of the enforcement of the mercantile program upon the colonies was to raise their scale of living more rapidly and to a higher level than otherwise would have been the case. Under this program, England discouraged the development of many colonial industries whose costs would have been higher than those of similar industries in England. Development of colonial industries

---

[1] See p. 55.

CHART 3-1
TRIANGULAR TRADE

FIGURE 1:

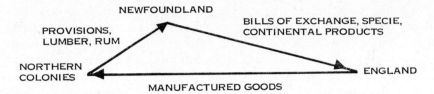

NEWFOUNDLAND

BILLS OF EXCHANGE, SPECIE,
CONTINENTAL PRODUCTS

PROVISIONS,
LUMBER, RUM

NORTHERN
COLONIES

ENGLAND

MANUFACTURED GOODS

FIGURE 2:

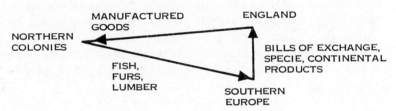

MANUFACTURED
GOODS

ENGLAND

NORTHERN
COLONIES

BILLS OF EXCHANGE,
SPECIE, CONTINENTAL
PRODUCTS

FISH,
FURS,
LUMBER

SOUTHERN
EUROPE

FIGURE 3:

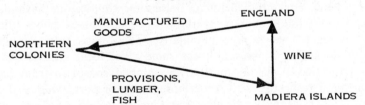

MANUFACTURED
GOODS

ENGLAND

NORTHERN
COLONIES

WINE

PROVISIONS,
LUMBER,
FISH

MADIERA ISLANDS

FIGURE 4:

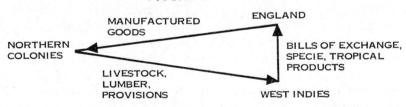

MANUFACTURED
GOODS

ENGLAND

NORTHERN
COLONIES

BILLS OF EXCHANGE,
SPECIE, TROPICAL
PRODUCTS

LIVESTOCK,
LUMBER,
PROVISIONS

WEST INDIES

FIGURE 5:

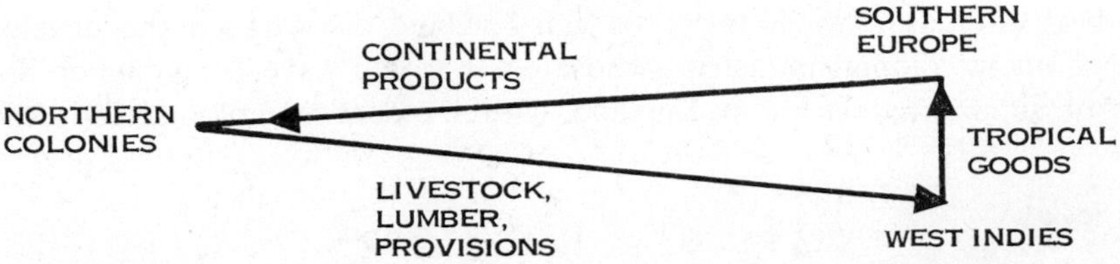

SOUTHERN
EUROPE

CONTINENTAL
PRODUCTS

NORTHERN
COLONIES

TROPICAL
GOODS

LIVESTOCK,
LUMBER,
PROVISIONS

WEST INDIES

was delayed until the industrial climate was more favorable. There has always been a tendency for talents and skills to express themselves in local markets even though the results are relatively high cost products.

Bills of Exchange. The extension of the English sphere of economic influence was manifest in the rather general use of London bills of exchange. Basically, a *bill of exchange* is an order by one person on a second person (bank) to pay a third person. The reader will recognize the similarity between a bill of exchange and an ordinary bank check. These credit instruments facilitated payments in London between buyers and sellers who were not only distant from each other, but also from England. One example will serve to illustrate their use.

A merchant capitalist carried a cargo of flour to a Mediterranean port where it was sold for £1,000. The purchaser paid for the flour by giving the merchant capitalist a bill of exchange on a London bank for that amount. The merchant capitalist now had an order that directed a London bank to pay him £1,000. After endorsing this bill he could use it in purchasing hardware, household goods, clothing, china, furniture, and other items. These items were then brought to the colonies and sold for more than they cost, if the venture was successful. Flour was thus used as a means of acquiring units of purchasing power in London. That type of transaction overcame the handicap of a shortage of gold and silver in the colonies.

The Extent of External Trade. Data from the Colonial Period are sparse, but enough exist to permit inferences concerning the level of trade and the importance of trading areas. Tables 3-1 and 3-2 present figures for colonial imports and exports in 1769, broken down by groups of colonies and major trading areas. Data for one year are ordinarily not a sound basis for generalization. Colonial trade followed such a constant pattern, however, that there is little reason to believe that 1769 was not a representative year. The general pattern for any other year would vary from this one only in aggregate value.

The figures show that New England found the West Indies a larger market for its exports and a larger source of imports than was Great Britain. They also reveal that New England was not able to take full advantage of the privilege of trading with continental countries of southern Europe. In the purchase of slaves from Africa, these figures seem to indicate that there was an intervening step by which the traders received trinkets, wines, and other products which were taken to Africa and used in the purchase of their human cargoes which were brought over to the western hemisphere. The New England economy was somewhat competitive with that of England. Most of its export trade was directed towards the West Indies, but not in large enough volume to offset an overall unfavorable trade balance. In fact, its imports from the West Indies usually exceeded in value its exports to that region. The only general area to which the value of New England exports was greater than its imports was southern Europe and Africa.

Table 3-1
Colonial Foreign Trade—1769
(Pounds Sterling)
Imports

Colony	Great Britain	Southern Europe	West Indies	Africa	Value by Colony	Total Value
New Hampshire	......	652	48,529	......	......	
Massachusetts	223,696	21,908	155,387	......	......	
Rhode Island	......	2,581	56,840	180	......	
Connecticut	......	267	53,994	......	......	
Total	223,696	25,408	314,750	180		564,034
New York	75,931	14,927	97,420	698	188,976	
New Jersey	......	327	1,664	......	1,991	
Pennsylvania	204,980	14,249	180,592	......	399,821	
Total	280,911	29,503	279,676	698		590,788
Maryland	......	4,683	32,198	5,400	......	
Virginia	714,944	9,442	77,454	7,020	......	
Total	714,944	14,125	109,652	12,420		851,141
North Carolina	......	933	10,604	1,080	......	
South Carolina	327,084	6,166	65,666	124,180	......	
Total	327,084	7,099	76,270	125,260		535,713
Georgia	58,341	547	9,408	13,440	81,736	
Total	58,341	547	9,408	13,440		81,736
TOTALS	1,604,976	76,682	789,756	151,998		2,623,412

Source: Timothy Pitkin, *A Statistical View of the Commerce of the United States of America* (New York City: James Eastburn & Company, 1817), p. 19, Adapted.

Table 3-2

Colonial Foreign Trade—1769

(Pounds Sterling)

Exports

Colony	Great Britain	Southern Europe	West Indies	Africa	Value by Colony	Total Value
New Hampshire	......	465	40,431	96	......	
Massachusetts	142,776	76,702	123,394	9,801	......	
Rhode Island	......	1,440	65,207	7,815	......	
Connecticut	......	2,567	79,395	......		
Total	142,776	81,174	308,427	17,712		550,089
New York	113,382	50,886	66,325	1,313	231,906	
New Jersey	......	......	2,532	......	2,532	
Pennsylvania	28,112	203,753	178,331	560	410,756	
Total	141,494	254,639	247,188	1,873		645,194
Maryland	......	66,556	22,303		......	
Virginia	759,961	73,635	68,946		......	
Total	759,961	140,191	91,249			991,401
North Carolina	405,015	3,238	27,944	72	......	
South Carolina	405,015	72,881	59,815	620	......	
Total	405,015	76,119	87,759	692		569,585
Georgia	82,270	614	13,286		96,170	
Total	82,270	614	13,286	......		96,170
TOTALS	1,531,516	552,737	747,909	20,277		2,852,439

Source: *Ibid.,* p. 20. Adapted.

Table 3-3
Principal Colonial Exports in 1770 to —

Great Britain	Southern Europe	West Indies	Africa
1. Lumber	Staves and Headings	Staves and Headings	Rum
2. Staves and Headings	Wheat	Beef and Pork	Hoops
3. Indigo	Fish	Corn	Spermaceti Candles
4. Whale Oil Fish	Corn	Spermaceti Candles	Lumber
5. Naval Stores	Beeswax	Fish	Sugar
6. Tobacco			

Source: Timothy Pitkin, *A Statistical View of the Commerce of the United States of America* (New York City: James Eastburn & Co., 1817), pp. 21-23. Adapted.

Trade with Other Colonies. Even though the external trade relations between the American colonies and England were the most important economic characteristic of Colonial America, internal or domestic trade did develop. Local trade was most common, with country stores and shops buying or accepting for credit the produce of the neighborhood, and selling or exchanging various other goods, some of them manufactured and many of them imported. In the growing seaport towns, well-organized markets dealt in all manner of goods, although household manufacture provided much that the colonist used even in these urban areas. Because of the high degree of self-sufficiency enjoyed by most colonial households, domestic trade did not develop as rapidly as external trade. And because both physical barriers and British colonial policy hindered the flow of goods in a north-south direction between the colonies, domestic trade tended to follow an east-west course. Raw materials, furs, and various other primary or extractive products flowed from the interior to the seaports, while desirable manufactured and luxury goods flowed in the opposite direction. It is easy to see that domestic trade was inextricably involved with external trade, and depended on external trade for much of its volume. This was true for all of the colonies, not those in New England alone. Several examples will illustrate this point.

Imports, Exports, and Domestic Trade. The exportation of naval stores, rum, flour, barrel staves, tuns, or fish was associated with a series of domestic exchanges, or domestic trade. Supercargoes, or ship captains in charge of tramp steamers, seldom, if ever, produced by themselves the commodities for which they sought foreign markets. From the standpoint of domestic trade, they were the buyers; from the standpoint of foreign trade, they were sellers or exporters. It is equally clear that, without an ensuing domestic trade, the importing of goods from the West Indies or England would have been folly on the part of the importer. He was not in position to consume the products imported, nor was he in a position to distribute them widely among the colonies. Shopkeepers, either general or specialized, bought them for the retail trade; and the money that was received from export balances was used to smooth the progress of domestic trade. Among the items of capital that were imported and became objects of internal trade were found mill machinery, ship iron, canvas, cordage, hardware, brick, nails, bellows, paint, and instruments of navigation. Farmers and artisans used spades, hoes, shovels, axes, saws, knives, chisels, grindstones, planes, cant hooks, hammers, trowels, and the iron parts of plows and other implements. Throughout the 17th century most of the cannon, shot, powder, and fire-arms were articles of import.

The colonial housewife used kettles, measuring cans, milk trays, bowls, ladles, sieves, pans, graters, funnels, paper boxes, flour boxes, punch strainers, woodenware, spoons, platters, porridge dishes, saucers, salts, tankards, and other pewterware. Buttons, needles, thimbles, pins, tape, ribbons, and filleting were also articles of import as were mouse traps, beer taps, lanterns, tinder-boxes, calendars, combs, basins, and inkhorns.

In spite of the development of household industries, many textiles, such as woolens, crepe, damask, lace, flannel, calico, gauze, cambric, gingham, cottons, and linsey-woolsey were imported; and wine, brandy, sugar, spices, books, paper, furniture, mirrors, candlesticks, snuffers, and curtain rings were products of foreign trade that became objects of domestic trade.

The Fur Trade. Furs and pelts were not only products of the forest and streams, they were articles of domestic and foreign trade and of domestic manufacture. Fur hats were worn in winter throughout the colonies; and since there were hat makers in Connecticut and probably elsewhere, the ban by the English on the manufacture of hats in the colonies was honored in the breach. Complaints were made to Parliament by hat manufacturers in England that their exports were declining in the face of an enlarging potential market in America, and pressure for suppression of the manufacture of hats in America was brought to bear.

In this case the domestic trade in furs affected the level of external trade, and invited regulation. Needless to say, the colonists continued their lucrative trapping pursuits, as well as their manufacture of fur hats. Apparently a decline in the supply of furs after the Hat Act of 1732 did more to suppress this industry than did the Act itself.

Money

The colonists were familiar with the use of money as a medium of exchange, but those who came over from England and other European countries brought little or no money with them. Since there were no native ores known to the colonists, much of the money that circulated in the colonies was of Spanish or French denomination that was obtained in trade with the Spanish and French West Indies, or with countries that border on the Mediterranean Sea. Even though there was a continual flow of money into the colonies, there likewise was just as continual a drainage of this money to England in settlement of unfavorable trade balances. The unfavorableness of these trade balances appeared in money values only, since they represented values of commodities imported into the colonies, many of which were sorely needed and which contributed to raising the economic level of living of these people.

Commodity Money. Adding to the problems caused by the unfavorable balance of trade was the English prohibition of bullion or coin exports to the colonies, a rational mercantilistic policy. Although trade with non-English areas brought in relatively large amounts of coin, there was never enough to take care of both domestic commerce and payments to England for imported goods and services. One widely used means of supplementing the metallic currency in circulation was commodity money. *Commodity money* was simply a commodity which, because of its common occurrence and value, served as a means of pricing goods and as a medium of exchange. It may have lacked uniformity, homogeneity, and relative stability of value, but it met at least one of the requirements of a good money, namely that of general acceptability. Salt, cattle, lead, corn, wheat, and Indian wampum were among the commodities used at one time or other as money.

Most of the colonists in New England were familiar with beaver skins, and they were given value equivalents in terms of other goods. They at least served as a common denominator of values, if not as a medium of exchange. When goods were exchanged directly for other goods, all that was necessary to effect an exchange was that the value of each be expressed in terms of the same thing. In the Southern Colonies, tobacco served as a common denominator of values. Since it was too fragile to circulate directly, *certificates of deposit* were issued. These were nothing but promises to pay the bearer a certain amount of tobacco that was in a bonded warehouse.

Paper Money. Another common supplement to the metallic currency was paper money, printed and issued in most cases by the individual colonies, and usually necessitated by colonial debts that could not be met in any other way. As early as 1690, the colony of Massachusetts issued bills of credit in order to pay some soldiers who had returned from an expedition to Quebec. A *bill of credit* was a promissory note that was issued by all of the colonies except Virginia in anticipation of tax receipts. Another form of paper credit money was the *loan bill,* which resembled a land bank note, with which many of the colonists were familiar. Some of these notes were issued by colonial governments, others by privately owned mortgage companies. There was little to choose between the bill of credit and the loan bill; both were paper credit money and in most instances were irredeemable in gold or silver. They probably contributed to the nonuse of metallic money once they were in circulation, but the original sequence of events seems to have been a shortage of hand-to-hand currency in any form followed by the issuance of paper money. The payments made in settlement of the balance of payments accounts were enough to create a shortage of metallic currency.

Inflation. Efforts by England to prevent, and the colonial governments to limit, the issuance and circulation of paper money were of no avail in the absence of adequate metallic money. Paper money first appeared in the New England Colonies, but by the end of the Colonial Period all thirteen colonies had issued it in varying amounts. In every case, the result was inflation—a rise in the general price level. One explanation for the price rise was that colonies issued paper money in excess of the economic need for currency. The amount of bills of credit and loan bills in circulation expanded faster than the production of goods and services, so that prices of the goods and services were bid up. Too much money was chasing too few goods.

Another reason why prices rose was that people lacked confidence in the ability of the government or the institution that issued the paper money to redeem it in specie. Both merchants and consumers were unwilling to accept paper money because of this doubt, and required more paper money than specie to complete the same transaction. Exchanges measured in paper money, therefore, had a higher nominal value than the same exchanges measured in specie. Suppose that a colonial merchant had imported some furniture from England. He would like to receive £2 in specie for it, in order to make a reasonable profit. But since he was required to accept paper money that had depreciated approximately 50 percent, he had to ask £4 for his furniture in order to receive purchasing power equal to £2 in specie.

The use of irredeemable credit money also contributed to the creation of inequity between debtors and creditors. A person who needed purchasing power would borrow a certain amount of money, measured in pounds sterling, from merchants or friends. The borrower would sign a contract calling for the return to the lender of the same number of pounds, plus an interest charge, at some time in the future. Suppose that the general price level rose 50 percent during the life of the contract. When the loan was due, the debtor repaid pounds that would purchase only half of what they purchased when he borrowed them. In other words, he returned money that was cheaper than the money he borrowed. Conversely, the creditor found that the money returned to him was worth only half as much as the money he loaned. Interest charges paid by the borrower helped to make up some of the difference, but interest rates were not usually high enough to compensate for price rises.

The viciousness of inflation lay in the fact that, once the process started and prices rose, more money was issued to cover prices and this made prices rise still higher. The end was repudiation and complete loss of money values by those who held money at that time. Wage earners, salaried persons, and government employees were all affected unfavorably by monetary inflation. Their incomes were relatively stable in comparison with those of merchants and businessmen who could charge higher prices for their commodities as inflation increased. Persons who receive relatively fixed incomes, in any form, lose some of the purchasing power of those incomes during inflationary periods. Any wage and salary increases they receive usually lag behind price movements.

Was the issuance of paper money beneficial to the colonies, in spite of the inflation it caused? Certainly a large number of transactions were carried out that might have been difficult to complete in the absence of paper money. And inflation in at least six of the colonies never reached really damaging levels. It seems probable that the advantages of colonial paper money did outweigh the disadvantages, particularly in terms of the long-run effects of the trade it facilitated.

Transportation

Because of the dependence of the New England Colonies on trade for both public and private revenues, transportation assumed a very important role in commercial life. Efficient means of moving goods to and from the hinterlands and through the ports along the coast were required for trade to grow and flourish. Waterways were the most commonly used of all means of movement, with land transportation serving a subsidiary connecting role.

Roads and Trails. Improved roads as we know them today were nonexistent in colonial New England. Such roads as did exist varied widely in condition and upkeep. Indian trails were commonly used, especially in the frontier areas, but their narrow width prohibited the passage of wheeled vehicles such as wagons and carts. The settlers did clear some frontier roads for vehicles, but only by removing the highest stumps and the largest stones. Passage was slow, hazardous, and uncomfortable, to say the least. Frontier roads were next to impassable in wet weather, even though logs and boards were laid in low places to prevent wagons from becoming mired in the mud.

In the more thickly settled regions of New England, roads were better developed and somewhat better maintained. Local traffic and commerce depended on land transportation to a large extent, since waterways did not extend throughout the settled areas. Town and local governments, therefore, sought to ensure an adequate road system by having roads cleared and then levying taxes for their maintenance. Farmers often paid the tax by working on the roads themselves. In spite of this attention, most New England roads were unsurfaced and suffered from neglect over much of their length. They, too, were often impassable in winter or wet weather.

A system of main roads connecting the major towns was developed by the end of the Colonial Period. Post roads were common, and highroads paralleling the coast permitted longer journeys by horsemen and light vehicles. Ultimately stage lines were introduced to provide scheduled transportation for both passengers and freight. Taverns, such as the Wayside Inn made famous by Henry Wadsworth Longfellow, were built along the more heavily traveled routes to accommodate drivers, passengers, and horses. After a long haul, horses had to be rested and new teams were made available at the stables behind the taverns. Passengers and drivers had to rest for the night or part of it. A day's journey started as early in the morning as daylight made its first appearance and continued until darkness put an end to further progress. After a hearty meal, the travelers gathered round the fireplace in the tavern's large parlor and exchanged stories of exciting adventure while freely imbibing "samples" of rum, gin, and other drinks that were available. The gay evenings served to make the weary sojourners forget the hardships they had endured the preceding day and braced them to withstand the trials of the following day's travel, which may have started as early as 4:30 A.M.

Land transportation remained relatively slow and expensive throughout colonial times. Not only were the roads themselves in bad shape most of the year, but the vehicles developed to carry passengers and freight over them never achieved a high level of efficiency. Large numbers of draft animals, along with their drivers, were required to pull heavy loads. Necessity alone stimulated the growth of the New England road system.

Waterways. Rivers were much more convenient to use for inland transportation than were roads. Large amounts of freight could be moved at low rates, and the rate of travel on the rivers usually exceeded that on land. In a period when time was not as crucial a factor as it is today, cost differentials probably determined that waterways would be the main arteries of commerce. For example, it was much easier and cheaper for goods to be shipped between settlements on the Connecticut River and Boston in either direction via water than to transport them overland for only a fraction of the distance. Indeed, it was often true that goods could be shipped to England more cheaply than they could be moved 100 miles inland by wagon or pack train. The New England rivers, flowing in a generally north-south direction, together with the coastal waters formed the avenues over which most of the regional trade was carried out.

Craft of almost every variety were used in water transportation, ranging from canoes and small skiffs on the frontier streams above the fall line, through riverboats and sailboats of medium size, to full-scale sailing ships that plied the coastal waters and the navigable larger streams. Steam power had not yet appeared on the scene, so wind and human muscles were the usual means of propulsion. Mules or horses were used to pull the boats on the few canals that were built.

Because trade was concentrated on the rivers, most inland towns and settlements were along river banks. Upstream navigation was unimpeded to the fall line, at which point a settlement was frequently found. This settlement served as a trading post for Indians and trappers who floated their pelts, hides, and furs downstream to the fall line. The presence of waterpower soon led to the erection of a sawmill and probably a gristmill, both of which were found in most of the frontier river settlements. Specialization of industry soon became apparent when men offered their services for pay in unloading and loading ships and barges. It was only accidental if a boat going upstream and one going downstream met at the fall line, and it was not long before someone erected a warehouse in which to store goods until they could be transported farther, either upstream or down. Farmers began to grow food to sell in these urban areas, and stores were opened to serve the people who engaged in specialized activities. It was not long before other people arrived to perform some simple banking functions and an interdependent population evolved.

The role of the New England trader, the man who supervised and fostered the movement of goods over the rivers and roads, cannot be overemphasized. The trader was not only interested in intracolonial trade, but he was also the prime instigator of intercolonial trade. He did more than sail ships around Cape Cod in carrying goods between Boston and Hartford. He extended his influence into the Middle and the Southern Colonies and initiated a relationship between them that continued throughout many years beyond the Colonial Period. The economic importance of that coastwise trade was not measured either by its value or by its volume. It was the principal means of communication between the colonies. Since very few rivers crossed colonial boundaries in their flow to the ocean, and roads were nonexistent or passable only under favorable weather conditions, coastwise shipping was the avenue of intercolonial communication, especially in the earlier part of the period and as late as 1750. By that time more or less regular water routes had been established for carrying passengers, mail, and small packages.

Industry

In order to develop manufacturing beyond the household stage, capital, machinery, raw materials, markets, a transportation system, currency, and a wage-earning segment of the population were necessary, as well as adequate supervision. British colonial policy included the suppression in the colonies of manufacturing industries that produced goods that were in direct competition with English manufacturers. But natural barriers raised by the absence of the foregoing essentials may have been more effective in preventing or delaying the development of manufacturing industries than the man-made laws of the British Parliament. As these handicaps were overcome in particular instances and for particular commodities, colonial industries appeared in spite of British restrictions.

Sources of power were found in the strength of animals and in the force of falling water. There was some mobility of animal power but none of waterpower which restricted the location of industry that needed such power to the immediate vicinity of waterfalls and rapids. Capital in the form of machinery was lacking, except for that amount that could be obtained from England or could be carved out of wood. It was contrary to English colonial policy to permit the exportation of machine capital, so only that which was smuggled or otherwise escaped the scrutiny of enforcement officers arrived in America. Since the origin of capital is savings, and the early colonists struggled to exist, let alone to save, it was not until possibly the 18th century that native capital began to appear, and that was primarily trading capital. This means that trading was lucrative enough in terms of financial returns to allow those who engaged in trade to cover all costs and to set aside sums for investment. The absence of money capital, again, was the result of English colonial policy, combined with the lack of natural deposits of gold or silver ores along the Atlantic plain.

Major New England Products. Goods produced by New England industry on a commercial scale were many and varied. Iron ores were found in many places, and pig iron was an important export. In recent years the restoration of one of the first ironworks at Saugus, Massachusetts, near Lynn, has been completed and is now open to the public. As early as 1642 kitchen ranges were being made at Lynn, and possibly at Saugus. Iron manufacturing soon spread over New England. It was this development that prompted a 1750 English law forbidding the processing of iron beyond the pig or bar iron stages. The law made the continued production of pig iron lawful, however, and tended to increase its export to England. According to mercantilistic policy, this arrangement was ideal: unfinished pig iron from the colonies was imported into England, where it was transformed into finished goods having a higher unit value. The sale of these iron goods outside England, often in the colonies themselves, contributed to a favorable balance of trade.

Refining iron ores in the colonies was a decentralized, small-scale industry, so strict enforcement of the law was difficult to achieve. Furnaces and forges were built near the basic materials for pig iron—bog or rock iron ore, limestone for a flux, and wood for charcoal—but were also near their intended markets, since the transportation costs for finished iron were high. The blast furnaces were primitive but effective. They looked something like huge fireplaces, with stacks extending twenty or more feet into the air. Ore, limestone, and charcoal were dumped in at the top. The charcoal melted the iron ore, the limestone removed many impurities from it, and the molten ore could be drained from the bottom of the furnace in a highly refined state.

Because of the severe winters in New England, clothing made of animal skins was used by the men to protect them from the wind and cold. Hats were made of beaver or of coonskin, and deerskin leggings and breeches protected the men in their outdoor activities. Their overcoats were lined with fur to afford additional protection against the elements. New York and New England teemed with furbearing animals which were trapped for their furs and skins and, incidentally, provided a source of food as a by-product. Why should a trapper send his furs to England, have them made into hats and other articles of clothing, and then sent back to New England with an added cost of transporting them 6,000 miles, when they could be processed at home without incurring the heavy cost of transportation?

Logging was carried on in the winter because of the comparative ease of dragging logs over snow and ice. Logs were piled on the riverbanks to wait for a thaw to float them down to a shipyard on or near the coast, or possibly to a sawmill that was located near the fall line.

Certain sections of Massachusetts, New Hampshire, and what are now Maine and Vermont contained forests of sugar maple trees. These trees were tapped in the early spring, and maple sugar was a home product of many New England farms. There are no records available to show how much this item was an object of trade, but there is little doubt residents of urban communities found maple sugar on the shelves of their food stores.

Even though shipping and shipbuilding have been discussed in terms of the Navigation Acts of the mid-17th century, mention of them should be made here in order to place them in context. New England shippers and shipping controlled most of the coastwise trade with the Southern Colonies. Ships were one of the principal exports to England as they were built here at lower cost than was possible in England.

Fishing and whaling have already been mentioned as the basis of much New England trade, but the reader should remember that a part of the products of this industry was consumed at home. Fish formed an important part of the diet of many New England families; and whale oil was widely used as a source of light, either in lamps or in candles.

Other products of New England industry were farm tools, furniture, and hardware. Gristmills and sawmills were found in all of the colonies. It was their presence near a waterfall that frequently gave rise to the settlement of a community. Frontier industries included blacksmithing and wagonmaking, although these activities were also common in the settled parts of the colonies.

In summary, those economic activities that depended heavily upon the products of extractive industries, and for which manufacturing processes added values that were greater than the costs of the labor and capital utilized, prospered in the New England colonies. To the extent that the economy was reliant upon a market situation or contributed to the furthering of one, the facts of a comparative cost or of an absolute cost advantage tended to cause the colonists to ignore, to evade, or to protest against an effort on the part of England to enforce mercantilistic policies against them.

Household Industry. It was in industry that competition with the mother country tended to create a degree of independence in the New England

Colonies that did not exist in the other colonies. Climate, natural resources, and skills of the colonists, together with their religious and moral outlook, contributed to this situation. It was considered sinful to be idle, and there were many days and weeks during the long and cold winter months when cold weather and deep snow prevented outdoor work. Spinning and weaving in the homes kept the women and children occupied. The products of this activity seldom found their way to the market, but they eliminated the need for buying imported British yarns and cloth. Farm tools were made and repaired by the men, and repairs to houses and barns were made when field work was impossible. Barns, corncribs, woodsheds, and carriage and wagon sheds were erected and repaired when the ground could not be worked, or crops cultivated or harvested. Boots and shoes for an entire family were made and repaired in the household. Shoes were made along a "straight" pattern or last. Shoes were not made to fit the right foot or the left, and sizing was not standardized. Before the Colonial Period came to an end shoe cobbling had become a specialized activity. Making and repairing harnesses was frequently a sideline activity of the cobbler.

THE MIDDLE COLONIES

The Middle Colonies—New York, New Jersey, Pennsylvania, Delaware, and Maryland—presented a more favorable set of conditions for agriculture · than did the New England area. Broad, fertile lands with adequate rainfall and a temperate climate were available to the land-hungry colonists for settlement. At the same time, the many navigable rivers of the region, as well as the wide bays and coastal waters, made transportation and trade an attractive alternative to farming. A profitable combination of the two occupations, supported by light industry, was to bring wealth and prominence to the Middle Colonies very early in the Colonial Period.

Agriculture

Farming in the middle region developed along distinctive lines, duplicating a few of the agricultural characteristics of other colonies, but generally following its own unique pattern. Apart from the normal factors of climate, soil fertility, farming techniques, and available markets that helped to determine the nature of agriculture in an area, land tenure and traditions from the Old World also played a formative role. Many of these traditions that were established during colonial times—including traditional crops—are practiced today, especially in those areas where the population is still of one national origin.

Land Tenure. It was in the Middle Colonies that attempts were first made to transplant the European feudal system to America. The growth of Dutch settlements in the New York area, beginning in the 1620's, resulted in the establishment of large estates along the Hudson River, owned and operated by landlords called *patroons*. In essence, the *patroon system* was a form of feudal organization in which the tenants on an estate rendered money payments and labor services to the patroon for the use of his land. Patroons had wide legal powers over both their lands and their tenants, being able to hold court and dispense justice without outside interference. When the English took over New York in 1664, they made few initial changes in the patroon system.

Large tracts of land that were later to become Pennsylvania, Delaware, and Maryland were granted by English rulers during the 17th century to William Penn, Lord de la Ware, and Lord Baltimore respectively. New Jersey was given by the Duke of York to his friends, Sir George Carteret and Sir John Berkeley. Ownership of the land remained in the hands of these titled proprietors, who were able to use and enjoy it as they saw fit. Tenants were welcome and necessary if the land was to be productive, but all worked the land at the pleasure of the landlord.

The principal obligation of tenants was the rendering of services two or three days a week for the proprietor and/or the sharing of crops on some agreed upon basis. In time, *quit rents* were paid and accepted in lieu of those services and sharing of crops. Ultimately, landlords found that they could not depend on quit rents for a reliable or sizable income, so they directed their energies toward trade and finance. Quit rents soon became nothing more than token payments, reminding tenants that they lived on the land because of the generosity of the landowner. In order to perpetuate the system, laws of entail and primogeniture were established in the Middle Colonies. They prevented an otherwise unrestricted ownership of land.

In order to be successful, the proprietorship system required a large number of farmers who were willing to work two or three days each week for their landlords, and who would accept regulation of their daily lives in sometimes minute detail. Unless they had been forced from their land by the enclosures in England or Europe, small farmers did not have to venture 3,000 miles across the ocean to work under these conditions. Indeed, many colonists came to the New World in order to escape the limitations placed upon them by the feudal system. They were, therefore, not attracted to the Middle Colonies until they were permitted to own their land, or at least to rent land and have the rights of free persons. Shortage of adequate farm labor was thus a primary problem for the proprietors. It was one of the forces that weakened but did not destroy the proprietorship system. Landlords were finally forced to offer leases on very favorable terms, but they retained ownership of the land in almost all cases.

Another means of alleviating the labor shortage was the importation of indentured servants from England and northern Europe. A group called "free willers" came from the Palatinate in the latter part of the 18th century. They were of sturdy German stock and settled in south central Pennsylvania, near what is now Lancaster County and counties to the northeast. They were the ancestors of the Pennsylvania Dutch, who still populate and cultivate some of the best lands in that state. Maryland was also a haven for many Germans who sought refuge from political and religious turmoil in their homeland. Other voluntary indentures were English who wanted to come to America but were not able to pay for their passage. Landlords met the ships carrying them and bought up their indentures, thus acquiring their labor services for the life of the indenture contract.

Partly because of the proprietorship system and partly because of the nature of the land, farms in the Middle Colonies were larger than those in New England. In Maryland, some plantations were to be found, worked by indentured servants, Negro slaves, or both. To be sure, small farms were found, but these were mainly in the frontier areas.

Major Crops and Livestock. The fertile lands of the Middle Colonies, together with a climate that favored tillable agriculture, provided the basis for a wide variety of farm products. Wheat was the principal crop, and wheat and flour were among the leading export commodities. Before the frontier passed west of the Appalachian Mountains, opening up other lands where wheat might be grown, the Middle Colonies were justifiably called the "Bread Colonies" of the New World. Other grains, including rye, barley, and oats, were grown for both commercial sale and fodder.

Farming was conducted on a scale somewhat higher than the subsistence level and, in addition to wheat and flour, exports consisted of smoked or packed meat, horses, mules, and goats. Surplus vegetables were taken to urban markets, and a pattern was established in this area which has been followed with few variations to the present time. Potash, that was a by-product of burning trees, was used as fertilizer by the more thrifty farmers, especially in their gardens which were planted in peas, beans, turnips, potatoes, tomatoes, and cabbage. Among the varieties of fruit trees found in these colonies were cherry, apple, peach, and pear; and the juices of at least three of these provided the basic ingredients for cider and wines.

Cattle, oxen, horses, mules, hogs, sheep, and goats were part of almost every farm, but very little or no care was taken of them. They were permitted to roam the fields and forest areas for food, and there was no selection in their breeding. The results of the lack of care were not conducive to the development of animals that had desirable characteristics.

While all farms had barns, smokehouses, and sheds for one purpose or another, those of the Pennsylvania Germans in the vicinity of Lancaster were unique in many respects. It was part of their way of life and their religion to take care of their farm animals, and they constructed barns that were large enough to house animals, farm crops, and some of their equipment. Since the winters were long and cold and outdoor pasturage was out of the question, hay mows were provided in the tops of the barns, which were frequently three stories high. They were usually built next to hills so that the second floors could be reached from the tops of the hills. On these floors were found hay wagons, rakes and other equipment, and sometimes stalls for horses. The lowest floors housed the cattle and opened into the barnyard. Characteristic of the barns was the stone construction, at least up to the hay mow, and the use of red paint on the wood structure. Barnyard fertilizer was used by many of these people, but the English, the erstwhile indentured servant, and others were more inclined to exploit their land to the utmost and then move west.

They followed the true pattern of the frontier farmer—exploit the cheap factor, land; economize on the scarce factors, labor and capital. Later generations have deplored the wasteful methods of the early settlers; but it is characteristic of any economy to exploit to the full that productive factor or the factors that are cheapest.

Trade

There is evidence that organized trade began in the Middle Colonies soon after the initial settlements and grew quickly in extent as the population expanded. Enough of the labor force avoided agricultural jobs to supply the tradesmen and merchants necessary for goods to move. Some of the settlers in the middle region had not been farmers in Europe, so they were less inclined to become farmers than to enter some commercial pursuit such as trade. Others found urban life more attractive than farming. Still others were attracted to urban communities by the lure of profits. Whatever the reasons, trade and tradesmen flourished from a very early time.

External Trade. The major characteristics of external trade have been described in the section on the New England Colonies, so only the pattern of participation by the Middle Colonies needs to be established. As the data in Table 3-2, page 57, show, almost 80 percent of the export trade of the Middle Colonies was with the West Indies, southern Europe, and Africa. Triangular trade obviously played an important role here, with some Middle Colony port serving as the beginning and end of the triangle. New York, Philadelphia, and Baltimore were the foremost port cities of the region, so that most of the import and export trade was funneled through their warehouses. Philadelphia also excelled in shipbuilding. A number of shipyards located around the city on the banks of the Delaware River were in competition with such New England shipbuilding centers as Newport and Boston.

The external trade of the Middle Colonies was doubly significant in that it provided much of the metallic currency needed to finance the unfavorable trade balance with England. The New England Colonies and the Southern Colonies traded largely with some part of the British Empire. It was the middle region that made contact with the outside world and brought new gold and silver into the colonies. There was a decided trend for English gold to be drained to the Middle East and the Orient through southern Europe and the Near East, due mainly to the desire of English consumers for exotic goods that could be obtained only in Eastern countries. Mercantilistic policy opposed such a drain. By permitting the Middle Colonies to trade with southern Europe, however, some of this gold was reclaimed.

Major export items from the Middle Colonies were almost completely the products of primary or extractive industries. Large amounts of wheat and flour were shipped from Philadelphia and Baltimore to the Mediterranean countries and to the French West Indies. Other items of commerce included pickled or smoked meats, barrel staves and hoops, tuns, horses and goats. Citizens in the Middle Colonies, like their colonial neighbors, enjoyed the manufactured goods of Europe, which formed a large part of their imports.

Internal Trade. Trade within the Middle Colonies was very similar to domestic trade in New England, except that agricultural goods played a larger role in exchange. Again, most domestic trade was ultimately connected with foreign trade, as primary goods flowed from the hinterlands to the seaports and finished goods moved in the opposite direction. Data are so meager that the extent of trade among the Middle Colonies cannot be measured. It was an important part of colonial economic activity, however. Retail stores were found in all of the towns, and the mere fact that towns existed and grew affords evidence of the increasing volume of domestic trade. By 1740 Benjamin Franklin was operating a printshop and retail bookstore in Philadelphia, about 100 years after the first printing press in English had been set up in Cambridge, Massachusetts.

Money

The Middle Colonies experienced the shortage of metallic currency that afflicted all of the English settlements in North America. Commodity money, including most of the staple agricultural goods, was used in various places as a supplement. In the early years of settlement, tobacco served as money. The tobacco itself was placed in a warehouse, and certificates of deposit were issued against it. These circulated as money, representing the value of the stored tobacco. When the tobacco harvests improved, increasing the supply of tobacco and lowering its price per pound, the certificates depreciated to such an extent that they ultimately were replaced by other money substitutes.

Loan certificates and bills of credit were also issued in the Middle Colonies, setting in motion inflationary pressures. Price increases may, therefore, be viewed as the cost of facilitating trade and finance. Additional relief for the strained colonial economy came from merchants themselves, including storekeepers and artisans in inland communities. It was common for these people to extend liberal credit to their customers, often for as long as a year. A local farmer would thus be permitted to buy manufactured goods on credit, and pay for them later by selling the merchant his farm produce. In the same way, tradesmen were able to finance imports through exports of goods, without the exchange of actual paper or metallic money.

Transportation

Early settlements in the Middle Colonies were made along navigable rivers. When land that fronted along rivers had been appropriated, settlers beat trails and roads into the hinterland. Most of the overland transportation was by horseback or wagons drawn by horses or oxen between farms and rivers. Since most of the rivers had a southeasterly flow, most of the overland transportation was carried on at some angle to the flow of the rivers. There was little or no movement of people or of goods between rivers. Roads were little more than Indian trails that had been widened to accommodate wagons. Planks may have been laid in marshes to permit the passage of wagons, especially in wet weather.

Settlements along the coast were connected with their hinterlands a distance of 30 or 40 miles inland by direct roads. Bridges were constructed over rivers and streams by the colonists, often in lieu of paying taxes.

Industry

New York was also the site of a shipbuilding industry that may have ranked next after New England and Charleston. It was not quite as near its hinterland that furnished it with naval stores, particularly lumber, and other occupations appeared to be more lucrative than building ships. The manufacture of iron became an important business in the colonies of Maryland, New Jersey, and Pennsylvania; glass was manufactured in New Jersey, and wool was an abundant raw material for household industries and for factory production. Sheep were grazed abundantly in these colonies, and lamb and mutton formed part of their diet as well as articles of export. Iron forges and foundries were widespread throughout the countryside. The largest operation was that of Peter Hasenclever in northern New Jersey. Sawmills were found near the rivers. Waterpower in these colonies was so abundant that it was also harnessed for use in the operation of gristmills and textile mills. Other frontier industries found in the Middle Colonies were blacksmithing and wagonmaking. The Conestoga wagon derives its name from the region in south central Pennsylvania where it was manufactured. Blacksmithing was important as the only ironworking unit in many communities. The blacksmith not only shod horses, he helped make and repair wagons, farm implements, hardware, and many household articles. Mention of *The Village Blacksmith* by Henry Wadsworth Longfellow is a sufficient reminder of the important role played by the "smithy."

Capital for those industries came from trading and commerce; and after the industries were in operation, profits were plowed back by their owners. Some of the capital came from Europe. The Europeans were a thrifty people, and profits of industry were large for the times. Labor for those industries was furnished by the many artisans who escaped from European countries, by indentured servants, and by those who were primarily engaged in agriculture and who could not work on farms because of the weather.

THE SOUTHERN COLONIES

Virginia, North and South Carolina, and Georgia constituted the southern group of colonies. The first permanent English settlement in North America was established at Jamestown, Virginia, in 1607. Rather than moving toward the south from this initial point, however, colonization spread along the Eastern Seaboard to the north of Virginia, in what were to become the Middle and New England Colonies. As a result, development of the Southern Colonies came late in the Colonial Period, with little time for a viable economic system to grow. At the time of the Revolution, the settlements in Georgia were barely 40 years old.

Apart from the late start, other factors in the Southern Colonies favored a nonindustrial economy. The wide coastal plain offered easily cleared and cultivated soil, plentiful rainfall, and a growing season that permitted two crops per year in the Lower South. The southern pine forests offered naval stores and building materials. Coupled with the mercantilistic policy of stimulating primary industries and agriculture in colonies, these conditions logically led to agriculture being the main occupation of most southerners.

Agriculture

All of the thirteen colonies had some agricultural characteristics in common, but each major group was in some way distinctive. The Southern Colonies produced many of the crops grown in other areas, and exhibited the small-farm culture which was so common to the North. What made the South different was its reliance on three or four basic money crops, widely grown and sometimes subsidized, and the use of plantations manned by Negro slaves. The haphazard method of settlement, which resulted in a disorganized pattern of land ownership and use, also set the Southern Colonies apart.

Land Tenure. Settlement in the South followed a distinctive pattern. Settlers tended to infiltrate along inland routes from other colonies farther north, rather than land directly from England or a continental country. Even Charleston, which had received some immigrants directly from Europe, was largely inhabited by colonists who had moved from Virginia. None of these people came in large, organized groups. For the most part, single families or a group of several families would migrate together. As a result, there was little formal surveying and laying out of the land on which they settled, unless the land was within the limits of an established town. Free and random choice of farm sites ultimately created a pattern of settlement which looked very much like a patchwork quilt. Plots were of varying sizes, and bore little organized relationship to each other. With no effective bounds on the size of a homestead, colonists who were able to utilize large amounts of land effectively could rather quickly achieve their aims.

The suitability of extensive agriculture in the South, coupled with available land, made the plantation system a possibility. A plantation was a large

farm which specialized in one or two major cash crops, using first indentured servants and later Negro slaves as a work force. Plantations were
meant to be efficient economic units, so they organized the work force for
year-round production. Such an arrangement was possible only in the
South where the climate made winter work a reality. Contrary to popular
opinion, a small or medium-sized farm was actually the most common
type of settlement in the Southern Colonies. Plantations required a sizable
capital investment, as well as a developed transportation system for supplies
and produce movement. Most of the plantations were, therefore, located in
settled areas, and were operated by relatively affluent persons. The great
majority of colonists, especially those in the frontier areas, could only afford
or could only operate small farms. Although the customs of entail, primogeniture, and quit rents paid to proprietors were introduced into the Southern
Colonies, their impact was minimal. This was particularly true in the frontier
areas, where enforcement of any law was difficult.

It was the Virginia migrants who established the first permanent settlements in the Carolinas. Labor on their plantations was provided by indentured
servants. When free of their servitude, the erstwhile indentured servants
became owners of small-sized farms. Lest they wrest political control of the
colony from the plantation owners, the latter took advantage of slave labor;
and by 1750 there may have been more than half as many slaves as there
were white people in the Southern Colonies.

Major Crops and Livestock. Southern farms produced a wide variety
of truck crops, similar to those in colonies farther to the north. Most of
these fruits and vegetables were consumed by farm families themselves or
were sold in local markets. Cows, pigs, sheep, and horses in varying numbers
were also common in the South, but were not usually produced in sufficient
numbers for the market. Most of the emphasis in agriculture was on the
important cash crops.

Rice, tobacco, sugarcane in certain regions, and hemp were the most
profitable crops to produce. Cotton did not become a major product of
the South until after the close of the Colonial Period. Tobacco was by far
the most important crop in Virginia, rice in North and South Carolina and
later in Georgia. The English attempted to subsidize the growing of indigo,
hemp, and the mulberry tree, but without much long-run success. Of these
products, indigo was the most profitable; and it was produced in all of the
Southern Colonies, until the colonists found that they could make more
money, even with the subsidy, in raising other crops. Though the colonists
could not formulate a statement of the principle of comparative costs as
applied to domestic industry, and the idea of *opportunity cost* [2] was unknown
to them, it was the operation of these two principles that turned their
attention to the planting of other crops.

---

[2] Opportunity cost of a productive agent is the value of that productive agent in
its best alternative use.

Unique in the marketing and shipping of tobacco to foreign ports was the lack of a highly concentrated tobacco market in the colonies. Tobacco planters in Virginia sought land along a river front and erected wharves along which ships moored to load for foreign ports. These ports were located in England because tobacco was an enumerated product and could not be sold or legally shipped directly to continental countries. Partly to compensate for the restricted but guaranteed market in England, and partly to produce more foodstuffs in England, Parliament forbade the growing of tobacco in England. This assured the colonists a market for their tobacco and one in which there was no competition with a home industry. But a buyers' monopoly is disadvantageous to the sellers, and the colonial tobacco growers were not pleased. Had continental markets been open to them, tobacco prices, undoubtedly, would have been higher. Not only would higher prices have been beneficial to the colonists, they would have been against British mercantile policy which dictated the importation of raw materials at the lowest possible prices.

It was in Virginia that one of the first attempts was made to control the prices of agricultural products. In the 17th century, when the crop was abundant and the price low, the colonial fathers thought that by restricting the land planted in tobacco, they could force the English to pay them a higher price the following year. An agreement was entered into and participated in by Maryland growers by which acreage planted in tobacco would be reduced the succeeding year. Maryland growers complained that some Virginia planters violated their agreements and, when word of this plan sifted into North Carolina, many farmers in that colony planted tobacco for the first time in order to benefit from its higher price. The result of all this is obvious: the total supply increased, and the price did not rise the next year.

Tobacco was cultivated extensively, and since it was to a rather high degree exhaustive of the natural ingredients of the soil, not many years passed by before the land became noticeably less productive. Farmers were faced with the problem of fertilizing the land, rotating crops, or taking up new lands to the west, some of which had to be cleared of trees. Because of the operation of the law of variable proportions and the farmers' desire to maximize profits, new lands were brought under cultivation and a new step was taken in the westward progress of the frontier. Old farms were either abandoned or they were occupied by a subsistence type of farmer, sometimes a poor white farmer, who worked closely with his labor, free or slave, and who planted more diversified crops, and possibly in rotation, than had formerly been done. The products of these farms did not find their way into foreign markets, and seldom were they found in domestic markets other than those nearby.

The Slave System. Negro slaves were first brought to the colonies by Dutch traders in 1619. From that time on, their numbers and their usefulness increased. It was the adaptability of the Negro to the wearisome cultivation of rice that gained a foothold for slavery in the coastal areas of the Carolinas and Georgia. Rice fields had to be flooded twice a year, and the workers were required to stand knee-deep in water for long hours under a hot sun. The Negro had developed a resistance to tropical fevers, and he could apparently withstand the ravages of malaria better than could white workers. Where white colonists would not or could not work, the Negro slave was forced to do so. Later, when cotton became the dominant crop, Negro slaves were able to undertake the intensive cultivation of the plants under a hot sun. It was through the process of economic selection rather than through a difference in attitude toward human bondage that slavery became established in the South.[3] Ultimately, great demand arose for slave labor to be used in the cultivation of rice and tobacco. Northern slave traders found a ready market for their human cargoes in the South.

Slave labor was cheaper than free white labor only when it could be utilized the year-round and in routine work where little or no supervision as to detail was required. Slaves had to be maintained whether or not there was work for them to do. They had not been trained to work in factories and mills where the pace was set by machines. Seasonal variations precluded their performing outdoor work the year-round. Factory and mill work was neither year-round nor routine. Slave labor could be utilized almost the year-round if rice and indigo or rice and tobacco were grown on the same plantation.

The fact that slave trading was engaged in by New England traders who outfitted ships and brought their human cargoes from Africa and the West Indies is prima facie evidence that New England, as a section, was not opposed to the idea of slavery. Again, household slaves were found in Northern and New England Colonies. Their work was year-round, indoors, and could be supervised closely. When rice and indigo, or rice and tobacco, were grown on the same plantation in the South, year-round work was provided and it was routine.

Slaves and indentured servants were found in the Middle Colonies, especially in Maryland; and it was their close proximity to each other that enabled writers to compare the life and lot of slaves with that of indentured servants.

Even in the Colonial Period, slaves were taught to use their hands; and many of them provided the artisan labor needed on their respective plantations. This eliminated the need for free white labor in nonfarming occupations, and served as a deterrent to the white immigrant moving to the South. To many of the immigrants, especially those of the later years of the Colonial Period, the idea of slavery was abhorrent; and the white immigrants did not want to compete with the slaves for a livelihood, whether on farms or

[3] The economic reasons for the growth of slavery in the South may be found in Kenneth M. Stampp, *The Peculiar Institution: Slavery in the Ante-Bellum South* (New York City: Vintage Books, Random House, 1956), *passim;* and in Ulrich B. Phillips, *Life and Labor in the Old South* (Boston: Little, Brown and Co., 1929), *passim.*

elsewhere. Outside of the Huguenots, who settled in North and South Carolina and some in Virginia and Georgia, very few non-English speaking immigrants were found in the South. This pattern of settlement established a precedent that was not broken until after the close of World War I.

Trade

Domestic trade and industry comprised a small portion of the economic activity in the Southern Colonies. Since many of the plantations were nearly self-sufficing as far as their relations with other plantations were concerned, most of the trade and trading was of an external variety. Of the American colonies, those in the South were the best suppliers of raw materials to England—raw materials that could not be produced in England, and hence did not compete with English goods. They were also the best customers of English manufactured goods because the skilled artisans did not settle there, and most slaves were capable of doing only coarse work. From that standpoint, the Southern Colonies fitted most satisfactorily into the scheme of British mercantilism. They were more dependent upon England for the sale of their products and as a source of household and domestic products and manufactured goods. Some of this trade, both outward and inward, appeared directly as coastwise trade, and Boston and New York served as *entrepôts* in this trade. It was the import of slaves and sugar directly from Africa and the West Indies that caused the Southern Colonies to experience an unfavorable trade balance.

Exports to those areas consisted of relatively small amounts of indigo, naval stores, tobacco, and large amounts of rice. This trade balance accentuated the debtor position of the Southern Colonies to other regions at home and abroad, a situation that continued to plague the South throughout the 19th century. Many of the imports from and exports to England appeared initially as coastwise trade with Northern and New England Colonies and helped place the South in debt to those regions.

Most, if not all, of the goods that partook of the triangular patterns of trade left the country through northern and middle colonial ports. On the return leg of a triangular pattern, the slave trade terminated in southern ports; commodities were landed in northern and middle colonial ports.

That the Southern Colonies were more dependent upon England than were any of the others is shown clearly by the data in Table 3-1, page 56. Making allowance for the reduced value of imports into New England does not alter this situation. The value of commodity imports does not measure the extent to which the Southern Colonies were dependent upon English manufactured goods. Many of the imports into New England and the Middle Colonies were, in turn, shipped coastwise to the South.

Money

The dominance of agriculture in the South and the frequency of relatively self-sufficient farm units did not diminish the need for money as a medium of exchange. Both external and internal trade required substantial amounts, and even the frontier farmer needed money from time to time for the purchase of necessities such as salt and gunpowder. Commodity money was common in the Southern Colonies, especially since the unfavorable balance of trade with England drained off most of the coin. Most staple goods served as money at one time or another. In Virginia and North Carolina, warehouse receipts for tobacco were circulated as money, ultimately meeting the same fate as those issued farther north in Maryland.

Loan bills and bills of credit also were issued as substitutes for metallic money. Some inflation resulted from their use, compounded by the instability of value of the warehouse receipts for tobacco. Book credit advanced by merchants served to fill the gap between the demand for purchasing power and the existing supply of money.

Transportation

Since plantations were settled along rivers and were relatively self-sustaining as far as relationships with other plantation owners were concerned, there was little need for overland transportation facilities other than roads that were found on given plantations. They were dirt roads that led from one field to another, and from rivers to plantation headquarters. Transportation north and south was along the coast, and inland from the coast, rivers sufficed.

Industry

Outside of agriculture and localized industries found on the plantations, the most important industry was that of building ships in Charleston, South Carolina. Charleston had a hinterland that was more productive of naval stores than was New England, and many of these products became objects of coastwise trade to the New England Colonies before they were exported to England.

Products of the plantation economy of the South that found their way to market were cattle, sheep, hogs, and horses, wheat, corn, and rye. Cotton and woolen clothing and coarse shoes for slaves, certain farm implements and utensils, cooperage stock, bricks, soap, candles, beer, and wine were sold to small farmers and to freed servants. Shipowners purchased cereal grains and meats.

QUESTIONS FOR REVIEW

1. Compare and contrast the development of agriculture in the New England Colonies with its development in the Southern Colonies.
2. Explain clearly what goals were achieved by means of external triangular trade. Outline two common patterns of triangular trade, one of which resulted in a flow of specie into the colonies.
3. England imposed few restrictions on internal colonial trade. Give several reasons why such trade, nevertheless, developed slowly.
4. Why was money scarce in the colonies? What steps were taken to overcome that scarcity?
5. What is inflation? How did inflation affect the colonial economy? What are the effects of inflation upon debtors and creditors?
6. Account for the presence of three industries that were found on the colonial frontier.
7. What were quit rents? How were quit rents used?
8. Why did proprietary farming along the Hudson River ultimately fail?

SUGGESTED READINGS

Bridenbaugh, Carl. *The Colonial Craftsman.* Chicago: Phoenix Books, University of Chicago Press, 1961.

Bruchey, Stuart. *The Roots of American Economic Growth, 1607-1861: An Essay in Social Causation.* New York City: Harper & Row, Publishers, 1965. Chapters 1 and 2.

Callender, Guy S. *Selections from the Economic History of the United States, 1765-1860.* New York City: Augustus M. Kelley, Publishers, 1965. Chapter 2.

Ferguson, E. James. "Currency Finance: An Interpretation of Colonial Monetary Practices," *American Economic History: Essays in Interpretation,* edited by Stanley Coben and Forest G. Hill. Philadelphia: J. B. Lippincott Co., 1966.

Gagliardo, John G. "Germans and Agriculture in Colonial Pennsylvania," *United States Economic History: Selected Readings,* edited by Harry N. Scheiber. New York City: Alfred A. Knopf, Inc., 1964.

Gray, Lewis C. "The Market Surplus Problems of Colonial Tobacco," *Issues in American Economic History,* edited by Gerald D. Nash. Boston: D. C. Heath & Company, 1964.

Land, Aubrey C. "Genesis of a Colonial Fortune: Daniel Dulany of Maryland," *American Economic History: Essays in Interpretation,* edited by Stanley Coben and Forest G. Hill. Philadelphia: J. B. Lippincott Co., 1966.

Sachs, William. "Agricultural Conditions in the Northern Colonies Before the Revolution," *Issues in American Economic History,* edited by Gerald D. Nash. Boston: D. C. Heath & Company, 1964.

Simkins, Francis B. *A History of the South,* 2d ed. New York City: Alfred A. Knopf, Inc., 1961. Chapters 3 and 5.

PART II

The Emergence of a New Nation—1763-1815

The termination of the French and Indian War initiated a new era of colonial unrest. The colonists gave turbulent expression to their dissatisfaction with England's regimentation of the colonial economy. Sectional differences in economic development caused uncertainty, and jealousies between sections endangered unity of purpose and action. Differences in climate, in the suitability of the soil to agriculture, distance from fishing banks, easy accessibility of forest resources, together with the exercise of the right of free enterprise that was guided by profit-making potentialities had resulted in an unconscious geographical specialization and division of labor.

In attempting to solve sectional differences, many political compromises were made, and a constitution that contained several references to economic organization and functioning of the federal government was adopted. The Constitution introduced guidelines for Congress to follow in its efforts to control and to stimulate economic activity.

Many economic aspects and relationships that were manifest during the Colonial Period were extended beyond the time of political independence. The importance of foreign trade and its nature as far as the kinds of goods that were exported and imported were concerned, the nature of the imbalance of the commodity trade account, the principal countries from which imports were received and to which exports were consigned—all continued the pattern established during the Colonial Period. The nature of hand-to-hand currency, the legal tender status of foreign coins, and the continued use of paper money followed patterns of colonial usage. The importance of England to the Southern States as supplier of manufactured goods, the use of slave labor, and the prevalence of plantation farming in the South; tillable agriculture on smaller farms in the North and West; the presence of wheat crops in frontier regions; the importance of naval industries to the people of New England; and the sources of relatively large personal incomes and the origins of money capital that was available for investment in American industries are some of the aspects of the colonial economy that were extended into later periods.

One of the challenges to the student of economic history is to discover when these relationships were severed, and, more importantly, what the conditions were that brought about their termination. At this point, the consideration of economic dislocations enters the study. New relations were established, the impacts of which fell unevenly on different economic groups. The transition period was extremely painful to labor, for example, when it was displaced in the short run by machinery. It was during this period, also, that American entrepreneurs, freed from British mercantilism, gave expression to their quests for profits by searching for new markets in far-off China.

From one point of view, this period was one of the most critical of our existence, because it was during these years that the pattern of our economic development was shaped. The incorporation at the state level of banks that issued circulating notes led to the chartering of a United States bank whose functions were to serve as fiscal agent of the federal government and to regulate bank note currency. A monetary system was devised under the guidance and influence of Alexander Hamilton, who also obtained the establishment of public credit at the federal level. A tariff program was embarked upon in order to give encouragement to manufacturing industries and to give balance to the economy. Albert Gallatin gave what proved to be a prophetic report to Congress on the need for the development of a transportation system. Congress adopted a policy of giving encouragement to the entry upon public lands by bona fide owners and settlers. The textile industry gave birth to the factory system. The principles of standardization and interchangeability of parts were introduced in the manufacture of firearms under government contract.

Chapter 4

DISCONTENT, DEFIANCE, AND

READJUSTMENTS—1763-1783

The Seven Years' War between England and France, 1756-63, was really a struggle over the establishment of their respective colonial empires that was manifested a hundred years earlier by the development of mercantilistic programs by both countries and by the passage of the Navigation Acts by England. The French and Indian War was the colonial phase of that armed struggle, during which the French are alleged to have goaded the Indians to making raids upon British frontier settlements. The terms of the Treaty of Paris, which terminated that war and which was signed in 1763, included what was thought to have been a settlement of the dispute between England and France over the disposition of lands west of the Appalachian Mountains. The French were pushed back into Canada north of the Great Lakes and the northern boundary of New York, and the Indians were not to inhabit the territory between the Appalachian Mountains, the Great Lakes, and the Mississippi River; however, they were given the privilege of hunting, trapping, and fishing in this territory. While the Treaty brought to a close one phase of the struggle for colonial empire between England and France, it marked the beginning of another period that has come to be looked upon as one of the most critical in American history. Had it not been for the successful termination of that struggle from the English point of view, the course of economic and political development of America would have been vastly different from that which led to the formation of a new nation. English influence was strong along the coastal plain, while the French had gone up the St. Lawrence River and into the territory west of the Appalachian Mountains. The French were engaged in hunting and trapping and in trading with the Indians, but had not expropriated the land for their exclusive use. They experienced little or no difficulty in aligning the Indians against the English who had begun to exert pressure as they moved westward beyond the Appalachians.

The Attitude of the Colonists Towards England

It has been estimated that there was a colonial population of 1,594,000 in 1760, about 80 percent of which was of English origin or descent. While that large percentage of colonists was English and their sympathies were with England, they no longer wanted to be subservient to England. They considered themselves to be citizens of England, even though they were removed some 3,000 miles from their homeland. As individuals, they had the rights of Englishmen. The industrial development of the colonies and their trade relations, internal and external, had been regulated for the benefit of the mother country. The colonists wanted their freedom extended throughout the entire area of their economic activities. They comprised the merchant, trading, and professional segments of the population in America and were looked upon as being the more conservative in their thinking. The other 20 percent of the people in the colonies were from other western and northern European countries—Germany, France, Spain, Portugal, Denmark, and the Scandinavian countries, primarily—and had no particular feeling of loyalty towards England. By 1770, possibly one fourth of the colonial population had no direct English connection; and for many of the remaining three fourths, their connections were little more than memories of past years, which had not been renewed by recent visitations to their mother country.

The Attitude of England Towards the Colonies

English attitudes towards the colonists, shared alike by members of Parliament and by the Crown, were that the colonists were English subjects and should be made to feel that they owed obeisance and respect to England. In addition to the policy of England exercising more control over her American colonies, there was the need to raise more revenue in the colonies to pay for their administration and supervision, as well as to provide more revenue for the mother country. To the extent that the cost of administering the colonies could have been provided by the colonists, just that much governmental money in England could have been released for other uses. That would have been tantamount to raising additional revenue in England.

DISCONTENT

In carrying out the program of exercising more control over the American colonies and of raising revenue in the colonies in order to make them pay their own way, England aggravated the colonists to the point of overt action. Law enforcement interferred with their freedom of enterprise which they zealously attempted to protect. Making the colonists pay their own way antagonized them because they deemed such costs to be entirely unnecessary.

Many grievances—some of which were political, some of which were economic in character—had a cumulative effect upon the discontent of the colonists. These grievances were not of the same intensity on the frontier as they were along the coastal areas. They were not the same in the New England Colonies as they were in the South. There was no one piece of legislation that, by itself, brought on rebellion; however, there was a series of enactments that were disconnected of themselves, but which were focused on law enforcement or raising revenue and which exhausted the patience of the colonists.

Proclamation of 1763

Since expanding the area of English settlement to the newly acquired territory west of the Appalachian Mountains would have made it more difficult to supervise and control the activities of the colonists, the Proclamation of 1763 restricted the western boundary of colonial settlements for the next ten years to a line connecting the headwaters of the rivers that emptied into the Atlantic Ocean. If nothing else had transpired at the time, that alone was enough to have aroused the ire of the colonists, many of whom were well aware of the richness of the land and of the abundance of natural resources in the region beyond the Appalachians. Those persons were settlers, hunters and trappers, and speculators in land values.

Settlers were those persons who, for one or more of many reasons, desired to move from the farms or lands east of the Appalachian Mountains to virgin land. Practices of land butchery had so depleted the soil in Virginia and the other colonies that continued extensive cultivation had lowered the level of crop yields. Many farmers found it easier to take up new lands a few miles to the west than to rehabilitate the soil by more intensive cultivation such as spreading natural fertilizer. Indentured servants whose terms of servitude had expired, or who had escaped from bondage, desired to settle upon new lands somewhat removed from their former environment. Hunters and trappers were not eager that permanent settlements be established in that territory, neither did they like the fact that the Indians had not been driven farther west and south. Probably the most vociferous objections came from that well-organized minority of land speculators, who now were required to obtain title to lands west of the Appalachian Mountains from England rather than from Governors of the colonies.

Depression

An economic depression set in shortly before the return of peace in 1763, and it was accompanied by a feeling of political and social unrest. The causes of that depression were not found in the enforcement of the Trade and Navigation Act against the colonies. They were inherent in the economic system within the framework of which adjustments to peacetime conditions were made following seven years of warfare against France. The depression was felt in all of the colonies through a slowdown in the pace of economic activity. Since foreign trade relations were probably the most important to all of the colonies, to the extent that they sold less overseas meant that they

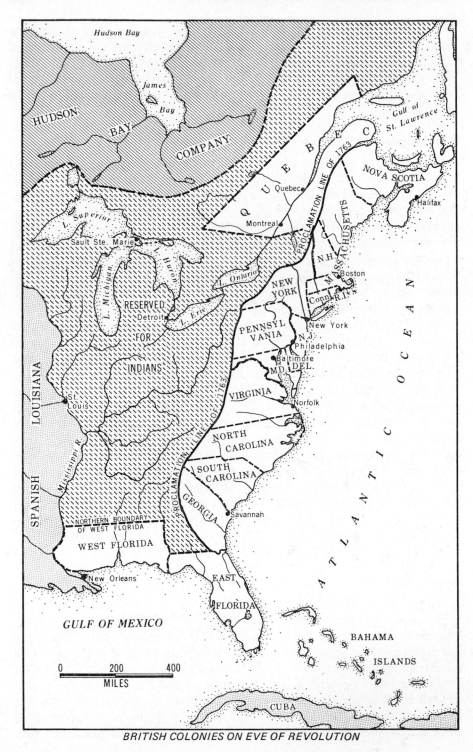

BRITISH COLONIES ON EVE OF REVOLUTION

purchased less from those markets. To the extent that domestic trade was closely related to overseas trade, local merchants experienced losses of business income. To the extent that businessmen could not pay their bills, members of the professions, bankers, and publishers were deprived of current income. Because economic development was not uniform throughout the colonies, the impacts of depression likewise differed.

Impact on the New England Colonies. New England felt the decline in the volume of foreign trade since it provided most of the physical facilities for overseas trade and the manpower to crew the ships. Ships were tied up to their wharves, sailors were idled, and artisans in shipbuilding were listed among the unemployed. Since the economies of towns and seaports were closely allied to the conditions of trade and commerce, local merchants suffered a decline in the volume and in the value of their retail trade. Prices of commodities fell, wages declined, and bill payments were difficult to collect.

Impact on the Middle Colonies. The volume of the import trade of New York alone declined from a peak of £630,785 in 1759 to a low of £98,047 in 1762. While the import level of 1759 was not attained again throughout the remainder of the Colonial Period, some recovery was measured after 1764; but there was no trend in the volume of trade, either on the increase or on the decrease. Native capital formation in the colonies, which had begun to appear as the result of trading with the West Indies and with European countries, was on the decline because of the rapid decrease in the volume and in the value of colonial external trade.

The Middle Colonies were the principal exporters of commodities to the West Indies; and with the decline in the price of sugar, both in America and in England, West Indian planters could neither buy nor pay for the same volume of goods at the same level of prices as formerly. That led to a decline in the incomes of those persons in the Middle Colonies who were engaged in either foreign or domestic trade or both. Unemployment increased; prices, including rents and wages, declined; and there was general suffering throughout the area.

Impact on the Southern Colonies. Declines in the price and in the volume of tobacco the Southern Colonies exported to England were disastrous to the economy of the South. Tobacco still was the principal crop; England was the only legal market under the principle of enumeration. The southern planter felt the brunt of the depression in his part of the country because his slaves had to be fed and clothed regardless of the prices of tobacco, rice, and indigo. Unemployment was not as severe in the South as it was in other colonies; and merchants did not feel the impact of the decline in cotton, only because merchandising was not as highly developed as it was in the other groups of colonies. The value of farmland declined, and the turnover of land ownership was low because the planter did not have funds with which to acquire more land to the west. The cotton planter was displaced at the prospect of not being able to expand his holdings when the overall price situation was favorable for such a move.

DEFIANCE

It was well known in England that the colonists were ignoring some of the restrictions laid down in accordance with mercantile doctrine and were evading others by smuggling or other means. One of those evasions was related to the importation of molasses from the West Indies, both French and British.

A New Enforcement Program

The costs of administering the American colonial program that had been increasing year by year had not been compensated for by increases in revenues collected from the colonists. The colonies were pushing their frontier settlements to the west and at no decrease in population along the coastal plain. In various ways the colonists began to protest their enforced dependence upon England. Before matters got out of hand, the mother country determined to make them conscious that they still were colonials.

Molasses Act of 1733. This Act levied an import duty of 6d. per gallon on molasses imported from the West Indies. The colonists honored this provision in the breach, and collectors of customs made little or no effort to enforce the levy.

Sugar Act of 1764. The Sugar Act was aimed more at the sugar trade with the French West Indies than it was at the British sugar trade; because, regardless of the tax, the colonists had been able to purchase sugar and molasses from the French at lower prices than they were charged by British planters. One of the principal industrial uses of sugar was in the manufacture of rum which was distasteful to the French. They preferred wines to rum, and sugar was not one of the ingredients of their favorite drink. But sugar was in great demand in England, the impact of which was felt in its sale by British planters and processors. In order to obtain sugar from the British West Indies, American colonists had to compete with the English market and pay a higher price than was asked by French planters and processors. Since the purchase of sugar and molasses from the French was contrary to the principles of British mercantilism, the Act of 1764 reduced the impost upon sugar from the French West Indies to 3d. per gallon, and customs officials made efforts to enforce its collection. To the British that was a reduction of 50 percent of the duty on sugar; to the American colonists it was the payment of a duty for the first time. That proved to be an irreconcilable difference in points of view, and one which was brought home to the colonist in the form of higher prices every time he purchased his rum. To the degree that the demand for rum was *inelastic,* that is to say that price increases within certain price ranges had little or no effect upon the quantity of rum purchased, retail merchants of other goods felt the impact of the impost in a decrease in volume of their sales. Thus importers of sugar from the West Indies, exporters of goods to the West Indies, merchants, shippers, and consumers were all opposed to the levy.

Legal Tender Act of 1764. The colonists had overcome to some extent the lack of a hand-to-hand currency by issuing bills of credit or loan bills,[1] neither of which circulated at face value, but they did facilitate the exchange of goods between the colonists. In order to discourage that kind of trade and to force the colonists to trade with English merchants, the terms of the Currency Act of 1751, which forbade the issuance of bills of credit in New England were extended in 1764 to the remaining colonies. While the main purpose may have been to protect English creditors, its impact fell upon all classes of persons, who raised their objections to that attempt on the part of England to stifle colonial internal or domestic trade.

Quartering Act of 1765. Another act of legislation that irritated the colonists and at the same time made them suspicious of England's intentions was the Quartering Act of 1765. Protecting the colonists from frontier raids by the French and Indians was more of a financial burden than the English wanted to bear, and since the colonists were English subjects it was quite proper for them to pay this cost. Accordingly provision was made for the colonists to be responsible for the housing and feeding of 10,000 soldiers who were sent over. Since the French had been pushed up into Canada and the colonists felt that they had been responsible for the frequent raids made by the Indians on the colonial frontier, in the minds of the colonists that hazard had been lessened to a large degree. The only other alternative for sending soldiers to the colonies was to make sure of more rigid enforcement of restrictive legislation, and that at a time when the colonists were desirous of more freedom, not less.

Stamp Tax of 1765. In order to raise more revenue within the colonies, Parliament enacted the Stamp Act in 1765, under the terms of which taxes were levied upon birth certificates, marriage certificates, legal papers of all kinds, college diplomas, playing cards, dice, leases, appointments to office, newspapers, and almanacs. While the impact of that tax was on all classes of people, the heaviest burdens were upon bankers, publishers, and members of the professions. These latter groups of persons were the leaders in their communities. They helped mold public opinion. They wrote editorials in the papers and gave expression to their thinking through the press and in the pulpit. They were the ones who publicized the slogan, "taxation without representation is tyranny."

[1] See Chapter 3, p. 60.

The Colonial Attitude Towards Taxation.

History reveals that lack of representation in legislative halls had little to do with the unpopularity of those taxes, although it was implied that the colonists would have paid them willingly had they been imposed by the duly elected representatives. There is another aspect to colonial objections concerning the manner in which the taxes were levied. Lack of representation in the law-making body in England confirmed the status of the American colonists as being subservient to England. Had the colonists been living in England, they would have had representation in Parliament. It seems doubtful, however, in the light of later developments that they would have accepted those levies any more graciously had they been levied by their own people. For example, a few years later when the Second Continental Congress (1775-76), which was composed of members who were duly elected by the colonists, requested the colonies to contribute money in order to finance the Confederation, the money was not forthcoming. The Continental Congress did not have the power to impose taxes; but on the occasion of its request for funds, the colonial governments could have levied taxes upon their citizens and turned the receipts over to the temporary Congress. But the people did not wish to pay taxes.

Again, in 1794, when the Congress of the United States levied an excise tax upon the manufacture and sale of whiskey, the farmers of northwestern Virginia, southeastern Ohio, and southwestern Pennsylvania, who had been selling their corn in eastern markets in the form of whiskey, rebelled to the point of forcing President Washington to send a contingent of the United States army to enforce the law. The economic principle behind that objection was more than an objection to paying taxes. Corn, as such, was too cheap and bulky to stand the heavy charge that was made to transport it to eastern markets. The process of transforming corn into whiskey added so much to its value that it could withstand the heavy transportation charge and still be sold at a profit. To the grower of corn that market was his livelihood, and cutting down on the sale of whiskey was depriving him of his livelihood. Frontiersmen were ignorant of the concept of inelasticity of demand. Within certain price ranges the demand for whiskey did not respond readily to price changes, but that pattern of consumer behavior was not generally known at the time.

It was only after overcoming strong opposition that Alexander Hamilton succeeded in having Congress levy the whiskey tax and other excise taxes, all of which were removed during President Jefferson's term of office. The colonists looked differently upon the use of external taxes or customs duties, partly because they had been accustomed to their use in England. They accepted them in principle because they felt that the tax burden did not fall on themselves as consumers. Customs duties were incorporated in retail prices, and the colonists were not aware of paying them when they purchased imported products. From Jefferson's time until 1861, with the exception of some temporary taxes levied to help finance the War of 1812, the only sources of governmental revenue at the federal level were from the sale of public lands and from customs duties. Unwillingness to pay taxes at the state level in the 1830's resulted in the inability of several states to pay interest on bonds that were issued for the purpose of financing internal improvements, which at the time were in the form of highways, canals, and railroads. The conclusion that must be reached from this analysis is that the colonists just did not wish to pay taxes to a central or state governmental unit even though they might have been levied by their duly elected representatives in Parliament or Congress.

Punitive Action by England—The Townshend Acts of 1767

The resistance to the payment of the stamp tax was so strong and violent that it was repealed the following year, 1766. Relief was not for long, however, as England was in need of funds both at home and to pay the costs of administering the American colonies.

The Townshend Acts of 1767 were a series of revenue acts which touched at the very heart of colonial life by taxing the importation of paints, painters' colors, lead, glass, and tea. Among the objections to those levies was the belief that they raised the cost of living at a time when the colonial economy was not very prosperous, combined with the fact that imports so far exceeded exports that the colonies had little gold with which to settle their obligations. A special provision was made for the East India Tea Company to sell tea in the American colonies for less than its price in England. As a matter of principle a tax of 3d. per pound was retained on its importation, but 12d. per pound was remitted by England on tea that was sent directly to America without first touching English shores. That procedure cut out two steps on the handling of tea and made it possible for tea to be sold for a lower price in the colonies than it sold for in England. To this there was no objection by tea drinkers, but it gave the East India Tea Company a monopoly on the sale of tea in America. Not only did that violate the principles of competition to which the colonists were committed, they thought it would pave the way for England to establish monopoly control in the sale of other products to and in the colonies. Another objection was raised by the smugglers of tea, who no longer found it profitable to engage in what had been a lucrative pursuit. While the number of merchants so engaged was not large percentagewise, they were among the colonial leaders and were in a position to voice their objections with telling effect. The reader is familiar with a tea party that was held in Boston harbor to which many of the uninvited guests were white men dressed as Indians, among whom was alleged to have been John Hancock.

Retaliatory Action by England—The Intolerable Acts of 1774

Parliament responded to the challenge to British authority by passing the so-called Intolerable Acts. The port of Boston was closed under the

Boston Port Bill until such time as the tea was paid for, and the terms of the Quartering Act were revived insofar as they applied to Massachusetts. In addition to those measures of economic impact, British agents who might be charged with violence in the performance of their duties were to be tried in English courts; and the power of the Governor was strengthened by taking away some power from the General Assembly and from the town meetings.

The Quebec Act of 1774, under the terms of which the territory east of the Mississippi River, north of the Ohio River, and south of the Great Lakes was annexed to Canada, caused great anxiety and unrest in the colonies of Virginia, New York, Connecticut, and Massachusetts, all of which laid claims to lands west of the Appalachian Mountains in that area. While the Quebec Act was not connected with the colonists' disregard for British authority, they resented it almost as much as they did the Intolerable Acts. Even though a few years of relative economic prosperity served to ease some of the pressure of discontent and defiance after 1770, the situation had developed too far and too deeply to be thrown off lightly by an improvement of business activity.

More effective than violence in opposing the oppressive tax measures was the refusal of the colonists to import goods from England, or to purchase them after they had been imported. This kind of opposition, however, may have done as much damage to colonial importers and to the economy in general as it did to British exporters. There was a rapid decline in the value of goods imported from England and in the volume of retail trade. An increase in unemployment was accompanied by a decrease in personal incomes. Just how much the series of events, the impacts of which were on tea, its importation, tea merchants, and tea drinkers, had to do with forming a preference that early Americans expressed for coffee is difficult to determine; but statistical data reveal that more coffee than tea has been imported since 1790. It is also known that consumption of tea in the colonies declined after the passage of the Tea Act in 1773, even though drinking tea was one of the habits or institutions the colonists brought with them to this country.

WAR PENDING

With the exception of men like William Pitt and a few others, English leaders in politics and trade did not realize the degree of solidarity and earnestness of purpose the colonists had attained. Freedom of enterprise, free pricing, competition, and the profit motive—all contributed to that condition; and it was in defense of those economic institutions as well as to obtain their political freedom that the colonists finally rebelled. Even so, it was not until England had taken drastic punitive action against them that they were driven to take extreme and violent measures. In spite of the boundary to western settlement that had been established by the Proclamation of 1763, many small towns, including Pittsburgh, had been established within the next ten years. Frontiersmen were more aggressive in their opposition to English rule than the more conservative tradesmen in eastern cities who had vested interests to protect. The Whigs stood to gain financially from the economic development of the colonies apart from any controls exercised by the English. The Tories thought their future lay in a continuation of the economic relationships into which they already had entered. Merchants and traders, shipbuilding and shipping interests, exporters and importers of commodities to and from England and English possessions were those who obtained their livelihoods from rather close economic contacts with England. They would suffer most from interrupting those relationships, at least in the short run.

Sectional Differences

Sectionally, the picture was a little more confused. There were frontiersmen in all of the thirteen colonies; but the nature of the vested interests was quite different, especially those of New England as compared with those of the South.

New England Colonies. Insofar as the people of New England wanted to engage in manufacturing or in trading with areas that were outside of the limited areas established in the terms of the Navigation Acts, they stood to gain by severing the shackles that restricted their economic development. While it is true that the New England economy was more competitive with that of England than were the economies of the other groups of colonies, it was in New England that most of the external trade, fishing, and shipbuilding were found. In terms of the percentage of the population that was engaged in those activities, it is impossible to draw any conclusions other than to remind the student that much of the support of the Revolutionary War came from New England, and that when the war had ended the Tories had suffered staggering losses of property and of personal belongings, and upwards of 20,000 persons had been driven to or had sought refuge in Canada. One reason why the Tories were so badly mistreated during and after the war was because they continued to sell their goods to the enemy. Food and articles of clothing, for the lack of which the soldiers in Washington's army suffered, were sold to the English, not entirely because of pro-British sympathy, but partly because the colonial merchants preferred English money and credit to that of the Continental Congress. Unfortunately, or otherwise, depending entirely upon a person's point of view as influenced by his economic status, there were many persons who stood to make money profits because of the war. Price inflation, scarcity of consumer goods, and competition between the Armed Forces and civilians for consumer goods and producer goods—all caused commodity prices to rise. Colonial merchants were able to take advantage of their fortuitous position.

There was no governmental organization to establish priorities and to enforce a program of economic control. The attempts of the New England

Colonies to establish maximum prices and wages were unsuccessful. Rent controls and rationing of consumer goods were not used to resist the forces of price inflation, nor to insure a steady flow of supplies to the Armed Forces. The profits that arose from smuggling goods into New England were large enough to offset the danger of loss or of confiscation.

Middle Colonies. There is little or no evidence to support the proposition that the people who lived in the Middle Colonies were any more loyal to the cause of the revolution than were the people of New England. The export trade to countries not under British domination was large, and it continued to be a source of profits during the war. Trade with continental countries of Europe and with those bordering along the Mediterranean Sea continued to bring in large profits, and here, too, the opportunity to sell supplies to the English for English money was more than the merchants could resist. English troops were subjected to the same weather conditions that caused so much suffering among the troops of the Continental Army, but they had more food and protective covering and suffered less. The shortage of food and of clothing was not absolute. It was one that could have been overcome by a more loyal effort on the part of the civilian population.

Southern Colonies. From one point of view, the southern planter had more to lose from a break with England than his brothers to the north. This was because his economy was tied more closely to that of England, as was manifest by the volume of imports and exports that passed through southern ports. However, there was another aspect of the southern plantation economy that was at least as important as its external trade relations, namely, the abundance of free land to the west. The Proclamation of 1763 appeared to remove western lands from within easy reach of the planter, and he may have known that the foreign market for tobacco and rice did not depend upon the continuation of his political allegiance to England. The deciding factor that swayed the southern planter to support the colonial cause was the desire for cheap or free land to the west. The only direction in which he could expand was towards the Mississippi River and beyond. The cultivation of tobacco was very exhaustive of the soil; and after a few years of repeated plantings, the output per acre began to decrease. Since the southern planter knew little about the uses of natural fertilizer, and if he did the cost of spreading it was too great, the only alternative was to move west.

The Declaration of Independence

Insofar as the attitude of the colonists was reflected in the Declaration of Independence in 1776, their political grievances were at least as numerous as those that carried economic implications. The following excerpts are not complete but they are indicative of colonial feelings toward King George III:

"He has endeavored to prevent the population of these States . . . .

"He has erected a multitude of New Offices, and sent hither swarms of Officers to harass our people, and eat out their substance.

". . . [giving] his Assent to their Acts of pretended Legislation: For quartering large bodies of armed troops among us: . . . For cutting our Trade with all parts of the world: For imposing Taxes on us without our Consent: . . . ."

The colonists were interested from an economic point of view in an increase in population. As landowners, that would tend to increase the value of their holdings; as speculators in western lands, or in frontier regions, growth in population was necessary for a successful outcome of their speculations. To merchants, a growing population meant larger markets for their wares; to traders with foreign countries, it meant an increase in the volume of imports and exports; and to shipowners, it meant an increase in the volume of goods transported. To manufacturers, a growing population not only meant a larger market, but an increase in the supply of labor and a possible decline in wages.

The "multitude of New Offices" and "swarms of Officers" meant more money had to be raised in the colonies with which to pay their salaries, and that meant increased taxation which was implied in the phrase to "eat out their substance." Another implication is that foodstuffs in New England, where many of those officers were located, were not as abundant as in other colonies; and insofar as those officers received salaries that were above the level of nongovernmental salaries in the colonies, their spending tended to raise the prices of consumer goods. The housing of those officers and their business quarters tended to compete with private enterprise, to the detriment of the latter.

The quartering of armed troops was not only an expense that had to be borne by the colonists, it meant stricter law enforcement, less smuggling, and a heavier tax burden.

"Cutting off our Trade with other parts of the world" was in violation of the principles of free enterprise and competition in seeking the most advantageous markets for the goods the colonists had to sell in world markets. It also narrowed the areas from which imports could be obtained, but the reader must be reminded that England and its colonial empire was the best supplier of commodity imports into the colonies.

". . . imposing Taxes on us without our Consent" was a restatement of the idea of taxation without representation. That statement was in accord with the general tenor of the entire Declaration. The statement, "imposing Taxes on us," was too prosaic for the purpose of obtaining the support of the colonists to such an important document. As has been brought out above, paying excise taxes was the thing to which they objected.

Financial Aspects of the Revolution

One of the time-honored problems of conducting a war is how to finance it with the least disturbance to the economy as a whole. That the colonies and the Continental Congress were hard pressed for an easy solution is manifest when it is remembered that one of the effects of the enforcement of British mercantile policy in the colonies was a shortage of money. There are only three ways to finance a war: (1) increase taxes and levy new ones that will yield revenues; (2) borrow from persons, institutions, and countries; and (3) print paper money.

Taxation. The antipathy of the colonists towards paying any kind of taxes, especially those levied by any form of central government, precluded that device as a source of any appreciable amount of revenue. Since the Second Continental Congress did not have the right to impose taxes, the best it could do was to requisition funds from the states and rely upon their willingness to comply with these requests. Though the newly formed states did impose new taxes upon their citizens and these taxes were productive of additional revenue, officials were loath to remit any of the proceeds to the federated government.

Borrowing. While the credit of the newly formed government had not been established, it was able to borrow funds from persons, from institutions, and from other countries. There were some loyal patriots who had amassed fortunes from the sale of western lands; from the profits of internal and of external trade; from the manufacture of iron, glass, and other articles; and from the conduct of financial transactions. Many of those persons lent their personal fortunes to the cause, partly for reasons of loyalty, and partly because they saw the promise of greater financial profits in the future as the country grew in population, in wealth, and in industry, and as more land was settled to the west. The name of Robert Morris stands out prominently among the financiers of the Revolution.

While France was not on the best of terms with England, she could ill afford another overt war. It was cheaper and would at the same time help to accomplish the same purpose to grant loans to the American Revolutionaries. Holland was still another country that had suffered more than mere loss of prestige upon the rise of the British Empire and was willing to extend financial aid to what she considered a just cause. In spite of the many difficulties and crises connected with the conduct of the struggle, a successful termination would open the doors of trade and investment to the nations of Continental Europe and would be a blow to the pride and prestige of the most powerful nation of Europe.

Printing Money. The most unsatisfactory aspect of financing the Revolution, as is always the case in any financial undertaking that involves the use of irredeemable paper money, was the issuance of continental currency by the Continental Congress, and of irredeemable credit money by the several states. Since that money was not issued in response to an economic need for units of purchasing power, nor were any provisions made for its ultimate redemption in gold or silver, it depreciated rapidly. An economic need for units of purchasing power would have been measured by an increase in the production of economic goods that would have operated on the demand side for money to offset its increase in supply, or in the rendering of services that would have satisfied people's wants more completely. The war was destructive of consumers' goods, of capital goods, and of manpower; and some actual increases in the production of goods were for the main purpose of being destroyed or of destroying other goods and persons. Under those conditions, it is little wonder that paper money depreciated rapidly and to a large extent.

Inflation. The American people found that one way to keep from incurring losses that resulted from the holding of continental currency was to spend it in the purchase of goods and services and let someone else lose because of its depreciation. That very action caused prices to rise more rapidly than they otherwise would have risen, and the currency to depreciate. Prices of commodities were quoted in terms of specie, and higher prices were quoted in terms of paper money. Farmers were somewhat loath to accept continental or colonial currency and much preferred the specie that the English had to offer them. Many of them refused to sell their products to urban dwellers who went hungry unless they had specie they could offer the farmers.

Rents, interest rates, wages, and prices rose in terms of depreciated money, but not in the same proportion. Commodity prices rose first and more rapidly than did rents, wages, and interest rates; and those persons whose incomes consisted in whole or in part of these relatively fixed types of incomes suffered to that extent. The phrase "not worth a continental" is not at all complimentary, since it derives its meaning from the almost complete worthlessness in exchange of the continental paper money.

Efforts were made by the Second Continental Congress and by the several states to exercise some kind of price control, which usually took the form of maximum prices that could be asked by dealers and by manufacturers for their goods. Since there were no effective means by which these controls could be enforced, they were entirely ineffective.

Impacts of War

The Revolutionary War was not a total war. It was a military struggle between two armies; and civilian activities were involved only as they felt the impacts of war, good or bad. There were no governmental controls over production, and no priorities were exercised in the distribution of scarce goods between war industries themselves or between war industries and those that produced for civilian consumption. Price and the kind of money used in paying for goods seemed to be the important considerations merchants and farmers gave in the market for their goods. As was true in almost all other economic relationships, the impacts of war were not uniform throughout all of the colonies.

The New England and Middle Colonies. In the early years of war, New England traders suffered financial losses, and unemployment figures soared to new heights. After a year or two of combat, England either permitted her goods to be sent to this country or she made little effort to prevent them from being shipped to enemy territory. The lure of money profits was too great to resist in the name of loyalty or of patriotism.

Manufacturing industries in the New England and Middle Colonies prospered as never before. During the early years of the war there was a decline in the importation of manufactured goods from England, along with an increase in the demand for them. The prices of these goods rose more rapidly than did their production costs. That combination of conditions was all that was needed to create a boom in manufacturing in the colonies. Manufacturing taboos set by England had been ignored to some extent throughout most of the Colonial Period, but now the lid was off. Textile and iron manufacturing may have prospered more than other industries and were common throughout the New England and Middle Colonies. The New England farmer was not able to take advantage of the wartime demand for his products, because he tended to operate just to supply his family. Conditions were such that he could not expand his output readily except in the production of livestock and meats. The farmer in the Middle Colonies was able to expand his activities to take advantage of the new demand for his products and their higher prices. Shortages of food in Washington's army were not due as much to actual shortages of foodstuffs as they were to unfavorable marketing conditions and inadequate transportation facilities that hampered the distribution of food. The same may be said for the lack of clothing for the soldiers of the Continental Army.

The Southern Colonies. The Southern Colonies may have fared worse than the others because of the lack of foreign markets and the inability of colonial markets to take up the slack. Blockades were effective in the early years of the war, and, when the British landed in southern ports, they not only destroyed cotton, tobacco, indigo, and hemp that were ready for export, but thousands of slaves were lost. Some rice continued to be exported to France and to the West Indies, but not in as large a volume as before the war, nor in large enough volume to make up for the reduction in the export of the other staples from the South. North Carolina and South Carolina were able to make a contribution to the food supply of the colonies when they increased their production of livestock and livestock products.

At no time were all of the colonies equally involved in warfare, nor was there a large standing army at the command of General George Washington. Transportation difficulties made it difficult or impossible to transport large numbers of men and large amounts of war materiel from one section of the colonies to another. Consequently, except for a nucleus of men and of supplies, battles were fought on somewhat of a local basis and food and supplies were obtained locally. The war opened with skirmishes in New

England in 1775. Many important battles were fought in the Middle Colonies by frontiersmen in those regions, and the war was brought to a close by the surrender of General Cornwallis in Yorktown, Virginia, in 1781. The war really was more involved than the foregoing account seems to indicate, but this is not a history of the military campaigns of the United States.

READJUSTMENTS

Many problems confronted the colonies upon the occasion of their gaining political freedom from England. They were not prepared to form a confederated government, and jealousies between the newly formed states made it difficult for them to arrive at policies that would apply to all of them alike. They differed in size of their populations and in their trade relations with other countries. Manufacturing and trade were more important than commercial agriculture in New England. Conditions were reversed in the South, and the thinking of the leaders in the Middle States was directed toward agriculture, manufacturing, and trade.

Public Land Policy

One objective of the Second Continental Congress was to draw up the framework of a federated government within which a central government could function. Claims to western lands by seven of the states had to be resolved before unanimity of action in Congress could be achieved.

One method of rewarding soldiers of the Continental Army was to give them claims to western lands to the west and north of the Ohio River. Many soldiers who did not want to exercise their claims to those lands sold them to speculators, who had already become interested in them. In order to lend support to their activities, speculators pressured members of the Continental Congress to pass legislation that would permit speculation; but it was not until some members of that Congress had been given land certificates themselves that they became interested in such legislation.

Congress was divided in its attitude towards the disposition of those lands. On the one hand, here was a possible source of revenue to the new and struggling central government, which at that time had been denied the right of taxation. On the other hand, an early settlement and development of the West would attract more people and would increase the productivity of the country and make it a richer and a stronger nation. The claims of Virginia conflicted with those of New York, Massachusetts, and Connecticut, and it was not until these states relinquished their claims that Maryland was willing to ratify the Articles of Confederation. North Carolina, South Carolina, and Georgia followed this precedent later and relinquished their claims to lands as far west as the Mississippi River. It was the ceding of these lands to the federal government that created the first public lands in the United States at the federal level. This accounts for the fact that there were

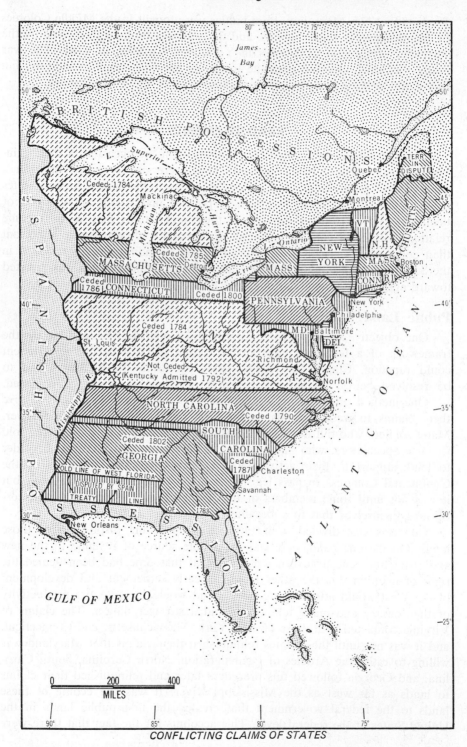

CONFLICTING CLAIMS OF STATES

no public lands in the original thirteen states, except those that had been owned by the Tories, the Crown, and the proprietors, and that which had been confiscated by the several states. In order to accomplish both objectives, legislation was passed to provide for an orderly settlement and political organization of the Northwest Territory.

Land Ordinance of 1785 and Northwest Ordinance of 1787

The Land Ordinance of 1785 provided for the survey of the land west of Pennsylvania into townships six miles square, which, in turn, were to be subdivided into 36 sections one mile square, which was the equivalent of 640 acres. One of these sections was to be set aside for the support of public education. After caring for the claims of the soldiers of the Continental Army, the remaining acreage was to be auctioned off at a price of not less than $1 per acre. It was thought that those terms were favorable to the farmer who wanted to settle upon a relatively small-sized farm, and they reflected the influence of New England upon that legislation. Since the proceeds from the sale of these public lands were not adequate to support the new government, Congress decided to encourage the sale of large tracts to land companies. The prospect of an early sale of large acreage to the Ohio Company spurred a hesitating Congress to the passage of the Northwest Ordinance of 1787, under the terms of which the territory north of the Ohio River and east of the Mississippi River was to be divided into at least three states, but not more than five.

Political Organization. While the settlement and economic development of western lands may have resembled the development of colonial empires of European nations in many respects, the Northwest Ordinance provided for an orderly progression from the status of territory to that of statehood on an equality with states that could boast of earlier settlement and organization. A temporary government was provided for the entire district by appointment by Congress of a governor, a secretary, and three judges. When any portion of that country had attained a population of 5,000 free male inhabitants, it was entitled to become organized as a territory with a governor and a legislative council of five members who would be appointed by Congress, an elected House of Representatives, and a nonvoting delegate to Congress. Eligibility to serve as a Representative was the ownership of at least 200 acres of land and residence in the district for a minimum of three years. Ownership of at least 50 acres of land and residence of two years entitled one to vote for a Representative. Upon reaching a population of 60,000 inhabitants, the territory would be eligible for admittance to the Union as a state "on equal footing with the original states, in all respects whatsoever." Among the guarantees that affected the economic development of that region were the obligations of private contracts; the encouragement given education; the exclusion of slavery or involuntary servitude, except in punishment of crimes; and protection of persons and property.

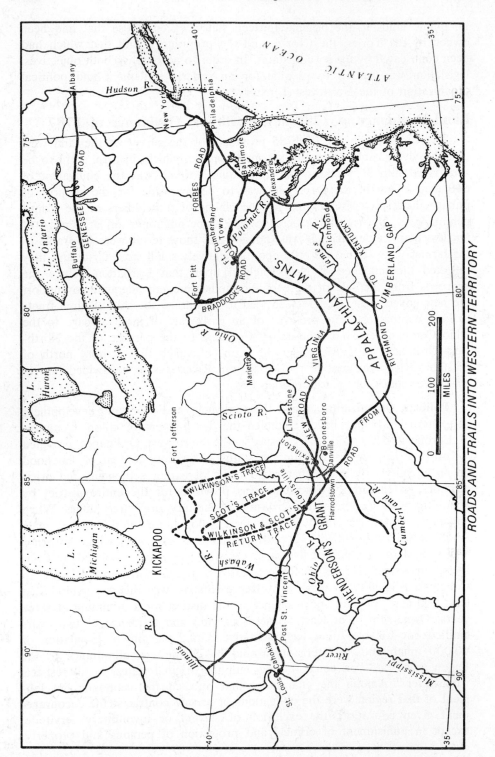

ROADS AND TRAILS INTO WESTERN TERRITORY

Impacts of the Land Ordinances. While the patterns laid down in the Ordinances of 1785 and 1787 have not been followed rigorously, the former did serve as a precedent that was followed in the surveying of much of the land west of the Mississippi River.

Road Construction. It was along section lines that states and counties first built dirt roads, and later improved them. Improvements were confined more to surfacing than to altering rights-of-way. Farmers naturally resisted efforts on the part of any organization to cut new highways across fertile fields, and for many, many years roads were of the farm-to-market type. The term *market* is used here to include railroad facilities and those for storing grain. Time was not of the essence, and the rate of travel was limited to the ability and endurance of horses and mules. Most roads were surfaced to accommodate one-way traffic; and the passing of wagons, carriages, and coaches often presented problems that broke the monotony of routine travel.

Balance of Power by Sections. The Northwest Ordinance of 1787 had provided that newly admitted states should have representation in government equal to that of the older, established states. This provision enabled the economy of the South to maintain its balance of power in the United States Senate with that of the free states until near mid-19th century. The same population ratio that determined representation in the House of Representatives for the original thirteen states applied to newly admitted ones. There could be no aristocracy of states founded upon the prestige of antiquity or upon economic resources and development, except as they might contribute to growth of population.

Land Ownership. Another influence that the Northwest Ordinance of 1787 had upon the economic development of the United States was in the matter of land ownership. Entail and primogeniture were abolished in the Old Northwest Territory, out of which were formed the states of Ohio, Indiana, Illinois, Michigan, and Wisconsin. This ordinance tended to assure a rather wide distribution of landholdings in those states, even allowing for the holdings of large land companies such as the Ohio Company's 1,780,000 acres and John Symmes' purchase of 250,000 acres between the Great and Little Miami Rivers. The Ohio Company founded Marietta, Ohio, in 1788; and shortly thereafter Symmes founded Cincinnati. In the 18th century, most, if not all, of the large land companies were formed for the purpose of buying large acreages in order to sell in smaller sized units at higher prices.

The Immediate Aftermath of War

The separation of the American colonies from England brought home to them in no uncertain terms what it had meant to be part of the British Empire, especially as concerned their trade relations. They had looked upon the Navigation Acts as repressive, as restrictive in limiting the scope and nature of their external trade. Much of what had formerly been ex-

---

ternal trade from the colonial point of view had been trade within the British Empire. It now became trade external to the British Empire. Whereas interpretations of many of the clauses and phrases of the Navigation Acts had been favorable to the colonies, they were now unfavorable to the states. American ships could no longer touch ports in the British West Indies, American seamen were no longer of English extraction for purposes of constituting three fourths of the crews of ships touching English shores, and much of the carrying trade that had been reserved for colonial vessels was now excluded from them. That was more serious than a mere decline in the statistics of commodity imports and commodity exports, as indicated in Table 4-1.

Table 4-1

**Value of Export-Import Trade with England
(Pounds Sterling)**

Year	Exports	Imports
1784	749,345	3,670,467
1785	893,594	2,308,023
1786	843,119	1,603,465
1787	893,637	2,009,111
1788	1,023,789	1,886,142
1789	1,050,198	2,525,298
1790	1,191,071	3,431,778
Totals	6,644,753	17,434,284
		6,644,753
Import Balance		10,789,531 (Unfavorable)

Source: Timothy Pitkin, *A Statistical View of the Commerce of the United States of America* (New York City: James Eastburn & Co., 1817), p. 30. Adapted.

The changed conditions meant a large increase in unemployment in America. It meant large numbers of idle ships and shipping facilities and of seamen. It meant a large decline in the volume of domestic trade with its complement of unemployed persons. It meant a decline in personal incomes and in wages; and had there been a method of calculating national income, it would have shown a large and sudden decline.

Postwar Depression

The commodities which had been on the enumerated list could now be sent to continental countries. Even though the wider market proved beneficial to the Americans, the inhabitants of Continental Europe enjoyed the same things from the former American colonies. They did not absorb the losses that resulted from the decline in sales of American exports to British markets. Commodity exports as well as commodity imports decreased in value to a large extent. That decline is usually discussed or described in terms of a business recession or depression, and it constituted an immediate postwar depression. Cyclical fluctuations, as we know them today, were not recognized as such in the 18th century, although the average American was aware of changes in prices, wages, and employment. In addition, the phenomenon known as an immediate postwar recession was not defined by the writers of the day.

The depression that came after 1783 was attributed to the break of the American states from the British Empire, and well it may have been. Nevertheless, the break followed a war, and probably would not have occurred in the absence of war, so the depression falls into the category of a postwar depression. One of the factors contributing to the depression was the unusually large volume of imports from England, the impact of which was to lower the prices of the imported products. Insofar as these products competed with the products of American industries that had been started during the war, their competition was ruinous to all of those persons who were connected with their original production and sale. This situation gave rise to pressure upon Congress for the tariff, which was being used as a source of revenue, to be made more highly protective. Among early American statesmen, Alexander Hamilton alone seemed not to have been impressed with the doctrine of free trade that was being promulgated by the noted economist Adam Smith. Hamilton argued strongly for tariff protection for infant American industries.

American export trade suffered more in volume than did the import trade, because of the loss of the market in the British West Indies. That loss was made up in part by an increase in exports to the French West Indies and by opening up an entirely new area of trade with China. Students of American history will remember the difficulties that were encountered by the representatives of the American government in their efforts to arrange trade treaties with European countries. The attitude of the representatives of foreign governments was logical: Why should we make treaties with this new government when it is going to have to trade with us anyway? That attitude proved to be correct. The freedom that had been won by the colonists was political rather than economic. England's trade with the United States became much more profitable after 1800 than it had ever been when the mercantile doctrine was enforced against the colonies. Many of the economic relationships that had been established during the Colonial Period continued to prevail for many years after the founding of the United States.

Two weaknesses of the American government under the Articles of Confederation gave rise to a demand that some other form of central government be instituted. Since those weaknesses were (1) lack of control over foreign commerce and (2) inability to take positive steps to collect revenue, it is natural that attention was focused upon those matters in the formulation of the Constitution.

ECONOMIC ASPECTS OF THE CONSTITUTION

When the Constitutional Convention was called to order in Philadelphia in 1787, its immediate objectives were to recommend such changes in the Articles of Confederation as would "render the constitution of the federal government adequate to the exigencies of the Union." The contributions of government under the Articles were two in number. First, jealousies between the several states made necessary a centralization of authority over such economic matters as commerce, internal and external; taxation, including import and export duties; the coinage system and the use of paper money. Second, and more positive in character, was the Northwest Ordinance under the terms of which the western lands were settled and organized into territories, later states.

Congress was given power to determine the monetary system and to regulate the value and use of foreign coins. This was of particular importance in the absence of any native ores of gold or silver. Foreign coins continued to have legal tender usage for many years. In fact, the last vestige of foreign legal tender coins was not removed until the mid-1850's.

The influence of the Southern States is seen in the prohibition against the use of direct taxes, except as levied in proportion to the population. The South wanted to protect itself against the imposition of taxes on land, which would fall heavily upon the plantation owner. Again, in barring the use of export duties, the southern planter and his representatives were assuring themselves of an export market for the products of the South not being restricted by the use of export tariffs. While the institution of slavery as such was not mentioned, provision was made that slaves could not be imported after 20 years from the date on which the Constitution was adopted. This proved to be 1808, and the inclusion of that clause reflected the thinking and general attitude of the South that, at the time of the drawing up of that document, the use of slave labor in southern agriculture was becoming unprofitable. Its principal use was in the cultivation of tobacco and rice, the planting of which was restricted to somewhat limited regions. The cost of cleaning cotton fibre from its seed was not conducive to making large profits in the growing of that product, and southern planters were far from unanimous in their attitudes towards the continuance of slavery.

In view of future developments, it may be well to remind the student that the Constitution made no mention of banks or of banking institutions or banking instruments. The Bank of North America had been founded by Robert Morris in 1781, and Massachusetts chartered the Bank of Massachusetts in 1784. Alexander Hamilton established the Bank of New York in the same year, but it was not until 1791 that New York granted it a charter. The successful conduct of these banks, all of which operated under the terms of state charters, may explain why the framers of the Constitution made no mention of the banking function. The only mention of the use of excise taxes was that they should be applied uniformly in all of the states. The government was also given the right and authority to establish a postal system and to build post roads. Encouragement was given to inventors and those who were mechanically minded by providing for patent rights for a limited number of years. Authors were given protection against plagiarism through the issuance of copyrights. The justification of these property rights was "to promote the progress of science and useful arts," rather than to create a monied aristocracy.

Little did those who were in favor of the Constitution realize the impact it would have upon the future development of the United States. It was drawn up in the light of the level of development at the time, and Article V set forth the conditions under which its terms could be amended to meet new situations and conditions as they might arise. Insofar as the amendments that have been made have arisen out of economic conditions, or insofar as they have had economic impacts, they will be discussed in connection with those conditions or those impacts.

QUESTIONS FOR REVIEW

1. (a) How do you account for the depressions of 1763 and 1783?
   (b) Explain the economic impacts of those depressions upon the colonial economy.

2. Why was the Sugar Act of 1764 objectionable to the colonists?

3. Of what economic importance was the Stamp Act of 1765?

4. Explain the attitude of the colonists towards the use of (1) excise taxes, (2) customs duties.

5. Explain the economic background of the war with England in 1776.

6. (a) Who were the Tories? (Give an economic interpretation.)
   (b) How did they fare when hostilities ceased? Explain the impacts of that treatment.

7. (a) What was the Northwest Ordinance of 1787?
   (b) What were the principal provisions of that Ordinance?

SUGGESTED READINGS

Beard, Charles A. "An Economic Interpretation of the Constitution," *Issues in American Economic History,* edited by Gerald D. Nash. Boston: D. C. Heath & Company, 1964.

Callender, Guy S. *Selections from the Economic History of the United States, 1765-1860.* New York City: Augustus M. Kelley, Publishers, 1965. Chapter 4.

Chamberlain, John. *The Enterprising Americans: A Business History of the United States.* New York City: Harper & Row, Publishers, 1963. Chapters 1-3.

Hacker, Louis M. *Major Documents in American Economic History.* Princeton, N. J.: D. Van Nostrand Co., Inc., 1961. Volume 1. Selection 1.

Jones, Peter d'A. *The Consumer Society: A History of American Capitalism.* Baltimore, Md.: Penguin Books, Inc., 1965. Chapter 2.

Lynd, Staughton. "Who Should Rule at Home?" *United States Economic History: Selected Readings,* edited by Harry N. Scheiber. New York City: Alfred A. Knopf, Inc., 1964.

McDonald, Forest. "Charles A. Beard's Pioneer Interpretation of the Making of the Constitution," *Issues in American Economic History,* edited by Gerald D. Nash. Boston: D. C. Heath & Company, 1964.

North, Douglass C. *The Economic Growth of the United States, 1790-1860.* Englewood Cliffs, N. J.: Prentice-Hall, Inc., 1961. Chapter 2.

——————————. *Growth and Welfare in the American Past: A New Economic History.* Englewood Cliffs, N. J.: Prentice-Hall, Inc., 1966. Chapters 3 and 4.

Ver Steeg, Clarence L. "The American Revolution Considered As an Economic Movement," *American Economic History: Essays in Interpretation,* edited by Stanley Coben and Forest G. Hill. Philadelphia: J. B. Lippincott Co., 1966.

Chapter 5

ESTABLISHING A NEW NATION

Following the adoption of the Constitution, Congress was confronted with the problem of implementing by statutory enactment the clauses that delegated to it the power to regulate or to control economic institutions and relationships. It was fortunate in having a man of the caliber of Alexander Hamilton to present to it some of the possible solutions to the problems in which he was particularly interested and in which he had some aptitude, even though Congress did not always adopt his programs.

Hamilton's Memorials to Congress

Hamilton favored the development of a national economy in which manufactures would be balanced with agriculture. There was no doubt in his mind that manufacturing was just as productive a pursuit as was agriculture, if not more so. He also knew that newly organized manufactures in this country could not compete on a cost basis with older established firms in Europe. Accordingly, he made his famous *Report on Manufactures* to Congress in December, 1791, in which he based his argument for protective tariffs upon the *infant industry* argument. *Infant industries* were those for which existed the necessary potentials for development, but in which certain cost disadvantages delayed their realization. A protective tariff had for its purpose overcoming some or all of those cost disadvantages in competition with similar products made in foreign countries. Early Congresses failed to give wholehearted support to the policy of protection.

Hamilton was also largely responsible for legislation that established a banking system and uniform money and currency. Those institutions were made necessary by the growth and westward expansion of population. Foreign and domestic trade increased rapidly after the American people had recovered from the shock of being outside the veil of the Navigation Acts.

Population Growth and Distribution

A population of approximately four million persons in 1790 was scattered throughout the Atlantic Coastal States and the District of Columbia.

Most of it was within 100 miles of the coast. Almost 50 percent of the people lived in the South, and the remainder was rather equally distributed throughout the Northern and Middle States. The westward movement of people from New England to the Middle States continued. In 1810 the Bureau of the Census reported a population of 7,239,881, and by 1815 it estimated than an additional million persons were living in the United States. These increases did not represent a corresponding increase in population density as they were spread over five additional states. Vermont, Tennessee, Kentucky, and Ohio had been admitted to the Union by 1810; and Louisiana became a state in 1812.

Leadership in population numbers in the South was not accompanied by a corresponding development of urban communities. Of the six cities of 8,000 or more population, Charleston, South Carolina, with 16,000 inhabitants, was the only one south of Baltimore which had 13,000. The other four such cities were Philadelphia (42,000), New York (33,000), Boston (18,000), and Salem (8,000). Albany was a frontier town; Pittsburgh was a pioneer settlement; and Lexington, Kentucky was still a battlefield on which the white man was struggling with the Indian for the right to live on lands west of the Appalachian Mountains—lands that had fertile soil and were rich and abundant in fish and wild game. The growth of coastal cities was due largely to an increase in the volume of external trade and to the continuation of coastwise trade which remained the principal means of transport between the New England States, the Middle States, and those of the South. The economic impacts of this coastal growth were felt in (1) increased specialization and division of labor of urban populations; (2) increased trade relations with their hinterlands; (3) demands for new and better roads; (4) greater interdependence between coastal towns and their hinterlands, which included inland urban communities.

BANKING

While there was no priority established in the Constitution concerning the order in which its provisions should be implemented by acts of Congress, it was to be expected that they would be acted upon as the needs for them presented themselves to the American people, or as Congress felt itself prepared to cope with the issues. One of the deficiencies of the colonial economy had been a lack of hand-to-hand currency. Paper money in the form of bank notes had a limited circulation and did not circulate at par in markets that were somewhat remote from the banks of issue. Between 1780 and 1790, the Bank of North America, the Bank of New York, and the Massachusetts Bank had been chartered with the privilege of issuing circulating notes. Those banks were granting commercial loans, the proceeds of which were taken in the form of circulating notes. Transportation and communication systems had not been developed to the point where they could facilitate establishing credit at places that were remote from the homes of debtors. Advantages in the use of demand deposits were known, and personal checks were used in local transactions.

State and Private Banking

Banking as a business presented an excellent opportunity for making profits. The number of state and private banks in 1811 numbered twenty-nine. Some banks permitted subscribers of capital stock to borrow from their banks and to receive circulating notes, which then were used to complete payments for their shares of stock. Since newly organized banks received their initial specie reserves from payments on shares of *capital stock,* that was not good banking, but neither were those banks sound. There was little specie available for the purpose of redeeming notes, and it is not surprising that bank notes did not circulate at *par,* or at *face value.* Circulating notes very similar in appearance to bank notes were issued by concerns that were not much more than printing companies. Those firms sent their representatives to distant places for the purpose of placing their notes in circulation, so they would not and could not be presented readily for redemption.

Parity of circulation was a *sine qua non* for the development of trade and commerce of which Hamilton was a strong advocate. Economic interdependence of persons and of regions was accompanied by an increase in the exchange of goods and services, and sound currency was essential to the accomplishment of such an economy.

The First Bank of the United States

Alexander Hamilton had been impressed with the organization and functioning of the Bank of North America and with the financial aid it had rendered the confederated government under the leadership of Robert Morris. The organization and functioning of the First Bank of the United States were the results of the influence of Hamilton, who was in favor of a strong central bank that would exercise control over private and state banks merely by the way it operated rather than by more direct means. The 20-year limit to the charter was a compromise with those who were not in favor of the bank. It was chartered in 1791 with a capital of $10 million, one fifth of which was owned by the Federal Treasury. Subscription to the other four fifths was thrown open to the public, and Robert Morris was among the largest individual stockholders. Foreign subscriptions were accepted, but it was clearly spelled out that foreign stockholders could not vote their shares of stock at the annual meetings.

The principal functions of the bank were (1) to serve as a fiscal agent of the government and (2) to regulate the note currency in circulation. As fiscal agent of the government, the bank made loans at times when other channels for receiving public monies were inadequate; it served as a depository for the federal government; it paid interest on the government debt; it accepted warrants drawn on it in payment of wages, salaries, and other governmental costs; and it transferred money from one part of the country to another at no cost to the government. In regulating the bank note currency, it was given no direct method by which this should be done. The procedure followed was to send the notes of state and private banks, which it had received in the process of transacting its business, to these banks for redemption, thus forcing them to keep adequate reserves for that purpose or admit failure. Such an action aroused the enmity of state and private bankers against the First Bank and ensured their opposition to a renewal of the bank's charter when that question came before Congress.

Branch Banking. The bank was permitted by its charter to establish branches as the need for them appeared. In the course of the 20 years of its operation eight branches were established, each of which performed locally the functions of the parent institution. The central office was located in Philadelphia and branches were found in Boston, New York, Baltimore, Washington, Norfolk, Charleston, New Orleans, and Savannah. The locations of these branches were important in that they indicated the need for banking services by commercial, industrial, and agricultural interests throughout the country. In terms of the functioning of the bank, these branches also tended to measure the need for currency to finance business transactions. Again, insofar as they acted as fiscal agent of the government, they point to the centers of import activity and to the collection of import duties which was the principal source of revenue to the federal government during that period. It was not until later that the westward movement had progressed across the Appalachian Mountains to the degree that central banking facilities were required in that region.

The bank engaged in commercial banking, and it was in that capacity that it aroused the opposition of private and state bankers. The bank paid an average of 8 percent per annum to its stockholders, much of which was derived from commercial banking practices. The members of the banking fraternity felt that the business that gave rise to such lucrative dividends should have gone to them.

Opposition to the Bank. Opposition to the bank from the time of Hamilton's first advocacy of a strong central bank to the day it closed its doors in 1811 came from different sources, several of which have already been indicated. Thomas Jefferson, James Madison, and many other prominent men of that day and age were opposed to it in principle; and they utilized the wording of the Constitution in support of that principle. Centralization and unconstitutionality were the focal points of their attack, and they had the support of those persons who felt the federal government should have limited powers. There were others who objected to the ownership of stock in the bank by Englishmen and investors in other European countries, even though such stockholders could not vote their stock unless they resided in the United States. When dividends of 8 percent per annum were paid on a par value share of $400, it meant an export, or its equivalent, of $32 per share at a time when our gold holdings were relatively low and to the very people with whom we were not on friendly terms. Had American capitalists subscribed to all of the stock in the bank, this objection could not have arisen.

Return to State and Private Banking

Upon the expiration of the charter of the bank, there was no central agency that had a stabilizing influence on banking and on the issuance of bank notes. State and private banking organizations increased rapidly, and circulating notes again depreciated. *Printing press money* that was issued in frontier communities appeared in large volume. Investigation usually revealed that the presses were located in dense woods accessible mainly to wildcats— hence the term *wildcat banking*.

The second war with England broke out in 1812, and the United States government had no central bank to which it could turn for aid in implementing its financial program. Speculation in land did not help the situation, neither did price inflation which accompanied the conduct of the war. The higher the price level the more bank credit was needed and issued; and, conversely, the more bank notes there were in circulation the higher prices rose. That vicious cycle went on uncontrolled, since there was no central bank functioning.

MONETARY SYSTEM

In recommending a monetary system that would fill the needs of the United States, acceptability and convenience seemed to be uppermost in the mind of Alexander Hamilton, whose recommendations were followed in large part by the Congress. He was familiar with the British system, also with the convenience of the decimal system, and was in favor of the latter.

Bimetallism

Bimetallism in which gold and silver were standard money materials had a theoretical advantage over the use of silver alone. Gold monometallism had not been adopted by any of the western European countries at the time. In the use of gold and silver, Hamilton knew that if the mint, or legal, ratio between the two metals was approximately equal to the market ratio, there would be no particular flight of either metal to or from the mint and the market; and the value of the dollar would be relatively stable, at least as far as the value of the basic metals was concerned. That fact or condition would also tend to keep the volume of coins in circulation in line with the need for them, as measured by the volume of exchanges to be transacted. Gold deposits had not been discovered in Africa, the United States, or Australia; and silver as a metal was much more plentiful. It was that kind of situation that gave rise to a market value ratio of something like 15 to 1, give or take a few points, during the latter part of the 18th century. At the time Hamilton made his recommendation regarding the adoption of bimetallism, the market ratio between silver and gold in Paris was 15½ to 1; in England it was 15 to 1. This meant that in the Paris market, 15½ units of silver by weight exchanged for 1 unit by weight of gold; and in the London market only 15 units of silver by weight were the value equivalent of 1 unit of gold by weight. Obviously, gold was worth more in terms of silver in the Paris market than it was in London. Conversely, silver was worth less in the Paris market than it was in London. Since Hamilton thought that our trade relations with England would be facilitated by adopting a legal ratio that was similar to the one in that market, he recommended a mint ratio of 15 to 1 which was incorporated by Congress into the Coinage Act of 1792 that established a bimetallic monetary system in the United States.

Silver Overvalued

The fact that trade with England was larger in dollar volume than it was with France had little or no effect in preventing a flow of silver to the United States mint. In accordance with the principle that when two monetary metals enjoy free coinage and are legal tender, the overvalued metal tends to displace the undervalued metal in circulation, there was much more silver money in circulation between 1792 and 1834 than there was gold money. Records reveal, however, that some gold bullion was taken to the mint, and there was coinage of some gold money. History does not explain the presence of the undervalued metal in circulation; but, undoubtedly, it was due to the imperfections of the market. Hamilton wanted the silver dollar to resemble the Spanish coin of that denomination, so the weight of 371.25 grains of pure silver was established, which meant that 24.75 grains of pure gold constituted a dollar. In spite of several changes in the mint ratio, and in the position silver has occupied in our monetary system, the silver dollar has always contained 371.25 grains of pure silver. Since standard silver money metal was .89243 fine, the silver dollar that circulated contained 416 grains of standard silver.

Traffic in Silver Dollars

Even though silver was the overvalued metal at the United States mint, a peculiar situation existed which caused the American dollar to be sent to the West Indies. The Spanish dollar contained approximately ten grains more silver than the American dollar, and either dollar was accepted at face value in both countries. In fact, the shiny American dollar was preferred in the West Indies to the Spanish coin. That afforded an opportunity for brokers and dealers to traffic in silver dollars by exchanging $100 in American silver, or 37,125 grains, for 100 Spanish dollars that contained 38,250 grains, thus gaining $3 by weight on the trade. This was legal in every respect; but Thomas Jefferson, who was President of the United States in 1806, stopped the coinage of the American dollar on the grounds that circumstances permitted only a few dealers to take advantage of that situation and enrich themselves. Jefferson was an agrarian at heart, and he wanted to protect the farmer from a situation that could not benefit him. Silver dollars were not coined again until after 1835. Stopping the coinage of the silver dollar by Presidential decree did not put an end to the exchange of American silver for the Spanish dollar, since trade was continued by using two 50-cent pieces instead of one dollar. That accounts for the prevalence of Spanish money in circulation in the United States for many years.

PUBLIC DEBT

One of the problems that beset the first Congress of the United States was how to settle the public debt, which consisted of $11,700,000 foreign debt and, according to Hamilton's estimate, something over $42,000,000 of domestic debt. Both of these figures include arrears on both principal and interest payments, with the former estimated at one third of the total indebtedness. With a total population of approximately four million persons in 1790 and total indebtedness of $54 million, the per capita federal debt amounted to $13.50. Most persons agreed that the foreign debt should have been funded and paid in full, but there were differences of opinion as to the ultimate disposition of the domestic or internal debt. Many of the evidences of indebtedness had been sold by their original owners at a discount, and to have paid them in full would have penalized those who had been patriotic enough to lend their funds to a shaky government but who for some reason had sold their bonds. Even though payment of face value would have rewarded speculation in government securities, which Hamilton and others did not want to encourage, they felt that any other settlement would reflect upon the credit of the United States. In due time the securities were paid in full to the holders.

State Debts

Another problem connected with the funding of the federal debt concerned the debts of the original thirteen states, most of which were incurred to finance the Revolutionary War with England. Since those debts were created to help finance the war, the successful outcome of which was necessary to the establishment of the federal government, Hamilton led a movement for the Treasury Department to assume that portion of the state debts that was incurred for the common cause. The fundamental basis for popular differences in attitude towards this question was found in the manner in which the several colonies had financed their war costs.

Attitudes Toward Debt Assumption

In general, debtors, farmers, and speculators in public lands and in government bonds favored the states issuing paper money in order to lighten the financial burden of retiring the debt, both public and private. On the other hand, merchants and creditors and those who had purchased government bonds in the expectation that they would be redeemed at face value opposed the issuance of paper money and favored the use of taxes to raise revenue for that purpose. The Southern States were opposed to the use of taxes that were based on population because of the large number of slaves therein, combined with a distrust on their part in the counting and weighting of slaves in proportion to their white populations. It was proposed that in assessing the states for funds that were to be used in retiring the public debt, slaves would be weighted at three fifths of their numbers in calculating the population base upon which taxes would be levied.

The unequal rate at which land values were assessed for tax purposes gave rise to inequities in the use of land taxes. Land in Virginia was assessed at one third more than was land in Pennsylvania, and it was thought that land in Pennsylvania was worth one third more than land in Virginia. Virginia had taxed landowners and had retired a large portion of its public debt. To have assessed land again at the federal level would have been inequitable to Virginia landowners, unless some kind of uniform assessment could have been made. It is striking to see how similar some of the fiscal problems of the 20th century are to those of the 18th century.

The Northern Colonies had financed the war by borrowing; most of the Southern and Middle Colonies had levied and collected taxes with which they had paid parts of their financial obligations, and seven of the colonies had issued paper money. The states of Rhode Island and Connecticut had not met any of their obligations of that sort, and Delaware and Pennsylvania had paid approximately two thirds or more of theirs. The Representatives of the states that had paid portions of their indebtedness felt that for the federal government to assume the debts of the states would mean that their people would be taxed a second time to pay the obligations. In order to obtain the votes of Maryland and Virginia, Hamilton made an agreement with Thomas Jefferson that, if the latter would use his influence to swing the votes of these two states in favor of the plan, Hamilton would use his influence in moving the capital city of the United States from Philadelphia to the banks of the Potomac River, which accounts for the selection and location of the District of Columbia. The passage of the Assumption Act of 1790 ensured both the building of Washington and the effective federal assumption of state debts.

SOURCES OF REVENUE

The experiences of the Second Continental Congress emphasized the need for sources of federal revenues that were more definitive than were available during the days of the Confederation. The terms of the Constitution provided several sources of revenue that required implementation by the Congress before a flow of funds was forthcoming. The sale of public lands, the levying of customs duties, and the imposition of excise taxes were those sources. Since the use of each one of those devices was incorporated into some program of development or of federal policy, the following presentation will be as much concerned with policy as with revenues received. The reader must remember that, if all of these sources proved to be inadequate in their yield of revenues, resort was had to borrowing, either from banks or through the issuance and sale of government stock. Lest there be confusion in terminology, government stock did not represent ownership rights to governmental income, nor did its ownership convey any rights of suffrage. It was nothing but a long-term bond, and evidence of government debt upon which interest had to be paid in order to maintain public credit standing. There were many occasions throughout the period under review when the Treasury Department borrowed funds for short periods of time from the Bank of the United States in anticipation of receipts from one or more of the sources of permanent revenue. While it was not absolutely necessary that the government have a fiscal agent to handle its finances, the use of a banking organization for that purpose was much less disturbing to the general business community than having the Treasury Department perform all of the functions.

Tariff of 1789

Since the Constitution forbade the use of tariff duties on commodity exports and reserved the use of import duties to the federal government, and since American people, in general, accepted the principle of external taxation, one of the first pieces of financial legislation was the passing of a tariff act. Alexander Hamilton used the infant industry argument in his campaign in support of the principle of protection. The United States had potentials of a labor supply and ample natural resources that were awaiting their utilization in industry. Capital of native origin and borrowed from other countries, plus entrepreneurial skills, were awaiting propitious times to be invested. American industry operated at a comparative cost disadvantage in competition with European industries largely because it was in its experimental and developmental stages. Given time those cost disadvantages would be overcome and infant industries then would be able to compete with foreign enterprise on a laissez faire competitive basis. Hamilton did not visualize that adult male labor would be available for or interested in factory work. He was influenced in his thinking by his knowledge of the labor segment in English industry. There women and children constituted the largest portion of industrial labor, and their incomes augmented family incomes. According to its preamble, Congress had in mind two objectives: namely, providing revenue for the federal government and protecting home industries. It is difficult to understand how the leaders of the period had the naiveté to think that the same piece of legislation could accomplish two such divergent objectives. Unless rates were applied differently to different kinds of goods, the result must have been either to afford protection to American industries or to yield revenue. To the extent that the government received revenue, protection was not provided. The degree of protection afforded by the levy of any tariff is difficult to measure because its effectiveness appears in a negative fashion—the absence of imports—or in an increase in prices of goods imported. The average level of duties in 1789 was approximately 8½ percent, which was probably insufficient to overcome any cost disadvantages American industries may have experienced at the time. It is likewise true that manufacturing in America was on the increase, but there were many factors that were external to the tariff that had an important bearing on that development, and it would be rather presumptuous to give sole credit to the tariff for it. Only 5 percent was levied on those goods for which individual rates were not provided and which were not admitted free of any duty.

From 1791 to 1811, the tariff was the largest single source of federal revenue, with an annual average of a little over $9 million. During the first half of that same period, internal revenue receipts accounted for an annual average of under $700,000 and the sale of public lands considerably less. However, during the latter half of that period, internal revenue, other than from the sale of public lands, became relatively insignificant, and the receipts from the latter amounted to a little over $700,000.

Table 5-1

Sources of Federal Revenue—1791-1815

Customs receipts	$229	million
Internal revenue	13	"
Sale of public lands	10	"
Direct taxes	6	"

Source: First through Nineteenth Congress, "Finance," *American State Papers* (Washington, D.C.: Gales and Seaton, 1789-1827) Vol. II, p. 919.

Less important sources of revenue during that period were loans, interest on the stock of the United States Bank, and the sale of postage stamps.

Internal Revenue

After the assumption of the state debts in 1790, it was apparent that the federal government would need additional revenue in order to service the debt. Accordingly, Alexander Hamilton recommended to Congress the use of excise taxes, the same kind of taxes to which the colonists had objected under British rule, and which they paid reluctantly during the period of the Confederation. One of the first such taxes imposed by Congress was upon whiskey, with the thought that it was in such general consumption that it would produce much needed revenues. Without going into detail on the numerous sources of objections to that tax, among which was the cost of setting up offices and personnel for purposes of enforcement and collection, there was an economic basis for the resistance to it on the part of many of the farmers who lived in southwest Pennsylvania, northwest Virginia (now West Virginia) and southeast Ohio. One of the better money crops produced by these people was corn, which was difficult to market in eastern communities because of the high cost of transporting it overland across the Appalachian Mountains in relation to its market value. Converting corn into whiskey added so much to its value that it could stand the cost of transportation to eastern markets and still return handsome profits to its producers. In order to quell a disturbance near Waynesburg, Pennsylvania, caused by the resistance to the efforts of federal officers to collect the tax, President Washington was forced to send federal troops to enforce the law. That was the first time federal troops were sent into a state in order to enforce a federal statute. Even though President Washington disliked the idea of sending troops to enforce compliance with the law, he felt that it was a necessary step in gaining respect for federal authority. Not long after that event the tax was repealed.

Other excises that were used for a few years were levies on carriages, on the manufacture of snuff, on the refining of sugar, and one on auction sales. Taken from the English law, but wholeheartedly supported by the farmers and others who had agricultural interests at heart, was the idea that wagons and carriages that were used directly or indirectly in carrying on agricultural pursuits were not to be taxed. The idea of exempting from taxation articles or commodities used in agriculture has been carried down through the years and has its latest application in exempting gasoline and fuel oil from sale taxes, provided they are used by farmers in the conduct of their business. This is a form of subsidy to agriculture that is as old as the United States, but one that is frequently overlooked (1) in measuring the farmer's contribution to the support of government and (2) in discussions that attempt to provide an answer to the question, "How much government aid is being given to the farmer?"

In spite of the leadership of Albert Gallatin, who had become Secretary of the Treasury in 1801 and who was concerned with the need for revenue to the extent that he tolerated the principle of excise taxes, both excise and direct taxes were abolished by Congress in 1802, not to be revived until 1861, except during the financial exigency created by the second war with England in 1812.

Sale of Public Lands

While the sale of public lands afforded some revenue during the period under discussion, revenue was not the main goal in such sales. Many classes of people, including those who were charged with determining public policy, were more concerned with the terms and conditions of the sale of land than they were with the revenue derived. Everybody except the speculators seemed to be in agreement that the land should be sold to bona fide settlers on the frontier, but they differed on other aspects of the program. The southern planter, who already was anticipating the day he would be forced to move west or accept a lower output on his land, was in favor of selling land in large acreages so as to accommodate the plantation type of farming. The northern and New England people, on the other hand, were accustomed to small family-size farms, and favored the policy of selling western lands in small amounts. Two dollars per acre was not a high price, especially in view of the value increment that would ensue in the near future; but it was more than many frontiersmen could afford to pay, even when considering the easy terms of payment, which in 1800 were one fourth down and the balance in four years. The purchase of 160 acres meant a down payment of $80 in cash; the immediate cost of 320 acres was a down payment of $160, which was more money than many of the frontiersmen handled in several years. The results of that policy were that (1) the government did not receive a dependable amount of revenue during any one fiscal year and (2) much of the land that was sold found its way into the hands of speculators. Speculators in western lands came to the rescue of would-be purchasers who could not complete their payments, and they also acquired land using fictitious names. In this manner they acquired thousands or millions of acres, instead of the few hundred, more or less, intended for them. There is also evidence that the Federal Land Agents themselves were not beyond overlooking some of the terms of sale if given the proper inducements. During that period, and later, the price of land and terms of sale were altered more in order to give encouragement to settling upon new lands than to raise revenue.

WESTERN EXPANSION

The westward movement that took place after 1789 was merely a continuation of the one that had its origin in the Colonial Period. While frontiersmen had penetrated the lands west of the Appalachian Mountains by the time of the Revolution, the pace of settlement and of the appropriation of land as far west as the Mississippi River and beyond was accelerated thereafter. The Ohio, Mississippi, and Missouri Rivers and their tributaries afforded easy means of transporting products of extractive industries downstream. Wheat, livestock, lumber, hides, pelts and skins constituted the cargoes of river barges bound for New Orleans.

The Louisiana Purchase

The acquisition of the Louisiana Territory from France in 1803 at a cost of $15,000,000, or something like three cents an acre, added more acreage to the expanse of the United States than lay east of the Mississippi River. In general, that extended the limits of the United States west and northwest from Louisiana to the Rocky Mountains and embraced the region that has come to be known as the Western Plains States, the granary of the United States. The talks that led to that acquisition had for their purpose opening up the Mississippi River to trade by Americans without paying tribute to another nation. They were held at a time when France was in dire need of money to finance its war with England and when it was in danger of losing the territory to England if France still owned it at the termination of an unsuccessful struggle. Even though President Jefferson was a strict interpreter of the Constitution, he supported James Monroe and Robert Livingston in their negotiations with France. At the time, Jefferson was more interested in depriving France of control over that territory than he was in adding to the extent and to the wealth of the United States. He lost no time in having Captain Meriwether Lewis and Lieutenant William Clark explore the territory. They not only went to the headwaters of the Missouri River but crossed over the mountains and went down the Columbia River to the Pacific Ocean. It was at the mouth of that river that Astoria was founded in 1810.

Exploitation of the Louisiana Territory

The opening of that vast area of virgin territory lent itself to exploitation by hunters and trappers, and that was the locale of the American Fur Company under the leadership of John Jacob Astor. When competition was taking its toll of profits out of the fur business, Astor sold his interest to the Western Fur Company which remained in competition with the Hudson Bay Company for another quarter century. Astor helped establish a pattern of capitalistic behavior that is still being followed by leaders with business acumen: namely, to sell a company or a business while it still shows profits on its books, in the belief that in the somewhat indefinite future not far away not only will profits decline but losses will ensue. Students of finance will recognize this as the process of *capitalizing profits*.

Transportation in the Louisiana Territory was by inland waterway, rivers, or via Indian trails. It was hazardous, to say the least, and only the hardy ventured far from the banks of the Mississippi River, the Missouri River, and their tributaries. While St. Louis had been founded during the Colonial Period, in 1764, it was furs brought from the Northwest Central States that contributed to its rapid development, long before railroads penetrated that territory. The bison was much sought after by the white man, and it was his greed for the products of that animal that brought him into conflict with the Indians. The Indians had learned to live with the bison, and they were loath to see its wanton destruction.

AGRICULTURE

Work was the order of the day; leisure time was almost unknown, and the idea of commercial entertainment had not crept into men's minds. Agriculture was the livelihood of nine out of ten families; land was cheap and could be purchased on credit. Even in the Northern States, where manufacturing industries had made their appearance, the value of lands that were devoted to agricultural pursuits was greater than the value of lands that supported manufacturing or were used in commerce. Except for plantation holdings in the South, farms were small and were cultivated largely by members of families. Farm labor was still scarce. Horses, cattle, and swine were found on almost all farms in all of the states; and sheep were most numerous in the New England and Middle Atlantic States.

New England and Middle Atlantic States

No pronounced changes had occurred in the pattern of agriculture in the North and West. To the extent that urban communities were being established and were growing in population, they provided markets for the products of the farm, particularly dairy products, poultry, eggs, and vegetables. That meant that farmers handled a little more money than formerly and could purchase in those same urban communities commodities that had been imported from Europe and some that were products of American manufacturers. Some of the goods they took off the market had formerly been products of domestic industries, while others represented a rise in the level of their consumption.

Wheat as a frontier product was grown in all of the states, and it was a product for export in Maryland, Pennsylvania, and New York. Richmond vied with Baltimore for the market in the West Indies. Hemp, flax, and wool were raw materials for manufacturing industries. Tobacco was widely grown from the southern border of Pennsylvania southward.

The South

Little progress had been made in cultivating new crops. Rice was still the principal crop and an export commodity of Georgia, North and South Carolina. These states also exported large amounts of indigo. Louisiana, Mississippi, Arkansas, Alabama, and Missouri were beginning to feel the impact of the westward movement of southern agriculture as more and more people migrated in an effort to find more fertile land on which to plant cotton, rice, and sugar.

During the latter part of the Colonial Period, the cost of cleaning cotton by hand was almost prohibitive. It has been estimated that one slave could clean about one pound of short staple cotton per day, or ten pounds of long staple cotton in the same length of time. In 1793, Eli Whitney invented the cotton gin which enabled one slave to clean about 300 pounds of cotton per day. Undoubtedly, there were many variations in the daily output of cotton, but the impact of the development of the cotton gin was that it reduced the cost of cleaning cotton to such an extent that it gave renewed life and energy to cotton's growth in the South.

Because of the apparent inefficiency of slave labor, a law had been passed by Congress, under the guidance of Representatives from Southern States, prohibiting the importation of slaves into the United States after 1808. It seemed that slave labor was becoming so unprofitable that the very people who stood to profit most by its continuance took steps to abolish it voluntarily. However, the results of the use of the cotton gin were so startling that cotton came to be the number one crop in the South and the slave system of labor received new support. Not only did the production of cotton make use of slave labor, but after about 1795, the planting of sugar-cane in Louisiana was stimulated by the discoveries of Etienne de Boré. By the introduction of new species of sugarcane, together with the development of a new process for refining it, he gave to the South another important crop, the cultivation of which required slave labor. It also increased the capital requirement of the planter because each sugar plantation had to have its own sugar mill, while cotton could be hauled long distances to a central cotton gin. One of the markets for sugar was the western settlements reached by steaming up the Mississippi, Ohio, and Missouri Rivers.

INDUSTRIAL DEVELOPMENT

The 18th century in England was a time of invention and mechanization of industry. The adaptation of water and of steam power to operate machinery may well have been more important than the inventions them-selves because it was the use of power other than hand or animal that made industrialization a reality. Wool and cotton textiles were made first in the home, and spinning and weaving had become important home industries. It was the application of waterpower to textile machinery that doomed the domestic system and made possible the factorization of textiles, boots and shoes, hats, the fabrication of iron, and many other industries.

England was engaged in a highly competitive struggle with France in the development of manufacturing industries. In order to keep new inven-tions and mechanical developments from falling into the hands of the French, British policy forbade the exportation of industrial equipment and the emigration of artisans who were familiar with either the construction of or the use of such equipment. In spite of many safeguards against such occurrences, one Samuel Slater found his way to Rhode Island where Moses Brown, a merchant, financed the erection of the first textile mill in Paw-tucket in 1790. Slater made blueprints of the Arkwright frame from memory and introduced several improvements in the spinning of cotton. Power for that mill, which was generated by a waterwheel, marks the beginning of the factory system applied to textiles; although the idea did not really take hold for another 30 years or more. In some districts, two thirds or more of the clothing worn in America was made in the home. The course of develop-ment of the textile industry was similar to that in Europe, in that woolen manufactures continued to be the products of the putting out organization of industry after cotton textiles had become factory made. Alexander Hamil-ton's *Report on Manufactures* in 1791 listed 17 distinct manufacturing industries, all of which depended upon the products of extractive industries for their raw materials.

Sources of Labor and Capital

The demand for industrial labor was met in part by natural increase, in part by the immigration of workers from England and continental countries, and in part by the exercise of latent skills of persons already resident in America. Female labor had always been more effective in textile mills than had male labor, and the wives and daughters of newly arrived immigrants augmented the numbers of women in immigrant families of years gone by in the labor force.

The priority of trading capital over industrial capital has already been established. Moses Brown was a successful merchant who visualized investment opportunities in industry. He invested in textile mills capital sums that had accrued from trading activities. To the extent that Brown's investment was just one instance of such a behavior pattern, the shortage of capital in America was being overcome in part by savings that were derived from American business.

Standardization of Parts

Eli Whitney has become well known for his invention of the cotton gin without which extensive cotton culture in the South would not have become established. He and Simeon North were the first persons to apply the principles of standardization and interchangeability of parts in American industry. Whitney's first test application of that principle was in fulfillment of a contract with the federal government in the manufacture of firearms. Simeon North, likewise, applied that principle in the manufacture and assembly of Colt revolvers. Even in the making of wooden, and later brass, clocks, manufacturers, such as Chauncey Jerome and Eli Tenny, introduced standardization and interchangeability of parts. Standardization and interchangeable parts required accurate tooling of machines, and thus was born the machine tooling industry which was located in the New England States near the mills and factories that utilized standardized parts.

TRADE

Specialization and division of labor continued to characterize the development of the American economy after 1789. Not for long, if ever, were pioneers of western lands economically self-sufficient above the subsistence level. Trade lines were established with eastern markets to which flowed the products of western farms and forests, and from which manufactured goods were obtained. Most of the latter had been imported from abroad to supplement the products of American manufacturing establishments. The latter did not have the capacity to meet the demands of the market. As some persons earned their initial incomes, and others had larger ones, specialization and division of labor created new interdependencies. As new families were formed and children born, an increased volume and variety of consumers' goods were incorporated into their scales of living. The latter were not uniform between or among urban and rural families, but they all increased in their own peculiar manner.

External Trade

Just as foreign trade relations with the mother country may have been the most outstanding characteristic of the American colonial economy, so did trade relations with foreign countries in general continue to be important throughout the entire period under observation. Here was a new nation still in its infancy in terms of economic development that had to "find its place in the sun," first, by dealing with England and France, which had the strongest national economies at the time, on a supplementary basis, and later, by competing with them. The degree of prosperity as measured by employment, wages, investment in capital, prices, and profits depended more upon external trade relations than upon the development of a domestic economy. In fact, it was the tempo of external trade relations that governed the level of internal trade. Persons living then should have realized the relationship between our economy and those of foreign nations, and how dependent they were upon these nations for the degree of activity with which the American economy functioned. Immediately following 1783, there was a rapid decline in the export-import trade that was conducted by American merchant vessels. The United States was then beyond the jurisdiction of the British Navigation Acts, and direct trade with England and its possessions became difficult or impossible.

Trade with China. Not to be outdone by that turn of events, American merchants sought trade relations with China. John Jacob Astor developed Astoria at the mouth of the Columbia River, in Oregon, as a port of embarkation for ships that sailed to China. Spices, Chinese yellowwood, silks, nankeens, and tea were found in the holds of his ships that docked at Astoria. Stephen Girard outfitted a fleet of ships that sailed to China from Philadelphia and to San Domingo from New Orleans. Tea, cotton, silk, nankeen, coffee, and spices were among the products in which he traded. Both Astor and Girard represented the merchant-capitalist class of entrepreneurs. They also were among the first to become millionaires in America. In both cases, after their fortunes had been made in trading, they were invested in financial institutions and in real estate. During the 1790's, crop failure in Europe brought prosperity to American farmers, as did their preoccupation with war. Had anybody been able to measure the national income for the years prior to about 1805, he, undoubtedly, would have recorded a large increase. It was during this period that many personal fortunes were created or enlarged. Mere mention of the names of Stephen Girard and John Jacob Astor should lend emphasis to this fact.

Prosperity. The span of years between 1793 and 1804 was one of unprecedented prosperity which was based upon a large and rapid growth in the volume and value of our external trade. During the Napoleonic Wars, merchant vessels of England and France were withdrawn from overseas trade with the western hemisphere nations. American merchant vessels sailed freely between the United States and South American countries, the West Indies, Europe, and China. When French merchant ships were driven from trans-Atlantic trade, American vessels almost monopolized the carrying trade between the French West Indies and France. Some products were carried directly from ports in South America and the West Indies to European ports; others were brought first to American ports whence they were reexported to their European destinations.

Boston, New York, Philadelphia, and Baltimore owed their rapid growth during that period to trade and commerce more than to the development of manufacturing. They not only became the largest export-import centers, they were the *entrepôts* of internal commerce. The number of wholesale and retail establishments increased, and their volume of business made a notable contribution to national income.

Trade with the West Indies had assumed its earlier importance and was providing the United States with exchange with which to pay for goods that were imported from England and from other European countries. In 1790 cotton had not made itself noticeable among the exports of the Southern States, but by 1815 it had forged ahead of all others and was beginning to shape the economic and political thinking of southern leaders. Because of the influence of cotton on the thinking of southern leaders, it also permeated the foreign policy of the United States, because southern leaders and thinkers were likewise national leaders and thinkers. While the principal item of export from the United States originated in the Southern States, the shipping facilities were in large part provided by people who resided in the Northern or New England States. As long as shipbuilding and shipping interests dominated New England industry, and as long as these industries were the main sources of income to those people, their attitude towards the export of cotton and towards the tariff supported that of the South. A few years later, in 1824, when manufacturing industries represented relatively large capital investments and employed a much larger proportion of the labor segment of the population, the tenor of thinking of the New England people became more favorable towards the use of protective tariffs. Sectional development was beginning to provide the basis for discussion and dispute. Differences in policies that were related to systems of agriculture and of labor, to public land policy, and to the tariff program were portents of things to come.

Internal Trade

Just as a pattern of external triangular trade had been developed during the Colonial Period, another pattern of internal triangular trade developed after 1790 with New Orleans, New York, and St. Louis each serving as a typical vertex. Barges on the Ohio, Missouri, and Mississippi Rivers were carried downstream, in part by currents, to New Orleans where the barges were broken up for firewood. Had trade gone upstream, the barges would have had to be poled, which was not only slow but expensive. It was much cheaper for furs and pelts, cereal grains, flour, lumber and lumber products, livestock, and many other products to be floated down the river to New Orleans, from where they were transported along the coast to New York or along the Eastern Seaboard. Sugar and cotton may also have been part of these cargoes. The proceeds from their sale in eastern markets were used to purchase manufactured imports or products of American manufacturers. Hardware, farm tools, salt, tableware, furniture, and kitchen utensils were shipped south to New Orleans by coastwise vessels and were carried overland to Pittsburgh, and then floated down the Ohio River to western markets to complete the triangle. Shoes, textiles, guns, ammunition, whiskey, and other articles of relatively small bulk formed the objects of overland trade. None of those products was easily perishable, and to all of them values large in proportion to their bulk had been imparted by their manufacture.

The introduction of steam on western waters in 1811 tended to break up the triangular trade and institute more direct trade between any two points, both of which were in the interior, or one of which was in the interior, the other along the coast. The steamboat also shortened the time of travel between points on inland waterways, and cheaper transportation costs attracted an increased volume of traffic. Cincinnati, Louisville, Indianapolis, Columbus, and Wheeling, among others, were beginning to take their places as *entrepôts* in the West.

TRANSPORTATION

Means of internal transportation and communication were undeveloped, with the Hudson, Delaware, Susquehanna, and James Rivers providing the principal avenues of transportation. Roads were scarcely worthy of the name, and postal communication was still in its infancy. By 1815 the Ohio and Mississippi Rivers were carrying tons of traffic on boats powered by steam, but the Cumberland Road had not reached Wheeling. Monopoly grants to control river transportation were difficult to enforce, and in 1824 the United States Supreme Court ruled in *Gibbons* v. *Ogden* that monopoly control of river transportation was in violation of the interstate commerce clause in the United States Constitution.

Albert Gallatin's Report

Albert Gallatin reported to Congress in 1808 the importance of constructing transportation facilities that would connect the cities along the Atlantic Coast with the hinterland. These facilities were roads, canals, and a combination of the two. Advantage would be taken of the rivers, by connecting those that emptied into the Atlantic Ocean with those whose flow was towards the Mississippi River and towards the Great Lakes. Canals were to be used as much as possible, because of the relative ease of transporting commodities by water compared with the difficulties of overland facilities, to say nothing of the relative costs of canal and overland transportation. Canal, or inland waterway transportation, met the requirements for carrying heavy, bulky, and relatively cheap products, most of which were raw materials, or those in the early stages of fabrication; time was not of great importance in transporting them from their sources to markets. At the beginning of the period, it was estimated that goods could not be transported profitably more than 150 miles unless demand conditions at their markets were such that they could bear a transportation cost of $15 per ton. Another estimate was that a distance of only 50 miles from a market made industrial independence expedient. One point is undeniable: the high cost of slow transportation lent itself to the development of an internal economy that attained a somewhat high degree of economic independence at the same time that transportation and communication facilities were being developed.

Post Roads

By 1800 Boston and Baltimore were each three days distant from New York, and Pittsburgh was reached in a week. Cleveland was two weeks distant from New York, and Richmond, Virginia, could be reached on the fifth day, if the weather was favorable. In 1790 there were 1,875 miles of post roads, and of the 75 post offices in the country, over one half of them were located in the South. The main post road extended from Wiscasset, Maine, in the North to Savannah, Georgia, in the South. The amount of postage usually depended upon the distance a letter was carried, and it was collected at the point of delivery. Rates were established for a single-page letter, and a two-page letter carried double the single rate. Every parcel was given the rate per ounce of four times a single-page letter. Newspapers were subsidized at the time with a rate of one cent for less than 100 miles; 1½ cents for greater distances.

Table 5-2
Scale of Postal Rates—February 20, 1792

Distance Carried	Postage Rate
not over 30 miles	6 cents
31- 60 "	8 "
61-100 "	10 "
101-150 "	12½ "
151-200 "	15 "
201-250 "	17 "
251-350 "	20 "
351-450 "	22 "
over 450 "	25 "

Source: U. S. Department of Commerce, Bureau of the Census, *Historical Statistics of the United States. Colonial Times to 1957* (Washington: U. S. Government Printing Office, 1960), p. 498.

PROGRESS v. GROWTH

There is no doubt that, in terms of population, landed area under cultivation, development of manufacturing, and other measures that may be applied, the United States made progress throughout the period, with the probable exception of the years of war and those in which the American economy was adversely affected by war in Europe. Data are too meager and unreliable to attempt a measurement of economic growth, which has come to mean an increase in per capita national income.

Economic Progress

Agriculture was still in a primitive state. Horsedrawn plows and wooden plowshares were in use. Crude, handmade cultivators were used in conditioning the soil for planting. Harvesting equipment consisted of the cradle and the flail. The benefits to be derived from fertilization and rotation of crops either were not known by American farmers, or were too costly to apply. Markets were not well enough established or sufficiently large to absorb increases in total output that might result from the use of more intensive methods of cultivation, had they been known.

Cereal grains from western farms did not measure increases in total output. Farms along the Atlantic coastal plain were abandoned entirely, or were put to other uses such as truck farming, raising fruit trees, and pasturage. Output per acre on many western farms exceeded the output of farms in New England and other Eastern States, except those that were situated along rivers that overflowed during the spring.

A Stage in Economic Development

Because of the scarcity of reliable data for the period, it is difficult to place an estimate on the amount of progress that had been made within the framework of the American economy. One estimate of the value of all real and personal property that was made by Samuel Blodget in his *Economica,* published in 1806, places a value of $600 million for 1774; $850 million for 1784, and by 1790 it had increased to $1,360 million. In the abstract, insofar as those estimates approached reality, they seem to indicate that the efforts of the colonists to harness the factors of production bore results that were favorable to them as a group, in that they measured progress. However, if these figures are reduced to estimated wealth *per capita,* quite a different situation is revealed. Using estimated population data for 1770 and 1780, extrapolation results in a per capita wealth of $267 in 1774, the same amount for 1784, and $346 in 1790. In view of the losses that were occasioned by the War, the figure for 1784 may not be far from right in its relation to that for 1774. The increase in wealth per capita by 1790 was a product of the resourcefulness and ingenuity of the American businessman of that era in overcoming the unfavorable impacts of (1) the exclusion of the United States from the veil of protection that had been afforded by the English Navigation Acts and (2) the depression that followed the close of the war.

WAR CLOUDS

The prosperity that emanated from United States shipping taking over the carrying trade between western hemisphere nations and Europe came to a sudden halt when England and France intensified their war efforts in attempting to blockade each other's ports. When England first attempted to invoke the Rule of War of 1756, which prohibited neutral nations from engaging in trade they had not enjoyed during peacetime, American nations circumvented its restrictions by bringing cargoes to American ports, paying customs on them, and then shipping them to their European destinations. After a series of diplomatic protests by England proved of little avail in preventing a flow of goods from America to France, England issued its Orders in Council, which had the effect of blockading the French coast to American shipping. France retaliated by issuing the Milan and Berlin Decrees, the enforcement of which denied to American ships entrance to British ports. Caught in the middle of the struggle between England and France, the importance of overseas shipping to the United States was revealed in a negative manner. Later, when nonimportation agreements were entered into and an Embargo Act was passed, not only was trade affected adversely, but the entire economy was thrown into reverse. Ships and shipping facilities were idled, sailors and longshoremen were unemployed, and internal aspects of our economy were likewise affected. The high degree of interdependence of the different segments of our economy was made manifest by the impact of decreased shipping.

The principles of *nonimportation* and *embargo* were not only abhorrent to the people of New England and New York, who were dependent upon foreign trade for their very livelihood, but their translation into overt action brought talk of secession. To the people of the West and to those who saw an opportunity to add new territory to the confines of the United States, the struggle in Europe afforded the occasion for pressing claims to western lands, whose boundaries, under the terms of the Louisiana Purchase, were in dispute. Indian raids on white settlements were being agitated by the British, and the pioneer settlers on the western front desired to dispose of that problem and to establish the boundary lines for West Florida. As far as disregard for the commercial rights of American vessels was concerned, the United States had as much provocation for declaring war against France as she had to fight England; in fact, both were equally guilty of confiscating American ships and/or their cargoes.

War of 1812

Sentiment was in favor of leniency towards France, and war was declared against England. The commercial interests in England were just as strongly opposed to that war as were similar interests in the United States. About the only thing that was settled by the struggle was the boundary dispute, which may have paved the way for the acquisition of Florida a few years later.

Since the United States Bank had been dissolved in 1811, the federal government had no fiscal agency to aid it in financing a war. The tax system was not one that could easily be adjusted to the needs of war. Main reliance was placed on the issuance of bonds to provide much needed revenues, and the New England States made manifest their position by purchasing bonds in the amount of only $3 million, while the citizens of New York and Maryland contributed $35 million. The war did not last long, nor were there any land skirmishes of any consequence. There were several forays attempted in an effort to capture Canada, but they terminated in dismal failure. The most spectacular success was that of Andrew Jackson's defense of New Orleans after the treaty of peace had been signed.

Two Economic Impacts of War

The war and its close had two significant impacts on the American economy, which form the subject matter for somewhat detailed discussion in the following chapters; but since the groundwork was laid during this period, they will be mentioned here. The lack of a fiscal agent for the federal government was so embarrassing to President Madison, who had led the opposition to the First United States Bank throughout its entire existence, that the functioning of a central bank became of more importance than its constitutionality, and he reported to Congress on the establishment of a second bank. The other impact was felt in the dumping of English manufactures on our shores as soon as the war came to an end. The term *dumping* is used advisedly, because in that process selling goods is more important than cost-price relationships. Many new manufacturing industries had been started during the war to counteract the shortages of imports from England. Because they had operated at a cost disadvantage compared with similar products that were manufactured in England and imported into the United States, they commanded higher prices than their imported competitors. The British manufacturers hoped to regain the markets they had lost during the war by underselling products made in the United States, and forcing manufacturers in the United States to close their doors. If successful, then the British exporters would raise the prices of the goods they sold in the United States. Agitation was strong for a protective tariff that would enable the manufacturers who invested risk capital during the war to continue to make profits afterwards.

QUESTIONS FOR REVIEW

1. (a) Why was the Bank of the United States established?
   (b) How did it exercise control over the note issues of state banks?
   (c) Why was its charter permitted to expire?

2. Describe the first monetary system of the United States.

3. Was the stoppage of the coinage of the silver dollar in 1806 related to a divergence between the legal ratio at which silver and gold were exchanged at the mint and the market ratio? Explain.

4. (a) Why did Alexander Hamilton want the federal government to assume some of the indebtedness of the several states?
   (b) On what bases did some of the states object to that program?

5. What sources of revenue were available to the federal government?

6. What was the infant industry argument for protection as used by Alexander Hamilton?

7. To the extent that Hamilton's program became a reality, how was the scarcity of industrial labor overcome?

8. Of what economic significance was the acquisition of the Louisiana Territory?

9. Of what economic significance was the standardization of machine parts and their interchangeability?

10. (a) Describe a triangular pattern of internal trade.
    (b) What was the impact of the introduction of the steamboat on western waters on internal triangular trade? Explain.

11. Is there any evidence to indicate that there was an increase in national income during this period? Explain.

SUGGESTED READINGS

Bogart, Ernest L., and Charles M. Thompson. *Readings in the Economic History of the United States*. New York City: Longmans, Green & Co., Inc., 1916. Chapters 6, 7, and 8.

Chamberlain, John. *The Enterprising Americans: A Business History of the United States*. New York City: Harper & Row, Publishers, 1963. Chapter 3.

Dillard, Dudley. *Economic Development of the North Atlantic Community*. Englewood Cliffs, N. J.: Prentice-Hall, Inc., 1967. Chapter 13.

Hacker, Louis. "Secretary of the Treasury," *Views of American Economic Growth: The Agricultural Era*, edited by Thomas C. Cochran and Thomas B. Brewer. New York City: McGraw-Hill Book Company, 1966.

Nettels, Curtis P. *The Emergence of a National Economy, 1775-1815*. New York City: Holt, Rinehart & Winston, Inc., 1962. Chapters 6-13.

North, Douglass C. *The Economic Growth of the United States. 1790-1860*. Englewood Cliffs, N. J.: Prentice-Hall, Inc., 1961. Chapters 3-6.

Redlich, Fritz. "First Period: General Characteristics," *Views of American Economic Growth: The Agricultural Era*, edited by Thomas C. Cochran and Thomas B. Brewer. New York City: McGraw-Hill Book Company, 1966.

PART III

The Rise of a New Nation:
Internal and External Development—1816-1865

The year 1816 marks the passage by Congress of what may be considered to have been the first protective tariff. While it was passed as part of the reconversion program following the close of the War of 1812, in New England it signaled the beginning of a new emphasis on manufacturing industries and the decline of shipping and shipbuilding as the leading type of activity.

Central banking was given another try, and while it may have been successful from one point of view, it may have been its very degree of success that, to a large degree, resulted in its demise. Free banking, a bond secured currency, a note guaranty plan—all at the state level—appeared, and Louisiana came through with a state banking law that established a precedent in placing banking on a high level of principle and practice. Branch banking at the state level appeared as a substitute for central banking at the national level.

Turnpikes, canals, and railroads not only provided improved means of transportation, but afforded outlets for the investment of funds, domestic and foreign. The westward movement was opening vast new areas of agricultural lands, later mining frontiers. The nation survived the most severe panic, recession, and depression of its young history and emerged from its demoralization in a stronger economic position than it had previously occupied; and when a second panic struck the country, it recovered in a much shorter period of time. Expansion of economic activity west of the Mississippi River went on with renewed vigor after the termination of the second war with England. The purchase of the Louisiana Territory in 1803 had opened up vast, unknown reservoirs of natural resources for exploitation by the American people. It was not until after 1816 that the surge of people and of agricultural activity made inroads on these resources. During the last decade of this period, land grants to railroads stimulated the development of transportation, agriculture, and commerce in this territory. Mining, except for the explosive development after 1849, and industrial activity had to wait until the close of the Civil War to penetrate the region.

A development, described as an agricultural revolution, had its fulfillment during this period. According to modern methods of agriculture, there was still much to be done. In terms of technologies that were available prior to this development, it truly was a revolution.

Industry commanded the attention of an ever increasing segment of the population and, at the close of the period, had reached a position of prominence at the consumers' goods level as a source of profits and national income.

Economic sectionalism was accentuating differences in thinking and in the formulating of economic programs by the leading politicians of the country. In addition to the specialization aspect of sectionalism, systems of labor, of landholding, and policies towards the disposition of public lands were in constant conflict with each other until the issues of the Civil War were settled.

Chapter 6

WESTWARD EXPANSION; PUBLIC LANDS; POPULATION GROWTH; AGRICULTURE

Two of the most significant facts of American economic development up to 1860 are a westward expansion and the growth of population. Even though there was little pressure of population upon landed resources along the Atlantic coastal plain, the very reasons why people left their homes in Europe to come to America predetermined a westward expansion in the United States. In fact, their coming to this country and their exploiting natural resources in Colonial America were the last stages of a movement that had started in Europe, and later was continued along a different pattern in the United States. The abundance of land together with freedom of enterprise and the absence of a social caste system were the permissive factors of that movement.

Throughout the years between 1820 and 1860, the population of the United States increased from 9.6 million to 31.4 million, an increase of approximately 230 percent, while the density of population increased from 5.6 per square mile to 10.6. Had the people who were here in 1860 been confined to the territory that was under settlement in 1820, the density of population would have been nearly 18 persons per square mile.

WESTWARD EXPANSION

The westward movement was more than a migratory movement of people from settled areas into virgin territory. The westward movement was more than an expansion of the territorial boundaries of the United States, and it was more than a movement of people into regions that were recently acquired by the United States. It was the initial stage of a larger development so complex in all of its facets that it defied analysis and comprehension until the closing years of the 19th century.

THE ADVANCE OF THE FRONTIER LINE

The people who participated in the westward movement did not isolate themselves from the rest of the country, nor were they aware of the fact that they were following a pattern or that they were initiating a movement of momentous consequences. They kept in contact with the regions from which they had moved through the media of trade and traders, later by using the transportation and communication facilities that were available.

Phases of the Westward Movement

The westward movement progressed by stages or phases, in distances possibly 20 to 40 miles, in time from three to five or ten years. There was nothing rigid about the patterns, and they were numerous in sequence followed, and in time.

Hunter or Trapper. The initial stage was more uniform than any of the later ones, and was manifest by the hunter and/or trapper seeking more distant sources of furs, skins, pelts, and hides, as well as wild game for eating. There may have been a trading post or a depot where he took the products of his hunting, but it had no permanency to which the word settlement could be applied. He moved on when the forests, streams, and plains had become nearly exhausted of wild animal life, or when the pressure of population was such that wild animals sought refuge in virgin areas.

Pioneer Farmer-Speculator. In either case, the hunter was usually followed by a farmer. Possibly, rancher is a more descriptive term. The latter made a clearing for his cabin, either for protection or for convenience, or both, and turned some soil for planting. He did not seek a large crop much beyond his needs, because there was no convenient market to absorb a surplus over the needs of his immediate family. He may have had some oxen, some horses, cows, hogs, and chickens. Even sheep may have been found among his livestock. Since he had no barns or barnyards or pens, his livestock roamed the woods and fields winter and summer, and they were given little care or protection. The family dog was trained to round up any strays that had wandered too far away from home. The livestock were not bred so as to develop any particular trait or characteristic that made the animals more adaptable to man's needs. Natural selection and survival seemed to determine which animals would procreate the following year's issue. That phase usually lasted until someone came along who wanted more permanent surroundings and who was willing to pay for them. The pioneer farmer may well have been a speculator who was more interested in making a profit from the sale of his holdings than he was in earning a living from the land.

Farmer. A farmer not only was more permanent than a rancher, he placed more emphasis on tilling the soil and on taking care of his livestock. He built barns and barnyards, a more permanent house in which to live and probably a larger one; he fenced a clearing and had carriages and wagons to suit his several needs. Some of his farm tools were horse drawn, but they were scaled to a small-sized farm. He brought furniture and other household wares with him; and he was prepared to raise a family or to enlarge upon one. In the absence of hired labor, children were an asset on a farm. When the farmer had outgrown that establishment, when the general community was becoming larger than he preferred, when another farmer offered him a price for his farm that he felt he could not refuse, or when a combination of two or more of these circumstances occurred, he moved another step toward the west.

Permanent Settlement. By that time a commercial center may have developed nearby, in which the farmer who had purchased the farm could sell his grain, his livestock, meat or dairy products, and in return obtain clothing, some of his food, possibly some seed and flour, and improved farm machinery. A railroad may not have been far away with a grain elevator on a siding to use in storing grain and in loading it on freight cars. By this time a bank usually offered its facilities to the farmer in accepting his deposits and in granting him loans. Professional services, such as those rendered by doctors, dentists, lawyers, and barbers, were also available, the effects of which were to raise his scale of living and to improve the general tenor of the community and to make it a more healthy and enjoyable place to live.

Mining Frontier. By the time the frontier of American life had reached the eastern edge of the Rocky Mountain plateau, gold had been discovered in California. That event altered the pattern of the westward movement. The prospect of sudden riches lured settlers to the West Coast, some of whom followed the Oregon Trail. Others sailed to Panama, crossed the isthmus by train or by wagon, and sailed again up the West Coast to California, at which place the westward movement took an easterly direction. In place of the hunter and trapper, then the rancher, followed by the farmer, was the prospector for gold. Since he took a supply of food with him, he did not have to take time out from his prospecting to grow it. Mining camps grew into mining towns, the culture of which serves as the setting for many western dramas as portrayed in movies and on television.

Not all prospectors for gold found it near Sutter's Mill, and some of them trekked eastward to stake out new claims. Others became discouraged or dissatisfied with life in mining camps and began to cultivate the soil. From that time until the close of the frontier 50 years or more later, there were two frontiers of settlement—one moving east from California, the other continuing its slow march across or through the Rocky Mountains.

PUBLIC LAND POLICY

After the close of the War of 1812 with England, there was a rush of pioneers to settle upon public lands. The word *pioneers* is used somewhat as a compromise to include all persons who settled upon public lands regardless of their objectives. Some were speculators who sought to acquire large acreages of land from the government at something like $1.25 an acre and after the passage of time sell to someone else at several dollars, more or less, per acre. These men may or may not have lived on some of their new holdings. Others among the pioneers were farmers who wanted land which they could cultivate and on which they could erect their homes and barns and possibly other farm buildings. Some of these farmers were speculators as well, and they hoped to sell their holdings after a few years at higher prices to other farmers who were moving west.

Conflicting Interests

A definite land policy was difficult to outline because of the conflicting interests of the members of Congress. Those who represented districts from the North and East were in favor of a policy that would return revenue to the Federal Treasury and at the same time would not drain the farm population or the labor force to the West. To the extent that farmers moved from New England to the West, farmland in New England tended to depreciate in value, and the local markets for goods that were manufactured in the cities or were imported from Europe decreased. Since farms in New England were relatively small, and were frequently described as family-sized farms, that pattern was advocated by their Congressmen. To the extent that labor from New England was attracted to the West for any reason or by any factor, it became that much more scarce in New England and wages rose. Other things remaining the same, increased wages meant increased production costs which, in turn, made it more difficult for the manufacturers to compete with similar goods that were imported. To state the situation in other words, New England wanted to protect its vested interests in land and in manufacturing industries. People in the Middle States tended to take sides with the people from New England in their policy determination and for many of the same reasons.

Table 6-1

Sales of Public Lands for Selected Years

Year	Acres
1835	12,564,500
1836	20,074,900
1837	5,601,100
1854	12,823,000
1855	11,959,800
1856	5,247,000

Source: U. S. Department of Commerce, Bureau of the Census, *Historical Statistics of the United States. Colonial Times to 1957* (Washington: U. S. Government Printing Office, 1960), p. 239. Adapted.

The southern plantation owners took an entirely different attitude towards the sale of public lands. First and foremost, they wanted to preserve and also to perpetuate and to extend the plantation system of agriculture, a one-crop system that depended upon the use of slave labor. Small-sized farms were not profitable to cultivate, and a high price would make it difficult for them to complete their payments. Consequently, they favored disposing of public lands in large acreages and at low prices per acre.

Somewhat opposed to either of the above plans were the westerners, most vociferous of whom were the speculators. They had purchased land for

quick turnover at a higher price. Attracting more people to the West increased the value of their holdings. Small to medium-sized parcels at low
prices on easy terms was what they advocated. After 1820, the sale of
public lands was second to the tariff as a source of income to the United
States Treasury. Even so, the importance of such sales was manifest in the
series of developments that led to the panics of 1837 [1] and 1857.[2]

The Second Bank of the United States was charged by President Jackson
with giving encouragement to speculation in public lands by its easy credit
policy; and it was his *Specie Circular* that precipitated the panic of 1837,
after several years of impending crisis, by requiring that payments on the
purchase contracts for public lands be made in specie.

More detailed analysis of the developmental aspects of this panic and of
the one that occurred in 1857 will be given in a later chapter. Suffice it to
say here that speculation in public lands in the 1850's was heightened by
the eagerness with which the fact of railroad construction caught the fancy
of farmers, businessmen, and speculators in public lands.

Henry Clay's American System

Henry Clay was sent to Congress by a constituency that lived in Kentucky, a state that was in a position to benefit by the migration of farmers
into its confines. Farmland in central Kentucky was extremely fertile; and
its limestone soil facilitated the growing of wheat, hemp, tobacco, and corn,
once it had been cleared of trees, or a heavy sod of grass had been plowed
under. Cotton was another crop that was cultivated in the western portion
of the state. A low wage labor was needed to cut hemp and break it, also
to grow cotton and tobacco, both of which required hand labor in their
cultivation as well as in their picking and cutting. Acreages for their most
profitable cultivation were somewhat larger than the family-sized farms of
New England.

In spite of these conditions in his home state, Clay appeared to be more
sympathetic with the overall program and policy that were advocated by the
vested interests in land, in manufacturing, and in commerce in New York
and New England. Not only did his attitude toward the disposal of public
lands seem contrary to the best interests of his constituents, but he favored
a high protective tariff on commodity imports, few, if any, of which were
products that offered competition to those that were produced in Kentucky.
On the other hand, to the extent that Kentuckians were purchasers of imported wares, they had to pay higher prices for those goods upon which a
tariff had been levied than they otherwise would have been compelled to
pay; and they were not given higher prices for the products they offered for
sale. To offset that apparent disregard for the economic welfare of his constituency, he developed a program which has come to be known as Clay's

[1] See Chapter 7, p. 175.
[2] See Chapter 11, p. 263.

"American System." It is better known in connection with a discussion of the tariff, and it will be referred to again in that connection in a later chapter. There were three facets to the system: (1) a protective tariff, (2) internal improvements, and (3) policy to govern the disposal of public lands.

Clay argued that the imposition of high customs duties that would encourage the development of domestic manufacturing industries would benefit the farmers by creating a home market for products of the farm. In spite of a certain degree of protection afforded by high tariffs, foreign goods that were subject to these rates would continue to enter ports of the United States, and revenue would accrue therefrom. The second facet to his system included the use of these revenues to help pay for internal improvements west of the Appalachian Mountains. Those improvements would be in the form of roads, canals, and making rivers navigable, all of which would tend to enhance the value of farmland in Kentucky and in other western states. These improvements would lower the cost of sending their products to market and would reduce the time en route.

Clay favored a policy of selling public lands in small to medium-size lots and at prices sufficiently high to discourage members of the laboring classes of the North and the East from acquiring them. Sales for cash rather than for credit would accomplish his purpose. That Clay was only partially successful in having the Congress accept his program is manifest in the terms that governed the sale of public lands under the Land Law of 1820.

The western influence was overcome by the North and the East in that preemption and donation were not accepted as valid claims to public lands. Lands could have been sold privately, but auctions of one-half and one-quarter sections were preferred. (A section consisted of 640 acres.) A minimum of $1.25 an acre was established for straight cash sales. This latter feature led the prospective purchasers of public lands to obtain bank credit. State banks and branches of the Second Bank of the United States extended credit in the form of bank notes to finance these purchases as well as the purchase of lands that had been acquired by speculators. Throughout the decade of the 1820's, government receipts from the sale of public lands averaged something over $1 million per annum, compared with an annual average of over $17 million of customs receipts.

Sales, Preemption, and Graduation

While the receipts from the sale of public lands increased after 1830, it was not until 1835 and 1836 that sales increased $10 million over the sales for the preceding year. In 1836, governmental receipts reached an all-time high of over $24 million from the sale of over 12,500,000 acres.

When President Andrew Jackson issued his *Specie Circular* in 1836, in conformance with which payments for public lands were made in specie, annual sales declined sharply, to a little over 5,600,000 acres, but those sales

Table 6-2

Federal Government Receipts from the Sale
of Public Lands and Customs—1821-1860
(000)

Year	Sales of Public Lands	Customs Duties
1821	$ 1,213	$13,004
1822	1,804	17,590
1823	917	19,088
1824	984	17,878
1825	1,216	20,099
1826	1,394	23,341
1827	1,496	19,712
1828	1,018	23,206
1829	1,517	22,682
1830	2,329	21,922
1831	3,211	24,224
1832	2,623	28,465
1833	3,968	29,033
1834	4,858	16,215
1835	14,758	19,391
1836	24,877	23,410
1837	6,776	11,169
1838	3,082	16,159
1839	7,076	23,138
1840	3,293	13,500
1841	1,366	14,487
1842	1,336	18,188
1843	898	7,047
1844	2,060	26,184
1845	2,077	27,528
1846	2,694	26,713
1847	2,498	23,748
1848	3,329	31,757
1849	1,689	28,347
1850	1,860	39,669
1851	2,352	49,018
1852	2,043	47,339
1853	1,667	58,932
1854	8,471	64,224
1855	11,497	53,026
1856	8,918	64,023
1857	3,829	63,876
1858	3,514	41,790
1859	1,757	49,566
1860	1,779	53,188

Source: *Historical Statistics of the United States. Colonial Times to 1957*, 1960,
p. 712. Adapted.

were not a measure of the rapidity with which western lands were being settled. Thousands of pioneers settled unlawfully upon millions of acres of public land before they had been surveyed and made available for legal entry. The Pre-emption Act of 1841 legalized the claims to such lands upon payment of $1.25 an acre for land upon which improvements had been made, provided the claimant did not own 320 acres elsewhere. That was another attempt on the part of the government to encourage early settlement by a large number of legitimate landowners and to discourage speculation.

The only other land act passed by the Congress prior to the Homestead Act in 1862 was the Graduation Act of 1854, under the terms of which the price of land that remained unsold at $1.25 an acre for ten years or more was reduced. The sliding scale of prices that applied to such lands was:

land on the market and unsold after							10 years	$1.00 an acre
"	"	"	"	"	"	"	15 "	.75 "
"	"	"	"	"	"	"	20 "	.50 "
"	"	"	"	"	"	"	25 "	.25 "
"	"	"	"	"	"	"	30 "	.125 "

Land Grants

In addition to giving encouragement to the westward migration of settlers by selling public lands in relatively small parcels at low prices, the government hastened the construction of internal improvements by granting land to encourage the construction of roads, canals, and railroads, and to make rivers more suitable for navigation. In fact, between 1820 and 1860, over 35 million acres were granted for those purposes as follows:

1823-1827	251,000 acres for wagon roads
1827-1853	3,898,000 acres for canals
1828-1840	1,405,000 acres for improvements of rivers
after 1847	29,756,000 acres to railroads

Land grants to railroads were much more spectacular in amount and in their political entanglements, but during the canal-building era competition was keen in the building of canals in order to facilitate the movement of goods from inland regions to coastal towns. Grants of land provided canal companies with a portion of their initial capital equipment.

Acquisition of New Territories

After the Louisiana Territory was added to the United States in 1803, the second largest single acquisition of new lands was that of Texas in 1845. The terms under which Texas was annexed to the Union forbade lands in that state from becoming public lands of the United States. The largest addition to the continental United States was the Mexican Cession of 1848 by which over 560,000 square miles of territory were added. It was from that acquisition that California, Nevada, Arizona, New Mexico, and parts of Colorado and Wyoming were formed. The ownership of the Oregon

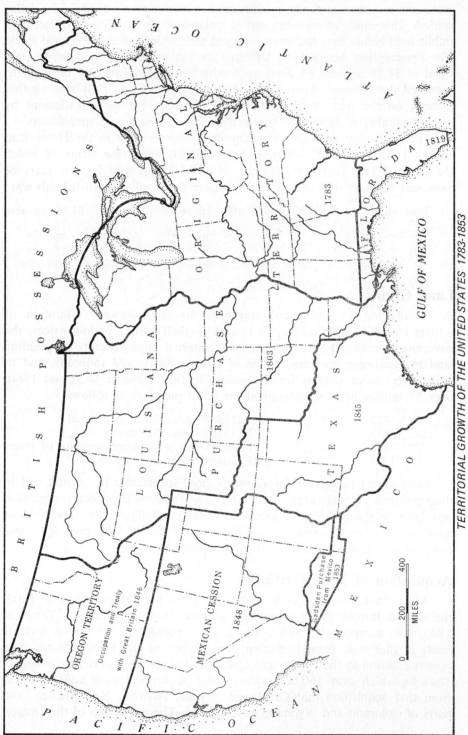

ATLANTIC OCEAN

FLORIDA 1819

1783

GULF OF MEXICO

ORIGINAL TERRITORY

BRITISH POSSESSIONS

LOUISIANA PURCHASE 1803

TEXAS 1845

M E X I C O

OREGON TERRITORY
Occupation and Treaty
with Great Britain 1846

MEXICAN CESSION 1848

Gadsden Purchase from Mexico 1853

PACIFIC OCEAN

MILES
0   200   400

TERRITORIAL GROWTH OF THE UNITED STATES 1783-1853

Territory was settled by treaty with England in 1846; and in the years to come Washington, Idaho, and Oregon were admitted to statehood. It remained for the Gadsden Purchase in 1853 to round out the territorial limits of the continental United States. It added 29,640 square miles to our domain and was acquired to facilitate the construction of a railroad over a southern route to the West Coast. Surveyors were seeking a means of access through the Rocky Mountains that would provide the most gradual elevations and reduce to a minimum the need for tunnels and trestles. Railroad men were talking in terms of a transcontinental line and a southern route, the eastern terminal of which would be New Orleans.

POPULATION GROWTH

Of the two factors—natural increase and immigration—that contributed to the growth of population between 1820 and 1860, the former exerted more influence until the Irish migration in the latter part of the 1840's which was followed by an influx of Germans the following decade.

Natural Increase

Although there are no reliable registrations of vital statistics for the early years of our development, it is known that birth rates prior to 1860 were much higher than they were after that year. Death rates also were higher, especially at childbirth and for children up to five years of age. It is known that the number of live births per 1,000 women between the ages of 15 and 44 was 260 in 1820. By 1860 it had declined to 184, and in 1900 it was only 130. Birth control measures were seldom used. Adults of both sexes were of the ages of greatest fertility. Children were looked upon as family assets. They were put to work at an early age, and they took care of their parents in sickness and in old age. Prior to 1860, life expectancy was approximately 20 years less than it is today.

It was not unusual for parents to have upwards of eight children. Death of the mother at childbirth and a high rate of infant mortality operated to keep down the number of children that attained the age of maturity or adulthood. Since every family needed the services of a mother and wife and since no one seemed to be responsible for taking care of widows, most of them remarried and began raising another set of children.

Immigration and Migration

The causes of the population increase throw light on one phase of the westward movement: namely, the migration of people to the west, or the relocation of the frontier of American life. Just as the first white settlers to America came from European countries, so did people from those same European countries continue to cross the Atlantic Ocean in search of an all-around politico-economic climate that was more suitable to their ideals and standards of life than were such climates in their home countries. As

Table 6-3

Population Growth and Density of Population—1820-1860

Year	Land Area in Square Miles	Increase in Square Miles of Land	Population	Population Increase	% Increase over Preceding Census	Population per Square Mile of Land
1820	1,749,462	. . . .	9,638,453	. . . .	. . .	5.6
1830	1,749,462	. . . .	12,866,020	3,227,567	33.5	7.4
1840	1,749,462	. . . .	17,069,453	4,203,433	32.7	9.8
1850	2,940,042	1,190,580	23,191,876	6,122,423	35.9	7.9
1860	2,969,640	29,598	31,443,321	8,251,445	35.6	10.6

Source: *Historical Statistics of the United States. Colonial Times to 1957*, 1960, p. 8. Adapted.

nearly as can be determined from census data, most of the immigrants who
came to the United States prior to 1860 were from the countries of northwestern Europe—the United Kingdom, Germany, the Scandinavian Countries, the Netherlands, Belgium, Luxembourg, Switzerland, and France. It
was not until 1845 that as many as 34,000 Germans emigrated to America
in one year. In 1852 and 1853, over 140,000 Germans emigrated each
year, and in 1854 over 215,000 Germans left the fatherland to start
life anew in the United States. After 1854, the German emigration
fell to less than one half of the average for 1852, 1853, and 1854. They
sought to escape from military and political disturbances. Coinciding with
the heavy German emigration from central Europe was that from Ireland in
the eight years commencing in 1847, during which span of years an average
of 148,366 Irish landed in America every year. Poverty, starvation, and
oppression by absentee English landlords caused them to seek better fortunes in Ameria. Free land and farming seemed to have little attraction
for those people, most of whom settled in urban communities in New
England, New York, New Jersey, and Pennsylvania where they performed
work that fell in the common labor bracket. Factory work also appealed to
them, and they became the mill hands in the textile industry in Massachusetts,
New York, New Jersey, and Pennsylvania.

For the entire period of 1816 to 1860, statistics reveal that over 60
percent of the immigrants were male. In those instances where age data
are available, over 70 percent of all new arrivals were under 40 years of age.
These data may throw some light upon the causes of the rapid growth in
population insofar as it was occasioned by natural increase, since these new
arrivals were in their most fertile span of years. These data also throw light
on the willingness of the people to move west and to settle upon new land.
They were not only youthful but were willing and eager to start life anew
on the frontier. While less than one half of the immigrants who were
admitted into the United States between 1847 and 1857 gave any occupation, of those who did, laborers, farmers, and skilled workers were most
numerous; and those who were engaged in commerce ranked fourth. There
is no reason for believing that those who did not declare any occupation
when they debarked on our shores were not members of the same working
groups as those who did declare their vocational preferences or affiliations.
One strong implication of the above data is that as population not only
increased but spread itself over a wider territory, internal trade increased
and was participated in by some of the new arrivals.

Composition

In 1820 the median age of the entire population was 16.7 years, with
that for the male portion being the same as for the female portion. By
1860 the median age had crept up to 19.4 years, with that of the male
population slightly higher than that of the female portion. The increase in
the median age of the male population could reflect the impact of immigra-

Table 6-4

Population of the United States by Regions—1820-1860
(millions)

Region	1820	1830	1840	1850	1860
New England (Maine, New Hampshire, Vermont, Massachusetts, Rhode Island, Connecticut)	1.7	2.0	2.2	2.7	3.1
Middle Atlantic (New York, New Jersey, Pennsylvania)	2.7	3.6	4.5	5.9	7.5
East North Central (Ohio, Indiana, Illinois, Michigan, Wisconsin)	.8	1.5	2.9	4.5	6.9
West North Central (Minnesota, Iowa, Missouri, North Dakota, South Dakota, Nebraska, Kansas)	.07	.1	.4	.9	2.2
South Atlantic (Delaware, Maryland, District of Columbia, Virginia, West Virginia, North Carolina, South Carolina, Georgia, Florida)	3.1	3.6	3.9	4.7	5.4
East South Central (Kentucky, Tennessee, Alabama, Mississippi)	1.1	1.8	2.6	3.4	4.0
West South Central (Arkansas, Louisiana, Oklahoma, Texas)	.17	.25	.45	.94	1.7
Mountain (Montana, Idaho, Wyoming, Colorado, New Mexico, Arizona, Utah, Nevada)	..	..	..	.07	.17
Pacific (Washington, Oregon, California)	..	..	..	.11	.44

Source: *Historical Statistics of the United States. Colonial Times to 1957*, 1960, pp. 12 and 13. Adapted.

tion, or it could be a measurement of an increase in the span of life of the American people. An increase in the national income could have contributed to increased longevity by enabling more persons to enjoy a higher scale of living than formerly. Without additional data, it is impossible to do more than to recognize both situations.

A study of Table 6-4 reveals the impact of population growth and its distribution throughout the United States. The South Atlantic States of Delaware, Maryland, District of Columbia, Virginia, West Virginia, North Carolina, South Carolina, Georgia, and Florida led in population in 1820, but gradually gave way to the Middle Atlantic States of New York, New Jersey, and Pennsylvania. The increase in the population of North Carolina and of South Carolina, Georgia, and Florida is a measurement of the increasing importance of plantation farming in those states. The accelerated increase in population growth in the Middle Atlantic States was due to the development of trade, manufacturing and industry, as well as agriculture, in New York and Pennsylvania.

Population increases in the East North Central and West North Central States give mute testimony to the strength of the westward movement in its extension into Ohio, Indiana, Illinois, Wisconsin, Missouri, and Iowa. While the population of the West South Central States of Louisiana, Arkansas, Oklahoma, and Texas was less than that of the sections to the north and to the east, the extension of the cotton kingdom into Louisiana and Arkansas conditioned the growth of those latter two states.

Distribution

The pattern of the westward movement west of the Mississippi River may be seen in the fact that California, then New Mexico, and later Utah displaced Arkansas as the frontier in the 1850 census. Montana, Wyoming, Nevada, Colorado, and Arizona were overlooked by the pioneers in their search for gold and other deposits of mineral wealth. The importance of Utah in that development reflects the impact of the Mormon migration which terminated at Salt Lake City.

Massachusetts, Rhode Island, and Connecticut contributed more to the population growth of New England than did the states of Maine, New Hampshire, and Vermont, in which farming continued to occupy the attention of a majority of their citizens.

Impact of Immigration

It has already been noted that the Irish who came to this country after 1845 did so in an effort to escape deprivation and starvation, due to the failure of the potato crop in Ireland. Since they brought with them little or no money, they tended to congregate in urban areas near the ports of their debarkation. Many of them were unschooled and untrained, and they comprised the common labor segment of the working population.

It is not surprising that those who came to America sought regions where they could continue to earn their livelihood in the manner to which they were accustomed. Many Scandinavians settled in northern Illinois, Wisconsin, and Minnesota where they engaged in dairying and other forms of agriculture. The Germans left a trail all the way across the country through Maryland, Pennsylvania, Ohio, and on out to Missouri, Iowa, Nebraska, and Wisconsin. Cincinnati, St. Louis, and Milwaukee have present-day cultural activities that reflect their German heritage.

Center of Population

Another approach to the study of population increase and its movement throughout the country is to trace the center of population from a point 23 miles east of Baltimore, Maryland, in 1790, to 20 miles south by east of Chillicothe, Ohio, in 1860, a distance of 356.7 miles to the west, or a straight line movement of 358.8 miles. In addition to the general movement to the west, there was a slight angle to the south of a net distance of 18.7 miles. The pull of the south reflects not only the force of the westward movement, but the growth and expansion of the plantation system of farming in the South.

Table 6-5

Center of Population of the United States—1790-1860

Year	Approximate Location	Direct Line	Movement in Miles		
			West	North	South
1790	23 miles east of Baltimore	...	...	...	...
1800	18 " west of Baltimore	40.6	40.6	...	...
1810	40 " northwest by west of Washington	36.9	36.5	...	.5
1820	16 " east of Moorefield, W. Va.	50.5	50.1	...	5.3
1830	19 " west-southwest of Moorefield, W. Va.	40.4	39.4	...	6.7
1840	16 " south of Clarksburg, W. Va.	55.0	54.8	4.7	9.0
1850	23 " southeast of Parkersburg, W. Va.	54.8	54.7	...	...
1860	20 " south by east of Chillicothe, Ohio	80.6	80.6	1.6	3.5
		358.8	356.7	6.3	25.0

Source: *The World Almanac* (New York City: Newspaper Enterprise Association, Inc., 1960), p. 267.

URBANIZATION

Not only did the population of the United States increase prior to 1860, it increased at the astounding rate of over 30 percent in each 10-year period as is manifest by a study of the decennial census data. Table 6-6 reveals

Table 6-6

Number of Places and Population (000) in Urban and Rural Territories

Population Size (000)	1820		1830		1840		1850		1860	
	No. of Places	Population	No. of Places	Population	No. of Places	Population	No. of Places	Population	No. of Places	Population
500-1,000	....	....	....	....	....	....	1	515.5	2	1,379.2
250-500	....	....	....	....	1	312.7	....	....	1	266.7
100-250	1	123.7	1	202.6	2	204.5	5	659.1	6	992.9
50-100	2	126.5	3	222.5	2	187.1	4	284.4	7	452.1
25-50	2	70.5	3	105.2	7	235.4	16	611.3	19	670.3
10-25	8	121.6	16	240.3	25	404.8	36	560.8	58	834.4
5-10	22	155.1	33	230.8	48	328.7	85	596.1	136	976.4
2.5-5	26	95.8	34	125.7	46	171.8	89	316.5	163	594.5
Total of Urban	61	693.2	90	1,127.1	131	1,845.0	236	3,543.7	392	6,166.5
Percentage of Total Population		7.2%		8.8%		10.8%		15.3%		19.6%
Total of Rural		8,945.1		11,738.7		15,224.4		19,648.1		25,226.8
Percentage of Total Population		92.8%		91.2%		89.2%		84.7%		80.4%

Source: *Historical Statistics of the United States. Colonial Times to 1957*, 1960, p. 14. Adapted.

not only the distribution of population between urban and rural areas, it measures the declining importance of agriculture and the increasing importance of commerce and industry after 1840. Another way of interpreting these data is that while more persons obtained their livelihood by engaging in agricultural pursuits, they comprised a smaller proportion of the total population. At the same time, the increasing number of urban dwellers represented a larger proportion of the total population. That trend in the development of the United States is usually thought of as having occurred after the Civil War, whereas, in reality, it started in an emphatic manner after 1840. It is safe to classify the rural population as farmers, because the suburban movement had not developed and people who lived on farms earned their livelihood by working the land.

Table 6-6 also reveals the growth of the number of urban areas, as defined by the United States Bureau of the Census. Communities having 2,500 inhabitants or more are classified as urban. It was not until 1850 that the urbanization movement resulted in a concentration of population of one million or more in New York City. During the next decade Philadelphia attained that distinction. By 1860, there were more than twice as many cities in the 10,000 to 25,000 classification as there were in the 2,500 to 5,000 group in 1820. From 1820 to 1860 the number of cities in the 25,000 to 50,000 category increased 8½ times, and those in the 10,000 to 25,000 category increased over 600 percent. By 1860, urbanization had become a reality and many of the economic problems of earning a livelihood and of utilizing the products and the services of urban economic activity presented themselves.

Economic specialization and occupational division of labor were aspects of a spontaneous organization of urban life—spontaneous, in that it was self-determined by the exercise of the privileges and opportunities of freedom of enterprise, rather than by central planning. Without making any effort to preview developments that comprise the subject matter for later chapters, an enumeration of some of the aspects of urban economic life and its organization will serve to differentiate the economics of urbanization from the economics of rural areas. City streets and sidewalks were adjuncts of urban life, and were classified as constituting a portion of social capital. Supplies of fresh, pure water were available by building reservoirs, digging wells, or by drawing it from lakes and/or rivers. Housing was more congested than it was in the country. Problems of protecting life and property were solved by providing specialty services that were paid for by cities and towns. The costs of providing services for their citizens were met by levying taxes at the local level. Except for the use of the special assessment device for raising revenue, which was somewhat in accordance with the benefit theory of taxation, the general property tax was widely used. While the corporate form of business organization was in general use after 1840, problems of taxing intangible property were not serious or complicated until a later period.

AGRICULTURE

While the Erie Canal itself was an engineering feat of great moment, its completion in 1825 had a greater impact upon the progress of the westward movement and upon the agricultural development of the United States north of the Ohio River to the east and to the west than any other single achievement. It made possible taking advantage of technological improvements in agricultural techniques. It furthered the development of specialization in agricultural production on individual farms. Regional or sectional specialization was intensified as a result of that inland waterway, the use of which lowered transportation costs on bulky products of relatively low unit value.

New England

Many changes in the organization of the economy of the New England States were among the impacts of the opening of the Erie Canal. Local farmers were unable to compete with those in the newly opened West on a cost-price basis in the growing of cereal grains. The New England farmers, therefore, took advantage of the larger concentrations of populations by providing them with dairy products. Urban populations also provided lucrative markets for fresh vegetables in season, poultry, and eggs. Truck farming areas were developed near cities, and they represented an aspect of a more intensive form of agriculture than was practiced in the cultivation of cereal grains. Fruit trees were planted, and apple orchards were rooted by hogs. Horses and cattle also fed beneath the trees, which were nourished by natural fertilizer at no cost to the farmer. At least two crops of hay were harvested, much of which was consumed locally, some of which found its way to urban markets.

Middle Atlantic States

Even though land in west central New York and in the valley of the Susquehanna River was more fertile than most lands in New England, the Middle Atlantic States did not escape the impact of the opening up of new lands farther to the west. Land in Ohio, Indiana, Illinois, Michigan, Wisconsin, and in the Blue Grass region in Kentucky was so much more fertile than land in New York, Pennsylvania, Maryland, Delaware, and New Jersey that farming in the latter group of states underwent many alterations. As was discussed in the previous section, farmers in New York, Pennsylvania, and to some extent in Maryland found the cultivation of apples, red cherries, and grapes more profitable than growing wheat and corn. As urban communities grew in those states, farming was adjusted to supply them with fruits, vegetables, poultry, dairy products, and livestock. The sale of money crops gave farmers the purchasing power they needed in obtaining from the market clothing, hardware, farm machinery, furniture, household wares, and sundry other products that contributed to making farm life less monotonous and more enjoyable.

Southern States

The westward movement of agriculture in the South extended the plantation system of cotton culture to the Mississippi River and beyond. Slavery flourished as never before, except in the border states of Virginia and Kentucky, where trading slaves took the place of using them in fields. In spite of the fact that slave trading was frowned upon by many persons and its practice was discouraged, it was engaged in by persons who were not recognized as belonging to the socially elite. To what extent slave breeding became a business has never been exactly determined. The principal investment of the southern planter was in land and slaves, and in Louisiana added to these investments were sugar mills. The market value of slaves rose and fell somewhat in line with the rise and fall in the price of cotton. Slaves were found on almost every southern farm. The average number of slaves per farm probably was between four and eight. Exact figures are difficult to obtain, but it has been estimated that not more than 1,733 white families owned more than 100 slaves. At the other end of the scale were the small yeomen farmers who farmed land that had been vacated by large planters when the latter moved to the West, or who tilled the soil in the upland regions that were not suitable to plantation farming. Those men were dirt farmers rather than gentlemen farmers, and they worked alongside the few slaves they might have owned. Most of them were Caucasians, although in some upland regions, free Negroes were found. Their land was poor and so were they; their crops were poor and so were the animals under their care. Theirs was a more self-sustaining existence, as they were in little or no contact with the outside world. Distant markets were rarely visited, and they developed a culture all their own. Emancipation of the slaves had little effect upon their mode of living, and they continued their crude existence until well into the 20th century.

THE AGRICULTURAL REVOLUTION

An increase in a population that was becoming more and more interdependent meant an increase in the need for more food to maintain a constant scale of living, let alone to permit a higher scale. If more people were to have more food and better food, the quantity available for sale had to be increased. That increase was provided, in part, by the people who moved west and who cultivated new lands extensively for the first time, lands that were more fertile than those in the Eastern States. Another type of development occurred during that period which, in some respects, was even more spectacular than harnessing new lands. It was also less wasteful of natural resources than was extensive cultivation of the soil. More intensive utilization of arable farmlands was the answer, and its impacts were so far-reaching and its results so astounding that it has sometimes been described in terms of an agricultural revolution.[3] The revolutionary aspect of the development is found in the results of the *initial* application of new technologies, rather than in the technologies themselves.

Scientific Farming

The wastes of extensive cultivation of the soil were found in the continual planting of the same crop on the same acreage, a procedure that has been designated as *soil butchery*. By that process, the ingredients of the soil that contributed to the growth of healthy plant life were drained from the land. Nitrogen, phosphorus, potassium, as well as iron and other minerals, were returned to the soil through the use of natural fertilizers and, later, chemically prepared mixtures under the name of commercial fertilizers. Experiments in soil analysis were conducted in Yale, Columbia, and other universities, by which the chemical composition of soil samples was determined. It was also discovered which proportions of nitrogen, phosphorus, potassium, and iron in the soil produced the best all-around results. The use of fertilizers made obsolete the practice of fallowing land in order to restore its fertility and the rotation of crops was not only not exhaustive of soil resources, it actually restored them. Root crops and legumes—turnips, beets, carrots, parsnips, alfalfa, beans, lentils, and peas—were found to loosen the soil and to restore the all-important nitrogen to it.

At the same time that chemists were learning how to improve the soil, other experiments were being conducted on the feeding and breeding of livestock. Bulls, rams, stallions, and boars were imported from European countries, and conscious efforts were made to develop definite characteristics in animal life. Some cattle were bred to produce larger quantities of milk, some to produce more butterfat in their milk. Steers were bred to improve upon their size as well as upon the quality of beef. Breeding alone would not accomplish these results; they had to be accompanied by balanced feeding. Sheep were bred to produce more wool and wool of better quality, and they were fed to yield more and better mutton and lamb meat. The razorback hog was not much better eating than were scrub cattle; and hogs were bred for shorter legs and rounder bellies, as well as for a better quality of pork. Draft horses and mules were needed to replace the slow and deliberate oxen in the fields and on the roads. Horses for driving and for riding were also developed, and a line of horses was bred whose utility lay in speed rather than in strength. Horse racing became a sport as well as a business and a source of income to many persons. On the other hand, horse racing afforded an outlet for many persons who derived pleasure as well as a livelihood from operating gambling facilities.

[3] Earle D. Ross and Robert L. Tontz, "The Term 'Agricultural Revolution' as Used by Economic Historians," *Economic Change in America,* eds. Joseph T. Lambie and Richard V. Clemence (Harrisburg, Pa.: Stackpole Books, 1954), p. 304.

Farm Machinery

Farm tools that had been brought over from Europe and used in this country for many years were not improved upon to any great extent before the first quarter of the 19th century. Cradles, rakes, scythes, sickles, pitchforks, spades, hoes, shovels, and crude plowshares that were made of wood with iron strips fastened along their cutting edges by local blacksmiths— all were powered by hand except the plow. Oxen were better suited than horses to pulling the plow in breaking up the ground the first time. The iron plowshare was being used in England; but it would poison the soil, or so thought the conservative farmers in America.

In the 1830's, experiments were conducted privately in attempts to perfect reapers to do away with cradles; mowers to improve upon scythes; rakes, seed drills, harrows, cultivators, and plows that would operate as horse-drawn machinery. Except for the plow, the rake, and the harrow, the general idea of them all was that the power generated by the axle turning was transmitted to the machine. Rivalry between inventors was as keen as it was between those who attempted to improve upon them, once an idea had become a reality. The superiority of one make over another was established in contests that were held in different sections of the country. Robert McCormick invented his reaper in Virginia; and his son, Cyrus H., seized upon the invention of his father, added a few improvements to it, and promoted its sales in Kentucky, Illinois, and other Western States. Meanwhile, Obed Hussey was exploiting a similar machine in New York and other Eastern States. Performance tests gave a slight advantage to the McCormick reaper; and when McCormick moved his plant to Illinois, his machine soon outsold its rival. Horse-drawn farm machinery was a form of operating capital that was necessary for successful farming. It was an important factor that made possible the winning of the West to agriculture.

Farm machinery provided one of the principal outlets for the iron industry prior to 1860. Much of the capital that was required was native capital. It came from the savings of those (1) who were engaged in mercantile operations and (2) who were operating textile mills in Eastern States.

In measuring the progress of the American economy, those developments represent (1) the operation of free enterprise, (2) the creation of native capital, (3) overcoming the labor shortage by substituting capital (4) greater development of specialization and division of labor—industrial and geographical, and (5) increased interdependence of and between different specialized segments of the American economy. The ultimate impact of all of that development was to make larger profits which were used in purchasing more consumer goods and in saving more capital.

Agricultural Education

Of what good were these technological and scientific developments in agriculture if there were not some means of spreading the good news about them, about their uses and the results attained therefrom? The development of educational and communication facilities was the answer. Some vocational classes in agriculture were offered in secondary schools; and in 1857 the first four-year college devoted to the teaching of agriculture was established in Michigan—Michigan Agricultural and Mechanical College, which now is known as Michigan State University. In addition to organized classes, fairs— state and local—were held, possibly once a year, at which farmers exhibited their livestock, grains, and other products of their farms. Since many farmers had to be shown to be convinced of the pragmatic side of scientific agriculture, that was an effective device for directing their attention to the benefits that could be derived from it.

Some Sunday newspapers carried a column, later a page, still later a section, that was devoted to expounding the gospel of scientific farming in one or more of its applications. An agricultural press that was devoted to some specialized activity was in circulation. The *Country Gentleman* was a weekly publication that enjoyed a national circulation. Other magazines were more specialized in that they concentrated their interest in one area or phase of agriculture, such as poultry raising, the breeding of livestock, or to the development and use of animal feed.

The immediate impact of the forces of the agricultural revolution was not the same in the different sections of the country. The cotton planters and those who were engaged in growing sugarcane and rice could make little or no use of farm machinery that was designed to be applied to the growing, cultivating, and harvesting of cereal grains; neither did they use commercial fertilizers. The capital equipment of southern farmers consisted of land and slaves and little else. New England farms were too small and the growing season was too short to justify a capital investment in large-sized farm machinery, but horse-drawn equipment was found on all of them. Again, since New England farmers found it unprofitable to compete in the market with cereal grains grown in the West, such of those crops as they grew were used locally for feed. Hay was an important crop; but the fields were relatively small, rough, and uneven. Fertilizers were used, crops were rotated, and livestock was bred for the qualities or characteristics the farmers desired. Because of the long winter season in New England, farmers improved upon the feeding and care of their farm animals. It was in the West that the full impact of the agricultural revolution was felt. Here the fields were large and relatively flat. Horses were needed to furnish the draft power essential to the operation of machinery. The larger the farms, the more horses were needed, the more natural fertilizer was available, the more land was planted in feed crops. The importance of the latter item was not fully appreciated until after the close of the first World War. By far the heaviest impact of improved techniques in agriculture was found in the reduction in the number of man-hours required to produce corn and wheat and cotton, each, on an acre of ground. The estimated yield per acre showed no change between 1820 and

1840, and in the production of cotton only was there an increase yield per acre by 1880. The principal effects of more enlightened agricultural techniques were (1) to permit the cultivation of vastly increased acreage and (2) to prevent a decrease in output per acre because of the operation of *diminishing returns.*

QUESTIONS FOR REVIEW

1. (a) Describe the pattern of the westward movement up to 1860.
(b) How did the mining frontier differ from the traditional pattern of frontier settlement?

2. Explain Henry Clay's American System.

3. Explain the migratory movement of peoples that may have stimulated our population increase.

4. What economic factors tended to cause an urbanization movement?

5. How did the opening of the Erie Canal affect agricultural development in the East? in the West? Explain.

6. (a) What was the agricultural revolution?
(b) What were the different phases or aspects of that revolution?

7. Did the impact of the agricultural revolution fall equally on all sections of the country? Why? Or why not?

SUGGESTED READINGS

Bogart, E. L., and C. M. Thompson. *Readings in the Economic History of the United States.* New York City: Longmans, Green and Co., Inc., 1916. Chapters 14 and 16.

Callender, Guy S. *Selections from the Economic History of the United States, 1765-1860.* New York City: Augustus M. Kelley, Publishers, 1965. Chapters 12 and 13.

Gates, Paul W. *The Farmer's Age, 1815-1860.* New York City: Holt, Rinehart & Winston, Inc., 1960.

Gates, Paul W. "The Role of the Land Speculator in Western Development," *Issues in American Economic History*, edited by Gerald D. Nash. Boston: D. C. Heath & Company, 1964.

Goodrich, Carter. "American Development Policy: The Case of Internal Improvements," *American Economic History: Essays in Interpretation*, edited by Stanley Coben and Forest G. Hill. Philadelphia: J. B. Lippincott Co., 1966.

Hacker, Louis M. *Major Documents in American Economic History*. Princeton, N. J.: D. Van Nostrand Co., Inc., 1961. Volume I. Selections 9 and 12.

Letwin, William (ed.). "Internal Improvements," *A Documentary History of American Economic Policy Since 1789*. Chicago: Aldine Publishing Co., 1962.

Ross, Earle D., and Robert L. Tontz. "The Term 'Agricultural Revolution' As Used by Economic Historians," *Economic Change in America*, edited by Joseph T. Lambie and Richard V. Clemence. Harrisburg, Pa.: Stackpole Books, 1954.

Chapter 7

MONEY, BANKING, AND FINANCE

The economic advancement of a country is affected by the nature of its monetary system, its banking structure, and the financial institutions that make short- and long-term credit available to businessmen. The risk of business enterprise, which normally would be borne by businessmen, can be shifted in part to insurance companies. Both fire insurance companies and life insurance companies perform a useful protective function through their assumption of risk and provide large sums of money that can be invested in land, mortgage bonds, and corporate securities.

THE MONETARY SYSTEM—1820-1860

The monetary system that this period inherited from that of 1792-1820 was anything but satisfactory. Homogeneity, convenience, and cognizability, all of which characteristics were essential to the general acceptability of money, were lacking in the metallic coins that were in circulation. "Chaotic" is mildly descriptive of the condition of the currency in 1816, only five short years since the stabilizing influence of the First Bank had been brought to a close. Bank notes prior to 1819 did not circulate at par. Langdon Cheves succeeded Commodore William Jones as President of the Bank of the United States in that year, and parity of circulation became a *fait accompli* for the notes of that bank. The legal ratio of 15 to 1 between silver and gold continued to overvalue silver so that only a small amount of gold money was in circulation. Silver coins that were comparable in value to the dollar were of French and Spanish mintage, but silver coins in value less than one dollar were coined in the United States and remained in circulation. Paper currency was in much greater abundance than was metallic money. Heterogeneous bank currencies circulated somewhat freely though they lacked uniformity of issue and parity of circulation.

Gold Overvalued

In an attempt to restore a balance between gold and silver money in circulation, Congress established a mint ratio of 16 to 1 in 1834. With a market ratio in the neighborhood of 15.6 to 1, gold was overvalued at the mint almost as much as the original ratio of 15 to 1 had overvalued silver. In response to the discovery of gold near Dahlonega, in north Georgia, and to the pull of the market for silver, silver coins soon disappeared from monetary usage and gold coins remained in circulation more or less permanently. To correct that situation, Congress altered the ratio again in 1837 to 15.988 to 1 by raising the fine gold content of the dollar to 23.22 grains. That ratio remained unchanged until 1934, although bimetallism was discontinued when the silver dollar was demonetized in 1873.

The overvaluation of gold at the mint, combined with the results of the discovery of gold in California in 1848, resulted in the coinage of more gold in the decade of the 1850's than during any previous 10-year period. In view of the reorganization of our monetary system in 1873, it is important that the reader keep in mind the fact that silver dollars virtually disappeared from circulation shortly after 1834.

The Subsidiary Coinage Act of 1853

Gold coins of small denomination had never been practical since they were too small in size to be convenient in handling. Coins of small denomination had always been minted from silver or other base metals. Disappearance of silver from monetary usage made it extremely difficult to complete exchanges in value other than those in even multiples of a dollar. Items that were priced for less than one dollar were difficult to obtain on a cash basis unless paper scrip or tokens were used. Foreign coins of low denomination were in demand to fill the void created by the disappearance of monetary silver. In order to make certain the continued circulation of fractional currency of American origin, Congress provided for the coinage of subsidiary coins in the Act of 1853, under the terms of which the silver content of 10, 25, and 50-cent pieces was reduced more than in proportion to their face value, so that there was less silver in each of ten dimes, four quarters, and two 50-cent pieces than there was in a silver dollar. These coins were given limited legal tender usage and were minted only on government account. They were not standard money, nor did they add any quality or characteristic to the monetary system other than convenience.

Paper Money

The Constitution of the United States forbade the state governments to issue paper money, but nothing was contained therein to prevent business firms—banks, railroads, schools, insurance companies, or industrial firms—from issuing circulating notes. Suffice it to say here that bank notes circulated in larger volume than did gold and silver money; and problems that were related to our monetary system, other than have been mentioned previously, arose out of the absence of uniform conditions under which bank notes were issued, circulated, and redeemed. Throughout most of the 20 years during which it operated, 1816-36, the Second Bank of the United States exercised a moderating influence upon the issuance and redemption of circulating notes that were issued by other institutions. Checks that were drawn against demand deposits were acceptable in settling monetary obligations in urban areas after about 1840, but their general usage was limited by the absence of communication facilities and of the means of establishing credit.

All of the developments that have been mentioned above had the effect of putting an end to the use of and the acceptance of foreign coins, and brought about the termination of the Colonial Period insofar as the use of money was concerned in the mid-1850's, when the Mexican dollar and the Spanish dollar were removed from legal tender status.

BANKING

The absence of a central bank proved to be such a handicap to the successful fiscal operations of the federal government that James Madison, who was President of the United States at the time, and who had been strongly opposed to extending the charter of the First Bank of the United States, selected a Secretary of the Treasury, Alexander Dallas, who would support his request to Congress to charter another central bank. Albert Gallatin, as Secretary of the Treasury, had been compelled to direct the fiscal operations of the federal government after 1811 without the benefit of a central bank. The issuance of bank note currency was under the control of state and private banks, and in the absence of effective controls, hand-to-hand currency was in a chaotic condition. Had the First Bank of the United States continued to function during the second war with England, resort to the issuance of Treasury notes might not have been necessary. The bank could have cooperated with the Treasury Department in financing the war program. Even though the war did not last long, its impact on the American economy was felt in many ways; and by 1816 the road to reconversion was made rougher by the absence of a central bank. Consequently, Congress chartered the Second Bank of the United States for a 20-year term that expired in 1836.

The Second Bank of the United States

In its organization and functions, the Second Bank of the United States resembled the prior bank. It was capitalized at $35 million compared with $10 million for the first bank, 20 percent of which, or $7 million in stock, was owned by the United States Treasury. As was true of the first bank, the Treasury could not vote its shares and the bank must be considered to have been privately owned and operated. It had a total of 28 branches, 23 of which were in simultaneous operation. Twelve of its branches were located in the South and west of the Appalachian Mountains. For both banks, circulating notes outstanding were limited to their respective capitalizations. The increase in the capitalization of the second bank, which made possible an increase in the maximum volume of circulating notes, together with the increased number of branches and their locations, may be considered as measures of the progress of the westward movement and of the increase in internal trade and commerce, since the proceeds of bank loans were taken in the form of circulating notes.

Functions. The functions of the second bank were to act as fiscal agent of the government and to regulate the bank note currency. It could deal in bills of exchange and in bullion. It was authorized to sell goods that had been pledged to secure loans that were in default, but it was not permitted to deal in public stock. Loans to the United States were limited to $500,000 at any given time, and to any state a maximum of $50,000 was effective. Its circulating notes of denominations under $100 were payable on demand and were legal tender in payments to the government. Up to 60 days notice could be required by the bank before redeeming notes of larger denomination. The bank was required to transmit public monies at par, and no charge could be made for that service. The Treasurer of the United States was authorized to deposit government funds in the bank. Upon occasion when he might do otherwise, he was required to report his reasons to Congress.

Difficult Years. As a commercial bank, the second bank operated in competition with state and private banks, whose officers and stockholders objected to that level of competition. The states of Maryland and Ohio attempted to levy taxes upon the operation of branch offices that were located in those respective states. Success in these efforts would have forced the branches to close; but in the case of *McCulloch* v. *Maryland* and again in *Osborn* v. *The Bank of the United States*, the Supreme Court of the United States upheld the constitutionality of the bank and ruled it to be exempt from state levy. Under the leadership of William Jones, who had been Secretary of the Treasury and earlier a naval officer, the bank got off to a miserable start. The Baltimore Branch engaged in some of the very practices the bank was organized to prevent, and the first three years of its operations were stormy ones.

To set the bank aright, Langdon Cheves, of South Carolina, was designated to succeed Jones and in three years restored the bank to a sound footing. While Cheves was a lawyer rather than a banker, he applied principles and practices that are accepted today by the members of the banking profession. He limited loans to the commercial type, with a maximum of 90 days maturity; and when they matured, the loans were to be retired and not renewed indefinitely. Collateral was exacted of borrowers in granting requests for loans; and the bank was required to maintain a cash reserve equal to one third of its demand obligations, most of which were in the form of circulating notes.

Speculators in public lands were opposed to Cheves' credit policies which made it more difficult to borrow from the Bank of the United States in financing their purchases. Pressure from that quarter, combined with the

fact of failing health and disagreement with his state over the right of states
to take separate action, led to Cheves' resignation in 1823. Nicholas Biddle,
of Pennsylvania, was appointed to lead the bank throughout the remainder
of its years of service. Biddle was an advocate of strong central banking
policies, policies which did not conform to political expediency. His personality led him into public dispute with his opponents.

Henry Clay was in favor of the bank; Andrew Jackson was opposed to
it and for many of the very reasons that Biddle favored it. Jackson's struggle
for the nomination to become leader of his political party, later President
of the United States, hinged on the issue of renewing the bank's charter. He
took the position that through its control over credit, the bank would
dominate entire communities. Unfortunately for the bank, the Cincinnati
Branch was compelled to foreclose on numerous mortgages that served to
illustrate the position that Jackson had assumed. The situation in Cincinnati
was somewhat typical of the control that Jackson feared:

> As a consequence of the transfer of real estate the bank owned a
> large part of Cincinnati: hotels, coffeehouses, warehouses, stores, stables,
> iron foundries, residences, vacant lots; besides over 50,000 acres of
> good farmland in Ohio and Kentucky. Its possession of this vast prop-
> erty maddened the former owners, now impoverished by a recklessness
> which they would not acknowledge . . . . Moreover, the situation gave
> to the politicians an opportunity too tempting to be neglected, and by
> a slight effort of the imagination one can almost hear the reverberations
> of "Old Bullion" Benton's voice startling the drowsy Senate as he
> thunders: "I know towns, yea, cities where this bank already appears
> as an engrossing proprietor. All the flourishing cities of the West are
> mortgaged to this money power. They may be devoured by it at any
> moment. They are in the jaws of the monster. A lump of butter in the
> mouth of a dog. One gulp, one swallow, and all is gone." [1]

Another of Jackson's objections to the bank was that it could be used
for political purposes; and when one or two of the presidents of branch
offices campaigned in their own right against him, they threw the bank
open to criticism in that respect even though they were careful to explain
that they were speaking as free men, not as representing any financial institution. In accordance with the terminology of modern usage, Jackson interpreted the results of the election of 1832 as a mandate to destroy the power
of the bank, which he proceeded to do before its charter expired. After he
found a Secretary of the Treasury who would deposit federal monies in
banks that were chartered by the several states, and which have come to be
known as Jackson's "pet banks," he continued to draw warrants upon the
bank in payment of government obligations. That man was Roger B. Taney,
who later became Chief Justice of the United States Supreme Court. He is
better known for his decision in the Dred Scott case. In that way Jackson

[1] C. H. Catterall, *The Second Bank of the United States* (Chicago: University of
Chicago Press, 1903), p. 67.

broke the power of the bank before its charter expired. In 1836 the bank was chartered by the state of Pennsylvania, and Nicholas Biddle continued to be its president. In fairness to Jackson, the "pet banks" were selected with a great deal of care, and conditions were imposed upon them that tended to protect government deposits. By November, 1836, over 80 such banks held government deposits that totaled just under $50 million.

Intolerable price inflation caused by persons speculating in public lands led to President Jackson's issuing his famous *Specie Circular.* Under the terms of that decree all payments to the government on the public land account had to be made in specie. A heavy withdrawal of gold from eastern banks followed. The Bank of the United States had become undermined by the withdrawal of government deposits from its vaults and was powerless to halt inflation. When specie payments were suspended by the banks, panic conditions swept the country.

The Independent Treasury

During the years of panic and depression of 1837-41, the United States lost heavily by the closing of state banks. Many of these losses, however, were not permanent, as the Treasury Department was a preferred creditor of the banks. Deposits in state banks that failed were made good with the exception of approximately $1 million, but the delay and ultimate losses were embarrassing to the Treasury to say the least. Since a movement in Congress to charter another central bank was vetoed by President Tyler, an Independent Treasury was established permanently in 1846. This was primarily an institution for the safekeeping of government deposits. It was not a bank, but the impacts of its operations were felt by the banks in the movement of currency to and from the Treasury. This movement was governed by the volume of taxes and customs duties collected in relation to the volume of governmental expenditures. The awkwardness of this situation to the banks and to the business community grew out of the fact that the receipts and expenditures bore little or no relation to the needs of private businessmen for money, but were solely dependent upon the fiscal operations of the federal government. The Independent Treasury was a warehouse for the storage of government monies until they were needed. These monies did not earn interest, nor did they enter into the reserves in support of demand obligations of the banks. While the Independent Treasury continued to function until 1920, national banks, later Federal Reserve Banks, were designated as depositories for government funds.

State Banking Developments

In the absence of an agency that could exercise control over banking operations, including the conditions under which circulating notes were issued, many people who wanted to get rich quickly laid aside their moral and ethical standards and began to print paper money which was similar to bank notes and which was often spurious. Some of these notes were issued by state banks, others by private corporations including railroads and insurance companies.

The Suffolk Banking System. Merchants of Boston, as well as banks, suffered losses because they accepted from their customers circulating notes which could not be redeemed at their places of issue. Under the leadership of the Suffolk Bank, a voluntary arrangement was made in 1818 under the terms of which the Suffolk Bank agreed to accept at par notes of other banks that maintained a redemption fund with it. Notes of other banks were accepted for collection only. In a comparatively short time, circulating notes that were issued by the banks in Massachusetts were accepted at par. That informal organization was really the first one to show the economic effects of the ready redeemability of circulating notes.

George Smith's Money. One of the more successful experiences in issuing circulating notes, in support of which there was little or no tangible security, was that of a company of which one George Smith was the principal owner. Smith had migrated to this country from Scotland and invested heavily in Chicago real estate. When he foresaw the coming of the panic of 1837, he sold his interests at a large profit and returned to Scotland. When payments on his land were in default, he returned to this country accompanied by Alexander Mitchell and a man named Scott. Together, they organized the Wisconsin Fire and Marine Insurance Company and began to issue certificates of deposit in small denominations. When the Illinois State Legislature outlawed the issuance of circulating notes of small denominations, Smith was instrumental in moving the company to Wisconsin, hence the corporate name. Since its charter forbade the issuance of paper money as such, it issued certificates of deposit which were similar to bank notes. These certificates enjoyed a wide acceptance from Buffalo to St. Louis and from Cincinnati to Detroit. They constituted the most prevalent form of "money" in Chicago and the Northwest. Two years after its charter was issued in 1838, certificates amounting to $4,819 were in circulation. When Smith sold his interest in the company in 1852, their value amounted to $1,470,000. Smith's severance of ownership of the company was due to the passage of a law by the legislature of Wisconsin that required a deposit of collateral with the State Banking Department to secure the ready redemption of circulating notes. To Smith, character was more important than collateral in providing ready redemption of notes, and it was ability to redeem all of his notes on demand even under the most challenging circumstances that caused them to circulate at par.

The New York Safety Fund System. New York passed a safety fund law in 1829 under the terms of which notes could be issued by banks in amounts not in excess of twice their capital. Each bank was assessed an annual fee of one half of 1 percent of its capital until 3 percent of its capital had been contributed. In cases of depletion of the safety fund, banks were subject to additional annual assessments of not more than one half of 1 percent of their capital. A few years later the maximum volume of the notes outstanding for one bank was limited to its capital, or to some multiple thereof. As the fund was used in meeting all of the demand obligations of banks that were in default, the remaining banks were forced to renew their one half of 1 percent annual contributions. Because of the banking crisis in 1837, no new banks were admitted to the system after 1838. Instead of having a salutary effect on bankers and banking practices, the safety fund caused some bankers to become careless and indifferent to their responsibilities because the system would take care of its creditors. To the extent that banks actually became unable to meet their demand obligations, their creditors did look to the system for payments. That system was strictly a guarantee plan at the state level and was in no way an insurance plan. The plan established a questionable precedent of having failed to provide effective deposit guarantee at the state level. However, it did make a contribution to effective control of commercial banking by authorizing quarterly examinations by three commissioners of banking. That was a decided improvement over the provisions governing the Second Bank of the United States under which the bank was subject to periodic examinations by an agent of the Secretary of the Treasury.

The New York Free Banking Act. The New York Free Banking Act of 1838 was important not only for its own provisions, but for the pattern it established for other states and for the federal government to follow. Not only did it provide for the general incorporation of banks by any group of persons who complied with the law, thus breaking up monopoly privileges in banking, it also provided for a bond secured bank note currency. Banks were permitted to issue notes upon the purchase and deposit of eligible bonds with the state banking agency. Bonds eligible to secure bank note circulation were those of the United States and of the states that were contiguous to New York, railroad bonds, utility bonds, and those of designated industries. The notes that were secured by those bonds lacked elasticity— the ability to expand and to contract in volume according to the needs of business—but they were safe and they circulated at par. In order to contribute to the stabilization of price levels, it was essential that bank note issues did not contribute to variations in the value of money. When the National Bank Act was passed by the Congress of the United States 25 years later, it likewise provided for the general incorporation of national banks and for a bond secured currency, although it defined eligibility to secure notes in different terms.

The Louisiana Banking Act of 1842. What may have been the outstanding example of state regulation of commercial banking prior to 1860 was the outgrowth of bank failures in New Orleans in 1837 and again in 1839 when local banks attempted to resume specie payments. Baring Brothers of London had a branch office in New Orleans, which, along with other banks in that city, financed a large volume of the cotton business. It was through that office of Baring Brothers that the financing of cotton was given an international flavor. Cotton was the most important product, not only of Louisiana, but of the entire South. Determined to take steps to prevent another wave of bank failures, the Louisiana State Legislature in 1842 passed an act that has come to be looked upon as a model of state banking legislation. It established banking in that state upon a sound footing by requiring (1) that the banks maintain a specie reserve equal to one third of their demand obligations; (2) that the banks maintain a deposit of collateral equal to two thirds of each commercial loan; (3) that the banks' commercial loans be restricted to maturities of 30, 60, and 90 days and that the loans be paid on their maturity dates, in order to apply the test of liquidity to them; (4) that the banks' directors be held responsible for losses and that they could not plead absence from a directors' meeting to escape liability, except in case of bona fide illness, or absence from the state on business.

Branch Banking. To fill the void in the performance of central banking functions and control that was created by the closing of the Second Bank of the United States in 1836, the states of Indiana, Iowa, and Ohio developed systems of statewide branch banking. Bank note currency continued to be the principal demand obligation of commercial banks, although after 1840 bank deposits subject to check were used in greater volume in urban areas and in the transaction of strictly local business. Transportation and communication facilities were too slow, too unreliable, and too infrequent to lend encouragement to the use of checks in intercity transactions. In terms of one-way travel from New York, Philadelphia was one day, Boston was over one day, Buffalo and Pittsburgh four days, Cincinnati one week, Detroit and St. Louis a little less than two weeks, and Chicago a little less than three weeks. New Orleans was two weeks distant from New York.

Branch banking in these three states did not follow the same pattern of organization and operation, but each one provided for the ready redemption of circulating notes in specie. Examinations of branch offices were provided, and a central voice was heard in formulating the credit policies of the branch offices. Indiana was the first state to prevent a return to *wildcat banking* after the close of the Second Bank of the United States, and in 1837 chartered a branch banking system for 20 years. That term was decided upon as one throughout which branch banking would be given a thorough trial and after which revisions could be introduced in a new charter in accordance with the development and demands of commerce, finance, and banking. A second bank of the state of Indiana was chartered in 1857, but the federal tax on the issues of state banks led to its ineffectiveness as a stabilizing factor in the issuance of circulating notes.

Other states were quick to authorize the establishment of state banks, some of which were sound, many of which were unsound. The test of soundness as applied to these banks was that of having been able to redeem their circulating notes on demand and in specie. Students who are interested in the development of commercial banking in states other than those mentioned here may obtain detailed information by turning to the reports of the state banking agencies.

FINANCE

Internal improvements were looked upon as quasi-governmental functions; and many canals, railroads, and highways were planned. The federal government lent money through the medium of purchasing bonds of states or municipalities in order to stimulate construction activity. Probably the first action to relieve a depression was the purchase of government bonds by the Treasury in order to put money in circulation after the panic of 1837.

Sources of Federal Revenue

Throughout the entire period under survey, the sources of revenue at the federal level were (1) receipts from the sale of public lands and (2) the collection of customs duties on imported products. The receipts from neither one of these sources could be adjusted to the governmental need for revenue as determined by the cost of operating the government in its several facets, nor could they be foretold with any degree of accuracy. Strange as it may seem to the reader in this day of Treasury deficits, between the years 1816 and 1860 inclusive there were 30 years of Treasury surplus and only 14 years of Treasury deficit. The year in which the largest surplus occurred was 1836 when it amounted to $19,959,000. Sales of public lands contributed more of the surplus than did customs receipts. The year of the largest Treasury deficit—$30,785,000—was 1847, and it reflected the increased spendings by the War Department in the expectation of overt action against Mexico.

Since tariffs form some of the subject matter of Chapter 9, they will be recognized here only as being unreliable sources of revenue. As far as revenues were concerned, tariff receipts seemed to depend as much on the value of imported products subject to levy as upon the size of the rate; and it is difficult to discern from the collections when changes in tariff rates were made, and if they were raised or lowered. Economic conditions in other countries, particularly those of western Europe, had about as much influence upon the nature of and the volume of our commodity trade as did internal factors. Neither did the level of tariff rates have much impact upon the degree of economic prosperity of the United States. The decade of the 1820's was an extremely prosperous one, and high protective tariff rates were in force. The 10-year period, 1846-56, likewise was one of a high degree of prosperity. The Walker Tariff of 1846, rightly classed as a low tariff, or one that was levied more for the purpose of raising revenue than to afford protection to American industries, exercised its influence through-

Table 7-1

Receipts, Expenditures, Public Debt of the Federal Government for Selected Years 1816-1860 (000)

Year	Receipts	Expenditures	Public Debt
1816	47,678	30,587	127,335
1820	17,881	18,261	91,016
1825	21,841	15,857	83,788
1830	24,844	15,143	48,565
1835	35,430	17,573	38
1836	50,827	30,868	38
1840	19,480	24,318	3,573
1845	29,970	22,937	15,925
1847	26,496	57,281	38,827
1850	43,603	39,543	63,453
1855	65,351	59,743	35,588
1860	56,065	63,131	64,844

Source: U. S. Department of Commerce, Bureau of the Census, *Historical Statistics of the United States. Colonial Times to 1957* (Washington: U. S. Government Printing Office, 1960), pp. 712, 719, 721. Adapted.

out this period. It is true that the ten years following the passage of the Compromise Tariff of 1833 were years of economic unrest and financial disturbance, but the reasons therefor were exogenous to the tariff.

Distribution of the Federal Treasury Surplus

Treasury surpluses were applied to reducing the size of the federal debt, which by 1836 had become practically extinct. That was the occasion for one of the most unusual actions ever taken by the Treasury: namely, to deposit the surplus with the states to be used by them in the financing of internal improvements, such as building roads and the construction of public buildings, libraries, and schools. Distribution of the surplus was made in proportion to population, which resulted in the states along the Atlantic seaboard receiving more than those west of the Appalachian Mountains. Most of the reserves of the United States Bank were in the western branches where they were being used to finance the sale of public lands and to make possible speculation in land. The distribution resulted in a physical transfer of funds to banks in the Eastern States, much to the dismay and chagrin of borrowers from western commercial banks and leading to the financial disorganization of these borrowers. After three fourths of the distribution had been effected, in the amount of a little over $28 million, the panic of 1837 put an end to the completion of that program. The surplus was *deposited* with the states, since there was no other channel under the terms of the Constitution of the United States under which such a distribution of funds could have been made. Senator Thomas Hart Benton, of Missouri, described the action in these words, "It is in name a deposit; in form a loan; in essential design a distribution." The Treasury has not been reimbursed by any of the states that were beneficiaries of these loans, and this fact is verified in the books of the Treasury which continue to carry the designation of unavailable funds. Many years later, Virginia laid claim to its share of the fourth installment in the amount of $732,809, but the Supreme Court ruled that the Treasury Department did not obligate itself when it deposited monies temporarily with the states.

Government in Relation to Business

That the federal government was not participating in economic activity, regulating it, or rendering services directly, is made manifest by a study of Table 7-2 on civilian employment. Including the executive, legislative, and judicial branches of government, there were only 36,672 civilian employees in 1861. The increase from 6,914 in 1821 is not a measure of government participation in economic activity. In addition to the size of the payroll, it shows that compared with the number of civilians on the government payroll in 1821, the number had increased over fivefold.

Table 7-2
Paid Civilian Employment of the Federal Government

Year	Total Employees	Executive Branch				Legislative Branch Total	Judicial Branch Total
		Total	Defense	Post Office	Other		
1816	4,837	4,479	109	3,341	948	243	115
1821	6,914	6,526	161	4,766	1,599	252	136
1831	11,491	11,067	377	8,764	1,926	289	135
1841	18,038	17,550	598	14,290	2,662	332	156
1851	26,274	25,713	403	21,391	3,919	384	177
1861	36,672	36,106	946	30,269	4,891	393	173

Source: *Historical Statistics of the United States. Colonial Times to 1957,* 1960, p. 710. Adapted.

Internal Improvements. In connection with the disposal of public lands, the interest of the government in education and in building roads has been mentioned; but no taxes were collected to finance either type of activity. The War Department was given the responsibility of constructing the Cumberland Road which started at Cumberland, Maryland, and passed through Wheeling, Virginia (it was then); Columbus, Zanesville, and Springfield, Ohio; Richmond, Indianapolis, and Terre Haute, Indiana; and on to Vandalia, Illinois, which city was reached in 1852. The reader will recognize that route as Highway 40. It was built for service, not for speed. It was paved with brick, and it followed rather closely the contour of the terrain over which it passed. Just west of Zanesville are two feats of engineering construction and design that are interesting. One is a Y bridge, in which the Y branches over the middle of the river; the other is an S bridge, the base of which is stone. The former is still in use, but the S bridge has been by-passed in the interests of speed and of safety; however, it has been preserved as an historic reminder of construction techniques and design of years gone by.

Distances between farms and local markets were longer in the West than they were in the East, and the market for cereal grains and for lumber products was in the East. Transportation was of prime importance in the development of the West, and it was there that public improvements were given the most attention. Public improvements were not only those that would be used by the public but those whose benefits would extend to the entire community, directly or indirectly, such as turnpikes and canals, and which, in turn, would promote settlement and the location of business activity. Not only were the costs of constructing public improvements larger than could be paid for out of ordinary tax receipts, but the feeling prevailed that their use could and would provide the means of servicing loans, the proceeds of which met immediate financial requirements. Tolls were collected from those who used the facilities. Toll schedules for turnpikes were not uniform. Rates were adjusted to the width of the tread of the wheels of wagons and of carriages, and the levy on wagons usually was larger than the levy on carriages. Two-horse teams were used to pull heavier loads than were pulled by one horse and caused more wear and tear on dirt and gravel roads. In general, wagons that were being used in conducting agricultural activities were not subject to paying tolls.

After 1830 competition in the construction of canals, turnpikes, and railroads led to the flotation of bonds to the amount of over $200 million, divided unequally between state, local, and federal governments in ratios of 11 to 1⅓ and 1 respectively. Following the successful operation of the Erie Canal, Pennsylvania and Maryland and municipalities therein became active in sponsoring public improvements, not because of the need for them, but rather to gain or to maintain prestige, prominence, and leadership in trade and travel between the East and the West. Revenues from the use of improvements were to be used in meeting interest payments on loans and ultimately to retire the principal sums when due. Toll receipts turned out to be entirely inadequate for those purposes, and delay and default in payments aggravated the feeling of uncertainty concerning the financial stability of the country.

Financing at the State Level. Activity at the state level was more spec-tacular in its impact on the American economy than it was at the federal level. The prevailing method by which the projects were financed was the issuance of bonds. Since the collection of tolls was relied upon to retire them, no new taxes were levied for that purpose. Canals, and later railroads, were constructed for competitive reasons and not because the volume of traffic justified them. Consequently, bonds were overissued by many states and were in default for many years. Repudiation by the states of Florida and Mississippi were brought to mind after World War I when England wanted to use those amounts to offset her obligations to the United States. The assumption of state debts by the federal government shortly after the War of the Revolution did not establish a precedent, and England's efforts in that direction came to naught.

While the financing of internal improvements was somewhat more spectacular, states and municipalities levied taxes for the purpose of raising revenue to enable them to perform their more ordinary functions. Probably the most significant activity entered into by some states, regulated by still others, was banking.

> From the facts which this table [page 174] displays, it appears that the cotton and tobacco-growing states expressed a decided preference for public banking, while the grain and metal-bearing states favored the building of canals and railroads. One may not, however, on this account, conclude that public sentiment in the North respecting banking questions was more highly educated than in the South, for the fact is that during this period the people of the North were provided with all the paper money they could desire. The Southern States did not so strongly feel the need of railroads and canals, for the nature of their produce, and the character of their industrial society, did not suggest the necessity of rapid inland communication. They regarded it as much more desirable to furnish the planter with 'capital' for the adoption of better methods in the culture of cotton, and to this end they established banks, or guaranteed the payment of notes issued by private associations. On the other hand, the great majority of the Northern States seems to have been completely mastered by the enthusiasm for public improvements. New York led the way by building the Erie Canal, and Pennsylvania and Maryland quickly followed, in order to protect their local interests. The lake states also, desiring to avail themselves of the benefits arising from direct communication with the Atlantic seaboard, and to open all parts of their territory to rapid settlement, adopted a similar policy. Other states, as for example, Kentucky and Tennessee, having no need for either cotton, banks, or canals, but influenced by the general enthusiasm for public improvements, set about building turnpikes and toll roads.[2]

Local Finance. Settlement of the West accentuated certain aspects of economic development that had been existent in the Eastern States where population was more dense and where distances between one urban center and another, between farmhouses and urban centers, and between one farmhouse and another were shorter. Roads had been built in the country; streets

[2] Charles J. Bullock, *Selected Readings in Public Finance* (Boston: Ginn and Company, 1920), pp. 889-90.

Table 7-3

Amount of State Debts in 1842 and the
Purposes for Which It Was Created

States and Territories	Internal and Public Improvements	Banking	Other	Total
New England (Massachusetts, Maine)	$ 4,105,000	....	$ 3,053,998	$ 7,158,998
Atlantic Coast (New York, Pennsylvania, Maryland, Virginia, South Carolina, Georgia)	77,865,162	595,811	8,882,390	87,343,363
Southern States (Louisiana, Alabama, Arkansas, Kentucky, Tennessee, Mississippi)	5,433,166	47,272,000	2,585,000	55,344,666
Midwest (Ohio, Indiana, Illinois, Michigan, Missouri)	38,436,417	4,424,259	745,000	43,655,676
Florida Territory	....	3,900,000	100,000	4,000,000
District of Columbia	....	....	1,316,030	1,316,030
TOTALS	$125,839,745	$56,192,070	$16,682,418	$198,818,733

Source: Charles J. Bullock, *Selected Readings in Public Finance* (Boston: Ginn and Company, 1920), p. 889. Adapted.

had been laid out in the cities. Counties and states were responsible for maintaining the roads; streets were maintained by the cities. Cities provided fire and police protection, but the farmer had no such organized protection upon which to depend. Sewers, storm and sanitary, were found in some urban areas; cesspools were used in others. Running water had been piped to town pumps; some houses and taverns provided the luxury of running water for their residents, though pumps in the kitchens or on back porches were used to raise water from cisterns or wells. Streets were lighted with oil burning lamps, and young boys were employed to light them every evening at dusk. Garbage collection was also a municipal function.

Schools were maintained by both cities and counties, and some states were supporting colleges. Teachers' salaries at any level of education were low, and unmarried teachers often boarded with patrons of the schools in which they taught. Hospitals were provided by both states and municipalities, though there was little or no duplication of services rendered. Hospitals for the mentally ill were operated by the states. Prisons were maintained at all three levels of government, and here again there was little duplication or overlapping of services. Counties maintained homes for the care of the poor and of the aged when there were no children or near of kin to shoulder this responsibility.

Enough has been said to point out the need for revenues at state, county, and local levels of government. Commutation of services for taxes was resorted to by farmers in many states, especially in New England. They had more time and equipment with which to work than money with which to pay taxes; and three days, more or less, per month working for the state or for the county was not burdensome. In northern climes, farmers were assigned certain sections of roads to keep open after snowfalls.

The General Property Tax. The general property tax was used by states, counties, and by local governments; and its burden fell somewhat equitably on taxpayers because most of their possessions were in the form of real estate or personalty that could not be hidden from tax assessors. That was the sole source of tax revenue to many states. The costs of maintaining the executive, judicial, and legislative functions were not burdensome; and militias were called out infrequently. Hospitals, charitable organizations, education, and the building and maintenance of roads were financed at the county level from the proceeds of the general property tax. In some states that tax was collected in the sheriff's office at no extra expense to the county organization. It was difficult for a taxpayer to evade it, unless by the device of relative undervaluation. Problems of assessment were relatively simple to solve as most of the property that was subject to taxation was not only tangible in character, but its value was comparatively easy to determine.

Municipalities used the general property tax as a means of having almost all of their citizens contribute to the support of local government. In addition, business license and occupation taxes brought in revenue from those who were utilizing municipal services and privileges in earning their livelihood. Special assessments were levied against real property to pay for improvements such as street paving, sidewalks, sewers—sanitary and storm—and the laying of water mains when providing water was a municipal function. Special assessments were justified on the grounds that those improvements enhanced the value of the abutting real property.

Panic and Despair

The panic of 1837 was the culmination of several developments or events, no one of which alone would or could have caused such a disturbance.

As is true of all panics, it was to a certain extent a state of mind—a state of mind regarding the ability of debtors to meet their financial obligations to their creditors. The bitter struggle between the President of the United States, Andrew Jackson, and the President of the Bank of the United States, Nicholas Biddle, over the very existence of the bank, shattered the confidence of people in banking institutions. That struggle terminated not only in the failure of the Congress to renew its charter, but in the weakening of its influence on the stability in the value of circulating notes after 1832 when Jackson's pet banks were favored with government deposits. The impact of Jackson's *Specie Circular* was more than the economy of the Western States could shoulder gracefully, so engrossed was so large a portion of its population in speculation in land and in public improvements. If people themselves were not participating in speculation, they were affected by the activities of those who were so engaged. Not only were commodity prices stimulated; but rents, interest, and wages likewise were inflated by the speculative mania. When the banking structure began to totter, rents started to come down, unemployment was on the increase, and wages fell. Default on public improvement bonds served only to fan the fire of failing faith in the soundness of a credit structure that had begun to crumble. That the crisis was not peculiar to the United States was manifest by the drop in the price of cotton in the London market. That made it difficult for the cotton planters in the South to pay their operating expenses, let alone to service their loans. Land values tumbled, as did the value of slaves. Banks, which had been financed in whole or in part by the issuance of bonds by some of the states, failed. Their circulating notes depreciated rapidly, which added to the confusion and to the financial losses in the South. Banks in New Orleans that had been financing not only much of the cotton that passed through that port, but that which was grown in Louisiana, were unable to withstand the pressure for specie and had to close their doors. That action threw the entire economy of New Orleans and of the state of Louisiana into a state of excitement and confusion. The banks in New Orleans were among the first to reopen their doors after the first phase of the panic. The pressure on their gold reserves was more than the banks could withstand, and they were forced to suspend specie payments again in 1839. The efforts of the State Legislature to prevent similar catastrophes in the future led to the passage of the Louisiana Banking Act of 1842.

Another factor that shook the confidence of creditors in their debtors' ability to meet their obligations was Old Man Weather, who engineered a crop failure. Since agriculture provided the principal commodity exports, this failure created an unfavorable trade balance and another demand for specie with which to pay for commodity imports.

On the material side, crop failures meant no shipments of grains; no shipments of grains meant idleness for railroad equipment, including labor, idleness for longshoremen and for the crews of oceangoing vessels. Unemployment in these segments of our economy added to the idleness of workers in domestic industries to make the coverage of the panic and of the depression more complete.

The panic of 1837 was the most severe one in over 50 years of constitutional government, not alone because every bank in the country suspended specie payments and bank note circulation dropped to one third of its amount in the six years preceding the break in 1837, but because of the business depression that ensued. Bank deposits were not a factor in this upheaval because they had not yet come into general use. The proceeds of commercial loans were still being taken in the form of bank notes. The change in the mint ratio of silver to gold that overvalued gold did little to provide specie. Gold had not yet been discovered in California and the deposits in Lumpkin County, Georgia, near Dahlonega, yielded only a limited amount of the metal. Unfavorable trade balances operated against a flow of gold to the United States mint; and it was not until 1842 that industrial activity absorbed most of the unemployed, banks were able to remain on a specie paying basis, and confidence in the integrity and soundness of our economic system had been restored.

Other Financial Institutions

The issuance of bonds by governmental units, later stocks and bonds by corporate firms, gave rise to the formation of organized security markets. It was in the use of those markets that much of the speculative activity of the 1930's, later of the 1950's, was carried on. In addition to the bonds of federal, state, and local governments, stocks and bonds of railroads, insurance companies, banks, gas and coal companies, and stocks of insurance companies commanded the attention of investors, speculators, and gamblers. In Boston, the securities of textile and of copper mining companies were prominent.

The principle of insurance, whereby uncertain, individual financial risks were transferred to groups and thus made certain, had been accepted during the Colonial Period. After the great fire in New York in 1835, many of the local insurance mutual organizations broadened their territorial coverages in order to permit the law of averages to function with greater accuracy.

Farmers' mutuals appeared about 1820; factory mutuals 15 years later. Marine insurance had long been accepted, but life insurance was still in its infancy in 1860.

QUESTIONS FOR REVIEW

1. (a) Describe the monetary system as it was constituted in 1816. How do you account for its characteristics?
   (b) What alterations were made in our monetary system between 1816 and 1865? What were the impacts of those alterations on our monetary system? Explain.
2. (a) Why was the Subsidiary Coinage Act of 1853 passed?
   (b) Did the results of the Subsidiary Coinage Act justify its passage? Explain.

3. What conditions gave rise to the formation of insurance companies?

4. (a) What was the Independent Treasury System?
   (b) What were some of the impacts of that system?

5. (a) What was the Suffolk Banking System?
   (b) What lessons were taught by the operation of that system?

6. What position in the development of banking does the Louisiana Banking Act of 1842 occupy? Explain.

7. Why was the general property tax more equitable prior to 1860 than it has become since that time?

8. How did the development of the corporate form of business organization give rise to speculation?

SUGGESTED READINGS

Callender, Guy S. *Selections from the Economic History of the United States, 1765-1860.* New York City: Augustus M. Kelley, Publishers, 1965. Chapter 11.

Gerrish, Catherine B. "Public Finance and Fiscal Policy, 1789-1865," *The Growth of the American Economy,* 2d ed., edited by Harold F. Williamson. New York City: Prentice-Hall, Inc., 1951.

Hammond, Bray. "Historical Introduction," *Economic Change in America,* edited by Joseph T. Lambie and Richard V. Clemence. Harrisburg, Pa.: Stackpole Books, 1954.

——————. "Jackson, Biddle, and the Bank of the United States," *American Economic History: Essays in Interpretation,* edited by Stanley Coben and Forest G. Hill. Philadelphia: J. B. Lippincott Co., 1966.

——————. "Public Policy and National Banks," *Issues in American Economic History,* edited by Gerald D. Nash. Boston: D. C. Heath & Company, 1964.

Hidy, Ralph W. "The Organization and Functions of Anglo-American Merchant Bankers, 1815-1860," *Economic Change in America,* edited by Joseph T. Lambie and Richard V. Clemence. Harrisburg, Pa.: Stackpole Books, 1954.

Johnson, E. A. J., and Herman E. Krooss. *The American Economy.* Englewood Cliffs, N. J.: Prentice-Hall, Inc., 1960. Chapter 10.

Schlesinger, Arthur M., Jr. "The Bank War," *Issues in American Economic History,* edited by Gerald D. Nash. Boston: D. C. Heath & Company, 1964.

Wright, Chester W. *Economic History of the United States,* 2d ed. New York City: McGraw-Hill Book Company, 1949. Chapters 24 and 25.

Chapter 8

TRANSPORTATION AND COMMUNICATION

In the 70-year period between 1789 and 1860, the westward movement of the frontier and the growth of both regional and national markets depended crucially on the means of transportation and communication available in the economy. The speed and efficiency of freight movement determined the types of goods that were distributed to consumers in newly settled areas, and at the same time influenced the levels of production in the supplying industries. Passenger transportation was necessary for the movement of business representatives, salesmen, and family members going to a new home. And it is obvious that the fastest means of transportation would be the fastest means of communication before electronic means of sending messages were devised. An understanding of the way in which our transportation systems developed is thus a key to many important economic changes.

ROADS AND HIGHWAYS

During the early national period, road and highway construction proceeded to keep pace with the movement of the frontier toward the Mississippi and the increasing density of settlement along the Eastern Seaboard. Less construction took place in the South than in the Middle States and New England, partly because of the rural nature of life in the region and partly because of the adequacy of natural waterways for much of the necessary transport of goods. In New England, however, communities embarked on a road-building program with almost feverish enthusiasm. By the close of the War of 1812, a network of roads and pikes traversed the area, varying in size and durability, but connecting dozens of towns and communities. Financing of the roads took place at both private and public levels, with townships bearing most of the costs of construction. Road lengths were normally much shorter than those found west of the Hudson River, and the high density of population spread the cost of construction over more persons. Some roads were built by free enterprise, the costs of which were recovered

by the collection of tolls. Companies were organized to furnish transportation
on schedule between two terminal cities in the East, and competition frequently appeared in the type of service rendered, rather than in rates.
Between any two given terminals, the routes of different companies varied
to a large extent, so that the principal competition appeared in rendering
through service rather than in serving local traffic. This situation prevailed
well into the era of railroad transportation.

Major Roads East of the Mississippi River

A number of wide and relatively clear roads were constructed in the
East before 1860. Running in a general east-west direction, they provided
easy access to the newly opened lands west of the Appalachian Mountains.
The Lancaster Turnpike, which extended west from Philadelphia to the
Susquehanna River, provided an artery for those who wanted to join the
westward movement, and they were legion. The Cumberland Road was the
first highway that was constructed with federal support. It connected Hagers-
town, Maryland, with Wheeling on the Ohio River, and afforded a direct
route to the West. Construction was begun in 1811, and six years elapsed
before it reached Wheeling. It was later completed to Vandalia, Illinois.

Another road, whose course lay entirely within the state of Kentucky,
but which was an important link in interstate traffic, was the Maysville
Road that wound its circuitous way from Maysville on the Ohio River to
Lexington in central Kentucky. This road was constructed in partial fulfillment of Henry Clay's plan for internal improvements, but it ran into the
stumbling block of an Andrew Jackson veto for the use of federal funds.
President Jackson's veto was based upon his belief that federal monies
should not be used in the construction of a highway that lay entirely in the
boundaries of one state. The fact that most of the goods transported over
that road came from Pittsburgh and points east, or were destined for those
markets, did not color his interpretation of the interstate commerce clause
of the United States Constitution. His action put an end to the development
of a road-building program at the federal level, and placed the burden for
financing the construction of roads upon the states. Under the circumstances,
it is not surprising that there was not only an absence of coordinated
highway-building programs at the state level, but that there were many
different approaches to solving the highway problem in the different states.

The first roads in frontier areas followed Indian trails or animal paths.
Since there was no road-making machinery available, constant travel was
relied upon to harden their surfaces. Where available, crushed rock or gravel
was used to make the roads more passable, especially in wet weather. In
some states north of the Ohio River and later in the Southwest, plank roads
were constructed through swamps, mires, depressions, and deep sand. Boards
and planks were cheap, and even though they were four inches thick, they
were quickly worn down by the constant pounding of hooves and the
passage of wagon wheels.

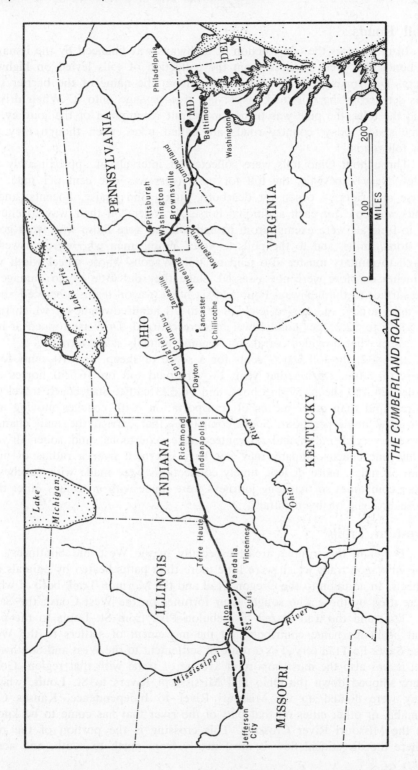

Toll Roads

In most cases the construction of highways was financed by the issuance of bonds that were serviced from the collection of tolls levied on highway users. Toll roads were called *turnpikes,* from the name of the barrier that was set across the toll road to prevent free passage onto it. When drivers paid the tolls, the pike was turned to permit resumption of the journey. In some states today, country roads are called pikes, even though they are not toll roads.

Throughout Ohio tolls were collected at intervals of approximately ten miles. Near Zanesville, the toll for passengers was one cent per mile; for horse and rider, 4 cents; for dearborn, sulky, and chaise, 8 cents; and 3 cents was paid for each additional horse. Travelers on their way to church or to funerals were exempt from paying toll, as were those who were going to stores, mills, and to the polls to vote. Young men who were answering a call to military muster also paid no toll. Wagons whose wheel width was 4 inches or more were not assessed, since they did little or no damage to the surface of the highway. Four and six-horse wagon teams advanced about 15 miles a day, and hauled loads of 60 to 70 hundredweight for which rates of $1.75 to $2.25 per hundredweight were charged. Drovers stopped at inns or taverns that provided corrals for keeping animals safe overnight.

In 1832, the toll was 5 cents for a score of sheep, and 10 cents for a score of cattle. During that year, drovers paid toll on 16,750 horses and mules, 24,410 sheep, 52,845 hogs, and 96,323 cattle. Stagecoach travel was more rapid than other means of transportation, with coaches moving at a rate of 7 miles per hour. Some companies that carried the mail changed horses every 5 miles, and guaranteed safe, courteous, and sober drivers. While one coach company may not have operated over a radius of more than 50 miles, more or less, timely connections were made with coaches of other companies so that long journeys were made with no delays other than those brought on by nightfall.

Western Trails

Travel in the frontier areas, especially in the West and Southwest, involved wagon trails which were little more than paths beaten by animals and wheels. In addition to the Oregon Trail and the Mormon Trail, both of which were used by those who sought their fortunes on the West Coast, the Santa Fe Trail and the trail blazed by Zebulon Pike from St. Louis to the peak that bears his name contributed to the movement of settlers to the West. The Santa Fe Trail served as a route of settlement to the West and Southwest, but it was also the most important avenue of trade with that region. Goods were shipped down the Ohio and Mississippi Rivers to St. Louis, whence they were floated up the Missouri River to Independence, Kansas City, Omaha, or other cities on that part of the river that has come to be known as the Missouri River Crossing. This crossing is the portion of the river where the directional flow is most nearly from north to south, and across

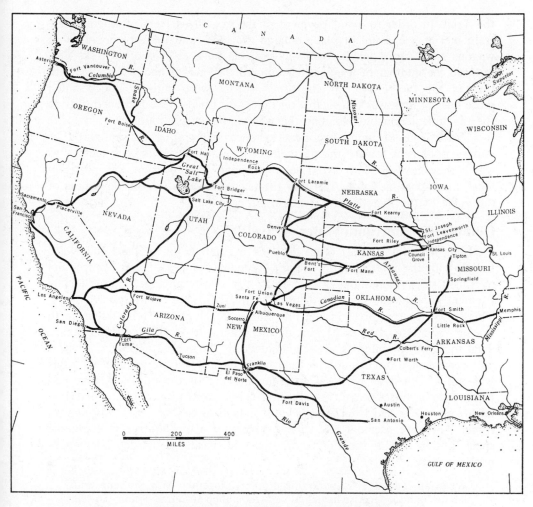

PRINCIPAL WESTERN TRAILS IN 1860

which much of the traffic from Chicago and St. Louis must pass on its
journey to the West. It has come to have significance in the setting of
railroad freight rates.

From Independence, the Santa Fe Trail wended its way to the south-
western city of that name, which was the major center of trade with Mexico.
Mexican traders set up shops in Santa Fe, and exchanges were made for
American goods that were brought there by trains of Conestoga wagons or
similar vehicles. The rise of Santa Fe as a trading center brought with it the
need for revenues to finance its governmental functions. It looked to trade
to satisfy this need, placing a tax on the wagons that brought in goods over

the Trail. In order to avoid payment of the tax, the drivers of wagons in a train met at a convenient place outside the town and loaded one or more wagons much more heavily than was possible for a cross-country trek. This reduced the number of wagons that entered the market and were subject to the tax. On the return trip, the same wagons were initially loaded much more heavily than was practicable on the Trail. Loads were lightened outside the tax jurisdiction by reloading the wagons that were waiting.

This is one of many historical instances illustrating the antipathy of American citizens toward the payment of taxes, and showing the lengths to which they have gone to avoid such payment. The evasion was perfectly legal, made possible by the fact that the tax base was a wagon, regardless of the value of the merchandise it might be carrying.

Combined Land and Water Travel

Long trips in the East often involved a combination of land and water travel, with the attendant miseries of frequent changes of conveyance and overnight stops. Conditions of such travel are clearly indicated by the advertisement published in the Philadelphia *National Gazette* on March 16, 1822. This typical excerpt gives insight into the approach that advertisers made to readers, and also gives some idea of the general level of advertising ethics. That there was mobility of women is shown by the special appeal of comfort and convenience the Columbian Line made to lady travelers. That all travel was not for business purposes is some measure of the advances that had been made in our economic organization. Some groups not only had acquired leisure time, but had been able to save enough money to enjoy this time in travel. The advertisement also gives evidence of a high degree of economic specialization and division of labor, in an increasingly interdependent economic society:

> When an individual embarks his property, together with his time and labour, in an enterprise having in view the public accommodation, as well as his own emolument, it cannot be thought impertinent or presumptuous, if he calls the attention of the public to his claims upon their encouragement and patronage; taking care that, in setting forth the peculiar advantages of his project, he does no injustice to others, but states his own pretensions with truth and accuracy, and treats his rivals with moderation and candour. It will be admitted that there are few things in which the whole community is more interested than an easy, safe, and expeditious communication between two great cities, whose inhabitants have daily occasion of intercourse, either for business or pleasure. Philadelphia and New York stand in this relation to each other; more, perhaps, than any other cities in the United States. In addition to their own residents, every traveller from the South and West to the North and East, or in the contrary direction, must traverse the space between these two cities, and has an immediate interest in the means provided for his conveyance. The importance of the object naturally produces attempts at improvement; and everybody knows how great the improvement has been within a few years.

The proprietors of the "COLUMBIAN LINE" offer themselves as candidates for the public favour, and believe that they can afford accommodations to travellers between Philadelphia and New York, greatly superior to any possessed by their rivals. They will briefly state the advantages of their establishment, and confidently appeal to experience for the truth of their representation.

TIMES OF DEPARTURE

By giving several departures daily from both cities, the Proprietors have peculiarly in view the accommodation of travellers; to some of whom it may be more convenient to leave early in the morning; and to others in the middle of the day. Those who go in the early line will arrive at the end of their journey in the afternoon of the same day, which, it is presumed, will particularly suit those who travel on business, and to whom expedition is of the greatest importance; and be also preferred by the ladies, to whom it is always unpleasant to lodge on the road at any inn, however commodious, especially when a great number of passengers crowded occasionally in the same house, render comfort almost unattainable. The fatigue of going through in a day in easy carriages and steam-boats is trifling compared to a division of a journey, and the necessity which must occur of riding late and rising early. This line wherefore will be particularly attended to, and everything done by the proprietors to make it worthy of a preference.

THE BOATS

The Steam Boats plying on the Delaware, both up and down the river, are surpassed by none in the United States for neatness, attention, accommodation and speed; and the PENNSYLVANIA and AETNA, belonging to the Columbian line, are upon a fair equality, in all these respects, with the others. Their tables are supplied from the Philadelphia Market, proverbial for excellence; and no pains will be spared to procure the best of any article as well as to serve it up in the best manner. Any reasonable complaint on this or any other head will be thankfully received and promptly redressed.

THE STAGE COACHES

The Traveller by this route to New York embarks on board a Steam Boat at Philadelphia which takes him up the river to Bordentown, where he finds the Coaches ready to receive him, without the least delay, and convey him to Amboy, where he again takes a Steam Boat by which he is landed in New York. The owners of the Coaches are some of the most experienced in our country, who understand thoroughly what is required, for the comfort, safety, and ease of the passengers, and have both the means and will to provide for them. Carriages, horses, and drivers will be furnished of the best kinds; and here also the Proprietors will be obliged to any person who will give information of any neglect or deficiency in the department. Intemperance, insolence or negligence in a driver; want of soundness or cleanliness in the Coaches, and defects in the horses, will be redressed as soon as made known; and information of such matters is earnestly desired and invited.

The advantages of this route, then, in general, are, that as compared with that by Trenton and Brunswick, the distance is shorter by

SEVENTEEN miles; and the obstructions of the navigation between Bordentown and Trenton, altogether avoided; and as compared with the route from Bristol to Powles Hook, the land carriage is considerably less than one half, the one having upwards of seventy miles of land carriage, and the other about thirty two. The journey will be made from 10 to 12 hours by the Columbian line, with little fatigue, and without any danger of disappointment except from accident, to which all lines are equally liable.

INLAND WATERWAYS

Just as in colonial days, rivers and canals served as highways of commerce over which both goods and passengers moved, providing efficient connecting links between communities in the interior and the bustling port cities. Wherever feasible, rivers were supplemented and connected by canals, so that excessive transshipment or transfer from land carriage to boats was avoided. Even the development of the railroad failed to mask the basic importance of these waterways. Their crucial role in the westward expansion of settlement is undisputed.

Rivers

Because of the rapid development of the westward movement after 1815, transportation facilities were utilized more extensively as well as more intensively. Steam power had been introduced on the Mississippi River in 1811, and two-way traffic had begun to replace simple downstream travel. The triangular pattern of trade among the West, the South, and the East was being discontinued in favor of the cheaper and more direct two-way traffic on navigable internal waterways. Products from the upper Mississippi and Missouri Rivers continued to find their way to New Orleans, and in addition were carried up the Ohio River, via Louisville and Cincinnati, towards Wheeling and Pittsburgh. From these points they found their way to eastern markets by turnpike and waterway or via river and canal to Lake Erie and Buffalo. Steam power also contributed to the expansion of commerce along the East Coast, as travel on navigable rivers such as the Hudson was made easier and more economical by the eastern steamboat.

It was possible to travel and to ship goods along inland waterways from New Orleans to New York, and to interchange goods at many intermediate cities. Profits were large, losses sometimes complete when riverboats hit snags or when boilers exploded. Traffic on the Ohio and Mississippi Rivers, and later the Missouri River, was heavy, as was traffic on the connecting canals. Freight that originated in the West to be carried east or south was of the heavy, bulky type and of relatively low value in relation to its size. In general, the largest portion of this traffic comprised products of extractive industries that would serve as raw materials of some processing industry and for which time in transit was not of the essence. Forest products and products of quarries and farms were found in great abundance; although pelts, hides, and furs must not be excluded, especially on the upper Mississippi and Missouri Rivers. Westbound cargoes consisted of manufactured products of both domestic and foreign origin. Cargo lists included household goods of all kinds—furniture, rugs, kitchenware, ranges and heating stoves —clothing for both sexes and for all ages, china and pottery, farm tools, building materials—nails, cordage, and shingles—and patent medicines.

Canals

Canals by their very nature must connect bodies of water. When the bodies of water so connected are navigable up to the points of connection, the result is often a vastly extended waterway system, capable of draining interior settlements of their surplus goods and equally capable of supplying them with needs available in more settled areas. Many of the canals constructed before 1860 had such an impact on the American economy. Their role in settlement and expansion is difficult to overstate.

The Erie Canal. Progress across New York State was facilitated by the opening of the Erie Canal in 1825. The Erie connected Albany on the Hudson River with Buffalo on Lake Erie. DeWitt Clinton's "Big Ditch" had been under construction since 1817, and its completion was one of the marvels of civil engineering. The only sources of power that were available were human, animal, and water. Steam power had not as yet been harnessed to construction equipment. Wheelbarrows and shovels initially were the major tools, but they gradually gave way to horse-drawn scoops, either dragged along the ground or suspended from axles between two wheels. The Erie provided the country's first engineering school, giving extensive experience to men who were later to guide the construction of the railroads.

The canal was an immediate success, quickly becoming the principal route between New England and eastern New York, and between Albany and points farther west. Cleveland, Toledo, Detroit, and Chicago on the Great Lakes; Cincinnati and Louisville on the Ohio River; and St. Louis on the Mississippi River—all benefited from the opening of the Erie.

The opening of the Erie provided an easier route over which both people and animals traveled, and goods were transported to the West. It afforded just as easy a route for transporting goods to the East, most of which were destined for New York City. There was no waterway east from Albany over which cargoes could be taken to Springfield, Worcester, or Boston; so the latter city was forced to give way to New York in the struggle for supremacy as the principal export-import city on the East Coast. The cost of transshipment to overland facilities was so much in excess of the cost of continuing down the Hudson River that the market voted for New York. Merchants of Boston and politicians in the state of Massachusetts promoted a canal from the Hudson River at Albany to the Connecticut River, but the cost of cutting through the Berkshire Mountains was prohibitive, and the canal was not constructed. From time to time over the past 150 years, this subject has been brought up; but the canal is still in the planning stage, if that far along.

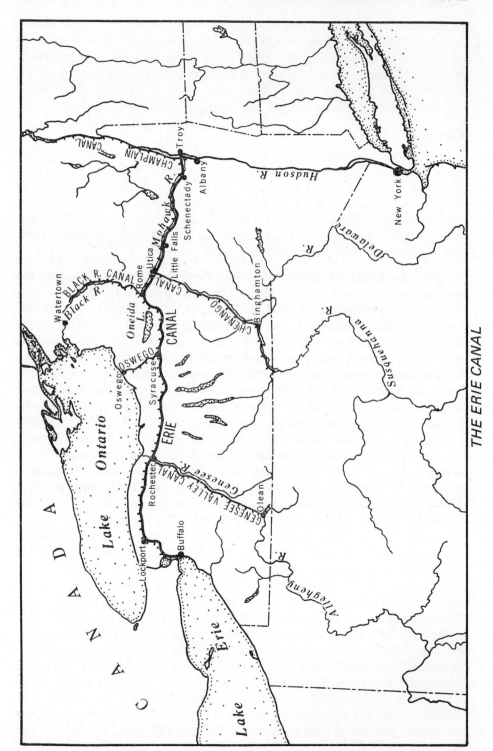

THE ERIE CANAL

As will be shown in the next chapter, the opening of the Erie Canal was only one of several economic developments that led to the rise of the port of New York. The new volume of agricultural products that passed through New York for the export market gave rise to the construction of new and larger port facilities—docks, wharves, piers, and warehouses. More work was provided for more longshoremen as well as for men connected with other levels of the export trade. Some of this work was done by newly arrived immigrants. Some of it was done by workers who were dislocated in New England or who found agriculture unattractive to them. Some men were attracted to New York because of the greater profit potential in urban, as opposed to agrarian, activity.

Competition from new agricultural areas because of the Erie Canal, and a shifting of the main east-west trade route for the same reason, caused severe dislocations in New England agriculture. While these were disturbing and disrupting to the farm population in the short run, they resulted in longer run advantages that followed a more intensive development of specialization and division of labor in industry, as well as in agriculture. Farmland in New England, except in localized areas, was not suitable for the growing of cereal grains on a commercial basis. Grains from across the Appalachian Mountains began to be sold in New York, and at a profit, at prices below the actual cost of producing those same grains in New England. As a result, farmers north of the Hudson River soon shifted production from grains to other salable commodities. The products of dairying, poultry raising, and truck farming found ready markets in nearby urban centers, aided by the lack of refrigerated transport that could have brought competition from western areas producing the same perishable goods. Eventually orchards producing apples, pears, cherries, and plums were to be found on most New England farms, adding to the diversity of foodstuffs the region sold. Fruit trees and cattle worked together in an economic way. Cows pastured in the orchards fed on the ground cover, and their droppings provided nutrients for both grass and trees. Hogs fenced in the same areas fed on the fruit that fell to the ground, and kept the soil loose with their rootings. The gradual adaptation of New England to the Erie Canal provided an economic base that was to benefit the region for years to come.

Canals in Other Areas. New England was not the only area vitally affected by the Erie Canal. The operation of the canal was so consequential to Philadelphia, to the entire state of Pennsylvania, and to the other Middle Atlantic States, that steps were taken to provide transportation facilities in those areas that would offer competition to it. These facilities were intended to intercept traffic from the West before it reached the Great Lakes or the Erie Canal, and to provide access to the West from Philadelphia, Baltimore, and other cities in the general vicinity.

One potentially competitive route was the Pennsylvania Cross State Canal, which was really a combination of railroad, riverway, and canal.

Philadelphia was already connected with the Susquehanna River at Columbia by the Union Canal, but this proved to be too small to carry the volume of traffic that was offered for transport. The state supplemented the Union Canal by constructing a railroad from Philadelphia to Columbia that was completed in 1834. From Columbia, a canal was built that followed the Susquehanna north to the mouth of the Juniata River, thence west to near Hollidaysburg. To surmount an elevation of 2,206 feet above sea level at that point, a series of inclined planes was constructed. Cable cars, designed to carry canal boats, were loaded in the river and hauled to the top of the incline. Attempts were made to schedule the movement of westbound and eastbound boats so that each could counterbalance the other on the inclines. On the western side of the ridge, the Conemaugh and the Allegheny Rivers were followed to Pittsburgh. While the Cross State Canal carried a large volume of traffic, delays caused by transshipments and high operating costs prevented it from becoming a serious competitor of the Erie Canal.

Not to be outdone by New York and Philadelphia, the citizens of Baltimore undertook to finance a canal that would connect the Potomac River at Georgetown with the Ohio River near Wheeling. It was completed by the Chesapeake and Ohio Canal Company as far as Cumberland, Maryland, which became its western terminal. It was used primarily to haul coal from Cumberland to Baltimore. Other canals of importance were the "anthracite" canals in Pennsylvania, New York, and New Jersey, and the tidewater canals in Virginia. The former provided easy access in shipping anthracite coal to its principal market. The James River was canalized some 200 miles up the river, a few miles beyond Buchanan. The original plan called for its connection with the Kanawha River, by which a continuous inland waterway would connect the Ohio River with the Atlantic Ocean via Richmond. This route was included in the Gallatin Report on Transportation in 1808. The James River improvement was a boon to tobacco growers along that river, but the connection with the Kanawha River was never made.

In 1826, a canal was constructed to bypass the falls of the Ohio River at Louisville. Ohio constructed several canals that connected rivers emptying into Lake Erie with tributaries of the Ohio River. Not to be outdone, Indiana built the Wabash Canal that directed inland traffic through that state. There was no alternative way of going from New York to Buffalo via Albany, but from there to the West or South there were several possible routes, all of which finally reached the Ohio and Mississippi Rivers. From Cleveland, water travel was continuous to Portsmouth, and Toledo was connected with Cincinnati and Evansville via Terre Haute and the Wabash River. Erie, Pennsylvania, was connected with Pittsburgh by means of canal and the Allegheny River. Chicago was afforded direct waterway connection with Rock Island on the upper Mississippi River and with St. Louis via La Salle and the Illinois River.

One route that connected the Ohio River with Lake Erie was the Ohio Canal that paralleled the Muskingum River for much of the distance be-

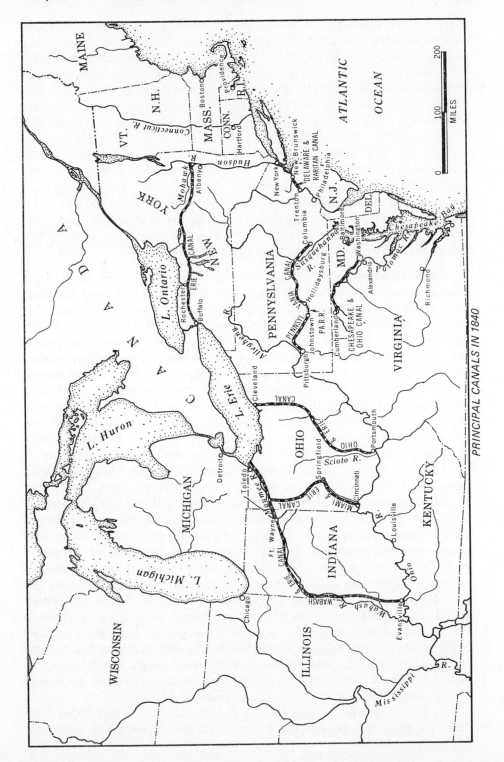

PRINCIPAL CANALS IN 1840

tween the two waterways. Zanesville was strategically located along its route, as well as along that of the Cumberland Road. While Zanesville received many benefits from both facilities, there was no particular advantage gained from being at their junction, as there was little or no interchange of traffic between them. Speculation in land and in business ventures in that area was disappointing, since it failed to yield the immediate large profits that were contemplated. The canal opened up new areas in competition with Zanesville, so the city never became the *entrepôt* for canal traffic between Ohio and eastern cities that many had desired. The Ohio Canal was 4 feet deep, 25 feet wide at the bottom, and 40 feet wide at the top. It was dug by shovel-wielding Irish immigrants who were paid 30 cents a day for working from sunup to dark. Farmers along the way provided teams of horses and mules hitched to wagons to haul away the dirt. All the towns along the canal route felt the impact of the spending of the wages paid for these services, low though they may seem when compared to modern wages.

Canal Financing. Profits from both domestic and foreign trade, from manufacturing, from agriculture, and from speculation in landed resources were not sufficient to finance the construction of the canals that were dug prior to 1860. Venture capital at the private level was also lacking. Public credit at almost all levels of government either came to the rescue of private construction companies by purchasing shares of stock in their enterprises, or provided the initial sums that were required to finance these improvements. To this extent, they truly were public improvements. By 1860, the federal government had granted approximately four million acres of public domain in the states that comprised the old Northwest Territory, in addition to sub-scribing to over $3 million of the capital stock of canal companies, of which the Chesapeake and Ohio Canal Company was the principal beneficiary.

The several states in which most of the canals were built were much more heavily involved than was the federal government. Over $60 million of state debt was incurred in 1835-37 alone for canal-building purposes. In addition to financing state canals, some of the states and the federal government became involved in the financing of several private ventures in canal construction and operation. This involvement took the form of investment in the shares of common stock of the companies, or of the purchase of bonds. Even the city of New Haven, Connecticut, aided in financing the New Haven and Northampton Canal, and the states of Maine and Rhode Island gave banking privileges to canal companies, as did several states in the Midwest. Least dependent upon public assistance were the anthracite canals in the Middle Atlantic States. Stephen Girard and John Jacob Astor were among those who invested family fortunes in canals, and it is not surprising that these canals attracted private venture capital because the density of their traffic gave the most promise of financial success.

In general, it was the lack of overall financial success that brought the canal era to an end, but the real causes of its closing are found among the factors that contributed to the financial losses. While there were canal boat and construction costs that burdened the canals with heavy fixed charges, density of traffic that varied widely, inability to operate year-round because of seasonal changes, and heavy repair and maintenance costs, the basic causes were only two: (1) speculation in canal building that resulted in overbuilding, in terms of the economic need for them based on the volume of freight offered for transport and (2) growing competition from the railroads.

In evaluating the success of the canal era, reliance must not be placed solely upon its financial aspects, important though they were. When state bonds were in default, individuals who had purchased them suffered financial losses, not only of interest income, but many times of capital itself—or at least unforeseen delays in recovering their capital investments. To offset individual losses and those of governments, account must be taken of the gains to the public that ensued from the economic development resulting from both the construction and the operation of the canals. True, these benefits were intangible and almost impossible to measure, but undoubtedly they contributed to national income and gross national product. The depression years that followed the years of greatest investment in canal construction contributed to their weak financial condition, but their contribution to the overall economic development of what some economists call *social overhead capital* was a positive benefit.

RAILROADS

Among the limitations to the use of canals were (1) variations in water supply or water level, (2) unsuitability for use the year-round in the northern temperate zone because of the severe, cold winters, and (3) the ability to extend transportation only from one waterway to another—lake to lake, river to river, lake to river, and lake or river to ocean. The railroad was to provide a practical means of overcoming these limitations. It could operate the year-round, it could go where canals could not, it could carry large cargoes of heterogeneous goods, and it could provide speedy transport for goods when time was a limiting factor.

Initial Functions

Arguments were many as to the relative merits of canals and railroads, and the vested interests in canals and turnpikes fought a losing battle in their efforts to protect their investments in the earlier forms of transportation facilities. The consensus seemed to be that canals would continue to be used to haul freight, largely because the railroads had no equipment for handling large, heavy, bulky items; and railroads would be superior for hauling passengers because of their greater speed. This prediction proved to be remarkably accurate, although the determining factor was freight rate differentials rather than lack of equipment.

One early use of railroads was to feed traffic to inland waterways. Another was to afford direct competition by paralleling canals. Eventually, railroads broke away entirely from the waterways and began to realize their potential in a period of rapid growth. As was the case with other transportation media, the new means of transport at first supplemented existing means, then competed with existing means, and finally supplanted them to a large degree. The 1840's and 1850's were thus distinguished by an increase in the relative importance of the railroad, and a decline in the relative importance of inland waterways. The absolute importance of both increased.

The first railroad in America was used to haul granite and stone from a quarry to Bunker Hill in 1826. The road was of narrow gauge, employed wooden rails, and used cars that were powered by either gravity or horses. This line was the first to use a turntable, a switch, and swiveling trucks for its eight-wheeled cars. Unfortunately for the inventor, these devices were not patented; and they became standard equipment on American railroads.

Power for the early railroads was varied. Most of the early ones were powered by horses or mules—some by treadmill, but more were directly horse drawn. Sails were even used in some instances. But the future of the railroad lay in the use of steam. After the engine "Tom Thumb" had been built by Peter Cooper in 1830, and had proved the practicability of the steam engine as a motive force, feelings were keen and intense as to the relative merits of horsepower and steam on the railroads. The only way to settle the argument was to stage a race. "Tom Thumb" got away to a fast start and was maintaining a comfortable lead over his animal rival, when a mechanical failure caused the engine to stop near the finish line, permitting the horse-drawn car to come in first. All this race really settled was the winning of that one event, because in a short time steam power had supplanted horsepower in all but frontier or underdeveloped regions.

The first successful steam railway was the result of frustration. Merchants of Baltimore became impatient over the delays in completing the Chesapeake and Ohio Canal, and subscribed to the capital stock of the new Baltimore and Ohio Railroad which was to be built between Baltimore and Wheeling. The canal was eventually completed, but so was the railroad, which began operations in 1828 as the nation's first commercial line. By the early 1830's railroads were being built all over the country as businessmen and merchants—not to mention state and local governments—began to realize their value to the economy. By 1833, the Charleston and Hamburg Railway had been completed from the seaport to Hamburg, South Carolina, a distance of 134 miles, which made it the longest railroad in the world at the time. To this line also goes the dubious honor of having had the first fatal accident, one that was brought about by the action of a fireman who was annoyed by the sound of escaping steam. He sat on the safety valve and thus assured himself of everlasting quiet. It was after this explosion that the manager of the railroad inserted a flatcar loaded high with cotton bales between the locomotive and the passenger cars to shield the passengers from harm during boiler explosions. Because most railroads operated for short distances, runs were completed by daylight. But at 20 miles per hour, the trip from Charleston to Hamburg and return could not be completed by daylight, thus necessitating a stopover. American ingenuity quickly brought forth the headlight, the first being a flatcar carrying a fire of pine knots or wood, safely burning on a bed of sand. Because of the short lines, early traffic was intrastate, and interchange of freights between lines was not provided for—indeed, the stimulus for such provision was yet to come.

Technological Change Before 1860

American capital was still in relatively short supply during the antebellum period, and while some of the railroad equipment was built in the United States, much of it was imported from England. The first locomotive to run on rails in America was built by John Stevens in 1825. Stevens operated his locomotive experimentally on a half-mile track near Hoboken, New Jersey. The locomotive "Stourbridge Lion" was imported from England in 1829, and was put into operation over a three-mile run out of Honesdale, Pennsylvania. Being of heavy British design, it proved too massive for the light American track, thus providing the stimulus for further development of American-oriented locomotives. Passenger cars were initially stagecoach bodies with flanged wheels. It was not until 1837 that the prototype of the modern passenger car appeared. Freight cars were usually flatcars upon which containers of boxes or barrels were placed to hold cargoes.

The first improvement in rails involved attaching long strips of iron along the tops of the rails. This created an unlooked-for hazard, as the ends of the strips would often come loose, curl up—becoming "snakeheads"—and pierce the floor of a coach where passengers might be riding. The original design from which the modern T-rail evolved came from the pen of Robert L. Stevens in 1830. In 1844, the first iron rails of American design came from the rolling mills, but steel rails were not to become common until the *Bessemer process* provided cheap and plentiful steel.

Wood was the first fuel used for steam locomotives. Sparks from the unscreened chimneys frequently burned passengers who may have been sitting on chairs or benches on open flatcars. Umbrellas were sometimes used to ward off the sparks, but they soon caught fire and created still another hazard. These and other stories of the development of American railroads are somewhat amusing in the light of modern railroading techniques, but they do point up the amazing progress that has taken place in 125 years.

The decade before the Civil War saw many improvements in railroad technology, along with the extension of the railway net. Oil lamps for night travel were introduced in 1850. Ten years later, gas was being used for the same purpose. Eight tons of butter were shipped from Ogdensburg, New York, to Boston in the initial trial of a refrigerator car. Ten inclined planes were used in linking Philadelphia with the Ohio River at Pittsburgh. The first vestibuled train was put into service in Connecticut. Wood gradually gave way to anthracite and bituminous coal as fuel for locomotives. And locomotives were redesigned to use the new fuels, including newly designed smokestacks without spark arresters.

Important technical developments of the Civil War years included the construction of a railway mail car, loading the first oil tank car at Titusville, Pennsylvania, and the operation of a block signal system through telegraphic communication media.

When American machine shops and foundries were not prepared to construct needed railroad equipment, designs for these were drawn by American engineers and then sent to England to be processed. Our imports from that country thus included capital equipment manufactured according to these patterns. Rails, track bed, lighter weight locomotives, swivel trucks, and many other features lent themselves to development by American ingenuity.

Spread of the Railway Net

The rapid increase in railroad mileage before 1860 probably overstated the demand for railroad transportation; but once the trackage was provided, the growth in other segments of the economy tended to absorb any surplus transportation facilities that existed. While the building of the Erie Canal provided the first instance of the use of mass labor in American construction, the railroads soon adopted the plan and depended heavily upon a stream of unskilled labor—mainly immigrant—to furnish the manpower needed for such extensive undertakings. There was obviously no organized planning of railroad construction and no central coordination. As an example, in the states of Ohio and Pennsylvania, a long trackage with seven different gauges was found, necessitating the unloading and reloading of cargo at each gauge change. Pennsylvania took the initial steps to correct this situation by requiring that all railroads within its boundaries use a uniform gauge of 4 feet 8½ inches, the standard English gauge. But another 30 years elapsed before this gauge became a national standard.

Railroads East of the Mississippi River. In 1830 there were 23 miles of railroad in operation. Thirteen miles were found in Maryland and ten miles in South Carolina, although histories of other states make mention of railroads operating within their borders about this time. By 1840 mileage had increased to 2,818, indicating strong support for the new mode of travel. Growth was geographically widespread. The Mississippi River was then reached at New Orleans, just north of Baton Rouge, and at Natchez. A line extended west from Springfield, Illinois, to the Illinois River not far above its confluence with the Mississippi River. It was not until after 1840 that lines were extended to the Mississippi at Memphis and again at New Orleans.

Regionally, the people of New England were quick to take advantage of a more rapid and flexible means of transportation than the canal had proved to be. Distances were relatively short, and offerings of freight were relatively large. Passenger traffic was also becoming important as a source of revenue to railroads. Passenger service was established between Boston and Newton in 1834, and between Boston and Providence in 1835. The latter line was the first to enter Rhode Island. The density of population and compactness of the region contributed to the profitability of railway transportation.

By 1840, passenger service had been established between Baltimore and Washington; between Winchester, Virginia, and Harper's Ferry; and between Toledo, Ohio, and Adrian in the Michigan Territory. The first sleeping car appeared on a run between Harrisburg and Chambersburg in Pennsylvania. Indiana felt the impact of the enthusiasm for railroad construction when nine miles of track were put into operation at Madison in 1838. Nine years later the first train puffed into Indianapolis. Nineteen states were listed in *Poor's Manual of Railroads* for 1840 as having railroad mileage, all of them along the Atlantic Coast except Alabama, Kentucky, Louisiana, Michigan, and Ohio. Pennsylvania led in mileage (754 miles) with almost twice as much as its nearest competitor, New York (374 miles). In order to participate in the trade between the East and the territory that lay west of the Appalachian Mountains, an all-rail connection between Boston and Buffalo was opened in 1842. By the close of that decade, Boston had been connected with New York, and Cincinnati with Sandusky, which was situated on the southern shore of Lake Erie.

An international flavor was given to the spread of the railway net in 1851 by the completion of a line between Rouses Point, New York, and La Prairie, Quebec. According to the first international agreement of its kind, rolling stock from each country was given free entry into the other. This made possible a continuous conveyance of both passengers and freight, without transshipment, between cities in Quebec and the cities of New York and Boston. The agreement permitting the free passage of rolling stock between the United States and Canada is still in effect.

By 1850, Pennsylvania, with 1,240 miles of track, was second to New York by only 121 miles, and was ahead of Massachusetts by 105 miles. A total of 9,021 miles of track included lines in six additional states: Florida, Illinois, Indiana, Mississippi, Vermont, and Wisconsin. Interest in the construction of railroads became more intense during the ensuing decade, in which 21,605 miles of track were added to existing facilities. The Mississippi River was crossed; and Arkansas, Iowa, and Missouri were added to the lists of states in which "modern" transportation facilities were being provided. Tennessee, Texas, and California also felt the contagious desire to build railroads. Minnesota and Oregon were the only two states of the 33 that had been admitted to the Union in which railroads had not been built by 1860.

Railroads in the South prior to 1860 were relatively short lines that were constructed to carry cotton from plantations to a navigable waterway—river, gulf, or ocean. Even before the completion of the Charleston and Hamburg Railroad, a short line out of New Orleans was put into operation, becoming in 1831 the first railroad in Louisiana. The first railroad in Alabama connected Tuscumbia with the Tennessee River at what is now Sheffield. Florida's first railroad connected Tallahassee with the Gulf of Mexico at St. Marks in 1836. In the same year, steam-powered locomotives were operating on a line that connected Lake Wimico with Port St. Joe, also on the Gulf. In the following year a steam railroad connected Natchez, Mississippi, with its hinterland; and Augusta, Georgia, became the eastern terminal of the first railroad in that state. Construction of the first railroad in Virginia was completed in 1831. Its function was to carry coal from the Falling Creek coal mines to tidewater at Richmond, a distance of about 12 miles. There was no railroad in the South worthy of being called a system. Passenger traffic was limited to planters and their families. When railroads were not available, horse-drawn coaches and riding horses were used.

North of the Ohio River, the general direction of the railroads was east-west, which followed the pattern of westward expansion. There were only one or two connections between cities in this region and those in the South. The first railroad running north and south that crossed state boundaries was opened from Petersburg, Virginia, to the Roanoke River in North Carolina in 1833.

Railroads West of the Mississippi River. The advance of the railroads west of the Mississippi River measures to a certain extent the progress of the westward movement, because in that region railroads were constructed in advance of or coincident with the movement of people. Although railroads were found on the Pacific Coast, there were many gaps to be filled in before settlement across the continent was uninterrupted. Speculation was rife concerning the construction of a transcontinental railroad that would receive aid from the federal government. The idea was taken up as a national project that would be of more benefit to the nation as a whole than to individual persons or regions. The discovery of gold in California in 1849 gave impetus, if not birth, to this idea. In projecting a route for this line, strife among three competing factions prevented any action from being taken. Chicago, St. Louis, and New Orleans were proposed as the eastern terminals of such a railroad. The political balance of power in Washington was too evenly divided to permit the road to get off the drawing board before 1862. In that year President Lincoln signed the act that authorized the construction of a railroad from the Missouri River to the Pacific Coast.

Land Grants

Railroad service seemed to be more important than immediate profits to many governmental bodies; and municipalities, states, and the federal government ultimately contributed heavily to its development. At first, stocks and bonds were purchased by governments. But soon governmental aid took more concrete form. President Fillmore signed the first Railroad Land Grant Act in 1850 in order to stimulate the construction of railroads in a somewhat unsettled region. Under the terms of this Act, the railroads received six sections of land for every mile of track that was completed. In return for the land, the railroads were required to haul freight, mail, and passengers on government account for one half the rates that were charged private shippers. Later the government discount was lowered from 50 percent to 20 percent, but commercial rates were not paid by federal agencies until 1946.

It was intended that the land granted to the railroads would serve as a basis upon which railroads could borrow money from the public. And, indeed, more ready cash was obtained by them from the sale of mortgage bonds than was furnished by their stockholders. Building railroads lent an air of speculation to the sale and settlement of public lands, but real benefits were evident. Current money income was received by the railroads from lands they rented to farmers. Businessmen flocked to the towns and terminals the railroads set up. Grain elevators were built along railway sidings to which farmers hauled their grain. Hardware and farm implement stores, grocery stores, general merchandise stores, and others were opened up. In time, banks were organized to provide financial support to the community. All of these commercial activities stimulated population growth in the emerging urban areas, and caused the rental value of land owned and leased by the railroads to increase.

Grains and produce from western farmers were shipped by rail to eastern markets. Westbound trains bore furniture, hardware, china, shoes, farm implements, clothing, drugs, proprietary medicines, and other articles for the home and farm. From the provision of these transportation services, the railroads were able to earn a continual, if not steady, income. That was their main function, after all. Owning, renting, and selling land were instrumental in getting them started.

The Illinois Central was one of the first railroads to receive land grants. In six years a continuous line from Chicago to Cairo had been completed, forming the first link in this important north-south interstate railroad. The line was the recipient of approximately three fourths of the four million acres of land granted during the 1850-60 decade. Eventually it was to extend its lines from Chicago to New Orleans and Mobile on the Gulf of Mexico.

COMMUNICATIONS

Methods of communication in the United States improved markedly as the transportation network spread and improved in efficiency. Before the 1830's, the speed with which a verbal or written message could be sent was limited by the fastest means of transportation available. Better land and water transport meant faster communication at the same time. The introduction of the electric telegraph broke this time barrier, however, permitting the almost instantaneous transmission of messages wherever telegraph lines were strung. By the time of the Civil War, telegraph lines extended all the way across the country.

Postal Service

Prior to 1860, mail was carried in a system financed by the federal government. Various means of transportation were used, including post riders and scheduled stagecoaches. Even after ships and railroads were used to carry the mails, they were not as dependable as the post rider and the stagecoaches until shortly before the Civil War. Coastwise shipping increased rapidly during this period, and ships engaged in such trade were used in carrying the mails. While there were some land routes to the south, ships from New York to Baltimore and ports on down the coast carried bags of mail, the contents of which were sorted and delivered locally. In South Carolina, mails were carried by rail as early at 1831. Seven years later, President Van Buren signed an act authorizing all railroads to carry the mail.

Since it was government policy to extend postal services to the public without regard to profit, it is not surprising that the number of post offices increased from 3,260 in 1816 to 28,498 in 1860. While newspapers were published in many communities, there was a tendency then, as now, for the larger urban papers to circulate widely, far beyond the immediate communities in which they were published. In 1850, the number of newspapers was 254 with a circulation of 758,000. Ten years later, 387 papers circulated 1,478,000 copies. Public policy encouraged the widespread circulation of newspapers, adding to the cost burden of the post offices and helping to creat large annual deficits. The papers were issued daily in many cases, and they carried announcements, advertisements, and news. Since more space was devoted to advertising than to news, it is evident that at this early date advertising supported the press—at the same time that it was subsidized by the federal government. There is no way of measuring the volume of trade generated by such advertising, but its existence is without doubt.

In 1816 the postal rate for single-page letters was 6 cents for distances of not over 30 miles. Above this minimum, rates were scaled upwards to 25 cents for distances in excess of 400 miles. Postal charges yielded a net surplus in 12 of the 23 years following 1816, amounting to $1.5 million. Beginning with 1838, there were 10 consecutive years of operating deficits for the post office department. These were not overcome by lowering the rates in 1845 to 5 cents a page for distances not in excess of 300 miles, and 10 cents a page for longer carries, until 1848, which ushered in a 4-year period of surplus earnings. However, the net deficit for the period 1816-51 inclusive was $224,000. In 1851, postal rates were simplified, with 3,000 miles the critical distance. Prepaid postage for shorter distances was 3 cents, and 6 cents for longer carries. If postage had to be collected on delivery, the rates were 5 cents and 10 cents. Increasing deficits from postal operations continued to burden the general Treasury through 1860. They were not reduced by another rate change in 1855 which abolished nonprepaid mail. That experience emphasized the fact that the use of the mails was independent of the cost of stamps. Private mail carriers in urban communities delivered mail to persons who were willing to pay 1 or 2 cents a letter for the service. Stamps were placed on sale for the first time in New York on July 1, 1847, and stamped envelopes were first issued in June, 1853.

The Telegraph

From its very beginning, communication has been tied closely to transportation, and developments in the two areas have been mutually stimulating. As transportation emerged into the railway era, communication was put to a new use—that of directly or indirectly controlling the operation of trains. Samuel F. B. Morse, an accomplished portrait painter and amateur inventor, developed a device during the early 1830's that used electrical impulses to transmit messages. Alfred Vail, Ezra Cornell, and other prominent men became enthusiastic over the prospects of promoting the new idea; and young Vail prevailed upon his father to put the apparatus into production in his factory in Morristown, New Jersey, in 1838. Reacting to slow public acceptance of the telegraph, Morse convinced Congress to appropriate $30,000 in 1844 for the purpose of completing a line from Washington to Baltimore, over which the first long-distance message was sent. In September, 1851, adoption by the transportation media permitted the first telegraphic dispatching of a railroad train from Turner (Harriman), New York. After 1844, private promoters took over the development of the telegraph. By 1852, 23,000 miles of wire had been stretched. By 1860, more than 50,000 miles of wire were in operation, and a year later the first transcontinental line was functioning. All of the large cities east of the Mississippi River were in direct connection with each other. In many of them the telegraph office was located in the railroad station, and there it has remained down into the 20th century.

In 1851, a group of men from Rochester, New York, led by Ezra Cornell, Hiram Sibley, and the Selden brothers, Samuel and Henry, incorporated the New York and Mississippi Valley Printing Telegraph Company with the right to extend its system throughout the entire United States. This company projected a line from Buffalo to St. Louis, but when it reached Louisville, lack of funds caused it to terminate there. It went into debt acquiring lines that extended from Buffalo to Detroit and from Cleveland to Pittsburgh, but it was still in better financial condition than were most of the 13 other companies operating in the five states north of the Ohio River. Under the guidance of Ezra Cornell, a consolidation of these companies was effected, and in April, 1856, the New York legislature authorized the chartering of the Western Union Telegraph Company. In such a fashion was the giant of modern telegraphy born.

QUESTIONS FOR REVIEW

1. (a) Where was the Cumberland Road located?
   (b) How was its construction financed?
   (c) How did its construction fit into the pattern of westward expansion?

2. Discuss clearly the economic impacts of the opening of the Erie Canal.

3. How was the construction of the Erie Canal related to the development of labor utilization in the United States?

4. To what extent did the federal government finance internal improvements?

5. (a) What were the initial functions of early American railroads?
   (b) How was construction of railroads east of the Mississippi River related to the general pattern of economic development of that region?

6. (a) Of what economic importance were railroads in the South?
   (b) What part did railroads play in the exchange of goods between the Northern and Southern States? Explain clearly.

7. How does an efficient transportation system affect the size and complexity of a market? If all of the railroads that existed in 1860 were suddenly destroyed, what would have happened to the national market for goods and services?

8. (a) What advances were made in the development of communication facilities before the Civil War?
   (b) How, or on what level of control, were communication facilities developed prior to the Civil War?

SUGGESTED READINGS

Callender, Guy S. *Selections from the Economic History of the United States, 1765-1860*. New York City: Augustus M. Kelley, Publishers, 1965. Chapter 8.

Chandler, Alfred D. (ed.). *The Railroads: The Nation's First Big Business*. New York City: Harcourt, Brace & World, Inc., 1965.

Fishlow, Albert. *American Railroads and the Transformation of the Ante-Bellum Economy*. Cambridge, Mass.: Harvard University Press, 1965.

Fogel, Robert W. "Railroads and the 'Take-off' Thesis: The American Case," *Views of American Economic Growth: The Agricultural Era*, edited by Thomas C. Cochran and Thomas B. Brewer. New York City: McGraw-Hill Book Company, 1966.

Goodrich, Carter. "American Development Policy: The Case of Internal Improvements," *American Economic History: Essays in Interpretation*, edited by Stanley Coben and Forest G. Hill. Philadelphia: J. B. Lippincott Co., 1966.

——————. (ed.). *Canals and American Economic Development*. New York City: Columbia University Press, 1961.

Jenks, Leland H. "Railroads as an Economic Force in American Development," *Economic Change in America*, edited by Joseph T. Lambie and Richard V. Clemence. Harrisburg, Pa.: Stackpole Books, 1954.

Stover, John F. *American Railroads*. Chicago: University of Chicago Press, 1961.

Taylor, George R. *The Transportation Revolution, 1815-1860*. New York City: Holt, Rinehart & Winston, Inc., 1951. Chapters 3, 4, and 5.

Chapter 9

MANUFACTURING; BUSINESS ORGANIZATION;
LABOR; THE TARIFF

While this period inherited some of the economic characteristics of the Colonial Period, it made rapid advances in the developing of manufacturing industries. Agricultural pursuits continued to attract and to support more persons than any others, but their percentage of superiority was declining. Manufacturing industries that utilized the products of the farm as raw materials were among the first to appear in the West.

MANUFACTURING

Labor became more plentiful later in this period, largely because of factors of push that were present in Ireland, later in Germany. Undoubtedly, pull factors directed thousands of immigrants to American shores, rather than to those of other countries.

The supply of native capital was on the increase due to higher earnings in the textile industry and in trade. Foreign capital was attracted to financing canals and railroads, and governments at all levels financed the construction of social capital. Other sources of capital accumulation were speculation in land and banking. It took more than earnings and savings to create capital. Investment of savings had to follow their accumulation, and profit potential had to appear before venture capital was committed.

Not only were the lack of markets and their localized nature disappearing, but they were expanding rapidly and becoming national in scope. National markets in 1860 were not as wide geographically as they became later; nevertheless, they were national in character. Highways and canals made their contributions to this development, but to the railroads goes the credit for nationalizing markets as far as their physical or material aspects were concerned. A sound monetary system, along with improved banking and credit structures, made financing the establishment of new markets relatively easy. Newspaper advertising and special low postal rates aided in the dissemination of knowledge about new products, where they could be obtained, and sometimes at what prices. By 1850, the spread of telegraph wires did much to nationalize markets and to facilitate the use of credit and credit instruments. The rapid increase in population and in per capita incomes tended to increase the sales of many varieties of consumers' goods.

Government Assistance

Government aid at any level of economic activity was prima facie evidence of the lack of private venture capital being directed into that activity. Governments purchased railroad bonds because there was an evident shortage of private capital. Governments granted land to canal and railroad companies in order to overcome a shortage of private venture capital or to eliminate the need for it in the creation of social capital. General incorporation was authorized for railroad companies and for banks, although prior to 1837, incorporations were effected by special *enabling acts* of legislatures or of Congress. Limited liability was granted to investors of venture capital in order to limit possible losses to the amount of capital "ventured." Encouragement was given to manufacturing through the medium of tariffs, and many and heated were the public and private discussions over that issue. True, some of the discussions hinged upon their revenue aspects; but more emphasis was given to the arguments, pro and con, on their creation of monopoly privileges, complete or partial, and to their effects upon prices.

Another encouragement to manufacturing was given indirectly through the creation of *patent laws*. Originally, patents were intended to encourage inventions by restricting the use of patented devices to those who paid for the privilege. While there is no way of measuring the positive effect that patent laws had in encouraging inventions, the fact that between 1816 and 1860 inclusive 38,516 patents on inventions were issued gives reason for believing that there was a positive effect. (See Table 9-1.) Patents and inventions were achieved largely on an individual basis. There were almost no organized departments of research in which full-time research specialists or technicians tested new devices and new techniques. One of the remarkable aspects of inventions and discoveries was that many of them were made by men who were not engaged in the industries to which they were related or in which they would be applied. Mechanical ingenuity, eagerness to experiment, and willingness to accept something new were given freer play during that period than ever before, and cumulative knowledge increased at a rapid rate. In searching for causes of that condition, place the opening of the West among the initial ones.

Free Enterprise Leadership

Among American businessmen and capitalists who contributed their capital to the development of American industries were John Jacob Astor, Stephen Girard, and Nathan Appleton. While their motive was individual gain or profit, rather than the general welfare of the people, the latter did

Table 9-1

Patents Applied for and Issued—1816-1860

Period	Applications	Issued
1816-1820	....	913
1821-1825	....	1,073
1826-1830	....	2,013
1831-1835	....	3,015
1836-1840 *	3,515	2,504
1841-1845	4,718	2,422
1846-1850	8,579	3,511
1851-1855	15,333	6,117
1856-1860	28,973	16,948
Total	61,118	38,516

* Time for reporting changed from calendar year to fiscal year in 1936. Figure for 1836 includes the number of patents issued between January 1, 1836, and July 4, 1837.

Source: U. S. Department of Commerce, Bureau of the Census, *Historical Statistics of the United States. Colonial Times to 1957* (Washington: U. S. Government Printing Office, 1960), p. 608. Adapted.

benefit from their enterprise. People were given employment, and wages were paid for their labor. Property values were increased to the advantage of many landowners who were remotely, if at all, connected with their projects. Urban rents were increased; stimulus was given to the construction industry and to the activities of concerns that provided manufacturing industries with raw materials. Opportunities were afforded businessmen to open small establishments at the retail level. All these factors had an impact on local urban rents and gave employment to local labor.

Qualities of Leadership. Many persons yielded to the challenges of entrepreneurial responsibilities, rather than work for others for wages. The evaluation of leadership, which may be considered in terms of management or of entrepreneurial skills, is difficult to present. The only training available to anyone was "on the job." Ambition, innate ability to organize, the courage of one's convictions, combined with a certain amount of daring and willingness to assume the risks of enterprise, together with faith in the product and confidence that the market would accept it, were traits and characteristics of successful businessmen. Pure, unadulterated luck may have entered into some successful and spectacular operations. The trial and error method was followed by many businessmen. Once they had decided upon a product, they were forced to make decisions on where to locate; how to combine the factors of production—land, labor, and capital; what volume or quantity of the product to make and for what price it should sell. The quantity that was produced in any given period was frequently decided by the market.

Orders for a certain quantity would be received by entrepreneurs in many industries before actual production occurred. This practice reduced the risk of the market, and, to some extent, the problem of price. After those decisions had been made, the entrepreneurs had to narrow the scope of their decisions as to which specific items or units of each to employ.

Location of Industry. Undoubtedly, location of a manufacturing plant was determined in many instances by where a person just happened to be living; and it is difficult to explain the location of many industries except in terms of where a particular artisan, an entrepreneur, or a capitalist happened to live. A notable exception to that principle is found in the decision made by Cyrus McCormick as to where to locate his plant in which to manufacture the reaper that bears his name. The reaper was invented and tested in Virginia, but McCormick realized that the market for it was in the Middle West and deliberately moved his factory to the state of Illinois. McCormick's chief rival and competitor, Obed Hussey, located his plant in Cincinnati, Ohio, and found his largest market in New York State. Hussey sold many more machines than did McCormick until the latter moved his plant to Chicago, which at that time, 1840, was a small country town. True, there were some mechanical advantages in favor of using the McCormick reaper, but nearness to market spurred the sales of that machine.

Sectional Development

Many industries were common to almost all sections of the United States and their products were sold locally. At the same time, there was a distinct trend towards a specialization of industries, one that was based upon the presence of natural resources or upon advantageous locations in respect to raw materials, transportation facilities, or markets. While most of the manufacturing industries depended upon the extractive industries for their raw materials, by-product industries had appeared. Other industries specialized in supplying parts that were complementary to other products. If local labor was not available, it was supplied by immigration. Much of the capital had local origins, but a portion of the venture capital that was invested west of the Appalachian Mountains was of eastern origin.

New England States. In comparison with other sections of the country, New England continued to have the heaviest concentration of manufacturing industries within its borders—textiles, watches and clocks, brassware, jewelry, paper, hardware, nails, wire, cordage, abrasives, shoes and leather goods, rifles and pistols, glassware, ships, and copperware, to mention some of the more important products. An abundance of water was available for power and other uses that were made of it in manufacturing, and later when steam supplanted water as a source of power it was also available. New England had a heavy concentration of urban centers that were not far distant from each other, some of which provided markets, while others were suppliers of workers. Bridgeport, New Haven, Waterbury, Hartford, and New London in Connecticut; Portland and many small towns in Maine that were located on or near rivers that had many falls and rapids in their rush to the ocean; Boston, Haverhill, Lawrence, Lowell, Holyoke, Springfield, Salem, Fall River, New Bedford, Lynn, Brockton, Worcester, and many smaller cities and towns in Massachusetts; and Providence and Pawtucket in Rhode Island were prominent among the cities in which New England industries were located. Transportation was adequate and both capital and entrepreneurial skills were native to the area. Newly arrived immigrants worked in the mills and lived in communities that were adjacent to them and within easy walking distance. Every town and hamlet had its blacksmith shop and lumbermill, and it was out of the former that many ironworks and metalworking factories or mills evolved.

Middle Atlantic States. The opening of the Erie Canal, the westward movement of wheat farming, and urban development in the East combined to give rise to a concentration of flour milling in west central New York State. Prior to the impacts of these developments having been fully realized, milling flour was a small-scale industry that catered to local markets. Local capital was invested therein, and wheat was obtained from nearby farms. When western farmers could produce and ship wheat cheaper via waterway to Buffalo and other cities along the Erie Canal than it could be grown locally for the market, venture capital was invested in flour mills along that waterway which became the first area of specialization in the manufacture of flour. Again, domestic capital was invested in what became one of the initial large-scale industries in the United States. Water was used to turn the mill wheels and to transport the product to market. Wheat in bulk was transported by water, but sufficient value was imparted by its manufacture into flour to enable the latter product to withstand the cost of transportation to markets by water and by rail and be sold at a profit.

The Middle Atlantic States became a beehive of industry that was unrelated to agriculture. Fuel was abundant in the forms of wood and coal—anthracite and bituminous. As long as the charcoal process for smelting iron ore remained in vogue, iron furnaces were found widely scattered throughout those states; but with the adoption of the coking process, together with the spread of the railway net, the industry became concentrated. Eastern Pennsylvania and New Jersey were the first centers of its concentration, but they gave way to the Pittsburgh area when bituminous coal was exploited in western Pennsylvania and what is now West Virginia. Bituminous coal produced coke better and cheaper than did anthracite. Limestone was abundant in West Virginia and Ohio, and the Ohio River and Ohio canals provided adequate transportation. The iron industry was slow in accepting the coking method of refining iron ore, but it followed the pattern that had been set by the industry in England.

In the early years of the 18th century, the English ironmaster, Abraham Darby, had made the first successful commercial application of the coking process to the smelting of iron ore. Just as English manufacturers of iron had attempted to protect their vested interests in the charcoal process, so did American entrepreneurs resist the displacement of charcoal by coke. It was not until American forests had been pushed into what was then the West and Northwest that charcoal became more expensive than coke. Comparative costs were not the only determining factors in the use of charcoal and coke in refining iron ore. Charcoal iron was superior to that made with coke in the manufacture of nails, hardware, and agricultural tools, because it could be worked more easily by blacksmiths and farmers. It must be remembered that the largest market for iron products was found in agriculture and domestic uses. When a market for iron was developed in industry and in railroading, blast furnaces were fired with coke to make a product that was highly suitable to those applications.

In the mid-1840's, Elias Howe invented a sewing machine. After Allan Wilson and Isaac Singer had improved upon the original model, it was introduced into the clothing and shoe industries. While it hastened the growth of shoe factories, it put new life into the domestic system in the ready-made clothing industry, the principal markets for which were seaport towns in supplying the needs of sailors and other workers. Sewing machines were powered with foot pedals, and tailors found that their wives and children could perform the less skilled work cheaper than they. They moved much of their work from their central shops to their homes and thus prolonged the domestic system as it pertained to the ready-made clothing industry.

The West. Glass continued to be one of the important products of American industry, and southwestern Pennsylvania and southeastern Ohio soon offered serious competition to New Jersey in its manufacture. Nearby deposits of silica sand were responsible for the westward movement of that industry, together with the opening up of new markets west of the Appalachian Mountains.

Meat Packing. The initial urbanization movement found slaughterhouses in or near almost every city. Meats were sold as freshly killed, since refrigeration techniques were limited to the springhouse and the icebox. As cities became larger, the market for meat became large enough to be supplied by other than local sources. As lands in western New York, Ohio, and Kentucky were settled, excellent grazing lands were found and were devoted to the raising and feeding of horses, cattle, and sheep, though not in the same pastures. Rail and water transportation facilities were entirely inadequate to haul cattle, and drovers were employed to drive herds to market. Taverns were built at convenient intervals along principal roads, and corrals were provided for feeding cattle and for keeping them from going astray at night. Even though cattle were fed en route to market, the drive which was often of several days duration caused them to lose weight. Since the drovers were paid in part on the basis of total receipts, they provided their cattle with large cakes of salt which made them thirsty. After drinking quantities of water, they were put on scales and sold as "watered stock." To this day, the term *watered stock* is used in corporation finance to refer to corporate stock behind which or in support of which are no real or existing values.

Hogs also were raised in abundance and fattened on corn. In addition to corn being an animal feed, it was a raw material in the distillation of whiskey. Distilleries produced a liquid drink for human consumption as their main product. An important by-product was mash, which made an excellent high protein food for fattening cattle in a short period of time after a long drive or after a winter of pasturage. It imparted a quality to beef that brought premium prices in the market. Lexington, in the center of the Blue Grass region of Kentucky, became one of the early centers for meat packing. Rich pastures and an abundance of corn also led to the breeding and racing of horses.

Cincinnati had the advantage of being located on the banks of the Ohio River, which offered ample and cheap transportation up and down the river. In the absence of refrigeration, fresh meats could not be kept long in an edible condition, especially in warm weather. Pork was pickled in brine, packed in barrels, and shipped to distant markets, hence the term *meat packing,* which no longer is descriptive of the actual process. Cincinnati was named "Porkopolis" and was said to have been the "most hoggish" city in the United States. From there, the industry moved to Indianapolis which, in turn, gave way to Chicago as the center of the meat packing industry shortly before the Civil War. Each move placed meat processing nearer to its sources of raw materials.

Diversification of Industry. The demand for barrels in which to ship and pack pork gave rise to the development and enlargement of a cooperage industry in Cincinnati, and that city became important in the manufacture of containers. Glue, oils, candles, soaps, bristles for brushes, and fertilizer were by-products of meat packing; and it was not long before they became the raw materials of major industries that contributed to the industrial development of Cincinnati.

That industry attracted industry is manifest by the development of Pittsburgh which was located at the confluence of the Monongahela and Allegheny Rivers. As early as 1820, Pittsburgh had become "the Birmingham of America," not alone because of its iron and steel manufacturing industries, but because of the wide diversity of manufacturing concerns found there. Census data show that Pittsburgh was a city of about 8,000 population and a company that employed 100 men to make steam engines was among the larger sized manufacturing units. Among Pittsburgh's manufacturers were a steamrolling and slitting mill, a steam flour mill, a steam paper mill, a steam cotton factory, a steam wool factory, a wire manufactory propelled by steam, three manufacturers of steam engines, two white and three green

glass manufacturers, three air foundries, two white and one white and red
lead factories, and three rope walk manufacturers. The city could also boast
of three banking houses.

Even though industry was moving west, it was not as much *from* industries in New England as it was *in addition to* industries in New England.

Southern States. While the Southern States were primarily agricultural
in thought, in organization, and in action, they were not devoid of industry.
Slaves were taught many handicrafts and produced many items for use on
their respective plantations. It is difficult to attempt any measurement of
their value or of their volume because these items did not reach a market.
Of those that did appear on markets, not only in the South, but in other
regions as well, tobacco, meal, flour, and lumber were of greatest importance. If ginning cotton were considered an industry, it would be among
the leaders. Cotton gins were numerous throughout the entire cotton growing
region and were located where they could easily be reached by wagons that
were drawn by mules. Grist mills and sawmills were small-scale operations
that required small amounts of capital per establishment, but there was a
tendency for establishments that processed tobacco and for those that
ground out flour to be on large-scale proportions. Capital for all of the
Southern industries tended to come from the North and from England, even
those amounts that were required for the growing and selling of cotton.

Successive years of cultivating land without either rotation of crops or
fallow had begun to take its toll of thousands of acres on which cotton and
tobacco had been grown for many years; and, as those farms were vacated
by plantation owners, they were broken into smaller sized units and were
occupied by yeoman type farmers, some of whom did not devote their entire
time to tilling the soil. Opportunities for many small-sized manufacturing
units were afforded those who could command sufficient capital and who
could utilize the labor, some of which was white, some Negro, in their
establishments. The development of the sewing machine made possible a
decentralization of establishments that made cotton and woolen goods.
Census reports reveal that while the Southern States had approximately the
same number of establishments as New England, in terms of capital invested,
number of employees, and value of the product, they were about one third
as important.

Leading Manufacturing Industries

Table 9-2 is revealing in many ways. To begin with, it shows that up to
1860, of the leading ten manufacturing industries, seven, and possibly eight
of them, were at the consumers' goods level; that is, they manufactured
goods that were used directly by consumers, rather than by other producers.
It reveals that there were many persons who did not depend upon the returns
from agricultural pursuits for their livelihood and that Alexander Hamilton's
plan for an economy that would be balanced between agriculture and manu-

Table 9-2

Leading Manufacturing Industries in the United States, 1860—(Adapted)

Item	I Value of Product (000)	II Value Added by Manufacture (000)	III Rank by Value Added	IV Employment	V Rank by Employment
1. Flour and Meal	$248,580	$40,083	4	27,682	8
2. Cotton Goods	107,338	54,671	1	114,955	2
3. Lumber	104,928	53,570	2	75,595	4
4. Boots and Shoes	91,889	49,161	3	123,026	1
5. Men's Clothing	80,831	36,681	5	114,800	3
6. Iron (Cast, Forged, Rolled, Wrought)	73,175	35,689	6	48,975	5
7. Leather	67,306	22,786	9	22,679	9
8. Woolen Goods	60,685	25,030	8	40,579	7
9. Liquors	56,589	21,667	10	12,706	10
10. Machinery	52,010	32,566	7	41,223	6

Source: U. S. Department of Commerce, Bureau of the Census, *Eighth Census, 1860: Manufactures*, pp. 733-42.

facturing was becoming a reality. Economic interdependence was on the increase. That interdependence not only described the relationships between the workers in an industry, but, more important, the interdependence that governed interchanges of goods in urban areas and between those who lived on farms and those who lived in cities. Regional interdependence unified the people in different sections of the country into more coherent economic units.

Implications that may be drawn from Table 9-2 are many, only a few of which will be mentioned here. Most of the products of these industries entered the market, and very few of the items were consumed by the workers themselves. There was a high degree of specialization and division of labor, both geographical and industrial. A labor segment of the population had become more permanent. The American people had incomes large enough to enable them to absorb market values that are indicated in Column I. The textile industry was by far the most important. One of the first reactions a person has to this table is that the country must have experienced a tremendous economic growth since the Colonial Period. Economic growth of the United States as such will be discussed in a later chapter.

Mechanization and Power

An industrial movement that has been described by some writers in terms of revolution was in progress in England after 1760. It was characterized by a number of important inventions that improved the productive efficiency of textile machinery and made possible a much larger output at lower unit costs in a given period of time with the use of a given amount of labor. Another aspect of that movement was the adaptation of steam power to machinery, one of the impacts of which, beyond the field of direct production, was to impart mobility to industry. Many of the new inventions were focused upon improvements in the machines that generated or transmitted power.

Economic Impacts of the Use of Power Machinery. One economic impact of these innovations in America was to mechanize many industries that traditionally had required the development of hand skills. Another impact was to require an accumulation of more capital and specialization in relation to labor. Labor could no longer own its own tools or instruments of production. That took industry out of the home and turned it into factory production. Many economic problems of organization and of management arose out of the factory type of organization. Taking labor out of the home and concentrating it in a factory called for many adjustments in the home and in home life. Problems arose out of the mere fact of people having to work alongside others. The workers no longer set the pace of production. Steadier concentration at work was required, compared with the relative freedom and absence of pressure under the putting out system. Industry was no longer supplemental to agriculture as a source of income to a family unit. It became a full-time operation and gave opportunity to women and children to contribute to the income of the family to a larger extent than formerly.

The organization of factory operations required the development of new skills of management and a breakdown of responsibility into department or division leaders—managers, superintendents, directors, overseers, and their assistants—some of whom were really in training to become heads of their respective division of operations, while others were given responsibilities that were in keeping with their abilities. Departmentalization in factory organization was an aspect of specialization and division of labor as applied to management. Labor itself became more highly specialized and performed only one step in the productive process, instead of carrying a product through all of its stages.

Since an increase in the volume of output was one of the most spectacular and most visible results of the mechanization of production and the development of specialization and division of labor, new markets had to be found that could and would absorb the increased product. The founding of the American colonies was spurred by the British Crown partially for that purpose. In spite of efforts by the English government and by English industrialists to prevent the spread of the component parts of their industrial organization to America, the record of its transposition across the Atlantic has already been chronicled in these pages.

Interchangeability of Standardized Parts. There remained one aspect of industrial development to be unfolded and perfected in the United States, one that differentiated growth in this country from growth in England and on the Continent. Eli Whitney and Simeon North had developed the technique of the interchangeability of standardized parts in assembling rifles and pistols. That principle was adopted by industrial leaders in this country, and it is the unique contribution of America to the world of production. Precision in machinery was essential to the interchangeability of parts, and it is not surprising to find that machine tooling industries were an integral part of the industrialization of New England. Initially, machine tooling was a relatively small-sized operation that was found in Vermont, Massachusetts, Connecticut, and Rhode Island. A pattern of economic development was established prior to 1860 that has been followed into the 20th century: namely, the development of a product industry is followed by the development of machine tooling to service the machine capital of that industry.

BUSINESS ORGANIZATION

Business organization followed the pattern of growth from single proprietorships to partnerships and ultimately to the corporate form of organization.

Sole Proprietorships and Partnerships

Small business units that utilized small capital sums, that employed few wage earners, whose influence on the market seldom extended beyond their immediate locality, and whose business affairs were tended to by an entrepreneur-owner did not require, nor could they utilize, a complicated organizational structure. The single enterprise form of business was well suited to the American economy until trade became interregional and wholesaling functions were performed by separate establishments. More capital and a slower rate of turnover of inventory required larger sums to be invested in inventories in relation to the total volume of business than were required by firms that operated at the retail level. As more capital was required, as the volume of business increased, as efficient management required more specialization, as division of labor resulted in more departmentalization of functions, the partnership form of business organization became more prevalent.

The Corporate Form of Business Organization

Transportation companies were quick to take advantage of the corporate form, particularly as it pertained to their financial structures. Corporate bonds that were issued to stimulate the building of canals and of railroads were found in investment portfolios in foreign countries, and financial transactions connected therewith helped balance the international payments account. In fact, the proceeds from the sale of those bonds made possible the importation of capital equipment from England and from continental countries. It was not until the state of New York passed the Bank Act of 1837 that the principle of general incorporation was accepted and applied to other types of businesses.

Manufacturing establishments were incorporated as their operations became too large and too complex for one-man control, or the financial responsibilities of their owners became too great to attract venture capital at the level of free enterprise. Legislatures were quick to see the necessity for granting limited liability to those persons who risked their savings in the purchase of shares of common stock in corporate enterprises. For those who were unwilling to assume risks of enterprise, but who wanted a share in the fruits of growth of American industries, corporate bonds were available for investment.

When the New York Stock Exchange was organized in 1817, seven firms and 13 individual brokers were admitted to trading in 30 listed issues of corporate securities, most of which were public stocks. It was another 20 years before trading in corporate issues of privately owned concerns occurred. Public stocks, those of private transportation companies, and those of a few banks and insurance companies were active on the Exchange by the middle of the 19th century.

Unaware of the possibilities of corporate development, legislators and others were loath to permit its spread to industries that were beyond the reach of their controls. Banks and transportation companies were controlled by legislatures passing specific enabling acts. They appreciated the advantages of the corporate form of business in those segments of industry. They also were aware of abuses of corporate power in railroading. Contemporaries who expressed themselves looked upon corporations as devices for making legal many acts that were detrimental to the public interest. Persons who were in control of corporations could use them to exploit labor, bondholders, and the general public.

The textile industry was one of the first to adopt the corporate form of business. The operation of textile mills under the *Waltham System* may have served to allay the fears of many persons, especially when that plan was compared with the *Fall River System,* as described later.

By 1851, the states of Connecticut, Massachusetts, New Jersey, and New York had passed general incorporation laws that applied to manufacturing, as well as to banking and transportation companies. It was in those same states that manufacturing industries were most highly concentrated.

LABOR

Throughout this entire period, labor continued to be in scarce supply in the face of a total population increase that was very rapid. While wages paid were at a higher level than were paid in England for similar kinds of work, they were low in terms of minimum requirements for subsistence living for an entire family. In order to overcome the shortage of labor in the textile mills north of Boston, a unique approach was made to attract women and young girls of American farm families. The form of business organization that was adopted by the Boston Manufacturing Company was corporate. Contrary to general statements concerning labor relations of corporations, the Boston Company assumed a solicitous and paternalistic attitude towards its female employees. To begin with, those women and young girls were available, in part, because agricultural pursuits did not occupy their whole time the year-round. To work in the mills was an opportunity for the women, many of whom came from Vermont, New Hampshire, and Massachusetts, to augment their family incomes that were received from farming. For the girls, the opportunity of earning additional money for dresses and feminine luxuries was a great attraction also.

People in America were aware of the unfavorable conditions under which factory labor lived and worked in England, and factory owners in America were compelled to provide living quarters and working conditions that would not stigmatize the women and young girls. The Waltham System, for such was the name given to the organization of the Boston Company, provided dormitories in which the women had to live. It provided a cultured atmosphere by establishing educational facilities and literary societies through which media the girls gave expression to their thinking.

The Lowell Offering, later The New England Offering, gives interesting insights into the cultural level on which those girls lived and worked. They were required to attend Sunday church services; they were chaperoned at all times and had to be in their rooms every night by nine o'clock. This latter requirement may not have imposed much of a hardship upon them, as there were no commercial amusements to attract them after dark, no electric lights and no automobiles. Entertainment was to be found in the parlors of their dormitories or in activities that were sponsored by the church.

To the south of Boston, the scarcity of mill labor was overcome in an entirely different manner. The Fall River System utilized the labor of immigrant families and the larger the family the more desirable it was in providing mill hands. Wages were scaled downward from the husband's and father's, then the mother's and down to the youngest, or until the age of seven or eight was reached. Adult male labor may have received $3.75 a week, adult female labor a little less, probably $3.25 per week. From there, wages were graduated downward, male labor at a given age receiving more than female labor at that same age. The few contemporary accounts that are extant indicate that the weekly earnings of an entire family that consisted of father, mother, and five or six children may have provided for a meager subsistence level of living, with nothing available for savings, for medical care, or for entertainment. Workers lived in houses that were provided by the companies, and they were paid in scrip that was redeemable only in company-owned stores. Parents were responsible for disciplining their children and for providing them with schooling after working hours at night.

Working hours in New England textile mills were from sunup to sundown. Workers who had migrated from the farm had worked these same hours, but they reacted unfavorably to working indoors and to having the pace of their work set by machinery and to working in relatively close quarters.

Immigrant laborers knew of no alternative opportunities for work, nor could they express themselves effectively to the smaller number of employers.

Second generation immigrants tended to join the westward movement and become laborers or farmers. Slum conditions around factories and mills began to blotch urban development; but in the absence of city planning or of zoning laws, free enterprise that was motivated by profit held the upper hand. When the textile industry itself moved into the Middle Atlantic States, it took with it the Fall River System of factory labor and tenement housing.

Labor Organization and Reform

Even though labor, as a productive factor, was in scarce supply, certain artisan groups became organized at an early date and, through the use of strikes and boycotts, were able to wrest higher wages and a shorter working day from their employers. Workers were much concerned with their social status, and they wanted themselves and their families to be accepted. Children of the entrepreneur class attended private schools; but tuition fees were higher than the workers could afford to pay, hence their advocacy of publicly supported educational facilities. In general, families of the working class were larger than were those of the capitalist or wealthy class; and as consumer units they could not afford the cost of maintaining the scale of living of the latter groups. Hours of leisure, educational experiences, subscriptions to newspapers and magazines, travel, medical care, and manner of dress set one group apart from the other. Fringe benefits were not part of the labor program, since pensions, hospitalization, paid vacations, paid holidays, and overtime pay were not the way of life for any group in the first half of the 19th century.

Early Labor Organizations. Carpenters, cordwainers, tailors, printers, and handloom weavers began to feel the impact of changes in market conditions; and in the late 1820's, effective labor organizations began to appear, but only for short periods of time for any given group. They followed the pattern of craft organization, and The Mechanics' Union of Trade Associations, formed in 1827 in Philadelphia, was the first known city central type of organization. The following year it entered politics and supported Andrew Jackson's candidacy for President of the United States. That was not a contest of labor against capital, as much as it was one of poor against rich. Workers wanted to curb the power of banks to issue notes that depreciated in exchange value in the interval of time they were accepted in payment of wages and when they were spent in the market place. They wanted a 10-hour day established by law; restriction of child labor; a system of free public schools; the abolition of sweatshops, of imprisonment for nonpayment of a debt, of contract labor; and the passage of mechanics' liens laws as a protection against the nonpayment of wages due them. Farmers and unskilled workers were invited to join the Workingman's Party, but they were not interested. The movement spread to include organizations in 15 states, and a labor press attempted to mold their thinking in terms of the interests of labor against the aristocracy, but four years later the Party disbanded. That is considered the first attempt of labor leaders to achieve their objective through the polls. True, Jackson was elected President of the United States, and democracy appeared to hold sway over aristocracy for several years, but labor was not ready to put up a solid front at the polls. The formation of The National Trades Union in 1834 was the first attempt to organize a national federation of labor, but it failed to survive the panic of 1837.

The 10-Hour Day. In March, 1840, President Martin Van Buren issued an Executive Order that established a 10-hour day for federal employees who were engaged in the construction of public works. Since the order included no reduction in pay, in reality it increased hourly wage rates at the same time that it reduced the number of hours worked per day, which were two of the objectives of organized labor. That was the first instance in which the federal government established a precedent in labor relations in order to justify and encourage similar action by free enterprise. That policy at the federal level was followed by New Hampshire in 1847 in establishing ten hours as a legal workday. However, that law was not effective in its results since it contained an escape clause—unless the parties to the contract specifically agreed to longer hours. Before 1850, Massachusetts, Connecticut, and Pennsylvania had passed child labor laws that established maximum hours of work per day at ten and a minimum age of employment at 12 and 13; and, in 1852, Ohio limited the employment of women to ten hours a day. Labor legislation between 1840 and 1865 had its greatest impact on women and children in industry, workers who were not strong enough from an economic point of view to bargain for themselves and whose wage incomes frequently augmented those of the principal wage earners—adult men.

Labor and the Courts. Strikes were the most effective weapon labor had in its struggle against employers. No one questioned the right of an individual to quit work when and if he wanted to, but *strikes* were collective work stoppages by workers who were not relinquishing their jobs and who attempted to prevent other workers from taking their places. Their effectiveness was curtailed by the attitude of the courts which ruled that labor unions as such were conspiracies against private property and were illegal. Membership in labor organizations included only some of the workers. When any objectives of such organizations that became realities applied only to them, the courts declared that the unions conspired against the nonmembers. It was not until 1842 that a Massachusetts court held in *Commonwealth* v. *Hunt* that labor unions per se were legal, as long as they were not organized to accomplish an unlawful purpose. The decision also included a denial that an attempt to establish a closed shop was unlawful, nor was it proof of an unlawful aim. A *closed shop* is one in which only members of the union may be employed and in which the selection of its employees is the responsibility of the representative of the union. It is his responsibility to furnish employees who are capable of doing the kind and the quality of work demanded by the job. *Collective bargaining* was entirely distasteful to employers, who insisted on their right to bargain directly with their own employees rather than with the union.

Programs for Social Reform

Another approach to providing a better life and living for wage earners and for eliminating inequalities in the distribution of wealth and in the receipt of incomes was in establishing entirely new types of societies that were composed of social and economic groups whose memberships were limited and in which cooperation replaced competition in economic activity. Among the more prominent colonies were Brook Farm that was established by Ralph Waldo Emerson and New Harmony in Indiana that was fashioned by Robert Owen. Arthur Brisbane, of the *New York Tribune* fame, was an ardent and zealous advocate of an idealistic societal organization in which equality would replace differentiation in the economic and social relationships of its members. The American people, as a whole, were not interested in reform movements that placed limitations on how much of this world's goods they could own and enjoy. Equality in the halls of justice and in social and economic opportunity was all that the majority of them sought. To them, the institution of private property in consumers' goods was not one that should be abolished; it was one whose benefits should be permitted to accrue to every person, regardless of his station in life. Manipulation and fraud were frowned upon; but free enterprise, freedom of contract, free public schools, suffrage not based upon the ownership of land and the alienation of land were principles and privileges they wanted to perpetuate.

THE TARIFF PROGRAM

Collection of customs provided one of the principal two sources of revenue drawn upon by the federal government prior to 1860, the other being the sale of public lands. As was the case in most developed countries of the time, internal taxation had not developed to the point that it contributed significantly to federal revenues.

Era of Protection

Alexander Hamilton's *Report on Manufactures* in 1808 helped to mold public opinion in favor of giving encouragement to the development of manufacturing industries. There was somewhat of a division of attitude towards the use of tariffs that was based upon the economic development of different sections of the country. The Southern States had a natural comparative advantage in the growing of many agricultural products which led to their exportation to foreign markets. Large imports from foreign countries into the Southern States were based upon the profitable sale of their exports. Shipping and shipbuilding were sources of income to many persons in New England who carried on and financed much of the trade to and from the Southern

States. Insofar as selfish economic interests colored their attitude towards the tariff, the following groups favored relatively low or revenue tariffs: the South, so that its cotton exports would not be curtailed and the prices of imported manufactured goods would not be raised; the shipping interests, so that they would have a large volume of exports and imports to transport.

Infant Industries Tariff of 1789. While the tariff of 1789 had failed to provide much protection to American industries, developments that occurred during the first years of the 19th century emphasized the need for it. Infant industries, which were stimulated by our troubles with England that terminated with the War of 1812, were operating at a cost disadvantage compared with similar industries in England and were in need of protection if they were to continue their productive operations. The tariff of 1816 was the first effective protective measure passed by Congress. It established a duty of 25 percent on cotton and wool textiles. At the end of three years the duty was to be lowered to 20 percent, but the 25 percent level was in fact extended for many years. Rates on other commodities were set to establish a general level of 20 percent which was needed to yield revenue with which to pay interest on bonds that were issued to finance the late war. A number of circumstances served to focus attention on a revision of the tariff within a few years. A strong foreign market for cotton and for food staples gave cotton growers high prices for their principal crop and gave the producers of wheat and provisions in the North high prices for their exports. Manufacturers in the Northern and Middle Atlantic States suffered from the competition of a large volume of British manufactured goods which were dumped on our shores after the Napoleonic Wars were over. British manufacturers thought that by dumping their goods in the United States they would be able to crush nascent industries. When competition with the products of local industries was eliminated, they would raise the prices of the goods that were sold in this country.

Development of Home Markets. One of the effects of the financial crisis of 1819 was to call attention to the importance of domestic manufacturing in balancing the agricultural segment of our economy. The decline in foreign demand for American goods that resulted in lower prices of staples paved the way for the development of home markets, and a protective tariff was one way to stimulate such a development. Tariffs on manufactured goods that were imported would tend to raise their prices in American markets to the level at or above which American manufacturers could sell similar goods and make a profit. Tariffs would tend to offset cost advantages of importing goods and of selling them in American markets. Encouragement would be given American capitalists to invest their capital in manufacturing enterprises. Employment would be given to factory labor, some of which might be drawn from farms; urban populations would tend to increase and would provide markets for farm staples and provisions. So went the argument that was championed by Henry Clay.

There is little evidence that the woolen industry was stimulated by the 25 percent rate that was established by the tariff of 1816. That industry had a good start and seemed to be firmly established. The minimum principle of applying a percentage rate to an arbitrarily designated minimum value did not afford the degree of protection to woolen manufacturers that it did to manufacturers of cotton. After the mechanization of the cotton industry, American manufacturers were most efficient in making coarse cotton fabrics of low value, the market for which was in the South and in the West Indies, where they were used in making loin cloths for slaves. The 25 percent rate was applied to 25 cents, even though the actual market value of coarse cotton goods was less than that. When the price fell to 12½ cents, the 6¼ cent tariff amounted to 50 percent protection; and when a low of 8½ cents a yard was reached in 1829, the degree of protection was 73.5 percent.

By 1824, American shipping and shipbuilding were not as important relative to other industries in New England, and entrepreneurs and capitalists were becoming more interested in manufacturing pursuits. This change in vested interests altered the attitude of the people of that section toward the tariff. As long as shipbuilding and shipping were leading occupations, people who were in any way connected with either one tended to be in favor of low tariffs or tariffs for revenue; but when manufacturing began to forge into the lead, vested interests supported the policy of protection. It is obvious that the votes of the New England delegation in Congress were divided when roll was called in voting on the Act of 1824 that raised the rates on iron, lead, wool, hemp, cotton bagging, and other articles whose protection was supported by the votes of delegates from the Middle Atlantic and the Western States.

The Tariff of Abominations. The country continued to grow and to develop diversified industries, and, rightly or wrongly, many people attributed a degree of prosperity that prevailed to the tariff. The highest level of rates in any act prior to 1860 was reached in the Act of 1828, which is known as the Tariff of Abominations, because no one wanted it even though a majority of Congress voted for it. The construction of that bill was a political maneuver that backfired when the John Quincy Adams Democrats of New England voted for it. The Andrew Jackson Democrats were opposed to it in principle, but at the same time they wanted to prove to the electorate in the Middle Atlantic and Western States that they had their interests at heart. The bill was introduced in Congress by John C. Calhoun, of South Carolina, who had the support of the southern delegation in Congress until it was brought to a vote. The rates were set at such a high level that the southerners thought the Adams Democrats would oppose them. When the bill came to a vote, the South was in solid opposition to it as planned, and the Jackson Democrats were in favor of it. The onus of its defeat was intended to fall on the Adams Democrats. They decided, however, that the manufacturing interests in New England would be better off with a high tariff that no one wanted than they would be if the level of the 1824 Act were continued and they voted for the bill. In carrying out its policy of protection it levied high rates on several raw materials that were used by American manufacturers, hemp and flax among others. Conditions in the United States were such that it took more than high customs duties to stimulate their production. Better grades of hemp that were suitable for making heavy rope and cordage were not grown in this country; and the impact of an initial rate of $45 per ton, plus three annual increments of $5, was to impose higher production costs on the producers of rope and cordage and eventually upon the builders and owner-operators of ships.

Lessening the Degree of Protection

Tariff rates on woolens were applied to minimum valuations of 50 cents, $1.00, $2.50, and $4.00 per yard, the effect of which was to force down declared valuations and to bring imported woolens into competition with the American product. Political attitude towards protection was modified during the following four years, possibly as a concession to the South. Henry Clay continued to be a staunch advocate of protection; and the 1832 measure returned the degree of protection to the 1824 level, which was decidedly protective. South Carolina voiced its objection and the dissatisfaction of the Southern States in passing its Nullification Act.

The Compromise Tariff of 1833. Clay and Calhoun met together and, with the approval of President Jackson, pushed the Compromise Tariff of 1833 through Congress. Under its terms all tariff rates over 20 percent were to be reduced by one tenth of that excess every two years for eight years, at which time one half of the remaining excess was to be removed on each of January 1 and July 1, 1842. Thereafter a uniform level of 20 percent on all commodities was to be maintained. During the time this Act was in force, the country passed through years of prosperity, years of crisis, and years of recovery, the causes of which were exogenous to the tariff. Not having any strong, clear issues on which to campaign for the 1842 election, the Whigs resurrected the tariff question and succeeded in obtaining support for increased rates. This support was based more on a split between President Tyler and the Whigs than on actual dissatisfaction with the 20 percent level that had been obtained under the Compromise Act of 1833.

The Walker Tariff of 1846. The Tariff of 1846 is best known for introducing the schedule principle upon the recommendation of Secretary of the Treasury R. J. Walker. Commodities were placed in categories or Schedules A, B, C, D through I, and to each schedule a given rate applied. Rates were scaled downward from 100 percent for commodities that were listed in Schedule A—brandies and spirits, to 40 percent for articles in Schedule B—tobacco, snuff, cigars, spices, preserved fruits, and meats. Raw materials that entered into the manufacture of products in this country were placed in Schedules C through H and carried rates that started at 30 percent and were scaled down by intervals of 5 percent. Commodities supposedly were graded according to their degrees of decreasing inelasticity of demand; but that is questionable when watches and diamonds were placed in Schedule G, to which a rate of 10 percent applied. The 1846 measure was designated as a revenue tariff, but coffee and tea were placed on the free list. Had revenue been uppermost in the mind of Secretary Walker, who practically wrote the bill, the importation of both tea and coffee could have been assessed a relatively high ad valorem duty without reducing their importation very much. Since those two items were purchased more because people wanted them for drinks than because of their cost, the demand for them was relatively inelastic. Had the tariff on one of them been higher than that on the other, consumer demand may have shifted to the item subjected to the lower rate. The Walker tariff in reality reduced the level of protection and introduced some free trade features. An innovation of convenience was the provision by which articles of import could be stored in government warehouses until their importers were ready to pay customs on them.

Prosperous was the term that best described the state of business in the early and mid-1850's. One cause of that prosperity was the rapid development of the West that gave rise to much speculative activity. Railroad construction went on at an accelerated rate. Much of that construction was stimulated by land grants to the Illinois Central Railroad and to others. A second cause is found in the large volume of imports, many of which were the end results of foreign investments in American enterprise. Some people prefer to discuss that phenomenon in terms of American entrepreneurs borrowing from abroad. Regardless of the phraseology, the economic impacts were identical. To avoid another embarrassing situation that could arise as a result of cumulative Treasury surpluses for the years 1850 to 1856 inclusive, the 1857 tariff rates were lowered to a level of 5 percent below the respective schedule levels that were established by the Walker tariff in 1846. A recession in our import trade was more effective in reducing Treasury surpluses than was the reduction in the tariff. Declining revenues and approaching war clouds not only averted continued Treasury surpluses but turned them into deficits.

Analysis of the Results of the Tariff Program

The most positive statement that may be made based upon the data found in Table 9-3 is that in only two years of the 45 years under consideration did the tariff fail to yield at least 50 percent of the total revenue at the federal level, and these were years of internal crisis and trade disturbances abroad. The year 1837 was the one in which total expenditures were at their peak until 1847, after which they failed to reach a level as low as that of 1837. That same year, 1837, tariff receipts were next to their low for the 45 years under analysis. In the first six months of 1843 the tariff yielded only $7,047 million, but that was 84.8 percent of total government receipts and 59 percent of total expenditures. In 21 of these years, the last of which was 1853, tariff receipts exceeded governmental expenditures and 15 of them were years in which so-called protective tariffs were in effect. It is apparent that the tariff was of much more interest to politicians than it was as a regulator of federal income and a guide for the development of domestic business.

Table 9-3

Government Receipts; Customs; Expenditures—1816-1860
(000)

Year	Total Receipts	Customs	Percentage of Customs to Total Receipts	Expenditures
1816	$47,678	$36,307	76.1	$30,587
1817	33,099	26,283	79.4	21,844
1818	21,585	17,176	79.5	19,825
1819	24,603	20,284	82.4	21,464
1820	17,881	15,006	83.9	18,261
1821	14,573	13,004	89.2	15,811
1822	20,232	17,590	86.9	15,000
1823	20,541	19,088	92.9	14,707
1824	19,381	17,878	92.2	20,327
1825	21,841	20,009	91.6	15,857
1826	25,260	23,341	92.4	17,036
1827	22,966	19,712	85.8	16,139
1828	24,764	23,206	93.7	16,395
1829	24,828	22,682	91.3	15,203
1830	24,844	21,922	88.2	15,143
1831	28,527	24,244	84.9	15,248
1832	31,866	28,465	89.3	17,289
1833	33,948	29,033	85.5	23,018
1834	21,792	16,215	74.4	18,628
1835	35,430	19,391	54.7	17,573
1836	50,827	23,410	46.0	30,868
1837	24,954	11,169	44.7	37,243
1838	26,303	16,159	61.4	33,865
1839	31,483	23,138	73.5	26,899
1840	19,480	13,500	69.3	24,318
1841	16,860	14,487	85.9	26,566
1842	19,976	18,188	91.0	25,206
1843 *	8,303	7,047	84.8	11,858
1844	29,321	26,184	89.3	22,338
1845	29,970	27,528	91.8	22,937
1846	29,700	26,713	89.9	27,767
1847	26,496	23,748	89.6	57,281
1848	35,736	31,757	88.8	45,377
1849	31,208	28,347	90.8	45,052
1850	43,603	39,669	90.9	39,543
1851	52,599	49,018	93.1	47,709
1852	49,847	47,339	94.9	44,195
1853	61,587	58,932	95.6	48,184
1854	73,800	64,224	87.0	58,045
1855	65,351	53,026	81.1	59,743
1856	74,057	64,023	86.4	69,571
1857	68,965	63,876	92.6	67,796
1858	46,665	41,790	89.5	74,185
1859	53,486	49,566	92.6	69,071
1860	56,065	53,188	94.8	63,131

* Data for 1843 are for January 1 to June 30. Henceforward, dates are for fiscal years beginning on July 1.

Source: *Historical Statistics of the United States. Colonial Times to 1957*, 1960, pp. 711 and 712. Adapted.

The condition of business in European countries was the factor that determined the volume of commodity exports and the prices Americans received for them. The rate of increase in population and the rate at which the westward movement occurred, together with domestic price levels, determined the volume of commodity imports. The investment of foreign capital in American enterprises influenced the importation of capital goods into the country.

Revenue v. Free Trade

A distinction must be made between a tariff whose objective was to raise revenue and one that revealed free trade tendencies. A tariff for revenue would place levies upon goods that were not produced in this country and those for which the demand was highly inelastic insofar as the rates were not high enough to give encouragement to the investment of capital in domestic concerns, or to motivate the purchase of substitute commodities. Tariffs on both coffee and tea were for revenue purposes, but when they were admitted free of duty, the trend was towards free trade. For the period under discussion, the tendency in starting a new industry was to adjust it to somewhat local markets. It was not until transportation facilities opened up what could be considered as national markets that the products of local industries ran into serious competition with imported products. When markets became larger than American industries could supply, imports from European countries appeared to compete with American products. The demand for manufactured goods was so large that there was room for domestic and imported wares. Table 9-3 on page 223 reveals clearly that even the Tariff of Abominations was not protective in the sense that it prevented the importation of foreign commodities. With levies subject to being raised or lowered every few years according to political influences of personalities in Congress, long-run investment of American capital in industries was influenced more by potential increases in demand, available supply of labor, and techniques of production than by the level of tariff rates at any given time.

Table 9-4
Average Level of Rates Under Tariff Acts, 1816-1857

Year	Level of Rate %	Tariff Acts
1816	20	First real protective tariff. Infant industries. Textiles and iron products.
1818	25	To offset dumping of English goods. Duty on iron raised; rates on textiles extended.
1824	40	Influence of Henry Clay.
1828	44	Tariff of Abominations.
1832	40	Followed by Tariff Nullification Act of South Carolina.
1833	20 (final)	Compromise Tariff. Gradually removed protection.
1842	40	Whig victory. Return to protection.
1846	35	Walker Tariff. Schedule principle. Government warehousing provided.
1857	30	To lower government surplus.

Tariff enactments have been classified as for revenue or for protection largely upon the so-called average level of rates that were established therein. Table 9-4 summarizes the level of rates for the major enactments prior to 1860. Allowances here are not made for modifications of rates on one or more products in the intervening years. For a person who wants to delve into the details of the provisions of the several tariff laws, a review of the articles listed and how they were treated may provide a better basis for designating any one as protective, for revenue purposes, or for free trade. Many enactments actually were a combination of the three. Any trend towards protection, towards free trade, or towards a revenue policy will be found by comparing preceding and succeeding bills and noting what treatment was given the respective schedules of commodities.

QUESTIONS FOR REVIEW

1. In what way(s) did government aid in the development of manufacturing industries?

2. What benefit(s) may the United States in its entirety have derived from the development of sectional specialization in industry?

3. (a) Discuss the important changes in economic organization that accompanied the growth of factories in American industry.
   (b) What were the alleged (1) advantages and (2) disadvantages of corporate organization?

4. At what level of production were the leading manufacturing industries in 1860?

5. (a) Contrast the Waltham System of factory organization with the Fall River System.
   (b) The features of which system have been perpetuated as industry moved west out of New England?

6. (a) What were the initial objectives of organized labor in the United States?
   (b) What level of workers first became interested in organizing? Explain.

7. What alternative steps were taken to alleviate some of the undesirable and unattractive aspects of American labor? What success did they have?

8. Outline the development of the tariff program of the United States from 1816 to 1860.

9. Were there any direct causal relationships between the level of tariff schedules and the degree of economic prosperity of the country? Explain clearly.

SUGGESTED READINGS

Callendar, Guy S. *Selections from the Economic History of the United States, 1765-1860.* New York City: Augustus M. Kelley, Publishers, 1965. Chapters 9, 10, and 14.

Davis, Lance E. "Stock Ownership in the Early New England Textile Industry," *United States Economic History: Selected Readings,* edited by Harry N. Scheiber. New York City: Alfred A. Knopf, Inc., 1964.

Dulles, Foster Rhea. *Labor in America,* 2d ed. New York City: Thomas Y. Crowell Company, 1960. Chapters 2-5.

Green, Constance M. "Light Manufactures and the Beginnings of Precision Manufacture," *The Growth of the American Economy,* 2d ed., edited by Harold F. Williamson. New York City: Prentice-Hall, Inc., 1951.

Harriman, D. G. "The Benefits of Protection," *Issues in American Economic History,* edited by Gerald D. Nash. Boston: D. C. Heath & Company, 1964.

Hunter, Louis C. "The Heavy Industries Before 1860," *The Growth of the American Economy,* 2d ed., edited by Harold F. Williamson. New York City: Prentice-Hall, Inc., 1951.

Kuhlmann, C. B. "Processing Agricultural Products in the Pre-Railway Age," *The Growth of the American Economy,* 2d ed., edited by Harold F. Williamson. New York City: Prentice-Hall, Inc., 1951.

Montgomery, R. E. "Evolution of American Labor," *Economic Change in America,* edited by Joseph T. Lambie and Richard V. Clemence. Harrisburg, Pa.: Stackpole Books, 1954.

Schafer, Joseph. "Was the West a Safety Valve for Labor?" *Issues in American Economic History,* edited by Gerald D. Nash. Boston: D. C. Heath & Company, 1964.

Shannon, Fred A. "A Post Mortem on the Labor-Safety Valve Theory," *Issues in American Economic History,* edited by Gerald D. Nash. Boston: D. C. Heath & Company, 1964.

Sullivan, William A. "The Industrial Revolution and the Factory Operative in Pennsylvania," *United States Economic History: Selected Readings,* edited by Harry N. Scheiber. New York City: Alfred A. Knopf, Inc., 1964.

Chapter 10

THE RISE OF DOMESTIC COMMERCE;

THE DECLINE OF FOREIGN COMMERCE

One of the most important characteristics of the early national period in American history was the changing relative importance of domestic and foreign trade. Although foreign trade had been the mainstay of the colonial economy, and continued strong after the Revolutionary War, the expanding internal markets of the new nation soon offered a multitude of outlets for domestically produced goods and services.

THE RISE OF DOMESTIC COMMERCE

The second war with England gave impetus to the spread of domestic commerce and to internal trade. When the war was terminated, American businessmen became active in their efforts to retain the trade they had won. Population had not only increased, it had spread out over a much wider expanse of land. It had become more specialized within areas and between areas. The level of money income had increased so that people could afford to satisfy their wants for scarce goods by trading for them. Roads had been constructed, inland waterways had been improved, steam power had been introduced on inland waterways. Later railroads facilitated the exchange of goods and services between communities. Money had been provided by banks, insurance companies, railroads, and industrial firms. The dollar was the almost universal unit of value, although foreign coins remained in circulation until shortly before the Civil War. Post roads had been established and mails were being carried out from urban center to urban center and into the sparsely settled frontier regions. The impacts of all facets of the westward movement stimulated internal trade and commerce. Internal trade is the result of division of labor as developed locally; internal commerce is the result of geographic specialization and division of labor. Population had increased from approximately 8.5 million persons in 1816 to over 31 million by 1860. While the census of 1850 did not enumerate any residents in North and

South Dakota, Nebraska, Kansas, Oklahoma, Montana, Idaho, Wyoming, Colorado, Arizona, and Nevada in the continental United States, all but Oklahoma, Montana, Idaho, and Wyoming had felt the impact of the westward movement of population by 1860. Urban areas of 2,500 or more people had increased from fewer than 60 in 1816 to 392 in 1860. That concentration of population in urban centers is prima facie evidence of an increase in the volume of trade and commerce; because, if nothing else is known about urban populations, it is known that they are mutually interdependent, not only among and between themselves but in their economic relations with rural peoples and those who live in other sections of the country.

River Traffic

Rivers that emptied their waters into the Atlantic Ocean continued to be important avenues of commerce. More than that, their importance increased with the passing of years. Now that steamboats were found on almost all navigable waterways, two-way traffic increased in volume. One effect of that development was to lower costs of water transportation which, in turn, served to attract still more traffic into its channels. Competition between companies that operated on inland waterways gave rise to keen rivalries in the rendering of services and in the charges made for carrying goods.

Among the more important rivers that carried large and frequent cargoes up and downstream were the Connecticut River in New England and the Hudson River in New York. The Delaware served Philadelphia and Trenton in good stead. Not to be overlooked was the Susquehanna River and its tributaries, along with the Potomac River that emptied into Chesapeake Bay. Other rivers along the Atlantic Coast were the James River, the Santee River, and the Savannah River to the south.

Across the mountains, the Cumberland and Tennessee Rivers made possible the portage of goods from eastern parts of Kentucky and Tennessee to New Orleans. The many tributaries to the north fed the Ohio River with a constant stream of valuable cargoes. The Missouri River and its tributaries made possible a large and continuous trade with that part of the Louisiana Territory that had been settled. Kansas City, Omaha, Sioux City, and Sioux Falls owe their importance to commerce up and down the Missouri River. Roads were almost impassable in wet weather, and cost factors prohibited their extensive use for any other than local travel. The importance of western rivers is easily seen by looking at a map which locates the larger commercial centers. Every one was located on a navigable waterway. It may truly be said that the rivers of the United States determined the principal routes of trade and commerce up to 1850. It was along those waterways that the West was settled first. Along their banks trading posts grew into commercial centers. Farm settlements radiated from those cities until the opening of the railroads established a new pattern of settlement. Steamboats distributed goods from the port of New Orleans to towns that lay along the banks of the Mississippi and Missouri Rivers and their tributaries. That merchandise consisted of foreign goods that had been taken directly to New Orleans and other items that had been the objects of a coastwise trade. Sugar and salt were added as products that originated in the South.

Canal Traffic

The increase in transportation facilities—highways, canals, and railroads —gives testimony to the growth of trade and commerce.

Table 10-1

Freight Traffic on the Sault Ste. Marie Canal, 1855-1865
(000 short tons; except grain, 000 bushels)

Year	Total Traffic	Iron Ore	Coal	Grain
1855	15	1	1	..
1856	34	12	4	82
1857	52	26	5	41
1858	57	31	4	21
1859	122	66	9	72
1860	154	120	..	133
1861	88	45	12	77
1862	162	113	11	59
1863	237	182	8	78
1864	284	214	11	144
1865	182	147	..	..

Source: U. S. Department of Commerce, Bureau of the Census, *Historical Statistics of the United States. Colonial Times to 1957* (Washington: U. S. Government Printing Office, 1960), p. 455. Adapted.

Table 10-1 reveals the increase in traffic on the Sault Ste. Marie Canal for the years 1855 to 1865 inclusive and isolates three products—iron ore, coal, and grain. Iron ore and grain were eastbound, coal was westbound. Since the figures given are in units of weight, it is impossible to make value comparisons of the volume of that two directional commerce. Other items entered into that trade, particularly westbound traffic. Another measure of the importance of commerce is the tonnage of freight on New York canals, as given in Table 10-2. Some of that traffic was the same as that charted in Table 10-1, especially grain.

It is well known that in specialized industries and in capital goods and raw material industries labor that is used in the production of the respective products does not consume them. When 6,811 employees at all levels received $4 million in wages in 1840 for mining 1,345 million short tons of bituminous coal and 8,129 million short tons of anthracite coal, not only was he coal an object of trade but much of the income received was spent at the retail level for consumers' goods that were obtained elsewhere than in the mining communities themselves. To a certain extent, increases in the

Table 10-2

Freight Tonnage on New York Canals—1837-1865
(short tons)

Time Period	All Canals	Erie Division Freight Originating
1837-40	5,356,066	3,086,966
1841-45	8,066,182	4,422,612
1846-50	13,906,051	7,783,481
1851-55	19,882,506	10,707,378
1856-60	19,557,233	9,448,793
1861-65	25,246,707	13,719,643

Source: *Historical Statistics of the United States. Colonial Times to 1957*, 1960, p. 455. Adapted.

production of each of the following commodities measured increases in trade and commerce.[1]

Coal Anthracite (short tons)	Bituminous (short tons)
1816 — 2,000	278,000
1860 — 10,984,000	9,057,000

Cement (000 barrels)	Pig Iron (000 short tons)
1818-29 300	1820 22
1850-59 11,000	1860 920

Iron Ore (long tons)	Zinc (short tons)
1860 2,873	1860 800

Copper (short tons)	Lead (short tons)
1845 112	1816 1,500
1860 8,064	1860 15,600

Another measure of domestic trade is found by examining the tonnage of documented merchant ships that were engaged in coastwise and internal waterway trade. As late as 1860, a large portion of the commerce between the Southern States and the Middle Atlantic and New England States is found in the statistics of coastwise trade.

Railroad Traffic

At the same time that traffic on inland waterways was increasing in absolute terms, it was decreasing in proportion to total domestic traffic. Between 1841 and 1861 inclusive newly constructed railroad mileage increased an average of 1,766 miles per year, most of which was single track east of the Mississippi River. Traffic was ready-made for the railroads as they

[1] U. S. Department of Commerce, Bureau of the Census, *Historical Statistics of the United States. Colonial Times to 1957* (Washington: U. S. Government Printing Office, 1960), pp. 357, 360, 364, 366, 368, and 370.

Table 10-3

Documented Vessels Engaged in Coastwise and Internal Waterway Trade

1816	522
1820	588
1830	517
1840	1,177
1850	1,798
1860	2,645

Source: *Historical Statistics of the United States. Colonial Times to 1957*, 1960, p. 445. Adapted.

connected established communities. Some of it was diverted from inland waterways, especially where the latter were paralleled by rails. By 1860, inland traffic east of the Mississippi River was about equally divided between waterways and railroads, but in terms of commodity values, the latter were foremost. Railroad terminals had been constructed at Chicago, St. Louis, and Memphis; and a large volume of traffic was carried between those cities and eastern cities. Even cotton that formerly was destined for New Orleans via the Mississippi River was carried by rail from Memphis to Savannah via Chattanooga and Atlanta. Grain was transported by rail to Chicago from where much of it was shipped to eastern markets on inland waters.

East of Pittsburgh most of the intercity traffic was captured by the railroads. Some river and canal traffic disappeared entirely and the Pennsylvania Cross State Canal became but a memory. The Erie Canal alone more than held its own in competition with the rails because of the large grain shipments from the West.

The discovery of gold in California and the Mormon settlements in Utah gave new life to trade over the Santa Fe Trail to the Southwest and over the Mormon Trail more directly to the West. Manufactured goods that entered the country through the port of New York became objects of domestic trade to the West and Southwest over those trails. European goods were reexported to Mexico at Santa Fe in exchange for silver. Drivers of Conestoga wagons traded household goods, articles of clothing, and hardware at trading posts for food, skins, and furs. Some of the caravans were one-way passages to the West; others returned to where they started, laden with precious metals, lumber, and ores.

Organization of Trade

Most common among the types of trade organizations were the wholesale, retail, and factor form, and their variations.

Wholesale Trade. Wholesalers were intermediaries between manufacturers and retailers. When manufacturers did not perform the storage function, wholesalers functioned in that manner until retailers were ready for the goods. This meant that, in addition to having had circulating capital represented by inventories, they had fixed capital in the form of storage facilities. The use of *circulating capital* provided money for its replacement; *fixed capital* represented a relatively permanent investment in assets that were not destroyed in their customary usages.

Sometimes wholesalers actually financed manufacturers and arranged for shipping, insurance, and other details. They collected accounts receivable and remitted payments. It was convenient for manufacturers to ship in bulk to relatively few dealers, to whom fell the duty of selling in smaller quantities to a larger number of retail establishments. Commission merchants were not unknown. They received goods from manufacturers on consignment and did not receive title to the wares they handled. They acted solely as middlemen between manufacturers and retailers.

In the Southern States, cotton factors were financed by northern capitalist-financiers. They, in turn, financed the planter in the growing and handling of cotton until it reached the mills or was exported. When crops failed or cotton prices were too low to support the servicing of the loans, more loans were granted for the following year, again secured by crop liens, and planters really were working for the factors.

Retail Trade. Peddlers continued to take their wares directly to consumers. Their heavily laden wagons that were usually drawn by two horses were really small rolling department stores. In frontier regions, they were more than sellers of merchandise: they also carried news. They handled mostly hardware, kitchenware, clothing, food staples, proprietary medicines, books, and magazines. They almost never carried perishable goods. The following passage describes peddlers as they were seen by Timothy Dwight,[2] who later became president of Yale University:

> For many years after tinned plates were manufactured in this place (Berlin, Connecticut) into culinary vessels, the only method used by pedlars for conveying them to distant towns for sale was by means of a horse and two baskets, balanced on his back. After the war, carts and wagons were used for this purpose, and have from that time to the present been the only means of conveyance which have been adopted.

> The manner in which this ware is disposed of puts to flight all calculation. A young man is furnished by the proprietor with a horse, and a cart covered with a box, containing as many tin vessels as the horse can conveniently draw. . . . Each of them walks, and rides, alternately, through this vast distance until he reaches Richmond, Newbern, Charleston, or Savannah. . . . Every inhabited part of the United States is visited by these men. I have seen them in the peninsula of Cape Cod, and in the neighborhood of Lake Erie; distant from each other no more than six hundred miles. They make their way to Detroit, four hundred miles farther; to Canada; to Kentucky; and, if I mistake not to New Orleans and St. Louis.

[2] Timothy Dwight, *Travels in New England and New York* (New Haven, Conn.: T. Dwight, 1822), Vol. II, pp. 43 and 44.

The General Store. Probably the most picturesque trade institution of them all was the general store, which had its beginning during the Colonial Period and which became more "general" as more kinds of goods were made available to consumers. If there was a post office, or a stagecoach stop, or both, in town or at crossroads, they were in the general store; and they added to the social atmosphere and cultural level of the institution. P. H. Nystrom described the general store in 1919 as follows: [3]

> The general store is perhaps the most typically American development in merchandising institutions, since very few like it are to be found anywhere else in the world. The old-time general store distributed dry goods, hardware, groceries, drugs, and even liquors. It was frequently the location of the post-office, and served as the village social center for the men. The old box stove, the rickety chair or two, the nearby barrels, and the sawdust spit box, were the almost universal furnishings that equipped it for its social services. Here politics, religion and neighbors were discussed. It may not be too much to say that here the tariff question, the government bank, internal improvements, foreign policies, and other important government matters were ultimately settled. Certainly statesmen had to reckon with the forces of public opinion generated and cultivated around the stove of the country store. With all its inefficiency, its wasteful methods, and its shortcomings as a retail establishment, it must be said that it successfully served its day as probably no other type of institution could. Many general stores still exist and will for years to come. But with increasing density of population and rising standard of living, the general store as such must give way to other types of retailing establishments.

Auctions. Auction sales were held at frequent intervals to attract potential buyers. That type of selling and buying had a special appeal to many persons. Some of the auctioneers were residents of the community, while others were itinerant vendors of specialty products. Jewelry, leather goods, furniture, and china were among the wares sold by that method. The overhead cost of this type of retailing organization was at a minimum, and buyers paid cash for their purchases. They were responsible for getting their purchases to their homes. Auctioneers were paid a percentage of the money value of their sales.

Specialty Stores. In urban areas where a continuous market had appeared, the curb markets that had been held in the early morning hours on Wednesdays and Saturdays gave way to retail stores in buildings that remained open all day, everyday but Sunday. The general store gave way to specialty retail stores. Furniture stores, shoe stores, china stores, jewelry stores, grocery stores, drugstores, and clothing stores—for men and for women—candy stores, and hardware stores were among the specialty stores that were found in almost all urban areas, both small and large. The one-price system was not always used and, within limits, clerks quoted such prices as were in accordance with their estimate of the customers' willingness and ability to

[3] P. H. Nystrom, *Economics of Retailing* (New York City: The Ronald Press Company, 1920), p. 23.

pay. Each of these stores was owned by someone who lived in the community in which it was located. Chain stores were unknown, and absentee ownership was seldom encountered. Most of them were single enterprise units in which their owners took an active part. Others were owned by partners who divided the duties of owning, managing, and operating between them. It was not until a much later date that the corporate form of business organization penetrated the organization of the retail trade.

The owners of retail stores did much of the work that had to be done. They employed very few people unless it was to perform salesclerk type of work. They were their own purchasing agents. Sometimes drummers called on them to take orders from samples or from catalog descriptions. Merchants, who were near New York or some other large commercial center, converged on wholesalers in those cities, possibly twice a year, to see what the market had to offer for the coming season. Cash sales were preferred, but open book accounts were kept for those customers who preferred to pay for their purchases once a month. Records are extant that reveal that some trade was conducted on a semibarter basis. Residents of rural areas would take eggs, fodder, flour, potatoes, and other commodities and exchange them for merchandise that was found in the stores. Records of these exchanges were kept in terms of money values. At regular intervals, balances were struck and final settlements were made in terms of cash, paper money, or by drawing a check on a bank in a nearby town. Store owners were also their own bookkeepers. Keeping books was relatively simple. Record keeping may be a more realistic term than bookkeeping, because in many instances the concepts of debits and credits were unknown. One page of a book was headed Sold To _____; the opposite page was headed Received or "Bot" From. Income tax records did not have to be kept, nor were sales taxes common at that time. The idea of cost accounting, not to mention systems of cost accounting, had not been accepted by owner-entrepreneurs. Partners frequently set up drawing accounts for themselves until profits had been determined at the close of the year. Close checks on inventories were not made. Clearance sales and special sales were not held in rural stores. Advertising was practically confined to signs and posters in stores and store windows. Exceptions were found in announcements that appeared in the weekly papers.

Department Stores. It was sometimes awkward and inconvenient for customers to move their horses literally from hitching post to hitching post. Getting in and out of buggies and carriages was not always easy, especially for the women, all of whom wore long dresses. The department store was the answer to those customer problems and to other problems with which owners of retail stores had to struggle. Alexander T. Stewart, in 1861, in New York and Jordan Marsh in Boston usually are given credit for implementing a new idea in retail marketing. A "one-stop" store offered many advantages to both the store owner and his customers. In effect, a department store was a combination of a number of different specialty stores under one roof. Stewart adopted the one-price system and attached a price to each item of merchandise. Some stores sold for cash only. Other stores permitted their customers to open charge accounts. Free home delivery was an added service that was rendered by some stores.

THE DECLINE OF FOREIGN COMMERCE

Available data on the respective values of domestic and international trade vary widely, and little will be gained here in attempting to present accurate figures. They are all in agreement on certain relationships which are the focal points of our attention in this chapter. The decline in foreign commerce was only in its relation to the value of domestic commerce. Allowing for dislocations due to wars and postwar efforts at reconstruction, data reveal that the values of goods and services that were imported and exported in 1860 were approximately double the value of goods that comprised domestic trade in 1820. By 1860 domestic trade may have been twice the value of foreign trade, and the general trend throughout this span of years was for foreign trade to increase in all of its facets. More ships were being constructed to participate in this trade; more frequent trips were made across the Atlantic Ocean not only because there were more ships, but there were faster vessels at the close of the period than at the beginning. They were also larger in size; and individual cargoes were larger and of greater values, allowing for fluctuations in prices of goods that were exported and imported.

Commodity Trade

The pattern of growth of our foreign trade is revealed by the data in Table 10-4 in which the commodity values are given for intervals of five years from 1820 to 1860 inclusive. Our leading exports in descending order of importance may be classified as (1) raw materials, (2) manufactures, (3) manufactured foodstuffs. Our imports in descending order of importance were (1) manufactures, (2) crude foods and raw materials, (3) manufactured foodstuffs. The United Kingdom was the destination for most of the American exports. While our products were marketed in continental countries in Europe, in Africa, Asia, Australia, and South America, the combined values of exports to those continents for most of the period were less than the values of the commodities that were absorbed in the United Kingdom. France and Germany were our best customers on the European continent.

American commodity imports came from around the world; but, again, most of them originated in the United Kingdom, France, and Germany. Tea from China, coffee from South American countries, and sugar from Cuba found large and growing markets in the United States.

The main conclusion that may safely be drawn from the data in Table 10-4 is that the total value of commodity imports exceeded the total value of commodity exports throughout the entire period covered by the table. The increase in the value of our exports was sparked by a spectacular increase in the export of cotton to England, which had pushed tobacco to

Table 10-4

Values of Domestically Produced Exports and Commodity Imports by Economic Classes, 1820-1860
(millions)

Year	Total Exports	Total Imports	Crude Foods and Raw Materials Exports	Crude Foods and Raw Materials Imports	Manufactured Foodstuffs Exports	Manufactured Foodstuffs Imports	Semimanufactures and Manufactures Exports	Semimanufactures and Manufactures Imports
1820	$ 52	$ 55 *	$ 33	$10 *	$10	$ 9 *	$ 9	$ 35 *
1825	67	91	46	19	9	11	12	61
1830	59	63	38	14	10	8	11	41
1835	100	137	77	28	9	16	14	93
1840	112 †	98 †	78	26	15	13	18	60
1845	98	113	63	27	13	11	22	75
1850	135	173	90	31	19	21	26	121
1855	193	258	119	60	33	34	40	164
1860	316	352	229	85	39	60	48	207

* Import data for 1821.
† Components do not sum to totals because of rounding.

Source: *Historical Statistics of the United States. Colonial Times to 1957*, 1960, p. 545. Adapted; Douglass C. North, *The Economic Growth of the United States, 1790-1860* (Englewood Cliffs, N. J.: Prentice-Hall, Inc., 1961), pp. 284, 285, 288, 289. Adapted.

second position. Cotton and woolen textiles, iron and steel products, followed by coffee, tea, and sugar led the parade of commodity imports.

As important as are the respective values of exports and imports and their trends in analyzing the American economy, mention of a few of the items in each of the above classifications affords an insight into the nature of the domestic activities that prepared items for export and that depended upon imports for further processing and trade. More important than total values in revealing the basic nature of our own economy are the products that were imported and exported.

Exports. As has already been mentioned, raw cotton headed the list of raw materials, followed by tobacco, livestock, wool, and hemp. Crude or raw foods of export were cereal grains, rice, potatoes, and apples. Prominent among the processed foods that were exported were dried and pickled fish; beef tallow, hides, and horned cattle; hogs, pork, bacon and lard; butter and cheese; flour and meal. In addition to whalebone and fish oils, naval stores, barrel staves, shingles, lumber products, pot and pearl ashes were exported in their semimanufactured state. In addition to processed food products, spermaceti candles, furs and skins, and miscellaneous items of manufacture were exported.

From 1821 through 1850, Cuba was a larger market for American merchandise, including reexports, than Germany; and after 1841 Canada and other British North American provinces passed Cuba as a market for American exports.

Imports. Space does not permit a listing of commodity imports in their entirety, even by economic classes, but the following items were piled high on American wharves. In addition to tea and coffee in their raw state, cocoa, cork, wool, spices, nuts, saltpeter, ivory, manila, and jute made the list of raw materials more complete. Manufactured foods of large volume and value were wines, distilled spirits, and beer; molasses, sugar, and cheese. The list of manufactured goods was much more varied and ranged through a long list of textiles—cotton and wool—iron and steel products, paints, chemicals, glue, books, quick silver, lead, and watches, to saddlery and arms.

Between 1820 and 1860, more imports by value originated in Cuba than in either Canada and other British North American provinces or Germany.

Table 10-5
Exports of Cotton—1821-1865

Years	Bales * (000)	Value (millions)
1821-25	1,524	$123
1826-30	2,546	133
1831-35	3,392	207
1836-40	5,244	321
1841-45 †	6,888	257
1846-50	7,102	296
1851-55	10,256	491
1856-60	13,344	744
1861-65 ‡	69	59

* One bale = 500 pounds.
† Data for 1843 are for nine months rather than for a year.
‡ No record of cotton exports for southern ports for the years 1862-65.

Source: *Historical Statistics of the United States. Colonial Times to 1957*, 1960, p. 547. Adapted.

Balance of Trade

As large as was the volume of our commodity exports they did not balance the value of our commodity imports. An international trade account was seldom, if ever, in balance; our international payments account was always in balance, allowing for errors and omissions. A shipment of gold may have been the final step in effecting a balance.

As was the case during the last 30 years of the Colonial Period, European peoples continued to sell goods of greater values to people in the United States than they purchased from them. Since the value of American commodity exports did not enable Americans to pay for their commodity imports, they were compelled to borrow from English banks. This is nothing but another way of saying that English investors lent their capital to borrowers in America to aid in the construction of canals and railroads, to finance the purchase of rolling stock for the railroads, and to provide capital for American industries. The United States continued to be a debtor nation, and in this respect or characteristic, the Colonial Period extended far beyond 1763.

Table 10-6

Value of Merchandise Exports and Imports
(millions)

Year	Exports *	Imports	Excess of Exports + or Imports —	Year	Exports *	Imports	Excess of Exports + or Imports —
1821	$ 55	$ 55	..	1844	106	103	+ 3
1822	61	80	— 19	1845	106	113	— 7
1823	68	72	— 4	1846	110	118	— 8
1824	69	72	— 3	1847	157	122	+ 34
1825	91	90	+ 1	1848	138	149	— 10
1826	73	78	— 5	1849	140	141	— 1
1827	74	71	+ 3	1850	144	174	— 29
1828	64	81	— 17	1851	189	211	— 22
1829	67	67	..	1852	167	207	— 40
1830	72	63	+ 9	1853	203	264	— 60
1831	72	96	— 24	1854	237	298	— 61
1832	82	95	— 14	1855	219	258	— 39
1833	88	101	— 14	1856	281	310	— 29
1834	102	109	— 6	1857	294	348	— 55
1835	115	137	— 22	1858	272	263	+ 9
1836	124	177	— 52	1859	293	331	— 38
1837	111	130	— 19	1860	334	354	— 20
1838	105	96	+ 9	1861	220	289	— 70
1839	112	156	— 44	1862	191	189	+ 1
1840	124	98	+ 25	1863	204	243	— 39
1841	112	123	— 11	1864	159	316	— 158
1842	100	96	+ 4	1865	166	239	— 73
1843	83	42	+ 40	....	...	...	..

* Exports include reexports.
Source: *Historical Statistics of the United States. Colonial Times to 1957*, 1960, p. 538.
    Adapted.

The United States as a Debtor Nation. The basic cause of the debtor position of the United States was the scarcity of native capital. That, in turn, was due to the fact that money incomes of the people and business firms were not sufficiently large to enable them to save enough to meet the demands of American businessmen for capital. The country was expanding, population was increasing in size and in density, and it was becoming more interdependent in its economic relationships—one group of people upon others, one section of the country upon others. Some of those groups of people were in close proximity to one another, others were more remotely situated. In both cases the fact of interdependence tended to enlarge upon the market for consumers' goods. To produce more consumers' goods required more capital. To have more money capital, people had to save more or borrow it from other people. The expansion of markets took place so rapidly and became so large that entrepreneurs were compelled to draw upon the savings of people who lived in older established economies within which the rate of economic growth did not absorb such savings. The relative scarcity of capital in the United States compared with its lesser degree of scarcity in older developed economies was manifest in higher rates of interest American borrowers were willing to pay and could afford to pay for the use of borrowed capital. They were willing to pay higher rates because they thought the actual added increment of return from the use of borrowed capital would be greater than the interest cost of that capital. They could afford to pay higher rates of interest because of the greater productivity of capital in the United States when it was combined with labor and land in proper proportions. Production in the United States, in general, had not been pushed as far into the stage of *diminishing returns* as it had in older economies. To look at the same problem from the point of view of foreign lenders of capital, they were willing and sometimes eager to invest their savings in American enterprises because they could receive higher rates of interest than their domestic borrowers could afford to pay.

Immaturity v. Maturity. The first economic impact of borrowing from abroad was the increase of American commodity imports on the balance of trade account. When there is no tangible commodity item of export to offset imports, the international trade account of a borrowing country shows a heavy import balance, or an *unfavorable balance of trade,* as the term has come to be used. During that phase of our economic development, the money value of new capital loans was greater than the cumulative interest payments due, combined with installment payments on the principal sums of loans of earlier years. That position or relationship is described in terms of immaturity as a debtor nation. In other words, the United States was an immature debtor nation throughout this entire period. The payments of interest and of principal sums operated to increase commodity exports over a period of time and when the total of these payments exceeded the value of new loans in any one year or period of time, the country was still a debtor nation but it had reached the stage of maturity. A mature debtor nation, as such, will have a commodity export balance, or a *favorable balance of trade.*

Financing Foreign Trade

From the standpoint of the manner in which foreign trade was financed, the Colonial Period had not terminated by 1860. The British pound sterling was the monetary unit in terms of which American exporters received payment for their goods, and American importers paid for theirs, and no money was shipped across the Atlantic Ocean in so doing. Important in the financing of both exports and imports were British firms, among which the House of Baring played a prominent role. That was an English investment firm whose partners became interested in extending credits that were used in financing the overseas trade of American business firms. Baring Brothers permitted *drafts* to be drawn against them, and they maintained an active market in *trade acceptances*. The name of Baring may be best known for its financing of the cotton trade, but trade between the United States and China, Cuba, and South American countries attracted Baring capital. When coffee, copper, dry goods, flax seed, hemp, breadstuffs, cloth, indigo, and mercury were added to the list of imports, American businessmen were indebted to Baring and similar investment firms for their successful operations.

Origins of International Payments

International transactions to which Americans were party may be classified as (1) shipments of merchandise, (2) service transactions, and (3) capital transactions.

Shipments of Merchandise. Shipments of merchandise consisted of the importation of commodities that could be obtained at lower cost from foreign producers than from domestic ones, or those which were not obtainable in this country. Commodity exports consisted of those items that were sold in foreign markets. The measurement of values of the commodity trade presented no particular problems.

Service Transactions. There were many transactions by number and by value that did not pertain to any physical or material goods. When American shipowners were reimbursed by English insurance companies for losses incurred on the high seas, a service export was added to the balance of payments account. Payments of premiums on such policies were tantamount to payments for the importation of protection. When American shippers paid transportation costs to owners of British ships, they paid for the importation of shipping services. Other service transactions consisted of immigrant remittances to home countries and donations to foreign relief. Interest on corporate bonds and dividends on corporate stock were other service payments. If Americans paid the items, they constituted imports; if Americans received payments, they were the equivalent of exports.

Capital Transactions. Until about 1900, foreigners invested more in American securities and physical properties than Americans did abroad, so there usually was a credit balance on the capital account. That situation was reversed when Americans began to invest more heavily abroad. Corporate securities and government bonds were attractive investment outlets for American capital.

Balance of Payments

A *balance of payments account* is a recording of the results of financial and service transactions between a given country and all others. A *trade account,* by itself, may never be in balance; but a balance of payments account, which includes all inflows and outflows of funds, will always be in balance, since it is essentially a double-entry bookkeeping system. When a country has a debit balance on its trade account (net inflow of funds), if its invisible trade does not establish compensating credit items, an outflow of gold will occur to balance the payments account.

Items that appear on the balance of payments account and that are not directly related to items found on the trade account appear on the capital account and are classified as *invisible items* of export or of import. As a general rule, any investment that, by itself and if the money were used, caused money to come into the United States was an export of securities or an *invisible export.* Such items as the investment of capital in the United States gave rise to the payment of interest and repayment of capital sums in later years. Costs of transportation, payments of insurance premiums and indemnifications for losses of assets, and other services which constituted the payments account made up imbalances on the trade account. The payment of transportation services that were rendered by American clipper ships loomed large on the balance of payments account. The United States was exporting transportation services. A smaller item, yet one that was not to be ignored, was money that immigrants brought with them into this country. When American shipowners were reimbursed by English marine insurance companies for losses that had been incurred on the high seas, an invisible export was added to the balance of payments account. *Invisible items of import* were payments for services that had been rendered by foreign ships; remittances of money by immigrants to their families in Europe, although that item did not become large until after 1870; and payments of insurance premiums, particularly for marine insurance, to foreign companies.

"Favorable" and "Unfavorable" Balance of Trade

In order to clarify the discussion of trade balances, a word should be said concerning the use of the terms *favorable* and *unfavorable* to describe export and import balances respectively. While our imports of capital goods from European countries led to what the mercantilists called an unfavorable balance of trade, from the standpoint of the economic development of the United States, those imports were decidedly favorable. Without them the development of natural resources would have progressed much more slowly. They served to support the rapid increase in population, in that this increase did not result in a lower scale of living, but in a higher scale. These imported goods made it possible for people to spread out over a wider range of territory, and to develop more, virgin, natural resources more intensively. They made it possible for the American people to enjoy goods and to satisfy their wants with goods that were not produced and could not be produced in the United States. The most favorable aspect of our commodity exports was that they helped pay for our commodity imports, and in the short run their being exported did not deprive the American people of particular quantities of goods that were needed to satisfy their wants.

A favorable commodity trade balance existed when the value of commodity exports exceeded the value of commodity imports. According to the mercantile doctrine, the difference in those values would cause a flow of money into this country. That this movement did not always actually occur, historical data clearly reveal. Commodity exports were related to commodity imports and the rendering of services by foreign peoples. An early export of naval stores may have been favorable to the colonies, or even to the United States in the early years of its existence and until the time when these products were needed to supply raw materials for the construction of clipper ships. Then to the extent that they continued to be found among our exports, they tended to raise the cost of building American ships. There is nothing "favorable" about that. The efforts to increase commodity exports resulted in a more rapid exhaustion and exploitation of our natural resources than otherwise would have taken place. There was nothing "favorable" about that. It should be clear to the reader that the terms *favorable* and *unfavorable,* as applied to foreign trade, refer solely to the imbalances of money values of commodity exports and of imports. There is no additional economic implication whatsoever.

Over a longer period of time capital goods that were listed among the imports for any given year contributed to the production of economic goods or the rendering of services in this country. Railroad capital may have been found among the imports for a given year. After the rails were laid, trains carried foodstuffs to New York at lower cost than formerly. Foodstuffs, then, were among the commodity exports that resulted from borrowing capital in years gone by. The value of the foodstuffs that had been exported may have constituted the interest payment on a capital loan, or it may have represented partial payment on a principal sum.

Shipping and Shipbuilding

Even though the manufacturing industries were demanding more economic resources after 1820 than formerly, shipping and shipbuilding continued actively as important industries, especially in the New England States and in New York. Wooden ships were constructed by skilled artisans who yielded to no others in their craftsmanship. That, together with an abundant supply of lumber, contributed to a lower cost of ship construction than in England. American shipyards built wooden vessels not only for use by American shipping companies, but to be sold to shipping companies in foreign countries. American seamen were exceptionally skilled in handling sailing vessels which resulted in fewer men crewing larger vessels than were required by foreign companies. Wages of American sailors were higher than were paid sailors of other countries, but because of greater skills and better seamanship in handling larger ships, American owned and operated ships were in direct and successful competition with vessels that were foreign owned and operated.

The American Clipper Ship. Sometime after 1830 a new design for sailing vessels resulted in their attaining greater speed and easier maneuverability in the water than their British counterparts. In the language of today, they were more streamlined, longer, more slender, and of narrower beam. It was the clipper ship that gave the United States supremacy on the high seas from about 1840 to 1860. That ship was found in all waters, and it made distances of well over 300 miles per day entirely with sail. It was not only engaged in overseas trade, it was found in coastal trade and it was ever present in the gold rush to California in 1848. Thousands of fortune hunters who did not want to brave the hardships of overland travel by stagecoach chose that mode of easy transportation on their journey to the West Coast.

The very reasons for the superiority of the clipper ship gave rise to the development in England of new techniques of building and of operating ships. Forests in England had long since been denuded of their best timber, and imports of timber from the Scandinavian countries added to their cost of construction. Masts, spars, and beams were found on ships leaving American shores for England. Iron was applied to shipbuilding and was found to have several advantages over the use of wood. In England, iron was cheaper, larger vessels could be constructed, heavier cargoes could be carried and, when powered by steam, an iron vessel was much faster than a clipper ship. All of these factors combined to cause the clipper ship to disappear from the high seas. Picturesqueness yielded to greater efficiency and lower costs in the race for profits. The Civil War hastened its displacement, and never again has an American merchant marine vessel been as majestic and as dominant.

Other Factors. The American government did not subsidize shipping to as large an extent as did England which was relatively more dependent upon overseas trade than was the United States. British policy was to subsidize both the construction of vessels and their operation. One impact of that policy is found in the rate structures of the British shipping industry. Operators of ships were not compelled to establish rates that covered the actual costs of carrying goods. Revenues that were collected from shipments did not have to cover all operational costs, fixed charges, and return a profit on the capital invested. Another competitive advantage that was enjoyed by the owners and operators of British vessels was in lower wages that were paid to the members of their crews. These conditions made possible the charging of lower rates and fares than were charged by American shipping companies. It was the advantages that were inherent in the clipper ship that enabled American shipping to survive.

Commercial ships that sailed the high seas were either tramp steamers or regular traders. The former were operated by merchant traders who owned the cargoes and the ships. They sailed wherever the lure for profits took them without any port schedule for departure or arrival. Their cargoes varied from time to time, but individual shipments usually were in shipload lots. Regular traders usually sailed between two ports and carried shipload cargoes. They did not attract passengers. They were strictly commercial vessels in that their owners transported freight for other persons for a price.

The coming of the packet liners, together with the development of the clipper ship, resulted in the disappearance of the merchant trader. No longer were the functions of foreign trading performed by one man. No longer did he start out with a cargo of his own goods to find a market in a foreign port and to obtain commodities for his return journey that he thought he could sell for a profit. Owners and operators of ocean liners were specialists in providing transportation. Other aspects of foreign trade were left for other specialists. Requirements were more stringent, techniques of trading and financing were more complex, and the volume of business was larger than one man could manage. Specialization was the order of the day; and economic interdependence required a degree of cooperation, much of which was unconsciously performed and hitherto unknown. Members of an economic society usually were not aware of the degree of cooperation until a crisis of some kind arose. One of those crises was a business recession, another was an epidemic of bank failures, and a third was war.

The Rise of New York Port. In 1818 an English concern, the Black Ball Line, started regularly scheduled sailings between Liverpool and New York. The impact of that innovation and the economic dislocations it created were not appreciated until Professor R. G. Albion, then of Princeton University, published *The Rise of New York Port, 1815-1860* in 1939.[4] He attributed the supremacy of New York City as an export-import center more to the establishment of regularly scheduled sailings of packet liners between New York and Liverpool than to the opening of the Erie Canal. Packet liners carried passengers, parcel post or express type of packages, and some heavier freight. Less than shipload shipments of freight increased in volume and contributed to the exchange of goods between persons and business firms in the United States and foreign countries. Packet liners plied the waters between designated ports and were powered at least partly by steam. Their contributions to the economic development of New York City lay beyond the ships and direct trade themselves and their schedules. Exporters who shipped goods from inland areas knew when their commodities had to reach New York in order to be shipped on a given scheduled liner. Importers of goods knew when to expect their shipments from abroad. The fact that the liners were able to maintain schedules of elapsed time in transit was important to shippers and passengers alike.

[4] Robert G. Albion and J. B. Pope, *The Rise of New York Port, 1815-1860* (New York City: Charles Scribner's Sons, 1939).

The natural advantages of location and a harbor that contributed to the growth of Boston as a seaport city no longer served that city in good stead. Of course, those aspects of Boston harbor were unchanged; but New York harbor was larger and just as good otherwise as was that of Boston. The Erie Canal, the operation of packet liners, together with the general economic development west of New England, gave to New York a locational advantage that Boston had enjoyed at an earlier date. Markets for imported products were found radiating from New York. Manufacturers and producers of commodities were in relatively easy contact with New York. Financial institutions that facilitated the movement of goods were found in New York. Brokers, commission agents, warehousemen, and wholesalers contributed to the handling of large volumes of bulky commodities; and transportation facilities were unexcelled. New York experienced a period of rapid growth and concentration of population, of industry, of capital, and of marketing facilities.

QUESTIONS FOR REVIEW

1. (a) What factors were responsible for the increase in domestic commerce after 1820?
   (b) What avenues of commerce were utilized in this development?

2. Beyond the realm of technological development, what were the economic impacts of the river steamboat upon the American economy?

3. What economic functions were performed by wholesalers?

4. Explain the manner in which the organization of retail trade developed.

5. (a) How was the cotton trade financed?
   (b) Did the method of financing the growing of cotton have an impact on the break between the North and the South? Explain.

6. How did the fact that the United States was an immature debtor nation prior to 1860 affect its balance of trade account?

7. (a) What are invisible exports?
   (b) What are invisible imports?
   (c) What are the functions of invisible items of foreign trade?

8. What invisible trade items loomed large on the balance of payments account prior to 1860?

9. (a) When is foreign trade "favorable"?
   (b) When is foreign trade "unfavorable"?
   (c) Criticize the use of favorable and unfavorable above from an economic point of view.

10. What factors gave rise to the superiority of the American clipper ship?

11. How do you account for the increasing importance of New York as a commercial center after 1825?

SUGGESTED READINGS

Callender, Guy S. *Selections from the Economic History of the United States, 1765-1860*. New York City: Augustus M. Kelley, Publishers, 1965. Chapters 6 and 7.

Davis, Lance E., Jonathan R. T. Hughes, and Duncan M. McDougall. *American Economic History*, 2d ed. Homewood, Ill.: Richard D. Irwin, Inc., 1965. Chapter 18.

Macesich, George. "International Trade and United States Economic Development Revisited," *American Economic History: Essays in Interpretation*, edited by Stanley Coben and Forest G. Hill. Philadelphia: J. B. Lippincott Co., 1966.

North, Douglass C. *The Economic Growth of the United States, 1790-1860*. Englewood Cliffs, N. J.: Prentice-Hall, Inc., 1961.

Taylor, George R. *The Transportation Revolution, 1815-1860*. New York City: Holt, Rinehart & Winston, Inc., 1951. Chapters 8 and 9.

Williamson, Jeffrey G. "International Trade and United States Economic Development," *American Economic History: Essays in Interpretation*, edited by Stanley Coben and Forest G. Hill. Philadelphia: J. B. Lippincott Co., 1966.

Chapter 11

INTERSECTIONAL DIFFERENCES; WAR. PERFORMANCE OF THE AMERICAN ECONOMY—1816-1865

BASIC ECONOMIC CONTRASTS

A technique used in the analysis of the economic development of the American colonies was to divide them into three groups or sections— Northern, Middle, and Southern. While land was in abundance in all of them, the manner in which it was appropriated and utilized in the various colonies differed widely, and that divergence in the patterns of land utilization widened throughout the first half of the 19th century. Land utilization was the basis for the formulation of attitudes and policies towards the disposal of public lands.

Land Policies

The people of the South were committed to an agricultural economy that was based on the plantation system. The perpetuation of that system depended on its ability to expand onto western lands. Expansion of the plantation system of agriculture depended upon the relatively easy availability of land, immediately in Alabama, Mississippi, and Louisiana, later in the vast area west of the Mississippi River. Vested interests in the easternmost regions of the Southern States had little to protect from the impacts of a westward movement of cotton and rice culture, since that movement usually did not occur until their continued plantings had begun to exhaust the soil to the point where crops became relatively unprofitable. Southern delegates in Congress favored selling public lands in large acreages and at low prices per acre so that the plantation owners would not have to compete with owners of small-sized farms for their land. The delegates from the Northern and from the Middle Atlantic States differed between themselves as to price policy, but were in agreement in favoring the sale of relatively small-sized farm parcels. The resulting policy was somewhat of a compromise in authorizing the sale of small-sized farms at low prices.

Towards the close of this period, the attitude of the people in the North and West changed somewhat to the extent that they advocated homesteading as an attraction to immigrants to settle upon land in the Northwestern and the Prairie States. The southern delegates in the United States Senate would not tolerate legislation of that nature, and it was not until their influence in Congress had been removed by the secession of the Southern States that such an act was passed by Congress. Rapid settlement of the North and the West would cause an imbalance between the representatives of the agricultural South, that depended upon slave labor and low tariffs, and representatives of other sections, in some of which manufacturing interests were dominant. West of the Appalachian Mountains and north of the Ohio River, agricultural interests were dominant; but they were not interested in a plantation type of farming, nor could they utilize slave labor efficiently. It is difficult to isolate the economic influences from those that were more political in motivation, but it is clear that the southern people did not want to relinquish control of power in Washington and become just another minority group.

Tariff Programs

Another reason for the South's struggle to maintain political balance in Congress was found in the tariff policy of the United States. As an agricultural section of the country and one that exported most of its money crop, the South was not interested in a tariff policy, except in a negative manner. The Northern and Middle Atlantic States were in favor of high protective tariffs in order to create home markets and to protect infant industries from competition in the sale of foreign manufactured goods. Until 1833 northern influence dominated the tariff policy of the United States; but from then to the close of the period under scrutiny, southern influence controlled that policy with the exception of one 4-year period, 1842-46. Not only was the South interested in maintaining a foreign market for its cotton, it was somewhat resentful of the fact that large amounts of its fluid capital were spent in northern markets for northern manufactures. Protective tariffs would serve only to aggravate that relationship or condition by providing an excuse to northern vendors to charge higher prices without having to face competition of imported goods.

In 1860, a writer in the *Boston Post,* in commenting on the size of southern markets, pointed to the fact that "the aggregate value of the merchandise sold to the South annually we estimate at some $60,000,000. The basis of the estimate is, first, the estimated amount of boots and shoes sold, which intelligent merchants place at from $20,000,000 to $30,000,000, including a limited amount that are manufactured with us and sold in New York. In the next place, we know from merchants in the trade that the amount of dry goods sold in the South yearly is many millions of dollars, and that the amount is second only to that of the sales of boots and shoes. In the third place, we learn from careful inquiry, and from the best sources, that the fish of various kinds sold realize $3,000,000, or in that neighborhood. Upwards of $1,000,000 is received for furniture sold in the South each year. The Southern States are much better markets than the Western for this article." Northern merchants were interested in tariffs as a means of keeping foreign competition out of a lucrative southern market.

Debtor-Creditor Relationships

In overcoming the problem of the scarcity of capital, the people of the Southern States had been unable to make much progress other than by borrowing from northern capitalists and from European banks. Most of the capital in the South that represented investments of plantation owners was in land and slaves. The planter had a cultural society that was unique in this country. Important in his scale of living was a large amount of free time—free, that is, from productive effort. He kept a stable of horses and a kennel of dogs, and the hunt was an important feature of his leisurely economy. He traveled abroad and educated his children in foreign schools. He entertained lavishly and his cupboards were well stocked with wines and liquors. He rode horseback and furnished carriages for his guests. His library was shelved with first editions and literary classics. Paintings adorned his walls. His mansion was the setting for debutante parties and other social events. His gardens were unexcelled in landscaping and in riotous colors in the blossoming season. His dress reflected that of the foreign gentleman, and his lady wore the latest Paris creations. He lived to enjoy life, and the abstinence required to save capital sums just was not to his liking.

Not only had the southerners been forced to borrow some capital from the North, but most of their shipping for overseas and coastwise trade was owned and operated by northern entrepreneurs. The cumulative effect of the dependence of the South upon northern capital had been to create and to perpetuate a debtor position of the South in its relations with the North. Financing of cotton crops from their planting to their export had been done with northern capital; and when crops failed or the price of cotton in world markets was low, again, it had been advances of capital funds from the North that carried planters over to the following year. Debtor peoples are somewhat prone to generate a feeling of ill will towards what appears to be their more fortunate creditors.

Internal Improvements

Another area of difference between the South and the North was in the allocation of federal monies for internal improvements. Henry Clay's system included the use of customs receipts to finance internal improvements; and, since the South voted heavily against protective tariffs, it could not expect to benefit directly by the allocation of the expenditure of such funds. Canals were not needed in the South and a plantation economy did not need the roads that were required to develop the trade and commerce of the North and of the Middle Western States.

Those differences, which were entirely honest and sincere, were the outgrowth of the socioeconomic climate of the respective areas involved. In a
republican form of government such as ours, it was not surprising that
those differences had their political implications and impacts. They revert
to the days of Alexander Hamilton and Thomas Jefferson who differed over
the degree of sovereignty the states should retain and how much power
should be vested in the federal government. The doctrine of States Rights
was a political weapon of a minority group, the delegates from the Southern
States, rather than a principal cause of internecine struggle.

Slavery

Initially, slavery had been the solution to the problem of labor shortage
in an agricultural and plantation type of economy. It had been tried in
the New England States and in the Middle Atlantic States and had been
found wanting. Some domestic slaves were found in those states at the
same time that sentiment was crystallizing against that institution. The slave
trade was entrepreneured almost entirely by New England traders who used
New England capital, and the profits from that trade accrued to New
England capitalists. There is no evidence that northern capital was used
to finance the internal slave marts that were located in the Southern States.
Slave owners in Virginia and Kentucky who had found the employment of
slaves in the cultivation of cotton and tobacco less profitable in the market
sold them on the auction block to the highest bidder. To the credit of
southern culture, let it be understood that breeding and slave trading were
frowned upon in the more elite social circles.

Census data record a white population in the South in 1860 of 7,033,973.
Allowing five persons to a family, they constituted approximately 1,406,794
families, 308,753 of which owned slaves. Slaves numbered 3,838,765 of a
total Negro population of 4,097,111. Most of the free Negroes were employed in urban areas though some were working with small yeomen farmers.
The average number of slaves owned was less than ten, and there may have
been ten or more planters who owned more than 1,000 slaves.

Slavery as a Cause of War. With only 25 percent of the southern
families owning slaves, why did almost the entire South rally round its cause
in 1861-65? Without attempting to list their order or priority, the answer
was found in (1) the fact that slavery provided an emotional appeal in
rallying people to support a cause—in the North, the cause of freedom; in
the South, the perpetuation of plantation farming. While slave labor had
been dominant in the growing of cotton, it had been used to a lesser extent
in the cultivation of tobacco, sugar, rice, and hemp. (2) The entire economy
of the South had been built around the plantation system of agriculture;
and the sale of cotton, tobacco, sugar, rice, and hemp to the world outside
the Southern States was the ultimate source of income to the South and to
its people, even to those who lived in urban communities and who were

not actively and directly engaged in any kind of agriculture. (3) While the percentage of Negro population to whites declined in the four census years of 1830, 1840, 1850, and 1860, Negroes constituted more than 25 percent of the total population in 1860. More alarming to the southerner of that day was the fact that in some counties in Alabama and Mississippi, Negroes actually outnumbered whites. *Manumission* with the right of free suffrage meant that political control would be in the hands of former slaves; many of whom had not been educated to the level where they could read and write. (4) On the other side were those persons who believed that it was morally wrong to enslave human beings and who had denounced the institution of slavery in such terms that there could be no compromising. Their campaign that spread propaganda of hate had forced the people into the camps of antislavery on the one hand, proslavery on the other. (5) The dispute over States Rights had been heightened by the Dred Scott decision in 1857. The Republican party, which had its origin in its opposition to the spread of slavery into western territories, assumed a more militant attitude towards the very existence of that institution, let alone its extension into new frontiers. (6) Many businessmen in the North had feared the financial consequences of a break with the South, and had opposed the nomination, later the election, of Abraham Lincoln. Many persons in the South had already given expression to their attitude by having freed their slaves and then having hired them back on a wage basis. Representative of the feeling of the poor whites of North Carolina was the condemnation of slavery as found in *The Impending Crisis of the South,* which was authored by Hinton R. Helper, who took the position that the system of slavery had plunged the South "into a state of comparative imbecility and obscurity." It was inflammatory statements such as this and others that were made by the abolitionists that removed the issue from settlement at the polls and carried it to the battlefield.

Political Balance of Power. When the Ordinance of 1787 provided that slave labor could not be introduced into the Old Northwest Territory, cotton had not become king in the South. Slavery had not become a burning issue. By 1818, the Missouri Territory had a population of more than 60,000 and applied for statehood. Many of those people had migrated from the Old South and were sympathetic to slavery. The ensuing struggle for control was settled for the time being by the Missouri Compromise in 1820. To maintain a balance of power in the United States Senate, Maine had been admitted as a free state, Missouri as a slave state. With the exception of Missouri, slavery had been prohibited in the Louisiana Territory north of parallel 36° 30'. Arkansas had been settled by plantation owners from east of the Mississippi River who used slave labor in the cultivation of cotton, tobacco, and corn. The extension of slavery was made an issue at the political level in the settlement of the far Western States. Economic conditions were not conducive to the use of slave labor in those states, but the politicians and reformers would not let the issue become dormant. The Compromise of 1850, followed by the Kansas-Nebraska Act four years later, only served to fan the flames of hatred and antagonism between the free states and the slave. Tempers were not mitigated by the decision in the Dred Scott case. By now the issue had taken hold at the political level and economic causes had become secondary. War was just beyond the horizon in spite of Herculean efforts to avert such a catastrophe.

WAR

Though the United States had been born from a war situation and it had been faced with several war crises at home and abroad in its first quarter century of national existence, those incidents were treated as temporary; and adjustments were made in the relationships between the central government and segments of the economy as exigencies required. While immediate, short-run results were uppermost in the minds of almost everyone, the impacts of those adjustments were felt in the ensuing years of peace. Needless to say, neither the North nor the South was prepared for civil strife to the extent that their resources had been developed to meet the demands of war. The economic relationships in the areas of finance, industry, transportation, and trade had been premised on a continuation of peaceful relationships not only between themselves, but between them and other nations of the world. Natural and industrial resources of all sections of the United States had been developed along the lines of the objectives of free enterprise and the profit motive; and their regimentation for welfare purposes or to attain military potentials had been given little or no consideration by American political and economic leaders.

Resources for Conducting the War

In terms of population numbers, natural resources and their development, agricultural development, diversification of crops and also of industry, and mineral resources, the North had a tremendous, almost overwhelming advantage over the South as they entered upon the conflict. The people in the Southern States had been using the money of the United States, and had none of their own except that issued by banks, railroads, lumber companies, and other types of concerns. There had been no necessity of financing a separate central government in the South, hence no revenues were available for such use. In only two areas did the South have an advantage over the North. Superior generalship on the field of battle turned the fortunes of war in favor of the South when all other odds were against it. The fact that most of the campaign activity took place on southern soil implanted a zeal and purpose in combat which the northern soldier did not seem to possess.

Population. While the 22 Northern States claimed a population of over 22 million persons, 5,700,000 of whom were males between the ages of

18 and 60, many people in the more Western and Northwestern States had not been much concerned over the struggle, its causes, its conduct, or its outcome; and the manpower they had contributed had done more to swell the size of the northern armies than to add zest to its purposeful fighting. Men of all nationalities were eligible to answer the call to battle. The South had a white population of a little over five million people, 1,300,000 of whom could be counted on for military service. The South had furnished the North with about one half as many soldiers as it had enlisted in its own army, hence the justification for the use of the term *civil* in referring to that struggle *in toto,* or in any of its phases. There was no immigrant population in the South from which to draw recruits for its forces.

Agriculture. It was in agriculture that the leaders of the southern cause thought they were more influential than the North in enlisting aid from European countries, particularly England. To them, cotton was king; and they thought the need for it as a raw material to keep the textile mills in England humming would influence the industrial and political leaders in England to throw their support to the South in its struggle to create a new nation. English cotton mills depended so heavily on cotton imports from the South that England would aid in rushing any blockade the northern navy might establish, or even destroy it; but, alas for the South, wheat crops failed in England, and, in a manner of thinking, it was pitting a hungry stomach against a cold back and the stomach won out. That was disappointing to the South, to put it mildly, because it had counted on British support not only to purchase its cotton, but to furnish it with many of the manufactured products it had been obtaining from northern manufacturers. Support by the British would have helped to keep the sea lanes open on which food and munitions of war could have been brought over to fill a void in southern resources. The continued sale of cotton would have furnished a supply of foreign exchange the South could have used in the purchase of food and munitions of war.

Good crop years, together with the loss of southern markets, enabled the United States to export wheat to England in larger volume than formerly and to offset the poor harvests there. In spite of farm labor having been drained into the army, increased use of farm machinery, newly arrived immigrant labor, the use of female labor, and the cultivation of new lands contributed to increasing the size of the harvest. Under the terms of the Homestead Act of 1862, free entry could be made on 160 acres of western lands to which title would be given at the end of five years residence upon it if permanent improvements had been made. In 1863, 8,223 entries were made upon a total of 1,315,680 acres, and in 1864 the corresponding data were 9,405 entries upon 1,504,000 acres. Because little preparation other than plowing and harrowing had to be made to bring them under cultivation, thousands of these acres were in production in wheat and corn during the war. In 1865, 8,924 entries were made upon 1,427,840 acres of homestead lands; but, since the war had terminated in April of that year, the impact of cultivating these acres was not felt until the years of reconstruction were in progress. During the war, there may have been some local shortages, but they were the result of failures in the distribution system and not in volume of production.

The South was not as fortunate as the North in its endowment of natural wealth and capital. To begin with, plantings in food crops were not sufficiently large to feed the southern people, and their imports from the North terminated with the outbreak of hostilities. Many planters had slaves cultivating gardens and cereal crops for local consumption; but after 1863 in particular, many slaves defected to the North or refused to work for their former masters, and some plantations were overrun with enemy forces. Small farms and those that were operated by poor whites produced diversified crops and foodstuffs, but not in large enough quantities to offset the loss of northern imports combined with the devastation of farms and plantations wrought by invading armies. One of the policies of the northern troops was to live off the bounty of the southern farms and to destroy any food and supplies that could not be confiscated.

Potential farm labor in the South had been drawn into military service, either voluntarily or involuntarily. When slaves refused to work or defected, farm work was seriously impaired. The strength and productivity of farm labor lay not alone in numbers of workers. Being inured to the hardships of farm work and applying labor intelligently were important factors. Young white men and women had not worked on southern farms. They could not become proficient workers spontaneously. While they were learning the hard way, the war continued to exhaust food supplies. Some food was obtained from border states. Other increments were obtained from the Southwest, which did not feel the early impacts of the war.

Transportation. The North had a tremendous advantage over the South in the realms of transportation facilities and in productive resources. East-west railway lines north of the Ohio River distributed food advantageously throughout the Northern States. Railroads also were utilized more in the movement of troops and supplies and facilitated their concentration in areas of prospective fighting. Probably the most important segment of railroad construction was the completion of a single gauge track between New York and Cincinnati. The Pennsylvania Railroad completed the first trunk line between the Atlantic Coast and Lake Michigan by acquiring the Pittsburgh, Fort Wayne and Chicago Railroad. Other improvements in railroad transportation included the extension of single gauge tracks, double tracking some lines, and erecting heavier bridges over some of the larger rivers.

At the outbreak of hostilities, railroads in the South were entirely inadequate to meet the demands of war. They continued to transport cotton to the nearest port where it could be shipped to England, but the northern blockade retarded that movement. One of the sagas of Civil War history is connected with the attempts to use the railroad between Atlanta and Chattanooga. The South was greatly handicapped in not having had through rail connections between its northern and its southern sectors. One of the objectives of the northern armies had been to destroy the railroads of the South, and the South had tried just as valiantly to rebuild them, or to construct new lines.

Industries. Again, the North had the advantage of iron mills and fabricating establishments. In 1859, the first commercial oil well had been put into operation near Oil City, northeast of Pittsburgh, Pennsylvania; and it was not long before there was a flourishing oil well supply industry. The making of pipes, barrels, derricks, and lamps enlarged upon the industrial activity of the North. Tank cars were designed and built to hasten the distribution of petroleum and its products throughout the North and East. Clothing factories in the North and in the South were adjusted to making military uniforms with the aid of newly installed sewing machines. Gordon McKay purchased the Benke machine for sewing leather soles to uppers and placed the boot and shoe industry on a larger scale operation.

Iron furnaces were in commercial production in the states of Maryland, Kentucky, Tennessee, and Virginia prior to the outbreak of hostilities. Since Maryland and Kentucky were border states in which allegiance was divided between the North and the South, their contributions in the form of iron products is questionable. Mills were operating in Tennessee and northern Georgia, which accounts for some of the military action in these regions. Early in the war, Virginia lost 55 counties in the northwestern part of the state, which became the state of West Virginia in 1863. That region was rich in mineral resources, coal, and timber. Again the South was lacking a distribution system, and northern armies made railroads and terminals prime targets for attack.

Finances. The leaders on both sides did not think the war would last very long, nor were they prepared to finance one of any appreciable duration. There was no revenue system of any sort for the Confederacy; and for the North, revenues from the sale of public lands and customs receipts were ill adapted to finance a war. There were, and are, only three ways by which wars are financed; and all three methods were used by both sides—taxation, borrowing, and issuing paper money.

Taxation. Among the first taxes imposed by the federal Congress were a direct tax of 22 cents per capita and an income tax of 3 percent on all incomes over $800 per year. By 1865, the personal exemption had been lowered to $600, and the rates of taxation graduated to 10 percent on incomes over $5,000. That tax yielded much more revenue after the war was over than during all of the war years put together. Its use was terminated by law in 1870. In 1817, the federal government had discontinued the use of excise taxes but the Act of 1861 imposed low and moderate rates on a large number of items rather than high rates on a few luxuries and necessities of inelastic demand. Among the classes of goods taxed were tobacco, liquors and beer, manufactured products, each at the several stages of production; railroads and steamboats; banking houses and insurance companies; legal documents of all kinds; legacies; and advertisements. Occupational licenses were issued and salaries of all officers of the United States were taxed. David A. Wells, a well-known writer in the area of public finance, expressed the idea in the following terms: "Wherever you find an article, a product, a trade, a profession, or a source of income, tax it." An upward revision of the tariff was made in 1862 and again in 1864 on the compensatory principle of protecting American manufacturers from foreign competition. The latter revision established an average rate of 47 percent on all imported commodities.

Loans. All told, the federal government borrowed $2,600,000 through the issuance and sale of bonds. When sales began to lag in 1863, one Jay Cooke was employed to organize a campaign beyond the institutional level and to appeal directly to the people to purchase them. His sales organization of several hundred persons literally combed the country on a door-to-door basis and sold the bonds.

Paper Money. United States notes were issued to the amount of $450 million to give the government some ready cash, and quickly. These notes were in the form of currency and were unsecured promises to pay their face values in gold. *Greenbacks,* as they were and still are called, comprised much of the hand-to-hand currency or government money; but they depreciated rapidly as their volume increased. That increase was not in response to or in proportion to an increase in the production of goods and the rendering of productive services, but in accordance with the government's need for units of purchasing power with which to pay for materials that were made to be destroyed or to destroy items of wealth. When it became questionable that they would ever be redeemed, either because the federal armies were not successful on the field of battle or because tax receipts were not of sufficient volume to redeem them, people lost confidence in the practical aspects of their redeemability and refused to accept them in trade at face value. At one time they depreciated to 38 cents on the dollar. Greenbacks were given full legal tender usage or privileges, public and private, and could be used in paying all debts and taxes to the United States, except the payments of customs duties. Also, they were not used in the payment of interest on the public debt.

By not accepting greenbacks in payment of customs duties, a flow of gold to the Treasury had been assured with which interest on the public debt could be paid as per contract. Legal tender did not then, and does not now, permit a substitution for gold when payment in that metal was designated in a contract. Prices of commodities were quoted in terms of standard money and also in terms of greenbacks. Thus, if a commodity had been priced at $1 in standard money, and the greenback was used at a time when it had depreciated 50 percent, $2 in greenbacks were required to complete the transaction. *Shinplasters* were a kind of fractional paper money that was issued to compensate for a shortage of fractional coins. They did not add anything to the monetary base, nor did they contribute to the inflationary trend of prices.

Banking Developments—The National Banking System

Since the close of the Second Bank of the United States in 1836, the federal government had had no fiscal agent. True, the Independent Treasury was the depository for government funds, but it had no other fiscal functions to perform. When the government was called upon a third time to restore order out of chaos in banking and in the issuance of circulating notes, it adopted an entirely different approach in the establishment of the National Banking System.

There was no semblance of central banking in the National Banking System. Branch banking was not mentioned, but, by rulings of the Comptroller of the Currency, it was prohibited. The government was unalterably committed to a policy of maintaining independent unit banking in the United States. Some centralization of authority was obtained through the office of the Comptroller of the Currency. As the principal executive officer of the National Banking System, he was in charge of accepting requests for charters for national banks. His office was responsible for seeing that the applicants had complied with all of the requirements of the law before charters were granted. He also established a system for examining the books of national banks at least four times a year. Government bonds which were owned by the banks were deposited with him to secure the redemption of national bank notes as well as to control the volume outstanding. In his vaults was the 5 percent redemption fund that was maintained by the issuing banks in order to guarantee the ready redemption of national bank notes in Washington. The government bonds assured their ultimate redemption; the redemption fund assured their circulation at par.

The immediate pressure for such an organization arose from the inability of the Treasury Department to float government bonds in its efforts to finance the war. Early successes on the field of battle were not such that instilled confidence in the government's ability to redeem them when they matured and to pay interest on them twice yearly until then.

In order to provide a market for government bonds and also to provide a uniform bank note currency, the National Banking System was authorized by act of Congress, February 25, 1863. The organization of national banking was patterned somewhat after the provisions of the New York Free Banking Act of 1838, in that general incorporation of banks was authorized and banks could issue bond secured circulating notes. Bonds that were eligible to secure national bank notes were certain long-term federal government bonds that were so designated. One third of the capital of each bank, or a minimum of $30,000, whichever was larger, had to be invested in government bonds. The banks were entirely independent unit banks with a Comptroller of the Currency as the principal executive officer. National bank notes were not given legal tender status, but they were made redeemable in lawful money on demand. Lawful money was defined by the Comptroller of the Currency as constituting legal tender money that was eligible to serve as bank reserves, and during the period under discussion, that meant government money.

Between February 25 and October 1, 1863, only 66 national banks were chartered; and they deposited less than $4 million in government bonds to secure national bank notes. Obviously, as a market for government bonds, national banks were found lacking. Under the terms of a revision of the Bank Act of June 3, 1864, 584 national banks had deposited approximately $65 million face value of government bonds by October of that year to secure their circulating notes. By the close of the war, national banks were furnishing a uniform bank note circulation, were absorbing a significant volume of government bonds, and some of them had been designated as depositories for government deposits, except customs receipts.

Confederate Finances

The approach that was made by the Confederacy to financing the war was not one of adjustment to an emergency situation. It was one of organizing an entirely new fiscal system that would finance an emergency situation. One of its most urgent needs was for money. The development of some kind of revenue system was a *sine qua non* in order to provide a continuous flow of income with which to finance the war. The first action that was taken was the seizure of something over $500,000 of Bullion Fund and customs receipts in New Orleans. A smaller sum was confiscated later, but these amounts were entirely inadequate to support the war program of the Confederacy. The most immediate source of funds was obtained by issuing bonds, some of which were collateralized by bales of cotton.

The constitution of the Confederate States of America provided for an export tariff on cotton, but the tariff yielded little or nothing to the Confederate Treasury. Other taxes included (1) an 8 percent property tax that excluded food for home consumption, personal and household goods; (2) a license tax imposed on most business establishments and professions; (3) a progressive earnings tax, graduated from 1 percent on $1,500 to 15 percent on earnings of $10,000 and over; (4) a tax on profits derived from the sale of designated items, first levied in 1863; and (5) a tax in kind taking one tenth of the volume of agricultural produce, based on the production levels of 1863. Needless to say, the volume of revenue that was received from those taxes was entirely inadequate to meet the war needs of the Confederacy; and it did not increase as the war years progressed. Loans and notes yielded most of the revenue, and they also contributed heavily to an inflation that tended to wipe out all property values and vested interests.

Currency was provided by the issuance of Treasury notes. Early issues were interest bearing and were fundable in bonds. Initially, they were issued as credit obligations, but as succeeding notes were put into circulation, they became *fiat money*. At the close of the war, they amounted to more than $1 billion.

Taxes were levied on income and profits. Licenses were imposed on business firms. Some of them were straight business licenses; others were combinations of a flat levy plus a percentage of gross sales. Total tax receipts during the war years were less than 10 percent of the currency notes that were issued and less than 25 percent of the receipts from the sale of bonds. Treasury notes amounted to 2½ times bond receipts.

Sums of money that were due northern people or northern concerns of any kind were made payable to the Confederate Treasury, but were difficult to collect. The entire economy of the South became so demoralized as the war progressed that only about 5 percent of the total receipts of the Confederacy were received through the channels of taxation.

PERFORMANCE OF THE AMERICAN ECONOMY—1816-1865

In approaching a study of how well an economy has functioned, it is necessary to establish certain criteria of measurement or evaluation. It also is essential that a distinction be made between the expansion of an economy and its growth. Expansion of the American economy could have taken place prior to 1865 with all of the outward appearances of economic growth. Closer scrutiny of the criteria may reveal that it was nothing more than an enlargement of the scope of activity that did not involve any change in the relationships between the factors of production, nor in the distribution of wealth among or between the people, most of whom occupied the double role of producers and consumers. Since the ultimate objective of all economic effort is to produce wealth that will satisfy man's wants, and to produce it with less effort, or lower cost per unit of output, unless these conditions are met, there most certainly is no growth.

An economic organization may operate for the benefit of landowners, or it may enable manufacturers to improve upon their economic status at the expense of other segments of the economy. When merchant traders were in control of an economic organization, they established a framework that enriched themselves at the expense of the members of other segments of the economy. To the extent that landowners were in control, they tended to emphasize the importance of land as the source of all wealth, to enforce laws of primogeniture and entail, to foster programs of free trade or low tariffs, and to construct a body of economic doctrine that tended to perpetuate and enhance their control over their economic society.

To the extent that manufacturers were in control, their economic doctrines tended to encourage savings and the investment of capital, and to eulogize the use of protective tariffs as a means not only of giving encouragement to the development of home industries and to the development of markets, but of benefiting those who belonged to other segments of the economy. Members of the working classes favored higher wages and shorter hours of work. They also wanted recognition at law and at the polls. They advocated the equality of the members of all segments of a free society in its educational and social institutions. In the development of the American economy to 1860, the influences of each of those groups were felt, and compromises were made from time to time in the various aspects or devices of control in recognition of their economic interests and objectives.

Modern economic relationships are described in terms of specialization, division of labor, and interdependence; and if the development of a complex economic organization of which these terms are descriptive has not resulted in raising the level of consumption of its people, little progress or growth has actually occurred. While the economic organization of New England, the Middle Atlantic States, the South, and the West was each somewhat unique and distinctive, each type of organization was dependent upon the ready but unconscious cooperation of the remaining sections for its ultimate success. The absence of trade barriers at state boundaries gave merchants new trading territory as the frontier of settlement was pushed westward. That enlarged upon their activities without necessarily implying economic growth. Increased business or larger profits were not per se measures of economic growth.

Tests of a Successful Economic Organization

Probably the first test of the operation of the American economic organization was the *support it provided for its people*. Population not only increased from almost 10 million persons in 1820 to a little over 31 million in 1860, but that 200 percent increase in population was accompanied by an increase in its density of about 100 percent, from 5.6 to 10.6 persons per square mile. That was due in part to the settlement roughly of 1,200,000 acres of land that counteracted a strong urbanization movement which was increasing the number as well as the size of cities, most of which were in the East.

Urban areas owed their growth to the development of commerce and of manufacturing. Reference to Table 11-1 reveals the part that manufacturing played in contributing to the growth and the size of the largest 15 cities in 1860. There were 126 other cities of more than 8,000 population, in several of which over 10 percent of the people were engaged in manufacturing. The gains from manufacturing were not equally distributed among those whose efforts made them possible. The factory system forced many alterations in the patterns of living and working, some of which were not entirely cultural in their impacts.

At the same time that factory organization displaced the domestic system, thousands of immigrants literally flooded our ports of entry, none of which were in the South. While many of the Germans and Scandinavians

Table 11-1

Leading Cities in 1860

Rank	Name of City	Population	Percentage of Population Engaged in Manufacturing
1	New York	1,080,330	9.5
2	Philadelphia	565,529	17.5
3	Baltimore	212,418	8.0
4	Boston	177,840	10.8
5	New Orleans	168,675	3.0
6	Cincinnati	161,044	18.3
7	St. Louis	160,773	5.8
8	Chicago	109,260	4.9
9	Buffalo	81,129	6.9
10	Newark	71,941	26.2
11	Louisville	68,033	9.8
12	Albany	62,367	9.3
13	Washington	61,122	3.9
14	San Francisco	56,802	2.6
15	Providence	50,666	22.0

Source: "Mortality and Miscellaneous Statistics," *Eighth Census of the United States* (Washington: U. S. Department of Commerce, Bureau of the Census, 1860), p. xviii.

went directly to farms in the West, thousands of others remained in eastern cities to add to the squalor of urban growth. Conditions of unemployment, low wages, unbelievably poor housing situations, poor working conditions, payments of wages in scrip, and exploitation of wage earners by owners of factories make it difficult and awkward to describe that kind of development in terms of economic growth, at least as far as sharing the products of that development was concerned. There is ample evidence to show that unskilled day workers, who may have constituted over 50 percent of the urban populations, were being paid little more than $1 per week; and the average earnings of journeymen printers in New York in 1845 were $6 a week, or $300 a year. That may have been the equivalent of about $1,500 in 1960. At the other extreme were the fortunes of Stephen Girard, who left $7 million when he died in 1831, and John Jacob Astor, who left $48 million when he passed away in 1848. There is no question that wealth had been produced, that its distribution was very unequal, and that the foundations of many millionaire fortunes had been laid. Many of those fortunes were the result of enlarged activities that had been brought under the control of one or a few men. There may have been no element of economic growth in those activities. Expansion, larger volume, and perhaps unethical practices contributed to the amassing of large fortunes. At the time, business was business, and frequently large money profits were enough justification for dishonest practices. No government agencies had been created to enforce fair trade practices.

Scales of Living. *Scales of living* are difficult to evaluate and to describe, data on that phase of living being so scattered and so meager. When prices are quoted for that early period, they are so ridiculously low that they are practically meaningless. It may not be far wrong to bridge the gap between 1860 and 1960 by multiplying wages and salaries by five. One item that does not appear in tables and budgets is the fact that there were fewer articles and varieties of articles to purchase then than now. Another factor is that little money, either absolutely or proportionately, was spent on commercial entertainment and amusements; these were provided in the home, by or in the church, or in the school. Reports on prevailing wage rates seldom mentioned commodity prices, so it is difficult to translate money incomes into real wages which measure scales or levels of living. Skilled workers, foremen, and supervisors in New England received $2.00 per day, give or take a few cents, when unskilled workers were being paid less than $1.00. Male schoolteachers in Boston received $2,267 a year, but women teachers were paid only $400. Baltimore paid its women teachers $292 a year, and men teachers received $1,267.

Leisure Time. One test that has been applied to economic systems is the fact of leisure time, its amount, and how it is spent. With a working day of from 12 to 14 hours, there was little leisure time during which workers could relax themselves in pleasurable activity. By 1860, a 10-hour day was rather common, and people were beginning to enjoy their leisure. Business and professional men, farmers, and southern planters had incomes that were sufficiently large to enable them to attend concerts, the theater, lectures, and to travel. Resorts were frequented in season by the socially elite. Every small city seemed to have its minstrel shows and vaudeville performances. Horse racing and prizefighting were the principal spectator sports of those that were held in the open.

Expansion of Economic Activity. Expansion of economic activity in the United States was somewhat phenomenal, especially compared with a much slower rate of expansion of the European economies. The most important factor in that expansion movement was the vast amount of new territory that was brought under settlement throughout all of this period, together with the fact of government encouragement, if not actual subsidization, of that movement. Of expansion there is no doubt, but was the rate of expansion healthy for the economy or for its people? The answer to that question depends partly upon the attitude of the person who is asked. From an economic point of view, the expansion of any economic activity was healthy and of overall benefit to the economy when the money income from that activity was sufficiently large to pay all costs involved and to return a profit to those persons who assumed the financial risks of enterprise. When the rate of expansion was unhealthy, financial losses became so large and the outlook for the future became so unpromising that prices fell, property values fell, banks failed, business firms failed, unemployment increased, interest rates were high, credit was contracted, and a crisis had turned into a panic and an industrial recession was in process. If the recession was serious or of a considerable duration, it developed into a depression.

Failures of Our Economic System

The first serious panic and depression occurred as a postwar phenomenon. One of the accompaniments of war has been, and still is, a sudden stimulus to industry and to general economic activity. Without going into an analysis of all of the causes of recessions and business depressions, the depression of 1819 was the culmination of a period of overexpansion of industry that had been stimulated by some of the conditions that grew out of war. Manufacturing industries increased rapidly and western lands had been settled more rapidly than the immediate short-run market situation warranted. Profits that might have arisen from the speculation in western lands were uppermost in the minds of those persons who participated in and were responsible for that phase of our development. The Second Bank of the United States, at that time, expanded its note issues and facilitated the speculation in western lands. When tariff legislation tended to retard the rate at which commodities were imported and new capital found its way into financing domestic manufacturing industries in the Northeast, business began to pick up, employment to increase, prices to rise, and business prosperity prevailed, although there were minor setbacks during the years 1820-37.

Panic of 1837. Speculation in western lands and in internal improvements increased toward the close of the decade of the 1820's and the early part of the 1830's. Debates and arguments over the fate of the Bank of the United States—discussions that amounted to severe disputes—lent instability and loss of confidence in the financial structure of the economy and in the role of the federal government. Jackson's *Specie Circular,* the closing of the Bank of the United States, and the distribution of the Treasury surplus among the states—all contributed to the panic of 1837 and to the depression that followed. The Treasury surplus was distributed on a per capita basis, which meant that most of it went to the Eastern States. Most of the surplus had been deposited in banks in Western States that were more sparsely populated. The movement of government monies from West to East was more than the economy could stand. The speculative boom in the West collapsed; banks closed their doors and suspended specie payments. The final installment of the Treasury surplus was not paid at that time, nor has it ever been paid. After several years of uncertainty and more or less floundering around from 1837 to 1843, the economy gained strength and its forward progress was accelerated.

Panic of 1857. The next serious setback occurred in 1857, the internal causes of which were overspeculation in railroad building and in railroad securities. The immediate and precipitating cause was the failure of the Ohio Life Insurance and Trust Company, which was actually a bank of deposit rather than an insurance company. Mismanagement of funds by the manager of its New York office resulted in its inability to meet some of its obligations on demand, and confidence in the entire financial system of the economy was shaken to the breaking point. War hysteria had the effect of stimulating trading and financial activities.

Most important in this respect was the fact that the American economy, which had been geared throughout almost its entire existence to conditions of peace, was able to adjust itself readily to the demands of internal strife and later to emerge from a war in better economic condition than before.

Causes of Economic Growth

Among the basic factors that contributed to the economic growth of the United States between 1820-65 was *innovation:* the introduction of new devices, or of new techniques of production, some of which resulted in lower unit production costs. For others the impacts were to open up entirely new channels of industry and of manufacturing and to make possible the production of entirely new products. It is not difficult to recall some of the new inventions, new techniques, or new devices that were made use of for the first time in the United States during this period and which provided stimuli to our economic development and, possibly, to our economic growth. Without giving them any priority of time or of importance, the following factors made direct contributions to the American economy by lowering unit costs of production as well as by making it possible to produce larger quantities of goods that were utilized directly by a larger number of people.

Agriculture. The developments that have been described under the guise of the agricultural revolution undoubtedly contributed to our economic growth by making possible larger output at lower unit costs. Horse-drawn farm machinery; the introduction and application of scientific farming, including the use of fertilizers; the rotation of crops; the introduction of new crops and scientific breeding of cattle, sheep, horses, and pigs loomed large in the development of agriculture, except in those states where plantation farming was practiced.

Business Organization. The development of the corporate form of business organization made it possible for some firms to operate on a larger scale and to combine more capital with land and labor in such a way that lower unit costs ensued. Corporations were recognized at law as legal entities. They had spans of life that were provided in the terms of their charters. Ownership interests were indicated through the ownership of shares of common stock. Railroad and canal companies raised more capital by borrowing through the instrumentality of bonds than through the sale of stock. Bondholders were creditors and had no ownership rights, privileges, or responsibilities. In case of corporate failures, stockholders were protected against the claims of their creditors. Through corporate organization the best men available were employed. Departmentalization tended to contribute greater efficiency of management and of operation. More capital was brought together than many individual enterprisers and partnerships could acquire or command. Within indeterminate limits, lower unit costs frequently followed increase in the volume of corporate activity. The factory system really was one of production, but its development never could have taken place as it did under the control of partnerships and single enterprise forms of business organization.

Manufacturing. Towards the close of this period, the increasing use of coke made from bituminous coal not only lowered the costs of producing iron and steel, it resulted in a better grade of steel. Meat-packing became a new industry after its entrepreneurs discovered some of the advantages of concentrating their efforts first in Cincinnati, later in Indianapolis, and finally in Chicago. Meat was produced in large packinghouses at lower costs than local butchers could handle it. It was in meat-packing that the discovery was made that it was cheaper to carry the product to the workers than it was to make the workmen move around in working on a carcass, and the endless chain method of production was the result. It was the meat-packers of Cincinnati who stressed the advantages of utilizing the by-products of a major industry. Lard, soap, candles, glue, and bristles shared the original cost of slaughtering hogs. The price of pork no longer had to cover the entire cost of processing the animals. Lard oil soon replaced whale oil for lighting and for lubricating purposes.

The introduction of the *Fourdrinier papermaking machine* marked the beginning of papermaking on a large scale, and lower unit costs were the result. It was not until after the process of *vulcanizing* rubber was accidentally discovered in 1839 that the rubber industry achieved *economies of scale*. The sewing machine as applied to the making of cotton and woolen goods took the manufacture of clothing out of the home and adapted it to factory organization. That reduced the time factor of the entire process and increased the productivity of the workers in terms of output. Unfortunately for the workers involved, the increase in their commodity productivity was not reflected in their wages. The application of the sewing machine to the making of boots and shoes was an important growth factor in trend, but its impact on the statistical measurement of growth was difficult to discern.

Power. The harnessing of steam power and the use of coal as fuel made the factory system of production possible and its substitution for horsepower or for waterpower added mobility to our industrialization in addition to lowering production costs. Mobility made it possible to locate industries near their sources of raw materials, near their markets, or near their labor supply as determined by the relative costs of transportation and wage rates.

Transportation. First canals and later railroads took the burden of moving goods and people off the roads and turnpikes at a mere fraction of the costs of highway transportation. They turned transportation from a factor that retarded the distribution of goods throughout the country into one that gave encouragement to it. The development of transportation, together with the burning of coal to produce steam, may have been the most important combination of factors that contributed to our economic growth.

Regionally, the impact of these and other technological improvements fell more heavily on the economy of those states that were north of the Ohio River, to the East and to the West, than upon the economy of the Southern States. If data were available from which to calculate the contribution to gross national product and national income by states, there is no doubt but that the contribution of the Southern States was the result of their expanded agricultural activity along traditional patterns rather than of increased efficiency of the productive factors, especially of land and labor, that operated to lower unit costs. Farm machinery, rotation of crops, scientific agriculture, and the importing and breeding of livestock just had no place in the South where heavy capital investment had been made in slaves in order to provide an ample, cheap, and continuous labor supply. While some manufacturing was found in the Southeastern States, the volume was not sufficiently large to offset the stabilizing effect that agriculture had upon the measurement of economic growth.

Estimated National Wealth

Insofar as the estimated wealth of the United States from the years 1825 to 1860 is correct, reference to the data in Table 11-2 reveals that it not only increased every year, but the increments of increase grew in every year with the exception of 1838, 1840, 1854, 1858, and 1860. The retarded increases for the years of 1838 and 1840 reflect the years of uncertainty following the panic of 1837 and the collapse of the cotton boom the following year. While the estimated wealth for 1854 was greater than that for 1853, the rate of increase over that for the preceding year declined. That was one of the impacts of a sharp but short-lived panic on the New York Stock Exchange in that year. The panic of 1857 retarded the rate of increase in wealth in 1858 and that, together with the impending sectional crisis, contributed to a similar reaction in 1860.

The impact of the California gold rush in 1849 was felt in the accelerated increase in the estimated value of wealth for that year, and an all-time increase for that period was recorded in 1851 when the estimated national wealth increased by $629 million. Increases in that total accelerated more rapidly during the decade of the 1850's than in any preceding similar period of time. For the entire span of 35 years covered by the table, the estimated total national wealth increased five times its value for the first year, 1825. On a per capita basis the estimated wealth in 1825 was approximately $300; in 1860 it was approximately $514. Most of this per capita increase in wealth occurred during the last ten years, for in 1850 the per capita figure was $307. These data are purely statistical concepts, and they must not

Table 11-2
Estimated National Wealth
(millions)

Year	Estimated Value	Increase in Increment	Increment of Increase
1825	$ 3,273	. . .	. .
1826	3,377	$ 104	$ 4
1827	3,484	107	3
1828	3,594	110	3
1829	3,708	114	4
1830	3,825	117	3
1831	3,946	121	4
1832	4,071	125	4
1833	4,200	129	4
1834	4,333	133	4
1835	4,470	137	4
1836	4,612	142	5
1837	4,759	147	5
1838	4,900	141	— 6
1839	5,066	166	15
1840	5,226	160	— 6
1841	5,392	166	6
1842	5,563	171	5
1843	5,739	176	5
1844	5,922	183	7
1845	6,109	187	4
1846	6,302	193	6
1847	6,501	199	6
1848	6,707	206	7
1849	6,918	211	5
1850	7,135	217	6
1851	7,981	846	629
1852	8,838	857	11
1853	9,708	970	113
1854	10,591	883	— 87
1855	11,488	897	14
1856	12,396	908	11
1857	13,318	1,022	114
1858	14,252	934	— 88
1859	15,200	1,048	114
1860	16,160	960	— 88

Source: U. S. Department of Commerce, Bureau of the Census, *Historical Statistics of the United States, 1789-1945* (Washington: U. S. Government Printing Office, 1949), p. 9. Adapted.

be construed as portraying conditions of reality. While data are incomplete, a conservative estimate of the number of millionaires in 1860 is 20; while at the same time there were thousands of workers who owned practically nothing of value. Be it good, or be it bad, the American economy had con-

tinued to function along the lines on which it had started out during the
Colonial Period and the first quarter century thereafter. It was that development that had given rise to the reform movements of the 1830's and 1840's,
but they were not sufficiently strong to do more than give weak expressions
to protests over the unequal distribution of wealth. Even many of those who
were in the lower income and wealth brackets at any given time aspired to
become members of a higher economic stratum in the years to come. Status,
immobility, and hopelessness in social and economic matters had given way
to mobility and hopefulness for social and economic betterment.

Sources of Income

Agriculture not only made the largest contribution to private income
throughout the first 70 years of the operation of the American economy,
it gave rise to more than twice the dollar volume that was contributed by
any other area of economic activity in the same span of years. While the
dollar volume that agriculture contributed to private incomes in 1859 was
five times its dollar contribution in 1799, percentagewise it declined from
39.5 percent to 30.8 percent. On the other hand, both manufacturing and
trade income as a percentage of private income increased, although their
combined dollar contribution throughout the period was a little less than
that of agriculture. Transportation and service industries made larger contributions to national income than did manufacturing and trade, but again
they declined percentagewise throughout most of the years.

In 1799 a larger portion of national income originated from trade than
from manufacturing, but after 1809 manufacturing forged to the front, and
it was not until after 1860 that a greater part of national income came from
trade than from manufacturing.

The impact of the California gold rush on national income was less
than it was in other areas of economic activity. While the dollar volume of
its contribution to national income more than doubled from 1849 to 1859,
and again from 1859 to 1869, all mining and quarrying activities accounted
for less than 2 percent of the total.

Power had not become enough of a separate industry by 1859 to become
much of a distinct source of national income. During the period under observation, power was more of an attribute of both transportation and manufacturing, and its contributions to the national income of the American
economy prior to 1860 are included in the figures for those industries.

Government and the Economy

Government was not entirely divorced from economic activity. Protection at local levels was afforded through the organization and operation of
police and fire departments, and at a higher level the United States Army
and Navy stood ready for action when and if necessary. Excise taxes were
collected at the local level and customs duties by the federal government.

Table 11-3

Realized Private Production Income, by Industries—1799-1869
and Percentage Contribution to Total Income (millions)

Year	Total Private Income	Agriculture		Manufacturing		Transportation		Trade		Mining and Quarrying		Construction		Service		Power		Other (Finance)	
1799	$ 668	$ 264	39.5%	$ 32	4.8%	$ 160	23.5%	$ 35	5.2%	$ 1	..	$ 53	4.8%	$ 64	9.6%	*	..	$ 59	10.5%
1809	901	306	32.2	55	6.1	236	26.2	41	4.5	2	..	72	8.0	110	12.2	*	..	79	10.8
1819	855	294	34.4	64	7.5	176	20.6	55	6.4	2	..	58	6.8	132	15.4	*	..	74	8.9
1829	947	329	34.7	98	10.3	143	15.0	61	6.4	3	..	66	7.0	163	17.2	*	..	84	8.8
1839	1,577	545	35.0	162	10.3	277	17.6	135	8.5	5	..	95	6.0	222	14.1	$ 1	..	135	8.5
1849	2,326	737	31.8	291	12.5	398	17.1	196	8.4	16	.7%	133	5.7	355	15.3	2	.1%	198	8.4
1859	4,098	1,264	30.8	495	12.1	694	16.9	494	12.1	44	1.7	184	4.5	572	14.0	6	.1	345	7.8
1869	6,288	1,517	24.1	1,000	15.9	718	11.4	1,039	16.5	102	1.6	387	6.1	968	15.4	23	.3	534	8.5

* Less than $500,000.

Source: *Historical Statistics of the United States, 1789-1945,* 1949, p. 14. Adapted.

The presence or absence of tariff duties on commodities provided hindrances or stimuli respectively to business firms that dealt locally in those goods.

The federal government gave encouragement and leadership to labor in providing a 10-hour day for its employees. The interstate commerce clause in the Constitution had not as yet been implemented by legislation by the Congress. Rivers and inland waterways had been kept open to transport services on a competitive basis. The monetary system had been strengthened and made more convenient to use. Encouragement had been given the westward movement through its public land policy and land grants to railroads.

State and local governments had purchased railroad bonds in order to aid in the financing of those speculative and competitive services. The federal government had purchased some of its own bonds before they matured in order to put money into circulation after the panic of 1837. Suffice it to say here that governments of many years gone by were interested in economic activities. This interest was revealed in many ways, which were not far different from methods used in the 20th century.

Changes in the Productive Factors

Absolute changes in the volume of the productive factors were no more important than were the changes in the proportion that each one bore to the others and to the demand for them. Increases in the amount of land, labor, and capital per se did not make any more plentiful, because of increases in the demand for them. There was no economic planning for the use of economic resources, except at the level of free enterprise. The absence of attempts to coordinate increases in their supply with demand for them resulted in many impacts that were disturbing, to say the least. There was no planning for population increases; and once they had become realities, adjustments had to be made either at the family level or at the level of free enterprise. The supply of land was fixed as far as its superficial area was concerned, but the boundary of the United States had been pushed across the continent. While that expansion was politically motivated, its economic impacts were not to be ignored. That capital was relatively scarce is manifest by the fact that its users were required to pay interest costs for amounts of capital they could not save.

Land. Land as a factor of production was measured in terms of acreage that had been appropriated for use in relation to the desires of persons who wanted to appropriate it. The economic rent of urban land tended to rise throughout the entire period, except during years of financial panic and industrial recessions. As the frontier had been pushed westward, no-rent land tended to become rent land, but that change did not take place with any degree of regularity. With the increase in acreage that was brought into use throughout this period, it is difficult to say that land in the abstract became scarcer than it was during earlier years. It is a fact, however, that from a locational point of view certain desirable sites became scarce. Testimony to that fact is given by reminding the reader that much of the increase in the fortune of John Jacob Astor arose from that condition. Astor owned valuable sites in New York City, and the competitive efforts of businessmen to transact their business on a limited number of sites imparted value to the land. It was that condition that caused buildings to be erected many stories high. In this way more persons could do business on the limited number of urban locations.

Labor. Labor was still in scarce supply, though much larger numbers of persons than formerly were in the laboring class. Immigration, especially in the years following the potato famine in Ireland and the years of social and political unrest in Germany, swelled the number of workers. Factors of push caused them to leave their native lands; factors of pull led them to the United States. To offset the increase in numbers of workers was the large increase in the demand for them in almost all areas of the productive segment of our economy. Factories had been increasing in size and in numbers; and in the era that was drawing to a close, both of these increases demanded more workers. Transportation facilities had expanded only because a supply of labor had been found to construct them. When laborers were not found in the United States, they were induced to immigrate from other countries.

Capital. Capital, as a productive factor, remained in scarce supply. Manifestation of that is found in the high rates of interest that borrowers were required to pay for its use. True, the risk factor contributed to the high level of interest rates; but the scarcity of capital, together with its rate of productivity, were the real causes of high interest rates. Native capital in large volume had appeared, but not in large enough amounts to begin to meet the demands for it. The answer to that state of disequilibrium had been found in borrowing from Europe. The immediate impact of those investments of foreign capital in the United States was to increase commodity imports. Their longer run impact had been to increase commodity exports.

Adjustments to War

From one point of view, the most remarkable aspect of our entire economic development was the relative ease with which an economy that had been erected on the basis of comparative freedom from government interference and regulation had adjusted itself to the needs of war. That was truer in the Northern States than in the Southern States. But remember that free enterprise had determined the most profitable uses for land, labor, and capital in both sections of the country on the presumption that they would remain at peace with each other. The economy had adjusted itself so readily and so completely that when the war came to an end the productive capacity of the North had been increased and more goods were being produced at the termination of the struggle than at its commencement, in spite of huge losses of manpower and of capital equipment.

QUESTIONS FOR REVIEW

1. What were the economic causes of the Civil War?
2. Develop the thesis that problems connected with the extension of slavery rather than the question of its existence were more important as a cause of the Civil War.
3. Why did England throw its weight in support of the northern cause?
4. To what extent, if at all, did the Civil War accelerate or retard the economic development of the United States?
5. How was the organization of banking altered during the course of the war?
6. (a) What was the office of Comptroller of the Currency?
   (b) What authority did the Comptroller of the Currency have?
7. What precedent was followed by the federal government in establishing the National Banking System?
8. (a) Distinguish between economic expansion and economic growth.
   (b) Does economic growth necessarily accompany expansion? Explain.
   (c) Is economic expansion necessary to economic growth? Explain.
9. Compare the economic causes of the panics of 1819, 1837, and 1857.
10. What part has capital accumulation played in overcoming a condition of underdevelopment in the United States?

SUGGESTED READINGS

Beard, Charles and Mary. "The Tariff as a Cause of Sectional Strife and the Civil War," *Issues in American Economic History,* edited by Gerald D. Nash. Boston: D. C. Heath & Company, 1964.

Bining, Arthur C., and Thomas C. Cochran, *The Rise of American Economic Life.* 4th ed. New York City: Charles Scribner's Sons, 1964. Chapter 14.

Bogart, Ernest L., and Donald L. Kemmerer. *Economic History of the American People.* 2d ed. New York City: Longmans, Green & Co., Inc., 1949. Chapter 18.

Faulkner, Harold U. *American Economic History.* 8th ed. New York City: Harper & Row, Publishers, 1960. Chapters 16 and 17.

Hofstadter, Richard. "The Tariff Issue on the Eve of the Civil War," *Issues in American Economic History,* edited by Gerald D. Nash. Boston: D. C. Heath & Company, 1964.

North, Douglass C. *The Economic Growth of the United States, 1790-1860.* Englewood Cliffs, N. J.: Prentice-Hall, Inc., 1961. Chapters 14 and 15.

Russel, Robert R. *A History of the American Economic System.* New York City: Appleton-Century-Crofts, 1964. Chapter 18.

Somers, Harold M. "The Performance of the American Economy, 1789-1865," *The Growth of the American Economy,* 2d ed., edited by Harold F. Williamson. New York City: Prentice-Hall, Inc., 1951.

Soule, George, and Vincent P. Carosso. *American Economic History.* New York City: Holt, Rinehart & Winston, Inc., 1957. Chapter 12.

PART IV

The Nation Matures: The Development of Economic Nationalism—1866-1920

Developments that were initiated before 1860 were stimulated by the Civil War, so that after 1865 new energies were released. These new developments reached their peak under the doctrine of laissez faire, and the results were so inequitable that measures were taken to control combinations and consolidations. In the enforcement of competition, the government was on the defensive. It was protecting society from what some people thought were undesirable social and economic consequences of monopoly control. At the same time, the courts were protecting vested interests.

The banking system was reorganized. National banks were given control over the issuance of bank notes, which declined in importance as deposit banking became more prevalent. Several changes were made in the monetary system, and in 1900 the United States formally declared for the gold standard. The Silver Bloc was organized during the years of falling prices in the 1870's, but its results were disappointing to the silver interests.

While the farm population continued to increase until after 1910, it constituted a progressively lower percentage of our total population. By 1920, more people lived in urban communities than lived and worked on farms. Falling prices of agricultural products placed farmers in an unfavorable position in the market place. They grasped at the idea of a protective tariff as the device that would restore some of the purchasing power of their dollars. The advantages of a market economy did not appear to accrue to farmers, and organized protests by farmers were made.

Effective entrepreneurial organizations of railroads and of manufacturers were becoming more and more oligopolistic in their controls over their respective market situations. These controls were realizations of the fears of the colonists a hundred years earlier when they had protested against the Tea Act of 1773, partly because they feared that the monopoly granted by England in the sale of tea would spread to other segments of the market. Labor organizations went through a period of organizational developments, the outcome of which was the triumph of the American Federation of Labor. The principle of union organization of labor had not been generally accepted, but progress towards this end was noticeable.

The 19th century came to a close with the rise of manufacturing industries at the expense of agriculture, the closing of the agricultural frontier, the start of a program of economic imperialism, and a change in the debtor-creditor relationships with foreign countries. Advances in technology altered radically the traditional economic relationships between agriculture, labor, transportation, and manufacturing after the turn of the century.

The early years of the 20th century were momentous ones for the American people. Since the western frontier had been closed, almost for the first time in history, they turned their backs on the West and focused their eyes across the Pacific Ocean and to the Caribbean Sea. As a prelude of dire things to come, Admiral Mayo shelled Vera Cruz and took charge of customs in retaliation for the arrest of some American sailors in Tampico. A punitive expedition into Mexico was led by General John J. Pershing.

Many segments of American life felt the impact of World War I. Of more significance than our entry into a world war was the fact that it was the first major conflict in which the United States had participated in over 50 years. The country had felt the impact of the European war for almost three years before she became actively engrossed in wartime activities. It was during this period of preparation that the tempo of our economic system was increased and its primary objectives altered.

Chapter 12

POPULATION GROWTH AND DISTRIBUTION.

PUBLIC LANDS

POPULATION GROWTH: FACTS AND CAUSES

By decades, the growth of population of the United States averaged 34.5 percent prior to 1860, 22.7 percent from then to 1920. Natural increase and unrestricted immigration were responsible for the high percentage of population increase that was revealed by each succeeding decennial census. Vital statistics are not entirely reliable for the earlier part of this period, but there is ample evidence that the birth rate was high. So was the death rate high, especially for infants under one year of age. By 1920, the rate of infant mortality in Massachusetts was less than 50 percent of the corresponding rate in 1870. Evidence of a high birth rate is found in the size of families, in which five children were considered a small family and 16 children may have been above the average but not at all uncommon. Families were not planned, and children were considered economic assets. If they lived on farms, they were used in jobs that were suited to their strength and skill. If they lived in urban areas, they went to work for wages and contributed their bit to the family income. Children also were relied upon to take care of their parents in case of sickness, accident, or old age. Retirement and old age pensions were not included in the standard of living of any class of people prior to the first World War; and retirement villages, cooperative apartments, and rest homes had not been devised.

Natural Increase

Birth rates were higher in rural areas than in urban communities, and first generation immigrant families had more children than did American families in the same general community. Second generation immigrant families tended to be smaller than the families from which the parents came.

Table 12-1

Rate of Population Growth by Decades—1790-1920

Year	Percentage Increase	Year	Percentage Increase
1790	..	1860	35 (34.5 average growth)
1800	35	1870	27
1810	36	1880	26
1820	33	1890	26
1830	34	1900	21
1840	33	1910	21.5
1850	36	1920	15 (22.7 average growth)

Source: U. S. Department of Commerce, Bureau of the Census, *Historical Statistics of the United States. Colonial Times to 1957* (Washington: U. S. Government Printing Office, 1960), p. 7. Adapted.

Since there are only two sources of population increase, immigration and natural increase, once the figures that denoted the total increase in population and those for immigration have been calculated for each successive decade, the numerical difference between them measures the natural increase for the respective decades. The results of such a calculation are found in Table 12-2.

Table 12-2

Increase in Population in the United States by Decades—1860-1920

Year	Total Population	Increase in Population	Immigration Total*	Average	Natural Increase
1860	31,443,321	....	....	......	....
1870	39,818,449	8,375,128	2,314,824	231,482	6,060,304
1880	50,155,783	10,337,334	2,812,191	281,219	7,525,143
1890	62,947,714	12,791,931	5,246,613	524,661	7,545,318
1900	75,994,575	13,046,861	3,687,564	368,756	9,359,297
1910	91,972,286	15,977,711	8,795,386	879,538	7,182,325
1920	105,710,620	13,738,334	5,735,811	573,581	8,002,523
Totals	74,267,299	28,592,389		......	45,674,910

* 10-year accumulative total.

Source: *Historical Statistics of the United States. Colonial Times to 1957*, 1960, pp. 8 and 56. Adapted. Also see Simon Kuznets and Ernest Rubin, *Immigration and the Foreign Born* (New York City: National Bureau of Economic Research, 1954), Occasional Paper 46.

By comparing the data on natural increase with those on immigration, the implication is strong that the natural increase for a given decade was dependent upon or affected by the immigration of the prior decade. Until

the census of 1890, the data for natural increase to those for immigration
were in a ratio of 3 to 1. The impact upon natural increase of the large
influx of foreigners throughout the decade of the 1880's was felt in its
increase in the following ten years. In spite of a decline in immigration for
the years 1891-1900 over that for the preceding ten years, the total increase
in population for the latter decade exceeded that of the earlier one.

The impact of the rush of immigrants to our shores from 1901 to 1910
was to provide the framework for an increase of almost one million in the
natural increase for the following decade over and above similar data for
1901-10. This occurred at a time when the birth rate was declining.

From 1860 to 1920 the total increase in population amounted to 74
million persons, of which natural increase provided 45 million persons and
immigration accounted for 29 million. This was a distinct departure from
the conditions that existed during the Colonial Period at which time immigration was the principal cause of population growth.

Immigration

The United States continued to be open to all peoples of other countries,
except to some of the Orientals, throughout most of this period. Noneconomic
reasons may have entered into the immigration movement prior to 1860,
but after the Civil War economic motivation caused hundreds of thousands
of people to leave their homeland every year in order to establish themselves
in the United States. Conditions of general poverty, hunger, inability to
own land, unemployment, low economic and social status, all of which could
be translated into terms of a lack of economic opportunity and security, were
the important push factors. Rumors of free land, fabulous wealth, an abundance of food, and rumors of plenty of work for all were among the factors
of pull that enticed thousands of persons to sever all ties with the known
and seek economic emancipation on a strange and unfamiliar continent.

Immigration Pattern. The early years of the Civil War did not prompt
foreigners to want to seek settlement in this country, and relatively few
immigrants were admitted to the United States during that period. In 1862,
91,985, most of whom were Germans, British, and Irish, journeyed to
this country; and in 1861 only 91,918 immigrants were counted. Immigrants
from the same three countries were in the majority and in both years over
55 percent of them were males. Over 70 percent of the entire group for both
years was between the ages of 15 and 40—the most productive childbearing
years. That pattern was followed rather closely throughout the entire period
under discussion and it explains in part why birth rates remained high.
The minimum figure for immigration of 1861 was not reached again until
1918, which was another war year. Starting with the year of the Mexican
War, every war in which the United States has been a participant has been
accompanied by a decline in immigration figures. In 1918, more immigrants
came from other countries of the western hemisphere than from Europe.

Another grouping that differs from that given in Table 12-2, one from 1905 through 1914, gives an all-time high average of 1,012,194 for a 10-year period. An average of 1,033,258 foreigners came to this country in the four years preceding the outbreak of World War I in Europe. The all-time high for any one year of 1,285,349 was reached in 1907, and 1,218,480 arrived here in 1914. Austro-Hungarians, Italians, and Russians, who comprised two thirds of the total, were responsible for those record-breaking figures. That was the climax of a movement that started in the 1880's and gained momentum as the years passed.

The "Old" Immigration. The "old" immigration, as it was called, had established, in many respects, a pattern of long years' standing. Those who came over prior to 1860 followed in the footsteps of the original settlers. They spoke the same language; they belonged to the same churches and many of them were Protestants; they had somewhat the same customs and ideals; and they engaged in similar economic activities. They were easily assimilated into the "American way of life." Many of them had some schooling and were eager to obtain more. They tended to settle in this country where they could continue to practice the occupations to which they were accustomed and in which they were more or less skilled.

Cincinnati, St. Louis, and Milwaukee had high concentrations of Germans, who also were found on farms in Iowa, Nebraska, and Wisconsin. They transplanted aspects of German culture; and turnvereins, musical activities, including symphony orchestras and conservatories of music, and beer halls were firmly rooted in the standard of living of those peoples. Scandinavians were concentrated in northern Illinois, Wisconsin, and Minnesota; and dairying and cheese making, as well as general farming, were carried on by them. Scandinavian women became domestic servants in Chicago and other midwestern cities and raised that activity to a new high level of respectability and dependability. Many of the Irish became mill hands, laborers, policemen, and politicians.

The "New" Immigration. Most of the immigrants from southern and eastern European and Slav countries belonged to the peasant class. Many of them could neither read nor write. They were economically depressed and would never have had an opportunity to own land or to improve themselves in their homeland in other ways. Most of them were members of the Roman Catholic Church. They brought with them few skills or talents that had been developed, and they tended to congregate in large numbers in the more populous cities of the East.

Once here, they tended to establish churches in which their own language was used. They made little or no effort to become acquainted with American ways of doing things. Their children did not attend schools regularly, if at all. Since they brought little or no money with them and had no friends or sponsors in this country to give them aid, they remained in or near their ports of debarkation. Were they unfortunate enough to have been brought

over under contract to some construction company, mining company, or
steel company, they were whisked away to some interior location where their
lives and levels of living were nothing of which Americans could be proud.
They had few or no cultural interests. In their extreme poverty and in ignorance of anything better in the United States, they became prey to employers
and exploiters of unskilled labor. Wherever they went they composed a
reservoir of common, unskilled labor, the turnover of which was rather high
in most industries. Women and children as well as adult males constituted
an ever-increasing supply of laborers. They were an important segment of
labor in textile mills and sweatshops. American industry expanded rapidly
during that period. Many industries that relied upon the use of mass labor
gave encouragement to the continued influx of immigrants. The marginal
significance of common labor was low, as was its productivity. Wages were
low. Minimum requirements for subsistence living were met only when all
members of families who were physically and mentally able were employed.

Those who were brought over under contract to construction companies,
and many who were not, were used in laying thousands of miles of railroad
track in the days when all work connected with laying roadbeds and trackage
was done by hand labor. They were also used as maintenance-of-way men.

Slum areas had already begun to blemish urban development, but it was
not until the enforcement of the military draft for World War I that persons
in general had their attention called to the almost desperate condition of
some of those people. Let it be said to the credit of the second generation
of these immigrants that many of them raised themselves to a higher level
of living and made positive contributions to the economic productivity of
the American people, for such they were by that time.

Surge from Southeastern Europe and Slav Countries. Immigration
from Italy experienced a large proportionate increase in 1880, but it was not
until 1900 that the per annum figure reached 100,000. It remained above
that figure annually through 1914. While they were at a low level of personal
income, the Italians had many admirable personal traits that made them
valuable additions to the melting pot of humanity. Many of them came to
this country in order to send money back home to support their parents
or other members of their families. Others sent money over to pay for the
passage of parents, wives, children, or brothers and sisters to this country.
Whatever the reason for so doing, those remittances loomed large on the
international balance of payments account of the United States as invisible
imports that helped compensate for a large export imbalance on the commodity trade account. The Italians were frugal people and usually had large-
sized families. They were not too proud to work, and many of them later
became merchants in a small way in vending staple and fancy fruits. Corner
fruit stands and two-wheel pushcarts were their vehicles of trade. The corner
stores usually handled tobacco products and candies in addition to fruits and
some vegetables in season.

Table 12-3

Foreign Born Population in the United States—1860-1920

Country of Birth	1860	1870	1880	1890	1900	1910	1920
All Countries	4,138,697	5,567,229	6,679,943	9,249,560	10,341,276	13,515,886	13,920,692
Northwestern Europe ..	2,472,211	3,124,638	3,494,484	4,380,752	4,202,683	4,239,067	3,830,094
Central and Eastern Europe	1,311,722	1,784,449	2,187,776	3,420,629	4,136,646	6,014,028	6,134,845
Southern Europe	20,365	25,853	58,265	206,648	530,200	1,525,875	1,911,213
Asia	36,796	64,565	107,630	113,396	120,248	191,484	237,950
Americas	288,285	551,335	807,230	1,088,245	1,317,380	1,489,231	1,727,017
All Others	9,318	16,389	24,558	39,890	34,119	56,201	79,573

Source: *Historical Statistics of the United States. Colonial Times to 1957,* 1960, p. 66. Adapted.

From 1900 to 1914 the rush of immigrants to America was unusually heavy, and the facilities at Ellis Island were taxed to capacity. Over 350,000 Greeks left their homeland in search of improved economic conditions in America. In terms of personal fortunes they were in the lower strata, but they were able and ambitious people. They operated small service businesses that did not require large amounts of capital, such as restaurants, shoe repair and shoe shining establishments, and used clothing stores. Second generation Greeks gave expression to their cultural interests and accomplishments and were easily absorbed into the American way of life. Throughout this span of years, the population of the United States was augmented by over 110,000 Austro-Hungarians every year and by an average of 150,000 Russians and others from the Baltic States of Latvia, Lithuania, and Esthonia. The peak year for Austro-Hungarian immigration was 1907 when 338,452 persons from that dual monarchy, which has since disintegrated into a number of smaller nations, entered the United States; and in 1914, 219,040 Russians cast their lot with the United States.

Many were the cultural, religious, social, and economic contributions that were made by these people who intermarried rather freely with peoples of other nationalities.

Distribution of Foreign Born Population. Data in Table 12-3 show the numerical growth of foreign born population from different regional foreign areas; and Table 12-4 discloses the proportion of our foreign born population whose origins were in those respective geographic areas.

Table 12-4

Percentage Distribution of Foreign Born Population—1860-1920

Country of Birth	1860	1870	1880	1890	1900	1910	1920
Northwest Europe	59.7%	56.1%	52.3%	47.4%	40.6%	31.3%	27.5%
Central and Eastern Europe	31.6	32.0	32.8	36.9	40.0	44.4	44.0
Southern Europe	.5	.5	.9	2.2	5.1	11.2	13.7
Asia	.9	1.2	1.6	1.2	1.2	1.4	1.7
Americas	6.9	9.9	12.1	11.7	12.7	11.0	12.4
All other	.2	.3	.4	.4	.3	.4	.6

Source: Derived from Table 12-3.

Table 12-5

Foreign Born Population and Native Population of Foreign or Mixed Parentage for Selected Countries

Selected Countries	1900		1910		1920	
	Number of Foreign Born	Native Population—Foreign or Mixed Parentage	Number of Foreign Born	Native Population—Foreign or Mixed Parentage	Number of Foreign Born	Native Population—Foreign or Mixed Parentage
Germany	2,663,418	5,340,147	2,311,237	5,670,611	1,686,108	5,346,004
Poland	383,407	326,764	937,884	725,924	1,139,979	1,303,351
Ireland	1,615,459	3,375,546	1,352,251	3,304,015	1,037,234	3,122,013
Italy	484,027	254,550	1,343,125	771,645	1,610,113	1,751,091

Source: *Historical Statistics of the United States. Colonial Times to 1957*, 1960, pp. 65 and 66. Adapted.

The foreign born population from northwestern Europe increased over 50 percent during that span of 60 years; but in proportion to the total foreign born persons who were living in the United States, it declined from 59.7 percent in 1860 to 27.5 percent in 1920. The 1910 census revealed that more persons from central and eastern Europe than from northwestern Europe had entered the country. Immigration from Germany was heavy throughout the entire period, but it was those from Poland who gave leadership in our foreign born population to central and eastern Europe. Italian immigration was responsible for southern Europe moving from fifth to third in importance of foreign born population in the United States in 1920.

By 1900 over five million of the total white population that was native to the United States had one or both parents born in Germany, and the progeny of foreign born Irish numbered over 1.5 million. It was not until 1920 that the foreign born Poles and Italians each were progenitors of over one million native children. From these data of selected countries, it is clear that once immigrants had arrived in the United States, they tended to lose their national identities and procreated a people who had traits and characteristics of all races and nations. These are the people we call Americans; it is they who are responsible for the economic productivity of the American people.

Resettlement of Immigrants in America

The pattern of distribution of the foreign born population in the United States that was established during the Colonial Period continued to prevail down through the years to the beginning of World War I. Just as most of the colonists first set foot on American soil in Virginia and to the north, so did the immigrants who arrived in the United States after 1865 disembark in New York, Boston, and Philadelphia. For our purposes the actual cities of debarkation are of less importance than the fact that they were located in the Northeastern and Middle Atlantic States. These are the very same states in which industry experienced its greatest development between the years of 1870 and 1914. It is a well-known fact that until after World War I there were few persons of foreign birth or even of foreign extraction south of the Mason and Dixon Line. Down to the turn of the century cotton culture continued to dominate the economy of the South, recognizing all of the time that agriculture in that region was becoming more and more diversified. Even so, European farmers were not attracted to that part of the United States in which sharecropping and the crop lien systems prevailed. Had they been satisfied to remain peasants, they would not have undertaken to resettle themselves in a new country after arduous and unpleasant voyages across the Atlantic Ocean.

After 1870 immigrant farmers ranked third in numbers among those who took up their homes in this country. Before 1860 they ranked second after unskilled laborers. Unskilled or common laborers continued to rank first after 1870, but skilled or artisan labor of the craftsman type advanced

Table 12-6
Population of the United States

Region	1860	1870	1880	1890	1900	1910	1920
New England (Maine, New Hampshire, Vermont, Massachusetts, Rhode Island, Connecticut)	3,135,283	3,487,924	4,010,529	4,700,749	5,592,017	6,552,681	7,400,909
Middle Atlantic (New York, New Jersey, Pennsylvania)	7,458,985	8,810,806	10,496,878	12,706,220	15,454,678	19,315,892	22,261,144
East North Central (Ohio, Indiana, Illinois, Michigan, Wisconsin)	6,926,884	9,124,517	11,206,668	13,478,305	15,985,581	18,250,621	21,475,543
West North Central (Minnesota, Iowa, Missouri, North Dakota, South Dakota, Nebraska, Kansas)	2,169,832	3,856,594	6,157,443	8,932,112	10,347,423	11,637,921	12,544,249
South Atlantic (Delaware, Maryland, District of Columbia, Virginia, West Virginia, North Carolina, South Carolina, Georgia, Florida)	5,364,703	5,853,610	7,597,197	8,857,922	10,443,480	12,194,895	13,990,272
East South Central (Kentucky, Tennessee, Alabama, Mississippi)	4,020,991	4,404,445	5,585,151	6,429,154	7,547,757	8,409,901	8,893,307
West South Central (Arkansas, Louisiana, Oklahoma, Texas)	1,747,667	2,029,965	3,334,220	4,740,983	6,532,290	8,784,534	10,242,224
Mountain (Montana, Idaho, Wyoming, Colorado, New Mexico, Arizona, Utah, Nevada)	174,923	315,385	653,119	1,213,935	1,674,657	2,633,517	3,336,101
Pacific (Washington, Oregon, California)	444,053	675,125	1,114,578	1,888,334	2,416,692	4,192,304	5,566,871
Total	31,443,321	38,558,371	50,155,783	62,947,714	75,994,575	91,972,266	105,710,620

Source: *Historical Statistics of the United States, Colonial Times to 1957, 1960,* pp. 12 and 13. Adapted.

Table 12-7

Distribution of Population by Sections, by Rank, and by Percentage

Section	1860 Rank	1860 Percentage	1870 Rank	1870 Percentage	1880 Rank	1880 Percentage	1890 Rank	1890 Percentage	1900 Rank	1900 Percentage	1910 Rank	1910 Percentage	1920 Rank	1920 Percentage
Middle Atlantic	1	23.7	2	22.9	2	21.0	2	20.2	2	20.4	1	21.0	1	21.0
East North Central	2	22.0	1	23.7	1	22.4	1	21.4	1	21.0	2	19.8	2	20.3
South Atlantic	3	17.1	3	15.2	3	15.1	3	14.1	3	13.7	3	13.3	3	13.2
East South Central	4	12.8	4	11.4	5	11.1	5	10.2	5	9.9	6	9.1	6	8.4
New England	5	10.0	6	9.1	6	8.0	7	7.5	7	7.4	7	7.1	7	7.0
West North Central	6	6.9	5	10.0	4	12.3	4	14.2	4	13.6	4	12.7	4	11.9
West South Central	7	5.5	7	5.2	7	6.6	6	7.5	6	8.6	5	9.6	5	9.7
Pacific	8	1.4	8	1.7	8	2.2	8	3.0	8	3.2	8	4.5	8	5.3
Mountain	9	.6	9	.8	9	1.3	9	1.9	9	2.2	9	2.9	9	3.2

Source: Derived from Table 12-6.

to second position. From 1906 to the outbreak of war, farm laborers and farm foremen arrived in larger numbers than did laborers in other fields of work. Craftsmen, foremen, and operators as a group ranked third. It was during that span of years that domestic servants were provided from among the most numerous classes of immigrants. Many of those were employed in private homes in urban areas; others found employment in large city hotels.

Density of Population

The first census in 1790 gave the United States a population of a little less than four million, and 100 years later almost 63 million persons were counted. In the 60-year span covered by this study, the population increased from 31 million to over 105 million persons in 1920. The density of population per square mile of landed area in 1790 was 4.5; and 100 years later it was 21.2. Population had grown 15 times in 100 years, increase in the density of population five times. In 1860 the density of population was 10.6; in 1920 it was 35.6. The spread of population throughout the continental United States is portrayed in Tables 12-6 and 12-7, in which the country is divided into New England, Middle Atlantic, East North Central, West North Central, South Atlantic, East South Central, West South Central, Mountain, and Pacific regional areas.

The New England States, which began to lose rank in population numbers during the Colonial Period, ranked fifth in 1860 and seventh in 1920. The South Atlantic States ranked third continuously throughout the period behind the Middle Atlantic and the East North Central States. Those two sections vied with each other for leadership. The former group of states led in 1860, lost to the East North Central States in 1870, and did not regain the prime position again until 1910. At the other end of the list the Mountain States were ninth and the Pacific States eighth. The impact of multiple increases in population of 19 for the Mountain States, 12 for the Pacific States, was lost by the extremely small population of those two sections in 1860. The westward movement had not penetrated Montana, Idaho, Wyoming, and Arizona in 1860, and ten years later Arizona and Wyoming had fewer than 10,000 population.

Urbanization. Not only was the rapid increase of the population of the United States after 1860 accompanied by a movement to the west and to the southwest, there was also a redistribution of the population between rural and urban areas throughout the entire country. That movement was partly the result of the development of manufacturing industries that required a concentration of population in order to furnish adequate supplies of labor. The mechanization of agriculture not only made possible the expansion of agricultural activities, but in a given area of operation it tended to release farm labor to become factory operatives in urban areas. The automotive industries in Michigan and in other Midwestern States drew heavily upon erstwhile farm laborers for their manpower. The development

Table 12-8

Distribution of Population Between Urban and Rural Territory—1860-1920

Class and Population Size	1860 No.	1870 No.	1870 % Inc.	1880 No.	1880 % Inc.	1890 No.	1890 % Inc.	1900 No.	1900 % Inc.	1910 No.	1910 % Inc.	1920 No.	1920 % Inc.
Urban Territory													
Places of 1,000,000 or more	...	...	..	1	..	3	200	3	..	3	..	3	..
Places of 100,000 to 1,000,000	9	14	56	19	36	25	32	35	40	47	34	65	38
Places of 10,000 to 100,000	84	154	83	203	32	326	61	402	23	547	36	684	25
Places of 2,500 to 10,000	299	495	66	716	45	994	39	1,297	30	1,665	28	1,970	18
Rural Territory													
Places of 1,000 to 2,500	...	...		...	..	1,603	...	2,128	33	2,717	28	3,030	12
Places under 1,000	...	...		...	..	4,887	...	6,803	39	9,113	34	9,825	8

Source: *Historical Statistics of the United States. Colonial Times to 1957*, 1960, p. 14. Adapted.

of horse-drawn machinery and its manufacture, principally in Illinois and Wisconsin, absorbed some immigrants who had recently arrived in this country; and farm labor found factory work and urban life more attractive than living and working on farms.

Growth of Urban Areas. The distribution of population between urban and rural areas is seen by studying Table 12-8. Percentagewise the most rapid urbanization occurred between 1860 and 1870. Compared with the number of urban areas in 1860, by 1870 the number of places of 100,000 population and over increased from 9 to 14, which was an increase of 56 percent. The number of places of from 10,000 to 100,000 population increased in the same span of years from 84 to 154, which was an increase of 83 percent. The number of places that could count from 2,500 to 10,000 people increased from 299 to 495, or 66 percent.

Since the number of urban areas in 1860 was smaller than it was in succeeding census years, a given numerical increase in the number of cities represented a decreasing percentage growth. Correspondingly, as the number of urban communities increased over the period under observation, a given numerical increase represented a smaller percentage growth. Thus, while an increase of 196 cities of from 2,500 to 10,000 population in 1870 over the number of such cities in 1860 represented an increase of 66 percent, an increase of 221 cities in that classification throughout the following decade represented an increase of only 45 percent. An increase of 368 such cities in the decade ending 1910 represented a percentage increase of only 28 percent. In studying Table 12-8 the student should make a similar analysis for each census classification of urban areas in order that he may really understand and appreciate the significance of the data given in the table.

Mechanization. Several factors were responsible for this movement, among which the mechanization of industry was foremost. New industries that were started during the Civil War were not only continued thereafter, they were expanded. The rapid increase in the construction of horse-drawn machinery demanded more laborers. The rapid increase in the size of horse-powered farm machinery made erstwhile farm laborers available for factory work. One of the impacts of the development of transportation and communication facilities was the growth of more towns and larger ones. The resumption of immigration towards the end of the war increased the available supply of labor. When soldiers returned to civilian life after 1865, many of them were somewhat restless and had no particular desire to return to the farm. True, many of them became homesteaders, but, as such, they were farm owners and not hired farm labor.

The South remained primarily rural until World War I, although industries had become more prevalent there after about 1890. The impact of the influx of immigrants was not felt in the South, and free white labor was reluctant to move where it would be forced to compete with the Negro. The Negro had not yet been trained to toil in factories or to work with

Table 12-9
Population in Urban and Rural Territory—1860-1920

Class and Population Size	1860	%	1870	%	1880	%	1890	%	1900	%	1910	%	1920	%
Urban Territory	6,216,518		9,902,361		14,129,735		22,106,265		30,159,921		41,998,932		54,157,973	
Places of 100,000 and over		8		11		12		15		19		22		26
Places of 10,000 to 100,000		7		9		9		12		13		15		16
Places of 2,500 to 10,000		5		6		7		8		8		9		9
Percentage of Total Population		20		26		28		35		40		46		51
Rural Territory	25,226,803		28,656,010		36,026,048		40,841,449		45,834,654		49,973,334		51,552,647	
Places of 1,000 to 2,500								4		4		5		5
Places of under 1,000								4		4		4		4
Other		..		..		..		57		52		45		40
Total		80		74		72		65		60		54		49

Source: *Historical Statistics of the United States. Colonial Times to 1957*, 1960, p. 14. Adapted.

machinery. The population of the 16 Southern States, which is found in Tables 12-6 and 12-7 grouped as South Atlantic, East South Central, and West South Central States, did not keep pace with the growth of population of the United States. In 1860, 35 percent of the total population of the United States was found in the Southern States; in 1900 the proportion had declined to 32 percent and in 1920 to 31 percent. That was due to the fact that the South still was primarily rural; and the rapid growth of population was taking place in cities, both in respect to their number and to their size.

Decline of Rural Population. In 1860, as Table 12-9 indicates, the rural population of the United States constituted 80 percent of the entire population; by 1900 it had dwindled proportionately to 60 percent; and in 1920 only 49 percent of our total population lived on farms and in places of less than 2,500 inhabitants. World War I was responsible for the continuation of the migratory movement of persons from rural areas to the cities. The war itself was responsible for resettling thousands of workers in urban areas where they were employed in war-essential industries. Shipyards, munitions plants, steel mills, chemical plants, textile mills, and many others attracted labor by offering higher wages than formerly and higher than nonessential industries could afford to pay. It was thought that when the war was over, those workers would return to their former homes, but this was not the case. Of course, many of them did, but still more remained in the cities and tried to find employment in other industries if they had to yield their jobs to soldiers who had exchanged their OD's (olive drab) for civilian clothes. Many of the erstwhile soldiers themselves did not return to rural living and became urban dwellers. One of the popular songs of that period carried the title "How're You Going to Keep Them Down on the Farm After They've Seen Paree." The strength of the urbanization movement from 1910 to 1920 is revealed in the figures that measure the growth of urban populations in comparison with the growth of rural areas. At that time, when the total population of the United States increased 15 percent, the urban population increased 28 percent and rural population only 3 percent.

Center of Population

The westward movement of population and of industry, together with the concentration of population in urban centers, had an impact on the center of population. The center of population at any given census date is that point through which a straight line may be drawn in any direction to divide the population of the United States in half. During the span of years under discussion, 1860 to 1920, the center of population moved a little over 210 miles to the west and about 12 miles southward. In 1860, the center of population was near Chillicothe, Ohio. In successive decades it moved to (1) northeast of Cincinnati; (2) southwest of Cincinnati; (3) east of Columbus, Indiana; (4) southeast of Columbus, Indiana; (5) in the city of Bloomington, Indiana; and (6) almost ten miles to the west, near

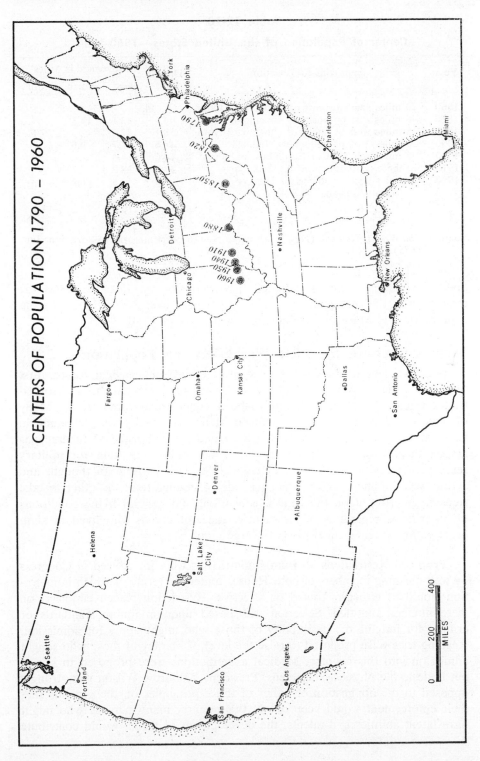

CENTERS OF POPULATION 1790 – 1960

Table 12-10

Center of Population of the United States—1860-1920

Year	Approximate Location	Direct Line	Movement in Miles		
			West	North	South
1860	20 miles south by east of Chillicothe, Ohio				
1870	48 miles east by north of Cincinnati, Ohio	44.1	42.1	13.3	..
1880	8 miles west by south of Cincinnati, Ohio	58.1	57.4	...	9.1
1890	20 miles east of Columbus, Indiana	48.6	47.7	9.0	..
1900	6 miles southeast of Columbus, Indiana	14.6	14.4	...	2.8
1910	In the city of Bloomington, Indiana	39.0	38.9	.7	..
1920	8 miles south-southeast of Spencer County, Indiana	9.8	9.8	.2	..
		214.2	210.3	23.2	11.9

Source: *The World Almanac* (New York City: Newspaper Enterprise Association, Inc., 1955), p. 267.

Spencer, Indiana, which is situated in Owen County. Prior to 1860 the movement of the center of population was a little over 350 miles west from near Baltimore, Maryland, which was its location in 1790.

Some Impacts of the First World War on Population

Selective service examinations for draftees brought to light for the first time how little of American culture and ways of living had been absorbed by thousands of immigrant families who lived in urban communities. Many of them could neither read nor write in their native language, let alone in English. They suffered from malnutrition and the incidence of tuberculosis among them was large. In general, they not only were unfit for military service, they really were unfit for civilian life. Two currents of thought and action were initiated: one to stem the tide of immigration; the other to take steps to improve upon the health, education, and general living conditions of all persons regardless of nationality, race, or creed, who lived in slum areas or in the tenement districts of large cities.

Proposed Restrictions on Immigration. Bills were introduced in Congress by well-meaning members of both Houses under the terms of which immigration would be either restricted or selective. Restriction placed emphasis on mere number admitted. Selection was based upon minimum standards or criteria for judging the desirability of those who might apply for admission. Reading tests were proposed to raise the level of literacy of those who sought admission into this country. Medical examinations were proposed to screen out undesirable physical specimens. President Woodrow Wilson was strongly opposed to the application of either of those principles on the grounds that their enforcement would keep out of this country many persons who might have latent abilities and talents, the development of which would contribute to our productivity or cultural accomplishments. After all, if similar tests had been applied to many of the settlers during the Colonial Period, some of the outstanding personalities of that period would have been excluded.

Again, the results of such tests could be used to bar admittance of qualified persons on political or other grounds. During the furor over women's suffrage, Emily Pankhurst had become a militant leader in Ireland. She planned a trip to the United States to further the cause of women's rights in this country. Many were the political and social leaders who did not relish even the thought of such a visit, much less its realization. When she applied for admission, someone was found who gave an unfavorable character testimonial against her—evidence that was based on hearsay and circumstances—that was sufficient on the part of the guardians of our morals to debar her from the United States. She was denied admittance on the grounds of moral turpitude. Literacy tests and medical examinations could be used in a similar manner to exclude otherwise intelligent and talented persons. Nothing along that line crystallized into definite legislation until a few years later.

Migratory Movement. One of the important migratory movements of population within the United States can be traced to the impact of World War I. That was the beginning of the movement of thousands of Negroes from southern farms to the cities, some of which were located in the North and the Middle West. The Armed Forces had trained Negro soldiers to use their hands and to become familiar with machinery. When those men returned to civilian life, thousands of them ventured into Pittsburgh, Chicago, Detroit, Cleveland, New York, Buffalo, St. Louis, and many other cities. Others sought farms north of the Ohio River and in the Middle Western States. Many of them did not fare much better in urban living than they had on southern farms. In fact, for the same amount of money, a family could have a higher scale of living in the country than in the city. Real incomes of farmers were larger than were those of urban dwellers, and rents in general were lower. Few urban dwellers raised their own food; it had to be purchased out of wages, salaries, or funded incomes. For some levels of living, clothing costs were higher in cities than in rural areas. Urban poverty has been described in very uncomplimentary terms, and as degrading to health and morals, but rural poverty frequently was very distressing. Educational opportunities were usually more numerous and better in northern cities.

Not only did Negro farmers and farm labor migrate to urban communities, farm labor in general, regardless of nationality or color of skin, converged upon cities in which war contracts were being filled. Urban wages were higher than were paid to farm workers. Farm machinery not only took the place of farm labor that had gone into the Armed Forces or that had been lured into urban communities by the promise of higher wages, its rapid adoption actually released farmhands to work in other segments of the economy. That urbanization movement was not accompanied by a corresponding increase in the construction of housing facilities. In order to accommodate these additions to urban populations, single family housing units became multiple housing facilities with few additions to living space or to plumbing and sanitary installations. These conditions stimulated the development of suburbia as places in which many families escaped from some of the more unpleasant aspects of urban living.

PUBLIC LANDS

One of the most impressive aspects of the development of the American economy after the Civil War was the westward movement of agriculture. That movement was stimulated by the increase in population and the accelerated rate of immigration, as well as by the difficulties that were encountered in their efforts to earn a livelihood by many farmers who tilled the soil in the regions of the United States that had been settled at a much earlier date. Probably even more important as a force that attracted people to the frontier was the availability of public lands, some of which were free, some of which were available at low cost, together with the building of many railroads, and laying out improved wagon roads.

The Homestead Act

The policy of giving encouragement to settling upon public lands rather than using their sale as a source of revenue that accrued to the federal government had long been advocated by Congressmen from the North and East. In 1862 the voice of the southern delegation was no longer heard in the halls of Congress, and the Homestead Act of that year provided that claims to 160 acres of land would be recognized five years after settlement. Commutation at $1.25 per acre was authorized at the end of one year if permanent improvements had been made thereon. The fact of permanent improvement was taken as prima facie evidence that the land had not been acquired for speculative purposes. In spite of the policy of disposing of public lands to legitimate homesteaders, there is ample evidence that speculators acquired title to thousands of acres by using aliases and fictitious names. The rapid increase in land values enabled them to make large speculative profits. Here was a manifestation of a willingness to assume a risk which has characterized our development from the Colonial Period down to the present. *Venture capital* has been and still is essential to economic progress in a system of free enterprise, and agricultural development proved to be an alluring adventure, if not always a profitable one.

Settlement Under the Homestead Act. It is not at all surprising to find that 8,223 homestead entries were made in 1863 which was the first full year following the passage of the Act. By 1866 such entries had increased to 15,355, and by 1870 they had more than doubled again when 33,972

Table 12-11

Total Number of Farms and Acreage in Farmland Combined with the Number of Homestead Entries and the Acreage Homesteaded—1870-1920

Year	Number of Farms (000)	Increase (000)	New Homestead Entries* (000)	Farm Acreage (000)	Increase (000)	New Homestead Acreage* (000)
1860	2,044	595	. . .	407,179	113,645	. . . . .
1870	2,660	616	142	407,723	544	22,754
1880	4,009	1,349	328	536,064	128,341	52,412
1890	4,565	556	497	623,207	87,143	69,773
1900	5,737	1,172	457	838,583	215,376	62,767
1910	6,406	669	832	878,792	40,209	130,737
1920	6,518	112	554	955,878	77,086	123,826

* Homestead Entries and Homestead Acreage are cumulative for 10-year periods.

Source: *Historical Statistics of the United States. Colonial Times to 1957*, 1960, pp. 237 and 278. Adapted.

entries were recorded. In the decade of 1881-90, a total of 497,083 entries was made upon public lands. A decrease of 40,140 entries the following decade did not establish a new pattern, for by 1920 another cumulative total of 1,385,867 entries had been recorded. It is apparent that the concept of the Bureau of the Census of a "closed" frontier was far from realistic except in terms of density of population. True enough, the new settlements were remote in space from urban centers to the east, but improved transportation facilities linked the two areas closer together in time.

Impacts of Homesteading. The data in Tables 12-11 and 12-12 reveal the effect that homesteading had upon the increase in the number of farms, together with the increase in acreage of farmland. After 1900 the increase in the total number of farms was less than the number of new homestead entries. Likewise, the new acreage that was homesteaded was in excess of the total increase in the acreage of farmland. The fact of the total increase in the number of farm units being less than the number of homestead entries may be explained in terms of two developments that took place during those years. One factor was an increase in the size of farm units. The data in Table 12-12 tell the story of the enlargement in the size of farm units.

A factor that tended to more than offset the impact of new homestead entries was an aspect of urbanization. There was a shifting of population out of urban areas that were noisy, dirty, and congested, into suburban areas. In expanding laterally, land that had been used for farming was appropriated for residential purposes. Other movements that made in-

Table 12-12

Number and Size of Farms—1880 to 1920
(000)

Year	Total	Acres						
		1–10	10–49	50–99	100–259	260–499	500–999	1000 and Over
1880	4,009	139	1,036	1,033	1,696	...	76	29
1890	4,565	150	1,168	1,122	2,009	...	84	32
1900	5,737	267	1,664	1,366	1,912	378	103	47
1910	6,362	335	1,919	1,438	2,051	444	125	50
1920	6,448	289	2,011	1,475	1,980	476	150	67

Source: *Historical Statistics of the United States. Colonial Times to 1957*, 1960, p. 279. Adapted.

roads on acreage devoted to agricultural uses and that reduced the number of farms were increases in the number and size of golf courses; enlargements of cemeteries both in size and in number; and, especially after 1910, farm-land that was appropriated for military uses—training camps and target areas, and for stockpiling ordnance and food rations.

Simultaneously with the opening up of new lands and the creation of new farms, a movement of consolidating land into a smaller number of larger sized farms prevented new homesteads from increasing the number of farms proportionately. Similarly, new lands that were homesteaded did not represent a net increase in land under cultivation. Data in Table 12-12 indicate that the trend towards larger sized farms that had commenced prior to 1900 progressed at an accelerated rate afterwards. That was made possible by the use of larger mechanized farm machinery and by the adaptation of the internal combustion engine to the needs of agriculture. Farming was becoming a larger sized operation.

Other Land Acts

Other acts of Congress that gave encouragement to early private appro-priation of public lands were the Timber Culture Act of 1873, the Stone and Timber Act of 1878, and the Desert Land Act of 1877. None of those Acts by themselves provided adequate acreage to suit the requirements of ranch farming. Under the terms of the Timber Culture Act, 160 acres of public land were given to settlers who agreed to plant trees on at least 40 acres of what turned out to be rather barren soil. The Stone and Timber Act made it possible to homestead timberlands in plats of 160 acres. Since this land was unsuitable to tillable agriculture it provided a channel through which richer timber resources were exploited by some of the large lumber companies of the West. The Desert Land Act was more realistic in that it provided that 640 acres of land could be purchased by settlers who agreed

to irrigate it. Much of the land in the 11 states to which the Act pertained
was fertile, but the average annual rainfall of less than 20 inches would
not support tillable agriculture. There were no large cities in those states
that could provide ready markets for the products of truck farming. If that
land were to be used in farming, it would have to be planted in cereal
grains—wheat, rye, barley, corn, and oats.

Settlement v. Speculation

It was the obvious intent of Congress to prevent public lands from
falling into the hands of speculators. Disposing of land in relatively small
acreages may have been one way to encourage the settlement of frontier
lands by permanent settlers and to prevent the lands from falling into
the hands of speculators; but those acreages were entirely unsuited to the
type of farming that was profitable, in general, west of the Mississippi River.
By taking advantage of the provisions of all of the public land acts, it was
possible for one homesteader to obtain under the provisions of the Homestead Act, 160 acres; Timber Culture Act, 160 acres; Stone and Timber
Act, 160 acres; and the Desert Land Act, 640 acres, for a total of 1,120
acres. When allowance is made for fraudulent entries, it is easy to understand how thousands of acres of public land fell into the hands of owners of
large farms, not of small ones; of speculators, not of settlers; of large land
companies whose purpose was to exploit resources and people rather than
to develop the land in a manner that was related to the general economic
development of the country. Suffice it to say here that, because of land grants
to railroads, the public lands that were available under the terms of the
aforementioned Land Acts were located 20 miles or more from railroads.
That fact, in itself, was a discouraging factor to many farmers who found
isolation an insurmountable problem. They could not haul their grain to
the railroads by means of horse-drawn equipment, neither could they drive
that distance for the goods that were obtainable only from eastern manufacturers. The result was that many settlers did not complete their applications for entry upon their lands. Discouraged, they returned to the East,
whence they had come, or found other employment in nearby communities.
Land fell into the hands of speculators, or of ranchers who acquired land
somewhat far removed from settlement. By combining the holdings of many
small pseudosettlers, thousands of acres were put to grazing cattle and sheep.

The Close of the Frontier and Its Impacts

The Bureau of the Census made a simple announcement in 1890 that
the frontier had been closed. Under the conditions that prevailed at the
time, there were no more free public lands upon which to settle. In reality
there were millions upon millions of public lands that had not been appropriated for use, but they required the application of social capital to make
them usable. The most important form of social capital was irrigation,
which was too costly for individual owners to provide. Not only was it too

costly, sources of surface water were too far removed from individual farms and problems of State Rights were involved in tapping them.

According to definition, a density of population of two persons or more per square mile identified frontier regions, and any lands upon which there were fewer persons were beyond the frontier. It remained for Frederick Jackson Turner in his essay entitled *The Significance of the Frontier* to describe the rhythm of the westward movement and the settlement of frontier regions. The enthusiasm with which he described the westward movement upon free lands and the impacts of that movement upon the remainder of the country led him astray in his interpretation of its significance.

One of the impacts of the close of the frontier was to terminate the expansion of land upon which extensive methods of utilization were profitable. A second impact was to compel farmers in the North and East to practice more intensive methods of cultivating their soil. Frequently, that involved the development of completely new uses for land in supplying urban markets with farm produce. Still a third impact was to call attention to the fact that our vast natural resources had been exploited almost to the point of foreseeable exhaustion. A movement for the conservation of natural resources led President Theodore Roosevelt to establish national forests and other reserves in order to conserve land and mineral wealth. In 1909, the Secretary of the Interior, acting upon the recommendation of a National Conservation Commission headed by Gifford Pinchot, withdrew 148 million acres of forest land, 80 million acres of coal land, 4.7 million acres of phosphate lands, and 1.5 million acres of waterpower sites from use by free enterprise.

QUESTIONS FOR REVIEW

1. (a) Compare the birth rates for rural areas with those for urban communities.
   (b) How do you explain the divergence between those data?

2. (a) Explain why immigrants came to America after 1870. What were the factors of "push" and "pull"?
   (b) Contrast the "old" immigration with the "new."

3. Why did newly arrived immigrants seem to avoid the South as an area in which to make their homes?

4. (a) Explain the migratory movement in the years just prior to World War I.
   (b) What was the impact of the war upon that movement?

5. What were the impacts of the results of the first selective service law and of the war itself upon the attitudes of Americans towards immigration? Explain clearly.

6. Outline the principal features of the public land policy of the federal government after 1862.

7. What were some of the economic impacts of the Homestead Act?

8. (a) What did the Bureau of the Census mean when it announced that the frontier had been closed?
   (b) What were the economic impacts of the disappearance of the frontier?

SUGGESTED READINGS

Benedict, Murray R. *Farm Policies of the United States, 1790-1950.* New York City: The Twentieth Century Fund, 1953. Chapter 1.

Dowd, Douglas F. "A Comparative Analysis of Economic Development in the American West and South," *United States Economic History: Selected Readings,* edited by Harry N. Scheiber. New York City: Alfred A. Knopf, Inc., 1964.

Gates, Paul W. "The Homestead Law in an Incongruous Land System," *United States Economic History: Selected Readings,* edited by Harry N. Scheiber. New York City: Alfred A. Knopf, Inc., 1964.

Hacker, Louis M. *Major Documents in American Economic History.* New York City: D. Van Nostrand Co., Inc., 1961. Vol. I, Nos. 16, 25, and 30.

Robbins, R. M. "The Public Domain in the Era of Exploitation," *Economic Change in America,* edited by Joseph T. Lambie and Richard V. Clemence. Harrisburg, Pa.: Stackpole Books, 1954.

Saloutos, Theodore. "Land Policy and Its Relation to Agricultural Production and Distribution, 1862 to 1933," *American Economic History: Essays in Interpretation,* edited by Stanley Coben and Forest G. Hill. Philadelphia: J. B. Lippincott Co., 1966.

Shannon, Fred A. "A Postmortem on the Labor-Safety Valve Theory," *Economic Change in America,* edited by Joseph T. Lambie and Richard V. Clemence. Harrisburg, Pa.: Stackpole Books, 1954.

——————. *The Farmer's Last Frontier: Agriculture, 1860-1897.* New York City: Holt, Rinehart & Winston, Inc., 1945.

Thomas, Brinley. "The Positive Contribution by Immigrants: The Economic Aspect," *United States Economic History: Selected Readings,* edited by Harry N. Scheiber. New York City: Alfred A. Knopf, Inc., 1964.

Wright, Chester W. *Economic History of the United States.* 2d ed. New York City: McGraw-Hill Book Company, 1949. Chapter 29.

Chapter 13

THE DEVELOPMENT OF AGRICULTURE—1865-1920

One of the aspects of the development of agriculture after 1865 was its adaptation to the market. In scope there really were three levels of markets: namely, local urban, national, and world. One adaptation took the form of ranch farming in the raising and feeding of cattle and sheep. Prairie grasses upon which bison had pastured for many years were low cost feed on the eastern slope of the Rocky Mountain plateau. A second adaptation was found in the development of wheat farming in the second tier of states west of the Mississippi River. A third adaptation was found in the raising of hogs in the states of Illinois, Iowa, and Missouri. All of these developments compelled farmers in the more eastern states to specialize in dairying, poultry raising, growing hay for the market, and in the growing of fruits and vegetables for urban markets.

Many and serious have been the dislocations in agriculture due to adaptations to markets. The dislocations have been felt in other segments of the economy. Landowners, capitalists, labor, and entrepreneurs felt adverse effects, many of which have tended to level off short-run gains.

RANCH FARMING

Much of the land that lies to the west of the first tier of states west of the Missouri River was covered with a heavy matting of grass that provided excellent pasturage for cattle, sheep, and horses. That grass performed an important function in the American economy that was not appreciated until after it had been plowed under in order to utilize the soil for tillable agriculture. East of the 98th meridian the average annual rainfall was in excess of 20 inches. That was ample to support tillable agriculture. West of the meridian, the average annual rainfall was too light to sustain arable farming.

The roots of that grass were interwoven in a complex fashion and were sufficiently deep to retard the flow of underground water on its way to a river. Water and grass, together, bound the soil so as to prevent erosion either from wind or from rainfall. Surface rainfall was not necessary for the grass to attain full, luxurious growth as long as water was available in the subsoil. Farmers found out the hard way that wooden plows and plowshares would not cut and turn that sod. It was not until James Oliver perfected a chilled iron plow in 1868 that it was possible and worthwhile from a cost standpoint to turn the sod and to plant the land in grains. Improvements in farm machinery, including attaching a seat on which the operator could ride, made possible the cultivation of larger farm units.

Cattle and Sheep Ranching

Land in Oklahoma, northern and western Texas, eastern New Mexico, Colorado, and Wyoming was too remote from railroad transportation for farmers to engage in arable farming on a commercial basis. Again, the cost of labor and of capital encouraged a more extensive utilization of that land. Ranching provided its own transportation. Labor was represented by cowboys and drovers. Once a capital investment in cows and bulls had been made, natural increase resulted in a relatively large supply of low cost capital. The initial scarcity of capital was overcome, in part, by English and Scottish cattlemen investing in American herds. They also were partly responsible for having meat shipped to England and to Scotland where it undersold meats that had been produced entirely in those countries.

The Long Drive. Regional specialization in raising cattle and sheep led to an exciting chapter in the development of the West. Cattle that were bred and pastured in the Southwestern States until they were ready to be fattened for the market were driven into Kansas and Colorado northward where pastures were abundant in grasses that made excellent cattle feed. The eastern slopes of the Rocky Mountains as far north as Montana were cleared of snow by the wind during the winter months. Here is the setting for the "long drive" from Texas to Montana. Transportation facilities had not been extended to that area, and the only means of reaching northern pastures was afoot. The drover-cowboy, who has been portrayed vividly in the movies and on television, originated in the need for having the cattle cared for on the ranges and for driving them from the southern regions to northern pastures for winter pasturage. When fattened, the cattle were shipped to market, probably in Chicago. That was one of the early influences that led to the supremacy of Chicago as the center of the meat-packing industry.

It was not until the wheat farmers had pushed into western Kansas and Nebraska that a conflict of interest occurred between drovers and ranchers, and wheat farmers. When lands in these states were planted in wheat and the route of the "long drive" went through them, much damage was done by cattle trampling wheat underfoot and eating it as they went along. Efforts of the cowboys to stimulate the forward movement of their herds did not lessen the damage done to growing crops. In self-defense, wheat farmers were forced to fence their fields with barbed wire. That was expensive, and it required an additional capital outlay on their part.

Barbed Wire. In 1874 the wheat farmers purchased 10,000 pounds of barbed wire at $20 per cwt., or 20 cents a pound. Six years later they acquired 80,500,000 pounds of wire. By 1897 the price had been reduced to $1.80 per cwt., or a little less than 2 cents per pound. In 1900 the owner of a large ranch in Texas stretched 247 miles of barbed wire at a cost of $37,250. At that rate the cost of fencing a section of land consisting of 640 acres with two strands of barbed wire was $1,200. To fence a square of four sections with two strands of barbed wire cost $2,400. That was an initial cost that was not incurred annually.

Not to be stalemated in their quest for better pastures, drovers supplied themselves with wire cutters; and the war between the rancher and the arable farmer was only intensified. That struggle terminated with the building of railroads to the west and southwest of Kansas City and Omaha. These railroads crossed the trails of the "long drive" and cattle towns sprang up along the way. It was at these crossings that cattle were put on board freight cars and hauled to greener pastures or to market. That not only saved time and damage en route, it prevented a loss of weight that resulted from driving cattle long distances on foot. Abilene, Dodge City, Ogalalla, and Miles City are among the better known cow towns; and oldtime residents of these cities have kept alive some of the traditions of the range country.

Table 13-1

Numbers of Cattle and Sheep and Their Respective Values per Head—1870-1920

Year	Cattle		Sheep	
	Number (000)	Value per Head	Number (000)	Value per Head
1870	31,082	$22.84	36,449	$ 1.87
1880	43,347	17.80	44,867	2.18
1890	60,014	16.95	42,693	2.29
1900	59,739	26.50	45,065	2.97
1910	58,993	24.54	46,939	4.06
1920	70,400	52.64	37,328	10.59

Source: U. S. Department of Commerce, Bureau of the Census, *Historical Statistics of the United States. Colonial Times to 1957* (Washington: U. S. Government Printing Office, 1960), pp. 289-290. Adapted.

Cattle Ranchers v. Sheep Ranchers

Another conflict arose between the cattle ranchers and the sheep ranchers. The cattle rancher and his drovers fought the sheep rancher and his tenders because cattle could not pasture after sheep had nibbled the grass too short for cattle to grasp with their tongues. Cattlemen also complained that the sharp pointed hooves of sheep dug up the turf; and, too, cattle would not drink where sheep had watered. Sheep were drowned, driven off cliffs, and destroyed by other means until a truce was called under the terms of which much of the grazing land was divided between cattle and sheep herders.

Individual ranchers grazed thousands of head of cattle or as many sheep. The latter were profitable because of the heavy demand for wool, mutton, and hides. Cattle were sold for beef, and their hides were tanned for leather.

ARABLE FARMING

Wheat and corn have always been the staple products of American agricultural pursuits north of the Ohio River and west of the Mississippi River. Cotton has occupied that position in the South. The degree of prosperity the farmer has enjoyed from year to year has depended, in large part, upon the prices the market offered for those crops. In more localized areas, prices of other crops have been the key to successful years, or years of failure. Tobacco in North Carolina, Kentucky, and Tennessee; sugar in Louisiana, and, later, fruit crops were grown locally. Watermelons, cantaloupes, strawberries, tomatoes, and peaches were grown for local consumption, later for regional and national markets. Truck farming was stimulated by the growth in the number and in the size of cities.

Extensive v. Intensive Cultivation

As long as there was an abundance of free land upon which to settle and cultivate in the growing of cereal grains, extensive was more descriptive of agricultural processes than was intensive, especially in the production

Table 13-2
Wheat Acreage, Production, and Prices, 1870-1920

Year	Acres Harvested (000)	Bushels Produced (000)	Price per Bushel
1870	20,945	254,429	$1.042
1880	38,096	502,257	.952
1890	36,686	449,042	.837
1900	49,203	599,315	.621
1910	45,793	625,476	.908
1920	62,358	843,277	1.827

Source: *Historical Statistics of the United States. Colonial Times to 1957*, 1960, p. 297. Adapted.

of staple crops. There was a strong tendency in the extension of arable farming to the west, for farming in the East to become more intensive, and for farmers east of the Mississippi River to devote less and less acreage to the planting of cereal grains. Eastern farmers became more attentive to the demands of nearby urban markets, less mindful of the development of world markets.

As farmlands were opened in the West, new acres were planted in wheat and corn. Some acreage on each farm was set aside on which to plant oats and other crops, such as rye, barley, buckwheat, flax, and later alfalfa. Corn, oats, and buckwheat were feed crops, as well as money crops; rye, barley, and flax found their way to the market. Alfalfa was used as a cover crop and alfalfa hay was fed to livestock.

Corn and Hogs

Wherever corn was grown in abundance, hogs were not far distant. That was true for small farms as well as for large farms, because the hog was a relatively efficient medium for turning corn and unedible refuse from the table into edible meat. He was a scavenger of a sort and tended to keep the soil loose where he rooted. The direct money outlay for his food was relatively low, and the corn he ate kept just that much from going to market on the cob.

On the smaller farms the hog may have been butchered for local consumption; from the larger farms he was sent to market and became a dependable source of money income. His meat was sold as ham, pork, or sausage; and many were the communities whose residents prided themselves in their making and cooking of country sausage and smoked ham.

Table 13-3
Production of Corn and Hogs—1870-1920

Year	Corn			Hogs	
	Acres Harvested (000)	Bushels Produced (000)	Price per Bushel	Number (000)	Value per Head
1870	38,388	1,124,775	.521¢	33,781	$ 5.64
1880	62,545	1,706,673	.390	44,327	4.40
1890	74,785	1,650,446	.496	48,130	4.80
1900	94,852	2,661,978	.350	51,055	5.36
1910	102,267	2,852,794	.515	48,072	9.05
1920	101,359	3,070,604	.638	60,159	20.00

Source: *Historical Statistics of the United States. Colonial Times to 1957*, 1960, pp. 289, 290, and 297. Adapted.

In the Middle Western States of Illinois and Iowa, corn was the leading cereal grain. It found its way to market on the hoof and was not processed by the farmers themselves. It was the slaughtering of hogs that gave renown to Cincinnati and Indianapolis, later to Chicago. For many years, more hogs than cattle were slaughtered in Chicago; and when some railroads banded together to finance the construction of the Union Stockyards, for which Chicago has become known the world over, ample space was allocated to the construction of hog pens.

Specialty Areas

Analysis and description of agriculture are facilitated and clarified by returning to a technique that was introduced in analyzing the economy of the Colonial Period. Agricultural environment was not uniform throughout the country. New England and the Middle Atlantic States developed their own patterns under the stimulus of free enterprise. The Southern States were confronted with unique problems that almost defied solution, but by the turn of the century, free enterprise had found ways of overcoming many of them.

New England. New England farmers felt the impact of the competition they encountered from western farmers in the markets of the East and in world markets. By the close of the century the production of wheat and corn in New England had declined 90 percent compared with figures for 1860.

The dislocation of farming in New England would have been much more serious had it not been for the development of urban centers. These centers functioned in two ways to relieve a difficult situation. First, they absorbed some of the surplus farm labor that was no longer needed on farms; second, when that labor was absorbed in commercial and industrial pursuits, it added to the market for the products of a new kind of specialized farming for which the New England States were adapted. New England towns provided lucrative markets for the products of dairy and poultry farming. In season beets, beans, carrots, cabbage, sweet corn, tomatoes, onions, turnips, parsnips, squash, and other vegetables were sold in stores and in roadside markets. Cranberries, currants, blackberries, blueberries, quinces, strawberries, and raspberries, in season, not only added to the incomes of rural families when sold, they gave savor and piquancy to tables when served fresh, or as jam, jelly, or preserves. Nothing was more delectable than a pie that was made from fresh berries. Fruit farmers took advantage of frost drainage on the hillsides to protect cherry, apple, pear, and plum trees in cold weather. These fruits were sold in wayside markets and in urban stores. Hotel dining rooms featured many of these delicacies on their menus.

The soil of the Connecticut River Valley was enriched every year by silt that was deposited by ebbing flood waters. Tobacco was the money crop upon which farmers in Connecticut and Massachusetts on both sides of the river depended for a flow of money income. Among the uncertainties of raising tobacco in New England were occasional hailstorms that slit the tender tobacco leaves into shreds. That was particularly disastrous to the growers because the principal market for the leaf was in its use as wrappers for cigars.

Potatoes became the specialty products of several counties in northern Maine, and the Bangor and Aroostook Railroad became known as the "potato railroad." Maine potatoes were sold in markets whose boundaries extended far to the west and south of the New England States. While the concentration of potato growing in Maine gave prominence to that state, other regions diversified their crops by harvesting thousands of bushels of potatoes for the market. New York, Pennsylvania, Maryland, Michigan, and later Idaho had regions in which Irish potatoes were among the principal crops. In fact, farmers in almost every state were able to raise them. Sometimes the comparative market prices of potatoes and other products were the factors that determined how many acres were planted in each crop. Farmers in Kansas and Iowa could raise excellent crops of potatoes, which they frequently did, so as to diversify the resources of their money incomes.

Middle Atlantic States. Farmers in New York could not compete with the farmers of more western lands in the growing, harvesting, and marketing of wheat. They turned their attention to growing vegetable and fruit crops. Apple orchards were planted across the central portion of the state, and vineyards were found along the banks of the Hudson River. The Susquehanna River Valley continued to be planted in wheat and corn on a commercial basis, but in much of the remainder of Pennsylvania apple and cherry trees dotted the hillsides. The products of truck farming and of poultry farms found ready markets in the industrial and commercial centers of that state. Under the conservative program of the Pennsylvania Germans, a unique agricultural economy developed in the south central portion of the state. The philosophy of life of these thrifty people was colored by their religious beliefs. They were not interested in amassing large amounts of personal wealth, and personal adornment was an expression of the vain desires of man which were sinful. Machinery was not accepted as a technique to be used in tilling the soil, neither was it incorporated into their standard of living in their personal lives. Since their personal wants were few and were for simple items, their earnings were almost literally plowed back into their farms. They took better care of their livestock and its housing than they did of themselves and their housing. Natural fertilizer, which was a by-product of their extensive use of horses and cows, was spread on their land every year to restore its fertility.

The South. If the economic fortunes of the South depended upon the market for cotton before 1865, they continued to be determined by that same market for many years thereafter. In terms of population as well as in terms of its distribution throughout more states, a larger area felt the economic impacts of changes in the cotton market after 1865 than before.

The Role of Cotton. It was not until 1878 that the production of cotton again reached the output of 1860. The years of reconstruction in the South were not kind to the growers of cotton. Sharecropping and crop lien systems were about the only organizations that provided labor on cotton plantations. There were no incentives to rotate crops, and fertilization was kept at a minimum. Even fallowing land was not practiced. Throughout the remaining years of the 19th century, exhaustion of the soil began to exact its toll. In 1879 the number of pounds of lint per acre was 294 in Louisiana, 292 in Arkansas. In 1909, the corresponding figures were 156 and 162 respectively. The production of cotton was maintained and increased only by bringing into cultivation new acres of land. Agricultural expansion knew no sectional boundaries except as to the manner by which it occurred and, possibly, in the forces that gave rise to it. Since immigrant farmers, who comprised a large class of new arrivals in this country, were not attracted by the prospects of farming in the South, any westward movement of cotton culture must have been instigated by the owners of southern plantations. By 1879, Texas ranked third after Mississippi and Georgia. Twenty years later it ranked first with a production equal to twice that of either of these two states and more than both of them put together. Between 1899 and 1919 Oklahoma increased its production of cotton from the tenth ranking state to the fourth. Texas was still in the lead, and South Carolina had advanced from sixth position in 1879 to fifth place in 1899 and third in 1919. The impacts of a more diversified agriculture in Alabama, Louisiana, and Mississippi are revealed in the decline in cotton output in these states in 1919.

As cotton planters moved west, their places were taken by yeomen farmers who owned and cultivated comparatively small-sized farms. They were working farmers. "Dirt" farmers is an expression that was frequently used to distinguish them from the gentlemen farmers of antebellum days. Since the land they occupied had been bled of its fertility by continued plantings of one crop, they found it necessary to fertilize the soil rather heavily. Natural fertilizer was used as far as it would go, but it may have lacked balanced ingredients because mules and cattle were not fed according to pattern until near the turn of the century. Commercial fertilizers that were mixed according to the needs of the soil as well as to the requirements of the various crops not only increased yields per acre but developed more nourishing crops. The costs of fertilizers were operating costs and were variable. These costs were subject to the dictates of the market for fertilizers as well as to variances in the needs of farmers. The use of commercial fertilizers was a step towards a more intensive cultivation of southern farms. It also represented progress in the conservation of natural resources.

While yeomen farmers may have grown some cotton, more diversified plantings appeared on small farms before they did on plantations. Corn, wheat, and oats were among the staple crops; peanuts, okra, field peas, beans and onions, sorghum, tomatoes, and potatoes were grown for local consumption in nearby communities. Roads were poor; canals were nonexistent;

Table 13-4

Production of Cotton in Leading Cotton-Growing States
(Bales of Lint, 500 lbs. Gross Weight)

State	1879	1899	1919
North Carolina	389,000	433,000	858,000
South Carolina	522,000	843,000	1,476,000
Georgia	814,000	1,232,000	1,681,000
Alabama	699,000	1,093,000	718,000
Mississippi	963,000	1,286,000	957,000
Tennessee	330,000	235,000	306,000
Louisiana	508,000	699,000	306,000
Arkansas	608,000	705,000	869,000
Oklahoma	......	227,000	1,006,000
Texas	805,000	2,584,000	2,971,000
Others	117,000	107,000	228,000
United States	5,755,000	9,444,000	11,376,000

Source: Compiled from United States Department of Commerce *Reports*. Cited in
Emory Q. Hawk, *Economic History of the South*. (Englewood Cliffs, N. J.:
Prentice-Hall, Inc., 1934), p. 454.

river travel was slow; and railroad managements were more interested in
through traffic from terminal to terminal than they were in serving way
stations or intermediate towns. Southern markets were strictly local, and
few products of southern farms found their way to northern marts.

As cotton culture spread to the Delta region and to the Southwest, the
newer lands excelled the older ones in productivity; and North Carolina,
South Carolina, Florida, Georgia, and Alabama lost rank among the leading
states in which it was raised. Mississippi, Louisiana, and Texas, not to
forget Arkansas, became the leading states for the production of cotton. It
was these states that provided the pathway for the progress of the boll weevil
from Mexico throughout the entire South.

Boll Weevil and Diversification. By 1870, the boll weevil had crossed
the Rio Grande River from Mexico into Texas. Traveling at the rate of
approximately 50 miles a year it wreaked havoc throughout the cotton
states by the outbreak in Europe of World War I. Disaster was turned
into victory that was memorialized by the erection of a monument in honor
of the boll weevil in Enterprise, Alabama. That pest did what man had been
unable to accomplish: namely, to force diversification of agriculture in the
South. Peanuts were grown for the nut and also for hay. Later peanut oil

was extracted from the nut, and the foundations of several by-product industries were laid. Corn was planted, and some livestock were pastured;
but another generation passed before new pasture grasses and hybrid corn
brought a new look to southern farms.

One of the important by-products of growing and ginning cotton was
cottonseed. Since it had no special cost of production it shared with the cotton
fiber the costs of raising, picking, and ginning. Looking at the matter from
one point of view, cottonseed did not become a separate product until the
ginning process had been completed. At one time it was crushed or mashed
and returned to the soil as fertilizer. Cottonseed contained a large percentage
of oil that was separated from the seed and sold as a commercial product.
By 1880 it had become the target for monopoly interests in controlling its
sale on the market. Since its processing was a manufacturing process rather
than one of agriculture, all we will do here is to recognize its existence as a
source of added income to the cotton grower.

Table 13-5
Cotton and Cottonseed—1870-1920

Year	Cotton			Cottonseed	
	Acres Harvested (000)	Bales Produced (000)	Price per Pound (Cents)	Tons Produced (000)	Price per Ton
1870	9,238	4,352	12.10	1,786	....
1880	15,921	6,606	9.83	2,822	....
1890	20,937	8,653	8.59	3,802	....
1900	24,886	10,124	9.15	4,500	....
1910	31,508	11,609	13.96	5,156	$26.11
1920	34,408	13,429	15.89	5,966	25.65

Source: *Historical Statistics of the United States. Colonial Times to 1957*, 1960,
pp. 301 and 302. Adapted.

DAIRY FARMING

While no one section of the country had a monopoly on dairying, it
contributed to the income of farmers in some regions more than in others.
A combination of circumstances in the New England States focused the
attention of farmers on that industry. Urban areas have always provided
concentrated and somewhat lucrative markets for dairy products and New
England cities were no exception. The Middle Atlantic States likewise presented markets for the products of dairy farms. No matter in what section
of the country urban areas developed, dairy farms were not far distant.

Milk, cream, butter, cheese, and ice cream are the products that are
usually classified as those of dairies; but, strictly speaking, milk and cream

have come to be the only ones that are produced in large volumes on farms. At one time the farmers in America made their own butter and cheese and some for the market. Throughout almost the entire period under review, butter, cheese, and ice cream have been products of manufacturing concerns rather than of farms. Even so, they are related so closely to the output of dairies that they are still classified as dairy products. Many dairies continue to furnish butter to local markets. In Wisconsin dairy farmers have formed cooperatives for the manufacture of butter and cheese. In addition to the sections of the United States that have already been mentioned, northern Illinois and Wisconsin have had a high degree of specialization in dairying. Not only did they produce large volumes of milk and cream, but butter and cheese in stores all over the country were identified by their packaging as having been processed in one of those states.

Table 13-6

Cows Kept on Farms for Milk, Milk Produced, By-Products—1870-1920

Year	Cows and Heifers Two Years Old and Older		Pounds of Butter (000)	Pounds of Cheese (000)	Pounds of Evaporated and Con-densed Milk (000)	Gallons of Ice Cream* (000)
	No. (000)	Value per Head				
1870	9,672	$31.89	412,130	180,780	3,786 †	24
1880	11,754	23.31	815,699	269,728	13,033 †	144
1890	15,000	22.30	1,171,211	318,458	44,867 †	851
1900	16,544	31.30	1,540,080	323,788	206,621	5,021
1910	19,450	35.40	1,706,076	355,000	555,938	29,637
1920	21,455	81.51	1,574,438	422,947	1,416,261	171,248

* 1869 and 10-year intervals to 1920.
† 1869, 1879, and 1889.
Source: *Historical Statistics of the United States. Colonial Times to 1957,* 1960, pp. 292-93. Adapted.

PROGRESS IN PRODUCTION

One way of measuring the progress of an industry is in terms of its total volume of output. However, an increase in volume could have resulted from greater activity at the same level of technology. Another measurement is in terms of yield per acre, and a third approach is in terms of man-hours per unit of output. According to some data that are presented by the Bureau of the Census, little progress was made between 1880 and 1920 in increasing the yield per acre of either wheat, corn, or cotton. In fact, the yield of lint per acre in 1920 was 10.6 percent less than it was in 1880.

Data in Table 13-7 reveal emphatically the advances that were made over a span of 40 years in reducing the number of man-hours per unit of corn, wheat, and cotton. In terms of man-hours to produce a given unit of output,

Table 13-7

Man-Hours to Produce Specified Amounts of Corn, Wheat, and Cotton—1880-1920

Crop	Item	1880	1900	1920
Corn	Man-hours per acre	46	38	32
	Before harvest	28	22	19
	Harvest	18	16	13
	Yield per acre (bushels)	25.6	25.9	28.4
	Man-hours per 100 bushels ..	180	147	113
Wheat	Man-hours per acre	20	15	12
	Before harvest	8	7	5.5
	Harvest	12	8	6.5
	Yield per acre (bushels)	13.2	13.9	13.8
	Man-hours per 100 bushels ..	152	108	87
Cotton	Man-hours per acre	119	112	90
	Before harvest	67	62	55
	Harvest	52	50	35
	Yield per acre (pounds)	179	191	160
	Man-hours per bale	318	280	269

Source: *Historical Statistics of the United States. Colonial Times to 1957,* 1960, p. 281. Adapted.

the greatest advance, 43 percent, was made in the production of wheat; the smallest advance, 15 percent, was made in the production of cotton. Man-hours saved per acre were greatest percentagewise in the production of wheat. These data confirm the analysis that has been made of the impact of the use of farm machinery upon the wheat farmers and others.

FARM POWER

The development and use of power on farms and in agricultural processes characterized farming from 1865 to 1920. Machinery could not have been adapted to farming unless power had been available with which to operate it. Without power, farmers could not have utilized improved technologies and operated larger sized farms.

Four sources of power energized American farms until the adaptation of the internal combustion engine to the needs of the farmer.

Wind Power

Wind power was used to provide water on farms where streams and springs were not available. Wells were dug and windmills erected to pump water from below the surface to tanks that were supported on stilts, after which the force of gravity made water available on tap. Some farmers were fortunate enough to have springs whose flows of water were in sufficient volume to meet the needs of the home, the barn and barnyard, or both.

Manpower

Manpower in the form of farm labor was used to perform chores around the house, in gardens, and in barns. Where acres of forests were found, saw-mills that were powered by water or by steam may have made easier the cutting of wood. Otherwise, axes were kept sharp. Horses, mules, and dairy cattle were cared for by hand labor. Large farms in the Middle Western States may have required the services of from 12 to 30 horses or more. They all had to be fed, curried, and harnessed by hand; and cleaning their stalls was a chore in every sense of the word. Dairy cattle were milked by hand, and dairy barns were not heated in cold weather. Corn picking contests were held annually to enliven an otherwise tedious task. To meet the seasonal needs for additional farm labor, transient workers were used to harvest wheat. When wheat ripened it had to be harvested at once to keep the grain from falling to the ground. Teen-age boys, college students, and grown men followed the harvest from Texas and Oklahoma northward through Kansas, Nebraska, South Dakota, North Dakota, Minnesota, Montana, and into Canada.

Horsepower

The continued use of farm labor in the cultivation and harvesting of cotton, rice, sugar, and tobacco did not preclude the use of horse and mule-drawn equipment in preparing the land for planting. No attempt is being made here to distinguish between the use of horses and mules, except to recognize the fact that mules were used extensively throughout the entire South. Breeding mules was a major activity in Kentucky, Tennessee, and Missouri. They were sold at auctions that attracted buyers from all over the South. They were transported by rail from the auction block to the farms, towns, and cities of their new owners. They were the principal draft animal in urban areas as well as on farms. Farm labor and relatively small-sized horse-drawn machinery continued to be used on farms in New England and the Middle Atlantic States long after farmers in Ohio, Indiana, Illinois, and the states west of the Mississippi River began to use larger sized equipment.

Utilization of farm machinery depended more upon the strength of horses and mules than upon some form of inanimate power. In order to get the work done in time, as farms increased in size they required more teams of horses and more units of farm machinery, later larger units. Larger sized farm machines did not eliminate the need for horsepower, as some of the larger combines that were in use towards the close of the century were powered by 30 horses or more. Plows, harrows, cultivators, rakes, tedders, and drills may have been pulled by teams of two or three horses abreast; but farmers used from six to ten units or more at a time staggered in tandem.

The increase in the number of horses and mules on farms from 1870 to 1920, as revealed in Table 13-8, was a product of the increase in (1) the number of farms, (2) the size of farms, and (3) the acreage of farmland under cultivation. The values of those animals represented investment values

Table 13-8

**Number of Horses and Mules on Farms
and Their Values per Head—1870-1920**

Year	Horses		Mules	
	Number (000)	Value	Number (000)	Value
1870	7,633	$ 66.69	1,245	$ 89.71
1880	10,903	53.74	1,878	61.74
1890	15,732	69.27	2,322	77.61
1900	17,856	43.56	3,139	51.46
1910	19,972	107.70	4,239	119.98
1920	20,091	96.45	5,651	148.29

Source: *Historical Statistics of the United States. Colonial Times to 1957*, 1960, pp. 289-90. Adapted.

rather than income values. Horsepower was efficient to the extent that its use was maximized throughout the year. It was inefficient in that its owners incurred a maintenance cost at times when it was not in use. Under ordinary circumstances it had little or no depreciation of capital value until it reached the age of 12 or 15, depending upon the care taken of it and its use. Farming may not have had all of the attributes of large-scale operation, but there is no question but that the farm unit in the Middle Western States and in Texas increased in size. That increase in size was accompanied by the introduction of the corporate form of organization. Shares of stock were sold, the proceeds of which were used to purchase costly farm machinery. By measuring acres in thousands instead of in hundreds, machines were used to capacity throughout a given year; and fixed costs were spread over larger bases thus lowering unit costs of production.

Steam Traction Engine

The most picturesque power unit found on American farms prior to World War I was powered by steam. Broad iron or steel tires and large lugs enabled the traction engine to travel slowly over almost any kind of terrain. It was noisy and dirty and from an engineering point of view it was extremely inefficient, but it performed all that it was supposed to do. It burned coal and wood, and on occasions it was cheaper to fire it with corn than to sell the corn and purchase coal with the proceeds. It was used in logging, in constructing roads, and in hauling several heavily laden wagons in tandem. As a unit that generated power, a belt that was stretched from its flywheel to one on another machine transmitted power for sawmills, for cutting ensilage and raising it to the tops of silos, and for threshing wheat.

One practice was for farmers to rent an engine by the day or week, for as long as it would take to thresh their wheat, or for whatever kind of work they wanted done. The operator was furnished by the owner. Then the owner moved on to another farm and repeated the process. That procedure made it possible for an owner to maximize the amount of capital investment necessary for individual farmers and reduced their fixed costs of farming which were so vulnerable in times of falling market prices. Farmers could obtain the use of that kind of capital equipment by increasing their operating expenses which increases were smaller than their fixed costs would have been. Because of the versatility of those engines, their overall costs were not a charge against any one kind of operation.

Internal Combustion Engine

A shortage of farm labor combined with an increase in the demand for foodstuffs provided the stimulus that may have been required to have the internal combustion engine accepted on the farm. Many farm boys had learned in army camps how to disassemble and reassemble automotive equipment. The development and operation of army tanks had taught the youth of America how to operate and take care of tractors. Near the close of the period under observation large tractors had begun to appear on large farms, small tractors on smaller size farms. Small tractors could be used to advantage on farms in the Appalachian region and in the New England States. They hastened the transition of farming from an activity that required a great deal of handwork, or human labor, to one that was destined to become rather highly mechanized. A much larger total population than formerly was being fed more and better food that was produced by a much smaller percentage of the total population than was required 50 years earlier.

Regional Use of Farm Machinery

Even though the McCormick reaper had been invented in a region of relatively small-sized units and Hussey took his reaper to New England, the greatest potential of the use of farm machinery was in the Middle West. In the East, farm machinery was a laborsaving device; in the West, it made possible the development of commercial farming without developing a peasantry. Without plows, cultivators, harrows, seed drills, rakes, tedders, hay loaders, threshing machines, reapers, balers, mowers, and binders, farming would have remained a family industry or one that was dependent upon the use of peasant labor. Threshing machines, later combines, that did away with the binders in cutting wheat, were powered by steam traction engines and made it possible to count acres in farm units in terms of hundreds and thousands instead of in terms of tens and hundreds. Surface terrain in Ohio, Indiana, and states to the west was more level and open, which condition made for an increase in the use of horse-drawn farm machinery. Larger sized farms were cultivated with more horse-drawn units of a given kind or with larger sized units. The latter made possible the cultivation of more acres without a proportionate addition of labor.

Farm Machinery Production

John Deere, Cyrus McCormick, and James Oliver located their manufacturing plants in Illinois and along the banks of the Mississippi River because of the availability of venture capital, much of which came from eastern
capitalists. Chicago, Peoria, Decatur, and the tri-cities of Davenport, Iowa,
Moline and Rock Island, Illinois, attracted manufacturers of farm machinery
partly because of the accident of an early start by McCormick and partly
because they were at the threshold of the farm country where the demand
for machines was greatest. Some of the labor that was needed to produce
and assemble the standardized and interchangeable machine parts consisted
of erstwhile farm labor that had been displaced or that found factory work
less drudging than toiling on farms.

FARM LABOR AND TENANCY

Farm Labor

One of the tasks of farm labor was to drive teams of horses that were
hitched to machines. Instead of being forced to plod on foot in the fields all
day in the hot sun, seats were built-in features of many units. Some drivers
stood on harrows and cultivators to add their weight to that of their machines
and thus increase their operating efficiency.

In New England, farm labor worked alongside farm owner-operators and
more handwork was involved. Since farming was less concentrated on given
crops, work was more diversified. In the Connecticut River Valley, the
cultivation of tobacco required a great deal of hand labor. No matter what
the section of the country, milking cows mornings and evenings seven days
a week was a hand chore. Where truck patches were measured in square
feet rather than in acres, most of the work was performed with hand equipment. Berry farming, fruit farming, and poultry raising required kinds of
operations that had not been transferred to machines.

Southern farm labor was completely disorganized throughout the Reconstruction Period, and immigrant labor was not attracted to the South
until a much later date. Plantation owners could not work in their fields,
and small yeomen farmers had all they could do to operate their own farms.
The best solution to the problem of supplying labor on southern farms was
found in the development of farm tenancy.

Farm Tenancy

Farm tenancy in the Southern States represented somewhat of a permanent status, and its increase did not indicate progress in any sense of the
word other than in overcoming a labor shortage. Owners of farms usually
furnished any equipment that was needed by their tenants, except the
horses or mules and possibly wagons that were required. Tenancy was created
more in meeting operating expenses than in providing permanent capital

equipment. The tenants usually shared their crops with the plantation owners on the basis of one third of corn or one fourth of the cotton crop. If the landowners furnished everything but the labor, they usually shared in 50 percent of the crops. Payment in kind seemed to be the only method that would work with southern farm labor, most of which was drawn from Negro families. There was a question of just who paid rent and who received rent or wages. From one point of view, the owners of farmlands paid their tenants in kind; from another point of view the tenants paid rents to their landlords in kind. In 1882 the Georgia State Supreme Court declared the system to be one of paying wages rather than one of true tenancy.

In the Northern and Middle Western States, farm tenancy was frequently a step to farm ownership. Capital requirements for owning and operating farms were such that almost all farmers were compelled to borrow at one time or another. Even though farmlands may have been paid for in full, the additional capital that was required to purchase farm machinery necessitated farmers borrowing for from one to five years, depending entirely upon individual circumstances. It was common practice for a dealer in farm machinery to carry his customers along for one year upon receipt of a down payment of 10 percent. Credit for periods in excess of one year had to be obtained from other sources.

FARM COSTS

Farming was not unique in the fact that costs were incurred before income from farming was realized. It was unique in the fact that farmers had less control over prices they received in the market than had entrepreneurs in nonagricultural pursuits. The high degree of competition in the sale of agricultural staples precluded the exercise of any restraints by individual farmers, and lack of organization prevented their collective action.

Fixed Costs

Fixed costs resulted from contractual relationships entered into when farmers borrowed money in order to purchase land and farm machinery and to make relatively permanent capital improvements. Installment payment and rates of interest were determined when loans were obtained and were influenced in part by prices of farm products at the time. They were rigid and inflexible throughout the loan period, even when future prices deviated from those that influenced the terms of payment.

Operating Costs

Operating costs were incurred in order to enable farmers to cultivate their land, to plant their crops, and to harvest them in due season. Until the close of the century, or after, western farmers spent little or nothing for fertilizer. Natural fertilizer was a product of farming, and if the land required such treatment, the only cost incurred, other than that of labor, was the initial cost of manure spreaders. It was not until near the close of the period under observation that natural fertilizers became scarce and farmers were forced to purchase commercial products. That situation was brought about by the internal combustion engine replacing horsepower on farms. Capital costs of tractors were large, but the upkeep was low compared to that of horsepower. The mechanization of farming released thousands of acres upon which feed crops had been grown for the planting of money crops. That was an aspect of the internal organization or management of farms by which the acreage that was planted in money crops was increased without appropriating any more land for farm use. That change also came at the very time that many acres of arable land had begun to show the effects of extensive methods of cultivation and required more fertilization to maintain the same rate of soil productivity as before. Some farmers grew their own seed for the next planting; others purchased theirs. That item of cost was incurred only once a year unless the first planting was washed away by heavy rains and by floods, was killed by frost, or was destroyed by drought, wind, or pests.

Labor costs were met by farmers providing places for the workers to live and offering some spending money in addition. Farms and farm homes were too far from urban communities for the workers to go back and forth every day. There was also lost motion and extra expense involved in providing such transportation. Horse and wagon teams would have been used because there were no other devices available in rural areas until after World War I. Roads were poor. Not many were better than graded dirt roads. Horsepower was the only motive power of practical use on country roads.

Living Costs

Living costs were limited by the somewhat plain subsistence of western farm households. There were no gasoline taxes, nor were there income taxes at any level of government to harass farmers at least once a year until after 1913. Because of high exemptions and deductions allowed in the early years of income tax payments, many farmers did not feel the impacts of that form of taxation until the effects of World War I were reflected in the prices of farm products. Property taxes were almost the only tax claim against farm incomes. Costs of entertainment were minimal. Country schools and country churches were centers of organized rural social activity. Problems of style and variety of clothing were easily solved. Succeeding children of the same sex inherited the clothing of their older brothers and sisters. Durable consumer goods were not available until after World War I. Radios, television sets, deep freezes, vacuum cleaners, electric toasters, electric fans, and electric hair dryers were not found in any homes until a later period. It was not until after 1920 that electricity was carried to farms. Before that time, only an occasional farm was wired for electricity. Wood, coal, and corn were fuels for heating and for cooking, and kerosene lamps provided a dim and flickering light. There were some years of such low prices for corn that it was cheaper for farmers to burn their corn directly rather than sell it and purchase coal with the proceeds. Telephones were found in many farmhouses in the latter years of the 19th century. Many and frequent were the visits between farm homes via the telephone. Multiple party lines were the rule, and families could ring their friends direct without going through a central exchange.

DEPENDENCE OF FARMERS UPON MARKET SITUATIONS

Ranch farming, in general, was less self-sufficient than was the more general type of farming east of the Mississippi River. It emphasized the dependence of the farmer on the market and on market situations over which he had no control. That dependence was on two kinds of markets.

The Markets

On one market he sold the products of his farm. From the other market he purchased most of his goods for domestic consumption as well as his capital equipment. Although the farmer did not understand much about the theory of price and of pricing, well did he understand the importance of price. The impacts of changes in prices in either market left their imprints upon his scale of living. It was only through the money that he received from the markets on which he sold his produce that he was able to purchase consumer goods and capital equipment from other markets. When prices were favorable to him and he had volume to sell, the farmer prospered. At least his money income generated within him a feeling of prosperity. It was through the use of that money income that he was able to meet his fixed costs, his operating costs, and the cost of living of his family.

Burden of Falling Prices

From 1873 to 1896 prices received in the market by farmers fell more rapidly than did prices of articles they purchased in other markets that were less competitive. That situation resulted in loss of purchasing power of farmers' dollars. The obligation of meeting fixed costs forced many farmers to become insolvent. After they had paid living costs and operating expenses, there was not enough left over to cover fixed costs.

Schedule A

Year	Amortization of Principal	Interest	Total Money Cost
1881	$480	$192.00	$672.00
1882	480	153.60	633.60
1883	480	115.20	595.20
1884	480	76.80	556.80
1885	480	38.40	518.40

As the price of wheat, for instance, fell, the sale of more bushels was required to meet operating and living costs, and proportionately fewer bushels remained to provide income with which to meet fixed obligations. Had Farmer Brown borrowed $2,400 for five years at 8 percent in January, 1881, in order to fence a square of four sections of land, his contractual obligations would have been in accordance with the data in Schedule A.

Assuming that he decided to plant wheat and that its average price throughout the loan period remained at $1.196 per bushel, the sale of 401 bushels per year would have retired one fifth of the principal of the loan. The number of bushels required to meet interest payments was 160 the first year, which number decreased by 32 bushels for each remaining year. In summary, the proceeds from the sale of 2,005 bushels would have retired the principal sum and an additional 481 bushels, the interest payments.

Based upon the average output per acre, that total of 2,486 bushels could have been grown upon 194 acres.

Had Farmer Brown been able to dispose of his wheat at its annual average price for each of the five years, his experience would have followed the pattern outlined in Schedule B. Instead of having been able to retire the

Schedule B

| Year | Annual Average Price per Bushel | Required to Amortize Total Fixed Costs | | |
		Bushels	Average Yield of Bushels per Acre	Number of Acres
1881	$1.196	562	11.3	50
1882	.888	714	15.1	47
1883	.914	651	12.3	53
1884	.645	863	14.9	58
1885	.772	672	11.4	59
		3,462		267

loan from the proceeds of the sale of 2,486 bushels of wheat, the sale of 3,462 was required. In terms of acreage planted in wheat, 73 additional acres were required. Farmer Brown may not have operated at or near the averages that were determined by the Bureau of the Census.

POSITION OF FARMERS IN MARKET SITUATIONS

One complaint of the farmer was that when crops were bountiful they brought a low price in the market and when prices were relatively high he did not have much to sell. That relationship was a true one for farmers as a class; but, of course, there were many exceptions to this general statement.

Market Dependence

It was difficult for many farmers to improve upon their scale of living because they, as individuals, had little or no control over the market situations with which they came in contact, and to which they were subject. As the 19th century progressed and railroad transportation facilities were improved, these markets became larger and larger until they attained worldwide proportions. Right at home, the only transportation facility that was available for use by the farmer was the railroad. This was true in all sections of the country, recognizing all the time that a large volume of wheat moved via the Great Lakes and the Erie Canal. These facilities were as foreign to the farmer as were those of ocean transportation. Horse-drawn wagons were used to haul wheat from the farms to railway sidings or to grain elevators. Railroads were used to transport wheat to lake ports or all the way to eastern markets, and railroad rates constituted a cost to the farmer of marketing his products. That cost was one of the first claims against the farmer's income from the sale of a given year's crops. To the extent to which their capital goods and consumers' goods were purchased from eastern producers, transporting those wares was an added cost to the farmer. Again, the matter of railroad rates was of great concern to him, but this time as an added cost of buying rather than as a cost of selling.

In general, the period from 1873 to 1896 was not kind to the American farmer from the point of view of the prices he received from the market for the commodities he sold. Not only did competition between farmers increase, what was more important at that time was the increase in the production of wheat from 236 million bushels in 1870 to 522 million bushels in 1900. For the same years the production of corn increased from 1,094 million bushels to 2,105 million bushels and cotton in pounds from 1,451 million to 4,757 million. These increases in output came from more than doubling both the number of farms in the United States and the acreage of land under cultivation. It was the number of bushels that were chasing after the dollar that was important in price determination. The numbers of bushels of wheat and of corn that were competing for the consumer's food dollar was the force that drove the prices of these products downward. The production of cotton in 1900 was three times the volume that was produced in 1870. This figure far surpassed the rate of population increase during that period. National income figures which are available reveal that the only way that the increased volume of cotton could have been absorbed was (1) at lowered prices per pound and (2) by increasing our exports of cotton to European countries. The answer as to how the increased volume of cotton was disposed of is found in the decline in its price to five and six cents a pound at a time when eight cents was considered as an average *break-even price*. The break-even price of an agricultural product is the same as it is in manufacturing or marketing. It is that price that will return to the grower all of his costs of production and nothing more. Thus, at an eight-cent per pound break-even price and a market price of five and six cents per pound, the plantation farmer in the South went into debt. That was not a new experience for the grower of cotton, but it served to emphasize his dependence upon the market and upon one crop.

European Markets

Fortunately for the midwestern farmer, several conditions prevailed that tended to give him a larger share of the markets of western Europe for grains and for meat. That new outlet tended to absorb what otherwise would have amounted to an overwhelming increase in the offerings of these products in American markets. There is no evidence that those new markets brought higher prices to American farmers, but they did serve to prevent prices from declining more rapidly and to a larger extent. Among the conditions that enabled American farm products to compete successfully in European markets were (1) reduced railroad rates from American farms to export cities along the Atalntic Coast, (2) the development of the refrigerator railroad car that made possible the shipment of fresh meats for long distances without danger of spoiling, and (3) the development of overseas transportation that reduced the time of crossing the ocean and reduced transportation costs. In Europe there was a movement of workers away from agriculture into manufacturing industries in urban communities. This not only reduced the amount of offerings of the products of local tillable agriculture, it created a greater dependence of European peoples upon the products of American farms. Greater urbanization of the peoples of western Europe created larger markets for the products of a highly specialized agricultural organization. The factorization of industries in western European countries, likewise, increased the dependence of European laboring segments of the population upon the products of specialized agricultural activities.

FARMERS' SEARCH FOR RELIEF

Following the reorganization of the monetary system in 1873, the amount of money in circulation did not increase along with the increase in commodity output and with population. Leaders of agrarian reform movements were convinced that a contraction in the volume of greenbacks outstanding, which was not offset by an increase in the volume of national bank notes, combined with the export of gold, was responsible for the fall in prices that commenced in 1873 and continued throughout most of the ensuing 20 odd years. Monetary reform that would serve to increase the amount of money in circulation and make credit easier to obtain was looked upon by them as a stimulant that would spark an upward movement of prices.

After it was apparent that the economic disadvantages of farmers in the market were aggregative rather than individualistic, and that they could not be remedied by the operation of the price system within the customary framework of the free enterprise system, farmers sought relief through the

channels of organization and politics. Since many of their efforts lay in the
areas of money and banking, transportation, and politics, only a brief summary of their programs will be given here.

The Granger Movement

Organizations of any kind are effective in direct proportion to the
homogeneity of their memberships. Traditionally, farmers have been difficult
to organize because of their inclination to giving individual expression to their
ideas and to their emotions. Again, they have been reluctant to accept ideas
and suggestions not of their own making. Economic, social, and political
conditions after 1875 were unfavorable to farmers in all sections of the
United States. Southern farmers were among the first to organize into alliances or granges. The former were local organizations that later became
affiliated with state organizations before national alliances were effected.
They were organized for fraternal, economic, educational, and political purposes. An economic grievance that was common to all farmers was the
price structure—low prices for the products they sold, relatively high prices
they were compelled to pay for the products they purchased from the
market. Add to this unsatisfactory terms of credit, and their principal
grievances could be found to have affected their pocketbooks.

The Patrons of Husbandry, better known as the *Grange,* was an organization of farmers in all sections of the United States, whose initial program
was to promote social and educational activities among its members. Granges
also carried the torch of economic reform, but along more or less conservative lines. They saw a distinct cleavage between them and the followers of
Wall Street and of manufacturing interests. They also felt that they were
mere pawns in the hands of unscrupulous railroad managers.

Outside of New England, the granges were strongest in the Middle
Western States of Illinois, Iowa, Nebraska, Minnesota, and Wisconsin.
Among the economic reforms advocated were more and cheaper money
in circulation and the abolishment of national banks. They also advocated
the organization of cooperatives in order to improve their positions in the
market. It was to sell to these cooperatives in Iowa that a mail-order house
in Chicago was organized early in the 1870's. Montgomery Ward sold
directly in wholesale lots to farm cooperatives, which, in turn, distributed
the merchandise to their members. Several years elapsed before Montgomery
Ward sold at retail directly to individual customers. In addition to their
social, educational, and fraternal activities, the granges triggered one of the
strongest protest movements of the time. They championed the farmer
in his protests against the discriminatory practices of railroads. These
practices were manifest in the structure of rates on freight to and from
midwestern farms. In fact, it was a series of protest cases against the
discriminatory pricing practices of the railroads that culminated in the
passage of the Interstate Commerce Act in 1887 and the organization of
the Interstate Commerce Commission that same year.

The Alliances

The programs of the Southern Alliance and the Western Alliance carried these organizations further into the realm of politics than the Grange was prepared to go. The principal bond of cohesion between these Alliances was "eight-cent corn, ten-cent oats, two-cent beef and no sale for butter and eggs." The attempt of the Western Alliance to affiliate with the Knights of Labor and to put up a united front at the polls sealed the doom of the former. Farmers were entrepreneurs, hirers of labor, and as such their interests just did not coincide with those of labor.

The Populist Party

Farmer unrest in Kansas gave rise to the formation of the Populist party which waved the banner of farm relief in its efforts to be heard in Congress. In 1892, it held its first national convention in Chicago. Among other things, it advocated a subtreasury system under which plan 1 percent would have been the interest cost of loans in amounts up to 80 percent of the value of nonperishable farm staples deposited with it. Other clauses in the program of economic reform included a flexible currency that was divorced from bank control; the return of free silver and bimetallism at a ratio of 16 to 1; a graduated income tax; postal savings banks; and government ownership of railroads, telegraph, and telephone systems. The protests of Populism were expressed in terms of over one million votes cast for James Weaver in the Presidential election of 1892. By 1896, the Populist party had decided to unite with the Democratic party which advocated bimetallism and other reform programs. In the election of that year, William Jennings Bryan in defeat received more votes than any winning candidate had ever received, but failed to carry his home state of Nebraska.

RETURN OF PROSPERITY

Throughout the first decade of the 20th century the American farmer received a larger portion of our national income than he had for many years, probably more than at any time since the United States had become industrialized, although accurate data in support of that statement are difficult to obtain. The productivity of industrial workers increased to such a level that they could purchase more of the products of the farm than formerly. Not only did they purchase more than formerly, they paid higher prices for their increased purchases. During this span of years the market was favorable to the farmer. True, the productivity of the farmer did increase during these years, but not as much so as did that of the industrial worker. It was that relationship that led to an increase in the real income of the American farmer. The market absorbed a larger volume of the products of American farms from the outbreak of hostilities in Europe until shortly after the termination of that catastrophe. There have been conflicting reports relating to the volume of output during these years, but they all are in accord with the fact that the market gave the American farmer the highest prices he had ever received since the close of the Civil War. This meant that these prices were the highest that the present generation of farmers had ever received during their entire careers of selling foodstuffs on the market.

It is a well-known fact that wage earners, particularly those in the lower income brackets, spend increases in their money incomes on food before they purchase the comforts and luxuries of life. This is the first step taken to raise the level of living of wage earners. Since urban workers did not raise their own foods, the impacts of increased consumption of food were reflected back to the farmer. Not only did wage incomes increase after 1900, the total number of persons who were employed in nonfarm occupations increased from 18 million in 1900 to 25 million in 1910 and to 31 million in 1920. Decennial increases of 40 percent and 25 percent respectively in the number of nonfarm employees, together with an increase in wages, brought a degree of farm prosperity to farmers they had not experienced for over a generation.

THE IMPACT OF WORLD WAR I ON AMERICAN AGRICULTURE

After the first fright of the uncertainties of war had subsided, American agriculture, in general, entered upon an era of apparent prosperity hitherto unknown and experienced by that generation of farmers. The impetus to increases in the prices of farm staples came first from the purchases of foodstuffs and cotton by European countries that were at war. A second cause of high and rising prices of the products of American agriculture was inflation. Rising prices were not confined or restricted to the products of American farms. Farmland itself increased in value in accordance with the principle of capitalizing the net product of land.

As money profits from farming increased, farmers purchased more land and at rising prices. They also purchased more farm machinery, not only to make it possible to cultivate larger acreages, but to take the place of farm labor that had donned military uniforms. The importance of these capital expenditures was found not so much in the short-run results of farming as in the long-run capital charges, or fixed charges, they incurred. At the time of purchase, neither the rate of interest nor the interest charge seemed out of line with the prices of wheat, corn, cotton, and other products, nor with land values. The servicing of these loans presented no problems until the prices of farm products began to fall a few years later.

In no manner of speaking can the war be held responsible for the mechanization of farms, because that process was well under way when the war broke out. The war may have been responsible for the rate at which farms were mechanized and for the adaptation of the internal combustion engine to farm use. Henry Ford had a small-sized farm tractor on the assembly line by 1917. This machine was adapted to the needs of farms east of the Mississippi River, where the topography was more irregular than to the west. Since farms in this region were in general smaller than those farther west, farmers could not afford the large capital outlay that was necessary to acquire the large, heavy tractors that were adapted to the needs of farms in the Middle West. The truck aided farmers more in marketing their products than in raising them. When roads were passable, trucks could carry heavier loads faster than could horse-drawn wagons. Their radius of operations was wider and not as much time was spent in going to and from marketing centers or loading stations as with horse-drawn equipment. Horses became surplus farm accessories just after the close of the war.

During the war years of 1915 to 1918, the United States not only fed itself but, in addition, it supplied the war-torn countries of Europe with food. War broke out in August, 1914, and it was not until the following year that American agriculture felt its favorable impacts.

FARM CREDIT

In 1916 the Congress of the United States provided for the establishment of Federal Farm Loan Banks and for Joint Stock Land Banks at the level of free enterprise. These banks came just in time to aid farmers in financing their purchases of additional farmland at high prices. The capital of those banks was owned by the Treasury Department and loanable funds over that amount were secured through the sale of bonds. Since the banks could not charge farmers more than 6 percent for borrowed monies, and they were limited to a profit of 1 percent over the cost to them of borrowing on a free market, the highest rate on the face of Federal Land Bank bonds was 5 percent. Thus, if the last bond issue bore 4 percent on the face, farmers were charged not more than 5 percent on loans obtained from the bank. These loans matured in from five to 40 years, and the proceeds were to be used in the purchase of farmland or in refinancing loans that bore higher rates of interest. The facilities of the Federal Reserve System were not adequate to meet the needs of farmers, except for their short-term loans of 90 days maturity, subject to renewal. Except for the definition of short-term agricultural credit for the use of Federal Reserve Banks, the Farm Loan Act of 1916 was the initial step taken by the federal government to provide for the credit needs of American farmers. While the provisions of the Act relieved the farmer of exorbitant interest burdens on long-term loans, it did not provide credit for maturities of more than one year and less than five. That kind of credit was not provided at the federal level until 1923.

POSITION OF AGRICULTURE IN THE AMERICAN ECONOMY

Despite the remarkable development that took place in agriculture or possibly because of it, it became of declining importance as a source of national income and as the direct support of labor and entrepreneurs. There was no guiding hand to direct the development of farming in general. The profit motive resulted in an imbalance between the demand for farm products and their supply. New supplies were relatively easy and cheap to produce, and guided by the forces of individual initiative and the short-run profit motive they tended to increase more rapidly than did the demand for them. With more farm products chasing after the consumers' dollars, there was no alternative to a fall in prices.

The trend toward larger sized farms that bordered on larger scale production resulted in larger volumes of farm products being produced with the application of fewer human hands. Larger sized farms have resulted in fewer farm entrepreneurs, and farm machinery has displaced farm labor and made the latter more productive.

QUESTIONS FOR REVIEW

1. (a) Describe the conflict between cattle ranchers and sheep ranchers.
   (b) What part did barbed wire play in (1) intensifying that conflict, (2) in resolving it?
2. What was the "long drive"?
3. In discussing the subject of specialization in agricultural activity, describe and account for (A) regional, (B) product specialization.
4. (a) What were the major sources of power found on American farms?
   (b) What economic dislocations were caused by adopting each successive form of power?
5. What was the Granger Movement? Was it successful?
6. What economic forces led to the Populist revolt?

SUGGESTED READINGS

Benedict, Murray R. *Farm Policies of the United States, 1790-1950.* New York City: The Twentieth Century Fund, 1953. Chapters 2 and 6.

Bogue, Allan G. and Margaret. " 'Profits' and the Frontier Land Speculator," *Issues in American Economic History,* edited by Gerald D. Nash. Boston: D. C. Heath & Company, 1964.

Farmer, Hallie. "The Economic Background of Frontier Populism," *Issues in American Economic History,* edited by Gerald D. Nash. Boston: D. C. Heath & Company, 1964.

Johnson, E. A. J., and Herman E. Krooss. "Emergence of a Chronic Farm Problem," *The American Economy.* Englewood Cliffs, N. J.: Prentice-Hall, Inc., 1960.

Krooss, Herman E. *American Economic Development.* 2d ed. Englewood Cliffs, N. J.: Prentice-Hall, Inc., 1966. Chapter 5.

Rothstein, Morton. "America in the International Rivalry for the British Wheat Market, 1860-1914," *United States Economic History: Selected Readings,* edited by Harry N. Scheiber. New York City: Alfred A. Knopf, Inc., 1964.

Saloutos, Theodore. "The Agricultural Problem and Nineteenth Century Industrialism," *Economic Change in America,* edited by Joseph T. Lambie and Richard V. Clemence. Harrisburg, Pa.: Stackpole Books, 1954.

Wiley, B. I. "Salient Changes in Southern Agriculture Since the Civil War," *Economic Change in America,* edited by Joseph T. Lambie and Richard V. Clemence. Harrisburg, Pa.: Stackpole Books, 1954.

Chapter 14

DEVELOPMENT OF INDEPENDENT

UNIT BANKING. TRIUMPH OF

THE GOLD STANDARD

THE NATIONAL BANKING SYSTEM

Even though the National Banking System was organized as a war measure, in the ensuing years of peace it played a much more important role. It is true that national banks were still required to purchase United States government bonds, but not because there were no other markets for them. Government bonds were deposited with the Comptroller of the Currency to serve as security for the holders of national bank notes. Security at the time the notes might be withdrawn from circulation was a long-run, situation. Short-run redeemability to assure parity of circulation was attained by requiring each of the issuing banks to provide the Comptroller of the Currency with a redemption fund that equalled 5 percent of the value of the notes outstanding.

National bank notes were absolutely safe, sound, and secure; but they lacked the characteristic of elasticity—the ability of a note issue to increase in volume when more money was needed in circulation and to contract in volume when the need for money declined. All other factors remaining the same, elasticity would tend to maintain the value of money at a relatively constant level; elasticity would tend to prevent deflation as well as inflation.

Banks could make commercial loans at 5 percent or 6 percent or even higher rates of interest, while government bonds that were declared eligible to secure national bank notes may have borne interest rates of 3 percent or 4 percent, seldom higher. When national banks had reserves in excess of the commercial requirements in their respective communities, rather than have these funds idle they purchased government bonds. That meant that more national bank notes were issued at the very time commerce and industry were not in need of funds, as evidenced by the decline in their borrowings from banks. Conversely, when the tempo of business activity increased, and there were additional needs for currency, commercial banks tended to sell their government bonds in the market in order to have reserves that were adequate to support an increased volume of commercial loans. *Perverse elasticity* is the term that has been used to describe this relationship between the needs for credit and the volume of bank notes outstanding.

As time went on, elasticity of bank notes became of less importance as demand deposits increased in use. The *fractional reserve plan* imparted a degree of elasticity to demand deposits that did not exist for bank notes. As communication facilities improved and credit information was more easily obtained, demand deposits became more significant in volume than bank notes. *Bank checks* tended to displace bank notes in the purchase of commodities and in the payment of monetary obligations.

Organizational Requirements

Minimum capital requirements of national banks were based on the population of the cities and towns in which they were located, rather than on the kinds of business done by them or the volume of their deposits. Banks that were located in places of 6,000 population or less were required to have a minimum capital of $50,000. Some years later this requirement was modified to meet competition from state banks. The capital requirement in towns of 3,000 population or less was reduced to $25,000. As many of these smaller banks were located in towns around which agriculture was the predominant economic activity, the fortunes of these banks were tied closely to those of agriculture. Banks that were located in cities in size from 6,000 to 50,000 population were required to have a minimum capital of $100,000, and banks in all cities of 50,000 population and over were given a minimum capital requirement of $200,000. All of these banks were independent unit banks, and no one of them occupied a more important place among banks on the basis of its functions or legal status than any of the others. Branch banking was not permitted, except that here, again, if any state banking laws permitted state banks to engage in branch banking, national banks could operate branch banks on the same level. As a matter of record, branch banking usually was confined to the establishment of multiple banking offices in one city in a given state. The remaining aspects of national banking will be given in a critical presentation. The remedies that were provided by the Federal Reserve Act will be indicated.

Reserve Requirements

For purposes of determining the reserve requirement against demand obligations of national banks, the cities of the country were divided into three classifications, which depended upon the existence of well-organized money markets, together with the financial relationships that existed between the banks in a given city and those in the surrounding territory.

Central Reserve Cities were New York, Chicago, and sometimes St. Louis. All national banks in these cities were required to maintain reserves of 25 percent in their own vaults. All reserve requirements were rigid and were instruments to safeguard the safety of demand deposits rather than to control the volume of bank credit. The *Reserve City* classification was composed of a variable number of cities such as Boston, Philadelphia, Pittsburgh, Baltimore, Cincinnati, Kansas City, New Orleans, San Francisco, Dallas, Portland, Seattle, and some 40 to 60 others, more or less. Legal reserve requirements for banks in that classification were 25 percent of demand obligations, one half of which had to be gold in the vaults of the respective banks themselves. The other one half of the reserves could have been deposited in banks in a city or cities in a higher classification. They usually were so deposited because they were permitted to receive an interest return of 2 percent per annum on such deposits, which otherwise would have been sterile. Competition compelled banks in the Central Reserve City classification to pay the 2 percent interest. The third and lowest classification, *Non-Reserve City*, was made up of all of the remaining cities and towns in which national banks were located. Other designations for that group were *country,* or *rural,* areas. The cities were given the designation but *not* the banks. There were banks in Central Reserve Cities, but there were *no* Central Reserve City banks. The same idea held true for banks in each of the other classifications.

Defects of National Banking

Defects of national banking hinged on the fact that it was patterned after past experiences. The immediate objectives were to meet the exigencies of a wartime economy. No one could foresee the rapidity with which transportation and communication technologies widened the area of economic activity. Local boundaries gave way to sectional ones, which, in turn, became national and international in scope. Certain built-in rigidities prevented adjustments in bank organization and procedures that prevented national banks from rendering the kinds of services that business interests required.

Pyramiding Bank Reserves. Banks in Non-Reserve Cities were permitted to place three fifths or 60 percent of their reserves on deposit in banks of a higher classification and to receive an interest income of 2 percent therefrom.

The process of placing part of their legal reserves in banks of higher classifications was known as pyramiding reserves. That procedure appeared on the surface to be advantageous to the banks in the lower classifications, because it afforded them an income from their reserves. On the other hand, when the depositors in banks in the lower classifications withdrew their deposits to a large extent, difficulties in obtaining adequate amounts of money were encountered by the banks.

Assume that Depositor D placed $10,000 in a bank in a Non-Reserve City. Immediately, a $1,500 reserve was set aside. The remaining $8,500 was loaned out at interest to local borrowers, or it may have been invested in the money market. Six hundred dollars of the reserve was kept in the bank; and the remaining $900 was deposited in a bank in a Reserve City,

Table 14-1
Pyramiding of National Bank Reserves

Banks	Legal Reserves Percentage	Deposits		Secondary*	Total Legal	Reserves †		
		Initial				In Bank	Deposits in Other Banks	Available for Lending
		Total	Available for Lending					
Central Reserve Cities	25	.....	.....	$112.50	$ 28.13	$ 28.13	None	$ 84.37
Reserve Cities	25	.....	.....	900.00	225.00	112.50	$112.50	675.00
Non-Reserve Cities	15	$10,000	$8,500	.....	1,500.00	600.00	$900.00	.....
						$740.63		$759.37

* A secondary deposit as used here is that portion of a legal reserve of a bank that could be deposited in a bank of a higher classification.

† Note that the sum of the Reserves in Bank and those Available for Lending are equal to the Total Legal Reserve of $1,500.

against which a reserve of $225 was established. One half of that amount, or $112.50, was deposited in a bank in New York City, which set aside a cash reserve of $28.13. The remaining $84.37 was loaned to brokers who were financing their customers in the purchase of corporate securities on margin. All told, there were cash reserves of $740.63 in banks in three cities in support of the initial deposit of $10,000. That was only 7.4 percent as against a legally required minimum of 15 percent. (See Table 14-1).

Several months later Depositor D might have decided that he needed the entire $10,000 in cash against which there was a total cash reserve of $740.63 in banks in all classifications. The original bank of deposit and its correspondents had to call in loans in the sum of $9,259.37. Assume that brokers had borrowed that amount of money in order to finance marginal transactions in corporate stock. Rather than request their customers to furnish more money, the brokers attempted to borrow that amount on call from other banks. If the latter banks were under similar pressure and were unable to extend more call loans, brokers requested additional money from their customers. If they were unable to meet those requests, the only recourse left to protect themselves was for the brokers to sell the securities whose purchase they had been financing.

Concerted efforts on the part of brokers to obtain funds in that manner resulted in declines in the prices of corporate stocks on organized security markets. Every decline of any significance tended to cause brokers to protect themselves against losses by calling upon their customers for additional sums of money. When the latter were unable to meet these demands, brokers sold them out and caused another dip in market prices. These were the initial steps that led to financial disaster. Pyramiding bank deposits resulted in entirely inadequate bank reserves, and the payment of 2 percent interest per annum by New York City banks compelled them to attempt to earn at least that much from their use. There were no central banks to which commercial banks could turn in their search for liquidity.

Federal Reserve banking remedied that defect—first, by reducing the reserve requirements of member banks and by requiring that all legal reserves be noninterest-bearing deposits in Federal Reserve Banks. Secondly, member banks were not permitted to pay interest on deposits made with them by other member banks.

Correspondent Relationships. A second defect of national banking was related to the correspondent relationships between banks. *Correspondent banks* are those that undertake to provide a variety of services for other banks, usually upon the understanding or requirement that the latter will maintain substantial deposit accounts with them. Checks on banks that were in correspondent relationships with each other were cleared at par, but other items had no par clearance. That meant that a depositor of a bank bore a charge by the bank of, possibly, 25 cents an item regardless of its face value. That charge was made because the drawee bank deducted that amount from the remittance that was due the bank that presented the item to the drawee bank. That practice grew out of the large volume of checks that were drawn on banks in Non-Reserve Cities and made payable to mail-order houses in Chicago. The volume was so large that rural banks incurred expenses in remitting money to Chicago banks. Again, because the rural banks were compelled to remit sums of money to banks in Chicago, they could not invest that money in interest-bearing bonds. In order to avoid the burden of no par clearing, banks would remit such items to their correspondent banks, until finally the item found its way to a bank that was a correspondent of the drawee bank. The process was costly and delayed the balancing of a customer's checkbook with the balance as shown by the bank. That defect was remedied in Federal Reserve banking by member banks being required to clear at par all items received by them from other member banks. That requirement did not pertain to clearing between member and nonmember banks. Again, Federal Reserve Banks were to act as clearing-houses for all member banks in the respective districts, and a gold settlement fund was established in Washington to facilitate interdistrict clearings.

No Monetary or Banking Policies. A third defect was the absence of any agency that had the power to determine monetary and/or banking policies. Since national banks were strictly independent unit banks, they could neither determine nor enforce such policies on other banks. There was no semblance of central banking, nor was there any coordination of banking services and policies. In fact, under national banking, it was considered a sign of weakness for one bank to have to borrow from another national bank. Federal Reserve banking has reversed that situation. It is now an element of strength of the banking system for one member bank to borrow from its Federal Reserve Bank. That defect was remedied by the establishment of a Federal Reserve Board (now called the Board of Governors of the Federal Reserve System) which was given the power to determine monetary and banking policies with which all member banks were required to conform.

Not Adapted to the Needs of Agriculture. One defect of national banking was that it was not adapted to the needs of agriculture. Loans granted by national banks were restricted to commercial loans that were self-liquidating within 90 days, or six months for agricultural paper. Large amounts of agricultural credit were not self-liquidating in 90 days, or even in six months. One renewal helped both the banks and the farmers. That was one level of the competition between state and national banks. Many agricultural communities could not support banks with a capital of $50,000.

State banking laws were realistic in permitting banks to be chartered with capitals of $25,000, $15,000, and even as little as $10,000. It was that competition that resulted in the minimum capitalization for national banks in towns of 3,000 population or under being reduced to $25,000. It is questionable that this modification of the capital requirements of national banks strengthened the system. In times of stress it was the state banks of small capitalization and the $25,000 capital national banks that failed first, except insofar as financial crises were phenomena of the money market rather than of the industrial and commercial segments of the economy.

Not a True System. It is questionable that the word *system* can be applied to the organization and operation of national banks. *System* implies some kind of coordination and cohesion among the banks. That did not exist, except at the organizational level. They did have to submit to examinations by the Comptroller of the Currency from three to five times a year. The Comptroller had no direct authority over the banks other than to advise and use moral suasion to correct what he deemed an undesirable situation.

The reader must not conclude from what has been said about national banking that it did not have its good features. Probably the most favorable aspect of national banking was the replacement of discount and issue by discount and deposit as the principal functions of commercial banks. Bank loans were discounted and the proceeds taken in the form of bank deposits instead of in the form of bank notes. Check currency came into more general use than bank note currency. It was that factor more than any other one thing that revealed the weaknesses of rigid reserves and the awkwardness and clumsiness of the method of clearing bank checks. Even when banks failed and bank deposits were frozen and sometimes eventually lost in large part, national bank notes continued to circulate at par, since their parity of circulation and ultimate redemption did not depend upon the degree of liquidity of any given national bank or banks. When the development of business and financial relationships required services that commercial banks could not perform, other types of banks were organized at the state level.

State Banks

Savings banks and trust companies were organized to perform some of the functions that were denied national banks. State banks were permitted to make loans to farmers in accordance with their needs for credit. That fact afforded them an advantage in competition with national banks and was one reason why the directors of state banks did not want their institutions to become national banks. Another deterrent to membership in the National Banking System was the fact that many state laws in regard to legal reserves were more liberal than were the requirements of the National Banking System. Many states permitted commercial banks to invest large portions of their legal reserves in bonds. For example, for every $100,000 of demand deposits in a state that required 20 percent reserves against demand deposits, $18,000 could be invested in bonds that might yield 4 percent or $720 per annum on its reserve alone. Multiply that income by the number of $100,000 units of deposits in a given bank, and the cost of becoming a national bank could well exceed the immediate financial gains therefrom.

It was once thought that when state banks were no longer permitted to issue circulating notes, they would petition the Comptroller of the Currency to become national banks. About the same time that state bank notes were taxed out of existence, demand deposits through the medium of checks came into general use throughout the United States. Now that commercial banks had become *banks of discount and deposit* instead of *banks of discount and issue*, loss of the privilege of issuing circulating notes came at a time when the privilege was less meaningful to the banks than formerly.

Commercial Banks—Discount and Deposit. As long as bank notes continued to be the principal form of hand-to-hand currency, their inelasticity was a serious defect. When, however, elasticity of the currency was obtained through the facilities of deposit banking, the inelasticity of bank notes was no longer such a significant defect. Data for a number of years prior to 1866 reveal that the volume of deposits exceeded that of bank notes. Checks were being used in making payments in urban areas before they were used in making payments between urban areas. The increase in the volume of bank deposits reflected the growth of commercial activities in urban areas. The student should be careful in drawing conclusions too hastily, however. Savings deposits and time deposits were not subject to being drawn on by the use of bank checks, and reports for the earlier years are both incomplete and do not distinguish between them. The figures for deposits also included government deposits and interbank deposits. Many of the interbank deposits were the result of pyramiding bank reserves, while others resulted from the maintenance of correspondent relationships. Data do not reveal the origin or sources of these classes of deposits, but neither of them was created by business concerns or by individual persons who were in the need for currency, and who found that bank credit was a convenient and safe form to use.

Data in Table 14-2 show the repressing effect the tax on state bank notes had upon the number of state banks, and not until 1873 did the number of such banks in operation more than double. That date also marked the beginning of the mail-order type of retail business. Payments were made by rural purchasers of goods remitting checks that were drawn against their local banks. That same year was characterized by an 80 percent increase in the volume of bank deposits, which was accompanied by a decrease of over 20 percent in the volume of circulating notes.

During the latter part of the 1880's, the number of commercial banks increased much more rapidly than did the volume of bank deposits. That situation reflected the increase in the volume of business that was transacted all over the United States. It also was a product of the increasing dependence of American farmers on the market and market situations, increased urbanization of population, and a growth of manufacturing industries, all of which resulted in a greater interdependence between persons in the different segments of our economy. In addition to providing agricultural credit, state banks were permitted to engage in trust banking which entered upon a period of growth and development, so much so, in fact, that national banking laws were revised to permit national banks to compete with state

Table 14-2

Total Number of State and National Banks, Together with Their Total Volume of Bank Deposits and of Bank Notes for Selected Years— 1866-1920

Year	Number of State Banks	Number of National Banks	Deposits (000,000)	Bank Notes (000,000)
1866	297	1,634	$ 759	$309
1867	272	1,636	743	330
1868	247	1,640	798	329
1869	259	1,619	772	329
1870	325	1,612	776	336
1871	452	1,723	888	370
1872	566	1,853	926	405
1873	1,330	1,968	1,625	339
1874	1,569	1,983	1,740	339
1875	1,260	2,076	2,008	318
1880	1,279	2,076	2,222	318
1885	1,661	2,689	3,079	269
1890	4,717	3,484	4,577	126
1895	6,103	3,715	5,539	179
1900	9,322	3,731	8,922	265
1905	13,103	5,664	13,772	445
1910	18,013	7,138	17,950	675
1915	20,420	7,597	22,504	722
1920	22,885	8,024	41,838	688

Source: U. S. Department of Commerce, Bureau of the Census, *Historical Statistics of the United States. Colonial Times to 1957* (Washington: U. S. Government Printing Office, 1960), pp. 626-629. Adapted.

banks on that level of operation. The authorization to perform fiduciary functions was included in the charters of state banks, while national banks had to make application to the Comptroller of the Currency to perform them.

Trust Companies. Trust companies became the department stores in the field of banking. Most of them engaged in commercial banking, and all of them performed fiduciary functions by the very nature of their charters. Some of them had investment banking departments; some engaged in mortgage banking; some of them had departments in which real estate transactions were handled. Insurance and bonding were other types of financial operations that were conducted by trust companies. All of them rented safety boxes for the safekeeping of valuables. One reason for their rapid growth was that they were not shackled at every move by state regulations. Their growth depended in part upon the acumen and integrity of their principal officers, together with the degree of confidence the general public had in them and in their institutions. Once personal or business credit had been established in one department of the company, entry was had into the channels of the others. Customers felt important when an officer of one department personally introduced them to an officer of another department. Trust companies were literally one-stop financial institutions that were established for the convenience of the banking public and for the profit of their stockholders.

Savings Banks. While the American people, in general, have not been considered as thrifty as their European cousins, the habit of saving some portion of their money income was ingrained in the standard of living of thousands of people. Mutual savings banks were established in the New England States, in Pennsylvania, and in Iowa, not to the exclusion of these institutions in other states. Outside of these states, corporate savings banks and savings departments of commercial banks were the principal institutions in which the small savings of large numbers of persons were deposited. Prior to World War I, the purchase of corporate and government securities was restricted principally to professional traders and to persons of relatively large incomes, who were somewhat familiar with the nature and characteristics of investments. Farmers, salaried persons, including schoolteachers and government employees, and small businessmen who were somewhat distant from the centers of finance found savings banks more attractive and secure than making direct investments. Then, too, the face amount of corporate and government bonds was seldom less than $1,000, sometimes $500, both of which denominations were too large to enable thousands of people to make direct investments, even if they had known something about bonds.

Growth in the number of depositors of savings banks and in the volume of savings deposits from 1866 to 1910 is shown in Table 14-3. The more rapid increase in the number of depositors that occurred after 1895 is a reflection of the increased tempo of business throughout the entire country. Except for the occurrence of some strikes on the part of labor, employment

Table 14-3
Number of Depositors and Savings Deposits in Savings Banks for Selected Years—1866-1910

Year	Number of Depositors	Amount of Deposits (millions)
1866	1,067,061	$ 282.5
1870	1,630,846	549.9
1875	2,359,864	924.0
1880	2,335,582	819.1
1885	3,071,495	1,095.2
1890	4,258,893	1,524.8
1895	4,875,519	1,810.6
1900	6,107,083	2,449.5
1905	7,696,229	3,261.2
1910	9,142,908	4,070.5

Source: *Historical Statistics of the United States, Colonial Times to 1957,* 1960, p. 641. Adapted.

was on the increase in urban areas; and the farmer was experiencing better times than he had enjoyed for many years. More people had larger incomes out of which they accumulated savings.

Data on savings and savings depositors are more complete for the years 1911-20, and Table 14-4 shows the participation played by mutual savings banks, by state banks, and by national banks in the savings process.

Table 14-4

Savings—Number of Depositors and Savings Deposits by Class of Bank—1911-1920

Year	Number of Depositors (000)		Amount of Savings Deposits (millions)			
	Mutual Savings Banks	National Banks	Mutual Savings Banks	State Banks	National Banks	Total
1911	7,691	2,341	$3,459	$3,024	$1,480	$ 7,963
1912	7,880	2,675	3,609	3,260	1,536	8,404
1913	8,034	2,965	3,812	3,368	1,369	8,548
1914	7,901	*	3,910	3,348	1,454	8,712
1915	7,643	*	3,945	3,541	1,321	8,807
1916	7,917	*	4,102	3,641	1,716	9,459
1917	8,651	*	4,339	4,364	2,173	10,876
1918	8,326	*	4,382	4,817	2,336	11,535
1919	9,040	6,763	4,732	5,532	2,776	13,040
1920	9,079	7,980	5,058	6,668	3,463	15,189

* Not available.
Source: *Historical Statistics of the United States. Colonial Times to 1957,* 1960, p. 640.
    Adapted.

After 1913 the interest that member banks could pay their depositors was controlled by the Federal Reserve Board, while nonmember state banks were not operating under similar restraint. Mutual savings banks were not admitted to membership in the Federal Reserve System.

The increase in total savings deposits after 1916 reflects the impacts of the European war on the American economy and the American people. After a slowing down of our economy in 1913, an acceleration thereafter tended to increase personal incomes more rapidly than the cost of living. Little did these persons realize at the time that in order to maintain a level of purchasing power of the interest increments on savings they would be compelled to increase the total amount saved. Another factor or condition that was not known to many depositors was that the inflation of the next few years of war would tend to erase much of the purchasing power of their savings. The generation of that day was much more familiar with falling prices than with rising prices and inflation. Statistics on savings, money, and prices were coming into existence, and more statistical studies were being made by more people than ever before; but there was a general feeling among persons that they were nothing more than mere statistics, and the analyses that were made did not and would not apply to them individually.

Postal Savings

Out of the unrest that developed over a period of years after 1873 arose agitation for some kind of savings institution, the most important feature of which would be safety of principal. No type or form of banking institution seemed to be immune from failing. The patrons of savings banks were as much interested in safety as in any other one aspect of banking. They were disturbed by the large number of bank failures and by the ultimate losses that resulted. Farmers in the Middle West and in the South, as well as those in other regions who had become dependent upon market situations, were much concerned over the loss of their deposits that followed the closing of state banks, national banks, and savings banks all over the country. They may have had just cause for believing that their fate was in the hands of the monied men of Wall Street. Their protests were heard through the medium of the Populist Party in their demands for the abolishment of the National Banking System and for the establishment of postal savings banks.

Table 14-5

Postal Savings System—1911-1920

Year	Number of Depositors	Deposits (000)	Withdrawals (000)
1911	11,918	$ 778	$ 101
1912	243,801	30,732	11,172
1913	331,006	41,701	28,120
1914	388,511	47,815	38,190
1915	525,414	70,315	48,074
1916	602,937	76,776	56,441
1917	674,728	132,112	86,177
1918	612,188	116,893	100,376
1919	565,509	136,690	117,838
1920	508,508	139,209	149,256

Source: *Historical Statistics of the United States. Colonial Times to 1957*, 1960, p. 641. Adapted.

It took the panic of 1907 to bring that issue to a head, and in 1910 the Postal Savings System was established. Depositors received certificates of deposit in convenient denominations. Interest at 2 percent per annum accrued at 3-month intervals. By cashing a $100 certificate at the end of one year for $102, the interest of that year became a principal sum on which interest was earned, if it was used in the purchase of a postal savings bank certificate. Table 14-5 reveals the rapidity with which the idea of postal savings was accepted by potential depositors. Among the patrons of postal savings banks were found immigrants and persons of foreign extraction who lacked confidence in free enterprise banking institutions. Farmers, laborers, and persons who had felt the impacts of the closing of commercial banks in which they had demand or savings deposit accounts patronized postal savings.

The volume of withdrawals in relation to the volume of new deposits seems to indicate that postal savings were used for temporary periods of saving. Savings banks calculated interest as of January 1 and July 1, and deposits made in the interim did not draw interest until the following interest paying date. Deposits in postal savings drew interest from the date on which they were made. The decline in the number of depositors and in the volume of deposits together with the increase in withdrawals after 1917 may have been the result of depositors taking advantage of higher rates of interest received by purchasing Liberty Bonds. Some of the withdrawals undoubtedly were made necessary by conditions that grew out of the war and its sudden termination in 1918.

Bank Failures

From the early years of the formation of the United States to 1933, the American people and business concerns had been subject to the losses and inconveniences caused by bank failures. Free, independent unit banking, as it had operated in the United States, undoubtedly had contributed to that situation. To reiterate, the National Banking System was hardly worthy of the name system. No qualifications or desirable characteristics of prospective bank officers were recognized at law; at least there was no agency established whose responsibility it was to evaluate the ability and integrity of prospective bank officials. While incompetent bank officials and fraudulent actions on the part of some of them may have contributed to the failure of some banks, the mere fact of independent unit banking together with the fact that commercial banks were not equipped and adapted to extend agricultural credit resulted in the failure of many banks.

The Comptroller of the Currency examined national banks at least three times a year. If the books were not in satisfactory condition for any reason whatsoever, the damage had already been done by the time the bank examiner made the disclosure. If the public or the depositors of such a bank became aware of the situation, they usually became panicky and started a run on that bank. A movement of that kind usually started a similar one by the depositors of other banks in the community just to see if they could get their money. If other banks were prepared for an unusual drain of cash all well and good; if not, they probably were brought to the brink of failure, if not actual inability to meet demands of depositors for cash withdrawals. Since there were no supporting financial agencies of any kind at any level, one of the theoretical weaknesses of independent unit banking became a reality.

Banks, both state and national, that served communities in which agriculture was the principal economic activity experienced a seasonal demand for loans, with a corresponding seasonal maturity of these loans. A better balanced situation, in which maturity dates were staggered throughout a period of time, provided banks with a test of liquidity, and enabled them to anticipate seasonal demands for cash by granting requests for new loans of smaller dollar volume than those that were maturing. Bank investment portfolios in multiple industry areas contained paper that matured at different times over a period of time rather than paper whose maturity dates were concentrated within an interval of a few weeks.

Promotions of bank employees have been notoriously slow. Many times employees of banks of long tenure at given positions in small banks realized their ambitions for promotions by organizing competing banks and having themselves appointed or elected to more responsible positions. That was a means by which cashiers became presidents or vice presidents and tellers became cashiers, regardless of their fitness for such positions or regardless of the need for additional banking capital in the community. It was more or less natural for business and personal friends of these men to patronize their institutions. In doing so they withdrew earning power from their former banks, and the same volume of loans was divided between more banks. Since new banks were not in answer to increased demands for bank credit, investment portfolios were diluted and the earning power of all banks in a given community was reduced. Loss of earning power was not the most serious result of that dilution from the standpoint of all banks. Loss of diversification of credit and inability to stagger maturity dates of loans were impacts that bore heavily on them.

Suspensions. The data in Table 14-6 must not be misconstrued by the student. At first glance the number of suspensions of state banks compared with suspensions of national banks might lead one to conclude that national banks were stronger than state banks. That may or may not have been the case, but not because of the origin of their charters. There were many more state banks to fail, and many were located in small communities in which there were no national banks. In 1871 and 1891 there were no failures among national banks. In each of the years 1869, 1870, and 1883, only one national bank closed its doors. In 1870 there were only three bank failures, one each of national, state commercial, and mutual savings banks. The years in which there were no failures among national banks were years of minimum failures among state banks, 7 and 9 respectively, which is prima facie evidence that general business conditions have been a more important cause of bank suspensions than defalcations of bank officials or incompetent officers.

Commencing with 1871 there was one year in each group of five years, as shown in Table 14-6, in which bank failures were much greater in number than in the other four years of the span. The greatest impact of the panic of 1873 on bank failures came the following year. The years of recession after

Table 14-6
Bank Suspensions—1866-1920

Year	Total	National	State Commercial Incorporated	State Commercial Private	Mutual Savings
1866–70	39	14	22	...	3
1868	14	6	7	...	1
1871–75	155	23	104	...	28
1874	57	10	40	...	7
1876–80	353	38	200	...	115
1878	140	10	70	...	60
1881–85	175	19	141	...	15
1884	63	6	54	...	3
1886–90	133	32	94	...	7
1890	37	6	30	...	1
1891–95	854	154	394	276	30
1893	496	69	228	194	5
1896–1900	439	88	171	151	29
1896	155	34	66	41	14
1901–05	383	68	145	163	7
1904	128	22	53	50	3
1906–10	441	51	252	129	9
1908	155	19	83	51	2
1911–15	575	59	384	124	8
1915	152	20	93	39	...
1916–20	379	24	291	62	2
1920	168	7	136	24	1

Source: *Historical Statistics of the United States. Colonial Times to 1957*, 1960, p. 636. Adapted.

the panic were more disastrous to the condition of commercial banks than the panic year itself. In 1878, out of a total of 140 commercial banks that suspended specie payments, ten were national banks and 60 were mutual savings banks. The latter institutions granted loans to railroads and invested rather heavily in farm mortgages, which fact may account for the large number of casualties. The most depressing year for commercial banks was 1893, in which year alone more commercial banks failed than in any 5-year span except one. Sixty-nine national banks, 228 incorporated state banks, and 194 private banks closed their doors, while only five mutual savings institutions were unable to meet the demands of their depositors for cash. The effects of the panics of 1904 and 1907 are revealed in the number of bank failures, in the latter instance not until 1908.

Monetary Commissions. The conditions of the last 25 years of the 19th century led to the appointment of the Indianapolis Monetary Commission in 1902 and the National Monetary Commission in 1908. These commissions were charged with the duty of coming up with some suggestions as to how the money and/or banking systems of the United States might be improved so as to soften the impacts of the business cycle. In 1910 a bill was presented to the Congress which included many of the reforms recommended by the Commission. Political considerations accounted for the fact that no action was taken by Congress because it was almost a foregone conclusion that the 1912 election would return a Democratic president to the White House. This did happen, and Woodrow Wilson wasted no time in presenting a banking reform bill to Congress. With some changes the Federal Reserve Act was passed on December 23, 1913, and the organization of the system was effected and the banks put into operation in August, 1914.

The Federal Reserve System

Federal Reserve Banks were regional central banks. One reserve bank and a desirable number of branch offices were located in each of the 12 Federal Reserve Districts. These were bankers' banks whose capital stock was owned by the member banks of the respective districts. National banks were required to subscribe to stock in their Federal Reserve Banks in an amount equal to 3 percent of their own paid-in capital and surplus. State banks could apply for membership in the Federal Reserve System by subscribing to the required amount of stock in the Federal Reserve Bank of their district, by agreeing to maintain the reserves that were required of member banks, by opening their books to examination by the Reserve Banks, and by clearing at par all items remitted to them by Federal Reserve Banks and by other member banks. The Treasury Department was authorized to subscribe to a sufficient number of shares to bring the minimum capitalization to $4 million. Since the subscriptions of member banks amounted to more than that minimum, the Treasury Department did not own and has not owned any equity interest in Federal Reserve Banks.

A Federal Reserve Board consisting of eight members, six of whom were appointed for ten years, was established as the ruling board for the entire system. It was not in charge of an operating bank. In order to assure and to insure control that was not biased towards Wall Street or towards the Treasury Department, the Secretary of the Treasury and the Comptroller of the Currency were made ex officio members, without power to vote. Six members of the Federal Reserve Board were to be appointed by the President of the United States with due regard to the financial, industrial, agricultural, and commercial interests of the country. A member of the Board to represent "dirt" farmers was not provided for until later. No two members could come from the same Federal Reserve District. One of the Board members was designated governor, another as vice-governor. The Board was charged with formulating the monetary and credit policies of the Federal Reserve System. In its control over credit, it was empowered to alter discount rates and to authorize open market operations.

An *Open Market Committee* was provided for to make a study of market and credit conditions and to determine the Board's policy. It was not until a later period that open market operations displaced changes in rediscount rates as the principal instrument of credit control. Open market operations are those purchases and sales of government bonds and bankers acceptances that are consummated on organized exchanges, or money markets. They are in contrast to the relationships that exist solely and directly between the Federal Reserve Banks and member banks.

Cities in which Federal Reserve Banks and their branches were located were given the designation of *Reserve Cities*, except New York and Chicago which were *Central Reserve Cities*. That designation or classification was carried over from national banking. Other features of Federal Reserve banking have been discussed in terms of how they improved upon the requirements of national banking, and they need not be repeated here.

Reserve Banks and the Business Cycle. It was the hope of its proponents that the operations of the Federal Reserve System would tend to smooth over the violent fluctuations of the business cycle that had proved to be so disturbing to all segments of the American economy. That was to be accomplished by divorcing its operations from those of the United States Treasury Department and from Wall Street. When the United States declared war on Germany in April, 1917, the Federal Reserve Board subordinated its policies to those of the government. It assumed the responsibility of selling Liberty Bonds and on such terms as to create an inflationary trend of prices, but winning the war was more important than controlling inflation.

In the first place, when bonds were purchased either by banks or by individuals and business firms, there was no loss of purchasing power by the buyers. Banks merely established deposit credits against which the government could draw checks. It was not until these checks were deposited in banks that the latter were required to maintain legal reserves against them. The buyers of bonds were enabled to borrow from their banks in order to pay for them. The bonds served as collateral for the loans, and the banks agreed to accept the interest on the face of the coupons as interest on their loans. That manner of purchase did not involve any loss of purchasing power to the buyers, nor did it appear that there was an interest cost to them. Over a period of time, the buyers could make installment payments to their banks when it was convenient for them and they had the money. The usual method of making payment was for the buyers to draw checks against their deposits and make them payable to the drawee banks. As fiscal agent of the government, the Federal Reserve System met its first crisis.

Circulating Notes. In order to bring greater uniformity in the issuance of bank notes, provisions were made under the terms of which all circulating notes would eventually be issued by Federal Reserve Banks. National bank notes would be replaced by Federal Reserve Bank notes. In addition, hoped for elasticity of bank note currency was provided for by relating the volume of Federal Reserve notes to the volume of commercial paper that was offered for rediscount. Commercial paper was self-liquidating and the volume of Federal Reserve notes in circulation would be adjusted to the requirements of the business world. Here, at last, was the degree of elasticity of the currency that had been so lacking in national banking. Before passing final judgment on the degree of elasticity which was really imparted to the currency, the reader will have to wait for further developments in the years to come.

It has sometimes been said and written that it takes a crisis of some kind to get a reform bill passed by Congress. The Federal Reserve Act was passed only after much thought and consideration had been given to it by specialists and by Congress. Senator Carter Glass of Virginia was one of the leading sponsors of the Act, and Professor Henry Parker Willis of Columbia University served as an expert consultant in drawing up the provisions of the bill and in working with the Board in developing some of the details in the organization and operation of the banks. Senator Glass was appointed by President Wilson as his Secretary of the Treasury, in which capacity he became an ex officio member of the first Federal Reserve Board. It may not be out of order to point out that the selection of Richmond over Baltimore to become the Federal Reserve Bank City of the 5th District may have been due to the influence of Secretary of the Treasury Carter Glass.

MONETARY DEVELOPMENTS

Two issues that were foremost in the minds of businessmen, farmers, and politicians were (1) the status of the greenback and bank note in our monetary system and (2) the silver question. In settling the silver issue a *de facto* situation was formalized by Congress in the passage of the Gold Standard Act in 1900. One of the most exciting political campaigns of the century was waged by William Jennings Bryan in which he pitted Wall Street against agriculture at the very time the agricultural frontier was being closed. Failure of the advocates of free silver and bimetallism at the polls was another measure of the penetration of business and business principles into other segments of the economy.

Greenbacks

The issuance of *greenbacks* created a problem of what to do with them after the Civil War. There is no doubt that they were inflationary at the time they were issued. Since they constituted approximately one fourth of the total amount of money of all kinds in circulation, their withdrawal would undoubtedly have resulted in a deflationary movement of prices, which was extremely unpopular at that time. There was so much interest shown in the ultimate disposition of the greenbacks that a Greenback party was formed. The platform of that party included putting more and cheaper money into circulation as a panacea for the farmer. There was a feeling that more or less continually rising prices would be good for the economy in general, the farmer in particular. A few years after the return of peace, Congress passed an act under the terms of which the greenback would never be redeemed; but the reaction was so strong and so unfavorable that Congress rescinded its action the following year but did not establish a date for such action.

In 1875 Congress provided for the redemption of the greenback at 100 cents on the dollar on and after January 1, 1879. After the Resumption Act was passed and until January 1, 1879, the value of the greenback appreciated as does a bond as it approaches its date of maturity. After resumption of specie payments all prices were quoted in terms of so-called standard money, which was gold. The last official action in relation to the greenback was taken in 1900 when one of the clauses of the Gold Standard Act of that year provided that the volume of greenbacks would be stabilized at the volume that was outstanding at that time, which was something over $346 million. By that time the volume of other kinds of money had increased to the extent that greenbacks constituted approximately 16 percent of total circulation. They were rapidly approaching the level of insignificance or of indifference in their effect upon prices. Whatever effect they may have had upon prices when they were first issued, they had become so stable in volume in the face of rapid growth of the economy and of other kinds of money that it is doubtful if they continued to have inflationary effects on prices.

Tax on State Bank Notes

In order to give encouragement to more banks joining the National Banking System, as well as to effect uniformity of bank notes in circulation, circulating notes of state banks were taxed 10 percent per annum. Since banks may not have netted more than 5 percent or 6 percent on that privilege it was no longer profitable for them to continue that practice, and in a few years state bank notes disappeared completely from use. They are found today in numismatic collections to which they lend color and interest because of the etchings that portray the economic activities that were conducted in the communities in which the issuing banks were located. Withdrawing state bank notes from circulation had little or no effect upon prices and the value of money because, if needed, they were replaced by national bank notes or by increases in demand deposits of commercial banks.

Demonetization of Silver

What may have proved to be the most disturbing adjustment to the currency system and one that passed unnoticed for several years was the Currency Act of 1873 which omitted naming the silver dollar as one of the coins that would be continued in use. Since the Act of 1834 first undervalued silver at the mint, few silver coins had been minted except under authorization of the Subsidiary Coinage Act of 1853. Again, after gold had been discovered in California in 1849, gold coins had come into general use, even though the United States still maintained a bimetallic monetary system. Silver had disappeared from use as standard money by default because it had been worth more in the market than at the mint. Shortly after the Currency

Act of 1873, a number of world events took place the effects of which were to lower the value of silver bullion in terms of gold.

Germany had adopted a gold standard, which meant that the silver that had been used as money found its way to markets in other countries. France was still on a bimetallic basis, but did not want its circulation to consist of an overabundance of silver. England was already on a gold standard, and when France followed suit, much of the silver was sold in the American market. About the same time that silver was demonetized in Europe, new deposits of silver were discovered in the United States. It was disturbing, to say the least, to the silver interests to have to stand by and watch the value of silver decline in terms of gold. A study was made of the entire market for silver, and disclosure of the fact that silver had been demonetized in the United States in 1873 resulted in loud and vigorous protests from the silver interests. Because the prices of agricultural products fell along with that of silver, farmers joined with the silverites in making their protests heard.

The "Crime of '73" was the designation that was given in 1875 to the demonetization of the silver dollar, and charges of chicanery were hurled against Wall Street and against politicians. There is ample evidence in the records of Congress that nobody was at all concerned when the silver dollar was not listed among the coins the Director of the Mint was authorized to strike. The silver dollar actually went by default. It was not until two years later when the market price of silver had declined that anybody became concerned about the position of silver in our monetary system. Silver no longer was standard money, nor was there free and unlimited coinage of silver. Except for the fact that specie payments were not being made, our monetary system had become a *de facto* gold standard. With the resumption of specie payments, the monetary system of the United States became one of monometallism in which gold was the sole standard monetary material.

Silver Purchase Acts. The "Crime of '73" became a battle cry to rally the followers of silver—the farmer, political reformers, anti-Wall Street people, and those who favored cheap money—behind the banner of silver. A Silver Bloc was formed in the United States Senate in order to do something for silver. The first step taken to create an artificial demand for silver was the passage of the Bland-Allison Act in 1878. The Secretary of the Treasury was authorized to purchase from $2 million to $4 million worth of silver per month and coin it into silver dollars. Actually, the minimum amount was purchased each month, and the new silver dollars accumulated in the Treasury. Silver certificates were authorized, but $10 was the smallest denomination. At the low level of prices that prevailed the next few years, a $10 minimum face value was too high a denomination to permit silver certificates to be used widely. Consequently, in 1886 bills in value of $5 and $1 were authorized, and the new silver dollars were put into circulation by proxy. Over 378 million silver dollars were coined in the twelve years during which that Act was in force, and the market price of silver continued its downward trend another ten cents an ounce. How much further the price of silver would have declined in the absence of Treasury purchases, no one knows.

In order to correct the downward trend in the market price of silver, the Silver Bloc succeeded in pushing through Congress the Sherman Silver Purchase Act of 1890, under which 4,500,000 ounces of silver were to be purchased each month. That silver was to be paid for in Treasury Notes of 1890, which were given full legal tender status and were made redeemable in either silver or gold. Only a sufficient number of silver dollars was to be coined to assure ready redemption of the Treasury Notes on demand.

Treasury Crisis. Shortly after the Sherman Act became effective, there was a strong export movement of gold to France which was not checked by the sale of several $50 million issues of gold bonds. It seems that the gold that was withdrawn from the Treasury through the redemption of Treasury Notes of 1890 left the country. Since no additional reserves had been set aside, when these notes were returned to circulation through the ordinary channels of fiscal operations, given notes could have been, and probably were, redeemed in gold a number of times. To the extent that gold was shipped to Europe, our gold reserves were reduced more or less permanently, and ultimately to such a dangerously low level that the Sherman Act was repealed in 1893.

That was a year of crisis for business, for banks, and for the United States government. Someone has estimated that the Treasury Department was within 48 hours of bankruptcy. President Cleveland was forced to choose either federal bankruptcy and repudiation of all government obligations or adoption of drastic steps to halt the outward flow of gold. He chose the latter course and entered into contractual relations with two Wall Street bankers. Although they acknowledged that they had nothing to do with its export, they agreed to purchase another $50 million bond issue with gold that was imported from France, and to attempt to prevent continued exports of gold. In that way the addition to our gold reserve represented entirely new gold in the country. As a result of these measures, new gold did come into the country, only a small amount of gold continued to be exported to Europe, and the gold reserves of the Treasury were raised to a level that was adequate to maintain the credit of the United States.

Banner of Monetary Reform

These were the years that gave encouragement to uniting the forces of Populism, Greenbackism, and Bimetallism in order to obtain some relief from falling prices, from failures of commercial banks, and from unemployment. That monetary reform would be a cure-all was the thinking of these people; and they rallied round the banner of William Jennings Bryan, who was the Presidential nominee of the Democratic party in 1896.

William McKinley carried the banner of Republicanism. Hot were the political battles that were waged between these two candidates for the highest office in the land. In his inimitable way, Bryan compared the likeness of his political foe to that of Napoleon Bonaparte; and when he discovered that the date of McKinley's nomination to the candidacy fell on the anniversary date of the Battle of Waterloo, Bryan predicted that McKinley would meet the fate of Napoleon. The issue was the choice between the gold standard and bimetallism. To quote Bryan, "Let me now come to the paramount issue. If our opponents ask us why it is that we say more on the monetary question than we say upon the tariff question, I reply that, if protection has slain its thousands, the gold standard has slain its tens of thousands. If they ask us why we do not embody in our platform *all* the things that we believe in, we reply that when we have restored the money of the Constitution all other necessary reforms will be possible; but that until this is done there is no other reform that can be accomplished."

Bryan went on to harangue "the idle holders of idle capital" and glorified "the struggling masses"—farmers and workers—and brought his speech to a close with, "Having behind us the producing masses of this nation and the world, supported by the commercial interests, the laboring interests, and the toilers everywhere, we answer their demand for a gold standard by saying to them: You shall not press down upon the brow of labor this crown of thorns, you shall not crucify mankind upon a cross of gold."

In spite of his brilliant oratory and the fervidness of his campaign, Bryan failed to carry the election. An improvement in prices, employment, and general business conditions eased the pressure for monetary reform; but it was not until 1900 that the Gold Standard Act was passed.

The Gold Standard Act

For the first time in our entire history, Congress passed legislation that based the monetary system upon gold. All other monies were to be kept at a parity with gold. The silver dollar was declared to be *standard* money, but silver was not given free coinage. The silver dollar had unlimited legal tender usage. The Act also provided a specific gold reserve of $150 million in support of approximately $346 million in greenbacks. If and when that reserve should reach a minimum of $100 million, the Secretary of the Treasury was authorized to sell United States government bonds in sufficient volume to restore it to $150 million. There was no question that the greenback had become credit money and that it would remain in circulation.

More About Silver

England had been on a free gold standard basis since 1820, but India was using the gold exchange standard in its trade relations with England. Briefly, that meant that while silver was the basis of the domestic system in that country, purchases from England were made in terms of gold. Again, English imports from India were paid for in terms of silver. During World

War I, because silver became in scarce supply in England, that country had difficulty in completing payments for goods she had purchased in India. Knowing that the United States had what amounted to a hoard of silver in the Treasury, England sought to acquire some of that metal to tide her over a critical crisis. The Pittman Act was introduced into Congress in 1918, under the terms of which the United States would melt down 350 million silver dollars and sell it to England at $1 an ounce. A corresponding value of silver certificates was to be withdrawn from circulation. If the need for currency arose, the certificates were to be replaced in circulation by Federal Reserve Bank notes. This was an opportunity for the United States to simplify its monetary system by disposing of an element that had not made a positive contribution to it since 1834. Before, however, the Silver Bloc would cast its votes for the Pittman Act, it succeeded in having a clause inserted that provided for the purchase after the war of the same amount of silver by weight at $1 an ounce and from American producers.

To complete the account of the Pittman Act, even though its effects continued into the following period, most of the silver dollars that were coined in the early 1920's were so-called Pittman silver dollars. The silver from which these dollars were coined was purchased from American producers at $1 an ounce according to the terms of the Act at a time when the market price of silver was in the neighborhood of 60 cents an ounce. In design they were just like any other silver dollar of different dates and were worth no more or no less than other silver dollars. Their return to circulation added nothing to the base of our monetary system, nor did silver dollars impart any value to the dollar. They continued to have the status of full legal tender.

Their actual circulation was widest in the Western States where silver ore was a commodity for the market. People in these states made an effort to keep people conscious of the silver dollar by using it themselves and by making change for tourists and visitors in terms of silver. They still felt that the monetary use of silver would add to the total demand for it and either tend to raise its market price or keep it from falling. There was no immediate agitation at the time for a remonetization of silver.

The next development in the history of silver relates to the provisions of the Inflation Act of 1933 and of the Silver Purchase Act of 1934.

QUESTIONS FOR REVIEW

1. State and explain any three defects of the National Banking System.

2. (a) What were banks of discount and deposit as distinct from banks of discount and issue?
   (b) Under a fractional reserve system of deposit banking, how did growth in the use of demand deposits tend to affect the degree of elasticity of the currency? Explain.

3. Explain why the number of state-chartered commercial banks has risen above the number of national banks since the early 1890's.

4. (a) What are member banks of the Federal Reserve System?
   (b) Under what conditions may commercial banks become member banks?

5. To what extent is the Federal Reserve System more of a system than was the National Banking System?

6. (a) What were greenbacks?
   (b) Why were they issued?
   (c) What effect did their use have upon prices?
   (d) What was their status after 1900?

7. (a) Why was silver demonetized in 1873?
   (b) How did the demonetization of silver affect our monetary system?

8. What was the monetary status of silver under the terms of (1) the Bland-Allison Act? (2) the Sherman Silver Purchase Act?

SUGGESTED READINGS

Gurley, J. G., and E. S. Shaw. "Money," *American Economic History*, edited by Seymour Harris. New York City: McGraw-Hill Book Company, 1961.

Hacker, Louis M. *Major Documents in American Economic History*. New York City: D. Van Nostrand Co., Inc., 1961. Vol. I, Nos. 19, 21, and 24; Vol. II, Nos. 3, 5, and 46.

Hammond, Bray. "Historical Introduction," *Economic Change in America*, edited by Joseph T. Lambie and Richard V. Clemence. Harrisburg, Pa.: Stackpole Books, 1954.

Johnson, E. A. J., and Herman E. Krooss. *The American Economy*. Englewood Cliffs, N. J.: Prentice-Hall, Inc., 1960. Chapter 10.

Poole, Kenyon E. "Money and Banking, 1865-1919," *The Growth of the American Economy*, 2d ed., edited by Harold F. Williamson. New York City: Prentice-Hall, Inc., 1951.

Redlich, Fritz. "Investment Banking," *Economic Change in America*, edited by Joseph T. Lambie and Richard V. Clemence. Harrisburg, Pa.: Stackpole Books, 1954.

Weissman, Rudolph. *The New Federal Reserve System*. New York City: Harper & Row, Publishers, 1913.

Chapter 15

NEW TECHNIQUES OF

TRANSPORTATION AND

COMMUNICATION

Foremost among the sectors contributing to the great surge of growth in the United States between the Civil War and World War I were those of transportation and communication. Expanding regional and national markets, which were requisites for the development of widespread mass production and higher levels of productive efficiency, depended crucially on the development of regional and national transportation nets. Means of communication which were far more rapid than the fastest locomotive or steamship were necessary for the emergence of unified national financial markets and for better industrial control over inventories and the flow of productive inputs. Although inland waterways and highways continued to be of importance during this period, the railroad was the dominant force, meeting little competition until the introduction of automobiles and buses after 1900.

ROADS AND HIGHWAYS

From the time of the Civil War until about 1900, there was little thought of a unified network of highways and roads crisscrossing the nation. Because of the widespread availability of railroad transportation, and because of the lack of road vehicles propelled by inanimate power sources, most roads remained local in nature and in upkeep. Burgeoning cities developed street plans and paved much of their street mileage, but unpaved or unsurfaced roads remained the rule for rural and suburban areas. Roads emerged simply to service the areas that could not be serviced by more efficient means.

The introduction of the internal combustion engine changed the situation completely. The first American motorcars or automobiles were produced during the 1890's for an essentially high-income market. In spite of their small numbers, however, car owners combined their efforts with those of the growing numbers of bicycle riders to press for more and better roads. With the advent of both mass production and mass consumption of automobiles after 1910, strong pressures at all levels of government resulted in more funds being allocated to the appropriate highway and road administrative boards. Registration figures indicate that 458,000 automobiles and 10,000 trucks and buses were on the roads in 1910, a situation which required immediate attention and action.

During World War I, the federal government finally decided to subsidize the individual states in their road-building efforts, thus establishing a precedent which has held to the present time. By 1920, when automobile registrations had climbed over the 8 million mark, and registrations of trucks and buses had passed 1.1 million, surfaced highways amounted to 387,000 miles. In comparison, total rural mileage was just over 2.9 million. Construction of all types of highways continued during the 1920's, as federal, state, and local programs were undertaken to meet the needs of the automobile age.

INLAND WATERWAYS

Until the construction of the railroads, the bulk of inland traffic moved over rivers, canals, and lakes. As the railroads first complemented and then supplanted some of the waterways, canals began to specialize in the movement of bulky, low unit value goods, for which speed of movement was not crucial. The average cost of freight per ton/mile was lower on a canal boat than on a railroad train, thus giving the canals a basic cost advantage. But for the movement of perishable goods, luxury items, or goods for which scheduling and speed of movement were important, the railroad was the logical means of transportation.

Some canals remained important over much of the 19th century. Traffic on the Erie Canal was increased when the New York system of canals was constructed, and the Hudson River became an important link in the entire state network. The rivers east of the Mississippi River continued to carry traffic, but the rapid increase in the volume of railroad traffic reduced the relative importance of these waterways.

With the development of the Mesabi Range of iron ore in Minnesota and the shipment of wheat from Duluth and Superior, the Sault Sainte Marie (Soo) Canal began to play a larger role in shipping. Coal and stone added their bulk to the traffic that flowed through the Soo. At one time there was a plan projected to develop Duluth and/or Superior into steel manufacturing towns that would supply a part of the steel demand in the Midwest and Northwest. Whalebacks that carried wheat to Cleveland and to other ports along the Great Lakes would transport coal on their return trips, thus providing fuel for blast furnaces. Wheat and coal were, therefore, to share the operating costs of each whaleback and lower the unit cost of transporting both products. While coal did share the costs of transportation with wheat, neither Duluth nor Superior ever competed seriously with South Chicago and Pittsburgh in the manufacture of steel.

The canal was closed to all traffic during four or five months of each year, depending on the timing and the severity of the winters. But the volume of traffic during the ice-free months more than justified its operation. Since 1885, more freight has passed through the Soo Canal each year than through any other single canal or system of canals in the United States. Indeed, during some years the Soo has carried more freight than either the Panama Canal or the Suez Canal. By 1890, traffic on the Soo exceeded by weight all of the traffic that was carried on the New York system of canals.

Among the more important rivers that continued to serve commerce and trade were the Hudson River in New York, the Delaware River between New Jersey and Pennsylvania, and several rivers in the Mississippi River basin. Coal was mined in the valley of the Monongahela River, and while much of it went to market via railroad, many cities and towns along this river and the Ohio River received their coal on barges that were pushed downstream. Some of the steel mills in Pittsburgh, Wheeling, Youngstown, and Ashland were stockpiled with coal that was floated down the river. Adding to the total flow of barges was coal that had been funneled down the Big Sandy River to the Ohio.

ELECTRIC URBAN AND INTERURBAN RAILWAYS

One factor tending to soften the impact of urbanization was the construction of urban transit systems. The evolution of these facilities from public omnibuses to horse-drawn rail cars to electric-powered streetcars constitutes one of the more exciting chapters in our economic history. To some writers, this development was associated with markets which were widening rapidly, but which were becoming more concentrated in the downtown sections of cities at the same time.

The spread of electric railways depended on efficient transmission of electrical power from central power stations. Overhead trolley wires were widely used for surface transportation, with trolleys and streetcars tapping the electrical power through connectors on the ends of long trolley poles. Overhead wires often created fire hazards, however, and were dangerous during ice storms and heavy snows. Third rails were also used to transmit power, but mainly in subways and on elevated railways where people were unlikely to come into contact with the rails.

Markets Served by Electric Railways

Housing problems presented themselves in almost every urban area where businessmen and employees had to live near their places of work. If they could not live near their work in terms of space, nearness in terms of time was even more essential. Electric railways were the answer to the problem of urban and suburban sprawl. By shortening the travel time between residential and business districts, they permitted workers to locate their homes in desirable residential areas outside the business complex.

As business districts expanded laterally, these same transportation facilities permitted customers to go from store to store quickly and cheaply, even when the stores were blocks apart. The normal fare was only a nickel. Surface transportation was much faster than walking, and faster even than driving a horse and carriage. Streetcars stopped at almost all street intersections and sometimes in the middle of blocks, adding convenience to their extensive list of virtues.

But the time came when surface transportation was no longer adequate for market. A more rapid means of transportation was necessary, one that could handle large numbers of passengers in a short period of time. Some cities found the answer in elevated railways, electrical railroads situated on tracks raised high above the normal traffic of city streets. Other cities were able to excavate passageways under their streets and install subterranean railways or subways. A few big cities, such as Chicago and New York City, used both systems. Depending in part on the nature of the areas that were served, stops on elevated railways and subways were less frequent than those on surface routes, and the distances between stations were generally longer than city blocks. Because of these arrangements, and because elevated and subway trains had unrestricted right-of-way, transportation was much more rapid than on surface electric railways. There was no pedestrian or horse-drawn traffic to retard the progress of the cars along the rails.

Fares everywhere were only five cents a ride, and transfers were given if a person's ultimate destination was on another route. But there were no transfers from one means of transportation to another. The low fare tended to compensate for traveling conditions, since all of the devices were noisy and dirty. The elevated structures created surface traffic problems that resulted from the heavy iron supports of the overhead tracks being anchored in the middle of busy streets. On some streets in New York City, shoppers could choose among surface cars, elevated or subway trains, and hansom cabs. The latter were the most stylish and aristocratic, and certainly in better condition than their electrically powered competitors. But they were really the forerunner of the modern taxicab, and cost more than other means of travel.

Profitability and Expansion

Power companies found that the electric transportation business was a profitable one. Once tracks had been laid and power stations constructed, an increasing volume of business up to the capacity of the fixed capital equipment was handled at lower unit costs. With fares still fixed at five cents, the profit was evident. Seeking wider markets, companies extended their tracks into suburban areas, thus becoming one of the first developers and promoters of suburban real estate. If companies did not engage in promotion themselves, they made it possible for others to do so. Lots were advertised for sale in terms of their distance from streetcar transportation, for instance. A location two blocks from a car line or less than two minutes' walk from a car stop was the lure used to attract prospective home owners. And as people moved out to these areas, additional transmission lines were installed to meet their other electrical needs.

After car tracks were laid to suburban areas, it was small matter to extend them to the next town—perhaps five or ten miles distant, or even forty miles in later days. Such lines offered little competition to steam railroads as they catered almost strictly to local traffic and made frequent stops between terminals. Fares were low and service was frequent. On some routes express packages and a limited amount of freight were carried, but passenger service remained the major function.

Economic Impacts of the Electric Railways

The interurbans were the means of extending the radius within which urban newspapers were read by rural subscribers and by those in neighboring towns on the same day the newspapers were published. Newspaper advertising was addressed to this group of readers, which was now within a short ride of the urban retail complex. This combination of events helped to bring on the decline of the country general store, and also damaged the trade of many small-town specialty stores such as those that dealt in clothing and furniture. It was easy, more satisfactory, and sometimes more exciting for the shopper to make her purchases in the central city. Only feed stores and hardware stores seemed able to withstand the impact of the new customer freedom of mobility.

Electric power plants were among the initial manufacturers and distributors of ice, and it was the electric cars that first transported ice to the country and to nearby small towns. In the country, the ice was thrown out of the cars along the right-of-way, and customers waited to pick it up in a wagon or buggy. In the outlying towns, the ice was kept in small storage houses where it could be picked up as needed.

Electric streetcars and interurbans were among the early means of finding amusements and entertainment outside the home. They made it possible for people to go somewhere at little cost within a short period of time. Amusement parks were developed near many large communities, many of them being located along the right-of-way of an intercity electric transportation line. This was another application of the principle of increasing returns. No new tracks had to be laid, unless there were sidings and switches. No new cars were required either, because the passenger load to amusement parks came at a time of low volume of traffic in and between urban areas. No additional car operators were required, and regular employees were afforded the opportunity of working a few additional hours per week and of increasing their earnings by that much. Amusements usually found in the parks included horseback riding, canoeing and boating, roller-skating, dancing, baseball, tennis, and various other games of the circus and county fair midway. Of course, every amusement park of any note provided an entirely new type of thrill for both children and adults with its roller coaster.

A special type of electric transportation was found in the form of inclined planes that were used in Pittsburgh, Cincinnati, and San Francisco, among other cities, to carry passengers up and down the sides of steep hills or mountains. Cars were driven onto horizontal platforms which were carried in that position up and down the inclines. Cables were sometimes used on both the upward and downward movements, and ratchets were dragged behind the cars on the upward climb as a safety measure. Many amusement parks and observation towers on the tops of mountains were reached by means of inclined planes.

RAILROADS

The period between the Civil War and World War I has been called the "Age of the Railroad," reflecting the dominance of that form of transportation in American economic life. Although barely 30 years old when conflict divided North and South, the railroad was firmly established east of the Mississippi River, providing speedy and regular access to major business centers from Florida to New England. With the changes initiated by the Civil War, the railroad was to expand not only in those areas of the East without rail service, but in the beckoning lands west of the Mississippi. The feeling of manifest destiny was to find concrete realization in a pair of rails stretching across the plains.

The Transcontinental Railroad

One of the major impacts of the Civil War was on the speed at which the railroad net was expanded. Plans for a transcontinental railroad had been held up for almost two decades as southerners and northerners argued over the location of its eastern terminal, each group favoring a location in its own region. Now that the voice of the South was silent in the halls of Congress, consideration of New Orleans or some other southern city was out of the question. Working quickly, in 1862 Congress chartered the Union Pacific Railroad to extend from the Missouri River to the eastern boundary of California. The Central Pacific Railroad was chartered to extend eastward from Sacramento, California. Construction was begun soon afterward.

Construction of the Railroad. Years of hard work and difficulty followed, as engineers and workers solved the problems of traversing new kinds of territory. Extensive use of immigrant laborers—mainly Irish on the Union Pacific and Orientals on the Central Pacific—helped to keep down labor costs, since the capital-intensive construction methods of today were not available. Some of the Irish hired to build the Union Pacific undoubtedly had gained their construction knowledge while helping dig canals, although the gangs of laborers used to dig the Erie Canal were generally too old by the time of the Civil War. Ultimately the two railroads joined at Promontory Point, Utah, on May 10, 1869. In a ceremony that befitted the occasion, a golden spike was used to join the last two rails, signaling the spanning of the continent. The golden spike, quickly replaced by one of iron, now rests in a vault at Stanford University.

Strictly speaking, the term *transcontinental* was a misnomer when applied to the Union Pacific-Central Pacific line. The railroad had no terminal on the East Coast, and the trip from Atlantic to Pacific could be made only by changing trains several times. But the trip could be made after 1869, so the Promontory Point ceremony did mark the joining of the two coasts. The eastern terminal of the Union Pacific was originally Council Bluffs, Iowa, just across the river from Omaha. A rash of railroad construction followed the joining of Council Bluffs and Sacramento, as lines in Chicago raced to be the first to connect Chicago and other eastern cities with the "transcontinental" railroad.

Grants of land were given to both railroads as a means of stimulating interest in their construction. Land itself was not adequate, however, since it did not provide ready cash with which to meet the current costs of construction. The government ultimately subsidized the Union Pacific and the Central Pacific to the extent of $16,000 per mile over level terrain, $48,000 per mile over and through the mountains, and $36,000 per mile in the valleys between mountain ranges. The subsidy money proved to be among the strongest stimuli leading to the completion of the railroad.

Impact on the American Bison. A sidelight on the construction of the transcontinental link was its impact on the American bison. To begin with, the bison or buffalo was a cheap source of meat for construction crews. Thousands of workers were fed buffalo meat at almost no cost to the construction companies. Secondly, the Union Pacific cut through the bison range and divided the animals into a southern herd and a northern herd, thus altering their migration patterns and the hunting habits of the American Indian. Once the railroad ran completely through buffalo country, the wanton destruction of these animals was almost a foregone conclusion.

For about 20 years the railroads promoted week-end excursions, the main features of which were bison hunts. The railroads provided transportation, sleeping quarters, food, rifles, and ammunition. In addition, they guaranteed bison. The hunting excursions were joined by those who wanted sport rather than meat or hides. Thousands of animals that were slaughtered were, therefore, left to rot on the plains. By the end of the century, the bison as a game animal had disappeared.

Again, the railroads were acting rationally in encouraging such parties. Railroad management had learned that railroads were operating under the principle of increasing returns within the limits that were set by rights-of-way and fixed capital equipment. Beyond a certain level of passenger and freight operation, additional traffic added much more to revenues than it did to costs. Hunting parties fell within this category.

Perhaps a more important impact of the bison hunts was the changes they brought about in the life of the American Indians. Bison were the basis of the living and the livelihood of the Indian. He ate buffalo meat, and buffalo hides kept him warm. Skins were used in covering his tepees, and served to carry his possessions from place to place. Sinews, bones, and other parts of the animal were also used in various ways by the Indian. His life on the plains was keyed to the life of the buffalo, with many of his religious ceremonies being addressed to the powers that controlled the movement of the herds. It was only when the bison were almost completely exterminated that the Indian resigned himself to life on reservations provided by the white man.

Demand by white people for buffalo robes eventually played a part in the disappearance of the bison. Such robes were in great demand, even by frontiersmen. Winters on the prairies were cold, and buffalo robes were quite warm. In some cases, rugs were made out of buffalo skins to keep floors warm underfoot. And local transportation, which was generally limited to horse and wagon or horse and sleigh when snow was on the ground, was made quite comfortable by huge, shaggy buffalo robes. In any event, buffalo robes were among the cheapest and warmest means of protection against cold weather and blustery winds.

Land Grants

Grants of land to the railroads followed several patterns, varying from state to state and from state to territory. All patterns were uniform in that they granted alternate sections of land in primary strips on opposite sides of the railroad. But the distance back from the railroad varied from six to 20 miles. If any of the granted sections had already been sold or otherwise appropriated, the railroads were given *lieu* lands, that is, lands that lay beyond the limits of six to 20 miles. In order to retain titles to these grants the railroads were required to meet certain specifications as to the mileage constructed within given periods of time. In return for the grants of land, railroads which received them were required to haul government personnel, commodities, and mail at one half the commercial rates. This requirement was not removed until 1946.

Authorities are in rather close agreement that a total of 131,350,534 acres of land were granted to railroads. Former Railroad Commissioner James B. Eastman estimated the value of this acreage at $126 million when the grants were made. A congressional committee report in 1945 estimated that the railroads had contributed over $900 million in payment for this acreage, reckoned in terms of the savings on freight and passenger rates on government business. That the government has been repaid for its original investment is without doubt. People do continue to differ on many problems concerning the land grants, however.

There have been no federal land grants to railroads in any of the states that grew out of the original thirteen colonies, nor in the states of Ohio,

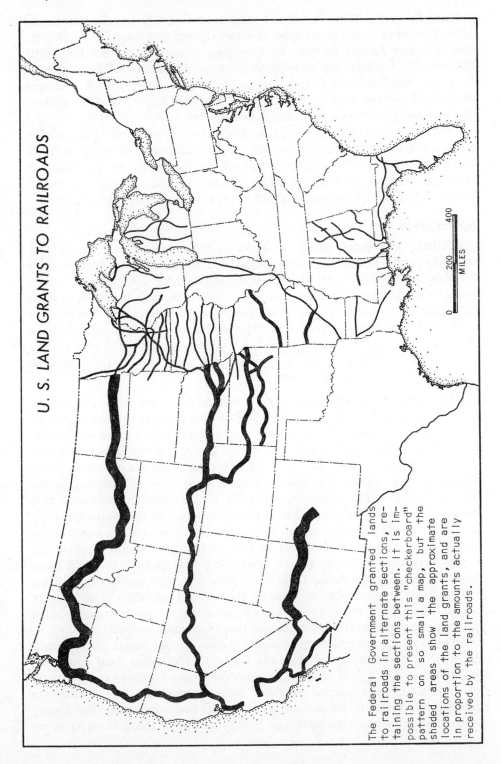

U. S. LAND GRANTS TO RAILROADS

The Federal Government granted lands to railroads in alternate sections, retaining the sections between. It is impossible to present this "checkerboard" pattern on so small a map, but the shaded areas show the approximate locations of the land grants, and are in proportion to the amounts actually received by the railroads.

Indiana, Kentucky, Tennessee, Oklahoma, and Texas. The largest percentages of land grants to total acreage were in North Dakota, Washington, Minnesota, Montana, and Kansas, in that order, ranging from 23.7 percent for North Dakota to 15.6 percent for Montana and Kansas. In none of the five Southern States in which railroads received grants of land was more than 8.3 percent of the total acreage used for that purpose. Alabama has the dubious distinction of leading the Southern States in that respect.

The chief interest in the land grant question is found in the attitude that railroad management takes concerning the "subsidization" of other forms of transportation in the 20th century. Competition is afforded by agencies that use highways and air transportation, not to mention internal waterways. Further discussion of this problem will be given in a later chapter.

Speculation

Federal land grants were not confined to stimulating either the first transcontinental railroad or any railroad that connected mid-America with the West Coast. They were also given to stimulate the construction of railroads before there was sufficient traffic to support them. Spurred on by such aid, railroads pioneered in the development of both farm and urban areas west of the Mississippi River, sometimes realizing substantial returns from the land given them. Speculators and speculation played a role in this development, but history has emphasized the speculation in the area of railroads rather than in public lands.

The Nature of Speculation. Such speculation was found in the handling of railroad securities and in the relationship between actual railroad construction costs and estimated costs. One of the most publicized cases of speculation involved the Credit Mobilier. Using the general laws of incorporation of the time, the members of the board of directors of the Union Pacific Railroad formed a construction company for the purpose of constructing the railroad facilities. This company, called the Credit Mobilier, submitted bids for construction to the railroad board of directors, and the board members awarded construction contracts to themselves as owners of the construction company. Since none of the directors were in the construction business, the actual work was contracted out to other firms. The element of profit arose from the fact that the actual costs of construction were much less than the bid made to the Union Pacific. Even so, the railroad paid the Credit Mobilier the full amount of the contract. Canny placement of stock bribes in high places helped to tone down the scandal that eventually resulted.

This was not the end of the incident, however. One result of the Credit Mobilier deal was to impose upon the Union Pacific higher fixed costs than it could pay. The Credit Mobilier accepted mortgage bonds in part payment of its contract. The interest on these bonds amounted to more than the railroad received in revenues over and above its operating costs, thus forcing ultimate foreclosure of the mortgage. Reorganization of the railroad squeezed out the former stockholders, who had purchased stock in good faith, and permitted the bondholders to take over the railroad for the amount of interest that was in arrears. Many of the smaller bondholders who had purchased railroad bonds for investment or speculation were unable to meet the conditions that were set for reorganizing the railroads and lost their entire commitments. Prominent promoters of railroads and railroad securities such as Leland J. Stanford, Collis P. Huntington, Mark Hopkins, and Charles Crocker seldom suffered such a fate.

Not many of the men whose names are connected with promoting railroads were actually builders. J. P. Morgan, E. H. Harriman, Jay Gould, James Fisk, Daniel Drew, and Cornelius Vanderbilt were financiers who were more interested in financial promotions and combinations of railroads than they were in actual construction or in operational efficiencies. James J. Hill may have been an exception to this generalization. He was concerned with the financial promotion of the Great Northern Railway, but not to the extent that he tried to inveigle land grants from the government. Construction of the Great Northern was carried out without benefit of such grants. Hill was an engineer as well as a promoter, and apparently was interested in constructing rights-of-way and operating trains in an efficient manner.

Jay Cooke and the Panic of 1873. Shortly after the success of the Union Pacific in linking up with the West Coast, the Northern Pacific Railroad, spurred by the enthusiasm of Jay Cooke, constructed a line to the West Coast on a route that lay north of the Union Pacific. Mountains were difficult to penetrate along this route, and construction costs were high. As a means of raising the necessary funds, Cooke underwrote a bond issue for the Northern Pacific through the medium of his investment bank. He used the same techniques that had been successful in marketing government bonds a decade earlier, but he apparently overestimated the willingness and ability of the public to absorb another capital issue of that kind. Perhaps he overestimated his own ability as an underwriter and a salesman. At any rate, when his bank failed to sell all of the bonds it had underwritten, it had to make good to the railroad. The bank did not have sufficient liquid funds to do so, and it failed.

The failure of Jay Cooke's scheme gave notice that all was not well with banks and with railroads in 1873. A general distrust of banks and financial institutions eventually grew into a full-scale financial panic. Depositors in growing numbers came to their banks to demand their deposits, not because they wanted to use the money for purchases, but because they were losing faith in the banks. When the banks could not pay and had to close their doors, the news spread quickly, and a financial panic was born.

Panic grew into recession and depression as other sectors of the economy were affected. Speculation in western lands had been heavy before 1873, purchases being made on the presumption that the same lands could be sold in a short time at higher prices. Speculation in railroad securities had been undertaken for much the same reason. When panic struck, land and railroad speculators attempted vainly to liquidate their holdings, often losing the greatest part of their investment. National banks were not permitted to grant loans on mortgages of farmlands, and state banks were of little help since they were declining in number and influences.

Since there were no bankers' banks, no lenders of last resort, commercial banks failed along with investment banks and railroads. When banks failed, business establishments failed, too, and had to close their doors. Employees were thrown out of work, and unemployment throughout the United States was on the increase. People did not have or could not obtain money with which to purchase commodities, and the volume of business contracted sharply. Depression was a reality.

The precise causes of any panic are very difficult to isolate, but it seems that the Panic of 1873 and the ensuing depression grew out of the economic dislocations of the Civil War. Every war has been followed by speculation in some parts of the economy. After the Civil War, it was speculation in western lands, railroad securities, and railroad construction that provided the proximate causes of the panic.

Expansion of the Railway Network

Apart from the spectacular success of the transcontinental railroad, there was significant but less spectacular growth in railway mileage both east and west of the Mississippi River. Gaps in eastern lines were filled in, as railroads in that area experienced a period of consolidation and change. And west of the Mississippi, construction crews raced to meet deadlines imposed by expanding markets and an ever-advancing frontier.

Railroads in the Midwest and the West. The pattern of railroads extending onto the plains was a complex one. West of Chicago, railroads fanned out like the spokes of a wheel to Minneapolis and St. Paul on the north to St. Louis on the south. Denver, Kansas City, Omaha, Des Moines, Salt Lake City, and Dallas had direct connections with Chicago. Seattle, Portland, San Francisco, and Los Angeles were the terminal cities along the West Coast. Railroads vied with each other in their attempts to control north-south traffic between these latter cities. The Southern Pacific Railroad constructed a line through Dallas to New Orleans to give this Louisiana city direct connection with the West. The Atchison, Topeka and Santa Fe Railroad followed the old Santa Fe Trail from Kansas City to the city of Santa Fe in New Mexico. It later extended its right-of-way to the West Coast, down to Fort Worth, and back to Chicago.

The Chicago, Rock Island and Pacific and the Chicago, Burlington and Quincy Railroads were other lines that extended their tracks into the Great Plains States. One of the last attempts to share the traffic west of Chicago was made by the Chicago, Milwaukee and St. Paul Railroad. Since it was the last railroad to survey rights-of-way over and through the Rocky Mountains on the northern sector, it was forced to lay out a route over lands that other roads had rejected for one reason or another. In crossing the Continental Divide its grades were longer and steeper and its curves sharper than those of the other lines. In order to save on fuel costs, its management decided to electrify its lines over the mountains. From an operational standpoint, the move was successful, since it permitted the trains to operate over the mountains without carrying fuel or requiring fuel stops. But it placed such a burden of overhead costs on the railroad that the line was forced into bankruptcy. When it was reorganized and rechartered as the Chicago, Milwaukee, St. Paul and Pacific Railroad, many of its bondholders were squeezed out.

Railroads in the East. At the same time that railroads were being constructed in the West more rapidly than traffic was growing, railroads east of the Mississippi River were experiencing their version of rapid development. Mergers and combinations of railroads were major features of this development, in addition to the construction of new lines. When several short lines were combined to form the New York Central Railroad, through service was provided between New York City and Buffalo, and later to Cleveland, Toledo, Detroit, and Chicago. In order to provide for continuous runs between these distant terminal cities, a standard track gauge of 4 feet 8½ inches was adopted. Branch and feeder lines adopted the same gauge so that railroad cars and locomotives could be interchanged between lines without the difficulty or delay that had been so annoying and costly before. Ultimately this gauge became the standard for the entire country. The Pennsylvania, the Baltimore and Ohio, and the Erie Railroads were formed by linking relatively short lines end to end. St. Louis, Cincinnati, and Louisville not only were connected directly with New York, but two or more railroads also vied with each other for their traffic, traffic which increased in volume at a rapid rate.

Urbanization and New Construction. Increases in population, increases in manufacturing output, more combinations of business firms, and new patterns of commerce focused attention on the urbanization movement during the late 19th century. Increased urban populations meant more economic interdependence between people in different urban communities, as well as between urban areas and rural areas. The exchange of goods and services and the transportation of passengers between such areas of specialization was facilitated by the expansion of the railway net. In the decade ending in 1880, 41,000 miles of new railroads were put into operation. But in the following decade, an astounding 70,000 miles of new track were laid.

Increases in railroad mileage were spectacular in some areas simply because the initial track figures were so small. In 1880, for example, there were fewer than 300 miles of railroads in each of Idaho and Washington, and only 106 miles in Montana. An increase of over 20 times the initial mileage in Montana during a decade was absolutely less than the increase in railroad mileage in such states as Colorado, Iowa, Kansas, and Nebraska.

But expansion was not confined to western railroads alone. Railway mileage in Florida more than quadrupled between 1870 and 1880, as industry, agriculture, and city life grew throughout the state. Railway mileage in Mississippi and North Carolina more than doubled. In Alabama, Georgia, Kentucky, Michigan, West Virginia, and Wisconsin, the increase in railway mileage was nearly twofold.

In terms of actual mileage constructed, the states of Illinois, Pennsylvania, and Ohio counted over 2,200 miles of new trackage; and New York was not far behind with 1,700 miles. The results of all the activity in railroad construction then and later were seen in the completion of five transcontinental lines, and others from Chicago, Detroit, Cleveland, and New York to the Gulf of Mexico and to the East Coast to Florida. Many miles of feeder lines were also constructed. By 1920, American railroads ran their trains over 252,000 miles of right-of-way. Truly it could be said that the level of living as well as the level of business activity were conditioned by the presence of railroads.

Passenger Traffic. While more has been written about the importance of freight traffic as a source of railroad revenue than about passenger traffic, for many years the latter was a source of revenue, especially for those railroads that could transport commuters to and from large cities. On most lines, passenger trains were given priority over freight trains, in spite of the fact that the latter may have been producers of more revenue.

Passenger fares were usually less than three cents per mile one way. A reduction of 20 percent was given for the purchase of a round-trip ticket. In order to accommodate passengers and to make them more comfortable on a long journey and one that extended through the night hours, the Pullman Company designed, constructed, and operated sleeping cars and diners. For those who wanted more luxurious accommodations than were to be had in ordinary passenger cars, chair cars and parlor cars were available for a price. Observation cars were attached to some trains that passed through scenic territory, and observation platforms were found at the rear of others. Officially, there was only one class of passenger service provided by the railroads, although the equipment and service differed between lines and between divisions on a given line.

The Twentieth Century Limited and the Broadway Limited may have been the most famous trains. They were luxury trains that operated between New York and Chicago with a minimum number of stops en route. Until 1920 they encountered no competition from automobile, bus, or air transportation. The demand for service was so great that both trains operated several sections daily between the two terminal cities.

Standard Time Zones. One important innovation brought about by the railroads was the adoption of standard time zones—eastern, central, mountain, and pacific. The zones were arranged to facilitate the scheduling of trains by abolishing the varying sun time used by almost all towns on an east-west route. Standard time was accepted officially by state and local governments in the respective time zones, each of which was approximately 15 degrees of longitude in width. From time to time as industrial and commercial conditions warranted, portions of states that were originally in the central time belt have been given eastern time without altering the official boundaries between these two zones. Such changes may have originated in the use of daylight saving time by some cities during World War I. This practice was meant to save fuel for lighting during the war, but it has been continued on a seasonal basis by many cities since then.

At first, many objections were raised to using daylight saving time, most of them hinging on the obvious break with habit and tradition. But when industry, commerce, and even agriculture had accustomed themselves to new schedules, they voluntarily voted to continue with it. Daylight saving time in the central time zone is the same as eastern standard time. In 1961, almost the entire state of Indiana was placed on eastern standard time, as was the north central portion of Kentucky, including the cities of Lexington and Louisville.

Government Regulation

Competition in operating the railroads led to many discriminatory acts by railroad managements. One condition noted before that contributed to questionable practices by the railroads was the high ratio of fixed costs to operating costs. In addition, total fixed costs bore no relation to the volume of traffic once these fixed costs had been incurred or once the railroads had been constructed.

Rate Discrimination. Discrimination in rate making took the form of setting different rates for different places, for different commodities, or for different firms. It is true that some variations in rates were justified on the basis of actual cost differentials in operation. For example, loading, unloading, and handling less than carload lots justified the charging of a higher rate than otherwise. But monopoly control of transportation facilities was frequently the cause or at least the justification for charging rates that were higher than those charged by the same railroad under competitive conditions. Rebates, discounts, short and long haul rate differentials, and deviations from published tariffs were common means of discrimination intended to increase railroad revenues. Under competitive conditions, traffic that was induced by charging rates that brought anything at all over operating costs was better than no traffic at all, because it left something to help defray fixed costs.

State railroad commissions were powerless to correct these situations in the absence of federal control. As long as most traffic was intrastate in character there was no pressure upon Congress to act under the interstate commerce clause of the Constitution. But as the railroad net became national in extent, the federal government was impelled to action.

The Granger Cases. Pressure for federal regulation of the railroads resulted from the decisions in a series of cases that dealt with their rate-making practices. Because the cases were originally brought by midwestern farm groups, they are generally called the Granger Cases. The first important case, *Munn* v. *Illinois* (94 U.S. 113), which was decided in 1877, established the right of a state legislature to regulate rates for rendering services by concerns that were affected with a public interest. Munn, who owned and operated a grain elevator in the state of Illinois, challenged the right of the Illinois legislature to establish the maximum rates he could charge farmers for storing their grain. The decision established the right of the legislature in that particular case, and established a precedent for regulation in similar situations.

Other Granger Cases established that the regulation of railroads by state legislatures was not subject to judicial review and that, in the absence of federal legislation, state legislatures could enact laws that indirectly affected interstate commerce. Ultimately, these rights of the states were abrogated. In 1886, the United States Supreme Court reversed an earlier ruling in *Stone* v. *Farmers' Loan and Trust Company* (116 U.S. 307-347) when it ruled that regulation of commerce at the state level was subject to review by the courts. In that same year, the Wabash case (118 U.S. 557-596) raised the issue of the power of a state legislature to regulate rates for transporting freight entirely within state boundaries, if the transportation within the state was part of an interstate movement. When the majority of the Supreme Court ruled against the power of a state to act in such cases, it practically forced Congress to enact the Interstate Commerce Act in 1887.

The Interstate Commerce Act. The Interstate Commerce Act provided for the establishment of an Interstate Commerce Commission consisting of five members appointed by the President and ratified by the Senate. The terms of office were for six years. Not more than three appointees could belong to the same political party. Appointees could not have been in the employ of any common carrier, nor could they have any financial interest in a common carrier, including the ownership of corporate stock. Salaries were set at $7,500 per year, and commissioners were not permitted to engage in any other business or employment.

Provisions of the Act. The Act provided that all interstate freight and passenger traffic was subject to federal regulation. The only reference that was made to rates was that they should be reasonable and just. The Commission was not given the authority to determine rates, nor was it empowered to establish levels above which rates could be declared unreasonable.

In correcting discriminatory practices by railroads, the Act forbade personal discrimination in the charging of rates and in giving rebates. It made it unlawful for the railroads to give preference or priority to any shipper, locality, or commodity. Railroads were required to provide proper and equal facilities for the interchange of traffic with other railroads. Carriers were not permitted to discriminate in rates between such connecting lines.

The long and short haul clause made it unlawful for a railroad to charge more "in the aggregate for the transportation of passengers or of like kind of property under substantially similar circumstances and conditions for a shorter haul than for a longer distance over the same line, in the same direction, the shorter being included within the longer distance." The Commission was empowered to authorize carriers to make exception to this rule, but only after careful investigation of the circumstances affecting each instance. This clause was inserted in answer to protests from the railroads which claimed cost differentials or other justifications for short and long haul discrimination.

Pooling traffic was forbidden, as was a division of either net profits or aggregate proceeds between railroads. Schedules of rates and fares were to be posted in public places, and increases in such rates and fares could be made only after ten days' notice. The public was to be given immediate notice of any rate reduction.

The Commission could hear complaints, and it was given power to initiate investigations of the management policies of common carriers. It was given the power to obtain such information from management as was needed to perform its duties, and it could require management to hand over books, contracts, and agreements that contained information pertinent to any inquiry that was being made.

Effectiveness of the Act. The Commission had to look to the courts to enforce its rulings as it was only a fact-finding body. Its findings, however, were to be considered as prima facie evidence in all judicial hearings. Since the courts permitted the railroads to submit additional evidence that had been withheld from the Commission, the effectiveness of the decisions of that body was lessened. In spite of the passage of the Compulsory Testimony Act in 1893, railroad officials continued to refuse to answer questions that were put to them by the Commission. The decisions of the Brimson case (154 U.S. 447-490) and the Brown case (161 U.S. 591-630) were required to establish the constitutionality of the Act.

In 1897 the Commission reported that the average time consumed in arriving at a court decision was four years. During litigation the railroads were permitted to continue whatever practice or procedure was being tested in the courts. Since the courts continued to permit railroads to submit evidence that had been withheld from the Commission, their decisions served to discredit the Commission in the eyes of the public, even though the rulings were sound in terms of the evidence that had been submitted. Two other situations rendered the Commission virtually powerless to prevent the practice of charging discriminatory rates. The first of these denied the Commission the right to establish maximum rates that it would consider reasonable; the other emasculated the short and long haul clause to the point of its annulment by the courts.

In 1903 Congress acted to prevent the delay in the courts hearing cases that arose under the Sherman Antitrust Act and the Interstate Commerce Act.

It required that Circuit Courts give precedence to such cases when the United States was a complainant and when the Attorney General certified that the suits were of public importance. It provided, further, that, if appeals were to be made, they be taken directly to the Supreme Court within 60 days following the entry of the decree of the Circuit Court.

The Elkins Act. In the same year Congress passed the Elkins Act to remedy a situation that injured both railroads and the public interest. Any departure from the published schedule of rates was to be considered as prima facie evidence of discrimination by the railroads involved. The railroads, along with their officers and agents, were made directly liable for violations of the Interstate Commerce Act. Receiving rebates was declared to be unlawful. Prison sentences for violators were replaced by a scale of fines reaching a maximum of $20,000. More important than any one of these provisions, however, was a clause giving the proper Circuit Court jurisdiction over cases that arose from public complaints that the law was being violated. District attorneys were authorized to prosecute such proceedings under the direction of the Attorney General and in the name of the Interstate Commerce Commission.

The Hepburn Act. In order to make the work of the Commission even more effective, its membership was increased by the Hepburn Act in 1906 to ten; and salaries of commissioners were raised to $10,000 per year. The term of office was extended to seven years. The jurisdiction of the Commission was extended to include express companies, sleeping car companies, pipelines, bridges, and ferries, if these media were utilized in interstate commerce. The Act also brought terminal facilities, including industrial railways, switches, spurs, tracks, freight depots, and yards under the control of the Commission, regardless of their ownership. Annual accounting reports that were required under the terms of the original Act were henceforth to be submitted to the Commission under oath. The Commission could require standard forms of all accounts, records, and memoranda to be kept by the railroads. It made it unlawful for the railroads to maintain any other set of accounts and records. Railroads were forbidden to give free transportation to passengers other than officers, employees, and their families. Other individuals explicitly permitted free transportation included employees of associated businesses, persons engaged in religious and charitable work, and persons who were too poor to pay the regular fare.

The Mann-Elkins Act. What may have been even more important in establishing respect for the Commission was the authority given to it to establish maximum reasonable rates. More teeth were provided for the enforcement of Commission rulings. The powers of the Commission were further extended by the Mann-Elkins Act of 1910 to include telephone, telegraph, and cable companies that were engaged in sending messages across state or national boundaries. The Commission was given the authority to suspend rates that might be proposed by the railroads until a hearing had been held. The short and long haul clause was clarified by removing the phrase "under substantially similar circumstances and conditions." The charge for a through haul between two points could not exceed the sum of the local rates over the same route. Once a railroad reduced its rates to meet competition with a water route, it might not increase these rates later on, if that water competition were eliminated, except for causes that did not arise from that elimination.

Smythe v. Ames. Decisions by the United States Supreme Court were often required on questions of public policy. In *Smythe* v. *Ames*, (169 U.S. 466-550) the Court established the principle that railroad rates were reasonable only when they permitted a railroad to earn a fair rate of return on the value of the property used in rendering transportation services. In spite of the fact that this decision was handed down in 1898, no provision was made by Congress to establish the value of railroad properties until the passage of the Railroad Valuation Act of 1913. In order to establish a schedule of rates that would yield a fair rate of return, a base upon which the rate could be calculated had to be established. Calculating this base was a problem.

One possibility was the calculation of market values of railroad properties from the market value of railroad securities. But this would not be realistic because the market values of railroad securities were derived from quotations on only a small portion of the total shares outstanding. Should the total number of corporate shares be offered for sale at one time, market quotations would decline drastically. A second defect of this method of property valuation lay in the fact that the values of shares traded were equivalent to their earnings capitalized at the current rate of interest. Obviously, the valuation of property had to be based upon some arbitrary criterion.

In *Smythe* v. *Ames*, the Supreme Court had decreed that the original cost of construction, the costs of additional capital equipment, the amount of and the market value of stocks and bonds, reproduction costs, the probable earning capacity of the property under given rates, and the sum of money required to meet operating expenses be considered in estimating the value of property upon which a fair rate of return should be calculated. The Court went on to say that other pertinent criteria might also be used. The Commission was ordered to begin the work of evaluation within 60 days, and to keep a continuing record of all changes made in railroads that might affect their values. Obviously, the Commission was not prepared to undertake such a colossal task, a task which included the establishment of the criteria under which it would operate. In 1920 not a single final valuation of any railroad had been announced.

Wartime Crisis

Soon after the outbreak of war in 1914, American railroads began to feel the strains of disrupted international trade. They found themselves unable to respond to the increased demands for service brought on by the war, reflecting major inflexibilities in organization and operation that had not been remedied by market forces. By 1917, when the United States finally entered the war, conditions in the industry had reached a crisis level. The federal government then was forced to intervene.

Prewar Competition. Prior to World War I, railroads had little or no effective competition from other forms of transportation. It is true that electric railway systems provided interurban transportation, but such service was slower than steam railroads, and it catered almost wholly to local traffic. The railroads did not object to the competition for local traffic because local service was costly to render unless its volume was large. Steam locomotives were fairly efficient once they were in motion, but starting them and stopping them involved a high consumption of coal and steam.

Railroads, therefore, aimed their competitive activities at attracting traffic from competing railroads, rather than towards creating healthy public relations that would engender more local traffic. If business firms or persons wanted to ship commodities, they had little choice other than to use one of the railroads serving their locality. If persons desired to travel long distances, railroad transportation afforded the only facilities. Although passenger traffic increased rapidly after the turn of the century, it was not as profitable as freight traffic for most railroads. A few lines did find passenger service profitable, however, including the Long Island Railroad and several other lines providing daily commuter service in and out of Boston, New York, Philadelphia, and Chicago. For persons who worked in large cities and lived in suburban areas, there were no adequate alternative rapid transit facilities to use in getting to and from work.

Terminal facilities, railroad trackage and right-of-way, railroad cars, and railroad services in general underwent only nominal improvements during the early years of the 20th century. In the absence of any overall planning, New York continued to be the export-import center for overseas trade and commerce. Harbor facilities and terminals at Boston, Philadelphia, Baltimore, and Norfolk could handle and were required to service only a limited amount of traffic. But as industries caught the spirit of westward expansion and growth, their products were funneled into the port of New York. From the Midwestern States, New York received freight and passengers on the New York Central lines, and Pennsylvania Railroad, the Baltimore and Ohio Railroad, and the Erie Railroad. Hinterlands closer to the port were able to move their goods to New York on the New York, New Haven and Hartford Railroad; the Central Railroad of New Jersey; the Delaware, Lackawanna and Western Railroad; the Delaware and Hudson Railroad; and the Philadelphia and Reading Railroad. The Southern Railway and the Chesapeake and Ohio Railroad channeled products from the Southern States into New York. Warehouse and storage equipment, docks, piers, wharves, and loading gear were adequate to handle the usual flow of goods into and out of New York. American shippers depended almost entirely upon bottoms of foreign registry to carry goods to and from foreign ports.

Initial Impacts of the War. After the United States had recovered from the initial shock of the war in Europe, the countries that were members of the Triple Entente and the Triple Alliance sent orders to American firms for supplies and material of all kinds. These orders caused the size of production units to be increased and the tempo of their operations to be quickened. The flow of goods to and through the port of New York was also increased.

Germany's submarine campaign played havoc with the merchant marines of England and France. Dozens of ships were sunk as they plied the Atlantic and connecting waters. Many of the ships that were not sent to the bottom were withdrawn from transoceanic trade and placed in direct war service by carrying men and goods across the English Channel. England and France were successful in their efforts to blockade German seaports, and few of their vessels cleared American ports after 1915.

The combined results of these developments were to decimate the merchant marine that plied the waters between the United States and the countries of western Europe. The remaining shipping space to Europe could not accommodate freight as rapidly as it arrived in New York. One result of this impasse was the storage of freight in railroad cars until they could be unloaded, since all of the warehouse and storage facilities in the city were full. The immediate effect of such storage was a shortage of cars that could be used for hauling freight and an overflow of idle cars from freight yards onto the main tracks. When the United States became an active participant in the war in April, 1917, the inland transportation system was jammed almost to the point of breakdown. Trains were not moving because tracks were being used for storage facilities, cars were not available, or there was insufficient locomotive power to pull them.

Government Control of the Railroads. President Woodrow Wilson acted upon the authority that had been given him by Congress and assumed control of the operational aspects of the railroads in December, 1917. While Secretary of the Treasury William Gibbs McAdoo was designated Director General of the Railroads, he depended upon the experienced personnel of the railroads to keep the trains moving. That was the principal objective of their "seizure," and all policies that were adopted and actions that were taken should be evaluated from that point of view. In order to protect the interests of the stockholder-owners, compensation that was the equivalent of the average railway operating income for the three years ending June 30, 1917, was guaranteed to them throughout the period of government control. This was a liberal settlement, since it reflected the financial results of railroad operations that had been stimulated by war orders from Europe. The government also agreed to return the railroads to their private owners in as good physical condition as they were in when the government assumed control of their operations.

Problems of Efficiency. It must be recognized that without the cooperation of railroad officials and operating personnel, the experiment would have been a complete failure. At the same time many railroad employees showed their resentment against the action of the government by maintaining a low level of public relations. They purposely attempted to strengthen any argument against government ownership and/or operation of American railroads. They did keep the trains running, but they were disrespectful and unaccommodating in their contacts with the public.

In keeping the trains running, many situations arose that would not have been condoned by the public had there not been a war. Passenger locomotives were attached to freight trains and freight locomotives failed to maintain the operating schedules of passenger trains. Yard engines were used in longer distance hauling of freight trains. Passenger cars, both day coaches and Pullmans, that had been withdrawn from service, were restored to use in order to meet the demands for space. When the railroads were returned to private control in 1920, managements complained bitterly over the poor condition of the rolling stock, terminal facilities, and trackage. They overlooked the fact that their own judgment had permitted the physical condition of their rolling stock to decline to a lower level than they were willing to admit. In evaluating the success or failure of the operation, these accomplishments must be kept in mind: (1) the blockade in New York was broken and the trains were kept running, (2) the government paid the rental that was agreed upon, and (3) maintenance activities kept railroad properties from deteriorating below the level of 1917. This point of view was strongly held by Walter D. Hines, who succeeded Secretary McAdoo as Director General of the Railroads. In his *War History of the American Railroads*, he wrote that future analyses and events would show conclusively that the government did maintain the physical properties of the railroads and did return them to private ownership in an acceptable condition.

Basic Changes in Operation. Director General McAdoo instituted a number of changes in the managerial and operational aspects of railroading in order to increase their efficiency, prevent unnecessary duplication of services, and expedite the movement of freight. Railroad executives were requested to route all traffic over the shortest distance to its destination. Under a program of unifying the physical facilities of all railroads, their locomotives, passenger and freight cars, terminals, ports, and other facilities were utilized alike, regardless of ownership. All ticket offices in a given city were consolidated into one, and that one was located in the passenger station. When track layouts permitted it, all passenger trains entered and departed from a central or union depot; and freight terminals were unified. Rolling stock and locomotives were assigned to railroads according to their respective requirements for such equipment. Passenger travel was discouraged through the imposition of a war tax on passenger fares. Competing schedules were reduced to one operation if it could accommodate all of the traffic. More rapid loading of freight cars was obtained by raising demurrage rates up to $10 per diem after the seventh day. Instead of allowing a consignee three days in which to pick up his freight, railroads made direct deliveries and charged the consignees for dray service. Under a *sailing day* plan, less than carload lots of freight were delivered to freight stations only on specified days of the week. Railroads were encouraged to make up solid trainloads of given commodities and to use the most direct route to their destination.

In order to expedite the movement of freight and to give priority to commodities that were essential to the war effort, the Car Service Section of the Division of Operations of the Railroad Administration issued permits for railroads to accept freight for shipment. Under this arrangement, shippers were required to deliver their goods promptly, and railroads were assured of cars in which to move them. Congestion at terminals and at export points was thus avoided. Cross hauls of bituminous coal were avoided under the terms of a Coal Zone plan. Twelve standard types of freight cars and six standard types of locomotives replaced over 2,000 styles of freight cars and nearly as many styles of locomotives.

The reason for going into this much detail on the plan of government control over the operations of railroads is that until the time of the war, the policy of Congress, of the Interstate Commerce Commission, and of the courts had been to enforce competition at all levels of operation and in all geographic areas. Economies that amounted to millions of dollars were realized in the span of 18 months of government control, simply because competition was avoided as much as possible. Government officials were so impressed with the results that the bill authorizing the return of the railroads to private management in 1920 also authorized many monopolistic practices in the name of increased efficiency and lower cost operations. Discussion of the Transportation Act of 1920 will be given in Chapter 22.

The Impact of Railroads on the Economy

The impact of railroads on economic development after the Civil War was probably as great as the influence of any other stimulatory factor. In previous sections their impact on the westward movement and on the settlement of farmland has been discussed. Some coverage has also been given to their contribution to the geographical specialization of industry and the expansion of markets. The remaining aspects of railroad influence concern finance, capital markets, and the demand for productive resources.

Derived Demand for Inputs. Railroads were the best customers of the iron and steel industry during the late 19th century. In operating over 250,000 miles of track, and in expanding the total railway net, the lines had a high level of demand for rails and railroad cross ties. A certain amount of these materials was needed to maintain existing trackage, while the remainder was used in laying new tracks. When justified by the volume of traffic, double tracks replaced single ones and four tracks augmented double-track systems. Heavier rails gradually replaced some of lighter weight. Wooden bridges and trestles gave way to those of steel construction. And shortly before World War I, cars of wooden construction were replaced by cars of steel, mainly to insure the safety of passenger and freight cargoes.

Railroads were among the first corporations to demand the services of secretaries, stenographers, typists, file clerks, and other types of office workers. To house the work and workers that were required by railroad managements, large office buildings were constructed in headquarters cities and at division points along their routes. Such construction created markets for materials and supplies and for labor that was not utilized directly by the railroads themselves. Millions of dollars in wages were paid to hundreds of thousands of workers, who in turn spent their wages on such consumers' goods as were available during the war. The economic impact of this spending, although it cannot be quantified, was substantial. For the railroads themselves employees at all levels increased in number from 749,000 in 1890 to 2,076,000 in 1920. Wages and salaries increased from $445.5 million to $3,754.3 million during the same period. Table 15-1 indicates clearly the high rate of increase.

Table 15-1
Railroad Employment and Compensation—1890-1920

Year	Number of Employees (000)	Compensation (000)
1890	749	. . . . . .
1895	785	$ 445,508
1900	1,018	557,265
1905	1,382	839,945
1910	1,699	1,143,725
1915	1,548	1,277,663
1920	2,076	3,754,281

Source: U. S. Department of Commerce, Bureau of the Census, *Historical Statistics of the United States. Colonial Times to 1957* (Washington: U. S. Government Printing Office, 1960), p. 437. Adapted.

Railroads were the largest consumers of bituminous coal throughout the entire 1865-1920 period. In fact, until after World War I, railroad locomotives were powered almost entirely by steam generated by burning bituminous coal. The first electrification of a main line road was for a distance of less than four miles through the Baltimore tunnel of the Baltimore and Ohio Railroad in 1895. A few years later trains that entered New York City were required to be powered by electricity. That policy resulted in the electrification of all main lines as far as Stamford, Connecticut, on the east; Harriman, New York, on the north; and Manhattan Transfer to the south and west.

Other than to power locomotives across the Rocky Mountains on the old Chicago, Milwaukee and St. Paul Railroad, these were the only major moves away from coal. Employment was given to coal miners whose services would not have been required otherwise. Rolling stock was required to haul coal from the mines to coaling stations along the main lines of railroads, especially those lines whose rights-of-way did not enter or border upon coal-bearing regions. Employment was provided in the construction and maintenance of coal cars, which increased the wages paid to labor. Increments to the national income that resulted from coal production were distributed to the company shareholders and bondholders. Since coal was the largest class of revenue traffic for some railroads, its contribution to national income was distributed to the holders of the securities of these lines. Looked at from this point of view, the production of coal and its distribution throughout the country made a contribution to national income that was not matched by any other one resource.

Table 15-2

Railroad Tax Accruals—1890-1920
(000)

1890	$ 29,806
1895	38,146
1900	44,445
1905	58,712
1910	98,035
1915	137,775
1920	279,272

Source: *Historical Statistics of the United States. Colonial Times to 1957*, 1960, p. 434. Adapted.

Taxes. Taxes paid directly by the railroads came to a total of $29.8 million in 1890. By 1920 they had increased to a total of $279.3 million. Table 15-2 itemizes tax accruals over this period. Note that these figures are for railroads alone. They do not include taxes paid by persons whose property was made more valuable by the presence and operations of railroads. The actual importance of these taxes did not lie in their absolute size or amount. It lay in the fact that many school systems, many counties, and many localities depended indirectly on the railroad taxes for much of their revenues. Railroad property was usually assessed on the basis of its total value in a given state, and then tax receipts were apportioned to the various counties on the basis of the proportionate amount of the property they contained. Cities and counties advertised the number of railroads that serviced them and the number of miles of track contained within their boundaries. These data were accepted as measures of dependable transportation services available to businesses. But they also may have indicated that other kinds of taxes were relatively low because of the traditionally high assessment of railroad property. Although the railroads may have been a major source of tax money, states, counties, and cities did little to promote their financial success once construction was completed.

Railroads as Investment Outlets. Railroad securities provided one of the largest outlets for the savings of the American people. Even so, without large amounts of foreign capital the railroads could not have been built as rapidly as they were. Though profits realized by American businesses were large, they were inadequate to meet the demands of the railroads for capital. An outlet was thus provided for the investment of foreign funds without in any way retarding the investment of domestic funds.

Investments of foreign capital in American railroads contributed heavily to the United States being an immature debtor nation. The investment of this very capital not only led to the exportation of foodstuffs and other raw materials, but also provided the physical equipment that lowered the costs of transporting commodities to cities along the East Coast to await their export. The impact of larger profits in American industry on the investment structure of railroads is shown in Table 15-3. These data show clearly the increasing reliance on domestic capital that helped in the transition from debtor nation to creditor nation by the end of World War I.

Table 15-3
Percentage of Foreign Stockholders in American Railways

	1890–96	1905
Louisville & Nashville	75	27
Illinois Central	65	21
New York, Ontario & Western	58	12
Pennsylvania Lines	52	19
Philadelphia & Reading	52	3
New York Central & Hudson River ..	37	9
Great Northern	33	2
Baltimore & Ohio	21	17
Chicago, Milwaukee & St. Paul	21	6

Source: Adopted from W. Z. Ripley, "Foreign Capital in Railways of the United States," *New York Journal of Commerce,* December 6, 1911.

COMMUNICATION

Communication media, like the railroads, had become national or even international in scope by the time of World War I. Apart from vastly improved postal service on the domestic scene, electronic marvels such as the telegraph and the telephone provided efficient, almost instantaneous communication across the country and even around the world.

The Telegraph

Although there was a rapid increase in the number of messages sent by wire after 1846, the telegraph industry experienced its most rapid growth and development after 1865. The name of Thomas A. Edison will be linked forever with that development, and not simply because he began his working career as a telegraph operator. Between 1860 and 1910 he applied for at least 1,000 patents to improve telegraph technology. His development of the quadruplex system that permitted the sending of four messages simultaneously over one wire made possible a rapid increase in the volume of business without a concomitant increase in equipment. Probably his most important contribution to the industry was the two-wire universal stock ticker, which continued in use with few alterations until well after World War I. Marshall Lefferts, head of the commercial news department of Western Union Telegraph Company, foresaw the importance of the invention and asked Edison to set a price on it. Edison thought that $3,000 was too much to ask, although he needed that amount to continue his experiments. But before he could make a decision, Lefferts offered him $40,000. Needless to say, Edison was overcome. He accepted the money, however, and put it to good use in the production of stock tickers and other electrical instruments.

Expansion of Telegraph Services. Because of the close tie-in between the telegraph industry and railroading, telegraph poles were set along railroad rights-of-way, and telegraph offices were found in almost all railroad stations. These offices handled commercial business as well as railroad messages. In some of the smaller towns in which offices were established, commercial messages were received and dispatched at railroad stations on Sundays, holidays, and after regular business hours when city offices were closed.

Miles of wire alone are not a good measure of growth in the telegraph industry, since technology made it possible to transmit many messages over the same mileage. But the number of telegraph offices and the number of messages do indicate the intensity at which the facilities were used once they were installed. Extension of telegraph service, which helped to determine this intensity, depended on a complex of factors including the mileage of wire, the acceptance of telegraph service as a commercial tool by the business community, and the adoption of the telegraph by the general public as a rapid and reliable means of communicating with their neighbors. Table 15-4 presents several time series for the period 1870-1920, showing clearly that acceptance and growth of the telegraph system was strong and widespread.

Individuals soon recognized the value of the telegraph, especially for sending messages over long distances in a far shorter time than by any other means of communication. Personal messages became common, typical among them being seasonal greetings, notices of times of arrival and departure, words of congratulation or of condolence, notices of accidents or illnesses, and notices of births and deaths. As a means of utilizing equipment and employee services that might be idle during certain hours, Western Union

Table 15-4
Western Union Telegraph Company—1870-1920

Year Ending June 30	Telegraph Offices	Miles of Wire (000)	Messages Handled (000)	Expenses (000)	Interest Expenses (000)	Dividends Declared (000)	Employees Number	Employees Wages & Salaries (000)
1870	3,972*	112	9,158	$ 4,539	$ 327	$1,035	. . . . .	. . . . .
1875	6,565	179	17,154	2,832	228	1,351	. . . . .	. . . . .
1880	9,077	234	29,216	5,863	435	3,280	. . . . .	. . . . .
1885	14,184	462	42,097	11,029	505	5,198	. . . . .	. . . . .
1890	19,382	679	55,879	13,701	898	4,955	. . . . .	. . . . .
1895	21,360	803	58,307	14,756	898	4,766	. . . . .	. . . . .
1900	22,900	933	63,168	16,934	991	4,867	. . . . .	. . . . .
1905	23,814	1,185	67,477	20,227	1,227	4,867	. . . . .	. . . . .
1910	24,825	1,429	75,135	24,544	1,951	2,987	. . . . .	. . . . .
1915	25,142	1,584	n.a.†	40,797	1,348	4,986	. . . . .	. . . . .
			Domestic Telegraph Industry					
1916	n.a.†	1,877	129,273‡	54,335	n.a.†	5,985	60,122‡	$46,953‡
1920	n.a.†	1,711	155,884	113,253	n.a.†	6,983	74,448	86,037

* Year ending December 31.
† Not available.
‡ Data are for 1917.

Source: *Historical Statistics of the United States. Colonial Times to 1957,* 1960, pp. 483-485. Adapted.

provided special services for customers in the form of night letters and day letters in which messages that did not contain more than 50 words were sent for the regular rate for a 10-word telegram. Night letters were delivered sometime during the following day, and day letters were delivered the same day they were sent, deliveries of both subject to priority of regular telegrams.

Results of sporting events were sent over the wires in time for them to appear in late evening editions of newspapers or in those of the following morning all over the country. The promptness with which the news was disseminated had much to do with popularizing sports, both amateur and professional. It also increased the sale of newspapers and provided employment for sportswriters. Insofar as advertising rates were based on total circulation, the extra sales could have carried the total circulation into a higher bracket.

Telegrams were delivered by young boys and men who might not have been employed otherwise. Except to nearby business firms, deliveries were made by bicycles or motorcycles. Since the messengers were familiar with the street plan of a given city, they were used by persons and by business firms that did not provide their own facilities to deliver packages and gifts. Telegraph delivery service obviously contributed to the demand for bicycles and motorcycles, and to the demand for repair and maintenance services. Before the automobile became generally popular, the bicycle industry constituted the largest market for rubber tires.

Impact on Economic Growth. The role of the telegraph companies in stimulating economic growth was an important one. For example, in 1920, 74,448 employees of such companies were paid a total of $86 million in wages and salaries. Another $7 million of dividends were distributed to shareholders. In that same year, operating expenses, including general property taxes, were $113.3 million. Implications are strong that the companies contributed heavily to the support of state and local governments through their tax payments.

Telegraph companies were among the larger outlets for various electrical appliances and equipment. Before the turn of the century, increases in the mileage of wire constituted a demand for iron wire. But after 1910 copper replaced iron as the conductor of messages via electrical impulse. The Western Union Telegraph Company alone was a borrower of large amounts of funds, and its interest expense of $2 million in 1910 shows the size of the income received by lenders.

The Telephone

Thirty-two years after the first message was flashed over telegraph wires, the human voice was transmitted by wire. Competition was keen, and technical problems were difficult, but Alexander Graham Bell was issued the initial patent for a telephone transmitter in 1876. Bell had become interested in transmitting the sound of the human voice via electrical impulses over wires in his efforts to teach deaf persons to talk. He discovered that if two reeds were tuned together, vibrations of one of the reeds could be transmitted to the other by electrical impulse. Once this fact was known, it was only a matter of time until the telephone became a reality.

Growth of the Telephone System. Not only was the first complete sentence transmitted by telephone in 1876, but a two-way transmission line was extended from Boston to Cambridgeport, a distance of two miles. From that small beginning, 47,000 phones were installed in the United States in four years, most of the phones belonging to the Bell System. In another year, wires had been strung the 45 miles from Boston to Providence. In that same year, a conversation was held via underground cable by persons who were a quarter of a mile apart.

In less than two years from the date the first patent was issued to Bell, people in Boston were talking to people in New York City, 235 miles distant. In 1892, telephone wires connected New York with Chicago, a distance of another 900 miles. But it was not until 1911 that wires were stretched from New York to Denver, 2,100 miles away, and it was two years more before they reached Salt Lake City, Utah. The first transcontinental line stretched a distance of 3,650 miles from Boston to San Francisco in 1915. Unlike its counterpart among the railroads, this line did extend from Atlantic to Pacific.

From the beginning of cable communication in 1881, the use of such media spread rapidly. The first long-distance cable between New York and Newark, New Jersey, was completed in 1902. Four years later it reached Philadelphia, 90 miles distant from New York. In 1913, the first conversation was carried on via underground cable between Washington and Boston, a distance of 455 miles. The extension of the cable to Washington was the result of a sleet storm that swept the Atlantic seaboard states on the occasion of the inauguration of William Howard Taft as President of the United States.

The distances over which the human voice was carried were impressive, but it must be remembered that the methods of erecting telephone poles and of stretching telephone wires were primitive compared with modern communications technology. Ditches in which cables were buried were dug by hand or by crude and relatively inefficient machines. Horses or mules were used in drawing plows or implements, and other teams were hitched to scrapers that moved the dirt back into place. Postholes were dug by hand and the labor of five or six men was required to set a pole. The crossbars on each pole were fastened securely by hand methods. Thousands of men were employed not only in installing the equipment, but in maintaining it. Various kinds of storms wreaked havoc on telephone and telegraph wires, and sometimes heavy rains interrupted service on underground cables.

Competition and Consolidation. The telephone industry developed under the aegis of free enterprise, and competition was a driving force that impelled rival companies to improve upon the quality of their services. When two or more local companies served a given community, duplication of facilities was an expense that was removed in time by the consolidation of the competing concerns. Before this event, if business firms wanted to be in contact with the maximum number of potential customers, it was necessary for them to have and to pay for the installations of each local company. These were the days when it was customary for housewives to order groceries and other items by telephone, and each store made one delivery or more by horse-drawn wagons every day. If the companies could not get together, several sets of telephone poles and several sets of wires where one of each would have sufficed detracted from the beauty of the streets and created fire and storm hazards. The telephone business was one that was suited by its very nature to a unification of its facilities and its services, if not to direct monopoly control.

When big business and large-scale operations were first analyzed, the telephone industry was included among those whose unit costs decreased as the volume of business increased. Some years later it was discovered that this condition prevailed only up to the limitations of a given switchboard. The next step forward in understanding telephone costs was to realize that the cost of making possible the connection of any given phone with all others increased as the number of installed phones increased. Larger sized switchboards cost proportionately more than smaller ones to construct. One reason for the continuing search for improvements in this industry has been the necessity of defeating the increasing unit costs that normally accompany an enlargement in the list of telephone subscribers.

That this list did increase is emphasized by a comparison of the number of phones in 1890, 227,900, with the number of installations in 1880, which was 47,900. During the last ten years of the 19th century, 658,000 new phones were installed. In 1910, a total of 4.9 million phones were in operation. The number of subscribers more than doubled in the next ten years, reaching a total of 12.6 million telephones in service. Note that these data apply only to the Bell System and to independent companies that had connected with Bell. The number of phones that were not connected with Bell reached a peak of 2.3 million in 1907. Their number declined steadily to 727,000 in 1920. These figures serve to verify the tendency for monopoly control to emerge in the telephone industry.

Postal Service

The fact that the telephone and telegraph businesses were conducted at a profit throughout this entire period, while the Post Office Department showed only nine years of profitable operations, does not justify saying that the Post Office was operated less efficiently than were privately owned businesses. In 1918 and 1919, when the federal government adopted a rate policy that would yield revenue for the war effort, the net return from rendering postal services averaged $69 million. The problem lies in the fact that postal rates are determined by the government, and not by a free market mechanism. During much of our history, rates have been set at levels that were too low to yield sufficient revenues to cover costs. Apart from the obvious political forces behind postal rates, other determining factors have included service, education, culture, and keeping people informed of national and international happenings. There is no way of measuring the profit that has accrued to the federal government from the sale of stamps that have not been used for postage and cancelled. Sales of stamps to philatelists must be measured in thousands of dollars each year.

Growth in postal services did not mean a concomitant growth in post offices. The number of post offices reached its peak in 1901 when 76,945 were in operation. The decline from that number to 52,641 took place during years in which postal services were being expanded. Urbanization outmoded some post offices, and others were closed in favor of an extension of rural free delivery services from fewer offices in more central locations. This service was initiated in 1896.

Table 15-5

Number of Post Offices and Number of Post Office Employees as Percentages of Total Paid Civilian Government Employees for Selected Years—1871-1921

Year	Number of Post Offices	Total Number of Paid Civilian Employees	Number of Post Office Employees	Percentage Post Office to Total
1871	30,045	51,020	36,696	72
1881	44,512	100,020	56,421	56
1891	64,329	157,442	95,449	61
1901	76,945	239,476	136,192	57
1911	59,237	395,905	211,546	53
1921	52,168	561,142	251,300	45

Source: *Historical Statistics of the United States. Colonial Times to 1957*, 1960, pp. 496, 497, 710. Adapted.

What may have been the most important postal innovation of this period was the institution of parcel post service in 1913. The service was long in coming, since it had been advocated by some of the rural reform movements 40 years before. Among the economic impacts of establishing the new service was the adverse effect on the volume of business handled by privately owned express companies, hence on their financial conditions. Beneficial impacts included the large increase in the volume of business done by mail-order houses, such as Sears, Roebuck and Co. and Montgomery Ward & Co., and the realization of a rise in the level of living of persons residing in rural areas.

Post Office Department workers formed one of the largest groups of civilians employed by the federal government. In 1871, they constituted 70 percent of all civilian government employees. During the next 50 years, their number increased from 35,696 to 251,300. But because of the rising importance of other governmental agencies, they made up only 45 percent of the civilian employees at the end of the period. These figures may be slightly distorted by the large number of war workers who were still on the payroll in 1921. After the sudden termination of the war in 1918, the government continued to perform many functions which required the retention of wartime help or even the addition of new workers to the payroll. A detailed view of Post Office Department growth is given by the data in Table 15-5.

QUESTIONS FOR REVIEW

1. (a) Explain the impact of the Civil War on railroad construction.
   (b) How did railroad construction west of the Mississippi River differ from that east of the same river in its relation to the economic development of the two regions?

2. What factors stimulated the construction of railroads west of St. Louis and Chicago?

3. (a) How were federal land grants related to the development of railroads?
   (b) Were land grants unilateral agreements? Explain clearly.

4. (a) How was railroad construction financed?
   (b) How did the level of fixed costs affect railroad rate policy?

5. (a) Why is *Munn* v. *Illinois* a milestone in the history of railroad regulation?
   (b) What conditions led to the passage of the Interstate Commerce Act?
   (c) Under what authority did Congress act when it passed such a bill?

6. (a) What was the decision in the *Smythe* v. *Ames* case?
   (b) What conditions brought about the passage of the Railroad Valuation Act in 1913?

7. (a) Why did the federal government take over the operation of the railroads in 1918?
   (b) How successful was the government in operating the railroads? Explain fully.

8. (a) Why was a federal tax placed on railroad passenger fares?
   (b) What is the present status of that tax?

9. (a) What forms of communication accelerated the development of domestic markets?
   (b) What other impacts on the economy resulted from the operation of systems of communication?

10. What were the economic impacts of the operation of parcel post service?

SUGGESTED READINGS

Arrington, Leonard J. "The Transcontinental Railroad and Mormon Economic Policy," *Views of American Economic Growth: The Industrial Era,* edited by Thomas C. Cochran and Thomas B. Brewer. New York City: McGraw-Hill Book Company, 1966.

Chandler, Alfred D., Jr. (ed.). *The Railroads: The Nation's First Big Business.* New York City: Harcourt, Brace & World, Inc., 1965.

Ellis, David N. "The Railroads and Their Federal Land Grants: A Critical Review," *Issues in American Economic History,* edited by Gerald D. Nash. Boston: D. C. Heath & Company, 1964.

Gilchrist, David T. "Albert Fink and the Pooling System," *Views of American Economic Growth: The Industrial Era,* edited by Thomas C. Cochran and Thomas B. Brewer. New York City: McGraw-Hill Book Company, 1966.

Greever, W. S. "A Comparison of Railroad Land Grant Policies," *Economic Change in America,* edited by Joseph T. Lambie and Richard V. Clemence. Harrisburg, Pa.: Stackpole Books, 1954.

Healy, Kent T. "Transportation," *The Growth of the American Economy,* 2d ed., edited by Harold F. Williamson. New York City: Prentice-Hall, Inc., 1951.

Henry, Robert S. "The Railroad Land Grant Legend in American History Texts," *Issues in American Economic History,* edited by Gerald D. Nash. Boston: D. C. Heath & Company, 1964.

Jenks, Leland H. "Railroads as an Economic Force in American Development," *Economic Change in America,* edited by Joseph T. Lambie and Richard V. Clemence. Harrisburg, Pa.: Stackpole Books, 1954.

Kirkland, Edward C. *Industry Comes of Age: Business, Labor, and Public Policy, 1860-1897.* New York City: Holt, Rinehart & Winston, Inc., 1961. Chapters 3-6.

Miller, George H. "Origins of the Iowa Granger Law," *United States Economic History: Selected Readings,* edited by Harry N. Scheiber. New York City: Alfred A. Knopf, Inc., 1964.

Chapter 16

INDUSTRIAL CLIMATE;

GROWTH OF MANUFACTURING

INDUSTRIAL CLIMATE

Throughout the Colonial Period, development of manufacturing industries was retarded (1) by attempts that were made by the English Parliament to enforce its mercantile program against its colonies and (2) by natural and economic conditions, many of which were more influential in preventing the birth of manufacturing in the United States than was British mercantilism. After the removal of man-made restrictions, many years were required to overcome these natural and economic barriers. To hasten the process, the federal government saw fit to pass tariff legislation that tended to give encouragement to the investment of capital by overcoming, in part, the cost disadvantages that beset many entrepreneurs in their efforts to organize land, labor, and capital into effective operating and producing firms.

Largely because of the influence of the southern delegation in Congress, the years of 1789-1816, 1833-42, and 1846-61 had been years in which tariffs had been used to yield revenue to the government rather than to afford protection to northern industries. Even tariffs that were intended to afford a flow of revenue to the government provided some protection to American industries, unless the tariffs were levied only and entirely on products which the United States was not suited to produce because of climate or lack of natural resources. The resourcefulness and enterprise of American businessmen overcame some of the economic factors that deterred the development of manufacturing, and the industrial climate was extremely favorable to such development. How industry developed prior to 1860 under the aegis of this climate formed the subject matter of Chapter 9.

Natural Resources

In searching for the basic reasons that accounted for the growth of industry in the United States after 1865, one concludes that it must have been a more favorable industrial climate that stimulated industry to extend itself beyond the horizons it had attained in 1860. In that climate natural resources were of the utmost importance. No matter what the population, the capitalist spirit, the potential market, without material resources upon which to work they would have been wasted. At best they would have remained as latent potentials. At the start of this period, the products of extractive industries became the raw materials of manufacturing industries and the fuel that powered them. Coal—anthracite and bituminous—which was the most important fuel in 1865 gradually relinquished its primacy to petroleum products, gas, and electricity. Wood, which had been basic to the construction industry, gave way in favor of iron and steel, brick, cement and concrete. The agricultural staples became the raw materials for diversified manufacturing industries. The products of mines were increased by developments in copper, lead, zinc, gold and silver, bauxite, silica, and cement. In addition to technological advances in these industries, there were developments of other industries and in other industries, the impacts of which were widespread.

Among the nonmetallic resources were stone, sand and gravel, marble, granite, salt, phosphate rock, sulphur, lime rock, and clay. These products became the cargoes of railroads and of inland waterways and were shipped to all corners of the country. As items of revenue freight, they were much sought after by the agencies of transport because they were shipped in bulk and required no special handling.

Population

Population was an important factor of industrial climate. Its growth tended to overcome the scarcity of labor, and simultaneously it provided an expanding market for the products of American industries.

An important aspect of the growth of population that made the industrial climate more favorable to employers was the immigration of thousands of people from European countries who came to join the working classes and not to become entrepreneurs or owners of farmlands. If these people had not already acquired the skills that would enable them to take their places in American factories, mills, and mines, it did not take long to teach them. Labor for transportation and service industries was equally as important as was an adequate supply of intelligent and capable industrial labor. From that population were drawn the entrepreneurial skills without which American industry could never have been organized.

The American people were imbued with the capitalist spirit, which meant that they were willing to take chances on the possibility of incurring losses as well as of receiving profits from the investment of their savings. The availability of risk capital was a *sine qua non* of our industrial development. Profits of successful enterprises became venture capital for others. To the extent that native supply of industrial capital overcame the traditional scarcity of that productive factor, the demand for foreign capital tended to decline. Stating it another way, opportunities for the investment of foreign capital in the United States tended to decline and to become less attractive to foreign investors. That development was one of the steps that led to the United States becoming a mature debtor nation. The increasing importance of commodity exports was concomitant with this relationship.

Markets

The westward movement was accompanied by an expansion of internal markets for capital goods and for consumer goods alike. The extension of the railway net not only served to open up new territory to settlement but also provided the connecting link over which the products of eastern manufacturing industries reached these new markets. If markets be considered a means by which buyers and sellers of goods were brought together, transportation and communication facilities were integral parts of the market and constituted a portion of the industrial climate. In discussing the expansion of markets that took place throughout this period, homage must be paid to the extent to which both geographical and industrial division of labor and specialization were extended. People themselves became more and more dependent upon the market for consumers' goods. As industrial firms became more highly concentrated they also became more specialized. Because of comparative cost situations, regions became specialized in their productive efforts. One of the impacts of the intensification of specialization and division of labor at the levels of labor, industry, and regions was to develop larger and more complex markets without any increases in population numbers.

Power

In the absence of cheap and ample sources of power, industry would never have come of age. Even today, in seeking new locations for industrial sites, one of the positive determining factors that molds decisions is that of power and its cost. The development of industry parallels the development of sources of power and making it available to industry at low cost. Steam power had already imparted mobility to industry. Petroleum, gas, and electrical energy were harnessed as never before during this period to power the wheels of industry. Industrial units could not have become as large as they did had it not been for power. Mechanical power needs no rest periods. Controlled correctly, nonanimal power is relentless in the force it exerts through the instrumentality of capital equipment.

Business Organization

The organization of business firms provided outlets for the investment of capital. The firms demanded some nonskilled labor and some labor at various levels of technological skills. Wages and other costs to these industries constituted incomes to the thousands of recipients of these payments. These incomes were spent in purchasing the products of an untold number and variety of other industries. Part of these incomes was channeled into taxes, interest, and savings. Sectional economic barriers were broken down. Geographic division of labor and specialization of industry were the outcome of the operation of free enterprise in which price and profit potential were the guiding lights. True, developments in the many areas of specialization were not always in balance with each other, or with the demand for their products, and improved technologies resulted in many economic dislocations. The results of these imbalances and of some of the problems that arose out of these economic dislocations furnish some subject matter for Chapter 21.

A favorable industrial climate was enhanced by the wide acceptance and use of the corporate form of business organization. That acceptance included (1) the business fraternity itself, (2) the courts, and (3) the general public. Business leaders were quick to grasp the advantages of the corporate form of business enterprise over either the single enterprise unit or the partnership. General incorporation laws made that form available to potential promoters and entrepreneurs on a competitive basis, although it was through the use of that same device that competition was restricted and monopoly control became a reality.

Financial Instruments. The general public had placed its stamp of approval on the corporate form of business organization when it (1) absorbed issues of corporate stock as evidences of ownership interest in them, and (2) accepted bonds as security for money that was lent to them. That the public had confidence in corporations, in the growth of the industries to which it lent money, in the men whose names were connected with the corporations, or in some combination of these factors, is manifest in the classification of bonds it absorbed—mortgage, debenture, and income.

Mortgage bonds were available for investors who were unwilling to assume entrepreneurial risks in corporations. Corporations gave as security to these persons a pledge of some property asset, either real or tangible. Land and buildings were pledged by industrial and commercial enterprises. Railroad terminals and way stations, railroad rights-of-way, and rolling stock were pledged to protect the holders of railroad bonds. *Debentures* were issued by corporations whose credit standing in the loan market was so high they were not required to pledge any asset values to protect bondholder-creditors. *Income bonds* carried a little more risk than either mortgage or debenture bonds, as interest on them was not payable unless it was earned currently. *Refunding bonds* were sold to refinance an entire issue or part of one that was not retired when it matured. *Reorganization bonds* were issued to enable corporations to continue to operate after they had gone bankrupt. These bonds were issued to reduce the fixed charges of corporations in their efforts to regain financial stability and liquidity. Refunding and reorganization bonds were accepted by people who desired a little more apparent security than was offered in the ownership of common and/or preferred stock.

Wage Policies. The mere fact of corporate organization was not a deterrent to the hiring of employees at any level of operation. Corporate firms, in general, were able to pay the competitive, going rates of wages. There are some indications that they may have paid higher salaries to top management officials than were paid by noncorporate firms. There also is evidence that, where corporate firms were the sole employers of labor in given communities, they paid their labor lower wages than were paid under more competitive conditions. That policy was by no means restricted or peculiar to corporate firms, but labor was frequently attracted to a community more because of the presence of a corporate business and the opportunity for employment it afforded than by a knowledge of the level of wages it paid.

Use and Abuse of Corporate Power. The creation of corporate entities meant that the continuity of their operations was not related directly to the continued existence of their officers or owners, nor to the connections of these persons with particular corporate entities. Some corporations probably were able to command more capital than any one person or small group of persons would have invested in one business situation. The reader may recognize immediately that this situation did not apply to Henry Ford and to the Ford Motor Company. This was one of the better known exceptions to the general principle that proved the rule. The corporate existence of the railroads, the steel companies, and the telephone and telegraph companies has transcended the lives of the men who first promoted them.

Anybody who is at all familiar with the development of the corporate form of business organization will admit that some fraudulent schemes have been perpetrated in the names of corporations against an innocent public, and millions of dollars have been lost thereby. Corporations did not always operate on the same level of ethics and morality that their individual officers and managers would have maintained had they been held responsible for their acts. The degrees of objectivity that governed the relationships between corporations and their employees and between corporations and the general public were modified after the turn of the century through the development of employee relations and public relations programs. As will be shown presently, the attitude of "the public be damned" as enunciated by William H. Vanderbilt in the 1880's was altered by the desire of corporate officials to vie with each other for the goodwill of the public as a form of corporate competition. After the government had made some disclosures via investigating committees or testimony in court actions, a certain amount of public resentment was created, one of the impacts of which showed up in a reduced volume of sales. Since these were the days before radio and television, the principal means of counteracting unfavorable publicity was through press releases, making after-dinner speeches, and in advertising copy.

The Tariff

An important aspect of the industrial climate in the United States after 1865 was its tariff program, if the use of the tariff could be dignified by that

Table 16-1

Tariff Receipts by the Federal Government—1856-1920
(000)

1856–1860	$ 272,443	Treasury surplus. Tariff lowered.
1866–1870	894,516	Continuation of wartime tariffs.
1871–1875	931,002	10 percent horizontal reduction in 1872.
1876–1880	732,971	As a whole, high level of rates was maintained.
1881–1885	1,009,816	
1886–1890	1,082,785	McKinley Act of 1890. Extension of protection.
1891–1895	884,308	1894. Moderation of protective principle.
1896–1900	925,444	Dingley Tariff, 1897. Highest level of protection yet reached.
1901–1905	1,300,584	
1906–1910	1,552,993	Payne-Aldrich Act, 1909. Downward revision not serious.
1911–1915	1,446,817	Underwood Tariff, 1913. Free list enlarged. Degree of protection lowered.
1916–1920	1,126,507	

Source: U. S. Department of Commerce, Bureau of the Census, *Historical Statistics of the United States. Colonial Times to 1957* (Washington: U. S. Government Printing Office, 1960), p. 712. Adapted and enlarged.

word. Just as the tariff was one of the important sources of revenue for the federal government prior to 1860, so it continued to be the channel through which the government received much of its revenue until after the adoption of the income tax amendment to the Federal Constitution in February, 1913, and its implementation later that year. From a strict economic point of view, tariff issues may have been given more consideration than was warranted by their impacts upon the American economy. There is no question but that the effects of tariffs or their absence were reflected on the balance sheets and income statements of many manufacturing firms, but their actual effects upon the entire country have not been given much emphasis. For instance, a tariff on the importation of certain iron and steel products that were made overseas by the use of modern (at the time) technologies made possible the continuance of the charcoal method of refining iron ores long after it had become a relatively high cost process in world markets. Not only did the protective tariff protect American producers of iron and steel products, it "protected" or perpetuated the use of high cost outmoded technologies. The impact of the situation was that it tended to raise prices of steel products to American consumers above what they otherwise would have been required to pay. That situation prevented consumers of steel from obtaining the utmost in commodity values out of the limited amounts of money they had to spend.

Impact on Railroads. Since railroads were the best customers of steel products in America, they were compelled to pay higher prices for their steel rails than if they had been able to import rails free of duty. To that extent their fixed costs were padded, and interest charges on bonded debt were higher than they otherwise would have been. Freight rates and passenger fares, undoubtedly, were raised to cover the high interest cost of railroad capital. Remembering that railroads were constructed largely with borrowed funds, that situation may have figured prominently in bankruptcies and financial reorganizations of American railroads.

The Tariff Act of 1870 imposed a duty of 1¼ cents per pound of steel, or $28 a gross ton. Since the price of Bessemer steel rails in England at that time was about $50 a ton, the cost of steel to American buyers was $78 a ton, neglecting the costs of shipping steel over 3,000 miles across the ocean. After 1873, as the price of steel fell in England, the levy of $28 a ton became a higher and higher percentage of its price. When the price of steel fell below $28 a ton, as it did in 1877, the tariff was more than 100 percent protective. In 1880 the average price of steel in England was about $36 a ton; in 1881 it was $31. In the United States railroad corporations were required to pay $67 and $61 per ton respectively. This explains one factor that contributed to the high construction costs and the overcapitalization of the American railroads which have become such troublesome items in attempts to establish fair and reasonable railroad rates that will yield a fair rate of return of investments in railroad capital.

Impact on Steel. Customs duties on imported steel products were lowered in subsequent acts of Congress, and improved technologies reduced the costs of manufacturing steel in the United States, but it was not until 1897 that the average price of steel in this country was less than its average price in England. Tariff legislation in 1894 imposed a duty of $7.84 a ton on imported steel, and it remained at that level until the passage of the Payne-Aldrich Bill in 1909. In spite of the fact that the duty on steel raised the cost of the imported product above the price of steel that was manufactured in this country, Americans continued to import steel. Whereas the largest market for steel had been the American railroads, steel was now being used in the construction industry; and the capacity of the American mills was not large enough to meet the market demand for it. Steel made the construction of skyscrapers possible. Engineers and designers found that bridges, tunnels, and tubes, in which steel replaced wood, were cheaper in the long run and more durable. Not to be overlooked was an increased margin of safety.

Impact on Wages. With protection, steel companies were enabled to pay wages that were competitive with wages that were paid by employers to workers who were employed in industries that operated at a comparative advantage over similar industries in foreign countries. To the extent that labor was lured away from industries that did not need and were not given protection into industries that were protected, employers in unprotected industries were compelled to pay wages above the level that otherwise would have prevailed. Other factors did not remain the same, and a large immigration of unskilled workers from southeastern European and Slavic countries provided a new source of relatively cheap labor with which to man new and expanding American industries. The emphasis that has been placed on the iron and steel industry in the above analysis does not imply that other industries did not feel similar impacts of protective tariffs.

Impact on Customs Receipts. Since the degree to which a tariff actually protected American industries should have been reflected in customs receipts, the fact that customs duties were large raises the question: How could commodities continue to be imported simultaneously with the protection that was afforded American industries? The answer to this perplexing question is explained in the realization that, while the general tone of tariff legislation was protective, products that either could not be grown or were not produced in this country continued to be imported and were a source of customs receipts. These particular levies were imposed for the purpose of obtaining revenue; at the same time they may have afforded some protection to producers of substitute products.

To illustrate the point—if the effect of the duty on tropical foods was to raise their domestic prices within price ranges for which their demands were elastic, American consumers substituted foodstuffs that were produced at home or upon which there was no levy. There is some question as to what extent a relatively high price for bananas will induce increased purchases of apples, oranges, pears, or other fruits in season. To the extent that the demands for imported foods were inelastic, American buyers paid higher prices for approximately the same volume of goods. Without casting any reflections or aspersions upon members of Congress, it is doubtful if the level of economic education had penetrated the Halls of Congress to the extent that the average member understood the concepts of *elasticity* or of *inelasticity of demand*. Tariff rates were determined on the basis of bargaining between members of Congress who weighed data that were presented by lobbyists who represented the industries whose participants were attempting to obtain legislation that was favorable to them individually and collectively. The impacts of such legislation upon the entire country were of little concern to them. There also was a certain amount of trading between the members of Congress—I will vote for the legislation of which you are in favor if you will support the bills I favor. None of these approaches to determining tariff rates or schedules was objective or scientific, but they were realistic.

Development of a Tariff Policy. Control of Congress passed from the delegates of the Southern States during the War between the States, and the years of carpetbag rule did not restore southern influence in Congress. It seems that a more or less permanent policy of protection was adopted by the Republican party which controlled the actions of Congress almost uninterruptedly from 1861 to 1910. There were some variations as to the respective tariff acts and the completeness with which the program of protection was implemented by act of Congress, but there was no question but that the idea of protecting American industries permeated the collective thinking of Congressmen throughout the entire period.

Compensatory Principle. Probably the most unique characteristic of American tariff policy was the retention of a protective tariff on wool. To compensate for a tariff of three cents a pound on raw wool, a rate of 12 cents a pound had been imposed on woolen goods in the tariff legislation of 1861. This compensatory principle was retained until 1894 when it was abolished. It was restored in the Dingley Tariff Act in 1897. By a combination of the use of ad valorem duties and specific duties, a "net" protection of 55 percent was given, compared with a 25 percent coverage only 30 years earlier.

Frequent alterations of the tariffs on wool were just as disturbing to the woolgrowers as they were to the manufacturers of woolens. Sheep ranchers had to adjust themselves to raising sheep for mutton when the price of wool was low. This tended to increase the supply of mutton on the market and to lower its price, not because of any active change in the demand for mutton but almost solely in response to the change in the price of wool. Given a certain elasticity in the demand for meat, a lower price for mutton tended to increase the purchases of that meat in consumer markets and to decrease the sales of beef and pork. There was one factor, in particular, that did not remain equal and that made it difficult for sheep ranchers and for meat-packers to adjust themselves to price changes. Many people just did not like the taste of mutton and lamb meat and did not react to changes in their market prices. Manufacturers of woolen goods in the United States were afforded protection of 100 percent or more until the Underwood Tariff of 1913, under the terms of which the *compensatory principle* as applied to wool and woolens was abolished.

Did Protective Tariffs Protect? Another explanation of why commodities continued to be imported from European countries in the face of high tariffs that presumably were protective is found in the limited capacity of American industrial firms to produce in relation to the overall demand for their products. The country expanded so rapidly in population, in expanse, in national income, and in disposable income per capita, that the American people demanded more of many kinds of goods than American industries could supply when they operated at capacity. This condition left room to absorb imported products that supplemented those that were produced at home, and served to raise the level of consumer satisfaction that was derived from spending disposable incomes. Again, in many instances the quality of imported products differed from the quality of the same products that were produced in the United States. Many technicians and others, too, were convinced that German cutlery steel was superior to cutlery steel made in the United States. Articles of clothing that were designed and made in France, Italy, or elsewhere were better than their facsimiles that were made in this country. Chemicals, perfumes, dyes, textiles, and many other articles were purchased as much according to where they were made as they were according to their retail prices.

The Dingley Tariff. At about the time the rates of the Dingley Tariff (1897) became effective, the downward movement of prices came to a halt. Throughout the first decade of the new century, consumer prices took a decided turn upward, and people complained about the high cost of living. Not many years earlier thousands of persons were unable to earn a livelihood with which to pay any cost of living. Salaried persons, schoolteachers, and government employees felt the strain of attempting to stretch the purchasing power of their dollars which did not increase in number as rapidly as did costs and prices. One of the reasons that was given as the cause of the rising cost of living was the tariff. Even though it was difficult to determine to just what extent the tariff was the culprit, not knowing how else to account for it, and knowing the Dingley Tariff had imposed the highest import duties in history, people in almost every walk of life could get a hearing by talking about the tariff. The effect of that talking was to initiate a demand for lower rates on commodity imports.

Even though William Jennings Bryan, who carried the banner for free trade, was defeated at the polls, pressure was so great that something be done that the Taft administration was forced to take action in the form of the Payne-Aldrich Bill in 1909. That Act was thrown together as a sop to the Democrats. Attempts were made by the Republicans to establish an "impartial" tariff board, whose members were to make a detailed study of the degrees of competition American goods encountered from imported wares and make recommendations accordingly. *Logrolling* was to become a thing of the past. Customs duties were to be based upon economic conditions, rather than upon the influence in Congress of professional logrollers. That change could not be made and was not made while President Taft held office. The Payne-Aldrich Bill was anything but a free trade bill. It can be said that it was less aggressively protective than had been the Dingley Bill.

Unrest Caused by Tariffs. Little did it matter to the American people that the rise in prices that was translated into a rise in the cost of living was worldwide, or that it may have been due to a rapid increase in the production of gold after 1898—they held the tariff responsible. There was a political upheaval in the complexion of the 60th Congress that reflected the dissatisfaction of the electorate with the conservative program under the leadership of President Taft. It was not until 1913 that the Underwood Tariff gave expression to those who favored a change in policy. Not since 1894 had such inroads been made against the policy of protectionism, and Professor Taussig brings out the fact that not since 1846 and 1857 had such low barriers been set up against a flow of commodity imports from foreign countries. The expectation by some that the cost of living would be lowered was "doomed to disappointment." Preparation for war in Europe, later, participation in World War I, disturbed the relationships upon which our export-import trade was based. International trade after the war was premised on foundations entirely different from those that prevailed before the war.

Banking Facilities and the Monetary Situation

One phase of the industrial climate in America that was much more favorable to the development of commerce and industry is found in the areas of money and credit. While the National Banking System was given to the country as a Civil War measure in 1863, it lent a certain amount of stability to the credit structure. It also contributed to the instability of the credit structure, as was presented in Chapter 14. While there was no aspect of central banking and many systemic features were lacking, national banking did result in a certain amount of uniformity of organization and operation of commercial banks. They received their charters from the Comptroller of the Currency and were subject to the provisions of the National Banking Act regardless of the respective states in which they were located. National banks were authorized to issue national bank notes, which turned out to be absolutely safe, sound, and secure, though they had some other defects. State bank notes were taxed out of existence, so that there was a uniform note currency the country over. The fact that national bank notes circulated at par facilitated the consummation of exchanges.

Commercial Banks. In addition to the national banks, there were several thousand commercial banks that received their charters from the respective states. These banks competed vigorously with national banks in the granting of commercial loans. Since the minimum capital for national banks was $25,000 in towns of 3,000 population or less, state banks were found in many smaller communities filling the needs for the extension of credit. While it is true that commercial banks had been organized primarily to extend short-term credits, it was the granting of credit that extended the markets for manufacturing concerns that were not able to extend credit directly to their customers, especially those at the consumer level.

Other Financial Institutions. Investment banks and insurance companies extended long-term credit to industrial concerns with which they financed their capital operations. Stockholder-owners of corporations either were unable to or did not desire to furnish all of the fixed capital of corporate organizations. Investment banks not only underwrote large capital issues, they sold them to the investing public in smaller amounts. Until about 1920, people with relatively small amounts of savings placed them on deposit in savings banks which were customers of investment banks. All in all, one set of financial organizations facilitated the raising of sufficient capital to organize and construct the productive facilities of industries; another set of financial organizations facilitated the day-to-day operations of these same industries, including sales of their products at the retail level.

Monetary Stability. In addition to a bank note currency that was relatively stable compared to the heterogeneity of notes that circulated prior to 1860, United States notes, or greenbacks, were issued by the federal government. While it is difficult to say that at first they added strength to the currency, they did add volume, and after 1879 they were made redeemable at 100 cents on the dollar. Any inflationary influences they may have exerted upon prices when they were issued were probably offset in later years by the over-all industrial development of the country, so that by 1900 when their volume in circulation was stabilized and a partial gold reserve was provided to secure their ready redemption, their presence may have prevented a deflationary tendency instead of inducing an inflationary one.

Most certainly the establishment of the Federal Reserve System in 1913 provided a still more favorable climate within which the American economy could function. It did more to systematize banking and credit at the commercial and consumer levels than had been done on a nationwide basis since the closing of the Second Bank of the United States in 1836. The adoption of the gold standard in 1900 formalized a situation that had existed since 1873, but it was the large amounts of new gold that found their way into the monetary system and caused prices to rise that did more to put an end to demands for monetary reform than any other factor. Rising prices are always favorable to the development of commerce and industry, and to tempering demands for economic and political reforms.

GROWTH OF MANUFACTURING

While manufacturing industries were not new at the time of the outbreak of the War between the States, that event served to stimulate activity in a number of industries, as is shown in Table 16-2 by the increase in the number of establishments between 1859, two years before the start of hostilities, and 1869, four years after their close. To complete war contracts before it was too late, textile mills increased in number and became more highly mechanized. To overcome the shortage of farm labor that resulted from the call for volunteers to enter the Armed Forces and the military draft, farm machinery was used more extensively and larger sized machines were used. The impact of an increase in immigrant labor was felt in an increase in the number of farm units, especially in the Middle Western States, and in the number of factory workers in urban communities in the New England States, and in New York, Pennsylvania, and New Jersey. Military forces made heavy demands upon the manufacturers of uniforms, caps and hats, boots and shoes, saddles and other harness wear, wagons, transport and supply trains, canvas goods—tents, tarpaulins, and other items—rifles, guns, mortars, cannon, caissons, and ammunition for them all. Production of all these items and many others was stepped up to new high levels of output. Railroad equipment of all kinds was in great demand—locomotives and tenders, boxcars, flatcars, passenger cars, rails, railroad ties, spikes, and bridges. Additions, replacements, and enlargements taxed the capacity of existing plants and hastened the construction of new ones. When the war was over, factories and mills that had been engaged in producing for the war effort were converted to providing goods for civilian consumption. As has always been the case in time of war, even prior to wars of the "all-out" variety, civilian goods were in short supply and had to be replenished.

Table 16-2

Growth of Manufactures—1859-1919
Factories Including Hand and Neighborhood

Year	Number of Establish- ments	Proprietors and Firm Members	Nonpro- duction Employees	Production and Related Workers (Average for Year)	Value Added by Manu- facturing (000)
1859	140,143	......	......	1,311,246	$ 854,257
1869	252,148	......	......	2,053,996	1,395,119
1879	253,852	......	......	2,732,595	1,972,756
1889	353,864	......	457,139	4,129,355	4,102,301
1899	509,490	......	380,739	5,097,562	5,474,892

Factories Excluding Hand and Neighborhood

Year	Number of Establish- ments	Proprietors and Firm Members	Nonpro- duction Employees	Production and Related Workers (Average for Year)	Value Added by Manu- facturing (000)
1899	204,754*	......	348,100	4,501,919	$ 4,646,981
1904	213,444	225,115	493,297	5,181,660	6,019,171
1909	264,810	272,421	750,330	6,261,736	8,160,075
1914	268,436	258,560	911,899†	6,602,287	9,385,622
1919	270,231	249,865	1,371,885	8,464,916	23,841,624

* A slight difference in identifying manufacturing establishments may account for some of the decline in the number of establishments that occurred in 1899 when hand and neighborhood establishments were excluded from enumeration. Prior to that time a minimum product value of $500 served as the criterion, after which the value of shipments from an establishment had to be $5,000 or more for it to have been counted.

† The increase in the number of nonproduction employees after 1909 may reflect the increase of office and bookkeeping clerks that were required to keep adequate cor- porate records for purposes of compiling corporate income taxes. After 1913 more employees were required to keep records for purposes of meeting individual income tax requirements.

Source: *Historical Statistics of the United States. Colonial Times to 1957,* 1960, p. 409. Adapted.

Some Impacts of the Civil War

The war made it possible to resolve the problems involved in locating the eastern terminal of the first transcontinental railroad, and four years after the return of peace that line became a reality with its eastern terminal at Omaha, Nebraska. Not only that, but land grants to railroads stimulated their construction west of the Mississippi River to new high levels. One impact of that activity was measured in terms of increases in the volumes of output of the many industries and business firms that furnished the railroads, railroad management, and railroad labor with supplies and equipment of all sorts. Another impact was felt in those industries whose raw materials were transported over the rails from their sources of natural deposit to factories where they were processed, whence the finished goods were transported to their respective markets. Still another impact was felt by those industries in the East which were brought into contact with new markets for their products in the West. New farms were opened up and grain elevators rose to new heights at convenient intervals along the railroad rights-of-way, breaking the monotony of the skyline in the Plains States.

Since the farm units west of the Mississippi River, in general, were less self-sufficient than had been those along the Atlantic coastal plain, grain elevators acted as nuclei for early settlements which later grew into towns and cities. Railroad sidings and loading platforms, general stores and post offices, barber shops and saloons, blacksmith shops and farmers' supply houses, and, in time, one or more banks constituted the business sections of those towns. Western farmers shipped their surplus farm produce to eastern markets in exchange for manufactured goods they could use in their homes and on their farms. Some of these goods had been imported from Europe; more and more of them were products of eastern factories and mills. Settling new lands in the West and Southwest continued to widen the markets for manufactured goods of the East. Many are the reasons for believing that the construction of the railway net between 1870 and 1910 was the most energizing factor that sparked the development of American manufacturing, trade and commerce, and of financial institutions that provided the necessary working capital as well as fixed capital.

To meet the demands of these new markets, industries in the East became larger in size and some of them of larger scale operations. The products of the combinations and trusts that were formed to combat the economic disadvantages of increasing competition could not and did not penetrate all of the local markets, nor were other markets saturated with them.

Rise of Capital Goods Industries

This period was characterized by a development that had a greater impact upon our international trade relations than did the increases in the size of the production units which led to increases in the volume of output. Between 1870 and the turn of the century, industries that produced capital

goods replaced those that produced consumer's goods among the largest ten
or fifteen industries in the entire United States.

The increase in the number of establishments is a measure of the increase in the demand for office equipment—typewriters, desks, chairs, tables,
filing cabinets, and other items. Elevators, both freight and passenger, eased
the burden of going up and down stairs. They became a necessity as office
buildings, factories, and warehouses were erected higher and higher above
their ground floors. Not to be forgotten are the many hotels that were erected
to accommodate not only commercial travelers but those persons who were
in attendance at business meetings and conventions. Since these latter were
held at the state, district, and national levels, and as there was a tendency
for the different organizations to select different sites in which to hold them
from year to year, transient and convention hotels were built in a large number of cities throughout the United States. Not only did the actual construction of these buildings channel orders to manufacturing industries, furnishing
them constituted large-sized orders for manufacturers who operated at different levels of production. Basements and subbasements became more than
mere cellars and storage rooms. These buildings created huge demands for
structural steel. Fire-resistant walls, window frames, and floorings replaced
more flammable materials. All these and many thousands of other items were
the products of manufacturing industries whose raw materials, in turn, were
the products of extractive industries.

The relative importance of the leading manufacturing industries is revealed in the changed position of their ranking among the leading industries
as shown in Table 16-3. Textile and textile products and food and kindred
products were in first and/or second rank throughout the entire period under
observation. Most, if not all, of the following leading twelve industries
operated at the producers' goods level. The manufacture of capital goods
that were used in making other capital equipment that was needed in the
production of consumers' goods surpassed in importance the industries that
produced consumers' goods. Capital goods industries made the physical,
mechanical, and material equipment that took larger sized production units
and those of larger scale proportions off the drawing board. Capital goods
industries increased in efficiency to the degree that their products were sold
in competitive markets in foreign countries as commodity exports of the
United States. One of the economic impacts of that development was the
disturbance of the traditional pattern of exporting foodstuffs and raw materials
and importing manufactured goods.

Approach to Economic Maturity

To the extent that the United States began to export manufactured goods
and capital equipment, similar items were not imported from European
countries. As the American market for the products of European manufacturers declined, so did the ability of these people to continue to absorb

Table 16-3

Rank of Manufacturing Industries by Book Value of Capital by Decades—1879-1919

Industry	1879*	1889*	1899*	1899†	1904†	1909†	1914†	1919†
Textile and Textile Products ..	1	1	2	2	2	2	2	2
Food and Kindred Products ...	2	2	1	1	1	1	1	1
Forest Products	3	3	3	4	5	5	5	5
Iron and Steel	4	4	5	5	3	3	3	3
Machinery (except Transportation)	5	5	4	3	4	4	4	4
Leather Goods	6	7	8	10	9	9	10	8
Chemicals	7	6	6	6	6	6	6	6
Nonferrous Metals	8	10	7	7	8	8	8	9
Stone, Glass, Clay	9	9	9	9	7	7	7	10
Printing and Publishing	10	8	10	8	10	10	9	12
Paper and Pulp	11	11	11	11	11	11	11	11
Petroleum Refining	12	12	13	13	13	13	13	13
Transportation Equipment	13	13	12	12	12	12	12	7
Rubber Products	14	14	14	14	14	14	14	14

* Covers factories having production of $500 or more.

† Includes custom and neighborhood shops.

Source: *Historical Statistics of the United States. Colonial Times to 1957,* 1960, p. 411. Adapted.

American commodity exports. From early colonial times British investors had invested large sums of capital in America on a free enterprise basis, partly because the rate of return on capital invested in the United States was higher than the return received from capital investments in England. These investments were among the factors that contributed to the debtor position of the United States in its relationship to that country. The fact that we were exporting manufactured goods and capital equipment to European peoples was a manifestation of our approach to the state of economic maturity as an industrial nation. This was the stage in which the investment of foreign capital in the United States was declining. In its relationships with other countries, the United States was altering its position from that of an international debtor nation to become an international creditor nation.

Fundamental Causes of the Increase in Manufacturing

Just as there were several natural and economic factors that were more effective in retarding the development of manufacturing industries throughout the Colonial Period than were man-made restrictions by the British, so were there several natural, economic, and political factors that provided stimuli to the development of manufacturing industries.

Natural Resources. The natural resources of the United States included almost every variety of soil and climate that are found north of the tropics. The combination of rich soils and abundant rainfall contributed to the growing of a wide variety of products. Sectional specialization in growing agricultural products was characteristic of our development after 1865. Among the market outlets for the products of commercialized farms were the manufacturing industries that used wheat, corn, barley, rye, oats, sugar, hemp, cotton, tobacco, dairy products, fruits, vegetables, hogs, cattle, and sheep as raw materials in the initial stages of their production processes. Almost all kinds of lumber that were used in woodworking and in construction were found in the vast forest regions of the United States. The one exception was trees that needed tropical climate, soils, and rainfall.

Mineral resources appeared to be inexhaustible. They were in large enough variety to support industry at its high level of technological development. They were obtainable at reasonable production costs, especially in comparison with their costs in areas that were external to the United States. Coal deposits were not only found in great abundance, they were so widely scattered throughout the United States that costs of shipping coal by inland waterway or by rail to manufacturing centers were little more than nominal. In 1859, the first well (Colonel Drake's) gushed oil near Titusville, Pennsylvania. That event marked the beginning of a rapid development of all aspects of the petroleum industry from the prospecting of new petroleum reserves, through its transportation to refineries, thence to market in the form of kerosene, gasoline, fuel oil, and its many by-products. Natural gas was discovered in or near deposits of petroleum. Gas not only was piped to cities where it was used for lighting, heating, and cooking, its use in industry provided a cheap fuel and steady heat, not to mention the time saved in obtaining instantaneous heat. The presence of gold and silver ores, copper, lead, zinc, and bauxite added to the stimulus afforded the industrial climate. Stone, marble, and brick clay deposits were found in widely scattered regions and served as the basis for the development of mining and manufacturing industries.

Table 16-4
Patents Issued by the United States Patent Office—1866-1920

| Five-Year Periods | Total | Individuals | Corporations | | To Residents of Foreign Countries |
			United States	Foreign	
1866–70	58,734	. . . . .	. . . .	. . .	1,877
1871–75	60,976	. . . . .	. . . .	. . .	2,706
1876–80	64,462	. . . . .	. . . .	. . .	3,392
1881–85	97,156	. . . . .	. . . .	. . .	6,222
1886–90	110,358	. . . . .	. . . .	. . .	8,599
1891–95	108,420	. . . . .	. . . .	. . .	10,667
1896–1900	112,188	. . . . .	. . . .	. . .	12,794
1901–05	143,727	20,896	4,370	280	17,241
1906–10	171,466	24,750	6,040	380	18,206
1911–15	185,981	24,756	7,580	520	21,688
1916–20	197,136	31,742	11,540	610	17,308

Source: *Historical Statistics of the United States. Colonial Times to 1957*, 1960, pp. 607-608. Adapted.

Attitude of Government. The government contributed to the creation and maintenance of a climate that was favorable to the development of industry (1) by protecting American manufacturers from competition with imported foreign goods, and (2) by stimulating invention and discovery through the issuance of patents. Undoubtedly, the tariff was a device used by Congress to give encouragement to the investment of industrial capital and to its profitable use. Just to what extent tariffs were the mothers of trusts prior to 1913 is somewhat of a moot question, but there is no question but that they created a favorable industrial climate. This is neither the time nor the place to discuss the desirability of the government issuing patents to protect the property rights of inventors in the uses of their inventions and dis-coveries. The fact remains that Congress did pass patent laws, and it may not be far from wrong to assume that in many instances they gave encourage-ment to experimentation and research. In instances where such encourage-ment was provided, patents tended to protect the property rights of those persons who made contributions to the economic processes of production. The fact that the United States Patent Office has made an effort to give patents only to those inventions that have given promise of having some practical application does not even imply that all such items have been exploited by some entrepreneur.

Attitude of the American People. The American people were ready and willing to accept the fact of industrialization and its economic, social, and political impacts. Among its economic impacts was the creation of a depen-dent wage earning class of people. These people found that it became more and more difficult to become landowners, farmers, and/or entrepreneurs, even in a small way. Individually they did not seem to share in the increase in the national income in proportion to the effort they expended. The gap in terms of income distribution as well as in the ownership of wealth between them and capitalist landowners was widening. They were forced to accept a low scale of living that was more or less taken for granted by the more wealthy classes.

Not only was the fact of urbanization accepted, the impacts of increasing densities of population were not disturbing to most people, at least not sufficiently so to arouse them to take any remedial action. The low scale of living of wage earners was made manifest in the growth of slum areas in which many of them lived. Lack of running water, heat, ventilation, light, fresh air, and sanitary facilities contributed to a low consumption level for large segments of urban populations, and raised the incidence of sickness and disease among them. Many wage earners did not exercise the right of suf-frage, let alone run for or hold public office. That resulted in officeholders representing the propertied classes. Many laws appeared to be more in the interest of property owners than in the interest of propertyless persons. All persons may have been equal in the eyes of the law, but wide divergencies existed between the economic opportunities of wage earners on the one hand and landowners and entrepreneurs on the other.

Localization of Industry

Many of the same factors that resulted in a localization of industry throughout the Colonial Period and in the first half of the 19th century continued to exercise their influences throughout the entire period under consideration. The westward movement had extended the geographical limits of agriculture, commerce, and industry to the West Coast; and new areas of localized economic activity appeared. No longer were areas in New England and other regions east of the Appalachian Mountains the only centers of concentrated industrial activity. Whether an industry located near the sources of its raw materials or near markets for its finished products depended largely upon the rate structures of transportation facilities.

Influence of Railroad Rates. In the latter half of the 19th century, railroad rate structures gave encouragement to the location of industries near the sources of their raw materials. This accounts for the movement of the boot and shoe industry away from Lynn and Brockton, Massachusetts, down to Brooklyn, then to St. Louis, Nashville, and to cities in Wisconsin. It was cheaper to ship the manufactured products to market than it was to transport cowhides longer distances. Values that were imparted to the hides by the manufacturing processes made the transportation costs small percentages of the values of the finished products, in this case, shoes. It is a fact, however, that the westward movement of the shoe industry did locate that industry near new centers of population. Cross freight charges from the West to New England and back again to the West were saved. Not only were freight rates saved, a more productive utilization of capital resources was effected by the move.

More Efficient Uses of Capital Resources. More efficient utilization of capital resources was brought about by the decisions made by the owners in an economic environment of free enterprise through the working of the profit system and not by some government planning commission. The iron and steel industry which had become localized in and near Pittsburgh, Pennsylvania, found new centers of activity in Cleveland, Ohio, and along the southern shores of Lake Michigan. After the coal resources of Colorado had been tapped, and iron ores were discovered nearby, Denver became the westernmost center for making iron and steel. In spite of the fact that iron ore, bituminous coal, and limestone were found near Birmingham, Alabama, the steel mills in that area produced only a small portion of the total amount of steel that was produced. High costs of mining the ore, difficulties that were encountered in refining the high phosphorous content ore, and a limited nearby market for finished steel—all worked against the mills in Birmingham producing more of that product. As the production of iron and steel moved westward, so did the industries that fabricated steel. Before some of the large steel companies undertook to fabricate their product in somewhat of a continuous process, separate plants were organized for that purpose. For all-round convenience and low cost operations they usually were located in the vicinity of steel mills.

Minneapolis and St. Paul became the flour milling capital of the United States because of their nearness to the wheat belt, their proximity to available waterpower that was harnessed to power the mills, and because of the development of adequate transportation facilities. In later years when the structure of freight rates was altered, it became more profitable to transport wheat in bulk near the markets where it was ground into flour. Rochester,

New York, benefited from this change in railroad rates. Fish canning industries were localized along the cities of the East and West Coasts. In earlier years that was accounted for in part by the difficulties that were encountered in keeping fish refrigerated until they could be processed. It also eliminated the necessity of paying freight or express charges on those parts of the fish that were inedible. Perishability was an important consideration in the localization of fruit canning and vegetable canning industries in California, New York State, and Maryland. Waterpower that was generated by many streams in the New England States in their dash for the ocean was harnessed by entrepreneurs in the textile industry as well as by those who operated vegetable canning mills. Atmospheric conditions and waterpower in addition to nearness to markets and the advantages of an early start were responsible for the localization of cotton textile mills in New England, particularly near Fall River, Massachusetts. The availability of risk capital and an adequate labor force exercised a positive influence in localizing textile mills in that region.

Machine Tooling. As long as manufacturing continued to be localized in New England, the machine tool industry was heavily concentrated in that area. Much of the work of machining tools required highly developed technical skills. Labor that had developed these skills was organized in relatively small-sized business firms, which were found in small towns in Vermont, Massachusetts, Rhode Island, and Connecticut more than in the remaining states in New England. When manufacturing moved westward, so did machine tooling in order to be near its markets. Cincinnati, Cleveland, and Toledo, Ohio; Detroit, and Chicago each listed machine tooling among the diversified industries that were found in these cities. Other smaller cities and towns were proud to count machine tooling among their industries that required highly skilled labor that enjoyed a relatively high scale of living among wage earners.

Established Reputation. Certain communities that had become well known for the excellence of their specialized, localized products attracted new firms whose products would compete with those that were already well established. These firms advertised that their shirts and collars were made in Troy, New York; their clocks and watches in Waterbury, Connecticut; their shoes in Brockton, Massachusetts; their flour in Minneapolis, Minnesota; their processed meats in Chicago, Illinois; their home insurance offices in Hartford, Connecticut; their writing paper was made in Holyoke, Massachusetts; children's games in Springfield, Massachusetts; mechanical toys in New Haven, Connecticut, and so on down the line of consumer products.

Prestige or the reputation of a community was not the only lure that attracted new firms to a given location. On the manufacturing and cost side of the question, such items as a well-trained labor force, available risk capital for investment, and transportation facilities each exercised its influence in determining the location of a new plant. The reserve labor force of firmly established industries became the nuclei of the labor forces of new concerns. People who had capital to invest had confidence in the stability and the success of given industries in respective communities. Bankers were accustomed to the peculiar credit needs of the industries they were accustomed to finance. Railroad transportation facilities had been provided in the way of railroad sidings, loading platforms, and other terminal facilities.

Concentration of Industry

A step towards the concentration of industries in localized areas was made when capital goods industries that were dependent upon the firms of localized industries for their markets began to locate near these markets. Cooperages that furnished hogsheads for the tobacco industry tended to locate near the markets to which tobacco farmers hauled their leaf. Companies that manufactured cigars and cigarettes tended to locate near the market for tobacco leaves. Another step towards the concentration of industry that localized still others was taken when the advance of technology made it possible to use the by-product waste materials of established industries as the basic raw materials of others. The meat-packers themselves used brains, livers, sweetbreads, tongues, and kidneys and sold them as "fancy meats." Other former waste products became the raw materials in the manufacture of bone meal fertilizer; brushes; toothbrushes; combs; casings for sausage, wieners, and frankfurters; cold meats; glue; lard; soap; and oleomargarine. Leather tanning and leather goods industries were established nearby. Shoe manufacturing also has followed somewhat the same pattern in locating near the centers of the meat-packing industry. Once it was said that every part of the hog except the squeal was being used in some product. Now that sounds are being tape-recorded, it is possible that even the squeal is used.

As long as slaughtering cattle, hogs, and sheep was done on a decentralized basis, by-products could not be utilized. Since the markets for home-killed meats, as they were called, was strictly local, not a sufficiently large number of animals was killed at any one place and at any one time for the waste materials to serve as raw materials for by-product industries. It was the fact of localization of meat-packing that yielded a sufficient and a continuously steady volume of waste products to support capital investment and business organization in by-product industries.

Not only did a reserve labor force influence the localization of industry, it contributed to the concentration of industries into what have become the industrial regions of the United States. These regions are characterized by the existence of a large variety of manufacturing, commercial, and service industries which have little or no relationship with one another. Diversification of industrial activity has lent stability to a regional economy. Industries that experienced different peak seasons drew upon the labor forces of industries that were operating at less than 100 percent capacity.

While many industries were becoming more and more highly mechanized by 1920, there was a large amount of heavy work and work that made little demand upon labor other than strong backs and hard muscles, which was performed by what was known as common labor. That labor shifted easily from one job to another, from one company to another, and any adjustments that were required in so doing were made in a short period of time. Wives and daughters of laboring men found it necessary or desirable to work in factories and mills; and, in many instances, it was the presence or the availability of that class of workers that attracted new firms to a given community. In those days it was common practice to pay women lower wages than were paid to adult men for doing the same kind of work. In some kinds of assembly work, women's fingers actually were more adept than men's and were preferred for that reason. Such preference, however, was not made manifest by the weekly contents of the pay envelope.

Growth of Selected Industries

The development of fuel constitutes the subject matter of a basic chapter in a treatise that describes the growth of manufacturing. While coal, oil, and gas are products of extractive industries, without them manufacturing would have remained a relatively small-scale enterprise that was located near sources of waterpower. It was the use of coal that imparted mobility to industry and that generated steam to power stationary and mobile engines. It was the burning of coal that made the manufacture of electricity a reality. Stretching ribbons of steel across the continent would have been futile without coal to burn in railroad locomotives.

Coal. Towards the close of the 18th century, a hunter camped for the night near Mauch Chunk, Pennsylvania. Before retiring for the night, he quenched his camp fire. Imagine his surprise the next morning to discover that the fire was still burning and at some distance from the bed of the original fire. The black rock upon which he had built his fire so that it would not spread turned out to be anthracite coal. Some years later, one Colonel Shoemaker hauled nine wagonloads of anthracite coal to Philadelphia but succeeded in selling only two of them. Rather than haul the remaining seven loads back home he gave them away. The firemen at a wireworks that had purchased his two wagonloads of coal tried for one day and a night to make it burn. They finally gave up in disgust and did not even take pains to close the furnace door. The following morning when they reported for work, they were amazed to find the firebox aglow with red coals. Left to itself and with air on the surface, the anthracite coal had ignited.

Anthracite. Anthracite coal was found in five counties in northeastern Pennsylvania. The restricted area in which it was found, together with the limited access to that region, made possible one of the most complete natural monopolies in the entire country. Five railroads controlled several canals that were dug in Pennsylvania and New Jersey, and the shipments of anthracite coal from mine to market were not permitted to reach competitive proportions. Because anthracite coal burned slowly with a blue flame at even temperatures and required little or no tending, it was in large demand as fuel for kitchen ranges and for heating purposes. Since it did not coke well, it contributed little to the development of iron and steel manufacturing. It burned with a clean low flame. A chimney was required to provide a draft but there was no smoke problem. Its cost, compared with that of other fuels, prevented volume sales in markets that were distant more than one hundred or two hundred miles from the mines, except along the southern shores of the Great Lakes to which markets it was transported by water.

Bituminous. Bituminous coal may have been the fuel that literally sparked American industry after 1870. Deposits of bituminous coal were distributed by nature over a much broader area than were those of anthracite coal. Monopoly control of its distribution as well as of its original production was impossible. One of the richest deposits of bituminous coal that was workable was found under the Appalachian Mountains in the states of Pennsylvania, eastern Ohio, West Virginia, Tennessee, Kentucky, and Alabama. Other deposits were found in Indiana, Illinois, and western Kentucky, all east of the Mississippi River. West of that river lower grades of coal were found in Minnesota, Iowa, Kansas, and Missouri. Still later, coal fields in Colorado and in other far Western States were mined. The product of these latter mines was used largely for local consumption.

Bituminous coal was burned in railroad locomotive fireboxes after the supply of wood for that purpose reached the stage of economic exhaustion. That stage was characterized by coal becoming cheaper to burn and more efficient than wood when used as fuel. In making coal available for (1) burning in fireboxes of railroad locomotives to keep trains in operation, (2) burning in furnaces in which heat was generated in public and in privately owned buildings to ward off the chills of winter, and (3) generating steam and electricity to turn the wheels of industry, transporting coal from mines to markets became one of the most important sources of operating revenue for many railroads. The Appalachian coal fields were penetrated by spurs of the Virginian, the Norfolk and Western, the Baltimore and Ohio, the Pennsylvania, the Louisville and Nashville, the Western Maryland and many other railroads for which coal became the principal item of revenue freight. The coal they could not deliver directly to consumers who were situated along their respective rights-of-way was delivered to connecting railroads. These latter lines shared in the revenue that was derived from transporting coal. Shorter lines penetrated the coal fields and carried this valuable product to tidewater, to the Great Lakes, and to other industrial centers. Compared with the tonnage that entered into domestic consumption, the exportation of coal throughout this period was relatively insignificant.

Impacts of Striking Miners. To guard against an interruption in the steady flow of coal to market caused by striking coal miners, power companies, manufacturers, and railroads stockpiled coal in order to protect themselves against a shortage of this important fuel. Otherwise, in case of a more or less prolonged interruption in the mining of coal, they would have been forced to close down their operations, or at best to operate on a reduced scale. To the railroads, loss of revenue was not the only economic impact of coal strikes. Reduction in the number of freight trains and in the frequency with which they operated caused unemployment of railroad employees and forced the railroads to operate at only a fraction of their capacity. Idle rolling stock, both locomotives and cars, was a heavy capital charge against their operations.

Other segments of the American economy felt the impact of coal strikes. Since unemployment insurance was not available to railroad employees upon whom idleness was forced, they were compelled to reduce their scales of consumption; and many of them resorted to the use of consumer credit. Merchants and professional men who depended upon the patronage of railroad employees found it increasingly difficult to collect payments for services rendered, and the volume of such services shrank. The reduction in the volume of transactions at the retail level of business was reflected in the reduction of business at the wholesale level, and ultimately the manufacturing segment of the American economy was retarded. These impacts brought about idle equipment and general unemployment all over the country due to the mutual interdependence of each segment of the economy upon all of the others. Communities that were strictly rural and agricultural felt them less severely than others.

Methods of Mining. Deep shaft mining proved to be more hazardous than strip mining. In mountainous areas some shafts were bored horizontally, others penetrated the bowels of the earth by more than 1,000 feet vertically. Ventilation, shoring up walls and ceilings, and preventing dust explosions posed problems for mining engineers. The Davey safety lamp was found on the visor of every miner's cap before a storage battery that could be carried in a coat or hip pocket was devised to provide current for an electric light bulb. Because of the highly competitive nature of mining coal and of selling it on the market, owner-operators of coal mines were compelled to keep operating costs at a minimum, frequently at the risk and cost of accident. It was not until the several states passed legislation that required the adoption of safety devices by the operators of all mines, and frequent inspection to enforce their use, that the toll of lives of miners was appreciably reduced.

Production Records. During the decade of the 1870's, more coal was mined in Pennsylvania than was produced in the two states of Illinois and Ohio, which ranked second and third respectively in coal tonnage mined. The five states of Pennsylvania, Illinois, Ohio, West Virginia, and Iowa produced

Table 16-5
Bituminous Coal Production—1870-1919
(000) tons

State	1870–79	1880–89	1890–99	1900–09	1910–19
Pennsylvania	130,601	277,782	509,276	1,114,774	1,608,720
Illinois	46,356	100,775	186,512	389,267	640,051
Ohio	41,150	79,738	132,535	252,327	334,143
West Virginia	14,027	37,442	123,157	355,951	750,309
Iowa	13,415	38,353	......	......	......
Alabama	.....	.....	55,379	115,297	......
Kentucky	.....	.....	......	......	221,375
Total	245,549	534,090	1,006,859	2,227,616	3,554,598
United States Total .	311,085	730,554	1,383,559	3,024,785	4,716,443
Percentage of Bituminous Coal Mined in Five States	66	73	73	73.5	75
Anthracite (Pennsylvania) ...	237,523	382,931	534,253	712,863	904,761

Source: *Bituminous Coal Annual, 1951* (Washington, D. C.: Bituminous Coal Institute [now National Coal Association]), p. 27. Adapted.

66 percent of the average total tonnage of 311,085,000 tons of coal that were produced in the United States throughout that decade. Throughout the following span of ten years, more than twice as much coal was mined in the entire United States, of which 73 percent was produced in these same five states. In 1890-99, the state of Alabama displaced the state of Iowa to become the fifth ranking coal-producing state, and in turn was outranked by the state of Kentucky in the second decade of the 20th century. By that time the leading five states produced 75 percent of the bituminous coal that was either raised to the surface or scraped from surface mines. It was in the opening decade of the 20th century that each of the leading five states yielded over 100 million tons of coal. Pennsylvania led them all with 1,114,774,000 tons. Indiana was a sixth state from which over 100 million tons of coal were mined during this decade. In the 10-year span that started with 1910, the state of Colorado joined this elite group.

Units of measuring quantities of coal, petroleum, natural gas, waterpower, and wood differ so widely that abstract numbers of the quantities of each of these fuels that were produced are somewhat meaningless. By reducing these divergent units to their equivalence in terms of bituminous coal, their relative participation in powering American industries is emphasized. At the same time the production of these fuels provided employment for thousands of workers and furnished outlets for the investment of capital. These industries provided new and larger markets for the products of capital goods industries, the growth of which was an outstanding feature of the overall economic development of the period under observation. (See Table 16-3, page 400) The anthracite coal industry participated in the growth of American industry between 1870 and 1900, after which it continued to expand in terms of output, but it declined in importance relative to the use of other fuels.

In 1910-19 it ranked second in terms of bituminous coal equivalent with a percentage of 11.9 of all fuels produced. Bituminous coal was far in the lead of all other fuels combined. In the decade 1910-19, 471,644,000 tons were produced which volume amounted to 63.7 percent of all fuels produced.

Competing Fuels. As important as coal was in contributing to the development of manufacturing industries, it encountered competition from petroleum, natural gas, and waterpower. Wood was still being used as fuel, but it was being rapidly replaced by the use of mineral and nonmineral fuels. While the use of waterpower in terms of bituminous coal equivalents increased, percentagewise its use remained fairly constant throughout the years 1870-1919. The use of wood as fuel to power industry and to furnish heat in cold weather declined absolutely as well as in terms of percentage to the total production of fuels. Reasons for this decline were (1) the exhaustion of forest resources, (2) its increased cost on the market, and (3) greater convenience and efficiency in the use of coal, petroleum, and natural gas.

Table 16-6 shows the volume of production of competing fuels in terms of their bituminous coal equivalents by decades from 1870 to 1920. The production of fuel wood was at its peak in 1870-79 at which time the production of natural gas was negligible, and petroleum was just beginning to be used to power industry. The use of anthracite coal reached its maximum in 1890-99 when its production amounted to 16.9 percent of the total production of fuels. In terms of volume produced, natural gas increased to a bituminous coal equivalent of over 25.5 million tons, but percentagewise it was approximately equal to the production of waterpower. In terms of the total amount of fuel that was produced in the first 20 years of the 20th century, coal constituted approximately 75 percent; but the output of anthracite coal had declined to 11.9 percent to offset the peak in the production of bituminous coal at 63.7 percent.

The production of fuel wood decreased from 64.0 percent of the total production of mineral fuels, waterpower and wood to 9.19 percent of that total in five decades; and the production of petroleum increased from 1.3 percent to 8.5 percent of that total in the same span of years. The production of all of these fuels increased 322 percent throughout the five decades for which data are given in Table 16-6 at a time when the production of fuel wood decreased by approximately 40 percent. Nothing is clearer than that fuel

Table 16-6

Production of Mineral Fuels, Waterpower and Wood in Terms of Their Bituminous Coal Equivalents (000 Tons)

Years	Bitumi- nous Coal	Per- centage of Total	Anthra- cite Coal	Per- centage of Total	Crude Petro- leum	Per- centage of Total	Natural Gas	Per- centage of Total	Water- power	Per- centage of Total	Fuel Wood	Per- centage of Total	Total	Per- centage Increase in Total
1870–79	31,109	17.7	23,038	13.1	2,336	1.3	n.a.*	....	6,755	3.9	112,556	64.0	175,797	....
1880–89	73,055	31.2	37,142	15.9	6,043	2.6	6,012	2.6	7,500	3.2	104,300	44.5	234,052	33.0
1890–99	138,356	45.0	51,819	16.9	11,848	3.9	9,218	3.0	9,014	2.9	87,019	28.3	307,274	31.2
1900–09	302,479	61.6	69,143	14.0	27,193	5.5	13,924	2.8	14,470	2.9	67,863	13.7	495,072	61.0
1910–19	471,644	63.7	87,756	11.9	62,862	8.5	25,657	3.5	24,752	3.3	67,625	9.1	740,625	49.5

* Not available.

Source: *Bituminous Coal Annual, 1950* (Washington, D. C.: Bituminous Coal Institute [now National Coal Association]), Table 7, pp. 26-27. Adapted.

wood gave way to other fuels during these years and by the close of World War I was no longer an important fuel that was used to power American industry. Even though the production of petroleum increased a little over 25-fold, it still ranked third, behind both coal and wood. In the following decade it was destined to take over second place as the source of fuel that was used to power American industry.

Power. One of the economic handicaps to the development of manufacturing industries during the Colonial Period was the absence of adequate and cheap power. By the close of World War I, sources of power competed with each other; and, insofar as state regulatory bodies permitted it, competition between them served to keep the rates within ranges that not only made them competitive it kept them at such levels that they were no longer handicaps to the development of manufacturing industries all over the United States. Most of the power companies operated at the level of free enterprise, although by the turn of the 20th century some municipalities operated their own electric light and power plants.

Electricity. In the earlier years of its use, electricity was generated in a large number of relatively small, local power plants. Experience, together with the development of technology, resulted in the construction of larger plants. Increased use of electrical energy was not accompanied by a proportionate increase in the number of generating plants. The use of electrical energy gave more mobility to industry than it acquired with the use of steam. Electrical energy could be transmitted miles, while steam power was used within a relatively short radius of the place where it was generated. The harnessing of waterpower with which to operate hydroelectric generating plants constituted one of the initial steps towards the production of electrical energy on a large-scale basis.

By 1920, 57,125,000 kilowatt-hours of electrical energy were consumed. Residential consumption amounted to 3,190,000,000 kilowatt-hours; 6,150,-000,000 kilowatt-hours were consumed by commercial enterprises, and the balance was consumed by industry. In 1912 the consumption of electrical energy by residential and commercial consumers was 910 million and 4,076 million kilowatt-hours respectively. In 1912 the annual average residential use per customer was 264 kilowatt-hours at the rate of 9.5 cents per kilowatt-hour for consumers of 25 kilowatt-hours per month. By 1920 the consumption per residence had increased to 339 kilowatt-hours, and the rate for consuming at the rate of 25 kilowatt-hours per month had decreased to 8.4 cents. In 1920, 34.7 percent of all dwellings received electrical service, but only 1.6 percent of farm dwellings were wired for electricity; 47.4 percent of urban dwellings were lighted by electricity. Electrical energy was not taken to American farms until the decade following the close of World War I. In 1902 the only publicly owned power plants were found at the municipal level, but by 1920 ten plants were owned and operated by the federal government. Approximately 10 percent of the 1,219 plants in 1902 were owned by municipalities, and in 1920 only 5 percent of 12,714 were publicly owned.

The names of two well-known men who were connected with the development of generating electricity are those of Thomas A. Edison and George Westinghouse. Every American is familiar with the saga of Thomas A. Edison. How he overcame the many obstacles to success is a Horatio Alger type story. There was one obstacle, however, that he was not able to overcome. Direct electric current (DC) with which he was experimenting when he introduced the incandescent lamp in the late 1870's could not be transmitted through wires for long distances. That fact alone prevented the development of centralized generating plants. Every community in which direct current was used for lighting purposes had its own independent generating plant. At about the same time, George Westinghouse was impressed with an invention in Europe of a secondary generator. This device made it possible to increase the voltage to send alternating current long distances, and then the voltage could be lowered by using another secondary generator near communities where the current was consumed. It was this transformer, as it is now called, that led to the wider use of alternating current, and to the erection of giant generating stations, some of which are hydroelectric. Edison Electric Companies in New York, New Jersey, Illinois, and elsewhere, still generate direct current for use within limited radii of the plants. Westinghouse triumphed over Edison, who was known as the "Wizard of Menlo Park," by improving upon the transformer and the use of alternating current.

Automobile. Mention of the names of Henry Ford, R. E. Olds, David Buick, and Henry Leland brings memories to those persons who witnessed the upsurge of the automobile and the decline of the horse as a draft animal. The Studebaker Company was one of the largest manufacturers of farm wagons whose management saw the handwriting on the wall and altered its capital equipment to get in on the ground floor in the manufacture of automobiles. Steam-powered automobiles had not proved to be practical and frequently gave trouble in cold weather. Electric power was not satisfactory, partly because storage batteries had not been perfected and voltage control devices were unheard of. The life of a battery was so short it limited the cruising radius of a car. At a time when car owners were demanding greater speed of locomotion, a car powered by electricity had no place.

The internal combustion engine was the answer to the power problem; gasoline proved to be the most satisfactory fuel; and pneumatic tires were more satisfactory than solid rubber or iron. Lack of good roads was a limiting factor to the general acceptance of the horseless carriage. Farm and country roads were in such poor condition that automobiles could traverse them in only the most favorable weather. City streets were being paved before 1910, and hitching posts and water troughs were becoming obsolete. Store deliveries were being made by truck, and businessmen were beginning to drive to their places of business. Patronage on streetcar lines was on the decline, and livery stables were becoming fire hazards in congested business areas.

Typical of the capital requirement of an automobile manufacturer was the $25,000 required by Henry Ford shortly after the turn of the century. Competition between inventors of automobile equipment was keen, and free enterprise made it possible for them to vie with one another for the favors of the motoring public. Many of the cars were not manufactured in the sense that rival "manufacturers" made all of the parts that went into the construction of cars. Many cars were the product of assembling parts that were made by different, and at first, independent firms. Different combinations of standard parts resulted in slight differences in different "makes" of cars.

Automobiles under the names of Brush, Knox, Reo, Cole, Marmon, Durant, Star, Locomobile, Stanley Steamer, Overland, Willys Knight, Chandler, and Apperson are found today only in museums. Some of them fell prey to competition; others were absorbed by other concerns when the combination movement hit the automobile industry.

Entertainment. Thomas Alva Edison developed a talking machine and a camera that photographed "moving" pictures. *Nickelodeons* [1] were the gathering places of old and young on Wednesdays and Saturdays until the moving picture theater displaced them in about 1910. The initial theaters were vacant storerooms in downtown areas of urban and rural communities alike. Indian, westerns, comic and travel pictures held their audiences spellbound. Howe's Tours took people on scenic tours at home and abroad for only 50 cents. Sound and motion effects lent atmosphere to the "tours" by simulating actual travel experiences.

QUESTIONS FOR REVIEW

1. What aspects of the industrial climate gave encouragement to the development of manufacturing in the United States?

2. How was the development of power related to the development of manufacturing?

3. How do you account for the prominence that was given to the tariff question after 1861?

4. What is the meaning of localization of industry? Illustrate and account for its existence.

5. What is concentration of industry? Why does industry concentrate in certain geographic areas?

6. What were the economic impacts of the development of the coal industry?

7. Has the automobile industry always been dominated by the Big Three? Why? or why not?

---

[2] A theater presenting entertainment for an admission price of five cents.

SUGGESTED READINGS

Bogart, Ernest L., and Charles M. Thompson (eds.). *Readings in the Economic History of the United States.* London: Longmans, Green & Co., Ltd., 1927. Chapter 21.

Chandler, Alfred D., Jr. "The Beginnings of 'Big Business' in American Industry," *United States Economic History: Selected Readings,* edited by Harry N. Scheiber. New York City: Alfred A. Knopf, Inc., 1964.

Kirkland, Edward C. "The Robber Barons Revisited," *American Economic History: Essays in Interpretation,* edited by Stanley Coben and Forest G. Hill. Philadelphia: J. B. Lippincott Co., 1966.

Kolko, Gabriel. "The Premises of Business Revisionism," *American Economic History: Essays in Interpretation,* edited by Stanley Coben and Forest G. Hill. Philadelphia: J. B. Lippincott Co., 1966.

Wright, Chester W. *Economic History of the United States.* 2d ed. New York City: McGraw-Hill Book Company, 1949. Chapters 33 and 34.

Chapter 17

INDUSTRIAL DEVELOPMENT,

CONCENTRATION, AND CONTROL

INDUSTRIAL DEVELOPMENT

Some of the factors that led to the extensive development of manufacturing, mining, commercial, and service industries likewise were responsible
for their intensive development. The rapid growth of the United States after
1870 was accompanied by an increase in the size of markets as well as by an
increase in their number. In some respects the increase in markets constituted
a widening of the areas within which goods were sold, as ribbons of steel
were laid across the country. In other respects the organization of a larger
number of outlets in local markets tended to increase their size. Urbanization in that era resulted not only in more people living and working in urban
areas, but more urban communities were created. That situation altered the
pattern of competition that had prevailed. Larger populations, larger and
wider markets, together with an extension of the railway net, permitted an
increase in the size of the firm. The business unit became larger. Sources
of dependable power aided in that development.

That the pace of economic activity after 1870 accelerated at a rapid rate
is revealed in terms of the *gross national product* of the combined efforts
of entrepreneurs at all levels of production and in all segments of the
economy. Even though the experiences of the Civil War emphasized the
importance of railway transportation from a military point of view, a rapid
development of the railway net took place under the stimuli that were found
within the framework of free enterprise. The formulation of what appeared
to be government policy at the federal level, by which grants of public lands
were used to stimulate the construction of railroads west of the Mississippi
River, was sponsored by those who stood to profit by that policy. Promotional
schemes, opportunities to realize speculative profits, and competition—all
served to hasten the laying of thousands of miles of steel rails across the
continent. Not only did the actual construction of railroads, railway rolling

stock, and terminal and way station facilities add to the gross national product of the United States, but extended transportation facilities widened the markets for goods that were manufactured east of the Mississippi River.

Increase in the Size of the Business Unit

The impelling motive to the size of the business unit becoming larger was the search for larger profits. These larger firms operated in mining, agriculture, lumbering, manufacturing, commerce, transportation, and in the generation and transmission of power. In transportation, short lines were united and combined end to end to become longer ones. In commerce and merchandising, specialty stores became larger; department stores were established; mail-order houses sent their catalogs to thousands of potential customers who lived in the Middle West, later in other regions; and chain stores covered the country so completely that scarcely a town of any size was without one. Firms that were engaged in manufacturing products for use by consumers increased the volume of their outputs. That was accomplished by increasing the use of machinery in production, by employing more workers, or by utilizing more machinery and more workers in combination. One measurable result of these developments was an increase in the value of the output of given firms or of given industrial organizations.

In the extractive industries, lumber companies purchased thousands of acres of land, some of which constituted reserves for future exploitation. Instead of only a few men cutting down trees on a few acres of land, hundreds of men cut down trees on hundreds or on thousands of acres. Here again, an increase in the size of the business unit was accompanied by the purchase of more land; by the employment of more labor; and by the use of more horses, saws, chains, and other equipment that was used in lumbering. The farm unit grew in size by tilling more land, by employing more horses and mules, by employing more multiple units of a given kind of farm machines and larger ones, and by employing more labor on the farms. Mining operations became larger by companies opening up new veins or more mines, by enlarging upon the area of underground activities, and by displacing hand-powered operations with horse or mule power and machinery. As new veins were opened up, more men and more equipment were required. More tonnage of coal, iron, copper, lead, and zinc per unit of operations was raised to the surface and readied for their respective markets.

When the size of the operating unit increased with little or no change in unit costs of production, it was merely a matter of a larger volume of business having been consummated at the same profit margin. Any increase in total net profits resulted from the same profit per unit of product having been multiplied by a larger number of units.

Large-Scale Production

Simultaneously with the increase in the size of the production unit and with the introduction of machine processes, a development toward large-scale production was taking place. When an increase in the volume of output of a production unit was accompanied by a reduction in unit costs of production, that firm was engaged in larger scale production. Large-scale production is a method of production the result of which is to lower unit costs. There is no absolute measurement of large-scale production. With improvements in technologies and in entrepreneurial skills, there is no limit to the extent of application of large-scale methods. Within the limitations of given technologies and of managerial skills at a given time, larger sized operations ceased to become of larger scale. Diseconomies of management were largely responsible for that condition. Profits of larger sized operations were not in proportion to increases in size because of leakages that management could not prevent.

Mechanization of Industry. The mechanization of industry was an approach to larger scale operations. All industries were not equally well adapted to the use of machinery. Actual processes of production had to be standardized because machinery could not readily adapt itself to irregular or to variable situations. Again, the product of machine production was somewhat uniform and standardized; and consumers had to accept a degree of uniformity and of standardization of the goods they purchased, consumed, and utilized.

One reason for the larger sized units of production was larger markets in which to sell their products. The reason for larger scale production, especially after 1870, was an effort by entrepreneurs to make profits in the face of falling market prices. Keen competition made it impossible for producers in many lines of activity to prevent market prices from falling. The best they could do in their efforts to maintain profit margins, let alone to increase them, was to attempt to lower unit production costs to counteract the effects of falling prices. Adopting large-scale methods of production was one of the efforts in an economic organization that continued to pay homage to free enterprise and in which the desire to make profits was the impelling motive that guided business leaders and inspired them on to greater efforts.

Limitations of Mechanization. One of the limitations upon the effectiveness of firms as they became larger was management. One of the factors that determined the degree of success of firms in lowering unit costs of production through the mechanization of industry was management.

Another limitation upon the extent to which industry was mechanized was the fact that all industrial efforts were not equally well adapted to the use of machine processes. The application of farm machinery to agriculture was a step toward larger scale operations in the short run; but there is some question that the operation of larger sized farms actually reduced the costs of producing cereal grains, tobacco, cotton, or whatever else was produced on them when figured on an annual basis. Not many, if any, farmers kept accurate accounts of costs, except total costs. Cost accounting systems were not applied to the operation of farms in general until after 1914.

Large-sized farm operations yielded larger incomes to their owners because larger quantities of farm products were sold rather than because of the lowering of their unit costs of production. In the long run, agricultural machinery of a given kind that was owned by individual farmers was used only a short time throughout a 12-month period, but its capital charges were incurred throughout the entire 12 months. When the fixed costs for an entire year were added to the operational costs (the variable costs that were incurred for a few days' or a few weeks' operation at most), unit costs were much higher. Farmers who operated relatively small farms in the Eastern States could not afford the heavy capital charges that accrued from the purchase of large-sized farm machinery. They could not take advantage of the use of farm tractors until Ford made a small-sized one that cost less, weighed less, and was more easily maneuvered than were large ones that were found on farms in the Plains States.

Just as Ford produced a motor car that "put every farmer and every laborer on the road" so did he make it possible for the small-scale farmer to derive the benefits that emanated from the use of the internal combustion engine as a power unit on the farm. Since the tractor was a mobile power unit, it was put to more uses than just pulling plows, harrows, mowers, reapers, and rakes. In the winter it was used in logging. It also generated the power that was used in cutting ice on lakes, rivers, and ponds, and in packing cakes of ice in sawdust in storage houses. The cost of these tractors was spread over activities throughout the year. In the Plains States the situation was somewhat different in that not only were the tractors much larger, much heavier, and less maneuverable, they could not be utilized for winter work. As with steam traction engines which they replaced, these new tractors were purchased by nonfarm entrepreneurs as capital equipment, and these entrepreneurs followed the harvest from Texas or Oklahoma to the Canadian border or beyond. Before tractors became a reality, 30-horse teams were used to pull large combines through the wheat fields in the Plains States. Mowing and threshing wheat in one operation was truly a large-scale operation, again not because of the large amount of wheat that was moved and threshed, but because of the saving of time and of money cost of production.

Cattle and sheep ranching were examples of large-scale operations in agriculture, not because of large numbers of heads of cattle or sheep that were herded on ranches, but because larger sized herds of cattle and of flocks of sheep were raised and tended at lower cost per head of each.

Retail Trade. One of the earliest attempts to apply large-scale production methods at the retail sales level of trade was the organization of department stores. It is difficult to say to just what extent that development was merely a form of integration of business at the retail level that was a step towards an increase in the size of the retail firm and to what extent it was a step towards larger scale production at the retail level. There is no doubt but that the potential for large-scale production was present; to what extent it became a reality is open to question. Management techniques were still hit-and-miss affairs, and accurate cost data were difficult to attain.

Department Stores. There is no doubt that, near the turn of the century or after, department store operations became of larger scale proportions. The notable feature of large-scale operations at the retail sales level was the absence of machinery. In some stores cashiering, making change, and wrapping packages were centralized in a business office; in others, packages were wrapped or put in bags in the respective departments, but money was handled in a central office. Wires or pneumatic tubes carried the small cash boxes back and forth between the sales counters and the cashier's office. Since salesclerks were departmentalized, they were familiar with their respective inventories; and little time was lost in locating the merchandise which the customer was interested in purchasing.

Chain Stores. By 1900 a strong movement to establish retail chain stores was in progress. Starting in 1859 with the founding of the Gilman & Hartford tea store in New York City, six years later it had expanded to 25 stores and had added a line of groceries. In a few years several chains of grocery stores had been organized. Prior to 1900, Jones Brothers Tea Company (later to become the Grand Union Company), Kroger Grocery and Baking Company, James Butler Grocery Company, five grocery companies in Philadelphia that merged to become the American Stores, H. C. Bohack Company, the Gristede Bros. of New York, The National Tea Company, The Jewel Tea Company, and many other food chains were organized.

The following chain stores were organized between 1900 and 1910:

1900—D. Pender Grocery Company (now Colonial Stores, Inc.); Hook Drugs, Indianapolis; Daniel Reeves (later acquired by Safeway stores); and Dockum Drug Stores, Wichita.
1901—United Cigar Stores; F & W Grand-Silver Stores (later H. L. Green Co.); Lane Bryant; A. L. Duckwall Stores Co.; Walgreen Co.
1902—J. C. Penney Company; Schultz Bros. (variety)
1903—Morris Stores (variety).
1905—Peoples Drug Stores.
1906—W. T. Grant.
1907—Louis K. Leggett Co.; Mading's Drug Stores, Houston, Texas; Fisher Brothers (grocery), Cleveland.
1908—A. S. Beck Shoe Corporation; Katz & Besthoff (drug), New Orleans.
1909—Western Auto Supply Company; Gallaher Drug Co., Dayton, Ohio; Hested Stores (variety), Fairbury, Nebraska.

Typically, chain stores undersold locally home-owned stores. They introduced the concept of cash and carry, no credit, no telephone orders, and no delivery. They depended upon low cost operations and a large volume of sales at low profit margins to bring financial success. Under the stimulus of making large profits, the chain store type of organization spread into the areas of drug, shoe, tobacco, variety, and apparel stores.

Variety Stores. Variety stores were known as "5 and 10-cent stores" for many years. Some of them extended their lines of merchandise to sell for from 25 cents to a dollar. These stores are usually thought of in connection with an increase in the size of the business firm, but they truly were large-scale operations because they operated at lower unit costs than did individually owned stores. In that period there was little talk of chain stores exercising monopoly controls in their respective areas of operations. They were in keen competition with home-owned stores and sometimes with other chain stores. Few closings of individually owned stores were traced to their failure to compete with chain stores. The home-owned stores still had something to offer their customers for which the latter were willing to pay. Telephone service, credit, and free delivery were still valued by many families who continued to patronize home-owned stores until after the close of World War I. If a family had a horse, it was not always convenient to hitch it to a carriage just to drive to a store to purchase a loaf of bread or a few other items. Streetcar service was awkward to use with a person's arms full of bundles, particularly if the cars were crowded. For people to carry packages home with them, even in their own cars, did not become a socially accepted practice in many walks of life until after 1920.

BUSINESS COMBINATIONS

The combination of business firms has been one way by which business units have become larger in size. Table 17-1 records the number of mergers

Table 17-1
Recorded Mergers in Manufacturing and Mining—1895-1919

Year	Recorded Mergers	Year	Recorded Mergers	Year	Recorded Mergers
1895	43	1904	79	1912	82
1896	26	1905	226	1913	85
1897	69	1906	128	1914	39
1898	303	1907	87	1915	71
1899	1,208	1908	50	1916	117
1900	340	1909	49	1917	195
1901	423	1910	142	1918	71
1902	379	1911	103	1919	171
1903	142	....	....	...	...

Source: U. S. Department of Commerce, Bureau of the Census, *Historical Statistics of the United States. Colonial Times to 1957* (Washington: U. S. Government Printing Office, 1960), p. 572. Adapted.

of manufacturing and mining establishments that took place between 1895 and 1919 inclusive. The impacts of the Sherman Antitrust Act and a depression are seen in the data for 1895-97. President McKinley's laissez faire policies toward combinations are reflected in the data for 1898-1902. The decision in the Northern Securities case combined with the fact that most potential mergers had become *fait accompli* by 1903 account for the decline in mergers through 1904. The panics of 1904 and 1907 discouraged the effecting of new mergers. The efforts of Presidents Theodore Roosevelt, William Taft, and Woodrow Wilson to keep business competitive are also reflected in the data.

Economic Causes

Since mergers were effected within the framework of free enterprise, the reason for mergers was, in general, to generate larger profits, allowing for the

Table 17-2

Gross National Product, Total and per Capita, in Current and in 1929 Prices—1869-1920

Years	Current Prices		1929 Prices	
	Total (billions)	Per Capita	Total (billions)	Per Capita
1869–1873*	$ 6.71‡	$165‡	$ 9.11‡	$223‡
1872–1876	7.53	171	11.2	254
1877–1881	9.18	186	16.1	327
1882–1886	11.3	204	20.7	374
1887–1891	12.3	199	24.0	388
1888–1893	13.1	204	26.1	405
1889–1893†	13.5	210	27.3	424
1892–1896	13.6	199	29.6	434
1897–1901	17.3	231	37.1	496
1902–1906	24.2	294	46.8	569
1907–1911	31.6	349	55.0	608
1912–1916	40.3	408	62.5	632
1917–1921	75.6	719	71.9	683
1919	78.9	755	74.2	710
1920	88.9	835	73.3	688

* Kuznets Concept figures.
† Department of Commerce figures.
‡ Average.

Source: *Historical Statistics of the United States. Colonial Times to 1957*, 1960, p. 139. Adapted.

fact that some business leaders sought more power in the realms of politics and economics.

Size of the Market. Under market conditions that were predominately competitive, one of the important factors that determined the total volume of output and the size of the production unit was the size of the market. That was determined, in part, by population numbers, in part, by that portion of the population whose consumption patterns included a given product. In addition to the latent desire for a commodity, people had to have units of purchasing power they could use and were willing to use in its procurement.

Increases in Gross National Product; Disposable Income per Capita. Increases in the national income that were distributed in such a manner that actual per capita incomes were likewise increased created a maximum potential to the expansion of markets. The data in Table 17-2 show that, in terms of 1929 prices, the gross national product increased somewhat steadily from a $223 average per capita for the years 1869-73 to a high per capita of $710 in 1919.

Disposable income per capita may be more pertinent in this connection. Disposable income per capita was the income out of which people purchased the products of the industries that had merged or that had become larger. In terms of 1929 prices (Table 17-3), disposable income per capita increased rapidly from an average of $427 for the 5-year period of 1897-1901 to $470 for the years 1902-06. These were the spans of years in which the merger

Table 17-3

Net National Product, National Income, and per Capita Disposable Income in Current Prices and in 1929 Prices—1897-1920 (Total Figures in Billions of Dollars)

Year or Period	Net National Product	National Income	Disposable Income		1929 Prices Per Capita
			Current Prices		
			Total	Per Capita	
1897–1901*	$15.8	$14.6	$14.1	$188.1	$427
1902–1906	22.1	20.7	20.0	243	470
1907–1911	28.9	27.2	26.4	281	500
1912–1916	36.9	34.8	33.3	349	538
1917–1921	70.3	66.9	61.0	578	548
1919	73.8	70.2	63.3	603	566
1920	83.0	79.1	71.5	672	688

* 5-year periods are annual averages.

Source: Office of Business Economics, *Survey of Current Business* (Washington: Department of Commerce, July, 1957), pp. 10 and 11.

movement was most concentrated. That movement slowed down after 1904, and so did the rate of increase in disposable income per capita.

More Distant Markets Closer Together in Time. Students of economic systems that have been referred to as capitalistic recognize at once that mergers, combinations, and larger sized production units were accompaniments of industrial and commercial expansion. Not only the fact of the extension of transportation facilities but their technological developments served to extend markets in space and to bring them together in time. In 1860 Charleston, Cincinnati, Louisville, Indianapolis, and Chicago were two days removed by railroad from New York City. No point along the entire length of the Mississippi River could be reached until the third day. By 1920 a two days' ride on the better trains took passengers from New York City to Denver, to all points in South Dakota and Nebraska, and to almost all points in North Dakota and Kansas. Cities that were situated along the West Coast were reached on the fourth day. Truly, in every sense of the word, the entire United States had become one large market and a free one in the sense that there were no trade barriers that hindered the movement of goods across state boundaries. Costs of transportation tended to increase prices or to reduce profits as commodities were sold at increasing distances from their places of manufacture. Reduced railroad rates for carload shipments tended to offset that influence.

Savings in Costs. Another cause of business combinations was the savings in overhead costs that resulted. Other factors remaining the same, the savings in cost resulted in larger profits. The profits of the combined business units were expected to be as large or larger than the sum of the profits of the smaller units had been before they were absorbed into larger ones. But, for many of their stockholders, profits of the larger units frequently were less than were the combined profits of the smaller units before combining. For any given management there appeared to be very definite limitations upon the size of the firm it could organize and operate efficiently. There may well have been limitations within the industries themselves.

Increasing Competition. Competition may have been the spice of trade, but many manufacturers learned the hard way that effective competition had had the effect of reducing prices and profits. Some of them learned that when prices of some commodities (those for which the demand was relatively elastic) were lowered, consumer response was somewhat pronounced in that the volume of sales increased in a proportion that was large compared with the percentage by which prices were reduced. Other manufacturers learned, also the hard way, that reductions in the prices of the goods they offered for sale gave little encouragement to prospective purchasers to buy more of them. Producers of commodities for which the demands were relatively inelastic discovered that the principal reaction of consumers to reductions in prices was such that they purchased these goods in very little larger quantities. In that manner consumers had more money out of their disposable incomes with which to purchase more items of some other goods, and some items of still other commodities. Small increases in the volume of sales of these goods were accompanied by declines in profits, and corporations were in business to make profits. It is not at all surprising that under these circumstances corporate managements sought means by which profits could be increased, or could be stabilized and not permitted to decrease.

Existence of a Capital Market. Another factor, and one that measured real progress of our economy, was the presence of a capital market, without which business combinations could not have been effected. When the required capital originated within the industries, the capital market was permissive in effect, as exemplified by the early oil and steel combinations. When the required capital arose external to the industry, the capital market may have been a causal factor, as exemplified by the J. P. Morgan Bank furnishing the capital required to organize the United States Steel Corporation.

Methods of Combining

One of the challenging factors in the study of mergers and combinations is the fact that they followed so many different patterns in arriving at somewhat similar objectives.

Horizontal Combination. *Horizontal combinations* were those of business firms that were operating on the same level or plane of activity—a union of retail firms, of wholesale firms, of railroads, of bakeries, of corporations that refined iron ore, and of many other firms that were engaged in similar or parallel activities. The formation of chain store organizations was one of horizontal combination and of horizontal expansion. The opening of new retail outlets by a grocery organization was an example of horizontal expansion and was an aspect of the growth in the size of the firm. There were more grocery stores at the retail level after the expansion than before.

Horizontal combination was brought about by the bringing together of business firms and business units that were already in operation. The fact of combination was accompanied by no immediate change in the number of locations at which business was done. A longer run impact may have been either an increase or a decrease in the number of retail outlets, depending entirely upon innumerable factors many of which were at the local level. Horizontal combination per se resulted in the concentration of business of a given kind into a smaller number of corporate owners. There may or may not have been an increase in the total volume of business that was transacted. If there were changes in the total volume of business transacted, they could have emanated from causes that were external to the organization of the firm. On the other hand, they could have been the result of changes in business policy within the organization.

Vertical Combination. Instead of increasing their capacities to produce at the same levels of operation, some firms undertook operations that were new for them and that were either a step forward or a step backward in the progress of commodities from their raw state to finished goods that were ready for the market. That process of development is described by the word *vertical* or by the phrase *integration of industry.* A steel company may have increased the number of blast furnaces from three to five, in which case its expansion was horizontal. On the other hand, and without entering into a discussion here of its reasons for so doing, it may have opened up a new coal mine and used its entire output in its own furnaces. By that development, the company became integrated; it had expanded vertically. Instead of expanding to a lower level of activity in relation to the production of iron and steel, the company may have added an entirely new unit in which iron and steel were fabricated into some product. That process was a forward step in the progress of iron and steel toward the market.

Again, the fact of vertical combination resulted in no immediate change in the number of production units. The same number of units was operating within the organizational framework of fewer corporate firms. To the extent that wholesale grocery firms absorbed retail outlets vertical combinations were effected. A grocery firm that integrated by opening up entirely new bakeries in which to bake the bread and pastries sold in its stores expanded vertically. If bakeries that were entirely independent of the ownership of a grocery firm were purchased by that firm, the latter became of larger size through the process of vertical combination.

Profit Results

The results of operating large combinations of industrial units were disappointing in terms of profits. Promoter-organizers of industrial combinations were those who profited the most and most often. A study made by the National Industrial Conference Board on Mergers in Industry arrived at the following conclusions: (1) Mergers were unable to increase profits or even to perpetuate them in industries that were subject to stagnation; on the other hand, an abnormal growth of new industries provided an industrial climate in which consolidated firms shared prosperity. (2) Industrial consolidations were not able to avoid sharp decreases in profits in years of general business depression. (3) When consolidations were handicapped by unmanageable financial structures which subjected them to fixed charges that were above their minimum earning capacities, they were unable to adapt themselves readily to new situations, or to take advantage of new opportunities, and were forced to relinquish their industrial leadership. (4) Business mergers offered no substitute for competent management.

Even though the profits of consolidated business units were disappointing in terms of what their integral components had realized in years gone by, they could have been higher than the profits of the latter would have been in the later years after consolidation. Competition became keener every year, and that condition would have lowered the sum total of the profits of the smaller firms that had entered into the combinations. There is no easy way of comparing the actual profits that were realized by the consolidated firms with the unrealized profits of the smaller companies had they been permitted to compete with each other, but the latter's profits probably would have been smaller.

Informal and Formal Corporate Control of Business

Many large corporations were loath to compete vigorously against one another and did not want to merge or to combine forces in a more formal manner. A solution was sought in an informal agreement between gentlemen; but when some of the parties thereto forgot these gentlemanly agreements and were taken to court futilely, a more complicated form of agreement was devised. When that form was declared by the courts to be illegal, still another arrangement was made that was legal. However, the courts reviewed the purposes for which holding companies were formed and found some to be against the public interest.

Pools. One of the first forms of business combinations, by which corporations attempted to control the intensity to which competition was given free play, was that of the *pool*. This was an informal agreement under the terms of which either business profits or the volume of business were "pooled" and distributed in some predetermined manner. For instance, the managements of two railroads that were in competition with each other for traffic that flowed between two given terminals could have agreed that 60 percent of the freight would be given to one railroad, 40 percent of the freight to the other one, regardless of the shippers' preferences as they were expressed in their deliveries to the terminal of one railroad or of the other. Under such an agreement it was the responsibility of the managements of the two railroads concerned to keep their respective operating costs below their operating revenues. Another pooling arrangement may have involved an arbitrary division of revenue between the two railroads, irrespective of which one actually transported the freight. Some five or six railroads that controlled the mining of anthracite coal in the five counties of northeastern Pennsylvania allotted to themselves respectively certain percentages of the total shipment of coal. Fines were exacted upon and collected from railroads that exceeded their allotments. In turn, the sums of money that were collected in that manner were distributed among the railroads that had carried less than their allotted portions of coal.

Pooling arrangements were not restricted in their use to railroads. They were used by manufacturers who attempted to control markets and market prices of their products. Rather than engage in devastating price wars, smaller concerns frequently accepted terms that were laid down by larger firms in order to assure their survival in the years immediately ahead. Among the better known industrial pools were those of the French Copper Syndicate, the steel rail pool, the Association of Wire Cut Nails, the one that was formed under the leadership of the Addyston Pipe and Steel Company, and the meat-packer pool. The French Copper Syndicate was organized in 1887 in order to purchase at higher than market price all the copper that was produced. That attempt to corner the world market for copper came to naught when the bank that was financing it closed its doors. Even though a steel rail pool produced over 90 percent of the total output of steel rails, it was unable to control the market and dissolved. It was reorganized twice before its final and permanent demise. The Association of Wire Cut Nails divided the market between its members. A committee met each month for the purpose of fixing the prices of nails for the following month. After a year and a half of futile efforts to regulate the level of competition in the sale of nails it was dissolved permanently. The Armour, Cudahy, Hammond, Morris, and Swift meat-packing companies formed a pool the effect of which was to limit the quantity of meat that each company could ship to the market and the prices at which it could be sold.

Even though these companies were counted among the largest in the business, competition from a large number of smaller concerns that operated in much smaller and more local markets served to make their agreements ineffective. When the objectives of the pool were given publicity in the press, the force of public opinion was brought to bear in breaking it up. The secretary of the pool immediately destroyed all his records so that no court action could be taken against any or all the member companies. The Addyston Pipe and Steel Company divided the market for its products with five other companies in order to avoid price competition between them within their respective spheres of influence. This pool was dissolved by order of the United States Supreme Court in 1899.

Trustee Agreements. A forward step in being able to control price and production policies of competing corporations was taken in the formation of trust agreements. The trustee device for corporate control was first used and made famous by the Standard Oil Company in 1879. Under a trust agreement, the stockholders of the companies whose boards of directors formed a trust deposited their certificates of shares of common stock with a board of trustees and received in exchange certificates of deposit from the trustees. Boards of trustees were invested with the power to vote the number of shares of the operating companies they held. In that manner, boards of trustees were able to elect members of the boards of directors of the operating companies whose common stocks were deposited with them, and thus control their policies. It sometimes happened that members of the board of trustees elected themselves to membership on the boards of directors of the operating companies. The only source of income that accrued to the boards of trustees was the payment of dividends by the boards of directors of the operating companies whose shares of common stock they held. After the expenses of the trustees were paid, any remainder of the income was distributed to the holders of their certificates of deposits.

Standard Oil Trust. One of the controls that was exercised by the Standard Oil Trust was to restrict the sales territories in which operating companies that were members of the trust could market their products so that they would not encounter competition from other operating members of the trust. Another control that was exercised by Standard Oil was in the field of pricing its products at the retail level. In areas where competition with the products of other oil companies was keen, Standard reduced the retail prices of its products in order to attract customers from competing retail outlets. Within customary ranges of retail prices of petroleum products, it was found that lowering prices had little effect in increasing total sales; but it did have the effect of redistributing the retail business in such a manner that the outlets that charged the lowest prices took business away from those outlets whose prices were above that level. In order to survive even in the short run, the latter outlets were compelled to meet the prices of their competitors. If the owners of the latter outlets did not have strong financial backing, sooner or later they succumbed to financial failure. They may have gone out of business entirely, or they may have sold out to Standard Oil at the latter's price, which many of them did. In either case, the outcome of price wars was (1) to reestablish prices at higher levels than prevailed during the competitive struggle and (2) to have little or no competition.

John D. Rockefeller. John D. Rockefeller, who was the guiding genius of Standard Oil, was not interested in controlling the original production of petroleum. There were too many oil fields and too many prospectors in petroleum production to attempt to control the industry at that level. The refining of petroleum required a large amount of capital, a great deal more than each prospector could have hoped to control. Since there was somewhat of a natural concentration or centralization of capital at that level of operation, Rockefeller sought to control it. Also, he was able to control the retail distribution of petroleum products, so the focal points of his organizational activities were directed towards the elimination of competition at these two levels of operation.

Control over Railroads. Rockefeller's control over industry appeared to know no limits. Since he controlled the refining of petroleum and also its retail distribution, his next effort lay in the direction of controlling the means of transporting petroleum and its products into his refineries, then from them to his retail outlets. Railroads were the principal means of transportation, with pipelines offering some competition. Since he did not own or control any of either of these facilities, he sought to gain his objectives by bargaining with the managements of these companies.

Several railroads served the territory, and they vied with each other for the privilege of transporting the bulk of the traffic that Standard Oil could give them. Rockefeller took advantage of his position and obtained rebates from them at the close of each month. He even went so far as to force a railroad to give Standard Oil a rate of 10 cents a barrel of oil and to charge other companies 35 cents a barrel, 25 cents of which went to Standard Oil. In addition, he forced the railroad to let the officials of Standard Oil see the bills of lading for the shipments of oil by his competitors so that Standard Oil knew at what points it would have competition at the retail level. Bills of lading also revealed the volume of business that competitors of Standard Oil were doing. The Pennsylvania Railroad was forced to make these concessions in order to prevent Standard Oil from giving its business to a competing railroad and also to prevent Standard Oil from carrying out its threat to construct a pipeline from Cleveland through western Pennsylvania and on into tidewater.

The Tobacco Trust. Prior to 1890, competition was active in all branches of the tobacco trade—snuff, plug, cigarette, and cigar. The Tobacco Trust differed from its contemporaries in that it was formed for the purpose of holding property while the others held securities. It exchanged its shares directly for the plants, business, brands, and goodwill of five companies that manufactured cigarettes. The fact that the trust was originally formed along the pattern of a horizontal combination does not imply that in its development and growth it did not become integrated to a high degree.

Nine tenths of the licorice that was made in the United States was used in the processing of tobacco, particularly plug, but also smoking tobacco and snuff. MacAndrews & Forbes Company which had an almost complete monopoly of licorice at the manufacturing level was absorbed by the Tobacco Trust, after which it continued to sell its product to independent tobacco manufacturing firms. Other concerns that did not process tobacco but that made related products which were bought by the trust were those that manufactured tin foil, cotton bags in which tobacco was packed, and wooden boxes. The trust controlled the companies that made the machinery that was used in the manufacture of tobacco and those that held patents for such machines. It controlled the Manhattan Brier Pipe Company and also a company that extracted nicotine from tobacco stems and sold it as the principal by-product.

Distributing concerns at the wholesale and retail levels were controlled by offering large discounts to jobbers who agreed to handle the products of the American Tobacco Company exclusively. A commission of 2½ percent was paid to jobbers who agreed to sell only to the retail trade and at prices that were fixed by the American Tobacco Company. They also had to agree not to discriminate against the products of that company. If they agreed to handle exclusively the products of the company, they received an additional 7½ percent. Since the 2½ percent commission was too small to allow the jobbers a profit, they were practically forced into handling American Tobacco Company products exclusively.

The only branch of the tobacco industry that was not rather completely controlled by the Tobacco Trust was the manufacture of cigars to which the application of machinery was not successful. In the 25-year period ending in 1895, the use of machinery in manufacturing cigarettes had reduced the labor cost from 96.4 cents per 1,000 cigarettes to 8.1 cents. No similar development had occurred in the manufacture of cigars. The Tobacco Trust was formed for the purpose of checking the decline in the prices of tobacco products, indirectly the decline in corporate profits. At the time of its formation, plug tobacco was the most popular form in which tobacco reached the consumer. When its prices commenced to fall in 1894, little did the officers of the Tobacco Trust realize how much of this was due to changes in consumer tastes, how much to competitive actions among the producers of plug. Both forces were focused on prices and when one popular brand was sold to jobbers at 13 cents a pound, that price did not cover production costs plus tax. For a number of years it was the profits from the cigarette trade that carried the struggle for the plug market along.

In 1870 the output of cigarettes was 16 million contrasted to 1,183 million cigars. It is also clear that smoking cigarettes was not as generally accepted as was smoking cigars. A cigar was more of a status symbol than was a cigarette; and as for women and young girls, and young boys, too, smoking cigarettes was almost unheard of except in brothels and saloons. By 1880 the market for cigarettes was about 20 percent of the market for cigars. It was not until 1895 that the production of 4,238 million cigarettes was greater by 139 million than that of cigars. From 1895 through 1898 the production of cigarettes was greater than that of cigars; however there was a lapse of another nine years before cigarettes became so popular that their production outnumbered that of cigars continuously.

The war years of 1918-19 provided a tremendous stimulus to the smoking of cigarettes. The peak of 53,865 million was reached in 1918 after which their production declined slightly for the next two years. One of the first advertisements of cigarettes that was directed to women smokers appeared about the turn of the century. It contained a picture of a pretty girl who held a wand on the far end of which sat a wise old owl that was doing the smoking. One of the freedoms that women gained after World War I was the right to smoke cigarettes, or it may have been merely an expression of a new freedom that was won at that time.

Cartel Type of Control. The Tobacco Trust controlled competition in foreign markets as well as in domestic ones. The principle of the cartel was used in apportioning markets within which the products of a given company could be sold. In the domestic market, price wars were entered into freely in order to force the manufacturers of competing products to agree to terms that were set by the trust. Some companies were absorbed. Some brand names of products were discontinued altogether, and competing plants were closed down after they had been acquired by the trust on its own terms.

After several years of litigation the trust was dissolved by order of the United States Supreme Court in 1911. Control of the operating companies that formed the trust was retained by the men who controlled it through the process of dividing the shares of the operating companies between them.

Other Trusts. The formation of 32 trusts prior to January 1, 1898, and 234 more between then and December 31, 1903, shows the extent to which there was a trust movement during these years. Business leaders were quick to see the advantages in the use of the trust device in their efforts to curb the repressing effects of uncontrolled competition upon prices and profits. The impacts of these controls were felt in the division of markets, in restrictions that were placed upon the production of commodities, and upon the rates at which they were placed on the market for sale. All these methods made it possible to control prices under conditions which were unfavorable to price control by more direct methods. Among the better known trusts were the Cotton Seed Oil Trust (1884), the Linseed Oil Trust (1885), the National Lead Trust (1887), and the Sugar Refineries Trust (1889) which was more frequently referred to as the Sugar Trust.

Financial Results. Of all the combinations that were effected between 1890 and 1903, 48 of them went into the hands of receivers before 1913. Some of them were reorganized at which time their capital structures were simplified and their fixed costs reduced. In some cases common stockholders were squeezed out entirely; in others the holders of mortgage bonds were compelled to accept junior securities in the reorganized concerns. Many of the companies were dissolved at tremendous financial losses to holders of both stocks and bonds. American La France, Worthington Pump & Machinery, General Asphalt, General Electric, Bethlehem Steel, United States Cordage, Corn Products Refining, and the American Seating companies were among the better known corporations that emerged from the financial ruins of companies that were formed by consolidating the resources of smaller operating concerns into larger ones.

Several of these companies, along with many others, have since lost their identities in the struggle for economic survival. Typical of a corporation that fought a losing battle against changes in mores and technologies was that of the American Bicycle Company. Out of its reorganization the Pope Manufacturing Company produced a chainless bicycle at a time when mechanized transportation facilities and forms of mass transportation were being developed and becoming more popular. The large degree of control the Pope Manufacturing Company exercised over the production and sale of bicycles that were of several different designs was fruitless in stemming the tide away from the bicycle as a form of transportation to more modern devices.

Trust Form Declared Illegal. No useful purpose will be served at this point in exposing some of the monopoly practices of other organizations. Suffice it to say here that they were frowned upon by the general public and by those who were charged with creating a favorable environment within which the forces of competition could operate. When the United States Supreme Court declared the trust form of business combination to be illegal because it operated in restraint of interstate trade and commerce, it was acting under the authority of the Sherman Antitrust Act of 1890, which will be discussed shortly.

Holding Company. The third step that was taken by American business leaders in their efforts not only to perpetuate profits but to make them and make them larger was to use the corporate device for the purpose of co-ordinating the practices and policies of business firms. *A holding company* was nothing but a corporation whose charter gave it the authority to purchase, to hold, and to control the corporate shares of a number of other corporations. As a distinct corporate entity, it could issue certificates of shares of stock; and it could borrow money through the issuance of corporate bonds. The proceeds from the sale of either or both of these types of securities were used to purchase shares of common stock of other holding companies and/or of operating companies it desired to control.

The courts could not rule adversely to the formation of holding companies per se, but they could and did look into the purposes for which holding companies were created. One of the more famous of such cases was that of the Northern Securities Company which was adjudicated in 1904. The Northern Securities Company had been formed by a group of men who were attempting to control the railroads that operated between Chicago, Omaha, and Denver. The United States Supreme Court found that the purpose for which the company was formed was illegal, as it operated in restraint of interstate trade, and the Court ordered it dissolved. In the dissolution that followed the Court order, the shares of common stock of the operating railroads were divided between the men who controlled the Northern Securities Company, thus forming what has come to be known as a *community of interest*. Since there was no formal organization as such and there was no legislation that covered such an informal arrangement, there was nothing the courts could do about it even though control of the operating railroads was in the same hands and centralization of authority remained as before.

Other combinations that were created by using the holding company device were The Diamond Match Company (1889), the United States Rubber Company (1892), the General Electric Company (1893), and the United States Leather Company (1893). Most of the industrial combinations that were incorporated after 1904 were concerned with areas of production that hardly existed when the Sherman Act was passed. Prominent among these are the Aluminum Company of America (1907), General Motors Corporation (1908), Paramount-Famous-Lasky Corporation (1916), Allied Chemical & Dye Corporation (1920), and the Radio Corporation of America (1920).

Combinations. Growth or enlargement in the size of firms that was accompanied by uniting two or more units already in operation was a combination of industry and has been discussed under that heading in an earlier part of this chapter. Many business firms became so large by the processes of expansion, combination, or of both expansion and combination, that they not only influenced or controlled retail selling prices and policies in their areas of activity, but also were able to control the prices which they paid local suppliers and others for their produce, foodstuffs, and other products. Large organizations became price leaders, if not outright dictators of prices.

The F. W. Woolworth Company may not have been the first of many variety stores in the United States, but it is one of the oldest organizations that has attained its position of leadership in its field both by expanding and by combining with other firms. When it opened new stores it expanded. When it combined with F. M. Kirby it became one of the largest, if not the largest, retail organizations of variety stores in the country. For many years, organizations of this sort were immune to governmental regulation at the federal level because Congress had not established a framework within which enforcement agencies could operate. It was not until after the passage of the Federal Trade Commission and the Clayton Acts in 1914 that the federal government was able to bring these large concerns and others similar to them under surveillance that later led to some semblance of regulation and control.

GOVERNMENT REGULATIONS AND CONTROL OF BUSINESS COMBINATIONS

It was not until American business and political leaders accepted the principle of social control that steps were taken at any level of government to protect consumers against the monopolistic practices of business firms that had consolidated their controls in one way or another.

Early Efforts at Control

Among the freedoms which the early colonists fought to establish and to perpetuate in America was the freedom of and in the market place. American common law sought to preserve the institution of free pricing in competitive market situations. The passage of free banking acts, including the National Banking Act of 1863, and the adoption of general incorporation acts by the several states were manifestations of attempts to discourage monopoly control of business and to give encouragement to competition. The Granger Acts were passed in the latter quarter of the 19th century by some of the Midwestern States in response to efforts on the part of railroad managements to stifle competition and to take advantage of a monopoly situation that was given to them through the terms of their charters and the nature of their corporate organizations. During these same years, manufacturing, mining, and industrial firms combined in many ways, the effects of which were, among other things, to place limits on the degree and scope of competitive activities and to substitute therefor one or more aspects of monopoly control. Controls were exercised over prices, over the volume of output, and over wages; also over the allocation of markets, employment practices, and aspects of competition at the retail level that were abhorrent to the principles, objectives, and ideals of a people to whom competition was such a basic institution it was almost sacred.

Consolidations, combinations, mergers, pools, trusts, and holding company organizations of business had advantages over smaller sized business firms that were not included in these categories. Their presence in the market restricted the opportunity for consumers to purchase their goods in freely competitive markets. Larger sized business firms, likewise, tended to limit the degree of competition in the marketplace. Insofar as these forms of businesses were purchasers of products that were further removed from ultimate consumers, they were *oligopsonistic*, in that they afforded somewhat limited markets for the goods they purchased for resale or which they processed before selling. Looking at their position in almost all market situations, it was one of advantage in its impact upon prices. They did not compete vigorously with themselves when they purchased goods, or when they sold them.

Control by States. By 1900 many states had attempted to regulate the operation of trusts either by statute or by constitutional provisions. The objects of the state statutes may be summarized as having (1) made criminal the making of many contracts and agreements that were not enforceable under the common law, and that were not positively illegal; (2) condemned certain practices that had been included under the term *monopoly* or *restraint of trade* or that had been held to be contrary to the principles of common law.

Among the practices that had been forbidden and made illegal by a number of states were price control, limitation of output, and division of sales territories. State statutes defined certain competitive methods that were to be considered as prima facie evidence that business firms were operating in restraint of trade. Penalties that were set for violations of those statutes varied widely between the several states. Among the more common penalties were fines and imprisonment of corporate officers; fines up to $1,500 a day against firms in Texas, in which state each day of operation constituted a separate offense; revocation of corporate charters; and voidance of contracts. In some states injured parties could claim damages and all court costs, including attorneys' fees; in others, double and triple damages could be recovered.

Federal Control. The problem of trusts and combinations soon became so complex that it reached far beyond the level of state control. Since the common law of the several states was not enforceable at the federal level, and the federal government had no common law, it became incumbent upon the federal government through the Congress to outlaw combinations and contracts the effects of which in operation were to restrain interstate trade and commerce. As early as 1884 the platforms of some of the minor political parties contained denunciations of pools and monopolies in general. They demanded that action be taken at the federal level to control them.

Sherman Antitrust Act. Early in July of 1890 Congress passed the bill that has come to be known as the Sherman Antitrust Act. In reality it was the cooperative effort of Senators Edmunds, Evarts, George, Hoar, and Ingalls. It made illegal "every contract, combination or conspiracy in restraint of trade or commerce among the states or with foreign nations." Enforcement was provided for in assessing fines upon firms, fines and imprisonment upon officers of firms that were found guilty of violating the terms of that Act. Injured persons could sue to recover three times the monetary damages they had sustained through these practices, plus all court costs including attorneys' fees.

Writing in 1904, John Moody, in his *Truth about Trusts,* listed 111 public utility trusts, 318 industrial trusts, and 16 trusts among the railroads that included consolidation of approximately 8,000 individual firms. Of the 318 industrial trusts all but 23 were formed after the passage of the Sherman Act. It is clearly evident that the government enforcement program was not equal to the task of enforcing the provisions of that Act, or that the several Presidents of the United States were not sympathetic to the idea of trust control at the federal level.

Within a few years after the passage of the Sherman Act, the decision of the United States Supreme Court in the Northern Securities case made it clear that its provisions did apply to the railroads. However, the decision of the same Court in the E. C. Knight case in 1895 tended to emasculate the Act. For all practical purposes the Sugar Trust had obtained a monopoly in the refining of sugar in Pennsylvania through the purchase of the E. C. Knight concern and three smaller firms. That action gave the American Sugar Refining Company, which was the core concern of the trust, control over approximately 98 percent of the sugar that was refined in the United States. The remaining 2 percent was refined by a company that was located in Massachusetts. When the Court ruled that manufacturing was not commerce, the government lost jurisdiction over combinations in the area of mining as well as of those in manufacturing.

Performance Record. The year 1903 is an important date in the economic history of the United States in that (1) it was the year in which the Bureau of Corporations was organized; and (2) it marked the termination of the second period of the concentration of the formation of trusts. Throughout the first 11 years following the passage of the Sherman Act, only 17 cases were instituted against combinations as against a record of 146 combinations having been effected in the short span of years, 1899-1901. It probably was the aggressive program of law enforcement by the Bureau of Corporations that discouraged the formation of additional trusts until the clouds of opposition had lifted. This program of law enforcement of the Bureau of Corporations seemed aggressive only because, prior to its establishment during the early years of President Theodore Roosevelt's administration, scarcely anything had been done to enforce the provisions of the Act. Court decisions, of which that on the E. C. Knight case was most discouraging, and apathy shown by political leaders in Washington, combined with the fact that no machinery had been established for gathering data on the subject, were responsible for the state of lethargy.

Bureau of Corporations. The Bureau of Corporations was established by Congress in 1903 for the purpose of investigating the actions of trusts and combinations. It was also authorized to advise the Department of Justice in cases that involved violation of the Sherman Act. While it initiated 42 suits during the Roosevelt administration, the President made it manifest that he did not intend to destroy big business when he gave encouragement to the ownership and control of the Tennessee Coal and Iron Company being taken over by the United States Steel Corporation in 1907. In fairness to the President it should be brought out here that the problem of this consolidation of two steel companies was combined with that of the impact of another corporate failure upon unemployment and upon the banking structure of the country in 1907. The Tennessee Coal and Iron Company was on the threshold of financial collapse at a time when such an occurrence would have shaken still more the confidence of the public in our industrial system and in commercial banks. Rather than have another corporate failure intensify an incipient panic situation, President Roosevelt let it be known that he would not institute suit against the United States Steel Corporation under the provisions of the Sherman Act should the latter corporation absorb the Tennessee Coal and Iron Company. That merger was effected, and it had a stabilizing effect on the American economy.

During President Taft's four years in office a total of 52 actions against trusts were initiated, 26 of which were begun in 1912. This activity reflected the movement for reform which swept the country, and which was revealed in the results of the elections that were held in 1910. That President Woodrow Wilson pursued a relatively vigorous course of action against monopolies is evidenced by the fact that in his first year in office 27 cases were carried to the United States Supreme Court. During his remaining seven years in office, action was taken against 68 other combinations. The number might have been larger had not problems connected with preparation for and the conduct of a world war been given priority over the internal problems of monopoly. It was during this period that the leaders of the Republican party did not advocate the destruction of big business if it was "good," and leaders of the Democratic party pledged themselves to compel big business to operate on a more competitive level.

Public Protests and Reform

The activity against trusts, combinations, and big business was the culmination of a protest movement that had its origin 30 years earlier and of
which the Populist revolt, the Greenback party, and the Socialist movement
were manifestations. Edward Bellamy's *Looking Backward* (1888) and
Henry D. Lloyd's *Wealth and Commonwealth*, published six years later, were
widely read. Their contents provided the subject matter for newspaper
editorials, lectures, and club discussions. Journalism had not developed the
techniques of the columnist, and radio and television commentators were yet
to be heard and seen. Before many of the writings appeared in book form,
they appeared as serials in popular magazines such as *Cosmopolitan, American, McClure's* and *The Saturday Evening Post.* Through these media, stories
were told to thousands of readers who would not have been reached in any
other way. Ida Ruth Tarbell, Lincoln Steffens, Burton J. Hendrick, Ray
Stannard Baker, and others revealed capitalism and big business, for such
they were, at their worst. They exposed some of the more intimate operations
of big business—the graft, the incompetence, the deceit, the immorality—and
other degrading features of doing business that were carried on in the name
of corporate enterprise.

Individual businessmen and corporate directors and officers would have
been horrified and insulted had their names been associated with such
patterns of behavior. They were leaders in churches and in financial circles.
Their names graced the membership roles of elite country clubs and other
social and political organizations. They operated under the legal concept of
a corporation—an artificial person, invisible, intangible, that existed only
in contemplation of the law. History had revealed the deplorable conditions
that had existed in mines, mills, and in factories in England and on the
Continent of Europe; but people were appalled to learn that similar conditions could be found in America.

One of the "muckrakers," for such they were, was Upton Sinclair, whose
exposures were made through the medium of his book entitled *The Jungle.*
His disclosures were in connection with the investigation that was being
made by the Bureau of Corporations of the functioning of the National
Packing Company which was owned jointly by the Armour, Swift, and
Morris packing companies. The unsanitary conditions that prevailed in
meat-packing plants were so revolting and so nauseating that the Pure Food
and Drug Act and the Meat Inspection Act were passed in answer to the
vigorous protests that were voiced by the general public.

The Bureau was active in bringing The Standard Oil Company and The
American Tobacco Company before the United States Supreme Court.
While many persons were not satisfied with the application of the *rule of
reason* when the law was written in terms of "all" contracts and combinations that operated in restraint of trade, these cases did serve the purpose of
broadening the interpretation of interstate commerce to include manufacturing

and mining corporate activities. They also reaffirmed the opinion that the holding company device did not provide an immunity from prosecution by the United States under the terms of the Sherman Act.

Prior to the presidential election of 1912, Woodrow Wilson campaigned on a platform that included reform of antitrust legislation. The electorate had become aroused by the writings of the muckrakers as well as by the interpretations of the courts in a number of important cases. In 1907, Judge Kennesaw Mountain Landis had acted on his convictions and assessed a fine of $29 million against the Standard Oil Company for accepting rebates from railroads. The immediate impact of that decision was to have Standard Oil shift the burden of the fine on the company to the consumers of Standard Oil products through the medium of higher prices. A few years later, another court reversed the decision that was handed down by Judge Landis, but Standard could not and did not remit the amount of the fine to these consumers from whom it had been collected. Judge Landis went on to become the first commissioner of major league baseball, a position that he held for many years. He conducted that office with the same fearless disregard for the power of money in and out of organized baseball that he had shown when he astonished the world with his decision in the Standard Oil case.

The Federal Trade Commission

After the election of 1912 in which the Democrats were put in control of Congress and in the executive mansion, they got to work at once on legislation that was intended to strengthen the antitrust laws by adding teeth to the enforcement program. The first legislative enactment was the passage of the Federal Trade Commission Act in September, 1914. That Act replaced the Bureau of Corporations with the Federal Trade Commission which was to consist of five members. The Commission was empowered to "prevent persons, partnerships or corporations, excepting banks, and common carriers that were subject to the acts to regulate interstate commerce, from using unfair methods of competition in commerce." In addition to the power to investigate the practices of combinations and to conduct hearings, the Commission was authorized to issue cease and desist orders and to apply to the United States Court of Appeals to enforce them. In addition to cease and desist orders, the Federal Trade Commission was given the power to negotiate terms of agreements that were known as *consent decrees*, violations of which were causes for court action initiated by the Commission.

Failure to define unfair trade practices made it difficult for the Commission to enforce its program. Courts were reluctant to enforce compliance upon concerns that willfully violated terms of consent decrees and cease and desist orders. Court judges who had been appointed by administrations that gave only lip service to the enforcement of antitrust laws found loopholes in actions that were initiated by the Commission. Members of the Commisson who were appointed by President Wilson were not reappointed by succeeding presidents when their terms expired. As a matter of political expediency new appointees were men who were more in sympathy with the platform of the party in power. With the return to office of the Republican party in 1920, the Federal Trade Commission together with the courts became more lax in their enforcement of fair trade practices.

The Clayton Antitrust Act

Shortly after the passage of the Federal Trade Commission Act, Congress strengthened the hand of the government in its efforts to curb the further monopolization of American industry by enacting the Clayton Antitrust Act. That Act forbade (1) the charging of prices that discriminated between purchasers when its effect was "to substantially lessen competition or tend to create a monopoly"; (2) the drawing up and the use of selling and/or leasing contracts of both patented and unpatented articles; and (3) interlocking directorates in competing concerns that were engaged in interstate commerce whose capital structures aggregated more than $1 million, and in banks when their deposits, capital, surplus, and undivided profits amounted to more than $5 million. The holding of stock by one corporation in another corporation for investment purposes was permitted but not when the effects of such holdings would be to lessen the degree of competition between them, or to create a monopoly.

QUESTIONS FOR REVIEW

1. (a) What evidence is there that industrial activity increased after 1870?
   (b) In what ways has that increase been measured?

2. (a) Explain the concept of large-scale production.
   (b) Is large-scale production always an accompaniment of an increase in size of a business firm? Explain.

3. (a) In what ways have firms become larger? Illustrate.
   (b) Distinguish between vertical and horizontal combinations in industry. Illustrate each form of combination.

4. (a) What were the reactions of the American people to the results of large industrial combinations?
   (b) How were these reactions implemented?

5. (a) What were some of the economic impacts of industrial and commercial combinations?
   (b) Were these impacts in accord with the principles upon which industry in America was founded? Explain clearly.

6. (a) How effective was the Sherman Antitrust Act of 1890 in accomplishing its objectives?
   (b) Explain your answer to Part (a).

7. (a) What and who were the "muckrakers"?
   (b) What useful purposes did they serve?

SUGGESTED READINGS

Bogart, Ernest L., and Charles M. Thompson (eds.). *Readings in the Economic History of the United States.* London: Longmans, Green & Co., Ltd., 1927. Chapter 31.

Edwards, George W. "Development of American Security Capitalism," *Views of American Economic Growth: The Industrial Era,* edited by Thomas C. Cochran and Thomas B. Brewer. New York City; McGraw-Hill Book Company, 1966.

Faulkner, Harold U. *The Decline of Laissez Faire, 1897-1917.* New York City: Holt, Rinehart & Winston, Inc., 1951. Chapters 5, 8, and 15.

Hidy, Ralph and Muriel. "Pioneering in Big Business," *Issues in American Economic History*, edited by Gerald D. Nash. Boston: D. C. Heath & Company, 1964.

Josephson, Matthew. "The Robber Barons," *Issues in American Economic History*, edited by Gerald D. Nash. Boston: D. C. Heath & Company, 1964.

Kirkland, Edward C. *Industry Comes of Age: Business, Labor, and Public Policy, 1860-1897.* New York City: Holt, Rinehart & Winston, Inc., 1961. Chapters 10 and 14.

Passer, Harold. "The Electrical Manufacturers," *Views of American Economic Growth: The Industrial Era,* edited by Thomas C. Cochran and Thomas B. Brewer. New York City: McGraw-Hill Book Company, 1966.

Warner, W. Lloyd, and James Abbeglen. *Big Business Leaders in America.* New York City: Atheneum Publishers, 1963.

Chapter 18

LABOR: ORGANIZATION AND

LEGISLATION

LABOR IN AMERICA

Growth of cities was accompanied by an increase in the number of wage earners, some of whom worked in factories and mills. Farm labor that was displaced by machinery, or that was attracted to urban living and working, comprised much of the original native supply of industrial labor. Many were the comparisons and contrasts that were made between the plights of farm and industrial labor. To some persons who were not familiar with the conditions of working and of living on farms, there was a strong appeal to live and to work in the great outdoors where there was plenty of room to move around without rubbing shoulders with someone else. The smell of new mown hay was contrasted to the foul odors of a paper mill or to the stench that characterized the Fulton Street Market, or to the putrid odors of slum areas that made persons want to hold their breath to avoid contamination. The croaking of frogs, the howl of the coyote, the noises of the barn and of the barnyard, the crowing of roosters and the cackling of hens were compared to the screeching and grinding noises of the factory and the mill.

Many men who worked on farms found the work long, hard, and monotonous. An 8-hour day was beyond their ken, and farm wages were low. The workday may not have been as long in the factory as it was on the farm, but a steady pace of work was set by machinery that was not under the direct control of its operatives. Farmers went to town on Saturdays and on some rainy days, but the latter were often spent in the repair and maintenance of farm equipment and farm buildings.

Milking cows was done by hand, and early morning hours in the North and Middle West were often dark and cold. Electricity had not reached the farm, and the automobile could not be driven on most country roads except under favorable weather conditions. Neither of these technologies reached rural areas in general until well after World War I. Entertainment centered around the home, the country church, and the country school; and members of school boards and church elders took their responsibilities seriously in seeing to it that their charges had wholesome entertainment. The development of transportation facilities and of systems of communication provided opportunities for farm labor to become aware of some of the variations of urban life. Many tasks were performed indoors where the workers were protected from the vagaries of inclement weather. Urban workers were paid in money rather than in kind. Associations with other persons of the same age and of the same or opposite sex were more frequent in the city and ofttimes more stimulating. Entertainment and amusements were more diversified than in rural areas. Some workers found it possible to save some of their earnings in order to get ahead in life and to raise their level of living.

Industrial labor, in general, was unskilled, uneducated, and unorganized. It was aware of the fact that it constituted the lowest bracket that measured the distribution of incomes and the ownership of wealth. Industries that required labor that acquired some skills were manned by workers who did not necessarily aspire to become entrepreneurs, but who wanted a larger share of the social dividends that were the results of the combined efforts of land, labor, and capital. They were beginning to develop a feeling of class consciousness, even if they lacked class solidarity. They desired standards of living that were higher than the levels upon which they actually lived. Included in their coveted standards were better housing, increased wages, shorter hours of work per day and per week, and more educational opportunities. They realized that the unequal distribution of wealth tended to perpetuate and to accentuate an unequal distribution of incomes.

Mechanization and Unemployment

Industry was becoming more highly mechanized, and new capital goods industries were springing up. Labor had always been confronted with seasonal unemployment. Cyclical unemployment was not a new phenomenon, but it became a more serious impediment to the progress of labor as industry became more highly mechanized. When depression conditions confronted consumers' goods and service industries, labor in capital goods' industries was forced into the army of the unemployed. Labor that had been displaced by machinery may have been absorbed by jobs that required lower levels of skills. As markets grew in size and in number, industries, likewise, grew in size and in number and employed more labor. The increase in the demand for labor is not substantiated in terms of wage rates. That labor was in greater supply is measured in terms of newly arrived immigrants from Europe after 1870, some of whom were imported under contract.

War, Economic Growth, and Employment

Had the rate of economic growth of the United States not been retarded by the forces of the Civil War, the 2.8 million immigrants who set foot on

American shores between 1863 and 1872 would probably have been absorbed by an increased demand for labor. As it was, unemployment that accompanied the postwar depression of 1873 was aggravated by their presence.

After their arrival, they constituted a portion of the American labor force. Insofar as they had been members of the labor force abroad, they were somewhat oriented by the facts of labor organization and legislation. In America, they were confronted with conditions of laissez faire in political philosophy and highly competitive conditions in finding employment.

Need for Organization

The fact that so many foreign workers and their families were being imported into the United States made it difficult for American workers, particularly the unskilled and semiskilled, to improve upon the conditions under which they worked. They had no bargaining power with employers nor with their representatives. Under the corporate form of business organization and in firms and plants that employed hundreds and even thousands of workers, employment managers were trained and paid to hire employees. They were not the real employers; they were the specialists who were paid by their employers to deal directly with applicants for jobs that were open. In the same departments were other specialists who were paid to deal with the employees and to hear any complaints that the latter desired to make. Here was an almost intolerable situation for labor but one about which it could do little or nothing in the absence of an effective organization. Workers even lost their individual identities and were given numbers by which they were known and identified.

One or two corporate employers of labor meant much more to a laborer than did a laborer mean to one or two corporate employers. If a laborer did not want to work for the terms laid down by the corporate employers, frequently there was nowhere else to apply for work. To a corporate employer it made little difference whether or not an applicant for work accepted his terms; there may have been several potential applicants for every opening in the plant. To a worker, it was a take-it-or-leave-it proposition, and taking it was frequently better than leaving it and having no work nor income at all.

Many workers lacked the mobility to move from one place to another. The result was that they, as individuals, were unable to maintain their economic status, much less improve upon it. If they approached the representatives of corporate employers to ask for higher wages, shorter working hours, better housing conditions, or more light in their area of work, they were considered to have been dissatisfied employees who were attempting to stir up trouble. They were discharged immediately, and their names were placed on a blacklist that was circulated among other employers of mass labor. With their names on the blacklist, it was impossible for them to obtain employment, and they became more or less permanently unemployed and as such were dependent upon charity, either organized or unorganized, for sufficient food and clothing to keep the bodies and souls of themselves, their wives, and children together.

Living conditions were almost beyond description. Housing, such as it was, was frequently provided by the manufacturers or the mining companies. It was below the minimum standard of decency and sanitation. Disease and drunkenness were rampant. Drink was almost the only release from fatigue and exhaustion after long hours of work in mills and mines. Undernourishment and malnutrition were not respecters of age or sex.

The Molly Maguires. The original Molly Maguires was an organization of Irish tenants who banded together to resist the evils of absentee landlordism in Ireland. The owners of Irish farms resided in England and dealt with their tenants through middlemen who were hired overseers. The leader of that protest movement was a woman by the name of Molly Maguire. To escape further prosecution in Ireland, many of the Molly Maguires escaped to the United States and settled near Shenandoah, Pennsylvania in the heart of the anthracite coal region. The rumor that Molly herself was in the group was never verified; nevertheless, her name was given to the organization that was founded in America.

The experiences of the Molly Maguires who, in America, were members of the Ancient Order of Hibernians, may or may not have been typical of labor conditions prior to 1886, but they have been given more publicity than the experiences of other groups.

The Ancient Order of Hibernians was an organization many of whose members were miners of anthracite coal in five counties of northeastern Pennsylvania. At first, it was a secret order and as such incurred the enmity of the Roman Catholic Church. Many of the Molly Maguires were of Irish descent and were communicants of the Roman Catholic Church, if they maintained any church affiliation. Even so, at one time the names of three Catholic priests were listed to be liquidated by the Molly Maguires. The anthracite mines were owned and operated by the managements of five railroads that maintained their headquarters in Philadelphia and other cities situated at some distance from the mines. All of the disadvantages of absentee landlordism were present.

Penetration into Politics. The Ancient Order of Hibernians was more than just a labor union. It was an organization whose membership consisted of law enforcement officers and judges at the municipal, county, and state levels. That was one reason it was so difficult to obtain a conviction in a court of law. Judges, members of juries, sheriffs—all were represented on the membership rolls of the A.O.H. Not only were they frequently sympathetic to the accused, but to defy or betray the Order was tantamount to signing their own death warrants.

Among the depredations committed by the Molly Maguires were bombings, shootings, killings, wrecking railroad trains, blowing up mine shafts, ventilator systems, and tipples, arson, and physical beatings. Many of these incidents occurred in broad daylight, and with many onlookers; but in court no one could be found who either could or would identify the culprits. Witnesses perjured themselves, but there was no one present in the courts to challenge them. The way the organization operated was to call upon strangers to a community to "pull" a job, after which they rode away on horseback amid the confusion and disorder that followed violence.

Dissolution. Finally a Pinkerton detective from Chicago by the name of James McParlan was employed by the Pennsylvania Railroad to attempt to penetrate the organization and to bring its leaders to justice. After many thrilling experiences and narrow escapes for his life, even before he was suspected of being a detective, he exposed many of the leaders who were finally convicted in court and sentenced to hang. The sentence was carried out on a dismal rainy day in the hanging of seven men. That put an end to the activities of the Ancient Order of Hibernians.

The mass hanging of the Molly Maguires may have put an end to their activities; it was only the beginning of many studies of the Ancient Order of Hibernians. There is now a theory that while the Molly Maguires were members of that Order, the members of the Order were not necessarily Molly Maguires. Doubt still encircles the real function of McParlan. What he did is an open book; why he did it is a moot question. The earlier theory that his participation in planning and in perpetrating the depredations against life and property was in order to establish his identity and his earnestness of purpose with other Molly Maguires has been superseded by the theory that he was a plant by the president of the Pennsylvania Railroad to make a case against labor in the eyes of the public. The facts of infiltration into government and into law enforcement agencies are firmly established as having occurred before the hiring of McParlan.

ORGANIZATION: THE EMERGENCE OF NATIONAL UNIONS

The war of 1861-65 caused prices to rise, and profits in many industries were larger than in prewar years. Many new firms and industries were organized in order to share in the larger profits of industry that were not only available but were being made by many firms at all levels of production—mining, manufacturing, wholesaling, and retailing. Labor had already attempted organization on a spot or local basis, but there was need for national unity among the workers. Because of competitive factors, labor organizations were compelled to place their demands before all producers of a product and before all producers of competing products.

Early Attempts at Organization

Unions increased in number from approximately 80 in 1863 to nearly 300 the following year. Local unions organized local federations that were called city centrals. The formation of city centrals led to statewide organizations and finally to national unions. Among the stronger national unions were those of plasterers, cigar makers, masons, and bricklayers. A union of typographers had been organized in 1852 and is the only labor union to have survived continuously to the present. The Brotherhood of Locomotive Engineers was organized in 1863, six years before completion of the first transcontinental railroad. Ten years elapsed before the Brotherhood of Locomotive Firemen and Enginemen was organized. The goals of these unions were increased wages, collective bargaining, shorter workdays, control over trainees and apprenticeships, and recognition. Not only was labor tending to lose its individuality, it was facing competition from recently arrived immigrants from northern and western European countries. Before many years had passed labor was to face competition from unskilled workers from southern and eastern Europe. During the first 15 years after the termination of hostilities, a total of 14 new national unions was organized, the membership in which varied from 300,000 in 1872 to only 50,000 in 1878. The pattern of union membership which fluctuated directly with the degree of industrial prosperity was unbroken by war years.

The National Labor Union. The National Labor Union, founded by William H. Sylvis in Baltimore in 1866, was in answer to demands for a unification of labor groups across the country. It gave encouragement to industrial peace through the channels of collective bargaining. After concentrating its efforts to obtain an 8-hour day, it attempted to stimulate interest in producers' cooperatives. In an effort to seek its objectives through the polls it became involved in the Greenback movement. As a result of its efforts Congress established an 8-hour day in 1868 which applied to laborers, workmen, and mechanics who were employed by the federal government or who were engaged in the fulfillment of government contracts. To establish a Bureau of Labor was included in the platform of the National Labor Union, but such a bureau did not become a reality until 1884.

Knights of St. Crispin. The Knights of St. Crispin were organized in 1867 in order to protect journeymen shoemakers against the competition that resulted from the adoption of machines in the manufacture of shoes. Skilled cordwainers were being replaced by machine operators in the march of economic progress as measured by the mechanization of industry, or by the use of more capital and more complicated capital in production. They were organized along industrial lines and fought for the principle of the *closed shop*. Most of their strikes were successful; they counted 50,000 members in the early 1870's.

As had happened so many times in years past, recession and depression wreaked disaster upon labor organizations and union membership; and the Knights of St. Crispin did not survive the depression that followed the panic of 1873. A few years later its membership was absorbed by the Holy Order of the Knights of Labor.

The Knights of Labor. While the Holy Order of the Knights of Labor was founded by Uriah S. Stephens in 1869, it was under the leadership of Terence V. Powderly that it achieved its greatest accomplishments. It started out as a local union of garment workers in Philadelphia, but the acceptance of other craftsmen was part of its expansion program. Membership was open to all wage earners irrespective of sex, race, color, or creed. Skilled and unskilled workers alike were to be welded together in order to put up a solid front to enforce their demands against employers.

The organizational structure of the Knights of Labor placed authority over local groups in the hands of its central governing body, but there was such a diversity of interests represented in its membership that the policy rulings of that body could not be enforced. Diversity did not end with membership; it boiled over into the determination of and carrying out of its programs. One group wanted to attain its ends through the process of collective bargaining; one group advocated the formation of cooperative organizations as a means of improving the scales of living of its members; still another group favored the polls as the best approach to the solution of its problems.

The leadership of the Knights of Labor was not sufficiently strong to weld those who held to these diversified opinions to put up a solid and unified front. Powderly had been a machinist but seemed unable to appeal directly to the workers. He was a highly cultured, idealistic leader who was not able to adjust himself readily to his surroundings. He was much too formal in his appeals to the workers to rally them to his support in a crisis. He could talk to employers and their representatives, political leaders, and government officials on their respective social and professional levels, but his formal attire and the atmosphere that surrounded his talks to labor created a schism between him and the workers. He could not enter a mill or a mine and talk to the workers in their own language. He could not get up on a soapbox on a street corner and rally his listeners to his cause. He wanted to be introduced to his audiences by an officer of a local group. He preferred to have a brass band play lively tunes before he gave his addresses in order to put those who were within earshot of his voice in the right frame of mind to listen to and digest what he had to say.

Program. The program of the Knights of Labor was idealistic rather than pragmatic. It sought to improve the environment in which the workers toiled and lived in the long run, while the workers themselves lived in the short run. They wanted to enjoy the fruits of their efforts rather than rejoice in the fact that their children and grandchildren might enjoy a shorter workday and a higher all-around level of living. Among the goals of attainment were to secure to the workers the full enjoyment of the wealth they helped create and sufficient leisure time in which to develop their intellectual, moral, and social faculties.

To these ends they demanded (1) the establishment of a Bureau of Labor Statistics at the federal level that would keep the public informed as to the needs of labor; (2) that public lands be sold to bona fide settlers rather than to speculators who would make profits from their resale to settlers; (3) the abrogation of all laws that did not bear equally upon capital and labor; (4) the adoption of measures that would promote the safety and health of those workers who were engaged in mining, manufacturing, and construction industries, and other measures that would indemnify workers for injuries that might be received through the lack of necessary and proper safeguards; (5) the recognition of and the incorporation of trade unions; (6) weekly pay in lawful money and the passage of laws that would give mechanics and laborers a first lien upon the products of their labor to the extent of their wages; (7) the abolition of the contract system on national, state, and municipal projects; (8) the substitution of compulsory arbitration for strikes wherever and whenever possible as a means of reconciling differences between labor and management, and the establishment of machinery for enforcing the decisions of the arbiters; (9) the prohibition of child labor under 15 years of age in workshops, mines, and factories; (10) the outlawing of the use of convict labor in fulfillment of contracts; and (11) a graduated income tax as a step towards equalizing the distribution of income and the ownership of wealth rather than as a device for raising revenue for government.

Of Congress, the Knights of Labor demanded (1) the abolition of national banks and the issuance of a national currency directly to the people instead of through the channels of banks and banking: this money should be given full legal tender privileges in the settlement of both public and private debt; the government should not recognize or create any private bank or banking corporation; (2) that monetary emergencies were to be met by the issuance of legal tender, noninterest-bearing money—the government should not issue bonds, notes, or bills of credit as devices for revenue when tax receipts were inadequate; (3) laws to prohibit the importation of foreign labor; (4) the establishment of a postal savings system and means within the organization of postoffices for the safekeeping of valuable papers, money, jewels, and other items of value; (5) laws that would nationalize the railroads, telephone, and telegraph systems.

The Knights of Labor for its part would endeavor (1) to establish consumer and producer cooperatives that would eventually supersede the wage system; (2) to secure equal pay for equal work by both sexes; (3) to obtain an 8-hour day; and (4) to influence labor to accept arbitration as a substitute for strikes in the settlement of disputes with management.

Activities. As many as 135 cooperative ventures were embarked upon by the Knights, most of them in mining, shoe manufacturing, and cooperage plants, all of which paid extremely low wages. These cooperatives were beset with internal dissension and inefficient management. In order to make up for a lack of capital, they were compelled to borrow at rates of interest that were above those paid by competitors and that precluded financial success.

Particularly frustrating to the efforts of the cooperatives to attain a measure of success was the opposition of the railroads, many of which were managed by men who had direct financial interests in manufacturing and in mining concerns. Railroads practiced methods of unfair competition in order to attract revenue traffic or to make it more productive of profits.

As an example of the extremes to which the managements of railroads went in their attempts to crush not only the cooperative form of business organization but the Knights of Labor in particular, the latter's experience in attempting to operate a coal mine at Cannelburg, Indiana, will be cited. The mine was purchased in order to sell coal to the Knights at prices that were lower than were charged by owners of mines that were operated by free enterprise for a profit. After the Knights had spent $20,000 in placing the mine in operable condition and another $1,000 in mining coal, they were forced to wait nine months before a railroad would construct a siding to the mine and connect it with the main line. After the connection had been made, the railroad refused to switch cars to and from the siding, and the cooperative was compelled to spend another $4,000 to acquire a switch engine. Then it was discovered that the coal could be used only for coking and for making gas and that contracts for such coal were signed in July only. That necessitated another delay of nine months. By that time the cooperative's funds were exhausted, and it was forced to sell to the competitor that had backed the railroad in its fight to preserve the capitalistic system of production for profit.

Strikes. In spite of the policy or attitude of the central authority towards the strike as a weapon of defense of labor against management, it was a strike that was called at the local level against the Wabash Railroad, which was controlled by Jay Gould, that lifted the Knights to their pinnacle of power and influence. The trouble really started in 1883 when the telegraphers struck the Western Union Company that was controlled by Jay Gould. They demanded 8-hour shifts, a 6-day week, and a wage increase of 15 percent. Even though the strikers appeared to have had the support of public opinion and of large segments of the public press, that effort bore no fruit for the workers except hatred for and distrust of labor organizations. To state the case mildly, Gould and the businesses he controlled became targets for labor to shoot at in the future. That opportunity presented itself two years later when the railroad shopmen struck the Union Pacific Railroad, which was owned by the same Jay Gould. With the assistance of the railroad trainmen, the shopmen won that struggle. Six months later members of the Knights of Labor were locked out of the shops of the Wabash Railroad, another Gould property. It was their victory in that struggle that attracted 600,000 new members to become Knights within a few months.

Opposition of Employers. Employers' associations became active in their efforts to crush organized labor and the Knights of Labor in particular.

The Gould system of railroads deliberately provoked another railroad strike in 1886. After a series of minor incidents that were intended to provoke the Knights of Labor to take overt action, a shopman was deliberately discharged in violation of an agreement with the union. The Knights rallied to his support and demanded recognition of the union and $1.50 a day for unskilled labor. About 9,000 railroad workers went out on strike, but management was able to crush it by using strong-arm methods and strikebreakers.

Strikes were not confined to just railroads during the formative years of labor organization. Unions were fighting for their very existence, and employers were just as determined to crush them. The railroad riots of 1877 that were accompanied by the wanton destruction of life and property in Pittsburgh weakened the cause of labor. To the general public it appeared that there were no limits to the actions that unions would take in their efforts to obtain recognition. Accounts of the disturbances were written up in a capitalistic press that was supported by advertising from privately owned enterprises. The newspapers themselves did not want to fall prey to the demands of organized labor. The freedom of the press seemed to preclude freedom in bargaining with its workers.

The International Harvester Company strike culminated in a riotous scene in Haymarket Square in Chicago in 1886. While a meeting of strikers was being held in the open, mounted police, fully armed for action, patrolled the outer edges of the crowd. Somebody threw a bomb and in the melee that ensued one policeman was killed, and several others were injured. The Homestead strike (steel) in 1892 was tantamount to open warfare with labor on the losing side.

Through distortion of reality and deliberate misrepresentation of the roles played by management, by armed troops, and by labor in these disturbances, the general public was led to believe that attempts to organize labor in reality were efforts to abolish the system of free enterprise and of private property and to destroy our form of government. Strikes were instigated by foreigners who were not sympathetic to the ideals and objectives of the Americans who united to quell that silent invasion of their institutions—economic, social, and political.

After the strikes failed, the railroad workers returned to work at reduced rates of pay. The average pay on the New York Central Railroad was $41.08 per month at the very time that dividends returned 8 percent on a capital of $90 million, one half of which was water. What may have been the worst effects of the strikes were a revival of the conspiracy doctrine in the courts; legislatures passed new anticonspiracy laws; and a precedent was established for the use of federal troops to quell so-called insurrection.

Decline. Even though industries were becoming more highly mechanized and human skills were in less demand in the performance of industrial processes, there were sufficient leaders within the organization of the Knights of Labor who were of the opinion that trade or craft organizations offered more for the workers than did the industrial type of organization. They felt, also, that labor did not have the solidarity that was required to weld the membership of the Knights of Labor into an organization of workers that could or would offer a united front in support of its demands against employers. As early as 1881, in their efforts to rally the cigar makers to support the cause of unionism, Adolph Strasser and Samuel Gompers, among others, supported measures that were introduced at the annual conventions of the Knights of Labor under the terms of which craft or trade unions would be admitted to full membership. Since Powderly and others of his ilk were adamant in their stand in favor of the industrial type of labor organization, the Cigar Makers Union withdrew its membership from the Knights and helped form the Federation of Organized Trades and Labor Unions. After untiring efforts to strengthen the Federation, Samuel Gompers was elected its chairman and president in 1883. That marked the beginning of a long and active career of leadership, unbroken except for one year, that terminated with his death in 1924.

The American Federation of Labor

The year 1877 was one of disaster for the Knights of Labor. Among the strikes that undermined the lifeblood of unionism was that of the cigar makers who sought to put an end to the tenement sweating system in the manufacture of cigars. When the strike failed, the labor movement appeared to have been crushed, but not in the minds of Strasser and Gompers. Strasser undertook to travel and to organize unions outside of New York; Gompers spent most of his spare time organizing workers in New York. They were strongly of the opinion that in order to be successful in attaining its goals, labor had to organize along national and international lines. They increased membership dues in order to build up a fund that was controlled by national officers, and they either adopted or prepared to adopt sickness, accident, and unemployment benefits. That Gompers was successful and foresighted in building and managing the fund was made manifest in the ability of the union to survive the trials and tribulations of the depression of 1893 to 1896.

Samuel Gompers. The American Federation of Labor was formally organized in 1886 with Samuel Gompers as its first president. He insisted that there be only one union for each trade in "all North America." Local unions entered the Federation through membership in their national unions. Each national union was to be completely self-governing over its own locals and free from domination by the Federation. Gompers would not tolerate the idea of workingmen becoming businessmen or professional men. He had seen the cooperative organization of the Knights of Labor fail, and he realized that the workers were not equipped by training or by point of view to become business managers. He opposed the entry of "theorizers" and of "intellectuals" into the Federation. They were "industrially impossible." The efforts of a united labor front were directed towards the attainment of higher wages, more leisure, and more liberty. Labor could have "moral power" only when it struggled for better living, better homes, and better citizenship. It was his firm belief that labor could best improve itself within the framework of economic capitalism. Gompers had experienced many injustices that had been perpetrated against labor in courts and by professional politicians, and he would have none of them. Labor would gain its objectives through the processes of collective bargaining with capitalist employers and not with politicians. To him politicians were not concerned with the public welfare and principles of citizenship.

Gompers led organized labor throughout the years of World War I and became a member of the Council of National Defense. He organized a War Committee on Labor and attended the peace conference in Paris as a member of the Commission on International Labor Legislation.

Influence of Peter J. McGuire. Among the men who exercised a great deal of influence on the thinking of Gompers was Peter J. McGuire who organized the English speaking branch of the Socialist party in 1876; who organized the Brotherhood of Carpenters and Joiners in 1881; who drafted the call for the convention that established the Federation of Organized Trades and Labor Unions of the United States and Canada; and who later was active in the American Federation of Labor. He was a man who had participated in the organization and operation of socialist groups in Europe, and who came to see the failure of socialism insofar as it improved the position of labor in society. It was McGuire who helped mold Gomper's thinking on improving the condition of labor within the framework of capitalism. It was this same McGuire who has been dubbed the Father of Labor Day.

Secret of Success. One factor that led to Gompers' success, in which Powderly had failed, was his ability to talk to prince and pauper alike. He could go into the mines and the mills and meet workingmen face to face, talk their language, and rally them round his banner—the banner of trade unionism. He could talk to mayors, to governors, and to Presidents of the United States and feel at ease. On all occasions he championed the cause of labor, even when the occasion did not call for it. In some circles Gompers was hated; in some circles Gompers was feared; in all circles he spoke his mind. In his zealous fight for the cause of labor, Gompers did not lose an opportunity to give labor credit for all it was due. Sometimes in his enthusiasm for his cause, he exaggerated to the point of arousing disgust and distrust of the man and of the movement for which he stood.

Membership. Membership figures for the American Federation of Labor and for independent unions alike are difficult to obtain. Union officers have always been reluctant to reveal membership data. Methods of reporting union membership have varied with the concept of what constituted actual union membership. Variations as to membership hinged upon the inclusion or exclusion of retired members, of those who were unemployed, apprentices, those who were out of work because of work stoppages, and in later years those who were members of the Armed Forces. Leo Wolman, in his studies made for the National Bureau of Economic Research,[1] based his figures on the reports of the unions themselves; while the Bureau of Labor Statistics (BLS) data are based on the per capita tax payments remitted by the affiliated unions.

Table 18-1

Labor Union Membership—1897-1920

Year	Total Union Membership (000)		American Federation of Labor			Unaffiliated Unions. Total Membership (000)
			Number of Affiliated Unions	Total Membership (000)		
	B L S	Wolman	B L S	B L S	Wolman	Wolman
1897	440	447	58	265	272	175
1900	791	868	82	548	625	243
1905	1,918	2,022	118	1,494	1,598	424
1910	2,116	2,140	120	1,562	1,587	554
1915	2,560	2,583	110	1,946	1,968	614
1920	5,034	5,048	110	4,079	4,093	955

Source: U. S. Department of Commerce, Bureau of the Census, *Historical Statistics of the United States. Colonial Times to 1957* (Washington: U. S. Government Printing Office, 1960), p. 97. Adapted.

Data for 1905 reveal the effect of the prosperity phase of a business cycle on the number of unions and on union membership. This phase of the business cycle continued to the outbreak of war in Europe in 1914. The data for 1920 are a measure of the results of the encouragement given by the federal government to the formation of labor unions and to labor's affiliation with the unions of their trade.

The American Railway Union

Some unions developed a program that was more belligerent towards employers, towards management, towards capital, and towards the capitalistic system than were the programs of the Knights of Labor and of the American Federation of Labor. To some persons the advancement of labor under the

[1] Leo Wolman, *Ebb and Flow in Trade Unionism* (New York City: National Bureau of Economic Research, 1936), pp. 16, 138, and 236.

guidance of Powderly and of Gompers was too slow. To others there was no compromising the points of view of labor and of capital. It was out of the action taken by the General Managers Association in 1886 in slashing the wages of the employees of 24 railroads that had terminals in Chicago that the American Railway Union was born.

Eugene V. Debs had been Secretary of the Brotherhood of Locomotive Firemen and had seen many strikes that were called by individual unions fail. He was convinced that the time was ripe to unite the railroad workers of America into one strong coherent union organization in order to combat the locking out and the blacklisting of railroad employees who had gone on strike.

The first opportunity for the American Railway Union to lock horns with the railroads presented itself in 1893, when George M. Pullman, a manu-facturer of railroad cars, discharged a large number of employees and reduced the wages of the remainder while the officers of the Pullman Palace Car Company continued to receive their salaries in full. This cut was made in anticipation of a decline in the profits of the railroads following the extremely profitable experience brought on by the operation of the Chicago World's Fair. To heap insult on injury, while wages of the workers were cut one fifth, rents on the company-owned houses in which the employees were compelled to live remained as they were. When a Committee of the American Railway Union called upon Pullman he fired three of them, contrary to his promise. The mayors of about 50 cities supported an effort to arbitrate the questions at issue but to no avail. Under the leadership of Debs the Railway Union called a strike. In effect, the members of the union would not operate a train to which was attached a Pullman car. Since the railroads insisted on attaching at least one such car to every mail train, there was complete stoppage of the movement of trains in the Middle West.

Debs had ordered his men to refrain from any overt violence, and much to the disappointment of the General Managers Association they obeyed their instructions implicitly. As had happened so many times, a group of ir-responsible men who were not members of the Railway Union stopped a mail train and damaged its locomotive. That was the opportunity for which the General Managers Association had been waiting, and it appealed to Washington for help. Contrary to constitutional authority, federal troops were sent to Chicago for the prime objective of keeping the mails moving. Governor John P. Altgeld, of the State of Illinois, protested vigorously that matters had not gotten out of hand at the state level, but to no avail. Debs was tried and sentenced to six months in prison for being in violation of the Sherman Act insofar as he had attempted to create a labor monopoly that interfered with the free flow of interstate commerce. While serving this sentence he was converted to socialism by Victor Berger, of Milwaukee, and in 1898 he organized the Socialist party and became its standard-bearer for many years. Five times he was the Presidential nominee of that party.

The Railroad Brotherhoods

The railroad brotherhoods were the most important unions of railroad workers outside the veil of the American Federation of Labor. They consisted of the Brotherhood of Locomotive Engineers, the Brotherhood of Locomotive Firemen and Enginemen, the Brotherhood of Railway Trainmen, and the Order of Railway Conductors.

Conservative Goals. Compared with the programs and policies of contemporary unions, their aims and objectives were much more conservative. They placed emphasis upon the unity of interests between limited groups of workers and their employers. They stressed the personal conduct of their members and made no complaints of exploitation against their employers. The cardinal principles of their personal behavior patterns were sobriety, honesty in all their dealings, justice, and morality, which led to their being called uplift unions.

The accident rate among railroad employees was distressingly high, and few workers could afford to pay the insurance premiums that were charged by privately owned and operated insurance companies. The incidence of deaths alone that resulted from accidents that occurred in the line of duty was nine a day or 3,000 a year. The average work life for railroad employees was only 17 years, by which time workers who had not been taken by death had become totally disabled in numerous cases. The railroad brotherhoods were more in the nature of mutual insurance societies than they were labor unions. Their annual premiums were approximately 75 percent of those charged by private concerns. Membership in the brotherhoods averaged about 90 percent of those who were eligible. To the brotherhoods, insurance was much more important than was collective bargaining as a method or process by which disputes between railroad employees and railway management were settled. In fact, they recognized that the responsibility for operating the railroads rested upon the shoulders of management.

Strike Policy. A unique arrangement within the Brotherhood of Railway Engineers and Firemen dealt with the behavior patterns of member firemen when their locomotive engineers might be on strike. Even though all of the firemen were either in training to become locomotive engineers or had already qualified as such, they were not permitted to do any kind of work during a strike of the engineers that they were not permitted to do before a strike was called. They were permitted, however, to fire locomotives that were engineered by nonunion men or by strikebreakers. That Brotherhood did not attempt to maintain a closed shop, neither did it subscribe to the principle of the boycott.

As late as 1913 the president of the Brotherhood of Railway Trainmen issued instructions to its membership that according to the strike rules of the Brotherhood its members were "expected to cease work at a given time and to peacefully and quietly depart from the company's property until the strike is settled or until you receive instructions from your general committee to return to service . . . . If the companies are able to secure the services of a sufficient number of men to operate their property *we must concede they have a right to do so.*" (Italics added.)

The Industrial Workers of the World

The unwillingness of the leadership of the American Federation of Labor to organize unskilled workers together with its stated policy of attempting to improve the status of labor within the framework of capitalism was, to some persons, a measurement of the insincerity of its program and of its objectives. To these persons, unskilled workers were more in need of organization than were the skilled. To such leaders as Eugene Debs and William D. Haywood, Gompers was a traitor to the cause of labor. The workers to whom these men appealed were transient agricultural workers, lumberjacks, longshoremen, textile workers, miners, steelworkers, and those who were engaged in constructing railroads and in maintaining them. These workers lacked leadership. Many of them were illiterate by American standards. Many of them were immigrants who had not learned to read, write, or speak English. Many of them had no permanent homes and wandered from place to place in search of employment, or in hope of finding employment that paid wages that were higher than they had received in their last jobs. All of them relied upon brawn more than upon brain. To many of them, life was a matter of the survival of the fittest.

Attempts had been made in the earlier years of the functioning of the American Federation of Labor to interest Samuel Gompers in organizing workers in some of the mass production industries along industrial lines on an industry-wide basis. Not only did Gompers himself oppose that form of union organization, but the officers of the respective craft organizations did not want to relinquish their authority. After the American Federation had ignored efforts to organize workers in the textile industry in the East and in some of the mining and lumber camps in the West, the Industrial Workers of the World championed the cause of these workers. Hesitancy to accept them into the American Federation was based as much on their radical approach to attain their ends as it was upon their form of organization. They were militant; they were aggressive; they were revolutionary in thought and action. They had as little patience with the basic philosophy of the American Federation as the latter had with industrial unionism.

Chicago Convention. Dissatisfied with the program of the American Federation of Labor, William D. Haywood, of the Western Federation of Miners, and Daniel DeLeon, of the Socialist Labor Party, along with several others, called a convention in Chicago in 1905. Haywood had been embittered by his experiences in conducting a strike of the Western Federation of Miners at Cripple Creek, Colorado, in 1903. That strike found each side committed to violence; and the struggle was marked by mine explosions, mob outbreaks, individual killings, the deliberate wrecking of trains, arrests, imprisonments, and the machine-gunning of miners' assemblies. After 12 months of open warfare, the miners bowed to the strength of vigilantes, deputized sheriffs, police, and the state militia. The miners had been battered and beaten into submission, but their spirit was still smoldering. That first convention of the Industrial Workers of the World was dominated by the overpowering personality of Haywood. He accepted violence as a necessary phase of the struggle of labor for freedom. He was in favor of direct action— strikes, sabotage, violence to property and to person. Nothing was sacred in the pitched battle between labor and capital. He was openly in favor of overthrowing the capitalistic system and substituting for it the ownership of the instruments of production by labor. The product of their toil should belong to the workers.

Militant Action. The most spectacular strikes instigated by the IWW were the strike of the textile workers against the American Woolen Company at Lawrence, Massachusetts, in 1912, which the IWW won, and the struggle it waged against the silk industry in Paterson, New Jersey, in 1913, which the IWW lost after six months of open warfare. The IWW engaged in scores of minor strikes, all of which were pitched battles. When war broke out in Europe, the *Wobblies*, as the Industrial Workers of the World were called, took a decided stand against their participating in it. Public reaction against that pronouncement, imprisonment of its leaders, and finally Haywood's jumping bail and escaping to Russia, sapped the lifeblood of the most revolutionary type of labor union that had appeared in the United States.

The impact of the IWW movement cannot be measured in terms of its membership. In 1913, which may have been the peak year of membership, popularity, and success, membership cards were issued to 120,000 persons, only 30,347 of whom paid membership dues. That factor or condition illustrates one of the reasons it has been difficult to obtain accurate data regarding union membership. If there was any positive result that emanated from the warfare that was conducted by the Wobblies, it was to call attention to the extremely low wages that unskilled and unorganized labor was being paid, and to the brutal methods with which police and militia handled strike situations. The complacency of conservative labor leaders may have been shaken but not to the point of substituting an industrial form of labor organization for that of trade unionism.

Force of Public Opinion. Probably the most important impact of the strikes in Massachusetts and New Jersey, which were marked by violence and wanton disregard for the sanctity of life or property, was the formulation of public opinion not only against the Industrial Workers of the World, but against all efforts to organize workers on industry-wide bases.

When the demands on the part of shipyard workers in Seattle, Washington, were rejected by their employers in 1919, the Central Labor Committee, which at that time was under the leadership of James A. Duncan, called a general strike. An estimated 60,000 workers responded to the call. Not only was the industrial segment of Seattle in turmoil for five days, but civilian life and living were deprived of most of their normal services. When the participating unions realized that they lacked the accord of public opinion, the withdrawal of their support from the Central Labor Committee caused the strike to collapse. Mayor Ole Hanson seized the opportunity to further his political cause by his defiance of Bolshevist influence and tactics.

Shortly after that display of disregard for authority and law and order, the Boston police went on strike. Calvin Coolidge may not have been waiting for an opportunity to put himself in the limelight, but his handling of that delicate situation as Governor of Massachusetts practically assured him of the nomination for the Vice-Presidency of the United States on the Republican ticket in 1920.

Union Program

One of the first demands organized labor made of employers was recognition of the union. That meant a willingness of employers to engage in collective bargaining and to accept the check-off system of collecting union dues of members.

Collective Bargaining. Collective bargaining was engaged in by representatives of the union, called *walking delegates*, and representatives of management. The former were especially trained, full-time employees of the union and were not on management's payroll. Representatives of management were usually employed in the Personnel Division and, likewise, were trained in their profession. Whatever terms of agreement were reached around the bargaining table usually were voted on by the employees who were affected. Management was in close contact with its representatives all the time, and an agreement was tantamount to acceptance by employers.

The Check-Off. Unions insisted that payroll officers withhold union dues from pay envelopes. That assured the unions that their members would pay their dues and that their membership rolls would be maintained. It also placed an added cost on management of administering payrolls.

Closed Shop. While employers usually objected to a *closed shop* in principle, in reality it was more practical than an *open shop*, in which non-union employees worked alongside members of the union. They received the same wages and fringe benefits without having shared the cost of obtaining them, to which union workers objected. Americans have never approved of the principle of free riding, and relationships between union and nonunion employees did not always lend themselves to the highest productivity. The responsibility of obtaining new employees was placed upon union officials. Only if they could not furnish workers who were qualified in all respects to do the work that was required of them, could employers select employees, and then the latter had to join the union. A modification of the closed shop was the *union shop*, in which case employers were permitted to select their employees. After a certain period, usually two weeks, such employees had to decide whether or not they wished to continue in their jobs. If so, they had to join the union and were subject to the identical terms and benefits outlined in the union contract.

Objections of Employers. Many employers objected to bargaining with men who were not on their payroll. Walking delegates were interfering with something that was not of their concern. Experience had proved the futility of regular employees complaining about working conditions or asking for higher wages. They created dissatisfaction among other workers and were fired from their jobs. Walking delegates could not be discharged by management no matter how objectionable they might become because they were not on the payroll.

Employers took the position that their employees should have the right to decide whether or not they paid union dues. They also thought employees should decide for themselves if union membership was desirable. One of the prerogatives of management was to select its employees, which made a union shop more acceptable than a closed shop.

Membership

The number of workers who have belonged to labor unions is difficult to obtain. Some reports on membership are based upon the number of membership cards that have been issued; others are based upon the collection or payment of membership dues. Transportation and communications industries have always been the most highly organized in the United States, at least in terms of memberships reported by Leo Wolman in his 1936 study.[2] In 1900, they reported memberships of 189,000 followed by 153,000 in building and construction, and 131,000 in mining, quarrying and oil. At the bottom of the list in membership totals were hotel and restaurant services with 5,000, domestic and personal services with 7,000, and textile workers with 8,000. By 1915 no alterations had occurred in the ranking of the first three industries but membership in the metals, machinery and shipbuilding trades had increased rapidly and by 1920 had a membership of 859,000, one that was much closer to the second place, building and construction, than it was to the fourth ranking, mining, quarrying and oil. Changes had also taken place at the lower end of the scale. By 1910 organized workers in hotel and restaurant services, with 61,000, had surpassed those in six other industries, and trades employees were last in membership with only 15,000.

Preparation for war in the United States and war itself established a framework of conditions within which labor was given encouragement to organize. A union membership that totaled 860,000 in 1900 had become

---

[2] *Ibid.*, pp. 232 and 237.

2,583,000 in 1915. In 1920 a peak of 5,048,000 union members was recorded. That figure was not to be reached again throughout the next 20 years.

Demands of Organized Labor

After recognition of the union had become a *fait accompli*, the next order of business was for the union to demand higher wages, shorter workdays and workweeks, rest periods, and improved working conditions. Many of the so-called fringe issues that comprise major portions of wage contracts did not appear until after the close of World War I. Before the war, demands for higher wages were foremost; and they usually included demands for shorter workdays and workweeks. Since many employers were calloused to the health of their workers, measures and devices to increase their safety and health were demanded of employers. Sanitary conditions were improved either by terms of labor contracts or by force of statutory enactment.

Weapons of Organized Labor

A *strike* is a temporary collective cessation of work by all employees concerned in a given dispute. When the dispute is settled the workers anticipate a return to their former jobs with no loss of seniority and no other discriminations by employers against them. To be most effective, places of the strikers must not be taken by any other workers, strike-breakers, or scabs, so that for the duration of the strike, industrial plants are forced to close their operations. Occasionally union officers permit maintenance men to remain at their posts, if that is necessary to the resumption of work when the strike is settled. Another weapon that has proved to be very effective is the *boycott*, which is a refusal of union members to purchase the product of the firm that is being struck. If that situation is not possible to carry out, or if it proves to be ineffective as a weapon of warfare against the employer, organized labor may refuse to patronize any firm that uses the product of the firm that is struck. Boycotts result in pressure on firms that are not being struck to be applied to those that are being struck to make some settlement with the dissatisfied segments of their employees. The *union label* is a device for which all loyal union men and women look when they purchase articles of clothing, furniture, shoes, tools, and other consumers' goods. Its influence is not confined to periods of strikes or tensions between labor and management. It creates markets for those products to which it is attached.

Methods of Enforcement

That union leaders were in earnest in their efforts to obtain higher wages for their members is made manifest by the number of work stoppages as revealed in Table 18-2. Some of these stoppages were lockouts by employers rather than strikes by employees, but the latter far outnumbered the former

Table 18-2

Work Stoppages, Workers Involved, and Major Issues—1881-1920

Time Period	Totals		Wages and Hours		Union Organization		Others Not Given	
	Work Stoppages	Workers Involved (000)	Work Stoppages	Workers Involved (000)	Number of Stoppages	Workers Involved (000)	Number of Stoppages	Workers Involved (000)
1881-1885	2,639	882	1,934	741	242	63	463	79
1886-1890	7,029	1,845	4,150	1,277	1,163	254	1,716	317
1891-1895	7,179	1,954	4,018	1,279	1,275	249	1,886	424
1896-1900	6,951	1,928	3,817	1,177	1,611	467	1,523	285
1901-1905	14,505	2,920	6,681	1,426	5,031	942	2,793	551
1906-1913	n.a.†	n.a.	n.a.	n.a.	n.a.	n.a.	n.a.	n.a.
1914-1915	2,797	n.a.	1,173	n.a.	565	n.a.	1,059	n.a.
1916-1920	18,633 *	n.a.	10,247	n.a.	3,595	n.a.	4,791	n.a.

* Count of stoppages derived from newspaper notices.
† Not available.

Source: *Historical Statistics of the United States. Colonial Times to 1957,* 1960, p. 99. Adapted.

both in their number and in the number of employees involved. That employers were just as determined not to yield to the demands made upon them by union leaders is made manifest by these same data. Wages and hours of labor per day or per week were the issues in a large majority of instances, larger than the data in the table reveal because of the many that were not reported.

Attempts were made to make strikes effective by picketing plants and properties of industrial concerns that were being struck. Loyal union men and women of any trade were instructed not to cross any picket line that had been formed. Employers usually attempted to hire nonunion men and women to replace members of unions who were on strike or who would not cross picket lines. If violence did not occur when workers attempted to cross picket lines, it frequently resulted in violence later to person or to property—to the persons of strikebreakers, to the property of both strike-breakers and of corporate employers. Violence may have been personal beatings or shootings. It may have been setting fire to someone's property. It may have taken the form of dynamiting, bombing, sabotage, and outright vandalism in the destruction of machinery, housing, mining facilities, factories, terminals, and storage facilities. Peaceful picketing and peaceful strikes were almost unknown. Destruction of life and property could not be condoned; but they were accompaniments of warfare, and strikes were manifestations of war—open war between employers and employees. To remove the fury from the struggle, troops, police, and state militias were called upon many times to quell disturbances and to maintain order.

Employers were determined to show striking employees that they—management—were in the saddle and were in position to make business decisions. It was the function of labor to carry out decisions and not to participate in their making. Labor was just as determined to show employers that they could not operate without labor and that labor would not work unless it were treated with consideration of its welfare and well-being. Workers were human beings, and they refused to continue to submit to terms of employment that were humiliating and degrading to mankind.

Opposition of Employers

Even as late in the development of employee relations as World War I many corporate employers were still fighting labor organizations. Employers in mass production industries were among the last to yield to the pressures of strikes, boycotts, and of public opinion. Large proportions of their employees were either unskilled workers or were in the lower brackets of skilled workers. Semiskilled was the term that was frequently used to classify those workers who were above the grade of common labor but who had not developed skills that were comparable to those required of carpenters, masons, electricians, paperhangers, plumbers, painters, roofers, tinners, machinists, and others. One of the impacts of the mechanization of industry was to lower the level of skills that were required of labor and to equalize them. In some respects labor was fighting a battle of survival.

Injunctions. One of the weapons of corporate employers whose employees were on strike was to obtain a court injunction. Judges were somewhat prone to issue injunctions against striking employees in order to protect the property and the property rights of employers, many of whom attempted to continue to operate with the use of nonunion employees. In polite circles these men were strikebreakers; in others they were tabbed *scabs*. Persons who violated the terms of injunctions were in contempt of court and as such could be punished by the judges who issued them without the benefit of trial by jury. The way it turned out was that if judges could be prevailed upon to issue injunctions, they were quick to uphold the dignity and authority of their respective courts, and labor did not have much chance.

Results of Strikes on Wages and Hours of Work

Perusal of the data that are presented in Table 18-3 reveals that progress was slow in advancing wage rates and in reducing the length of the workweek. The most noticeable advance was made between the years 1915 and 1920. Data reveal the impacts of war and to some extent the policy and influence of the federal government regarding wages and hours of labor per week. What isn't shown in the table is the length of the basic workweek for which contractual base wage rates were paid. Pay for hours worked beyond the basic workweek was compensated for at the rate of one and a half times the base rate. That plan became common during the war as a means of increasing the volume of output of goods that were consumed at home as well as those that were sent to Europe either in support of American troops who were stationed on foreign soil or in support of our Allies.

Postal employees have enjoyed a 48-hour week longer than other workers who are represented in Table 18-3. The impact of effective organization is revealed in the 43.8 average workweek for building tradesmen when union employees in manufacturing industries averaged 47.5 hours work per week. Both the hours worked per week and the average hourly earnings of bituminous coal miners throw light upon the need for effective organization among coal miners. This segment of the laboring population proved to be one of the most difficult of all to organize effectively. Not only was bituminous coal sold in highly competitive markets, it was mined by workers who were just as highly competitive. Unskilled workers lacked a champion when the Socialist party and the IWW's passed into oblivion, until the United Mine Workers rose within the ranks of the American Federation of Labor. A weekly pay of $10.65 for unskilled employees was totally inadequate to support them and their families after 1910. It was in this segment of the population that the largest sized families were found.

While data in Table 18-3 show that an increase in wage rates was accompanied by a decrease in hours worked per week, all these advancements

Table 18-3

Hours and Earnings in Manufacturing, in Selected Manufacturing Industries, and for Unskilled Labor—1890-1920

Year	Manufacturing Total		Manufacturing Union		Manufacturing Payroll		Bituminous Coal Mining		Railroads Full-Time Weekly Earnings	Building Trades		Postal Employees		Unskilled Average Full-Time Weekly Earnings
	I*	II†	I	II	I	II	I	II		I	II	I	II	
1890	60.0	$0.199	54.4	$0.324	62.2	$0.149	60.0	$0.180	$11.38	51.3	$0.341	48.0	$0.352	$ 8.71
1900	59.0	.216	53.0	.341	62.1	.152	52.6	.204	11.43	48.3	.374	48.0	.371	8.83
1910	56.6	.260	50.1	.403	59.8	.188	51.6	.299	14.07	45.2	.520	48.0	.420	10.65
1915	55.0	.287	48.6	.439	58.2	.212	51.6	.337	15.78	44.8	.569	48.0	.466	10.65
1920	51.0	.663	45.7	.884	53.5	.561	48.2	.784	34.14	43.8	1.052	48.0	.739	25.98

* Columns I. Average weekly hours

† Columns II. Average hourly earnings

Source: *Historical Statistics of the United States. Colonial Times to 1957*, 1960, p.91. Adapted.

may not rightly be attributed to the efforts of organized labor. When entrepreneurs were making profits—and making still larger profits necessitated the hiring of more labor—they entered the labor market by offering higher wages than formerly. Many employees in the lower wage brackets did not have any particular feeling of loyalty to their corporate employers and did not hesitate to move on to better jobs if the actual moving was not complicated and if it did not involve much of a cost on their part. Labor turnover has been costly to corporate employers, and raising wages voluntarily tended to make laborers more contented where they were employed and tended also to reduce labor turnover.

A glance at Tables 18-4 and 18-5 lends confirmation to the fact that prior to World War I American labor was not well paid on an annual basis. Seasonal unemployment, cyclical unemployment, illness and accident—all served to interrupt the continuity of laborers' services throughout a given 12-month period. The data in these tables also confirm the statement that has been made before, namely that the first 10 to 15 years of the 20th century were relatively prosperous for labor. Beyond that period the impact of war distorted the relationships that determined the economic status of labor. In view of what has been said before, it is not at all surprising to find that farm workers were paid much less on an annual basis than were wage earners in any of the industries and public utilities for which data are given in the table. Judging from the wages they received, public schoolteachers either were not considered as having been very productive or their services were held in low esteem by members of school boards who were appointed by elective officials or who were elected directly by the voters. They must have had dedicated professional concern for the youth of America. Their financial rewards were not much above the level of those of farm workers. Ministers, too, received meager and entirely inadequate salaries. They were compelled by force of circumstances to accept charity from members of their churches. The aristocrats among wage earners were railroad employees, with those of street railways not far behind. White collar workers in manufacturing industries and in railroads by 1905 had average annual incomes in excess of those that were received by federal employees in the executive departments and by postal workers. These jobs were created by the combination and merger movements that became somewhat strong after 1870. Railroads became larger by end-to-end combinations. Freight traffic was shipped longer distances, and the revenues therefrom had to be shared with other railroads, rather than remain for the use of those upon which traffic originated. This work required the services of bookkeepers and clerks—both record and file.

Industries in which wage earners in 1920 tended to receive more than double their 1915 wage incomes were manufacturing, steam railroads, street railways, gas and electricity, and bituminous coal mining. Occupational workers, those who worked for telephone and telegraph companies, and white collar employees were not so fortunate. The average wage of telephone

Table 18-4

Average Annual Earnings in All Industries and in Selected Industries and Occupations—1890-1920

Year	All Industries—Nonfarm	Wage Earners—Manufacturing	Wage Earners—Steam Railroads	Clerical Workers—Manufacturing and Steam Railroads	Street Railways	Telephone	Telegraph	Gas and Electricity	Bituminous Coal Mining	Farm Labor
1890	$ 486	$ 439	$ 560	$ 848	$ 557	...	...	$ 687	$ 406	$233
1895	468	416	546	941	509	...	...	640	307	216
1900	490	435	548	1,011	604	...	...	620	438	247
1905	554	494	589	1,076	646	$401	$ 581	543	500	302
1910	630	558	677	1,156	681	417	649	622	558	336
1915	687	568	815	1,267	748	529	792	644	589	355
1920	1,489	1,358	1,817	2,160	1,608	980	1,145	1,432	1,386	810

Source: *Historical Statistics of the United States. Colonial Times to 1957*, 1960, pp. 91, 92. Adapted.

employees was lowered by including the very low rates of pay that were received by switchboard operators. Many of these operators were young girls whose pay contributed to enlarging family incomes rather than constituting them.

Table 18-5
Average Annual Earnings of Selected Occupations—1890-1920

Year	Federal Employees *	Postal Employees	Public School-teachers	Ministers
1890	....	$ 878	$256	$ 794
1895	$1,104	935	289	787
1900	1,033	925	328	731
1905	1,072	935	392	759
1910	1,108	1,049	492	802
1915	1,152	1,162	578	984
1920	1,648	1,844	936	1,428

* Executive departments

Source: *Historical Statistics of the United States, Colonial Times to 1957*, 1960, pp. 91, 92. Adapted.

LABOR LEGISLATION

One difficulty that was encountered in several attempts that were made to obtain court approval of laws that regulated the terms and conditions under which labor accepted employment was the clause in the Constitution of the United States that guarantees the freedom of all persons to enter into contractual relationships with other persons. Laws that shortened the length of the workday were infringements upon the freedom of workers to contract for longer workdays than might be provided for in the law. Minimum wage laws prevented workers from entering into wage agreements whereby they might express a willingness to work for wages below the legal minimum.

Another legal barrier that had to be overcome in the thinking of the judges and in their interpretation of the law was that any kind of labor legislation was a form of class legislation, and as such was unconstitutional. Until the courts became more social minded, or until they became aware of the social impacts and implications of excessively long hours of work per day or per week at wages which did not permit workers and their families to maintain scales of living that measured up to the minimum of health, sanitation, and decency, they had difficulty in finding legal precedents for declaring such laws valid. After they became aware of the social impacts, they had to be concerned with them and the effects they had, not only upon present generations of society, but upon future generations. Slum areas were the breeding places of filth, malnutrition, and disease. Contagion was impossible to control, and the incidence of communicable diseases was high. Many crimes against property and against persons were bred by the conditions under which workers—factory, mill, mine, transportation, trade, and commerce—were compelled to live. Forces of circumstances overpowered those of personal pride, morality, and ethics. Laws had been framed to protect property and property rights. For many years the rights of persons were subordinate to the rights of property.

The voice of adult male labor as it was expressed through the channels of trade unions did not give encouragement to legislation that would tend to curb labor's power and influence in bargaining collectively with employers and their representatives. The feeling was widespread among union leaders that they could take care of themselves without the aid of the law, and they might gain more than the law would give them at any given time.

Provisions of Early Legislation

Early legislation that had for its purpose (1) limiting the length of the workday or of the workweek and (2) establishing minimum wage rates that could be paid in certain industries was difficult to enforce partly because of the interpretations of the law by judges at both the state and federal levels. The opening wedge to placing restrictions upon the terms of the labor contract by law was upheld in the name of protecting those who were too weak to protect themselves—women and children. That weakness stemmed from lack of effective organization as well as from their physical condition. Some consideration was given to protecting future generations of persons yet unborn. When a man's work was done he could rest, relax, and recuperate before the next day's task was begun. That was not so with women. When their work in factory or mill was done, their work at home began and they might work 20 hours or more in a continuity of 24 hours. It was to protect their health that laws were passed at the state level, the effects of which were to restrict the hours per day that they could work.

Laws that restricted the hours children were permitted to work per day were justified from the point of view that the children of today are the progenitors of the children of tomorrow. If their growth were stunted or their health and physical condition were impaired by strenuous labor and by their mothers having worked in unhealthy and unsanitary environments, their children would be weaklings and undernourished at birth. There was no uniformity in the setting of minimum age requirements in the several states. The range was wide, varying from a minimum of 12 to a maximum of 21. They were all in agreement in one respect: agricultural labor was exempt from their provisions. This was in recognition of the fact that child labor on farms worked out-of-doors; the work was under parental supervision, and there was not the drive to keep up with the pace that was set by power-driven machinery. Farmers could not afford to pay high wages for work that was done by members outside their own immediate families. Work on farms did not have the same undesirable effects upon the health of children that factory, mill, and mine work had.

Federal Child Labor Legislation

In the name of equalizing competition between firms in a given industry that were subjected to different state laws in respect to the use of child labor, attempts were made to have Congress pass a child labor law that would place all employers, regardless of the states in which they operated, on the same basis. In 1916, Congress passed an act which prohibited the transportation across state boundaries of products of mines or of factories in which children under the age of 14 had been employed, or between the ages of 14 and 16 had been permitted to work over 8 hours a day or 6 days a week within 30 days prior to delivery of the products to common carriers.

In 1918 in *Hammer* v. *Dagenhart* (247 U.S. 251), the Supreme Court held that the law, in reality, was an attempt to control the conditions under which goods were manufactured before they entered into interstate commerce. Responsibility for regulating conditions under which goods were produced lay with the states and not with the federal government and the law was declared to be unconstitutional.

Not to be thwarted in its efforts to control child labor, Congress passed another bill that placed a tax of 10 percent on the net income of employers of child labor within the limitations cited above. In *Bailey* v. *Drexel Furniture Company* (276 Fed. 452) the Court held again that the tax, in reality, dealt with conditions under which goods were manufactured which was the responsibility of the states. The tax was declared to be a penalty that was imposed upon manufacturers in order to coerce them to act as Congress wished them to. Since it was not an act to regulate interstate commerce, it was declared to be null and void.

Length of the Workday

The opening wedge to the acceptance of laws that restricted the number of working hours per day for adult male labor was a provision that placed government employees and those who had been working a 10-hour day in the fulfillment of government contracts (in the early years of the 20th century) on an 8-hour day. As early as 1888 the number of hours that a mail carrier could work was reduced from ten hours to eight hours per day with no decrease in pay. In 1912 the 8-hour day was made to apply to clerks in the first and second-class post offices.

Long hours of work not only caused a high incidence of fatigue among the workers, they were the cause of industrial accidents and of accidents in which the general public suffered injury. It was in the name of accident prevention and of safety to the general public that the hours of adult male labor were restricted in steam railroad, street railway, and other industries with which the public came in direct contact. Union officials did not wax enthusiastic over that type of legislation, as they felt that it weakened the cause of organized labor. They had to justify the very existence of union organization and its cost to their memberships. Any development that brought benefits to labor by processes other than collective bargaining was frowned upon by labor leaders.

Concern over Health and Safety

The impacts of labor legislation were felt in restrictions that were placed on night employment of women and children, rest periods, and lunch hours during the workday. Saturday afternoons and holidays were given recognition in the name of conserving the health and strength of the labor force. Health—public and individual—and safety to the public and to the workers were the justifications of labor legislation. When it was found that immigrant families and others were given homework in cigar wrapping (1885) and in the many branches of the textile industries, laws regulating the operation of *sweatshops* were passed in the name of preserving the health of the public. Instances were discovered in which persons with tuberculosis, typhoid fever, and other highly contagious diseases were given piecework to do in their tenements. Materials were spread out on the beds of sick persons where they became infiltrated with the germs of disease. As these materials passed through many hands on their way to ultimate consumers, they left trails of infection on many innocent and unsuspecting persons. As early as 1885 New York attempted to put an end to sweatshops by prohibiting the manufacture of cigars and other tobacco products in tenement houses in first-class cities. The law was declared unconstitutional in that it was an abuse of the police power and an infringement on the freedom of cigar workers, who, under the law, were forced from their homes and the beneficient influences there in order to find employment in their chosen trade (*In re Jacobs*, 98 N.Y. 98, 1885).

The next approach that was made in attacking the sweatshop system of work was to license places where homework could be performed. Certain standards of health and sanitation were established. In New York City alone there were 15,000 licensed operations and over 9,000 other homes in which work was being done. Working eight hours a day, it was estimated that it would have taken three inspectors to enforce the terms of the law in each tenement, or a total of 45,000 inspectors to keep an eye on these places day and night. In 1913, New York turned from issuing licenses for such work to prohibiting it entirely for food products, dolls or doll clothing, and children's and infants' wearing apparel.

It was the influence of safety that induced public opinion and the courts to accept laws that established minimum hours of work for adult males in the field of public transportation. It was in the name of the general welfare and health factors that brought the acceptance of minimum wage laws. Minimum wages were those that were necessary to enable a worker to maintain himself and his family at a minimum level of health and decency. If the support of his family did not measure up to that elusive standard, not only that family but others would be contaminated and they would become burdens on the public purse.

Responsibility for Industrial Accidents

In order to stave off a social and political revolution in Germany, which would have been spearheaded by the Socialists, Chancellor Bismarck was responsible for having some laws pushed through the Reichstag in 1884 that were in the nature of workmen's compensation laws. The need for some such legislation was found in the low wages that were paid to labor. They were entirely inadequate to provide medical care of the crudest sort to the sick, or to pay the costs of industrial accidents and illnesses. Unemployment was an ever-present threat to industrial workers, particularly to those who possessed no skills, and fortunate was the family whose breadwinner found steady and continuous employment throughout the year and throughout his years of active service.

Theory held that the wages that were paid to workers who were engaged in seasonal occupations were sufficiently high to tide prudent families over or through the seasons of no work. The hazards of some jobs were compensated for by wage differentials over and above the wages that were received by the same grade of labor that was not exposed to the same hazards. These ideas may have been good in theory, but workers just were not compensated in proportion either to the unsteadiness of their jobs or to the degree of hazard involved. Workers did not hestitate to accept employment just because it was seasonal, or because the risk of accident was greater than it was in other kinds of work. As for accidents, they might occur to others but not to any given employee. He was calloused and indifferent to the possibility of his being injured or killed on the job. Then, too, there were many more applicants or candidates for jobs than there were jobs to be filled. The greater the degree of mechanization, the less was the absolute demand for both employees of low level skills and employees who had acquired skills of higher levels. Machinery set the pace for labor, not vice versa. Long hours created fatigue, loss of sensitivity to risk, lack of attention, and slower reflexes. Even drowsiness and catnapping were frequent occurrences, especially after a man had worked 12 hours on a day shift and then was forced to change to the night shift and work another 12 hours without rest. This condition prevailed in the steel industry and others.

Common Law Defenses Against Employer Liability. There were no statutory provisions at state or federal levels that protected employees against losses incurred because of industrial accidents over which they had no control. If employees or their heirs wanted compensation for financial burdens they had incurred, they were compelled to bring suit in state courts against the persons whom they thought were responsible for the accidents. Since most judges gave little recognition to the social responsibilities of corporate employers, plaintiffs at court seldom were given relief.

Contributory Negligence. Under the doctrine of contributory negligence, if an injured worker in any manner had contributed to the cause of an accident, his employer was not financially responsible. During a moment of inattention a worker may have contributed to the cause of an accident as a result of which he was injured or killed. He may have suffered from industrial fatigue, or a tireless piece of machinery may have continued to operate at a pace more rapid than the worker could maintain. He may have been just plain careless. In any similar case an individual or corporate employer was not liable in the eyes of the courts.

Assumption of Risk. In mining and mechanized industries, in particular, there were many kinds of accidents that seemed inherent. Dust explosions, falling slate, and accidents in elevator shafts were of such frequent occurrence as to warn men that when they accepted employment in coal mines, they exposed themselves to these and other hazards. Other men who worked with machinery were presumed to be aware that mechanical failures, many of which inflicted injury or death upon employees, could not be prevented. Courts held that since men had accepted employment voluntarily, they assumed the risks of industrial hazards; and employers could not be held financially responsible in case of accident.

Fellow Servant Rule. In many instances, when accidents are the result of negligence or ignorance of certain employees, other workers suffer injuries or death. Employers were not responsible, and relief should be sought from the persons who were directly responsible. The utter futility of obtaining such relief is evident. Also, under corporate organization all officers, administrators, and supervisors are employees, or fellow servants; and corporate employers were exonerated of all blame.

Workmen's Compensation Laws. With these three defenses available to employers and with current wages so low that even prudent employees could not possibly save enough out of current income to provide the funds that were necessary to pay the costs of industrial accidents, something had to be done to protect wage earners. As was to be expected, state laws ran afoul the barrier of unconstitutionality; and it was not until 1917 that the United States Supreme Court laid down the criteria for approving them; namely (1) the exercise of the police power of the state, (2) the reasonableness of the law in imposing charges upon employers, (3) the object of the legislation must be in the interest of the general public rather than of private or particular concern, and (4) the burden must be equitably distributed. It was estimated that by the end of 1917 the compensation laws of 40 states and territories covered over 8½ million workers, or nearly 40 percent of the total number of workers. These laws were not compulsory to the degree that employers could not use some other form of protection; but if they did so, the common law defenses were not available to them.

Public employees, those who were engaged in interstate commerce, domestic servants, agricultural workers, and workmen in establishments that employed fewer than a stated minimum number of employees, were among the classifications of workers who were not covered by compensation laws.

Federal Legislation

Beyond regulating the hours and conditions of its own employees and those who were working to fulfill government contracts, the federal government had attempted no legislation that interfered with the prerogative of the states in determining the conditions under which commodities might be manufactured. The United States Department of Labor was established by law in 1913. It included the Bureau of Labor Statistics, the Bureau of Immigration and Naturalization, and the Children's Bureau. The Secretary of Labor was authorized to act as mediator and to appoint commissioners of conciliation in labor disputes. A Conciliation Service was established as a separate division of the Department in 1918. President Wilson appointed William B. Wilson, who was a trade unionist, to become the first Secretary of Labor, which office he held until 1921.

Under the terms of the Clayton Act of 1914 labor was declared not to be a commodity, and as such it became exempt from the provisions of the Sherman Antitrust Act of 1890. It also limited the use of injunctions in labor disputes and declared that picketing was a lawful activity. During the following year the La Follette Seamen's Act was passed, the effect of which was to place seamen on a level with other segments of labor in the United States. Among other provisions it guaranteed them a minimum wage of $45 a month at a time when Chinese and Japanese crewmen were receiving anywhere from $7.50 to $9.00 for the same period of time. At least 75 percent of the crews of ships that were owned and operated by Americans were to be capable of understanding any and all orders given by the ship's officers; a minimum of 64 percent of the deck crews shall have passed physical and professional examinations to assure their fitness for their jobs; one half of the wages that were due at the time were to be paid to members of the crews while they were in any port; and the crew of any vessel could leave the service at any time the vessel should tie up in an American port. There were other provisions that governed the hours of work members of crews could be required to work per week, and lifeboats had to be carried on all ships.

About the only legislation prior to 1920 whose impact was on unemployment was in connection with the establishment of employment offices. They were set up at the state level to correct the evil of privately owned and operated agencies as much as they were intended to fit unemployed workers into available jobs. While the federal government first used such a plan in placing farm labor and in attempts to settle newly arrived immigrants where there was work for them to perform, it was the pressure of war that led to the organization of the United States Employment Service in 1918. In the 15-month period that ended in March, 1919, that Service registered over 5¼ million workers, 5 million of whom were referred to employers who were in need of additional workers. In spite of many shortcomings in developing that Service in such a short time, over 3¾ million positions were filled. In August, 1918, all employers of more than 100 persons who were engaged in war work were required by Presidential proclamation to obtain their un- skilled workers through the facilities of the United States Employment Service. When the pressures of war eased in 1919, the Service became entangled in politics, and it lost its effectiveness except for supplying infor- mation to local public officers. There was a strong feeling in both official and unofficial circles that such service should be performed at the state level rather than by the federal government.

The most important piece of labor legislation at the Federal level prior to 1920 may have been the Adamson Act which was passed by Congress under pressure of a threatened strike by the Railroad Brotherhoods. President Wilson did not want our transportation facilities to be tied up at such a critical time in our nation's history. We were on the brink of a world war, and a strike of the Railroad Brotherhoods would have been fatal to a successful struggle against the Central Powers. The provisions of that Act, which were carried over into the years of peace that followed the signing of the Armistice in November, 1918, were the establishment of a basic 40-hour week for railway labor, with time and a half paid for hours worked over and above that base.

QUESTIONS FOR REVIEW

1. What economic developments, the impacts of which were upon the labor segment of the population, encouraged the formation of labor unions?
2. (a) Who were the Knights of Labor?
   (b) What was the program of the Knights of Labor?
   (c) Why did the Knights of Labor fail to survive?
3. What factors contributed to the longevity of the American Federation of Labor?
4. (a) What was the attitude of the American Federation of Labor towards labor legislation?
   (b) How were early state laws that attempted to regulate conditions of em- ployment justified?
5. Who was Eugene V. Debs? Samuel Gompers? William D. Haywood? Terence V. Powderly?
6. How did the organization and program of the Railroad Brotherhoods differ from those of other labor organization?

7. Why was the federal government unsuccessful in its efforts to legislate child labor out of existence?

8. Explain the common law defenses once used by employers to avoid financial responsibility for accidents and injuries to their employees.

9. What was the Adamson Act of 1916? What was its significance?

SUGGESTED READINGS

Bogart, Ernest L., and Charles M. Thompson (eds.). *Readings in the Economic History of the United States.* London: Longmans, Green & Co., Ltd., 1927. Chapter 22.

Grob, Gerald N. "The Knights of Labor and the Trade Unions, 1878-1886," *Views of American Economic Growth: The Industrial Era,* edited by Thomas C. Cochran and Thomas B. Brewer. New York City: McGraw-Hill Book Company, 1966.

Faulkner, Harold U. *The Decline of Laissez Faire, 1897-1917.* New York City: Holt, Rinehart & Winston, Inc., 1951. Chapters 21 and 22.

Hardman, J. B. S. "From 'Job Consciousness' to Power Accumulation," *Issues in American Economic History,* edited by Gerald D. Nash. Boston: D. C. Heath & Company, 1964.

Kirkland, Edward C. *Industry Comes of Age: Business, Labor, and Public Policy, 1860-1897.* New York City: Holt, Rinehart & Winston, Inc., 1961. Chapters 27 and 28.

Montgomery, Royal E. "Evolution of American Labor," *Issues in American Economic History,* edited by Gerald D. Nash. Boston: D. C. Heath & Company, 1964.

Perlman, Selig. "The Basic Philosophy of the American Labor Movement," *Economic Change in America,* edited by Joseph T. Lambie and Richard V. Clemence. Harrisburg, Pa.: Stackpole Books, 1954.

Taft, Philip. "A Theory of the American Labor Movement," *Issues in American Economic History,* edited by Gerald D. Nash. Boston: D. C. Heath & Company, 1964.

——————. "The I. W. W. in the Grain Belt," *American Economic History: Essays in Interpretation,* edited by Stanley Coben and Forest G. Hill. Philadelphia: J. B. Lippincott Co., 1966.

Wright, Chester W. *Economic History of the United States.* 2d ed. New York City: McGraw-Hill Book Company, 1949. Chapters 35 and 36.

Chapter 19

MARKETS AND TRADE:

DOMESTIC AND FOREIGN

One of the most important aspects of the growth of the American economy after 1865 was its orientation to market situations. The days were long past when production was undertaken in the home for the home. Local markets were expanded into national and international markets as transportation and communication facilities were developed. Most of the larger firms produced for the market rather than in response to specific orders on hand. Financial organizations were adjusted to the needs of larger and more distant markets, both domestic and foreign.

DOMESTIC TRADE

Industrial specialization and division of labor sparked the development of local trade. Regional specialization in agriculture and in manufacturing sparked interregional domestic trade. The slight decrease in the portion of our national income that was generated by domestic trade operations does not measure its importance in terms of its volume, the number of establishments, or the number of persons who obtained their livelihoods from such domestic operations.

Settlement of the West

After the termination of hostilities in 1865, the principal business of the people of the United States appeared to be the settlement of the West and the exploitation of the natural resources that were in that region. Through its public land policy as was revealed through the passage of the Homestead Act, the Timber Culture Act, the Desert Land Act, and the Timber and Stone Act, the federal government facilitated, encouraged, and stimulated the appropriation and exploitation on a free enterprise basis of the natural resources that were found west of the Mississippi River. Land grants to railroads combined with a liberal immigration policy and financial aid in the construction of railroad rights-of-way resulted in a much more rapid rate of construction of the railway net than otherwise would have taken place.

Railroads without traffic to transport were superfluous. Railroad managements promoted the settlement of frontiersmen along their rights-of-way. Settlement itself gave rise to one-way passenger traffic. The economic impact of settlement was found in the stimulation of two-way freight traffic. These frontiersmen were economically self-sufficient only at a low level of living. They increased the degree to which division of labor and regional specialization were intensified on a voluntary, free enterprise basis. Specialization was along regional lines; division of labor was along industrial, commercial, and mercantile lines. Any enhancement of specialization or division of labor gave rise to new trade relations and to the exchange of commodities for commodities, services for services, or commodities for services.

The Investment of Eastern Capital in Western America. By 1865 some well-defined regional specializations of economic activity had bestowed their benefits upon the American people. Manufacturing and commerce were heavily concentrated in the New England States and in New York, New Jersey, and Pennsylvania. While the Southern States still were predominately agricultural in character, they were engaging in a more diversified type, which in itself stimulated trade between the people in this region and those who lived in the North and East. People who lived in the states that lay west of the Mississippi River traded the products of their farms, their ranches, their mines, and their forests for the products of the other regions of the country. Interregional trade had become truly intersectional in character.

As the pace of the westward movement increased, extensive agriculture, mining, and lumbering pursuits required more financing than did the settlements east of the Mississippi River, partly because the activities were carried on on a much larger scale, partly because the settlements, or the people in them, were less self-sufficient. Capital that was required to develop any industrial activity of necessity had to be obtained by borrowing from those persons and financial institutions that had venture capital to lend. While some of this capital came from European countries, more correctly from persons and financial institutions that were located in Europe, it is that portion of the capital that had its origin in the United States with which we are now concerned.

In all places and at all times there has been a certain amount of savings which has found investment outlets away from the regions in which it originated. Industrialists, financiers, and officers of financial institutions tended to seek channels for investing their loanable capital from which they would receive the highest rates of interest that were available at the time the investment decisions were made and that were compatible with safety. Rates of interest on investments that were made west of the Mississippi River tended to be higher, in general, than were those that were made in the Eastern States. Part of the interest differential was accounted for in the greater element of risk involved in not being able to supervise its use as well as or as closely as capital invested nearby or at home. Again, capital tended to be more productive as an initial dose in an extensive investment than it was as an additional dose of an intensive application of capital. It was partially a matter of the operation of that inexorable law—the law of *diminishing productivity* as applied to land and capital.

Flow of Goods. The initial impact of an investment of capital in the West was to cause a flow of goods from east to west; the payment of interest and installments of the principal sums when due tended to cause a flow of goods from west to east. The western flow of goods consisted largely of manufactured goods, durable capital goods, as well as consumers' goods; the eastern flow of goods was one of foodstuffs, lumber, and mineral products. As industry itself participated in the westward movement, as it did towards the close of the 19th century, there was a flow of heavy durable capital goods to the west, a flow of manufactured goods that were ready for consumption to the east.

There was another type of development that followed the flow of capital goods to the west. The immediate products of the capital goods industries were sold in the West and then raw materials, foodstuffs, and consumers' goods flowed to the east. One form of such capital goods was horse-drawn farm machinery, much of which was manufactured in the states of Illinois and Wisconsin. Binders, reapers, mowers, threshers, cultivators, rakes, manure spreaders and hay loaders, among others, were sold to farmers in all the Middle Western and Western States; later, combines and tractors were added to the list and manure spreaders were dropped. There were several large manufacturers of farm wagons of all types that were used to meet the requirements of western farmers. This capital equipment was the object of much trading between farmers and retailers, after the latter, in turn, had purchased it from the manufacturers.

Every time there was a flow of goods of any kind in either direction, it represented either the initial transaction to a trade or the final one. As explained in these terms, it took two transactions to consummate a trade. Each transaction was completed with the use of money or credit, and it was the use of this same money or credit in another transaction that wrote *finis* to the trade.

Banking Structure

Sound monetary, banking, and credit systems oil the wheels of exchange. The use of the word *system* in referring to bank organization and practice prior to 1914 is an anomaly. Banks were chartered at the level of each of the several states and by the Comptroller of the Currency. There were more state banks than national banks. State laws established a structural framework within which the state banks operated, but they had no bearing upon bank or credit policies. State banks were permitted to establish savings departments and to grant real estate loans and loans to farmers. National banks, at first, were restricted to the area of financing commerce and trade. Commercial loans were intended to be self-liquidating within a maximum period of 90 days. State and national banks were independent unit banks that were not subject to policy programs that might have been imposed upon them by some central banking authority. They were free to grant short-term commercial loans subject only to the policies of their respective boards of directors and within the limitations that were established by their respective reserve situations.

In spite of the handicaps of independent unit banking insofar as their impacts were felt in the conduct of interregional trade and commerce, the acceptance of deposit banking and the development of correspondent relationships between banks facilitated the settlement of interregional obligations. Improved communication services that were provided by telephone and telegraph companies under the stimulus of free enterprise augmented the extension of postal services by the government.

Monetary System

While there were some changes and short-run disturbances that gave rise to feelings of uncertainty as to the soundness of our money, in the long run throughout the entire period under consideration, the monetary, banking, and credit systems facilitated trade—local, regional, national, and international. After 1879 government and bank paper money alike circulated at face value the country over. While some economic segments of the population—those persons who were engaged in agricultural pursuits, for example—were placed at a long-run disadvantage in terms of the purchasing power of their incomes, there is no evidence that trade and commerce were stifled on that account. In fact, the long period of falling prices may have contributed to an increase in trade by volume because the farmer attempted to maintain the level of his dollar income by producing and selling more products of the farm at lower prices. The increased prosperity of urban workers after 1900 enabled them to make purchases and to pay prices for them that were beyond their reach prior to that time.

Transportation

Transportation of commodities and of persons was speeded up. By 1920, Chicago and Cincinnati were one day distant from New York; St. Louis, New Orleans, and Denver were reached the second day. The Rocky Mountain States, central and west Texas were reached the third day; Seattle, Portland, San Francisco, and Los Angeles the fourth day. Freight service was a little slower. Automobile, truck, and air facilities provided only local service, if they were operated at all.

Extension of the railway net and the improvement of transportation facilities led to a higher degree of economic interdependence between the different segments of the American economy. This, together with an increase in disposable incomes, gave rise to a larger volume of trade. Corporate profits were distributed as dividends to the holders of common stock, or they were reinvested directly by the corporations that earned them. In either case they were returned to the stream of trade and commerce in the circular flow of money throughout the economy. Tax collections at the state and local levels gave way in dollar volume to tax collections at the federal level after 1909 with the institution of the corporate income tax, which was followed in 1913 by the tax on personal incomes. Money that flowed into government coffers was paid out directly for goods and services, even though there were some years in which the fiscal operations of the Treasury Department revealed a surplus. That amount that was used in the purchase of government supplies took part in trade directly; that portion that was used to compensate for services rendered supported trade indirectly.

ORGANIZATION OF MARKETING AND TRADE

It should be clear by this time that the process of trade, direct or indirect, became more complex as markets were widened and as specialization and division of labor were developed to higher levels. Increasing interdependence among and between the various elements of our economic society demanded a larger volume of trade and a more complex business organization. It is on some of these organizations or institutions that our attention will now be focused.

Direct Selling

Direct selling by the original producer of any given line of producers' and consumers' goods had almost disappeared except for some lines of agricultural produce that were bartered with local merchants or were sold directly to consumers. In season, strawberries, tomatoes, apples, pears, plums, cherries, peaches, peas, beans, beets, carrots, cucumbers, cauliflower, cabbages, and egg plant, among other vegetables, were sold in roadside markets and to local grocers. Costs of refrigeration, packing, and transport kept these items off distant markets. Dairies were of local ownership and operation except in and near the largest cities. The pounding of horseshoes on dirt and pavement could be heard early in the morning as horse-drawn wagons carried fresh milk, cream, eggs, and butter direct from farm to consumer. In warm weather these products were packed in chopped ice. Most of the work was completed by nine o'clock so the customers could have fresh milk and cream for breakfast, so the bottles could be taken into the houses and refrigerated before the sun became hot, and so the drivers and horses could be used for other work on farms if needed.

Bread and other bakery products and yeast cakes were sold via direct selling. Bakery bread was not comparable in taste and texture to homemade bread, and many housewives baked bread in their kitchens. One of the millionaire fortunes of the century was made by the makers of Fleischman's yeast cakes in Cincinnati, Ohio.

Curb Markets

In areas that were settled heavily by Germans, curb markets were held twice a week on Wednesday and Saturday. Fresh fruits and vegetables in season were hauled to city markets where the wagons were backed up to the curbs of the streets, so the prospective buyers could see and frequently handle what they were purchasing. Buyers for restaurants and hotel dining rooms frequently stocked their storerooms with the produce from these markets. Again, these markets were usually closed by 8 A.M. so that both buyers and sellers could go about their daily routines without having to stop to shop for food.

An outgrowth of this technique was found in many other cities in which curb markets at the retail level were not found. Produce merchants, many of whom purchased their commodities from distant markets, sold their fruits and vegetables to stores, hotels, restaurants, and to vendors who stocked their wagons with choice produce. Italian fruit vendors pushed two-wheel carts through residential streets calling out their items.

Hucksters

Hucksters, who retailed perishable fruits and vegetables, obtained their foodstuffs from curb markets or at wholesale establishments before sunrise. They developed regular routes and called on regular customers usually three times a week. In this manner they covered one route on Mondays, Wednesdays, and Fridays, another one on the other three weekdays. On request they would obtain special items for individual customers, such as bakery products, brooms, pails, aprons, kitchenware and other household products. This method of buying appealed to many housewives who did not or could not frequent retail stores and who did not want to order over the phone.

The day of the automobile and the time when housewives going to market and carrying bags of groceries home with them was the accepted thing to do were yet to come. Status did not permit personal shopping and carrying packages home.

The Market House

From the curb and early morning shopping twice a week, markets went under cover in a large "market house" which may have been municipally owned. The market house usually extended the length of an entire block so that shoppers could enter and exit at either end. Some meats and fish may have been under cover, fish and oysters in season were packed in ice but the produce was shelved in open stalls. Dealers in fish and oysters seldom carried other lines of food. Some dealers specialized in fresh fruits and vegetables in season, some in home-butchered meats; and there were some that carried both fresh meats and vegetables, though either one or the other department may have been leased to another operator. Canned goods, preserves, and jams were found in limited quantities in these stalls.

Each dealer usually had his own telephone, two if there were two local systems, and his own delivery equipment. Depending upon the volume of business and the nature of his trade, his equipment consisted of one or more bicycles or a horse-drawn wagon. Stalls were frequently tended by husband and wife, or by either one alone, if the other had a better paying job elsewhere. Sanitary provisions did not measure up to the highest standards. Screens may have covered windows and doors; but, with the constant coming and going of customers and delivery boys, opportunities were ample for flies to enter the building and to swarm on meats, fruits, and vegetables. Many stalls lacked running water, and other sanitary facilities were entirely lacking. Most communities appointed inspectors whose function it was to enforce the sanitary and health codes. Shortly before closing time, attendants in each stall swept the dust and dirt that had accumulated into the main aisle from where the caretaker of the building picked it up later. Dust in the air that was not breathed by last-minute shoppers remained to settle on the produce and be delivered to customers the following day.

Communication Facilities Related to Markets

Communication facilities were means by which buyers and sellers in distant places were brought together. In local markets the telephone was an important medium by which this was accomplished. In wider markets the telegraph carried many commercial messages. There is no way of breaking down the uses that were made of either the telephone or the telegraph systems of the country. There is little doubt but that the largest volume of business done by telegraph companies was of commercial origin. There is also no doubt but that a large volume of local trade at both the retail and wholesale levels was consummated over the telephone. Personal use of telegraph service was restricted by custom to notices of births, illnesses, and deaths; dates and times of arrivals and departures by train; and congratulatory messages upon occasions that called for such greetings.

Postal Services. Development of postal services was a measure of the widening of markets and also of their intensification. From a market that was restricted to the Granges and to their memberships in 1872, Montgomery Ward and Company expanded its mail-order business to include deliveries direct to consumers. Rural customers found it much easier and convenient to shop by mail-order catalog where selections of merchandise could be made to suit their needs than it was to drive to town, which may have been an all-day experience, and then be confronted with very limited variety, styles, and sizes of goods. Sears Roebuck and Company was the other mail-order house that furnished competition in the mail-order business at the national level.

Table 19-1 provides some data that are useful in measuring both the intensive and the extensive development of domestic markets. It is readily recognized and understood that the number of stamps, stamped envelopes, and wrappers sold by post offices the country over was not an accurate measure of the expansion of markets; nor were they precise measurements of the growth in their size. While much first-class mail was motivated more by social reasons than business or commercial, friendly letters contained much information that led directly or indirectly to the purchase of one or more commodities. Even when business transactions were consummated by long-distance telephone or by the use of telegrams, they almost invariably were confirmed by correspondence. Circulars, brochures, mail-order catalogs, and newspapers have been sent through the mail in large volume, much to the disgust and annoyance of many of their recipients.

Table 19-1

Number of Post Offices and Postal Services—1865-1920

Year	Number of Post Offices	Ordinary Postage Stamps Issued (000)	Stamped Envelopes and Wrappers Issued (000)	Pieces of Mail of All Kinds Handled (000)
1865	20,550	387,419	26,206	. . . .
1870	28,492	468,118	26,289	. . . .
1875	35,547	682,342	149,766	. . . .
1880	42,989	875,682	207,137	. . . .
1885	51,252	1,465,122	322,751	3,747,000 (1886)
1890	62,401	2,219,737	513,833	4,005,408
1895	70,064	2,795,424	598,848	5,134,281
1900	76,688	3,998,544	707,555	7,129,990
1905	68,131	5,751,017	1,074,918	10,187,505
1910	59,580	9,067,164	1,506,861	14,850,102
1915	56,380	11,226,386	1,793,764	18,567,445 (1913)
1920	52,641	13,212,790	2,350,073	n.a. *

* Not available.

Source: U. S. Department of Commerce, Bureau of the Census, *Historical Statistics of the United States. Colonial Times to 1957* (Washington: U.S. Government Printing Office, 1960), pp. 496-497. Adapted.

The decline in the number of post offices after 1900 was the result of reorganization within the Post Office Department, one aspect of which was the closing of a number of offices in small towns that was accompanied by an extension of rural free mail delivery service. A total of 28,685 miles of rural routes in 1900 was increased to 993,068 miles in 1910 and to 1,151,832 miles in 1920. By the latter date some routes had been motorized. Prior to the establishment of parcel post service in 1912, express companies that were operated at the level of free enterprise carried most of what is now the fourth-class mail. The volume of mail at the Christmas season was given a new look with the realization by the people that shipping gifts via United States mail was cheaper in many instances than shipping by express. Seasonal employment was afforded thousands of young men, and owners of horse and wagon teams rented them to augment the delivery facilities that were in use the year-round. It is impossible to say how much of the additional earnings of the persons who rendered these temporary services went into channels of trade, but the presumption is that not much of their income was hoarded and that its impact was directly or indirectly felt on the volume of trade at the retail level.

Advertising. From the point of view of economic history, advertising has been communicating to the masses of potential buyers the availability of merchandise. Some advertising copy has described the commodity; some has told of the uses to which it could be put; some has given the list price; some has attempted to list the names of stores or the kinds of stores where the product could be purchased; and some has combined two or more of the above approaches in its effort to lure the dollar of the American buying public. Some of the advertising has been addressed to retailers; some to manufacturers; and some to potential consumers. Much of the space that has been devoted to newspaper advertising has dealt with on-the-spot purchases of consumers' goods that have been consumed rather completely in a short period of time. For the retailers they have been goods for which the rate of turnover has been comparatively high.

Media. In order to get word to the people before the days of radio and television, billboards were erected parallel to railroad rights-of-way so that passengers could be made aware or reminded of the advertised products at times when they had little else to do other than to read billboards. Streetcar and subway car cards were used to remind those who were going to work or going shopping to be sure to obtain X product before returning home. Magazines were also used, but they were issued weekly or monthly and found their way into the homes of their subscribers, where they were read somewhat leisurely.

Newspapers were the media through which advertisers' messages reached thousands of readers daily; many more thousands read the Sunday papers. When daily papers sold for two cents and three cents each, as many of them did prior to 1920, the sale price of a newspaper did not pay for the newsprint and handling charges, let alone the cost of obtaining the news items, setting up the type, operating large and complex printing presses, and distributing them to their readers. Advertising carried the cost of almost every daily and Sunday newspaper, as well as the weekly and monthly magazines.

One measure of the number of people that were reached through newspaper advertising alone is arrived at by remembering that each newspaper was read on the average by two or more adults. Weekly newspapers circulated principally in small towns that were not able to support daily issues, and in surrounding rural territories. Many subscribers to weekly home newspapers also subscribed to a daily and possibly a Sunday issue of a metropolitan paper. That vendors thought that advertising was a worthwhile expenditure is the only conclusion that can be drawn from a glance at the increase of such expenditures over a span of some 50 years.

Table 19-2

Newspapers—Daily, Sunday, and Weekly—1860-1920

	Total		Daily		Sunday		Weekly	
Year	Number	Circu-lation (000)	Number	Circu-lation (000)	Number	Circu-lation (000)	Number	Circu-lation (000)
1860	....	....	387	1,478	....	....	....	....
1870	....	....	574	2,602	....	....	....	....
1880	....	....	971	3,566	....	....	....	....
1890	....	....	1,610	8,387	....	....	....	....
1900	....	....	2,226	15,102	....	....	....	....
1909	17,023	58,505	2,600	24,212	520	13,347	13,903	20,946
1914	16,944	67,108	2,580	28,777	571	16,480	13,793	21,851
1919	15,190	73,139	2,441	33,029	604	19,369	12,145	20,741

Source: *Historical Statistics of the United States. Colonial Times to 1957*, 1960, p. 500. Adapted.

Advertising as a Business. From an expenditure of $50 million in 1867, a total of $200 million was spent for advertising in 1880 and $542 million in 1900. By this time 12,000 agents and salesmen were engaged in the advertising business. In another ten years 11,000 agents and salesmen handled over $1 billion worth of advertising material. By 1920, 25,000 agents and salesmen handled over $2.25 billion of advertising material. People were beginning to question the functions of a service that commanded such a large volume of the productive resources of the country. The conclusion was reached that from the social point of view competitive advertising was wasteful, although it may have been extremely profitable for certain advertisers and for the media in which advertisements were placed. On the other hand, informative advertising was considered to have been educational in character. It played an important role in increasing the level of living of thousands of people by merely informing them of consumers' goods that were available and to what uses they could be put.

Advertising undoubtedly increased the volume of trade over what would have taken place in its absence. In so doing, it contributed to increased employment and increased wages as the volume of manufactured goods produced and sold, particularly of those at the consumers' goods level, increased. The impact of advertising was also felt in the volume of traffic— freight and express.

Wholesaling Practices

Manufacturers found it utterly impossible to attempt to sell their products directly to their ultimate consumers. They produced their commodities in bulk, and this was the easiest and cheapest form in which to sell them. On the other hand, consumers found it convenient to purchase their goods in relatively small quantities and possibly at more or less frequent intervals of time. To narrow the gap between the needs of manufacturers and those of consumers a group of middlemen began to function. There were so many patterns and so many variations of a given pattern that it would serve no useful purpose to attempt to describe or explain all of them. Typical or generally prevailing types of trade organizations will be related to each other in the following paragraphs.

Some industries were organized in such a way that buyers from all over the country would assemble in some large centralized city to attend a kind of fair or exhibit at which the manufacturers of consumer goods would show their products for the coming season. As a service to all persons who needed it, the newspapers in these cities carried a column which listed the kinds of goods that were on display at a particular time. The names of buyers, the stores they represented, and their headquarters while in the city were listed in detail and in alphabetical order, sometimes by cities, sometimes by industries. The buyers purchased their goods directly from the manufacturers or from their representatives, and the merchandise was shipped directly from the manufacturers to the retail stores in bulk. Ladies' hats, dresses and ready-to-wear, and furniture were among the consumer goods that reached the retailers through these channels. Items of food, in general, were distributed through the medium of wholesalers, thence to retailers. In some cases separate items of food were repackaged in retail sizes by the wholesalers and delivered by them upon call. There were wholesale houses for packaged candies, others for fruits and vegetables, still others for canned goods and food staples.

Traveling Salesmen. Shoe salesmen carried samples with them in huge boxes that were shipped by express and taken to a suite of rooms in a prominent, centrally located hotel where they were placed on display for the benefit of buyers for stores in the city and in surrounding cities and towns. One general order per season was placed by each store, and shipments were sent in their entirety to each store. Sometimes special orders were taken for shoe styles or sizes that were not in stock, and frequently a special handling charge was assessed the customer. Retail stores under a name such as The Sample Shoe Store were the outlets for sample shoes when they had served their purpose.

Men's clothing—suits and coats—were sold by sample and by sample squares of different patterns of cloth and pictures of various styles. These, too, were sent direct from the manufacturer to the retailer once a season. Wholesale establishments for drugs, hardware, chinaware, and piece goods received shipments of their merchandise from manufacturers. The wholesale houses had their own salesmen who called on the retail trade, displayed samples, and took orders. Some stores that posed primarily as retail stores also did a wholesale business, but only to other retail outlets. Competition among wholesale grocers was more apparent than it was in other commodities or classes of consumers' goods. They had corps of salesmen who had established routes and were scheduled to visit some retail stores once and some of them twice a week. They had regular visitation days in a community so that retailers knew when to expect them and also for how many days to stock up.

Variations in Wholesale Distribution. Changes in the organization of retail stores called for changes in the methods of distributing goods from manufacturer to retailer. The development of the department store amounted to nothing but the combination of a large number of retail stores and departments under one roof. Some of them had large warehouses in which supplies of goods were kept until needed. To this extent some of them did their own wholesaling. In some cases departments that handled hats, or shoes, or novelties, for instance, were rented out to specialty dealers in these commodities. There were no outward manifestations of such arrangements, and relatively few customers were aware of them.

Chain stores, which have already been discussed as a marketing phase of large-scale production, performed their own wholesaling functions. One of the basic reasons for the development of the chain store organization was to enable it to take advantage of prices that were quoted for purchases in large volume. If the organization was one that sold groceries, regional or district warehouses served as distributing centers in which some of the items may have been placed in smaller sized packages before they were delivered to the many retail outlets. In respect to the cost of goods, each retail outlet had the advantage of lower wholesale costs which were passed along to consumers in the form of lower retail prices, without any reduction in the quality of the product.

Functions of Other Middlemen. Brokers, commission merchants, jobbers, and manufacturers' outlets were other forms of middlemen, all of whom furthered the progress of consumers' goods from their original producers to their ultimate consumers. Brokers and salesmen required very little capital to enter business. Their main forte was their ability to make contacts. They had to sell themselves almost as much as the products they handled. Usually they were paid on a commission basis. Many manufacturers obtained consumer acceptance of their products through some form of national advertising which lightened the task of the salesmen. In some instances they functioned more as order takers at regular intervals than as salesmen. Salesmanship entered into their activities when they first introduced a product in an area or to an individual merchant and also when they were forced to compete with another brand of goods that had proved to be popular in a community or among the customers of a store. They had to convince the managers of retail stores of the quality of their products. They provided window and counter cards that called attention to the brand name of the product they were selling. Folders, pamphlets, sample packages, and give-away gadgets were used to overcome customer resistance to a new product.

Customer Services at the Retail Level

In addition to the rent of land and the cost of capital that was tied up in inventories and delivery equipment, owners of food stores and others at the retail level of operation had to employ clerks and front men in accordance with their volume of business. In the days before centralized telephone service, and before personal shopping became popular and accepted, particularly in the grocery line, each store owner was compelled to install a minimum of the same number of phones as there were telephone companies serving the community. Some of the larger stores required more than one installation that was connected with a local switchboard to handle their volume of business during rush hours, which usually came before the noon hour.

Housewives relied upon store owners and their clerks to give them quality products. Items were identified by name, and clerks selected brands and placed them in boxes identified by the customers' names. When it came time for delivery, the boxes were placed on the floor or shelves of delivery wagons and were taken to the back doors of the customers' houses.

Most of the business was credit and delivery rather than cash-and-carry. Systems of bookkeeping were installed, and bookkeepers were employed to post items from journals to ledgers and to make out customer statements at the end of each month. All the work connected with keeping books and financial records was done by hand, since business machines beyond the level of typewriters and cash registers had not been invented.

Practically all kinds of retail stores maintained their own customer delivery service. This service required the purchase and maintenance of as many horses and delivery wagons as were necessary to render prompt service to their customers, and a driver for each delivery unit. About the time of World War I, or a year or two later, automobiles began to displace horse-drawn equipment; and as delivery service became more rapid, fewer delivery units were required to service the same volume of business. Entrepreneurs now were subjected to court costs for speeding and to the costs of accidents. Automobile insurance was in its infancy, and premiums on policies were set by "guestimate" rather than by statistical calculation.

A New Look at Costs and Prices. When commodity prices began to rise after 1900, much attention was given to the spread between prices that were paid original producers of foodstuffs by so-called middlemen in the merchandising process and prices consumers were required to pay for these commodities. Because of an increase in competition in the sale of many consumers' goods, owners of retail stores were not able to raise their prices to consumers in proportion to the increases in their costs. More producers of a larger variety of consumer goods were competing for the consumers' dollars. Many consumers received fixed incomes in the nature of salaries, pensions and retirement compensations, payments from insurance companies, and interest on bonds, and could not continue to purchase the same quantities of goods they acquired when prices were lower or when there were not so many commodities competing for their dollars. One form of adjustment that was made to the situation was the effort that was made to reduce the costs of selling consumer goods.

Chain stores were organized in order to take advantage of discounts that were given them for purchases in volume from manufacturers. Chain store organization also had the effect of standardizing the packaging and labeling of consumers' goods which tended to lower their production costs. The next step was the introduction of self-service in order to lower the cost of handling goods—labor costs. Cash-and-carry did away with the need for taking orders over the telephone and having store clerks fill them and then make out charge slips. Bookkeeping was simplified, delivery equipment was eliminated, and telephones were removed. Postage costs were greatly reduced when monthly statements were no longer mailed to each individual customer. Retail stores continued to require the services of employees, but they were fewer in number and they received lower wages than did the clerks who had to meet their customers, create goodwill, and maintain favorable customer relations. A shortage of labor that was brought about by war conditions may have hastened some of these changes. Again, owners of retail establishments were unable to pay wages comparable to those that were paid in other industries. The impact of the corporate income tax law was being felt in the increase in the demand for bookkeepers and the development of an accounting profession.

Some Dislocations at the Retail Level. Many types of specialty stores tended to disappear entirely or to become much fewer in number. Glass and china stores, and confectionery stores, especially those that sold "homemade" candies, tended to disappear and their merchandise was found in department stores and in drugstores. Owners of jewelry stores felt the impact of the increasing popularity of costume jewelry and many of them were forced out of business. These developments serve as an excellent illustration of an increase in one kind of economic activity causing a dislocation of another kind of economic activity which made necessary adjustments in the capital structure of our economy as well as in the labor segment.

Neighborhood Stores. Because populations were living farther and farther away from downtown centers of retail trade, neighborhood stores began to appear in many places. Neighborhood stores were in no sense of the word shopping centers. Grocery stores and drugstores were among the first to leave the downtown sections, in some cases in order to escape the higher rents that were being exacted by owners of such lands from their tenants. These rents were determined by the net return from urban sites when put to their most productive uses rather than by the abilities of individual tenants to pay for the privilege of occupying them. When land-owners raised their rents and store owner-managers could not increase their net returns accordingly, there was nothing to do but move to other locations.

Frequently, though not always, they sought locations on or near the corners of the intersections of two or more important thoroughfares. This made it convenient for persons who alighted from streetcars to make last-minute purchases before proceeding to their homes. Many drugstores already had soda fountains which soon became lunch counters, and their display counters and windows began to resemble variety stores, so wide was the line of goods they carried. Barber shops, ice cream parlors, and, occasionally, other types of retail outlets found it to their advantage to become neighborhood stores. As more automobiles came into use at the family level at the close of World War I, customer parking became a problem. Hitching posts and watering troughs became items of historical interest only.

Other Impacts of Progress. Many persons who were engaged in trade and commerce were dislocated by the march of economic progress. Store clerks, stock clerks, delivery boys, bookkeepers, and salesmen found themselves out of jobs because the positions they occupied had been abolished. As chain store operations increased and individually home-owned stores became fewer in number, the wholesale functions of the marketing process were absorbed by the parent organizations and local wholesale outlets were dislocated. Not only was there a dislocation of labor, but the capital requirements of merchants underwent many changes. As telephones and delivery equipment were released entirely, as capital was concentrated, altered, and later more highly specialized, operating capital in merchandising became available for different uses or was more highly concentrated in larger production units.

Trade Markups

There were many costs that were incurred in handling a product between the time of its original production and the time it reached the home of its

Table 19-3
Retail Trade Margins, by Kind of Store—1869-1919
(Percentage of Retail Value)

Year	Grocery		Ap-parel	Shoes		Farm Imple-ments	Hard-ware	Drugs	Dry Goods	Meat	De-part-ment	Mail Order	Fur-ni-ture*
	Inde-pen-dent	Chain		Inde-pen-dent	Chain								
1869	18.0	...	21.1	21.4	...	23.0	...	...	...	...	...	...	...
1879	18.5	...	23.2	23.1	...	21.4	25.2	28.4	18.7	...	...	...	30.0
1889	19.0	...	25.4	24.7	...	19.6	23.7	30.2	19.2	29.0	22.2	24.4	30.6
1899	19.5	...	27.5	26.3	...	18.0	22.2	31.8	21.4	28.0	25.6	25.0	31.2
1909	19.5	17.0	29.6	28.0	33.5	18.0	23.6	33.6	27.0	26.8	29.3	25.6	31.2
1919	19.5	18.0	31.8	29.5	32.0	19.2	25.0	34.6	29.0	25.8	32.8	26.2	39.0

* Independent

Source: *Historical Statistics of the United States. Colonial Times to 1957*, 1960, p. 523. Adapted.

consumer. Some idea of the cost at the level of the retailer alone can be had by glancing at the margins of markup over wholesale cost that were made at the retail level. It was out of these markups that all overhead and operating costs were paid, after which the entrepreneur counted his profits. Costs of handling goods at the retail level were much greater than those at the wholesale level. Where comparable data are obtainable they reveal this fact not only in terms of percentage markups but also in the fact that the markups at the retail level were on higher monetary bases than were the markups at the wholesale level. Data in Table 19-3 for department stores and for mail-order stores are interesting when compared with the markups for those that were independently owned. Prices at department stores included costs of transportation and delivery, while similar costs had to be added to the prices that were quoted by mail-order houses to obtain the actual cost to the consumer. When some of the mail-order houses began to open retail outlets in some of the larger cities, the retail prices for certain goods were somewhat above the quotations for the same or similar goods by mail order. The price differentials were necessary to cover the additional overhead costs of operating the retail stores plus the costs of transporting the merchandise from factory to store.

Table 19-4

Wholesale Trade Margins of Independent Wholesalers—1869-1919
(Percentage of Wholesale Value)

Year	Dry Goods	Furniture	Lumber	Hardware	Drug (General Line)
1869	14.0	14.0	10.0	19.0	10.0
1879	15.0	14.0	10.0	19.0	11.0
1889	16.0	14.0	10.0	19.0	12.2
1899	17.0	14.0	10.0	19.0	13.6
1909	18.0	15.0	11.5	20.0	15.2
1919	18.0	16.2	13.0	22.0	16.6

Source: *Historical Statistics of the United States. Colonial Times to 1957*, 1960, p. 525. Adapted.

Trade as Origin of National Income

The estimates of Harold Barger in Tables 19-5 and 19-6 are useful in comprehending the contribution that wholesale and retail trade has made to the development and progress of the American economy. The persons who have been employed in trade have contributed to the volume of trade and commerce through the spending of their incomes on commodities that were produced by other persons.

Table 19-5
Employees and Proprietors in Wholesale and Retail Trade—1869-1929
(000)

Estimated Employment	1869	1879	1889	1899	1909	1919	1929
Wholesale							
Employees	208	321	529	704	955	1,142	1,631
Proprietors	52	65	83	92	97	103	113
Retail							
Employees	196	349	698	1,132	1,857	2,480	4,215
Proprietors	429	602	862	1,073	1,302	1,485	1,862
TOTAL	885	1,337	2,172	3,001	4,211	5,210	7,821
Total Population (000)	34,051	49,208	61,775	74,779	90,492	105,063	122,000
Percentage Population Engaged in Trade	2.59	2.69	3.51	4.01	4.65	4.95	6.41

Source: Data on Employees and Proprietors in Wholesale and Retail Trade, 1869-1929 taken from Harold Barger, *Income Originating in Trade, 1869-1929*, in *Trends in the American Economy in the Nineteenth Century: Studies in Income and Wealth*, Vol. 24 (New York City: National Bureau of Economic Research, 1960), p. 327. Copyright by N.B.E.R. in 1960. Data on Population compiled by the authors.

The increase in total population of the United States from 38 million in 1870 to 122 million in 1929 was accompanied by an increase in the number of wholesale houses and retail establishments. The number of proprietors does not measure precisely the number of establishments at any level of operation because of the use of the partnership and corporate forms of business organization, but it does measure the production level of the contribution they made to the productive process. Throughout the entire period the number of employees at the wholesale level exceeded the number of proprietors and this same relationship between employers and employees did not prevail at the retail level until the turn of the century. For 30 years the number of employees had been increasing more rapidly than had the number of proprietors. This was an accompaniment of the merger movement and of the increasing size of the business unit at the retail level.

Table 19-6 reveals how persons who were employed by retail stores made their living, the number of hours they worked per week, and the average wage they received. The census reports of the state of Indiana for 1879 indicate that there was a definite relationship between the annual incomes that were received by employers and those that were received by their employees.

That relationship was the basis upon which a multiplier was obtained to calculate the annual incomes of proprietors once the annual incomes of wage earners had been determined.

Table 19-6

Average Annual Incomes Received by Employees and by Proprietors—1869-1929

	1869	1879	1889	1899	1909	1919	1929
Retail Trade							
Hours per Week	66	66	66	65	59	56	54
Hourly Wages							
Retail	$0.167	$0.130	$0.154	$0.175	$0.209	$0.480	$0.543
Wholesale Trade							
Annual Income							
per Employee	$ 783	$ 610	$ 722	$ 809	$ 875	$1,911	$2,083
Assumed Multi-							
plier	2.9	2.7	2.5	2.3	2.1	1.9	1.67
Annual Income							
per Proprietor	$2,271	$1,647	$1,805	$1,861	$1,838	$3,631	$3,479
Retail Trade							
Annual Income							
per Employee	$ 533	$ 415	$ 491	$ 551	$ 596	$1,301	$1,418
Assumed Multi-							
plier	1.5	1.4	1.3	1.2	1.1	1.0	0.94
Annual Income							
per Proprietor	$ 800	$ 581	$ 638	$ 661	$ 656	$1,301	$1,333

Source: Harold Barger, *Income Originating in Trade, 1869-1929. Trends in the American Economy: Studies in Income and Wealth*, Vol. 24 (New York City: National Bureau of Economic Research), p. 329. Copyright by N.B.E.R. in 1960.

The effect of competition within the areas of wholesale trade and retail trade respectively is shown by comparing the average annual incomes received by the employees and by the employers at both levels of trade. Competition has been much more keen at the retail trade level than at the level of wholesale trade. Retail stores were where the ultimate consumers went to purchase goods that would satisfy their wants directly. They were the stores that were played off against each other in the buyers' efforts to get the most for their dollars. They were the stores that were closest to the pulses of the buyers and were forced to adjust retail prices in line with total demand and the elasticities of demand for the various lines of goods they handled.

Table 19-7 approximates the amount of the national income that originated in trade, both wholesale and retail, and shows the percentage relationship between the incomes that originated in trade and total national income.

Table 19-7

Income Originating in Trade—1869-1929
Percentage of National Income
(billions)

	1869	1879	1889	1899	1909	1919	1929
Wholesale Trade							
Employee Compensation	$ .16	$ .20	$ .38	$ .57	$ .84	$ 2.18	$ 3.40
Unincorporated Profits	.12	.11	.15	.17	.18	.37	.38
Retail Trade							
Employee Compensation	.10	.14	.34	.62	1.11	3.23	5.98
Unincorporated Profits	.34	.35	.55	.71	.85	1.93	2.48
Wholesale and Retail Trade Combined.							
Employee Compensation	.27	.34	.72	1.19	1.94	5.41	9.38
Unincorporated Profits	.46	.46	.70	.88	1.03	2.31	2.87
Corporate Profits	. . .	. . .	. . .	. . .	0.60	1.23	0.76
Interest	. . .	. . .	. . .	. . .	. . .	0.04	0.08
Income Originating	$ 0.73	$ 0.80	$ 1.42	$ 2.07	$ 3.57	$ 8.98	$ 13.08
* National Income (millions)	$6,827	$7,227	$10,701	$15,364	$26,456	$62,945	$79,498
Percentage of Income Originating in Trade to National Income	10.7	10.36	13.27	13.4	13.8	14.2	16.4

* These income payments to individuals are found in *The Economic Almanac* (New York City: Thomas Y. Crowell Company, 1953-54), p. 505.

Source: Harold Barger, *Income Originating in Trade, 1869-1929. Trends in the American Economy: Studies in Income and Wealth,* Vol. 24 (New York City: National Bureau of Economic Research), p. 329. Copyright by N.B.E.R. in 1960.

Government and Trade

If there was any government policy the impact of which was felt on internal trade and commerce it centered around (1) making available on easy terms settlement upon public lands, and (2) the maintenance and support of competition in the conduct of interstate trade in particular and overall trade in general. The former policy was made manifest in a series of laws in the period under observation in which the Homestead Act was the initial one. The latter policy was manifest in the passage of the Interstate Commerce Act, the Sherman Antitrust Act, the Clayton Act, and the Federal Trade Commission Act, and modifications and amendments to all of them that have been made from time to time as the need arose. State banking and the National Banking System gave encouragement to competitive banking policies and practices, which in turn facilitated the obtaining and use of bank credit in the conduct of trade—wholesale and retail, local and regional.

These Acts were referred to in the paragraph that treated the framework within which trade was developed. They are referred to here as stimulants to trade and commerce. They expanded areas within which domestic trade was conducted and between which interregional trade was featured. They widened the doors through which passed a larger volume of trade.

FOREIGN TRADE

While the volume of foreign trade and its value increased throughout almost the entire period under observation, it never was as important a source of income nor did it support as many people as did domestic trade and commerce. The United States Department of State, Congress, or any other body or group of leaders did not formulate any definite foreign economic policy, nor was any continuity given to any policy that may have been enunciated at any given time because of some particular circumstance. Our tariff program, or "policy," was a result of political sophistry in the attempts that were made by candidates for political office to obtain sufficient votes to send them to Washington in the first place, or to return them to the halls of Congress where they could continue to represent their constituents in framing the laws of the land. Fortunately for them and more so for the United States, their errors of judgment or of ignorance were covered up by the rapid economic growth and development of the country. The country developed so rapidly that domestic or home industries did not have the capacity to produce the volume of commodities that was demanded by the American people. This condition gave rise to the import of commodities from other parts of the world. From the point of view of those persons who were directly or indirectly connected with foreign trade, it was important to them as a means of earning a living.

New Patterns of Foreign Trade

While some aspects of American export and import trade resembled the pattern that had been established prior to 1860, some important changes took place around the turn of the century that had tremendous impacts upon the position of the United States in its economic relations with foreign countries, especially those of western Europe—England, France, and Germany. The economies of these countries were much older than was the American economy. One measure of the maturity of these economies was found in the large amounts of capital their citizens had accumulated and were willing to invest in industries in America. From their points of view they were foreign investments. From our point of view they were capital sums that American business firms and corporations borrowed from foreign countries. It is much more realistic to say that they were capital sums that were borrowed by American businessmen and corporations from foreign banks and businessmen.

Many of the investments of foreign capital were portfolio investments rather than direct ones, the impacts of which were to aid in the development of many phases and many segments of American industry. *Portfolio investments* were those that were made through the purchase of corporate securities without any intent of acquiring majority ownership or control. *Direct investments* were made for the purpose of owning, operating, and controlling industrial organizations. Interest income, dividend returns, and profits were the ultimate reasons that impelled foreign capitalists or businessmen to invest their money in this country.

Agriculture, mining, manufacturing, and transportation—all attracted foreign capital not alone because capital that was invested in these industries was productive. The fact that rates of return on capital investments in the United States tended to be higher than rates of return on capital invested in England and in Continental countries lured large amounts of venture capital to American shores.

Portfolio Investments. Much of the foreign capital that found its way into the United States was in the form of portfolio investments in American railroads, most of which ran in an east-west direction. These capital investments tended to lower transportation costs on commodities that were shipped from states that lay west of the Appalachian Mountains to the coastal ports on the Atlantic Ocean. British capital contributed to making possible the exportation of cereal grains, foodstuffs, cotton, tobacco, coal and related fuels, meats, and later a wide assortment of manufactured goods and machinery. Until 1900 exports of nonmanufactured goods were of greater value than were the exports of manufactured goods, although the values of the latter were increasing steadily up to World War I. After the close of the war, in fact after 1916, the value of manufactured goods of export increased very rapidly. During the 5-year period of 1916-20 the values of finished manufactured goods including foodstuffs that were exported exceeded the values of all our commodity imports.

Nature of Commodity Exports and Imports. Before undertaking an analysis of commodity exports and imports of crude materials, foodstuffs, semimanufactures, and finished manufactured goods, an explanation of the nature of the commodities in each classification is in order. Among the more important crude materials that were exported were raw cotton, leaf tobacco, coal, and later petroleum; whole raw silk, hides and skins, and crude rubber were found among the largest of our imports. Coffee, tea, tropical fruits and nuts were among the leading crude foodstuffs of import; while grain, fruits, and vegetables were found in the holds of ships that sailed from American ports. Large quantities of lard were exported to Italy and to other countries. Other manufactured foodstuffs that were exported included meats and prepared fruits. Sugar has been an important commodity import ever since the Colonial Period. Meat and wheat flour also were found on ships that

Table 19-8

Value of Merchandise Exports and Imports by Economic Classes—1871-1920
(millions)

Years	Total		Crude Materials		Crude Foodstuffs		Manufactured Foodstuffs		Semi-Manufactures		Finished Manufactures	
	Exports	Imports	Exports	Imports	Exports	Imports	Exports	Imports	Exports	Imports	Exports	Imports
1871-1875	$ 2,429	$ 2,889	$1,092	$ 467	$ 376	$ 408	$ 476	$ 580	$ 113	$ 392	$ 373	$1,043
1876-1880	3,319	2,463	1,070	456	795	446	809	530	151	308	493	724
1881-1885	3,873	3,337	1,308	665	813	496	987	638	185	459	578	1,077
1886-1890	3,628	3,585	1,384	812	543	565	909	591	200	566	594	1,052
1891-1895	4,381	3,925	1,475	928	753	733	1,192	704	276	564	683	1,001
1896-1900	5,680	3,708	1,483	1,093	1,074	559	1,364	590	547	494	1,213	971
1901-1905	7,134	4,861	2,161	1,623	870	627	1,581	601	806	810	1,718	1,200
1906-1910	8,755	6,724	2,774	2,325	779	739	1,586	794	1,245	1,197	2,369	1,671
1911-1915	11,659	8,561	3,583	2,988	1,029	1,095	1,671	1,076	1,796	1,497	3,578	1,914
1916-1920	33,471	17,557	6,127	7,034	3,073	2,115	5,941	2,882	5,160	3,017	13,169	2,513

Source: *Historical Statistics of the United States. Colonial Times to 1957*, 1960, pp. 544-545. Adapted.

entered home ports. Lumber, iron and steel plates, and refined copper typified the semimanufactured goods that found ready markets abroad; while copper in bars, tin in bars, and wood pulp were readily absorbed by American industries. Wood and iron products, textiles, and later cigarettes were among the leading manufactured goods that were exported; while woolens, cotton textiles and lace, newsprint, iron and steel products, and manufactured fur products found ready markets in the United States.

An export ratio by value of 15 percent of finished manufactured goods to total commodity exports in 1871-75 became 30 percent in 1911-15, which was the last 5-year period just prior to our entry into a world holocaust. For the same span of years, the importation of finished manufactures declined from 36 percent to 22 percent of total commodity exports. In 1871-75 crude materials constituted 48 percent of our commodity exports and only 16 percent of our commodity imports. For the period 1911-15 these figures had become 30 percent for exports and 35 percent for imports. These data reveal in somewhat vivid fashion the metamorphosis through which our international trade has passed. They are much more meaningful in describing the growth to maturity of the American economy than are data that measure increases in volume or in value only. Again, these data are important in explaining some of the problems that have arisen in connection with maintaining a balance of international payments without experiencing a loss of gold. European countries were the workshop of the world throughout this period; and as long as the principal imports of the United States continued to consist more of manufactured goods than of raw materials, the origin of commodity imports into the United States was Europe.

Sources of Imports; Destinations of Exports. In contrast to later developments, western European countries were more productive sources of American imports than were all the other countries in the world from which we obtained commodities of any and all classifications. Until 1910 over one half of all American imports came from Europe. Something less than one half of the goods that were imported from European peoples were purchased from the United Kingdom. Not only were European peoples the best providers of American commodity imports, they constituted the best market for American commodity exports. Consistently, the United Kingdom was our best customer in absorbing more of our exports than Germany and France combined, which countries were our second and third best customers respectively until 1912, after which time Canada purchased more goods by value than did Germany. Until 1888, China constituted the largest market in Asia for American exports, after which time the Japanese economy absorbed more American products than did China.

In the Western Hemisphere, Canadians were the purchasers of by far the largest amount of American exports. Starting in 1912, they absorbed more exports by value than any other area in the world except the United Kingdom.

Table 19-9
Value of Exports of United States Merchandise by Country of Destination
1871-1920
(millions)

Period	Total Value	America *		Europe		Asia		Australia and Oceania	Africa
		Total	Canada	Total	United Kingdom	Total	Japan		
1871-1875	$ 2,804	$ 490	$ 171	$ 2,253	$ 1,517	$ 24	$ 6	$ 23	$ 14
1876-1880	3,513	479	166	2,919	1,872	54	10	39	21
1881-1885	3,960	577	201	3,209	2,098	87	13	64	22
1886-1890	3,692	570	185	2,928	1,907	102	20	76	18
1891-1895	4,462	718	238	3,547	2,183	103	20	70	26
1896-1900	5,786	907	392	4,437	2,476	227	87	132	87
1901-1905	7,270	1,343	611	5,253	2,764	384	138	148	140
1906-1910	8,894	2,090	886	6,065	2,793	486	167	162	93
1911-1915	11,853	3,207	1,660	7,586	3,244	666	240	257	134
1916-1920	34,014	8,637	4,027	21,388	10,061	2,999	1,313	563	428

* Total figures include Central and South American countries.

Source: *Historical Statistics of the United States. Colonial Times to 1957*, 1960, pp. 550 and 551. Adapted.

Table 19-10

Value of Imports by Country of Origin—1871-1920 (millions)

Period	Total Value	America *		Europe		Asia		Australia and Oceania	Africa
		Total	Canada	Total	United Kingdom	Total	Japan		
1871-1875	$ 2,889	$ 965	$ 168	$1,606	$1,042	$ 276	$ 34	$ 19	$ 21
1876-1880	2,463	912	137	1,237	664	279	61	22	12
1881-1885	3,337	1,070	208	1,839	859	349	66	58	22
1886-1890	3,585	1,107	200	2,009	861	371	89	81	17
1891-1895	3,925	1,406	180	1,988	800	426	113	81	24
1896-1900	3,708	1,055	183	1,950	725	541	135	115	49
1901-1905	4,861	1,520	259	2,492	841	748	210	46	55
1906-1910	6,724	2,084	390	3,448	1,126	1,024	326	83	82
1911-1915	8,561	3,001	652	3,991	1,380	1,355	458	96	120
1916-1920	17,557	8,410	2,210	3,481	1,557	4,816	1,563	369	483

* Total figures include Central and South American countries.

Source: *Historical Statistics of the United States. Colonial Times to 1957*, 1960, pp. 552 and 553. Adapted.

Balance of Payments

Throughout much of the period under observation, the value of American commodity exports exceeded the value of commodity imports. One factor that may have contributed to this situation was the increasing volume of manufactured goods that was exported in relation to the volume of raw material exports and a corresponding decline in the volume of manufactured goods in relation to raw material imports. Commodity trade accounts are seldom, if ever, in balance. The United States had a large favorable balance on its commodity trade account and an unfavorable balance among the invisible items of foreign trade.

Since the American merchant marine carried little of our commodity exports and imports after the termination of the internecine struggle in 1865, smaller payments for overseas transportation services were paid by foreign shippers to the owners of American vessels and correspondingly larger payments were made by American shippers to the owners of foreign merchant vessels. In other words, Americans imported transportation services that formerly had been rendered by Americans, and they ceased to export these same services to foreigners. Included in the payments for transportation were wage payments made to merchant seamen who largely were inhabitants of foreign countries. Wages of American seamen were higher than were those of the seamen of foreign nationals. In accordance with the principle of least cost, Americans imported the services of the crews of foreign merchant ships.

One of the economic impacts of the immigration of thousands of Italian nationals after 1880 was related to one of the reasons for their coming over. Many of them came first and obtained work afterwards. In these days sponsorship was not required, neither was admittance into the United States based upon any kind of quota. After they had found employment and had accumulated sufficient savings in banks, they remitted the cost of transportation to America to members of their families they had left in Italy, in order that they, too, might enjoy the privileges of living in the United States. Other remittances were made at more or less regular intervals to augment the incomes of relatives in Italy, who, for reasons known best to them, did not wish to leave their homeland. All of these remittances were American invisible imports which declined in importance with the start of World War I.

English insurance companies underwrote many risks in America and for Americans. Practically all the marine insurance prior to 1916 was obtained from English companies. Lloyd's of London underwrote many risks other companies would not assume. Fire, property, and casualty insurance policies, business and individual, were carried with English concerns. Payments of annual premiums constituted invisible imports. These payments were cumulative in effect; and insofar as insurance companies experienced underwriting profits from their business that was done in the United States, they amounted to more than the payments they made to policyholders here who suffered losses. When these companies were called upon to reimburse Americans for loss of life or property damage that resulted from the occurrence of some disaster, such as the Chicago fire or the San Francisco earthquake, the United States experienced a net "export" of losses.

From Pound Sterling to Dollar Exchange. It took more than mere authority or permission for American banks to establish operating branches in foreign countries. The pound sterling had long been the monetary unit in terms of which the values of foreign transactions were expressed; and banks and businessmen all over the world were more or less familiar with the uses of sterling exchange, its convenience, its security, and its relative stability. The impacts of World War I provided the framework within which American banks established branches in foreign cities. Whereas American banks and businessmen had been importing the banking services of English banks, they were in a position not only to cease importing these services but to export them. Dollar exchange became more acceptable than sterling exchange in the settlement of obligations that arose out of international transactions—both commodity and financial.

Impacts of World War I upon Foreign Trade

The impacts of war in Europe were felt in the United States before we became active participants. As early as 1913 the shadows of war began to descend over Europe. American industry—manufacturing and transportation —increased the tempo of its operations in order to take care of the large orders for all kinds of commodities—capital goods and consumers' goods— for the military and for civilian populations. This stimulation to industry may have checked the severity of an industrial recession which loomed over the horizon at that time. Exports of food and clothing for both soldiers and civilians, munitions and ordnance materials, were on the increase. American industries increased their operations to capacity, and new establishments were erected to accommodate the increase in the volume of business.

From Debtor Nation to Creditor. When foreign countries had exhausted their bank balances that were available for the purchase of American war supplies, they fell back on the device of liquidating corporate securities and government bonds in American financial marts. Foreign holders of American securities were required to exchange them for bonds that were issued by their respective governments. Up to this point foreign governments undertook to provide their citizens with at least a portion of the current incomes which they had been receiving from the United States.

Governments then sold these securities in the New York money market. With the bank balances so obtained they were able to pay American dollars for the commodities they obtained from this country. A long-run impact of this expediency was its effect upon the balance of payments account. Simultaneously with an increase in commodity exports, invisible imports decreased. American corporations were no longer required to make interest and dividend payments to foreign holders of their securities which meant a sudden decline in American invisible imports. As serial bonds became due they were payable within the United States and no longer appeared as invisible imports for the years in which they matured. The repatriation of American corporate securities was instrumental in the United States becoming a creditor nation after being a debtor nation for well over a century. By the turn of the century American investors had begun to invest their savings in foreign securities, but all this had done was to reduce the degree to which we were a debtor nation. At the same time that American securities were repatriated, American banks, individual persons, and the government extended credit to foreign governments and to foreign corporations. This was the first time that the federal government, as such, had given direct financial aid to foreign governments. Truly, and for the first time, the United States government had become a creditor to foreign governments.

Adjustments to War Conditions. In order to provide shipping facilities to replace those foreign vessels that had been destroyed in the German submarine campaign or had been interned in neutral ports, and others that had been withdrawn from overseas trade and put into across-channel service, the United States Shipping Board was established by Congress in 1916. Its purpose was to subsidize the construction of American ships in order to provide an adequate and an effective American merchant marine. This represented a displacement, to some extent, of invisible imports with invisible exports in the international balance of payments account. In other instances, invisible imports were replaced by domestic payments that did not appear on this account. When Lloyd's of London and the other insurance companies refused to underwrite marine insurance policies, the federal government through the agency of the War Risk Insurance Corporation performed this function. Later, privately owned insurance companies were organized in the United States for this purpose, and a business that had given rise to a portion of our invisible imports no longer loomed large. Payments of premiums to marine insurance companies and payments of losses by them to American policyholders had become in large part domestic transactions.

The Webb-Pomerene Act of 1916 authorized the organization of export companies into cartels in order that American exports would no longer compete with themselves in the sale of similar or substitute products in foreign markets. This had the effect of maintaining the values of exports of American products in foreign markets.

Neutrality and Trade. During the early months of the European war the United States maintained a policy of strict neutrality. Sales of American products to European countries were governed almost entirely by the ability of each country to pay for them and to transport them safely across the ocean. Since the blockade of the German coast by the British and

French navies had the effect of making it almost impossible to reach German ports, American business firms exported much larger volumes and values of goods to the Allied Powers than they did to the Central Powers. This aspect of our trade relations seemed to lend color to the degree of neutrality that was observed by the United States. Not only was the state of neutrality affected by trade, the sympathy and support of the American people may have been swayed by the trade factor to the cause of the Allies.

QUESTIONS FOR REVIEW

1. In what ways was the investment of eastern capital in western America similar to the investment of British capital in America? In what ways was it different?

2. Explain clearly how the banking structure of the United States contributed to the development of internal markets and marketing.

3. What developments in the United States postal system contributed to the enlargement and widening of domestic markets?

4. What were the functions of wholesalers during this period?

5. (a) What conditions led to the disappearance of many independent wholesalers?
   (b) Was the disappearance of the independent wholesaler prima facie proof of the fact that his functions were no longer performed? Explain clearly.

6. What became of the specialty stores, such as china and glass, jewelry, and local candy retailers, in the march of progress?

7. What changes were beginning to appear by 1900 in the origin of our commodity imports? in the destination of our commodity exports?

8. What economic impacts did the outbreak of the European war in 1914 have upon our foreign commodity trade account?

SUGGESTED READINGS

Andreano, Ralph L. (ed.). "Four Recent Studies in American Economic History," *New Views on American Economic Development.* Cambridge, Mass.: Schenkman Publishing Co., Inc., 1965. Part I, No. 3.

Barger, Harold. "Distribution's Place in the American Economy Since 1869," *Issues in American Economic History,* edited by Gerald D. Nash. Boston: D. C. Heath & Company, 1964.

——————. *Income Originating in Trade, 1869-1929 Trends in the American Economy: Studies in Income and Wealth,* Vol. 24. New York City: National Bureau of Economic Research, 1960.

Faulkner, Harold U. *American Economic History.* 8th ed. New York City: Harper and Row, Publishers, 1960. Chapter 25.

Faulkner, Harold U. *The Decline of Laissez Faire, 1897-1917.* New York City: Holt, Rinehart & Winston, Inc., 1951. Chapter 3.

Kirkland, Edward C. *Industry Comes of Age: Business, Labor, and Public Policy, 1860-1897.* New York City: Holt, Rinehart & Winston, Inc., 1961. Chapters 13 and 14.

Marburg, Theodore. "Domestic Trade and Marketing," *The Growth of the American Economy*, 2d ed., edited by Harold F. Williamson. New York City: Prentice-Hall, Inc., 1951

Rezneck, Samuel. "Light Manufactures," *The Growth of the American Economy*, 2d ed., edited by Harold F. Williamson. New York City: Prentice-Hall, Inc., 1951.

Stewart, Paul W., and J. Frederick Dewhurst, "Does Distribution Cost Too Much?" *Issues in American Economic History*, edited by Gerald D. Nash. Boston: D. C. Heath & Company, 1964.

Chapter 20

MATURATION: PERFORMANCE

OF THE AMERICAN ECONOMY

The word *maturity* as used in an economic sense refers to that stage of economic development that no longer has the characteristics of under-development. In applying this test to the American economy, maturity was reached when external trade relations were no longer the most important characteristic and when relationships between the productive factors no longer resembled those that prevailed throughout the Colonial Period.

The facts of an intensive utilization of land and more reliance upon nonextractive industries in the production of wealth that would satisfy their wants and as sources of national income were prima facie evidences of the emergence of a more mature economy. The passage of the American economy from one that was primarily agricultural to one in which agriculture was balanced with manufacturing industries and with commercial activities was a phase of its maturation. The growth and development of a distinct labor segment of the population and one that acquired a certain amount of mobility was another manifestation of its maturation.

Maturation was a gradual process that was motivated by profit-making potentials at the level of free enterprise. Only when the operation of an unrestrained capitalism resulted in extremely one-sided benefits to certain segments and corresponding harmful impacts on others from a social point of view did government establish new rules for making a living.

TESTS OF ECONOMIC MATURITY
IN A FREE ENTERPRISE ECONOMY

It is difficult, if not impossible, to fix a date after which the economy became mature; however, there are tests that may be applied, the outcomes of which indicate that progress towards maturity had been made.

Use of Land and Natural Resources

In terms of the number of acres of land in the United States, land has appeared to have been abundant at all times; however, correct judgment cannot be based upon acreage alone. By 1900, the continental United States as it is now constituted became a reality. The real test of the degree of abundance of land must be derived from the size, composition, and concentration of the population of the United States in relation to the need for lands that could be put to different uses and on which or in which there were different kinds of natural resources. The quantity of farmland has to be considered in terms of the most profitable uses to which it could be put. One almost infallible test of the growth of a country or of a portion of it towards maturity is the phenomenon of economic rent. When land was in absolute abundance, it was a free good and economic rent did not exist. When marginal lands were pushed farther away from concentrations of population, and when their intensive utilization gave rise to new marginal costs of production, land as a productive factor had become more scarce.

From Extensive to Intensive Utilization. When the agricultural frontier moved westward, land in older regions either was abandoned or was used more intensively. A more intensive utilization of land was not only an indication of its having become scarce in certain uses, it was a test of increasing maturity. Agricultural areas in New England and other eastern states matured before those west of the Mississippi River.

Timberlands and those in which mineral deposits were found were exploited to the point of exhaustion. The exploitation of natural resources was spearheaded by the profit motive which made it appear that lands that were in great abundance became relatively scarce or disappeared absolutely. On the other hand, the impact of using brick, concrete, and steel in building construction was to give an appearance of greater abundance to timberlands, although there may have been no increase in their acreage. When the charcoal process of refining iron ores was replaced by the coking process, timber from which charcoal could be made appeared to become more plentiful.

Densities of urban populations, together with the radii of urban areas, are measures of the abundance of land in restricted areas. During the period under observation, the outward expansion of some urban areas was retarded by the presence of natural phenomena, in which case expansion was upward instead of outward. Skyscrapers, large apartment houses, and office buildings were manifestations of the growing to maturity of local communities. They were demonstrations of more intensive utilizations of urban sites. There is only one intersection of Wall Street and Broadway in New York City; only one intersection of Fifth Avenue and 42nd Street in the same city; only one loop district in Chicago; only one Golden Triangle in Pittsburgh, Pennsylvania; and only one locality of its kind in each and every metropolitan district in the United States. In terms of the numbers of persons who want to transact some kind of business in these areas, they are extremely scarce.

Disappearance of the Agricultural Frontier. One of the conditions that led to a more intensive utilization of farmland was the closing of the agricultural frontier in 1890. The Bureau of the Census announced that closing in terms of a population density of two persons per square mile. More important from the point of view of economic history is the fact that it amounted to the end of free farmland. This was the end of the colonization of western lands by eastern people. This, in itself, was a measure of economic maturity as it pertained to settlement upon land and the exploitation of other forms of natural resources in western America. Gone were the days when land could be put to productive use without cost or man-made improvements. While the closing of the frontier was more of a statistical concept than it was economic or realistic, it did call attention to the fact that the United States had grown out of the years of economic adolescence into the stage of economic adulthood. The people of the United States were reluctant to accept this status. They were just as reluctant to accept the responsibilities of economic adulthood as are some individuals to admit to adulthood in their physiological and psychological development.

Opening New Frontiers. In addition to the mining frontier that was exploited on the western slope of the Rocky Mountains following the discovery of gold, there was another similar frontier on the eastern slope and in the Rocky Mountain plateau. Coal, iron ore, lead, copper, and other minerals were found in abundance. The greatest handicaps to their exploitation were the costs of mining and their distance from markets. The former was overcome in part by the development of new technologies; the latter, by the spread of the urbanization movement to include the establishment of new centers of manufacturing, trade, and transportation in this locale. The discovery of oil in Pennsylvania may not be worthy of being designated as a new frontier, but portions of the states of Kansas and Oklahoma were concentrated locales of this frontier.

Conservation of Natural Resources. During the Colonial Period and for many, many years thereafter on into the 19th century, while it may not have been a positive governmental policy to exploit our vast stores of natural resources, little or nothing was done to discourage it. Commencing with the passage of the Homestead Act in 1862 pressure groups in Congress were responsible for the passage of legislation that gave encouragement to, if it did not actually promote, the wasteful exploitation of western lands and natural resources. Sometimes it was the laxness of enforcement officers in the field, sometimes it was their vulnerability to offers of bribes that led to a more exhaustive exploitation of natural resources than was intended by the Congress. The fact remains that lumber and mineral resources were developed more in conformity to the individual profit motive than they were in line with public policy. President Theodore Roosevelt's concern over the conservation of natural resources in the early years of the 20th century was another measurement of the maturation of the American economy. Timberlands and mineral deposits were being depleted in order to bring profit to an individual person or to a corporate group. In the absence of technological advances in construction and in industry that might alleviate the need for these resources, future generations of Americans as yet unborn would suffer from this folly.

National Parks and Forests. Yellowstone, Yosemite, and Sequoia National Parks were among the first that were established to preserve the beauty and grandeur of nature. Later other forests were removed from private and commercial exploitation, and national forests were added to the program. No section of the country had a monopoly in their location. They were havens for bird and animal life. They also attracted thousands of vacationers and travelers who sought to get away from the humdrum of urban life. There is no way of measuring the contribution these areas made to the conservation of health and life.

The disappearance of the frontier made necessary a more all-inclusive approach to the successful utilization of our landed resources. Irrigation and power dam facilities were forms of *social capital,* and the investment of public funds in social capital is one manifestation of economic maturity. There were millions of acres of land in the continental United States that had not been settled, nor had they even been appropriated by private owners in 1890. These were acres upon which labor and capital had to be expended in order to make them productive. Irrigation was a solution to one of the problems that was connected with the creation of social capital.

Irrigation of Arid Lands. In the name of conserving water supplies and of controlling floodwaters, giant power dams have been erected at strategic places across rivers. Not only have these projects retarded the flow of water to the ocean, they have utilized waterpower in the generation of electrical energy and in so doing have saved coal and petroleum for other uses. The costs of constructing any of these improvements upon land were greater than free enterprise could shoulder as long as the making of profits was the test of successful enterprise.

Prior to 1920 much more social capital in the form of dams had been constructed from the Rocky Mountain area to the West Coast than had been constructed in the Eastern States. Five rivers had been dammed in the state of New York to provide a water supply for New York City, and one river each in New Hampshire and North Carolina had been dammed in order to develop power. The story is entirely different in the West and Southwest where six dams had been constructed in order to conserve water with which to irrigate fertile but arid lands. All of the dams had been completed shortly before the United States became actively engaged in war. Eight dams had been constructed to generate power, two to control flood-waters, and three to furnish a water supply to urban areas. At the close of

World War I, land was offered free to soldiers in return for loyal services they had rendered their country, but there were few takers of few acres. Most of this land was in the Far West and Southwest where lack of rainfall and isolation from other people and activities made it unattractive to persons who had only recently returned from the intense heat of war. How social capital was applied to these lands forms the subject matter of Chapters 23 and 24, which examine the New Deal program.

External Trade Relations

The traditional pattern of our export-import trade was for products of extractive industries to dominate our exports; manufactured products to dominate imports.

Changes in Exports and Imports. One indication of our maturing economy was less dependency upon other countries for manufactures and greater utilization of raw materials that were basic to our production of manufactured goods, many of which were producers' goods. In spite of our large increase in population and an increase in its ability to consume, especially after 1900, we continued to sell cereal grains and cotton in world markets.

By 1876 this country was exporting more manufactured foodstuffs by value than it imported. In 1877 American exports of crude foodstuffs were greater by value than were the imports of similar commodities. It was not until 1898, however, that the value of our exports of manufactured goods, including semimanufactures, was greater than was the value of those goods that came into this country. *Semimanufactured goods* were those that had been processed from basic raw materials and which, in turn, became raw materials for manufacturing and fabricating industries in this country. All these changes in the relationships between the kinds of commodities that were imported and those that were exported were indications of an increasing maturity of the American economy.

Tariff Legislation. Regardless of the argument pro and con, the fact remains that after 1865 the general trend of tariff legislation was to provide greater and greater protection to American industries. Tariffs may have been levied to develop home markets; they may have been accepted in the name of affording protection to *infant industries* in their struggle for survival in competition with more mature industries in European countries. Some people fell for the argument that protective tariffs enabled American entrepreneurs to pay their laborers high wages. Other purposes for which tariffs may have been justified in the eyes of the public were to develop a greater degree of economic self-sufficiency than otherwise would have existed and to strengthen our military position among the nations of the world. All these arguments may have had some small degree of validity during the developmental stages of our nation or of particular industries.

However, by 1910 the United States had reached the status that England had attained in 1846. Unit costs of many American manufactured products were lower than the costs of similar goods that were produced in European countries. American industries were in need of foreign markets to absorb those portions of their products that could not be sold in the United States at a profit. Industrial technology had developed to the point where it needed raw materials that were not found among the natural resources that were indigenous to the United States. Lowering import duties would encourage other countries to reduce or to remove their duties on goods that they imported from the United States. In this manner American industries and the people of the United States and foreign industries and the inhabitants of foreign countries would mutually benefit from the program. The Underwood Tariff of 1913 was the first such enactment since 1861 that could be termed a revenue tariff or one in which the *principle of free trade* was given more than token expression. Since so-called protective tariffs had yielded considerable amounts of revenue to the federal government, an income tax law was passed. This law was passed as a rider to the Underwood bill. It implemented the sixteenth amendment to the United States Constitution that had been ratified in February of that same year.

Capital

One of the measures of the approaching maturity of the American economy was found in the increase in native capital that was available for investment, first in domestic industries, later in industries in foreign countries. Venture capital was of two kinds: namely, that which was available in pioneering the development of an industry, and that which was used to enlarge upon the organization and operation of industrial enterprises that had stood the test of time and which were in need of additional capital.

Sources. By 1860 a large amount of native capital was available for investment in manufacturing, in mining, in transportation, in lumbering, and in trade and commerce. Whereas prior to this time much of the native capital had originated in profits that were made in successful ventures in foreign and domestic trade, foreign trade was much less important in this respect after 1860. Domestic trade contributed a larger share of capital accumulation after 1860 than before, as did manufacturing, which included food processing. Extractive industries other than agriculture contributed increments of capital. Risks of capital were greater in pioneering industrial development than they were in enlarging upon it. The national income of the American people had become large enough and was distributed in such a manner that large capital sums were available for investment in American industrial development. Much of the so-called risk capital came from individual capitalists and entrepreneurs.

The desire for power to control corporations through the ownership of shares of common stock was a determining factor that led certain business entrepreneurs to purchase large blocks of shares of such securities in certain growing firms.

Investment of Savings. Savings banks, savings departments of commercial banks, and insurance companies were the financial institutions through which capital was accumulated. They were the principal investors in government and corporate bonds. Their executives were interested in a comparative stability of business and of prices, and they sacrificed large potential profits and losses for continuity of income and safety of principle. They abhorred price competition that assumed the nature of price wars of the cutthroat variety. Large portions of shares of common and preferred stock were held somewhat closely by the promoters and organizers of corporate firms, but there were many individuals towards the close of this period who were lured by attractive brochures and the glib tongues of salesmen into investing in the future development of their country. To them, and at this time, the real lure in the short run was to be able to share in the initial developmental profits of growing enterprises. Interest rates, profit potentials, and the prospects of capital gains channeled capital first into industries, secondly into individual corporate firms in these industries.

Investment Banks. Investment banks underwrote entire capital issues of corporate securities on the expectation that they, in turn, would be able to sell them to institutional or to individual investors. Among their regular customers were savings banks and savings departments of commercial banks, and the directors of endowment funds of colleges, universities, and other types of institutions and foundations, as some of them were designated. In addition to institutional purchasers of corporate securities from investment banks, individual persons whose monthly or annual incomes were larger than they needed for the purchase of consumers' goods and services invested their savings in securities that had been investigated and approved by the officers of those institutions in whom they had the utmost confidence.

Many more persons owned corporate securities than traded in them actively in order to make what is now called capital gains. Participants in trading activities on organized security and/or commodity exchanges were mostly those persons of relatively large money incomes and holdings of wealth who won and lost large monetary fortunes due to the vicissitudes of the markets, for which they themselves may have been in part responsible, and of which others were innocent victims. Small amounts of these capital gains found their way into more permanent and more economically productive channels. Investors, other than professional traders, had not reached the level of sophistication that gave them any confidence in investing in corporate equity securities.

Investment services had not developed to the extent that they were available to casual investors. Market information was not readily available to the masses of people who were able to save small sums of money out of current income. Another deterrent to wage earners and salaried persons owning government and corporate bonds was the prevailing minimum denomination of $1,000. Some bonds were outstanding that had face values of $500, but they were in decidedly limited volume. It remained for the federal government to reduce the face value of its Liberty Bonds to $50 in an attempt to make it possible for most of the civilian population to participate in financing the war effort. For the very first time in their lives, many thousands of persons who had been using the facilities of savings banks and savings departments in commercial banks came in direct possession of bonds and they liked it. But more of this in another chapter.

Capital Movements Related to Economic Maturity

During the latter half of the 19th century the United States became a mature debtor nation. This status was the culmination, in part, of efforts of American businessmen to borrow capital from banks and from persons in western European countries. In part it was brought about by the efforts of European capitalists and capitalistic institutions to find investment outlets for their loanable funds that would return higher rates of interest than were being received from domestic investments of comparable safety and maturity. Except in rare instances, these were portfolio investments, not direct ones. Throughout the years of immaturity as a debtor nation, commodity and service imports into the United States had exceeded the value of similar exports. Maturity as a debtor nation had the effect of reversing the flow of commodities to a net export balance. These exports represented payments of interest and repayments of principal sums as they became due and payable.

From Debtor to Creditor. Toward the close of the 19th century, American capitalists and financial institutions began to make investments abroad and for reasons that were similar to those that had attracted European capital to the United States. It may be more proper to say that at the same time that European capital was being invested in the United States by individual capitalists and by capitalistic institutions in western Europe, capitalists and capitalistic institutions in the United States were investing capital sums in Canada, in Mexico, and in the West Indies. As a point of departure, whereas most of the investments of European capital in the United States were portfolio investments, most of the American capital that was invested in the Western Hemisphere was direct. It was not until the pressures of a shooting war placed heavier demands for capital upon the countries involved in war than these countries could meet that American capital was invested in Europe. There were practically no direct loans made by American corporations, nor did the United States government lend directly to the governments of western European countries until the outbreak of hostilities in 1914 and prior to our active participation therein. Until this development took place, the cumulative total of American commodity exports that represented payments of interest, payments on principal sums borrowed as they became due and payable, and the investment of American capital abroad were not as large as our interest obligations alone; therefore, we were forced to borrow additional capital sums in order to meet these obligations.

Cleona Lewis, in her book entitled *America's Stake in International In-vestments*,[1] estimated that our net debt increased from about $2,710,000,000 in 1897 to $3,686,000,000 in 1914. The excess of exports over imports on our commodity trade account was a measure of our maturity as a debtor nation. The investment of American capital in foreign countries, by itself, was indicative of the fact that the United States had arrived at the stage of immaturity as a creditor nation. The commodity exports that followed these investments only served to increase the excess of our commodity exports over our commodity imports. Shortly thereafter, foreign investments in the United States began to decline and American investments abroad continued to increase. The impact of these movements was to cause a relative decline in commodity imports and to alter their character, to increase the value of commodity exports and to alter their composition. We were now lending to people or to firms in the same countries from which we formerly had borrowed.

Rehabilitation of American Securities. One very serious dislocation in the long run was brought about by the selling in New York City of American corporate securities that were owned by Europeans. The immediate trans-actions were initiated by the need on the part of foreign governments for dollar balances in New York City banks that they could use in the purchase of war materiel. The efforts to turn foreign investments into bank balances reduced the degree to which the United States was a debtor nation, the immediate effects of which were to increase commodity exports. This increase in commodity exports was extended to a long-run situation when these dollar balances were exhausted by setting up new balances when Americans began to lend extensively to the Allied Powers. The J. P. Morgan Bank in New York City organized a syndicate of investment bankers that spear-headed this activity. Incidentally, these very loans may have been instru-mental in swinging the support of the United States to the Allies in 1917. By 1920, the United States had been catapulted into the position of a mature creditor nation without its people having had time to adjust them-selves to this status. In 1920 the thinking of our industrial and political leaders continued to reflect a philosophy that had been induced by long years of debtorship to European countries.

The Development of Economic Imperialism

What may have been one of the most convincing demonstrations of the fact that the American economy was approaching the stage of maturity was the appearance of some of the symptoms of economic imperialism. From time to time there were personalities in government who favored expanding our sphere of economic influence beyond the borders of continental United States, but these persons did not receive the wholehearted support of our

[1] Cleona Lewis, *America's Stake in International Investments* (Washington, D.C.: The Brookings Institution, 1938), p. 445.

industrial or financial leaders. The latter could obtain just as large and as spectacular profits from exploiting natural resources and in constructing railroads in the western United States as they could from exploiting the resources and people of some extraterritorial country, and without encountering the political hazards that might have led to military consequences.

Purchase of Alaska. One of the first manifestations of imperialism on the part of the United States after 1860 was the purchase of Alaska from Russia in 1867. There may have been some political implications connected with the acquisition of this Territory, and there may have been some military aspects or influences that were brought to bear, but we are concerned with the economic background that led to such a departure from any policy or program we had developed nationally up to this time.

There was a surplus of Treasury funds over and above those needed to carry on the customary and traditional functions of government at the federal level. The last time such a situation confronted government officials was in 1837 at which time it was decided to distribute the surplus to the several states in proportion to their populations. The difficulties that were encountered at this time following the initial attempts to carry out this policy were so untimely that the program was not pushed to completion. Neither persons nor agencies in Washington wanted to assume the responsibilities for any unfavorable economic impacts that might ensue if a similar course of action were to be taken. Another alternative was to open the "pork barrel" to the wanton spending of government monies for purposes of financing alleged internal improvements. Still another possibility of disposing of the Treasury surplus was to vote more and higher pensions to veterans of the Civil War. The solution that was found at the time was the purchase of Alaska at a cost of $7,200,000.

Russia had obtained large amounts of fish and furs from the Alaskan peninsula, but the Russians knew little or nothing about the vast stores of timber and mineral resources that were to be found therein. The people of the United States were not known as a fish-eating people; and there were many, untouched virgin forests within Alaskan boundaries. Twenty years went by before gold was discovered in the valley of the Klondike River. Other minerals that were exploited by capital that came from the United States were silver and coal. Fishing provided large incomes even before Alaska became a Territory of the United States. Alaskan waters abounded in salmon, halibut, herring, and cod fish. Spruce, red and yellow cedar, hemlock, and birch trees were found on 44 million acres of forest land. Among furbearing animals that were much sought after and whose skins and furs were marketed in the United States and elsewhere were seal, sable, ermine, otter, wolverine, beaver, muskrat, mink, lynx, fox, and marten.

Citizens of the United States, in general, were so preoccupied with internal problems that grew out of the development of agriculture, corporate combinations and trusts, railroads, and some aspects of their monetary system, they had little time to devote to the external expansion of their economic activity until near the close of the 19th century.

Investment and Control. Judging from what has been written so far, economic imperialism seems to have had something to do with the investment of capital in foreign countries. A portfolio type of investment of capital in any country did not lead to economic imperialism, nor was it to be considered by anyone as being imperialistic because of the fact that no controls at any level of operation were exercised by the investors. Even the direct investment of capital in foreign countries was not considered as being imperialistic unless it was accompanied by efforts by the investors to exercise some control over the economies and/or the governments of the countries in which the investments were made.

Prior to World War I, individual and corporate capital of American origin was invested in other countries. Some of it was invested in the sugar industry in Cuba; some of it was used to promote the development of the banana industry in Central American countries. American capital was invested also in the mining of gold and other metals in Canada, in the production of pineapples in Hawaii, and in the mining of silver, copper, and other metals in Mexico. Insofar as the mere investment of capital in a foreign country in order to obtain profits was concerned, there was nothing any more "imperialistic," nothing more aggressive or expansionist than there was in the investment of capital in American coal mines or in American railroads. Just as did the investment of capital in American industries have political impacts and repercussions, so did the investing of American capital abroad lead to political complications and crises.

Need for Foreign Economic Policy. The investment of capital abroad by American capitalists or industrialists called for the development of a foreign economic policy, which was a phase of our development that lacked consistency and continuity and something with which American statesmen and politicians had had no experience or background. They had been concerned with the development of policies according to which titles to public lands were distributed to private interests. They also had been concerned with giving encouragement to the extension of the railway net throughout the Middle West and the Far West. For many years their attention had been called to the need for strengthening our monetary and our banking systems and to ways of controlling consolidations and combinations the results of which operated in restraint of interstate trade and commerce. Little thought had been devoted to external economic relationships other than to those that had arisen from applying the provisions of the several tariff laws.

Political Aggression. International conflicts of interest had arisen from the fact that after capital investments had been made in foreign countries, governments came into power that were not sympathetic to the industries of their respective countries being controlled by foreign industrialists.

Treaties have been abrogated, industries have been nationalized, and real property has been confiscated. There is an important question that may be posed at this juncture, to which the finding of an answer offers a challenge to every reader. It is a well-known fact that when the Northern Pacific or some other railroad company, or the Anaconda Copper Company or some other industrial concern, was unable to meet its financial obligations in the form of interest on borrowed money, the American government was not called upon to operate the company for the benefit of bondholders until all the payments that were in arrears had been paid in full. Why, then, when foreign corporations have been unable to meet their interest obligations to American bondholders, has the American government been called upon to administer the collection and utilization of customs duties until the financial obligations of these foreign corporations have been met in full?

Military Intervention. Probably a more prevalent approach to the accomplishment of economic imperialism, and one that has given rise to more political or international crises than any other, has been the lending of capital by banks or by governments directly to other governments on terms that the latter could not carry out in full and on time. The nonpayment of interest by a debtor government to its creditors has been made the excuse for landing military and/or naval forces in order to force the payments of such obligations.

Individual governmental administrations in Spanish-speaking countries in the Western Hemisphere have been notoriously unstable ever since they obtained their political freedom. On many, if not all, of these occasions detachments of United States Marines, or of other branches of the Armed Forces, have been landed either to maintain order or to restore it. Some so-called yellow journalists have been very militant in their urgings that overt action be taken against the offenders. Others have been a little more naive in their attempts to justify such action after it has been taken. The United States went to the aid of a people that were being oppressed by Spain; it was going to Christianize the Philippines, many of whose peoples had known Catholicism for 300 years, more or less.

There were other instances of imperialistic expansion or overt acts of intervention by the United States; but since many of them were instigated by persons in government office or by newspaper owner-editors, there is some question as to the extent to which they were motivated by economic considerations, how much by political and/or military influences. The mention of a few names will serve to freshen the memories of all Americans who have studied United States history at the secondary level. "We point with pride" to the exploits of Theodore Roosevelt at San Juan Hill, to Admiral Mayo at Vera Cruz, to General Pershing in pursuit of Pancho Villa in Mexico, and to the feats of Admiral Dewey in Manila Bay. In attempting to avoid intervention in Mexico, President Wilson went on to say, "I have to pause and remind myself that I am President of the United States and not of a small group of Americans with vested interests in Mexico." The implications of this statement point out the relationships between economic penetration by a group of vested interests and the involvement of the United States in crises of international import.

Surge of Nationalism. Hemispherical defense, or it may have been a surge of nationalism, justified the purchase of the Virgin Islands from Denmark and the construction of the Panama Canal. It was the enforcement of the principles that had been established in the Monroe Doctrine that motivated Theodore Roosevelt to protect Venezuela from the naval strength of Germany. The mere mention of the blowing up of the battleship Maine in Havana Harbor, in which many Americans lost their lives; the Spanish-American War; Cuba; Puerto Rico; and the acquisition of Samoa, Hawaii, and the Philippine Islands arouses a feeling of patriotism and of nationalism in the bosoms of all red-blooded American youth. These events were of as much political and military significance as they were economic in their causation and much more so in their settlement. To the extent that economic relationships were involved, they pertained to relatively small groups of persons or corporations who made American dignity, American supremacy, and American nationalism issues in support of which the power of the American government was sought. Dollar diplomacy was used in place of bullet diplomacy, and it spoke with almost as much authority as the latter.

Agriculture Becomes Balanced with Industry

Between 1870 and 1920, percentage declines in agriculture, construction, transportation and public utilities, and service industries as sources of national income were offset by percentage increases in manufacturing and finance. (See Table 20-1) Incomes from mining industries were spectacular, but so were losses, and mining did little more than hold its own in contributing to national income throughout the years under consideration. Agriculture continued to decline percentagewise as a source of national income until the influence of World War I restored it to its former level. The influence of the war was likewise seen in its failure to reverse the downward trend of trade as a source of national income. Manufacturing activities originated continuously larger percentages of national income.

By the turn of the century, manufacturing was contributing a larger share of our national income than was agriculture. What all this means is that agriculture no longer occupied the prime position among occupations that it did in former years. Alexander Hamilton's goal of balancing agriculture with industry finally had been attained. This did not mean that people had less food to eat at the close of the 19th century than they had at its beginning. On the contrary, 30 times as many people had more to eat per capita than they had during Hamilton's day. Not only did people eat more food, they had a greater variety of food from which to select their menus for each meal. It is an aphorism to say that just as farmers depended upon the market for the sale of their produce, so did other segments of the population depend upon that same market to obtain their foodstuffs.

Table 20-1

Percentage Contribution of National Income by Industry—1869-1948 (Based on Values in Current Prices)

Period	Agriculture	Mining	Manufacturing	Contract Construction	Transportation and Other Public Utilities	Trade	Service	Government	Finance and Miscellaneous
Martin's Estimates—Aggregate Payments									
1869 and 1879	20.5	1.8	13.9	5.3	11.9	15.7	14.7	4.4	11.7
1879 and 1889	16.1	2.1	16.6	5.5	11.9	16.6	13.6	4.9	12.6
1889 and 1899	17.1	2.5	18.2	4.9	10.7	16.8	11.8	6.0	12.0
1899—1908	16.7	3.1	18.4	4.5	10.7	15.3	9.6	5.6	16.0
1904—1913	17.0	3.3	18.9	4.3	11.0	15.0	8.9	5.4	16.2
1909—1918	17.7	3.3	20.8	3.2	10.7	14.5	8.2	6.3	15.4
1914—1923	15.2	3.3	22.2	3.0	11.0	14.0	8.3	7.9	15.0
1919—1928	12.2	3.1	22.2	3.9	11.3	13.7	9.4	8.6	15.7
National Bureau of Economic Research Estimates—National Income									
1919—1928	10.5	2.5	21.9	4.4	9.8	13.6	11.6	9.6	16.1
1924—1933	8.7	1.9	19.6	4.2	10.4	13.3	13.4	11.8	16.7
1929—1938	8.5	1.7	19.4	2.9	10.0	13.6	13.9	14.4	15.6
1934—1943	9.2	1.7	24.2	2.9	8.5	13.2	12.1	15.4	12.7
1939—1948	9.4	1.6	27.1	3.4	7.3	13.3	10.5	17.2	10.2

Source: U. S. Department of Commerce, Bureau of the Census, *Historical Statistics of the United States. Colonial Times to 1957* (Washington: U. S. Government Printing Office, 1960), p. 140.

Central Banking

The champions of independent unit banking had strong enough representation in Congress to forestall any and all efforts to introduce some kind of central banking legislation until the need for it was so imperative that positive action was finally taken. The attitude of the people towards banking was an outgrowth of the stage of economic development of the United States. As long as business, commerce, and finance were conducted on local or regional bases there may have been no particular need for the determination of any particular monetary, banking, or credit policies.

Long after railroads had served to connect the economic regions of America, long after telephone and telegraph systems had spread their wires across the nation and had made direct communication possible between persons separated by hundreds or thousands of miles, long after nationwide markets were a *fait accompli*, banking authorities were still struggling to adjust their operations through the establishment of correspondent relationships between banks. They could not effectuate banking policy; they could not determine the bases upon which they dealt with their correspondent banks and with their own customers. On occasions the Comptroller of the Currency may have issued words of suggestion or advice to the boards of directors of individual national banks or to banks in general, but as long as national banks operated within the reserve limitations of the National Bank Act, he could not exert any overall positive policy control. Again, the fact that there were more state banks in the country than national banks prevented him from having even a salutary effect upon the operations of commercial banks.

Apathy of the American People towards Central Banking. Banks failed; business experienced its good times and bad; our commodity export and import trade was subject to wide variations; internal commodity prices varied widely; unemployment brought hardship and suffering to millions of workers and their families; gold reserves in banks and in the United States Treasury fluctuated widely, but there were no serious demands for the adoption of central banking. When the Populist and the Greenback parties advocated abolishing national banks and issuing more greenbacks, they revealed how little they really understood the operations of banking and of monetary institutions. They clung to the devices that had become traditional before the country had become an integrated economic unit. By 1900 the economic status of the farmer was on the upgrade, and his voice of dissension mellowed as his money income increased. The adoption of the gold standard in this year may be considered as a sign of maturity, even though it merely gave formal recognition to a situation that had existed since 1873.

Positive Action. Competitive actions and competitive policies on the part of individual banks had been the cause of many banking crises since the establishment of national banking in 1863. Finally it dawned on some of the men who had given the matter a great deal of thought and consideration that a study should be made of the entire banking structure. Canada, England, France, and Germany all had some kind of central banking, and they had not experienced the large number of bank failures, even on a proportionate basis, as had the United States. Banks in these countries had responded to the needs of business and had not, by their own actions, contributed to or brought on critical financial situations. The passage of the Federal Reserve Act in 1913 must be considered to have been one of the measures of a maturing economy.

Taxation

By 1913, costs of operating government had increased to the level that required a more business-like approach to the problem of how best to raise more revenue. Gone were the days when the sale of public lands was an important source of revenue to the federal government, and time had proved the difficulty or impossibility of coordinating the collection of customs duties with the need for them. Some of the increased costs at the federal level were the result of the assumption of functions that formerly had been performed at the state level, or had not been performed at all. President Wilson had in mind the development of still other programs at the federal level that would have required additional increments of income to cover their costs.

Failure of the General Property Tax. The development of the corporate form of business organization gave rise to tax paying ability that emanated from the ownership of intangible property. The general property tax had been adopted and accepted at a time when the ownership of land and of other tangible assets was a measure of one's tax paying ability. By the dawn of the 20th century the ownership of tangible property alone had proved to be entirely inadequate and unfair as a measure of tax paying ability. More and more of the nation's income was being distributed on the basis of the ownership of corporate stocks and bonds. Few taxpayers declared their ownership of clocks, watches, and other items of personal property; still fewer persons declared their holdings of intangibles. The idea was preached that every person owed something to the support of government, and that as governmental functions were broadened, personal income had become the basis upon which the amount he owed should be calculated.

Ability-to-Pay Principle of Taxation. Economists had been developing a faculty theory of taxation, in line with which taxes should be levied upon and collected from taxpayers in accordance with their ability to pay. The income tax had been advocated in fulfillment of the idea that a person's income was a measurement of tax paying ability. The idea was based upon the principle of the decreasing marginal utility of the dollar. The inheritance tax also conformed to this principle and was used by the federal government largely as a source of revenue, although there had been some agitation for using both it and the income tax as means for equalizing the distribution of wealth and of incomes. Corporations had been subjected to an income tax since 1909. State governments had passed income tax laws as their needs for revenue increased; and landowners were loathe to be the sole bearers of increased tax burdens when millions of persons who did not own land had tax paying ability as measured in terms of money incomes.

The Federal Income Tax. The acceptance of direct taxation in the form of an income tax was a test of the fact that maturity had been attained in our attitude towards federal taxation. People were no more anxious or eager to be taxed in 1913 than they had been in the Colonial Period, but they had matured in their thinking about taxes. They also had lived long enough with a federated government to know more about it.

The use of an income tax gave promise of Congress being able to adjust revenue to the needs of government rather than vice versa.

The 16th Constitutional Amendment. While the Supreme Court had declared the corporate income tax of 1909 an excise tax and hence constitutional, it required an amendment to the Constitution before it would accept a direct tax on persons that was not levied in proportion to population.

The First Income Tax Law of 1913. As might be expected, Congress had to move slowly in its use of an income tax before it could become the principal source of federal revenue. In the first place, the Department of Internal Revenue was not staffed to handle a burden of personal tax returns that were complicated and involved. In the second place, taxpayers had to be educated slowly into the mysteries of such a tax, including keeping accurate records of incomes and expenditures. In the third place, there was no corps of experts trained in income tax accounting; and in the fourth place, there were no court decisions to serve as precedents in handling borderline cases and those in which there were honest differences of opinion.

Earned incomes consisted of wages and salaries and were taxed less heavily than were unearned incomes that consisted of interest, dividends, and similar incomes.

All persons with net incomes of $3,000 or more were required to file income tax returns. Tax rates were graduated from 1 percent on the first $20,000 of taxable income to 7 percent on taxable incomes over $500,000. Taxable incomes were less than total incomes by the amount of deductions that were specified by law. In 1916 rates ranged from 2 percent on the first $20,000 of taxable incomes to 15 percent on such incomes over $2,000,000. Other changes in income tax rates will be presented under the heading of "War Finance" on page 538.

Fewer than 400,000 returns were made until 1916 when 437,036 were filed. In this year the tax from 362,907 taxable returns amounted to $173,387,000 compared with $225,962,000 from customs and $635,979,000 from other internal revenue sources.

Need for Government Regulation

The growth of industrial and commercial firms led to the formation of organizations which protected the public from the impacts of competition. No longer could employees and consumers protect their own interests. Objectivity replaced subjectivity. Individual employees lost their identities. Individual consumers lost any influence or control over production they once exercised. Custom-made items cost more than similar ones in mass markets. Profits were uppermost in the minds of producers and their managements which became objective. Employees became labor. Customers became the market. Producers were much fewer in number than were labor and consumers. In order to protect the masses of people from exploitation by a relatively few, government at respective levels has seen fit to establish new rules that govern the relationships between different members of the business fraternity and between these members and consumers, but without destroying the basic, fundamental motive of those who choose to continue in or to enter the business world. It has attempted to develop teamwork among the members of our economic society, rather than to develop individual star performers.

In order to establish the pattern which was followed by the federal government in developing its policies for regulating business activity, a word concerning the development of the commercial food industry is in order.

Pure Food and Drugs Act. Prior to 1860, the preparation of food as well as its production was carried on largely at the family level. After they had become directed towards the market, consumers had no way of protecting themselves from the avidity of corporate entrepreneurs whose interests were more in the search for profits than in producing and serving food that was not contaminated in any way. They were so far removed from the marketplace that matters of sanitation and of health and cleanliness were of little concern to many of them. Competitive conditions were such that they could not have been regulated at the local level, but it was not until after Theodore Roosevelt had succeeded William McKinley that he was able to enlist congressional support in passing a pure food and drug act.

By this act the adulteration and misbranding of food and drugs were prohibited. Adulteration occurred if a foreign substance had been introduced into a product, the effect of which was to lower the strength or the quality of the product, or if a valuable ingredient of a product had been removed. Misbranding occurred if a product were an imitation of another product; if it had been labeled so as to mislead or to deceive its purchaser; or if the package or label bore any misleading statement, device, or design. Dr. Harvey W. Wiley's *An Autobiography* [2] tells of the trials and tribulations of the first United States Commissioner of Food and Drugs. The program had

[2] Harvey W. Wiley, *An Autobiography* (Indianapolis: The Bobbs-Merrill Co., Inc., 1930).

been strengthened by the authority that had been given to the Federal Trade Commission, but still there were many loopholes in its enforcement. Publicity was depended upon to create public opinion, but publicity was not always forthcoming when corporate managers threatened to withdraw their advertising from those portions of the public press that printed information that was unfavorable to the corporate advertisers.

Social Insurance

Insofar as the mechanization of industrial processes was a measurement of economic maturity, social legislation was one of its concomitants. As late as 1920 the United States was not ready for an all-out program of social insurance at any level of government. Workmen's compensation laws had been enacted by several of the states and by the federal government to take care of some of the financial burdens that were imposed upon employees through no fault of their own. There was a feeling in some circles that unemployment was just as much a product of our industrial organization as were industrial accidents and deaths, but expression of this idea was not voiced in legislation until a later period.

Old age and retirement, as we know them, were not social problems in any segment of our economy until after 1860. When the problems of old age did arise they were settled at the levels of county and state governments through media of institutionalized homes that were operated as charitable institutions. One of the functions of children was to care for aged, sick, idle, and incapacitated parents. It was only when there were no living children or when they were financially unable or unwilling to care for their parents that the latter were institutionalized and became public charges. State and county homes for the aged served one useful purpose for which they were not intended. They were used to illustrate the futility of attempting to levy taxes on the basis of benefits received from government, at least as far as the residents of these institutions were concerned.

Labor Legislation

Closely allied to social legislation from the point of view of its development and its acceptance by the people was labor legislation. Government at any level did not pass labor laws until our industrial organization had become so complex that workers themselves were not able to do anything to improve the conditions under which they worked, even though the latter might have been injurious to them. Legislation was accepted first in those industries whose work endangered the health and lives of the workers. More personal attention was given to workers in food industries—processing, baking, and serving—in the name of health and welfare of their patrons. More attention was given to the cleanliness and sanitation of the premises and to the health and physical condition of the employees themselves. Physical examinations and health records were required at regular intervals for the protection of the public.

In industries that endangered the health of the workers, such items as hours, ventilation, rest periods, lunch hours, and the application of safety devices and sanitation facilities were the focal points of regulation. When textiles were not permitted to be worked on in crowded tenements and by persons who had tuberculosis or other contagious diseases, the American economy revealed signs of maturity in that, in addition to considerations of immediate short-run profits to the entrepreneurs, the welfare and well-being of their employees and of the public that consumed the end products were objects of attention. Industrial immaturity was characterized by short-run, individual considerations that yielded profits to entrepreneurs. Industrial maturity was reached when entrepreneurs considered long-run impacts, and society established a framework within which they could earn their profits.

One of the manifestations of economic maturity was the passage by Congress of the Adamson Act in 1916. This Act did not abolish collective bargaining between management and employees as a process of settling disputes, but it did protect the general public and the country as a whole when this process had broken down.

Other Indexes of Economic Maturity

Recognition of economic maturity is found in the fact that government undertook to establish rules for making business profits and earning a living. As was the case in the passage of social insurance and of labor laws, these rules had for their purpose protecting those persons who could no longer protect themselves against encroachments on their rights and freedom.

Railroad Legislation. The passage of the Interstate Commerce Act of 1887 was manifestation that a certain stage of maturity had been reached in the development of railroad transportation. Regulation at the state level was no longer adequate. It did not satisfy either the railroads or its patrons. It did not solve the problems that arose out of interstate traffic which was becoming a larger and larger portion of the total traffic of railroads. Additional legislation such as the Elkins Act, the Hepburn Act, and the Mann-Elkins Railroad Act were the result of maturity in handling some of the problems that were connected with regulating railroads. The Railway Evaluation Act of 1913 was passed in recognition of the fact that a more mature approach to the regulation of railway rate making was essential to the attainment of the objects of regulation. At the termination of the period under observation, the Transportation Act of 1920 gave recognition to the fact that railway transportation had matured to the stage at which there should be more cooperative competition and less uncoordinated free competition. Competition was not confined to rate making; it could appear in the quality and convenience of the services that railroads rendered.

The Regulation of Monopoly and Enforcement of Fair Trade. Just as the policy of the Interstate Commerce Commission had been to enforce competition between the railroads, so did the Sherman Antitrust Act of 1890 outline provisions for the enforcement of competition between industrial and commercial firms. Regardless of what a person may think about the manner in which the *rule of reason* was introduced into the deliberations of the United States Supreme Court and of the instance of its first application, there is no doubt but that it gave expression to the maturation of American industry, or at least in certain segments of it. It recognized that a change had taken place gradually as a result of which absolutely free and unfettered competition was harmful to the economy as a whole as well as to some of the components of combinations. The Clayton Act of 1914 and the Federal Trade Commission Act of the same year were further manifestations of a maturing economy.

Leisure Time. The concept of leisure time is that amount of time that is not devoted directly and immediately to earning an income, or to obtaining a livelihood. Unless it resulted from enforced unemployment, it did not mean idleness. It gave rise to an exceedingly large variety of activities, which, in turn, gave rise to the production of wealth and the rendering of services that were utilized during this time. Increase in leisure time was indicative of a maturing economy.

Education. Not only were more youth of America extending their years of scholastic attainment into and beyond the secondary level of education, professional and graduate programs of 4-year colleges and universities attracted more of them. To make this possible, their parents not only had increased their annual incomes beyond their immediate needs, they had been able to save out of their incomes in order to support their children in their extended years of unproductiveness. The experiences our young men had in World War I did as much or more than anything else to impress upon them the urgency and importance of at least a college education. As someone stated, in the short run if a boy wanted to become a second lieutenant in the United States Army, he would have to have graduated from college. When this statement was made, there were no indications that the war would terminate in a little over 18 months after we formally declared that our support would be thrown on the side of the Allies in their struggle against the Central Powers. Even so, after the war was over, and before there were indications that another catastrophic struggle was lurking over the horizon, young boys and girls swarmed onto college campuses in larger numbers than the then existing facilities were capable of accommodating. Girls had gained a new freedom during the war, and going to college and preparing themselves to earn a livelihood was an expression of the freedom.

Commercial Entertainment. Schools and churches ceased to function as centers of entertainment outside the home. In the home, the magic lantern and stereopticon were displaced by the cinema, which required a theater instead of a parlor in which it could be shown. It was viewed by hundreds of people instead of by a few invited guests. It required the employment of people who were paid wages for their work. Those persons who preferred live entertainment found it in the minstrel show, vaudeville performances, and opera. Professional baseball provided relaxation to those interested persons who could take afternoons off from work and who had the price of admission. Bowling, roller skating, and amusement parks offered a variety of entertainment to those who were interested in participating. Public dance pavilions, band concerts, midway type games and entertainment, boating and canoeing, merry-go-rounds, and roller coasters attracted thousands of pleasure seekers every week; and on holiday occasions crowds in attendance made it difficult for everybody but the concessionaires.

Organized Research. As the size of the industrial unit became larger and competition between giant corporations became keener, firms no longer could afford to depend upon casual discoveries and inventions or upon those that were purely accidental. Top management was confronted with problems of production, the solutions to which were essential to the continued successful operation of the business within the established framework. Research departments or divisions were organized. They employed hundreds of research scientists, such as chemists, physicists, and engineers—civil, electrical, industrial, and mechanical. Thousands of dollars were budgeted to research in the competitive race to lower unit costs of production and to devise new products and new packaging for old products. Research programs were coordinated with the needs of business rather than with the whims and fancies of the individual researchers themselves. Efforts were also made to devise ways of producing larger volumes of goods without duplicating smaller production machines. Therein was found the key to large-scale production.

PERFORMANCE OF THE AMERICAN ECONOMY—1866-1920

After Appomattox the United States experienced a rapid growth in most, if not all, of the segments of its economy. Where growth did not occur, changes took place, the effects of which were to alter the status quo of each industrial or economic segment in its relation to each of the other segments individually and to all of them collectively. It may have been the irregular and uncoordinated development of economic segments that gave rise to some of the inequalities, if not inequities, in the distribution and receipt of incomes and in the concentration of wealth in the hands of a relatively few persons. Monopoly control of industry may likewise have contributed to these same conditions. There was no economic planning at any level of government. What planning there was occurred at the level of free enterprise and was entirely within economic segments and not at all between them.

Cyclical Fluctuations

The American economy was not spared what has turned out to be one of the most disturbing developments of an industrial society—the business cycle. Little was known about the origin of this phenomenon; much more was known about its economic impacts or consequences. Nobody seemed to be responsible for its occurrence; nobody could do much in the way of preventing it. It appeared to have a monetary aspect, an agricultural phase, and an industrial circumstance. War appeared to have had such disturbing and disrupting effects upon our economic organization that had been geared to peacetime conditions and that was premised upon the continuation of peaceful relations with other countries that the cessation of military programs invariably led to industrial recessions or depressions. Sometimes it was easier to find the spark that set off a recession than it was to discover what had brought about a turn for the better unless it was something that was akin to self-exhaustion. The failure of the Jay Cooke investment bank in 1873, the gold crisis in 1893, and the closing of the Knickerbocker Trust Company in New York in 1907 appeared to have precipitated panic situations. For some reason the latter disturbance (1907) was felt more in the form of a decline in prices than it was in a decline in industrial activity. While prolonged periods of declines in industrial activity had caused many unpleasant and discouraging events to happen, the low levels of each succeeding downward trend tended to be higher than the preceding low point. This condition gave rise to what statisticians called an upward secular trend, which was the long-run trend that developed after 1896. Before this year the country had experienced approximately 20 years of a downward secular trend.

After a panic situation had subsided somewhat, unemployment tended to increase; and bank rates of interest on commercial loans declined in response to a decline in the volume of such loans. This decline was brought about by commercial loans maturing more rapidly than new loans were either requested or granted, and excess reserves of commercial banks tended to increase. Railroad car loadings declined; fewer and shorter freight trains were operated. Prices, both wholesale and retail, declined. The volume of business or the rate of turnover of inventories in foodstores remained relatively constant, but profit margins declined. Capital goods industries suffered larger losses in volume; and it was at this level that unemployment was most serious, along with railroad transportation. It was to correct this pattern of the business cycle, the canker of our capitalistic economic organization, that the Federal Reserve System had been organized. Just how well the dreams of its proponents were realized forms the thesis of a later chapter's discussion.

National Income

In 1889 national income in terms of current dollars amounted to $6,827 million or $180 per capita. By 1900 these figures had reached $16,158 million and $212 respectively, and by 1920 they were $68,434 million and $642 respectively. In terms of 1926 dollars, the per capita incomes were $237, $480, and $567, respectively. Compared with 1870, population had increased 90 percent by 1900, national income per capita, 102.5 percent, which is not at all startling when one recalls the tremendous overall industrial development that occurred throughout this span of years. On the other hand, from 1900 to 1920 when population increased 39 percent, per capita income increased only 18 percent. This is not surprising either considering that 1920 was only two years removed from the most destructive war the country had ever known although this war had not been fought on home soil. On a per capita basis adjusted to 1926 prices, a peak of $646 was reached in 1918. In addition to the retarding effects of war, inflation had taken its toll. By extrapolation, population increased 34 percent between 1900 and 1918 as against an increase in adjusted per capita income of 35 percent.

Distribution of Wealth and the Receipt of Income

Tables that were drawn to reveal the inequalities in the distribution of the ownership of wealth and of the receipt of personal or family incomes were disturbing to some young minds. It was not that young people had not been aware of them in the communities in which they lived. Their attention had not been attracted by graphic methods, nor had they stopped to realize the extent or the extremes to which these inequalities were found. It was disturbing to become aware of the fact that the upper 20 percent of the families in the United States had more than twice the incomes of the lowest 40 percent and that the upper 20 percent of the families received 50 percent of the total income, while the lowest 40 percent distributed only 15 percent of the total income among them. These figures changed in detail from year to year, but there were few alterations in the general pattern.

As startling as these figures are, it must be remembered that a dependent wage class and an unequal distribution of the ownership of wealth and unequal annual incomes are basic to a capitalistic economic organization. Concentration of wealth in the hands of a relatively few persons gives proof that the capitalistic system had been functioning as was to be expected. Prior to the analysis of individual income tax returns at the federal level, data of this nature had to be obtained from probate courts or from the research studies of sociologists or economists. Sampling was inadequate and somewhat unreliable; but insofar as taxpayers were conscientious in making out their returns, data after World War I were much more reliable and authentic than had theretofore been the case. A feeling of "social responsibility" of wealth had spread among the members of most of the wealthy families, except for the *nouveaux riches*, who had attained their wealth from the control of oil fields and other newly exploited natural resources, and others who were in position to profit financially because of some fortuitous circumstances in the years of war.

Persons who were dissatisfied with the manifestations of the lack of social responsibility of wealth advocated an increase in progressive income tax rates and inheritance taxes in order to prevent the perpetuation of large concentrations of wealth, if not their formation. This agitation also came at a time when the financial obligations of government were larger than could be met from the revenues of customary sources of governmental funds. There is little evidence to show that either of these devices was used for purposes other than to yield revenues to government. Inequalities in the economic strength of different classes and groups of persons undoubtedly gave rise to the passage of laws that fell in the category of social legislation. The functioning of our capitalistic economy was recognized as having brought about these inequalities; and attempts were made to correct them, but within the basic framework of capitalism.

Government Employment

Just as enlargement in the size of business units and their incorporation increased the need for white collar workers, so did the enforcement of government regulations, including the corporate and personal income tax laws, result in a large and rapid increase in the number of government civilian employees. In 1900, there were 94,893 civil service employees; in 1910, 222,278; and in 1920, 427,603. The war necessitated the employment of 326,899 in 1917 and of 642,432 in 1918. As war agencies were phasing out in 1919, employees with civil service status declined to 592,691. These persons rendered services that had to be paid for out of increased taxes. They represented an increment of society whose consumer goods were produced by farmers, factory and mill workers, while the scale of living of the American people was on the increase.

Advances in Levels of Living

Equal advances in levels of living were not experienced by persons in all walks of life. In general, farmers and urban workers fared better in the decade prior to the outbreak of war in Europe than they had for 30 years, and during the war their incomes soared to heights unknown. There were, however, submarginal farmers who lived on submarginal land who did not participate in farm prosperity. Likewise, there were many persons in urban areas who lived in abject poverty. If they worked at all, their jobs were menial and their pay substandard.

Data in Tables 20-2 and 20-3 afford a comparison of average wages and hours worked per week in several industries. Union employees enjoyed shorter work weeks and received higher wages; but since they constituted only a small percentage of total workers, except in Building Construction and Railroads, the data are more representative of reality, insofar as averages are real. Annual increases do not measure net gains in scales of living because of increases in the cost of living. Based on 1913 prices, the cost of living index increased from 67.7 in 1900 to 93.1 in 1910, and from 101.1 in 1915 to 203.7 in 1920.[3]

[3] U. S. Department of Commerce, Bureau of the Census, *Historical Statistics of the United States. Colonial Times to 1957* (Washington: U. S. Government Printing Office, 1960), p. 127.

Table 20-2

Hours and Earnings in Manufacturing and Selected Nonmanufacturing Industries, and for "Lower Skilled" Labor—1890-1920

Year	Manufacturing		Bituminous Coal Mining		Railroads	Building Trades		Postal Employees		"Lower-Skilled" Labor
	Average Weekly Hours	Average Hourly Earnings	Average Weekly Hours	Average Hourly Earnings	Average Full-Time Weekly Earnings	Average Weekly Hours (Union)	Average Hourly Earnings (Union)	Average Weekly Hours	Average Hourly Earnings	Average Full-Time Weekly Earnings
1890	62.2	$.149	60.0	$.180	$11.38	51.3	$ .341	48.0	$.352	$ 8.71
1895	62.3	.141	60.0	.158	11.22	50.3	.341	48.0	.375	7.45
1900	62.1	.152	52.6	.204	11.43	48.3	.374	48.0	.371	8.83
1905	61.1	.168	51.6	.276	12.45	46.1	.454	48.0	.375	9.91
1910	59.8	.188	51.6	.299	14.07	45.2	.520	48.0	.420	10.65
1915	58.2	.212	51.6	.337	15.78	44.8	.569	48.0	.466	10.65
1920	53.5	.561	48.2	.784	34.14	43.8	1.052	48.0	.739	25.98

Source: *Historical Statistics of the United States. Colonial Times to 1957*, 1960, p.91. Adapted.

Table 20-3

Average Annual Earnings in Selected Industries and Occupations
1890-1920

Year	Manu-factur-ing	Steam Rail-roads	Street Railways	Tele-phone	Tele-graph	Gas and Electri-city	Clerical Workers, Mfg. and Steam R.R.'s	Bitumi-nous Coal Mining	Farm Labor	Postal Employ-ees	Public School Teach-ers	Min-ist-ers
1890	$ 439	$ 560	$ 557	...	...	$ 687	$ 848	$ 406	$233	$ 878	$256	$ 794
1895	416	546	509	...	...	640	941	307	216	935	289	787
1900	435	548	604	...	...	620	1,011	438	247	925	328	731
1905	494	589	646	$401	$ 581	543	1,076	500	302	935	392	759
1910	558	677	681	417	649	622	1,156	558	336	1,049	492	802
1913	578	760	704	438	717	661	1,236	631	360	1,124	547	899
1915	568	815	748	529	792	644	1,267	589	355	1,162	578	984
1920	1,358	1,817	1,608	980	1,145	1,432	2,160	1,386	810	1,844	939	1,428

Source: *Historical Statistics of the United States. Colonial Times to 1957*, 1960, p. 91. Adapted.

Persons who held responsible positions in schools and colleges, in industry and government received salaries of $5,000 or more per annum. Higher level corporate, business, and government personnel who held elective offices received higher pay. Vested interests in urban land and bankers were among the more affluent members of any community.

Housing construction; paving of streets and sidewalks; laying storm and sanitary sewers, gas lines and water mains; extending electric light and telephone services provided employment for skilled and unskilled employees alike. When these facilities had been provided, additional work remained to be done in enabling customer-consumers to raise their scales of living. Extended urban areas demanded more police and fire protection.

In 1920 the United States had more telephones than any country in the world. Long-distance service made it possible to carry on direct conversation via telephone with thousands of subscribers all over the United States. The human voice was not always distinct and clear, and many conversations left their participants more confused than completely satisfied.

Competition in rendering telephone service had yielded to monopoly control in the name of accommodating more customers, greater efficiency, and lower operating costs. It had been established that the telephone industry was operating under conditions of increasing cost in enlarging the size of switchboards, which were still manned by human labor.

Rates for ten-word telegrams or 50-word night letters were cheaper and more satisfactory than were many long-distance telephone calls. If messages could not be wired directly to their points of destination, telephones were used to complete their deliveries.

Competition had narrowed to the level of two large operating companies that duplicated services and facilities in many communities. It resulted in a plethora of unsightly telegraph poles and wires that were stretched along or across city streets. Besides being unsightly, they created hazards to life and property on occasions of large fires and severe storms of wind and ice.

War

One of the most crucial tests that the American economy had faced, certainly since the dark and discouraging days of the early 1860's, was that of having participated in a world war. The war was not one between armies; it was one between entire national economies in which natural resources played an important and determining role. Given abundant resources, it required an effective organization to utilize and to coordinate them in a war effort. Effective leadership and morale were important subjective factors that pointed to ultimate success.

Involvements. By 1914 different facets of the American economy had become so intertwined with the economies of European and other countries that it was next to impossible for the United States not to have been drawn into a conflict that was worldwide in its impacts. Commodity exports and imports, investments of foreign capital in the United States and those of American capital in foreign countries, the financial obligations that arose out of these investments, marine insurance and the operation of overseas transportation facilities—all were affected by the outbreak of hostilities in 1914, and in turn, affected the attitudes and sympathies of the American people and of the American government towards the nations at war. One of the more immediate impacts was the stimulation of American industries and the entire American economy that was brought about in the filling of contracts to supply munitions of war, food, and clothing to all countries impartially. *Impartially* did not mean in equal quantities, because the British blockade of the United States as well as of the coast of Europe made it difficult for vessels of the Central Powers to enter or leave our harbors.

German Ingenuity. German ingenuity accomplished a feat of daring which at the same time was of great economic significance. Early in the war, Germany felt the pinch of the lack of food, clothing, and munitions while at the same time she had an abundance of chemical dyes. The United States had been importing German chemical dyes in large volume for many years. Due to the effectiveness of the British blockade, Germany ran out of balances in American banks with which she could purchase war materiel that was badly needed to bring the war to a short and successful conclusion. The world was startled to learn one morning that a German submarine had crossed the Atlantic Ocean successfully and had landed in Chesapeake Bay not far from Baltimore. Its cargo consisted of chemical dye products for which there was a brisk market in the United States. The proceeds of their sale were used to pay for food, clothing, and munitions of war. Not to be outdone a second time, England increased its efforts to blockade the Atlantic Coast south of New Jersey. Before many weeks had passed, another German submarine had landed off the north shores of Long Island Sound, its cargo again chemical dye products. Not only were they the last of such voyages, since England redoubled her vigilance in blockading the Atlantic Coast off the United States, they were the only commercial uses that any nation has made of submarines. It has never been revealed how much of the distance that was covered by either or both of these submarines on their round trips was made underwater; neither has it been revealed if either or both of them returned to Germany successfully.

Industrial Prosperity. Prosperity in industry and in urban areas was reflected in years of relative prosperity in the agricultural segment of our economy. Unemployment was decreasing; employment was on the increase. More urban workers received some money income; the incomes of others increased. White collar workers at both corporate and government levels were becoming more numerous. Corporations were required to maintain better and more accurate systems of record keeping which gave rise to the study and principle of accounting. Simple single or double entry bookkeeping was no longer adequate for the purpose of keeping corporate financial records and later for calculating corporate income taxes.

Government at all levels was expanding its activities, and increases in public payrolls were mute testimony of the need for additional public revenues. Shortly after Woodrow Wilson was elected President of the United States the tempo of business activity began to decline. Following the passage of the Underwood Tariff Act in 1913, businessmen began to complain that they could no longer compete with lower cost commodity imports from European countries. The volume of business declined, unemployment increased, and commodity prices fell. There was talk of an industrial crisis, and when war broke out in Europe in 1914 there was an immediate sharp decline in business and in the production of goods. When the country had recovered from the first shock of war, increased orders from western European countries instilled new life and vigor into the American economy. American commodity exports increased, and imports from the belligerent nations decreased.

Ocean Shipping. Ocean shipping was in a chaotic condition. German submarines sank commercial vessels of almost all nations, many of them without warning. England stopped American ships on the high seas to prevent their cargoes from reaching Germany. Merchant vessels of the belligerent powers were withdrawn from overseas commercial trade in order to meet more pressing and short-run immediate needs of war. Foreign marine insurance companies refused to underwrite either vessels or their cargoes, and American exporters refused to ship goods unless insurance protection was given. Congress provided a Bureau of War Risk Insurance one of whose functions was to insure American exports until they had arrived safely at their ports of destination. A system of convoying merchant vessels from the United States and return, together with camouflaging them, tended to reduce the loss of ships that plied the waters between the United States and France and England.

In order to relieve the shortage of overseas transport facilities, the United States Shipping Board was charged with having ships constructed and put into service with a minimum of delay. Principles of mass production and the assembly line method were introduced into the construction of ships. Inland waterways that were navigable became beehives of activity in constructing ships. Because of the shortage of iron and steel, all-wooden ships were designed; and Liberty ships slid down their stocks into the water at an amazing rate.

War Finance. The Federal Revenue System was entirely inadequate to meet the needs of war. The Treasury established a plan whereby 40 percent of the costs would be paid out of tax receipts, 60 percent out of borrowings. In reality about one third of the costs were met from tax receipts, two thirds from the proceeds of the sale of bonds. The interest-bearing public debt rose from $1,023 million, or $12.36 per capita on March 31, 1917, to a peak of $26,348 million, or $250.18 per capita on August 31, 1919. The income tax soon became the principal source of tax revenue. In 1917 personal exemptions were lowered to $1,000 for single persons, $2,000 for married ones. Allowable deductions were $200 per dependent. Tax rates started at 2 percent on the first $2,000 of taxable incomes and were graduated upward to 67 percent on incomes of $2 million and over. The following year Congress raised the minimum rate to 6 percent on the initial $4,000 and levied 77 percent on incomes of $1 million and over. In 1919 rates of 5 percent to 73 percent were made to apply to the same income brackets. Excise taxes on tobacco products and liquor were raised, and it was hoped that higher postal rates would more nearly cover the costs of carrying the mail.

New Taxes. An inheritance tax was introduced in 1916, as was an excess profits tax, in an effort to raise one third of the cost of the war from tax receipts. The excess profits tax was an adaptation of a war profits tax.

In calculating their excess profits, businessmen were permitted to use their average profits for the years 1911, 1912, and 1913 as the base. Profits over and above this average were subjected to a graduated scale of rates that ranged from 20 percent to 60 percent. In addition to yielding revenue, the excess profits tax was a sop to those persons who were not in position to increase their money incomes because of the war effort.

Amusement taxes and taxes on luxuries not only were imposed for the first time at the federal level, their rates were increased as the needs for additional revenue became more urgent. Theater tickets and admissions to the cinema, club dues, chewing gum, telephone and telegraph messages, and phonograph records were taxed. While these taxes yielded large revenues in terms of dollars, they fell short of the expectations of the tax authorities. In order to conserve space on trains, railroad and sleeping car tickets were taxed. In reality these taxes seemed to increase the cost of railroad transportation more than they served to retard the use of railway facilities by the civilian population. They were such a lucrative source of revenue that when the emergency that led to their use had subsided the taxes were retained.

Bonds. Five Liberty and Victory loans were floated to make up the difference between current war needs for revenue and tax yields. Responsibility for floating these loans was assumed by the Federal Reserve Banks as fiscal agents of the government and at no cost to the government. For purposes of administration only, each Federal Reserve District was divided into hundreds of county and local districts, each one of which was given a bond quota in dollar volume. Local committees then determined the money value of the bonds that were to be purchased by each firm and each person. Woe to the business firm or person who did not subscribe to its or his quota! Pressure was terrific and many a purchaser bought more bonds than he could really afford. These were the first to sell their bonds after the Armistice was signed in November, 1918.

Corps of three-minute speakers were organized in every community, whose duties consisted of appearing at public meetings of all kinds and giving loyalty sales talks for Liberty bonds. Performances and public gatherings of all sorts were interrupted for three minutes during which speakers spoke their lines. Purchase plans were made easy, and denominations were low enough to be within the reach of members of low-income groups. Subscribers could borrow from their banks at which time government deposits were increased by the full amount of the purchase against which no legal reserves had to be maintained by the banks. These loans did not appear on the surface to cost the subscribers anything, because the banks agreed to accept the coupon rates of interest as the cost of the loans. Not until the subscribers had paid the banks in full did they receive the coupon rate of interest on their savings.

Rationing. The demand for foodstuffs of all kinds increased tremendously, not only because the United States was shipping food to Europe, but because men in the armed services ate more food than they did while they were engaged in peacetime activities, which for many men were more sedentary in character. Again, farm laborers who formerly helped raise their own food and who became urban industrial workers then were required to purchase their food from the market. To help make our food supplies last longer than they otherwise would have, "wheatless" Mondays, "meatless" Tuesdays, and "porkless" Thursdays were instituted. The force of public opinion combined with a feeling of helping to win the war were relied upon to enforce these programs.

Fuel became scarce, not because it wasn't being mined but because of the increased industrial use of coal in plants that were actively participating in the war effort. Railroad facilities also presented some difficulties in the form of car shortages, inadequate locomotive power, and inability to keep trains moving. At one time all manufacturing plants east of the Mississippi River were ordered to close down for a 5-day period, after which "fuelless" Mondays were proclaimed. Attempts to avoid cross hauls of coal were made by decreeing that communities should be served with coal from the mines that were nearest them, rather than by the mines of their choice.

Daylight saving time was introduced into this country for the first time in order to conserve light and fuel as well as to extend the working day if necessary without working long hours after dark. Long and loud were the wails and protests of farmers who maintained that they could not teach their cows to give their milk an hour earlier twice daily. They also claimed there was too much dew and moisture on the ground early in the morning to permit them to work on their farms. City folk didn't like to get up in the dark and to eat their evening meals in broad daylight. To make matters worse, the winter of 1917-18 was one of the coldest and most severe in every way on record at the time, and much suffering was brought on by the inability of local dealers to fill their orders for coal. Restrictions upon the shipment of coal and in its consumption were eased up to lighten the suffering that was caused by the shortage.

Inflation. One of the most disturbing accompaniments of World War I upon the civilian segment of the economy was the high level of price inflation which completely altered traditional relationships between different segments of the economy. Wartime activity increased the demand for many kinds of goods and services, decreased the demand for others. Even though there was no diminution in the volume of production of some products, a more powerful increase in their demand caused their prices to rise. Again, many products and services were diverted from peacetime use to meet the demand of an all-out war and their prices rose in the domestic market.

In the past, wars in the United States and in Europe had always caused inflation partly because of the changes in the demand for goods, partly because of the manner in which wars had been financed. Even though the United States did not resort to the issuance of fiat money, or credit paper money, in the financing of World War I, bank credit was of major importance in its fiscal operations. Approximately 70 percent of the monetary cost of the war was financed through the use of credit. It is a well-known fact that in wartime the government was much more interested in obtaining goods than it was in paring down costs. Again, individual firms and contractors took advantage of their opportunities to gain larger margins of profits than they made during times of peace. All these patterns of behavior added up to price inflation. While the conduct of the war itself may have been a measurement of economic maturity, the failure to control inflation was a continuation of economic immaturity in this sector of the economy.

No one in a position of authority or in a position to know about it had the slightest idea that the war would terminate so shortly after the formal entry of the United States into the conflict. One of the measurements of economic immaturity was the failure of the government to plan for the return to peacetime conditions. When the Armistice was signed in November, 1918, the United States had geared its war machine and the several facets of its production machinery to their highest levels of output. Then, with almost no warning at all, the German army collapsed, and the war was brought to a conclusion. Nobody wanted the war to continue unnecessarily longer, but our economy was entirely unprepared for the reconversion to peacetime pursuits. This explains the economic chaos that prevailed for a year or more and the occurrence of an immediate postwar recession.

Postwar Recovery

When one stops to consider that our entire development and growth almost from our very beginning had been premised upon the existence of peaceful international relations and upon their continuation into an indefinite future, the harnessing of our economy to meet the needs of war was a tremendous task and one that was not accomplished without many trials and errors before it became a *fait accompli.* Something less than 5 million men had been dressed in uniform and another 6 million supported them behind the front line. To have had 11 million men withdrawn from production without causing a complete organizational and functional break-down was one of the marvels of the operation of a free enterprise economy.

When the war came to a sudden and unforeseen end in November, 1918, government agencies had not been established to control the reconversion of our human and industrial resources to a peacetime basis. Consequently, the economy suffered a shock in the nature of an immediate postwar industrial recession. Unemployment was rife, prices fell rapidly, and industrial activity suffered a noticeable decline. Persons who had incurred debts and financial obligations at inflated monetary values were unable to meet their obligations as they became due.

In a more cheerful vein, private building construction was resumed readily, once restrictions and priorities had been removed. The Emergency Fleet Corporation continued its program of completing the construction of vessels that were well on their way towards completion. In the manufacture of men's clothing, few alterations had to be made in the changeover from turning out O.D.'s to civilian clothing, for which there was an unusually brisk market. Manufacturers of army shoes found that the market continued to absorb them as well as dress shoes. The export of food and of capital equipment continued at an unabated pace, and the Baldwin Locomotive Company alone sold over $11 billion worth of locomotives to Belgium in the one year, 1919.

There was a rearrangement of the labor force internally. Two million or more women and older men who had been lured into industry by op-portunities to earn high wages, together with an urge to do their bit in the war effort, retired when the emergency had passed. This helped absorb some of the men who had been released from military service, and it kept down the number of men who could not adjust readily to peacetime efforts.

As the period drew to a close, partial recovery had been made. Our economy had displayed remarkable resilience following material, business, and psychological reverses.

Spanish Influenza

Not only had the United States been through the agonies of war, the casualties that followed the ravages of an epidemic of Spanish influenza were even larger than those that resulted from war. In 18 months of active war-fare, the Armed Forces of the United States suffered casualties of 320,518, while the toll from influenza in the winter months of 1918-19 totalled 548,000. At this time, medical practitioners were not prepared to combat the disease, which may have been imported by prisoners of war or by wounded soldiers who had been repatriated. There is no evidence to prove that the epidemic was a result of thousands of members of the medical pro-fession being pressed into military service. Their presence in military camps at home and abroad was no deterrent to the spread of this dread disease. In addition to the direct casualties of influenza were the many cases of tuberculosis, pneumonia, kidney trouble, heart condition, and other organic ailments that were among its after effects. The economic impacts of this disaster were added on to the more direct burdens of war.

QUESTIONS FOR REVIEW

1. (a) Explain the concept of economic maturity in the internal development of the United States.
(b) In what ways may the nature of commodity exports and commodity imports indicate a measure of economic immaturity or economic maturity?

2. (a) What is economic imperialism?
(b) What was the first manifestation of economic imperialism on the part of the United States? Defend your position.

3. Did the acquisition of Alaska and the Panama Canal Zone follow the pattern of imperialistic development or expansion? Why or why not?

4. How do you account for the increased direction given to business toward the close of the 19th century and thereafter?

5. Why were social insurance measures not accepted in the United States until near the turn of the 20th century?

6. Taking into consideration periods of crisis as well as more normal periods, how well did the American economic organization perform prior to 1920?

7. State clearly what factors you think were responsible for whatever level of success had been attained by the American economy by 1920.

SUGGESTED READINGS

Faulkner, Harold U. *The Decline of Laissez Faire, 1897-1917.* New York City: Holt, Rinehart & Winston, Inc., 1951.

Johnson, E. A. J., and Herman E. Krooss. *The American Economy.* Englewood Cliffs, N. J.: Prentice-Hall, Inc., 1960. Chapter 14.

Letwin, William, (ed.), *Documentary History of American Economic Policy Since 1789.* Chicago: Aldine Publishing Company, 1961. Sections H, I, and J.

Lewis, Cleona. "Wartime Liquidation," *Views of American Economic Growth: The Industrial Era,* edited by Thomas C. Cochran and Thomas B. Brewer. New York City: McGraw-Hill Book Company, 1966.

Ratchford, B. U. "History of the Federal Debt of the United States," *Economic Change in America,* edited by Joseph T. Lambie and Richard V. Clemence. Harrisburg, Pa.: Stackpole Books, 1954.

Somers, Harold M. "The Performance of the American Economy, 1866-1918," *The Growth of the American Economy*, 2d ed., edited by Harold F. Williamson. New York City: Prentice-Hall, Inc., 1951.

Syrett, Harold C. "The Business Press and American Neutrality, 1914-1917," *Issues in American Economic History*, edited by Gerald D. Nash. Boston: D. C. Heath & Company, 1964.

Van Alstyne, Richard W. "Private American Loans to the Allies, 1914-1916," *Issues in American Economic History*, edited by Gerald D. Nash. Boston: D. C. Heath & Company, 1964.

Wiebe, Robert H. "Business Disunity and the Progressive Movement, 1901-1914," *American Economic History: Essays in Interpretation*, edited by Stanley Coben and Forest G. Hill. Philadelphia: J. B. Lippincott Co., 1966.

Wright, Chester W. *Economic History of the United States*. 2d ed. New York City: McGraw-Hill Book Company, 1949. Chapters 41 and 42.

PART V

The United States in a World Economy—1921-Present

The entry of the United States into World War I in 1917 accelerated greatly the development of new technologies. Machinery had displaced thousands of workers, many of whom had been absorbed by the industrialization of new areas. New economic relationships had been entered into and new techniques developed.

World War I plunged the United States headlong into a world economy it had entered less spectacularly a generation earlier. Immigration was being retarded, first by the war and its aftermath, later by legislative processes. Prices continued to rise; banks and commercial and industrial firms were failing in the midst of unprecedented prosperity; farming as a whole was becoming depressed. Prices of farm products were not keeping pace with rising prices of industrial and manufactured goods.

Shipbuilding had been reactivated on a large-scale production basis for the first time in over 50 years. Another impact of the war in Europe had been to alter the investment position of the United States in relation to other countries from that of mature debtor to that of immature creditor nation. Still another impact of the war on the United States resulted from the Treaty of Versailles in 1919, under the terms of which the Central Powers were required to make reparation payments to England and to France. These countries, in turn, were expected to pay principal sums they had borrowed from the United States, together with the interest when due.

Many of the economic developments that took place throughout the decade of the 1920's were a direct outcome of the war and its sudden termination. While the subject matter of this book deals mainly with economic matters, changes in mores and in social organization must be recognized as having made possible some of the economic developments of the period.

Lawlessness in some areas rose to new levels. Though it may not have been the most important factor, the passage of the Volstead Act of 1919, together with the attitude of the people that led to wholesale violations of its terms, provided a framework within which much economic activity was carried on.

After the war the economy had to adjust to the fact that women had gained new freedom, both economic and social. An adjustment also had to be made for the great numbers of soldiers who had once lived on farms, but had decided on resuming civilian life in the city. A restless spirit existed in many people and was reflected in various ways, such as the many get-rich-quick schemes that were promoted throughout the 1920's.

The decade of the 1920's was followed by a decade of depression and despair. Not until there existed the threat of another war in Europe was the economic despondency lifted in the United States. Four years of war were followed by renewed economic activities, some of which were reminders of the 1920's, others which were entirely new and different. For one thing, the problems of reparations and payments of war debts did not throttle economic progress.

Since World War II the economy of the United States has experienced continuous growth except for short periods of relatively minor recession. Following the last of these periods, the economy entered into a period of sustained growth, facing in the late 1960's and early 1970's a resulting problem of inflation.

Chapter 21

THE AFTERMATH OF WAR

Just when the American people had built the economy to its highest level of production and had adjusted themselves to wartime regulations and restrictions, World War I came to a sudden termination. Neither our government nor industry had made plans for a reconversion of productive resources, including manpower, to peacetime objectives.

When the nation recovered from the initial shock caused by the war's abrupt termination, there was a release of economic energy that carried the economy to new levels of activity. No new money or banking institutions were introduced, but the Federal Reserve Board was given an opportunity to use its instruments of credit control. All segments of the economy except agriculture were stimulated by the cessation of war and the release of wartime controls.

One of the problems that faced the nation at the end of the war was the rapidity with which men in uniform were returned to civilian life, many of whom had lived in rural communities. The growth pattern of our population created many problems, some of which will be presented in the following pages.

POPULATION GROWTH AND DISTRIBUTION

As important as was the growth of population after 1920, its movement into urban centers was even more so. The census of 1920 revealed for the first time that a majority of our people lived in urban areas—those in which 2,500 or more persons resided in incorporated communities. Table 21-1 shows the distribution of population between urban and rural areas, together with the percentage increases in total, urban, and rural populations respectively. The depression decade of 1930-39 was not representative of the period after 1920 in any respect.

In 1950 urban areas were redefined [1] by the Bureau of the Census to include unincorporated parts of urbanized areas. In that census year, the population of these unincorporated areas totaled approximately 7 million; in 1960, 10 million. People moved from incorporated cities to obtain relief from taxes, congestion, noise, and dirt. They were served by public transportation systems and by public utilities. The impact of the movement was to lower the populations in hundreds of large incorporated cities, to enlarge the size of metropolitan areas, and to increase the number of persons living

Table 21-1

Growth of Population, Urban and Rural—1910-1950
(1940 Urban Base)
(millions)

	Total Population			Urban			Rural		
Year	Total Popula-tion	Increase	% Increase	Total	% of Total	% Increase	Total	% of Total	% Increase
1950	151	19	14	89	59	20	62	41	9
1940	132	9	7	74	56	7	57	43	6
1930	123	17	16	69	56	28	54	44	4
1920	106	14	15	54	51	29	52	49	4
1910	92			42	46		50	54	

Source: U. S. Department of Commerce, Bureau of the Census, *Historical Statistics of the United States. Colonial Times to 1957* (Washington: U. S. Government Printing Office, 1960), p. 14. Adapted.

in urban areas. The absolute as well as the relative decline in rural population that is revealed by the census data for 1950 (Table 21-2) is the result of enlarging the base for urban populations. Confusion over reality and interpretation usually follows a change in a statistical base. One interpretation is as valid as the other, once a person knows the bases on which the data are classified.

[1] According to the definition used in 1940, basically, urban populations were limited to those living in incorporated places of 2,500 population or more. In 1950, the concept of urban population was broadened to include (1) all inhabitants of incorporated places, except those living in incorporated "towns" in New England, New York, and Wisconsin; (2) densely settled urban fringe areas around cities of 50,000 or more inhabitants; and (3) unincorporated places of 2,500 or more inhabitants outside any urban fringe area.

Table 21-2

Distribution of Population Between Urban and Rural Areas—1940-1960* (1950 Urban Base) (millions)

Year	Total Population		Urban			Rural		
	Total Popula- tion	% Increase	Total	% of Total	% Increase	Total	% of Total	% Increase
1960	179	18	125	70	30	54	30	..
1950	151	14	96	64	30	54	36	—4
1940†	132	7	74	56	7	57	43	6

* Alaska and Hawaii not included.
† 1940 Urban Base.

Source: *Historical Statistics of the United States, Continuation to 1962 and Revisions,* 1965, p. 3.

The population groups used by the Bureau of the Census reveal that while cities of from 2,500 to 5,000 population were the most numerous between 1920 and 1960 the 25,000 to 100,000 population class has contained the largest total populations of urban communities that contain less than one million residents. Students of municipal finance have pointed out that after cities have exceeded 25,000 population they have operated under conditions of increasing cost. Urbanization, therefore, has presented many fiscal problems that have challenged equitable solutions. Cities have been limited to the sources of revenue permitted by their charters; and finding additional tax money to pay for paving and maintaining streets, expansion of police and fire departments, garbage disposal, storm and sanitary sewers, and inspection services has challenged the resourcefulness of tax authorities. Heavy tax burdens have been one of the causes of a general movement of urban peoples to suburban districts, some of which have been unincorporated.

Causes of Urban Growth

The close of two world wars stimulated the movements of people from farms to cities at unprecedented rates. In the 1920's, the automobile industry centered in southern Michigan, northern Ohio, and Indiana. It was not only the actual assembly of automobiles that demanded labor, the manufacture of automobile parts did also. The motion picture industry attracted accomplished and aspiring performers, writers, directors, producers, and technicians to the Los Angeles area. In more recent years, the latter region has become a center of diversified industries that have experienced rapid growth and development. Detroit and Los Angeles joined New York, Chicago, and Philadelphia in the over one million population class.

Public acceptance of the automobile necessitated the development and expansion of the petroleum industry at all levels of production and marketing. Cities in Texas, Oklahoma, Kansas, and California owe their growth to the accident of oil pools having been exploited in these locales.

Activity in building construction, road and street paving, the expansion of water and gas mains, storm and sanitary sewers, and the stretching of telephone and power lines attracted skilled and semiskilled workers into urban areas.

Many of the men who had recently returned to civilian life after both wars were absorbed by the acceleration of industrialization that characterized the economies of those years. Men who had learned the fundamentals of mechanics and electronics in service and did not want to return to farm life provided a ready supply of labor to the automotive, farm machinery, electrical, construction, and other industries.

After the close of World War I, durable household goods industries attracted thousands of workers into factories and other thousands of persons into the marketing of these products. Following the close of World War II, electronics and related industries and air conditioning at all levels of production attracted thousands of workers, skilled and unskilled, including managers and entrepreneurs.

Not to be overlooked among the causes of urban growth was the policy of decentralizing defense industries. Some workers have been moved from large communities to less populous ones; others have been recruited from nearby rural peoples.

Population Growth

The rate of population growth was less spectacular than was urban growth in the 1920 decade. The decrease in the birth rate alarmed students of population who promulgated dire forecasts of race suicide and the attainment of a maximum population of 165 million by 1960. There was no similar decline in the birth rate after 1945; in fact, it increased. The excess of births over deaths remained at a low level until near the close of the depression decade, or until impending war in Europe lent encouragement to a more rapid formation of families and to the rate of natural increase.

CONSTRUCTION ACTIVITIES

After the war, the construction industry experienced a period of adjustment. The adjustment, however, was not felt by the shipyards engaged in building ships under government contracts. The fact that ships for which contracts had already been let and whose construction was underway were completed meant that employment in shipyards continued unabated. These workers received relatively high wages, the spending of which kept the economies in shipbuilding areas operating at high levels. Industries that were sources of supply to shipbuilding likewise were kept active.

Eventually other construction activity began an upward surge in response to the changing needs and activities of the American public.

Multiple Housing and Dining Facilities

During the war years, practically all civilian construction had ceased. When priorities were abolished and construction workers became available for civilian employment, there was renewed activity in the construction of residential, business, and industrial buildings. At first the level of construction was more in the nature of maintenance and replacement than it was in providing entirely new and expanded facilities.

In the early years of the 1920's, construction took on the nature of expansion. Domestic servants who had entered war service earned so much more and their lives were so much freer and exciting that they did not return to their former work. At the same time, wives who had never done their own housework did not intend to commence doing it. Many housewives who had worked for pay during the war years were loath to relinquish their jobs in order to return to full-time housekeeping. Others who felt the pinch of price inflation on their housekeeping budgets were impelled to add a second increment to the family income. One impact of inflation was that large houses and apartments were no longer in great demand. The small efficiency apartment and resident hotel were the answers. In either situation, families had no responsibilities of mowing lawns, raking leaves, or shoveling snow from sidewalks in winter. Neither did they have to fire furnaces in cold weather. Maid service was provided by managements of apartment buildings and of hotels. Families who lived in residence hotels frequently ate their meals in their dining rooms. Restaurants, coffee shops, and cafes multiplied rapidly in number in response to the demand for high quality public dining rooms. Cafeterias met the need for more rapid service than could be obtained in establishments that served *table d'hôte* style, and tipping was not required to obtain service. For those who were price conscious, cafeteria service was usually cheaper than other levels of public dining room service.

Amusement Places

Less time than formerly was spent in the home. Places of amusement and of public entertainment were frequented in the evening hours, Sundays, and on holidays. Moving picture palaces in downtown areas and neighborhood theaters in outlying districts were constructed to accommodate the thousands of patrons who enjoyed this form of relaxation. Vaudeville circuits were operated by Keith, Orpheum, Loewe, and others; and many a local musician found ready employment in their orchestra pits. Several troupes of minstrel shows toured the country and kept their audiences in laughter with light entertainment. To meet the demand for spending less time in shopping and in preparing food, neighborhood stores were erected and delicatessens catered to apartment dwellers.

Competitive Construction

Construction of moving picture theaters, neighborhood mercantile facilities, and chain stores was conducted at a highly competitive pace. Members of the building and construction trades had all the work they could do, and their wages tended to creep upward. Before many years had elapsed this competition began to take its toll of many properties. More seats had been provided in moving picture theaters than there were patrons to occupy them, and price cutting was not the answer to a shortage of receipts. More apartments in more apartment buildings were provided than there were families to occupy them, and here, too, a reduction in rents was not the answer. The opening of neighborhood mercantile establishments did not attract sufficient customers, and it was not long until distress sales were held in order to raise money with which to meet the demands of creditors.

Corporate Mortgages

In financing the construction of these facilities, advantage was taken of the corporate mortgage plan. Borrowers obtained corporate mortgages that covered the total amounts borrowed, and deposited them in trust with real estate mortgage companies. The latter issued serial bonds in denominations as low as $100. Prospective investors were urged to subscribe to their purchase for possibly 10 percent down payments and balances on installments, and were given attractive bond purchase record books. Interest rates on mortgage bonds were higher than those on government bonds or on savings deposits, but their owners thought they were the result of the inflationary trend of the decade rather than warnings of sad days to come. When surplus apartments, business houses, and theaters began to appear, their managers began to reduce rentals; theater managers, to reduce prices of admission. The only effect the reductions appeared to have was to draw patronage away from other similar facilities, which, in turn, were compelled to lower their rentals and prices. It was not long before gross incomes at reduced prices did little more than cover operating expenses, and some operations did not even cover these. Delays in receiving interest payments, or defaults thereon, caused bondholders to question the integrity and sincerity of businessmen and of bankers, and even to lose confidence in our economic system.

Residential Property Values

The movement of lower income farm labor into the cities of the North and Middle West resulted in the degeneration of many residential areas. Since these people had neither money nor industrial skills, they moved into low rent residential areas that were already crowded. New York had its Harlem; Chicago its Southside; and Pittsburgh, St. Louis, Cleveland, and Detroit, to mention only a few, had similar areas. To make room for these people, housing facilities that formerly had been occupied by middle and upper income people were taken over for housing the newly arrived migrants.

As this movement progressed, owners of individual housing units and those tenants of apartment houses financially able moved farther out from town, or at least into other neighborhoods, and rents on many of the buildings that had been financed by the issue of mortgage bonds began to fall. Even with lower rents, capacity occupation of apartment houses was difficult to maintain. Slum areas were extended outward; and vested interests in urban land and buildings were hard pressed to maintain customary incomes, let alone to participate in rental increases.

MANUFACTURING AND INDUSTRY

One of the impacts of World War I was to alter the tempo of the business world as well as that of living. Electrical energy not only displaced other forms of energy in many uses, but entirely new applications were made of it. The development of and greater dependability of the internal combustion engine gave an amazing degree of mobility to American industry and to the American people. The war not only had made people restless, it had made them more daring in all phases of their life. This daring was revealed in their style of dress; it was revealed in their desire to be on the move, to visit places, to see new things, and to encounter many new experiences. It was expressed in the many new business ventures that were embarked upon in the expectation of making large and easy profits. Status seemed to have become a symbol of antiquity and of decay. New ideas were introduced into almost all segments of society. The art of journalism was developed to new levels of expression. Advertising techniques carried people away with their new appeals to the unsuspecting and unsophisticated public. They became more daring and straightforward. Competition was the watchword of business. New products appeared on the market so rapidly that patents and copyrights afforded little protection to their holders.

The Automobile Industry

The automobile industry provided one of the sparks that set the economy aflame as nothing had since the development of the railroads. Henry Ford took the lead in providing a car that laborers and white collar workers could afford to own and to operate. In getting people to and from work, the automobile was replacing the bicycle. Motorcycles were replacing bicycles in rendering many kinds of delivery services. Automobile trucks and vans were displacing horse-drawn equipment and were beginning to participate in longer haul traffic. Buses were competing with electric urban and interurban transportation facilities. They likewise were competing with steam-powered railroads, particularly in rendering commuting services. Accessories that were responsible for a more rapid and general acceptance of the automobile were the self-starter that did away with the need for cranking cars by hand to get them started and the storage battery that replaced the magneto as a source of electrical energy. The former made it possible for women to drive cars that were powered with gasoline-fueled internal combustion engines. The latter device not only was accessory to the self-starter, but it made night driving safer by eliminating acetylene lighting.

In the early years of automobile manufacturing, not many kinds or makes of cars were actually manufactured. They were assembled. Different automobile parts were manufactured by corporations that were independent of those that assembled them into completed cars. The Ford Motor Company took the lead in producing parts for its cars. Ford also adopted the policy of producing its Model T in such a manner that the earlier models would not be out of style when compared with later ones. One of the sources of large fixed costs in manufacturing automobiles were and are in the costs of tooling and retooling plants. This accounted for the general policy that was followed by many manufacturers of adopting a basic design for, say, three years, then making improvements within the general design the second and third years of its production. Ford went further than this in designing all improvements and new parts in such a manner that they could be installed in models of any previous year.

Another factor that enabled the Ford Motor Company to sell its cars for such a low price, $294 in 1924, compared with other makes of cars was that it was the first manufacturer of automobiles to introduce the assembly line method of production and to take advantage of lower costs and increased volume of production that resulted from such a huge development of division of labor. Ford also gave to owners of its cars a wide choice of body colors as long as they chose black. The clutch system of control was simple to operate. The entire mechanism was relatively as simple. People used to joke about the Ford and say that all that was needed in its repair kit were a few hairpins and safety pins. In fact, the countless number and frequency of Ford jokes were one of the best and cheapest forms of advertising the car.

Mass Production and Integration. In the early 1920's, the Ford Motor Company was considered to have been one of the largest, if not the largest, industrial kingdoms in the world. The River Rouge plant extended over almost two square miles and employed over 100,000 men. The company owned and operated 31 branch assembly plants and four other branch production units. It was one of the more highly integrated industrial corporations in the world, whose holdings extended to 13 foreign countries in Europe and South America. It owned timberlands, coal and iron mines, railway transportation facilities, subsidiary manufacturing plants, and a six-million acre tract of rubber trees in Brazil. It has been estimated that in 1923 at a time when 125,000 employees were on Ford's payroll in the United States and 8,000 were abroad, another 500,000 men were indirectly dependent upon the company for employment.

In order to show the remarkable degree to which the different manufacturing processes were integrated and coordinated, the story is told that on a given day of the week a shipload of iron ore was delivered to the docks at the River Rouge plant. It was cast, machined, assembled as a unit, and shipped to a branch plant 300 miles distant where it was assembled into a finished car, sold to a dealer, and by him to a customer four days later. This type of organization and operation of production units explains why unit production costs in the United States were lower than they were for similar products that were manufactured in European countries. Standardization had been developed greatly, and consumers liked the results.

While the Ford, Chevrolet, and more ephemeral makes of cars, such as the Star, depended upon volume of sales to the masses, the aristocrats of the industry, such as Locomobile, Packard, Pierce Arrow, and Cadillac, were much larger cars and heavier and were more comfortable to ride. These cars cost at least two or three times more than the lowest priced automobiles. Their manufacturers attempted to impart to them prestige values, with distinction, and probably a higher quality of workmanship.

Some Economic Impacts of the Automobile. The automobile freed people from a rigid pattern of mobility that followed the scheduling of trains which had come to be the traditional mode of transportation. Long-distance intercity travel had been made by rail; local urban transportation was by electric streetcar. Some of the larger cities had horse-drawn cabs or hansoms to accommodate strictly local passengers. By 1920 electric interurban systems had been established which may have competed with railroads for through traffic, but not for traffic to and from intermediate points. All these modes of transportation were well patronized, but there were individual and personal limitations to their usage. These were overcome by the popularity of the automobile, the bus, and the motor truck. Where trains may have operated one or two times a day, buses operated every hour. Where electric interurban cars may have had runs scheduled at intervals of an hour, automobile owners could come and go at their convenience. Automobile owners were no longer compelled to arrange their activities according to transportation schedules. Where electric streetcars could operate only on those streets on which steel rails had been laid, motor buses were flexible both as to their routes and schedules. No switches were required to make two-way traffic possible on given streets.

Scrap Iron. In view of the scarcity of scrap steel at the opening of World War II, it may be in order to point out here that when buses displaced electric city and intercity transportation facilities, labor costs prohibited taking up the rails. In many cities they were overlaid with new paving materials when street improvements were made. The exigency of the war demand for scrap iron, which was needed in the open hearth process of manufacturing steel that was used in the fabrication of ordnance and other war materiel, overcame the high cost of removing them, and many rails, amounting to thousands of tons of scrap iron, were reclaimed.

Increased Mobility. Mobility of people was accompanied by the development of organizations and institutions that rendered personal services to their patrons who were en route to and from terminal cities. Parking spaces and garages replaced hitching posts and livery stables. Filling stations sprang up like weeds along well-traveled highways. Needs for zoning of property had not arisen previously and few, if any, restrictions governing the use of land had been established. Tourist homes were of mutual gain to owners and to patrons. A home atmosphere appealed to many persons. Homeowners received auxiliary incomes that were large in relation to particular cost outlays and ofttimes associations were pleasant. Many families provided tourist accommodations only until mortgages had been cleared.

Auxiliary Services. Gasoline filling stations that were located on highways were likely to have automobile mechanics on call; some of them had tow trucks and service cars, and practically all sold new automobile tires or repaired old ones. Dining rooms and lunch counters proved to be profitable ventures and frequently were tended by members of the operators' families. Soft drinks and candy bars, crackers and chewing gum were placed in view and within easy reach of the occupants of cars that stopped for service and large profits were derived from their sale.

Census data on the number of managers of gasoline filling stations are criteria of the number of filling stations in operation. The data do not include the pumps that were operated in conjunction with country stores and whose volume of sales did not require special attendants. They increased in number from 15,000 in 1920 to 89,000 in 1930. During the same span of years employment of managers of motor vehicle and accessory establishments increased from 29,000 to 62,000. Managers of garages and automobile repair shops increased from 56,000 in 1920 to 93,000 in 1930. The number of operatives in motor vehicle and motor vehicle equipment establishments increased from 125,000 to 170,000 and laborers in these same establishments from 93,000 to 124,000 in the same span of years. From these data it may be deduced that employment in the automobile and allied service industries increased from 564,000 in 1920 to 1,448,000 ten years later.

The economic impacts of these developments were still more far-reaching when consideration is given to the employment that was afforded in the construction of the buildings that were used to house these establishments and of the employment of still other workers who provided the materials out of which they were constructed and furnished and in transporting them to their building sites. No estimate can be made of the amount of land and its value that was utilized by automotive industries and of the rental incomes that were received by its owners. Taking every facet of its development into consideration, it is conservative to say that the automobile and related industries made major contributions to the national income and to the general level of prosperity.

Marketing Motor Cars and Fuels. While petroleum products were not new and the Standard Oil Trust had already been legally dissolved, the new market for gasoline and fuel oil imparted new life to the industry. Long-distance movement of oil and gasoline was by tank car and pipeline. Over 33,000 miles of pipeline were constructed during the 1920's to total 88,728 miles in operation in 1930. Again, the impact of this development was far-reaching into other segments of our economy. The iron and steel industry went into high gear in providing sections of pipe and tank cars, as well. Railroads were called upon to transport pipe from points of their production to the localities of their utilization. After tank cars had been put into use, railroads had a large volume of revenue traffic in carload or even trainload lots.

Factory sales of passenger automobiles more than doubled throughout the decade of the 1920's, as did the production of motor trucks and buses combined, but their factory values did not increase in the same proportion. The first three-million car year was 1923, but it was six years later when four million automobile passenger cars were produced. Over twice as many automobile trucks and buses were produced in 1929 as in 1924 compared with an increase in passenger cars of 39 percent in the same period.

Perusal of the data in Table 21-3 seems to indicate that the oscillations of the business cycle had greater impacts upon the sale of automobile cars, trucks, and buses than they had on the gallons of gasoline and motor fuel consumed. The sale of trucks and buses did not always conform to the pattern of sales of automobile passenger cars. While the sales of new automobiles declined in each of the years 1921, 1924, 1926, 1927, and 1930, only in 1921, 1927, and again in 1930, did the sales of trucks and buses decline. This is a measure of the increasing acceptance of the motor truck in replacing horse-drawn delivery trucks, transfer wagons, and moving vans, and of the motor bus in replacing electric transportation facilities.

A decline in the sale of new passenger automobiles, trucks, and buses was accompanied by a greater consumption of gasoline and motor fuel and this in the face of greater mileage that was obtained from gasoline motors of the same horsepower. Towards the close of the decade there was a trend away from the four-cylinder motor in favor of a six or an eight-cylinder. Other factors remaining the same, gasoline consumption increased in direct ratio with increases in the number of motor cylinders and the horsepower they generated. Improved roads made it possible, as well as tempting, to travel at higher speeds and at the cost of a greater consumption of gasoline. The first four-million car year, 1929, was followed by a heavy decline in the sale of new cars in 1930. A decline of 37 percent in new car sales was accompanied by a decline of 41 percent in their wholesale values, and a decline of 34.7 percent in the sale of new trucks and buses was accompanied by a decline of 37 percent in their wholesale values. In the absence of pertinent cost data, it is easily understood why the prices of new automobiles at the start of the depression are described as having been sticky.

The most significant impact of reasonable decreases in wholesale car prices was reduction in the total gross income of their manufacturers.

Table 21-3

Motor Vehicle Factory Sales: Motor Fuel Usage—1920-1930

| | Motor Vehicle Factory Sales | | | | Motor Fuel Usage (000 gals.) | | |
| | Passenger Cars | | Trucks and Buses | | | | |
Year	Number	Wholesale Value (000)	Number	Wholesale Value (000)	Highway	Non-highway	Total
1920	1,905,560	$1,809,171	321,789	$423,249	3,346,000	102,164	3,448,164
1921	1,468,067	1,038,191	148,052	166,071	3,935,000	129,824	4,064,824
1922	2,274,185	1,494,514	269,991	226,050	4,841,000	173,035	5,014,035
1923	3,624,717	2,196,272	409,295	308,538	6,078,000	235,177	6,313,177
1924	3,185,881	1,970,097	416,659	318,581	7,497,000	312,186	7,809,186
1925	3,735,171	2,458,370	530,659	458,400	8,749,075	394,890	9,143,965
1926	3,692,317	2,607,365	608,617	484,823	10,063,951	488,210	10,552,161
1927	2,936,533	2,164,671	464,793	420,131	11,331,326	605,570	11,936,896
1928	3,775,417	2,572,599	583,342	460,109	12,361,460	728,822	13,090,282
1929	4,455,178	2,790,614	881,909	622,534	14,139,301	911,735	15,051,036
1930	2,787,456	1,644,083	575,364	390,752	14,753,911	1,023,796	15,777,707

Source: *Historical Statistics of the United States. Colonial Times to 1957,* 1960, p. 462. Adapted.

Rubber and Automobile Tires. The Hevea tree, which was and still is one of the best sources of natural rubber, grew wild in the valley of the Amazon River. Sir Henry Wickham, an Englishman, succeeded in smuggling some 70,000 seeds of the tree from Brazil by having crates sent to the Botanical Gardens in Kew, near London. Since the seeds were extremely perishable, only a few thousand of them sprouted after they had been planted. These trees were shipped to Ceylon to form the nucleus of the rubber plantation industry in the Malayan Peninsula, Indo-China, the East Indies, and other Far Eastern Islands. Under a plan by which the shipment of rubber to Western countries was strictly controlled, its price soared to $1.21 a pound in this county in 1925. To offset this monopoly other rubber plantations were planted in Africa and Mexico. Thomas E. Edison and Henry Ford combined their talents and their resources in search of a method of converting the common goldenrod into rubber. This experiment was conducted on the west coast of south Florida. Needless to say, these efforts came to naught.

The large rubber tire manufacturers competed against themselves and their franchised dealers in the sale of their tires by manufacturing tires of equal quality for mail-order houses and oil companies. The tires were sold under different brand names and at prices that were lower than those that carried their own brand names. Since these so-called off-brand tires carried the same guarantees as the standard brands, dealers in the latter tires suffered large financial losses. When automobile tire repair shops refused to service off-brand tires, mail-order houses in large cities and filling station operators all over the country were compelled to provide road service for their customers.

The development of the automobile and accessory industries came at an extremely opportune time from the standpoint of the general health of the American economy. Farm workers were being displaced by farm machinery, and thousands of filling station owners and attendants and employees in automobile and automobile parts manufacturing plants absorbed them and prevented an otherwise serious condition of unemployment. Mechanical and technical improvements on railroads likewise displaced railway labor, much of which was absorbed in the automotive industry. The decline of passenger and freight traffic that resulted from competition with the automotive car, bus, and truck threw thousands of railway employees out of work. Again, many of them found employment in automotive industries, and their period of economic inactivity was only transitory.

The Highway Movement. People who owned automobiles had a yen to go places and to see and do things that were beyond their traditional horizons. The experiences of many young men during the war made them restless, and they enjoyed some of the new contacts and travels they had made at government expense. Mechanical improvements made automobiles more dependable and more durable than formerly.

Many roads that had accommodated state and local traffic were called upon to carry much larger volumes of traffic that consisted of heavier loads than those for which they had been constructed. Streams that had been forded in low water by local traffic had to be bridged. Wooden bridges that had been built to bear up under relatively light local traffic had to be strengthened and rebuilt. Where bridges had not been constructed over wider and larger rivers, ferries were provided, some of which operated on schedule, others only when there was traffic.

Even though the several states increased assessments, levied automobile license taxes and taxes on the sale of gasoline that was used to propel motor vehicles on highways, current income did not prove to be adequate to cover the costs of construction. Long-term bonds were issued and retired out of tax receipts, and were given a high investment rating. Since the income from the bonds was exempt from liability to pay federal income taxes, the market for them was rather active, and they were much sought after by persons who were in the upper income brackets.

Irrespective of the level of government that had undertaken to construct improved roads and highways, the immediate impact of their financing was the issuance of bonds which were paid off over a period of years out of tax receipts. State debts that had been incurred in the financing of roads increased from $372,945 in 1921 to $933,066 in 1926, to $1,879,797 in 1931, to $2,210,385 in 1936, and declined to $1,159,025 four years later.

In order to accelerate the improvement of major highways, Congress in 1921 authorized the designation of a system of principal interstate and intercounty roads that was limited to 7 percent of the total rural mileage then existing. The use of federal money was restricted to the system and could not be used to construct or to improve roads in incorporated places. As a general rule, federal funds were to be matched by state funds. Gradually over the years more public monies were made available for the construction of farm to market roads and for others that were not strictly main ribbons of pavement across the continent. The National and Lincoln Highways could not be routed to include all of the interior cities in the country whose chambers of commerce and city officials thought that they should have been honored by having one or the other designated highways routed through them. Jealousies between cities were settled only in the designation of other federal highways. Consequently other routes were laid out that included as many of these cities as could be accommodated. This settlement turned out to be satisfactory from the standpoint of the increased volume of traffic and the demand by tourists for alternate routes. It was only by taking alternate routes that people could visit different parts of the country. The cities that were not located directly on one of the federal highways were connected with them by improved roads, and directions were set up on the former telling how to reach these cities and the distance to them.

The Electrical Appliance Industry

One of the postwar developments that sparked industrial activity was the wider acceptance of electrical energy by consumers. Electricity had been used in lighting streets, houses, stores, and office buildings for many years; but household appliances had not been adapted to its use. "Going electric" was part of the new pattern of living, in which housekeeping chores were minimized and housewives were given more freedom. Convenience was the watchword, and status was attained by using electric household appliances.

The adaptation of electrical energy to the operation of household appliances gave rise to the concept of durable consumer goods. Not only this, but it afforded new outlets for capital investment at the manufacturing, wholesale, and retail levels. New opportunities were afforded for giving expression to entrepreneurial skills, and new channels were provided into which labor was attracted.

Vacuum Cleaners. The suction principle of picking up dust was rather new in its application to vacuum cleaners. As has been true for many new products, there was a hesitancy by housewives in accepting the suction principle of cleaning rugs. Someone started a rumor that continuous suction would loosen the nap on rugs, to which there may have been some truth if the cleaners were rubbed "against the grain."

Vacuum cleaners were sold by house-to-house salesmen who gave demonstrations of performance in the homes of prospective customers. Cleaners were found on display in furniture stores, hardware stores, variety stores, department stores, mail-order retail outlets, and electrical appliance stores. They were also sold via mail-order catalogue.

Refrigerators. By 1920, few alterations had been made in the basic designs of ice refrigerators. Housewives did have a choice between a top icer and another which had the ice compartment on one side. In the latter models there was a choice between a right-hand ice compartment and one that was on the left. In many respects the models with side ice compartments were more convenient to service as well as to use. In parts of the country where natural ice could not be cut each winter and stored in sawdust in vast storage buildings, many families were denied ice refrigeration. Years ago shiploads of natural ice were shipped from New York City and other northern ports coastwise to Jacksonville and to other southern ports, whence it was redistributed to surrounding towns. Country households kept perishable foods and dairy products in spring houses. Many families were not fortunate enough to have any refrigeration facilities at all, and in warm weather they were compelled to purchase perishable foods on the basis of one day's needs.

When the cost of manufacturing ice had been lowered to the point where it could be retailed at a price of 50 cents a hundred pounds, or less, artificial or manufactured ice was produced on large-scale proportions and retailed sometimes by independent peddlers as well as by the companies that manufactured it. Horse-drawn wagons that were covered to keep the direct rays of the sun from melting the ice were used in retail delivery, which usually was made in the mornings in order to find housewives or their maids at home.

Electric refrigerators were sold as much on convenience and appearance as they were on performance. Housewives or maids did not have to stay at home until the iceman came, nor did they have to clean up dirty foot tracks and drops of water after he left. Instead of chipping ice from large cakes to use in cooling drinks, ice cubes were made in trays. Defrosting at irregular intervals was one of the offsetting disadvantages in using electric refrigerators. Their prices were sufficiently high to have them sold on a class market according to sizes of family incomes. Competition between electric refrigerators and ice boxes compelled manufacturers of the latter to modernize their designs in attempts to hold their customers. Mechanical refrigerators were on display in the same outlets in which vacuum cleaners were dispensed. Generally, such household appliances were available from the same sources.

Kitchen Ranges. About the only variation in styles of kitchen ranges, other than in size and in the location of their ovens, was found in the fuel they burned. Wood, anthracite coal, bituminous coal, gas, and kerosene all had their day of popularity and customer acceptance. To some extent customer selection depended upon the ready availability of the respective kinds of fuel and upon their local costs. Families that were located in rural communities frequently had wood available for the cutting. Families in the New England States, that did not burn wood, preferred anthracite coal because of its cleanliness, relative ease of tending, and its constant heat. In other parts of the country bituminous coal was much cheaper than anthracite coal and did not require as much attention as wood fires. One advantage of kerosene was that it did not require any fixed installation, and it could be purchased in local stores and in small quantities. The most modern and convenient ranges to use were those that burned gas, either natural or manufactured. Heat was instantaneous and was easily regulated. Pilot burners did away with the need for keeping boxes of matches in the kitchen and in using them to start fires.

Electric ranges made their appeal on convenience and appearance. They usually were finished in enamel or in porcelain and looked better than the dark and sometimes dingy looking iron ranges; neither did they have over-hanging heating ovens which gave iron stoves an appearance of imbalance and cumbersomeness.

Washing Machines. The advent of mechanical washing machines that were powered by electricity made washing clothes a much easier chore than formerly. Clothes could be cleaned at home by rotation, by agitation, or by suction cup, but they still had to be hung outside on a line to dry and were ironed by hand. Electric mangles were being used, but they were not in common use.

Since prices of electric washing machines were high at first, they appealed only to the more well-to-do housewives. As the market was saturated and improved processes of production had lowered costs, manufacturers went out for volume and got it. The profits that were made in the manufacture and sale of electric washing machines were offset from a social point of view by losses that were incurred by steam laundries, some of which were forced to close down entirely. Others had to release some of their contact men and delivery equipment. There was, however, little or no permanent unemployment caused by these changes in our economic organization and its functioning because of the expansion of many other areas of activity in the production and marketing of washing machines.

Because of the traditional pattern of having clothes washed by hand in the Southern States, the mechanical washing machine was accepted more slowly there than it was in other sections of the country. When southern farm labor began to move into northern cities, the women went along sooner or later, and washwomen either became more scarce in the South, or they wanted more money for their work, either one of which developments helped eventually to create a demand for electric washing machines.

Other Electric Appliances. Among other durable consumer goods for which there was a large sale in the 1920's were electric irons, electric toasters, electric clocks, and electric cake mixers. None of these appliances consumed much electric current, and their use in individual homes made little impact upon the monthly bill for electricity. Not so with the refrigerator, the vacuum cleaner, the kitchen range, and later the hot water heater. Convenience and cleanliness were the intangible benefits that were related to the use of electric household appliances. Status was an important consideration within given circles of friends, especially for the housewives. Push-button controls were becoming popular, as were all forms of labor-saving devices, at least labor of the old kind. Electric toasters were of many designs and in the early days of their usage were operated by hand. Later, automatic toasters appeared on the market, and the modern housewife dared not be caught with an old-fashioned one on her table or in her kitchen. A conscious effort was made by the manufacturers of electric appliances to introduce new designs in rather rapid succession in order to appeal to the vanity and pride of their customers. Volume of sales was kept high in this manner, and older models were discarded before they wore out. There were no trade-in values for small appliances because there were no markets for used models.

The stimuli to the American economy were found at the levels of electric appliance manufacture, their distribution, and their retail sale outlets. Thousands of workers found employment in each stage of the movement of these goods from their original producers to their ultimate consumers. The value of electric appliances that were made for domestic consumption is shown in Table 21-4. The highest total value of such goods produced prior to 1921 was $82.8 million in the year 1920. From 1921 to 1929 such values increased over one and one half times, or from $63.2 million to $176.7. There were two years in this span of ten years in which such values of output declined, namely, 1922 and 1930. Inventory turnovers were large, the volume

Table 21-4

Value of Electric Appliances for Domestic Consumption at Current Producers' Prices—1921-1930
(millions)

1921	$ 63.2
1922	58.6
1923	76.3
1924	83.4
1925	106.3
1926	137.5
1927	146.3
1928	152.7
1929	176.7
1930	160.0

Source: *Historical Statistics of the United States. Colonial Times to 1957,* 1960, p. 420. Adapted.

of sales was larger, and the velocity of money increased. By 1929 the volume
of sales of household appliances and radios amounted to $942 million in
retail prices.

Methods of Financing Consumer Expenditures

The student may well wonder how people could pay for so many relatively costly items out of current incomes. The answer is that they didn't.
Pianos, organs, and suites of furniture had been sold on terms for many years.
Installment buying or selling, depending upon how a person looks at the
matter, came into its own after the war. It was a tool by which merchants
of durable consumers' goods competed with each other for the bonus dollars
and others that found their way into circulation after 1918. It gave consumers opportunities to derive the benefits from using commodities before
they were paid for. Because of accidents or other unforeseen events, some
consumers entered into contracts that extended beyond the lives of the goods
they were purchasing. Looking at the problem from one point of view,
installment buying was a kind of forced saving at an interest cost instead
of an interest income, except that the money went into the purchase of
consumers' goods and did not become an investment.

There was one aspect of installment about which there was no question.
Insofar as it increased the demand for an article, other things remaining the
same, it tended to increase the price. Add to this the interest cost of extended
payments, and consumers' goods cost more than they would have, had
everyone waited until they could have purchased them on a cash basis.
Commercial credit companies were organized to finance installment sales
so that the merchants who sold the time payment contracts to them at a
discount could receive their money. Not many retail dealers had sufficient
capital to enable them to finance their own installment sales. Sales of
electric refrigerators, radios, pianos, combination radio and phonograph sets,
furniture, vacuum cleaners, ranges, washing machines, rugs, carpets, automobiles, and other consumer durables were financed in this manner.

Advertising

One of the problems that confronted manufacturers, wholesalers, and
retailers was how to dispose of the largest national commodity output the
country had ever produced. A problem that was closer to the individual firm
and to the businessman was how each one could appropriate the largest
possible share of the national market. In part, the problem was for the
leaders of industry to educate the public in the use of new consumers' goods.
Acceptance of a product or its incorporation into the standard of living was
the initial task of its promoters. Once a product had been accepted by consumers, the next step was to make more persons want to actually include
the product in their scales of living.

The use of competitive advertising increased in an effort to establish
brand preferences on the part of consumers. Another change in the com-

plexion of advertising was the effort made to tailor advertising to specific consumer groups within the mass market. Also the psychology of consumers as individuals was studied, and persuasive appeals to real or imagined needs increased. For example, people were encouraged to place radios in their kitchens, living rooms, and bedrooms. Consumers were informed that if children had a radio in their rooms, they could tune in programs in which they were interested without being in conflict with their parents' preference of programs.

THE ENTERTAINMENT INDUSTRY

The entertainment industry rapidly became a significant part of the economic growth in the 1920's with the advent of commercial radio and the talking movies.

Commercial Radio

The first commercial radio station was licensed to broadcast its first program in 1920. While radio station KDKA, Westinghouse Electric and Manufacturing Company, Pittsburgh, had the distinction of having broadcast the first program, it was not permitted to occupy the unique position of being the only broadcast station in the United States for long. Data in Table 21-5 reveal how rapidly the radio was accepted by the American

Table 21-5

Number of Broadcast Stations, Radio Sets Produced, and Families with Radio Sets—1921-1930

Year	Operating Standard Broadcast Stations (AM)	Radio Sets Produced (000)	Families with Radio Sets (000)
1921	1	. . . .	. . . .
1922	30	100	60
1923	556	500	400
1924	530	1,500	1,250
1925	571	2,000	2,750
1926	528	1,750	4,500
1927	681	1,350	6,750
1928	677	3,250	8,000
1929	606	4,428	10,250
1930	618	3,789	13,750

Source: *Historical Statistics of the United States. Colonial Times to 1957*, 1960, p. 491. Adapted.

people. From one broadcasting station in 1921, the number increased to 681 in 1927, after which date there was a decline to 618 in 1930. One hundred thousand receiving sets were produced in 1922, two million in 1925 after which there was a shrinkage in production for two years, only to pick up with increased vigor to reach a maximum of 4,428,000 in 1929.

While there was a fluctuation in the number of broadcasting stations and in the number of receiving sets that were produced, not so with the number of families owning radios. From 60,000 families in 1922, the number increased to 13,750,000 in 1930. Since the use of earphones had given way to loud speakers, the number of families that owned receiving sets no longer measured the size of listening audiences. Friends and neighbors were invited by owners of radios to listen to an evening of entertainment. In this manner millions of people were able to enjoy the novelty programs that were sent over the air. They became potential purchasers of radios in their own right. It is somewhat difficult to analyze the economic impacts of radio broadcasting on other forms of entertainment. There is no question that it decreased the demand for local bands and orchestras. Musicians became unemployed at a time when members of many other occupations were in great demand. When the piano industry felt the unfavorable impact of radio, piano dealers and music teachers were also adversely affected.

Motion Picture Industry

Radio was not the only form of entertainment that was enjoyed by millions of people in the 1920's. The motion picture industry experienced boom times, and sound pictures almost completely replaced silent pictures toward the close of the decade. Trick photography caught the fancy of movie goers. Also the plots of the stories that were portrayed on the screen gave expression to the new freedom that was being experienced and enjoyed.

The Wurlitzer Company and other manufacturers of pipe organs for theaters experienced good times as organs displaced orchestras in motion picture theaters. As an added attraction, the showing of pictures was interrupted in favor of a singfest that was led by the organist. Words to the music were thrown on the screen so that everybody in the audience could participate. The data in Table 21-6 make it clear why the number of motion picture projectionists doubled throughout the decade. It required 20,000 operators to project pictures on screens from noon until midnight, six or seven days a week. There were many communities that did not permit the showing of moving pictures on Sundays. Fines were not effective in enforcing Sunday closing laws, because theater owners could more than pay their fines out of the receipts for the one day.

Economic Impacts

Considering all the aspects of producing commercial entertainment, there is no question but that it had become big business. The hundreds of millions of dollars that were spent by those who sought admission to motion picture

Table 21-6

Average Weekly Attendance at Moving Picture Theaters; Total Cost of Admissions to Moving Picture and to Other Theaters—1921-1930

Year	Average Weekly Attendance at Moving Picture Theaters (millions)	Total Cost of Admissions (millions)	
		Motion Pictures	Other Theater Entertainment
1921	..	$301	$ 81
1922	40	....	....
1923	43	336	146
1924	46	....	....
1925	46	367	174
1926	50	....	....
1927	57	526	195
1928	65	....	....
1929	80	720	127
1930	90	732	95

Source: *Historical Statistics of the United States. Colonial Times to 1957*, 1960, pp. 224 and 225. Adapted.

productions found their way into many channels of utilization. Moving picture theaters had to be constructed and paid for; rent had to be paid for their usage. Light, heat, and electric fans had to be installed to make them useful and comfortable for their patrons; ushers were provided to escort patrons to their seats. Theaters had to be cleaned and fumigated every day. Taxes which went towards paying for the general costs of orderly government were paid to urban governments. When personal appearances were made by actors, singers, and other artists, employment was provided for these kinds of services. Moving picture reels were shipped by express from one city to another, which provided a constant traffic of this nature to a kind of agency that had felt the impacts of competition with parcel post.

Add to these impacts others that followed the spending of other hundreds of thousands of dollars to those who performed on the legitimate stage. Repeat the same expenses to entirely different groups of people and some idea may be obtained of the magnitude of the entertainment business. Moving picture actors and actresses and those who appeared on the legitimate stage were not noted for their frugal habits. They not only spent their incomes rather freely but in a somewhat luxurious and extravagant manner, at least according to the standards that were set by schoolteachers, government employees, and other salaried persons.

One of the impacts of the new kinds of entertainment that were enjoyed after the war, many of which were found or enjoyed outside the home, was found in the manufacturing and sale of pianos. Prior to the war a peak volume of 364,200 pianos were produced in 1909. This production figure has not been reached again, even in the more affluent years that followed a second war when the ownership of pianos became a status symbol. The year 1904 also was the year in which the largest number of reed organs was produced. In 1929 only 2,700 were produced compared with the 113,000 that were produced in 1904.

LABOR IN MECHANIZED INDUSTRIES

Mechanization of industry was not new after the close of World War I, but it did develop at a greatly accelerated rate. The assembly line method of mass production had undergone a thorough testing and was being applied in automotive plants more intensively than elsewhere. The industries that were antecedent to automobile manufacturing proper had already progressed through the process of replacing both skilled and unskilled labor with machine methods. The results of the alterations in the proportions in the use of labor and capital had been made manifest in (1) the elimination of much of the physical labor that formerly had been used in lifting, moving, and the general handling of materials, both raw materials and finished goods; (2) a greatly increased demand for machine operators and machine tenders whose tasks required diligence, alertness, and dexterity; and (3) in higher hourly wages for shorter workdays and weeks. For a given output per week, the total payroll actually was less than formerly due to the fact that machinery was performing tasks that had been done by hundreds, more or less, of common, unskilled workers and a smaller number of highly skilled employees.

Hundreds of job classifications in the automotive industry had been reduced to six—machine tenders, assemblers, skilled workers, inspectors and testors, helpers, and laborers. See Table 21-7. Possibly 60 percent or more of the employees of a given plant were classified as machine tenders and assemblers, and only from 10 to 15 percent of the employees were unskilled. At the time, not more than one employee in ten belonged to a trade such as blacksmith, die sinker, machinist, painter, and varnisher. Differentiation of work and of workers by trade was disappearing. Graduations in human labor were being leveled off at positions that were lower than those of highly skilled labor, above that of common labor. Work of the highly skilled and of the completely unskilled worker had been transferred to machinery. The changes in the composition of the labor force in mass production industries emphasized (1) the importance of the effectiveness of, and the almost necessity of, an organization of labor that was industry wide in scope and coverage and (2) a decline in the need and effectiveness of craft unions.

Changes in the Demand for Labor

While the mechanization of industry had been taking place for many decades, expansion of markets and developments of new processes more

Table 21-7

Group Classification of Workers and Average Hourly Earnings (Male Employees Only)

Group Number	Type of Operation	Number of Representative Establishments	Number of Workers	Average Hourly Wage Rate	Increasing or Decreasing Proportion of Working Force
I	Machine Tenders	39	12,332	.68	Increasing
II	Assemblers	40	4,631	.66	Increasing
III	Skilled Workers (Trade)	34	2,360	.84	Decreasing
IV	Inspectors and Testers	31	4,043	.61	No conclusive data
V	Helpers	23	653	.56	No conclusive data
VI	Laborers	24	2,307	.46	Decreasing

Source: *Wages and Hours in the Automobile Industry,* Bulletin 348 (Washington: U. S. Bureau of Labor Statistics, October, 1923).

than absorbed workers who had been displaced. Now it appeared that while the displacement of workers by machinery may have been transitory in its impact upon unemployment, periods of transition had become of longer duration than formerly and unemployment became a problem of national concern. New industries that were developed throughout the 1920's were more extensively mechanized in their initial stages of development than had been true before the war.

Agriculture. Agriculture was becoming of larger scale and was more highly and completely mechanized. Even the skill of milking cows had been imparted to pneumatic suction machines; and many hand milkers had been released from their tedium twice daily, early in the morning and in late afternoon, in daylight and in darkness, seven days a week in winter and in summer, in below freezing weather and when temperatures were excessively high. No longer could a Chicago fire be started by a recalcitrant cow. Much of the field work was being done by mechanical devices, and much labor on farms had become in the nature of driving tractors or other forms of farm machinery. That unemployment was not much more serious during the 1920's is due to the rise of automobile manufacturing and that of durable consumers' goods. The decline in the number of farm workers in no way measured a decline in the productivity of American farms.

Mining. Mining had become a highly mechanical process, whether it was coal, lead, copper, stone quarrying, or other minerals. Increases in the production of manufactured goods made their impacts felt in increases in mining basic raw materials. Mining activity was actually on the increase throughout the decade; but very little of it was powered by hand, and the employment of miners, in general, declined.

Railway Transportation. Railroads were in serious competition with motor trucks, buses, and automobiles; but the competition showed up more in the reduced utilization of the capacity of railway facilities than in an actual reduction of trains that were in operation and in the number of stations, both freight and passenger, that were discontinued. Railroads laid heavier rails, constructed stronger bridges, used more powerful locomotives, and purchased cars of larger capacity, so that they could haul longer and heavier trainloads with fewer operating personnel. Not only were trains longer than before, but elapsed time between terminals was reduced and equipment was used more efficiently. Automatic controls replaced hand controls in general; even automatic signals and protective devices at railroad grade crossings in urban communities were installed.

Building Construction. While the mechanization of building construction may have displaced labor of given job classifications, the increase in total construction activity tended to absorb those who adjusted themselves to other routines of work. Concrete was being mixed by machinery, although ready-mix machines had not come into general use. Hod carriers were being replaced by hoists and by elevators. Larger and heavier materials were being raised by derricks rather than by hand-turned windlasses. One effect of these labor-saving devices was to hasten the completion of new buildings; another one was to lower costs of construction and in this way encourage the construction of more buildings.

Trade and Service Industries. Trade and service industries not only absorbed some of the workers from other industries who had been displaced by machinery, they provided outlets for segments of the population that had not sought work before the war.

Office work of many kinds became available to women and to young girls. Record keeping, stenography, filing, and duties of receptionist were performed by women who usually were preferred to men in filling these positions. Business schools and colleges trained girls for office work and acquainted them with the nature of their duties. Many women found opportunities to become waitresses.

The construction of tall office buildings, apartment houses, and hotels after the war created a demand for elevator operators. Some of these jobs were filled by men and boys; more of them by young girls who could learn their duties in a short period of time and with little supervision. As department stores became larger and ground space became more costly, they expanded upwards rather than outwards, and customer elevators were installed to facilitate the movement of shoppers from one floor to another. The installation of escalators did not eliminate the need for elevators.

Many general department stores were clerked by women, although many of the supervisors were men. Variety stores, drugstores, specialty clothing stores, and chain stores opened their doors to more clerks during the 1920's. Not only did the volume of trade increase, the increase in the number of stores at the retail level increased the job opportunities for both men and women. Hardware stores and furniture stores were clerked almost entirely by men. The ideas of cash-and-carry and of self-service had not permeated the thinking of management. Wages were not high in relation to percentage markups on merchandise, and personal service and attention to customers' needs were the levels on which competition was based.

Impacts of Larger Family Incomes

Many families enjoyed two or more sources of regular income. In some instances, the additional incomes permitted their recipients to maintain their accustomed scale of living in the face of rising costs and expenses. For others, additional incomes enabled families to raise their scales of living. A second wage earner in a family may have been one of the intangible real costs of owning an automobile, of owning a home, an electric refrigerator and/or other durable consumers' goods. New furniture, new china, new silver, more and better clothing, fur coats, ability to travel, attending operas and concerts—all were made available to many persons and families by having more than one source of wage or salary income. There may have been some moonlighting, but it was not as prevalent or as much publicized as it was in later years. All of these activities not only contributed to a feeling of prosperity and of good times, they provided employment in other lines of work; they may have contributed to an inflationary trend; they did contribute to the realization of large business profits that entrepreneurs earned during the prosperous 1920's. Some of the increased activity on organized stock and commodity markets may easily be attributed to the fact that people and families had larger incomes than formerly. If these activities increased risks of loss of capital sums, they only added to the period's excitement, which people seemed to demand in one form or another.

Decline in Influence of Organized Labor

A situation that was inherent within the organization and operation of industry undoubtedly contributed to the weakening of organized labor during the 1920's. The introduction of more machinery, along with the extension of the principles of mass production into many of the newer industries that experienced rapid growth in this decade, resulted in a less than proportionate increase in the employment of skilled craftsmen. This factor, combined with the reluctance of the American Federation of Labor to make an appeal to nonskilled workers, did as much to weaken the bargaining power of organized labor as did the growth of company unions. The latter appealed more to those segments of labor that were not included in the program of the American Federation than to craftsmen. The real economic impact of the organization and functioning of company unions was to postpone the initiation of a drive to organize noncraftsmen along some pattern of industrial organization.

Labor as individuals fared much better than did labor organizations during the 1920's. After the effort to organize the steel and coal mining industries had failed, entrepreneurs made concerted efforts to crush all labor organizations by sponsoring and promoting company unions.

One purpose of the company union was to prove to labor that wages and conditions could be improved without labor having to incur the heavy costs of formal organization; management and labor were working together in order to accomplish a common objective. Under this arrangement labor did not have to contribute to paying large salaries for professional labor organization officers at the national level, smaller salaries for officers at the local level. Transportation and other expenses were not charges against the take-home pay of labor. Company employees, usually those who were in public relations or personnel departments, were paid by management to promote programs that presumably were in the interests of employees.

Real Wage Increase

In spite of the weakening in strength and power of organized labor, workers gained more in terms of real income than they had in many corresponding spans of years in the past. Paul Douglas in his *Real Wages in the United States, 1920-1926* [2] revealed that real incomes to labor increased 13 percent from 1920 to 1923 and another 11 percent from then until 1928. Productivity in manufacturing industries increased even more rapidly and to a larger extent so that increases in wages that were paid to labor not only did not decrease net earnings of industry, they came at a time when earnings increased.

Prelude to New Deal Labor Legislation

During the Hoover administration, Congress revealed its sympathy towards the principles of organized labor in passing the Davis-Bacon Act in 1931 and the Norris-LaGuardia Act the following year. They evidenced a more positive attitude on the part of Congress towards labor that culminated in the labor program of the New Deal.

The Davis-Bacon Act. The federal government assumed leadership in attempting to raise wages in the construction industry in the passage of the Davis-Bacon Act in 1931. The terms of the Act did not guarantee to anyone the right to organize, nor did it compel the use of collective bargaining in

[2] (Boston: Houghton Mifflin Company, 1930).

the settlement of wage disputes or in reaching agreements over the terms of a labor contract. It did provide that workers who were engaged in the construction of public works for which federal appropriations had been made were to receive prevailing rates of pay. These rates were resolved in terms of union wages that were effective in the respective localities where such work was in progress.

The Norris-LaGuardia Act. Rule by injunction was terminated by the terms of the Norris-LaGuardia Act of 1932. Under its terms restraining orders could be issued by federal courts only after findings that were based upon testimony of witnesses for both sides of the disputants that (1) unlawful acts had been or will be threatened or committed unless restrained; (2) substantial and irreparable injury to employers' properties will follow; (3) greater damage will be inflicted upon employers by denial of relief; (4) employer-complainants had no other remedy at law; (5) public officials who have the obligation of protecting employers' properties have been or are unwilling to furnish adequate protection to such properties. Within a few years, many states had enacted anti-injunction laws.

Equally as important as a reform measure was the provision in the Norris-LaGuardia Act that outlawed *yellow dog contracts,* under the terms of which workers agreed not to affiliate with any labor union during their tenure of employment. Most of the states that enacted antistrike legislation also prohibited the drawing up of similar contracts. The Act also limited the liability of unions, their officers, and members for damages that might be caused by unlawful acts of individual officers, agents, and members.

IMMIGRATION

Since the movements of people are sensitive to the phases of the business cycle, the immediate postwar depression and the one in 1920-21 were accompanied by sharp declines in the number of persons who arrived on our shores. For a number of years Samuel Gompers and the American Federation of Labor had agitated in favor of some kind of restriction being placed on the number of persons coming to this country to make their homes and to earn their livelihoods in competition with American workers. In 1921 Congress passed an act that limited the number of such new arrivals to 3 percent of the nationals enumerated in the 1910 census.

Some authorities claimed that the law discriminated against countries of southern and eastern Europe. To the extent that they may have been right, how much more did the 1924 Act discriminate against the same countries when the percentage was lowered to 2 percent and applied to the census data of 1890! Technically there was no element of discrimination in either provision because the percentages were applied uniformly to the nationals of each country in determining the number of persons who would be permitted to pass through the gates of Ellis Island. Still too many people were entering the United States in terms of the number of unemployed persons in the 1920's. Provision was made that after July 1, 1927, only 150,000 immigrants per year would be admitted as permanent residents. The quota for any given country was that portion of 150,000 that the nationals of the country bore to the entire population of the United States based on the 1920 census. While immigrants from Western Hemisphere countries were not subject to quota restrictions, the same conditions of eligibility applied to them as to the others. These restrictions were applied during a decade in which our people seem to have decided in one way or another to retard the rate of population increase.

EARLY RETIREMENT OF UNITED STATES WAR DEBT

By the end of the war the federal debt had reached a peak of almost $26 billion, which was considered a staggering burden at the time. The Liberty Bond issues and the Victory Bond issue that was floated after the Armistice was signed were 25-40 year bonds, which meant that they could not be redeemed for at least 25 years.

The continued use of income, inheritance, and excess profits taxes after the war yielded budgetary surpluses for the federal government. Andrew Mellon, who was Secretary of the Treasury at the time, took advantage of the discount at which government bonds were selling, due solely to a market price situation. Inflation, combined with a relative scarcity of loanable funds, caused market rates of interest to rise when Federal Reserve Banks no longer supported the market for government securities. Mellon used some of the Treasury surplus in purchasing government bonds in the open market at a discount and reduced the federal debt at a rate of almost a billion dollars a year for ten years. In doing so, he saved millions of dollars of interest cost. It was in connection with his debt retirement program that Mellon was criticized very harshly. His many critics and opponents brought out the fact that the Treasury Department retired the debt by paying less than par for the bonds, which was tantamount to default. The bond indenture said nothing about the government not being able to buy them back in the open market and at market prices before they matured. The only time the government promised to redeem $1,000 bonds for $1,000 was on their respective dates of maturity. There was absolutely no reason why the Treasury should not have taken advantage of an open market situation, when bondholders offered to sell holdings at less than face value.

The retirement of the debt in the early years of the 1920 decade and the selling of bonds by individual owners increased the cash holdings of former bondholders. There were several opportunities that were available to them in the ultimate disposition of the new money. Deposits in savings banks were on the increase, and sales of life insurance and endowment policies rose to new heights. Real estate mortgage bonds that bore from 5 percent to 7 percent interest were made attractive to former holders of

government bonds and the depositors in savings banks. Other millions of
dollars undoubtedly found their way into speculative markets, both commodity and corporate security markets. There is no way by which the distribution of the money can be calculated, but it is generally recognized that
the partial retirement of the federal debt before its maturity was a major
factor in developing the speculative mania of the 1920's.

FOREIGN WAR DEBTS

One of the legacies of the late war was the change in the financial
relationship between the United States and European countries. Normal
trade relations and motives that guided the direction of free enterprise both
here and abroad had resulted in trends that had begun to lessen our position as a debtor nation. Financial relationships had been initiated which,
if carried to extremes, would have resulted over a period of years in the
United States losing its net debtor position and becoming a net creditor
of other countries. This transition was hastened by the conditions of war
during which nonbusiness considerations superseded those of prudent investment, and the search for profit potentials in the investment of venture capital.

Loans Between Governments

Large sums of money were lent by the United States government to
governments of European nations that were at war. The principal sums
that were lent came from savings from the productivity of capital. Since
before the war the borrowing nations had not been actively engaged in
owning and in operating business enterprises, they were forced to impose
heavy tax burdens on private industry, or, as an alternative, to nationalize
industries in order to derive incomes with which to repay borrowed capital
and to pay interest obligations thereon. Another source of funds that might
have been available to England and France to retire their indebtedness was
the payment of reparations by the Central Powers. Even though the German
delegates to the peace conference had been forced to sign a statement that
included the acceptance of responsibility for having started the war, a great
number of Germans, including one Adolf Hitler, vehemently denied any and
all such responsibility.

It was finally recognized by officials of the United States (1) that the
economies of the defeated nations were in a state of turmoil, (2) that
political conditions were so unstable it was difficult, if not impossible, to
collect the war debt in full even if their national incomes had been sufficiently
large to have permitted them to do so. The Dawes Plan, later the Young
Plan, established annual payments on reparations that presumably were
based on the ability of the defeated nations to pay, instead of upon the
values of property and of human lives that had been destroyed. Profits that
were derived from basic industries, such as coal mining, the manufacture
of iron and steel, railroads and public utilities were to be turned over to

the reparations committee and by it to England and France. The United States did not submit any claims to the committee.

Loans in Default. When Germany failed to make payments to compensate for damage suffered by England and France, the latter countries refused to repay the loans they had obtained from the United States. Not only did they refuse to make payments on the principal sums of their debts, they did not even meet their interest obligations.

England and France exerted tremendous pressure upon the United States to have it cancel all of their indebtedness to compensate for the United States not having suffered any direct losses or damage to property or lives at home. This statement was not exactly true, if damage that was caused by sabotage at shipyards, piers, and ammunition dumps be taken into consideration. President Coolidge and most, if not all, government officials, bankers, and businessmen took the position that since the loans had been granted in good faith they were to be repaid in full when due. They were in no sense gifts or donations, nor did they represent to any degree our share in the participation in the war effort. Our insistence that the war debts be repaid was not at all consistent with other developments, the impacts of which were measures of the ability of the debtor nations to pay. Immediately after the termination of the war, Congress made an upward revision of tariff rates on specific commodity imports. In 1922, it passed the Fordney-McCumber tariff "in order to do something for agriculture." Leaving this aspect of the bill for later discussion, any increase in tariff rates tended to make it more difficult for European peoples to sell their goods in the United States.

A Frequently Overlooked Aspect of Debt. There is another angle to the debt question that frequently is overlooked. The capital sums that were lent by the United States government to foreign nations were, in turn, borrowed from the American people. Most of the proceeds of these loans had been spent in this country. The impacts of such spending were to operate on the demand side for American commodities that were in scarce supply because of the war and to force their prices higher than they otherwise would have been had the demand for them been measured by prewar conditions. Not only this, but when foreign governments repudiated their debts to the United States, the latter government continued to honor its obligations to American holders of government bonds. This was done only by using tax money for the purpose. Many of the government bonds had found their way into the investment portfolios of the more wealthy persons who were in the upper income tax brackets. Since the bonds were tax exempt, the people in the middle and lower income tax brackets were taxed to retire evidences of government indebtedness that were in the hands of persons who had more tax paying ability than they. Again, some of these wealthy persons could well have added to their wealth by having sold goods and supplies to the very nations that were in default on their indebtedness to us.

QUESTIONS FOR REVIEW

1. What was the most perplexing problem in the area of population growth during the 1920 decade? Explain your answer fully.

2. How did construction activity contribute to (1) the creation of good times? (2) a recession of economic activity towards the close of the decade?

3. Explain how the debt policy of the Secretary of the Treasury contributed to the inflation of stock prices.

4. (a) Why was immigration into the United States finally restricted?
(b) Explain the present immigration laws of the United States.

5. (a) What conditions gave rise to a new demand for labor?
(b) What conditions gave rise to a new supply of labor?

6. Why did women who were not from families in lower income brackets enter industry?

SUGGESTED READINGS

Barnes, James A. *Wealth of the American People.* Englewood Cliffs, N. J.: Prentice-Hall, Inc., 1949. Chapters 28, 29, and 31.

Borden, Neil H. "The Economic Effects of Advertising," *Issues in American Economic History,* edited by Gerald D. Nash. Boston: D. C. Heath and Co., 1964.

Dillard, Dudley. *Economic Development of the North Atlantic Community.* Englewood Cliffs, N. J.: Prentice-Hall, Inc., 1967. Chapter 31.

Krooss, Herman F. *American Economic Development.* 2d ed. Englewood Cliffs, N. J.: Prentice-Hall, Inc., 1966.

Letwin, William (ed.). *Documentary History of American Economic Policy Since 1789.* Chicago: Aldine Publishing Company, 1961. Selection 21.

Leuchtenburg, William E. "The Second Industrial Revolution," *American Economic History: Essays in Interpretation,* edited by Stanley Coben and Forest G. Hill. Philadelphia: J. B. Lippincott Co., 1966.

Levy, Lester, and Roy J. Sampson. *American Economic Development.* Boston: Allyn & Bacon, Inc., 1962. Chapter 16.

Paxson, F. L. "The Highway Movement, 1916-1935," *Economic Change in America,* edited by Joseph T. Lambie and Richard V. Clemence. Harrisburg, Pa.: Stackpole Books, 1954.

Pontecorvo, Giulio. "Investment Banking and Security Speculation in the Late 1920's," *United States Economic History: Selected Readings,* edited by Harry N. Scheiber. New York City: Alfred A. Knopf, Inc., 1964.

Soule, George. *Prosperity Decade: From War to Depression, 1917-1929.* New York City: Holt, Rinehart & Winston, Inc., 1947. Chapters 6-10.

Stocking, Collis A. "Modern Advertising and Economic Theory," *Issues in American Economic History,* edited by Gerald D. Nash. Boston: D. C. Heath and Co., 1964.

Wright, Chester W. *Economic History of the United States.* 2d ed. New York City: McGraw-Hill Book Company, 1949. Chapter 43.

Chapter 22

MORE ON PROSPERITY

AGRICULTURE

American agriculture felt the shock of the sudden termination of war as much as or more than any segment of our economy. In gearing agricultural production to the point where it would be large enough to feed the peoples of European countries whose farms had been devastated by war and whose agricultural labor forces had been drawn into military service or into industrial production, American farmers had attempted to engage in larger scale operations. This meant capital investment in the form of more farm machinery and the combining of small farm units into larger units without loss of acreage that was under cultivation. Since farmers never had large savings out of current income that they could have used for the purpose, they were compelled to enter the free market for capital funds and to borrow sufficient sums of money to enable them to accomplish their objectives.

When prices of agricultural commodities began to fall later in the 1920's, contract rates of interest remained constant. This relationship placed farmers in the position of having to meet constant fixed costs out of the proceeds of the sales of their cereal grains and other farm products at falling prices. In order to have incomes that were adequate to meet these fixed costs and then to maintain their living at the accustomed levels, they were compelled to attempt to produce larger outputs. Increased production involved the purchase of more commercial fertilizer and increases in other of their operating costs, along with more complex utilization of certain of their farm machines which required the purchase of more fuel and the payment of more wages to labor. Undoubtedly the increased output of farm products forced prices downward, and individual farmers were powerless to do anything about it. Agricultural products were highly competitive in the home market, all the more so because of the loss of some of the foreign export markets that resulted when European farmers put their farmland to productive use in much less time than our people thought they either could or would be able to. Though some progress was made in organizing cooperatives, farmers in the United States were more successful in controlling the sale of dairy products than they were in restricting the acreage that was planted in any particular crop or in all crops. In the absence of controls at some local level, the individual farmer would have harmed only himself had he restricted the output of his land voluntarily.

Farmers did receive some relief from having to pay high interest rates on loans they had obtained from free enterprise sources when Federal Intermediate Credit Banks were authorized in 1923. These banks were empowered to finance and to refinance the farmers through the granting of loans that would mature from six months to three years from date. Under conditions of risk that were acceptable to bankers, credit that was needed for the purchase of feeder cattle, to repair barns and equipment, to erect fences, to drain pastures, and to acquire machinery could be obtained through the facilities of Intermediate Credit Banks. Longer term capital costs could be financed by obtaining credit of five to 40 years from Federal Land Banks.

Changes in Farm Organization

Changes that occurred in the size of farms are revealed in the data that are contained in Table 22-1.

Table 22-1
Farms and Land in Farms, by Size of Farms—1920-1930
(000)

Year	Total	Under Ten Acres			10 to 49 Acres	50 to 99 Acres	100 to 259 Acres	260 to 499 Acres	500 Acres and Over
		Total	Under 3 Acres	3 to 9 Acres					
1920	6,448	289	20	269	2,011	1,475	1,980	476	217
1925	6,372	378	15	363	2,039	1,421	1,887	440	207
1930	6,289	358	43	315	2,000	1,375	1,864	451	241

Source: U. S. Department of Commerce, Bureau of the Census, *Historical Statistics of the United States. Colonial Times to 1957* (Washington: U. S. Government Printing Office, 1960), p. 279. Adapted.

The increase in the number of farms of 500 acres and larger was effected by entrepreneurs having combined a number of smaller sized farms, or by owners of large farms having brought smaller ones together, rather than having appropriated virgin lands to farm uses for the first time. It was to be expected, therefore, that the number of farms larger than ten acres but of less than 500 acres would have decreased. In order to farm larger acreages when additional farmhands were not available, farm owners purchased more

farm machinery. The purchasing power with which to do this could well
have been borrowed from Intermediate Credit Banks.

Increase in Use of Mechanical Power

Data in Table 22-2 indicate that the number of tractors on farms
increased 2.68 times in ten years, the number of motor trucks increased
over four times, and the number of automobiles over one and one-half times
throughout that same span of years. The total value of farm implements and
machinery did not keep pace with these increases because of changes in the

Table 22-2
Farm Machinery and Equipment—1921-1930

Year	Motor Vehicles and Specified Machines on Farms (000)			Value of Farm Implements and Machinery (millions)
	Tractors	Motor Trucks	Automobiles	
1921	343	207	2,382	$3,551
1922	372	263	2,425	2,900
1923	428	316	2,618	2,832
1924	496	363	3,004	2,985
1925	549	459	3,283	2,955
1926	621	559	3,605	3,042
1927	693	662	3,820	3,126
1928	782	753	3,820	3,088
1929	827	840	3,970	3,178
1930	920	900	4,135	3,302

Source: *Historical Statistics of the United States. Colonial Times to 1957,* 1960,
p. 285. Adapted.

retail prices of the other items. Competition between the manufacturers of
farm machinery was extremely keen in these years, and the same degree
of competition was in evidence at the retail level. At the same time that the
numbers of tractors, motor trucks, and automobiles on farms were on the
increase, the number of horses and mules on farms declined. The number of
farm horses decreased from 19,369,000 in 1921 to 13,384,000 in 1930,
while the number of mules on farms declined only 384,000 in the same span
of years. Mules were more prevalent on farms in the Southern States than
elsewhere and farm machinery either had not been as well adapted to use
in cultivating and in harvesting crops that were grown on these farms, or
southern farmers had difficulty in obtaining the necessary capital funds with
which to purchase it. Again farm labor in the South was more productive
when it was applied to hand tools or horse- and mule-drawn equipment.

The index of the consumption of feed by farm horses and mules, based on the average for the years 1947-49, declined from 297 in 1921 to 263 in 1925 and to 219 in 1930. While these changes were taking place, farmland that was planted in feed crops for farm horses and mules decreased from 87 million acres in 1921 to 78 million acres in 1925 and to 65 million acres in 1930. Since farming was highly commercialized and farmers were forced to sell more crops to offset the decline in prices they were compelled to accept for farm produce, the 22 million acres were seeded in crops that found their way to the marketplace. To the extent that these lands were planted in crops that could have been used for animal feed and which found their way to the market, prices of these crops fell. To the extent that these lands were planted in other crops, again an increase in their supply was not in response to an increase in a demand for them and their market prices fell.

Lower Property Values; Higher Taxes

The increase in the mechanization of farm processes and of farm equipment was accompanied by a decrease in the value of farmlands, building, machinery, equipment, and livestock. Average values per acre of farmlands and buildings declined at a time when taxes on farm property increased. Real estate taxes increased from a total of $510 million in 1921 to $517 million in 1925 and to $567 million in 1930. Taxes per acre of farmland for the same years were 54 cents, 56 cents, and 57 cents, respectively. In 1928 and 1929 real estate taxes reached a maximum of 58 cents per acre. Added to real estate taxes were those on personal property and on automobiles. Personal property taxes that had amounted to $72 million in each of the years 1924 and 1925 went to a high of $84 million in 1929. By the following year, the personal tax burden had declined $3 million. Increases in automotive taxes that were paid by farmers were more spectacular. The totals included payments of all registration and tag fees for automobiles and motor trucks and for permits for farmers to drive either or both. These taxes increased from $55 million in 1924 to $127 million in 1930. The increase in automotive taxes was offset, in part, by decreases in labor costs and increases in the productivity of labor and of land.

Increased Productivity

If the mechanization of farming and improved technological processes were not effective in increasing farm net incomes, they did result in saving the amount of time that was required to produce basic units of given products. Whether the savings be measured in terms of the number of man-hours that were required to produce 100 bushels each of wheat and of corn, and a bale of cotton, or in terms of the number of man-hours that were applied to an acre of land that was planted in wheat, in corn, and in cotton, respectively, they loomed large in reducing the drudgery of farming. Fewer man-hours per acre were spent in producing wheat and cotton combined than in producing cotton. To measure the progress made in increasing

Table 22-3

Farms, Land in Farms, Value of Farm Property, and Taxes Levied on Farm Property—1921-1930

Year	Number of Farms (000)	Land in Farms (000 Acres)	Total Value Farmland, Buildings, Machinery, Equipment, Livestock (millions)	Farmland and Buildings		Taxes Levied on Farm Property			Automotive Taxes Paid by Farmers (millions)
				Total Value (millions)	Average Value per Acre	Real Estate Total (millions)	Amount per Acre	Personal Property (millions)	
1921	6,511	949,566	$71,401	$61,523	$64.79	$510	$ .54	...	...
1922	6,500	943,253	61,982	54,050	57.30	509	.54	...	...
1923	6,492	936,941	60,902	52,629	56.17	516	.55	...	...
1924	6,480	930,628	58,519	50,487	54.25	511	.55	$72	$ 55
1925	6,471	924,316	57,439	49,463	53.51	517	.56	72	72
1926	6,462	936,806	57,412	49,000	52.31	526	.56	73	83
1927	6,458	949,297	56,393	47,680	50.23	545	.57	75	94
1928	6,470	961,787	56,727	47,532	49.42	556	.58	80	102
1929	6,512	974,277	57,738	47,985	49.25	567	.58	84	119
1930	6,546	986,768	57,689	47,873	48.52	567	.57	81	127

Source: *Historical Statistics of the United States. Colonial Times to 1957*, 1960, pp. 278 and 282. Adapted.

the productivity of labor, data that pertain to the number of man-hours required to produce 100 bushels of wheat, 100 bushels of corn, and a bale of cotton that contained 480 pounds of lint are most revealing.

Table 22-4

Man-Hours Used to Produce Specified Amounts of Wheat, Corn, and Cotton—1900-1950

	1900		1920		1940		1950	
	Wheat	Corn	Wheat	Corn	Wheat	Corn	Wheat	Corn
Man-hours per acre	15	38	12	32	7.5	25	4.6	15.2
Before harvest	7	22	5.5	19	3.7	15	2.6	9.9
Harvest	8	16	6.5	13	3.8	10	2.0	5.3
Yield per acre (bushels)	13.9	25.9	13.8	28.4	15.9	30.3	16.6	39
Man-hours per 100 bushels	108.0	147.0	87.0	113.0	47.0	83.0	28.0	39.0

Cotton			
Man-hours per acre	112	90	98	74
Before harvest	62	55	46	33
Harvest	50	35	52	41
Yield of lint per acre	191	160	245	283
Man-hours per bale	280	269	191	126

Source: *Historical Statistics of the United States. Colonial Times to 1957*, 1960, p. 281. Adapted.

Need for Parity Prices

Farmers were plagued by a price-purchasing power relationship that was not new, but it was one that made a bad situation worse because of the increase in prices that had occurred prior to 1925. It was the same old story over again—the purchasing power of the dollar they received from the sale of their produce was greater than that of the same dollar when they later took that dollar to market.

For farmers to have had as much purchasing power in any given year as they had on the average of 1910 to 1914, the parity ratio would have to have been 100. The fact that at no time throughout the decade to which the data in Table 22-5 pertain was the parity ratio this high means that they were unable to maintain the standard of living with the same money incomes they had enjoyed during the base period. Taxes and interest costs rose more rapidly than did wage costs, production costs, and living costs. Of these three types or classes of costs, production costs rose least, wage rates the most.

At no time during the entire decade was total cash income equal to what farmers had received in 1920. In 1921 total cash income received by farmers was only two thirds of their 1920 income.

Table 22-5

Index of Prices Received and Prices Paid by Farmers and Parity Ratio— 1921-1930

Year	Prices Received by Farmers	Prices Paid, Including Taxes, Interest, and Wages	Parity Ratio (1910-14)
1921	124	155	80
1922	131	151	87
1923	142	159	89
1924	143	160	89
1925	156	164	95
1926	145	160	91
1927	140	159	88
1928	148	162	91
1929	148	160	92
1930	125	151	83

Source: *Historical Statistics of the United States. Colonial Times to 1957*, 1960, p. 283. Adapted.

Nonstaple Farming

Many persons think of farming in terms of wheat, corn, and other cereal grains, and cotton, but this is not at all the true picture. Almost all farmers kept some livestock, even though raising animals for the market may not have been their major activity. Cows, pigs, and chickens were kept for domestic reasons, and their increases were sent to market. Incomes from the sale of these increases augmented incomes from major sources. Little pigs often were purchased and fattened on slop and garbage at almost no cost. When they were sold on the market, any price they brought over and above their original costs was a source of income their vendors would not otherwise have enjoyed. Cows contributed to the real incomes of farmers, as did poultry of all sorts. Milk, butter, cheese, and eggs were major items of food on farmers' dining room tables; and broods of chickens were hatched for home consumption. Sheep were raised in some regions for meat, in others for wool; and the prices of lamb meat, mutton, and wool were no exception to the downward trend of prices that were received by farmers for their produce. In raising livestock for the market, farmers were confronted with the problem of having to sell it on markets that were relatively lower than those from which it had been purchased. Livestock may well have been bred on the farms on which it was raised, in which case there were no market prices involved as original cost items. The situation was that raising livestock for the market was not as profitable as it had been in the years prior to 1921, but raising livestock was part of farming.

The production and sale of butter, cheese, evaporated and condensed milk, and ice cream increased in volume throughout the decade; but farmers received somewhat lower prices for them. Producers of butter on a commercial scale encountered serious competition from margarine, whose market prices were approximately one half those of butter. The price differential between butter and margarine was such as to attract purchasers, even though they were compelled to add coloring matter to it if they preferred their spread to have a yellow color. This competition brought no ill to producers of cotton seed, soybeans, and peanuts, whose oils were used in the manufacture of margarine. Corn oil was another vegetable oil that went into the manufacture of this butter substitute.

Price Situations

Prior to 1920 American farmers had received over $2.00 a bushel for wheat and as high as $1.50 a bushel for corn. After 1921, the price of wheat at the farm fell below $1.00 a bushel for four of the next ten years, and ranged between $1.03 and $1.43 a bushel for the remaining six years. The price of corn went from 51 cents per bushel in 1921 to a high of $1.06 in 1924, after which it fell back to between 70.1 cents and 84.7 cents per bushel until it hit a new low of 59.8 cents in 1930. Prices for oats, barley, and rye, all for grain, followed the same pattern and were much lower during the 1920's than they had been in the years just prior to this time. Soybeans became an important crop for many farmers in some of the Middle Western States by 1924. Even though their prices dropped from an average of $2.458 per bushel in 1924 to $1.368 per bushel in 1930, between the years of 1926 and 1929 the demand for them was elastic from the farmers' point of view, so that even though their prices declined to an average at the farm of $1.879 in 1929, the gross income farmers received from their sale was larger than it had been in 1926 when the average price they received was $2.009 per bushel. Without going into detail over the price situation of each of these grains, the price pattern for rye will serve to illustrate the impact upon farmers during the 1920's of declines in prices of some of their minor crops. From 1916 to 1920, prices of rye for grain ranged between $1.124 and $1.733 per bushel at the farm. Between 1921 and 1930 the range in prices at the farm was from a low of 44.4 cents per bushel to 95.3 cents per bushel.

Rice, Sugar, and Tobacco. Changes in price patterns for rice, sugar, and tobacco were important to those farmers who either could not or did not depend as much upon the production and sale of wheat and corn and other cereal grains as did the farmers in Middle Western States and those of the Far Northwest. In 1919 the price of rice was $5.46 per hundred pounds. In the space of only two years, it had fallen to $2.18 a hundred pounds, after which it recovered to $3.30 a hundred pounds in 1925, only to fall again to $1.74 in 1930. In 1919, the price of sugarcane at the farm was $14 a ton. From a low of $3.63 a ton in 1921, it recovered to $7.09 a ton in 1923, after which it declined to $3.31 in 1930. The story of tobacco is a tragic one for the farmers who relied upon the sale of this product as their principal source of income. A combination of influences had carried its average price to a record high of 31.2 cents a pound in 1919. The following year saw a larger crop produced on 24,000 fewer acres of land that sold for only 17.3 cents per pound. In 1922 the price of tobacco had recovered to 22.8 cents per pound after which it declined to 16.8 cents in 1925 and to 12.8 cents a pound in 1930.

Potatoes. Potato growers did not escape the wide and sometimes disastrous fluctuations in the prices of their product that were experienced by other farmers. The low price for Irish potatoes at the end of the decade was only one third of their highest price of a few years earlier. Prices of sweet potatoes at the farm fluctuated from $2.53 per cwt. in 1920 to a high of $2.96 per cwt. in 1925 after which year they fell to a low of $1.93, in 1930. Hay was grown and cut on a commercial scale by many farmers in the New England States, in New York, in Pennsylvania, in Ohio, and in other East Central States. From $20.90 a ton in 1919, the price of hay fell to $13.30 a ton in 1926 and to $10.30 a ton one year later.

Cotton. Cotton growers received 35.34 cents per pound of cotton, and $65.79 per ton of cottonseed in 1919, but not for long. The price of 28.69 cents per pound of cotton and $41.23 a ton for cottonseed were the highest prices they received for these products respectively during the decade, at the close of which the market gave them 9.46 cents a pound for cotton and $22.04 a ton for cottonseed. In 1926 increases in the number of cotton bales combined with tons of cottonseed that were sold, yielded a larger gross income to farmers than they had received in 1921, even though the price of cotton had declined 4.53 cents per pound and that of cottonseed $7.10 a ton. The amount of cotton and of cottonseed produced more than doubled which more than compensated for the decline of approximately 25 percent each in the prices of cotton and cottonseed respectively. When the costs of planting, cultivating, and harvesting approximately 16 million acres of cotton, in addition to the 28,678,000 acres that were so planted in 1921, are taken into consideration and added to the costs of ginning an additional 125 percent of cottonseed, the increase in the gross income of 42 percent that cotton growers received over these same years shrinks to insignificance.

Perishable Fruits. Prices of perishable fruits, such as apples, peaches, pears, grapes, oranges, and grapefruit, all of which were sold in markets that were more local in character than were markets for the more staple crops, were subject to price fluctuations that were almost as spectacular and uncontrollable as were those for the staples. Other factors remaining the same, the growth of young fruit trees to maturity was accompanied by an increase in their output without the necessity of new capital expenditures for additional trees.

Impacts of Prices Not Uniform. Since all the prices that have been cited above were average prices at the farm level, some farmers received more than these averages, others received less. Neither do these prices mean that all farmers in all parts of the United States lost money every year, nor do they indicate which ones may have found that farming was profitable. They conceal the fact that many individual farmers were able to maintain their accustomed standards of living, and that others were able to improve upon theirs. Farmers who were fortunate enough to have land that was well above the margin of cultivation enjoyed standards of living that were well above their customary levels of living. They were the ones who were enabled to enjoy the benefits and pleasures that were to be derived from owning and utilizing the affluence of the postwar period, and who shared new-found leisure time that resulted from the introduction of new technologies in the production of both consumers' and producers' goods.

TARIFFS

Irrespective of the position of certain farmers in relation to margins of cultivation, all of them were affected to some extent by the parity situation that is portrayed in Table 22-5. Voluntary efforts to regulate the acreage that was planted in a particular crop in a given year, or to control the rate at which farm produce was sent to markets, have brought only failure. The formation of alliances, granges, new political parties, and attempts to bring price relief through the enactment of monetary measures—all had failed to provide any price relief to those who needed it most. The political party that was in control of Congress turned to the tariff in order to do something for agriculture.

The Fordney-McCumber Tariff

Accordingly, the Fordney-McCumber Tariff Act was passed by Congress in September, 1922. Of especial concern to farmers was the treatment that was accorded products that were produced on American farms, and farm machinery that was used in their production. Since the Payne-Aldrich Tariff of 1909 was the last Act that incorporated the principles of protection, some of the rates contained therein will serve as the base with which the rates in the Fordney-McCumber Act will be compared.

The rates on wheat and rye, very little of which products were imported, were raised five cents a bushel. Corn remained at 15 cents a bushel. Three cents a pound was levied against beef, and lamb meat was raised two and

Table 22-6

Prices Received by Farmers for Selected Money Crops for Years 1919-1931
(Averages in Dollars)

Commodity	Unit of Pricing	1931	1929	1924	1919
Dairy Products					
Butter	lb.	$ .272	$ .422	$ .395	$ .503
Butterfat in Cream	lb.	.248	.452	.404	.533
Whole Milk					
Wholesale	100 lbs.	1.69	2.53	2.22	3.29
Retail	quart	.101	.115	.111	.119
Shorn Wool	lb.	.136	.302	.366	.495
Poultry and Eggs					
Chickens	lb.	.158	.228	.194	. .
Eggs	doz.	.176	.298	.267	.413
Turkeys	lb.	.193	.245	. .	. .
Staples					
Corn—all purposes	bu.	.321	.799	1.063	1.513
Wheat—for grain	bu.	.391	1.036	1.247	2.163
Oats—for grain	bu.	.213	.418	.478	.767
Barley—for grain	bu.	.328	.539	.742	1.244
Flaxseed	bu.	1.167	2.812	2.179	4.407
Soybeans for beans	bu.	.498	1.879	2.458	—
Rice	100 lbs.	1.08	2.22	2.99	5.46
Rye for grain	bu.	.341	.857	.953	1.459
Sugarcane	ton	3.21	3.73	5.58	14.00
Hay	ton	8.73	10.90	12.70	20.90
Cotton	lb.	.0566	.1678	.2291	.3534
Cottonseed	lb.	8.97	30.92	33.26	65.79
Tobacco	lb.	.082	.183	.19	.312
Potatoes—Irish	cwt.	.763	2.18	1.14	3.23
Fruits					
Apples	bu.	.64	1.39	1.23	1.78
Peaches	bu.	.60	1.49	1.31	1.86
Pears	bu.	.77	1.71	1.57	2.02
Grapes	bu.	22.60	27.30	37.90	. .
Oranges (tangerines)	box	1.22	3.59	2.85	3.11
Grapefruit	box	.80	1.89	.96	1.60

Source: *Historical Statistics of the United States. Colonial Times to 1957*, 1960, pp. 294-297, 299-304. Adapted.

one-half cents per pound. In order to appease California growers, rates on lemons, nuts, and similar products were returned to near their levels in 1909. Agricultural implements were placed on the free list, which was merely a gesture since they were being produced and sold more cheaply in the United States than in other countries. Also, imported farm implements were not as efficient when applied to American farms as were American-made implements. The tariff on sugar was placed at 2.206 cents per pound, but sugar that was imported from Cuba was assessed 20 percent less than this. To compensate for an increase in the rate of raw wool, rates on clothing wool were raised from 50 percent to 100 percent. Raw wool was given a rate of 31 cents a pound, but wool in the form of cloth was given a rate of from 37 cents to 45 cents on its wool content plus an ad valorem duty of 50 percent. In general and in the long run, farmers were worse off in terms of purchasing power after the passage of the Act than before, because they had had little competition from imported grains and other farm commodities and were compelled to pay higher prices for many items they purchased from the market. Another abortive attempt to help farmers was the passage of the Hawley-Smoot Bill in 1930, the effects of which will form the subject matter for discussion and analysis in the following chapter.

Attempts at Regulation

In the meantime, several attempts were made in Congress to pass legislation the result of which would have been to enable the export of agricultural staples to have subsidized farmers. Five times was a McNary-Haugen Bill passed by the Congress and vetoed by President Coolidge on the grounds of unconstitutionality and also because it provided no real solution of the basic problem. Carrying out its provisions would have prolonged the imbalance between production costs, volumes of commodities produced, and the prices received by farmers for the commodities they sold. It would have encouraged a continuation of large volumes of output when reductions were needed to effect higher prices at farm levels.

Finally, in 1929 the Agricultural Marketing Act provided for the establishment of the Federal Farm Board which was given a revolving fund of $500 million to lend to farmers' cooperatives at low interest cost and to remove so-called exportable surpluses of selected commodities from the market. Loans were granted to farm cooperatives for the purpose of delaying the movement of wheat and other commodities to the market. Two fifths of the revolving fund was used to support the price of wheat alone. Other cooperatives to which loans were extended were The National Cotton Cooperative Association, and associations that were organized to market beans, livestock, dairy products, Texas figs, Florida and Texas citrus, California grapes, potatoes, apples, pecans, sugar beets, tobacco, and rice. Since most of the activities of the Board extended into the following decade, no further analysis will be made here except to say that while the proponents of the Agricultural Marketing Act were sincere of purpose, they failed to get at the core of the problem which was the supplying of agricultural commodities to markets that could not absorb them at prices favorable to farmers.

BANKING AND FINANCE

Banking made two contributions to the economy after 1920, one of which contributed to and measured a degree of prosperity; the other was an element of weakness that contributed to the depression that followed the stock market crash in October, 1929, and to the collapse of our banking system in 1932. Not all commercial banks were national banks, or even members of the Federal Reserve System. Throughout the decade, there were approximately twice as many nonmember banks as there were member banks, although the total assets of the latter, in general, amounted to two and one half times the total assets of the former. The nonmember banks were state and private banks, many of which were located in small, rural communities. Many of them were capitalized for amounts below the minimum that was required of member banks. In their loan portfolios were found evidences of loans to farmers some of which were for relatively short terms. Others were loans that were secured by real estate and were for longer terms than national banks were permitted to grant. Both state and private banks granted more mortgage loans than national banking permitted.

Competitive Banking

In order to compete successfully with state and other nonmember banks, member banks were permitted to grant more loans on real estate throughout the 1920's. Implementations of this permission led to their loan portfolios becoming less liquid. Inability to liquidate farm mortgage paper readily was one of the causes of bank failures in the decade.

Competition between banks was keen, and since their earnings were relatively large they erected new and imposing structures to house their activities. By their appearance of luxury and strength they imparted, or so it was thought, confidence and trust in the banks themselves. As a competitive factor, elaborate and imposing new banking offices attracted new customers, both depositors and borrowers. The architectural designs of bank buildings, both exteriors and interiors, did not lend themselves readily to other kinds of occupancies. When banks were in distress, disposal of their buildings added little to the cash holdings of receivers in bankruptcy or of bank conservators. Liquidation values of bank office buildings were small percentages of their original costs of construction.

The impact of the unfavorable position of American farmers in the market was felt in their inability to repay their bank loans. Foreclosures by banks did not help matters at all; in fact, they made bad matters worse. Extensions of credit were given that were far beyond the dictates of law and principle, in hopes that in the following years, farmer borrowers might be able to reduce their bank indebtedness. Only too frequently were bankers forced to grant additional credit as an alternative to operating farms that could have been taken over in foreclosure proceedings.

Unfortunately, as it turned out in the long run, when bankers began to loosen up on their criteria of sound investments, they added to their holdings of corporate stock at the expense of lower percentage holdings of bonds—government, public utility, and industrial, including railroad. When capital gains were turned into capital losses, real or potential, commercial departments of banks exchanged their corporate stock for government bonds that were in the portfolios of their respective investment departments, then sold them in order to meet demands of depositors for cash. It was this behavior pattern of bankers that led to one of President Roosevelt's bank reform measures—separation of commercial and investment banking functions.

Bank Failures

One of the occurrences that annoyed many depositors of commercial banks was the frequency with which the latter closed their doors. The annoyance came from the practice of depositors of carrying only small amounts of money on their persons. They had found that writing checks against their demand deposits was safer and more convenient than carrying money with them. Cancelled checks also offered evidence of payments having been made and when they were made. The fact of bank failures tended to weaken the confidence of depositors in our banking structure. The announcement of the closing of one bank in a community raised doubts in the minds of depositors of other banks concerning the soundness of the latter institutions. Many of these depositors withdrew their deposits and placed their temporary surplus funds in postal savings, or they may have hidden them somewhere in their homes. Banks in larger cities felt the impact of these withdrawals, the cumulative effect of which was to place a strain on them. Membership in the Federal Reserve System did not per se assure the liquidity of the assets of member banks, nor did it prevent bankers from assuming larger risks of investment than the principles of conservative banking practice dictated. Commodity prices were rising, security prices were rising rapidly, and bonds of public utility holding companies offered rates of return that were attractive. While member banks were not immune to failure, their record was much more favorable than that of state nonmember banks. Banking laws had not made good bankers or good banking. They were needed to protect an innocent public against the wiles of clever men who were in positions to influence banking policy and practice.

Member Banks Not Immune. Before drawing any conclusions too hastily from the data in Table 22-7, there are several facts which should be kept in mind, the first of which is that, in general, nonmember banks outnumbered member banks by a ratio of approximately 2 to 1. Secondly, more banks that were capitalized at $25,000 or less suspended their operations than did banks in any other classification according to capitalization. During the period 1921 through 1936, 1,700 member banks of this size suspended, while 7,000 nonmember banks of the same classification closed their doors. Largeness of bank capital appears to have added strength to banks, since the least number of failures during these years occurred in banks that were capitalized at $500,000 or more. Even so, good banking practice was better security for depositors than was the amount of bank capital.

Table 22-7
Bank Suspensions: Member and Nonmember—1921-1933

Year	Member Banks			Nonmember Banks		
	Total	National	State	Total	State	Private
1921	71	52	19	434	390	44
1922	62	49	13	305	282	23
1923	122	90	32	524	501	23
1924	160	122	38	615	578	37
1925	146	118	28	472	433	39
1926	158	123	35	818	766	52
1927	122	91	31	547	514	33
1928	73	57	16	426	407	19
1929	81	64	17	578	547	31
1930	188	161	27	1,164	1,106	58
1931	516	409	107	1,778	1,698	80
1932	311	276	35	1,125	1,088	37
1933	1,275	1,101	174	2,729	2,620	109
Totals	3,285	2,713	572	11,515	10,930	585

Source: *Historical Statistics of the United States. Colonial Times to 1957,* 1960, p. 636. Adapted.

An analysis of bank failures that may be more revealing than that of abstract numbers is the percentage of banks of all classifications that failed, followed by a breakdown of the percentage of failures of national banks, state member banks, and nonmember banks in each of these categories. These data include mutual savings banks, against whose deposits checks could not be drawn.

Losses of savings deposits were significant in framing attitudes towards banks and banking institutions. Many depositors had been looking to the future and had accumulated and deposited savings in the banks that would have enabled them to accomplish various objectives. Among these objectives were financing the college education of children, building or purchasing homes, financing vacation trips, helping to establish new homes for married sons and daughters, taking care of unexpected hospital and medical expenses, and providing income after retiring from years of active service. Losses of

Table 22-8
Bank Suspensions During Significant Periods

Period of Time	All Banks		National Banks			State Member Banks			National and State Nonmember Banks		
	Number	% of Banks, in Operation	Number	% of Suspensions	% of All Operating Banks	Number	% of Suspensions	% of All Operating Banks	Number	% of Suspensions	Operating % of All Banks
1921-29	5,411	19.8	766	14.1	9.6	229	4.2	15.6	4,416	81.6	24.7
1930-33	8,812	42.9	1,947	22.1	29.0	363	4.1	37.9	6,502	73.8	50.6
1921-36	14,344	61.6	2,719	18.9	37.9	592	4.1	47.8	11,033	76.9	74.2

Source: Basic data adapted from Federal Reserve *Banking Studies* (1941), p. 419.

savings made impossible the spending of money for any of these purposes, and probably for just as many more, and to this extent served to lower future demands for materials and services.

Losses of some savings, especially those that were in savings departments of commercial banks, contributed to the serious loss of confidence that depositors had in their banks and in banking in general. When commercial banks began to place charges for handling demand deposit accounts, some tellers in some banks told some of their customers who objected to having to pay these charges that they could transfer their accounts to the savings department and escape such payments. After complying with these suggestions, savings depositors could no longer use checks. They went on a cash basis. Imagine their reaction to having been told when they went to their banks to withdraw some of their savings that they would have to wait possibly 30 days to obtain their cash, because such notice was almost always

Table 22-9

Deposits of Suspended Banks
(000)

Year	Total	National	State Member	Nonmember	Private
1921	$ 172,188	$ 20,777	$ 17,363	$ 125,159	$ 8,889
1922	91,182	20,197	7,113	61,964	1,908
1923	149,601	34,244	12,559	101,025	1,773
1924	210,151	64,890	13,645	123,888	7,728
1925	167,555	55,574	9,883	94,547	7,551
1926	260,378	43,998	23,466	183,517	9,397
1927	199,329	45,547	17,942	131,503	4,337
1928	142,386	36,483	10,247	92,710	2,946
1929	230,643	41,614	16,459	164,858	7,712
1930	837,096	170,446	202,339	448,989	15,262
1931	1,690,232	439,171	293,957	935,957	21,157
1932	706,188	214,150	55,153	429,079	7,806
1933	3,596,698	1,610,549	783,399	1,189,469	13,281

Source: *Federal Reserve Bulletin,* Vol. 23 (September, 1937), pp. 873-877.

given before payments to depositors were completely suspended. Bank officials were only doing what they were empowered to do. The very nature of true savings deposits precluded their being withdrawn on demand, but competition among banks and between banks and other financial institutions at times when prices were rising and bank assets were easily liquidated appeared to have overcome the inherent dangers of such practice.

Some Impacts of Failures of Commercial Banks. The suspension of commercial banks had greater impacts upon the American economy than did suspensions of savings banks. More deposits had been created in the Federal Reserve System through borrowings by businessmen, firms, and corporations, than by deposits of actual cash. When these deposits were not available, thousands and thousands of depositors, firms and persons alike, were denied at least the temporary use of their money. The circulation of money and credit was slowed to a standstill, and the volume of business transactions declined rapidly and to a large extent. The fractional reserve plan to secure deposits had worked well when business had run along smoothly and people had confidence in banks and in the banking system. When, however, the confidence was lost, fractional reserves proved to be entirely inadequate to support deposit credit.

Brokers' Loans. A weakness that had existed for many years, but which had not been recognized as such, was the true position of brokers' loans in relation to the degree of liquidity of the banking system. For many years, banks throughout the nation had established correspondent relationships with banks in New York City. One reason for so doing was the large and active money market there. Banks that had cash reserves over and above their legal minimum requirements and that were not needed as *till money* deposited them in their correspondent banks in New York City. These banks lent their excess reserves on call or demand to brokers who were financing marginal transactions on the New York Stock Exchange for their customers. Such loans were and still are subject to renewal daily. If for any reason at all a bank refused to renew a loan, the broker or brokers who were affected borrowed from other banks in order to pay their loans to the initial bank. By this process reserves were really shifted from one bank or banks to others, the result of which was to redistribute excess reserves between New York City banks; and no new money was introduced into the banking system. The situation had been thought of in terms of liquidity—to a bank, yes; to all banks, no.

This fact was driven home in no unmistakable manner in 1929 when brokers were unable to borrow from other banks in order to repay call loans they had obtained from given banks. When their customers whom they were financing were unable to supply additional margins, their only recourse was to sell the securities that had been purchased on margins and which they held as collateral to protect their loans. When one or a few brokers sold such securities their volume was not sufficiently large to depress their market prices. However, when surplus reserves could not be shifted, and all brokers were compelled to unload their collateral holdings, the pressure of sales forced market quotations downward. The downward movement of stock prices forced brokers to sell additional securities, which action forced prices down still further. This behavior pattern contributed to the stock market crash in October, 1929, and others in former years. Had bankers appreciated the difference between the liquidity of a given bank and that of a system of banks, or that the liquidity of a given bank was attained only by shifting cash out of other banks, they might have been more cautious.

Federal Reserve Credit Policies

When World War I was over, the Federal Reserve Board began to exercise its right of control over bank credit which was one of the principal reasons why the system had been organized. The only instrument of credit control with which American banking authorities had had any practical experience was the discount rate. Moral suasion had been used with only moderate degrees of success. Open market operations had been authorized by the Federal Reserve Act, but American bankers were hesitant to engage in them for purposes of credit control because they did not know what impacts they would have either on the banks themselves or upon the American economy. Individual banks had been buying and selling government bonds throughout their entire years of existence, but these activities had been governed entirely by consideration of individual bank reserves and earnings potentials. There had been no systemic policies or concerted uniform actions by individual banks.

In order to encourage the use of *bankers' acceptances* in place of individual open book accounts, the Federal Reserve Board adopted a policy of always being ready and willing to purchase these instruments even at times when broader policy considerations had dictated otherwise. Federal Reserve Banks had never been ordered to sell bankers' acceptances from their investment portfolios in order to contract bank credit.

After prices had fallen and the country appeared to be on the threshold of an economic recession, the level of economic activity responded somewhat readily to a lowering of the rediscount rate at the opening of the 1920 decade. A year or so later the Board saw fit to raise the rediscount rate in order to check what it thought was an incipient inflationary trend. The tempo of the economy slowed down, and the Board was given a severe tongue-lashing by its critics for having put a stop to a nascent period of prosperity. There was direct and forceful evidence of the effectiveness of the Board's action in its control over bank credit.

Qualitative Control of Credit. The next development was an attempt to control bank credit qualitatively rather than quantitatively because of the feeling that quantitative controls that would permit inflationary or deflationary influences to operate in certain segments of the economy might become general. If investigation revealed that the resources that were available in the construction industry, for example, were being utilized to capacity, banks were instructed to limit the granting of additional credit to members of this industry. On the other hand, if a condition of excess capacity were found to exist in furniture manufacturing, directing additional bank credit into this channel might stimulate industrial activity therein. The presence of a time lag between the appearance of an adverse condition and action by the Board, combined with harsh criticism of the policy, caused the Board to give up qualitative methods of credit control.

Open Market Operations. The Board began to feel its way in the development of the other instrument of control that was given to it, namely, open market operations. These consisted of purchasing and selling government securities in the open market. It was found that when Federal Reserve Banks sold government bonds in the open market, member bank deposits in Federal Reserve Banks declined. Individual deposits in member banks likewise declined, and depositors had smaller balances against which they could write checks. Conversely, when Federal Reserve Banks purchased government bonds in the open market, both member bank deposits in Federal Reserve Banks and individual deposits in member banks increased. Here was an instrument of credit control that was *active*. Federal Reserve Banks could force member banks into certain reserve situations. Changes in rediscount rates were *passive* in that they gave encouragement to certain changes in the volume of bank credit, but could not enforce or compel them. If businessmen borrowers did not respond either to increases or decreases in discount rates, no changes in loans and in deposits ensued.

By 1926 the index number of wholesale prices had become somewhat stable, but thereafter prices of shares of corporate stock rose rapidly in response to an unprecedented wave of speculation at this level. Prior to the raising of the rate of discount on call loans by the New York Federal Reserve Bank, Montagu Norman, who was long time governor of the Bank of England, came to the United States for the sole purpose of trying to discourage such a move. England had returned to the prewar gold standard in 1925. Because the pound sterling was highly overvalued in the market and in terms of other currencies, the Bank of England was experiencing difficulty in retaining a gold reserve that was adequate to assure ready redeemability of the pound. Had the Federal Reserve Bank of New York raised its rediscount rate, its level would have been higher than that in England; and encouragement would have been given to the export of gold from England to New York at the very time England wanted to retain what it already had and to import more. The Federal Reserve authorities were torn in policy between attempting to prevent further stock market inflation in the United States and aiding England to remain on the gold standard with a highly overvalued currency. The decision was made to raise the rediscount rate. England remained on the gold standard for only another two short years. The United States passed through one of the most highly speculative eras the New York Stock Exchange had ever experienced.

Life Insurance

While life insurance in the United States is by no means a 20th century phenomenon, it has received greater and more general acceptance since World

War I than it experienced prior to this event. Selling insurance was strictly
a business at the time, and few efforts had been expended to elevate it to
the status of a profession until 1927, when the American College of Life
Underwriters was organized. Prior to 1910, insurance companies operated
on somewhat questionable levels of ethics as was revealed by the Armstrong
investigation in 1908. Since the publication of the report of this committee,
the several states had undertaken to regulate the organization and operation
of life insurance companies within their respective geographic boundaries.

For many years the insurance business was frequently combined with
selling real estate at the local level of operation, and there was a tendency for
agents to accept business when it was presented to them instead of their
taking the initiative to sell it. In fact, many local agents really did not know
what they were selling other than by name. Provisions of policy contracts
had been drawn up in legal terminology which only trained lawyers could
understand or interpret, and even they were sometimes confused. There was
no such thing as programming life insurance to meet the requirements of
policyholders. Life insurance policies were contracts to pay certain sums of
money to the beneficiaries named therein upon the death of the insured for
which the latter were required to pay regular premiums throughout the terms
of the contracts.

Public Awareness and Acceptance of Life Insurance. Several million
American men and boys took out government term insurance in amounts of
$10,000 during World War I. While some of the men permitted their policies
to expire after they returned to civilian life, many others converted their
policies from term contracts to some kind of reserve life insurance. Conversion had to take place within the organization of the government, but
additional insurance could be had only from free enterprise companies. The
awareness of insurance, together with new scales of living after the war,
new concepts of financial responsibilities towards families, new attitudes
towards the importance of educating children beyond the high school level,
and larger family incomes—all contributed to a greater acceptance of the
principles of life insurance by the American people than ever before. Some
persons were attracted to life insurance from the point of view of its investment potential. The rate of return was at least as high as it was on savings
accounts in banks; and, in addition, there was a contractual obligation to
pay premiums regularly, which feature was lacking in savings deposits.
There is no way of measuring their influences, but tying life insurance to
mortgage and installment transactions undoubtedly helped to popularize the
insurance principle.

The Status of Life Insurance Companies. In 1920, there were 335 life
insurance companies operating in the United States. They sold more than
four times as much insurance as 284 companies had sold in 1910. While
group insurance was not written until 1911, in 1920 a total of $441 million
was written to bring the total amount of group insurance in force to $1,570

million. The census reported 120,000 life insurance agents and brokers in
1920 and 258,000 in 1930. Not only did more people purchase more life
insurance throughout this span of ten years, more than twice as many persons
earned their livelihoods, in whole or in part, by selling it at the close of the
decade than did so at its opening. For some persons, selling insurance was a
part-time vocation in order to add to the amounts they earned from their
principal jobs or positions. Insurance companies became employers of thousands of white collar workers, not only in their home offices but also at the
district and local level. Typists, filing clerks, stenographers, receptionists,
statisticians and statistical clerks, actuaries, medical examiners, investment
experts, lawyers, credit men in many areas of specialty, and others found
employment in insurance company offices and many of the latter at relatively high salaries. Starting with statisticians, employee lists were scanned
for officer material; and promotions were more rapid than in other financial
institutions.

It was during this period that investments of life insurance companies had
a larger impact on the capital market than ever before. Insurance companies
not only became larger buyers of the offerings of investment banks, but they
began to absorb entire issues before they even arrived on the market and
had been given tests of the market. Prior to the war, life insurance companies had been making capital commitments quietly and without large or
disturbing impacts on capital markets. The upsurge in their business that
followed the return of peace provided them with large capital sums which,
by the very nature of their business, they were compelled to invest in
competition with capital that came from other sources.

Investment Trusts

There were thousands of persons of relatively small incomes and small
capital savings who were envious of other persons who were daring enough
to make direct investments in corporate common stocks, preferred stocks,
and bonds. A type of financial institution that had been known in Europe
for a number of years, but which had never been popular in the United
States, called the investment trust, was organized for the benefit of those
who were timid of the market, who did not have large sums to invest at
any one time, and who did not know how to manage their investments.
Shares in investment trusts were sold to such persons, whose incomes came
from the distribution of earnings income received by the managers of
investment trusts. These institutions were organized for the purpose of
buying stocks and/or bonds in operating concerns and holding them in
order to receive income. They differed from the holding companies that
were organized for the purpose of exercising control over operating
companies, in that they—the investment trusts—were not permitted to vote
the shares of common stock that were in their investment portfolios. The
holders of shares of investment trusts did not receive as large incomes as
did those who owned corporate shares directly due to the fact that the

managers and owners of the trusts deducted their salaries and costs of operation from their total income before distributing any income to the shareholders of the trusts.

Some investment trusts held widely diversified investments in their portfolios; others specialized in the holding of shares of specified types of companies, such as railroads, public utilities, mining companies, oil refining companies, and industrials. Some were permitted to make trading profits; others were restricted to purchasing and holding securities merely for the purpose of receiving income from them. Sometimes the investment of new capital sums was required to follow a definite pattern in maintaining a designated proportion of the securities of different kinds of companies in their portfolios. There were customer advantages and disadvantages to the several kinds of trusts according to the terms of their organization, so that all persons who were attracted to this kind of investment institution could find one or more to their liking.

PUBLIC UTILITIES AND RAILROAD REGULATION

The presentation of public utilities at this level will be confined almost entirely to electric light and power companies, recognizing all the time that water companies and gas companies are included in the category of public utilities. The developments that took place in these areas were largely internal as far as company organizations were concerned. Operating companies were combined at the level of ownership, and holding companies formed large networks of operating companies. It was difficult to make tie-ins in supplying water, and gas companies were organized that distributed gas to municipalities whence it was distributed locally by a local company. The impacts of financing these companies were not as forceful on the investing public as were the impacts of financing electric light and power companies.

Some Operating Principles of Public Utilities

The movement by which small generating plants were merged into large organizations was accelerated after the war. Small plants were either done away with entirely, or were kept to serve on a standby basis to help out during hours of peak load consumption or in times of emergency when service might otherwise have been interrupted. Economy of operation was found to exist in large-sized plants. Some municipalities undertook the function of supplying electric power to their citizenry. They had been furnishing supplies of water; and controlling the generation, distribution, and sale of electrical energy was merely an extension of an idea rather than the implementation of a new one. Many privately owned power companies operated retail outlets for the sale of electric appliances and durable consumer goods in order to promote a greater acceptance and use of electrical energy.

Within the limitation of capacity of a given generating plant, the industry was one of decreasing costs, and it was only natural for the companies to promote the use of their product. In the early years of the industry, generating plants were among the larger industrial users of bituminous coal. Even after the conservation movement dictated the construction of hydroelectric generating plants, steam power continued to generate more electrical energy than did waterpower. The capacity of a production unit had to be sufficiently large to provide the growth beyond the peak load of consumption at the time it was erected. The peak of consumption may have been for only a few hours of the 24 in a day. In order to increase the consumption of electrical energy at so-called off peak hours throughout the day and night, rate differentials were scheduled in order to encourage not only a greater use of electrical energy but a more even rate of consumption throughout a 24-hour cycle. Since the hours of peak load in one community did not always occur simultaneously with the hours of peak load in other communities, economies of operation were effected by providing for an interchange of energy between two or more communities. The next step in organizational development was the merging of small concerns into larger ones that resulted in the formation of giant light and power companies.

Holding Companies

Accompanying the physical tying together of generating plants and the merging of small operating units into larger ones was a unique development of public utility holding companies, one of the main features of which was their financial structure. The issuance of voting and nonvoting shares of common stock, together with the use of preferred stocks and bonds in the financing of these companies, kept their control in the hands of a relatively few men who furnished a small percentage of the capital required. From another point of view it resulted in investment opportunities to many who either did not care to or who could not exercise any control over the companies in which their capital was invested. Pyramiding corporate issues in public utility companies channeled power and control over vast corporate empires into the hands of a few promoter utility magnates.

The success of such financial operations depended upon the existence of a ready market for public utility stocks and bonds, and such a market did exist throughout most of the years of the decade of the 1920's. To start with, let us assume that the management of a public utility holding company issued as many shares of Class B common stock as it issued of Class A common stock, the latter carrying no right to vote at stockholders' meetings. Nonvoting preferred stock was frequently issued in amounts equal to the cumulative total of Class A and Class B common stock. To complete the financial structure, bonds equal in face value to twice the amount of corporate stock may have been authorized. At this level of organization the financial structure may have been similar to the following pattern:

Capitalization of a utility holding company—

Common stock:

Class A (Nonvoting)	$ 1,000,000
Class B (Voting)	1,000,000
Preferred stock	2,000,000
Bonds	8,000,000
Total	$12,000,000

Control of this hypothetical concern could be obtained through the ownership of $501,000 of Class B common stock. Now assume that the directors of this holding company authorized the purchase of Class B voting shares of common stock in one or more holding companies and operating companies as well whose capital structures conformed to the pattern shown above. At this level of organization, the financial structure of the holding company would then appear as follows:

Class A Common Stock	$ 12,000,000
Class B Common Stock	12,000,000
Preferred Stock	24,000,000
Bonds	96,000,000
Total	$144,000,000

At this point, an original investment of $501,000 controlled an empire that was capitalized at $144,000,000. The possibilities of expansion were unlimited, and in practice they turned out exactly that way. The names of a few of the more spectacular utility holding companies may serve to bring to mind others that collapsed under their own weight and added to the loss of confidence the American people had in their industrial leaders and in their economic organization. Electric Bond and Share, Associated Gas and Electric, United Corporation, and Mid-West Utilities were a few of the corporate bodies whose names were prominently and frequently spread across financial and news pages.

Railroads and the Transportation Act of 1920

The control of railroad operations by the federal government in 1918 was intended to continue throughout the remaining years of war. After the armistice became effective, public opinion favored the return of the railroads to private management. Pressure was also brought by railway labor and by investors in railroad securities, neither of whom wanted government control to remain in effect long enough for it to become in the nature of permanent policy. The terms of the Transportation Act of 1920 unveiled entirely new objectives of railroad regulation, most of which were the outgrowth of experiences of the Railroad Administration. The Act authorized the Interstate Commerce Commission to consolidate the railroads in such a manner that the strong ones, financially, would absorb the weaker ones. Rates were to be adjusted to yield a fair rate of return on the value of railroad properties. One half of the excess earnings over the fair rate was to be "re-captured" by the Interstate Commerce Commission to serve as a fund from which weak roads could borrow. The tenor of the investment market made it difficult for railroad managements to attract outside capital in order to finance improvements to their properties. The re-capture clause was repealed in 1933.

Pooling was permitted with the approval of the Interstate Commerce Commission. Wasteful practices of competition were abolished. Where practical, the joint use of railroad terminals was required. The Commission was unable to present a plan of consolidation that was acceptable to the railroads and the initiative for so-doing was returned to free enterprise.

Railroad bonds had lost much of their attractiveness to conservative investors and railroads were unable to borrow in the open market without adding more to fixed costs, which were already too high in terms of operating revenues that were available to finance them. Capital improvements were financed out of earnings and at the expense of lower rates of return on equity capital.

Many improvements on the physical capital of railroads were made in the name of increased efficiencies. In order to operate longer and heavier trains, heavier rails were laid, bridges were widened and strengthened, and heavier locomotives with added horse power were constructed. New freight cars with increased capacity, and longer passenger cars enabled railroads to transport more traffic without increasing the number of trains and the amount of labor employed. Railroad managements were burdened with increased costs of labor at a time when operating revenues were decreasing, or at best remaining constant. Motor transportation facilities had begun to capture a sufficiently large proportion of total traffic to offer serious competition to the railroads for the first time in over 70 years.

AMERICAN INVESTMENTS ABROAD

By the turn of the 20th century, American investors had become interested in investing some of their loanable funds in securities of foreign corporations and of foreign governments. Insofar as savings were invested through the media of corporate stock, the investments were portfolio in character; and any rights of control that accompanied the ownership of such instruments were not exercised. Insofar as loanable funds were invested in corporate bonds, they returned contractual rates of interest, and they represented savings out of personal incomes that had found outlets in foreign industrial channels.

Need for Capital in Europe

After the war a functional approach to the analysis of the investment of American capital in foreign countries reveals the fact that foreign peoples not only no longer had capital of their own which was available for investment abroad, they lacked sufficient savings to meet the requirements of their own domestic economies. Deficiencies in the volume of domestic capital were made up by borrowing from investors in other countries. Insofar as they borrowed capital from residents or institutions of the United States, these capital sums became American investments in foreign countries.

Among the causes of the deficiency of domestic capital in foreign countries was the decline in the national incomes of these countries out of which savings could have been effected. Foreign economies were so badly disorganized by the war and the ensuing unrest that production did not meet their own requirements, let alone produce surpluses that were available for export to foreign markets. This was, therefore, the background for European countries ceasing to be creditors of the United States and of their becoming debtor nations. This meant that the United States had given up its traditional role of debtor nation for that of creditor. Just as the English people had formerly lent to people in the United States in order to finance commodity exports from England to the United States, *so did American investors lend to buyers in foreign countries in order to finance our commodity exports to them.* The continuation of a large volume of exports throughout the decade of the 1920's depended upon the continued investment of American capital in foreign securities.

Based upon average unit values of exports and imports for 1923-25, the index of exports declined from 100 in 1925 to 87 in 1929; the index value of imports declined from 105 in 1925 to 87 in 1929. The decline in the value of imports did not support the former high level of exports. The decline in foreign trade penetrated our domestic economy, the impact of which was felt in manufacturing, transportation, and domestic trade. This decline was among the early indicators of a slowdown of the pace of economic activity.

There is no evidence to support the thesis that American savings became available for investment abroad because of a reduction in the need for capital in the United States. It was a matter of our national income having become so large that persons were able to save larger capital sums than could be invested profitably in the United States. Again, it was not an absence of profit potentials in the United States as much as it was the presence of greater interest return on foreign investment.

The above presentation is necessary to understand the real impacts of the default of foreign bonds in later years. American investors provided foreign concerns with dollar balances in American banks that were used in paying General Motors Corporation, Du Pont, General Electric, and other American corporations that exported their products to foreign countries throughout the decade. They had been paid before any of the bonds were in default. It was the American bondholders, banks, and other institutions and individuals that failed to receive further interest income and returns of principal sums that had been invested.

MARKETS

In addition to changes in housing patterns, in family work patterns, in recreational interests and opportunities, in the manner of dress, in the financial structure, and in means of transportation, changes in market organization and in marketing functions added to the excitement of the decade. Competition by retail merchants for the consumer's dollar resulted either in an actual lowering of prices or, as was more frequently the case, in not raising prices to conform to increases in wholesale costs, or at least to increases in the costs of making their goods ready for consumers. Some of these costs were commodity costs, others were at the levels of services and labor. In many instances rents were raised at the termination of lease contracts that ran for definite time periods. Interest on borrowed capital also tended to rise. The net result of all these cost increases was to narrow the margins of residual income that belonged to the owner-operators of retail outlets.

Price Differentials

In the sale of many farm products in which there was little processing done between farms and ultimate consumers, other than packaging, the gap between consumer prices and farm prices was widening. This was the result of several conditions, all of which were disturbing to farmers and consumers alike. The farmers complained because they received such low prices, especially in comparison with prices at the retail level, and consumers complained because they were required to pay prices that were so much higher than the farmers received. Some seasonal situations arose during which lower prices at the farm level were not reflected in lower prices at the consumer retail level. In other situations when farm prices rose, consumer prices rose still more. Middlemen somewhere up and down the line appeared to have contributed to rising prices and to have resisted falling prices. Incomes received from the sale of farm products were not distributed equally among persons at all levels at which the commodities had been handled.

Chain Stores

Some retail store employees found that they could obtain higher wage rates of pay in other lines of work. Rather than increase the wages of such employees in order to keep them, store managers sought new patterns of organization that did away with their performing certain functions that had become somewhat traditional and simultaneously decreased their need for such employees. Among the reorganizations that were effected was reducing delivery service, and having this service performed by parcel delivery companies. Sometimes small fees were charged per package delivered, and the service was organized in such a manner that only one delivery per day was made in a given quadrant in a city. Other store managers rearranged their goods on their shelves in order to permit a greater selection of items by their customers. This was also a device by which the volume of retail sales was increased. Telephone services were reduced or abolished entirely, and open book charge accounts were discouraged by giving small discounts for cash purchases. This increased the flow of cash income and decreased the cost of bookkeeping and collection of accounts. The organization and operation of chain specialty stores became popular with everybody except the owners of homeowned stores who found it difficult to compete with them. Chain stores usually did their own wholesaling and operated their own trucks in delivering their goods to their retail outlets. Some of them sold items that were packaged and labeled with their own brand names. Other items that traditionally had been sold in bulk were prepackaged with their weights and prices stamped thereon.

New Patterns of Shopping

Patterns of shopping by housewives underwent significant changes. When wives and mothers worked all day, they had little time and less inclination to prepare meals, and delicatessen stores thrived on their patronage on workdays. Wives and also husbands began to bring their groceries and other purchases home with them after their working hours were over. Since deep freezes and freezing compartments in refrigerators either were unknown or were not in general use, only two or three days' supply of perishable foods was purchased at one time.

Working husbands and working wives, or working husbands driving to work in their family automobiles, set the pattern for two-car families. This level of living was memorialized in the latter years of the decade when President Coolidge set the goal of attainment for the level of living of the American people to include not only a two-car garage in every yard, but two cars in it. Forms of public transportation were giving way to privately owned and operated automobiles. Streets were being used for parking. Parking lots and parking garages came to the rescue of persons who went shopping in their cars and others who drove to work in their automobiles. Livery stables and hitching posts gave way to automobile service stations and garages. Horse-drawn vehicles disappeared from the streets, but policemen continued to cover their beat on horseback. Mounted policemen were much more mobile than patrolmen, and they were able to handle traffic congestions and other difficult situations more easily.

Store personnel and shoppers were caught in the throes of heavy traffic jams. Downtown city traffic always had been dense, but now it called for some rearrangement of business locations. When people rode public transportation facilities and stores provided free delivery of purchases, the advantages of store locations on busy streets were many. Under the new patterns that have been described, downtown locations were becoming outmoded. Shopping areas were being extended. They began to encroach upon traditional residential areas. In some cities there were some definite trends towards a regrouping of stores in given neighborhoods, which became the first neighborhood shopping centers, but they were of an entirely different organizational setup and pattern from those that sprang up after World War II.

THE STOCK MARKET CRASH

It is unfortunate to have to close the analysis and description of the economic development of an era that was as exciting and apparently as prosperous as were the 1920's on a discordant note, but the sudden turn of events makes this necessary. In the spring of 1929, there was a rather violent reaction in the stock market, but most well informed persons seem to think it was the result of speculators attempting to realize some of their paper profits. This may have been the case, but the action was much stronger than any similar profit taking in past years. This was the proving ground for the liquidity of brokers' loans. This was the time when people in banking circles learned the difference between true liquidity for a system of banks and the shiftability of reserves from certain banks to others.

Business indicators pointed to conditions of recession all through the summer months. It is difficult to measure how much the stock market reflected business conditions and how much it may have caused them. Undoubtedly at a time like 1929 there was a mutual reaction. Several events had occurred in both the business and the financial world that had shaken the confidence that people had placed in men of prominence and leadership. The thinking seemed to have followed a pattern of, "If we can't trust these men to be honest, straightforward, and sincere in their business and financial relationships, what about men of less prominence, but who at the same time occupy positions of responsibility?"

Once the movement got started there seemed to be no question but that the inability of marginal buyers of securities to furnish additional margins, combined with brokers' inability to shift bank reserves from certain banks to others, forced a wholesale and unprecedented selling of securities. Each fall in the market forced brokers to call for additional margins that were not forthcoming, and more forced sales ensued. This round of affairs could not continue forever, and the complete collapse occurred on Tuesday, October 29, 1929. Time and space do not permit a long, detailed description and analysis of what happened prior to and after the collapse. Should the reader be interested in and concerned about these events, he is referred to a book entitled *The Great Crash*, by Professor John K. Galbraith.[1] The aftermath of the crash was unemployment, falling prices, business failures, bank failures,

---

[1] John Kenneth Galbraith, *The Great Crash* (Sentry ed.; Boston: Houghton Mifflin Company, 1961).

and a general stagnation of business. Conditions did recover for a short time, only to experience a relapse which comprises the general topic of discussion in the following chapter.

QUESTIONS FOR REVIEW

1. To what extent did the mechanization of the American economy extend to farms?

2. How did the mechanization of farms contribute to lower prices of cereal grains?

3. How did the federal government come to the aid of farmers in providing financial assistance to them after 1920?

4. Explain the statement that farmers were experiencing conditions of depression when members of the industrial and commercial segments of our economy were experiencing prosperity.

5. Explain clearly why brokers' loans were shiftable but not liquid as far as Federal Reserve member banks were concerned.

6. Explain clearly the economic impacts of open market purchases by Federal Reserve Banks.

7. In what different ways may the growth and development of life insurance companies have contributed to conditions of prosperity in the 1920's?

8. Show how and why one segment of the American economy financed commodity exports to Europe after 1920.

9. Account for two significant changes in the organization and functioning of markets.

SUGGESTED READINGS

Barnes, James A. *Wealth of the American People.* Englewood Cliffs, N. J.: Prentice-Hall, Inc., 1949. Chapter 32.

Dillard, Dudley. *Economic Development of the North Atlantic Community.* Englewood Cliffs, N. J.: Prentice-Hall, Inc., 1967. Chapter 32.

Jones, Peter d'A. *The Consumer Society.* Baltimore, Md.: Penguin Books, Inc., 1965. Chapter 9.

Letwin, William (ed.). *Documentary History of American Economic Policy Since 1789.* Chicago: Aldine Publishing Company, 1962. Section K.

Range, Willard. "The Landed and the Landless: Georgia Agriculture, 1920-1940," *United States Economic History: Selected Readings,* edited by Harry N. Scheiber. New York City: Alfred A. Knopf, Inc., 1964.

Simonson, G. R. "The Demand for Aircraft and the Aircraft Industry, 1907-1958," *United States Economic History: Selected Readings,* edited by Harry N. Scheiber. New York City: Alfred A. Knopf, Inc., 1964.

Soule, George. *Prosperity Decade: From War to Depression, 1917-1929.* New York City: Holt, Rinehart & Winston, Inc., 1947. Chapters 11-15.

Wright, Chester W. *Economic History of the United States.* 2d ed. New York City: McGraw-Hill Book Company, 1949. Chapter 43.

Chapter 23

CRISIS, PANIC, AND RELIEF

CRISIS

Several indications of impending economic disorganization were casting their shadows on the horizon of the American economy in the closing years of the most prosperous and exciting decade the United States had experienced. According to the Bureau of the Census, with a labor force of approximately 46 million people in 1927, and 47 million in 1928, unemployment increased from 1,890,000 in 1927 to 2,080,000 the following year. Many persons thought that the reduction in the number of unemployed in 1929 to 1,550,000, accompanied as it was by an increase in the labor force to 48 million persons, showed the economy was operating on a sound basis.

The most spectacular manifestation of impending economic disaster was the stock market crash in October, 1929. It was followed by months of uncertainty that bordered on recession, later by increased unemployment, falling prices, and lower wages. Banks continued to fail. The continuation of our large volume of commodity exports depended upon the continued investment of American capital in foreign securities. Production of commodities that comprised our exports depended upon the same factor. Continued production of these commodities meant continued employment of labor, payment of wages, distribution of corporate dividends, and payments of interest on borrowed capital. Volume of transportation, sales of automobiles and durable consumers' goods, the completion of installment purchase contracts, and payments on mortgages on land and on buildings—all depended to a large extent upon the continued investment of American capital abroad. In addition, the financial success of foreign shipping, shipbuilding, the operation of overseas vessels, the employment of ship crews and of longshoremen, depended upon the level of foreign investment. Other weaknesses in agriculture, in building construction, and in banking continued to harass the American people and to shake their confidence in the continued growth of the American economy.

Herbert Hoover had been elected President of the United States after a campaign that was hotly contested over the radio. He had revealed his organizational ability in feeding the starving peoples of Europe during and after World War I. His term of office as Secretary of Commerce in the cabinets of Presidents Harding and Coolidge had enhanced his prestige among the electorate. In his religious affiliation he was not a Roman Catholic as was his opponent, the former Governor of New York, Alfred E. Smith. He had been selected as the man who was best qualified to continue the programs of Harding and Coolidge under whose guidance the American economy had performed on unprecedentedly high levels. The graft at high levels of administration in Washington during Harding's administration had not gone unnoticed, but the real impacts of maladministration were salved over by high levels of profits and of employment.

Resort To Tariffs

Since the terms of the Fordney-McCumber Act of 1922 had not provided the degree of relief for American agriculture that had been promised by its advocates, another tariff measure was in order; at least it was consistent with the program of the Republican party since it gained power in Washington in 1861. The idea was to keep imported products out of American markets in order to create home markets for the products of American farms and to provide employment for American labor. There was nothing original in these ideas. That it might make consumers pay higher prices for food and for manufactured goods was looked upon favorably by many authorities.

The Hawley-Smoot Tariff. The effects of raising tariff rates on imported commodities in accordance with the terms of the Hawley-Smoot Bill were not overlooked. They were ignored. A memorial was drawn up in which were shown the probable effects of raising tariff rates on commodity imports at a time when the American export-import trade had begun to decline. It brought out the fact that retaliatory measures probably would be taken by Canada and by European countries, the effects of which would be to lower their levels of commodity imports from the United States. This memorial was signed by over 1,000 professional economists and presented to President Hoover for his consideration. He ignored the warnings as being of academic concern only and proceeded to sign the Tariff Act of 1930 which raised rates even higher than they had been under the Fordney-McCumber Act of 1922, and to the highest level in history. This was a return to a program of economic nationalism and isolation at a time when world conditions demanded economic international cooperation to raise the level of activity at home and abroad. Reaction to this most untimely measure was immediate, and countries that had been accepting imports from the United States raised their import duties on these commodities. Signed by the President on July 17, 1930, the Hawley-Smoot Bill has been labeled one of the most serious blunders of the Hoover administration.

Decline in Export-Import Trade. In 1929 commodity exports amounted to $5,157 million. In 1930 they declined to $3,781 million, or by 26.6

Table 23-1

Value of Merchandise Exports and Imports by Economic Classes— 1929-1940 (millions)

	Merchandise Exports						Merchandise Imports						
		Foodstuffs		Manufactures				Foodstuffs		Manufactures			
Year	Total	Crude Mater- ials	Crude	Manu- factured	Semi-	Fin- ished	Total	Crude Mater- ials	Crude	Manu- factured	Crude Mater- ials	Semi-	Fin- ished
1929	$5,157	$1,142	$270	$484	$729	$2,532	$4,399	$1,559	$539	$424	$885	$994	
1930	3,781	829	179	363	513	1,898	3,061	1,002	400	293	608	757	
1931	2,378	567	127	247	318	1,120	2,091	642	305	222	372	549	
1932	1,576	514	89	152	197	624	1,323	358	233	174	217	341	
1933	1,647	591	48	155	237	617	1,450	418	216	201	292	322	
1934	2,100	653	59	168	342	879	1,636	461	254	264	307	350	
1935	2,243	683	59	157	350	994	2,039	582	322	319	410	406	
1936	2,419	670	58	144	393	1,154	2,424	733	349	386	490	466	
1937	3,299	731	105	178	669	1,617	3,010	971	413	440	634	551	
1938	3,057	607	249	184	494	1,523	1,950	576	260	311	385	418	
1939	3,123	545	111	202	599	1,667	2,276	745	291	313	487	440	
1940	3,934	464	74	167	900	2,330	2,541	1,011	285	277	559	409	

Source: U.S. Department of Commerce, Bureau of the Census, *Historical Statistics of the United States. Colonial Times to 1957* (Washington: U.S. Government Printing Office, 1960), p. 544. Adapted.

percent. Exports of crude materials, excluding foodstuffs, declined 27 percent; those of crude foodstuffs declined 34 percent, and of manufactured foodstuffs, 25 percent. Exports of manufactured goods, finished, declined 25 percent, of semimanufactured goods, 29.6 percent. These data indicate that of all segments of our economy that participated in our export trade, agriculture was harmed more than were manufactures, and the Act was passed in order to give aid to American farmers.

The decline in commodity imports in 1930 compared with those for 1929 was 29 percent. Broken down into classes of commodities, the imports of manufactured goods declined 20.7 percent; those of finished manufactures, 23.8 percent; of semimanufactures, 31.6 percent. Imports of foodstuffs declined 28 percent and those of crude materials—nonfoods—declined 35 percent. If the impact of the Hawley-Smoot Bill did not create a home market, it at least was partially successful in keeping foreign manufactured goods away from our shores. The importance of our foreign trade was not found in its volume in absolute numbers; it was found in the manner in which it had been stimulated by the investment of American capital abroad and in the interdependence between it and aspects of our domestic economy—manufacturing, trade, and the employment of labor.

Default of Foreign Obligations, Debt Moratorium

By 1930 the failure on the part of foreign nations to pay their international obligations was more than a manifestation of their feeling of animosity towards the United States. It was brought on by the fact that commodity prices in foreign countries had fallen so far below the price level which existed when the debts were created that it was impossible for these nations to service their debts. Added to this was the decline in their commodity exports, due to some extent to the fact that the United States had taken over some of the markets to which European countries had formerly exported. Their situation was similar to that of the American farmers ten years earlier, at which time the latter lost their foreign markets and prices fell to levels that made it impossible for them to service their debts.

International financial obligations were ignored. Germany had not been making payments to the Reparations Committee. Other European countries that were debtor to the United States—with the sole exception of Finland—were not remitting capital sums when due. In order to relieve the pressure on gold and the anxiety that arose from nonpayment of obligations to the United States, President Hoover declared a 1-year moratorium on the payment of international obligations. This action relieved pressure on the balances of foreign nations in American banks and delayed a further movement of gold into the United States. It also legalized the nonpayment of capital sums that were due the United States and removed any unfavorable impacts of the situation. The impacts of having become a mature creditor nation were new to the United States.

Unemployment

The whistling-in-the-dark policy of giving publicity to statements of leading bankers and industrialists in an effort to bolster confidence in the soundness of the American economy and to check the trends towards increased unemployment and reductions in wages and salaries was entirely unsuccessful and ineffective. Corporate employers could not afford to continue to pay the same wage rates to the same number of employees in the face of declining volumes of business. The impacts of unemployment were felt beyond the level of unemployed workers themselves. Persons who were kept on payrolls did not know how long it would be until they were listed among the unemployed, and they became cautious in spending their wage and salary incomes. Unemployment was no longer endemic; it had become epidemic.

Inadequacy of Relief. Charitable organizations that were supported by voluntary contributions were unable to meet the demands that were made upon them for relief of all sorts. Breadlines formed daily in communities both large and small. Physical facilities were taxed to the limit. County and municipal agencies got into the act of providing relief, but their financial resources were unable to stand the strain, as their fiscal programs in years past had not included such items for relief. Tent villages and "Hoovervilles" sprang up along railroad rights-of-way, under bridges over streams of water, in twilight zones near the outskirts of cities and towns. In coal mining communities they were found on slag piles where heat from the ashes provided warmth for the squatters. Packing boxes, piano boxes, old streetcars and buses provided bases upon which many shanty towns were built. Their inhabitants were unwashed; they were hungry and cold in season; and with it all, they were surprisingly orderly for persons who were in such desperate and destitute circumstances. They scavenged garbage cans and trucks, dumping grounds, and refuse matter to salvage any little bits of fuel, clothing, or food. They walked along railroad tracks to pick up lumps of coal that may have fallen from locomotive tenders. Other people slept in public parks, in subways, and in railroad stations. Some even rode subway trains all night because they offered shelter and warmth. Any shelter was better than none at all.

Associated charities, church organizations, county and city poor farms, YMCA's, and similar organizations were not equipped financially or physically to handle the volume of charitable work that was in urgent need of being done. Bread lines were many and lengthy before government relief agencies were organized and made effective. Individuals were licensed to sell apples on street corners or to peddle them through office buildings to salaried persons who still had employment. They were found at entrances to buildings, to stores, and to subways in large cities. Selling apples may not have yielded net returns as large as the peddlers had received when they worked on a hourly basis in industry, but at least they were making honest efforts to earn some kind of money income. One reason many people fell into the spirit of this kind of merchandising was because they themselves may have been compelled to cut down on their expenditures for food, for snacks, or for lunches; and apples were good eating.

Table 23-2
Unemployment in the United States—1927-1940

1927	1,890,000		1934	11,340,000
1928	2,080,000		1935	10,610,000
1929	1,550,000		1936	9,030,000
1930	4,340,000		1937	7,700,000
1931	8,020,000		1938	10,390,000
1932	12,060,000		1939	9,480,000
1933	12,830,000		1940	8,120,000

Source: *Historical Statistics of the United States. Colonial Times to 1957*, 1960, p. 73. Adapted.

The Administration's Philosophy on Relief. The economic philosophy of the administration in Washington precluded the taking of any direct action at the federal level to bring about either relief or recovery. The several states, counties, municipalities, and free enterprise had these responsibilities, and there was no valid reason for the federal government assuming them. Appeals were made directly to corporate officers and boards of directors not to create situations of worsening unemployment and to maintain levels of wage payments. The psychology of the program was that when people read in the papers that our industrial leaders gave expression to their confidence in the American economy on a free enterprise basis, people would not panic and would continue their respective economic programs at the same levels as theretofore. Committees were appointed by the President to make thorough investigations and studies of certain aspects of our economy and to report directly to him. Publicity that was given to the contents of these reports was intended to instill confidence in people and to give direction to measures that might be taken at the level of free enterprise to bolster the economy.

One of the most essential steps that could have been taken, according to President Hoover, was to balance the budget. Pressure had been placed on him to undertake a program of public works in order to create employment, to put money into circulation, and to produce activity at the level of construction. This would have stimulated orders for heavy earth-moving equipment, for iron and steel, for cement and concrete work, for stone, heavy timber, and sand, for automobiles and motor trucks, and for railway transportation. In line with his policy of not having the federal government go into debt in order to provide relief, the President hesitated to borrow money unless its use provided income with which to service and eventually retire the debt.

The Reconstruction Finance Corporation

In accordance with the philosophy that prevention of further economic disaster was better than cure, Congress, as an emergency measure, authorized the organization of the Reconstruction Finance Corporation, whose charter would expire in two years, or in 1934.[1] In addition to its capital of $500 million, which was provided entirely by the government, it was authorized to issue tax free debentures to a maximum of $1,500 million that were guaranteed by the government. Capital sums were to be loaned to certain firms and organizations to keep them from failing. It was hoped that, in this manner, confidence in the American economy would be restored more positively. Prevention of business and financial failures and bankruptcies would avoid delays or actual default in the payment of interest obligations. Other positive benefits might be the maintenance of levels of employment and of wage rates as well as those of total wage payments. Bonds that had been issued in prior years and at rates of interest that were current at the dates of issue could be refinanced in line with the lower rates of interest that were current after 1932. This was an opportunity that was offered to business firms to lower their fixed charges that had to be met out of incomes that were lower than those at the times of original issue. Railroads, public utilities, banks, insurance companies, and industrial concerns were the direct beneficiaries of the activities of the Reconstruction Finance Corporation.

Extension of Activities. In July, 1932, the lending power of the Corporation was increased by $1,800 million. Its area of influence was extended to include loans to states and to public and private agencies in order to promote the construction of self-liquidating projects that were of public benefit. Some idea of the extent to which its credit helped bolster concerns that were on the brink of financial collapse may be gained from the fact that during the first 18 months of its operations it loaned a total of $3 billion. In order to prevent any collusion in the granting of loans the names of corporate borrowers were to be made public. This part of the program boomeranged because it made people aware for the first time that the borrowers were in financial straits. Instead of borrowing from the Corporation having been regarded as an element of financial strength, it was interpreted in terms of financial weakness.

The Dawes Bank Incident. Charles G. Dawes, formerly Vice President of the United States during the Coolidge administration and later president of a large commercial bank in Chicago, Illinois, was the Corporation's first President. Shortly after he resigned as President of the Reconstruction Finance Corporation to return to the bank in Chicago, the bank obtained a $90 million dollar loan from the Corporation. When this revelation was made in the press in the latter part of 1932, a scandal appeared to be in

[1] Its charter was renewed until 1953, at which time the RFC was reorganized to become The Small Business Administration.

the process of being exposed. The Dawes bank in Chicago was a correspondent to hundreds of smaller banks throughout the entire Middle Western States, many of which were located in agricultural regions. Had it been permitted to close its doors, these correspondent banks would have been forced to suspend payments to their depositors; and thousands of the latter would have had still more thousands of dollars of demand deposits frozen to them. Had this event been permitted to occur, a bank crisis undoubtedly would have occurred, the likes of which were unknown in American history. In justice to Mr. Dawes, to his bank, and to the Corporation itself, it must be stated that the bank not only paid the principal of the loan in full, but the $23 million interest obligation.

PANIC

Unemployment and its relief, failures of business firms, defaults of interest payments and of principal sums when due, and falling prices were aspects of economic recessions. When the weight of their cumulative impacts brought about a collapse of our banking structure panic conditions ensued.

Bank Failures

Outside of the psychological factor, loss of the use of bank deposits was the most serious impact of the failures of commercial banks. The failure of over 5,000 such banks in 1930-32 inclusive resulted in at least a temporary loss of over $3 billion in deposit currency. Fear swept the country; and customers of banks that had not failed began to wonder if, perhaps, some of them eventually would do so in the indefinite future. To guard against this possibility becoming a reality, depositors began to withdraw their deposits and by so doing brought failure to some banks that from almost every kind of credit analysis were sound institutions. The money that was withdrawn was placed in safety deposit boxes, deposited in Postal Savings, or was carried on the persons of former depositors. Deposit banking, in which fractional reserves were maintained, required and depended upon about as large a volume of new deposits being made as were withdrawn. When cash withdrawals greatly exceeded new deposits, and investment portfolios had to be liquidated at large losses in order to have cash with which to meet withdrawals, many banks were forced to close their doors. State and national banking laws required banks to remain open every regular business day throughout regular banking hours.

Bank Holiday. In order to assist the banks and to ease the pressure of depositors upon their reserves and to give them time to liquidate some of their assets, Governors of several states, including those of Michigan, Ohio, and Illinois, decreed that holiday hours be observed for several days in early 1933. In addition to banks, other types of business firms closed their doors. The frequency of urban transportation services was reduced; all factories, wholesale and retail establishments were closed, except those that traditionally remained open on these days. People did not need pocket money because there were no ways of spending it, and the need for writing checks on their banks did not exist. Contract payments that fell due during these days were extended without penalty to the next regular business day.

During the closing days of the Hoover administration conditions continued to grow worse, and by the time Franklin D. Roosevelt was inaugurated as President of the United States they had become so critical that one of his first official acts was to close all banks on March 6. One week later the sound banks began to open on an unrestricted basis. To state the facts a little more accurately, the banks closed for the weekend on Saturday, as usual, while Hoover was still President. They failed to open on Monday which was the first complete business day of the new administration. In order that the onus of the collapse of the banks rest on the shoulders of the previous administration, President Roosevelt made it clear that it was his job to reopen them. People were surprisingly calm throughout the crisis, during which the Comptroller of the Currency was in charge of all national banks.

Banks Reopened. Only those banks that were or had become 100 percent liquid during the holiday were given licenses to open on an unrestricted basis. About 2,000 others that were temporarily short of cash in relation to their volume of demand deposits were placed in charge of *conservators*, who "conserved" the assets of their respective banks in the interests of depositors. These banks were opened on a restricted basis. They could accept new deposits, against which 100 percent reserves were maintained; and depositors were permitted to draw against them freely. Deposits that were in these banks when the holiday was declared were frozen against their being used until their conservators were able to liquidate investment portfolios in more leisurely markets.

About 3,000 banks failed to open, and after a reasonable length of time, restricted banks whose conservators had been unable to restore liquidity to their assets were either merged with other banks or were closed permanently. All possible steps were taken to reopen as many banks as could reasonably be expected to meet their depositors' demands for cash. Some banks that should have been closed permanently were licensed to reopen on a restricted basis. That some of the latter institutions turned out to be in sound condition is attested to by the few bank failures that occurred throughout the first seven years of the operation of the Federal Deposit Insurance Corporation. The *Federal Reserve Bulletin* of June, 1933, reported that 1,163 member banks with total deposits of $1,856,427,000 were still operating on a restricted basis at the end of May of that year.

Bank Reform Legislation

In his preelection campaign speeches, Franklin D. Roosevelt expressed his bitterness towards members of the banking profession, particularly those who had broken faith with their customers who had given expression to their confidence in banks by relying upon the judgments of their officers and by maintaining deposit balances in their banks. Since he placed much of the responsibility for the failure of many banks directly on their shoulders, bank reform legislation was given high priority on his legislative calendar and in June, 1933, the Emergency Banking Act was passed by Congress. Since this legislation was recognized as a temporary measure that was drawn up somewhat hastily, it was superseded by the Bank Act of 1935, which incorporated and made permanent many of the provisions of the earlier Act.

Bank Acts of 1933 and 1935. In order to extend the benefits of membership in the Federal Reserve System, Morris Plan Banks were made eligible for membership upon application. In order to meet the minimum capital requirements for membership, mutual savings institutions whose surpluses and undivided profits equaled the capital requirements for corporate institutions were made eligible for membership.

The Reconstruction Finance Corporation was authorized to subscribe to and to purchase, when called upon to do so, preferred stock, capital notes, and debentures of banks and trust companies. In implementing this authority the RFC authorized or made agreements to purchase the preferred stock of 3,278 banks and trust companies in the amount of $659,380,000; capital notes of 183 institutions that amounted to $165,790,000; and debentures of 2,452 institutions in the amount of $225,811,050. Of the total sum of $1,050,981,050, only $640,033,292 was actually expended. In addition to these subscriptions to bank capital, loans in an aggregate amount of $762,487,050 were authorized to reorganize or liquidate 2,028 institutions.

Deposit Insurance. Deposit insurance was provided through the organization of the Federal Deposit Insurance Corporation. The Treasury Department was authorized to subscribe to stock of the corporation in the amount of $150 million. The remainder of its capital was provided in part by assessing Federal Reserve Banks in amounts equal to one half of their respective surpluses as of January 1, 1933, one half of which was due and payable at once. Member banks were assessed ½ of 1 percent of their total deposits, one half of which was payable at the time of their acceptance as members of the Corporation. Insurance coverage was provided initially for individual deposits up to $2,500; six months later coverage was extended to protect individual accounts up to $5,000 and in 1950 coverage was increased to $10,000. A graduated scale of coverage was provided so that deposits in excess of $50,000 were insured 50 percent. For purposes of administering the Act, different accounts that were held for the benefit of a given depositor were to be treated as a single deposit. All national and state member banks were required to become members of the FDIC after July 1, 1934, or relinquish their membership designation and affiliation.

That deposit insurance was effective is attested to by the small number of bank failures between 1933 and 1941. On the other hand, the decline in the number of banks that failed after 1935 was due, in part, to the fact that only the strong banks had been permitted to reopen on an unrestricted basis. Weak banks had been merged with strong ones, and the public was none the wiser. Only 16 national banks and six state member banks failed in this span of years. Many of them were banks that never should have been reopened after the banking holiday. The record for nonmember banks is not nearly as impressive, except in comparison with the number of such failures prior to 1934. A total of 207 insured nonmember banks and 86 noninsured nonmember banks closed during these years. Ninety-four of the 207 insured nonmember banks closed in the two years, 1937 and 1938.

Evaluation of Deposit Insurance. From the description of the terms and conditions of deposit insurance, it is clear that it in no way resembled insurance. There is no relationship between the rate of contribution or assessment of a member bank to the Federal Deposit Insurance Corporation and the degree of risk of a particular bank not being able to pay its depositors' claims on demand. The principle of insurance is the shifting of individual, indeterminate risks to a group (the insurance company) through the payment of annual premiums. The latter are determined in accordance with the probability of losses befalling insured persons and/or firms. The greater the factor of safety, the lower the cost to the individual; the greater the degree of individual hazard, the larger is the contribution of the individual to the total cost. Large uncertain losses to individuals are prepaid and made certain for the group. In the deposit insurance plan of 1935, banks were assessed on the basis of their total demand deposits rather than on the basis of a given bank's susceptability to closing. A bank with a reserve of 5 percent above its legal minimum would contribute no more than another bank that maintained a reserve equal to 50 percent above the legal minimum.

Plans for guaranteeing demand deposits had been evolved by several states in years gone by, and every one of them failed. The word *insurance* instills more confidence in risk bearers than does the word *guarantee*. There was no unsavory background at any level of operation of deposit insurance. A guarantee plan on a nationwide basis is much more sound in principle than is one that is restricted to statewide operations. This evaluation is in no way intended to detract from the effectiveness of the FDIC. It is intended more to point out the fact that a nationwide deposit guarantee plan has succeeded when a number of statewide plans have not. The latter did not provide adequate security for deposits.

Other Provisions for Strengthening Bank Organization and Operations. National banks were permitted to establish branches in states on the same level at which banks that were chartered by the respective states were permitted to do so.

Bank holding companies were not permitted to vote their holdings of common stock of operating banks unless they obtained permission from the Federal Reserve Board of Governors.

Limitations were placed on the investment securities that member banks could have in their investment portfolios. On and after the date of approval of the Act, minimum capitalization of national banks was to be $50,000 even in towns of 3,000 population or less. Member banks were prohibited from paying interest on demand deposits, and the Board of Governors was given power to establish the rate of interest on time and on savings deposits. Since deposit insurance protected depositors, the Act removed the double liability obligation from the owners of the common stock of member banks.

In order to prevent a recurrence of speculative transactions in corporate securities, real estate, and commodities that were being financed by member bank credit, officers of Reserve Banks were charged with the duty of keeping informed on the use of member bank credit, and of reporting such information to the Board of Governors. In cases of continued misuse of member bank credit, the Board was authorized to deny such banks further use of Reserve Bank credit facilities. In addition to obtaining Federal Reserve credit by the rediscount process, member banks were permitted to obtain direct advances from their respective Reserve Banks for 15 days on their promissory notes when the latter were collateralled by government securities.

An Open Market Committee was created whose membership was to be constituted by the members of the Board of Governors and five other persons, not more than one of whom could be selected from any one Federal Reserve District. This Committee was to meet in Washington four times a year and was given complete control over open market policy.

The Secretary of the Treasury and the Comptroller of the Currency were no longer to be ex officio members of the Board of Governors of the Federal Reserve System, which was the new designation given to the former Federal Reserve Board.

Commercial banks no longer were permitted to engage in investment banking. The hour of decision presented itself to the Board of Directors of the J. P. Morgan Bank, which was an investment bank that engaged in commercial banking. Prospects of making profits from investment banking were so remote at the time that the Board decided in favor of commercial banking.

Whereas the legal reserve ratios had been reduced from the scale that was determined in the original Act, or from 18 percent, 15 percent, and 12 percent, on demand deposits in banks in Central Reserve Cities, Reserve Cities, and Nonreserve Cities and 5 percent on savings deposits, regardless of the classification of the city in which banks were located, to 13 percent, 10 percent, 7 percent on demand deposits and 3 percent on savings deposits, respectively, the Act of 1935 empowered the Board of Governors to determine the actual reserve ratios within a range of the above schedule of rates as minimums and not more than twice these percentages as the maximums, or more accurately 13 percent and 26 percent, 10 percent and 20 percent, 7 percent and 14 percent against demand deposits respectively and 3 percent to 6 percent on savings deposits in all classifications of banks.

RELIEF

Relief measures were of two kinds: those whose initial impacts were to relieve conditions of poverty and lack of money income; and those that mitigated panic conditions and loss of confidence in our economic institutions. Many writers treat the banking legislation of 1933 and 1935 as part of the program of reform. Reforms they were, especially the Act of 1935 that made permanent the terms of the Act of 1933. Their immediate objective was to allay the panic conditions that had gripped the nation. Once confidence in banks and banking had been restored, Congress went about its business of implementing the President's program of relief and reform at other levels of economic organization.

President Roosevelt had stated in outlining his relief and recovery programs that he was going to do something for the forgotten men of the American economy. They were "forgotten" in the sense that they had received very little or no positive benefits of legislation at the federal level. True enough, tariff legislation that had had the support of American farmers had passed Congress, but the positive and direct benefits that accrued to them were decidedly nebulous. Some United States Supreme Court decisions had been rendered that appeared to place labor in a more favorable position in the eyes of the law, but again direct and positive benefits are difficult to trace. Legislation in 1914 and again in 1932 had clarified the position that organized labor occupied in relation to antitrust legislation and to the use of injunctions by employers in combating efforts on the part of labor to strike, but nothing grew out of these enactments directly that tended to raise the level of living of workingmen. Roosevelt attacked the farm problem first and discovered that he did not have the wholehearted support of Congress. Sentiment in the Senate was so evenly divided pro and con that the Senators from seven of the Western States formed a silver bloc, the purpose of which was to force some monetary legislation through Congress that would benefit their constituents. The result took the form of the Thomas Amendment to the Agricultural Adjustment Act of 1933, commonly called the Inflation Act of 1933.

The Thomas Amendment to the Agricultural Adjustment Act of 1933

President Roosevelt was not averse to "doing something for silver" because of the effect he thought it would have upon the general level of prices. According to the findings of the Twentieth Century Fund, the long-term debt of public agencies—local, state, and federal—amounted to $33 billion, while the debt of business firms and of individuals totaled $100 billion. These debts had been incurred in the 1920's when prices and interest rates were much higher than they were after 1930. Prices had fallen to such a low level, and the volume of trade, including our export trade, had declined to such an extent that it was impossible for debtors to service their debts. It was that relationship between the internal debt structure and prices that lay behind the emphasis the New Deal placed upon raising the general level of prices as a means of restoring a degree of prosperity to the economy that had not existed for a number of years.

The production of gold had declined somewhat steadily since 1915, and the average price of silver in New York had declined from $1.11 an ounce in 1919 to 27 cents an ounce in 1932. The decline in the rate at which gold had been produced was held responsible for the increase in its value not only in terms of silver but in terms of almost all commodities and services. Not enough new money had been put into circulation to sustain the price level, and prices dropped somewhat precipitously. It was at this point that President Roosevelt began to talk about restoring a "sound" dollar to our monetary system. He had attended a world monetary conference in London, and pledged to return the United States to a "sound" monetary system and to maintain it thereafter. To the surprise of many persons, he walked out of a meeting of the conference when it discussed ways and means of returning to the traditional gold standard and of maintaining it with respect to both internal and external transactions. *Sound* money for years had referred to money that was readily redeemable in gold at its face value and on demand of the people, not at the will of government. Without letting people know at the time of the change in his usage of the term, *sound* money to him was one whose value or whose purchasing power was constant throughout a period of time. It existed when the debtor returned the same dollar value to the creditor that he had borrowed from him at an earlier date. To put it in common language, sound money existed when the general level of prices remained constant; when the index number of commodity prices remained constant.

The decline in prices since 1929 was due in part to the use of unsound money, to the President's way of thinking. With the decline in the production of gold occurring at a time of increase in population, an increase in the production of commodities and in the number and frequency of transactions, the dollar had to be redefined in more realistic terms and its value established in harmony with economic conditions that prevailed after a world war had been fought and won. The traditional American dollar had to be abandoned when the economy broke away from its traditional pattern.

Two provisions were made in the Inflation Act of 1933 which it was thought would increase the monetary demand for silver, hence its price. The President was given the authority to return the country to a bimetallic monetary standard, using gold and silver at any ratio he might choose. The United States had not been able to collect much of its World War I debt from foreign countries in terms of gold, so the Act authorized the Secretary of the Treasury to accept for a period of six months up to $200 million in silver to be valued at not more than 50 cents an ounce in payment thereof. England immediately took advantage of the alternative and paid a $10 million installment on her war debt in silver purchased at 50 cents an ounce and by so doing saved approximately $2,750,000, but our monetary base was not affected.

In addition to attempting to restore silver to the monetary base, a position it had not occupied since 1873, the Federal Reserve Banks were authorized to purchase an additional $3 billion of government securities, and the Treasury was authorized to print and issue a like amount of United States notes.

Devaluation of the Dollar. The Inflation Act of 1933 had authorized the President to reduce the gold content of the dollar by not more than 50 percent. Over a period of time the gold content of the dollar was stabilized at approximately 13.71 grains which was a reduction of approximately 41 percent of the traditional 23.22 grains to the dollar that had been established by Congress in 1837. The fact that contracts were made payable in legal tender and that all monies and government paper money were declared to be legal payment compelled creditors to accept legal tender in the dollar amounts that were specified in their respective contracts in place of the gold equivalent of these dollars on the date the contracts were signed. The former gold content of the dollar was the equivalent of $1.69 in terms of the devalued dollar.

The Gold Stabilization Fund. One of the results, if not an immediate objective of devaluing the dollar, was the establishment of a $2 billion stabilization fund which was to be used in stabilizing the value of the dollar in the foreign exchange market. The fund was provided in somewhat of a burdenless fashion, in that whatever the reserve was by weight at the time the gold content of the dollar was reduced, it was the equivalent of that many more 13.71 grain dollars.

Objectives of the Devaluation Program. President Roosevelt outlined two objectives of his devaluation program: namely, to raise internal commodity prices and to increase commodity exports. At the same time the President wanted to raise internal commodity prices, he did not give people any more dollars with which to pay them. For almost 20 years gold coins had had very limited circulation in the United States. Paper money and bank deposits subject to check were the currencies with which the American people were most familiar. They were decidedly conscious of how many dollar units they had; the gold content of a dollar they hadn't used for 20 years meant little or nothing to them. They had no more dollars to spend after devaluation than they had before, and to the extent that they had been required to pay higher prices for some of their daily requirements they would have had less money with which to purchase others. The general level of internal commodity prices could not have been pushed upward because there were insufficient dollars to support a higher level.

Other factors remaining the same, the reduction in the gold content of the dollar did stimulate the export of commodities to other countries. Assuming the gold content of the British pound sterling to have been 113 grains of gold, reducing the gold content of the American dollar from 23.22 grains of pure gold to 13.71 grains made it possible for English buyers of American goods to command approximately 8.24 American dollars with one of their monetary units instead of the traditional 4.86 units. In this manner they were given more American dollars with which to pay for their imports from the United States without having had to relinquish any more units of their own money.

As a matter of fact the volume of American commodity exports did increase as did the prices of some of our agricultural products. However, had price increases responded in proportion to the amount of the devaluation of the dollar, American commodity exports would not and could not have increased. There was a slight increase in the level of internal commodity prices that bore little or no relation to the devaluation of the dollar and that would have occurred had devaluation not taken place.

Prolonged Drouth. In the closing years of the 1920's and early 1930's, there was a prolonged and serious drouth in the states that lay north of the Ohio River from the Middle West to New England. The impact of the drouth was to reduce the volume of farm staples, of dairy products, and of meats that reached the market. Springs that had never been known to have gone dry furnished little or no water. River beds and streams dried up. Reservoirs were depleted. Artesian wells were deepened and new ones were dug in search for new channels of underground water. Railroads hauled water from the Missouri River in tank cars to destitute communities where it was rationed cautiously to consumers. Washing automobiles and sprinkling lawns were prohibited and people were asked to take fewer baths per week.

Louis M. Hacker, in his *Short History of the New Deal*,[2] wrote:

> Nothing was more unsettling to the New Deal than the drouth and hot weather which scorched the agricultural sections of the country in the late spring and the midsummer of 1934. Centering first in the Dakotas and Minnesota the drouth moved through the Middle West and the Central South, leaving no important growing area untouched. The effect on crops and livestock was dismaying. The corn yield was estimated at 1,607,000,000 bushels on August 10, as compared with 2,344,000,000 bushels for the year previous; wheat production was placed at 491,000,000 bushels, as compared with 528,000,000 bushels for the year before; the cotton forecast was the lowest in a generation, being 9,195,000 bales, as compared with 13,047,000 bales in 1933. The Department of Agriculture anticipated that the production of oats, barley, flaxseed, and buckwheat, in addition to corn and wheat, would be the smallest in thirty years or more; the hay and tobacco crops also were seriously affected; the government was compelled to buy up 2,600,000 head of cattle for slaughter because of the parching of wide belts of pasturing areas. The estimated damage was $5,000,000,000; some 5,300,000 people were involved; hundreds of thousands of persons were already destitute and being supported by federal relief.

Abrogation of the Gold Clause in Contracts. On March 10, 1933, the President issued an executive order to stop the exportation of gold except

[2] Louis M. Hacker, *A Short History of the New Deal* (New York City: F. S. Crofts & Co., 1935), p. 26. Permission granted by Appleton-Century-Crofts, Division of Meredith Corporation.

under license from the Treasury. A month later he forbade the hoarding of gold coin, gold bullion, and gold certificates; and on April 19 he stopped the free movement of gold, which gave formal recognition to the United States departure from the gold standard. In June, Congress cancelled the gold clause in all contracts, public and private, and made contracts payable in legal tender.

Holders of several types of contracts that specified payment in gold coin of former weight and fineness tested the constitutionality of the abrogation of the gold clause in the Supreme Court of the United States. In the cases brought by holders of gold certificates and government bonds, the Court ruled that the Resolution of June 5, 1933, was unconstitutional. At the same time, had holders of gold certificates been permitted to redeem them in gold, the gold would necessarily have been turned in to the Treasury in exchange for paper money in a ratio that was based on the former gold content of the dollar. As for the holders of government bonds, since the plaintiffs had not shown that they had suffered any loss of purchasing power in having been compelled to accept paper currency, they were not given any relief. Had the gold clause in government contracts not been abrogated, the principal of the public debt would have increased to $169 million for each $100 million of debt outstanding, and the interest burden would have increased likewise annually. This was the last thing that the President wanted to have happen. Shortly thereafter, President Roosevelt closed the Court of Claims to cases that involved the payment of gold in domestic contracts. The constitutionality of the Resolution was upheld by the Court insofar as it applied to the gold clause in private contracts. To have done otherwise would have subordinated the constitutional right of the government to control the value of money to the right of individuals to enter into contractual relationships, the terms of which were inimical to the constitutional rights of the government.

The Silver Purchase Act of 1934

Shortly after the passage of the Inflation Act and the Gold Reserve Act, the passage of the Silver Purchase Act (1934) authorized the Treasury to purchase silver bullion until there was one third as much silver bullion on reserve by weight as there was gold. Another way of expressing the same goal was to have one fourth of all monetary reserves in terms of silver. This meant that every time there was addition to our gold reserves the Treasury was authorized to purchase one third as much silver. At the time the Act was passed, an addition of approximately 1,308 million ounces of silver was needed to attain the ratio of 3 to 1. Nineteen months later and after having purchased over 843 million ounces of silver, it still lacked 1,075 million ounces because of the inflow of gold reserves. On July 10, 1939, after the purchase of nearly 2,100 million ounces of silver at a cost of $1,150 million, the quantity of silver still required to attain the 3 to 1 ratio was approximately 1,410 million ounces, or more than when the program began. Gold reserves in 1934 were expressed in terms of $7,856 million; in 1939 they amounted to $16,135 million. The addition of all of this silver to our monetary reserves was meaningless as far as adding silver to our monetary base was concerned because silver was not basic standard money material. In the early years of the program, in addition to an added cost to the Treasury of approximately $16 million a day, it stimulated the world market for silver and attracted silver from Mexico and China to the extent that these two countries had to suspend specie payments in terms of silver.

Retirement of National Bank Notes

In keeping with the policy of lowering the interest burden of the Treasury, the President called in the Panama Canal 5 percent bonds of 1905 for retirement and refinanced them at a saving of about 2 percent per annum. Since these bonds were the last ones that had been made eligible to secure national bank notes, retiring the bonds automatically retired the circulating notes. Since June 12, 1935, national bank notes still outstanding have been direct obligations of the United States Treasury, the respective national banks of issue having deposited with it sufficient funds for their redemption in full. In this manner, not only was a somewhat disturbing element in our monetary system—one that had outlived whatever useful purposes it may have performed—removed, but our currency system was simplified by the elimination of one kind of inelastic note.

Plan for Subsistence Homesteads

In 1929, out of a total of six million farmers in the United States, the average income that was derived from the sale of cash crops for almost one half this number amounted to not more than $356. Almost three million farmers had between them the sum of $1,041,517,000 out of which to make their mortgage payments, pay their taxes, pay for any improvements to farmlands and/or equipment, after having paid for household goods, clothing, and many other items of comfort and luxury which the American system of mass production and interchangeable parts had placed within the cost-price range of the masses. The other three million farmers derived something over $8.5 billion from the sale of their cash crops. A little more than 50 percent of the farmers received almost 90 percent of the value of the country's cash crops.

If these conditions had been permitted to continue, the forces of competition in free markets would have forced many of the three million less efficient farmers to relinquish their farmlands and to join the army of from 11 to 15 million unemployed industrial workers. The sum of $25 million was granted to the President, under Title II of the National Industrial Recovery Act, "for making loans for and otherwise aiding in the purchase of subsistence homesteads." The fund was to be used to establish demonstration projects that would add to the development of a permanent program of this nature. At an estimated cost per family of $2,500, only 10,000 families could be resettled on homesteads. About 2,000 families actually were settled in fewer than ten demonstration projects, and the problems that arose were so insurmountable that the idea was given up in a few years.

The Agricultural Adjustment Act

The first part of the farm relief program is found in the Agricultural Adjustment Act that passed both houses of Congress and was signed by the President on May 12, 1933. It was intended to "re-establish prices to farmers at a level that will give agricultural commodities a purchasing power with respect to articles that farmers buy equivalent to the purchasing power of agricultural commodities in the base period." This was the enunciation of the principle of parity prices and was made to apply to the basic crops of wheat, cotton, corn, hogs, rice, dairy products, and tobacco. The following year, after farmers had shifted their plantings from the controlled, basic crops to the uncontrolled crops, controls and benefit payments were extended to include growers of beef and dairy cattle, peanuts, rye, barley, flax, grain sorghum, sugar beets, and cane sugar. Farm incomes were to be raised by one or more of the three methods that are explained in the following paragraphs. The subsidies that were financed by the imposition and collection of taxes placed on the processors of the enumerated farm products were to be passed on to consumers in the form of higher prices.

Methods of Raising Farm Incomes. There were three principal ways by which the farmer was to be aided under the Agricultural Adjustment Act.

Cotton Option Contracts. The Secretary of Agriculture was authorized to enter into contracts with cotton growers under the terms of which the latter were to reduce the acreage planted in cotton in 1933 to at least 30 percent below the acreage they planted in 1932, and no commercial fertilizer was to be applied to the reduced acreage. The land that was withdrawn from cultivation was not to be planted in any other cash crop. In return, the growers were to receive options on the amount of cotton which was held by the old Federal Farm Board that corresponded to the size of their reductions. If the price of cotton rose, the farmers were permitted to make a profit by exercising their options. If the price of cotton did not rise, their options would not be exercised.

Benefit Payments. The Secretary of Agriculture was authorized to make agreements with the growers of basic cash crops under the terms of which the latter would receive cash payments for the acreage that was removed from cultivation.

Marketing Agreements. Producers, processors, and distributors of agricultural products were authorized to present plans to the Secretary of Agriculture that would (a) eliminate wastes of competition, (b) improve upon trade practices, (c) raise prices at the producer level, and (d) provide for the orderly disposal of surplus products in consumer markets.

Results of Reduction in Acreage. In spite of the support of the administration's program by the farmers in reducing the acreage that was planted in basic crops in 1933, nature failed to cooperate as wholeheartedly. Reduction in acreage turned out to be not synonymous with reduction in crop yield; neither did higher prices at the farm bring increased purchasing power to farmers. A 25 percent reduction in acreage that was planted in cotton in 1933 compared with the 1932 acreage was accompanied by an increase in yield per acre from a 5-year average of 174 pounds to over 209 pounds or 20.1 percent. The year's crop in 1933 was the equal of that of 1932, and the carryover of 11½ million bales was lessened only slightly. To make matters worse for the successful operation of the program, the administration was unsuccessful in obtaining the cooperation of foreign countries. In 1933 production of cotton outside the United States reached a peak since the predepression season of 1928-29. In terms of farmers' purchasing power, it remained the same in May, 1934, as it had been in May, 1933.

Efforts to decrease the production of the other basic crops and to raise the purchasing power of the farmers who grew them were as fruitless as they were in the area of cotton. The figures were different, but the ultimate results were almost identical. The extent to which intensive methods of cultivation had been pushed may have carried the cultivation of farmland so far into the stage of diminishing returns that when land was cultivated less intensively, or more extensively, productivity actually increased. Little pigs were slaughtered to reduce the rate at which pigs were sent to market. When rows of basic crops were planted farther apart, productivity per row increased. Many were the caustic remarks about turning back the pages of progress in agriculture and about the false economy of paying farmers not to produce, rather than in proportion to their positive contributions.

Legality of the AAA. When the Supreme Court ruled that the Constitution did not authorize any federal controls over agricultural pursuits, the President presented a similar act to Congress in 1938 in the name of conservation. Reduction in acreages under cultivation are now made in the name of conserving agricultural resources, and impacts upon production and price are legally incidental.

Frazier-Lemke Bill

The farm mortgage situation had plagued farmers in the 1920 decade; it buried them in the early years of the 1930's. The Frazier-Lemke Farm Bankruptcy Bill was passed by Congress in June, 1934, the purpose of which was to facilitate the refinancing of farm mortgages somewhat in line with the low levels of prices that debtor farmers received in the market for their products. Efforts were made to modify the terms of the original mortgage indentures by reducing the rate of interest and granting extensions of time throughout which reduced payments were to be made while the debtor farmers remained in possession of their farm properties. Farmers could request reappraisals of their farms and farm properties which were to be "fair and reasonable, though not necessarily their market value," and methods were established by which farmers could repurchase their properties at their newly appraised values with interest at 1 percent and amortizations over periods of six years. If creditor mortgagees objected to this form of adjustment, farmers were to be permitted to retain possession of their farms under reasonable rental agreements for five years, during which time bankruptcy proceedings were to be held in abeyance. This was strictly an emergency provision. Similar legislation at the state level was accepted by the courts provided the preambles made reference to an emergency situation.

The National Industrial Recovery Act

The National Industrial Recovery Act (NIRA), which became the law of the land in June, 1933, consisted of three parts or titles, the first of which was concerned with the organization of industry and was to remain in force two years. The second title had to do with the creation of public works programs, and the third called for a revision of the Emergency Relief and Construction Act and included a number of miscellaneous activities. Among the more important provisions of the Act were (1) the delegation of the powers and functions that were indicated in the Act to an agency the President was empowered to establish; (2) codes of fair competition were to be drawn up by trade or industrial associations and submitted to the President for his approval. These codes were not intended to "promote monopolies or to eliminate or suppress small enterprise"; (3) after approval by the President, the codes were enforceable at law and the courts could issue injunctions against violations thereof; (4) if industries did not submit codes of their own making, the President could prescribe them; (5) to aid in the enforcement of code practices, the President was empowered to license firms in industries that could not agree upon code practices that would apply to them; (6) every code of fair competition was to contain the following conditions affecting labor.

Section 7-A of Title III. These conditions were found in Section 7-A, which is quoted in full:

> (1) That employees shall have the right to organize and bargain collectively through representatives of their own choosing, and shall be free from interference, restraint, or coercion of employers of labor, or their agents, in the designation of such representatives or in self-organization, or in other concerted activities for the purpose of collective bargaining or other mutual aid or protection; (2) that no employee and no one seeking employment shall be required as a condition of employment to join any company union or to refrain from joining, organizing, or assisting a labor organization of his own choosing; and (3) that employers shall comply with the maximum hours of labor, minimum rates of pay, and other conditions of employment approved or prescribed by the President.

Machinery was provided to enforce compliance with codes of fair competition. A blanket code, called the President's Reemployment Agreement, was drawn up and was made effective until the respective industries agreed upon their own. For clerks, a 40-hour week was established with minimum wages of from $12 to $15 a week. Industrial workers were given a 35-hour week at a minimum pay of 30 cents to 40 cents an hour. Children under 16 years of age were not to be employed, except that those between the ages of 14 and 16 might be employed in other than mechanical and manufacturing industries not longer than three hours daily between the hours of 7 A.M. and 7 P.M. Signers of the blanket codes were to display an emblem of a Blue Eagle, as were employers in those industries for which code practice agreements had been accepted. By the middle of 1934 more than 400 codes had been signed and an additional 300 codes had had their hearings completed. It was estimated that over 20 million workers were protected by the Blue Eagle. A year later the NIRA was declared unconstitutional by unanimous decision of the United States Supreme Court, first, on the grounds that the poultry business of the New York City metropolitan area could not be regulated under the interstate commerce clause of the Constitution. More important for the entire program was the ruling of the Court that Congress had delegated legislative authority without specifying how it should be exercised, and that the authority had been exercised by voluntary associations (the code authorities) which sought to give their mandates the force of law.

Title II. Under Title II of the NIRA, the Public Works Administration was established to aid recovery by providing work for some of the unemployed and by setting the wheels of industry turning once more. The program was to include among other things (1) the construction, repair, and improvement of public highways and parkways, public buildings, and any publicly owned instrumentalities and facilities; (2) the conservation and development of natural resources, including control, utilization, and purification of waters, prevention of soil erosion, development of waterpower, transmission of electrical energy, and the construction of river and harbor improvements and flood control; (3) any projects of a character heretofore constructed or carried on either directly by public authority or with public aid to serve the interests of the general public; (4) the construction, reconstruction, alteration, or repair under public regulation or control of low cost housing and slum clearance projects; (5) any project of any character heretofore eligible for loans under the provisions of the Emergency Relief and Construction Act of 1932. This last was to include loans for the completion of hospitals, the operation of which was partly financed from public funds, the construction of naval vessels under the terms or limits of the London Naval Limitation Treaty of 1930, aircraft required for this purpose, as well as army housing and the mechanization and motorization of army equipment.

While a detailed plan for public works was being drawn up, the President was authorized and empowered through the Administrator or through such other agencies as he might designate or create (1) to construct, finance, or aid in the construction or financing of any public work projects included in the comprehensive plan referred to above; (2) to make grants to states, municipalities, or other public bodies upon such terms as he, the President, might prescribe, for the construction, repair or improvement of any projects included in the enumeration in the preceding paragraph, but no such grant should be in excess of 30 percent of the cost of labor and the materials employed upon such projects; (3) to acquire by the purchase or the power of eminent domain any real or personal property in connection with the construction of any such project; (4) to aid in the financing of such railroad maintenance and equipment as may be approved by the Interstate Commerce Commission; and (5) to advance the unappropriated balance of the sum authorized for the construction and equipment of an annex to the Library of Congress.

Though employment was given to several million persons who otherwise would have been unemployed and over $3 billion was spent, the results were disappointing based upon the criteria that were outlined at the beginning of the program. The Civil Works Administration, the Civilian Conservation Corps, the Works Progress Administration, and the Public Works Administration, among other alphabetical agencies, were established. Though not the largest by any measure of comparison, the Civilian Conservation Corps and the National Youth Administration may have done more real and permanent good than many of the other agencies.

The Civilian Conservation Corps

The CCC enrolled 2¼ million young men between the ages of 17 and 25 who otherwise might have caused problems of delinquency, and placed them in 1,500 camps that were widely scattered throughout every state. None of them could remain in camp over two years. Hard physical labor was required, organized recreation facilities and activities were provided, and the cultural development of these young men was not neglected. While the camps were placed under the supervision of the military and military discipline was maintained, strict orders were given that absolutely no military training of any kind or degree was to be given. Enrollees were given $30 monthly of which $22 were sent to their parents or other dependents. The work done by these boys was all outdoors and consisted of constructing fire towers and bridges; cutting logging trails, building roads and landing fields; erosion and flood control; forestry and forest fire prevention; making recreation facilities; and conservation of wild life. The work of planting millions of trees by Tennessee Valley Authority was performed by boys from 20 CCC camps. In terms of personal benefits, good food, plenty of fresh air and exercise, medical care and regular hours of living combined to increase the health, vigor, and vitality for the 2¼ million young men.

Other work that was accomplished by CCC labor was laying out roadside parkways, and clearing and beautifying rights-of-way along highways.

A measure of conservation and also of fire prevention was found in the clearing of underbrush in forest lands. Small and undesirable trees were removed in order to provide more room for growth and development of others. Dead limbs and branches were trimmed from trees, and real progress was made almost for the first time in beautifying and conserving natural resources on a large scale.

The National Youth Administration

The National Youth Administration made possible the extension of high school and/or college and university education to between four and five hundred thousand young men and women who otherwise would have been compelled to forego their pursuit of their education for economic reasons. High school students were permitted to work no longer than three hours per day on school days and seven hours on Saturdays for which they received a maximum of $6 a month. Undergraduate students were permitted to earn from $10 to $20 per month at the rate of from 25 cents to 35 cents per hour. Graduate students could earn from $20 to $30 per month at little higher hourly rates of pay. They performed clerical duties, served school lunches, raised and canned food, built and repaired schools, libraries, hospitals, swimming pools, bandstands, tennis courts, stadiums, roads, airports, levees and dams, and made and repaired furniture and tools.

Maximum earnings do not seem adequate for the purchase of necessities at prices that have prevailed since 1945, but in terms of prices that prevailed in depression years they enabled thousands of students to meet many or most of their current financial obligations. Textbooks may have cost from $3.50 to $5.00 each, and other school supplies were priced at correspondingly low levels. Men's suits were available within a range of $20 to $30, and $10 was a high price for shoes. Student rooms may have cost $10 a month and board $4.50 per week. *A la carte* prices were mythical compared to those with which readers of this page are familiar. Thousands of men and women who occupy responsible positions today owe their education and training to opportunities given them by the National Youth Administration.

Cultural Programs

Along more cultural lines artists were employed to paint murals on walls of post offices and other public buildings. Authors were employed to write histories that otherwise might never have been written. One of the more popular and widely read of such histories was a series that portrayed the historic importance of the principal rivers in the United States. Important cartographical projects were completed, and surveys of public and private tracts of land became matters of public record.

The Tennessee Valley Authority

Muscle Shoals had been developed during World War I under President Wilson's administration in order to generate electric power that could be used in the fixation of nitrogen for use in the manufacture of explosives and of commercial fertilizers. Its location was in northern Alabama on a bend of the Tennessee River. Political factors, the opposition of the privately owned light and power companies, and a feeling on the part of thousands of persons that the federal government should not own and operate a facility that would offer competition to free enterprise resulted in a failure to develop its economic potentials. In the early 1930's during the administration of President Hoover, Boulder Dam was constructed on the Colorado River as a measure of relief and in the name of conservation of natural resources. The name of this dam has been changed to Hoover Dam in honor of the President who initiated its construction. Since the New Deal program included the development of resources, the conservation of natural resources, and the investment of federal funds in such a manner that employment would be given to persons and to capital that otherwise would be unemployed, it is not strange that the Tennessee Valley Authority was created to expand upon the operations at Muscle Shoals.

Social Planning. One objective of the Roosevelt administration was to utilize to the greatest extent the potentialities of the Muscle Shoals development in the generation and sale of electric power in order to establish a rate standard against which rates of privately owned and operated light and power companies could be compared. As an experiment in social planning, the Authority was empowered to construct dams, power plants, and transmission lines; to develop and manufacture fertilizers; and to outline a general program for promoting and improving upon the general welfare, both social and economic, of the people in the areas of the seven states of Alabama, Tennessee, Georgia, Virginia, North Carolina, Kentucky, and Mississippi that comprised the Tennessee Valley region.

This marked the first effort at the federal level to rehabilitate an entire region—its people and its industries. In order to raise the level of income and the scale of living of the inhabitants of the area, efforts were made to introduce more modern methods of cultivating the soil and controlling soil erosion. Fertilizers were adapted to the conditions of the soil and to the needs of crops for minerals in their optimum proportions. Mixtures were designated by the proportions in which nitrogen, phosphorus, and potassium were present, to which ferrous and nonferrous metals were added in smaller quantities. Manpower from CCC camps was utilized in carrying out its reforestation program. Agriculture was balanced with industry to add stability and diversity to the economic activities of the area.

Test of Elasticity of Demand for Electricity. One of the most enlightening results of the generation, transmission, and sale of electricity by the Tennessee Valley Authority was the disclosure that the demand for electric power was decidedly elastic within certain rate ranges. When the Alabama Power Company reduced its rates 31 percent the residential use of electricity increased 44 percent. A reduction of 35 percent in its rates by the Georgia

Power Company was accompanied by an increase in the consumption of current of 47 percent, and the most surprising result of all was obtained by the Tennessee Electric Power Company when a rate reduction of 46 percent was followed by an increase of 92 percent in the consumption of electric current. Prior to this experiment, the traditional procedure in rate-making practice was for a company to wait until the consumption of electricity had increased, then to ask for a reduction in its rates.

Residents of the Tennessee Valley area previously had not constituted a market for durable electric household appliances. Privately owned electric light and power companies had not seen their way to render service in this area. In addition, the original purchase terms of this kind of equipment were more burdensome than these people with relatively low incomes could bear and their operating costs were prohibitive. As incomes of these people were raised, the terms of purchase contracts for electric appliances were made easier and costs of consuming electric current were lowered. Not only were the residents in the TVA area the beneficiaries of this program, merchants, servicemen, banks, agencies of transport and manufacturing—not only of electrical appliances but of multitudinous other consumer goods—felt the impacts of the higher scales of living that were effected in the area. Improved roads were constructed, libraries were established, and programs of public education—vocational, technical, and traditional—were raised to higher levels. Better physical facilities for schools were also provided.

Impacts of the TVA. The transforming effects of the development of TVA penetrated other regions. Incomes were raised and larger volumes of business were transacted. Portions of the Valley were regions whose people had had relatively few contacts, cultural or physical, with people in other regions. The penetration of railroads into this region had provided access and egress to coal mines and to forest lands. Values of commodities that were transported into these regions were not commensurate with the values of raw materials extracted therefrom. There was little or no exchange of culture and of ideas via telephone or telegraph, mail or personal visitations. These regions had been described by historians and by sociologists as being inhabited by the purest strains of Anglo-Saxon blood found in the United States. Economists had described these areas as excellent places in which to make a poor living and poor places in which to make a good living. The coming of TVA altered for the better many of the traditional and historical patterns of living.

Evaluation of TVA Program. The rates that TVA charged for electric current were not required to cover all the overhead costs of this organization; nor did TVA pay any taxes. Privately owned light and power companies were critical in the use of TVA to set standards of rates for privately owned and operated companies for this reason. However, there is one incontrovertible fact that must be taken into consideration in the evaluation of the program, and that is that the profits that were made by TVA over and above its operating costs were larger than the taxes it would have been required to pay had the same tax rates been applied to the same tax base that applied to privately owned companies. Electric current was distributed locally through cooperatives which purchased current from TVA at wholesale rates and sold to their customers at retail rates which were lower than the rates that were charged by privately owned concerns.

The fears of many persons in business and out that TVA might establish a precedent for the federal government taking over the ownership and operation of all electric light and power companies have been unfounded. Except in the short run, when privately owned and operated light and power companies have been compelled to lower their rates, they have not suffered financial losses. Privately owned companies in the past have advertised and emphasized the convenience factor in the use of electricity. To many potential consumers the costs of convenience were in excess of what they felt they could afford to pay. To their way of thinking there were many other items of necessity that had priority over the convenience factor in the use of electricity. Now that rates have been lowered in many communities, these potential customers have become active ones, and they have been enjoying the conveniences that accompany the use of electric power in addition to the necessities that formerly were given priority.

Housing Finance

The Home Owners Refinancing Act (June, 1933) authorized the establishment of the Home Owners Loan Corporation (HOLC) with an original capital of $200 million that was provided entirely by the United States Treasury. Additional capital was obtained through the issuance of bonds of not more than $2 billion. Its function was to refinance mortgage debts which had become due or which had been foreclosed within two years from date of their application. Refinancing was done by the HOLC offering in exchange its bonds that carried the guarantee of the government both as to principal and interest for the instruments of mortgagees. The latter were required to accept bonds of face value that did not exceed 80 percent of the appraised value of the property as determined by appraisers who represented the Corporation. The maximum value was not to exceed $14,000. Previous mortgages and all liens against a property were thus merged into a single first mortgage that was held by the Corporation and was secured by the home. Interest was at the rate of 5 percent, and the bonds matured in not more than 15 years, which term could be extended by the Corporation upon just cause. Since the original bonds were guaranteed as to interest only, mortgagees were somewhat hesitant to accept HOLC bonds; but by June, 1934, the Corporation had financed 340,000 home mortgages on total advances of $1,028 million, 99 percent of which involved mortgages that were past due.

Federal Savings and Loan Associations. Federal Savings and Loan Associations were organized under the authority of the Home Owners Loan Act of April, 1934. They were local, mutual thrift, and financing agencies that were sponsored by the federal government. Funds were obtained to finance the construction of new homes from the sale of shares which served as security for the money the shareowners borrowed. As agencies of thrift, they accepted deposits from persons who were attracted to them by higher rates of interest return than were paid by savings banks or by savings departments of national banks. Deposits of this nature were insured up to $10,000 per account by the Federal Savings and Loan Insurance Corporation which had a capital of $100 million that was subscribed to entirely by the United States Treasury.

Slum Clearance. The Public Works Administration initiated a program for the improvement of housing conditions both urban and rural. While the PWA was more of a relief agency than anything else, its housing division subordinated make-work aspects for actual improvements in housing and in housing conditions. The general idea was for PWA not to construct any public housing facilities in urban areas until there was an actual shortage that was not being relieved by free enterprise. Conditions were so critical in a number of areas that public housing was provided first, then other facilities were torn down.

The program was as much or more one of social betterment than it was a matter of relieving a housing shortage. Restrictions were laid down as to the financial status of persons to become eligible to occupy public housing. They could not receive incomes of over $800 per annum, which minimum was raised a few years later. They were charged lower rentals than individual owners could afford to accept, because the loans were amortized over a period of 60 years instead of 20 or 30 years, and the rate of interest was lower. Personal habits of applicants were examined before they were accepted for tenancy, and they were required to keep the exterior as well as the interior of their housing neat and trim. Some of them were given an incentive to meet such standards which were entirely lacking when they occupied privately owned housing. They were given hot and cold running water, sanitary sewage disposal, and garbage and trash collections at frequent and regular intervals. Playground and playground facilities were provided to keep the children of occupants of public housing off the streets and to guide their energies into somewhat useful channels.

An Evaluation of the Impacts of Relief Measures

All the measures that have been discussed in this chapter had aspects of relief and reform, but few of recovery. Public authorities at all levels of government shied away from direct methods of relief, partly because of the overwhelming costs involved, more so because of their degrading effects upon the morale of the recipients. Morale already was at a low ebb without making it worse by handing out relief gratis, or such was the thinking of many of our leaders. It had been hoped that measures of relief would lead to recovery; but, again, the psychology of depression had such a hold on most persons that the low levels of monetary relief precluded any such stimulation to economic activity.

Since devaluation of the dollar and the agricultural program had a common objective—to raise prices—it is fitting to close this chapter with an evaluation of the New Deal in terms of its impacts on the price structure. It is well agreed that the failure to place additional monetary units in circulation kept general prices from rising. Then, too, several independent studies of the factors that affected prices of agricultural products were made in widely separated regions of the country, and they all came out with surprisingly similar results; namely, that not more than 10 percent of price increases may have been due to the efforts of the New Deal, while the operation of natural forces, including the drouth, accounted for the remaining 90 percent.[3]

QUESTIONS FOR REVIEW

1. (a) What were some omens of economic disaster that appeared on our economic horizons prior to 1929?
   (b) What is the meaning of the phrase "economic imbalance"?

2. (a) In what manner and to what extent was the dollar devalued?
   (b) Was the dollar devalued in terms of its power in exchange? Explain carefully.

3. (a) Why was the dollar devalued?
   (b) Did devaluation of the dollar accomplish its intended objectives? Why or why not?

4. What aspects of bank legislation of 1933 and 1935 were of a reform nature? Explain.

5. (a) What was the Agricultural Adjustment Act of 1933? Was it a measure of reform or relief?
   (b) Why was the AAA declared unconstitutional?

SUGGESTED READINGS

Arnold, Thurmond. *The Folklore of Capitalism.* New Haven, Conn.: Yale University Press, 1937.

Burck, Gilbert, and Charles Silberman. "Why the Depression Lasted So Long," *American Economic History: Essays in Interpretation,* edited by Stanley Coben and Forest G. Hill. Philadelphia: J. B. Lippincott Co., 1966.

---

[3] Before studying the contents of Chapter 24, students should read *The Great Depression* by David A. Shannon. Please bear in mind that all the excerpts are contemporary writings of life and experiences in the early and mid-1930's.

Coben, Stanley, and Forest G. Hill (eds.). "No One Has Starved," *American Economic History: Essays in Interpretation*. Philadelphia: J. B. Lippincott Co., 1966.

Faulkner, Harold U. *American Economic History*. 8th ed. New York City: Harper & Row, Publishers, 1954. Chapter 29.

Fisher, Irving. "The Great Stock Market Crash of 1929," *Issues in American Economic History*, edited by Gerald D. Nash. Boston: D. C. Heath and Co., 1964.

Galbraith, John K. *The Great Crash: 1929*. Boston, Mass: Houghton Mifflin Company, 1955.

Shannon, David A. (ed.). *The Great Depression*. Englewood Cliffs: Prentice-Hall, Inc., 1960.

Wright, Chester W. *Economic History of the United States*. 2d ed. New York City: McGraw-Hill Book Company, 1949. Chapter 43.

Chapter 24

THE NEW DEAL:

REFORM AND RECOVERY

REFORM

The philosophy of the New Deal included the idea that some of our economic institutions permitted practices that contributed to the collapse of our economy. Again, the lack of institutional controls was permissive of actions that were unethical and had undesirable impacts on our economic development. The bank legislation that was presented in Chapter 23 as relieving weaknesses in our banking structure contained measures of reform that may have been essential antecedents of well-grounded recovery. To classify a measure as one of reform is one thing; just how much it contributed to recovery is another. Similarly, it is extremely difficult to detect what factors spearheaded permanent recovery, but it appears that exogenous factors were more significant than were endogenous ones.

Banking and Finance

There is no quantitative measurement of the impact of the work of the Federal Deposit Insurance Corporation and of the Federal Savings and Loan Insurance Corporation upon the economy other than what is found in the reduced number of bank failures that followed their initial period of functioning. More important than the mere reduction in the frequency of bank failures was the confidence that was instilled in depositors that their banks would not fail. The FDIC also took steps that strengthened banks. Investment portfolios of member banks were scrutinized carefully for the purpose of maintaining a high degree of liquidity in order to prevent bank failures, rather than to offer a cure afterwards. Life insurance companies had weathered the storm in commendable fashion, and the volume of their business increased in response to their record of comparative soundness and stability. Patrons of Postal Savings gained sufficient confidence in commercial banks to return to the use of demand deposits.

Bankers themselves who had cringed under the tongue-lashing of the President took a new outlook on the prospects of commercial banking and began to chafe at the new restrictions that had been imposed upon them. They had forgotten that only a few years earlier he had saved them from suffering even larger financial losses than they actually incurred.

The separation of investment banking operations from those of commercial banking removed a source of income for commercial banks, but undoubtedly this action was a measure that resulted in strengthening commercial banks at a time when they needed bolstering. Many depositor-customers of banks were unaware of the reform. Its success was reflected in the greater soundness and stability of banks.

Neither were many depositors aware of the limitations that had been placed upon the control of banking operations and policies by bank holding companies, but again the strength that was imparted to the banking system probably justified the action that was taken. Bankers, in general, have never been much concerned with the operation of a banking system. They were the products of the philosophy and the operations of independent unit banking, and they adhered to their individuality so strongly that it required the Act of 1935 to make the officers of Federal Reserve Banks realize that the Board of Governors had definite authority over their activities and the determination of the credit policies of the Reserve Banks. One of the outcomes of these disturbing years was to strengthen systemic banking without undermining the most desirable features of individual unit banking.

Federal Securities Act of 1933; Securities Exchange Act of 1934

What may have been the most significant reform measure of these Acts was the protection that was afforded the general public, particularly the potential investors in corporate securities. All securities that were listed on organized security exchanges were to be registered, and in the future they must be registered before they are listed on such exchanges. Information was to be furnished about the organization; the nature of the business performed and its financial structure, including the kinds of securities that were outstanding; the names of the men who served on the Board of Directors; and the number and value of the company's shares that were owned by its officers, by members of the Board, and by the underwriters of its securities. Bonus and profit-sharing plans were to be outlined; management and service contracts were to be bared; and balance sheets, and profit and loss statements were to be filed with the Commission. Standards of corporate management may have been raised, and corporate accounting practices were made uniform and possibly more enlightening and intelligible to the layman. There was no guarantee of financial soundness or security, nor were prospective investors compelled to resort to SEC files for information that pertained to corporate patterns of organization and behavior, but at least such data were made available for those who were interested.

Other purposes of this legislation were (1) to restrict the amount of credit that was available to support trading in securities and to restrict the volume of speculative trading on organized security markets; (2) to restrict the extent to which officers could manipulate the values of their corporate securities by disseminating inaccurate or incomplete information concerning them, or by engaging in *wash* sales or in other fictitious transactions for purposes that were not beneficial to the public.

The Board of Governors of the Federal Reserve System was given the power to regulate the margin that speculators had to provide in purchasing corporate securities on margin through brokers. The higher the margin required, the lower were brokers' loans in relation to the total value of marginal transactions. Margin requirements have been raised when the Board deemed it desirable to reduce the volume of speculative credit.

Transportation

The framers of the Transportation Act of 1920 could not foresee the many developments that would occur during the following two decades and its provisions were soon outmoded. Competition with motor transport, later air transport, placed the railroads in a precarious position from which they could not extricate themselves within the existing framework of legislation.

The Emergency Transportation Act of 1933. Since railroad rates, as controlled by the Interstate Commerce Commission, were not flexible, railroad managements could not adjust either passenger or freight rates commensurate with reductions in commodity prices and personal incomes. Consequently, traffic managers, in their search for lower rates, sought motor carriers and air transport. The railroads competed with motor carriers and air transport, and there was likewise competition among all three—all resulting in chaos and needless, high cost duplication of services. The initial effort to restore order to unbridled competition was found in the provisions of The Emergency Railroad Transportation Act of 1933. Its departures from traditional patterns of government policy and control were found in the purposes for which the Act was passed. It was intended to encourage and promote or require action on the part of the carriers and their subsidiaries that were subject to the authority of the Interstate Commerce Commission which would avoid the unnecessary duplication of services and facilities of any nature and which would permit the joint use of terminals and trackage incident thereto or requisite to such joint use, except that no routes in operation at the time were to be discontinued without the consent of all participating railroads or upon order of the Coordinator. All wasteful practices in the rendition of transportation services were to be eliminated.

Financial reorganization of the railroads was encouraged, with due regard being paid the legal rights of security owners, so as to reduce fixed charges as were deemed to be in the public interest and to improve the credit rating of the railroads. Finally, a study was to be made of other means of improving transportation in all its forms, and plans were to be prepared for implementing such improvements.

The Office of Coordinator of Transportation was established and Joseph B. Eastmen, long a member of the Interstate Commerce Commission and one of the leading authorities in the area of railroad regulation, was appointed to the office. One of his early reports to Congress indicated his belief at the time that government ownership and operation of the railroads was the only effective solution to the railroad problem. Railroad holding companies were placed under the jurisdiction of the Commission, and the recapture clause of the Transportation Act of 1920 was repealed. Thus was brought to an end one of the most controversial matters in the whole area of railroad regulation. Short lines and electric railways, which were disappearing rapidly, were represented on regional committees that met with the Coordinator, but motor and air transport agencies were bypassed.

Motor Transportation. Competition was taking its toll in economic segments other than in marketing. The automobile, motor bus, and motor truck had offered competition to railroads and to electric interurban and street railway facilities. Urban communities had long since restored some semblance of order out of chaos by granting franchises to urban motor bus companies which restricted the operation of buses to certain streets, established fares, and designated regular stopping places where passengers could board and leave buses. Licenses were required of the operators of taxicabs as well as of the companies that furnished them. This level of competition combined with the ownership and use of individual motor cars on city streets and on highways had serious impacts on the financial aspects of other companies that offered public transportation service.

Intrastate transport services, both passenger and freight, were regulated at the state level, but no effective regulation of motor carriers had been imposed at the federal level. It remained for the Motor Carrier Act of 1935 to restore a semblance of order to interstate motor transport service. Regulations that were imposed were similar to those that had been applied to the railroads 50 years earlier in the Interstate Commerce Act. In one important respect there was a point of departure. Since competition took care of the maximum rates motor carriers could charge, they were not brought under the scrutiny of the Interstate Commerce Commission.

Air Transport. Aviation had come a long way since Kitty Hawk. It had passed through the stages of stunt flying, air show spectaculars, offering sightseeing rides at county and state fairs, and of carrying the mail. Engineering designs had improved to the level where planes could carry large numbers of passengers per plane. Freight and express services were available. All planes were powered by propellers. In design, the biplane was being superseded by the monoplane. Lighter-than-air transport facilities had become memories, and not always pleasant ones at that. The Shenandoah and the Akron dirigible disasters had taken their tolls of lives, and the spectacular explosion of the

Hindenberg as it neared its mooring at Lakehurst, New Jersey, wrote finis to trans-Atlantic service in a sausage type balloon. Many improvements had been made in heavier-than-air machines and accepted in the name of military defense. Numerous and costly accidents, many of them fatal to human lives, marred the development and public acceptance of the airplane as a medium of public transport. Federal control of aviation as far as rendering mail service was concerned was removed from the Department of Commerce to the Army. The safety record of the military was vastly better than that of commercial flying, and mail reached its destination with fewer delays.

The very nature of aviation predetermined its regulation at the federal level. There was little or no resistance by the states to the passage of the Civil Aeronautics Authority Act in 1938. Two years later the Civil Aeronautics Authority was reorganized. Within the Authority, which was an agency within the Department of Commerce, Congress established the Civil Aeronautics Administration and the Civil Aeronautics Board. The former office was to administer all matters that pertained to the airways system, the enforcement of safety rules that were laid down by the Civil Aeronautics Board (CAB), and the promotion of airline traffic. The CAB was placed in charge of economic regulation and the issuance of all rules that would enhance the safety of flying. It took over the task of attempting to reconstruct the causes of all accidents that happened to civilian commercial planes.

The CAB assured the airlines of profitable operations by determining the amount of airmail subsidy which would be paid by the Post Office Department. In establishing rates, it took into consideration the financial needs of each carrier under efficient management, over and above its receipts from free enterprise commerce, that were essential to rendering the services required of it. Efficiency of management and of operation was not measured in terms of profits. Need was not cumulative for the industry in its entirety. It was determined by the flow of money income to each line in relation to its costs. Lines for which commercial operations were profitable were given low mail subsidies. Lines for which the needs were greater received larger mail subsidies. In 1948 these subsidies ranged from a low of 60 cents per mail ton mile to $70 for the same unit of measurement.

Social Insurance

The industrialization of the United States presented many social and economic problems that either had not existed when agricultural activities were the principal origins of our national income or had not become of nationwide concern. Unemployment on a seasonal basis had always presented somewhat of a problem, but the use of family labor on farms and the localization of farming held this problem to minimal proportions. There had been no particular problem of old age, as most workers had not lived long enough to retire. When they had lived to retirement, or when they became permanently disabled, their children assumed the responsibility of caring for them. Some of them were cared for in county, city, or state institutions. The relationship between parents and their children was altered by new patterns of social behavior that came into vogue after World War I.

The problem that was related to the incidence of industrial accidents, namely, how to provide financial assistance to those persons who had become totally or partially incapacitated, had not been and probably could not be solved at the level of free enterprise. Solutions to this and other problems of a similar nature added increments to production costs, and competitive conditions made individual firms somewhat reluctant to add increments to their costs which they could not pass along to consumers in the form of higher prices. State authorities were hesitant to impose constitutional or statutory requirements upon industry, lest the latter be driven from their states, or lest the requirements prove to be deterrents to new industries locating therein.

Old Age Pensions. The states of California, Maryland, Minnesota, Montana, and Wyoming had passed old age security laws by 1930; but the pensions that were paid were woefully inadequate even to sustain persons at a minimum of comfort and decency level of living when they had attained the age of 65 or 70. The costs of these plans were borne entirely by taxing the public, irrespective of the relationship of individuals and firms to respective industries or their products. In December, 1933, the average pension that was paid by 23 states whose legislatures had passed old age security laws ranged from a minimum of $7.69 in the state of Colorado to a maximum of $29.35 in Maryland. Several states provided maximum monthly payments of $35; but in Massachusetts and Montana where no maximums were provided, the December, 1933, pension payments averaged $25.02 and $12.51 respectively. In December, 1934, Nebraska paid persons who had passed their 65th birthday an average of $3.88 compared to upper limits of $30 a month for single persons, $50 a month for a couple. Despite the fact that pensions were paid by eight states in December, 1934, that had not paid any such increments during the corresponding month in 1933, and that nine states paid larger average pensions than they had paid in December, 1933, the average payment by 23 states was $16.16 in December, 1934, compared with an average pension payment of $19.34 one year earlier by 15 states.

The following states had county optional pension plans that had been provided in the years indicated, but at the close of 1934 no pensions had been paid: Nevada (1925), Kentucky (1926), and West Virginia (1931). All the counties in each of the following states participated in pension plans: Arizona, California, Delaware, Iowa, Massachusetts, New Hampshire, New York, North Dakota, and Ohio. The addition of six states to the list that paid pensions in December, 1934, added only .08 percent of the population that lived in counties in which pensions were paid to the list of those receiving payments. Suffice it to say that the American people were not being taken care of adequately, even in the states and counties in which some provision had been made for them. Basic to any program of social reconstruction and reform was the financial security of all persons. Insurance plans differed from direct relief in that the funds that were necessary to carry out the programs were to be obtained from contributions made by the benefactors. Relief payments were made from the revenues that flowed into the Treasury in the collection of taxes.

Need for Expanding Coverage. Many were the interpretations of the causes of the slowdown in production in 1929. One explanation was in terms of overproduction; another was in terms of underconsumption, and it was to correct the latter that much attention was given and much energy expended. Regardless of the validity of either or both of these approaches in finding the cause of the slowdown, the fact remains that the productive capacity of the capital resources of the United States was not being used to full extent. The Brookings Institution estimated that in 1929 the United States was capable of producing as much as $110 billion a year and that the rate of growth since 1900 had been 5 percent per annum. At this rate, by 1930 the annual output would have amounted to $170 billion.

In 1929 the total output amounted to $87.4 billion, and by 1933 it had fallen to $39.6 billion. By 1937 the output had increased to $74 billion, only to fall the following year to $67.2 billion. Eight million families, more or less, had annual incomes of less than $800; clothing manufacturers were making one suit of clothes per year for each three men in the country; in 1935 two thirds of working families subsisted on less than $14.50 a week. Obviously there was something wrong with our economic organization that had such a large production potential and such a low volume of actual output. Men and machines were idle, and there appeared to be no way to ignite the spark of recovery other than to put more units of purchasing power into the hands of the masses.

Inadequacy of Relief Programs at State Levels. State pension plans had failed to accomplish this purpose, and there were no plans at state and local levels for providing compensation to the unemployed. Even so the problem was national in scope, and a solution had to be found at the national level. Senator Huey Long, of Louisiana, and the Reverend Charles E. Coughlin, a Roman Catholic priest from Detroit, each formulated different plans for getting the wheels of industry to turning again. It remained for Dr. Francis E. Townsend, of California, to come up with a plan that appealed to thousands of voters but one which was never adopted. He was a retired physician, who at one time had been comfortably well off but who had been ruined financially by the depression. The spending of $200 per month by all persons who had attained the age of 60 was his approach to putting idle resources back to work. Under his plan, over $32 billion, which was 40 percent of the income for 1929, would be spent annually by 13 million persons. The average income per family in 1929 was $2,700, some of which was saved; while under the Townsend Plan, husband and wife, each of whom had attained the age of 60, together would receive $4,800 all of which had to be spent at the rate of $400 per month. He proposed to finance the program by placing a tax of 2 percent on all transactions.

If the several plans did nothing more than focus the attention of the electorate upon the inadequacy of state and private plans for providing relief to the aged and to the unemployed, they served a useful purpose. Private pension plans that had been adopted by some corporate employers proved to be fair weather schemes that collapsed in time of real need.

Social Security. In August, 1935, Congress approved its first social security plan, one that provided pensions for persons above 65 years of age and unemployment compensation for certain classes of workers. No provisions were made to cover agricultural workers, casual laborers, domestic servants, employees of the several states or of the federal government, or officers and crews of ships that plied navigable waters. Employees of nonprofit organizations, such as churches, schools, charitable and scientific institutions, were excluded from receiving social security benefits. Immediate payments of up to $15 a month were to be paid to needy persons who had already attained the age of 65 and who lived in states that would at least match this amount. Future payments were to be assured by the collection of payroll taxes that started at 1 percent and were graduated upwards to reach 3 percent in 1948. Employees were assessed similar amounts which were withheld from their weekly paychecks. This procedure lowered the cost of collecting social security taxes and also assured that all persons who were covered by the law in receiving compensation paid their proportionate share of the costs of the program.

Unemployment Insurance. In 1933 the Wagner-Peyser Act had authorized the establishment of the United States Employment Service as a bureau within the Department of Labor. The Service coordinated the activities of similar state organizations; it prescribed standards of operation; and it collected statistical data that pertained to the general problem of unemployment. In order to be eligible to receive unemployment benefit payments, applicants not only had to be registered at one of the public employment offices, they had to have exhausted the facilities of these offices in their search for employment. Unemployment compensation was to be paid for from 12 to 26 weeks in amounts that were equal to not more than one half of the weekly wage rates of the respective beneficiaries. Employers were assessed initially at the rate of 1 percent of their payrolls, and individual employees had like amounts withheld from their weekly wages. This withholding rate was graduated upward to reach 3 percent by 1938. Since the amounts that were collected from the respective states were to be spent elsewhere unless the states matched the benefit payments of the federal government, all the states enacted laws that met federal requirements, and benefit payments were made uniform the country over. The states were likewise given federal aid in providing payments to dependent children, to provide for carrying on programs of maternal care, child welfare, and public health work.

The only part of the social security program that was administered solely by the federal government was old age benefits or insurance. The states were required to establish public employment offices and to disburse the benefit payments to the unemployed, to the blind, and to the other recipients of social security benefits.

Few persons appeared to understand how the reserves that would be created by the collection of taxes from employer payrolls and from wage earners would be handled. Most persons thought that money would be hoarded in safe places and would be paid out in the future as the occasions arose. Far from being hoarded, these reserves were used in retiring the federal debt on occasions and in the purchase of new issues of federal bonds. In the early days of the program, appropriations were made by the Congress to meet the payments that were anticipated by the director of the program. After the program had been in force for several years and collections were in excess of current obligations, government bonds were purchased, the interest from which strengthened the reserves and tended to reduce the amounts that had to be appropriated in future years in order to meet current obligations.

Built-in Corrective to Instability. Unemployment insurance, in particular, has become one of the built-in correctives to prolonged periods of recession and depression. The program has been extended so that many of the classes of workers that were excluded from the original program have been covered either on a compulsory or on a voluntary basis. The exclusion of state and federal employees was not a serious omission; nor did it cause injustice or create inequities, since these persons were included in civil service programs, merit systems, or retirement programs as they are called in various instances. Many white collar workers and those of religious institutions have been afforded the opportunity of having the protection of the federal social security program. While some of these workers have been covered in the past by other programs, the latter have proved to be unstable and inadequate in time of greatest need.

Benefit Payments. Payments of social security benefits from 1935 to 1940 to the aged, to the blind, and to dependent children were much more important to the individual beneficiaries than they were to society in its entirety. Working persons were relieved of some, if not all, of the financial burdens that had been imposed upon them of caring for dependent aged parents and relatives and for the blind. Widowed mothers found living made less burdensome by the receipt of monthly checks to care for their dependent children. These checks may well have been the means of keeping families together, children in school, and of maintaining approximately the standard of living to which the families were accustomed. The use of savings may have been postponed to a later date during which time the additional interest payments could have been compounded. Since payments to the aged and to the blind may have reduced the need for institutional care, at least at the level of public expense, they did not represent proportional increases in the cost of public welfare either at the state or federal levels.

During the first 17 months of operation of social security, a total of $334,405,977 was paid out to the following classes of beneficiaries:

Old Age	$277,524,116
Blind	10,815,299
Dependent Children	46,066,562
Total	$334,405,977

Throughout the first six months of 1938, $179,508,721 was paid in unemployment relief. For the fiscal year that ended on June 30, 1939, such benefit payments amounted to $446,147,697; and for the fiscal year that ended on June 30, 1940, unemployment benefits amounted to $482,510,753. Payments to the unemployed were made too late and they were too small in dollar values to be of any use in stimulating recovery at this particular time. The psychology of unemployment could not be overcome merely by the payment of a few dollars to possibly one fifth or less of the unemployed. By the time they were first paid in 1938 the country had passed through a period of noticeable recovery only to suffer a violent reaction in late 1937 and early 1938. After the impacts of war in Europe were felt in many segments of the American economy, recovery appeared to be on its way, but this is a topic that forms the subject matter of a later paragraph.

Pains of Economic Progress. Social security and unemployment insurance rank alongside workmen's compensation as forward steps that were taken to relieve some adverse economic impacts on some segments of our population that had become victims of economic, social, and industrial progress. Economic progress always hurts some people. Unemployment compensation is not true insurance, in that contributions are not graduated according to the degree of risk; but the bearers of the risk pool their contributions and are paid therefrom when the risks become realities. A strict application of insurance to group risks does not itself prevent losses, nor does the payment of unemployment insurance prevent unemployment of those who are eligible to receive the payments. The hope and expectation of the New Dealers was that the payment of unemployment compensation to those who had become unemployed would prevent others from becoming unemployed. The theory was that by maintaining the purchasing power of those who no longer were receiving wages, declines in the level of operation of other industries in which the incidence of unemployment had not become noticeable would be avoided. Unemployment compensation as a preventive of widespread unemployment was much more effective than were such payments after unemployment had been experienced by 20 to 25 percent of the working population for a period of several years.

Labor Reforms

After the nullification of Section 7 of the National Industrial Recovery Act, it was evident to Senator Wagner, of New York, and others that if the government were going to make good on its promise to do something for labor, more positive action than relying on court decisions would have to be taken. He was largely responsible for drawing up the terms of the National Labor Relations Act in 1935 to which reference is made in terms of its sponsor. It embodied and enlarged upon the desirable features of Section 7 of the National Industrial Recovery Act that were based upon the premise that collective bargaining was socially desirable and necessary in order to overcome the inequality of bargaining power between employers and their employees. It also recognized that approximately 25 percent, almost 5,900, of the strikes that had been called between 1919 and 1934 inclusive, were called in attempts to obtain recognition of unions, of which collective bargaining was and still is the basic manifestation.

The National Labor Relations Act. The Act restated the principles that had been enunciated in Section 7 of the National Industrial Recovery Act. The general right that employees had to organize had long been recognized in common law and had been proclaimed in the Erdman Act, the Railway Labor Act, and others. The Wagner Act confirmed and extended rights that had been affirmed to employees of the American railroads to workers in all segments of American industry. The statement that "employees shall have the right to self-organization, to form, join, or assist labor organizations, to bargain collectively through representatives of their own choosing, and to engage in concerted activities, for the purpose of collective bargaining or other mutual aid or protection" was followed by defining unfair labor practices that were in violation of these rights. Legal machinery was created by which these rights could be enforced.

Unfair Labor Practices. In order to prevent any misunderstanding of the intent of Congress either by the National Labor Relations Board or by the courts, the Act went on to say that "it shall be an unfair labor practice for an employer to interfere with, restrain, or coerce employees in the exercise of the rights" that have been stated above. Espionage is one form of "restraint, interference or coercion." Physical ejection of representatives of unions from properties of employers is coercion, as is the hiring of men to work their way into union offices for the purpose of undermining their organizations. Discriminatory practices in hiring, firing, and in promoting employees have been declared to be unfair labor practices. Employers may not advise their workers in matters that pertain to union membership. Company unions were outlawed as an unfair labor practice that interfered with the formation or administration of labor organization. In order to make the Act effective, provision was made that employers could not take any kind of action against any of their employees who might have filed charges or given testimony under the Act.

The unfair practices that have been listed in the preceding paragraph on page 651 are somewhat negative in character, in that they state what employers may not do. The most positive requirement of the Act is that which compels employers to meet with representatives of unions that have been chosen by the exercise of the ballot. It should be noted here that while employers are required to meet with the duly elected representatives of their employees, they are not compelled to reach agreements with them. In order to assure that elections are carried out in conformity to law, representatives of the National Labor Relations Board organize and supervise all such elections. Employees must be given time off from their work to cast their ballots.

Jones & Laughlin Steel Corporation v. N.L.R.B. It was not to be expected that employers would yield without a struggle what they had considered to be their rights in bargaining with their employees and in their efforts to maintain open shops. What may have been one of the most concerted efforts to forestall the purposes and objectives of the National Labor Relations Act was exerted by the Jones & Laughlin Steel Corporation which had been one of the strongest opponents of unionism. In fact, it was the challenge of this steel company to the National Labor Relations Board that led to the Supreme Court's decision that upheld the provisions of the Act. Industrial leaders were confident that the Court would follow the precedent that was established in the Schechter case, namely, that the labor policies of the defendent did not have an impact upon interstate commerce. On the contrary, the Court held that in view of the far-flung activities of the Jones & Laughlin Steel Corporation, their stoppage would have "a most serious effect upon interstate commerce. . . . When industries organize themselves on a national scale, making their relation to interstate commerce the dominant factor in their activities, how can it be maintained that their industrial labor relations constitute a forbidden field into which Congress may not enter when it is necessary to protect interstate commerce from the paralyzing consequences of industrial war?"

Sit-down Strikes. It was during the period in which corporations were in noncompliance with the provisions of the Wagner Act that sit-down strikes were staged. One of the initial uses of this technique was in connection with the efforts of John L. Lewis to organize the Fisher Body Plant Division of General Motors Corporation in Flint, Michigan, in the fall of 1935. Steel plants in Gary, Pittsburgh, and South Chicago had already been seized by workers who engaged in sit-down strikes. Not only did employees occupy factories and mills, they turned them into armed fortresses that defied efforts of any agency to dislodge them. It was the episode at Flint that broke the resistance of General Motors to the principles of organized labor. After a few years of the application of this technique, the Supreme Court declared that it was an unlawful seizure of corporate property and ordered union officers to cease and desist from the practice.

That the passage of the National Labor Relations Act in 1935 did not put an end to strikes is evident from the data that constitute Table 24-1. The data belie the statement that it is futile for organized labor to call strikes during periods of unemployment and falling prices. More strikes were called and more workers were involved after 1933 than during many of the allegedly prosperous years of the 1920's.

Table 24-1
The Number of Strikes and Related Data—1930-1941

Year	Number of Strikes	Number of Workers Involved	Man-days Idle	Percentage of Workers Involved
1930	637	182,975	3,316,808	.8
1931	810	341,817	6,893,244	1.6
1932	841	324,210	10,502,033	1.8
1933	1,695	1,168,272	16,872,128	6.3
1934	1,856	1,466,695	19,591,949	7.2
1935	2,014	1,117,213	15,456,337	5.2
1936	2,172	788,648	13,901,956	3.1
1937	4,740	1,860,621	28,424,857	7.2
1938	2,772	688,376	9,148,273	2.8
1939	2,613	1,170,962	17,812,219	4.7
1940	2,508	576,988	6,700,872	2.3
1941	4,288	2,362,620	23,047,556	8.4

Source: *Monthly Labor Review,* 1942, p. 1109.

The Walsh-Healey Act. The Walsh-Healey Act, 1936, also called the Public Contracts Act, provided the conditions under which supplies and materials were to be purchased on government contracts entered into for such purposes, and for other purposes. It authorized the Secretary of Labor to determine the prevailing rates of wages that were being paid in the respective communities in which government contracts were being fulfilled. Manufacturers of supplies and materials, articles and equipment, were required to pay these wage rates to all employees who were employed in the performance of government contracts. No person was to be permitted to work more than eight hours in any one day, or more than 40 hours in any one week. No male employee under the age of 18, no female employee under the age of 16, and no convict labor was to be employed by such manufacturers. Working conditions had to meet the safety, sanitation, and inspection laws of the respective states in which such contracts were being fulfilled. Under certain conditions, and they were stated in Section 6 of the Act, the Secretary of Labor was authorized to permit exceptions to be made concerning the payment of prevailing wage rates by employers who were performing under government contracts "as he may find necessary and proper in the public interest or to prevent injustice and undue hardship." The rate for overtime pay "shall not be less than" one and one-half times the basic rate of pay for any employee affected.

That the provisions of the Act were not to be applied universally was made clear in Section 9 of the Act. They were to apply only to the purchase of materials, supplies, articles, or equipment the contracts for which were let after receiving sealed bids. The purchase of perishables, including dairy, livestock, and nursery products, or of agricultural or farm products that were processed for sale by their original producers were exempt from the provisions of the Act.

The Act provided the opening wedge by which some of the principles that were first laid down in the Adamson Act in 1916, and made to apply to railway labor only, were extended to manufacturing industries and to commercial organizations. In the absence of other reliable data concerning the prevailing rates of wages in different communities, the Secretary of Labor looked to the terms of union contracts for such wage rates. In so doing, employers were not permitted to underbid their competitors solely on the basis of existing wage rate differentials that might arise from their paying nonunion wages. The Act accomplished what had not been done through the channel of a constitutional amendment: namely, it abolished child labor in the fulfillment of government contracts. Organized labor in America had always been opposed to child labor because it was thought that to the extent that children were employed in industry, adult male labor was deprived of an opportunity of holding jobs. The years of depression emphasized this fact more than ever; and people came to accept the principle that fathers, mothers, and adults, irrespective of their marital status, should be given preference in filling the limited number of jobs that were available in the years of industrial recession and of depression.

As for regulating wages, the Walsh-Healey Act did not establish an arbitrary floor below which it was against the law for employers to pay. Prevailing wage rates presumably had been established by the process of collective bargaining between employers and their employees, and they need not have been at the same level in different manufacturing industries in a given location, nor were they necessarily uniform in the same industries in different areas. Prevailing wages had been set with due regard to the marginal productivity of labor. Industry-wide scales of pay were not recognized until a later date.

The Fair Labor Standards Act. It remained for the Fair Labor Standards Act of 1938 to extend the 8-hour day, the 40-hour week, and the principle of one and one-half times the base rate of pay for hours worked in excess of 40 in any one week to employers or firms that were engaged directly or indirectly in interstate commerce. Child labor was abolished. Exempt again were operatives in agriculture, dairying, fishing, and retailing and service establishments whose principal activities were local or intrastate in nature rather than interstate. Executives and members of the professions also were exempt from the requirement of being paid one and one-half times the base rate of pay for hours worked in excess of 40 in any given week. The Wages and Hours Division of the Department of Labor was charged with enforcing the provisions of this Act, which has come to be known more popularly as "The Wages and Hours Act."

The purpose of the Act was to establish a minimum wage of 40 cents an hour in the industries to which its terms applied; at the same time it did not want the payment of this wage to work an undue hardship upon employers who had been paying less than 40 cents an hour and who had to meet competition in the sale of their products. A statutory minimum of 25 cents an hour could be paid for one year; 30 cents an hour could be paid for the next six years, so that by 1945, at most, a uniform minimum wage of 40 cents an hour would prevail in all industries to which the terms of the Act applied. Provision was made for the appointment of industry-wide tripartite committees composed of representatives of employers, of employees, and the public. These committees were to investigate conditions in the respective areas of industrial activity and to recommend minimal scales of wages for the various classes of employees. In no case were wage classifications to be determined solely on the basis of either age or of sex. Among the conditions that were to be considered by the industry committees were the prevailing wage rates for work of like character, the wages that were paid by other employers who voluntarily maintained fair minimum wage standards, and the cost of living. The committees were to establish the highest minimum rate that could be enforced without creating any additional unemployment that might result from the payment of these minimums in their efforts to attain the 40-cent standard minimum wage in the shortest possible time.

Minimum Wages and Marginal Productivity. In the enforcement of the standard minimum wage, there was an awareness of the influence of marginal productivity in the determination of wages. At the same time the implication was strong that some rates of wages were actually below this level and could be raised without affecting commodity prices. Insofar as wages were raised to comply with the standard minimum wage, the incomes of workers were increased, their purchasing power was increased, and the volume of sales of necessities responded accordingly. The receipt of minimum wage incomes did not permit workers to enjoy many comforts or luxuries. The impact of paying higher minimum wages than had formerly prevailed was felt by those who had received wage differentials above the respective minimums in different industries.

Minimum wages were paid to and received by what has traditionally been called common labor. Common labor was that type of work that was physical rather than mental. It involved little or no responsibility or decision making.

It did not come into direct contact with the public. It functioned with little or no capital equipment of any kind beyond a hand-powered tool or implement. Responsibilities and skills that were required of semiskilled workers were compensated for by the payment of wage differentials that were added to the wages of common labor. In turn, other rate differentials were added to the wages of semiskilled workers of higher levels to arrive at the wages that were paid to members of the skilled classifications of labor.

Economic Impacts of Minimum Wage Laws. One important impact of the enforcement of a standard minimum wage was that increased purchasing power was given to all workers and the volume of business consummated increased accordingly. Another important economic impact of the enforcement of any wage minimum was that the payment of wages at all levels of performance depended less and less upon marginal productivity of the workers. Instead of employers relating their numbers of workers and their wages to respective marginal utilities, they had to adjust marginal utilities and the number of employees so that the present values of their respective marginal products were not higher than the required minimum wage rates. Still another impact of laws or contracts that determined wage rates has been to hasten the introduction and use of more capital equipment that has displaced labor in the short run. The expansion of the economy, that has produced larger and larger national incomes, has served the important function of absorbing labor that has been displaced in the short run by the introduction of machinery, or the intensification of its use in industry.

The Coal Conservation Act of 1935

Two situations gave rise to unstable conditions in the mining and marketing of bituminous coal that led to periods of boom and bust as measured in terms of profits. To start with, deposits of bituminous coal were so extensive that it was extremely difficult to control the rate at which it was mined and sold in market places. Coal that was mined from a given vein was homogeneous, a fact which made it almost entirely impossible to impart to it a brand name by which the product of a given operator could be identified. Ofttimes purchasers specified that they wanted coal that had been mined in Kentucky, in West Virginia, in Pennsylvania, in Alabama, or elsewhere. Even so they were compelled to take whatever a local dealer had stored in his bins or in his yard.

A second factor that contributed to the instability of coal mining was the fact that some operations were organized, while others were not. There were many operations that were conducted on relatively high levels of safety, health, and sanitation. Many were the operations, however, that were relatively small as measured in terms of the number of employees; in terms of the value of capital that was utilized in the mining processes; and in terms of the tonnage of coal that was raised to the surface, processed, and sold on the market. Cumulative totals of these items were large, and the coal that was produced from the small operations competed successfully with the product of larger mines, especially in nearby markets.

When the National Industrial Recovery Act failed to survive the test of the Supreme Court, Senator Guffey, of Pennsylvania, sponsored a bill in Congress that has come to be known as the Guffey Act of 1935. Although the terms of the Act were intended to evidence the importance of imposing standards that should govern or control the conditions under which bituminous coal is mined in the name of general welfare, the Supreme Court reiterated its position that had been so well expressed in the E. C. Knight sugar case and in the two cases that were taken before it that arose out of attempts to regulate the employment of child labor, namely, that the mining of coal may not be regulated by the Congress under the power given it by the interstate commerce clause of the Constitution. Because price fixing features were tied in with the labor provisions of the Act, they could not be approved by the Court. However, the decision did contain an implication that the Court might look more kindly upon an effort to establish federal control over prices and trade practices if they were divorced from interstate commerce. Accordingly, the Guffey-Vinson Act was passed by Congress and signed by the President in April, 1937. The effect of its passage was to extend to mining operations the same levels of control that already had been exercised over railway, manufacturing, and interstate commerce.

Production data reveal that less bituminous coal was produced in 1938 and 1939 than in 1937, but it is difficult to determine that the decrease was due to the enforcement of or to the impacts of the Coal Conservation Act. The entire economy of the United States was feeling the impacts of pending war in Europe that was coming nearer and nearer to one of realization for the United States. Internal economic conditions were anything but stable during these years of anticipation. Too many other things did not remain the same to permit any objective evaluation of the economic impacts of that Act upon the tonnage of coal that was mined.

Birth of the Congress for Industrial Organization

Many labor leaders thought the time had come for the American Federation of Labor to champion the cause of the unskilled workers and at the same time to organize labor along industrial lines instead of continuing to adhere to a craft type of organization at a time when craft skills were losing much of their traditional distinctiveness. William Green, who had succeeded Samuel Gompers as president of the American Federation of Labor, felt just as strongly as the latter towards craft organizations. Green showed his disdain for industrial unionism by refusing to approve this form of organization on the occasions of the annual conventions of the American Federation of Labor in San Francisco in 1934, and in Atlantic City in 1935.

A group of leaders led by John L. Lewis formed a Committee for Industrial Organization in November, 1935, and shortly thereafter Lewis wrote a letter to William Green in which he resigned his office of vice-president of the American Federation of Labor. In 1938 the rift in the ranks of labor was made permanent by the organization of the Congress for Industrial Organization. Unlike earlier advocates of industrial unionism, the CIO advocated the use of collective bargaining within the existing framework of a capitalistic order in its efforts to improve upon the status of wage earners. While the CIO was prepared to exercise more political pressure than was advocated by the American Federation of Labor, it did not advocate an alteration in our political system, nor did it advocate the organization of a separate labor party.

The unique aspect in the break in the ranks of organized labor is not found in the advocacy of industrial unionism; it is found in the organization of a new labor union at a time when unemployment was at a high level in the American economy. Almost one fourth of the civilian labor force was unemployed in 1933. By 1935 conditions had improved to the extent that one fifth of the civilian labor force was unemployed. Partial recovery appears to have been incipient in 1937 when the percentage of unemployed workers reached a low of 14.3 percent for the decade. (See Table 24-2.) Unemployment increased by approximately 30 percent in 1938, but declined again the following year in response to an increase in orders from European countries, who either were at war or were preparing for another holocaust.

Table 24-2

Unemployment for the Years 1929-1940
(Annual Averages in Thousands of Persons over 14 Years of Age)

Year	Unemployed	Percent of Civilian Labor Force
1929	1,550	3.2
1930	4,340	8.7
1931	8,020	15.9
1932	12,060	23.6
1933	12,830	24.9
1934	11,340	21.7
1935	10,610	20.1
1936	9,030	16.9
1937	7,700	14.3
1938	10,390	19.0
1939	9,480	17.2
1940	8,120	14.6

Source: U. S. Department of Commerce, Bureau of the Census, *Historical Statistics of the United States. Colonial Times to 1957* (Washington: U. S. Government Printing Office, 1960), p. 73. Adapted.

Other Accomplishments of Labor

The Goodyear Rubber & Tire Company was forced to recognize the United Rubber Workers (CIO) after the latter staged its first successful large sit-down strike in 1936. The Anti-Strike Breakers Act, sometimes known as the Byrnes Act, made it unlawful "to transport or aid in transporting strikebreakers in interstate or foreign commerce."

The year 1937 was a memorable one in the history of the Congress of Industrial Organization. The CIO succeeded in its efforts to organize two of the mass production industries it had endeavored so long to organize. General Motors Corporation and the United States Steel Corporation recognized CIO unions as the bargaining agents for their respective employees. United States Steel finally accepted the principle and fact of an 8-hour day and a 40-hour week.

Progress of the Depression

Progress of the depression is frequently presented in terms of unemployment, in terms of foreign trade, in terms of price trends, and in terms of the utilization of our productive resources. Another vivid portrayal of the depression is obtained from observing per capita national incomes, not that they measure actual incomes each person received. They do distribute

Table 24-3

National Income and Disposable Income—1929-1940
(In Billions of Dollars, Except per Capita Figures in Dollars)

Year	National Income Total	National Income Per Capita	Disposable Income Total	Disposable Income Per Capita
1929	$87.7	$720	$83.1	$682
1930	75.7	615	74.4	604
1931	59.7	487	63.8	521
1932	42.5	340	48.7	398
1933	40.2	321	45.7	363
1934	49.0	387	52.0	410
1935	57.1	448	58.3	457
1936	64.9	506	66.2	511
1937	73.6	570	71.0	550
1938	67.6	520	65.7	519
1939	72.8	555	70.4	537
1940	81.6	617	76.1	576

Source: *Historical Statistics of the United States. Colonial Times to 1957*, 1960, p. 139. Adapted.

equal shares of total national incomes between all persons who rely upon income in a market-oriented economic society.

National Income; Disposable Income. In 1929 gross national product reached an all-time peak of $104.4 billion; per capita it measured $857. For the same year national income equaled $87.8 billion and disposable income $83.1 billion. Reduced to a per capita level, national income was $720; disposable income $682. The depth of the depression was reached in 1933, by which time national income had declined to $40.2 billion or $321 per capita; and disposable income amounted to $45.7 billion, or $363 per capita. The course of the depression is sketched in the data that constitute Table 24-3.

National income is composed of the aggregate earnings of labor and property which arise from the current production of goods and services. *Disposable income* is the amount received by persons from all sources inclusive of transfers from government and business but exclusive of business transfers, minus deductions for taxes. For years in which government transfer payments exceeded tax withholdings and nontax payments to general government, disposable income was larger than national income. In terms of national income and of disposable income per capita, the depth of the depression was reached in 1933. The per capita disposable income of $363 for that year does not mean that every person had $22 more than one half of what they had to spend in 1929. This item is solely a statistical average,

Table 24-4
Wholesale Price Indexes (BLS)—1929-1940
(1929 = 100)

Year	All Commodities	All Commodities Other than Farm	Farm Products
1929	95.3	91.6	104.9
1930	86.4	85.2	88.3
1931	73.0	75.0	64.8
1932	64.8	70.2	48.2
1933	65.9	71.2	51.4
1934	74.9	78.4	65.3
1935	80.0	77.9	78.8
1936	80.8	79.6	80.9
1937	86.3	85.3	86.4
1938	78.6	81.7	68.5
1939	77.1	81.3	65.3
1940	78.6	83.0	67.7

Source: *Historical Statistics of the United States. Colonial Times to 1957,* 1960, p. 116. Adapted.

but as such it is a useful concept for purposes of comparison. The data for 1937 indicate that economic activity had increased noticeably. This statement is borne out by the data on unemployment which are given in Table 24-2 and those on the movement of wholesale prices which appear in Table 24-4. More people had more money to spend on consumers' goods in 1937 than they had for this purpose in 1933, but the following year witnessed a sharp decline.

Foreign Trade. The first impression a student receives in glancing at the data in Table 24-5 is the rapid decline in the values of both commodity exports and commodity imports from 1929 to 1932 and the slow rate of recovery from 1933 through 1940. A second impression is that for every year the value of commodity exports exceeded the value of commodity imports. The cumulative total of the excess of export values for the 12 years was $6,870 million. This imbalance in the commodity trade account was made up by the shipment of gold and some silver, and by the movement of financial capital, so that the international payments account balanced. Lacking in this presentation, but of no particular significance, are the items of invisible export and invisible import. So much gold was shipped into the United States in settlement of these balances that the Board of Governors undertook to sterilize it, i.e., to keep it from supporting additional bank credit.

Even though our foreign trade constituted a smaller percentage of our total trade than did our domestic trade, declines such as are revealed by the data in Table 24-5 were tremendously significant to all of those persons

Table 24-5

Merchandise Exports and Imports—1929-1940

Year	Exports	Imports	Excess of Exports
1929	$5,241	$4,399	$ 842
1930	3,843	3,061	782
1931	2,424	2,091	333
1932	1,611	1,323	288
1933	1,675	1,450	225
1934	2,133	1,655	478
1935	2,283	2,047	235
1936	2,456	2,423	33
1937	3,349	3,084	265
1938	3,094	1,960	1,134
1939	3,177	2,318	859
1940	4,021	2,625	1,396

Source: *Economic Almanac* (New York: Thomas Y. Crowell Company, 1954), p. 54.

and business firms that were in any manner connected with the latter. Much of the unemployment and idle resources of the period may be attributed to the decline in our foreign trade. That part of the decline in national income that was caused by the decline in foreign trade was reflected in the decrease in the disposable incomes received by labor and by management personnel in that segment of our economy.

RECOVERY

The recovery of our export volume that occurred in and after 1934 may be attributed in part to the devaluation of the American dollar in 1933. Devaluation enabled foreign purchasers of American goods to obtain more American dollars with which to pay for their purchases without being required to relinquish any more of their own monetary units. The value of commodity imports recovered more slowly than did the value of commodity exports partly because the lower weight dollar made imports cost more to American buyers unless prices in European countries declined approximately the same proportion. As the values of American exports increased there were larger dollar balances in foreign banks that could be utilized by American importers. In the area of foreign trade and for the decade, recovery seemed to stem, at least in part, from the stimulus afforded by the implementation of the terms of the Inflation Act of 1933.

Reciprocal Trade Agreements

To repair the damage that was wrought by the passage of the Hawley-Smoot Act of 1930 required that some drastic action be taken. Congress relinquished its power of tariff making to the President in 1934 in order to make our tariff program more flexible and timely in terms of the need for adjustments in rates. The Reciprocal Trade Agreements Act of 1934 was really an amendment to the Hawley-Smoot bill.

The President was empowered to modify existing duties by not more that 50 percent, except on imports from countries that discriminated against American exports. The era of competitive tariff making became a thing of the past. Modifications of tariff rates were permissible when they would assist (1) in restoring the American standard of living; (2) in decreasing unemployment and in overcoming economic depression; (3) in increasing the purchasing power of the American people; and (4) in establishing and maintaining a better relationship between the agricultural, industrial, mining, and commercial segments of our economy.

Even though the value of our commodity imports increased by over $950 million between 1934 and 1940, customs receipts decreased over the same period from $372 million to $331 million. Individual and corporate income taxes had replaced customs duties as major sources of federal revenue.

Partial Recovery, 1936-1937

An examination of the data in Tables 24-3 through 24-5 reveals the fact that the American economy was staging a comeback. So well founded did the recovery appear to be that federal authorities decided it was time to withdraw some of the government supports and to give market forces freer play. In line with the stated policy of maintaining and sustaining overall economic stabilization, the Department of Agriculture in 1937 announced that it would reduce its volume of purchases of basic commodities. The Board of Governors of the Federal Reserve System announced that it would authorize an increase in the rediscount rate and an increase in the reserve requirements of member banks. The idea was to curb what appeared to be an inflationary trend. It seems that the confidence of the people in the operation of their economic system had not been restored to the level whereby they could take in stride announcements of such steps being taken in the near future. Immediately there was a precipitous downward movement in the business cycle, but not for long.

Reasons for Slow Rate of Recovery

The question frequently has been asked why all of the relief measures that provided work for several million persons and that required the expenditure of billions of dollars of public monies were not more effective in overcoming the blight of economic and industrial depression. More than 30 years of retrospection have failed to uncover a definitive answer unless it is found in terms of depression psychology. Putting people to work on a government project and letting them earn up to $30 a month or more, or sending $22 a month to parents of CCC boys may have given people some money to spend on necessities of life, but they were not happy or elated over it. Neither did they know how long they would receive this money. Many such beneficiaries saved as much of their earnings as they could, not knowing when they again might join the army of the unemployed.

Some persons who received incomes that were larger than needed to provide minimum daily necessities used at least some of their surpluses in paying long overdue bills to owners of grocery stores, drug stores, clothing stores, and others who had carried them along until better days. Paying monthly bills was not popular, and neither was having the ability to pay them. Many persons who continued to receive monthly salaries fell in line with those who had no incomes or whose incomes were inadequate to pay current obligations and made all kinds of excuses for not paying theirs. Members of the medical, dental, and legal professions endured financial hardships. People no longer had badly needed dental work done; or if they did, they did not or could not pay for it. Landlords experienced difficulty in collecting rents, and rentals on many properties were reduced. When evictions were made, houses and apartments remained vacant unless tenants from higher rental properties moved into lower rental ones.

Failure of PWA and WPA to Stimulate Recovery. Some reasons for the slow rate of recovery are found in the organizations of the PWA and of the WPA. The former utilized the industrial organization of free enterprise and made no effort to utilize unemployed resources. The latter agency organized its own firms to carry out projects that were awarded to them. Managerial talent that had been idle was utilized, and employment was given to men and women whose names were not found on anybody's payroll. Both agencies placed emphasis on utilizing as much labor and as little capital machinery as possible. Analysis of the business cycle has revealed the important role played by capital investment in its relation to economic activity and to stagnation. When public buildings were constructed, emphasis was placed on hiring as many men as possible, doing as much of the work as possible by hand labor with the use of hand tools, and in drawing out the period of construction over as many days as possible in order to keep the men at work.

Earning potentials on the investment of new private capital were so weak that the flow of new capital to the market was at a standstill.

Capital Investment. New capital investment is essential to maintain a given level of economic activity; its increase spurs activity to higher levels. Publicity given to the Morgan Bank having relinquished its investment banking functions only served to prolong the psychology of depression.

Price Policies. A partial answer to the question of how to explain the slow rate of recovery in the 1930's is found in the price policies of leading corporations. Prices of manufactured goods were sticky; they remained at their former levels when prices of agricultural products and other consumers' goods were at lower ones. Manufacturers of heavy, durable capital and consumers' goods tended to maintain prices even at a cost of laying off some of their employees. Automobile owners wanted to replace their depreciated cars at lower prices, but manufacturers gave them more car for the same amount of money which the buyers would not pay or could not afford to pay. This policy may have been proper in the short run and in times of no particular stress or strain on the economic system for an individual manufacturer; but, collectively, in the long run and in times of serious maladjustments and off-balances in an economic system, it undoubtedly delayed recovery if it did not actually intensify the degree or level of economic depression.

Estimates of unemployment were as high as 15 million. Granted that this figure may have been high by as much as three or four million persons, providing relief work for no more than four or five million workers at subsistence wages did little to overcome unemployment, to put employment on a sound footing, and to surmount or to make much headway against the psychology of depression.

The reform measures were more of a long-run significance, except as they served to prevent further incidents that would have undermined confidence in our economy. They did little to stimulate economic activity in increasing productive effort, in decreasing unemployment, and in causing the productive capacity of our industries to be more completely utilized.

Profits can be made at any level of prices as long as total unit costs are kept below prices. Operating or variable costs were reduced, but fixed costs were less flexible. Like it or not, the impelling motive to industrial effort in an economy that is oriented to the market is profits. It was not until profit potentials appeared in the industrial horizon that effective recovery became a reality.

Accomplishments of the New Deal

The results of the New Deal program were disappointing to its proponents in that the various measures that were taken did not provide any permanent stimulus to economic recovery. To those who had advocated greater government controls over economic activity at the federal level, the program was more successful. There seems to be no question that actions were taken in the name of an economic emergency which at any other time and under different economic conditions would have required years to have been accepted by the people and adopted by Congress. In this respect the depression years may be considered to have effected an economic and social revolution. In spite of reforms or changes in our monetary system and more particularly in our banking structure, people were slow in reassuring themselves as to the soundness and stability of our economic system.

Attempts that were made to pack the Supreme Court with judges who were somewhat sympathetic to the social and economic philosophy of the New Deal may have raised some doubts in the minds of many people concerning the ultimate outcome of the efforts of President Roosevelt to eliminate some of the influences and relationships that he felt were not in the best interests of the people. They did not understand why he had encouraged the adoption of code agreements in all segments of industry and the formation of trade associations in the early years of the New Deal and later had become almost violent in his opposition to them and to big business. Many merchants thought that he was undermining the very foundations upon which business had been built and which had prevented the forces of competition and free enterprise from driving them out of business. Many contracts and agreements had been entered into in the name of preserving profits or of creating them and profits were necessary adjuncts to free enterprise. It was disturbing to businessmen and to thinking people to have well-established economic relationships that had been entered into in the name of orderliness and of free enterprise declared unlawful by Congress or by the Supreme Court.

Business had become so large and competition so keen that free pricing alone no longer served to allocate productive resources among or between segments of the economy or between business firms. Leaders of big business had sought to control prices in one manner or another in the name of profits to themselves. They had long since learned the hard way that under con-

ditions of free competition profits had tended to disappear. Their goal of
attainment was larger profits not smaller ones. They emphasized the importance of production even at the social cost of excluding many consumers
from enjoying the pleasures and benefits that came from owning and consuming many items of consumer goods. Class distinctions had become more
pronounced. The fulfillment of property rights that were established in the
ownership of corporate stocks and bonds played an important role in distributing national income to the members of society. Inequities that were
legal in all respects had resulted from the controls that had been exercised
by a small percentage of the population, the impacts of which were felt by
all persons, directly or indirectly.

Business organizations had made successful efforts to obtain legislation
that was favorable to their owners. Agriculture and labor had not been able
to organize effectively and freely for the purpose of enabling them to obtain
larger shares of the national income which had increased over the years.
From the point of view that the New Deal program directed a larger proportional share of the national income to labor and to agriculture, the program
was successful. Insofar as the program had for its objective breaking the
grip that big business had obtained on manufacturing, trade, and commerce,
it had met with a large measure of success. Insofar as it had attempted to
break the hold that financiers, bankers, and insurance companies had on
the economy, it had met with a measure of success. Insofar as the program
had for its purpose raising internal commodity prices and putting men back
to work, the program fell far short of success.

Europe Prepares for War

Hitler had obtained control over Germany when von Hindenberg abdi-
cated on account of his advanced age. Almost immediately it became evident
that Hitler had no intention of being bound by the terms of the Treaty of
Versailles insofar as they pertained to the rearmament of Germany. From
the very beginning of the problem he had disclaimed any intention of paying
the German debt to the American people. The Ruhr and Saar valleys became
beehives of activity in the production of iron and steel and in the mining of
coal. While Hitler encountered some labor problems, unemployment was not
one of them. After 1937, the increased tempo of the German economy was
reflected in similar increases in the production of heavy, durable goods in
other countries. Since factories in European countries could not turn out
goods rapidly enough, orders were given to American firms by England and
France who were stockpiling many kinds of commodities that would become
in short supply in case war should break out in Europe. Few people either
in Europe or in America were naive enough to believe that Munich had
prevented war; it merely postponed the day when the German army would
again be on the march. It also gave more time for preparing for a struggle,
the like of which the world had never experienced.

Revival of American Railroads. American railroads had suffered financial losses since competition with vehicles that were powered by internal combustion engines became a reality. All the depression did was to accentuate these losses rather than to create them. Had it not been for the assistance granted them by the Reconstruction Finance Corporation they would have been in a much worse condition. Astute managements of one or two railroads enabled them to take advantage of low market rates of interest on long-term capital investment, low wages, and low prices for materials that entered into the construction of railway equipment.

The Pennsylvania Railroad had completed the electrification of its main line from Washington to New York at a time when current volume of traffic did not seem to justify such expenditures. Five railroads that entered Cincinnati and which had maintained their separate terminal facilities finally reached an agreement under the terms of which they combined to construct a new union passenger terminal that served all of them jointly. Again it was low interest rates, low wages, and low prices of building materials combined with the savings to each of the participating railroads that motivated this capital improvement. The Chesapeake and Ohio Railroad constructed new terminal facilities at Newport News, Virginia, in order to provide a new port through which goods and commodities from the Middle West could be channeled to European destinations. This railroad had direct connections with St. Louis, Chicago, Detroit, and Cincinnati from which cities foodstuffs and manufactured goods could be sent to Europe without being funneled through the port of New York. The Norfolk and Western Railroad constructed huge coal terminal facilities at Norfolk, Virginia.

These and other similar capital improvements proved of immense value during the buildup for war because they tended to relieve New York from the congestion from which it suffered prior to and during World War I. Other railroads constructed larger and heavier bridges and laid heavier rails in anticipation of being able to handle larger volumes of traffic at lower unit costs. Revenue traffic increased in such proportions that railroads which were in arrears in their interest payments on bonds were enabled to make these payments current. The market in railroad bonds became livelier than it had been for years, and speculators expressed renewed interest in them in their efforts to become the beneficiaries and the recipients of cumulative interest obligations that were in arrears, and were becoming payable. More conservative investors who continued to hold railroad bonds in their portfolios found renewed sources of income.

Production Increases. Before the impact of war orders from Europe resulted in the construction of additional and enlarged capital facilities, filling these orders absorbed the slack of idle equipment and tended to cause American firms to increase their output to near 100 percent of capacity. By operating longer hours per day and per week and by working more intensively, output in some cases actually exceeded normal rated volume.

Preparation of European countries for war is what really reduced unemployment in the United States. It also geared production and management to levels that enabled American manufacturers to adjust themselves to the needs of war when the United States became actively engaged. The data in Table 24-2 reveal decreases in unemployment that occurred prior to 1941. The data for 1939 reflect the uncertainties that existed in a neutral nation and which always accompany the actual outbreak of hostilities. Most of the workers who were unemployed from 1942 to the close of the war were those persons who had been employed in industries or by firms that had been closed because they were not deemed essential to the war effort and who had not found employment in an industry or in a firm whose product contributed to the war effort.

QUESTIONS FOR REVIEW

1. Describe the activities of the Securities Exchange Commission.

2. (a) What was a sit-down strike?
   (b) Why did organized labor give up the technique of the sit-down strike in its protests against corporate employers with which it was in dispute?

3. Describe two impacts of the mechanization of industry upon labor.

4. How did Congress modify its tariff policies to meet depression conditions?

5. What was responsible for the increase in commodity exports in the latter half of the 1930 decade?

6. How did some segments of free enterprise industry take advantage of depressed economic conditions to improve their capital equipment?

SUGGESTED READINGS

Cochran, Thomas C. "Business and the Public," *United States Economic History: Selected Readings,* edited by Harry N. Scheiber. New York City: Alfred A. Knopf, Inc., 1964.

Dulles, Foster Rhea. *Labor in America.* 2d ed. New York City: Thomas Y. Crowell Company, 1949. Chapters 25 and 26.

Fite, Gilbert C. "Seven Months in the A. A. A.," *Views of American Economic Growth: The Industrial Era,* edited by Thomas C. Cochran and Thomas B. Brewer. New York City: McGraw-Hill Book Company, 1966.

Hacker, Louis M. (ed.). *Major Documents in American Economic History.* Vol. II. New York City: D. Van Nostrand Co., Inc., 1961. Selections 11-20.

Johnson, E. A. J., and Herman E. Krooss. *The American Economy.* Englewood Cliffs, N. J.: Prentice-Hall, Inc., 1960. Chapter 13.

Kimmel, Lewis H. "Keynesian Theory, Public Opinion, and the New Deal," *United States Economic History: Selected Readings,* edited by Harry N. Scheiber. New York City: Alfred A. Knopf, Inc., 1964.

Letwin, William (ed.). *A Documentary History of American Economic Policy Since 1789.* Chicago: Aldine Publishing Company, 1961. Part III, Section L.

Means, Gardiner C. "A Critique of Professor Smithies," *Issues in American Economic History,* edited by Gerald D. Nash. Boston: D. C. Heath & Company, 1964.

North, Douglas C. *Growth and Welfare in the American Past.* Englewood Cliffs, N. J.: Prentice-Hall, Inc., 1966, pp. 167-180.

Saposs, David J. "Voluntarism in the American Labor Movement," *United States Economic History: Selected Readings,* edited by Harry N. Scheiber. New York City: Alfred A. Knopf, Inc., 1964.

Smithies, Arthur. "The American Economy in the Thirties," *Issues in American Economic History,* edited by Gerald D. Nash. Boston: D. C. Heath & Company, 1964.

Wright, Chester W. *Economic History of the United States.* 2d ed. New York City: McGraw-Hill Book Company, 1949.

Chapter 25

THE WAR YEARS

NEED FOR PREPARATION

Even though the United States had participated successfully in a war "to make the world safe for democracy," there were doubts in the minds of many persons that the world had been made safe, let alone safe for democracy. The attitude of many European peoples was that they had suffered enough from the atrocities of war and wanted no more of it. These attitudes were reflected in high level government offices. To many political, civilian, and military leaders the Treaty of Versailles not only did not settle many of the important economic and political issues, it created more than it resolved. The creation of many small and independent nations disturbed the balance of power that England, France, and Germany had maintained for 50 years, more or less. While the United States was not and never had been an aggressive nation, it realized soon after the signing of the armistice in November, 1918, that it would have to be better prepared for defense than it was in 1917.

Not only must the country be better prepared for war, it must be prepared for total war. As defined by the Germans, the aim of *all-out* or *total* war "is the utter destruction of the vanquished nation and its final and complete disappearance from the stage of history." It is unrestricted in its means and may be fought on land, at sea, and in the air with weapons that have been and are being developed during the conflict and which are the product of modern technology.

Since total war was to be waged by entire populations, civilians had to be trained and disciplined in how to conduct themselves in their participation in the war effort. Ordnance depots had to be established throughout the country for the storing of foodstuffs, uniforms, ammunition, and ordnance items of all kinds. The Maritime Commission continued to subsidize the building of merchant ships, many of which were so designed that they could be converted to the needs of war with little effort. Reserve Officer Training Corps programs had to be enlarged and young men encouraged to engage in healthful sports and body-building exercises that would prepare them for the strenuous duties of the military. The Air Force was also enlarged and trained in the maneuvers of war.

Profits v. Neutrality

To ensure the neutrality of the United States upon the outbreak of hostilities abroad, to prevent a recurrence of the problems that arose when foreign nations defaulted on their obligations to us, and to take some of the profits out of war, Congress in 1935 passed the Johnson Neutrality Act, under the terms of which sales of commodities to nations who were engaged in war were placed on a cash-and-carry basis. It was sales of war materiel by American firms to European firms and governments, particularly after 1937, that did much to absorb thousands of unemployed persons, to accelerate the production of American mills and factories, and to strengthen the financial structures of American railroads. If the government had plans for taking the profit out of wars in which we might be engaged, it had done nothing to prevent American corporations in almost all segments of industry and at almost all levels of operation from profiting from wars which other nations waged provided they purchased goods on a cash-and-carry basis. More important, from the standpoint of the economic preparation of the productive machinery being readied to meet the demands of war, was the fact that much of the preparation was effected at the level of free enterprise, motivated by the prospect of making profits. This degree or level of preparation proved to be at least as effective as preparations later on that were prompted by government action.

Obstacles to Production for War

The largest obstacle to organizing the war was not one of production; neither was it one of manpower nor of technology. It was how to gear an economy, which from its infancy had been fed and nourished on the fruits of free enterprise in its search for profits, for all-out war. Prices and profits had been relied upon to allocate natural resources and other productive factors to the different channels of industry. Labor had been lured from agriculture when industry offered higher wages. Capital had been directed into the manufacture of farm machinery by larger profit potentials than prevailed in the furniture industry and many others. Capital and labor had seldom been attracted into the channels of shipbuilding or of owning and operating overseas shipping facilities, because they were more productive when applied to railroading, to the production of iron and steel and of steel products, to the manufacture of shoes, glassware, textiles, ready-made clothing, and of many other products. The aim of warfare was not to make profits. It was to destroy wealth and capital goods, and to remove manpower from active participation in the war effort, and in producing the instruments of warfare.

Raw materials could not be diverted from peacetime industries to provide materials of war through the medium of price. Not that price would not have accomplished this result, but inflation would have occurred with all its impacts, thus undermining the economy and breaking down the *esprit de corps* of the people.

Problems of Preparedness

One of the lessons the United States learned from its experience in World War I was that it must never let itself fall into the state of unpreparedness in which it found itself in April, 1917. The danger lay at the level of trained personnel as much as it did at the level of supplies and the organization of industry. Mobilization of supplies proved to be the most serious bottleneck, if there was such, to the successful termination of the war. War was no longer one soldier, one gun; it was ten or more civilian workers in support of one man at the front. One gun was no longer adequate in an age of mechanized warfare, an age in which the application of new technologies was the *sine qua non* of success. Natural resources that had contributed to the attainment and maintenance of a high scale of living were diverted to the war effort which meant that they entered into the production of items that would be destroyed or else would aid in the destruction of wealth and of human lives. In either case, win or lose on the field of battle, the country would be the loser in terms of available natural resources and of manpower. By the time the United States entered the war, rubber, steel, manganese, cork, zinc, and nickel, among other metals that were basic raw materials in the manufacture of machines of destruction, were in short supply. The problems created by the shortage of these products included (1) how and where to obtain new sources of supply; (2) how to give direction to their use in products that were essential to the war effort and to establish priorities in these uses; (3) how to reduce dependence upon the price system to allocate them to industries or to product use; (4) how to discover and to use substitute materials that would serve in their stead.

Manpower. Manpower in the Armed Forces and in industry had to be maintained at high levels of efficiency if the war was to be brought to a successful conclusion. In a way, it may have been fortunate that there were seven or eight million persons who were unemployed when we entered the war. Enlisting their services in industry or in the Armed Forces did not result in any direct dislocation nor did it have an inflationary effect. There was an entirely different problem after the unemployed had been absorbed, but this will be discussed later in this chapter.

Transportation. Transportation had been one of the bottlenecks in 1917-18. Coordination of overland facilities and of inland waterway facilities with overseas shipping was essential. Again, a shortage of overseas shipping facilities should not be permitted to interfere with, to handicap, or to delay carrying out the programs of the Armed Forces abroad.

Finance. How to finance the war and at the same time control price and credit inflation were important questions the answers to which would affect the morale of civilians whether or not they were engaged in the war effort.

In March, 1941, Congress passed an act that is commonly referred to as the Lend-Lease Act, which authorized the President to "sell, transfer title, exchange, lease, lend, or otherwise dispose of" whatever articles he chose to any country whose defense he deemed vital to the defense of the United States. This was an effort to prevent the rise of huge international war debts which could never be retired in later years, and at the same time to render aid to our allies. It obviated the difficult problem that defaulting on international financial obligations would create. Within the year, two appropriations that totaled $13 billion were made by Congress, most of which was used to finance shipments to Great Britain and to her allies, the remainder being loaned to Brazil and to other Latin American countries.

COORDINATION OF ECONOMIC RESOURCES

After many attempts to organize the resources of the entire country for the war effort, by January, 1942, a fairly distinct and definitive organization had been established. Within the Executive Offices of the President, an Office of Emergency Management was created which was under the direction and supervision of the President. The Office was charged with coordinating the operations and policies of the following defense agencies:

A. The Office of Civilian Defense which organized defense activities at the level of civilian activities and civilian population

B. The Defense Housing Division

C. The Defense Communication Board which allocated and coordinated communication facilities among civilian and military organizations

D. The Office of Defense Transportation which coordinated the services of transportation facilities and assured their maximum utilization

E. The Office of Scientific Research and Development

F. The Lend-Lease Administration

G. The Office of the Coordinator of International Affairs

H. The National War Labor Board whose duty it was to settle industrial disputes and to keep the wheels of industry turning

I. The Office of Defense, Health, and Welfare Services whose director was the Federal Security Administrator

J. The Office of Price Administration

K. The Supply Priorities and Allocations Board which determined (1) the requirements for goods that were in scarce supply for military, for civilian, and for other purposes, and (2) the policies that governed priorities and the allocation of such goods among their competing uses

L. The Office of Production Management

Outside of the Office for Emergency Management the following agencies engaged in important defense activities:

A. The Board of Economic Welfare
B. The Departments of Interior, Army and Navy, Agriculture, and the
    Treasury each of which was assigned specific coordinating and advisory
    functions
C. The Council of National Defense, which was composed of the Secretaries
    of War, Navy, Interior, Agriculture, Commerce, and Labor

The chief problems that confronted these Boards were how to coordinate
their policies and directives and how to prevent the issuance of contradictory
orders.

Manpower for Armed Forces

In order to build up a defense army that would be trained in newer
methods of warfare, Congress passed a Selective Service Act in September,
1940, which required all men between the ages of 21 and 35 to register
for one year of military service. Plans were laid to increase the regular
army from 250,000 to 1,418,000, excluding members of the National Guard
and the Reserves, by June, 1942. Men were to be called into service at the
rate of 900,000 per annum and members of the National Guard were enlisted
in the federal army. Since the close of World War I, members of the National
Guard had been receiving field training in summer camps.

There was a serious shortage of supplies with which to arm and to equip
these recruits. Army camps and cantonments were not large enough to house
and feed such numbers of men. Cantonments were located at strategic places
according to the type of military training for which the men were being
prepared. In most cases, entirely new facilities had to be constructed literally
from the ground up. Water and gas pipes had to be paid; storm and sanitary
sewers had to be provided; streets, sidewalks, and recreation areas had to
be constructed, not to mention barracks for enlisted men and for draftees,
houses for commissioned officers, mess halls and storage facilities for food,
arms, and all kinds of ordnance material. One idea of the draft was not to
press men into service more rapidly than there were supplies and accommodations for them; but as time became more and more important, and
unavoidable delays slowed down the processes of construction, pressures of
manpower upon physical facilities almost reached the bursting point.

Civilian Manpower

As was discussed earlier in this chapter, many were the estimates of the
number of men at home who were needed to support one man at the front.
Mr. William S. Knudsen estimated this ratio to be 10 to 1 and other estimates
were even higher. At this ratio, an army of four million men required a force
of 40 million civilian workers to sustain it. The reserve of unemployed labor
was drawn upon and unemployment in the civilian labor force had decreased
from 17.2 percent in 1939 to 1.2 percent in 1944, or to only 670,000 persons.

In spite of the increase in the number of men in uniform, the civilian labor force increased steadily throughout the war years. Data in Table 25-2 indicate that hundreds of thousands of persons who had not constituted part of the labor force prior to 1940 contributed their services for a price. There was some decline in the number of housekeepers, which seems to indicate that many wives entered industry for the first time. Many of these women

Table 25-1

Unemployment—1939-1945
(000's of persons 14 years of age and older)

Year	Unemployed	Percentage of Civilian Labor Force
1939	9,480	17.2
1940	8,120	14.6
1941	5,560	9.9
1942	2,660	4.7
1943	1,070	1.9
1944	670	1.2
1945	1,040	1.9

Source: U.S. Department of Commerce, Bureau of the Census, *Historical Statistics of the United States. Colonial Times to 1957* (Washington: U.S. Government Printing Office, 1960), p. 73. Adapted.

Table 25-2

Labor Force Status of the Population—1940-1945
(000's of persons 14 years of age and older)

Year	Total Civilian Labor Force	Not in Labor Force			
		Total	House-keeping	In School	Other
1940	47,520	45,380	. . . . .	. . . . .	. . . . .
1941	50,350	45,170	. . . . .	. . . . .	. . . . .
1942	53,750	43,410	28,690	6,370	8,350
1943	54,470	40,280	27,320	5,100	7,860
1944	53,960	39,770	27,350	4,540	7,880
1945	52,820	41,410	27,760	4,830	8,820

Source: *Historical Statistics of the United States. Colonial Times to 1957*, 1960, p. 70. Adapted.

were wives of men who were in uniform and who were serving overseas. For them, hard work helped to alleviate worry or boredom. All of them found that a second income would enable them to finance projects after the war that had previously been denied them. Even more pronounced was the decline in the number of persons who attended school. College and university campuses were almost deserted of students, except those who had been classified in the draft as 4-F, which was the designation given to those who had been found unfit for military service, and to others who had been assigned to do experimental work in mathematics and in the natural and biological sciences. Since the number of persons in the labor force included those who were in the Armed Forces, it is impossible to calculate how much of the decline in the number of persons who were in attendance at school represented those who donned uniforms and how many of them became wage earners.

Table 25-3

Labor Force by Age and Sex—1940-1945
(000's of persons 14 years of age and older)

	TOTAL	MALE				FEMALE
Year		Total	14-19	45-64	65 and over	Total
1940	56,180	42,020	3,270	12,170	1,950	14,160
1941	57,530	42,890	....	....	....	14,640
1942	60,380	44,260	....	....	....	16,120
1943	64,560	45,750	4,700	13,200	2,320	18,810
1944	66,040	46,670	4,950	13,300	2,430	19,370
1945	65,290	46,020	4,530	13,370	2,460	19,270

Source: *Historical Statistics of the United States. Colonial Times to 1957*, 1960, p. 71. Adapted.

Because the figures for employment in Table 25-3 include those who were in the Armed Forces, data for the age groups that were subject to military duty are excluded from this analysis. Even so, many young men who were in the 14 to 19 age group, especially those who were 18 and 19 years old, we know were in uniform. Some men between the ages of 45 and 64 were in uniform, but the total increase in the number of workers in this age bracket may safely be assumed to have represented those who became civilian employees. Five hundred thousand men aged 65 and over entered the labor force between 1940 and 1945, and undoubtedly most of them came out of retirement in order to make their contribution toward winning the war. Incidentally, the wages and salaries these men received must have made life a little more enjoyable. This experience proved that in many instances workers' years of productivity had not come to an end at age 65. Not only were their incomes increased, but the fact that they were doing something added to their enjoyment of living. In spite of war shortages and the rationing of many kinds of consumers' goods, they must have become consumers of goods they otherwise would not have purchased; and when the war was over many of them undoubtedly spent some or all of their savings that were accumulated during their period of employment. More striking than changes in the pattern of employment of male workers was the increase in the number of female workers that occurred during the years of war. The increase amounted to over five million women and young girls, over 50 percent of whom were in the age group 25 to 64.

Urban Concentration. The location of the supply of labor was as important as its size. Farm labor, casual labor, white collar labor, schoolteachers, and others were attracted to urban centers in which government contracts were being filled. Cities and towns mushroomed in terms of population growth as well as in the values of goods that were produced therein. At the time of the redistribution of the labor force between rural areas and those that were urban, it was thought that when the exigencies of war were over, workmen would return to their former homes, as many of them did. Accommodations and arrangements were somewhat temporary in character, which added to the seriousness of the situation when the movement of population did not reverse itself.

Length of the Work Period. An increase in the labor force, as far as its productivity was concerned, was accomplished by increasing the length of the workday and of the workweek. While there was no set pattern that was followed by industry in this respect, 48 and 52-hour workweeks were common, and 72-hour workweeks were not unknown. In addition to longer workweeks per given shift of employees, entire plants or plant sections were in operation around the clock. Employees did not object seriously to lengthening the workweek or to night work, as either was accompanied by increases in the rate of pay over the customary number of hours worked. Hours of work in excess of the former standard or basic workweek were paid for at the rate of time and a half the base rate, hours on the night shift received a differential of several cents per hour, and hours worked on the owl shift were compensated for by still another wage rate differential. The extra rates of pay for war work did not narrow the profit margins of employers, most of whom were paid in terms of cost plus a fixed fee per unit of output. The government had learned that a cost plus percentage plan that had been used in World War I only served to raise the cost of war unnecessarily.

The Federal government felt that it could not request or demand that industry lengthen its workweek without itself setting an example. Consequently, government employees were required to work several hours of overtime per week at one and a half times their base rates of pay. The impact of paying these wages extended beyond the time when the workweek was reduced to its prewar status. The government again took the lead by maintaining its schedules of take-home pay for reduced workweeks. This was tantamount to a wage increase; but what was more important from the standpoint of the economy as a whole, disposable incomes remained constant, except as they were affected by workers returning to civilian life.

Transportation

Except for transoceanic ships, transportation facilities were in much better physical condition at the start of the war than they had been 25 years earlier. Railway locomotives, cars, tracks, bridges, trestles, and terminals were much more adequate and better prepared to handle the rapid increase of freight and passengers that were in need of transport services.

Military Priority. Priority of freight and of passenger space was given to the shipment of war materiel and to those who were in uniform or who were certified as traveling in the war effort. Old freight cars that had stood on sidings for years were reconditioned and pressed into service. Passenger coaches, Pullman cars, and dining cars that had been considered obsolete were reconditioned and used regularly. Entire passenger trains were devoted to the movement of troops, and some freight trains hauled nothing but ordnance materiel and other items that were destined for military establishments both in this country and abroad. Civilians traveled at the risk of being put off trains and/or planes at some intervening station, if any military officer or person with certified priority awaited accommodations. Many of the latter traveled by airplane; and many were the civilians who were "bumped" by men with prior claims to seats, and long and tedious were the delays in awaiting other opportunities to complete trips.

Sales of new automobiles for all practical purposes were restricted to the military, to essential governmental agencies, or to those persons who were given certificates of necessity by a governmental defense agency. Since gasoline was rationed, individual persons did not enjoy the freedom of movement from one city to another they had enjoyed for over 20 years. If they wanted to travel, they went by motor bus, train, or airplane.

Nonfreight Services. Passenger trains that had moved little but mail and express for years were crowded to the level of no more standing room available. People learned that they could travel all night without the comforts of Pullman car accommodations. Because dining cars were not large enough to serve all passengers, most travelers took lunch boxes or snacks with them. Mail, parcel post, and express shipments were heavier than they had been for many years. Passenger, mail, and express terminals almost literally burst at their seams. Trains were late in arriving and in departing from terminals because of the crowded conditions that delayed loading and unloading activities. More trains entered and left terminals than could be cleared in the yards without delays.

Not only were the facilities of railroads taxed to capacity by carrying traffic that was generated by the war effort and by limitations that were placed upon the utilization of privately owned automobiles in intercity travel as well as in commuter service, but the facilities of airlines and motor transportation companies were expanded and used to capacity. There may have actually been an increase in the number of persons who traveled during these years. On the other hand, it may have been their concentration in the three means of transport that resulted in congestion at almost all terminals giving the appearance that more persons were traveling. There are no means of measuring the volume of traffic that used public facilities during these years that formerly had found their individually owned cars more convenient to use. This expansion is evidence of the fact that gasoline was not in short supply. In 1940 there were 19 concerns operating 369 aircraft; in 1945 there were 421 planes in service, operated by 20 concerns. These companies employed 15,984 persons in 1940 and 50,313 in 1945, and this increase occurred at a time when civilian workers were being drafted into the military and into civilian war work. Draft boards were urged not only to defer draftees who were engaged in essential war services, but to give direction to others who had been trained and were qualified to render such services.

Over 2.5 million passengers were flown 1,052,156,000 revenue miles in 1940 which figures were more than tripled in 1945. In 1940, 3,476,224 tons of freight and express and over 10 tons of mail were flown the equivalent of 1 mile. By 1945, air service had increased to where it transported over 6.5 million revenue passengers a total of 3,362,455,000 miles. Over 22 million tons of freight and express were flown the equivalent of 1 mile, and ton miles of mail had increased to 65,092,921. In other words, air mail carriage compared with that for freight and express increased at a ratio of 5 to 6 in a span of 5 years. Since time was so important in the war years, the development of air transport service made a direct contribution to winning the war. The impact of this development carried over into the years of reconstruction and reconversion to the extent that many persons who had been compelled to patronize air transport services during the war chose to continue to do so afterwards. Many pilots who were discharged from military service chose to continue to use their skills in piloting cargo planes for private industry. Many were the plane loads of cargoes that were flown from points of original production or of concentration to distant market centers or to points from which they were distributed more locally at wholesale and retail levels.

Overseas Shipments. Overseas freight was handled more efficiently than it was in World War I, when almost all of this kind of traffic was funneled through the port of New York. Freight from Detroit, Chicago, St. Louis, and other points in the West was diverted from New York into the ports of Baltimore, Norfolk, Newport News, Philadelphia, and other seaports south of New York. Some traffic left the country through the port of Boston. Facilities at New Orleans, Mobile, Jacksonville, Savannah, and other southern ports were used to relieve congestion at New York. The use of these ports made it more difficult for the enemy to blockade ships and to intercept them en route to foreign waters.

Germany's unrestricted submarine campaign spared no waters. Raw materials from South America, from Africa, from the Near East, from the Far East, and from North America were intercepted on their way to England or to France. It was not until airplanes and blimps were used to detect the presence of alien submarines that even convoys were safe. In an effort to counteract the loss of tonnage that went to the bottom, German vessels that had been impounded in ports of the Western Hemisphere were added to the American fleet of merchant vessels. Four hundred and twenty-five thousand gross tons were thus added to the merchant marine of the United States, and a like amount to the merchant fleets of Latin American republics.

Under the neutrality legislation as amended in 1939, foreign trade with belligerent nations had to be conducted on a cash-and-carry basis; ships of American registry were not permitted to carry either cargoes or passengers to the ports of any nation that had been designated as belligerent by the President of the United States; and American vessels could not carry arms or enter zones that had been declared by the President to be combat areas. In order to make deliveries of supplies to the belligerent nations of Europe possible, more than 80 vessels were transferred from United States to Panamanian registry after war broke out in Europe in 1939. This action helped to sustain a flow of goods to Europe, and under the protection of the United States Navy. In 1942 and 1943 the construction of 12 million gross tons of shipping was planned, compared with less than 750,000 gross tons actually completed in 1941. In 1939 the merchant marine of the United States totaled 8,909,000 gross tons.

Transportation and the Decentralization of Industry. In order to safeguard against concentrated centers of production becoming deactivated because of sabotage, bombing, or some other unforeseen event, industrial leaders were encouraged to subcontract portions of their work to smaller sized production units that were scattered throughout the countryside. Inability to produce or to process primary materials in certain geographic regions of the United States was no reason why products could not be assembled there. The success of this program depended, in part, on the adequacy of transportation, and of labor and its housing. In implementing the program, a continuous, reliable, and adequate system of transportation had to be developed and maintained. The availability of transportation facilities had to be coordinated with schedules of factory production in order not to interrupt the processes of assembly line production. Managerial skills were taxed to the utmost in order to maintain a steady flow of supplies to the front.

Finance

The implications of a statement that appeared in *The London Economist* on May 3, 1941, are manifold: "The task of finance in war is to see that nothing is decided on financial grounds."

The financial plan that was outlined but not realized was to meet 40 percent of the monetary costs of the war with tax revenues, and 60 percent of the costs with revenues from loans. Let it be understood clearly that the proportionate use of taxes and borrowing was *not* determined on the basis of what generation of people should bear the cost or the burden of financing the war. In either case, the generation that fought the war paid for it. This is not to say that future generations did not feel a burden, but it was not shifted to them. Any war that was as destructive of human lives and of wealth as was World War II was bound to leave its impacts upon future generations as well as upon the present one. Had the war been financed by floating external loans and had it been fought by mercenary soldiers, part of the financial burden could have been shifted to the future, but neither of these methods was used.

Taxation. The income tax was capable of being adjusted more readily than were other forms of taxes; and with the adoption of the principle of withholding taxes from pay envelopes, tax revenues were collected on a current basis. This provided a steady flow of tax income to the government and made it easy for taxpayers to contribute their support to the war effort.

Corporate Income Tax. Corporate incomes were subject to a normal tax to which an excess profits tax was added in 1940. Excess profits taxes were applied to adjusted excess profits net income, which was $5,000 less than excess profits net income. Excess profits net income could be derived by one of two methods: (1) If invested capital was taken as the base upon which such taxes were calculated, excess profits net income was that portion of total net income that was in excess of 8 percent on invested capital. In 1941, the tax was graduated to the extent that a base rate of 8 percent was applied on the first $5 million of capital investment and 7 percent was applied on capital investments over $5 million. (2) If average earnings were selected as the base upon which excess profits were calculated, excess profits net incomes were those profits that were in excess of 95 percent of the average net incomes from 1936 to 1939. This method enabled many corporations whose earnings were far greater than they had been prior to the impact of European war orders upon American business activity either to avoid payment of this tax or to reduce the amount of their tax liability.

Personal Income Tax. Progressive taxation of personal incomes that fell within given brackets was attained by applying surtax rates to the normal rates of taxation. In 1940 normal tax rates were 4 percent on all taxable incomes; the Revenue Act of 1942 raised the tax to 6 percent, while the level was lowered to 3 percent for 1944 and 1945. Table 25-4 presents

Table 25-4

Normal Tax Rates, Personal Exemptions, and Exemptions Allowed for Each Dependent—1940-1945

Normal Tax	1940 4%	1941 4%	1942 6%	1943 6%	1944 3%	1945 3%
Personal Exemptions						
Single Persons	$ 800	$ 750	$ 500	$ 500	$ 500	$ 500
Married Persons	2,000	1,500	1,200	1,200	1,000	1,000
Exemptions for Each Dependent	400	400	350	350	500	500

Source: *Historical Statistics of the United States. Colonial Times to 1957*, 1960, p. 703. Adapted.

the basic tax schedule of normal tax rates, personal exemptions, and exemptions for each dependent that was in effect throughout the war years. The combination of increases in incomes and the lowering of personal exemptions made many more people subject to paying income taxes throughout the war years, and in this way to make their contribution to the war effort. In 1940 a total of over 14.5 million tax returns with taxable incomes were filed. In 1942 incomes on which net returns were taxable numbered over 36.5 million; and in the final year of the war, 1945, taxable incomes were found in 49.75 million returns. Not only did many persons pay larger taxes, more persons paid some taxes as the war years progressed. Three and one-half times as many persons paid income taxes in 1945 as compared with the number of persons who contributed to the war effort in 1941. The true picture of the income tax burden upon taxpayers is revealed much more vividly by giving consideration to the combined normal tax and surtax rates for the same span of years, which data are given in Table 25-5. By applying these rates to the maximum income in each of the tax brackets that have been selected, the reader will obtain the money equivalent of each tax rate.

Defense Taxes. A number of defense taxes were levied that were added to tax rates that were already in effect. Their purpose was to raise additional tax money at the beginning of the war emergency and at the same time to reduce the number of dollars people had with which to purchase consumers' goods that were becoming progressively scarce. The War Revenue Act of 1942 levied a new kind of tax on individual incomes called a Victory Tax. It was a 5 percent levy on all wages and salaries over $624 per annum. It was collected at the source from all workers except those who were in the Armed Forces, domestic servants, and farm and casual laborers. These who were exempt from having this tax deducted at the source paid

Table 25-5

Federal Individual Income Tax: Combined Normal and Surtax Rates—1940-1945

Taxable Incomes (000)	1940 %	1941 %	1942 %	1943 %	1944 %	1945 %
$ 0–2	4	10	19	19	23	23
2–4	4	13	22	22	25	25
4–6	8	17	26	26	29	29
6–8	10	21	30	30	33	33
8–10	12	25	34	34	37	37
18–20	25	42	52	52	56	56
44–50	40	59	69	69	75	75
90–100	60	68	83	83	90	90
300–500	70–72	75–76	88	88	90	90
1,000–	77–79	79–81	88	88	90	90

Source: Tax Foundation, *Facts and Figures on Government Finance,* 12th ed., 1962-1963, p. 115.

it along with their regular income taxes on their due dates. Wages and salaries were not to be increased in order to counteract the impact of the Victory Tax. A plan was devised by which a refund of 25 percent for single persons, 40 percent for married persons, and 2 percent for each dependent would be credited against income tax obligations after the war. If these credits were used to reduce debts that were outstanding on September 1, 1942, life insurance premiums on policies that were in force on the same date, or to purchase government bonds, they could have been deducted in 1944.

In order to raise more money from the estate tax, the minimum rate of 2 percent was raised to 3 percent and the bracket range to which this rate applied was lowered. At the same time, the total exemption of $40,000 was raised to $60,000 before the new rate was applied. The purpose was to obtain more revenue from this source, but at the same time there was no desire to penalize the inheritors of estates unduly merely because their benefactors happened to pass away during the years of war.

Excise Taxes. Excise taxes were increased on some items of luxury, while on others, taxes were levied for the first time. There was an element of inflation control when taxes were levied on such items as jewelry and watches, cameras and photographic supplies, furs, toilet preparations, luggage and leather goods, telephone charges on local and long-distance calls, all messages that were sent by telegraph, cable, and radio, and on admissions to all forms of sporting events and other entertainment, except for benefit performances. Documentary and stamp taxes on alcoholic liquors, tobacco, playing cards, deeds and conveyances, and the issuance and transfer of cor-

porate stocks and bonds were raised. Manufacturers' excise taxes were levied
on sporting goods, firearms, motor oil and gasoline, diesel fuel, automobiles,
motor trucks and buses, motorcycles, automobile parts and accessories,
matches, radios, electric refrigerators, fountain pens and mechanical pencils,
and business office and store machines, except cash registers. Almost every
person in every walk of life made financial contributions in support of
the war at many levels of economic activity and of consumption. Automobile
owners were required annually to purchase stickers at their post offices for
$5, and place them on their car windshields. In addition to the sticker
indicating the year, easy identification by enforcement officers was made
possible by the use of different colors each year.

In order to discourage the civilian use of public conveyances, a transportation tax was added to regular fares. In reality this tax did not serve
as a deterrent to civilian travel. It was productive of so much revenue that
it was retained for many years after the war came to an end against the
vigorous protests of railroad managements.

Table 25-6
Federal Tax Receipts—1940-1945

Year	Total Tax Collections	Income Taxes		Employ-ment	Estate and Gift	Excise
		Individual	Corporate			
1940	5,340,452	982,017	1,147,592	833,521	360,071	1,884,512
1941	7,370,108	1,417,655	2,053,469	925,856	407,058	2,399,417
1942	13,047,869	3,262,800	4,744,083	1,185,362	432,540	3,141,183
1943	22,371,386	6,629,932	9,668,956	1,498,705	447,496	3,797,503
1944	40,121,760	18,261,005	14,766,796	1,738,372	511,211	4,463,674
1945	43,800,388	19,034,313	16,027,213	1,779,177	643,055	5,944,630

Source: *Historical Statistics of the United States. Colonial Times to 1957*, 1960 p. 713.
Adapted.

Table 25-6 affords the reader a comparison of the results of the new
taxes that were collected during the war years. Until 1942 excise taxes
yielded larger total revenues than did either the corporate income tax or
the tax on individual incomes. Corporate income tax receipts were greater
than those from taxes on individual incomes for another year, since which
time the ranking in terms of receipts has been (1) individual income tax,
(2) corporate income tax, (3) excise taxes, (4) employment taxes, and
(5) estate and gift taxes. Employment taxes comprise employer, employee,
and self-employed taxes for the federal old age, survivor and disability
insurance system, the federal unemployment insurance tax on employers,
and the railroad retirement tax on employers and employees.

Loans. The purchase of government bonds appealed more to most people than did paying taxes, although both of these actions deprived them of spending current incomes in the purchase of consumers' goods which they could enjoy immediately. Federal fiscal authorities had learned from the experience of the other world war, and issued a new class of bond whose purchase would not set inflationary forces in action. This was an interest accrual bond, designated Series E, that matured ten years from the month of purchase. The purchase price was in multiples of $18.75 for each $25 of principal, or $750 for a $1,000 bond. Schedules of cash values after certain lengths of maturity were printed on the reverse of each bond. They could be cashed at banks at these respective values any time after six months from date of purchase, which represented low interest accruals until the maturity date at which time the interest return amounted to approximately 3 percent. These bonds were nonnegotiable, and could not be used as collateral for bank loans. They were purchased out of current income, and the government was not given deposit credit in a bank until they had been paid for in full. Their purchase did not represent an increase in dollars that were chasing after scarce goods because their purchasers relinquished a corresponding number of dollars. The transaction was strictly that of a transfer of purchasing power rather than one that resulted in additional bank credit being put into circulation. In addition to Series E bonds, several other types were issued that business firms could acquire. Again, while revenue was an important consideration in their sale, the control of bank credit and of inflation was uppermost in the minds of Treasury officials.

The Federal Debt. By 1940 the debt of the federal government was just short of $43 billion. In 1945 it had become $258 billion. The interest

Table 25-7

Gross National Product, National Income, Federal Debt—1940-1946
(Per capita in current dollars)

Year	Federal Debt	Gross National Product	National Income
1940	325	761	617
1941	367	943	781
1942	537	1,180	1,021
1943	999	1,408	1,245
1944	1,452	1,527	1,319
1945	1,848	1,526	1,295
1946	1,905	1,490	1,279

Source: *Historical Statistics of the United States. Colonial Times to 1957*, 1960, p. 139. Adjusted.

on this principal sum was just under $5 billion which was more than the total debt at the federal level in 1918. In 1917 the debt amounted to $2,975,619,000. A better way of measuring the growth and size of the debt and one that may indicate to what extent it represented an economic burden is to compare it on a per capita basis with the size and rate of growth of gross national product and of national income. The data in Table 25-7 make these comparisons from which the reader may draw his own conclusions. The amount of the federal debt is important only in its relation to national income. As long as national income increases more rapidly than does the cost of servicing the debt, there is no increase in the real burden of the debt. President Roosevelt was insistent that the rate of interest be kept at a low level, partly in order to lighten the burden of the debt. The decline in gross national product after 1945 undoubtedly reflects the loss of capital goods and the exhaustion of natural resources that occurred directly as a result of the war effort.

Effect on Consumption. We have already brought out that the purchase of government bonds by the civilian population was a means of extending financial support to the government. Just as important an impact on the economy was exerted by the accompanying increase in savings and the retirement of units of purchasing power from the chase after scarce consumers' goods.

Savings alone, however, were not sufficient to prevent price increases, particularly when consumers' goods were purchased and hoarded because they were becoming more scarce rather than because they were needed in the immediate satisfaction of human wants. In this category were coffee and tea, sugar, candy bars, facial tissue and tobacco products, to mention only a few. One reason for the scarcity of some of these items was not found at the level of production. Rather it was due to the direction given their sale in outlets that were located in military establishments in this country and abroad.

Federal Reserve Credit Policy. The Board of Governors of the Federal Reserve System yielded to the authority of the Treasury Department in formulating its open market policies. It agreed to have Federal Reserve Banks purchase United States government bonds regardless of the impacts of these purchases upon the volume of credit outstanding in relation to seasonal or cyclical fluctuations of business. The object was to maintain the market for government bonds at high price levels and their interest yields low.

Effects of the Credit Policy. Not only did the Federal Reserve credit policy make it possible for the Treasury to continue to issue government bonds at lower interest rates than otherwise would have been possible, it tended to keep market rates of interest correspondingly low. A longer run effect of the policy was to reduce the monetary value of the interest on the federal debt in later years. Market quotations on government bonds were above par, which fact instilled confidence in the participants in the money market that the credit rating of the government was not being impaired by its efforts to finance a world war.

Margin Requirements. The Board of Governors of the Federal Reserve System did not alter the requirements for purchasing corporate securities on margin on organized security exchanges until a few months prior to the termination of the war. The rates of 40 percent under Regulation T for extensions of credit to brokers and dealers, of 50 percent for short sales, and of 40 percent under Regulation U for loans by banks on stock were effective until February 5, 1945, at which time all margin requirements were raised to 75 percent. Sales of corporate stock continued to increase in volume until 1946 during which year the decline amounted to 14 million shares under the total for 1945 in response to an increase of required margins to 100 percent that was effective from January 20, 1946, to January 31, 1947. The decline in stock market activity continued throughout the remaining years of the decade even though lower required margins of 75 percent were in effect after February 1, 1947. From these data it appears that factors that were external to the money market itself exercised more influence over the volume of sales of corporate shares than did margin requirements.

Control of Inflation

Inflation is confiscatory; it redistributes wealth and incomes among the members of society. It weakens morale and causes suffering, deprivation, and loss of purchasing power, especially to those persons who depend upon funded incomes, salaries that are traditionally fixed, and those that are determined by law at some level. In addition, it adds to the costs of war at a time when costs are not determining factors in the choice of goods that are used in the war effort. The increasing scarcity of consumers' goods causes prices to rise. More persons having larger incomes during war than those to which they are accustomed causes prices to rise. Put the two causal conditions together and substantial inflation results. Inflation occurs when employment and wage costs rise under conditions which make it impossible to increase the production of consumers' goods. The extent to which consumers' purchasing power is not restricted is a cause of higher prices.

Office of Price Administration. The functions of the Office of Price Administration included (1) the prevention of unjustified price increases, rising costs of living, profiteering, and inflation; (2) the prevention and hoarding of commodities; (3) the stimulation of the production of supplies for civilian use after military requirements had been met, and the allocation of the civilian supplies of goods among their competing uses; and (4) the determination of maximum prices for finished goods and for any factor of production. Its duties were so broad in scope and so vast in volume that the OPA had to depend upon voluntary compliance and cooperation of the business firms concerned, and upon consumers not offering to purchase commodities under black market conditions.

Price Controls. On April 28, 1942, retailers, wholesalers, manufacturers, and producers, with some exceptions, were prohibited from charging more for their goods and services than the highest prices they had charged during the preceding month. Prices of millions of articles, domestic and imported, were placed under control. Included were almost all processed foods— bread, sugar, coffee, beef, pork, fresh milk and cream, all articles of apparel including shoes and dry goods, soap, fuel, drugs, furniture and furnishings, and hardware. Various types of services such as laundry, dry cleaning, shoe repair, automobile repair, funerals, and the storage of furs were included.

Initially, farm products were exempt from price controls at the farm level; but as their prices continued to mount, the President asked Congress to authorize controls over the prices of butter, eggs, poultry, cheese, evaporated and condensed milk, flour, onions, potatoes, fresh and canned citrus fruit, lamb meat and cornmeal.

Ceiling prices were determined at the level of each retail outlet, and the owner of each store was required to post in some public manner ceiling prices that pertained to every item in his store. One reason for this was the magnitude of the problem; another was in order to permit as much price competition as prevailed during the month of March, 1942. Prices could be lowered, but quality and weights had to be maintained. Later on in the program, ceiling prices were established for such commodities as vacuum cleaners, mechanical refrigerators, automobile tires—new, used, and recapped—silk and nylon hose, and used typewriters. The latter was made necessary by the strict controls that were placed over the manufacture of new machines. Both the capital and labor of typewriter manufacturers were easily and readily converted to the manufacture of guns.

Rent Controls. Rent controls were first applied in some 70 cities that had been designated as defense areas and in which large manufacturing plants were located that were involved with the production of items especially designed to further our defense program. They were applied to areas in which shipping facilities were being constructed and operated, partly to prevent landlords from separating large portions of wage incomes from civilian war workers, partly to control price inflation. High rentals would have given landlords more money with which to chase scarce consumers' goods. Rent controls did not serve their purpose entirely well. Owners of rental properties who could not charge higher rents after maintenance costs had been incurred often preferred to withdraw them from the market entirely. Many houses that formerly had been rental properties were put up for sale, but takers were few. Restrictions on rents and upon maintenance and improvement costs went with the building and not with its owner.

Rent controls were indirectly responsible for the construction of many housing projects all over the country to make up for the housing shortage that reached an acute stage when war workers and civilian employees in governmental war agencies continued to move into cities in the face of fewer rental housing properties. Costs of construction were under control as was the square footage of floor space in each house. Housing that contained something close to 1,000 square feet and which cost approximately $5,000 rented for $50 per month. The general plan was a rental charge that equaled 1 percent per month of the cost of construction of the house. Mortgages were guaranteed by the government, and occupants at the time the war housing emergency was declared to be no longer existent were given options to purchase their homes at an increase of 10 percent over original construction costs. These houses were constructed with a minimum of waste space in the form of hallways, storage space, cellars, and porches; but they were places in which workers and employees, who could be certified as being engaged in the war effort, could live without having to pay outrageous rents. Storage space in attics consisted of nothing but a few wide boards laid down on the ceiling rafters to meet the minimum requirement of 100 square feet.

Between July 1, 1940, and October 1, 1942, the combined efforts of private industry and the government resulted in the completion of 500,000 war housing units, some of which were single family units, while some were dormitory type and apartments and some were trailers. Over one and one-half million additional war workers required over one and one-quarter million living accommodation units between July, 1942, and July, 1943. One half of these were found in existing structures, many of which were remodeled; about one third were provided by the erection of public housing units while the remainder was provided at the level of free enterprise.

Some landlords attempted to evade OPA restrictions on rents by evicting tenants who refused to pay amounts that were above established ceilings and then entering into pseudo sales contracts, with no down payment required and for which principal sums were paid off in monthly installments that were above the established rental payments for the respective properties. The OPA put a stop to this practice by requiring that a down payment of one third of the "purchase" price be made by the "buyer" who could not borrow the amount of his down payment.

Rationing. Rationing programs were introduced in order to relieve the pressure of price upon scarce goods. The OPA issued books of ration coupons in which designated coupons were made eligible for the purchase of stated items within specified periods of time.

Products and Services Effected. Such coupons were required to accompany the purchase price of sugar, gasoline, shoes, meat, and other items. While there was no shortage of gasoline for civilian use there was a shortage of natural rubber and of rubber tires which were conserved for use by the military. By cutting down on the amount of gasoline the owners of automobiles could purchase, wear and tear on tires were reduced to a minimum. A maximum rate of speed of 35 miles per hour was established. Gasoline coupons A, which permitted the purchase of three gallons of gasoline per week, were issued to owners of automobiles the operation of which was in no way connected with the war effort. B coupons which permitted the purchase of five gallons were issued to those who participated in the war effort and for whom private transportation was essential. Other coupons were issued to truckers and to operators of vehicles for hire.

The use of public transportation facilities was not only encouraged it was forced on many persons who had become accustomed to driving their own cars. Electric street railway companies dug deep into their reserves of discarded streetcars and employed maintenance crews to service them every night to keep them from breaking down rather than to repair them afterwards. Cars were one-man operations with the motormen in control of all phases of their operations. Because of the shortage of manpower, combined with the increase in the number of cars in service and of their frequency of making runs, women were trained to take over an operation that traditionally had been restricted to males. Subway trains, surface and elevated cars, and commuting passenger railway trains, not to mention buses, had more traffic than they could accommodate comfortably. Even standing room was at a premium during the rush hours of the morning and again late in the afternoon. Patrons of sporting events, of opera productions, and of all kinds of public entertainment utilized the facilities of public transportation. The problem was not one of inadequate parking, it was one of gasoline.

The rationing of sugar was not permitted to interfere with home canning of fruits and vegetables. Extra sugar was available with the use of special coupons that were released by the OPA for this purpose.

The consumption of fuel oil for the winter of 1942-43 was rationed on the basis of gallonage that had been consumed the preceding winter, the number of persons living in a house, particularly invalids and small children, the square footage of floor space and the heat zone, of which there were four, in which a person resided. Thirty states from North Dakota to Florida were divided into four heat zones for this purpose and records of the Weather Bureau for the past 43 years were used in determining the boundaries of the zones and the amount of fuel oil that was rationed. The government laid 3,800 miles of pipelines at a cost of $180 million in an attempt to assure a steady flow of oil and gas into the industrial areas of the North and East. Big Inch, a 24-inch line 1,340 miles long, was constructed from the oil fields of Texas to New York and Pennsylvania. Little Inch, 20 inches in diameter, was constructed from Louisiana, across the states of Mississippi, Alabama, Georgia, and north to industrial areas. Four smaller and shorter lines were laid in order to conserve tank car space and railroad facilities.

Ration Banking. A system of ration banking was borrowed from England where it had operated successfully. After a trial period in Albany, Schenectady, and Troy, New York, it was extended to other parts of the country. Under this plan all merchants and dealers in rationed commodities deposited in their local banks the ration coupons they received from their customers. When they were in need of new supplies, in addition to drawing money checks against their banks to pay for the goods, these checks were accompanied by checks in terms of ration coupons drawn against their deposits of these items in their local banks. These checks were cleared in the same manner as were checks that were drawn against ordinary deposits.

Wage Control. By an executive order of the President issued on October 3, 1942, basic wage rates were frozen at their levels of September 15, 1942. Adjustments were permitted to be made after this date to correct maladjustments, inequalities, and gross inequities; to eliminate substandards of living; and to aid in the prosecution of the war. Employees could be promoted to higher paying jobs, and they could continue to be paid time and a half the base rate of pay for overtime.

Wage earners were not entirely free to move from one job to another higher paying one. They had to obtain certificates stating that they were not engaged in work essential to the war effort, or if they were so employed, adequate replacements were available. Scarcity in the supply of labor was overcome in part by an order of the President in which a minimum 48-hour workweek was established early in 1943. The order applied to civilian government employees as well as to wage earners in industry.

Little Steel. Between January, 1941, and May, 1942, the cost of living index as measured by the Bureau of Labor Statistics increased 15 percent. This percentage increase was the basis upon which the Little Steel Case was settled. Wage increases to correct maladjustments were permitted if the average straight-time wage rates in a plant or in a separate bargaining unit had not increased 15 percent since January, 1941. This increase was not applied to an individual wage rate; it was applied to the unit of employment of which the individual was a part. After wages had been adjusted under Little Steel, advances in wages were permitted to correct inequalities and inequities and to maintain traditional wage rate differentials between jobs that required different levels of skills. For example, when the minimum rate for the common labor classification was raised to 50 cents an hour, other adjustments were made in the wages of workers who had acquired higher levels of skills in order to maintain traditional patterns of the wage structure.

Some Impacts of Wage Control. When minimum wage rates were raised to 40 cents an hour, later to 50 cents, increases in weekly pay envelopes before taxes amounted to $4.80 and $6.00, respectively, for just overtime for thousands of workers whose basic workweek consisted of 40 hours, and who worked 48 hours. This meant increases in the pay envelopes of tens of thousands of employees who were in the semiskilled and skilled labor job classifications. Another factor that must be considered in the overall analysis of wage control is that these controls were applied to more than one wage earner in many families. Not only did husbands and wives work, but their teenage and older unmarried daughters joined the labor force. Boys who were too young to volunteer for military duty or to be drafted also went to work either on a full-time or a part-time basis. No matter whether family incomes are considered or total wages to all workers, more wage dollars were paid to and received by thousands of persons than ever before. Other things remaining the same, this meant that more dollars were chasing consumer's goods that were continually becoming more scarce, which made the control of price inflation just that much more difficult.

Much of the increases in family incomes and in farm incomes were used to retire mortgage or other indebtedness before it actually matured. Farmers were shown that while it had been more difficult for them to service their mortgage obligations during periods when the prices of farm commodities were falling, it was correspondingly easy for them to service these obligations and even to retire them when the prices of farm commodities were rising. Payments to Federal Land Banks and to Land Bank Commissioners broke all records. During the first six months of 1942, a total of $131,346,000 was paid on principal sums of farm mortgage loans; while only $106,861,000 had been paid in all of 1940 and $125,589,000 in 1941. Loans that were paid back entirely amounted to $80 million during the first six months of 1942 compared with $79 million and $51 million for the entire years of 1941 and 1940, respectively.

Banking

It is not surprising to find that the business of commercial banking increased rapidly during the war years. War contracts for all the branches of the Armed Forces were awarded with the understanding that subcontractors would be given opportunities to partake of the war effort. This policy was followed in order to bring about a maximum utilization of our productive resources. Commercial banks, large and small, felt the impact of the policy. Total deposits in all banks increased from $70,854 million in 1940 to $159,293 million in 1946, of which United States government deposits amounted to $824 million and $13,415 million, respectively. Government deposits reached their peak of $24,385 million in 1945 compared with a high of $1,542 million in 1918. Such deposits in 1945 were distributed between national banks and all others in a ratio of 13 to 11. The number of insured banks decreased by 5 between 1940 and 1945, while the number of uninsured banks decreased by 318. Total assets of insured banks more than doubled; of uninsured banks assets declined 25 percent. A total of 48 banks closed their doors in 1940, and 47 more failed throughout the next 5 years; 39 of these failed in 1941 and 1942. The number of depositors in the Postal Savings System increased over 1 million in the war years. As of January 1, 1940, time and savings deposits in all banks that totaled $27,729 million by the end of 1945 had become $48,452 million. These data illustrate vividly the position that banks occupied in collecting relatively small savings from large numbers of persons and making them available to borrowers of capital—both short term and long term.

Communication

Communication services expanded more intensively than they did extensively during the war years. No new telephone exchanges were established. From 1941 through 1945, 4,701,000 miles of telephone wire were strung by the Bell System compared with 3,901,000 and 5,995,000 miles of wire in the single years of 1939 and 1940 respectively. In 1941, 321,422 employees within the Bell Telephone System received average annual wages of $1,823; and in 1945, 396,198 employees received an annual average wage that amounted to $2,296. This increased average could have been attained and probably was by employing more new men in the higher wage brackets than in the lower. Average annual wages of $1,257 in 1942 that were paid to 32,196 employees of telephone companies that were independent of the Bell System had become $1,513 for 36,000 such employees in 1945. Direct dialing had not become nationwide, and the average annual wages revealed the impact of the low wages that were paid to telephone exchange operators. Linemen and repair mechanics undoubtedly were among those whose annual incomes were above the average for the industry. While the number of independent telephone companies increased slightly, by only 17, from 1941 to 1945, miles of wire were actually fewer by 192,000 miles in 1945 than they had been in 1942.

An increase of 50 percent in average daily long-distance calls compared with only a 5 percent increase in the number of local calls measures to some extent the more intensive use that was made of the telephone. That people had become even more accustomed to the convenience of the telephone, or to the long-distance aspect of it, is evidenced by the increase in the average number of local calls and of toll messages, each of which increased 50 percent from 1945 to 1956 inclusive. The technical difficulties that produced indistinct and far-away tones of voice had been overcome and long-distance messages had become as distinct and clear as local calls and almost as easy to make. The demand for telephone service appeared to be elastic in nature. As rates for 3-minute daytime calls between New York and Chicago dropped from $1.90 in 1940 to $1.50 in 1957, between New York and Denver from $4.40 to $3.25, between New York and San Francisco from $4.00 to $2.50, and other tolls were correspondingly lowered, operating revenues increased rather than decreased, which is evidence supporting relative elasticity of demand.

The number of phones per 1,000 of population was 165.1 in 1940, 198.1 in 1945, and 354.5 in 1956; and it is to be remembered that there were 7,806 more units of 1,000 population in 1945 than there were in 1940, and that there were another 29,246 additional units of 1,000 population in 1956 than there were in 1945.

Agriculture

War activities abroad focused attention upon the United States as the one neutral nation that could and would assume the responsibility of feeding the war-stricken peoples of Europe. The impact of the war demand for the products of American agriculture came at a time when the restrictive measures of the New Deal program were still in effect. Even so, the carryover of wheat, corn, and cotton had remained large each year; and the United States entered the war with ample reserves of the principal food and fiber crops and with a production potential that far exceeded the requirements of peacetime at the levels of economic activity of the immediate prewar period.

Conditions that resulted in large reserves of underemployed labor were altered to those in which farm labor became more completely utilized and more expensive. Farm operations were planned with a view to lengthening the work period in seasonal activities. Power machinery was used more extensively, animal power less so, partly to conserve the use of farm labor some of which was migratory workers. The overall output of agricultural products increased between 1940 and 1945 by almost 25 percent at a time when total employment [1] at the farm level actually decreased by about 7 percent. Longer hours of work, greater use of farm machinery, and a more efficient use of farm labor more than made up for a decrease of 19 percent in the number of hired workers on farms in this span of years.

In the initial stages of price control, prices of agricultural products were exempt; however, a few months later these prices seemed to be getting out of hand. In order to implement the President's order to hold the line, on April 30, 1942, retail prices of meat, butter, and coffee were "rolled back" about 10 percent, which resulted in consumers paying less for these products than they had been paying in the immediate past. To protect the prior handlers of these products, an equivalent subsidy was given by the government to those who operated at the food processing level. During the months of May and June the prices of 39 additional farm commodities were rolled back, and in August prices of the more important fresh fruits and vegetables and most kinds of fresh fish were brought under control. The implication here was that if more incentives were needed to stimulate the production of farm products, it was the policy of the President that they would not be permitted to take the form of higher prices at the retail level.

Records indicate that in spite of scarcities of food, in spite of rationing of basic commodities and of control over their prices, the American civilian population consumed the largest amount of food per capita in its entire history. Rationed foods at controlled prices enabled thousands of workers who had been unable to purchase many quality foods to do so for the first time with their wartime earnings which were larger than ever before. When meat rations were not adequate to feed hungry mouths, people relied upon pressed

---

[1] Includes owner-operators of farms and members of their families.

canned meats, cold cuts, and sandwich fills, none of which were rationed and all of which were sold at or under ceiling prices.

At the close of the war, American farmers had increased their bank deposits and holdings of currency from $3.9 billion on January 1, 1940, to almost $14 billion on January 1, 1946. They owned $5 billion of United States savings bonds, a form of savings they were slow to accept. Farm mortgages had been reduced $1.5 billion, and their total debt had been lowered from $10 billion to $8.3 billion. On the other hand, values of farm real estate had increased from $33.6 billion to $56.5 billion; and the value of their livestock was $9.6 billion compared with $5.1 billion in 1940, in spite of a decline in the number of horses and mules in amounts of 2 million and 1 million respectively.

Production

The story of how readily America adjusted to production for war would not be complete without reference to *The Arsenal of Democracy: The Story of American War Production* by Donald W. Nelson.[2] This probably is the most authoritative and interesting account that has been written dealing with the conversion of industrial effort from peacetime commodities and peacetime objectives to those that were needed to support the war effort. The conversion was nothing short of a revolution; but the element of profit was not only retained, in some instances it loomed up larger than ever before.

Airplane Production. One of the miracles of production during the war was the annual output of airplanes. The largest number of planes that had been produced in any one year prior to the emergency was 6,193 in 1929. In 1940 the entire industry turned out 12,804 planes, 6,019 of which were destined to see military service. Some of the latter were sent to European countries on lend-lease terms. When President Roosevelt made known the need for 52,000 new planes in one year, production managers threw up their hands in horror. Never could the industry accomplish such a stupendous task; but the President told them it not only could be done but would be done. In 1942, 1943, and 1944, all of the planes that were produced were pressed into military action. In the first of these years, 47,836 planes rolled off the assembly lines; the second year saw 85,898 planes put into service, and 1944 topped them all with a record of 96,318. These totals include some that were made in Canada but were financed by the United States. To accomplish this remarkable feat, old factories were reconditioned, entirely new plants were constructed, and most automobile and many other factories were converted to specifications of the aircraft industry. All of them were operated 24 hours a day with three shifts of labor. Basic wage rates were paid for the 8 A.M. to 4 P.M. shift; a night shift differential was added to earnings of those who worked from 4 P.M. to midnight; and those who

[2] Donald W. Nelson, *The Arsenal of Democracy: The Story of American War Production* (New York City: Harcourt, Brace & World, Inc., 1946).

worked the owl shift from midnight to 8 A.M. received still another wage differential. This was only one way by which weekly pay envelopes were fattened without altering base rates of pay.

Other War Production. Since the automobile manufacturers were not only the champions of but the best exemplifiers of mass production in which the assembly line had been incorporated into its most important component, they were called upon to produce for war instead of for peace and they met the challenge. One of them alone produced not only armored cars, ambulances, tanks and army trucks, but aircraft engines, airplanes and some of their parts, such as propellors, wings, fuel pumps, instruments, landing gears and automobile pilots; Diesel engines for ships, tanks and trucks; carbines; anti-aircraft guns and aircraft cannon and machine guns; radios; parachute flares, and many other items.

The facilities of watch manufacturers, including their skilled workers, were converted to the production of instruments of precise measurement and exactness of performance that were used in all branches of the United States Armed Forces.

Landing craft and Liberty ships rolled off the assembly lines of Andrew Higgins and Henry J. Kaiser at unprecedented rates. Assembly line methods of constructing ships were unheard of, but if they were going to be put afloat before it was too late, this method had to be developed and its product accepted. Instead of ten months or more that had lapsed between laying keels and delivering ships in 1917, vessels were turned out in 40 days or less. Two hundred Liberty ships grew to almost 3,000. They were not objects of beauty or of grace. Substitute materials were used whenever and wherever possible without loss of strength or of efficiency.

Even though there were many types and models of war vehicles, such items as door handles, spark plugs, batteries, belts, generators, and other items were standardized not only to reduce their costs of production but to facilitate their repair and replacement. One concern that had obtained a contract to deliver 20 specimens of weapons within a year at a cost of $667 each actually produced more than 28,000 at a unit cost of only $141. Other incidents of unbelievable accomplishments occurred, but to enumerate them here would only result in proliferation.

QUESTIONS FOR REVIEW

1. (a) Had American industries had an opportunity to adjust themselves to the needs of war before 1942? Explain.
   (b) What were some of the impacts of war in Europe upon our railroads, and upon the labor and agricultural segments of our economy?

2. What were some of the obstacles to developing a preparedness program?

3. (a) In what ways was the supply of labor increased to meet the exigencies of war?
(b) Were these sources of labor supply retained after the close of the war? Explain.
(c) Use your answer to (b) above to explain some of the impacts these forces had upon our postwar economic development.

4. (a) How well did the railroads meet the demands of war in the 1940's?
(b) How did developments in the 1930's contribute to the degree of success or failure of the railroads to contribute their share to the war effort?

5. (a) Explain in some detail the efforts of the federal government to control price inflation during the war.
(b) Were these efforts successful? Explain why or why not.

6. (a) What was the Little Steel decision in the settlement of a wage dispute?
(b) Of what importance was Little Steel in stabilizing wages?

SUGGESTED READINGS

Barnes, James A. *Wealth of the American People*. Englewood Cliffs, N. J.: Prentice-Hall, Inc., 1949. Chapter 38.

Bining, Arthur C., and Thomas C. Cochran. *The Rise of American Economic Life*. 4th ed. New York City: Charles Scribner's Sons, 1964. Chapter 27.

Clough, Shepard B. *The Economic Development of Western Civilization*. New York City: McGraw-Hill Book Company, 1959. Chapter 20.

Krooss, Herman E. *American Economic Development*. 2d ed. Englewood Cliffs, N. J.: Prentice-Hall, Inc., 1966. Chapter 16.

Robertson, Ross M. *History of the American Economy*. 2d ed. New York City: Harcourt, Brace & World, Inc., 1964. See also index references to World War II.

Williamson, Harold F. (ed.). *The Growth of the American Economy*. 2d ed. Englewood Cliffs, N. J.: Prentice-Hall, Inc., 1951. See also index references to World War II.

Wright, Chester W. *Economic History of the United States*. 2d ed. New York City: McGraw-Hill Book Company, 1949. Chapter 44.

Chapter 26

RECONVERSION

WITHOUT DEPRESSION

IMMEDIATE POSTWAR DEVELOPMENTS

High-level administrators in the Truman administration remembered the chaotic conditions that followed the release of controls and restrictions upon prices and uses of commodities after the armistice was signed in November, 1918. They were also mindful of the high degree of unemployment that was caused by the hasty return of soldiers to civilian life. A plan had been devised according to which price and rent controls would be released gradually over a period of time, and men in uniform would not be discharged from service more rapidly than they could be absorbed into industry. They had been guaranteed their old jobs back, but some of the latter were no longer existent.

Some of the men did not want to return to their old jobs. They wanted something better, at least as far as wage rates were concerned, than the wages they had been paid before they were inducted into service. Pressures from the men in uniform, from their parents and wives, and from the people in general were so intense that neither the President, the members of his cabinet who were concerned with the matter, nor the military leaders could carry out their plans for an orderly release of men from service. Pressures were just as strong to remove all priorities, price and rent controls, and the rationing of consumer goods. Rationing and controls over prices of most consumer goods were abandoned immediately following VJ day. A ceiling on the price of sugar was maintained until its market supply could be brought closer to its market demand.

Release of Savings

Pent-up savings were used to purchase consumers' goods that had been rationed and others that had almost disappeared from the counters of retail stores in order to make them available in PX's. Industry reconverted its capital equipment and assembly lines to turn out consumers' goods for millions of persons who had been deprived of them throughout the duration or who had been able to purchase them only on a rationed or restricted basis. More workers had more money than ever before in their whole lives with which to purchase food, clothing, and luxury items. Among foods, the cumulative effects of purchasing fresh meats by those who had been deprived of them for over three long years and the new market demand from thousands of workers whose weekly wages were large enough for the first time to permit them to do so caused prices of meats to soar and market supplies to become low. There was no less meat being put on the market, but it was being taken off meat counters much more rapidly.

Demand for Motor Equipment

Many automobiles and motor trucks that were not new when the war broke out and all new cars that were channeled into the military had become more run-down and physically depreciated when the war was over. Prospective purchasers of new cars were required to wait their turn. Waiting lists were long, and the same names appeared on the lists of more than one dealer. This was an opportune time for the Kaiser-Frazer Company to market its new cars. Many prospective customers of dealers of one of the Big Three automobile manufacturers purchased the newer makes of cars and found them acceptable. Competition between them and the older makes of cars became so keen that the Kaiser-Frazer Company found it increasingly difficult to obtain coal for fuel, iron and steel, and automobile parts from established manufacturers. When Kaiser-Frazer could no longer purchase its basic raw materials in the market, it appealed to and obtained a loan from the Reconstruction Finance Corporation of sufficient value to enable it to construct mills and to become more completely integrated so that its supplies would come within its own organizational setup. The loan was justified by the government in the name of promoting and maintaining competition in the manufacture and sale of automobiles. This use of the RFC was far from any of the original purposes for which loans were extended in 1932 and the ensuing years of the New Deal.

Automobiles appeared on city streets and on highways, and patronage of public transportation facilities declined rapidly. Electric streetcars gave way to electric trolley buses and to those powered by internal combustion engines. City bus lines were extended, and fares were raised. The immediate effect of higher bus fares was the use of more private automobiles on city streets and a heavy demand for parking spaces. A solution to this problem provides the subject matter for discussion later in the chapter.

Employment

The rapid rate of return of GI's to civilian life was not accompanied by an increase of unemployment. Labor at many levels of skills was in scarce supply. The retooling of capital goods machinery in factories and mills absorbed some of the workers whose skills enabled them to perform this kind of work. Manufacturers of thousands of articles increased the productive capacities of their establishments in order to obtain their share of the pent-up savings that were being released.

Building Construction

The building construction industry was one of the largest employers of ex-service men. At the level of free enterprise, it had been at a standstill for several years. Fires had destroyed thousands of buildings—residence, business, and factory—many of which had not been restored for one or more of several reasons. Thousands of new families had been formed during the war years, and the size of existing families had increased. In most instances, when the new husbands and potential fathers went off to camp, the new wives and children moved in with parents or with in-laws. Living was not comfortable, but it was tolerated. When husbands and fathers returned home, they were forced to join an already overcrowded household until separate residential facilities could be constructed.

Extensive Expansion. In most urban communities the expansion of housing facilities was along extensive lines, though there was considerable intensive growth. Extensive development took the form of opening new housing subdivisions which required extensions of storm and sanitary sewers, new pavements, curbs and sidewalks, new gas mains, water mains, and extensions of electric light and power lines. Financing the new housing construction was no problem to former GI's, who were given special terms of low down payments, or none at all, and up to 30 years to pay principal sums at low rates of interest.

Intensive Expansion. Intensive expansion in building construction took the form of new and larger apartment buildings and hotels, enlargements in the floor space of office buildings, restaurants, and theaters. There were many reasons that entered into the preference that many families expressed for the apartment mode of living, one of which was the factor of safety. The war may have encouraged a disrespect for law and order which was revealed in an increase in violence against property and against persons. Many families who did not want to assume the responsibility of maintaining yards and gardens, shoveling snow in winter, doing the chores of keeping house, and firing furnaces in winter sought relief in apartment living.

New Methods of Construction. Machinery was used in construction to speed up the work of making new quarters for housing families, new business firms, and new factories. Bulldozers and heavy earth-moving equipment displaced more primitive methods that harnessed the strength of men and of animals. Electric saws displaced the hand-powered type, and the sound of power hammers and riveters pierced the air. Ready concrete mixers transported concrete to sites where it could be used upon arrival without loss of time in the mixing process. Brick was no longer a pavement surface, nor was it used for sidewalks, and concrete blocks largely displaced brick in the construction of outer walls for all kinds of structures.

While there was an overall increase in the demand for lumber, its use in permanent construction and in interior finishing gave way in large measure to iron and steel, and to concrete, tile, and terrazzo floors. These substitute materials were not only cheaper than wood, but they were also fireproof and were incorporated into building codes for public buildings and commercial establishments. Owners found additional savings in the setting of lower premiums on fire insurance policies.

Demand for Complementary Services

With the expansion of areas of business and of living, cities and governments were called upon to expand their areas of services. New sewage disposal plants were constructed; more firemen and policemen were required to protect property and person; additional fire-fighting equipment had to be purchased, and new fire stations were constructed adjacent to new areas of development. Additional costs to municipalities that were incurred in financing these developments were partly offset by reductions in insurance premiums that were paid by property owners. Members of sheriffs' staffs were increased, and counties were compelled to provide fire protection to those who resided beyond the areas of urban responsibility.

The federal government employed more men to deliver mail and parcel post packages, more clerks were required to work in post offices, and branch offices were opened in outlying districts in order to take postal services nearer to those who used them. Rural routes and some city routes were motorized, and more mail drop boxes were placed at strategic intersections of important streets.

All these activities were among the many ways by which people made their living after the war. While they took place at or near the consumer level, they were reflected back to the first stages of production. From the extractive industries of mining, agriculture, and lumbering, over agencies of transport to manufacturing, processing, and fabricating, materials and commodities were distributed to wholesalers, thence to retailers until finally they reached the hands of ultimate consumers. One of the demands for services and for goods was complementary to the completion of new apartments and new houses. At our level of living it was almost a joint demand. It was the demand for the installation of new telephones. Telephone companies were almost compelled to ration their services. Four-party lines were used until adequate switchboard space and new wires could be strung. Names were placed on waiting lists until new central exchanges could be constructed or expanded. Branch exchanges were erected to relieve the load at central offices. Telephone companies and their suppliers had never experienced such booming expansion as took place after the war. Vacations with pay were cancelled, and employees received time and one-half rates for working through them in an effort to reduce the backlog of orders for installations and to render more complete and more adequate service to subscribers of telephone service.

NO IMMEDIATE POSTWAR DEPRESSION

From what has been written so far the reader must have concluded that conditions were not ripe for a serious recession or for a prolonged economic and industrial depression to develop. Most certainly there were not the slightest indicators of a financial panic. Economic activity at the level of free enterprise saw to that with the support of substantial governmental measures. Before mentioning other forces or factors that contributed to the maintenance of a high level of economic activity, a recount of some developments that have been presented in other frameworks is in order.

1. The release of pent-up purchasing power.
2. The opportunity to purchase durable consumers' goods that had been in scarce supply for several years, or which had not been available at all.
3. The demand for automobiles, automobile tires, and gasoline.
4. Unprecedented activity in the building construction industry in erecting housing—single and multiple family units, and business establishments at the levels of retail, wholesale, and manufacturing.
5. The tasks of reconverting wartime production lines in factories to the requirements of production for peace.
6. The rapid growth of residential subdivisions with all of its economic implications.
7. The expansion of governmental services—federal, state and local.

Wage Patterns

When wartime urgencies for volume production were over, the President urged industrial leaders and managers to return to their traditional shorter workweek without any reduction in take-home pay. This was tantamount to a wage increase, but business and industrial communities cooperated wholeheartedly with the President who led the way in maintaining salaries of government employees at the levels they had reached during the war when they returned to a 40-hour workweek. This plan was effective in preventing a reduction in wage and salary incomes from their high levels when production was slowed down somewhat immediately following VJ day. The plan had the effect not only of maintaining wage and salary payments for those who had been employed, but also of setting new and higher levels of beginning pay scales for new employees who were added to payrolls. To the extent that lowered incomes had antedated earlier recessions, they did not put any pressure on prices, nor did they have the effect of reducing the volume of business transactions after 1945.

Street and Highway Improvements

New and larger concentrations of populations in urban areas created new levels of congestion on city streets and on highways. Municipal administrative officers were compelled to designate certain streets as through streets and to widen them and to improve and repave others. Counties and states undertook the construction of four-lane highways to relieve congestion on two-lane roads and to make them safer. The impacts of these types of road construction on employment in the construction industries and in their lines of supply added to the total wages and salaries that were received by employees. To service the large number of motor trucks and passenger cars that appeared on the highways, filling stations and repair garages were erected at strategic locations on city streets and alongside country roads. To accommodate truck drivers and persons who were traveling by car, restaurants and motels were constructed and sleeping accommodations were built in connection with eating facilities. To accommodate the patrons of motor buses, new terminals and facilities at rest stops were constructed.

People had been deprived of driving their automobiles and of going somewhere in them for so long that they gave vent to their feelings and to their new freedom by driving to restaurants and cafes that had been built along highways or in nearby cities and towns. They drove to distant athletic contests, to theater productions, to concerts, lectures, and did not hesitate to spend the night away from their homes. Life was different. Life was free, and living was comparatively easy.

Capital Investment and Unemployment

One of the most significant factors that determined a high level of economic activity following the close of the war was the level of capital investment. During years of war private capital investment remained at a low level. Total investment was high, but the federal government was responsible for a large percentage, and private capital investments were at a minimum.

Data in Table 26-1 reveal the pattern of investment of private capital and the portion of it that was invested in producers' durable goods. The impact of capital investment on employment is seen by comparing Column 3 and Column 4 with Columns 1 and 2. From the point of view of individual workers, the fact of unemployment, and its increases and decreases, are important if these workers are involved. From the standpoint of the American economy, the percentage of unemployed in the civilian labor force is more significant. In the darkest two years of the Great Depression, unemployment accounted for 23.6 percent and 24.9 percent of the civilian labor force. In 1942 it was 4.7 percent and in 1944 it was 1.2 percent. Absolutely, unemployment after World War II was serious; relatively, it was not alarming.

Table 26-1

Gross Private Investment, Unemployment, and Government Expenditures—1945-1955

Year	Gross Private Investment (billions)		Unemployment (000)		Government Purchases of Goods and Services (billions)
	Total	Producers' Durable Goods	Total	Percentage of Civilian Labor Force	
	(1)	(2)	(3)	(4)	(5)
1945	$17.0	$12.7	1,040	1.9	$131.2
1946	42.4	16.1	2,270	3.9	43.9
1947	41.5	21.7	2,142	3.6	37.2
1948	49.8	22.8	2,064	3.4	42.1
1949	38.5	19.8	3,395	5.5	47.2
1950	55.9	21.3	3,142	5.0	45.1
1951	57.7	22.0	1,875	3.0	63.3
1952	50.4	21.8	1,673	2.7	77.7
1953	50.6	22.5	1,602	2.5	84.3
1954	48.9	20.8	3,230	5.0	75.3
1955	62.5	22.5	2,654	4.0	73.2

Source: U.S. Department of Commerce, Bureau of the Census, *Historical Statistics of the United States. Colonial Times to 1957* (Washington: U.S. Government Printing Office, 1960), pp. 73 and 143. Adapted.

Efforts on the part of government to counteract the failure of private capital investment to increase steadily, or even to maintain a given level, are measured in Column 5. Authority for these variations in government expenditures will be discussed later in this chapter. There always is a time lag between governmental expenditure and its impact on employment.

THE LABOR FRONT

The termination of hostilities was the occasion for organized labor to make concerted drives, or all-out efforts, to obtain wage increases and extended fringe benefits, particularly in the mass production industries. Labor leaders took the position that, if they could not obtain higher wage rates for workers who were organized at the time, they never would and never could obtain them. They drove what appeared to be hard bargains in the steel, meat-packing, automobile, and coal industries. The usual pattern was to establish an industry-wide contract by bargaining with the larger firms in the respective industries and then make adjustments in contracts with smaller firms when necessary. The assumption was that the larger firms were the most efficient: they had the lowest average unit costs of production; and they controlled prices, or at least established price leadership.

New Labor Program

Union leaders no longer based their arguments for increased wages on the increased productivity of labor. They based their demands for increased wage rates and for fringe benefits upon the profit and loss statements of corporate employers.

They made strenuous efforts to organize plant foremen and plant superintendents, but in general met with defeat. The latter groups of employees were in a position to enforce programs and policies of employers and to take steps to increase production rather than to protect employees from actions of employers that might be detrimental to employees. They were presumed to have more the point of view of employers than that of employees, but insofar as they were organized there was a tendency on their part to lose this perspective.

Labor did not object to reductions in the age of compulsory retirement, or in the minimum terms of service and age combined, after which retirement would be on a voluntary basis. This support was given in the name of accelerating the rate of promotions from lower paying to higher paying jobs, thus providing employment to some men who had recently entered the labor market, and to others who may have been recently unemployed. Severance pay was demanded when such a benefit was not already provided. This form of compensation became increasingly significant at a time when an accelerated tempo of automating industrial processes created temporary unemployment for some workers, longer run or more permanent unemployment for many of those workers who were in the older age brackets, and among those who could not easily adjust themselves to more completely mechanized operations. Unfortunately for some workers, new employment was found only at the cost of lower rates of pay in jobs that required less highly developed skills or degrees of manual dexterity.

Wages and Profits. Employers took the position that wages were determined in part by the productivity of labor and in part by opportunity wage rates (the rates of pay that their workers could and would receive from other employers for doing the same kinds of work, and what other employers were paying their own employees for performing identical tasks, or those that required the same degrees of dexterity, training, strength and endurance). They went on to say that, if labor wanted wage adjustments to conform to the pattern of corporate profits, wage rates should be lowered when profits declined as well as raised when profits increased. Labor, in general, refused to accept this philosophy, although in a few instances employees of some firms accepted lower wages when the income statements of employer firms revealed financial losses. The alternative was for them to close down their operations entirely and for their employees to become unemployed.

Again, to have based wage rates upon profits would have created unstable conditions in the labor market, so the employers claimed. Workers would want their names on the payrolls of the most profitable firms and would shun the less profitable ones. Workers countered that overall industry profits were the criteria, not those of individual firms.

Corporate managers admitted profits in some instances, but in all instances they denied that their existence gave them (the corporations) comparable ability to raise wages. Profits were necessary to attract free capital to industry with which to finance its growth and expansion, so went the argument. The result of this conflict in the interpretation of the existence and functioning of profits was that wage increases that were won by labor around the bargaining table were almost invariably followed by price increases. In many struggles between organized labor and corporate employers, the former appeared to have the sympathy of government officials, or their outright support, if their efforts to obtain wage increases did not result in price adjustments. Since "other factors did not remain the same," these price increases had little effect in reducing either the volume of sales or their values, and profits continued to be made. They, in turn, gave rise to another round of wage increases, and a spiral of wage-price inflation was truly in effect. There seemed to be no limit to the upward trend of prices until prices in the steel industry were rolled back under Presidential pressure.

Industry-wide Wage Contracts. The basic philosophy upon which industry-wide bargaining was based was that, insofar as both profits and marginal productivity entered into the determination of wages, they should be measured on the performance of the industry collectively, rather than upon the experience of each individual production unit. Labor should not be penalized for the inefficiency of management, whether it was due to the size of the plant, to its location, or to differences in the talents and capabilities of plant managers. If certain producers could not follow the industry-wide wage pattern, their problem was to increase their productive efficiency, to merge with larger and more efficient firms, or to close down entirely. That labor did not look kindly upon the latter eventuality is shown by its willingness to compromise with Southern coal, iron, and steel producers rather than have these corporations shut down their plants.

Fringe Benefits. Not only was labor determined to obtain what it thought was its share of our national income, it wanted to share in fringe benefits that other segments of the population enjoyed. In general, fringe benefits tended to increase the degree of economic security of employees; to increase their take-home pay under certain circumstances; and to increase the amount of time in which employees could engage in leisure time activities. Many disputes between labor and management were settled by extending to labor the benefits of group hospitalization and life insurance policies and also shorter periods of employment to establish eligibility for longer vacations with pay. Severance pay before reaching the age of retirement and retirement programs and pensions were given more attention in collective bargaining than ever before. Labor talked about a guaranteed annual wage, but mainly as a matter of indoctrination.

Strikes

Despite the policy of the National War Labor Board of not considering applications for wage adjustments when employees were on strike, and the pledge of union officials not to call strikes during war years, the number of strikes that occurred during the war was not much lower, except for 1942, than the number called immediately thereafter. Union leaders strove to get the participants in "wildcat" strikes to return to work as soon as possible. The average length of strikes dropped from 18.3 days in 1941 to 11.7 days in 1942 to only 5 days in 1943 and 1944. The increase in the average duration of strikes in 1945 reflects the readiness with which labor seized the opportunity to enforce its demand for higher wages, shorter hours, and union recognition, when the stresses of war were no longer present.

There is little argument that strikes that are of short duration and are successful are well worth the effort on the part of the striking workers. When strikes are long and drawn out, it is another matter from a financial point of view to those who are out of work.

In the steel strike of 1952 there were approximately 500,000 members of the United Steel Workers of America out on strike. At the time the average steelworker earned $3.10 an hour, $124 a week, and was demanding an additional 15 cents an hour, or $6 a week. After a walkout that lasted almost 8 weeks, the average steelworker had lost almost $922 in wages. At the rate of increase in pay of 15 cents an hour or $6 a week, and assuming continuous employment at the new rate of pay, it would take 3 years, 9 weeks, and 1½ days just to recover his loss. Of course, during the walkout he could have moonlighted, as many did. He also could have received benefits from the strike fund the union had established. In addition, he might have drawn unemployment compensation under Social Security, so that he was not entirely without money income.

In coal mining, strikes that have been successful in winning higher wages and/or shorter hours of work per day or per week have been followed by greater uses of machinery in the mining process and by the need for the services of fewer miners, so that many of the latter have become permanently unemployed in their chosen field of work, and in the only kind of work many of them knew how to perform. In addition, the miners that are employed have become more machine tenders than coal miners, in the traditional meaning of the word. John L. Lewis obtained for these men an unemployment increment of 60 cents per ton, or some other amount, from the sale of each ton of coal at the mine, which amount usually has been added to the price of coal. Then as the retail price of coal exceeded the cost of other fuels to consumers, gas, oil, and liquid petroleum were substituted for coal, and its consumption tended to decline. Little matter did this make to Mr. Lewis, who was much more concerned with obtaining for coal miners their share of an increasing national income, their share of leisure time, and a scale of living comparable to that enjoyed by workers in other segments of the economy.

Strikes among employees of urban transportation companies were frequently followed by upward adjustments in passenger fares. These adjustments, combined with the formation of car pools, increased uses of individual cars, and other devices resulted in lower volumes of passenger traffic and in reduced services rendered by urban transportation companies. Management appeared not to understand the principles of elasticity of demand for urban transportation services, or if they did understand such principles they had difficulty in formulating rate schedules to conform with them. Strikes of railroad employees have meant more business for pipeline companies and for motor truck and bus transport lines.

The material benefits that have followed the successful termination of strikes of short duration undoubtedly have accrued to those who participated in them, especially if they increased their tenure of employment in the same concerns. New employees in these concerns derived the same material benefits without having had to incur any of the cost of getting them. Just as important to many of the individual workers was a gain in self-respect, in prestige, and a feeling of success in the bitter struggle with employers.

An Attempt to Organize an Entire Community

In the spring of 1952, Central City, a coal mining town of 4,000 inhabitants in western Kentucky, received the attention of the officers of District 50, United Mine Workers of America. District 50 was and is a catchall for many kinds of workers who are not found in large enough numbers to justify separate organizations and to support their own independent officers, and who have not become affiliated with any other labor organization. An effort was made to sign up every businessman in town even if he were the sole proprietor of a one-man business firm. Employers were asked to sign an agreement requiring them to recognize District 50's bargaining agent for their employees and to negotiate with the agents of District 50 over wages and working conditions of their employees. The pattern appeared to be to sign employers first, then their employees, just the reverse order of the traditional approach union representatives make in the efforts to organize a firm or an industry. Attempts were made to sign up the owner-operator of a one-chair barber shop on the pretense that he might install a second chair sometime in the future, at which time he would be compelled to bargain with the union over the operator's wages and working conditions.

Shops of owners who did not cooperate with the union in this respect were picketed and instances of violence occurred. Since all of the miners who lived in Central City were members of the union they would not cross picket lines that had been established. Loyalties of members of miners' families were divided; and the wives, sons, and daughters of some miners refused to trade at union stores. To avoid dealing with proprietors who had not signed up, miners themselves drove miles to surrounding towns rather than cross picket lines. Because the chief of police was a former coal miner and a member of the union, he refused to take action against coal miners in protecting the properties of storeowners. Special law enforcement officers were deputized both by city and by county authorities to maintain law and order.

After a struggle that lasted for eight months, damage had been done that amounted to thousands of dollars. Reports of union officials as to what was actually accomplished vary widely from the reports of those who were nonunion sympathizers. Since all the reports were made by persons who were strongly biased, they likewise undoubtedly reflected these attitudes. One thing is certain—the first attempt on the part of organized labor to organize an entire community met with dismal failure, but not until an immeasurable and in some instances an irreparable amount of damage had been done, and ill will among former friends, between members of given families, and between members of the same churches had been created.

The Taft-Hartley Act

The large number of strikes that occurred after the war, combined with the fact that the terms of the Wagner Act made it extremely difficult for industrial leaders to counteract the increase in the powers of organized labor, gave rise to many expressions of dissatisfaction with the limitations that had been placed upon employers by the terms of the Act. Labor seems to have been given unfair advantages in its dealings with employers. The latter had been hamstrung and made powerless in their efforts to retain some of the functions that had been theirs traditionally. Many persons of influence were vitally concerned that the many interruptions in production would at least retard economic growth, if not lead to an actual decline in physical output that could reach the proportion of an economic depression.

The answer was found in the passage of the Taft-Hartley Act, which was passed by Congress in 1947 over the veto of President Truman. Most important in assuring the continuity of production were two provisions of the Act that dealt with conditions under which strikes could be called. Labor was required to give management 60 days notice before a potential strike. Throughout these 60 days both management and labor were required to make honest and urgent efforts to agree upon terms of a new contract. Failure to do so could justify the calling of a strike except in an industry which the President might designate as necessary to our national defense. In a case in which the welfare of the entire nation was at stake, the President might declare a national emergency to exist and invoke a clause in the Act which established a cooling-off period of 80 days during which the offices of the Federal Mediation and Conciliation Service were to be brought to bear upon the representatives of labor in an effort to avert a strike. If an agreement could not be reached at the end of the 80 days, labor had the right to strike, except that in case of dire emergency the President might nationalize the industry until terms acceptable to both sides were reached.

Amendment to the Wagner Act. The Act was really an amendment to the Wagner Act of 12 years earlier and as such forbade some unfair labor practices against employers thus matching the unfair labor practices that employers could not engage in under the terms of the Wagner Act. Other provisions of the Act that were particularly obnoxious to labor were (1) the requirement that labor leaders must take an anti-Communist oath or lose the protection of the National Labor Relations Board; (2) labor must not contribute to the election campaign of any candidate for office; (3) labor organizations are required to submit financial statements annually to the NRLB; (4) labor is forbidden to engage in boycotts against firms or products; and (5) employers who have been damaged by the unlawful practices of organized labor may sue in the courts to recover the monetary equivalent of the damages plus court costs. The closed shop was abolished, but on vote of the employees involved a union shop could be continued except in the states that have enacted right-to-work laws. The check-off could not be enforced against the desire of an employee.

Labor Objects. It is not surprising that labor was and is strongly opposed to the terms of the Taft-Hartley Act. How frequently the 80-day cooling-off period has been invoked seems to have depended as much or more upon the politico-economic philosophy of the administration in Washington than upon any other one factor. Labor has not looked kindly upon the requirement that its leaders take an anti-Communist oath, even though some of the unions themselves have done what they could to eliminate subversive elements from among their officers. Labor has objected even more vigorously to the clause that permits right-to-work legislation at the state level, and pressure is being exercised on Congress to abolish it.

The first important modification of the Act was made in 1959 by passage of the Labor-Management Reporting and Disclosure Act (or Landrum-Griffin Act). The Act attempted to provide members of organized labor greater protection against financial mismanagement of union funds; clarified procedures for holding union elections; gave added protection to business firms against the use of secondary boycotts; and placed added limitations upon the use of organizational and jurisdictional picketing.

Even though President Truman vetoed the Taft-Hartley Act, he saw fit under his own liberal interpretation of its terms to nationalize the steel industry in 1952 when a dispute over wages had not been settled within the 80-day cooling-off period. The strike was resumed after the Supreme Court ruled that the President had exceeded his powers when he ordered the seizure.

Wage Adjustments

In 1946, the United Steel Workers (CIO) ended a strike of one month's duration and established a *first-round* pattern of wage increases of 18½

Table 26-2

Average Earnings of Production Workers in Manufacturing—1946-1960

Year	Durable Goods		Nondurable Goods	
	Average Weekly Hours	Average Weekly Earnings	Average Weekly Hours	Average Weekly Earnings
1946	40.2	$46.49	40.5	$41.14
1947	40.6	52.46	40.1	46.96
1948	40.5	57.11	39.6	50.61
1949	39.5	58.03	38.8	51.41
1950	41.2	63.32	39.7	54.71
1951	41.6	69.47	39.5	58.46
1952	41.5	73.46	39.6	60.98
1953	41.3	77.23	39.5	63.60
1954	40.2	77.18	39.0	64.74
1955	41.4	83.21	39.8	68.06
1956	41.1	86.31	39.5	71.10
1957	40.3	88.66	39.1	73.51
1958	39.5	90.06	38.8	75.27
1959	40.8	97.10	39.6	79.60
1960*	40.1	98.25	39.1	81.33

* Data not available on comparable basis after 1960.

Source: *Historical Statistics of the United States. Colonial Times to 1957,* 1960, p. 92; and supplement, *Continuation to 1962 and Revisions,* 1965, p. 15. Adapted.

cents an hour. This was followed by a strike by the United Automobile Workers (CIO) against General Motors Corporation that lasted 3½ months and which came to an end only when both parties to the dispute accepted a wage increase of 18½ cents an hour. These wage adjustments were given as reasons for or justifications of price increases, and they set the pattern for similar wage adjustments in other industries. After having been threatened with a military draft of striking employees in order to keep the trains running, the Locomotive Engineers (Independent) accepted an 18½ cents an hour increase after a strike that lasted only two days.

Data in Table 26-2 reveal to what extent organized labor succeeded in obtaining wage increases through 1960. Since these rates are averages that were received by groups of employees, many individual rates were above these given in the table, while others were lower. Average weekly wages for both groups represented in the table increased every year, even when average hours worked per week declined. Variations in average hours worked per week were minimal and could not have been the reason for increases in average weekly wages. While not all labor in manufacturing industries was organized, the impact of wage increases that were the result of collective bargaining was felt by employers of nonunion labor. Since wage rates received by the latter were, in general, lower than those whose wages had been determined by collective bargaining, nonunion and unskilled workers benefited more from minimum wage requirements and from the signing of new union wage contracts than did union workers. In order to retain full complements of nonunion workers, their employers were required to raise their wages to conform more closely to union patterns.

Wages Paid to Farm Workers. Farm workers may have received 50 percent more wages per month than industrial workers received per week. This fact may help explain why transient workers from Mexico and some Caribbean countries have been imported on a temporary basis to pick fruits, berries, and vegetables on occasions when American farm workers have been unemployed. Unemployment compensation or social security payments have been more acceptable to many men and women than have stooping, bending, or kneeling several hours a day or all day at such low rates of pay.

Fringe Benefits. How the new program of labor in respect to fringe benefits was implemented in wage contracts is shown in the terms of settlement of an industry-wide strike of the United Steel Workers (CIO) that included noncontributory pensions of $100 a month at age 65, plus death, sickness, and accident benefits. That the public concurred in these terms was manifested in the recommendations of a fact-finding board that was appointed by the President: employers were to contribute 6 cents an hour towards a pension for each employee and 4 cents an hour to provide social insurance for him.

In 1956, the United Mine Workers of America established ten new hospitals to serve miners and their families in cities and towns in Kentucky, Virginia, and West Virginia. Bituminous coal mine operators agreed to contribute to the U.M.W.A. Retirement and Welfare Fund at the rate of 40 cents for each ton of coal that was mined under the terms and conditions of union contracts. Five of the hospitals were sold in 1963.

In 1960 employers on the West Coast attempted to introduce labor-saving equipment in loading and unloading cargoes on ships and in moving items of freight on piers and into and out of warehouses. Collective bargaining resulted in the Longshoremen and Warehousemen's Union permitting the use of labor-saving equipment only after the Pacific Maritime Association had agreed to contribute $5 million a year to a fund that would provide annual pensions of $7,920 to each of 5,000 registered longshoremen when they reached the age of 65, and after 25 years of service. These examples are sufficient to establish the nature and degree of economic security that organized labor has been demanding of employers in order to permit its members to enjoy the better life that persons in other segments of the economy had been enjoying for a number of years.

Success Not Universal. That not all of the efforts of organized labor to attain greater degrees of economic security have been successful is manifested by some of the experiences printers, lithographers, and typographers have had in their organized efforts to preserve their jobs in the newspaper industry. Competition with radio and television media in advertising, combined with rising costs of newsprint and other items of expense, has caused newspaper publishers to seek ways of reducing costs of publishing in order to maintain desirable and necessary profit margins. Strikes have been called against newspaper publishers in New York, Cleveland, Portland (Oregon), Brooklyn, Miami, Baltimore, and other cities not only to enforce demands for wage increases, but also in protest against the adoption and use of printing processes that did not require the traditional services of labor and that reduced the number of employees required to put out an edition of newspapers. Some of these strikes resulted in a permanent suspension of some papers; others were merged in order to save on both labor and capital costs; and still others adopted new processes that did not require the services of linotype operators, typographers, and other traditional classes of employees. Some employees were compelled to accept work in job classifications other than those in which they were accustomed to working.

Minimum Wage Legislation

Even though the War Labor Board had permitted wage adjustments up to 50 cents an hour in 1943, provided those increases above the 40 cent an hour maximum that had been established by the Fair Labor Standards Act in 1938 would not be used as justification for price increases, the terms of the latter Act were not amended until 1949, when the minimum wage was set at 75 cents an hour. In 1955 the minimum wage was again raised to $1.00 an hour, effective March 1. In September, 1961, the coverage of the Fair Labor Standards Act was extended to approximately 3.6 million additional workers, most of whom were employed in the retail trade and construction industries. These workers were given an initial minimum wage of $1.00 an hour, which became $1.15 in September, 1964, and $1.25 one year later. The minimum wage for workers who were already covered in 1961 was raised to $1.15 an hour and to $1.25 an hour in 1963. All workers who were covered by the terms of the FLS Act were given time and a half their base rate of pay for all hours worked per week in excess of 40 by September, 1965. On January 1, 1968, a minimum of $1.65 an hour became effective, and its coverage of job classifications was broadened.

Merger of AFL and CIO

What was hailed at the time as one of the momentous actions of the century was the merging of the American Federation of Labor and the Congress of Industrial Organization in December, 1955. The actual merger had been preceded by a no-raiding pact covering the two years ending on January 1, 1956. Officers of both unions took steps to bring about an effective merger that would be implemented within two years at the state, territorial, and local levels. Approximately 16 million worker-members, who constituted 85 percent of membership in all unions in the United States, were brought into the fold. The Constitution of the AFL-CIO provided for an industrial union department, with which 69 unions affiliated, 38 of which were formerly affiliated with the AFL. In its first year of organization, former AFL and CIO organizations in ten states merged. Jurisdictional strikes were no longer to be an issue unless they involved the rights of independent or unaffiliated unions. What may have been the most notable development in the trend towards unification of labor union organization in the United States was the affiliation of the Brotherhood of Locomotive Firemen and Engineers with the merged group. For 83 years the B.L.F. & E. had remained an independent and a powerful organization. In 1957 the Brotherhood of Railroad Trainmen, the American Train Dispatchers Association, and the American Railway Supervisors Association followed the B.L.F. & E. into the fold. In 1958 the AFL-CIO took disciplinary action against several union officials who refused to answer questions that were posed by a United States Senate board of inquiry, on the grounds that the answers might be self-incriminatory.

GOVERNMENT CONTROLS OVER ECONOMIC ACTIVITY

Economic history had for many years explained variations in the tempo of economic activity and the level of employment in terms of speculation in the sale of public lands and in internal improvements, together with structural weaknesses in our monetary and banking systems. As the United States became more highly industrialized and less dependent upon agricultural pursuits as the principal means of earning a livelihood for a majority of its citizens, periods of relative economic inactivity were accompanied by larger numbers of unemployed workers, absolutely and relatively speaking. People adopted a rather fatalistic attitude towards the fact of unemployment as a phenomenon with which they had to live. Government at any level did not adopt any policy of action, although relief may have been afforded at the local level and by charitable organizations.

Philosophy of Government

The basic philosophy of the federal government was that of *laissez faire*; and when it became necessary or politically desirable to modify this philosophy, the government took measures to enforce competition in almost all segments of economic activity. There was a strong feeling that conditions created by World War I were the basic and fundamental causes of the Great Crash and of the Great Depression that ensued. Implementing the instruments of credit control that had been given the Board of Governors of the Federal Reserve System had proved to be ineffective in controlling business fluctuations and reviving a flagging economy.

Economic organization for war in 1941 was much more complex and more complete than it had been in 1917-18. Nobody wanted to experience another postwar depression that could be proportionately greater than the one from which the country had recently emerged. In fact, no one wanted to experience a postwar depression of any degree of severity. Since the impact of the war was felt in every segment of the economy, and since it was not fought to bring profit to any industry or to any segment of the economy, congressional leaders felt that the federal government should take steps to adopt measures to stabilize the economy, not only in the years immediately following the end of hostilities, but for years thereafter.

The Employment Act of 1946

Many people felt that the economy had become so large and so complex that it was a function of government to step in where no profit-making concern could tread. This idea was formalized in the context of the Employment Act of 1946, the purpose of which was to "declare a national policy on employment, production and purchasing power, and for other purposes." In Section 2 of the Act, Congress declared:

> . . . that it is the continuing policy and responsibility of the Federal Government to use all practicable means consisting (sic) with its needs and obligations and other essential considerations of national policy, with the assistance and cooperation of industry, agriculture, labor and State and local governments, to coordinate and utilize all its plans, functions, and resources for the purpose of creating and maintaining, in a manner calculated to foster and promote free competitive enterprise and the general welfare, conditions under which there will be afforded useful employment opportunities, including self-employment, for those able, willing, and seeking to work, and to promote maximum employment, production, and purchasing power.

A Council of Economic Advisers was provided for, which was to make a continuing study of the American economy. It was to assist the President in the preparation of a report on the state of the nation which he was to deliver within 90 days after the opening of each regular session of Congress. Among its other functions were those of gathering

> . . . timely and authoritative information concerning economic developments and economic trends—to analyze and interpret such information in the light of the policy declared in Section 2 for the purpose of determining whether such developments and trends are interfering or are likely to interfere, with the achievement of such policy, and to compile and submit to the President studies relating to such developments and trends.

The Council also was charged with evaluating the numerous programs and activities of the federal government for the purpose of determining to what extent they do or do not contribute to the attainment of such policy. It was to recommend to the President steps that he might take in the promotion of economic stability and to maintain full employment, production, and purchasing power. It also was to study and report on matters of economic policy and federal legislation that the President might request.

GOVERNMENT ACTIVITIES: EMPLOYMENT AND FINANCE

Units of government at all levels experienced financial problems that were on a vastly larger scale than they had ever been. Population had migrated from rural areas into urban, and urban peoples had partaken of suburban movements. Some of these suburban developments were within the established patterns of city limits and were near their peripheries. In many locations city limits were extended; and in still others, which were situated entirely in county domain, property owners received some of the benefits of municipal services.

Employment and Payrolls

Municipalities that operated their own water systems, sewage disposal plants, and generated their own electrical energy frequently extended their areas of influence to peripheral areas. Regardless of the reasons for so doing, municipal payrolls increased and capital expenditures did likewise. When the latter were financed from the proceeds of the sale of bond issues, increased interest costs were a charge against tax revenues. Additional men were employed to man the expanded services. Another outgrowth of the increase in urban population was that larger police forces were required to patrol densely settled areas and to provide initial protection to peripheral areas either within city limits or without. In the latter instances, additions were made to county patrols or to sheriffs' staffs. Again, to offset the added drain on tax revenues there was the volume of business that was given to free enterprise in the manufacture of more uniforms and other equipment that these men required in the performance of their regular lines of duty.

In addition to the expanded payrolls for numbers of employees, governments at all levels were compelled to raise wage rates and to make upward adjustments in pay scales in order to compete with free enterprise for the limited manpower that was available. Some government officials realized that there was an ethical or a moral issue involved and initiated movements to raise the levels of civil service or merit system schedules of pay. Even so, the almost universal pattern of pay increases seemed to have been to raise top salaries and wages more than lower level ones, even on a percentage basis. Another condition that was disturbing, to say the least, to employees of some years standing was that when civil service requirements did not pertain, new employees with no experience were paid as much as or more than was paid employees of years of service and experience. Conditions were such in the labor market that older employees could not afford to give up tenure and start over somewhere else, and new employees could not be obtained unless they were paid wages that were competitive.

Table 26-3

Number of Civilian Employees and Payrolls of Federal, State, and Local Governments for Selected Years

| | Federal | | State and Local | | | |
| | | | Schools | | Other | |
Year	Numbers (000)	Monthly Payroll (millions)	Numbers (000)	Monthly Payroll (millions)	Numbers (000)	Monthly Payroll (millions)
1940	1,128	$ 177	1,320	$ 175.3	2,026	$ 213.5
1949	2,047	539.2	1,658	384.8	2,497	481.9
1961	2,484	1,213.6	3,050	1,204.6	3,566	1,215.3

Source: *Facts and Figures on Government Finance, 1962-1963* (New York City: Tax Foundation, 1963), p. 36.

New Sources of Tax Revenue for State and Local Governments

Property taxes were the principal sources of revenues at the city and county levels of government. Because of the difficulties involved in placing intangibles on tax rolls when they were declared voluntarily by taxpayers, they were taxed at lower millage rates than was real estate. Voluntary declaration failed to disclose most of the intangibles that were held and owned by taxpayers, and federal income tax reports were made available to local and state assessors. This eliminated some of the inequities in tax paying burdens that existed between taxpayers who were honest enough to declare their intangible holdings of taxable property and those who had attempted to evade their tax obligations by failing to declare theirs. As real estate values increased after the return of peace, so did assessed values of property for tax purposes. This took place without any increases in the proportions that assessed values bore to real values. Some communities increased their tax revenues by raising the percentages that assessed values of real estate bore to their market values. When urban communities extended their city limits, thousands of dollars worth of real estate was placed on their tax rolls for the first time, and counties were in some cases deprived of these values on which to levy taxes.

Income Tax. Taxes that had come to be considered as reserved for use by state and federal governments respectively were adapted to use by local governmental units. Among some of the larger cities that imposed local income taxes are Detroit, Philadelphia, St. Louis, Pittsburgh, Louisville, Cincinnati, and Columbus. In many places these taxes are withheld by employers and are adjusted after personal declarations have been made.

Miscellaneous Sources of Revenue. Business and license taxes have been broadened in some cities, while in others they have been increased. Many communities have voted "wet" on the liquor question in order to obtain tax revenues from the sale of alcoholic beverages. Some cities resorted to the use of sales taxes—special, general, or both—which usually were lower than similar taxes that were levied by state and federal governments. Parking meters originally had been installed in order to control the parking of automobiles on city streets. Rates varied, in general, from one cent for ten or twelve minutes of parking to five cents for one hour, sometimes for two. Proceeds from parking meters originally were intended to be used in enforcing parking restrictions and traffic regulations, but they soon became larger than the costs of enforcement and contributed to the costs of the general operations of governments.

Costs of tapping sanitary sewers and water mains were raised, as were costs of building permits and inspection fees. Property owners were assessed the costs or partial costs of paving city streets. If garbage and trash collections were functions of city and county governments, householders were charged monthly fees which were based on the frequency with which these services were rendered. If these services were let out on bid to private or to individual collectors, contracts were awarded to the highest bidders rather than to the lowest except when charges were billed directly to householders. Minimum rates were charged for the consumption of water and electrical energy when they were performed by municipally owned facilities.

Many cities throughout the country levied admissions taxes, except to charitable events, and also taxes on the sale of cigarettes.

Sources of Federal Revenue

The federal government retained most of the excise taxes it had imposed during the war, partly to obtain revenue and partly as a check to further inflation. These taxes tended to reduce the number of dollars that continued to chase after scarce goods. Even though there was no need to conserve space in transportation facilities and to reserve what space there was to the military or to the officials of civilian government, the 10 percent tax on the sale of transportation tickets was retained for approximately 20 years after the war.

An offset to tax revenues derived from the tax on the cost of passenger fares was the repeal of a provision that required the railroads to charge less than commercial rates for traffic they hauled for the federal government. Under the terms of land grants to railroads, the latter had been required to haul all government traffic—passenger and freight, during both peacetime and wartime at less than commercial rates. This provision was removed in the mid-1940's as a means of affording financial relief to the railroads which were in dire need of additional operating revenues.

At the same time that relief was afforded the railroads, added costs were imposed upon the federal government insofar as railroad transport continued to be used. Motor and air transport were used more and more for both convenience and saving time. No study has been made of the added costs of railway transportation to the federal government that followed the termination of the land grant preferential rates, but whatever they amounted to they came at a time when governmental costs were rising rapidly.

The Federal Debt

Since only about 40 percent of the costs of the war had been met with tax receipts, it was necessary for the Treasury Department to issue bonds. Their sale served the double purpose of raising revenue and of controlling inflation. In order to keep the cost of borrowing to a minimum, the Board of Governors agreed to subordinate the regulatory functions of the Federal Reserve System to the policies of the Treasury in carrying out its policies of war finance. In supporting the market for United States government bonds, the Federal Reserve kept their market quotations above par and the net yield to their purchasers below the interest rates that appeared on their faces. This policy tended to facilitate the sale of government coupon bonds as there was a ready market for them if purchasers anticipated reasons for increasing the degree of liquidity of their assets. Also, keeping the yield on investment in government bonds low aided in the continued sale of Series E savings bonds.

Growth of the Debt. The size of the federal debt itself had grown to an almost incomprehensible amount at the close of the fiscal year, June 30, 1946. A peak debt up to this time of over $269 billion was reached, after which it was reduced to $253 billion in 1948. The 1946 debt level was not reached again until 1954, at which time it amounted to $271 billion. The debt was reduced slightly in 1956 and again in 1957 after which it began to rise again. The principal problem that was connected with the national debt was not its size but its servicing. As was learned in England over 100 years ago, a public debt need not be an economic burden. Insofar as the debt contributed to an increase in the productivity of a national economy, it represented no burden if the national income had increased more rapidly than the costs of servicing the debt.

Federal authorities have been aware of this relationship between the cost of debt service and national income and have concerned themselves with how to increase the flow of national income as much as or more than the rate of increase in the cost of servicing the national debt. That they have been successful is made manifest by the fact that our national income has been increasing more than have the costs of debt service and that the level of living has been increasing throughout the years in which the national debt has risen. Another testimonial to the fact that the increase in the federal debt has not placed a correspondingly heavier economic burden upon the American people is the fact that while prices have risen slightly their increase has not triggered an uncontrolled price inflation.

The End of Treasury Domination Over the Credit Policies of the Board of Governors. Seven years after the cessation of hostilities, the Board of Governors asserted its right of control over open market operations, the rediscount rate, and the reserve requirements of member banks. The Board took the attitude that the rate of increase of commodity prices should at least be retarded if not brought to an end. The immediate effect of implementing this policy in 1951 was a decline in the market prices of government bonds, which is tantamount to saying that the investment yield to the purchasers of these bonds increased. The days of artifically low interest rates were over. Thereafter bank rates of interest tended to equilibrate the supply of loanable funds with the demand for them.

INTERNATIONAL CONSIDERATIONS

The American economy was not immune from the impacts of economic conditions in foreign countries after the war. Immediate recovery of their economic organizations was essential to the return to a state of mutual economic interdependence. Since the nations that had been actively engaged in war were devoid of financial resources, capital goods, and many natural resources that were essential to the progress of recovery programs, the responsibility for stimulating their return to production for nonwar purposes was assumed by the United States.

The Marshall Plan

While the Marshall Plan usually is thought of as part of the European Recovery Program, our interest is not with the degree of economic recovery of European nations but with the economic impacts of the plan itself and the economic impact of the recovery these nations made upon the American economy. It really matters little how many millions of dollars were lent to this or that country. The importance of these loans is found in the fact that most of the Marshall Plan dollars were spent in the United States in paying wages to American labor, in the purchase of raw materials, fuel, and for the generation of electrical and/or mechanical energy. Transportation agencies likewise felt the impact of the plan in the increase of commodities that were presented to them to transport to a port of embarkation. People became so concerned with the fact that the United States gave financial aid to foreign nations they overlooked the effects of the aid-giving upon American industries. Manufacturers of such heavy durable goods as railroad locomotives and other forms of rolling stock, heavy earth-moving equipment, farm machinery, and textile machinery—all participated, although not alike, in the production of capital equipment and in its export.

The Dollar Shortage in Foreign Exchange

When price was the principal influence upon both the volume of trade and the direction of the movement of commodities between countries, there was no particular problem either of a shortage of exchange or of a surplus. Starting about 1920 or shortly thereafter, a serious problem of international exchange arose out of the fact that an unusually large percentage of the world's monetary gold supply found its way into the United States. At the time, our problem was that we already had so much gold, in terms of which international balances were settled, that other countries could not purchase commodities from us on a pay-as-you-go basis. Our banks and financiers came to the rescue in the short run and lent foreign buyers funds with which to pay for the goods they purchased from us—their commodity imports, our commodity exports. What it amounted to was that one segment of the American people was providing the means for paying another segment for the goods the latter sold and shipped abroad. This was splendid in the short run, but it created another longer run problem of how foreigners were going to repay their loans to us and in what form we would accept payment.

Controlled Exchange Rates. By the time war broke out in 1941, most of the European countries and others, too, had inaugurated some kind of controlled exchange, barter or quota systems or limitations placed on their imports of commodities, hence indirectly upon their exports. These systems were brought about by the maldistribution of monetary gold and by limitations that had been placed upon its movement between countries.

The International Monetary Fund had been created in 1945 in order to stabilize the foreign exchanges, but its operation was no guarantee that gold would seek its own level of distribution between nations. The IMF operated more on the principle of bank balances than upon an equitable distribution of gold. The principle of making international payments by using bank balances was not new. It was the exhaustion of bank balances in some countries and their accumulation in others that gave the gold points their significance in confining rates of exchange between them and in controlling the distribution of gold between countries. More disturbing to trade relations between the United States and western European nations, including England, was the fact that while European nations wanted to import commodities from the United States, the latter country found the sources of most of its imports in other parts of the world. The United States had reached the stage in its economic development where it was manufacturing within itself many or most of the commodities it formerly had imported from Europe. Not only was it manufacturing these commodities, it was exporting them to Europe and to other countries that formerly had been market areas or outlets for European products.

New Pattern of Foreign Trade. Larger portions of our imports than formerly were composed of tropical foods, fruits, and spices, none of which were native to Europe. American industry thirsted for petroleum products, for precious metals, and scarce raw materials that were required by manufacturers who wished to impart certain desired qualities or characteristics to iron and steel, or which were used as basic raw materials by American industries. Table 26-4, which is not intended to be complete, affords the reader some idea of the diversified and widely scattered sources of raw materials that are imported into the United States in order to manufacture better, safer, and more attractive automobiles.

Table 26-4

Sources of Raw Materials That Went into the Manufacture of American Automobiles in 1954

Country	Raw Materials of Export to the United States
Belgian Congo	Diamonds, tin
Bolivia	Antimony, asbestos, tin
Brazil	Diamonds, mica, tin
Canada	Copper, lead, mica, nickel, zinc
Chile	Copper
Cuba	Manganese
French West Africa	Diamonds
Gold Coast	Diamonds, manganese
Guiana {British	Bauxite, diamonds
Guiana {Dutch	Bauxite
India	Manganese, mica
Indonesia	Bauxite, tin
Malaya	Tin
Madagascar	Mica
Mexico	Antimony, copper, lead, manganese, zinc
Morocco	Manganese
Nigeria	Tin
Peru	Lead, zinc
Philippines	Chromite
Portugal	Tungsten
Southern Rhodesia	Asbestos, chromite
Spain	Tungsten, zinc
Thailand	Tin
Turkey	Chromite
Union of South Africa	Antimony, asbestos, chromite, manganese
Yugoslavia	Lead

Source: Automobile Manufacturers Association, *Automobile Facts* (April, 1954), p. 8.

The same kind of table could be constructed for other industries, or for all industries combined. The point is that the principal reason there was a shortage of dollar exchange that European importers could use in paying for American exports was the fact that changes had taken place within the American economy, thus throwing the force of foreign buying to areas other than to Europe.

During the war the flow of natural rubber from the Far East was cut off and the United States government subsidized the development of a synthetic rubber industry. Many of the desirable qualities of natural rubber had been imparted to the synthetic product. This fact together with the monetary investment in the industry created a problem after the war when the flow of natural rubber to the United States either was or could be resumed.

The question that required an answer had a political impact as well as an economic one. Should the United States return to the practice or policy of importing natural rubber and scrap the synthetic facilities that had been erected in this country? Or should American industries continue to use synthetic rubber to the exclusion of importing natural rubber from the Far East? The former course involved huge capital losses which could be added to the cost of war; the latter would make it more difficult for England to pay for imported goods from the United States. The first question was one that involved the operation of a national economy; the other, one that recognized a high degree of international economic interdependence. In the latter instance, the chain of events was that the money that was used to pay for natural rubber from the Far East contributed to the profitableness of an industry which was financed very heavily with British capital. Income that was received by the exporters of natural rubber was used in paying interest on the investment of British capital, which in turn established bank balances (dollar exchange) in England that were available to the purchasers of American products. The question was resolved in favor of easing international economic relationships, and we returned to the former practice of importing natural rubber. Cost-price relationships were subordinated to maintaining cordial economic and political relationships with England, which in turn encouraged continued export of American goods to that country.

The Korean Incident

The economic importance of the Korean incident, or police action, as it was called at the time, is found in the stimulus it provided those industries that were involved in the fulfillment of government contracts to supply war material—food, clothing, ordnance, airplanes, and other means of transport. It came at a time when the domestic economy seemed to be lagging. Employment in capital goods industries and in those that felt the impact of government orders increased. National income was maintained at a high level, and disposable incomes likewise were large. Railroads were offered loads of freight that were destined for overseas shipment. To the extent that some of the military reserve forces were called back into service, at least temporary employment was provided to their replacements. Extra compensation that was paid men who saw foreign service added to the cumulative savings that were spent on consumers' goods after they returned to civilian life.

QUESTIONS FOR REVIEW

1. Explain clearly why there has *not* been a major post-World War II economic or industrial depression.

2. (a) How did the Taft-Hartley Act fit into the overall program of labor legislation?
(b) What is the status of the Taft-Hartley Act today?

3. Insofar as organized labor was successful in obtaining wage increases in each of several cycles of efforts, how were employers able to pay these increases?

4. (a) Of what economic significance was the Employment Act of 1946?
(b) What were the principal provisions of the Employment Act of 1946?

5. (a) In what ways may government at all levels have contributed to the growth of the American economy after 1945?
(b) How did each of the local, state, and federal levels of government obtain revenue with which to finance their activities after 1945? Be specific.

6. What position did the general sales tax occupy in programs of governmental finance after 1945?

7. (a) What was (A) the general level, (B) the general pattern or trend of the federal debt after 1945?
(b) Check with some reliable source for data that reveal the amount of the current federal debt. What source did you use?

SUGGESTED READINGS

Barnes, James A. *Wealth of the American People.* Englewood Cliffs, N. J.: Prentice-Hall, Inc., 1949. Chapter 39.

Bining, Arthur C., and Thomas C. Cochran. *The Rise of American Economic Life.* 4th ed. New York City: Charles Scribner's Sons, 1964. Chapter 28.

Dillard, Dudley. *Economic Development of the North Atlantic Community.* Englewood Cliffs, N. J.: Prentice-Hall, Inc., 1967. Chapters 36 and 37.

Hacker, Louis M. (ed.). *Major Documents in American Economic History.* New York City: D. Van Nostrand Co., Inc., 1961. Vol. II. Selections 21-23.

Johnson, E. A. J., and Herman E. Krooss. *The American Economy.* Englewood Cliffs, N. J.: Prentice-Hall, Inc., 1960. Chapter 14.

Krooss, Herman E. *American Economic Development.* 2d ed. Englewood Cliffs, N. J.: Prentice-Hall, Inc., 1966. Chapter 16.

Syrett, Harold C. "The Business Press and American Neutrality," *Issues in American Economic History,* edited by Gerald D. Nash. Boston: D. C. Heath & Company, 1964.

Wright, Chester W. "The More Enduring Economic Consequences of American Wars," *Issues in American Economic History,* edited by Gerald D. Nash. Boston: D. C. Heath & Company, 1964.

Chapter 27

POPULATION

The increase in the population of the United States since the close of the war is not a new phenomenon. There have been variations in the rate of increase, however. Census data for 1940 reveal an increase of only 7 percent throughout the depression decade. The following decade witnessed an increase of 14 percent, while the 28 million additional persons who were counted in 1960 represented an increase of 18 percent in ten years. These persons had to be housed, clothed, fed, and educated. The opportunities for employment combined with the level of wages and salaries determined the level of living the entire population experienced.

Changes in Composition

In 1956 the total population of the United States was estimated to have been 168,221,000, of which more than 28 percent were 14 years of age and younger and 8.8 percent were at least 65 years of age. In 1968 estimated population was 201,087,000, which represented more than normal growth, due to the fact that the population of Alaska and of Hawaii were added to that of the continental United States in 1959. This accretion added approximately 3,000,000 persons to the citizenry of the United States. That the population was becoming older is borne out by a breakdown of data. In 1956, 17.6 percent of the population was 55 years of age and over. While the 1967 data revealed a numerical increase of persons in this age bracket of 6,648,000, this was 18.3 percent of our total estimated population.

The same trend is discovered in analyzing data of persons 65 years or older. In 1956 they constituted 8.8 percent of our total estimated population, while in 1967 the figure had become 9.1 percent. An increase of $3/10$ of a percentage point in 11 years represented a numerical increase of 3,891,000 persons 65 years of age and older. The latter figure is much more meaningful when consideration is given to taking care of these persons, housing them, and providing something for them to do. Also the money they spent on consumers' goods and recreation was of more significance when stated in numerical terms rather than in percentages of total populations.

A more significant fact from the standpoint of productivity, general welfare, and scale of living was that the number of persons 55 years of age and over increased more rapidly between 1956 and 1967 than did those in the most productive span of years, ages 25 to 54. Many persons were productive prior to their 25th birthdays, and still others continued working beyond the age of 55 and even 65. Thousands of men and women under the age of 25 were still in school, and many men had retired before they had become 55. The fact remains that people attained their 55th birthdays more rapidly than they were replaced by persons who entered the 25-year age group, and yet the scale of living of the American people continued to increase. The answer to this condition is found in the fact that the increase in gross national product and in national income more than compensated for the loss of the productive efforts of those who attained the upper age brackets. The productivity of younger workers had been increased by combining their efforts with more efficient tools and machines.

Decline in Rural Population. Not only did total population increase rapidly, its distribution between urban and rural areas created many economic problems. Despite the overall increase in total population of over 18 million persons between 1950 and 1960, there were almost 200,000 fewer people living in rural areas in 1960 than in 1950. The impacts of urban migration are revealed in Table 27-1 which gives data on increases in the number of cities in the respective population categories, together with the increased number of persons living in these places. It is not surprising that the numbers of urban residents in given population brackets increased more in the lower ranges than in the upper ones.

It was in the smaller cities that public utility and sanitary installations and streets were most inadequate in meeting the pressures placed upon them by the rapid growth of the population they served. School buildings were too few in number and too small in size to accommodate the thousands of children of new families who moved into the respective cities, let alone to take care of the natural increase of the families that were more firmly established in these cities.

Move to Suburbs. The migration of rural peoples into urban areas was offset, in part, by a movement of urban residents into suburban areas, a fact revealed rather conclusively by the 1960 census. At the time, the population of many urban areas had declined, but metropolitan areas housed more persons than formerly. This movement to the suburbs was counteracted by an extension of urban spheres of political influence to conform more closely to economic boundaries. Increases in the number of cities that ranged from 10,000 population to 100,000 reflected the trend toward expansion of large corporate firms. Instead of enlarging the size of operations in their most centralized locations, they established branch units in smaller cities. Factors

Table 27-1

Increases in the Number of Places in Urban Areas by Population Groups with Increases in Population That Resided in These Respective Groups

Population of Urban Areas	Number of Places in 1960*	Increases in Number of Places since 1950	Population in Urban Areas	
			1960 Census	Increases since 1950
1,000,000 or more	5	0	17,484,059	79,609
500,000 to 1,000,000	16	3	11,110,991	1,924,046
250,000 to 500,000	29	6	10,471,687	2,230,127
100,000 to 250,000	81	16	11,652,426	2,173,764
50,000 to 100,000	201	75	13,385,902	4,905,079
25,000 to 50,000	429	177	14,854,787	6,047,066
10,000 to 25,000	1,131	353	17,513,223	5,646,718
5,000 to 10,000	1,388	212	9,738,502	1,599,906
2,500 to 5,000	2,140	294	7,541,910	1,051,504

* Alaska and Hawaii omitted from 1960 data.

Source: U. S. Department of Commerce, Bureau of the Census, *Historical Statistics of the United States. Colonial Times to 1957; Continuation to 1962 and Revisions* (Washington: U. S. Government Printing Office, 1965), p. 3. Adapted.

that brought about this pattern of development include (1) efforts of corporations to improve their tax positions; (2) problems of the labor market; (3) transportation rates; (4) relocation of markets; (5) educational, recreational, and cultural considerations; and (6) managerial inefficiencies of larger sized production units.

Housing

To take care of the thousands of new families that had been established, as well as to meet the changing needs of families that had already been established, 10 million homes were constructed during the 1950's. In order to accommodate the thousands of retirees, retirement villages and retirement homes were built. Such developments in Arizona, California, Florida, and in other states catered to the needs of retired persons at costs that were commensurate with retirement incomes.

Some of the retirement incomes were at the level of social security payments; some were combinations of salary base plus years of service; some had been purchased through the medium of endowment policies; others were at the levels of executive salaries, which in some respects were deferred salary payments; and some were determined by what people had accumulated in savings institutions. Other retirement incomes were combinations of two or more of the above sources.

Schools

The only limit that was placed on the construction of new schools seems to have been the amount of tax money the school authorities could and would appropriate for this purpose. Volumes have been written about increases in enrollments that have made new schools inadequate the day they opened. Grammar schools, junior high schools, senior high schools, junior colleges, and regular 4-year colleges and institutions have felt the impact of increases in school populations. Politicians and educators have waxed eloquent over the crowded, intolerable conditions that were found in some school systems as well as in institutions of higher learning, but little has been said or written about the economic impacts of the widespread increases in school enrollments.

Increase in Number of Teachers and Teacher Salaries. Attention has been given to crowded classrooms that have affected adversely the learning potentials of children.

More new teachers have been employed, many of whom have been second wage earners in hundreds or thousands of families. Family incomes have thus been augmented, however inadequate salaries may have been compared with certain standards of remuneration. In 1956, 1,213,459 elementary and secondary schoolteachers, principals and other supervisors, and consultants received average annual salaries of $4,156. In 1968, an average annual salary of $7,296 was paid to and received by 1,837,926 persons in the above categories. Not only was the average salary $3,140 more than in 1956, it was paid to 624,467 more persons than received the lower pay in 1956. It is erroneous to assume that none of the increased number of teachers had incomes in the earlier year. Some of them had taken up work in education after having found some other vocation unsatisfactory. It must be remembered, too, that public school superintendents and principals were paid much higher salaries than were paid classroom teachers. In 1956 there were 50,973 principals of public schools, and in 10 years this number had been augmented by 28,000 and this in the face of a decline in the number of one-teacher public schools from 34,964 in 1956 to 13,333 in 1962 and to 6,491 in 1966.

Colleges and Universities. A significant impact of larger disposable family incomes was that they made it possible for more students to enroll in and to graduate from secondary schools. Increasingly large numbers of them sought admission into 4-year colleges and universities. Despite the construction of new dormitories, classroom buildings, laboratories and libraries, and the hiring of additional members to their teaching staffs, most institutions of higher learning were compelled to restrict their enrollments. So great was the rush of students to their campuses that their faculties increased from 38,249 in 1962 to 46,539 in 1964.

Not to deny students the opportunity to obtain higher levels of education, municipalities, counties, and states established 2-year junior colleges, some of which offered liberal arts subjects. In line with the adage "you can't perform today's work with yesterday's skills," some junior colleges offered vocational training to those not desiring scholastic disciplines.

In conjunction with these expanding education programs came the demand for more administrators, clerks, and teachers. Increased growth and development soon occurred in such concerns as supply houses, microfilm companies, and paperback publishers. New national income and disposable incomes were generated by these activities.

Immigration

The impacts of immigration upon native populations were not heavy except, possibly, in locales where new arrivals may have concentrated. An offset to the quota arrivals in 1956 were those who left the country voluntarily. The net immigration of that year was only about 9,000 persons. In each of the years between 1956 and 1967, craftsmen, foremen, operators, and kindred workers led the parade into this country although their numbers declined from 44,950 in 1956 to 30,148 in 1962 and to 18,921 in 1967. Laborers, except in farms and in mines, declined from 27,807 in 1956 to 11,100 in 1958 and to 10,129 in 1967. Almost twice as many farm laborers and farm foremen reached our shores as farmers and farm managers during the years when a net of 2,808,000 persons left American farms for life in urban communities, including those in Alaska and Hawaii. An average of about 31,000 professional, technical, and other such workers left their home countries between 1963 and 1967 to pursue their careers in America. As of December, 1965, as amended in 1967, the quota system as applied to those of national origin was abolished, and a quota of 158,261 was established. Other criteria of eligibility for admittance were not altered. In 1967, 153,079 persons were admitted against quota on a first-come-first-serve basis, and 209,000 nonquota immigrants were admitted. With curbs on emigration from Europe and other countries, the importance of the removal of the quota system could well lie in the sphere of politics rather than in economics.

AGRICULTURE

Many trends in agricultural development that had become clearly defined after World War II continued throughout this period. Simultaneously with a decline in the number of persons who were employed on farms from 6,449,000 in 1955 to 3,164,000 in March, 1967, the wage rate per day, without room and board, increased from $5.30 to $9.00. Trite though it may sound, increased wages that were received by farm laborers were increased costs of producing farm products.

Increased Productivity of Farm Labor

At least some of the wage increases were compensations for increases in the productivity of farm labor, as is suggested by scanning the number of man-hours that were required to produce certain crops.

Table 27-2

Man-hours Required to Produce Selected Crops, and Yields per Acre

Crop	Item	1950	1960	1963-67
Wheat	Man-hours per acre	4.9	3.1	2.9
	Before harvest	2.7	1.9	
	Harvest	2.2	1.2	
	Yield per acre (bushels)	16.6	24.9	25.9
	Man-hours per 100 bushels	30.0	12.0	11.0
Corn	Man-hours per acre	15.5	7.9	6.1
	Before harvest	10.0	5.1	
	Harvest	5.5	2.8	
	Yield per acre (bushels)	39.7	56.9	71.1
	Man-hours per 100 bushels	39.0	14.0	9.0
Cotton	Man-hours per acre	72.0	54.0	38.0
	Before harvest	33.0	23.0	
	Harvest	39.0	31.0	
	Yield of lint per acre (lbs.)	283.0	454.0	505.0
	Man-hours per bale	122.0	57.0	36.0

Source: *Historical Statistics of the United States. Colonial Times to 1957,* 1960, p. 281.
Adapted; and United States Department of Agriculture, *Agricultural Statistics*
(Washington: U. S. Government Printing Office, 1968), p. 461.

Increased productivity of farm labor was not unique for those who worked in growing wheat, corn, and/or cotton as attested to by data on total farm output. Based on production data using 1957-59 as the base period, the index number of farm output per man-hour in livestock and products increased from 89 in 1956 to 127 in 1962 and to 171.2 in 1967; that for output per man-hour in crops increased from 83 in 1956 to 124 in 1962 and to 155 in 1967.

Cash Position of Farmers

Cash incomes received by farmers were not adequately measured by incomes they received from the sale of crops and livestock because of additional payments by the government for withholding land from production. Dairy and/or poultry farming was a supplementary activity for some farmers; others specialized almost entirely along these lines.

The declining purchasing power of the farmer's dollar is shown by comparing indexes of the prices received by farmers with indexes of prices farmers paid for goods and services. Based upon 1910-14 prices, the price index of all farm products increased from 230 in 1956 to 253 in 1967. The cost of living index of prices that were paid by farmers in the same years increased from 274 in 1956 to 322 in 1967. The index of prices that were paid for production items such as feed, livestock, motor vehicles, farm

Table 27-3

Cash Received by Farmers from Crops, Livestock, and Governmental Payments—1956-1967
(millions)

	1956	1958	1960	1962	1967
Crops	$14,252	$14,182	$15,103	$15,935	$18,220
Livestock	16,312	19,223	18,909	19,986	24,365
Governmental Payments	553	1,089	693	1,736	3,071
Totals	$31,117	$34,494	$34,705	$37,657	$45,656

Source: *Historical Statistics of the United States. Colonial Times to 1957; Continuation to 1962 and Revisions,* 1965, p. 43. Adapted; and United States Department of Agriculture, *Agricultural Statistics* (Washington: U. S. Government Printing Office, 1968), p. 479.

machinery, farm supplies, fertilizer, seed, and building and fencing materials increased from 250 in 1956 to 287 in 1967. The ratio of prices received from the sale of all products of the farm to all expenses including taxes, interest, and wages (parity prices) was 83 in 1956, 85 two years later, and 74 in 1967. Capital costs of farmers continued to rise with the purchase, not only of tractors, motor trucks, and automobiles, but of grain combines, corn pickers, milking machines, pickup bales, and field forage harvesters. The value of farm implements and machinery in 1966 was $29.4 billion, which represented an increase of $12.9 million in such values since 1956. Taxes per acre of farmland rose from an average of 92 cents in 1956 to $1.86 in 1967. Taxes on personal property that was owned by farmers increased from $204 million in 1956 to $337 million in 1967. The costs of fire insurance in farmers' mutual fire insurance companies increased 2.8 cents per $100 of value between 1956 and 1962.

Increased Costs of Intensive Cultivation

One measure of the extent to which farms have become mechanized is found in the comparison of the 4 million horses and mules on farms in 1962 with the 1.6 million "working animals" found on farms in 1967. Only 4 million acres of land were required for the growing of feed crops.

Potatoes, cotton, tobacco, and celery, among other crops, are now harvested by machinery; and other machines are used in seeding most farmlands regardless of the crops that are planted. Electrical energy and internal combustion engines generate most of the power that is used on farms.

The use of machinery is only one factor in a more intensive cultivation of American farms. When western lands were first opened to farming, they did not require the use of any fertilizer. When the fertility of these lands had been reduced and fertilizer was needed to restore some of the elements of the soil that had been bled from it by constant, repetitive plantings, the fertilizer was a by-product of the farms, and the only cost of natural fertilizer was the labor cost of spreading it after an initial capital outlay had been incurred in purchasing a spreader. In 1967, however, farmers spent a total of $2,048,000,000 on the purchase of commercial fertilizer and lime. These are annual, variable costs of farming and are charged against current revenues. The purchase value of farm machinery is a fixed cost; and only interest, depreciation, and operating costs are charges against current farm incomes.

Government credit agencies provide tailor-made credit to fit the needs of farmers; even so, life insurance companies are granting larger dollar volumes of loans to farmers than are Federal Land Banks and all other government credit institutions combined. Wealthy individuals are still important sources of loans to farmers.

Reduction of Farm Acreages Under Cultivation

Ever since the Great Depression, efforts have been made to remove farmers and farming from the forces of pure competition. Programs that have been developed for limiting the acreage that has been planted in basic or selected crops have been only partially successful. Rainfall, floods, drouth, and variations in temperatures had combined their cumulative effects on the volume of crops that were harvested once they had been seeded. Land that has been withheld from production usually has been of the poorer grades, some of which never should have been cultivated in the first place. This fact alone has increased average outputs per acre without any increases in the productivity of lands that have remained in use. A few data that have been taken from the reports of the Bureau of the Census illustrate the point.

Impacts on Corn. In 1956, 75.2 million acres of land that were planted in corn yielded a total of 3.4 billion bushels that sold for $1.29 per bushel. The average yield per acre for that year was 45.7 bushels. In 1967, when 14.9 million fewer acres were planted in corn compared with such acreage in 1956, the average yield was 78.2 bushels per acre. Total output for 1967 was 1.3 million bushels in excess of the 1956 crop, and it sold for an average of $1.07 per bushel. Marginal costs of producing corn were lowered, and total output was increased. How much of the decrease in price of 22 cents per bushel was represented by lower marginal costs and how much by the increase in the amount of corn produced is impossible to determine in a study of this nature. Since the price of corn is determined in a world market, it may not be far from right to attach more importance to world conditions of supply and demand for corn than to its marginal cost in the United States. The average return per acre of corn land in 1956 was $53.49; in 1967 it had increased to $83.67. Economic prosperity of farmers who planted large acreages of land in corn has been determined more by increases in the productivity of this land than by increases in the physical production of corn.

Impacts on Wheat. The wheat farmer did not fare as well as did the growers of corn. In 1956, wheat was grown on 49.8 million acres of land at an average yield of 20.2 bushels to the acre. Total yield was slightly over 1 billion bushels for which the market paid $1.97 per bushel. Productivity per acre was $49.79. In 1967, and after almost 10 million acres of wheat land had been added to cultivation, the average yield was 25.8 bushels. Total yield was 513 million bushels in excess of the 1956 harvest, and at the price of $1.41 per bushel the productivity of wheat land on the average amounted to $36.38. Insofar as lower grades of land were withdrawn from cultivation, marginal costs were lowered, and the 1967 price was less than that for 1956. In this case, however, it is clear that marginal costs of growing wheat had little to do with price determination. World factors, external to growing wheat in the United States, exercised a greater influence on the price of wheat than did costs of production and the supply of domestic wheat.

Impacts on Oats. The analysis of the production of oats for grain serves to show the futility of attempting to draw any conclusions about the effect reductions of crop acreage have upon the volume of these crops and their prices in a dynamic economic organization—and a worldwide one at that. In 1956, 33.3 million acres of land that were planted in oats for grain yielded 1.1 billion bushels, for an average yield of 34.5 bushels per acre. Productivity at the average price of 69 cents per bushel amounted to $23.74 an acre. In 1967, a total of 782 million bushels was harvested from 15.9 million acres for an average yield of 49 bushels per acre. At 66 cents per bushel the productivity of such land was $32.34 an acre.

Impacts on Other Crops. Other products of the farm for which the effects of reductions in acreage planted were more than overcome by increases in output per acre were barley, hay, cotton, tobacco, and Irish potatoes. Of these products, only cotton and tobacco were priced higher in 1967 than in 1956. Apples, plums, peaches, cherries, grapes, oranges, grapefruit, and lemons were among the major fruit crops that were produced on a specialty basis and which in successful years returned large money incomes to their growers. Add to the list strawberries, blueberries, cantaloupes, and watermelons and you have a list of farm products that formerly were sold on local markets but which now are for national markets. When the production of beans, peas, tomatoes, cabbage, lettuce, peppers, celery, radishes, onions, and potatoes were restricted to the environs of large urban populations, they were available strictly on a seasonal basis.

Development of National Markets

When transportation facilities equipped with mechanical refrigeration created one huge national market for perishables, as well as for staple products, fruits and vegetables that had been available only in certain seasons of the year in local markets were marketed on an almost year-round basis. The development of agricultural resources in California, Arizona, New Mexico, Texas, Oregon, Washington, Florida, Louisiana, and other Southern States has made year-round production and consumption of fresh fruits and vegetables a reality. Frozen foods and concentrates have all but driven some canned goods off the market; and many small, local canneries of fruits and vegetables have been forced to cease operating. While these local canneries were in operation only a few weeks each year, they provided sources of supplementary incomes to thousands of workers collectively.

Canned orange juice and canned grapefruit juice all but gave way to frozen concentrates. Watermelons and cantaloupes are now sold in northern markets weeks or months before local crops are harvested, and they are found in southern markets long after local crops have been sold. For many years, new potatoes from Florida have been marketed in so-called normal years before the crops from Maine and Michigan have been harvested. Costs of growing them in Florida are much greater than costs in these other regions largely because of the large amounts of commercial fertilizer that must be applied to the soil. On occasions when the Florida crop has over-lapped those of Maine and Michigan, potato growers in all regions have suffered large financial losses or have not made as large gains as they other-wise would have made. Tomatoes have been grown all the way from the southern part of Florida up the Atlantic Coast to New England. They have also been produced in greenhouses out of season. Crops from California, Texas, and even Mexico, have been assuring American housewives of year-round supplies of fresh fruits and vegetables. Since the Castro revolution, Cuban fruits and vegetables have been scarce in American stores.

Cattle Raising

A review of cattle markets affords an answer as to why many farmers have entered the business either of raising cattle or of feeding them for the market. The high price of cattle food has discouraged many persons from continuing to raise them; nevertheless, thousands of acres in Southern States have been cleared and sown in pasture grass, and previous idle acres have been made productive. Not as much artificial feed has to be fed cattle that graze southern pastures. Warm temperatures and ample rainfall have contributed to making it possible to graze more head of cattle per acre than in other regions in the United States. "Western beef," a name given to the quality of meat rather than to the geographic region in which cattle have been fed, has been a product of the South for many years.

Because of state and federal requirements for handling edible meats, local home-killed meats, as such, have long since disappeared from meat markets. Increases in numbers of cattle slaughtered have been absorbed, in part, either by almost entirely new consumers of meat products or by those in former low-income brackets whose take-home pay has been increased as the direct or indirect result of new floors on wages having been imposed by law or by action of organized labor. As happened during and immediately following both world wars, it was a matter of more persons eating some meat as much as it was the same consumers eating more. Rationing during World War II entitled thousands of workers to purchase more meat than they had been able to purchase out of their prewar incomes. The levels of disposable incomes for workers continued to rise, with few and temporary interruptions, all through the period.

Price Supports and World Markets

Government price supports resulted in pricing many of our agricultural staples, including cotton and rice, out of foreign markets. Had their prices been permitted to remain at levels that were determined in free markets, thousands or millions of bushels of cereal grains and cotton would have sought foreign outlets. In order to stimulate the export of products of American farms, the Brannan Plan proposed to withdraw all government price supports from agricultural staples and to permit prices to settle at their competitive levels in domestic as well as in world markets. American farmers were to have been reimbursed for differences between parity prices or certain percentages thereof and those at which they actually sold their products. This would have enabled domestic consumers to obtain their farm products at lower prices, which in turn would have left them more money out of their disposable income to purchase other nonfarm products. The plan probably would have resulted in larger volumes of commodity exports which would have reduced the quantities of goods that were sold in domestic markets. Prices of agricultural products probably would have risen over the years, and subsidies would have decreased. The plan had little support outside the Department of Agriculture and was defeated in Congress when put to a vote. It was made clear that once a government had entered the business of influencing prices, it was and is extremely difficult to remove these or substitute influences.

GOVERNMENT FINANCE

Instead of government revenues and expenditures being tolerated, they became instruments of control. Government at all levels of operation undertook new functions and performed old ones on much larger scales. Rising prices also contributed to an increase in government expenditures incurred in performing traditional functions at former levels. Constitutions of some states and some municipal charters contain clauses that prevent these governments from creating bonded debts. Revenue certificates have been useful in financing capital improvements when their costs could not be raised by selling long-term bonds.

Statutory Limitations to the Federal Debt

At the close of World War II, the federal debt limit had reached $300 billion, after which it was reduced to $275 billion. From 1946 to 1954 it remained at this figure. In order to finance postwar programs at home and abroad without exceeding the debt limitations that had been imposed by Congress, the Treasury Department used the technique of establishing temporary debt that carried total indebtedness above statutory limitations.

Since 1954 the general trend of the statutory limit to the guaranteed federal indebtedness has been upward, although there have been some interruptions in this trend. At the close of the war, it stood at $300 billion. Since this time, limitations on the permanent debt have been lowered at one time to $275 billion; at other times they have been established at $283 billion, $285 billion, and $287 billion. Effective July 1, 1965, the statutory limitation was lowered to $285 billion. Over and above the maximums to the permanent debt, temporary additions have been authorized. The latter amounts have been influenced by the fiscal programs of the United States at the respective dates of authorization. Congress has been reluctant to establish a ceiling on the permanent debt in excess of $285 billion. It has held that a figure in excess of this total could be inflationary. On June 16, 1965, the Senate passed H. R. 8464, which was signed by the President on June 24 and became Public Law 49 of the 89th Congress. Its terms reduced the permanent debt by $2 billion to $285 billion to which was added a temporary debt of $43 billion to set an all-time record of $328 billion,[1] an amount $1 billion less than the President had requested through the Treasury Department and which he thought was essential to the financing of some emergency situations that had arisen.

The increase of $4 billion (the total debt was $324 billion in 1964) in the over-all maximum debt came after a reduction of income tax rates and either the removal of or reduction in the rates of excise taxes that had been levied as wartime measures. It had been anticipated that decreases in personal income tax rates would increase spending for commodities on which excise taxes had been lowered. Increased volume of such sales would not only compensate for lower taxes thereon but would stimulate business activity of all firms that handled these products from the retailer back to the manufacturer and producers of the raw materials out of which they were made. Middlemen would feel the impact of increases in their volumes of business, and employment would be increased. All these impacts would focus on larger personal and corporate incomes which would be subject to taxation at the lower rates and make no new financing necessary. There is no direct evidence to date that the reduction on the tax on transportation fares has stimulated either railroad or airway passenger traffic. It did release money that had been used in paying the tax to be spent on consumers' goods.

[1] In March, 1967, a temporary debt of $51 billion raised the all-time upper limit to $336 billion, for which the war in Vietnam was largely responsible.

Fiscal Operations

Taxes took larger amounts out of personal incomes in the 1960's than ever before. Federal personal income taxes were withheld by employers from salary checks in order to keep payments at least partially current. Other tax obligations and additional income tax payments were paid out of take-home pay which made taxpayers more conscious of their amounts.

Sources of Federal Revenues. Since 1910 income taxes—corporate and personal—other forms of internal revenue taxes, and customs receipts have been the principal sources of revenue to the federal government. The extent to which income taxes have displaced excise taxes and customs receipts is made manifest by the data in Table 27-4.

Table 27-4

Sources of Federal Government Tax Receipts for Selected Years (millions)

Kind of Tax	1913	1956	1959	1962	1968
Internal Revenue	$344	$75,109	$79,798	$99,441	$153,073
Personal Income	....	35,338	40,735	50,650	78,219
Corporate Income	....	21,299	18,092	21,296	29,889
Employment Taxes	....	7,296	8,854	12,708	27,576
Estate and Gift	....	1,171	1,353	2,035	3,076
Excise	307	10,004	10,760	12,752	14,313
Customs	319	705	948	1,171	2,113
Other	....	3,006	3,158	3,206	9,675

Source: *Historical Statistics of the United States. Colonial Times to 1957*, 1960, pp. 712 and 713; supplement, *Continuation to 1962 and Revisions*, 1965, p. 97. Adapted; and *The World Almanac* (New York City: Newspaper Enterprise Association, Inc., 1969), p. 131.

Sources of State Revenues. Since the receipts from the collection of unemployment taxes have not been available for the payment of governmental operating expenses, they have been excluded from all considerations in the following presentation.

In 1967 general sales and gross receipts or use taxes were levied by all but six states. Personal income taxes were imposed by all states except Connecticut, Florida, Illinois, Maine, Michigan, Nebraska, Nevada, Ohio, Pennsylvania, Rhode Island, South Dakota, Texas, Washington, and Wyoming; but Connecticut, Pennsylvania, Rhode Island, and South Dakota collected income taxes from corporations. West Virginia and New Hampshire taxed personal incomes, but not those of corporations. In 1962 New Jersey levied income taxes on its residents whose incomes originated in New York and on incomes that originated in New Jersey and were received by residents of New York.

Oklahoma, Rhode Island, and Tennessee which did not tax property in 1956 were joined by Alaska and Hawaii in this respect in 1959. South Dakota collected $747,000 from property taxes in 1956, but only $2,000 in 1962.

As sources of state revenues, property taxes ranked first until 1929 when the receipts from the collection of motor fuel taxes surpassed them. In that year, property taxes ranked second, motor vehicle and operators' licenses a close third, and income taxes fourth. Nineteen twenty-nine was also the first year in which motor fuel tax receipts exceeded those that were derived from motor vehicle and operators' licenses. These two taxes continued to be the best two sources of state revenues until 1942 when revenues from the collection of general sales taxes were greater than those from motor vehicle and operators' licenses. In 1942 the ranking taxes in terms of state revenues were motor fuel; general sales, use or gross receipts; income taxes and taxes on motor vehicle and operators' licenses. In 1943 and again in the following year, state revenues that were derived from ownership and operation of motor vehicles declined sharply because gasoline was rationed and new cars were practically unavailable to civilians.

From 1956 through the fiscal year that ended June 30, 1966, ranking sources of state revenues are given in Table 27-5.

Table 27-5

Importance of State Taxes, by Rank, as Sources of State Revenues—1956-1966

Kind of Tax	1956	1958	1960	1962	1966
General sales, use or gross receipts	1	1	1	1	1
Income	3	3	2	2	2
Motor vehicle fuel sales	2	2	3	3	3
Motor vehicle and operators' licenses	4	4	4	4	4
Sales of tobacco products	6	6	5	5	5
Alcoholic beverage sales and licenses	5	5	6	6	6
Property	7	7	7	7	7

Source: *Facts and Figures of Government Finance, 1967* (New York City: Tax Foundation, 1967), pp. 174 and 175. Adapted.

Sources of Revenue for Local Governments. The property tax has been and still is the principal source of tax revenue to governments at the local level. Because expenditures on the local level outran revenues from the property tax, business and license taxes, sales and gross receipts taxes, and others were imposed. The property tax has been declining as a source of revenue in proportion to the returns received from other sources. Cities have been compelled to increase their fees for tapping water mains and sanitary sewers. When the collection of garbage and trash has been a function of city governments, the latter have been compelled to increase their fees or charges for such services. The importance of income tax receipts to the individual cities in which they were imposed is lost in the aggregate data shown in Table 27-6. While utility taxes were not part of general revenue, the increasing importance of such taxes is shown in this table. Collections of utility taxes have not increased as much as have charges and miscellaneous taxes, hence the lower percentages of the collections of such taxes in 1965 compared with such collections in 1950.

Table 27-6

Percentage Distribution of the Revenue of Local Governments According to Its Source

Year	Total General	Property	Sales and Gross Receipts	Income	Licenses and Others	Charges and Miscellaneous	Utility Taxes
1922	92.6	77.7	0.5	...	2.0	12.4	7.0
1940	86.4	72.0	2.2	0.3	3.1	8.8	12.2
1950	82.1	60.3	4.1	0.6	3.3	13.7	15.5
1961	84.7	58.7	4.9	0.9	2.5	17.6	12.9
1965	84.8	57.4	5.3	1.1	2.1	18.8	12.7

Source: *Facts and Figures of Government Finance, 1967* (New York City: Tax Foundation, 1967), p. 231. Adapted.

In order to add adjustability and flexibility to local tax revenues in addition to adding to their total sums, cities in six states have been empowered to levy income taxes on their citizens. Among the larger cities that have been using this tax since Philadelphia and Washington, D. C. first adopted it in 1939 are Baltimore, Cleveland, New York, Detroit, St. Louis, Pittsburgh, and Cincinnati. Nine cities in Kentucky, four in Michigan, one in Missouri, 72 in Ohio, and 370 in Pennsylvania have also been compelled to use it.

As of September 1, 1966, a general sales tax has been collected in Washington, D. C., and counties in seven states derived revenue from this source. All the counties and 361 cities in California were relying upon collections of sales taxes to augment collections from other sources.

Nine counties in Alabama, one county in Tennessee, almost all of the municipalities in Florida, together with cities in nine other states were taxing the sale of cigarettes in 1966, while New Mexico was remitting one percent of the state tax to local governments. On July 1, 1966, sales in Atlantic City, New Jersey were exempted from the state sales tax. Counties in four states and cities in four other states were adding from $\frac{2}{10}$ of one cent to five cents to the gasoline taxes that were being levied by the state and federal governments.

Expenditures

Expanding activity at the federal, state, and local levels of government has resulted in increasing expenditures at all levels.

Federal. The level of financial operations by the federal government gave no indication that the government had either relinquished or decreased the volume of any of its activities. Between 1966 and 1968, wages and salaries of military and civilian employees were raised. It is impossible to interpret services rendered in terms of increasing expenditures alone. Intergovernmental payments almost doubled from 1963 to 1967, which indicates that the federal government was exercising more influence or control over what formerly had been functions of states and local governmental units. The cost of maintaining the nonmilitary operations increased from $36,417 million in 1959 to $55,040 million in 1967.

Before the Great Depression, the general plan or procedure in formulating a government budget was first to determine the costs of operation and then to find the revenue to cover them. Deficit financing was unavoidable during the depression, and war came along before any readjustments could be made. If any real efforts have been made to balance the federal budget since the war, they have not been effective except in very few years. In order to make conditions appear better, the budget was divided into ordinary and extraordinary items of expenditure. The former include those items that are necessary to the performance of the constitutional functions of government. Extraordinary expenditures are those that are directly related to the conduct of war both present and past, to complementing relief programs, and to rendering foreign aid. After so many years of deficit financing, many persons have come to deem it necessary to the full utilization of productive resources of the country. Other persons have voiced just as strong opinions that the American economy could have carried its own load and has not needed government financing in order to provide full employment and maximization of the utilization of productive factors and a growth experience of at least 3 percent per annum. Students of economic history have more and more data at their command to enable them to draw their own conclusions.

State and Local Governments. Past experiences with debts at state and local governmental levels have been so very unfavorable, not only to creditors but to taxpayers, that constitutional or other limitations have been placed on the amount or fact of bonded indebtedness. There have been no legal objections to the use of certificates of indebtedness that have been self-liquidating. State road departments have issued bonds in order to finance the construction of roads and have retired them with the proceeds of gasoline taxes. Cities have borrowed money for the construction of streets when they have been empowered to levy special assessments against abutting property owners to repay the loans. States have issued bonds for the construction of school buildings, dormitories, and other buildings, the incomes from the use of which have been employed to retire the principal sums when due and to pay the annual interest obligations until then. Municipalities have constructed schools and have made other capital improvements when they have been able to add millage to the local tax rate to cover such costs.

Civilian Employment and Government Payrolls. More and more persons have made their livelihood by working for government, as shown by the data in Table 27-7. For many years government has been in competition with free enterprise for the services of persons of widely different abilities and skills. Wages and salaries of government employees traditionally have been more stable at all levels of government and at all levels of pay than have wages and salaries paid by free enterprise. This relationship has resulted in free enterprise complaining of a shortage of applicants to fill jobs during periods of recession, while government agencies have complained of their inability to employ persons during periods of rising prices and economic prosperity.

Regardless of the outcome of this competition, government payrolls have been met out of tax receipts. As the number of government employees at given levels of wages and salaries has increased, more tax money has been appropriated to assure the payment of their wages. Increases in governmental functions have been accompanied by increases in civilian employment. During periods of rising commodity prices, which have entailed rising costs of living, total wage and salary bills have increased that have not been caused by, nor have they represented, expansions of governmental functions. Since 1946 Presidents of the United States have recommended wage and salary adjustments for federal employees more frequently than in earlier years. There has been no firm policy in respect to wage adjustments at lower levels of governments; but pressures have been exerted at these levels to follow federal policies, especially during periods of expansion of federal functions in order to retain full complements of employees.

Origins and Impacts of Government Payrolls. The economic impacts of public employment and of their pay have fallen more heavily upon local governmental units than they have upon higher levels of government. The economic impacts of federal employment and payrolls were more widely spread over the 50 states, while the impacts of state employment and payrolls were largely confined within state boundaries. The economic impacts of employment and payrolls of local government units were even more highly concentrated than those of the various states. Revenues out of which federal employees were paid came from widely scattered regions all over the United States and payments received were just as widely spent. State employees were paid from revenues that had been collected within the states, but expenditures were made far beyond these boundaries. Employees of local units were paid out of revenues that had accrued from the collection of local taxes.

Table 27-7

Public Employment of Civilian Workers and Payrolls
for Selected Years (October)

	1954		1960 *		1965 *	
	Employ-ment (000)	Payroll (millions)	Employ-ment (000)	Payroll (millions)	Employ-ment (000)	Payroll (millions)
Federal Total	2,373	$ 784.8	2,421	$1,117.8	2,588	$1,483.7
State Total	1,198	314.6	1,592	544.9	2,028	849.2
All Local Total	3,661	1,003.6	4,795	1,670.1	5,973	2,551.1

* Includes data for Alaska and Hawaii.

Source: *Facts and Figures of Government Finance, 1962-1963* (New York City: Tax Foundation), p. 36; and *1967*, p. 26.

Impacts of Government Expenditures and Receipts. While per capita data are purely statistical concepts and are not related directly to individuals, they are convenient media of economic analysis. This presentation would be incomplete and entirely inadequate without having made an examination of governmental expenditures and receipts in order to understand how taxpaying citizens have been affected. In calculating per capita disposable incomes, tax obligations have been deducted from gross incomes.

Careful perusal of the data contained in Table 27-8 reveals some interesting and important facts pertaining to the relative importance of federal, state, and local governmental units in regard to the collection of taxes and their disposal. In addition to the relative importance of the different levels of government, the sum total of their tax collections and of their expenditures measures the impacts of the financial aspects of government upon the American economy and upon its individual constituents.

In 1927 tax receipts at all levels of government constituted 10.7 percent of net national product; in 1950, 25.3 percent; and in 1965 the total tax take of government at all levels amounted to 29.3 percent of net national product. This meant that taxpayers were denied the opportunity to enjoy directly over one fourth of the net national product their cooperative efforts produced. However, in the circular flow of money the tax receipts of all levels of government were returned to circulation through the medium of

Table 27-8

Federal, State, and Local Tax Receipts and Expenditures: Total, per Capita, and Percentage Distribution for Selected Years

	1927	1940	1950	1966
PART A—Receipts				
Totals (millions)				
Federal	$ 3,364	$ 5,583	$37,853	$116,500
State	1,608	4,157	8,958	31,300
Local	4,479	4,503	7,988	27,400
Totals	$ 9,451	$14,243	$54,799	$175,200
Per Capita				
Federal	$ 29	$ 43	$ 255	$ 598
State	14	32	60	161
Local	38	34	54	141
Totals	$ 81	$ 109	$ 369	$ 900
Percentage Distribution				
Federal	35.6	39.2	69.1	66.5
State	17.0	29.2	16.3	17.9
Local	47.4	31.6	14.6	15.6
Totals	100.0	100.0	100.0	100.0
PART B—Expenditures				
Totals (millions)				
Federal	$ 3,533	$10,061	$44,800	$137,800
State	1,882	4,545	12,774	38,200
Local	5,805	5,811	12,761	43,500
Totals	$11,220	$20,417	$70,335	$219,500
Per Capita				
Federal	$ 30	$ 77	$ 301	$ 707
State	16	35	86	196
Local	49	44	86	223
Totals	$ 95	$ 156	$ 473	$ 1,126
Percentage Distribution				
Federal	31.5	49.3	63.7	62.8
State	16.8	22.3	18.2	17.4
Local	51.7	28.5	18.1	19.8
Totals	100.0	100.0	100.0	100.0

Source: *Facts and Figures of Government Finance, 1967* (New York City: Tax Foundation, 1967), pp. 19, 20, 22, and 23.

wages or in the payment of materials and services that have been rendered for governments.

In any event, sooner or later most government expenditures have had their impacts on employment and on wage payments. Most government employees have rendered services. Relatively few of them have been engaged in what might be called direct production. Exception must be made for employees who have operated publicly owned public utilities and for those who have operated municipally owned transportation facilities and who have conducted publicly owned stores such as retail liquor establishments. The more employees who have withdrawn from direct production and entered government service the greater has been the productivity of labor and other productive factors. Scales of living and national incomes have increased, concurrently with increases in the number of government employees.

TRANSPORTATION AND COMMUNICATION

In the 1950's and 1960's, significant changes have taken place in the transportation and communication industries. The interstate highway system, revitalization of the railroads, increased passenger and freight traffic of the airlines, and expansion of our communication facilities evidence our continuous progress.

Federal Aid Highways and Their Impacts

In the name of national defense, Congress in 1958 revised its policy of giving aid to the construction of highways. By 1972, 41,000 miles of interstate highways were to be constructed, with 90 percent of their costs financed at the federal level. "It (the system) should be so located as to connect by routes as direct as practicable, the principal metropolitan areas, cities, and industrial centers to serve the national defense." In 1969 there was some doubt as to the completion of the entire system by 1972. Reduction of internal expenditures for budgetary reasons and control of inflation may take precedence over its completion.

Nevertheless, the system has already had widespread impacts on transportation and the economy in general. Motels, restaurants and quick lunch stands, and gasoline filling stations, which were in operation to serve an increasingly larger number of motorists on state and federal highways, suffered when longer and longer sections of the interstate system were opened to travel. Tourists were attracted from other highways in such large numbers that the aforementioned accommodations suffered losses in patronage sufficient to force some to close and others to be sold at losses. To meet this competition, state road departments have initiated improvement programs that had for their goal reclaiming some of the lost traffic. Except within metropolitan areas, traffic moves almost as rapidly on state highways as it does on interstate highways, and there is a lower traffic count.

Railroads

One of the undisputed facts about railroad transportation was the continued decline in revenues that were derived from rendering passenger service. True enough, revenue per passenger mile increased from 2.685 cents in 1956 to 3.19 cents in 1966, but the number of passengers carried decreased at the same time from 429.9 million in 1956 to 307.5 million in 1966. Total revenue to the railroads derived from rendering passenger services declined from $757.6 million in 1956 to $547.1 million in 1966.

Railroads in all sections of the United States petitioned the Interstate Commerce Commission for permission to withdraw passenger trains from service. Frequently, they requested permission to discontinue service to stations that either did not originate revenue traffic or to which only small volumes and values of freight were shipped. Similar petitions were presented to State Railroad Commissions when they had jurisdiction. The criterion upon which decisions were based was the adequacy of alternate transportation services for carrying mail, as well as freight and passenger cargoes. Many trains were discontinued, others were merged, and still others were permitted to operate less frequently.

Revenue received from rendering freight services increased from $9,089 million in 1956 to $9,487 million in 1966. The low point in freight revenues was reached in 1961 when $7,859 million was received. Freight revenue per ton mile in 1960 was 1.417 cents; in 1965 it was 1.28 cents, but the revenue tonnage that originated on railroads increased from 1,301 million in 1960 to 1,479 million in 1965. By 1962, the railroads had more than recovered freight that had been lost to motor trucks and to airplanes. Tons of freight carried one mile in 1965 were 135,345 million greater than in 1960. The decline in revenue from rendering passenger services after 1960 was more than compensated by the increase in revenue from rendering freight services. At the time railroads incurred losses of $85 million in passenger revenues, they earned $885 million more of freight revenues. This gain supported the payment of increased dividends to holders of railroad common stock that amounted to $121 million, or a total of $553 million in 1965.

Traditionally, railroads have paid property taxes based on assessed valuations that were higher in relation to *true* or *market* values than were the assessed values of nonrailroad properties. In July, 1965, the Illinois Supreme Court ordered Cook County to refund $325,000 in taxes which the Burlington railroad had paid in 1957 on properties that had been assessed at 100 percent of value compared with 50 percent assessments on nonrailroad properties. The avoidance of high taxes combined with savings in maintenance and upkeep compelled railroad managements to reconsider their programs of owning real estate with the result that many railroad companies have sold their stations—passenger and freight alike—then leased them back from their new owners.

Passenger Traffic. Commuting trains were no longer profitable, and their patronage continued to decline. Data for 1957 showed a slight increase over the 4,841,000 commuters who were carried in 1956. But by 1966 such patronage had declined to 2,104,000 passengers. That revenues from rendering longer haul passenger service did not compensate for losses that accrued from commuter traffic is not surprising when it is realized that the volume of Pullman traffic declined from 6,882 million passenger miles over 89,124 miles of railroad in 1956 to 1,967 million passenger miles over 42,713 miles of railroad in 1967. In 1950, these data were 10,588 million passenger miles over 102,722 miles of railroad.

Cars of new design were pressed into service in hopes of luring passengers back to the railroads, but to no avail. Thousands of commuters were transported in one direction in a rush period in the mornings and in the opposite direction in the afternoons. Relatively little traffic was carried either way between rush hours and in the evenings, and the revenues from one-way traffic were totally inadequate to cover costs of return trips from which little revenue was received. Some railroads increased fares, but they only served the purpose of driving patrons to some substitute facility, and the financial results were disappointing to railroad managements. Seasonal traffic to resort areas continued to be profitable to the relatively few railroads that shared in it. Three or four railroads east of the Mississippi River enjoyed a lucrative north-south traffic, and approximately the same number of railroads between Chicago or St. Louis and the Far West were able to show profits from passenger services only by merging so-called crack trains and by being less competitive as to train schedules.

Railroads lost a large volume of interterminal passenger patronage to air service, to bus lines, and to the use of privately owned and operated automobiles. They willingly relinquished short-haul traffic to substitute carriers—although the use of diesel electric locomotives reduced noticeably the costs of frequent stops and starts.

Freight Traffic. After the termination of hostilities in 1945, the railroads lost valuable revenue-producing freight to motor trucks, air transportation, and privately owned operations. They even lost some of the heavy long-distance hauls when buyers began to accept shipments from manufacturers in truckload lots instead of in carload lots. One reason for this change was that the buyers did not want to incur the expense of financing and storing carload shipments. They did not want to have large sums of money tied up in inventories. An impact of this situation was to force steel companies and others to warehouse their own products until their customers were ready to receive them in truckload lots.

Trailer-on-Flatcar Service. Prior to the Great Depression, railroads had been the principal carriers of automobiles that were distributed from manufacturers and assemblers to dealers all over the country. During the depression, cars were delivered by trailer truck over the highways, and railroads lost a profitable, net revenue-producing freight. After the war, distribution of automobiles by trailer truck was resumed. In an effort to reclaim a portion of the revenue that railroads had lost to competing facilities, some of them began to experiment with trailer-on-flatcar (TOFC) or "piggyback" service. Freight schedules were speeded up so that truck transportation via TOFC was faster than was service over the road. TOFC service has proved to be extremely profitable to the railroads, and its use has been extended to include almost all the important trunklines, both east-west and north-south.

Unit Trains. Another experiment that has proved to be profitable to the railroads was the development and use of unit trains. Initially they hauled coal from mines to large consumers, such as public utility generating plants. The President of the Southern Railway System reported in *Railway Age* on August 2, 1965, that his system was the first to inaugurate the idea of a unit train in January, 1960, when it began to haul coal from mines to a plant of the Southeastern Electric Generating Company near Wilsonville, Alabama. The service that began with 56 car trains five days a week has been expanded to trains of 120 cars. In 1965 coal shipments on this train alone were at the rate of three million tons per year.

More publicity was given to the unit train that was organized to haul coal from mines in West Virginia to a public utility facility in New Hampshire, since which time its use has spread to include much wider coverage. Railroads gave special low rates for such hauls that did not permit or involve cut-offs or cut-ins. Through passage was arranged if two or more railroads were involved, with stops permitted only to change crews and locomotives. Cars were deadheaded empty on the return trip. One of the impacts of the use of unit trains was to compete successfully with other forms of transportation and to return to the railroads some of the traffic they had lost.

Several years ago a continuous rubber sluice stretched from near Cambridge, Ohio, to Cleveland over which coal was carried as sludge directly from the mines at rates with which the railroads could not compete at carload rates. Coal via unit train could be delivered in Cleveland cheaper than could coal via sluiceway; and the latter facility became obsolete, a victim of technological and managerial organizational improvement. At their terminals, cars were unloaded via rotary dumping which has resulted in turn-around times of four and five hours instead of the four or five days under the old methods. Grain from the Middle West was transported to New York via unit trains and dumped directly into the holds of the ships that were going to take it overseas without any intermediary time-consuming, costly handling.

The operation of unit trains gave rise to the design and construction of hundreds of new and larger freight cars in order to transport heavier revenue shipments at less than proportionate increases in operating costs. These orders came at a time when steel fabricating manufacturers were suffering from a lack of new orders. Thousands of employees were given employment at different levels of production, including basic steel and mining companies, in order to fill orders for the special types of cars that were adapted to unit train hauls. The new concentration of the steel industry in the Middle Western States within a short radius of Chicago has required special cars to haul the hot steel slabs or billets from the Pittsburgh area to the midwestern plants where they were fabricated according to the demands of the market. Heavier diesel electric locomotives have been designed to meet the needs of unit train services in order to replace multiple power units that were not heavy enough to pull the added tonnage of unit trains alone.

Central Traffic Control. The principal problem that confronted railroad managements in recent years was how to reduce operating costs in the face of declining operating revenues. Before they made any alterations in service schedules and before they could change their rates for services rendered, they had to petition the Interstate Commerce Commission for permission. In some instances, the ICC acted favorably upon such petitions, but in others the Commission acted only after long delays. In former times when the volume of traffic became too large to operate trains in two directions on one track, a second track was laid that was parallel to the first, and switchovers were installed at strategic locations for use in case of emergencies. The development and installation of central traffic control systems permitted railroads to operate as many trains over single tracks in both directions as they had formerly operated over two tracks and at lower maintenance costs. Push-button controls at one central location made it possible for one or two men at a signal panel to control the operation of both freight and passenger trains throughout an entire division.

Air Transport

In 1956, 41.7 million domestic revenue passengers were flown 22.4 billion miles, and in 1967, 142.5 million passengers were flown 75.5 billion miles. Among these were some of the passengers that the railroads had lost during the same span of years. A more significant development and one that had an adverse effect on railroads was the increase in mail, express, and freight shipped by air. The latter consisted of valuable but small pack-ages—those on which railroads charged rates that yielded surplus revenue over costs. It was not so much the fact that tonnage was lost by the railroads to airlines as it was that they lost the most profitable items. If there was economy to passengers in air transportation, it was found in the saving of time and in the cost of meals. In 1956 the revenue per passenger mile for railroads was 2.685 cents; for airlines it was 5.32 cents. In 1966 these revenues had increased to 3.19 cents and 5.83 cents respectively.

During the first half of 1968, airlines flew 41,385 million revenue pas-sengers compared with 35,262 million in the first half of 1967. Available seat miles increased 25.6 percent in the same period, and the percentage of available seats sold was 56.9 in 1967, 53.1 in 1968. For the same periods of time, air cargoes on regularly scheduled planes were 21.9 percent larger in 1968 than in 1967.

Mail Service

For several years the post office department has been concerned with the amount of time that elapsed between the receipt of mail and its delivery at points of destination. More and more persons have been utilizing airmail service even though it costs more than train mail. The post office department has been dispatching mail by air when regular airmail has not been of sufficient volume to constitute full loads. It also has been dispatching mail via motor truck between mail train schedules and from locations that are no longer serviced by railroads. One issue of *Railway Age* (1965) reported that New Bedford, Massachusetts, with a population of 102,000, was the largest independent community without rail passenger service, hence without train mail service. That motor trucks and airlines have been carrying larger percentages of mail than formerly is revealed by the increase in the ton-miles of mail flown in 1967 compared with the ton-miles flown in 1956. In the latter year mail was flown a total of 90.3 million ton-miles, and in 1967 this figure became 567.7 million. Loss of mail contracts, which amounted to subsidies, accounts for the discontinuance of passenger trains in all sections of the United States.

Communication

Miles of wire over which the Bell Telephone System carried messages increased from 220 million in 1956 to 480 million in 1967. That the telephone industry was geographically competitive during these years is evidenced by the growth in the number of independent companies from 550 that had installed 9.7 million telephones in 1960 to 666 that had installed 14.7 million telephones in 1967. Operating revenues of the Bell System increased approximately 84 percent between 1960 and 1966, compared with an almost 100 percent increase in the operating revenues of independents. Stockholders in the latter companies received 96 percent more dividends in 1966 than they received in 1960.

Impacts of Automation

The effects of automation are more noticeable in the employment data for the Bell System prior to 1962 than they are for the independent companies. Between 1956 and 1962, the number of employees in the Bell System declined by 75,000, or 12 percent, but 666,982 employees in 1966 received an average wage of $6,853, whereas 653,074 employees in 1956 had received an average wage of $4,416. Independent telephone companies paid an average wage of $5,563 to 25,000 more workers than had received an average wage of $2,772 in 1956. The combination of an increase in the number of installations and direct dialing for both local and long distance calls has resulted in a large increase in daily telephone calls and a relative decrease in the number of telegraph messages that have been transmitted. Extended telephone services combined with a greater acceptance of air mail have displaced the services of telegraph companies. The latter have attempted to regain their popularity by offering special rates for transmitting code messages on days of the year when greetings are in order.

QUESTIONS FOR REVIEW

1. (a) What was the trend of population growth after 1946?
   (b) What changes occurred in the composition of our population after 1946?
   (c) Explain some of the impacts of these changes.

2. What factors were responsible for increases in productivity per acre of land that was planted in corn, wheat, and oats?

3. How could the production of agricultural products increase in the face of restrictions of acreage under cultivation?

4. What methods were used in cultivating land more intensively?

5. (a) What has been the pattern of total federal debt since 1946?
   (b) How effective were the statutory limitations Congress placed on maximum indebtedness? Explain.

6. (a) What were the principal sources of state revenues after 1946?
   (b) What were the needs of the states for additional revenues after 1946?

7. (a) What were the needs for additional local revenues after 1946?
   (b) How were these needs met?

8. (a) What has been the experience of railroads regarding passenger traffic since 1956?
   (b) When commutation trains are crowded both mornings and evenings, why do they *not* yield net revenues to the railroads?

9. Explain why greater personal mobility today is accompanied by declines in railroad passenger revenues.

10. Is the decline in the number of employees of telephone companies a measure of the decline in communication services? Explain clearly.

SUGGESTED READINGS

Bernstein, Irving. "The Growth of American Unions, 1945-1960," *Views of American Economic Growth: The Industrial Era,* edited by Thomas C. Cochran and Thomas B. Brewer. New York City: McGraw-Hill Book Company, 1966.

Bining, Arthur C., and Thomas C. Cochran. *The Rise of American Economic Life.* 4th ed. New York City: Charles Scribner's Sons, 1964. Chapter 30.

Bowen, William G. *Labor and the National Economy.* New York City: W. W. Norton & Company, Inc., 1965.

Clark, Colin. "The Danger Point in Taxes," *Issues in American Economic History,* edited by Gerald D. Nash. Boston: D. C. Heath & Company, 1964.

Dillard, Dudley. *Economic Development of the North Atlantic Community.* Englewood Cliffs, N. J.: Prentice-Hall, Inc., 1967. Chapter 37.

Fite, Gilbert C., and Jim E. Reese. *An Economic History of the United States.* 2d ed. New York City: Houghton Mifflin Company, 1965. Chapter 33.

Hacker, Louis M. (ed.). *Major Documents in American Economic History.* New York City: D. Van Nostrand Co., Inc., 1961. Vol. II, Selections 24-27.

Hardman, J. B. S. "Labor in Midpassage," *Views of American Economic Growth: The Industrial Era,* edited by Thomas C. Cochran and Thomas B. Brewer. New York City: McGraw-Hill Book Company, 1966.

Hecht, Reuben W., and Eugene G. McKibben. "Efficiency of Labor," *Views of American Economic Growth: The Industrial Era,* edited by Thomas C. Cochran and Thomas B. Brewer. New York City: McGraw-Hill Book Company, 1966.

Heller, Walter W. "The Myth of Tax Limits," *Issues in American Economic History,* edited by Gerald D. Nash. Boston: D. C. Heath & Company, 1964.

McGuire, Joseph W. *Business and Society.* New York City: McGraw-Hill Book Company, 1963. Chapter 13.

Phelps, Edmund S. (ed.). *Private Wants and Public Needs.* Rev. ed. New York City: W. W. Norton & Company, Inc., 1965.

Vatter, Harold G. *The U. S. Economy in the 1950's.* New York City: W. W. Norton & Company, Inc., 1963.

Chapter 28

POSTWAR PROGRESS—PART II

CORPORATE DEVELOPMENTS

As industrial processes have become more highly mechanized and markets have become larger, industrial concerns have grown larger and relatively fewer in number. Competition in the areas of quality and performance has replaced price competition. Since many boards of directors have hesitated to dilute the interests of existing holders of common stock, capital structures have been enlarged by the issuance and sale of preferred stock and of long-term bonds. Working capital has been obtained from commercial banks through the medium of term loans. To remain competitive, banks have been compelled to enlarge their capital structures. This has been accomplished largely through the process of merging. Commercial banks do not issue long-term bonds.

Mergers

The movement toward industrial concentration was not new to the 20th century, although its pattern of accomplishment was somewhat different from that of an earlier one that terminated shortly after the turn of the century. The movement that gave birth to the Sherman Antitrust Act of 1890 was motivated almost entirely by the desire and intent of the owners of large corporations to escape from the profit-leveling effects of competition by obtaining control of firms that manufactured similar products. Control of price through control of production was the object of attainment.

Industrial. The Great Depression put an end to an extensive merger movement that began during the 1920's. Between 1919 and 1929 there were 270 mergers of iron and steel companies alone. In 1926, 1,029 local public utility corporations merged into larger companies; and 1,268 other mergers in manufacturing and mining resulted in 8,000 other corporations losing their identities. Mergers were not restricted to smaller concerns being absorbed by larger firms as shown by the Dodge automobile becoming a Chrysler product in 1928 and the Big Five meat-packers becoming the

Big Four through the merging of Morris and Company into Armour five years later.

Vertical Mergers. The merger movement that occurred after the close of World War II followed an entirely different pattern. This movement was one of integration of industry and a union of companies whose products were entirely unrelated. Corporations that were heavily involved in defense contracts sought concerns that made products that were in civilian use. Firms that were in regions whose markets were not growing rapidly sought others in regions in which markets were developing rapidly. In 1960, there were 877 mergers of mining and manufacturing firms, and in 1967 there were 1,317, for an increase of 484 percent. In other areas of business activity, mergers in 1967 were 159.4 percent greater than those that were effected in 1960—179 compared with 69. The total number of mergers in 1967 compared with their averages for 1948-57 in 11 manufacturing industries is shown in Table 28-1.

Table 28-1

Mergers in Manufacturing and Nonmanufacturing Industries, Other Than Mining, in 1967 Compared with Their Ten-Year Average, 1948-1957, by Industry Group of Acquiring Concerns

Lines of Manufacturing	1948-1957 Average	1967 Total
Nonelectrical Machinery	58.7	155
Food and Kindred Products	46.5	95
Chemicals	37.5	123
Fabricated Metals	31.7	87
Transportation Equipment, including Parts	31.3	103
Textiles and Clothing	25.0	67
Electrical Machinery	34.8	257
Primary Metals	21.0	65
Stone, Clay, and Glass Products	14.5	35
Paper and Allied Products	17.7	36
Professional and Scientific Instruments	13.1	92
Other	42.6	146
TOTALS	374.4	1,261
Nonmanufacturing (excluding Mining)	27.2	179

Source: United States Department of Commerce, Bureau of the Census, *Statistical Abstract* (Washington: U. S. Government Printing Office, 1968), p. 487.

Probably the most important single cause of such activity was a desire to stabilize corporate earnings over a period of years and throughout years of cyclical fluctuations. A company that manufactured cordage [1] purchased two concerns that supplied accessories to manufacturers of shoes; a maker of machine tools absorbed a manufacturer of machines for cutting masonry brick, tile, and refractories. A food processing company purchased control of a steel manufacturing company because management of the former claimed management of the steel company was inefficient. Life insurance companies broadened their underwriting coverage to include hospitalization, fire, casualty, and automobile insurance. The owner of a moving picture theater corporation acquired three soft drink bottling plants and three vending machine companies. A maker of cosmetics, industrial chemicals, and sanitation products broadened its lines of merchandise in acquiring a company that manufactured disinfectants, deodorizers, and other "industrial sanitation maintenance" products.

One of the better examples of product diversification brought about by the process of industrial mergers is that of one of the larger tobacco manufacturing companies. Since 1957 it has acquired Milprint, Inc., a producer of flexible packaging; Polymer Industries, Inc., a producer of industrial adhesives and textile chemicals; and the American Safety Razor Company, which had begun to manufacture stainless steel blades. Early in 1963 it acquired the Burma-Vita Company of Minneapolis, which manufactured Burma Shave; and one of its most recent acquisitions has been that of the Clark Brothers Chewing Gum Company of Pittsburgh. The Nicolet Paper Division of this tobacco company has commenced making a new type of aluminized paper which was intended to compete with household aluminum foil. It appears that at least one tobacco company has attempted to insure itself against losses that might follow a change in the smoking habits of the American people.

In 1964 one of the large radio and television networks acquired 90 percent control of a major league professional baseball franchise. In order to avoid antitrust action, it scheduled telecasts of ball games in which its own team was not a participant.

How Financed. Post-World War II mergers have involved little or no refinancing on the part of the concerns that have retained their corporate identities. Large corporate surpluses had been built up out of earnings that had not been distributed to common stockholders in the form of dividends. In many cases they have been used to purchase controlling shares on the market. Some mergers have been effected by the boards of directors of acquiring concerns offering to purchase designated numbers of shares of stock that might be presented by stockholders of the companies they desire to control on or before designated dates. Other mergers have been effected by making direct exchanges of treasury common stock of the acquiring

---

[1] More recently this company sold all its plants in the United States that manufactured cordage and is operating only at that level in Canada, where labor and other costs are lower than in this country.

corporations for shares of the others at ratios that have been determined by the ratios of the market prices of the respective shares on the dates of the original offers.

A Unique Dissolution. A reverse pattern was established by the Supreme Court in 1957 when the Du Pont Corporation was ordered to divest itself of some 63 million shares of common stock of General Motors Corporation, or 8 percent of the latter's total number of shares outstanding at the time. Evidence in court did not support the charge of collusion between the two corporations, and the ownership of 8 percent of the shares of common stock did not carry with it control of General Motors Corporation, but the latter corporation had purchased its automobile body paints from Du Pont. Divestiture was made by Du Pont distributing these shares among its own shareholders in proportion to the number of shares of Du Pont common stock they held. There were no immediate impacts on the market, although there was a larger potential number of shares available, assuming that Du Pont had not traded actively in General Motors.

Banks. Bank mergers are one aspect of a general merger movement, but they have been determined more by industrial mergers than by conditions that have arisen within the structures of individual banks themselves. Increases in the size of industrial, manufacturing, and commercial corporations, together with their increased requirements for working capital, have compelled commercial banks to become larger in order to accommodate their borrowing customers. The quickest way to become larger and that which was least disturbing in capital markets and to equity interests was through the acquisition of the assets of other going concerns. Merging of banks was a way of establishing branch offices in states in which this kind of expansion was difficult to accomplish.

The initial movement was restricted to banks that were located in a given area. Recently it has extended to banks that have served entirely different geographic areas, such as banks in New York City merging with banks in Schenectady, Rochester, Albany, or some other upstate community. Such developments can occur only in those areas within which branch bank offices may be established. The Board of Governors has consistently followed the policy of granting member banks the same privileges in this regard that state nonmember banks have enjoyed. One of the most important tests that has been applied by the Board has been the possible effects of each merger upon competitive conditions in the area of influence of the banks that were included in each request.

Two bank mergers that had been approved by the Board and which were effected by the managements of the respective banks have since been ordered dissolved by the Department of Justice on the ground that they were in violation of the Sherman Act. One of these banks was located in Lexington, Kentucky; the other, in New York City. The banks were ordered to redistribute their deposits, depositors, loans, and the contents of their investment portfolios among and between the former two banks respectively within a specified period of time subject to a fine of $100 per day for noncompliance. The very size of such a task precluded its completion within the allotted time, and the banks appealed to the court for relief from the penalty. The court suspended payment of the penalty when the banks presented evidence of their earnest intention of compliance. A later ruling permitted these two mergers to remain effective. The Department of Justice now rules upon the monopoly aspects of proposed mergers before the Board of Governors considers them. There have been a number of Board denials of applications that have had Department of Justice approval, and in the name of decreased competition between banks.

While merging of commercial banks has left much to be desired, the implementation of the credit policies of the Board of Governors appears to have become more effective, especially when nonmember banks have merged with member banks.

Holding companies have been formed to effect consolidations, since they do not come under the jurisdiction of the Comptroller of the Currency, nor are they subject to rulings of the Board of Governors. One of the impacts of the functioning of bank holding companies is to circumvent restrictions against branch banking.

Railroads. By 1960 it had become unmistakably clear that the only way to salvage the railroads was to permit steps to be taken that would result in drastic reductions in operating costs as well as in overhead. Passenger trains had been discontinued or consolidated. Longer and heavier trains were being operated. New and specialized types of freight cars were being purchased in order to accommodate shippers and to lure them away from competing modes of public transportation. One victory for the railroads that was not directly connected with mergers was the acceptance of a plan under which wages of locomotive firemen would no longer be claims on operating incomes.

In 1959 the Interstate Commerce Commission had approved the merger of the Virginian Railway into the Norfolk and Western. The following year its approval of the Erie-Delaware—Lackawanna and Western merger was intended to help solve each road's problem of insufficient revenues and heavy losses that accrued from their passenger divisions, especially from their rendering commuter services in New Jersey. That same year the Minneapolis & St. Louis Railroad merged with the Chicago & Northwestern; and the Minneapolis, St. Paul and Sault St. Marie, the Duluth, South Shore and Atlantic, and the Wisconsin Central became the Soo Line Railroad.

Other Mergers. In 1962 the Pennsylvania Railroad obtained control of the Lehigh Valley; the Chesapeake and Ohio Railway obtained control of the Baltimore and Ohio; and the Central of Georgia became part of the Southern Railway System. After years of negotiations and hearings, the merger of the Atlantic Coast Line Railroad with the Seaboard Airline was approved in 1963. Another consolidation made the Norfolk and Western Railroad one of the largest lines in the entire United States. It has acquired control of the Nickel Plate, the Wabash, the Pittsburgh and West Virginia, the Akron, Canton and Youngstown, and finally the Sandusky Division of the Pennsylvania Railroad, which gave the parent railroad direct connections between the Eastern Seaboard at Norfolk and several terminals on the Great Lakes, Chicago, St. Louis, Omaha, Kansas City, and Des Moines in the Middle West. This merger was directly in accord with the policy of diverting traffic that originated in the Middle West and was destined for overseas markets out of trunk line territory to more southern ports. The New York Central and the Pennsylvania Railroads have merged to form the Penn-Central Railroad, which, in turn, is now operating the New York, New Haven and Hartford Railroad, whose officers had threatened to cease operating unless financial relief was forthcoming.

Proposed Mergers. Awaiting the approval of the Interstate Commerce Commission in 1969 were the Great Northern, Northern Pacific and Burlington lines, which in turn would lease the Spokane, Portland and Seattle Railroad; and the Santa Fe and the Southern Pacific Railroads which were vying with each other for control of the Western Pacific. Other proposals that were awaiting decisions of the Interstate Commerce Commission were the Chicago, Rock Island and Pacific to become part of the Union Pacific line or of the Chicago and Northwestern; the Missouri Pacific or the Illinois Central to obtain control of the Chicago and Eastern Illinois Railroad; and finally the Chesapeake and Ohio to control the Western Maryland.

Some of these proposals were to unite highly competitive railroads; others were to extend lines end-to-end in order to save on interchanges and to shorten distances and times of shipments between two terminals.

Publishing. The publishing industry had been confronted with rising cost of materials, increasing demands by labor for higher wages and more fringe benefits, and a decreasing volume of advertising. Radio and, more recently, television have proved more effective in reminding listeners and viewers many times daily of the advantages they would derive from using X product. Visual and verbal presentations were more effective than the printed page in getting their messages across to the public. Advertising money that newspapers and magazines had been receiving was being diverted into other channels of communication.

Book publishers were faced with rising costs, some of which were eliminated or reduced by the merging process.

Newspapers. Publishers of daily newspapers have not escaped the trend towards combination. In June, 1964, 130 companies published 640 dailies. In 1964, only 66 cities had two or more papers printed by different publishers, a decline of 50 in ten years. In the 1920's, New York City had 14 daily and eight Sunday papers; Chicago had 14 daily papers. In 1967, the former had three dailies and one Sunday paper; Chicago had four dailies published by two different publishers.

Among the reasons given by newspaper publishers for merging are (1) the growth of suburbia, accompanied by an increase in the number of dailies in cities of less than 250,000 population; (2) competition with radio and television; (3) the changing nature of the press; (4) the power of advertisers; and (5) the high cost of printing. In 1966, joint ventures in publishing newspapers numbered 25. A joint venture exists when two papers function as one except in the area of editorial coverage. They usually involve a common printing plant, common distribution and circulation facilities, and a common advertising department and business office. Each paper contributes to total costs in accordance with contract terms and receives revenue on the basis of its own sales and advertising revenues.

The Department of Justice has looked askance upon mergers of newspaper publishers. It has concerned itself with monopoly control as evidenced by unreasonable restraints of trade, unfair competitive practices, and control over advertising and subscription rates. United States courts have been realistic in holding that antitrust legislation does not prevent a lessening of competition by merger when one party thereto has been losing money.

Another trend that has been gaining strength in recent years has been for operator-owners of television broadcasting stations to acquire control of newspapers. Regardless of the monopolistic impacts of such combinations, the fact remains that many television stations have showed profits which have been used to offset losses from publishing newspapers. Tax loss influences have been brought to bear in consummating some of these mergers.

Books. Publishing books at all levels of sophistication has been a highly competitive activity. Many such firms have been owned and managed by members or descendants of the founding families. Caught in the wave of rising costs of newsprint, printer's ink, and labor at a time when competitive forces in the market did not permit commensurate price increases, individual firms experienced declining profits, in some instances to the point of complete disappearance or the realization of losses. As family heirs became fewer in number or as they lost interest in publishing, as costs rose more rapidly than did the selling prices of books times volume of sales, as more books in certain areas of intellectual interest were published by more publishers, the latter tended to control smaller portions of their markets, and profits began to decline to the level that caused the owners of some firms to be willing to sell to others that desired to become larger.

Whatever the reason or reasons for so doing, publishing houses became fewer in number and larger in size. One feature of these mergers was that firm names that carried goodwill did not disappear. Hyphenated corporate names have become more numerous proportionately in book publishing than in other industrial segments of our economy. Even The Macmillan Company has lost its corporate identity, but its name has been preserved for reasons of goodwill. Firms that formerly confined their titles to fiction have entered the textbook field and vice versa. Other firms that specialized in business and economics, in science, in engineering, or in management have published titles of books in other areas of intellectual interest. Firms that were located in the eastern United States have entered more western markets by obtaining control of firms in these areas. The rapid growth in the Pacific Coastal States has opened up new markets for books at all levels of learning and in all its branches. The rapid growth in the number of schools and colleges and in school age population in these states has increased the demand for literature in its broadest sense. Despite the large and rapid growth of markets, high labor costs have compelled publishers of books and of newspapers to raise the levels of productivity of their employees by combining fewer of them with more highly efficient mechanized processes.

Impacts on Banks. Mergers, consolidations, and internal expansions of business and industrial firms had their impacts on their needs for services of banks, both commercial and investment. As large and financially successful commercial and industrial units built up larger corporate surpluses out of earnings, they relied, proportionately, less and less upon banks to finance their current operations and more upon their corporate surpluses to finance longer run capital improvements and expansions. Instead of relying upon the market to determine the status of their instruments of finance, loans were obtained directly from insurance companies that collectively had millions of dollars to invest. Term loans from commercial banks tended to replace the traditional self-liquidating commercial loan of 30, 60, and 90 days maturity. They gave rise to the use of certificates of deposit by state banks and national banks that bore interest rates above those that were paid for passbook savings. These rates were lost if their holders redeemed the certificates before their expiration dates.

Corporate Profits

The economic concept of profits is that they are portions of business incomes that are over and above all business expenses, fixed and variable, explicit and implicit. They accrue to the owners of business enterprise. Corporate development over the last 100 years has removed from the stockholders, who are the corporate owners, the function of decision making and has delegated it to management and to boards of directors who have been paid salaries as part of operating costs. Decisions have been made at one of these levels to "plow under" certain amounts of earnings each year instead of having asked common stockholders to provide additional new capital, or of having borrowed more capital in the open market. Amounts of net earnings that have not been returned to operate the firms have been paid to their owners who had assumed the risks of enterprise.

Functions. Profits are the criteria of the financial success of corporations, and of corporations grouped according to the levels of activity upon which they operate. Profits may be considered as rewards for risk taking, and they may be either positive or negative. That there have been risks of enterprise is shown by data on the number of firms that have been discontinued over the years. The one cause of the largest number of firms going out of business each year has been the failure of receipts to cover all costs of doing business. In 1956, 342,000 firms discontinued operations, of which 148,000 were operating at the level of retail trade. In 1960 out of a total of 384,000 firms that went out of business, 157,000 had been in retail trade. It may not be surprising that more new establishments were opened up at the retail level than at the levels of construction, manufacturing, wholesale trade, and rendering services.

Table 28-2

The Number of New and Discontinued Firms in All Segments of Industry—Selected Years

Business Firms *	1956	1960	1967
New Business Firms	431,000	438,000	n.a. †
Corporations	141,163	182,713	206,569
Discontinued Firms	342,000	384,000	n.a.
Corporations	12,686	15,545	12,364

* Alaska and Hawaii not included.
† Not available.

Source: U. S. Department of Commerce, Bureau of the Census, *Historical Statistics of the United States. Colonial Times to 1957; Continuation to 1962 and Revisions* (Washington: U. S. Government Printing Office, 1965), p. 79; and *Economic Report to the President* (Washington: U. S. Government Printing Office, 1969), p. 316.

Insofar as the movement of firms into and out of business may have been a test of the degree or intensity of imperfect competition, data for recent years indicate that it is still the prevailing framework within which business firms operate. Only at the level of wholesale trade have more firms been discontinued than were newly organized. This is in accord with an earlier analysis of trade which revealed that the functions of wholesaling were being and have been assumed by many of the large integrated firms.

Reasons for Becoming Stockholders. Only a relatively few of the corporate stockholders bought stock because of their desire to control corporate policies and to make corporate decisions. Depending upon their financial status, which included their financial responsibilities present and future, people who were not speculators purchased shares of corporate stock either for their probable increases in capital values, to receive current income therefrom, or both. If they were building estates for the future, corporate earnings and probable growth were more important than dividends. Particularly since 1946, people have sought dividend incomes to counteract losses of purchasing power of wages and salaries resulting from inflation.

Corporate Dividend Experiences. Manufacturing industries, which have ranked third in number of firms in the economy, have ranked first in the payment of cash dividends for years; and trade, which has ranked first in the number of individual firms, has lagged behind manufacturing and finance, insurance, and real estate in the distribution of cash dividends.

Looking at cash dividends that have been paid in relation to the capitalization of firms, corporations that have been capitalized at $100 million or more have distributed dividends in dollar volume in excess of those that have been paid by all other corporations combined. Trends of dividend payments have been far from uniform in the ten classifications of corporations according to size of capitalization that constitute the object of attention in Table 28-3. Undoubtedly, the level of the area in which corporations have operated has had as much influence on their earning as has their size. Some industries, regardless of their size, have been more susceptible to cyclical fluctuations, major and minor, than have others.

Efforts to Maintain Earnings. In recent years corporate profits have, in general, been on the increase. Many corporations have reported that increases in sales have not resulted in corresponding increases in earnings. That costs have risen more rapidly than earnings has caused many boards of directors to review their organizational setups in efforts to check the trend. Some highly integrated companies have sold subsidiaries or divisions that have retarded their overall financial progress. Some corporations have decentralized their lines of control; still others have effected greater degrees of centralization of control in their efforts to stop leaks or seepages of incomes. There did not appear to be any one answer to the problem. It was found within the internal organization of many corporations. Many others introduced entirely new blood into their organizations, some of which came from competing firms and some of which represented experience and success in entirely unrelated lines of business.

Costs of opening up new retail outlets, especially in communities in which the particular firm had not been established, have constituted drains on incomes from sales of many chain store types of variety and specialty stores. Long-range programs of expansion have included the opening of new stores successively for several years, the costs of which have offset the financial gains that were made in many of the older stores in the chains.

Larger disposable incomes, combined with more people receiving them, resulted in increased sales of most kinds of consumers' goods, durable as well as nondurable. These increases redounded to supplier levels, and business firms in general had never had it so well. In 1961 the American Telephone and Telegraph Company reported net earnings of $2,049,400, followed closely by General Motors Corporation which earned $1,627,276. In 1961,

Table 28-3

Number of Corporations by Total Assets and Cash Dividends They Have Paid—1956-1966

(Dividends in millions)

All Industries Total Assets	1956		1958		1960		1966	
	Number	Divi-dends	Number	Divi-dends	Number	Divi-dends	Number	Divi-dends
Less than $50,000	332,685	$ 82	370,757	$ 66	499,163	$ 141	276,298	$ 194.0
$50,000-$99,999	150,165	84	166,581	74	190,316	114	167,724	208.6
$100,000-$249,999	171,122	190	195,025	201	229,142	285	215,943	483.1
$250,000-$499,999	76,929	197	88,311	188	105,174	252	112,153	480.8
$500,000-$999,999	41,366	249	46,346	236	54,991	319	61,513	468.3
$1,000,000-$4,999,999	39,861	843	43,321	756	47,983	894	54,298	1,082.1
$5,000,000-$9,999,999	7,295	491	7,870	462	8,280	485	9,972	557.7
$10,000,000-$49,999,999	6,547	1,769	7,220	1,580	7,912	1,650	9,778	2,652.6
$50,000,000-$99,999,999	896	1,178	1,001	1,152	1,145	1,211	1,470	1,325.7
$100,000,000-Over	1,080	9,274	1,203	10,171	1,333	11,649	1,873	19,766.0

Source: *Historical Statistics of the United States. Colonial Times to 1957; Continuation to 1962 and Revisions,* 1965, pp. 82-84. Adapted; U. S. Department of the Treasury, Internal Revenue Service, *Statistics of Income, Corporation Tax Returns, Preliminary,* 1966 (Washington: U. S. Government Printing Office, 1968), p. 30.

Table 28-4

Number of Corporate Firms by Function and Total Cash Dividends Paid—1956-1966
(Dividends in millions)

Corporations	1956 Number	1956 Dividends	1958 Number	1958 Dividends	1960 Number	1960 Dividends	1966 Number	1966 Dividends
Agriculture	9,892	$ 44	12,618	$ 53	17,139	$ 50	16,667	$ 86,309
Mining and Quarrying	10,861	837	10,971	758	13,071	814	7,363	1,061,749
Manufacturing	128,457	7,121	145,531	7,239	165,862	8,028	134,683	12,794,944
Trade	270,951	1,060	294,629	982	355,613	1,232	197,980	1,143,490
Service	74,372	189	89,494	181	121,024	277	116,105	423,472
Finance, Insurance, and Real Estate	244,755	2,491	272,305	2,780	334,388	3,466	251,037	6,202,201
Public Utilities	32,895	2,535	35,161	2,802	43,852	3,199	39,456	4,963,275
Construction	45,223	80	56,181	89	72,332	116	70,470	191,979

Source: *Historical Statistics of the United States. Colonial Times to 1957; Continuation to 1962 and Revisions,* 1965, pp. 80-82. Adapted; U. S. Department of the Treasury, Internal Revenue Service, *Statistics of Income, Corporation Tax Returns, Preliminary,* 1966 (Washington: U. S. Government Printing Office, 1968), p. 30.

Delta Airlines earned $4,652,000; 1968 earnings were $36,134,000, down from $49,190,000 the preceding year. In 1967, Continental Airlines earned $17,310,000 which was three times its earnings in 1964.

Price Fixing. Complaints were registered at the Philadelphia office of the Antitrust Division of the United States Department of Justice in 1957 over what appeared to be price fixing in the heavy electrical equipment industry. Again in 1959 the Tennessee Valley Authority reported the fact of identical price quotations when it opened sealed bids on some of its equipment. A grand jury was called into session in July of that year, and three additional such bodies interviewed more than 100 witnesses. Out of these hearings came the indictments of 29 firms and 45 of their executive officers. The defendant companies and their officers pleaded guilty or *nolo contendere;* and early in February of 1961 Judge J. Cullen Gainey, of the United States District Court in Philadelphia, made history when he fined the corporations a total of $1,787,000 and 44 of their corporate officers $137,500. In addition to the personal fines, seven executives were sent to prison for 30 days each, and 21 others were placed on probation.

This was the first time corporate officers had been held individually responsible for the actions of their corporate entities. It was merely the beginning of trouble for the defendant corporations, which since have been sued in the courts by municipalities and public utility companies for triple the damages they were alleged to have incurred; and many individual settlements have been made out of court. To the credit of the corporate officers of the defendant companies, they expressed a willingness to look into the terms of any and all contracts that had been consummated over the past several years and to make restitution for damages when it was evident that they had been incurred. Board chairmen and executive officers denied knowledge of what had taken place, and many of the division heads who had been responsible for violating the Sherman Antitrust Act were relieved of their connections with their employer corporations.

Control Devices. Evidence showed that representatives of the defendant companies met periodically and allocated bids on "power switch gear" in the proportion of 39 percent to General Electric; 35 percent to Westinghouse Electric; 11 percent to I-T-E Circuit Breaker; 8 percent to Allis Chalmers; and 7 percent to Federal Pacific Electric Company. In their efforts to control price quotations, a plan of rotating bidding positions was adopted. Another control device had been to divide the United States into four quadrants, each of which had a secretary who allocated business within his territory. Still other devices were revealed for the first time in court hearings, none of which had been approved or even known by top management of some of the companies. They were schemes that had been evolved by division managers in order to impress their superior officers and at the same time to appear competitive in their efforts to obtain volume of business and profits.

LIFE INSURANCE

Insurance companies have come to occupy a more important place in the American economy than ever before. In March, 1967, they employed a total of 1,310,000 persons of whom 450,000 constituted just the sales personnel of life insurance companies. Of this group 220,000 earned over 50 percent of their total incomes from such sales; another 230,000 earned less than 50 percent of their incomes from this source. Nonsales personnel that worked in home offices, agencies, brokerages, and in other phases of insurance constituted another 860,000 employees. Most of the selling personnel were men; most of the nonsales force were women.

Assets

The total assets of life insurance companies alone in current dollars are shown in Table 28-5. The figures in the column headed "Industrial and Miscellaneous" show the extent to which life insurance companies have become suppliers of long-term capital to industrial firms. Not only did the percentage of such loans to total assets increase from .7 of 1 percent in 1920 to 25.2 percent in 1967, the base to which these percentages applied increased from $7,320 million in 1920 to $177,361 million in 1967. The importance of having replaced railroad bonds with those of public utilities is revealed by comparing data in the columns under these heads. That life insurance companies supported the government in its war effort is emphasized by the large percentage of holdings of government bonds in 1945. Life insurance companies as well as the owners of 167 million life insurance policies in 1945 had much at stake in the outcome of the war.

Table 28-5

Assets of Life Insurance Companies for Selected Years and Their Distribution Between Important Classes

Years	Amount (millions)	Percentage Distribution of Investments							
		U. S. Bonds	Rail-road Bonds	Public Util-ities	Industrial and Miscellaneous	Corpo-ration Stock	Mort-gages	Other	Total
1920	$ 7,320	11.3	24.3	1.7	.7	1.0	33.4	27.6	100.0
1930	18,880	1.7	15.5	8.6	1.9	2.8	40.2	29.3	100.0
1940	30,802	18.7	9.2	13.9	5.0	2.0	19.4	31.8	100.0
1945	44,797	45.9	6.6	11.6	4.3	2.2	14.8	14.6	100.0
1950	64,020	21.0	5.0	16.5	14.9	3.3	25.1	14.2	100.0
1955	90,432	9.5	4.3	15.5	20.1	4.0	32.6	14.0	100.0
1960	119,576	5.4	3.1	14.0	22.4	4.2	34.9	16.0	100.0
1965	158,884	3.2	2.1	10.7	24.2	5.7	37.8	16.3	100.0
1967	177,361	2.6	1.9	9.6	25.2	6.1	38.1	16.5	100.0

Source: *The Life Insurance Fact Book* (New York City: The Institute of Life Insurance, 1968), pp. 65 and 66.

Payments

In 1957, the average amount of life insurance per family was $8,000; in 1967 this figure was $17,200. Related to disposable incomes per family in 1957 of $5,600 and in 1967 of $8,700, insurance protection per family not only was greater, but it increased more rapidly. Life insurance benefit payments in 1967 were $13,293,600,000, of which death benefits amounting to $5,665,300 were paid to 2,613,000 claimants. The living benefit payments on life insurance amounted to $7,628,000 compared with social security payments for old age, survivor benefits, and disability payments of $21,406,455,000. In addition to meeting death claims and living insurance benefits payments, health insurance benefit payments in 1967 amounted to $5,178,000,000, of which 48.6 percent went towards meeting hospital expenses: 16.0 percent was for surgery; 20.7 percent compensated, at least in part, for loss of income including accidental death and dismemberment payments; and 14.7 percent helped defray medical expenses.

Casualty and other types of insurance companies paid another $1,008 million in health benefits excluding payments that were made by Blue Cross, Blue Shield, and other similar organizations. All insurance companies paid their policyholders health benefits that amounted to $6.2 billion.

LEISURE TIME

Many years ago organized labor advocated shorter work weeks for certain employees without reducing the number of hours per week that factories, mills, mines, stores, and other forms of businesses operated. One reason for this program was to enable workers to receive time and a half the base rate of pay for all overtime employment. Another reason cited was to stagger the limited amount of work or the limited number of jobs among a larger number of employees. One of the results of this program has been to afford workers more time in which to spend their earnings. Vacations with pay, in addition to longer vacations, have enabled workers and others, too, to take trips via air, automobile, train, or steamship.

Vacation periods are usually one week or more, depending largely upon individual employee rank and years of service with present employers. Some industrial firms close down their operations entirely for all employees during designated vacation periods. More common is the practice of staggering vacations between the months of June and September or some other period. Concerns that do not want work to pile up until their office employees return from vacation, or whose policy does not permit employees who are working to perform the extra duties of those who are on vacation, take advantage of opportunities to employ temporary help from companies that operate specifically for this purpose. These girls are paid by the companies that serve as clearing houses for part-time employees and not by the employers to whom they are assigned.

Paid Vacations

Closely related to tourism for thousands of employees is the length of paid vacations as well as the amounts of money vacationers have to spend. The latter are functions of savings that have been accumulated out of wages and salaries for such occasions. In addition, are vacation plans that are incorporated into wage agreements, especially those with organized labor. Prior to World War II one such pattern may have provided a one-week paid vacation per year after ten years, two weeks per year after 15 years of continuous employment. Since World War II more liberal terms in vacation plans are among the fringe benefits for which labor has bargained.

It makes little difference here if a company's vacation program was devised around the bargaining table with representatives of organized labor, or if similar programs were entered into in order to provide additional employment for younger worker replacements. The fact remains that some of these vacationing employees may have taken trips to Europe and aided in the furtherance of a balance of international payments that was unfavorable to the United States. Others remained in this country and helped populate resort areas. In any case, they increased the demand for leisure time products and provided employment for thousands of workers in leisure time industries. The sale of automobiles, new and used, and their accessories were boosted by those persons who did not trust their old car or their tires to carry them safely long distances. Motels and hotels, public eating establishments of all kinds, sporting goods and equipment, sports clothing, boats and boating, fishing tackle, travel by air, by train and by bus, racetracks, theaters, and other forms of leisure time institutions all felt the impacts of these new and expanded vacation programs. Not only have leisure time industries felt the impacts of these programs, but the manufacturers of consumers' goods, in general, that satisfied less exotic wants felt the impact of increased payrolls that resulted from replacing those who were on vacation. Some workers established new homes, still others established new and larger families, and all of them demanded more consumers' goods and had larger disposable incomes with which to acquire them.

All these developments were forces that were let loose at the level of free enterprise that tended to keep the operation of the American economy in high gear.

Tourism

When tourist motoring was first encouraged, the philosophy was to route cars through the main streets of cities and towns all across the country. Motorists themselves did not object to this because of the many types of services they and their cars required. Merchants felt that tourist trade increased their volume of sales and brought new money into their communities. When the volume of through traffic became so large that it interfered with local traffic and tended to cause accidents, policemen were assigned to important street intersections to direct traffic. Later traffic lights were installed, and manpower was conserved for other aspects of law enforcement. Roads and streets that had been constructed to accommodate horse-drawn vehicles became entirely inadequate for motor vehicles; and bottlenecks to a continued forward movement of cars presented problems to city, county, and state authorities. One solution was to designate one-way streets; another was to widen them, and still another was to reroute motor trucks to keep them out of congested areas. Off-street parking was another partial solution to relieving congestion on city streets. Finally, some authorities saw the necessity for widening streets and highways to four lanes with parking prohibited on them. Highways were divided not only to make possible greater speeds without sacrificing safety, but to reduce the number of accidents.

Revenues to cover the costs of these improvements were derived immediately from the sale of bonds which were retired more gradually over a period of years by the collection of gasoline taxes which ranged from three cents per gallon to seven cents at the state level to which the federal government added one cent, or sometimes two, to cover its costs of constructing highways. Local governmental units have succeeded in shifting some of the costs of widening and paving streets by having some of them designated as either federal or state highways. Streets that have been so designated have been maintained by the local authorities once they have been constructed. It seems that each new improvement tended to create its own new traffic hazards as rapidly as it relieved old ones.

The next approach to relieve congestion and to enable cars to keep moving on the streets was the construction of throughways in cities, superhighways in the country. The former usually were elevated above the street level so that there was no cross traffic; neither were there signal lights to impede progress. Entrances and exits were provided at strategic intervals, and minimum speeds of 40 miles an hour were required.

The Interstate Highway System. As was discussed in Chapter 27, the federal government became involved in highway construction on a new level when it charted an interstate highway system in the name of national defense. The only time these roads have been needed for this purpose was on the occasion of the Cuban crisis in 1962 at which time the construction of the interstate highway system was too spotty to be of much assistance. However, highways that had been given federal designation were used; and local traffic suffered much inconvenience, many accidents, and some loss of life. If nothing else, this crisis served to emphasize the need for a federal system of highways upon which high speeds could be maintained without the hazards of cross traffic and frequent stopping and starting.

State Superhighways. In addition to the interstate (federal) highway systems, many states have constructed systems of superhighways. The mention of the Pennsylvania Turnpike, the New Jersey Turnpike, and the Garden State Highway will serve to define this level of highway construction and operation. Massachusetts, Connecticut, New York, New Jersey, Ohio, and many other states to the west and south have their own state highway systems and still others are under construction. Some of them have air spotters to detect cars that are in distress and to dispatch service trucks to their assistance. States have permitted filling stations, restaurants, and motels along their rights-of-way; and some states have charged tolls for driving on these roads.

Impacts of Tourism. At many of the important highway interchanges, motels, restaurants, and filling stations have been erected. Depending upon many indeterminate factors, three or more filling stations have been erected at interchanges. Likewise, chain motels and restaurants have been located nearby in order to attract tourists. The impacts of interstate highways by-passing many communities entirely and circumventing others have not been determined with any degree of certainty, except in some few localities. One thing is certain: other routes through cities have been cleared for more strictly local traffic, and accident hazards have been reduced.

In recent years there has been a mushroom growth of hamburger, sandwich and soft drink stands throughout the countryside and along streets over which some through traffic has been routed. Tourists have saved time and money, and their children have eaten more en route than had they patronized regular dining rooms or cafes. Another impact of the automobile and tourism has been the decline in the patronage of hotels. Tourists have found that motels have offered many conveniences that hotels could not offer and at no sacrifice of quality of accommodations and service.

An impact of tourism and the proliferation of motels, restaurants, and filling stations has been felt by the construction industry and by the manufacturers of the equipment and furnishings for these types of establishments. Additional employment has been provided those who have wanted full-time and part-time work in staffing these new business establishments.

Sports

Thousands of employees of firms that manufacture sports equipment and uniforms and those who sell these products owe their full-time employment to the fact that their customers have leisure time. If sports enthusiasts did not have the time to witness such events, to read about them in the press, to watch televised games, and to listen to radio broadcasts, not only would their participants not have jobs, but all of those who are connected with their management, their promotion, and their administration would be compelled to seek employment in competition with others who are gainfully employed in other lines of work.

Amateur and professional sports are attracting more and more of the services of manpower, both in direct participation and indirectly in management and in public relations. Capital investments in sports arenas and in manufacturing capital have reached major proportions. Sporting events are attracting larger crowds than ever and this in spite of increases in prices of admission. In addition, radio and television networks are spending several million dollars annually for the privilege of broadcasting and televising such events as professional golf, bowling, basketball, wrestling, hockey, baseball, and football. In the latter sport, post-season bowl games of college football and championship games of professional football climax the regular seasons of broadcasting and televising games weekly. In baseball, World Series broadcasts and television presentations are heard and seen by additional millions of persons. The costs of such programs are paid for by producers of soft drinks, shaving equipment, tobacco products, and other consumers' goods that appeal more to men than to women.

Professional Baseball and Its Impacts. Professional baseball has expanded its major league teams to 12 in each of two leagues. Televising major league games has resulted in a reduction in the number of minor leagues. Over a span of seven months each year, 29 players on each team participate in 162 games. Each team, of necessity, plays 81 games away from the cities in which they have been awarded franchises. Since these games usually are played in series of three or four games each, over 290 players, managers, and other team personnel make several visits to each of the other 11 cities in their respective leagues. For doing so, they are paid salaries that range from the required minimum of $10,000 a year to an estimated $70,000 or $80,000 or more for exceptional players whose talents are an attraction. In addition, they receive a per diem stipend while away from their home cities. Many players receive additional compensation for endorsing such goods as soft drinks, hair tonics and shampoos, tobacco products, and deodorants.

In order to accommodate the patrons of professional baseball, 22 stadiums have been constructed with seating capacities that range from 30,000 to 77,000. The need for parking space nearby has involved the relocation of housing and business facilities. In some cities, the construction of new stadiums and adequate parking areas has been incorporated in urban redevelopment and rehabilitation programs. Major league baseball has attracted not less than 18,600,000 persons per season since 1960, and a record number of 25,203,229 enthusiasts passed through turnstiles in 1966. Attendance at World Series games varies with the size of the parks in which they are played and with the number of games played. In 1968, a total of 379,670 persons spent $3,018,113 for tickets to seven games. In addition, untold thousands of persons traveled hundreds of miles to witness these events and spent thousands of dollars on travel, overnight accommodations, eating, and incidental expenses.

Recognizing that attendance at sporting events varies widely from city to city and from year to year, figures gathered several years ago showed that in all cities having major league teams, over $180 million of business per year owes its origin to baseball. In addition, the salaries of all the players and those who are connected with major league teams carry the total for one season to gigantic proportions.

Football. Professional football has reached a peak of popularity with fans and players alike. Many athletes who have earned college and professional degrees have been lured into the game by the prospect of relatively large salaries to augment their starting compensations in their chosen fields. Their years of actual play are few, and the danger of injury is ever present.

From August through December and sometimes into January, six to ten major professional games are played each week. They draw from 20,000 to 60,000 or more persons per game. As with professional baseball, transport agencies, restaurants and refreshment dispensaries, hotels and motels derive the largest financial returns. Not to be overlooked is the extra consumption of gasoline and the payment of gasoline taxes into state treasuries.

College and university football seasons consist of from seven to ten games a year. Every weekend from the middle of September to December several hundred thousand spectators witness college football on a hundred or more college campuses. Traveling squads consist of from 30 to 50 or more active players, several coaches and trainers, cheerleaders and, for many games, large college bands—all of whom have to be transported, fed, and housed over weekends.

Football fans have been notoriously free spenders, especially those who are away from their homes. An estimate of $20 per day over and above the cost of admission has been considered conservative. It is not surprising that chambers of commerce vie with each other in their efforts to schedule college and university football games in their own cities. Just one game a year that is played before a full stadium of 100,000 persons causes $2,000,000 of "new" money to be put into circulation locally. In addition to regular season games there are five post-season bowl games, each of which is played before from 60,000 to 100,000 fans. Ten lesser bowl games attract in excess of 10,000 spectators each. Senior bowl, East-West, North-South, and Shriner benefit games are witnessed by from 20,000 to 60,000 or more each. Consider the fact that members of these squads are rewarded for their services by receiving gold watches, luggage, or some other suitable items of value, and the local merchants from whom they are purchased profit handsomely from such business which incurs no overhead costs to supply.

High School Sports. High school football and basketball games that are played all across the country attract millions of supporters. Many of these games have been played at night on fields that have been lighted brilliantly for the occasion. Electric light and power companies have found that consumption has compensated somewhat for a decline in the industrial and commercial use of electrical energy after six o'clock. The principal impact of midget and little league football is felt by the suppliers of uniforms and equipment. Local business may be funneled to one or two retail stores which may be called upon to equip a hundred or more players.

Horse Racing. If horse racing ever was the sport of kings, its patrons no longer are restricted to royalty. In 1966, over 23 million persons made the turnstiles at racetracks click during 3,454 days of harness racing in 16 states. Over one and a half times that many persons, 37,891,966, attended race meetings in 27 states in 4,292 days of thoroughbred racing. Over 61 million racing enthusiasts placed $5,539,595,735 in pari-mutuel machines, of which $385,732,930 went into the coffers of state treasuries. In addition to the revenue that 27 states derived from major racetracks, 12 states collected an additional $5,856,497 from racing events that were held in connection with county fairs.

Considering horse racing solely as a source of revenue to the states in which racing has been legalized, in 1966, 27 states collected a total of $385,733,000 from the operation of pari-mutuel machines. Assuming that this amount of money, had it not been derived from the operation of race-tracks, would have been raised from levies upon property, Table 28-6 reveals that in New Jersey, property owners were relieved of an additional millage of 1.1 or $1.10 per thousand dollars of assessed property valuation. Property owners in the state of New York were relieved of an additional burden of $2.73 per thousand dollars of assessed valuation. This helps explain the tendency to authorize more days of racing per year, or to open new tracks.

Table 28-6

Millage on Assessed Property Valuations Represented by the Receipts of Pari-mutuel Taxes in Selected States and Totals in 27 States—1966

State	Assessed Valuation of Real Property (millions)	Property Tax Collections (000)	Pari-mutuel Tax Collections (000)	Property Assessments Represented by Pari-mutuel Collections	
				Per $100	Per $1,000
California	$ 33,508	$188,688	$ 46,806	$0.131	$ 1.31
Florida	26,928	571	37,757	0.140	1.40
Illinois	31,072	789	31,005	0.099	.99
Kentucky	11,811	22,573	4,118	0.034	.34
Massachusetts	13,837	431	15,558	0.113	1.13
New Jersey	26,767	2,228	29,418	0.110	1.10
New York	51,469	7,958	140,906	0.273	2.73
Totals	195,392	223,238	305,568	0.900	9.00
Totals—27 States	292,650	575,318	385,733	1.390	13.90

Source: U. S. Department of Commerce, Bureau of the Census; Census of Governments, *Taxable Property Values* (Washington: U. S. Government Printing Office, 1968), p. 33; and *Facts and Figures of Government Finance, 1967* (New York City: The Tax Foundation, Inc., 1967), pp. 181 and 205. Adapted.

MARKETING PATTERNS

Shopping Centers

One of the most spectacular patterns in the development of markets, particularly after 1950, was the construction of shopping centers in areas that are some distance from downtown shopping districts. Neighborhood store sites were expanded to shopping centers, and entirely new shopping centers were laid out with an indefinite number and variety of retail stores signed up to become tenants. The core store was almost always a huge supermarket type of grocery or food store. Others may have been drug, variety, hardware, bakery, shoe, department, men's wear, ladies' specialty, paint, or package store that dispensed liquors; cafeterias and retail outlets of mail-order firms were also common. Downtown department stores have found that branch stores in shopping centers have helped them retain their customers in competition with other stores that dealt in like quality merchandise. A customer lure was not only ample free parking space, but parking without a time limit. Another attraction to shopping centers was an expansion of the one-stop idea that aided in the promotion of supermarkets.

Trading Stamps

Trading stamps had been used on a rather limited basis for many years, but by the 1950's they became one of the most competitive tools at the retail level. Department stores may have been the principal outlet that gave trading stamps to their customers; but they were being used by supermarkets and small grocery stores, filling stations, and stores that retailed many other kinds of goods. Strong were the arguments for and against effectiveness of their use, but the fact remains that many store managers arrived at decisions that their use cost more than the value of the added volume of business they attracted. Several studies have been made in order to determine the conditions under which their use was profitable. Such studies revealed that the volume of business had to increase at least 15 percent in order for the cost to be returned in terms of net revenue from sales. Some organizations used stamps purely as a defensive gesture to hold their customers rather than to obtain new ones. In many instances such use was at the cost of raising retail prices slightly. Stamps have been used on special occasions to promote quick and ready sales of automobiles and to promote sales of houses by their owners. Their effectiveness in overcoming buyer resistance on such occasions has never been proved and is open to question.

QUESTIONS FOR REVIEW

1. How do you account for the large number of industrial mergers that have taken place in recent years?

2. (a) Why have banks been compelled to become larger?

(b) Explain the role of bank mergers in the process of their becoming larger.

(c) How has the Department of Justice looked upon bank mergers? Explain some of the complications that have arisen out of the enforcement of this viewpoint.

3. Why have railroads merged in recent years?

4. Come to a definite conclusion regarding the influence of trading stamps and their impacts upon retail outlets.

5. Why do individual persons purchase shares of corporate stock?

6. How have the existence of interstate highways affected business in local communities?

7. How has tourism affected business in cities that are located on important state and national highways?

8. Why do large cities vie with one another to become sites of sporting events that will attract large crowds?

9. (a) What has been one of the outstanding developments in the organization of marketing since about 1950?

(b) How do you account for this development?

SUGGESTED READINGS

Bining, Arthur C., and Thomas C. Cochran. *The Rise of American Economic Life.* 4th ed. New York City: Charles Scribner's Sons, 1964. Chapter 32.

Dillard, Dudley. *Economic Development of the North Atlantic Community.* Englewood Cliffs, N. J.: Prentice-Hall, Inc., 1967. Chapter 38.

Fite, Gilbert C., and Jim E. Reese. *An Economic History of the United States.* 2d ed. Boston: Houghton Mifflin Company, 1965. Chapter 33.

Galbraith, John K. *The Affluent Society.* Boston, Mass.: Houghton Mifflin Company, 1958. Chapter 24.

Krooss, Herman E. *American Economic Development.* 2d ed. Englewood Cliffs, N. J.: Prentice-Hall, Inc., 1966. Chapter 7.

Larrabee, Eric, and Rolf Meyersohn (eds.). *Mass Leisure.* New York City: The Free Press, 1958.

Leuchtenberg, William E. "The Second Industrial Revolution," *American Economic History: Essays in Interpretation,* edited by Stanley Coben and Forest G. Hill. Philadelphia: J. B. Lippincott Co., 1966.

McGuire, Joseph W. *Business and Society.* New York City: McGraw-Hill Book Company, 1963. Chapter 9.

Oswald, Rudolph. "The Growth of Longer Vacations," *The American Federationist* (November, 1967), pp. 19-22.

Chapter 29

THE PERFORMANCE OF THE

AMERICAN ECONOMY

There is no absolute measurement of how well the American economy has functioned. If the standard of evaluation be in terms of full employment, it has not functioned well. If the standard be in terms of equality of incomes and in the ownership of wealth, there remains much to be desired. If economic imperialism be the goal of attainment, the sphere of economic influence has not been extended far beyond the horizons that had been laid out by 1914. Statehood for Alaska and Hawaii has incorporated these areas more solidly into the structure of the American economy; on the other hand, the Philippines have been given their political independence.

More detailed analyses will be made in this chapter on (1) how well the American economy has utilized the basic institutions of capitalism; (2) how smoothly or how evenly our economy has functioned; (3) how well our economy has functioned to prepare for war and to wage warfare; (4) why government, particularly at the federal level, has participated more and more in establishing a legal framework within which economic enterprise must function; (5) how well the economy of the United States has become integrated with the economies of other nations; and last but by no means least, (6) how well our economy has generated a national income that has enabled its people to enjoy higher levels of living and more leisure time.

CAPITALISM

Since the economy of the United States, from the early Colonial Period down to the present, has developed within the framework of capitalism, one measure of its performance may be made in terms of the extent to which its fundamental institutions have functioned, together with the psychological attitude of the people. The economy has passed through the trading, industrial, and financial phases of its development and has arrived at or entered into the security stage. The acceptance of the corporate form of business organization was accompanied by the issuance of corporate stocks and bonds, with which financial instruments people gradually are becoming familiar. Attempts by persons or groups to obtain control of corporate managements via stock market transactions rather than by making direct approaches to managements they wished to control is evidence of the capitalist spirit.

Private Property

That private property has been sacred is evidenced by the emphasis the courts have placed upon it in rendering decisions in which rights of persons and rights of property have been in conflict. Since the New Deal Program, rights of persons have been given more consideration by the courts.

Dependent Wage Earning Class

Basic to the successful operation of a capitalistic system is the presence of a dependent labor class. Lack of such a segment of the population was one of the early barriers to the industrialization and commercialization of our economy. How this void in our economic organization has been overcome constitutes an important chapter in our development. Labor at some levels may still be in short supply, but not because of a shortage of people or because they aspire to becoming entrepreneurs. Social security and unemployment insurance have made idleness more attractive to some persons than earning their own way in the world. Government at all levels has become interested in increasing the skills of our youth in order that they may become adjusted to the requirements of a highly mechanized system of production. Vocational training is being urged upon high school students who do not intend to graduate and upon those who are not going to attend institutions of higher learning. Service in all branches of the Armed Forces prepares young men to find places in civilian life. Many are the men who have re-entered civilian life at higher levels of technology and of training than they were qualified for when they entered service.

Even though labor has become more class-conscious than formerly and has acquired a higher degree of class solidarity, it is no longer as completely a nonvested interest group as it was prior to World War I. Many workers own land and improvements thereon. Wage earners are registered owners of corporate stock. Many of them own corporate and government bonds, and insurance companies list wage earners among their policyholders.

Production for Market

No fact that is related to our economy is more generally accepted than that it is dominated by the market. Transportation and communication technologies have widened markets; and at the same time they have consolidated small, separate markets into larger, more homogeneous ones. They have done away with space, and they have reduced the time factor in the marketing process.

Money

The profit system presupposes the use of money as a medium of exchange, as a standard of value, and as a store of value. Most of these functions have been subrogated to bank deposits; but the dollar continues to function as the standard of value, which is that thing in terms of which the values of all commodities and services are expressed. The dollar still lacks stability of value, which it should have if it is to function smoothly as a store of value. Its lack of this quality has given rise to business cycles, which topic will be presented to the reader later in this chapter.

At the consumer level, the credit card has come to occupy an important place, not only in enabling producers to capture the trade of consumers, but in doing away with the hand-to-hand use of money. Bank credit has been substituted therefor, and the dollar is being used more efficiently. Less actual cash has to be carried by individuals whether they are on tour or are buying in communities in which they reside and are well known.

Alterations have now been made in the composition of our subsidiary coins, but they are not basic to our monetary system, and they do not impart any value to our monetary base. These changes were made in order to release government silver for use in industry. There are no more, no fewer standard monetary units—dollars—in circulation because of them.

The United States has evolved some kind of managed currency system with the Board of Governors of the Federal Reserve System at the helm. Free coinage of standard monetary metals is a thing of the past. Monies of all denominations are issued on government account. There is nothing alarming about this as long as the Board remains politically independent of government control, or of domination by Treasury fiscal policy. Call it government control, if you prefer, but the fact remains that, except in time of the two world wars, and up through the Korean action, Federal Reserve policies have not been formulated to augment fiscal policies or to aid the Treasury Department in carrying out its fiscal operations.

Banking

Our banking system has not functioned, nor is it functioning now, as a homogeneous system of banks. As long as more than 50 percent of the commercial banks of the United States are nonmember banks there is an element of weakness and of potential danger, even though collectively they own only 15 percent of the assets of all commercial banks, make only 15 percent of the loans, and have only 16 percent of the demand deposits against which checks can be drawn. Even though the proportions of nonmember banks, their assets, loans, and deposits to member banks differ from those of the 1920's, it was the steady and continual withdrawal of deposits of the nonmember banks throughout the decade that weakened the position of member banks in larger cities which served in correspondent relationships to these banks.

The strength of our banking system may no longer be measured or evaluated entirely in terms of membership of commercial banks in the Federal Reserve System. The primary function of the Federal Reserve System is to implement the money and credit policies that have been delineated by the Board of Governors and thus impart stability to the entire system.

Federal Deposit Insurance Corporation and Insured Deposits. Membership in the Federal Deposit Insurance Corporation has imparted strength to banks and confidence of depositors in their banks that did not ensue from membership in the Federal Reserve System. The number of individual accounts that have been covered by bank insurance has been proportionately larger than the number of insured banks. On the occasion of each of eight random call dates from October, 1934, to September, 1955, over 96 percent of the deposit accounts in commercial banks were fully protected. For the same dates, the percentage of total deposits that were insured varied from a low of 37.7 percent on September 24, 1941 to a high of 55.1 percent on September 21, 1955. Except for September, 1941, the percentage of insured deposits to total deposits increased from 44.1 in 1934 to 55.1 in 1955 and to 97.2 in 1967.

Table 29-1

Accounts Fully and Partially Insured and Deposits Insured in All Banks in Continental United States—1955 and 1964

Date	Number of Banks	Number of Accounts (000)			Percentage of Accounts	
		Total	Fully Insured	Partially Insured	Fully Insured	Partially Insured
Sept. 21, 1955	13,476	129,308	127,027	2,281	98.2	1.8
Nov. 18, 1964	13,787	174,202	169,264	4,938	97.2	2.8

Table 29-1 (Continued)

Year	Total	Deposits Insured (000)			Uninsured (000)	Percentage of Total Deposits	
		Total Insured	In Fully Protected Accounts	In Partially Protected Accounts	In Partially Insured Accounts	Insured	Not Insured
1955	$202,396	$111,535	$ 88,720	$22,815	$ 90,861	55.1	44.9
1964	336,847	183,739	134,359	49,380	153,108	54.5	45.5

Source: *Annual Report* (Washington: Federal Deposit Insurance Corporation, 1955), p. 62; and *Statistical Tables* (Washington: Federal Deposit Insurance Corporation, November, 1955), p. 2.

Insured Accounts. From the psychological point of view, the percentage of individual accounts that were completely insured may have been more significant than the percentage of commercial banks that were insured.

Since complete coverage of deposits in commercial banks was extended to $10,000 in 1950 and to $15,000 in 1966, increases in the number of accounts that were fully protected reflect the increases in maximum coverages more than they do increases in the number of new accounts of less than $5,000. In 1955, approximately 55 percent of total deposits in insured banks were insured. On December 30, 1967, complete coverage of deposits was estimated to have been 58.2 percent. The 45 percent of total deposits that were not insured were found in the 1.8 percent and 2.8 percent respectively of the accounts that were partially insured. Of the insured deposits, 43.8 percent and 39.8 percent were found in the 98.2 percent and 97.2 percent respectively of the accounts that were fully protected. Twenty percent and 24.3 percent respectively of the deposits in the accounts that were partially protected were fully covered. On October 16, 1966, maximum coverage was raised to $15,000, and complete coverage was extended to 99 percent of all accounts.

Table 29-2

Bank Suspensions in the United States—1964-1967

| Year | Total | Number of Banks | | | | Total | Deposits (000) | | | |
| | | Member Banks | | State and Private | | | Member Banks | | State and Private | |
		National	State Member	In-sured	Non-insured		National	State Member	In-sured	Non-insured
1964	8	1	..	6	1	$22,022	3,419	..	$18,174	429
1965	7	2	..	1	4	44,857	41,952	..	434	2,471
1966	1	..	..	1	..	669	..	..	669	..
1967	4	1	1	2	..	10,802	3,814	3,839	3,149	..

Source: U. S. Department of Commerce, Bureau of the Census, *Statistical Abstract of the United States: 1968* (Washington: U. S. Government Printing Office, 1968), p. 447. Adapted.

Bank Suspensions. Membership in the Federal Deposit Insurance Corporation has not been an ironclad guarantee against bank failures, but it has served somewhat effectively to soften their impacts. It has helped, also, in preventing serious runs on other banks due solely to a lack of confidence in banks and not because of any known weaknesses in particular ones. Many developments within our banking system have taken place, one effect of which has been to strengthen individual banks. It must be kept in mind that it takes good bankers to operate banks successfully in the long run and from the point of view of sound banking. In the years 1964-67 inclusive, only five member banks suspended payments. In 1964-67, four member banks actually closed their doors. By contrast, there were ten closings of state banks that were insured. Five banks that had not protected their depositors by becoming members of the Federal Deposit Insurance Corporation closed their doors during this same period. Table 29-2 indicates the volume of deposits in the banks in each of the respective categories that failed.

Instruments of Credit Control. Basically, commercial banks are still independent unit banks. Systemic features have been introduced through the organization of the Federal Reserve System. Impacts of open market operations and implementations of Regulations T and U of the Securities and Exchange Commission have fallen on all commercial banks. Moral suasion affects member banks directly, and changes in rediscount rates and legal reserve requirements may indirectly affect nonmember banks as well as member banks. Changes in instruments of control that compel banks to alter their volume of credit outstanding are active; those that permit such changes are permissive in their effects. Table 29-3 affords a summary of the level of degree of effectiveness of the several instruments.

Table 29-3

Instruments of Credit Control Together with the Degree of Effectiveness of Each

Instruments of Credit Control	Active		Permissive	
	Increase	Decrease	Increase	Decrease
Moral suasion			x	x
Change in rediscount rate			x	x
Change in legal reserve requirements	x			x
Open market purchases			x	
sales	x			
Changes in margin requirements	x			x

Freedom of Enterprise and the Profit System

Freedom of enterprise exists more in theory than it does in practice. Capital requirements have become so demanding that they restrict both the entry and departure of persons into and out of business. Even though farm staples are still sold on highly competitive markets, high costs of land and of financing mechanized farming make it more difficult for persons to take up farming. Difficulties in liquidating farm values in land and capital equipment create situations in which farm operators strive to reduce negative profits (losses) instead of making positive ones.

State and local governments have placed many restrictions upon freedom of enterprise in the name of protection and safety. Zoning laws and long-range planning by municipal and county boards restrict the uses to which land may be put. Examinations and other requirements limit the movement of persons into occupations and professions.

One of the deterrents to the exercise of free enterprise in entering any of the professions is the cost of preparing for the respective profession. Length of training is an additional cost over and above the monetary expense for tuition, books, and supplies, and possibly special uniforms when and where required. Basic college training is essential to entering upon advanced programs that are required in all specialty areas. Advanced degrees are required for those who enter the teaching profession. In addition to professional degrees, in some areas years of internship equivalent to apprenticeship are required. After basic degrees have been acquired, one or more years of specialized study and experience are required before the specialist is prepared to meet his clients at the level of sophistication they expect.

Except for business operations that are owned and operated by government, such as the postal system, and others that are subsidized, profits are measures of success or failure. Even in times of rising prices, business firms fail because their costs rise more than do their gross receipts, both of which are functions of price.

CYCLICAL FLUCTUATIONS

Our economy is always in one phase or another of a business cycle, and at any given time it is sometimes difficult, if not impossible, to discern just what phase is in progress. Even since 1946, when Congress passed the Employment Act, we have experienced several periods of relative recession that have been accompanied by increases in the number of unemployed persons. Unemployment is the tragedy of an economic depression, the same as it is at any other time. It may occur in an individual form; it may occur in any given industry; it may be prevalent in regional areas; and its existence may not recognize any of these boundaries or limitations, in which case it may point to a depression, or a recession. The latter is a milder form of the former, and there is no known line of demarcation between them.

While the existence of unemployment has been known at any given time, sometimes it has been difficult to designate it as denoting a recession or a depression until after the slowing down process of the economy has been checked and a turn for the better has manifested itself. Only then and in terms of the decline in prices, increases in unemployment, increases in the volume of bank reserves, decreases in business profits, and increases in business failures have certain phases of the business cycle been designated as depressions. Interest rates have not always been satisfactory criteria of phases of business cycles, nor have they had the influence that governmental fiscal policies have had upon them. Business failures have not always been satisfactory criteria because they have occurred during periods of prosperity as well as in periods of depression or recession. Causes of business failures have been more reliable criteria than the fact itself. Even there, confusion may result from the fact that insufficient capital has caused failures during periods of accelerated activity as well as during periods of slowdowns.

It may be well to bring out again that several correctives to cyclical fluctuations have been built into the American economy which have tended to stabilize the pace of economic activity throughout the years, at least since the close of World War II. Other correctives have been applied to stabilize the economy. Years ago Dr. Wesley Clair Mitchell called attention to certain forces, which he called *self-generating,* that were inherent in a system of free captialism and that tended to correct cyclical trends, but not until after much damage had been done.

Social security payments to the unemployed and to retirees have put money into circulation that has not measured degrees or facts of productivity. The fact is that these payments have been paid when their recipients have become unproductive. For these persons the power to consume has not depended upon their power to produce; and the fact of continued consumption has not only shortened the duration of unemployment for many workers, it has prevented additional slowdowns or shutdowns of other business firms which would have increased the extent and seriousness of unemployment.

Since 1946 the application of the instruments of credit control that have been presented in Table 29-3 have proved to be effective in stabilizing the growth of the American economy.

Programs of public works, including flood control, roadbuilding, and public health and sanitation, have offered opportunities to correct slowdowns of the American economy and will continue to do so.

Higher levels of communication techniques must be considered to be among the forces that have exerted control over cyclical fluctuations. They are intangible forces that have defied measurement. Radio broadcasting and news programs over television, personal interviews with prominent personalities over both media, the writings of newspaper columnists, financial and business services whose information has been spread far beyond the limits of their subscription lists when cited by business, and news media that have been read by millions of persons have become instruments of social control, whether intended or not.

PREPARATION FOR WAR

If the test of preparation for war be applied to the functioning of the American economy, let it be remembered first that from its very beginning our economy has been organized along the lines of freedom of enterprise. The profit motive was the impelling incentive that gave direction to the facets of our economic organization. Organization for war has been limited to the needs of an adequate defense.

By 1917, when the United States became an active participant in a conflict of worldwide proportions, the wheels of American industry had been oiled by the impacts of orders from European countries which had been at war for three years. Entrepreneurs had hesitated to expand the capacities of their plants because of uncertainties concerning the duration of hostilities and the problems that were connected with writing off capital outlays that had been incurred because of the war. Since the demand for war materiel exceeded the capacities of American industrial units, time was consumed in constructing the additional equipment that was needed to increase volume of output to the levels that were dictated by the needs of our military forces both here and abroad. The government gave encouragement to this expansion by permitting an accelerated depreciation of such values for income tax purposes. A similar situation confronted the government in 1941 and a similar solution was effected. In both instances, organized labor, or at least its most influential segment, pledged itself to support the war effort. Following the successful termination of both conflicts, many of the facilities that had been constructed by government and by industry were dismantled. Others were placed on a standby basis until they had become obsolete due to the development of new and higher levels of technologies.

Even though there have been no formal declarations of war since 1945, commitments were made to the governments of Korea and of South Viet Nam under the terms of which men and materiel were sent to these countries. While heartaches and inconveniences have resulted from these actions, the problems of organizing the productive factors were met successfully although, again, somewhat tardily. The demands of our Armed Forces overseas have been met without disturbing the levels of living of the American people. In fact, these levels have continued to rise.

GOVERNMENT IN RELATION TO BUSINESS

Just as nongovernmental associations have made rules and regulations to govern the conduct of their members, so has government been compelled to regulate the patterns of behavior of its members. All persons in all walks of life and at all ages have not been able to take care of their own interests and of their own welfare with equal degrees of success. Government has stepped in to lighten the economic impacts of the operations of our complex capitalistic economy upon those who have been victimized by it. On the other hand, many persons have found themselves in fortuitous situations that enabled them to benefit greatly at the expense of others. Corrective federal legislation has been more concerned with relieving the "expense of others" than it has with reducing the benefits of the relatively few.

Welfare and Defense

Even when situations have arisen that have affected the general welfare of the people and the economy, Presidents of the United States have hesitated to intervene in disputes between organized labor and management. When national defense has been threatened by interruptions in transportation or industrial production, Presidential interventions have been effective in restoring industrial peace.

Inflation Control

Uncontrolled inflation is just as dangerous in undermining the morale of the masses and in injuring their general welfare as is some less subtle force. Following announcements that prices of some basic commodities would be raised, government has been successful in preventing such increases from taking effect. In other instances, it has pressured management to roll back price increases that had been put into effect. Stockpiles of copper, aluminum, and silver have been liquidated in whole or in part when the flow of these metals to the market has been retarded or stopped entirely.

Inflation is inherent in the market system of the United States. The increases in disposable income, which reflect higher productivity, the independent bargaining position of labor, the increased level of management proficiency, and the achievement of profits for entrepreneurs generate such a tendency toward inflation. The individual in his dual role as producer and consumer is more able over a period of time to pay higher prices for goods out of the increased earnings he receives from producing those goods.

The persistent decrease in the dollar's value in the waning years of the 1960's has created much concern in both the private and public sectors of the economy. In an attempt to restore price stability without a disproportionate increase in unemployment, the federal government has taken several steps. The surtax of 1968 and the increase in the discount rate and reserve requirements of commercial banks by the Federal Reserve Board of Governors are examples of the government's attempt to restore price stability. The following are suggestions that have been made for restoring reasonable stability of costs and prices: (1) alter interest rates and build confidence in the dollar by creating a budget surplus; (2) continue the 1968 surtax and prevent increases in spending; (3) restrict the use of credit; (4) schedule annual meetings of the representatives of labor, management, and government to agree upon policies that are needed for growth without inflation; (5) add federal resources to the efforts of business to reduce unemployment; and, (6) reactivate federal agencies to deal with cost, prices, stability, and economic growth.

Minimum Wage Legislation

While it has been the expressed policy of government that increases in minimum wages not be used to justify increases in prices, industrial leaders have found that when these increases were not related to increases in productivity of their employees, unit costs of production increased. Margins of prices over costs represented profits which were the impelling motive to entrepreneurial efforts. As these margins were lowered, profits declined and producers were compelled to raise prices. This was not difficult to accomplish in the face of rising disposable incomes to the masses. Legal minimum wages applied to unskilled workers, many of whom were unorganized. Even so, in order to maintain traditional differentials between their wages and those of many grades of semiskilled and skilled workers, wages of the latter groups were raised upon the expiration of existing wage contracts.

Minimum wage legislation has accomplished its objective of increasing wage incomes of both unskilled and skilled workers who are employed. Lines of people awaiting job offers at employment offices all over the country give mute testimony to the fact that many persons are idle because they will not work for less than minimum wages, even though they are not covered under the law. Potential employers reorganize their labor forces, obtain machines to do the work, or leave it undone. Minimum wages have not guaranteed jobs to all workers.

In February, 1969, the minimum wage was $1.60 an hour. Labor leaders have already announced that they will strive for $2.00. Commodity prices have been rising ever since minimum wages have been effective, so that increases in wage incomes have not represented or permitted proportionate increases in the levels of living of their recipients.

The student will recognize that the protective function has motivated government in its efforts to regulate the economic activities of its citizens.

Fiscal Policies

There has been no evidence that fiscal policies at the state and local levels have been related to or determined by efforts to stimulate the tempo of our economy or to retard its rate of growth. The same cannot be said in describing or analyzing fiscal policies at the federal level. The Employment Act of 1946 made the federal government responsible for preventing serious inflationary movements and for providing stimuli for a laggard economy. The government has attempted to prevent uncontrolled expansion or inflation, as well as periods of falling prices, increased unemployment, and business recessions.

Budget Considerations

Balancing the budget at the national level is no longer an objective of fiscal authorities. Federal expenditures have been lowered on occasion more in line with lowered costs of national defense and of the functional requirements of the government than to bring them within the limits of tax receipts. Tax authorities at state and federal levels have found that given rates of taxation have yielded progressively larger tax revenues as national income has increased and as commodity prices have risen. Gross receipts have increased; commodity prices to which sales taxes have been applied have risen; more gallons of gasoline have been sold because more families had one car, more families had two cars, and more trucks and buses were on the road. Electric-powered streetcars have all but been replaced by gasoline or diesel-powered buses. People have become more mobile; they have moved their residences from urban areas into suburban communities. More gasoline filling

stations have been put into service than have been withdrawn, which has increased the values of properties on tax roles of state and local governments.

Included in the fiscal policies of government has been the movement to
increase the wages and salaries of government employees who numbered
approximately 3.25 million more in 1967 than in 1960. This trend must
be borne in mind when considering the aspects of total employment regardless
of who pays wages and salaries and from what sources they have been
derived.

Whether the decision to aid in the construction of an interstate highway
system was made in the name of national defense, whether it was made in the
name of aiding our economy by stimulating those industries that are
related directly or indirectly to the construction of highways, of giving employment to thousands of workers, of welding the American people into a more
homogeneous populace, of relieving traffic congestion on state and local highways and on city streets, or of increasing the factor of safety in driving, the
entire program has had fiscal consequences. If tax incomes have not been
sufficiently large to cover their costs, increments have been added to our
debt structure.

Tax policy has developed along the line of making more people contribute to the support of government rather than to levy taxes in accordance
with the ability-to-pay theory of taxation. This trend has been justified on
the premise that capital accumulation has resulted from high-level net incomes and not from low-level ones; and in order to assure the rate of
capital investment that is essential to the minimum rate of growth that will
promote economic prosperity and keep unemployment to a minimum, high-
level incomes should not be impaired by the application of high rates of
taxation to them. The implementation of this policy has placed the burden
of taxation upon those in the lower and middle-income brackets, say of
$25,000 and under.

INTEGRATION OF THE AMERICAN ECONOMY WITH
ECONOMIES OF OTHER NATIONS

The importance of our foreign trade has never been found in its volume
or in its value but in its marginal aspects. Foreign trade has been important
to those enterprises that have been individually affected by it. In 1953,
American steel was competitive in foreign markets in the sale of steel sections,
plate and cold rolled sheets, but not in the sale of merchant bars. By
January 1, 1961, it was not competitive in foreign markets in any of these
products, and the United States was a net importer of steel. The extent to
which the export of selected classes of commodities declined in world markets
between 1953 and 1961, expressed in round numbers, was: electrical
machinery, 11 percent; other machinery, 10 percent; transportation equipment, 12 percent; chemicals, 2 percent; textiles, 4 percent; and manufactures,
7 percent.

During the period in which the United States was sharing less and less in the world export trade, Germany and Japan increased their shares in the world export of the foregoing classes of commodities.

Losses of foreign markets for American manufactures have resulted in American manufacturers establishing branch plants in the Common Market area, which have been direct investments of American capital.

The exportation of finished products from the United States to this area were subject to the imposition of protective tariff rates upon their arrival at ports of entry. Since lower duties had been imposed upon raw materials and semimanufactured goods, the latter goods were exported from this country to branch plants that had been established abroad, where they were processed into completed products and distributed throughout the Common Market countries without being subjected to the protective rates that applied to similar products obtained directly from the United States. The exportation of these materials to foreign branch plants provided employment for American workers who otherwise may have been unemployed or who may have been compelled to work at lower wages in other domestic industries.

Portfolio investments abroad were dominant prior to 1920 and consisted of the purchase of foreign securities of foreign corporations or governments and in time deposits in foreign banks. For the entire decade of the 1950's, except for 1953, more American dollars were sent abroad in portfolio investments than were returned to this country in the form of interest payments thereon. On the other hand, throughout this same decade, the inflow of income from direct investments of American capital abroad was greater than the outflow of new capital investments. Most of the direct investments of American capital abroad since 1956 have been made in Canada. Manufacturing and mining segments of the economy have attracted almost one half of the $16,840 million that were invested in that one country in 1966 alone. The search for oil in Canada, its extraction and refinement, attracted an annual average of over $2,500 million of American capital from 1956 to 1962 inclusive and $3,606 million in 1966 alone.

Direction of American Foreign Trade

The pattern of American foreign trade in the span of years from 1946 to 1955 inclusive did not lend itself towards the restoration of prewar balances of commodity trade between the United States, and Europe and Africa. During these years our import trade with African countries became larger in values than our import trade with European countries and made the settlement of balances with Great Britain, France, and Germany difficult to attain. Since 1955, however, our import trade with these three countries has increased noticeably on the basis of comparative advantages that they have enjoyed in the production of manufactured products. Great Britain, France, and Germany no longer had many of the raw materials needed by American industries which then had to be obtained from other countries. This is where Africa came in. It still is true, however, that we continue to sell more commodities in these countries than we purchase from them.

In recent years our merchant marine, including ocean liners, has become smaller; and we have been forced to rely more and more upon ships of foreign registry to transport both our commodity imports and exports and our foreign tourist trade. The establishment of branches of American banks in foreign countries has made us less reliant upon banks of British charter in financing our foreign trade and in accommodating tourists. This is tantamount to a decrease in commodity imports on the balance of international payments account.

Direct Investment of Foreign Capital in American Industries

Foreign countries whose individuals and business firms have made direct investments in American industries, and which are still current, are the United Kingdom with $2.8 billion, Holland with $1.4 billion, and Switzerland with $949 million. West Germany is far behind with direct investments in the United States that total $247 million. Among the better known products that are made by companies in which large amounts of foreign capital are currently invested are those that carry the brand names of Nestle's Chocolate, Twenty Mule Team Borax, and the Crosse-Blackwell variety of canned foods, jams, and jellies. Raleigh cigarettes are made by Brown & Williamson Tobacco Company of Louisville, Kentucky, which is a subsidiary of a British concern. Dunlop Tires, Capital Records, the Volkswagen, and Shell Petroleum products are other well-known import commodities the purchase of which tends to lead to an unfavorable balance of international payments. The sale of Bayer aspirin, of the products of Dow Chemical Company, of Pittsburgh Coke and Chemical Company, and of Brown and Company, a producer of pulp and paper products in New England, supports the principle that, in a free competitive economy, price and the ability to satisfy wants are more significant in the marketplace than is the source of capital. There is a long list of American companies in which foreign investments loom large even to the extent of complete ownership and control.

NATIONAL INCOME

National income has become a statistical tool. Its use has made possible the measurement of many facets of our economy about which conjectural statements formerly were made, that could be supported only by citing data from the reports of the Bureau of the Census. Not only has the size of our national income in the abstract been of much concern, but the proportion which different segments of the economy have generated has facilitated a more accurate analysis of the American economy. The data that are presented in Table 29-4 confirm the amounts of our national income that were generated in selected years by each of ten segments of our economy, together with the relative importance of each segment in making these contributions. The relative decline of agriculture, fisheries, and forestry has been presented in terms of the number of people who made their livelihoods from

Table 29-4

National Income by Industry
(billions)

Industry	1929 Amount	Rank	1956 Amount	Rank	1960 * Amount	Rank	1967 Amount	Rank
Total National Income	$87.8		$349.4		$414.5		$649.6	
Manufacturing	21.9	1	109.3	1	125.8	1	196.3	1
Trade—Retail and Wholesale	13.4	2	57.3	2	64.4	2	95.9	2
Government and Government Enterprises	5.1	7	40.3	3	52.9	3	93.9	3
Services	10.3	4	37.0	4	44.4	5	74.7	4
Finance, Insurance, and Real Estate	12.7	3	32.1	5	45.9	4	70.4	5
Contract Construction	3.8	8	19.1	6	26.5	6	40.3	6
Transportation	6.6	6	16.8	7	18.2	7	26.1	7
Communications and Public Utilities	2.9	9	12.5	9	17.1	8	25.8	8
Agriculture, Forestry, and Fisheries	8.3	5	16.1	8	16.9	9	21.8	9
Mining †	2.0	10	6.3	10	..	..	..	..
Originating Outside United States	.8	..	2.0	..	2.3	..	4.5	..

* Alaska and Hawaii included first time in 1960.
† Included with Contract Construction in 1960 and 1967.

Source: U. S. Department of Commerce, Bureau of the Census, *Historical Statistics of the United States. Colonial Times to 1957*, 1960, p. 140. Also, U. S. Department of Commerce, Bureau of the Census, *Statistical Abstract* (Washington: U. S. Government Printing Office, 1968), p. 318.

these activities—the number of owners and of employees; but the national income approach to this analysis made the results even more convincing.

Sources

Much has been written over the years about the increases in government payrolls at all levels of government, but not until the national income analysis had been perfected were people able to determine just what government and government enterprises really contributed to the development and growth of the economy. In this respect, its importance is measured by its increase in rank from seventh place in 1929 to third position in 1956 by which time it had surpassed agriculture, fishing, forestry; finance, insurance, and real estate; transportation; and services in generating national incomes. Government payrolls have increased not only because additional names have been added, but also because wages and salaries of government employees have been increased. The impacts of raising minimum wage rates have been felt first by those workers who have been employed in government industries and in performing the functions of government.

Types

Since 1929 over 40 percent of our national income has emanated from activities in manufacturing and trade—both wholesale and retail—and agriculture, forestry, fishing has dropped in rank from eighth to ninth. In 1929, the latter ranked fifth. Even though mining activities have been contributing over twice as much per year since 1929 as they did in that year, they accounted for less than 2 percent of our total national income in 1963.

Data in Table 29-5 bring out very clearly and emphatically that almost two-thirds of our national income was and is distributed in the form of wages and salaries. At the same time it still is true that more individual

Table 29-5

National Income by Type of Income
(billions)

Type of Income	1929		1960 *		1967 *	
	Amount	Rank	Amount	Rank	Amount	Rank
Compensation of Employees	$51.1	1	$293.6	1	$469.7	1
Proprietors' Income	14.8	2	46.2	2	58.4	3
Rental Income of Persons	5.4	5	12.1	5	20.1	5
Corporate Inventories and Capital Adjustments	10.1	3	44.5	3	79.0	2
Net Interest	6.4	4	18.0	4	22.4	4

* Alaska and Hawaii included in 1960 and 1967.

Source: *Historical Statistics of the United States. Colonial Times to 1957*, 1960, p. 141; and the supplement, *Continuation to 1962 and Revisions*, 1965, p. 15. Adapted; U. S. Department of Commerce, Bureau of the Census, *Statistical Abstract* (Washington: U. S. Government Printing Office, 1968), p. 317.

savings are made out of the other three categories in this table than are made from wage incomes. It likewise is true that the receipt of wage incomes individually has not led and does not lead to the establishment of outstandingly large fortunes or estates. Wages and salaries have always loomed large because of the millions of persons who have been remunerated for their productive efforts as employees compared with much smaller numbers of persons who have received incomes in the form of business profits, rents, and increases in corporate increments.

A wider acceptance of the necessity for higher education rather than its desirability has had the effect of postponing the years of entry of thousands of teen-agers into the labor market from the time they have graduated from high school, or earlier, to from two to four years or more later, after they have received higher levels of education and of technical training. Some persons have completed two years of junior college work, some have obtained four years of college and university experience, and more and more students who have displayed capacities for still higher learning have attained one or more years of additional specialized and technical training. When these latter persons have entered the labor market they have been able to command wages and salaries that have been above the levels they would have received had they entered the market prior to the receipt of these added years of training. As teen-agers and untrained workers, they would have been subject to the minimum wages that have been paid unskilled persons. As more skilled employees, they have received differentials above these minimums which have represented larger contributions to national income.

This situation is reflected in part in terms of the increased percentage of national income that wages and salaries have contributed to the total national income for selected years, and the smaller percentages of national income that have had their origins in other segments of activity. Fifty-eight percent of our national income appeared in the form of wages and salaries in 1929; in 1967 this percentage had increased to 72.3. Corporate inventories and capital adjustments increased from 11.5 percent to 12.2 percent. Over the same span of years, portions of national income that originated in other forms of contributions to our productive efforts declined: rentals from 6.1 percent to 3.1 percent; proprietors' incomes from 16.8 percent to 9.0 percent; and net interest from 7.4 percent to 3.4 percent. The new percentage of national income that has appeared in the form of wages has reflected the policy of organized labor in its attempt to have wages adjusted on the basis of corporate profits instead of upon the marginal productivity of the workers. However, it has been claimed that profits have been large because some of the productivity wages have not been paid to labor.

An analysis of the performance of the American economy in 1967 would not be complete without a consideration of the per capita personal incomes that have been received by the residents of the respective states and regions of the United States.

Per Capita Personal Incomes

One of the statistical impacts of Alaska and Hawaii attaining statehood has been to raise the level of per capita personal income for the entire United States. In 1960, which was the first year in which economic data for these areas were incorporated into data of the United States, the per capita income of Alaska was $2,760, and that for Hawaii was $2,274, both of which were above the average of $2,217 for the United States. With respect to this measurement of economic accomplishment, Alaska ranked above all of the states in the East North Central, West North Central, South Atlantic, East South Central, West South Central and Mountain regions. Connecticut, New York, the District of Columbia, California, and Nevada were the only states in the other regions whose per capita incomes were higher than that of Alaska. In the same year the per capita incomes of the states in the West North Central, South Atlantic, East South Central, and West South Central regions were lower than that of Hawaii. Only those of Connecticut; Massachusetts; all of the Middle Atlantic States, except Pennsylvania; Illinois; Michigan; Ohio; Colorado; Washington; Wyoming; California; and Nevada were higher.

By 1967, the per capita incomes of Delaware, Maryland, District of Columbia, and Washington had increased by more than the $1,082 increment by which income increased in Hawaii, to rank ahead of the latter state. While the per capita income of Alaska in 1967 was $879 above the level it had attained in 1960, larger increases in the per capita incomes of Connecticut, New York, Delaware, Illinois, and California enabled them to outrank Alaska in that year. In terms of per capita personal incomes, the youngest and the noncontiguous states more than held their own among those of much greater political maturity and were in no way detrimental to the overall development of the United States.

Both the size of the per capita personal income in the District of Columbia and its rank among the states reflected the increase in the number of federal government employees who resided there as well as the increases in salaries they had received. All doubts concerning either the fact of or the amount of the contribution that government has made to our national income should be erased by these data.

Any historical analysis of the performance of the American economy would be incomplete without an evaluation of the per capita income in relation to the existence of poverty or affluence. Since both concepts are valid only in a relative sense, some more or less arbitrary yardsticks for their measurement must be accepted. The study of the Conference on Economic Progress previously referred to in this chapter defined "modest but adequate" budgets in terms of annual incomes of $6,000 for families and of $2,750 for unattached persons. The reader must not compare these standards with the per capita incomes either of regions or of states and draw any conclusions which may not be valid. Per capita calculations took into consideration the

reach a total of 78 million in 1967, and union membership jumped from 2.7 million to 15.6 million in 1968.

These abstract figures fail to register gains that have been made in organizing production workers in mass production industries and among those at the lower levels of manual skills in all industries. They likewise fail to measure a trend of a decline in the employment of unskilled workers. In 1913 employment in manufacturing industries accounted for 40 percent of nonfarm workers on payrolls. In 1967 this figure was 28.8 percent. Trade and service industries have expanded rapidly and have absorbed large percentages of workers who were formerly engaged in manufacturing.

Mechanization of processes that formerly were manual in nature combined with higher levels of technical efficiencies of workers, not only has reduced the length of the workweek, it has reduced the amount of time that is required to produce a given volume of output. Increases in money wages have tended to lag behind increases in industrial efficiencies of workers and production costs have declined.

Comparative Efficiencies

A capitalistic economy has its advantages and its disadvantages from many points of view, but so does every other type of economic order. A study was made in 1955 that compared the approximate work time required to buy selected commodities in Moscow and in New York City. At a time when an average worker in New York City received $83.58 for working 42 hours a week, an average industrial worker in Moscow was paid $37.50 for 48 hours of work. Table 29-7 contains a few comparisons which are quite impressive.

Table 29-7

Approximate Work Time Required to Buy Selected Commodities (Fixed State Store Prices in Moscow, April 1, 1954; New York City Store Prices, March 15, 1954)

Commodity	Approximate Work Time		
	Average Worker in New York City	Industrial Worker in Moscow	Percent Moscow Work Time is of New York City
A 6-tube radio	13 hours	32 days	2,000
A man's woolen suit	3 days	47 days	1,600
A cake of toilet soap	3 min.	24 minutes	800
1 pound of sugar	3 min., 15 sec.	84 minutes	2,600
1 pound of beef	22 min.	117 minutes	500
1 ounce of tobacco	3 min., 30 sec.	9 minutes	250

Source: U. S. Department of Labor, Bureau of Labor Statistics, Foreign Labor Information, *Labor Conditions in the Soviet Union: Selected Studies* (Washington, October, 1955), p. 50.

LONGEVITY AND RETIREMENT

It was not until the census of 1830 that persons were on record as having attained the age of 60. In 1900 the Bureau of the Census reported that there were approximately three million persons 65 years of age and older. In 1880 it had reported 958,000 persons 60 years of age and over. In 1960 there were 16.5 million people in this age bracket. These data serve to illustrate, not only the magnitude of the problem, but its relative recency in developing. In 1950 there were 10.5 million persons, aged 15-19, members of which group had increased to 13 million in 1960. Recognizing all the time that all persons did not retire upon attaining the age of 65 and that all persons did not enter the labor market at age 15, it appears that persons were reaching the age of at least potential retirement more rapidly than they were being replaced by younger persons entering the labor market for the first time. Insofar as this relationship actually existed, it would have created a scarcity of labor had it not been that other factors did not remain the same.

Society was presented with a problem of automation in industry which did away with certain labor skills. Jobs that required lower labor skills were being eliminated more rapidly than older persons were retiring and being replaced. This technological unemployment problem has been met partly by free enterprise, partly by the government, in providing new opportunities for persons to acquire new skills in on-the-job training programs and in schools that offer training at the levels of new technologies.

Some retired persons are recipients of social security benefits only. Others receive incomes from endowment policies, pension plans, and retirement programs. Some draw on savings accounts, and many thousands are receiving incomes from many combinations of two or more of these sources. Retired persons who have had leisure forced upon them have accepted part-time or even full-time employment as much to help pass the time away as to earn additional income. They are much more consumers of goods than they are producers, and they no longer depend upon their children or upon county homes to provide for them. Retirement villages have been planned with the requirements of senior citizens in mind. Condominium apartments have been erected, the managements of which have attempted to furnish all the material needs of their residents.

Before retirement, men and women now work five days a week and live and consume seven days. Many of them enjoy pleasures on Saturdays and Sundays that are denied them the other five days. The time has come when almost every kind of sport and recreation calls for its own special kind of attire from head to foot, and businessmen have been quick to exploit the potentials in every area of activity. Agencies of the federal government have made it possible to reclaim swamp and wastelands in order to make them available for golf courses, wild life and game reservations, and fishing camps. Leisure time industries truly have become big business.

MEDICAL SCIENCE

Advances in the medical sciences do not fall directly within the sphere or scope of economic analysis, but their impacts on the American economy have loomed large. One of the more successful conquests over diseases has been the almost complete eradication of poliomyelitis and other diseases of the spinal cord. Thirty years ago their attacks on human life struck in the most unexpected places and at the most crucial stages in the lives of their victims. There were no known cures, and the treatments that were given to sufferers, if they survived, varied widely. If they did not kill outright, they deprived their victims of their ability to earn their livelihoods in whole or in part. Frequently they left permanent marks on their survivors in the weakening of one or more of their vital organs that shortened the years in which they made positive contributions to society. Millions of dollars were spent in financing scientific research that led to the discovery of the Salk serum.

Both hospitalization and major medical insurance have become available to millions of persons of all ages and in all walks of life. These kinds of insurance have resulted in the utilization of hospital facilities more frequently and more completely than formerly. New hospitals have been erected, old ones have been enlarged, and all of them have required more expert, better trained personnel to staff them.

Many participants in hospital and major medical programs have taken advantage of group plans which provide benefits similar to those in individual plans but at much lower costs. Persons who have suffered much illness have received treatment, including surgery, which they could not have afforded to pay for out of savings or out of their current earnings. Economic benefits that have accrued to society as well as to individuals have been manifold and are found in the return of many workers to full status as producers in some cases; in others this return has occurred after shorter periods of interruptions or enforced idleness. Hospitalization and major medical programs are found among the fringe benefits that have accrued as a result of collective bargaining.

ADVENTURES IN SPACE

When scientists and engineers had made great inroads toward understanding the mysteries of the earth, outer space offered challenges that all but defied solution. Costs were astronomical, and the government, along with foundations for the advancement of science, undertook to underwrite them. Billions of dollars have been spent in developing communication systems between continents via Telstar. Solo flights in orbit via one-man space capsules have yielded to multi-modual spacecraft. It is too early to know what the economic impacts of such accomplishments are or will be; but the effects of having devoted billions of dollars to such efforts have been felt in wages, employment, and in particular in the metallurgical, electronic, and steel industries. Land values near Cape Kennedy, Florida, and Houston, Texas, have soared. Other areas in New Mexico, Kentucky, Maine, and Nevada, to mention only a few, have felt the impacts of government research in space projects. Entire new communities have been planned and laid out. Construction workers and employees of electronics firms have never lived better. Tourists have been lured to centers of research and development by "open houses" on certain occasions which have given additional volumes of business to the builders of motels and restaurants and to their owner-operators. The dollars that have been spent in developing the space age have penetrated almost every segment of our economy.

QUESTIONS FOR REVIEW

1. Are there any reasons for believing that cyclical fluctuations may be less frequent and/or less severe in the future than they have been in the past? Explain carefully.

2. How has increased government regulation of the American economy fit into the framework of economic capitalism?

3. What is the prevailing attitude of governments towards a balanced budget?

4. Does the pattern of foreign trade follow that which had been established prior to 1914? Explain.

5. (a) How has the Common Market affected American exports? Explain.
   (b) How have American manufacturers attempted to overcome this situation?

6. Was the investment of European capital in American industry peculiar to the Colonial Period? Explain in some detail.

7. In light of the affluence of the 1950's and the early 1960's, have conditions of poverty been overcome? Explain carefully.

8. Is per capita national income evenly distributed throughout the United States? Explain or illustrate your answer.

9. To what extent have adventures in space had impacts upon the American economy?

SUGGESTED READINGS

Arnold, Thurmond. *The Folklore of Capitalism.* New Haven: Yale University Press, 1962.

Balassa, Bela (ed.). *Changing Patterns in Foreign Trade Payments.* New York City: W. W. Norton & Company, Inc., 1964.

Bolino, August C. *The Development of the American Economy.* 2d ed. Columbus, Ohio: Charles E. Merrill Publishing Co., 1966. Chapter 15.

Bowen, William G. (ed.). *Labor and the National Economy*. New York City: W. W. Norton & Company, Inc., 1965.

Budd, Edward C. (ed.). *Inequality and Poverty*. New York City: W. W. Norton & Company, Inc., 1967.

Chandler, Alfred D., Jr., and Fritz Redlich. "Recent Developments in American Business Administration and Their Conceptualization," *American Economic History: Essays in Interpretation,* edited by Stanley Coben and Forest G. Hill. Philadelphia: J. B. Lippincott Co., 1966.

Clough, Shepard B. *The Economic Development of Western Civilization*. New York City: McGraw-Hill Book Company, 1959. Chapter 21.

Davis, Jerome. *Capitalism and Its Culture*. New York City: Holt, Rinehart & Winston, Inc., 1935.

Dillard, Dudley. *Economic Development of the North Atlantic Community*. Englewood Cliffs, N. J.: Prentice-Hall, Inc., 1967. Chapter 38.

Hacker, Louis M. (ed.). *Major Documents in American Economic History.* New York City: D. Van Nostrand Co., Inc., 1961. Vol. II, Selection 27.

MacDonald, Dwight. "Our Invisible Poor," *American Economic History: Essays in Interpretation,* edited by Stanley Coben and Forest G. Hill. Philadelphia: J. B. Lippincott Co., 1966.

Mansfield, Edwin (ed.). *Monopoly Power and Economic Performance.* New York City: W. W. Norton & Company, Inc., 1964.

Mason, Edward S. "Interests, Ideologies, and the Problem of Stability and Growth," *American Economic History: Essays in Interpretation,* edited by Stanley Coben and Forest G. Hill. Philadelphia: J. B. Lippincott Co., 1966.

Monsen, R. J. *Modern American Capitalism*. Boston: Houghton Mifflin Company, 1963.

Phelps, Edmund S. (ed.). *Private Wants and Public Needs*. Rev. ed. New York City: W. W. Norton & Company, Inc., 1965.

Index

A

Ability-to-pay principle of taxation, 524, 786
Absolute cost advantage, 9
Act of 1834 (silver), 345
Adamson Act
  as evidence of national maturation, 528
  labor legislation, 476
Advertising
  as a business, 487
  media, 486
  trade, 486
  after World War I, 564
Age of the Railroad, 356
Agricultural Adjustment Act of 1933
  acreage reduction, results of, 630
  cotton option contracts, 629
  farm incomes, methods of raising, 629
  legality of, 630
  marketing, agreements in, 629
  parity prices, principle of, 629
  payments, benefit, 629
  Thomas Amendment to, 623
Agricultural Revolution, 6, 154
  education in new technologies, 156
  impacts of, 157
  machinery, farm, 156
  McCormick, Cyrus H., 156
  science in farming, 155
  soil butchery, 155
Agriculture
  acreages under cultivation, reduction of, 732
  Agricultural Revolution, 154
  Brannan Plan, 735
  cash position of farmers, 730
  cattle, 734
  cattle ranchers v. sheep ranchers, 302
  Civil War, importance to South in, 253
  costs, farm, 316
  credit, farm, 325
  cultivation, increased costs of intensive, 731
  dairy farming, 309
  development of, 300
  economic growth, indication of, 264
  Erie Canal, 153
  farmers, organization of, 321
  farm labor, increased productivity of, 729
  Grange, 322
  labor, farm, 315
  labor for, after World War I, 569
  machinery, farm, 314
  markets, adaptations to, 300
  markets, farmer dependence upon, 318, 320
  market situations, position of farmers in, 319
  Middle Atlantic States, 153
  National Banking System, 332
  national markets, development of, 733
  New England, 153
  position of, in the American economy, 325
  power, farm, 311
  price supports, 735
  production, progress in, 310
  prosperity, return of, 323
  ranch farming, 300
  ranching, cattle and sheep, 301
  relief, farmers' search for, 321
  Southern States, 154
  tenancy, farm, 315
  westward movement of, 294
  world markets, 735
  World War I, impact of, 324
  World War II, 694
  See also Farming
Agriculture after World War I
  Agricultural Marketing Act, 590
  farm organization, changes in, 580
  mechanical power, increase in use of, 581
  nonstaple farming, 585
  parity prices, need for, 584
  price fluctuations, 586
  price situations, 586
  productivity, increased, 582
  property, higher taxes on, 582
  property values, lower, 582
Agriculture during the early national period
  importance of, 121
  Middle Atlantic States, 122
  New England States, 122
  slavery, 122
  Southern States, 122
  westward movement of, 122
Agriculture in the Middle Colonies
  Bread Colonies, 69
  crops and livestock, 69
  entail, 68
  feudalism, 67
  free willers, 68
  indentured servants, 68
  land tenure, 67
  patroon, 68
  primogeniture, 68
  proprietorship system, 68
  quit rents, 68
Agriculture in the New England Colonies, 47
  conditions, basic, 48
  land tenure, 49
  major crops and livestock, 49
Agriculture in the Southern Colonies
  comparative costs, 74
  cotton, 74
  crops and livestock, 74
  land tenure, 73
  opportunity cost, 74
  plantation system, 73
  price control, 75
  settlement pattern, 73
  slavery, 75
Agriculture Marketing Act
  Federal Farm Board, 590

Air, transportation by, 748
Airplanes
  production of, during World War II, 695
Alaska, purchase of, 518
Alliances, farmer, 322
American College of Life Underwriters
  organization of, 599
American economic history, *see* Economic
  history
American Federation of Labor (AFL)
  Congress of Industrial Organization,
    merger with, 713
  Gompers, Samuel, 453
  membership, 454
  organization of, 453
American Fur Company
  Astor, John Jacob, 121
  Louisiana Purchase, 121
American Railway Union
  birth of, 455
  Debs, Eugene V., 456
  Pullman, George M., struggle with, 456
American System
  Clay, Henry, 140
  facets of, 141
  public lands, 140
Ancient Order of Hibernians
  dissolution of, 447
  Molly Maguires, 446
  politics, penetration into, 446
Anthracite coal, 407
Anti-Strike Breakers Act, 659
Arkwright frame
  Slater, Samuel, 123
Articles of Confederation
  governmental contributions, 106
  public land policy, 99
Assistance by government
  enabling acts, 204
  patent laws, 204
Assumption Act of 1790
  assumption of state debts, 116
  Washington, D. C., 116
Astor, John Jacob, 121, 125
Atlantic Coastal States
  growth of population, causes and impacts
    of, 110
Auctions, 233
Automobile
  economic impacts of, 555
  fuel, marketing, 557
  industry, growth of, 414
  industry, integration of, 554
  industry after World War I, 553
  marketing, 557
  mobility, increased, 556
  movement, the highway, 559
  production, mass, 554
  production of first, 351
  services, auxiliary, 556
  tires, rubber for, 558

B

Balance of payments
  English insurance companies, payments to,
    504
  immigration, effect of, 504

  pound sterling to dollar exchange, 505
  World War I, 505
Balance of trade
  favorable, 34
  unfavorable, 34, 60
Baltimore, Lord, 68
Bank Act of 1933, 620
Bank Act of 1935, 620
Bank deposits, 4
Banking, 160
  banks, state, 333
  branch, statewide, 168
  capitalism, as an institution of, 777
  capital stock, 111
  central bank, absence of, 162
  checks, 328
  circulating notes, 111
  Civil War, 257
  commercial banks, impacts of failures of,
    596
  competitive, 591
  credit control, instruments of, 780
  failures of banks, 339, 592
  Federal Deposit Insurance Corporation,
    641
  Federal Deposit Insurance Corporation,
    coverage by, 778
  federal reserve, 331
  Federal Reserve Board, credit policies of,
    597
  Federal Reserve member banks, failures
    of, 592
  Federal Reserve System, 342
  First Bank of the United States, 111
  fractional reserve plan, 328
  function of Federal Reserve System in,
    778
  Independent Treasury, 165
  independent unit, development of, 327
  loans, brokers', 596
  Louisiana Banking Act of 1842, 167
  monetary commissions, 341
  monetary developments, 344
  National Banking System, 257, 327
  National Banking System, defects in, 329
  national banks, organizational require-
    ments of, 328
  national banks, reserve requirements of,
    328
  New Deal, under the, 641
  New York Free Banking Act, 167
  New York safety fund system, 166
  private, 111
  savings, postal, 338
  Second Bank of the United States, 162
  state, 111, 165
  Suffolk Bank, 166
  suspensions of banks, 779
  trade, importance to, 480
  War of 1812, 113
  World War II, 692
Banking, central
  apathy toward, 523
  maturation, national, 523
  positive action, 523
Bank notes, 4
Bank of New York, 110

Bank of North America
Bankers' acceptances, 597
Banks, 106
  currency, 110
  American branches in foreign countries, 788
  Bank Act of 1933, 620
  Bank Act of 1935, 620
  commercial, 334, 395
  conservators, 619
  correspondent, defined, 331
  of discount and deposit, 334
  of discount and issue, 334
  failures of, 339, 618
  Federal Deposit Insurance Corporation, 620
  holiday, 618
  industry, 395
  insurance, deposit, 620
  investment, 515
  mergers of, 755
  mergers on, impacts of, 759
  provisions for strengthening, 621
  reform, legislation for, 619
  reopened, 619
  Reserve, 343
  savings, 336
  state, 333
  suspensions of, 340
  trust companies, 335
Baring Brothers of London, 167
Barter in colonies, 37
Baseball, 770
Bell, Alexander Graham, 379
Berger, Victor, 456
Berk, Lord, 28
Berkeley, Sir John, 68
Bessemer process
  railroads, 195
Biddle, Nicholas
  Second Bank of the United States, 164
Bill of credit, 89
  definition of, 60
  Middle Colonies, 71
  Southern Colonies, 78
Bill of exchange, 53, 55
Bimetallism, 345
  advantage of, theoretical, 113
  Coinage Act of 1792, 114
  market value ratio, 113
  monetary system, 113
  monometallism, 113
  reform, monetary, 347
Bison
  American Indians, 358
  railroads, 357
Bituminous coal, 408
Bland-Allison Act (1878), 346
Blockade of the South
  Revolutionary War, 98
Blodget, Samuel
  Economica, 129
Boll weevil, 308
Bonds
  income, 388
  mortgage, 388
  refunding, 388

  reorganization, 388
  World War I, 539
Book credit in the Southern Colonies, 78
Book publishing, mergers in, 758
Borrowing war finances, 96
Boston Port Bill, 92
Boston Tea Party, 91
Boycott, 216
  colonial defiance, 92
  definition of, 462
Brannan Plan, 735
Bread Colonies, 69
British colonial policy
  mercantilism, 34
  mercantilistic attitudes and laws, 34
  Navigation Acts, 35
  privateering, 34
  regional differences, 36
Broadway Limited, 364
Brook Farm, 218
Brotherhoods, railroad
  goals of, 457
  list of, 457
  strike policy, 457
  uplift unions, 457
Brown, Moses, 123
Bryan, William Jennings, 347
Budget, national
  balancing the, 785
Bureau of Corporations
  dissolution of, 440
  organization of, 438
Business
  government's relation to, 783
  organization of, 203
Business organization
  corporations, 213, 264
  economic growth, indication of, 264
  partnerships, 213
  proprietorships, 213
Business unit
  combinations, 422
  increase in size of, 418
By-products
  concentration of industry, 406
Byrnes Act, *see* Anti-Strike Breakers Act

C

Calvert, George, 28
Canals
  anthracite canals, 190
  Erie Canal, 187
  evaluation of success of the era of, 193
  financing of, 192
  important, 189
  reasons for end of the era of, 192
  Sault Sainte Marie, 352
  tidewater canals, 190
  traffic on, 229
  usage, limitations of, 193
Capital
  banks, investment, 515
  direct investment in American industries of foreign, 788
  direct investments, 499
  investment after World War II of, 703
  investment in the west of eastern, 479

lack of Southern, 249
for manufacturing, 203
maturation, national, 514
movements related to economic maturity,
  516
portfolio investments, 499
productive factors, changes in, 271
savings, investment of, 515
scarcity of native, 238
social, 512
sources of, 514
Capital account
  invisible items, 241
Capitalism
  banking, 777
  evaluation of the institutions of, 775
  freedom of enterprise as an institution of,
    780
  private property, 776
  production for market through, 776
  profit system as an institution of, 780
  role of money in, 777
  wage earning class as an institution of,
    776
Capitalizing profits, 121
Capital stock, 111
Carteret, John, 28
Carteret, Sir George, 68
Cash-and-carry, 491
Cattle
  raising of, 734
  Western beef, 734
Center of population
  definition of, 290
  movement of, 290
Central Pacific Railroad, 356
Central Reserve Cities
  Federal Reserve System, 343
  National Banking System, 328
Certificate of deposit
  definition of, 60
  Middle Colonies, 71
Chain stores, 491
Charles II of England, 28
Charleston, South Carolina, 28
Check-off
  union program, 460
Checks, 328
Cheves, Langdon, 163
Chicago
  meat packing, 209, 301, 305
Circulating notes, 4
  bank notes, 111
Circulation, currency
  parity of, 111
Cities
  growth of, 44
  important, 44
  urban occupations, 45
  westward movement, 45
City centrals, 448
Civil Aeronautics Act, 645
Civil Aeronautics Administration, 645
Civil Aeronautics Authority, 645
Civil Aeronautics Board (CAB), 645
Civilian Conservation Corps (CCC), 633

Civil War, 247
  agriculture, importance of, 253
  banking, development of, 257
  economic adjustments to, 271
  finances, 255, 258
  Homestead Act of 1862, 253
  industries, 255
  labor, effect on, 444
  loans, financing by, 256
  manufacturing, impact on, 396, 398
  North, advantages of the, 252
  Panic of 1873, 362
  paper money, financing by issuing, 256
  population, Northern and Southern, 252
  railroads, impact on, 356
  resources for, 252
  slavery as a cause of the, 250
  South, advantages of the, 252
  taxation, financing by, 255
  transportation, 254
Clark, William, 121
Clay, Henry,
  American System, 140
  markets, home, 219
  public lands, 140
  Second Bank of the United States, opinion
    on, 164
Clayton Antitrust Act (1914), 435, 441, 529
Clipper ship, 243
Closed shop
  definition of, 217
  Knights of St. Crispin, 448
  union program, 460
Coal
  anthracite, 407
  bituminous, 408
  miners, striking, 409
  mining, methods of, 409
  production records, 409
  railroads, usage by, 374
Coal Conservation Act (1935), 656
Coffee, 92
Coinage Act of 1792
  bimetallism, 114
  Hamilton, Alexander, 114
Coking
  Darby, Abraham, 208
  Middle Atlantic States, 207
Collective bargaining
  labor, 218
  National Labor Union, 448
  walking delegates, 460
Colleges
  enrollment, increase in, 728
Colonial attitude toward England
  origin of population, 84
Colonial defiance
  Boston Tea Party, 91
  Intolerable Acts, 91
  Legal Tender Act of 1764, 89
  Molasses Act of 1733, 88
  Quartering Act of 1765, 89
  retaliation by England, 91
  Stamp Tax of 1765, 89
  Sugar Act of 1764, 88
  taxation, attitude toward, 90
  Townshend Acts, 91

Colonial development
  Middle Colonies, 67
  New England Colonies, 47
  Southern Colonies, 73
Colonial discontent
  depression, 85
  law enforcement, 84
  Proclamation of 1763, 85
  revenue, 84
Colonial economic institutions
  division of labor, 31
  economic specialization, 31
  freedom of enterprise, 31
  free pricing, 32
  private property, 30
Colonial economy
  British colonial policy, 34
  characteristics of, 30
  economic institutions, 30
  growth and development of the population, 39
  growth of cities, 44
  labor supply, 42
  production and consumption, 37
  sectional differences, 32
Colonial production and consumption
  barter, 37
  commercial activities, 38
  household activities, 37
Colonial sectional differences
  Middle Colonies, 33
  New England Colonies, 32
  Southern Colonies, 33
Colonization of America
  characteristics of the colonial economy, 30
  early American settlements, 27
  early colonial policies, 26
  English colonial policies, 26, 34
  growth and development of population, 39
  growth of cities, 44
  growth of trade, 23
  immigration, causes of, 28
  labor supply, 42
  nature of trade, 24
  profits, quest for, 27
  trade and change, 24
  trade and trade routes, 25
Columbus, Christopher, 25
Combinations
  Bureau of Corporations, 438
  business, 422
  business, economic causes of, 423
  business, formal corporate control of, 428
  business, informal corporate control of, 428
  Clayton Antitrust Act (1914), 435, 441
  competition, increasing, 425
  control, federal, 436
  control of, early efforts at, 435
  control by states of, 436
  costs, savings in, 425
  Federal Trade Commission, 440
  government regulation of, 435
  holding company, 434
  horizontal, defined, 426
  industry, integration of, 427
  market, existence of a capital, 426

  market, size of, 424
  methods of combining, 426
  oligopsonistic, 436
  pools, defined, 428
  profits, 427
  protests, public, 439
  reform, 439
  Sherman Antitrust Act, 437
  Sinclair, Upton, 439
  strength of, 435
  trusts, 429
  vertical, defined, 427
Commerce
  canals, traffic on, 229
  domestic, rise of, 227
  foreign, decline of, 227, 235
  payments, balance of, 241
  payments, origins of international, 240
  railroads, traffic on, 230
  rivers, traffic on, 228
  shipbuilding, 242
  shipping, 242
  trade, balance of, 237, 241
  trade, commodity, 235
  trade, financing foreign, 239
  trade, organization of, 231
Commissions, monetary, 341
Commodity money
  Middle Colonies, 71
  Southern Colonies, 78
Commodity money in the New England Colonies
  certificates of deposit, 60
  definition of, 60
Common Market
  American investments in, 787
Communication, 179, 351, 376
  automation, impacts of, 749
  postal service, 200, 381, 748
  telegraph, 199, 201, 377
  telephone, 379, 749
  Telstar, 797
  transportation, relation to, 199
  World War II, 693
Community of interest
  holding company, 434
Comparative cost advantage, 9, 31
Comparative costs, 74
Compensation
  fellow servant rule, 474
  liability, law defenses against employer, 473
  negligence, contributory, 474
  risk, assumption of, 474
  workmen's, 474
Compensatory principle
  Dingley Tariff Act (1897), 393
  Underwood Tariff of 1913, 393
Competition
  business combinations, 425
  Revolutionary War, 92
Compromise of 1850, 252
Compromise Tariff of 1833, 170, 221
Comptroller of the Currency
  Federal Reserve System, 342
  National Banking System, 327, 333, 339

Congress of Industrial Organization (CIO)
  American Federation of Labor, merger with, 713
  birth of, 657
Consent decrees
  Federal Trade Commission, 440
Conservation of soil, 85
Conservators, 619
Constitutional Convention
  objectives of, 106
Constitution of the United States
  amendments, provision for, 107
  aspects of, economic, 106
  Constitutional Convention, 106
  copyrights, 107
Construction, building
  after World War I, 550, 552, 570
  after World War II, 700
Consumer goods
  definition of, 210
  durable and nondurable, 5
Consumption, 5
Continental currency
  finances, Revolutionary War, 96
Continental Divide
  railroads, 363
"Continental, not worth a," 97
Cooke, Jay
  Panic of 1873, 361
Copyrights, 107
Corn and hogs, 304
Cornwallis, 99
Corporations
  bonds, income, 388
  bonds, mortgage, 388
  bonds, refunding, 388
  bonds, reorganization, 388
  branches, establishment of, 726
  business, organization of, 213
  debentures, 388
  manufacturing industries, 213
  mergers, 752
  officers, liability of, 764
  organization, business, 264
  power, abuse of, 389
  power, use of, 389
  profits of, 759
  textile, 214
  transportation companies, 213
  wages, 388
  Waltham System, 214
Costs
  combinations, savings effected by, 425
Cotton
  Baring Brothers of London, 167
  boll weevil, 308
  cotton gin, invention of, 122
  cottonseed, 309
  rise of importance of, 122
  role of, 307
  spread of, 308
  trade, effect upon, 126
Council of Economic Advisers, 715
Credit control
  instruments of, in banking, 780

Credit, farm
  Federal Farm Loan Banks, 325
  Joint Stock Land Banks, 325
Credit Mobilier, 360
Crime of '73, 346
Crisis, economic
  debt, moratorium on, 614
  foreign obligations, default of, 614
  panic, national, 611
  Reconstruction Finance Corporation, 617
  stock market crash (1929), 611
  tariffs, resort to, 612
  unemployment, 615
Crisis, treasury (1893), 347
Crops
  Middle Colonies, 69
  New England Colonies, 49
  Southern Colonies, 74
Cultivation
  extensive v. intensive, 303
Cumberland Road, 180
Currency Act of 1751, 89
Currency Act of 1873, 345
Currency in the colonial economy, 110
Customs duties, 169
Cycles, business
  Federal Reserve System, 343
Cyclical fluctuations
  correctives to, 782
  depression, 781
  unemployment, 781

D

Dairy farming, 309
Darby, Abraham, 208
Davis-Bacon Act, 572
Dawes bank
  Reconstruction Finance Corporation, 617
Debentures, 388
Debs, Eugene V.
  American Railway Union, 456
  Berger, Victor, influence of, 456
  Socialist party in the United States, 456
Debt, federal, 685
  growth of the, 719
  statutory limitations to the, 736
Debt, foreign
  default on, 614
Debt, public
  amount of, 115
  Congress, first, 115
Debt, state
  assumption, attitudes toward, 115
  assumption, methods of, 115
  Assumption Act of 1790, 116
  bargaining for an agreement on, 116
  Hamilton, Alexander, 115
  incurrence of, 115
  paper money, issuance of, 115
  Revolutionary War, 115
  slaves, concession for, 116
  taxation, 115
Debtor nation, 238
Declaration of Independence
  George III, 94
  quartering of troops, 95
  trade limitations, 95

Deere, John, 315
Defense, national
  government intervention in business for, 783
  role of interstate highway system in, 744
Deflation
  note issue, elasticity of, 327
De la Ware, Lord, 68
Demand deposits, 4
Depression
  identification of a, 781
  income, disposable, 660
  income, national, 660
  progress of the, 659
  trade, foreign, 661
Depression, colonial
  cause of, 85
  impact on the colonies, 87
  trade, domestic, 87
  trade, foreign, 85
Depression after the Revolutionary War
  causes of, 105
  recession, 105
Desert Land Act of 1877, 296
Differences, intersectional
  improvements, internal, 249
  land policies, 247
  relationships, debtor-creditor, 249
  slavery, opinions concerning, 250
  tariff programs, attitudes toward, 248
Diminishing productivity, law of, 480
Diminishing returns, 158, 239
Dingley Tariff Act (1897)
  compensatory principle, 393
  cost of living, rising, 394
Discontent, defiance, and readjustments, 83
  Constitution of the United States, 106
  defiance, 88
  discontent, 84
  readjustments, 99
  war pending, 92
Dividends, corporate, 761
Domestic system, fall of the, 123
Drafts, 53, 240
Dred Scott, case at law, 251
Drouth
  New Deal, effect on, 626

E

East India Tea Company
  Townshend Acts, 91
Economica, 129
Economic activity, expansion of
  American economy, tests of the success of, 262
Economic history
  American, 2
  consumption as a factor in, 5
  definition of, 2
  distribution as a factor in, 4
  economic theory in, 8
  exchange values as a factor in, 4
  general trends in economic progress, 5
  lessons of, 10
  nature and content of, 1
  production as a factor of, 3

Economic progress
  specialization, 7
  stimulatory changes, basic, 6
  trends in, 5
Economics
  definition of, 1
  nature of, 1
Economics and economic history, 1
Economic significance of geographic and demographic factors, 10
  economic dislocations, 17
  geographic determinants, 11
  regional differences, 13
  role of people, 15
  technology as a modifying factor in, 17
Economic theory
  economic history, uses in, 8
  economic principles, illustration of, 8
  knowledge, practical, 9
Economies of scale
  rubber, manufacturing of, 265
Economy, American
  agriculture in, position of, 325
  capitalism, 775
  Civil War, adjustments to, 271
  cyclical fluctuations in, 781
  economic activity, expansion of, 262
  failures of, 263
  government, relationship of, 268
  government's relation to business, 783
  growth of the, 211
  income, sources of, 268
  integration of, with economies of other nations, 786
  labor, accomplishments of, 794
  leisure time, 262
  longevity of populace, 796
  medicine, 797
  national income, 788
  national wealth, estimated, 266
  Panic of 1837, 263
  Panic of 1857, 263
  performance of the, 247, 259, 775
  productive factors, changes in, 270
  retirement, 796
  scale of living, 262
  space adventures, 797
  success, tests of, 260
  war preparations, 782
Economy, American (1866-1920)
  cyclical fluctuations in, 530
  employment, government, 533
  income, national, 531
  income, receipt of, 532
  levels of living, advances in, 533
  performance of, 530
  wealth, distribution of, 532
  World War I, 536
  World War I, recovery from, 541
Edison, Thomas A.
  electricity, 414
  telegraph, improvement of, 377
Elasticity
  of demand, 392
  of Federal Reserve notes, 344
  of note issue, 327
  perverse, 328

Electrical appliance industry, 560
Electricity
    Edison, Thomas A., 414
    industry, 413
    Westinghouse, George, 414
Elkins Act, 368, 528
Embargo
    War of 1812, 130
Emergency Transportation Act of 1933, 643
Employment
    government, 533
    labor, 444
    after World War II, 699, 716
Employment Act of 1946
    Council of Economic Advisers, formation
        of, 715
    provisions of, 785
    purpose of, 715
Enabling acts, 204
Engine
    internal combustion, 314, 351
    steam traction, in farming, 313
English attitude toward the colonies, 84
Entail
    definition of, 28
    Middle Colonies, 68
Entertainment
    industry, economic impacts of the, 566
    industry, growth of the, 415
    motion pictures, 566
    nickelodeons, 415
    radio, 565
Entrepreneurs, qualities of, 205
Enumeration, principle of, 36
Erie Canal
    agriculture in New England, 189
    importance of, 187
    New York port, opening of, 189
    railroads, competition with, 231
Exchange values, 4
Expansion westward, 135
    gold, discovery of, 138
    Louisiana Purchase, 120
    phases of, 136
Exports
    commodity, nature of, 499
    destinations of, 501
    invisible items, 241
    trade, commodity, 236

F

Face value, 111
Fair Labor Standards Act, 654
Fall line of rivers, 64
Fall River System, 214
Farming
    arable, 303
    corn and hogs, 304
    costs of living in, 317
    costs of operation of, 316
    credit for, 325
    dairy, 309
    engine, internal combustion, 314
    engine, steam traction, 313
    fixed costs of, 316
    horsepower in, 312
    labor for, 315
    machinery, production of, 315

    machinery, regional use of, 314
    manpower for, 312
    markets, European, 321
    in Middle Atlantic States, 306
    in New England, 305
    Populist party, 323
    prices, falling, 318
    ranch, 300
    in the South, 306
    specialty areas of, 305
    tenancy, 315
    wind power in, 311
    See also Agriculture
Father of Labor Day, 454
Federal Deposit Insurance Corporation
        (FDIC)
    bank suspensions, influence on, 779
    coverage by, 778
    evaluation of, 621
    New Deal, 641
    organization of, 620
Federal Farm Board, 590
Federal Farm Loan Banks, 325
Federal Reserve Act
    banking, national, 328
    passage of, 342
Federal Reserve banking
    World War I, 5
Federal Reserve Banks
    circulating notes, issuance of, 343
    strength of, 332
Federal Reserve Board
    bankers' acceptances, 597
    credit, qualitative control of, 597
    credit policies of, 597
    establishment of, 332
    membership of, 342
    open market operations, 598
Federal Reserve Districts, 342
Federal Reserve System, 396
    Board of Governors, 332
    Central Reserve Cities, 343
    circulating notes, 343
    credit policy during World War II, 686
    cycle, business, 343
    function of, 778
    margin requirements during World War
        II of, 687
    membership requirements for, 342
    National Banking System, remedies for
        defects in, 331
    Open Market Committee, 342
    organization of, 342
    Reserve Cities, 343
Federal Savings and Loan Associations, 638
Federal Savings and Loan Insurance Cor-
        poration, 638, 641
Federal Securities Act of 1933, 642
Federal Trade Commission
    consent decrees, 440
    establishment of, 440
Federal Trade Commission Act, 435, 440,
    529
Federal Treasury
    surplus, distribution of, 170
Federation of Organized Trades and Labor
    Unions, 453

Fellow servant rule, 474
Feudalism
  colonial, 67
  See also Patroon system
Fiat money, 259
Finance, 160
  Civil War, 255
  debt, statutory limitation to the federal, 736
  expenditures, federal government, 740
  expenditures, government payroll, 741
  expenditures, state and local government, 740
  federal revenue, sources of, 169
  Federal Savings and Loan Insurance Corporation, 641
  Federal Treasury surplus, distribution of, 170
  government, 735
  institutions of, 177
  insurance, life, 598
  New Deal, under the, 641
  relationship of government and business, 171
  revenues, sources for local government, 738
  revenues, sources for federal, 737
  revenues, sources for state, 737
  trusts, investment, 600
  after World War II, 716
  See also Banking
Finance during the Revolutionary War
  borrowing, 96
  continental currency, issuance of, 96
  France, 96
  Holland, 96
  inflation, 97
  means of attaining, 96
  Morris, Robert, 96
  price control, 97
  taxation, 96
Finance during World War II
  Federal Reserve System, credit policy of, 686
  loans, 685
  taxation, 681
Financiers
  manufacturing, 204
  railroads, early, 361
Financing at the state level
  banking, public, 173
  bonds, issuance, 173
First Bank of the United States
  branch banking, 112
  centralization, 112
  central office, 112
  charter, 111
  commercial banking, 112
  expiration of, 113
  foreign stock, 111
• functions of, 111
  Hamilton, Alexander, 111
Fisheries, colonial, 50
Fishing and whaling
  New England Colonies, 66
Fluctuations, cyclical, 530
Football, 771

Ford, Henry, 553
Fordney-McCumber Tariff Act, 588
Foreign exchange
  dollar shortage after World War II, 720
  exchange rates, controlled, 721
  International Monetary Fund, 721
  trade, new pattern of foreign, 721
Fox, George, 28
Fractional reserve plan, 328
France
  Louisiana Purchase, 120
Frazier-Lemke Farm Bankruptcy Bill, 630
Freedom of enterprise
  as an institution of capitalism, 780
Free pricing
  Revolutionary War, 92
Free willers, 68
French and Indian War, 83
Fringe benefits, 706, 712
Frontier, close of the, 297
Fuel
  automobile, marketing of the, 557
  industrial, 411

G

Gadsden Purchase, 145
Gallatin, Albert, 162
  internal revenue, 119
  transportation, 127
Gauge, standard
  railroads, 363
George III of England, 94
Gold
  discovery in California of, 138
Gold Reserve Act, 627
Gold standard, triumph of the, 327
Gold Standard Act, 344, 348
Gompers, Samuel
  American Federation of Labor, 453
  Federation of Organized Trades and Labor Unions, 453
  McGuire, Peter J., 454
  success of, 454
Gould, Jay
  Holy Order of the Knights of Labor, 451
Government
  budget considerations of the, 785
  business' relation to, 783
  combinations, early efforts to control, 435
  debt, federal, 719
  defense, national, 783
  economy, relationship to the, 268
  Employment Act of 1946, 715, 785
  expenditures, 742
  fiscal policies, 785
  inflation control by, 784
  legislation for minimum wages by, 784
  manufacturing, attitude toward, 402
  payrolls, 716, 741
  philosophy of, after World War II, 714
  railroads, control of, 371
  railroads, regulation of, 365
  receipts, 742
  revenue, sources of federal, 718
  state and local, new sources of tax revenue for, 717
  welfare, national, 783

Government stock, 117
Graduation Act of 1854, 143
Grange
  alliances, 322
  Interstate Commerce Act, 322
  Interstate Commerce Commission, 322
  See also Patrons of Husbandry, The
Granger Cases, 366
Grants of land to railroads, 358
Greenback
  definition of, 256
  Gold Standard Act, 345
  party, formation of, 344
  redemption of, 345
  Resumption Act, 345
Greenbackism, 347
Gross national product (GNP)
  economic activity, 417
  markets, 424
Growth, U. S. economic
  agriculture, 264
  business, organization of, 264
  causes of, 264
  manufacturing, 265
  power, harnessing of, 265
  transportation, 265
Guffey Act of 1935, 657
Guffey-Vinson Act, 657

H

Hamilton, Alexander
  banking, 109
  Coinage Act of 1792, 114
  Congress, 109
  currency, 109
  First Bank of the United States, 111
  infant industry, 109
  parity of circulation, 111
  Report on Manufactures, 109
  state debts, 115
  taxation, 90
Hats and clothing in the New England
  Colonies, 66
Hawley-Smoot Tariff, 612
Haywood, William D., 458
Headright system, 29
Hepburn Act, 368, 528
Highways
  improvements after World War II on, 703
  interstate, impacts of, 744
  need for more, 559
  tourism on interstate, 768
  transportation, 351
  See also Roads
Hogs and corn, 304
Holding companies
  community of interest, 434
  definition of, 434
  important, 434
Holy Order of the Knights of Labor
  activities of, 450
  birth of, 449
  decline of, 452
  Gould, Jay, 451
  opposition of employers to, 451
  Powderly, Terence V., 449
  program of, 449

  railroads, 451
  strikes, 451
Home Owners Loan Act (1934), 638
Home Owners Loan Corporation (HOLC),
  637
Home Owners Refinancing Act (1933), 637
Homestead Act
  homesteading, impacts of, 295
  settlement under the, 294
  terms of, 294
Homestead Act of 1862, 253
Homesteading
  Northern and Western attitude toward,
  248
  Southern attitude toward, 248
Homesteads, subsistence, 628
Horizontal combinations, 426
Horses
  racing of, 771
  as a source of power on farms, 312
House of Baring, 240
Housing
  Federal Savings and Loan Associations,
  638
  Home Owners Loan Corporation
  (HOLC), 637
  Home Owners Refinancing Act (1933),
  637
  population, growth of, 727
  slums, clearance of, 638
  after World War I, 551
Hudson Bay Company, 121
Huguenots, 30

I

Immigrants
  as labor in industry, 386
  settlement of, 260
Immigration
  composition of, 729
  Europe, Southeastern, 279
  foreign born, distribution of, 281
  impact of, 149
  "new," 278
  "old," 278
  pattern of, 277
  population growth, 145, 275
  push factors, 277
  resettlement in America, 283
  restrictions on, 292
  Slavic, 279
  South, effect on the, 288
  World War I, 292
  after World War I, 573
Immigration to the colonies
  causes of, 28
  contribution of immigrants, 41
  nature of, 41
  pull forces, 28
  push forces, 28
Imperialism
  aggression, political, 519
  Alaska, purchase of, 518
  economic, development of, 517
  foreign economic policy, recognition of
  need for, 519
  intervention, military, 520

investment and control, 519
nationalism, surge of, 521
Imports
    commodity, nature of, 499
    important, 237
    invisible items, 241
    sources of, 501
Improvements, internal
    sectional differences, 249
Inclined planes, 356
Income, disposable
    definition of, 660
    per capita, 424
Income, national
    definition of, 660
    for 1866-1920, 531
    by industry, 789
    measurement of American economy
        through, 788
    personal incomes, distribution of, 793
    personal incomes, per capita, 792
    sources of, 268, 789
    types of, 790
Income, personal
    distribution of, 793
    per capita, 792
    poverty in America, 794
Increase, natural
    population, growth of the, 275
Indentured servants
    kidnapping of labor for colonies, 29
    Middle Colonies, 68
    voluntarily and involuntarily, 43
Independent Treasury
    establishment of, 165
    function of, 165
Indians, American
    bison, disappearance of the, 358
Industrial Workers of the World (Wobblies)
    action, militant, 459
    convention in Chicago, 458
    organization of, 458
    public opinion of, 459
Industry
    automobile, 414
    banking facilities, 395
    banks, commercial, 395
    business organization, 387
    business unit, increase in the size of the,
        418
    by-products, use of, 406
    Civil War, 255, 396
    climate, industrial, 385
    coal as a fuel for, 407
    colonial restrictions, 64
    concentration of, 406, 417
    control of, 417
    corporate, 388
    decentralization of, during World War II,
        680
    development of, 417
    diversification of, 209
    electrical appliance, 560
    electricity, use of, 413
    entertainment, 415
    financial institutions, 395
    foreign capital in American, 788

fuels, 411
gross national product, 417
industries, growth of selected, 407
industries, rise of capital goods, 398
infant, tariff legislation to protect, 513
integration of, 427
labor, immigrant, 386
leading ones, 210
localization of, 403
location of, 206
markets, 387
mechanization of, 288, 419
monetary stability, 396
population, 386
power for, 387, 413
primacy of, as evidence of national
    maturation, 521
production, large-scale, 418
prosperity in, as a result of World War I,
    537
railroad rates, 404
resources, capital, 404
resources, natural, 385
in the South, 288
strikes in the coal, 409
tariffs, 389
tooling, machine, 405
after World War I, 553
See also Manufacturing
Industry during the early national period
    capital, sources of, 123
    domestic system, fall of the, 123
    labor, sources of, 123
    Slater, Samuel, 123
    standardization, 124
Industry in the Middle Colonies, 72
Industry in the New England Colonies, 64
Industry in the Southern Colonies, 78
Inelasticity of demand, 392
    definition of, 88
Infant industries
    definition of, 109
    Hamilton, Alexander, 109, 117
    tariff legislation to protect, 513
Infant Industries Tariff of 1789, 219
Inflation
    causes of, during wartime, 687
    government attempts to control, 784
    New England Colonies, 61
    note issue, elasticity of, 327
    Office of Price Administration, 687
    price controls during World War II, 688
    rationing during World War II, 689
    rent controls during World War II, 688
    Revolutionary War, 97
    Southern Colonies, 78
    wage controls, 691
    World War I, accompanying, 541
Inflation Act of 1933, *see* Thomas Amend-
    ment to the Agricultural Adjustment
    Act of 1933
Influenza, Spanish, 542
Injunctions, 465
Installment buying after World War I, 564
Insurance
    American College of Life Underwriters,
        599
    fire, 160

life, 160, 598
life, assets of, 765
life insurance companies, status of, 599
life, payments of, 766
public awareness and acceptance of life,
　599
Insurance companies, 177, 599
Insurance, social, 527
pensions, old age, 646
problems necessitating, 645
social security, 648
Integration
automobile industry, 554
Internal improvements
bonds, flotation of, 172
tolls, 172
Internal revenue
excise taxes, 118
exemptions, agricultural, 119
Gallatin, Albert, 119
Hamilton, Alexander, 118
whiskey, 118
Whiskey Rebellion, 119
International Monetary Fund (IMF), 721
Interstate Commerce Act, 528
effectiveness of, 367
Grange, 322
passage of the, 322
provisions of the, 366
Interstate Commerce Commission
appointees to, 366
Grange, 322
organization of, 322
Intolerable Acts, 91
Boston Port Bill, 92
British agents, trial of, 92
Governor, power of, 92
Quartering Act revived, 92
Quebec Act, 92
Investments
abroad, 604
direct, 499
Europe, need for capital in, 605
foreign portfolio, 787
portfolio, defined, 499
in railroads, 376
Invisible items
capital account, 241
definition of, 241
Iron industry
coking, effect of, 208
Middle Atlantic States, 207
New England Colonies, 65
Irrigation, 512
Italian dominance, reaction to, 25

J

Jackson, Andrew
Battle of New Orleans, 131
pet banks, 164
Second Bank of the United States, objec-
　tions to, 164
Specie Circular, terms of, 165
Jefferson, Thomas
First Bank of the United States, 112
Louisiana Purchase, 121
silver dollars, 114

Johnson Neutrality Act, 671
Joint Stock Land Banks, 325

K

Kansas-Nebraska Act, 252
Kidnapping of labor for the colonies, 29
Knights of Labor, *see* Holy Order of the
　Knights of Labor
Knights of St. Crispin
closed shop, 448
Korea, police action in, 723

L

Label, union, 462
Labor
accomplishments of, 659, 794
American Federation of Labor, 453
Civil War, 444
class of people as an institution of capi-
　talism, 776
closed shop, 217
collective bargaining, 218
division of, 478
efficiencies, comparative, 795
employment, 444
Fair Labor Standards Act, 654
under the Fall River System, 215
farm, 315
farm, displaced, 443
farm, increased productivity of, 729
farm to industrial, comparison of, 443
female, 214
growth, economic, 444
immigrant, 271, 356
increase in the supply of, 203
legal actions of, 217
legislation, 443, 469
living conditions of, 215
mechanization, 212, 444
Molly Maguires, 446
National Labor Relations Act, 651
National Trades Union, The, 217
organization, need for, 445
organization of, 443
organizations, early, 216
organized, demands of, 462
organized, weapons of, 462
productive factors, changes in, 271
provisions of early legislation, 470
reform, 216, 218
strikes, 217
unemployment, 444
unions, emergence of national, 447
unions, legalized, 217
Walsh-Healey Act, 653
under the Waltham System, 215
working hours, regulation of, 217
Labor after World War I
agriculture, 569
construction, building, 570
Davis-Bacon Act, 572
demand for, 568
incomes, impacts of larger, 571
industries, mechanized, 568
industries, trade and service, 570
mining, 570
New Deal legislation, prelude to, 572

Norris-LaGuardia Act, 573
organized, decline in the influence of, 571
railroads, 570
real wage increase, 572
Labor after World War II
    AFL and CIO, merger of, 713
    community organization, attempt at, 708
    corporate profits, wages based on, 705
    fringe benefits, 706, 712
    minimum wage legislation, 713
    program, new, 705
    strikes, 707
    Taft-Hartley Act, 709
    wage adjustments, 710
    wage contracts, industry-wide, 706
Labor-Management Reporting and Dis-
    closure Act, 710
Labor supply
    definition of, 42
    indentured servants, 43
    scarcity of, overcoming, 42
    slavery, 43
Lakes, 352
Land
    agricultural frontier, disappearance of,
        511
    arid, irrigation of, 512
    frontiers, opening new, 511
    grants for internal improvements, 143
    homesteading, 248
    maturity, economic national, 510
    Middle Atlantic States, policy of the, 247
    Northern policy, 247
    productive factors, changes in, 270
    Southern policy, 247
    utilization, extensive to intensive, 510
Land Law of 1820, 141
Land Ordinance of 1785, 103
    impacts of, 103
    provisions of, 101
    road construction, 103
Lands, public, 275, 294
    acts passed concerning, 296
    frontier, close of the, 297
    Homestead Act, 294
    settlement of, 297
    speculation, 294, 297
    venture capital, 294
Landrum-Griffin Act, see Labor-Manage-
    ment Reporting and Disclosure Act
Leadership, free enterprise
    financiers of industries, early, 204
    industry, locating, 206
    qualities of, 205
Legal Tender Act of 1764
    colonial defiance, 89
    Currency Act of 1751, 89
    loan bills, 89
    purpose of, 89
Legislation concerning labor, 443, 469, 527
    Adamson Act, 476
    of children, 471
    compensation, workmen's, 473
    federal, 475
    health and safety, 472
    minimum wages, 473
    provisions of early, 470

sweatshops, control of operation of, 472
workday, length of the, 471
Leisure time
    American economy, tests of the success
        of the, 262
    definition of, 529
    education, effect of, 6
    production, effect on, 5
    sports, 769
    tourism, 767
    vacations, paid, 767
Lend-Lease Act, 673
Lewis, John L., 657
Lewis, Meriwether, 121
Liberty Bonds, 339, 343, 516
Lieu lands, 358
Little Steel, 691
Livestock
    breeding of, 155
    in Middle Colonies, 69
    in New England Colonies, 49
    in Southern Colonies, 74
Livingston, Robert, 121
Loan bill, 89
    definition of, 60
    Southern Colonies, 78
Loan certificates, 71
Loans
    Civil War, financing, 256
    during World War II, 685
Loans, brokers'
    source of, 596
    stock market crash (1929), 596
Logrolling
    tariffs, 394
Long drive, 301
Longevity of American people, 796
Louisiana Banking Act of 1842, 167
    passage, reason for, 176
    requirements of, 168
Louisiana Purchase
    American Fur Company, 121
    boundaries, extension of, 120
    Clark, William, 121
    cost of, 120
    exploitation of, 121
    Jefferson, Thomas, 121
    Lewis, Meriwether, 121
    Livingston, Robert, 121
    Monroe, James, 121
    negotiators for, 121
Lumber industry in the New England Col-
    onies, 66

M

Machine tooling, 405
    birth of, 124
    standardization, 213
Machinery, farm
    cultivation, intensive, 731
    names in, famous, 315
    production of, 315
    usage, regional, 314
Machinery, power, 212
Madison, James
    banking, 131, 162
    First Bank of the United States, 112

Mail service, 748
Malthus, Thomas, 8
Mann-Elkins Railroad Act, 368, 528
Manufacturing
    American people, attitude of, 403
    Appleton, Nathan, 204
    assistance by government, 204
    Astor, John Jacob, 204
    capital, increase in the supply of, 203
    Civil War, impact of, 396
    Colonial Period, 385
    development by sections, 206
    economic growth, indication of, 265
    economies of scale, 265
    enabling acts, 204
    financiers, early, 205
    Fourdrinier papermaking machine, 265
    Girard, Stephen, 204
    government, attitude of, 402
    growth of, 385, 396
    increase in, causes of, 401
    industries, capital goods, 398
    industries, leading, 210
    industries, locating, 206
    leadership, free enterprise, 204
    markets, national, 203
    maturity, national economic, 399
    meat packing, 208
    mechanization, 211
    Middle Atlantic States, 207
    Middle Colonies, 98
    New England Colonies, 98
    New England States, 206
    patent laws, 204
    resources, natural, 401
    Southern States, 210
    standardization, 212
    in the West, 203, 208
    after World War I, 553
    See also Industry
Marketing
    organization of, 482
    shopping centers, 773
    stamps, trading, 773
Markets
    advertising, 486
    capital, 426
    chain stores, 606
    communication facilities related to, 484
    curb, 483
    dependence of farmers on, 318, 320
    domestic, 478
    European, 321
    farmer position in market situations, 319
    foreign, 478
    gross national product, increases in, 424
    growth of national, 203
    home, development of, 219
    income, disposable per capita, 424
    industry, 387, 406
    market hours, 483
    national, for agricultural products, 733
    postal services, 484
    price differentials, 606
    production, large-scale, 419
    production for, as an institution of cap-
        italism, 776

    proximity in time of, 425
    shopping after World War I, new patterns
        of, 607
    size of, 424
    world, for agricultural products, 735
    See also Trade
Market value ratio, 113
Marshall Plan, 720
Mash, 209
Massachusetts Bank, 110
Maturation (national)
    agriculture balanced with industry, 521
    American securities, rehabilitation of, 517
    banking, central, 523
    capital, 514
    capital movements related to, 516
    debtor to creditor, 516
    definition of, 509
    education, 529
    entertainment, commercial, 529
    fair trade, enforcement of, 528
    Federal Reserve Act, 524
    government regulation, need for, 526
    imperialism, economic, 517
    insurance, social, 527
    land, use of, 510
    legislation, labor, 527
    legislation, railroad, 528
    leisure time, 529
    monopoly, regulation of, 528
    natural resources, use of, 510
    research, organized, 530
    semimanufactured goods, 513
    social capital, investment in, 512
    taxation, 524
    tests of economic, 509
    trade relations, external, 513
    United States, 509
McCormick, Cyrus
    machinery for farms, 315
    reaper, 156
    reaper industry, location of, 206
McGuire, Peter J., 454
McKinley, William, 348
Meat packing, 208
    "watered stock," 209
Mechanization
    labor, effects upon, 212, 444
    limitations of, 419
    power machines, impacts of, 212
    South, effect upon the, 288
    specialization, 212
    standardization, 212
    urbanization, 288
Medicine, 797
Mercantilism, 34
Mergers
    banks, 755
    banks, impact on, 759
    financing of, 754
    industrial, 752
    publishing, 757
    railroads, 756
    vertical, 753
    See also Combinations
Mexican Cession, 143

Middle Atlantic States
  farming in, 306
  manufacturing in, 207
Middle Colonies
  agriculture in, 67
  colonies included in, 33
  depression, impact of, 87
  features of, 33
  industry in, 72
  money, 71
  physiography of, 67
  Revolution, impacts of, 98
  Revolutionary War, potential impacts of,
    94
  trade, 70
  transportation, 72
Middlemen, 488
Mills, flour, 207
Mining
  labor for, after World War I, 570
Mint ratio, 113
Missouri Compromise of 1820, 251
Molasses Act of 1733, 88
Molly Maguires
  Ancient Order of Hibernians, 446
  original, in Ireland, 446
Monetary system
  bimetallism, 113
  decimal system, 113
  dollars, silver, 114
  Hamilton, Alexander, 113
  money, paper, 161
  overvaluation of gold, 160
  overvaluation of silver, 114
  Subsidiary Coinage Act of 1853, 161
  trade, importance to, 481
Money, 160
  in a capitalistic system, 777
  Gold Standard Act, 348
  greenbacks, 256, 344
  managed currency system, 777
  monetary system, bimetallic, 345
  notes, tax on state bank, 345
  paper, 161
  Pittman Act, 349
  reform, banner of, 347
  shinplasters, 257
  silver, demonetization of, 345
  substitutes for, 777
Money in the Middle Colonies
  bill of credit, 71
  certificates of deposit, 71
  commodity money, 71
  loan certificates, 71
Money in the New England Colonies
  bill of credit, 60
  certificates of deposit, 60
  commodity money, 60
  inflation, 61
  loan bill, 60
  paper money, 60
Money in the Southern Colonies
  bill of credit, 78
  book credit, 78
  commodity money, 78
  inflation, 78
  loan bill, 78

Monometallism, 113, 346
Monopoly, 127, 436
Monroe, James, 121
Mormon Trail, 182
Morris, Robert
  Bank of North America, 111
  finances for Revolutionary War, 96
  First Bank of the United States, 111
Morse, Samuel F. B., 201
Mortgages
  corporate, after World War I, 552
Motor equipment
  demand for, after World War II, 699
Muckrakers, 439

N

Nation, establishing a new
  agriculture, 121
  banking, 110
  expansion westward, 120
  Hamilton, Alexander, 109
  industry, 123
  monetary system, 113
  population, distribution and growth of,
    109
  progress, 129
  public debt, 115
  revenue, 116
  trade, 124
  transportation, 127
  War of 1812, 130
National Bank Act, 167
National Banking System
  agriculture, 332
  Central Reserve Cities, 328
  Comptroller of the Currency, 327
  correspondent banks, 331
  defects in, 329
  establishment of, 257, 327
  monetary or banking policies, lack of, 332
  Non-Reserve City, 329
  notes, national bank, 327
  requirements, reserve, 328
  Reserve City, 329
  reserves, pyramiding bank, 329
  system, not a true, 333
National bank notes, retirement of, 628
National income
  trade as origin of, 495
National Industrial Recovery Act (NIRA)
  provisions of, 631
  Public Works Administration, establish-
    ment of, 632
  Title II, 632
  Title III, Section 7-A of, 631
Nationalism, 521
National Labor Relations Act
  Jones & Laughlin Steel Corporation **v.**
    N.L.R.B., 652
  labor practices, unfair, 651
  strikes, sit-down, 652
  terms of, 651
National Labor Union
  collective bargaining, 448
  Greenback movement, 448
  organization of, 448
National Monetary Commission, 341

National Trades Union, The, 217
National wealth
  estimated for 1825-1860, 266
National Youth Administration, 634
Navigation Acts (English), 35, 83, 103, 109
  colonial violations of, 52
  principle of enumeration, 36
Negligence, contributory, 474
New Deal
  accomplishments of, 665
  banking, 641
  Coal Conservation Act (1935), 656
  Congress for Industrial Organization
    (CIO), 657
  depression, progress of the, 659
  drouth, effect of, 626
  evaluation of, 639
  Federal Securities Act of 1933, 642
  finance, 641
  insurance, social, 645
  labor, accomplishments of, 659
  labor reforms, 651
  recovery, 662
  recovery, reasons for slow rate of, 663
  reform, 641
  Securities Exchange Act of 1934, 642
  Tennessee Valley Authority, 635
  trade agreements, reciprocal, 662
  transportation, 643
  World War II, European preparations
    for, 666
New England
  farming in, 305
  manufacturing, 206
New England Colonies
  agriculture in, 47
  colonies included in, 32
  depression, impact of, 87
  features of, 33
  money, 59
  physiography, 47
  Revolution, impacts of, 98
  Revolutionary War, potential impacts of,
    93
  trade and industry in, 47, 50, 64
  transportation, 62
New Harmony, 218
New Jersey, 28
New Orleans, Battle of, 131
Newspapers
  joint venture, 758
  mergers in, 757
New York City, rise of port of, 244
New York Colony, 28
New York Free Banking Act
  importance of, 167
  provisions of, 167
New York Stock Exchange, 214
Nickelodeons, 415
Nonimportation
  War of 1812, 130
Non-Reserve City
  National Banking System, 329
Norris-LaGuardia Act
  New Deal, prelude to, 573
  yellow dog contracts, 573
North, Simeon, 124

Northwest Ordinance
  contracts, private, 101
  education, 101
  entail, 103
  impacts of, 103, 106
  Ohio Company, 101
  power, balance of, 103
  primogeniture, 103
  protection, personal, 101
  provisions for political organization, 101
  requirements for statehood, 101
  roads, construction of, 103
  slavery, 101
  terms of, 101
Northwest Territory
  government of, 101
  organization of, political, 101
  requirements for statehood, 101
  settlement of, 101
Notes
  circulating, 343
  state bank, 334
Nullification Act, 221

O

Office of Emergency Management, 673
Office of Price Administration, 687
Ohio Company, 101, 103
Oligopsonistic
  combinations, 436
Oliver, James, 315
Open Market Committee
  creation of, 622
  Federal Reserve System, 342
Open market operations
  definitions of, 343
  Federal Reserve Board, instruments of
    control for, 598
Open shop, 460
Operational costs, 420
Opportunity cost, 74
Ordinance of 1787
  slavery, 251
  See also Northwest Ordinance
Oregon Territory, acquisition of, 143
Oregon Trail, 182
Organization, business
  corporate, 388
  financial instruments, 388
  labor, division of, 387
  specialization, 388
  wage policies, 388
Overvaluation
  gold, 160
  mint ratio, changes in, 160

P

Panic, 611
  bank reform, legislation for, 619
  banks, failures of, 618
Panic of 1837
  American economy, failures of, 263
  causes of, 175, 263
  Second Bank of the United States, 176
  severity of, 177
  Specie Circular, 140, 176

Panic of 1857
  American economy, failures of, 263
  causes of, 263
Panic of 1873
  causes of, 362
  Cooke, Jay, 361
Panic of 1904, 423
Panic of 1907, 423
Paper money in the New England Colonies
  bill of credit, 60
  loan bill, 60
Par, at
  definition of, 111
Partnerships
  business, organization of, 213
Passengers on railroads, 364
Patent laws
  effect of, 204
  manufacturing, encouragement to, 204
Patents, 107
Patrons of Husbandry, The, 322
Patroon system, 68
Payments, balance of
  balance of payments account, defined, 241
  invisible items, defined, 241
Payne-Aldrich Bill (1909), 391, 394
Penn, William, 28, 68
Pennsylvania, 28, 30
Pensions, old age, 646
  Townsend Plan, 647
Perverse elasticity, 328
Petroleum
  fuel, industrial, 411
Philadelphia
  Constitutional Convention, 106
  First Bank of the United States, 112
Picket, 464
Piggyback railway service, see Trailer-on-
    flatcar (TOFC) service
Pike, Zebulon, 182
Pioneer, 138
Pitt, William, 92
Pittman Act, 349
Pittman silver dollars, 349
Plantation system
  description of, 73
  expansion of, 247
  labor, 74
  South, importance to the, 250
Pools
  definition of, 428
  examples of, 429
Population
  of American colonies, 40
  Atlantic Coastal States, 109
  banks, national, 328
  center of, 150, 290
  climate, industrial, 386
  colonial (1760), 84
  composition of, 147, 725
  density of, 286
  distribution after World War I, 547
  distribution at time of Civil War, 252
  distribution between urban and rural, 286
  distribution of, 109, 149, 275, 281, 283
  distribution of colonial, 40
  District of Columbia, 109

  foreign born, 280
  growth after World War I, 547, 550
  growth and development, 39
  growth of, 109, 145, 275
  growth rate of, 276
  housing, 727
  immigrants, contribution of, 41
  immigrants, resettlement of, 283
  immigration, 145, 149, 277, 729
  immigration, nature of, 41
  increase, natural, 145, 275
  migration, 145
  Negro ratio before Civil War, 251
  rural, decline in, 290, 726
  schools, 728
  South, 110, 290
  spread of, in U. S., 227
  suburbs, move to, 726
  urban growth after World War I, causes
    of, 549
  urbanization, 286
  urbanization caused by World War II,
    677
  westward movement, 110
  World War I, 290, 292
Populism, 347
Populist party, 323
Postal Savings System, 338
Postal service
  early means of, 200
  growth of, 200, 381
  markets, widening of, 484
  newspapers, as added cost burden, 200
  parcel post, 382
  postage, methods of collecting, 200
  postage, rates of, 200
Postal system
  Constitution of the United States, 107
Potato railroad, 306
Poverty in America, 794
Powderly, Terence V., 449
Power
  factory system, development of, 265
  horse, in farming, 312
  for industry, 387, 413
  manpower, in farming, 312
  wind, in farming, 311
Pre-emption Act of 1841, 143
Price control
  Revolutionary War, 97
  Southern Colonies, 75
  World War II, 688
Prices
  differentials in, 606
  fixing, 764
Price supports
  agricultural produce, 735
Primogeniture
  definition of, 29
  Middle Colonies, 68
Prince Henry of Portugal (the Navigator),
    25
Principles of free trade, 8
Printing press money, 113
Privateering, 34
Proclamation of 1763
  discontent with, 85

hunters and trappers, 85
indentured servants, 85
Southern Colonies, 94
speculators, 85
terms of, 85
violation of, 92
Production
effects of education on, 6
mass, in automobile industry, 554
nature and systems of, 3
Production, large-scale, 418
costs of operation of, 420
definition of, 419
markets, 419
mechanization, limitations of, 419
mechanization of industry, 419
trade, retail, 420
Productive factors
capital, 271
changes in, 270
labor, 271
land, 270
Profit motive, 31
Revolutionary War, 92
Profits
banking, 111
combinations, business, 427
quest for, 27, 29
types of, 4
World War II, 671
Profits, corporate
definition of, 759
dividends, 761
earnings, efforts to maintain, 761
price fixing, 764
stockholders, 760
Profit system
as an institution of capitalism, 780
Progress
agriculture, measuring production in, 310
Blodget, Samuel, 129
Economica, 129
evaluation of, 129
Promontory Point, Utah
railroad, transcontinental, 356
Property
institution of private, 776
values of, after World War I, 552
Property tax, general
uses of, 175
Proprietorships
business, organization of, 213
Proprietorship system
Middle Colonies, 68
Prosperity
return of, to farmers, 323
Prosperity after World War I
agriculture, 579
banking and finance, 591
investments abroad, 604
markets, 606
railroads, regulation of, 601
stock market (1929), crash of, 608
tariffs, 588
utilities, public, 601
Public Contracts Act, *see* Walsh-Healey Act

Public land policy
Articles of Confederation, 99
public lands, first, 99
after the Revolutionary War, 99
soldiers of the Revolutionary War, 99
speculators, 99
Public lands
American System, 140
attitudes toward sale of, 119
Clay, Henry, 140
federal revenue, source of, 169
Gadsden Purchase, 145
Graduation Act of 1854, 143
grants, 143
interests, conflicting, 139
Land Law of 1820, 141
Mexican Cession, 143
Oregon Territory, 143
pioneers, 138
Pre-emption Act of 1841, 143
price of, 120
sales of, 119, 141
settlement upon, unlawful, 143
speculation in, 120
territories acquired, 143
Texas annexed, 143
Public Works Administration (PWA)
program of, 632
slum clearance, 638
Publishing, mergers in, 757
Pull, forces of
definition of, 28
entail, 28
headright system, 29
immigrants to America, 42
primogeniture, 28
Pullman, George M., 456
Pullman Company
railroads, 364
Pure Food and Drugs Act, 526
Push, forces of, 29

Q

Quakerism, 28
Quartering Act of 1765
colonial defiance of, 89
purpose of, 89
revived, 92
Quebec Act, 92

R

Railroad, transcontinental
bison, impact on, 357
construction of, 356
Promontory Point, Utah, 356
Railroad Land Grant Act, first, 198
Railroads
"Age of the Railroad," 356
Bessemer process, 195
Broadway Limited, 364
brotherhoods, 457
canals, triumph over, 193
change in technology before 1860, 195
Civil War, impact of, 356
coal, 375
commercial, first, 194
competition before World War I, 370
Continental Divide, 363

control by government, 371
Cooke, Jay, 361
Credit Mobilier, 360
crisis, wartime, 369
developments in, during Civil War years, 196
dominance of, 351
East, 363
economy, impact on, 373
efficiency, problems of, 372
Elkins Act, 368
expansion of, 362
financiers, early, 361
first one, 194
function, initial, 193
gauge, standard rail, 196, 363
Granger Cases, 366
hazards in early, 195
Hepburn Act, 368
improvements, early, 195
inputs, demand for, 373
Interstate Commerce Act, 366
investments in, 376
labor for, after World War I, 570
land grants to, 198, 358
legislation concerning, as index of economic maturity, 528
lieu lands, 358
Mann-Elkins Act, 368
markets, national, 203
mergers of, 756
Midwest, 362
Mississippi River, east of, 196
Mississippi River, west of, 198
operation, changes in, 372
Panic of 1873, 361
power for early, 194
Pullman Company, 364
Railroad Land Grant Act, first, 198
rates, discrimination of, 365
regulation of, 365, 601
Rockefeller, John D., 430
rolling stock, Canada, 197
sailing day plan, 373
sleeping car, first, 197
Smythe v. Ames, 369
speculation, 360
spread of, 196
Stevens, John, 195
Stourbridge Lion, 195
taxes paid by, 375
telegraph, 377
time zones, standard, 364
Tom Thumb, 194
traffic, 230
traffic, centrally controlled, 748
traffic, decline in passenger, 744
traffic, freight, 746
traffic, passenger, 364
trailer-on-flatcar (TOFC) service, 746
Transportation Act of 1920, 603
Twentieth Century Limited, 364
unit trains, 747
urbanization, 363
West, 362, 479
World War I, initial impacts of, 371
Railroad Valuation Act (1913), 369

Railway, electric
expansion of, 354
impacts of, economic, 355
markets served, 353
Railway Evaluation Act, 528
Ranchers
cattle v. sheep, 302
farmers, conflict with, 301
Ranching
barbed wire, 302
cattle and sheep, 301
the long drive, 301
Rationing
World War I, 540
World War II, 689
Reaper, 156
Reciprocal Trade Agreements Act (1934), 662
Reconstruction Finance Corporation
activities, extension of, 617
Dawes bank incident, 617
Reform
combinations, business, 439
Refrigeration
agricultural produce, national market for, 733
railroads, 195
Relationship of government and business
finance, state level, 172
improvements, internal, 171
property tax, general, 175
Relief, 611
Agricultural Adjustment Act of 1933, 629
Amendment to the Agricultural Adjustment Act of 1933, 623
Civilian Conservation Corps (CCC), 633
cultural programs, 634
Frazier-Lemke Bill, 630
homesteads, subsistence, 628
housing, financing, 637
measures of, 623
measures of, evaluation of, 638
national bank notes, retirement of, 628
National Industrial Recovery Act (NIRA), 631
National Youth Administration, 634
Silver Purchase Act of 1934, 627
Tennessee Valley Authority (TVA), 634
Rent controls during World War II, 688
Report on Manufactures, 218
Hamilton, Alexander, 109
infant industry, 109
Reserve City
Federal Reserve System, 343
National Banking System, 329
Reserves
pyramiding, defined, 329
Resources, capital
use of, 404
Resources, natural, 401
conservation of, 511
exploitation of, 510
maturity, national economic, 510
parks and forests, national, 512
Restraint of trade, 436
Resumption Act, 345

Retail
  costs and prices, a new look at, 491
  customer services, 490
  dislocations at that level, 491
  neighborhood stores, 492
  progress, impacts of, 492
Retirement
  American economy, effect on, 796
Revenue
  customs duties, 116
  excise taxes, 116
  government, sources for local, 738
  government stock, 117
  Internal Revenue, 118
  provisions for constitutional, 116
  public lands, 116, 119
  Second Continental Congress, 116
  sources of, 116, 118
  state, sources of, 737
  Tariff of 1789, 117
Revenue, federal
  customs duties, 91, 169
  lands, public, 91, 169
  sources of, 737
  Walker Tariff of 1846, 169
Revenue Act of 1942, 681
Revolutionary War
  aftermath of, 103
  aspects of, 97
  competition, 92
  Cornwallis, 99
  Declaration of Independence, 94
  finances, 95
  freedom of enterprise, 92
  free pricing, 92
  impacts of, 97
  Middle Colonies, 94, 98
  New England Colonies, 93, 98
  Pitt, William, 92
  Proclamation of 1763, 94
  profit motive, 92
  sectional differences, 93
  Southern Colonies, 94, 98
  state debts, 115
  Tories, 93
  Whigs, 93
  Yorktown, Virginia, 99
Revolutionary War, readjustments after the
  depression, postwar, 104
  Land Ordinance of 1785, 101
  Northwest Ordinance, 101
  public land policy, 99
  war, aftermath of, 103
Rhode Island
  settlement of, 27
  textile mill, first, 27
Rice in the Southern Colonies, 74
Risk
  assumption of, by employees, 474
Rivers, 352
  Delaware River, 353
  freight carried on, 186
  Hudson River, 353
  important ones in commerce, 228
  steamboat, 228
  trade, patterns of, 186
  traffic on, 228

Roads
  Constitution of the United States, 107
  Cumberland Road, 180
  engine, introduction of the internal com-
    bustion, 351
  federal aid, 180
  financing early, 179
  first, 180
  Lancaster Turnpike, 180
  Maysville Road, 180
  Mississippi River, east of, 180
  Mormon Trail, 182
  New England, 179
  New England Colonies, 62
  Oregon Trail, 182
  post, 128
  Santa Fe Trail, 182
  subsidation, federal, 352
  surfaces of early, 180
  toll, 182
  tolls, exemptions from, 182
  trails, western, 182
  transportation, 351
  turnpikes, defined, 182
Rockefeller, John D.,
  railroads, control over, 430
  Standard Oil Trust, 430
Roosevelt, Franklin D.,
  banks, reopening of the, 619
Rubber
  automobile tires, 558
Rule, fellow servant, 474
Rum
  inelastic demand, 88
  Sugar Act of 1764, 88

S

Sailing day plan, 373
Santa Fe Trail, 182
Sault Sainte Marie (Soo), 352
Savings
  postal, 338
  released after World War II, 698
Scabs, *see* Strikebreakers
Scale of living
  American economy, tests of the success
    of, 262
  as evidence of progress, 5
Schedule principle
  explanation of, 221
  Walker Tariff of 1846, 221
Schools
  colleges and universities, 728
  teacher numbers, increase in, 728
  teacher salaries, increase in, 728
Second Bank of the United States
  Biddle, Nicholas, 164
  branches, location of, 162
  cases at law, 163
  characteristics of, 162
  charter, reasons for, 162
  Cheves, Langdon, 163
  Clay, Henry, 164
  difficulties of, 163
  First Bank of the United States, similari-
    ties to, 162
  functions of, 163

Jackson, Andrew, 164
Jackson's "pet banks," 164
Jones, William, 163
Panic of 1837, 176
Securities Exchange Act of 1934, 642
Security markets, 177
Selective Service Act (1940), 674
Selling, direct, 482
Semimanufactured goods, 513
Services, complementary
    demand for, after World War II, 701
Settlements, early American, 27
Seven Years' War, 83
Sewing machine, invention of, 208
Sherman Antitrust Act (1890), 434, 437,
    529
    Bureau of Corporations, 438
Sherman Silver Purchase Act (1890), 347
Shinplasters, 257
Shipping and shipbuilding, 242
    clipper ship, impact of the, 243
    colonial, 52
    commercial ships, 243
    New England Colonies, 66
    New York, rise of, 244
    packet liners, 244
    Southern Colonies, 78
    subsidization, British, 243
Shopping
    centers, growth of, 773
    new patterns of, after World War I, 607
Silver
    Bland-Allison Act (1878), 346
    "Crime of '73," 346
    crisis, treasury, 347
    Currency Act of 1873, 345
    demonetization of, 345
    overvaluation of, 114
    Pittman Act, 349
    Pittman silver dollars, 349
    Sherman Silver Purchase Act (1890), 347
    Silver Purchase Acts, 346
Silver dollar
    coinage, stoppage of, 115
    Jefferson, Thomas, 114
    Spanish dollar, 114
    traffic in, 114
    West Indies, 114
Silver Purchase Act of 1934, 627
Sinclair, Upton, 439
Singer, Isaac, 208
Slater, Samuel
    Arkwright frame, 123
    textile mill, first, 27, 123
Slavery
    Constitution of the United States, 106
    cotton, 122
    growth of, 76, 154
    growth of, reasons for, 250
    indentured servants compared to, 43
    Missouri Compromise of 1820, 251
    origin of, 75
    politics, 251
    slave trading, 76, 154
    sugarcane, 123
    war, cause of, 250
Small Business Administration, 617

Smith, Adam, 8, 105
Smith, George
    banking, 166
    Wisconsin Fire and Marine Insurance
        Company, 166
Smythe v. *Ames,* 369
Social overhead capital, 193
Social security
    insurance, unemployment, 648
    payments, benefit, 649
    plan, first, 648
    progress, economic, 650
Soil butchery, 155
Soo Canal, *see* Sault Sainte Marie
Sound money, 624
South
    antebellum, description of, 249
    boll weevil, 308
    cotton, role of, 307
    farming in, 306
    farm tenancy in, 315
    manufacturing, 210
Southern Colonies
    agriculture in, 73
    blockades of, 98
    depression, impact of, 87
    features of, 33
    industry in, 78
    money, 77
    physiography of, 73
    Revolution, impacts of, 98
    Revolutionary War, potential impacts of,
        94
    trade in, 77
    transportation in, 78
Space, adventures in, 797
Specialization, 7
    industrial, by sections of country, 206
    mechanization, 212
    trade, domestic, 478
Specie, 37
Specie Circular
    Panic of 1837, 176, 263
    public lands, 141
    terms of, 165
Speculation
    in public lands, 297
    railroads, 360
Sports
    baseball, impacts of professional, 770
    football, 771
    high school, 771
    horses, racing of, 771
    leisure time, 769
Stamps, trading
    impact of, 773
Stamp Tax of 1765
    colonial defiance, 89
    levy of, 89
    purpose of, 89
Standardization
    in industry, 212
    Whitney, Eli, 124
Standard of living
    definition of, 2
    as opposed to scale of living, 2
    scarcity as a factor in, 2

Standard Oil
  Rockefeller, John D., 430
  trust, 430
Standard time zones
  railroads, 364
State
  combinations, control of, 436
Steamboat
  river traffic, effect upon, 228
  triangular trade, 127
Steampower in railroads, 194
Steam traction engine, 313
Stephens, Uriah S., 449
Stevens, John, 195
Stevens, Robert L., 195
St. Lawrence River, 83
Stock market
  crash of (1929), 608, 611
Stone and Timber Act of 1878, 296
Stores
  chain, 421, 606
  department, 234, 420
  general, 233
  specialty, 233
  variety, 422
Stourbridge Lion, 195
Streetcars, 353
Streets
  improvements after World War II, 703
Strikebreakers, 465
Strikes, 216
  definition of, 217, 462
  hours of work, results on, 465
  sit-down, 652
  wages, results on, 465
  World War II, during and after, 707
Subsidiary Coinage Act of 1853, 161
  silver, 345
Suburbia
  move to, 726
  railways, expansion of electric, 354
Suffolk Bank, 166
Sugar Act of 1764
  colonial defiance of, 88
  purpose of, 88
  rum, 88
Sugarcane
  importance of, 123
  Southern Colonies, 74
Sugar industry
  New England Colonies, 66
Superhighways, state
  tourism, 768
Sweatshops, 472
Symmes, John, 103

T

Taft-Hartley Act
  labor, objections of, 710
  Labor-Management Reporting and Dis-
    closure Act, 710
  terms of, 709
  Wagner Act, amendment to, 710
Taney, Roger B., 164
Tariff Act of 1870, 391
Tariff of Abominations, 220

Tariff of 1789
  Hamilton, Alexander, 117
  infant industry, 117
Tariffs, 203
  analyzed, 222
  attitude of Middle Atlantic States toward,
    248
  attitude of Northern States toward, 248
  attitude of Southern States toward, 248
  compensatory principle, 393
  Compromise Tariff of 1833, 221
  crisis, during economic, 612
  customs receipts, impact on, 392
  Dingley Tariff, 394
  Fordney-McCumber Tariff Act, 588
  free trade, defined, 224
  Hamilton, Alexander, 109
  Hawley-Smoot Tariff, 612
  home markets, development of, 219
  infant industries, 513
  Infant Industries Tariff of 1789, 219
  kinds of, 225
  legislation effecting national maturity, 513
  logrolling, 394
  policy, development of a, 392
  protection, evaluation of, 393
  protection, lessening of, 221
  protective, 218, 385, 389
  railroads, impact on, 391
  regulation, attempts at, 590
  revenue, 224
  steel, impact on, 391
  Tariff of Abominations, 220
  trade, decline in export-import, 612
  Underwood Tariff of 1913, 514
  unrest, 394
  wages, impact on, 391
  Walker Tariff of 1846, 221
Taxation
  ability-to-pay principle of, 524, 786
  Civil War, financing, 255
  colonial attitude toward, 90
  Confederation, financing the, 90
  Constitution of the United States, 106
  Constitution of the United States, 16th
    amendment to, 525
  Declaration of Independence, 95
  general property tax, failure of, 524
  income, 717
  income tax, federal, 525
  Income tax law of 1913, 525
  maturation, evidence of national, 524
  railroads, paid by, 375
  revenue, federal, 91
  revenue, miscellaneous sources of, 718
  state and local governments, new sources
    for, 717
  war finances, 96
  Whiskey Rebellion, 90
  for World War I, 539
Taxation during World War II
  corporate income, 681
  defense, 682
  excise, 683
  personal income, 681
  Revenue Act of 1942, 681
  Victory Tax, 682

Tea Act (1773), 92
Teachers
    number of, increase in, 728
    salaries of, increase in, 728
Telegraph
    communications, effect on, 199
    Edison, Thomas A., 377
    growth, impact on economic, 379
    markets, national, 204
    Morse, Samuel F. B., 201
    services, expansion of, 377
    Western Union Telegraph Company, 201
Telephone
    Bell, Alexander Graham, 379
    competition, 380
    consolidation, 380
    system, growth of the, 380
    use of, increase in the, 749
Telstar, 797
Tenancy, farm, 315
Tennessee Valley Authority (TVA)
    elasticity of demand for electricity, 635
    evaluation of, 636
    impact of, 636
    New Deal, 635
    social planning, 635
Texas, annexation of, 143
Theory of population, 8
Thomas Amendment to the Agricultural Ad-
        justment Act of 1933
    devaluation program, 625
    dollar, devaluation of the, 625
    drouth, 626
    gold clause, abrogation of the contractual,
        626
    gold stabilization fund, 625
    terms of, 623
Three-cornered trade, see Triangular trade
Till money, 596
Timber Culture Act of 1873, 296
Tobacco
    control, cartel type of, 432
    Southern Colonies, 74
    Tobacco Trust, The, 431
Tom Thumb, 194
Tories, 93
Tourism
    highways, interstate, 768
    impacts of, 767, 769
    superhighways, state, 768
Townshend Acts
    articles taxed, 91
    Boston Tea Party, 91
    East India Tea Company, 91
    objections to, 91
    tea smugglers, effect on, 91
Townsend Plan, 647
Trade
    account, 237, 241
    auctions, 233
    balance of, 237
    balance of, favorable, 239, 241
    balance of, unfavorable, 77, 239, 241
    balance of, with U. S. as debtor, 238
    balance of payments, 504
    banking structure, importance of a sound,
        480

capital, direct investments of, 499
capital, portfolio investments of, 499
commodity, 235
commodity exports and imports, nature
    of, 499
customer services in retail, 490
division of labor, 478
domestic, 478
exports, 236
exports, destinations of, 501
exports and imports, changes in, 513
foreign, 478, 498
foreign, customers for, 235
foreign, direction of American, 787
foreign, financing, 239
foreign, growth of, 235
foreign, impacts of World War I on, 505
foreign, importance of, 786
foreign, new patterns of, 498, 721
government and, 497
House of Baring, 240
hucksters, 483
imports, 237
imports, sources of, 501
market house, 483
markets, curb, 483
markups, 492
monetary system, importance of a sound,
    481
Navigation Acts, 103
neutrality during World War I, 506
organization of, 231, 482
as origin of national income, 494
payments account, international, 237, 241
principle of free, 514
retail, 232, 420
after the Revolutionary War, 103
rivers, along, 228
selling, direct, 482
specialization, 478
stores, department, 234
stores, general, 233
stores, specialty, 233
tariffs, legislation on, 513
transportation, 481
Webb-Pomerene Act, 506
West, settlement of the, 478
wholesale, 231, 488
Trade acceptances, 240
Trade and change, 24
Trade and service industries
    labor for, after World War I, 570
Trade and trade routes
    Italian dominance, reaction to, 25
    nature of, 24
    westward movement of, 25
Trade during the early national period
    with China, 125
    cotton, importance of, 126
    external, importance of, 125
    internal, 126
    labor, division of, 124
    prosperity of, 125
    steamboats, 127
    specialization, 124
    trade centers, important, 126
    triangular, internal, 126

Trade in the Middle Colonies
  currency, new, 70
  exports, 70
  external, 70
  growth of, reasons for, 70
  internal, 71
  port cities, 70
  triangular, 70
Trade in the New England Colonies
  bills of exchange, 55
  external, 50, 55
  fur trade, 59
  hat industry restrictions, 59
  imports and exports, 58
  industries associated with, 50
  internal, 58
  triangular, 52
  types of, 50
Trade in the Southern Colonies
  England, dependency on, 77
  external, 77
  self-sufficiency, domestic, 77
  trade balance, unfavorable, 77
  triangular trade, 77
Trailer-on-flatcar (TOFC), 746
Trains
  trailer-on-flatcar service, 746
  unit, 747
Transactions, international
  merchandise, shipments of, 240
  transactions, capital, 240
  transactions, service, 240
Transportation
  air, 644, 748
  banking, 110
  Civil Aeronautics Administration, 645
  Civil Aeronautics Authority, 645
  Civil Aeronautics Authority Act, 645
  Civil Aeronautics Board (CAB), 645
  Civil War, 254
  developments in, importance of, 265
  economic growth, indication of, 265
  Emergency Transportation Act of 1933, 643
  highways, 179, 351
  highways, impacts of federal aid, 744
  inclined planes, 356
  land-water combination, 184
  motor, 644
  railroad, 193, 351, 356
  railroads, decline in passenger traffic on, 744
  railroads, efforts to increase freight traffic on, 746
  railways, electric, 353
  roads, 179, 351
  roads, toll, 182
  trade, 481
  trails, western, 182
  waterways, inland, 186, 352
Transportation Act of 1920, 528, 604
Transportation during the early national period
  Gallatin, Albert, 127
  rivers, principal, 127
  roads, post, 128

Transportation during World War II, 672
  industry, decentralization of, 680
  military, priority of the, 678
  nonfreight, 678
  overseas, shipments for, 679
Transportation in the Middle Colonies, 72
Transportation in the New England Colonies
  roads and trails, 62
  trade, 62
  waterways, 63
Transportation in the Southern Colonies, 78
Treasury surplus, distribution of the Panic of 1837, 263
Treaty of Paris, 83
Triangular trade
  bills of exchange, 53
  drafts, 53
  Middle Colonies, 70
  patterns of, 52
  Southern Colonies, 77
Trust companies, 335
Trusts
  cartel, principle of the, 432
  explanation of, 429
  financial results, 433
  as illegal, 433
  important, 433
  investment, 600
  Rockefeller, John D., 430
  Sherman Antitrust Act, 434, 437
  Standard Oil Trust, 430
  Tobacco Trust, The, 431
Turnpikes, 182
Twentieth Century Limited, 364

U

Underwood Tariff of 1913
  compensatory principle, 393
  revenue, 514
  unrest, expression of, 394
Unemployment
  cyclical, 444
  degrees of, 781
  labor, 444
  relief, administration's philosophy on, 616
  relief, inadequacy of, 615
  after World War II, 703
Union Pacific Railroad, 356
Unions
  American Federation of Labor, 453
  American Railway Union, 455
  boycott, defined, 462
  brotherhoods, railroad, 457
  check-off, 460
  city centrals, 448
  closed shop, 460
  collective bargaining, 460
  Commonwealth v. *Hunt,* 217
  employers, objections of, 461
  employers, opposition of, 451, 464
  enforcement, methods of, 462
  Holy Order of the Knights of Labor, 449
  Industrial Workers of the World, 458
  injunctions as employer weapon, 465
  Knights of St. Crispin, 448
  label, union, 462

labor, demands of organized, 462
labor, national organization of, 447
labor, program of organized, 460
membership in, 461
National Labor Union, organization of, 448
open shop, 460
organization, early attempts at, 447
picket, 464
strikebreakers, 465
strikes, 462, 465
union shop, defined, 461
weapons of, 462
Union shop, 461
United States Employment Service
activities, 648
organization, 476
United States Shipping Board, 506
Universities
enrollment increase in, 728
Uplift unions, 457
Urban areas
definition of, 548
growth of, 260
growth of, after World War I, 549
Urbanization, 150
aspects of, 152
attitudes toward, 403
growth of, 260, 288, 549
homesteading, offset to, 295
mechanization, 288
population, density of, 286
railroads, 363
World War I, effect of, 290, 293, 549
Utilities, public
holding companies, 602
operating, principles of, 601

V

Vacations, paid, 767
Variable proportions, law of, 9, 75
Venture capital
public lands, 294
Vertical combinations, 427
Victory Tax
World War II, 682

W

Wabash Railroad
Gould, Jay, 451
Holy Order of the Knights of Labor, 451
Wages
adjustments in, after World War II, 710
contracts, industry-wide, 706
controls on, during World War II, 691
labor, demands of, 705
legislation for minimum, 713, 784
minimum, 5, 473
minimum, economic impacts of laws concerning, 656
patterns of, after World War II, 702
productivity, marginal, 655
Wages and Hours Act, *see* Fair Labor Standards Act
Wagner Act, 710
Wagner-Peyser Act, 648
Walker Tariff of 1846
federal revenue, 169

protection, lessening of, 221
schedule principle, 221
Walking delegates, 460
Walsh-Healey Act, 653
Waltham System, 214
War
all-out, defined, 670
finances for, attaining, 96
preparations for, as test of economy's performance, 782
total, defined, 670
War debts, foreign
aspect of, frequently overlooked, 576
loans between governments, 575
loans in default, 576
War Between the States, *see* Civil War
War of 1812
causes of, 130
central banking, lack of, 113
embargo, 130
financing, 131
impacts of, 131
inflation, 113
nonimportation, 130
speculation, 113
trade, internal, 227
War Revenue Act (1942), 682
Washington, George, 98
Washington, D. C.
location, reasons for, 116
Wash sales, 643
Water
fuel, industrial, 411
Watered stock
definition of, 209
origin of name, 209
Waterways
canals, 187, 229
inland, 352
New England Colonies, 63
rivers, 186, 228
Wealth
accumulations of, 261
distribution of, for 1866-1920, 532
Webb-Pomerene Act, 506
Welfare, national
government intervention for, 783
West
flow of goods to and from the, 480
investment of eastern capital in, 479
manufacturing in, 208
meat packing in, 208
railroads, as important to settlement in the, 479
settlement of, 478
Western beef, 734
Western Union Telegraph Company, 201
Westinghouse, George, 414
Westward movement
commerce, internal, 227
rivers, importance of, 228
Whaling, colonial, 50
Whigs, 93
Whiskey Rebellion
Hamilton, Alexander, 90
internal revenue, 119
taxation, 90

Whitney, Eli
  agriculture, 122
  standardization, 124
Wholesalers, 231
Wholesaling
  distribution, variations in, 489
  middlemen, 488
  salesmen, traveling, 488
Wildcat banking
  definition of, 113
  printing press money, 113
Williams, Roger, 27
Wire, barbed, 302
Wobblies, *see* Industrial Workers of the
  World
World War I
  adjustments to, 506
  aftermath of, 547
  agriculture, impact on, 324
  bonds, 539
  creditor, U. S. becomes a, 505
  finances, 538
  foreign trade, impacts on, 505
  German ingenuity, 537
  immigration, restrictions on, 292
  industry, prosperity in, 537
  inflation, 541
  involvements, 536
  migration as a cause of, 293
  neutrality and trade, 506
  population, impacts on, 292
  railroad competition, prewar, 370
  railroads, crisis for, 369
  railroads, initial impacts on, 371
  rationing, 540
  recovery from, 541
  shipping, ocean, 538
  taxes, new, 539
  United States Shipping Board, establish-
    ment of, 506
  urbanization, 290
World War I, after
  advertising, 564
  amusements, places of, 551
  automobile industry, 553
  construction, 550, 552
  consumer expeditures, methods of financ-
    ing, 564
  dining facilities, 551
  electrical appliance industry, 560
  entertainment industry, 565
  housing, multiple, 551
  immigration, 573
  labor in mechanized industries, 568
  manufacturing and industry, 553
  mortgages, corporate, 552
  population, growth and distribution of,
    547
  property, values of residential, 552
  war debts, early retirement of U. S., 574
  war debts, foreign, 575
World War II
  agriculture, 694
  armed forces, manpower for the, 672, 674
  banking, 692
  communication, 693
  economic resources, coordination of, 673
  finance, 673, 681
  inflation, control of, 687
  Johnson Neutrality Act, 671
  Lend-Lease Act, 673
  manpower, civilian, 672, 674
  neutrality, American, 671
  Office of Emergency Management, 673
  population, urban move of, 677
  preparation for, in Europe, 666
  preparation for, work period in, 677
  preparation in the U. S., need for, 670
  preparedness, problems of, 672
  production, airplane, 695
  production, increases in American, 667
  production, obstacles to, 671
  production, readiness for, 695
  profits, 671
  railroads, revival of American, 667
  scrap iron, use of, 555
  Selective Service Act (1940), 674
  transportation, 672, 678
  years of war, 670
World War II, after
  agriculture, 729
  capital, investment of, 703
  communication, 744, 749
  considerations, international, 720
  construction, building, 700
  corporate developments, 752
  dollar shortage in the foreign exchange,
    720
  economic activity, government controls
    over, 714
  employment, 699
  employment, government role concerning,
    716
  finance, government, 735
  finance, government role concerning, 716
  insurance, life, 765
  Korea, police action in, 723
  labor, demands of organized, 704
  leisure time, 766
  marketing, patterns of, 773
  Marshall Plan, 720
  motor equipment, demand for, 699
  population, 725
  progress, 725
  reconversion without depression, 698, 702
  savings, release of, 698
  services, demand for complementary, 701
  streets and highways, improvements on,
    703
  transportation, 744
  unemployment, 703
  wages, patterns of, 702

Y

Yellow dog contracts, 573
Yorktown, Virginia, 99